Apple Hill
Left - right
View Ridge Dr
6. apt E

INTRODUCTION TO PSYCHOLOGY
Second Edition

Linda L. Davidoff

McGRAW-HILL BOOK COMPANY

New York   St. Louis   San Francisco   Auckland   Bogotá   Hamburg
Johannesburg   London   Madrid   Mexico   Montreal   New Delhi
Panama   Paris   São Paulo   Singapore
Sydney   Tokyo   Toronto

INTRODUCTION TO PSYCHOLOGY

Copyright © 1980, 1976 by McGraw-Hill, Inc.
All rights reserved. Printed in the United States of America.
No part of this publication may be reproduced, stored in a retrieval system,
or transmitted, in any form or by any means, electronic,
mechanical, photocopying, recording, or otherwise,
without prior written permission of the publisher.

1234567890 V H V H 89876543210

See Acknowledgments on pages 640-643.
Copyrights included on this page by reference.

This book was set in Century Expanded by Black Dot, Inc.
The editors were Janis M. Yates and Laura D. Warner;
the designer was Ben Kann;
the production supervisor was Joe Campanella.
The photo editor was Linda Gutierrez.
New drawings were done by J & R Services, Inc., and Ed Malsberg.
The cover photograph was taken by Ben Kann.
Von Hoffmann Press, Inc., was printer and binder.

Library of Congress Cataloging in Publication Data

Davidoff, Linda L
    Introduction to psychology.

    Bibliography: p.
    Includes index.
    1. Psychology. I. Title.
BF121.D326 1980   150   79-18732
ISBN 0-07-015504-6

To some very special friends:

my father, *Samuel Bert Lee*, in memory
my grandmothers, *Anna I. Litwack* and *Pauline Weisman*
my grandfather, *Charles Litwack*

Contents

To the Student

I want to tell you about the learning aids that were built into this text, and to make some suggestions for their use. The Study Guides following each chapter should be particularly helpful for reviewing. Typically, the guides contain these sections:

1. *Lists of key terms, important research, basic concepts, and people to identify.* Your teacher is likely to hold you responsible for items on these lists, along with other italicized words and expressions. As you study a chapter, test yourself to see whether you can define, discuss, describe, or identify these items. Then review any material that gives you difficulty. The order of items in these lists generally follows the order of the chapter. The page numbers (in parentheses) following the key terms tell where the relevant text discussions begin.

2. *Self-Quiz.* Once you feel that you have mastered the material in the chapter, try answering the multiple-choice questions of the Self-Quiz. If your answers differ from those in the Answer Keys (at the end of the Study Guide), review the appropriate information (beginning on the pages listed). Keep in mind that the Self-Quiz only *samples* the important topics of the chapter.

3. *Exercises.* The Exercises were designed to give practice on difficult or potentially confusing material. Answer Keys are provided; so are the page numbers of sections that should be reviewed if you experience problems.

4. *Suggested Readings.* For additional information about topics mentioned in a chapter, these readings—chosen because they are both informative and enjoyable—are a good place to begin.

The chapters themselves contain a number of features that may be helpful to you. The opening *outline* gives an overview. Reminders telling where we are headed are scattered throughout the chapter. Psychological research suggests that people learn more when they know in advance what to expect. Every time you come to a red triangle, you will find a block of *Using Psychology* questions (also marked with a red triangle) on the same or a neighboring page. These sections provide both a break and an opportunity to mull over what you have read. You will be asked to explain fundamental information in your own words, generate examples, apply concepts to your own life, debate controversial issues, or think about implications. Using psychology is probably the best way to learn it. A *summary* concluding each chapter reviews the most important points covered.

The *captions* accompanying many of the illustrations and photographs supplement information provided in the body of the text. In some instances, examples, applications, or related materials are described. Be sure to find out whether you are responsible for this information.

Like a dictionary, the *Glossary* (at the back of the book) defines important terms that are used repeatedly. If you come across a technical word that is not immediately defined or described, assume that it was used in an earlier chapter and look in the Glossary. If you need further information, find the topic in the *Index* and read the appropriate portion of the text. When previously covered materials are essential for understanding concepts or findings, a chapter reference and/or summary is usually provided.

I have one additional suggestion. Before starting, jump ahead to the section entitled "Improving Long-Term Memory," in Chapter 8. While you will probably encounter a few unfamiliar technical words, you should be able to use many of the practical tips on learning and remembering discussed here.

I hope you find your introduction to psychology rewarding and enjoyable.

Linda L. Davidoff

Like so many other human undertakings, writing a text involves approximating a set of ideals. Revision provides an opportunity to move closer to those goals. I researched and wrote for more than two full years for the second edition of this book, working particularly hard on these features.

Clarity One major goal of this revision was improvement in the clarity of descriptions, explanations, examples, and organization. Many texts present materials in an abbreviated fashion, omitting logical steps that may be obvious to someone who already understands the topic at hand. I have tried to track down and include these intermediate stages of reasoning. Technical terms are defined—at least roughly—when they first appear and again in the Glossary. When material discussed elsewhere in the text is essential for understanding a given topic, a brief summary or chapter reference is provided. Because the book is clear, it should be easy to read.

Consideration of complexities Though easily read texts are often overly simplistic, the two characteristics are not necessarily associated. In describing what is known about psychological issues, I have tried to be mindful of problems, complexities, remaining puzzles, and the tentative, evolving nature of current information. You will also find that most assertions are documented, though the references are unobtrusive and do not interfere with readability. There are several arguments for rigorous documentation: Students and instructors may check out sources of interest. And students are shown that the author's contentions and conclusions must be supported.

Interest and relevance This book should be enjoyable to read for several reasons. I included inherently interesting material with educational integrity. Chapters frequently begin with short, engrossing case histories. The writing style is informal. Because many human examples are used and everyday applications and implications are highlighted, readers should feel that psychology has a lot of relevance to life.

Cohesiveness Many introductory psychology books ramble; some shift abruptly from topic to topic without trying to tie the material together. I have attempted to be concise and to integrate coherently the diverse findings that are described. The text is cohesive in another sense: the elements of each chapter fit together sequentially. Case studies, research investigations, and controversial issues are treated in context. Readers are directed to relevant illustrations. *Using Psychology* questions (signaled by red triangles) appear after major sections at natural resting places.

Comprehensiveness with a selective focus The second edition of this text contains a greater number of traditional topics than the first edition did. There is more material, for example, on memory, language, thought, ordinary waking consciousness, the brain and behavior, personality theory, personality assessment, abnormal syndromes, sex differences, adjustment throughout the life cycle, adolescence, death, attribution, helping, and love. While the second edition is more comprehensive than the first, the number of topics was deliberately limited. I resisted the temptation to say something about everything because a brief text, such as this one, cannot possibly cover every psychological topic in a meaningful way. Concentrating on fewer subjects gives space for explanations (as well as descriptions), quotations, paraphrased readings, and discussions of applications, implications, controversies, historical perspectives, and key investigations. This focused approach conveys insights into how psychologists explore the issues that interest them, and it portrays psychology as a vital, dynamic enterprise.

Pedagogy Pedagogical devices of various types have been worked out with care and built into this second edition. Because the headings are simple and descriptive, chapter-opening outlines provide an overview that may be useful for review. Advanced organizers—frequently in the form of questions—appear before major text sections, suggesting where we are heading. The Using Psychology exercises (a new feature) can aid learning in several ways. Students answering the questions on their own will see how psychological materials apply to themselves; and they will find it easier to retain important information. Specific Using Psychology questions might be assigned for homework, extra credit, or class discussion. Each chapter ends with a Summary. The Study Guide following the Summary contains lists of key items (terms, research, concepts, and people) as well as a multiple-choice Self-Quiz, Exercises on difficult or potentially confusing materials, Suggested Readings, and Answer Keys. Because the Study Guides are convenient, students are more likely to take advantage of them. The Self-Quiz and Exercise questions have been refined; specific page references for review have been added. The listings in the Suggested Readings sections have been updated and described in some detail to make them enticing. For students who require extra help, the Active Learning Resources Manual contains learning objectives, mastery check questions on text and figures, and formal grass-roots psychology research projects. All this material is either new or extensively revised. The format of the manual makes it easy to reproduce specific items for class handouts.

Educationally oriented illustrations The figures in the second edition were selected for their educational merit. Most of the photographs provide supplementary information, often new perspectives on issues, additional research, examples, or applications. You will also find a relatively large number of charts contrasting approaches that are likely to be confusing. Figure-related questions are included in the Test File so that students may be held responsible for such information.

Sexual, cultural, and racial balance This book avoids sexist language and stereotypes. Masculine and feminine designations are used generically only in quotations from other sources. Feminine and masculine examples alternate. In Chapters 10 and 17, physical and social bases of gender-related behavioral differences are treated at some length; known sex differences in conduct are mentioned in many chapters. The book has ethnic-racial diversity as well, in terms of names, photographs, and illustrations.

Currency A great deal of recent material has been incorporated into the second edition. Still, I have tried not to neglect important historical and classical studies.

Flexibility A number of features make this text adaptable to differing needs. Chapters may be assigned out of order, and many may be omitted entirely. This flexibility exists because necessary background material is summarized and/or referenced by chapter number and because the Glossary and Index are very comprehensive. The most fundamental information, which appears, I believe, in Chapters 1, 2, 3, and 5, should be assigned somewhere near the beginning of the course. And certain material is far more easily understood in a fixed sequence. Motivation should precede Emotion; Personality should precede Abnormal Behavior; Abnormal Behavior should precede The Treatment of Abnormal Behavior. If the topic of statistics (Appendix) is assigned, it probably fits in most logically following Chapter 2.

I have had a vast amount of assistance with this revision. Students in my introductory classes at Essex Community College were astute critics, pointing out unclear or confusing explanations. My colleagues and friends—especially Elaine Bresnahan, Barbara McClinton, Al Marshello, Ann Meier, Jim Sherry, and Ann Kaiser Stearns—provided a great deal of helpful feedback. A number of other instructors who had used the first edition critiqued it or commented on early drafts of second-edition chapters or on an elaborate outline-summary of plans for the second edition. I am grateful to these people for many excellent suggestions: Victor Agruso, Drury College; R. T. Bamber, Lewis and Clark College; John Barlow, Kingsborough Community College; Susan Bennett, Pennsylvania State University, Beaver Campus; Lemuel Cross, Wayne County Community College; C. Edwin Druding, Phoenix College; Judy Hix, Southern Oklahoma City Junior College; Philip Klingensmith, Southwest Missouri State University; Judith Larkin, Canisius College; Anne Maganzini, Bergen Community College; Ruth Maki, North Dakota State University; Wayne Maples, University of Texas, Arlington; Robert Martin, Ball State University; David Miller, Bob Jones University; Rick Mitchell, Harford Community College; Jay Moore, University of Wisconsin, Milwaukee; Cecil Nichols, Miami-Dade Community College; Keith Owen, Austin Community College; Robert Pitcher, Baldwin-Wallace College; Retta Poe, Western Kentucky University; David Quinby, Youngstown State University; Lyle Smith, Dyersburg State Community College; Robert Thibadeau, Rutgers University, Livingston College; David Thomas, Rutgers University, Livingston College; Steven Vincent, Eastern Michigan University; William Wagman, University of Baltimore; and Carol Weiss-Dethy, Tunxis Community College.

The book also benefited greatly from the expertise of the following psychologists, who reviewed early drafts of at least one second-edition chapter: Arthur Bachrach, U.S. Naval Medical Research Institute; John Bare, Carleton College; James Coleman, University of California, Los Angeles; Martin Covington, University of California, Berkeley; Gerald Davison, State University of New York, Stoney Brook; Daniel G. Freedman, University of Chicago; Richard Kasschau, University of Houston; Robert Kozma, University of Michigan; Geoffrey Loftus, University of Washington; Fay-Tyler Norton, Cuyahoga Community College; James Phillips, Oklahoma State University; John Popplestone, University of Akron; Michael Spiegler, Providence College; Timothy Teyler, Northeastern Ohio Universities College of Medicine; and Wilse Webb, University of Florida.

All the McGraw-Hill staff and associates working with me have been pleasant and patient. Jan Yates, Laura Warner, Linda Gutierrez, and Ben Kann have been most closely involved in producing the second edition. The Baltimore County Libraries provided an indispensable interlibrary loan service. I am especially obliged to the librarians at the Cockeysville branch of the Public Library and to Darlene Little of Essex Community College for procuring hundreds and hundreds of books and journals for me. Audrey Eick has been the platonic ideal of a typist, producing almost perfect copy in the least possible amount of time and managing to remain warm, cheerful, conscientious, and entirely reliable.

My friend and husband Martin Davidoff worked diligently and devotedly from beginning to end as editor, critic, consultant, designer of figures, and draftsperson. I am grateful, too, for his continuing encouragement and support. Finally, I want to thank Tillie Davidoff and Alan Davidoff for coming to my aid at numerous points in this project.

Linda L. Davidoff

Psychology: Present and Past

What is psychology all about? Throughout this chapter we focus on this question as we explore the nature and roots of modern psychology. Students come to a first course with varied expectations. Are your ideas about psychology realistic? We begin with a quiz—to give you some information about your current knowledge.

An Introductory Quiz

1. What is the primary subject matter of psychology?
  a. Adjustment and abnormality
  b. Personality, emotion, and motivation
  c. All *human* behavior and mental processes
  d. All behavior and mental processes

2. Psychology overlaps with sociology but not with biology.
True   False

3. How do the majority of psychologists characterize psychology?
  a. Commonsense
  b. A humanitarian endeavor
  c. A philosophical enterprise
  d. A science

4. What is the population that psychologists usually study?
  a. Cats and dogs

b. Monkeys
c. People
d. Pigeons and rats
5. Psychologists are in agreement about the goals of psychology and the methods that should be used to pursue those goals.
True   False

6. Psychologists understand a great many phenomena quite completely.
True   False
7. What activity do psychologists engage in most frequently?
   a. Application and practice
   b. Management and administration

c. Research
d. Teaching
8. Psychologists tend to be specialists in particular subject-matter areas.
True   False
9. "Psychoanalyst" is another name for a psychologist.
True   False

These questions will be answered as we examine the nature of modern psychology.

THE NATURE OF MODERN PSYCHOLOGY

In this section we consider psychology's subject matter, scientific status, use of animals in research, unity, and completeness. We then explore the roles currently played by psychologists in the United States and the differences between psychologists, psychiatrists, and psychoanalysts.

The Subject Matter of Psychology

Psychology (derived from the Greek words meaning "study of the mind or soul") is usually defined today as the science that studies behavior and mental processes. The topics that psychologists investigate include all those listed in the Table of Contents, and then some: development, physiological bases of behavior, learning, perception, consciousness, memory, thought, language, motivation, emotion, intelligence, personality, adjustment, abnormal behavior, treatment of abnormal behavior, social influences, and social behavior. Psychology is often applied in industry, education, engineering, consumer affairs, and many other areas.

Note that psychologists study both biological and social topics. Unlike biologists, *physiological psychologists* or *psychobiologists* focus on *relationships* between behavior and mental functioning on the one hand and biology on the other. And whereas sociologists direct their attention to groups, group processes, and

social forces, *social psychologists* focus on group and social influences on individuals.

Students sometimes view psychologists as primarily concerned with questions about particular people, such as: "Is Molly Jonas capable of doing college-level work?" and "How can Roger and Emma O'Leary solve their marital problems?" While some psychologists fit this image, many are searching for general knowledge and are more likely to be investigating impersonal issues such as: "What conditions improve memory?" "What are the effects of losing sleep?" "Does intelligence decline in old age?" and "Can anxiety lead to illness?" (In later chapters we will look at the tentative answers to these questions.)

Psychology as a Science

We all use what might be called a psychology of commonsense as we struggle along from day to day. We observe and try to explain our own behavior and that of others. We attempt to predict who will do what and when. And we often hold opinions about gaining control over life—the best approach for rearing children, making friends, impressing people, and controlling anger, for instance. But a psychology built from casual observations has some critical weaknesses. Our discussion will be more understandable if you try using commonsense to evaluate the statements in Table 1-1, before reading further.

The type of commonsense psychology that people collect informally leads to an inaccurate body of knowledge for several reasons. Commonsense provides no sound guidelines for evaluating complicated questions. To judge the statements in Table 1-1, you proba-

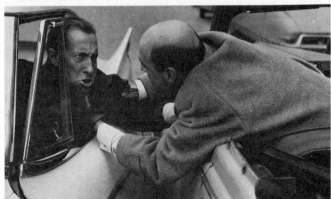

FIGURE 1-1 Psychologists use human and animal research participants to study a wide range of topics, including parent-child relationships, aggression, anxiety, and sex-role behavior. [(a) *R. D. Nadler, Yerkes Primate Research Center*; (b) *de Sazo/Rapho Photo Researchers*; (c) *Ed Lettau/Photo Researchers*; (d) *Elaine M. Ward.*]

a

c

d

b

bly relied on intuition, memories of several personal experiences, or the words of some authority (say, a teacher, friend, or TV celebrity). These are not reliable sources of information, of course. Commonsense principles tend to accumulate haphazardly and uncritically too. People do not systematically evaluate their beliefs to identify the principles that hold true generally and to discard the others. There is evidence, in fact, that ordinary human beings tend to go through life gathering confirming support for beliefs they already

hold and discounting or ignoring negative data [1].

Science provides logical guidelines for evaluating evidence and well-reasoned techniques for verifying principles. Consequently, psychologists usually rely on the *scientific method* for information about behavior and mental processes. They pursue *scientific goals* such as precise description and explanation and ultimately the accumulation of an integrated and internally consistent body of knowledge. They use *scientific procedures*, including sys-

TABLE 1-1 Does "Commonsense" Make Good Psychology?

Use "commonsense" to evaluate these statements:
1. The baby's love for its mother is based on the fulfillment of physical needs, especially hunger. T F
2. People have only five sensory capacities: sight, hearing, touch, smell, and taste. T F
3. Infants are blind at birth. T F
4. Every normal human being dreams. T F
5. Going to sleep after learning is likely to result in better retention than engaging in another activity following learning. T F
6. The more a person memorizes by rote (mechanically by repetition), the better she or he becomes at memorizing. T F
7. The more highly motivated people are, the better they do at solving complex problems. T F
8. People are the only animals that can use a language. T F
9. Individuals with very high intelligence are almost always very creative. T F
10. As a group, women are consistently more romantic than men. T F

The correct responses appear in the Answer Keys of the Study Guide, which will also direct you to the chapter in which each topic is discussed.

tematic observation and experimentation, to gather publicly observable data. They attempt to abide by *scientific principles*. They try, for example, to shield their work from their personal biases and to remain open-minded. We will look more closely at scientific goals, methods, and principles in Chapter 2. While you may not have expected to find psychologists so concerned about being scientific, there are excellent reasons for this approach, which should be clear once you've finished Chapter 2. Incidentally, because psychologists see themselves as scientists, we will use the terms *psychologist* and *behavioral scientist* interchangeably. The broader label *social scientist* refers to all who study society or social behavior: psychologists, sociologists, anthropologists, historians, and others.

Psychology and Animals

Goldfish, cockroaches, worms, crabs, bats, rats, pigeons, armadillos, dogs, cats, monkeys, people, and many other animals serve as *subjects*, or research participants, in psychological investigations. Rats and pigeons are probably the most prevalent participants in laboratory research [2]. Students are often surprised and sometimes disheartened to find so many studies on such animals. Behavioral scientists use simple organisms as research subjects for a number of reasons. Sometimes they are genuinely interested in the conduct of the gerbil or the dove or the stickleback fish or the chimpanzee. These are legitimate concerns. As we defined it, psychology is the science of *all* behavior and mental functioning.

Many, perhaps even most, psychologists who study nonhuman animals are interested in understanding people but choose to work with simpler organisms instead. Why? One reason is ethics. There are many types of research that cannot morally be conducted with human beings. To understand how the brain affects behavior and functioning, behavioral scientists sometimes remove specific parts of it—in nonhuman animals, of course—and observe the results. Through breeding programs researchers can arrange the genetics of certain animals and see how heredity influences particular characteristics. Similarly, using laboratory animal subjects, psychologists can systematically explore the consequences of potentially destructive experiences, such as isolation, crowding, punishment, malnutrition, and stress. When behavioral scientists observe people who have endured brain damage, malnutrition, crowding, or a catastrophic flood, say, many factors are mixed together. In such cases, it is often impossible to be certain that a particular effect is due to a particular cause. (See Figure 1-2.)

Nonhuman animals have undeniable practical advantages as well. They are cooperative, convenient, and easily studied for long periods. The big brown bat, for example, weighs 25 grams (nearly an ounce), eats very little, has minimal housing requirements, demands no salary, needs no deception, and arrives on time. If the psychologist goes on vacation, the bat can be boxed (a cigar box will do) and stored several months in a refrigerator with a little water. When the researcher returns, the bat is easily thawed in an hour and ready for study [3]. Further, specific animals have advantages for particular kinds of research. Pigeons, for instance, have excellent vision, especially color vision. Consequently, they make good candidates for studies of perception. Rats are fine subjects for genetic research because a new generation appears approximately every three months. Even the most enthusiastic and dedicated behavioral scientist could not study more than three generations of people in a lifetime.

Finally, some investigators argue that basic behavioral and mental processes are easier to detect in simple creatures than in complex ones. They assume that many psychological principles apply to all animals, including people. To put it another way, findings about less complicated organisms may *generalize* to human beings. Undoubtedly, some principles do have general value. For example, rats, pigeons, and people condition in similar ways, as we will see in Chapter 5. But few psychologists believe that principles derived from nonhuman animal research can explain complex types of human functioning such as abstract reasoning, language, personality, and social behavior.

Throughout this text we will be concerned primarily with people. We will examine research on less complex organisms only when it advances our understanding of human beings.

Psychology: A Unified, Complete Science?

Psychology is neither a unified nor a complete body of knowledge. Consider unity first. Behavioral scientists do not agree on fundamental assumptions about goals, primary subject matter, and ideal methods, as we will soon see. What's more, the diverse subjects that psychologists research are hard to tie together neatly. Like other sciences, psychology is far from being complete. There are many important phenomena that we do not understand. So do not expect to find in

FIGURE 1-2 Many interacting conditions influence behavior in natural settings. This Indian family of twenty-one members lives together in a single room in Bombay. Competiton for available resources, lack of privacy, poverty, and the diverse stresses associated with poverty probably accompany the high-density living arrangement. By studying simpler animals in controlled environments, psychologists attempt to isolate the effects of specific influences. [Top: *John Oldenkamp*; bottom: *Silverstone Magnum*.]

psychology a single approach to the subject matter or answers to all your questions.

American Psychologists Today

More than 47,000 Americans (perhaps as many as 70,000) currently identify themselves as psychologists [4]. As pictured by a survey of the American Psychological Association in the early 1970s, behavioral scientists are a varied group. They range widely in age and reside in every American state and possession. Close to 70 percent of them hold the doctor of philosophy or a similar professional degree; another 30 percent hold a master's degree. About 25 percent are women [5].

TABLE 1-2 Major Specialists in Psychology

Specialist	Percentage of total (approximate)	Primary activities
Clinical psychologist	33	Assesses and treats people with psychological problems; conducts research on normal and abnormal behavior, diagnosis, and treatment.
Counseling psychologist	12	Counsels people with mild adjustment problems and promotes achievement in educational and work settings; combines research, consultation, and treatment.
Experimental psychologist	9	Designs and conducts research in a specific area, such as learning, sensation, motivation, language, or the physiological bases of behavior.
School psychologist	9	Increases the intellectual, social, and emotional development of children in schools by establishing programs, consulting, doing research, training teachers, and treating youngsters with problems.
Educational psychologist	7	Develops, designs, and evaluates materials and procedures for educational programs.
Industrial and organizational psychologist	6	Combines research, consultation, and program development to enhance efficiency, satisfaction, and morale on the job.
Social psychologist	5	Studies how people influence one another.
Developmental psychologist	4	Studies changes in behavior with age.
Personality psychologist	2	Studies how and why people differ from one another and how those differences may be assessed.
Community psychologist	2	Treats people with psychological problems within the community; initiates community action and develops community programs to enhance mental health.
Psychometric (quantitative) psychologist	1	Develops and evaluates tests; designs research to measure behavioral and mental functions.
Engineering psychologist	1	Designs and evaluates environments, machinery, training devices, programs, and systems to improve the relationship between people and their environment.

Sources: Boneau, C. A., & Cuca, J. M. An overview of psychology's human resources: Characteristics and salaries from the 1972 APA survey. *American Psychologist,* 1974, **29**(11), 821–840; *Careers in psychology.* Washington, D.C.: American Psychological Association, 1975.

Do psychologists specialize? Generally, they must. As we mentioned before, psychology is a large collection of subjects. The research literature on each topic is vast and grows larger each year. No single person could possibly master all of psychology. It is doubtful, in fact, that any individual could fully master even one area. So behavioral scientists concentrate on one or two subjects typically. They are often known, incidentally, by the topics which they study or the settings where they work (as shown in Table 1-2).

What do psychologists usually do? Close to 39 percent apply psychology in practical settings (offering counseling, rehabilitation, psychotherapy, and diagnosis, for example, or designing programs for mental health clinics, schools, industrial plants, or prisons). About 25 percent primarily teach. Another 17 percent mainly do research. Some 19 percent direct clinics, research projects, consultant agencies, training programs, and the like. Figure 1-3 shows the major settings where behavioral scientists work.

Psychologists, Psychiatrists, and Psychoanalysts

Many people confuse psychologists, psychiatrists, and psychoanalysts. It should now be clear that psychologists play various roles, and many do not fit the popular stereotype at all. Clinical psychologists, psychiatrists, and psychoanalysts often fill similar jobs. All three professionals may work in mental health settings, diagnosing and treating people with mild and severe psychological problems. The major differences among these specialists come from their training. *Clinical psychologists* usually hold a doctor of philosophy (Ph.D.) degree in psychology and serve a one-year internship in a mental health setting. Generally, they spend about five years in graduate school learning about normal and abnormal behavior, diagnosis (including testing), and treatment. They are trained to conduct research to further the understanding of these subjects too. After completing their education, clinical psychologists work as prac-

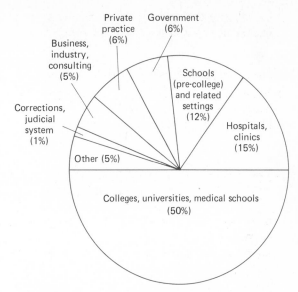

FIGURE 1-3 Major employment settings of psychologists.

titioners in clinics, hospitals, and private practice and as teachers and investigators of behavior in colleges, universities, and medical schools.

Psychiatrists, in contrast, go through medical school and emerge with a doctor of medicine (M.D.) degree. Then, to qualify as psychiatrists, they serve an approximately three-year residency in a mental health setting, typically a hospital. There they are trained to detect and treat emotional disturbances, using psychological methods as well as drugs, surgery, and other medical procedures.

About 10 percent of all psychiatrists in the United States call themselves *psychoanalysts*. In addition to their psychiatric training, they have intensively studied Freud's personality theories and treatment methods (known as *psychoanalysis*) in a recognized training institute and have been psychoanalyzed themselves. In theory, anyone can become a psychoanalyst by graduating from a psychoanalytic institution and participating in psychoanalysis. In practice, most training schools accept only physicians. Consequently, in America psychoanalysis is essentially a subdivision of psychiatry. ▲

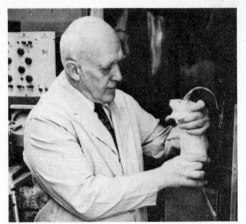

FIGURE 1-4 Psychologists play varied roles, including those of researcher and psychotherapist. Psychologist Neal Miller is shown working in his laboratory at Rockefeller University. Psychologist Ann Stearns counsels a patient in her office in Baltimore. [Left: *Dr. Neal E. Miller, The Rockefeller University*; right: *Dr. Ann Kaiser Stearns*.]

▲ USING PSYCHOLOGY

1. Check your answers to the introductory quiz. Were your ideas about psychology realistic? (The answers are given in the Answer Keys.)

2. Explain in your own words what's wrong with using commonsense alone to build a body of accurate information about behavior.

3. People sometimes contend that psychologists should quit studying the behavior of animals because no useful information can be obtained. Argue against this position.

4. Ask several friends or family members if they know the differences between psychologists, psychiatrists, and psychoanalysts. If they don't (and few people seem to), enlighten them.

FIVE MOVEMENTS THAT SHAPED MODERN PSYCHOLOGY

People, as we know them today (*homo sapiens*, to be precise), appeared on earth about 100,000 years ago [6]. They have probably been trying to understand themselves ever since. Aristotle (384–322 B.C.), the Greek philosopher, is sometimes called the Father of Psychology. But speculation about psychological matters did not begin with the Greek thinker. Hundreds of years before Aristotle, the earliest philosophers on record were dealing with these topics.

We begin our brief survey of the shaping of psychology at a much later point in history—in the last part of the nineteenth century, when the field called psychology emerged. Physiologists were just beginning to use scientific methods to study the brain, nerves, and sense organs. Most important, perhaps, the philosopher and physicist Gustav Fechner (1801–1887) had shown how scientific methods could be applied to the study of mental processes. Early in the 1850s Fechner became interested in the relationship between physical stimulation and sensation. He was especially fascinated by the sensitivity of the human senses. How bright must a star be to be seen? How loud must a noise be to be heard? How heavy must a touch be to be felt? Fechner devised the necessary techniques to find precise answers to questions like these. When Fechner's major work, *Elements of Psychophysics*, was published in 1860, it showed how experimental and mathematical procedures could be used to study the human mind. About twenty years later, a German physiologist, Wilhelm Wundt, founded a discipline that he eventually called psychology.

Wilhelm Wundt, Edward Titchener, and Structuralism

Originally trained as a physician, Wilhelm Wundt (1832–1920) (shown in Figure 1-5) taught physiology for seventeen years at the University of Heidelberg in Germany. Early in his career he showed an intense interest in mental processes. At this time the field of psychology had no domain of its own; its subject matter belonged to philosophy. Wundt's ambition was to establish an independent identity for psychology. With this goal in mind, he left Heidelberg to accept the chairpersonship of the Philosophy Department at the University of Leipzig in Germany. Four years later, in 1879, Wundt founded the first experimental psychology laboratory in the world, thus conferring on psychology full-fledged scientific status.

Wilhelm Wundt was a solemn, scholarly man who published more than 50,000 pages before he died. He believed that psychologists should investigate the *elementary processes of human consciousness* (immediate experience), their combinations, and relationships much as chemists study the fundamental elements of matter. What did Wundt mean by elementary processes of human consciousness? In the words of Edward Titchener, a British psychologist and one of Wundt's ablest students:

The world of psychology contains looks and tones and feels; it is the world of dark and light, of noise and silence, of rough and smooth; its space is sometimes large and sometimes small, as everyone knows who in adult life has gone back to his childhood's home; its time is sometimes short and sometimes long. . . . It contains also the thoughts,

FIGURE 1-5 Wilhelm Wundt, a physician who taught physiology, established in 1879 what is considered the first experimental psychology laboratory in the world. [*The Bettmann Archive.*]

emotions, memories, imagination, volitions [choices] that you naturally ascribe to mind. . . . [7]

Wundt felt that it was particularly important to study central mental operations such as attention, intentions, and goals.

How were psychologists supposed to study these elementary processes of consciousness? Wundt and his followers devised a method called *analytic introspection*, a formal type of self-observation. Observing scientists were carefully trained to answer specific, well-defined questions about their own experiences in the laboratory. They were considered unfit to provide data for publication until they had made 10,000 observations [8]! What do we mean by the term "observation"? Consider an example. In one study Wundt and his colleagues listened to the beats of a metronome, the mechanical instrument, pictured in Figure 1-6, that clicks repeatedly at an adjustable pace and is used by music students to help

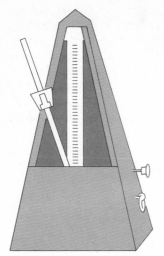

FIGURE 1-6 A metronome.

them hold specific rhythms. As soon as a pattern of sounds ended, the psychologists immediately reported their perceptions. Wundt recorded that he had a feeling of slight tension while waiting for the clicks to begin, a sense of mild excitement when the rate increased, and the sensation of an agreeable whole when the sounds ended [9]. Proceeding in this general way, Wundt and his followers analyzed many kinds of sensation patterns into their component parts. Titchener eventually published a summary of the basic "sensation qualities" that had been discovered. The list included 32,820 sensation qualities for the eye, 11,600 for the ear, 4 for the skin, and 1 for the joints. Presumably, each element could be blended with others in varied ways to form perceptions and ideas [10].

In 1892 Titchener migrated to the United States and took charge of a new experimental psychology laboratory at Cornell University. There he spread Wundt's ideas and became the leader of the movement known as *structuralism*. The structuralists held these beliefs: (1) psychologists should study human consciousness, particularly sensory experiences; (2) they should use painstaking analytic introspective laboratory studies; and (3) they should analyze the mental processes into

elements, discover their combinations and connections, and locate related structures in the nervous system.

Structuralism had some clear limitations. First, structuralist psychologists emphasized one method of study, formal introspection. It was a dull, unreliable procedure. Moreover, it automatically excluded from study the experiences of children and nonhuman animals, since they could not be properly trained. Second, structuralist psychologists considered complex phenomena such as thinking, language, morality, and abnormality inappropriate for introspective studies and consequently outside the realm of science. (They did believe that complicated topics like these could be handled by logical analysis or casual observation.) Third, the structuralists were unwilling to address themselves to practical issues. Other movements arose to remedy these shortcomings.

William James and Functionalism

William James (1842–1910), one of the most influential of American psychologists (pictured in Figure 1-7), taught philosophy and psychology at Harvard University for thirty-five years. James did not identify with any movement. His special "system" of psychology evolved from keen observations of himself and others. He opposed structuralism because he saw it as artificial, narrow, and essentially inaccurate. Consciousness, James argued, is "personal and unique," "continually changing," "evolving over time," and "selective" in choosing from among the stimuli that bombard it. Above all, it helps people *adapt* to their environments [11].

In the early 1900s several psychologists at the University of Chicago (including John Dewey, the famous philosopher and educator) were strongly influenced by James's views. Like James, they were interested in the mental processes, particularly in how they *functioned* to help people survive in a dangerous world. Although the *functionalists*, as are attractive characteristics, they make it hard for movements to survive intact. Eventually, functionalism was replaced by a new American movement, *behaviorism.* Many of the functionalists' assumptions survived and are incorporated in the current approach known as *cognitive psychology*, which will be discussed later.

John Watson and Behaviorism

John Watson (1878–1958), pictured in Figure 1-8, completed his doctorate in the field of

FIGURE 1-7 William James, an outstanding figure in the history of psychology, believed that psychologists should study the functioning of mental processes. James wrote beautifully and vividly about many psychological concepts. His introductory textbook, *Principles of Psychology*, has been a source of inspiration for several generations of behavioral scientists. [*Culver Pictures, Inc.*]

they were called, disagreed with one another on many issues, they were strongly united in their opposition to structuralism. They shared these additional beliefs: (1) psychologists should study the *functioning* of mental processes and many other topics, including the behavior of children and simple animals, abnormality, and individual differences between people; (2) they should use *informal introspection* (self-observation and self-report) and *objective methods* (those relatively free of bias) such as experimentation; and (3) psychological knowledge should be applied to practical matters such as education, law, and business.

On many basic issues the psychologists in the functionalist movement went their separate ways. Although diversity and flexibility

FIGURE 1-8 John Watson, the founder of behaviorism, was determined to make psychology into a respected science. His position about the environment's impact on the individual is expressed in his famous declaration: "Give me a dozen healthy infants well formed and my own specified world to bring them up in and I'll guarantee to take any one at random and train him to become any type of specialist I might select—doctor, lawyer, artist, merchant-chief, and yes, even beggarman and thief, regardless of his talents, penchants, tendencies, abilities, vocations, and race of his ancestors [13]." [*Historical Pictures Service.*]

animal psychology at the University of Chicago under a functionalist professor. As a young man, he was one of numerous behavioral scientists dissatisfied with the prevailing practices of American psychology. One of Watson's major complaints about structuralism and functionalism was this: Facts about consciousness could *not* be tested and reproduced by all trained observers, because they depended on each person's idiosyncratic impressions. He felt that introspection was a serious bar to progress. He expressed himself colorfully:

All that introspective psychology has been able to contribute is the assertion that mental states are made up of several thousand irreducible units like redness, greenness, coolness, warmth, and the like. . . . Whether there are ten irreducible sensations or a hundred thousand (even granting their existence) . . . matters not one whit to that organized body of world-wide data we call science. [12]

Watson resolved to make psychology a respectable science like the physical sciences. He felt psychologists should study *observable* behavior and adopt *objective* methods. In 1912 when Watson began lecturing and writing to publicize his views, the movement known as *behaviorism* is said to have been born.

Many young American psychologists were attracted to the behaviorist movement—partly because of Watson's forceful prose and flamboyant manner. In some form or another, behaviorism dominated American psychology for about thirty years. The early behaviorists subscribed to these beliefs:

1. Psychologists should study environmental events (*stimuli*) and observable behavior (*responses*).
2. Experience is a more important influence on behavior, abilities, and traits than heredity. For that reason, learning is an especially significant topic for investigation.
3. Introspection should be abandoned for objective methods (namely, experimentation, observation, and testing).
4. Psychologists should aim at the description, explanation, prediction, and control of behavior. They should also undertake practical tasks such as

advising parents, lawmakers, educators, and business people.
5. The behavior of lesser animals should be investigated (along with human behavior) because simple organisms are easier to study and understand than complex ones.

Behaviorism began as an angry movement. As it evolved, its philosophy was broadened. The behavioristic approach shaped modern psychology and continues to exert a profound impact. You may have noticed that our discussion of the nature of modern psychology was strongly influenced by behavioristic ideas.

Max Wertheimer and Gestalt Psychology

While behaviorism was flourishing in America, gestalt psychology (*gestalt* is the German word for shape, pattern, or structure) was growing up in Germany. As the name suggests, the gestalt psychologists believed that experiences carried with them a quality of wholeness or structure. Like behaviorism, gestalt psychology arose, in part, as a protest against structuralism, particularly the practice of reducing complex experiences to simple elements. (In their obsession with precision and observable behavior, the behaviorists were guilty of this policy as well.)

The gestalt movement had a number of leaders, including Wolfgang Köhler, Kurt Koffka, and Max Wertheimer. The movement began, most historians claim, in 1912 when Max Wertheimer (1880–1943), a German psychologist then at the University of Frankfurt (see Figure 1-9), published a report on studies of *apparent movement*, perceived motion where none is present in actuality. The "moving" news bulletin in Times Square in New York City provides an example of apparent movement. In reality, thousands of lights are flashing on and off; nothing is moving. Motion pictures are a more common illustration of this phenomenon. Here a rapidly presented series of still photos gives the illusion of continuous, uninterrupted action. To demonstrate apparent movement, Wertheimer stationed two electric light bulbs several feet apart on the edge of a table, then mounted a vertical rod near the center of the table. The setup is shown in Figure 1-10. When both lights were turned on in a dimly lit room, two separate shadows of the rod were cast on the wall. But if the lights were alternately switched on and off at certain speeds, observers reported seeing a single shadow moving back and forth.

What do Wertheimer's studies of apparent movement have to do with gestalt psychology? For the first time, presumably, it had been asserted and demonstrated that the whole is different from the sum of its parts and that the parts have to be "seen in terms of their place, role, and function in the whole of which they are parts [14]." Apparent movement could not be understood simply by analyzing its components. At any given instant one light bulb was on, the other off, and only one fixed shadow existed. Yet observers saw motion. To understand the illusion, all the interacting elements in the situation (including the physiological functioning of the observer's eyes and brain as well as the light pattern) had to be taken into account. The whole was clearly different from the sum of its parts. This statement became the slogan of gestalt psychology.

The study of apparent movement reveals some additional distinguishing characteristics of gestalt psychology:

1. Apparent movement occurs when people interpret sensory data. The meanings that human beings impose on the objects and events of their world *(subjective experience)* is a theme that was emphasized by gestalt psychologists. In the beginning they were especially interested in understanding perception, problem solving, and thinking.

2. To investigate apparent movement, Wertheimer had his research subjects report what they saw (a type of *informal introspection*). Gestalt psychologists believed that behavioral scientists had to study people's conscious subjective experiences. They encouraged the use of objective methods too.

FIGURE 1-9 Max Wertheimer's studies of apparent movement supported the gestalt belief that the whole is very different from the sum of its parts. [*United Press International Photo.*]

FIGURE 1-10 The apparatus Max Wertheimer used to demonstrate apparent movement.

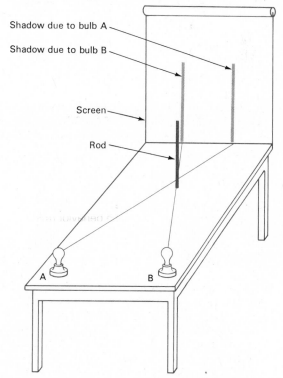

Shadow due to bulb A

Shadow due to bulb B

Screen

Rod

A   B

The gestalt movement was a strong, unified one. Its philosophy shaped the direction of psychology in Germany and later influenced American psychology (particularly, the study of perception). As we will soon see, two contemporary approaches—humanistic and cognitive—show gestalt psychology's unmistakable imprint.

Sigmund Freud and Psychoanalytic Theory

If you've never studied psychology before, the chances are you have not heard of Wundt, Watson, or Wertheimer, and maybe James until now. But you're probably acquainted with Sigmund Freud (1856–1939), the Viennese physician who specialized in treating problems of the nervous system, particularly neurotic disorders. Neurotic disorders, as you may already know, are characterized by excessive anxiety and, in some cases, by depression, fatigue, insomnia, paralysis, or other

symptoms related to conflict or stress. Freud's photograph is shown in Figure 1-11. His name and ideas are so familiar to the general public that psychology is sometimes equated with *psychoanalytic theory*, the general name for Freudian ideas about personality, abnormality, and treatment. Psychoanalytic theory is, of course, only one psychological theory. The psychoanalytic movement did not resemble the others that we have described because Freud never attempted to influence academic psychology. His aim was to provide aid for suffering people. Since psychoanalytic theory has been immensely influential inside psychology and has attracted a large following among behavioral scientists, we will consider it a psychology movement.

In Freud's day, medical doctors did not understand neurotic problems or know how to treat them. Freud soon discovered that ministering to the neurotic person's physical symptoms was useless; he began looking around for an appropriate psychological therapy. Several

FIGURE 1-11 Sigmund Freud, the originator of psychoanalytic theory, in his study with his chow dog. While psychoanalysis began as a way of treating neurotic patients, it developed into a new conception of human nature. [*Historical Pictures Service.*]

colleagues were hypnotizing their neurotic patients and encouraging them to "talk out" their problems. When these patients discussed and relived the traumatic experiences that seemed to be associated with their symptoms, they frequently improved. Freud adopted hypnosis for a while but found it unsatisfactory. Not everyone could attain a trancelike state; and hypnosis appeared to result in temporary cures with new symptoms breaking out later on. Eventually, Freud developed a new procedure, *free association,* which served many of the same purposes while having fewer problems. Patients relaxed on a couch and were encouraged to say whatever came into their minds. They were also asked to report their dreams. Freud analyzed all the material that emerged, looking for wishes, fears, conflicts, thoughts, and memories which were beyond the patient's awareness. In Freud's words:

When I set myself the task of bringing to light what human beings keep hidden within them, not by the compelling power of hypnosis, but by observing what they say and what they show, I thought the task was a harder one than it really is. He that has eyes to see and ears to hear may convince himself that no mortal can keep a secret. If the lips are silent, he chatters with his finger tips; betrayal oozes out of him at every pore. And thus the task of making conscious the most hidden recesses of the mind is one which is quite possible to accomplish. [15]

In sum, we might say that Freud treated his patients by trying to bring what was unconscious to consciousness.

Drawing on thousands of hours of careful listening and analysis (and self-observation, as well), Freud formulated hypotheses, or hunches, about personality. He attempted to test his ideas as he treated people—by comparing his hypotheses with further observa-

tions. Freud tried to explain every fact, no matter how trivial it appeared. He insisted that all the details fit together tightly. Proceeding in this manner, he formed comprehensive theories about normal and abnormal personality, which he continued to revise throughout his lifetime as clinical observations warranted. (We will look at Freud's ideas in more depth in Chapters 13 through 16.)

In the meantime, you should know that Freud's followers held these general beliefs:

1. Psychologists should study the laws and determinants of personality (normal and abnormal) and devise treatment methods for personality disorders.

2. Unconscious motives, memories, fears, conflicts, and frustrations are important aspects of personality. Bringing these phenomena to consciousness is crucial therapy for personality disorders.

3. Personality is formed during early childhood. Exploring memories of the first five years of life is essential for treatment.

4. Personality is most suitably studied within the context of a long-term intimate relationship between patient and therapist. During the course of that association, patients report thoughts, feelings, memories, fantasies, and dreams (*informal introspection,* once again) while the therapist analyzes and interprets the material and observes the patient's behavior.

Psychoanalytic theory created a revolution in the conception and treatment of emotional problems and generated interest among academic psychologists in unconscious motivation, personality, abnormal behavior, and child development. As we will see, psychoanalytic ideas are still very much alive today in both their original form and numerous modifications.

Table 1-3 compares the past movements that have been described. ▲

TABLE 1-3 A Comparison of Five
Past Movements in Psychology

Structuralism
Subject matter: Elementary processes of consciousness (especially sensory experiences), their combinations, and relationships to nervous systems structures
Major goal: Knowledge
Research methods emphasized: Analytic introspection
Population studied: Trained observers (psychologists themselves)

Functionalism
Subject matter: The functioning of mental processes, particularly as they help people survive and adapt
Major goals: Knowledge, application
Research methods emphasized: Informal introspection; objective methods
Population studied: Primarily human adults; occasionally children and less complex animals

Behaviorism
Subject matter: Stimuli and observable responses; learning emphasized
Major goals: Knowledge, application
Research methods emphasized: Objective methods
Population studied: People and other animals.

Gestalt psychology
Subject matter: Subjective whole human experience; perception, thinking, and problem solving emphasized
Major goal: Knowledge
Research methods emphasized: Informal introspection; objective methods
Population studied: People (occasionally other primates such as chimpanzees)

Psychoanalytic theory
Subject matter: Normal and abnormal personality (laws, determinants in early childhood, and unconscious aspects emphasized); treatment of abnormal behavior
Major goals: Service, knowledge
Research methods emphasized:
  Patients: Informal introspection to reveal conscious experiences
  Therapists: Logical analysis and observation to uncover unconscious materials
Population studied: Patients (usually adults)

FOUR CURRENT VIEWS OF MODERN PSYCHOLOGY

The science of psychology continues to grow and change; and it cannot yet be cast into a single mold. Although contemporary psychologists rarely follow specific movements, they disagree on some fundamental philosophical issues and approach psychology in distinctly different ways. Even today there is no consensus on goals, appropriate subject matter, or the best methods for studying psychological phenomena. Many behavioral scientists identify to some degree with one of four major points of view—psychoanalytic, neobehavioristic, cognitive, or humanistic. Some favor an *eclectic approach* or a combination of viewpoints.

The Psychoanalytic Point of View

Many psychologists, especially those who study personality, adjustment, abnormality, and treatment and those who work in clinic settings with psychologically troubled people, take the psychoanalytic point of view. Although there are wide individual variations in their specific beliefs, psychoanalytically oriented psychologists usually hold the views discussed in the preceding section. In the words of Erich Fromm, a psychologist and psychoanalyst:

The essence of psychoanalytic procedure . . . is observing facts. Nobody is as minutely observed as is a patient during hundreds of hours of psychoanalytic interviews. The procedure of psychoanalysis is to draw inferences [conclusions] from the observed facts, to form hypotheses, to compare the hypotheses with further facts which one finds, and eventually to coalesce [bring together] a body of material sufficient to recognize the possibility of the hypotheses, if not their verification. [16]

The following excerpt from Sigmund Freud's *Psychopathology of Everyday Life* illustrates the psychoanalytic approach. As you read, try to pinpoint the distinctive features of the psychoanalytic perspective.

Studying Slips of the Tongue: The Psychoanalytic Approach of Sigmund Freud

"Among the examples of the mistakes in speech collected by me I can scarcely find one in which I would be obliged to attribute the speech disturbance simply and solely to [the] contact effect of sound. Almost invariably I discover, besides this, a disturbing influence of something outside of the intended speech. The disturbing element is either a single unconscious thought, which comes to light through the speech blunder, and can only be brought to consciousness through a searching analysis, or it is a more general psychic motive, which directs itself against the entire speech." [Freud discusses twenty-three examples, including the following.]

"(*d*) A woman, speaking about a game invented by her children and called by them 'the man in the box' said 'the manx in the boc.' I could readily understand her mistake. It was while analyzing her dream, in which her husband is depicted as very generous in money matters—just the reverse of reality—that she made this speech blunder. The day before she had asked for a new set of furs, which her husband denied her, claiming that he could not afford to spend so much money. She upbraided him for his stinginess. 'For putting away so much into the strong box,' and mentioned a friend whose husband has not nearly his income, and yet he presented his wife with a mink coat for her birthday. The mistake is now comprehensible. The word manx reduces itself to the minks which she longs for, and the box refers to her husband's stinginess."

"(*e*) A similar mechanism is shown in the mistake of another patient whose memory deserted her in the midst of a long forgotten childish reminiscense [memory]. Her memory failed to inform her on which part of the body the prying and lustful hand of another had touched her. Soon thereafter she visited one of her friends with whom she discussed summer homes. Asked where her cottage in M was located, she answered 'Near the mountain loin' instead of 'mountain lane.' . . . Hence I find that it is not the contact effects of the sound but the thoughts outside the intended speech which determine the origin of the speech blunder [17]."

The Neobehavioristic Point of View

Today the behavioristic approach is broader and more flexible than in Watson's day. Modern behaviorists still investigate stimuli, observable responses, and learning. They also increasingly study complicated phenomena that cannot be directly observed, such as love, stress, empathy, trust, and personality. This new type of behaviorism is sometimes called *neobehaviorism* ("neo" means new) to distinguish it from Watson's orthodox approach. (We will use the terms "neobehaviorism" and "behaviorism" interchangeably throughout the text.) The major characteristic of the neobehavioristic position is its insistence on asking precise, well-delineated questions, using objective methods, and doing careful research.

In the following passage Jay Weiss, a neobehavioristic psychologist at Rockefeller University in New York City, describes how he researched the question, "How does the psychological factor, predictability of stress, affect the formation of stomach ulcers?" As you read, try to specify the distinctive characteristics of the neobehavioristic philosophy.

Investigating Ulcers in the Laboratory: The Approach of a Neobehaviorist

An intriguing medical idea is that psychological processes affect disease. "Recently I have been studying the influence of psychological factors on the development of gastric lesions or stomach ulcers," Weiss writes. "[In one study] two rats received electric shocks simultaneously through electrodes placed on their tail, while a third rat served as a control and received no shocks. Of the two rats receiving shocks, one heard a beeping tone that began 10 seconds before each shock. The other rat also heard the tone, but the tone sounded randomly with respect to the shock. Thus both these animals received the same [identical] shocks, but one could predict when the shocks would occur whereas the other could not. Since the physical stressor was the same for the two animals, any consistent difference between them in the amount of ulceration would be the result of the difference in the predictability of the stressor, the psychological variable being studied."

"As was to be expected," Weiss continues, "the control rats that received no shock developed very little gastric ulceration or none. A striking result of the experiment was that rats able to predict when the shocks would occur also showed relatively little ulceration whereas those that received the same shocks unpredictably showed a considerable amount of ulceration." Figure 1-12 illustrates this finding. In short, Weiss's results support the idea that the psychological variable of predictability was the main determinant of ulcer severity, not shock itself [18].

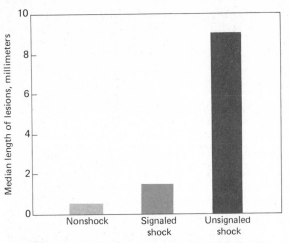

FIGURE 1-12 Rats that can predict when shocks will occur develop less gastric ulceration than animals that receive the same shocks unpredictably. [*Adapted from Psychological factors in stress and disease by J. M. Weiss. Copyright © 1972 by Scientific American, Inc. All rights reserved.*]

The Cognitive Point of View

From the 1930s to the 1960s "respectable" American psychologists talked little and cautiously (if at all) about the mind, imagination, thinking, making choices, solving problems, and similar *cognitive processes*, or mental activities. Watson's behaviorism made these topics taboo. The early behaviorists treated people as if they were "black boxes" which could be understood simply by measuring the stimuli that went in and the responses that came out. In the early 1960s *cognitive psychologists* began to rebel against the old behavioristic model. They insisted that psychologists had to come to understand what was going on inside the black box—particularly, the operations of the mind.

Cognitive psychologists hold these beliefs:

1. Behavioral scientists should study mental processes such as thought, perception, memory, attention, problem solving, and language.
2. They should aim at acquiring precise knowledge of how these processes operate and how they are applied in everyday life.

3. Informal introspection should be used, particularly to develop hunches, whereas objective methods are preferred to confirm these impressions.

Note that cognitive psychology clearly combines aspects of functionalism, gestalt psychology, and behaviorism. The paraphrased account that follows describes the cognitive research of Ulric Neisser, William Hirst, and Elizabeth Spelke on dividing attention and doing several tasks at once. As you read, try to identify the characteristic features of the cognitive approach.

Dividing One's Attention: The Approach of Cognitive Psychologists

Is it possible to attend at the same time to two very different things? Or can a second task be carried out only automatically, outside of consciousness? In a recent study, two college students worked an hour a day for an entire semester to help us answer this question. They read stories silently while simultaneously copying words that the experimenter dictated. Each word was presented as soon as the preceding one had been copied. At first the students found the dual task difficult; and they read much more slowly than previously. But, after about six weeks of practice, reading speeds returned to normal. Careful tests showed that the subjects fully comprehended what they read.

Not only did the research participants learn to read and write at the same time, but also to understand what they were writing—while reading. In a later phase of the experiment, the subjects were given lists of words which fell into one of two categories—say, animal and furniture names. The students were asked to write down the category from which the dictated word had come, rather than the word itself. After a great deal of practice, this task could be combined with reading at normal speed and comprehension.

Carefully controlled experiments with additional subjects confirmed that (1) people were not merely switching back and forth quickly between the two tasks and (2) individuals were actively absorbing information during both reading and writing.

These studies probably don't have any practical applications. Simultaneous reading and writing is just too difficult to ever become a popular pastime. But the investigation does have theoretical implications. The fact that it is possible to perform two complicated mental procedures simultaneously suggests that human cognitive activity is usefully thought of as a collection of acquired skills, rather than as the operation of a fixed mechanism. So far as we know, no

FIGURE 1-13 As long as activities are fairly simple and relatively automatic—such as walking, singing, and talking—people have little trouble combining them. The research of Ulric Neisser and his colleagues suggests that people can be trained to perform complex actions simultaneously too. In real life, this same type of learning sometimes occurs. Translators at the United Nations, for instance, learn to divide their attention between translating and reporting one idea while listening for the next one. [*M. Tzovaras/United Nations.*]

rigid machinery limits the amount of information that can be picked up from one source while attending to another. Performance depends instead on learned skills. Practice, in this instance, can enable people to do what seems impossible at first glance.

"In retrospect, perhaps we should not have been surprised by this result. Equally dramatic improvements occur in more mundane skills. When one first learns to drive, for example, control of the car requires one's full attention. Later, the practiced driver can shift gears and turn corners and overtake trucks while arguing vigorously about (say) psychological theory. Many skilled typists can carry on a conversation while typing from copy, but it seems unlikely that they could do so without practice; certainly I can't [19]." (See Figure 1-13.)

The Humanistic Point of View

Humanistically oriented psychologists are united by a common goal: they want to humanize psychology. That is, they want to make psychology the study of "what it means to be alive as a human being [20]." They come from diverse backgrounds and vary considerably in their individual beliefs. Still, most humanistically oriented psychologists share these general attitudes.

1. Although behavioral scientists must gather knowledge, their major goal should be service. Psychologists should help people understand themselves and develop to their fullest potential. They should aim at expanding and enriching human lives.

2. Behavioral scientists should study living human beings as wholes, rather than compartmentalizing functioning into categories such as perception, learning, and personality. (Note the gestalt influence.)

3. Significant human problems—including personal responsibility, life goals, commitment, fulfillment, creativity, spontaneity, and values—should be the subjects of psychological investigations.

4. Behavioral scientists should focus on subjective awareness (how people view their own experiences) since interpretation is fundamental to all human activity. (This emphasis also reflects the influence of gestalt psychology.)

5. Behavioral scientists should strive to understand the individual, the exceptional, and the unpredictable, as well as the general and universal. In contrast, psychoanalytic, neobehavioristic, and cognitive psychologists are most interested in discovering general laws of functioning.

6. The specific methods that behavioral scientists adopt should be secondary to the problems they choose to study. Accordingly, humanistic psychologists use many kinds of research strategies: objective methods, individual case studies, informal introspective techniques, and even the analysis of literary works. Because humanistic psychologists believe that intuitive awareness is a valid source of information, they do not hesitate to rely on their own subjective feelings and impressions.

In the following excerpt, Abraham Maslow (1908–1970), an important figure in the humanistic movement (see Figure 1-14), describes the beginning of his *self-actualization* (roughly, self-fulfillment) research. Note how Maslow's study exemplifies the humanistic approach.

FIGURE 1-14 Abraham Maslow was a leading spokesperson for humanistic psychology, which he called the "third force" (along with behaviorism and psychoanalysis). [*Brandeis University.*]

The Beginning of Self-Actualization Research:
The Approach of a Humanistically Oriented Psychologist

"My investigations on self-actualization were not planned to be research and did not start out as research. They started out as the effort of a young intellectual to try to understand two of his teachers whom he loved, adored, and admired, and who were very, very wonderful people. . . . I could not be content simply to adore, but sought to understand why these two people were so different from the run-of-the-mill people in the world. These two people were Ruth Benedict and Max Wertheimer. They were my teachers after I came with a Ph.D. from the West to New York City, and they were most remarkable human beings. My training in psychology equipped me not at all for understanding them. It was as if they were not quite people but something more than people. My own investigations began as a pre-scientific or non-scientific activity. I made descriptions and notes on Max Wertheimer, and I made notes on Ruth Benedict. When I tried to understand them, think about them, and write about them in my journal and my notes, I realized in one wonderful moment that their two patterns could be generalized. I was talking about a kind of person, not about two noncomparable individuals. There was a wonderful excitement in that. I tried to see whether this pattern could be found elsewhere, and I did find it elsewhere, in one person after another.

"By ordinary standards of laboratory research, that is, of rigorous and controlled research, this simply was not research at all. My generalizations grew out of my selection of certain kinds of people. Obviously other judges are needed. So far, one man has selected perhaps two dozen people whom he liked or admired very much and thought were wonderful people and then tried to figure them out and found that he was able to describe a syndrome—the kind of pattern that seemed to fit all of them. . . . The people I selected for my investigation were older people, people who had lived much of their lives out and were visibly successful. . . . When you select out for careful study very fine and healthy people, strong people, creative people, saintly people, sagacious [wise] people—in fact, exactly the kind of people I picked out—then you get a different view of mankind. You are asking how tall can people grow, what can a human being become [21]?"

Eventually Maslow studied forty-nine apparently self-actualized persons whom he admired (including personal acquaintances, friends, living and dead public figures, and college students). He gathered his data by obtaining biographical information, questioning friends and relatives, and in some cases by questioning and testing the subjects themselves. Gradually Maslow formed global, or general, impressions of each person, which he later analyzed for common themes. He concluded that these exemplary human beings shared fifteen characteristics, including an accurate perception of reality, the ability to accept themselves and others, naturalness, problem-centeredness rather than self-centeredness, a positive liking for solitude and privacy, resistance to conformity, and a deep feeling of sympathy for people. Self-actualized individuals were not entirely angelic. On occasion they could be obstinate, cold, irritable, boring, selfish, and depressed [22].

Four Perspectives

The ideas of psychoanalytic, neobehavioristic, cognitive, and humanistic psychologists are summarized in Table 1-4. Each perspective provides important insights. The neobehavioristic approach offers psychology objective ways of investigating the functioning of people and other animals. The cognitive view reminds behavioral scientists that mental processes are among the most fascinating and important of topics. The psychoanalytic tradition points to the many mysterious aspects of personality that need thorough exploration. Finally, the humanistic philosophy offers important goals by insisting that psychologists research meaningful questions and use their knowledge for serving human beings. ▲

▲ **USING PSYCHOLOGY**

1. Carefully reread the passages by Freud, Weiss, Neisser and colleagues, and Maslow, and pick out the statements that illustrate each author's philosophical approach.

2. Do you find any single current view of psychology more appealing than the others? Which one? Why?

3. If you could create an eclectic psychology, what aspects of each viewpoint would you select? Would you add anything else?

TABLE 1-4 A Comparison of Four Current Views of Psychology

Freud

Psychoanalytic view *still maintained by some*
Subject matter: Normal and abnormal personality (laws, determinants in early childhood, and unconscious aspects emphasized); treatment of abnormal behavior
Major goals: Service, knowledge
Research methods emphasized:
  Patients: Informal introspection to reveal conscious experiences
  Therapists: Logical analysis and observation to uncover unconscious materials
Population studied: Patients (usually adults)

Neobehavioristic view *Watson — include thought as area of study.*
Subject matter: Any well-defined question about simple or complex animal or human behavior—including functions that cannot be observed
Major goals: Knowledge, application
Research methods emphasized: Objective methods
Population studied: People and less complex animals

Cognitive view *Thinking*
Subject matter: The functioning of mental activities (perceptual processes, problem solving, memory, etc.)
Major goal: Knowledge
Research methods emphasized: Objective methods, informal introspection
Population studied: Primarily people (occasionally lesser animals)

Humanistic view *Abraham Maslow, Carl Rogers — living up to your potential*
Subject matter: Questions about the whole person, subjective human experience, and significant human problems; the extraordinary and individual as well as the usual and universal
Major goals: Service and enrichment of life, primary; knowledge, secondary
Research methods emphasized: The observer's intuitive awareness is considered important. All procedures—objective methods, informal introspection, case study, analysis of literature, etc.—are acceptable
Population studied: People

SUMMARY
Psychology: Present and Past

1. We defined psychology as the science that studies behavior and mental processes. It focuses on both social and biological topics. It is neither unified nor complete.

2. Psychologists specialize in particular subject matter. The largest number apply psychology in practical settings. Many teach, do research, and serve administrative functions.

3. Clinical psychologists, psychiatrists, and psychoanalysts may all work in mental health settings diagnosing and treating people with psychological problems. Major differences between these professionals come from their training.

4. Five movements—structuralism, functionalism, behaviorism, gestalt psychology, and psychoanalytic theory—shaped modern psychology. Each advocated specific goals, subject matter, and procedures for psychology.

5. Many psychologists today identify with one of four viewpoints—psychoanalytic, neobehavioristic, cognitive, or humanistic. Each approach emphasizes particular goals, procedures, and subject matter.

A Study Guide for Chapter One

Key terms psychology (2), scientific method (3), behavioral scientist (4), social scientist (4), subject (4), generalize (5), psychiatrist (7), psychoanalyst (7), analytic introspection (9), objective method (11), informal introspection (11), stimulus (12), response (12), subjective experience (13), eclectic (16), cognitive process (18), and other italicized words and expressions.

Important research animal participants in psychological research, characteristics of American psychologists, slips of the tongue (Freud), predictability of stress and ulcers (Weiss), divided attention (Neisser, Hirst, Spelke), self-actualization (Maslow).

Basic concepts structuralism, functionalism, behaviorism (neobehavioristic approach), gestalt psychology, psychoanalytic theory, cognitive approach, humanistic approach.

People to identify Aristotle, Fechner, Wundt, Titchener, James, Watson, Wertheimer, Freud, Maslow.

Self-Quiz

1. How is psychology defined today?
   a. The science of behavior and mental processes
   b. The science of *human* behavior and mental processes
   c. The science of the mind
   d. The study of motivation, emotion, personality, adjustment, and abnormality

2. Which of the following populations participates most frequently in psychological studies?
   a. Cats and dogs *b.* Monkeys
   c. People *d.* Rats and pigeons

3. Which occupation attracts the largest number of psychologists?
   a. Administration and management
   b. Application and practice
   c. Research
   d. Teaching

4. What is the major difference between psychiatrists and psychoanalysts?
   a. Psychiatrists have an M.D. degree while psychoanalysts rarely do.
   b. Psychoanalysts are better qualified than psychiatrists to treat severe mental disorders.
   c. Psychoanalysts place greater emphasis than psychiatrists do on experimental research.

   d. Psychoanalysts receive intensive training in Freud's theories, while psychiatrists may not.

5. Who wrote the book *Elements of Psychophysics*, demonstrating for the first time how scientific principles could be applied to questions about mental processes?
   a. Gustav Fechner *b.* William James
   c. Edward Titchener *d.* Wilhelm Wundt

6. What is analytic introspection?
   a. A formal type of self-observation
   b. An informal type of self-observation
   c. Any self-report method
   d. A technique of recalling childhood events

7. Who is credited with founding "the first psychology laboratory in the world" in 1879?
   a. Gustav Fechner *b.* William James
   c. Edward Titchener *d.* Wilhelm Wundt

8. Which question would have been most likely to interest William James?
   a. How bright must a light be to be seen?
   b. How do animals learn?
   c. How do people adapt to the world?
   d. What are the elementary processes of human consciousness?

9. Which is one of structuralism's major limitations?
   a. Excluding children and animals
   b. Focusing almost exclusively on practical matters
   c. Overemphasizing environmental influences on behavior
   d. Using informal research techniques

10. Which modern approach was most clearly influenced by functionalism?
   a. Cognitive *b.* Humanistic
   c. Neobehavioristic *d.* Psychoanalytic

11. Which goal is most closely associated with the name of John Watson and behaviorism?
   a. Complexity *b.* Flexibility
   c. Objectivity *d.* Unity

12. Which statement summarizes one of the most basic beliefs of the gestalt psychologists?
   a. Events must be analyzed into their component parts.
   b. One cannot understand human experience simply by studying isolated elements.
   c. Psychologists should use only objective methods.
   d. Psychology should focus on emotion, motivation, adjustment, personality, and abnormality.

13. Which movement both created a revolution in the conception and treatment of psychological problems and generated great interest in child development?
   a. Functionalism *b.* Gestalt psychology
   c. Psychoanalytic theory *d.* Structuralism

14. On which point do neobehaviorists differ from behaviorists?

    a. Neobehaviorists no longer argue that psychologists must ask precise, well-delineated questions.

    b. Neobehaviorists no longer insist that only observable phenomena be studied.

    c. Neobehaviorists no longer investigate stimuli.

    d. Neobehaviorists no longer measure responses.

15. Which philosophy is most likely to be held by a psychologist studying autobiographies of unusually creative people?

    a. Cognitive   *b.* Humanistic

    c. Neobehavioristic   *d.* Psychoanalytic

Exercise

PAST MOVEMENTS AND CURRENT VIEWPOINTS IN PSYCHOLOGY. It is easy to confuse the ideas of the various past movements and current viewpoints in psychology. This exercise should help you decide whether you have them straight. Match the movements or viewpoints with the statements that characterize them. A single statement may characterize more than one movement or viewpoint. If you make many mistakes, review pages 8 to 22.

PAST MOVEMENTS: behaviorism (B), functionalism (F), gestalt psychology (G), psychoanalytic theory (P), structuralism (S)

_____ *1.* Analyzed elementary processes of human consciousness.

_____ *2.* Focused on the *functioning* of mental processes.

_____ *3.* Concentrated on normal and abnormal personality.

_____ *4.* Urged psychologists to study stimuli and responses.

_____ *5.* Developed from clinical experiences with neurotic people.

_____ *6.* Stressed the environment as the most important influence on development.

_____ *7.* Assumed that much human behavior is caused by unconscious motives, conflicts, and fears.

_____ *8.* Claimed that the whole was very different than the sum of its parts.

_____ *9.* Advocated the use of analytic introspection.

_____ *10.* Believed that psychology should be applied to practical problems such as education and business.

_____ *11.* Published a list of sensation qualities.

_____ *12.* Wanted to relate mental elements to nervous system structures.

_____ *13.* Assumed that studies of simple animals could provide information about people.

CURRENT VIEWPOINTS: cognitive (C), humanistic (H), neobehavioristic (N), psychoanalytic (P)

_____ *14.* Emphasizes the study of functioning mental processes.

_____ *15.* Advocates enriching human lives as psychology's primary goal.

_____ *16.* Assumes personality is formed during early childhood.

_____ *17.* Studies patients.

_____ *18.* Assumes psychologists should study whole human beings.

_____ *19.* Uses methods developed by Freud.

_____ *20.* Insists on precise questions above all else.

_____ *21.* Believes methods are a secondary concern.

_____ *22.* Emphasizes objective methods.

_____ *23.* Most likely to study simple animals.

Suggested Readings

1. Fancher, R. E. *Pioneers of psychology.* New York: Norton, 1979 (paperback). An introduction to the lives and works of some individuals who shaped modern psychology. Fancher "attempts to illustrate how several fundamental ideas and theories actually came into being by presenting them in the contexts of the lives and perspectives of the individuals who first grappled with them."

2. Keller, F. S. *The definition of psychology.* (2d ed.) New York: Appleton-Century-Crofts, 1973. Keller provides a vivid and exciting account of the early psychology movements.

3. *Careers in psychology.* Washington, D.C.: American Psychological Association, 1975. This career information pamphlet was prepared for students who may be interested in majoring in psychology. It includes "some typical job advertisements, coupled . . . with fictitious descriptions of persons who might successfully do the job." Single copies are free to students from: American Psychological Association, Publication Sales Department, 1200 17th St., N.W., Washington, D.C. 20036.

4. Evans, R. I. *The making of psychology: Discussions with creative contributors.* New York: Knopf, 1976 (paperback). Evans interviews important contributors to psychology, emphasizing their research and ideas. The dialogues convey insight into the interviewees' personalities too.

5. Cohen, D. *Psychologists on psychology: Modern innovators talk about their work.* New York: Taplinger, 1977 (paperback). Here are thirteen in-depth interviews with prominent psychologists on their personal careers and on what psychology ought to be. Though the author comes to some very debatable general conclusions, the interviews themselves and the issues raised are interesting ones well worth reading about.

6. A fascinating way to learn more about the history of psychology is by reading autobiographies. Beginning in the late 1920s, distinguished psychologists were asked to contribute their career-related memoirs to a series of books entitled *History of psychology in autobiography.* As of 1979, six volumes of brief autobiographies had been published. A number of different editors (including C. A. Murchison, E. G. Boring, and G. Lindzey) and several publishers (notably, Appleton-Century-Crofts and Prentice-Hall) collaborated in this effort. The books are not difficult to track down by title.

7. Wollheim, R. *Sigmund Freud.* New York: Viking, 1971 (paperback). This biography looks at how psychoanalytic thinking evolved to solve specific problems. It is clearly written and very interesting.

Answer Keys

Introductory Quiz

1. *d* **2.** F **3.** *d* **4.** *d* **5.** F **6.** F
7. *a* **8.** T **9.** F

Table 1-1

1. F (Chapter 3) **2.** F (Chapter 6) **3.** F (Chapter 6)
4. T (Chapter 7) **5.** T (Chapter 8) **6.** F (Chapter 8)
7. F (Chapter 9) **8.** F (Chapter 9)
9. F (Chapter 12) **10.** F (Chapter 17)

Self-Quiz

1. *a* (2) **2.** *d* (4) **3.** *b* (7) **4.** *d* (7)
5. *a* (8) **6.** *a* (9) **7.** *d* (9) **8.** *c* (10)
9. *a* (10) **10.** *a* (11) **11.** *c* (12) **12.** *b* (12)
13. *c* (15) **14.** *b* (17) **15.** *b* (20)

Exercise

1. S **2.** F **3.** P **4.** B **5.** P **6.** B
7. P **8.** G **9.** S **10.** F, B **11.** S **12.** S
13. B, F **14.** C **15.** H **16.** P **17.** P
18. H **19.** P **20.** N **21.** H **22.** N, C
23. N

CHAPTER TWO
Psychology: The Scientific Approach

We can learn something about how and why people think and behave as they do from looking at paintings and reading literature. Religion and philosophy give perspectives on human nature. Introspection is another source of information. But, as we mentioned in Chapter 1, the great majority of psychologists endorse the ways of science as the most appropriate ones for achieving a thorough, well-organized body of accurate information about behavior and mental functioning. Most of the findings that will be discussed in this text were established by the scientific approach. In this chapter we focus on the scientific method—its goals, principles, and research techniques. Our account of science will not emphasize the day-to-day details. Still, you should know that psychologists, like other scientists, do a lot of muddling around. They get started, have to stop, try, err, try again, overlook the obvious, happen by chance on promising ideas, and compromise because of convenience and budgetary concerns. In actuality, then, "people don't usually do research the way people who write books [or chapters] about research say they do research [1]." Be warned at the beginning: Science is not all clarity and light, and "scientific progress is often made through capitalizing on misconception, error, ambiguity, and accident [2]."

In the late 1950s Lewis Thomas, a prominent medical researcher, accidentally discovered how an enzyme (papain) affects cartilage tissue in rabbits' ears. Thomas's account of his own progress clearly reveals how scientists, including psychologists, frequently grapple with problems. As you read, focus on Thomas's practices and procedures. The biological details are not important for our purposes.

The Case of the Floppy-Eared Rabbits

"For this investigation I used trypsin, because it was the most available enzyme around the laboratory, and I got nothing. We also happened to have papain; I don't know where it had come from; but because it was there, I tried it. . . . What the papain did was . . . produce these bizarre cosmetic changes [the rabbits' ears flopped]. . . . It was one of the most uniform reactions I'd ever seen. It always happened and it looked as if something important must have happened to cause this reaction. . . . I chased it like crazy. . . . I did the expected things. I had sections cut, and I had them stained by all the techniques available at the time. I expected to find a great deal. . . . I hadn't thought of cartilage. You're not likely to, because it's not considered interesting. . . . I know my own idea had always been that cartilage is a quiet, inactive tissue."

After a few months Thomas abandoned this research because he was "terribly busy working on another problem," one on which he was "making progress." Besides, Thomas had "already used all the rabbits he could afford." Several years later while teaching medical students, Thomas stumbled back onto the floppy-eared rabbit phenomenon. This time he discovered that papain changed the structure of cartilage tissue. Thomas achieved the insight because he was teaching students and for that reason following correct scientific procedure [3].

Consider the following questions:

1. Why did Thomas choose papain? Trypsin?
2. How did Thomas "chase the cause" of floppy ears?
3. Why didn't Thomas think of cartilage initially?
4. For what reasons did Thomas abandon the research on floppy-eared rabbits?
5. What led to Thomas's discovery?

Thomas's self-description is anything but glamorous. It highlights the idea that scientific research is a human enterprise. Like other human undertakings, science depends on availability and accident and is frequently limited by stereotyped notions, preconceptions, conventions, and mundane realities. As you read, try to keep in mind that scientists are people. For more information about the human aspects of science, see the Suggested Readings at the end of this chapter.

We turn now to the scientific approach of psychology, beginning with its goals.

GOALS OF PSYCHOLOGICAL RESEARCH

Behavioral scientists aim at four basic goals: description, explanation, prediction, and control.

Description is the basic goal of any science. Psychologists gather facts about behavior and mental functioning in order to put together precise, coherent pictures of these phenomena. Whenever possible, they observe or measure directly. When direct strategies are either impossible or extremely difficult, they turn to tests, interviews, questionnaires, and other indirect tactics which are less likely to be accurate. Consider aggression. Psychologists could directly observe fighting and destructive behavior in three-year-olds in a nursery school. But, if they were interested in learning more about battered wives, they'd probably have to use interviews or questionnaires. Self-report measures, like these, have severe problems that will be discussed later.

Once a phenomenon has been described accurately, behavioral scientists usually try to explain it. *Explanation* consists of establishing a network of cause-and-effect relationships. Generally, plausible explanations called *hypotheses* are proposed and tested by controlled experimentation. (More on controlled experiments later.) An example of a hypothesis is: Watching violence on TV increases aggression in children. Though they're frequently phrased as statements, hypotheses are simply possible explanations that need to be tested.

Hypotheses which receive some support are checked out further. One powerful test is *prediction*. If a hypothesis is accurate, it should be able to describe what will happen in related situations. Suppose that psychologists discover that watching war movies increases children's aggressive acts. We might then predict and expect to find that observing assaultive parents makes youngsters more combative as well.

Control is another powerful test of a hypothesis. The conditions that are thought to cause a behavior or mental process are al-

FIGURE 2-1 In many cases, control simply means that psychologists apply their knowledge to solve practical problems. Attempts to "control" learning have resulted in improved teaching techniques. Efforts to "control" prejudice have produced more acceptance among members of different races. [Left: *Department of Health, Education and Welfare*; right: *Ginger Chih/Peter Arnold*.]

tered, or controlled, to see if the phenomenon changes accordingly. While control for its own sake is frightening, in the majority of cases control in psychological research is essentially *application*. Psychologists are applying their knowledge to solve practical problems. If watching violence really increases children's fighting, for example, we should be able to reduce aggression by restricting television and film violence and by training parents and others to use nonviolent techniques. Gaining "control" over aggression shows that we understand the important conditions that produced it. Figure 2-1 illustrates additional examples of control.

Laws and Theories in Psychology

While individual psychologists work to understand limited aspects of conduct, they hope to amass a unified body of information that can explain all behavior and mental functioning. Eventually, systematically ordered knowledge results in laws and theories. In psychology and other sciences, *laws* describe regular, predictable relationships. *Theories* provide explanations of experimental findings, or *data*. Some theories involve a simple hypothesis, while others integrate a great deal of information. Whatever their scope, theories

serve a gap-filling function. They say how findings fit together and what they mean. Scientists prefer *testable* theories, those that can be confirmed or disproved by further research to check on the theory's usefulness. In sum, theories serve two roles. They provide the understanding that is the ultimate goal of research. And, they stimulate further investigations, leading to new knowledge.

PRINCIPLES THAT GUIDE PSYCHOLOGICAL RESEARCH

"Science," it has been observed, "is first of all a set of attitudes [4]." Numerous attitudes or principles give the scientific enterprise its distinct flavor. We describe the most important ones: precision, objectivity, empiricism, determinism, parsimony, and tentativeness.

Precision Psychologists attempt to be *precise* in several ways. First, they clearly define what they are studying. Second, they try to put their results in numerical form, instead of relying on personal impressions. You will find behavioral scientists making measurements on such seemingly immeasurable phenomena as love, anxiety, and marijuana intoxication. Third, after their research is complete, psychologists write detailed reports describing subjects, equipment, procedures, tasks, and results. Precise research reporting allows other behavioral scientists to repeat, or *replicate*, one another's studies to make certain the findings are consistent.

Objectivity Like all other human beings, psychologists have biases. When we say that they strive to be *objective*, we mean that they try to keep their biases from influencing their studies. In some cases, behavioral scientists arrange for assistants who do not know the hypotheses being tested and feel fairly neutral about the topic under study to conduct the actual investigation. We will have more to say about minimizing the effects of experimenter bias later in the chapter.

If you're skeptical about human nature, you may wonder if there are any checks on the objectivity of psychologists. One of the strengths of the scientific method is its built-in, self-regulating nature. Behavioral scientists are continually scrutinizing one another's research and replicating one another's studies, so the anticipation of criticism probably encourages many psychologists to guard their work from bias. From time to time, cases of bias, and even deliberate dishonesty, do crop up. But because so many people work on similar problems, what holds true and when is eventually sorted out.

Empiricism Like other scientists, psychologists believe that direct observation is the best source of knowledge. Speculation by itself is considered inadequate evidence. This "look and see" attitude is called *empiricism*. No one is exempt. Even the most distinguished authorities must back up their hunches with data. Psychologists investigating the effects of sleep loss, for example, must conduct careful studies and *observe* the results. They *should not advance as evidence* popular notions, their own plausible ideas, the speculations of eminent scientists, or surveys of people's opinions on this topic. All these strategies rely on conjecture and not on direct observation. Empiricism does not require that psychologists make all observations for themselves. It specifies only that assertions be backed up by somebody's empirical studies, which may be known through written reports, speeches, or personal correspondence.

Determinism *Determinism* refers to the belief that all events have natural causes. Psychologists believe that people's actions are determined by huge numbers of factors—some from within (such as genetic potentialities, motives, emotions, and thoughts) and some from outside (for instance, pressures from other people and current circumstances). If conduct is determined by natural causes, then it can be explained eventually.

Determinism is sometimes confused with *fatalism*, a belief that behavior is established in advance by outside forces beyond the person's control. The following example contrasts the two beliefs and makes their differences clear:

Charlie Green is a very rigid individual. He eats lunch at the same café at the same time every day. At precisely 12:03 each day he turns the corner at Second and Main Streets on his way to the café. On February 2 a new company is moving into an office on the third floor of the building at Second and Main. They start raising a 300 pound safe, using a block and tackle, at precisely 12:00. It just so happens that the rope is fraying and will be able to hold a 300 pound weight for only three minutes. Now a fatalist watching this scene might say that poor Mr. Green is doomed to be smashed. A determinist, on the other hand, might say that if everything remains the same with relation to Mr. Green, he is likely to round the corner and be killed. The determinist also thinks he can be of help, so he tells Green that a safe is being lifted and that it is dangerous to walk under it. Mr. Green says 'Thank you,' looks up (for the first time in five years), sees the safe, and detours into the street as the safe falls harmlessly. One of the determinants of Green's behavior is the verbal information he receives. [5]

A belief in determinism does not necessarily rule out a belief in freedom of choice, as is sometimes supposed. As one psychologist has put it, "One of the determinants of our choices is our mental machinery which is not some predictable . . . cogwheels revolving in our heads," but rather a collection of different possible modes of thought which we can adopt or ignore, depending on our purposes, desires, feelings, and drives [6]."

We might say, then, that determinism boils down to certain attitudes about explaining and predicting. The more we know, the more we understand and the more we can predict. Psychologists cannot currently predict people's behavior with complete accuracy because there are too many determining factors to take into account and too much that is not understood.

We stated before that psychologists look for *natural* explanations. No matter how mystifying something is, psychologists assume that there are natural causes that may be discovered eventually. They do not consider magic, fate, luck, evil spirits, God, or other supernatural forces as influences.

Parsimony Many psychologists try to be *parsimonious*. Literally, the term means stingy. In scientific usage, "parsimony" refers to a standard policy on explanations: simple explanations that fit the observed facts are preferred and should be tested initially. Complex or abstract explanations are advanced only when less complicated ones have proven inadequate or incorrect. You might think of scientists as being "stingy" with their thoughts. Consider the observation that certain people eat with great gusto, relishing every morsel of food. Here is a parsimonious explanation: Sensitivity to the taste of food and degree of inhibition about expressing these perceptions vary a great deal. Enthusiastic eaters tend to be both very sensitive to the taste of food and very uninhibited about revealing their feelings. A nonparsimonious explanation might offer this relatively complicated account: People who savor eating were not breast-fed for a long enough time to satisfy their oral needs. Subsequently, they developed obsessive drives for eating and all other oral activities. Eating, as well as smoking, gum chewing, talking, and similar actions, brings such individuals a primitive type of infantile joy. Figure 2-2 presents a second example of parsimonious and nonparsimonious explanations.

Tentativeness Psychologists try to be open-minded, accepting of criticism, and ready to reevaluate and revise their conclusions if new evidence warrants it. In other words, they regard their findings as *tentative*. This attitude is realistic for many reasons. Even though behavioral scientists try to perform the most careful observations that they are capable of, they cannot eliminate every potential source of error. Mistakes can creep in because of complications in the real world, faulty instruments, or improperly designed procedures. More frequently than not, behavior and mental processes turn out to be

FIGURE 2-2 Hockey star Gordie Howe is flanked by sons Marty (left) and Mark, also outstanding players. Can you think of a parsimonious explanation for the adage, "Like father, like son?" One possibility is that fathers often teach and encourage their sons in activities that they themselves are interested in. Compare this explanation with a nonparsimonious one: Without realizing it, the son competes with the father for the mother's love. To win the mother's affection, the son continually attempts to outperform the father. [*Wide World Photo*.]

more complex than they initially appear. You may want to keep in mind the words of one distinguished psychologist:

My effort . . . in trying to make psychological research more scientific . . . has convinced me of our need to be modest about the scientific validity of our present conclusions. *Psychology could be wrong* even on issues on which we now seem to have a scientific concensus. [7] ▲

PRELIMINARIES: BEFORE THE RESEARCH BEGINS

Before psychologists begin to investigate a topic, they refine their questions, define their terms, and select their participants.

The Questions Psychologists Ask

Psychologists begin their research with general questions about behavior and mental functioning that arouse their curiosity. Such questions may include: What does stress do to people? What makes adolescents turn to crime? What happens to personality in old age? As a rule, psychologists select questions that can be answered by empirical, or observational, procedures. A question such as "What are the psychological effects of cohabitation?" can be investigated by observing or interviewing couples who are living together without religious or legal sanctions. But the issue "Is cohabitation wrong?" depends on judgments, not on observations. See Figure 2-3. Similarly, nothing can be observed that

FIGURE 2-3 While the rightness or wrongness of cohabitation cannot be established by empirical methods, the feelings of cohabiting couples can be investigated by such procedures. For one study of this topic, psychologist Eleanor Macklin had about 300 unmarried student couples who were living together fill in questionnaires. About 70 percent of the respondents said that emotional attachment was the most important reason for choosing to live together. Parents appeared to be the most frequent source of outside problems. The tendency to become too involved—to feel excessively dependent on the relationship with loss of identity and reduced activity—turned out to be the most commonly reported emotional problem [29]. [*Peter Southwick.*]

enables us to examine questions such as "Do fish in a dream symbolize unfulfilled sexual desires?" or "Do people have the right to mercy-kill another human being?"

General questions about psychological issues are often ambiguous (unclear) and enormous in scope. Consider the question "What

▲ USING PSYCHOLOGY

1. Suppose that a classmate argues, "Psychologists are interested in gaining control over people's behavior." Explain what is meant by the goal called "control."

2. How are fatalism and determinism similar? Different?

3. Give an example of a parsimonious and a nonparsimonious explanation for the popularity of rock-and-roll music.

4. As you informally accumulate a body of psychological knowledge in everyday life, are there any scientific principles that you either observe or violate fairly consistently?

does stress do to people?" There are hundreds of stresses. They affect different persons at different times in different ways. Our general question, then, is really many questions. Each must be tackled individually. We might change "What does stress do to people?" to the clearer, more specific question "How does a natural disaster like a hurricane [a particular stressor] affect the desire of adults to seek others out [a particular effect]?" The question "What makes adolescents turn to crime?" might be narrowed to "Do the majority of juvenile delinquents in Boston come from families with only one parent?" General questions must usually be restated to remove ambiguities and to limit their scope so that a systematic investigation may be possible.

After formulating a researchable question, behavioral scientists define their terms.

Operational Definitions

Consider the statement, "We studied crime." "Crime" could refer to jaywalking, parking in a no-parking zone, smoking marijuana, shoplifting, armed robbery, rape, and/or murder. In other words, "crime," like most other words that we use every day, has multiple meanings. If psychologists are going to understand one another and if the public is going to understand psychologists, then terms must be pinned down precisely. One way to do that is to relate all terms to the procedures that are

used to observe or measure them. The resulting definitions, called *operational definitions*, are widely used in research for clarity. We might operationally define crime as acts listed as felonies by federal law, for instance. Table 2-1 presents several additional illustrations. Note that operational and formal definitions are very different. Operational definitions are distinctive in several ways. First, they are never abstract. They are always tied to observations or measurements—frequently to physiological, self-report, or behavioral measures. Second, there are many possible operational definitions for any concept, process, or phenomenon. Third, operational definitions are narrow and apply to limited situations. When defining terms for research purposes, psychologists typically sacrifice generality for precision.

As psychologists are refining their questions and defining their terms, they must decide whom they are going to study.

Selecting Human Subjects for Psychological Research

Behavioral scientists may be interested in discovering general psychological laws that apply to all people. Or they may want to explore questions about the functioning of specific types of persons, for instance, neurotics, youth-gang members, individuals with terminal cancer, migrant laborers, adult

TABLE 2-1 Sample Operational Definitions

Term	Operational definition(s)	Formal definition
Work	Eating with chopsticks rather than silverware in a Chinese restaurant; number of pecans shelled	The expenditure of energy
Stress	Exposure to noise or shock of a particular intensity and duration; amount of defecation after five minutes in a new situation (in rats)	Sense of inner turmoil
Love	Amount of time spent clinging to mother or mother substitute	Feeling of profoundly tender, passionate affection
Learning	Performance on a specific test	A change in behavior or mental functioning due to experience

women, or newborn babies. The entire group that the psychologist wants to understand is called the *population*. Practical considerations make it impossible to study all people, all neurotics, all youth-gang members, or almost any other entire population. Inevitably, investigators pick *samples*, portions of the population for study. These samples should mirror the entire population of interest.

There are two ideal strategies for choosing samples: representative sampling and random sampling. In representative sampling, subjects who reflect the important characteristics of the relevant population are chosen. Suppose that you are studying the effects of TV advertisements on Americans. You might decide that age, intelligence, sex, geographical location, and religious affiliation are likely to influence reactions to ads. You could go to U.S. census data and similar sources to see what percentage of people falls within the various categories of age bracket, IQ range, sex, geographical region, and religion. Then, in selecting your sample you might include similar percentages of individuals to *represent* the entire population.

Random sampling means picking subjects in such a way that each and every person in the population under consideration has an equal chance of being selected for the research. As long as the sample is large, this strategy also results in a group that mirrors the general population. To randomly sample Americans (an exceedingly difficult task), you might place the names of all United States citizens on slips of paper, mix the slips thoroughly in some enormous vessel, and draw 2,000 names.

When relatively large representative or random samples are carefully chosen, different samples from the same population yield similar results. They produce essentially the same findings that would be obtained from the entire population.

In reality, behavioral scientists rarely study representative or random samples of an entire population because their time, money, and resources are limited. Instead, they try to assemble a random or representative sample

of a *portion* of the population that is *readily available* and *cooperative*. Psychologists interested in eight-year-olds might choose a random sample from P.S. 105 in Brooklyn. Behavioral scientists curious about married women might study a representative sample of faculty wives at Upswitch University. A recent cataloging of the samples behavioral scientists use for social and personality research suggests that college students are by far the most popular subjects. They play the role of "guinea pig" for nearly 80 percent of all social and personality investigations. First- and second-year students in introductory psychology courses are especially likely to be involved [8]. Research on males alone is twice as common as that on females alone [9]. We may conclude, then, that behavioral scientists frequently study comparatively bright, well-educated, young, well-to-do, white people (especially men) and that we must be exceedingly careful about assuming that our findings are generally true.

THE PSYCHOLOGIST'S RESEARCH TOOLS

In this section we examine five commonly used research techniques: direct observations, assessment devices, case studies, experiments, and correlational studies. Each of these tools is suited to particular types of questions. Just as in carpentry, the "best" one depends on the problem.

Direct Observations

Psychologists who choose to observe or measure a phenomenon directly often face a conflict. They want both to make precise, objective observations and to view realistic behavior. It is hard to do both simultaneously. Precision and objectivity are more easily achieved in artificial settings like laboratories, whereas authentic responses are more apt to be seen in natural situations. In the end, some compromise must be reached.

To conduct *laboratory observations*, behavioral scientists create a standard setting which stimulates the behavior of interest and allows exact, unbiased measurements to be made. Because subjects are all exposed to the same situation, it's relatively easy to compare their responses. Research participants may be aware of the observers' presence, but they rarely know precisely *why* they are being studied. For example, as part of an investigation of mothers' behavior toward first- and later-born children, laboratory observations were conducted at Columbia University. Mothers believed that they were participating in a study of independent thinking. Each parent observed her nursery school–aged child solving puzzles for five minutes, heard an evaluation of the youngster's performance, then was left alone to interact with the child. The mother-child interactions were observed, coded, and rated by three independent observers [10].

In making *naturalistic observations*, the psychologist is primarily interested in viewing behavior in a natural setting and in disturbing it as little as possible. Though considerations of precision and objectivity may be important, they are secondary. The collection of naturalistic observations poses a difficult problem at the outset. How can the behavioral scientists' presence be disguised or concealed so as to distort minimally the conduct being viewed? Sometimes psychologists watch from the sidelines. They might observe people's reactions to a beggar requesting money while they are sitting on a park bench pretending to be absorbed in a book. In some situations, hidden movie or videotape cameras or tape recorders record events. *Participant observation*, actually joining the activities that are being watched and consequently being mistaken by the subjects for members of their own group, is a less commonly used tactic. In one such study, observers had themselves admitted to various mental institutions by claiming to hear voices. The hospital staffs, considered

the record keeping of the observers symptomatic of their psychological problems [11]. In another participant observation, social scientists posed as "true believers" in order to be accepted by a religious cult. The group's leader had prophesied that the world would be destroyed by a flood and earthquake on a particular December day and that the faithful group members would be rescued beforehand by a flying saucer. The investigators wanted to see how the zealots coped with the failure of their predictions [12].

Participant observation has one important advantage; close contact with subjects. But, as scientists become involved, they lose their capacity to record events in an unbiased manner. Since the observers in the mental hospital study had agreed beforehand to work for their own release by acting sane, none of them knew when they would be freed. Being awakened on the fifteenth or sixteenth morning by the greeting, "Come on you m———— f————s, out of bed!" must have heavily taxed their powers of impartiality. Participant observations have another problem. Observers may unknowingly influence subjects' behavior. The "true-believing" social scientists found that their presence bolstered their subjects' self-confidence. When all things are considered, then, participant observation is probably not the best way to make naturalistic observations if there is a choice.

After finding a way to observe research participants without influencing them unnecessarily, psychologists try to devise accurate, systematic techniques for recording information. Sometimes this is impossible. Observations on the religious cult members often had to be written hastily in summary form three or four hours after the fact. The following example illustrates how observations in a natural setting can be recorded in an orderly, dispassionate way.

Naturalistic Observations of Childbirth

As part of an effort to learn more about the influences on and consequences of childbirth, Barbara Anderson, Kay Standley, Joanne Nicholson, and their colleagues at the National Institute of Child Health and Human Development are observing women in active labor and their husbands in the hospital. The observation period occurs before anesthetics are administered. Guided by stopwatches, the psychologists view events, such as those shown in Table 2-2, for thirty seconds. They allow an additional thirty seconds to record their perceptions. The observers rate the laboring woman's social interactions too, including the physical intimacy of the wife-husband relationship and the effectiveness of the couple's interactions in alleviating the woman's physical distress. When two observers used this system to gather information on ten labors, they agreed with one another 90 percent of the time or more.

Precise observations like these will allow behavioral scientists to see which personal and social characteristics are associated with pain and pain reduction during labor. Since experiences during childbirth are related to attitudes toward infants and feelings of confidence as a caregiver, this information has far-reaching practical applications [13].

TABLE 2-2 Some Observational Categories Used in a Naturalistic Study of the Delivery Process

Physical state of the laboring woman			
1. Contraction: Contraction Resting Both	**2.** Vocalizations: Laugh or smile Cry Scream Moan	**3.** Body tension: Relaxed Tense Very tense	**4.** Body movement: Movement Stable

Content of conversations			
1. Well-being **2.** Breathing	**3.** Baby **4.** Relationship	**5.** Labor **6.** Pain	**7.** Medication **8.** Procedures

Source: Adapted from Anderson and Standley, 1977.

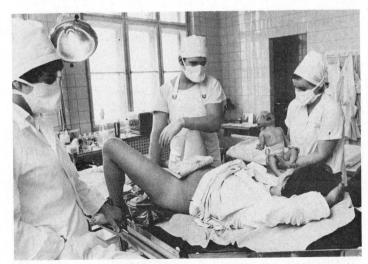

FIGURE 2-4 Before psychologists can investigate influences on, and consequences of, the childbirth experience, they must be able to measure its important dimensions. [*Eastfoto.*]

Assessment Devices

Behavioral scientists cannot always make direct observations. Very few investigators will be able to observe human beings committing crimes or falling in love, for example. Inner experiences, such as beliefs, fantasies, and feelings, cannot be seen or measured directly. Limitations on time, money, and staff prohibit the direct observation of very large numbers of people. In all these instances, psychologists turn to assessment devices: questionnaires, tests, and interviews. We focus on questionnaires and tests, two commonly used assessment procedures, in more detail.

Questionnaires Questionnaires allow psychologists to collect information *quickly* and *inexpensively* on the thinking and behavior of *large numbers* of individuals. Typically, a questionnaire asks questions that require readily available information and a minimal amount of soul searching. To answer, subjects simply mark the appropriate response.

The wording of the questions is one key to a questionnaire's success. Please examine the items listed in Table 2-3 before reading further. Are these satisfactory questions? Good questionnaire questions have several virtues.

1. The wording is simple and specific so that the meaning is clear. When questions are ambiguous, they may be read differently by various subjects. The final results are, consequently, uninterpretable. The first question in Table 2-3 is unclear. Because the precise meaning of the word "happy" is not defined, the term may be perceived in several ways. Does "happy" mean "ecstatic"? Or, does it mean "free from excessive problems and worries"? Further, if you've had ups-and-downs over the past six months (as almost everybody does), you may not find any of the response options entirely appropriate.

2. Good questions do not convey bias for or against particular response options. The question "Don't you feel that people should express their feelings honestly?" conveys the author's belief that people should be open. The questions in Table 2-3 are not at fault on this account.

3. Good questions attempt to eliminate careless responding, including agreement to be helpful, and disagreement for its own sake. In answering the

TABLE 2-3 Questions from a Questionnaire on Happiness*

In general, how happy or unhappy have you been over the last six months?

1. Very happy   **5.** Slightly unhappy
2. Moderately happy   **6.** Moderately unhappy
3. Slightly happy   **7.** Very unhappy
4. Neither happy nor unhappy

For each of the following issues, indicate how important it is to your own happiness.

	Not at all important	Slightly important	Moderately important	Very important
Recognition, success	1	2	3	4
Children and being a parent	1	2	3	4
Your financial situation	1	2	3	4
Your health and physical condition	1	2	3	4
Your house or apartment	1	2	3	4
Your job or primary activity	1	2	3	4
Personal growth and development	1	2	3	4
Exercise and physical recreation	1	2	3	4
Religion	1	2	3	4
Being in love	1	2	3	4
Your sex life	1	2	3	4
Marriage	1	2	3	4
Your spouse's or partner's happiness	1	2	3	4
Friends and social life	1	2	3	4
Your body and physical attractiveness	1	2	3	4
The city or town you live in	1	2	3	4

*The results of this survey were summarized in *Psychology Today*, August 1976.

Source: Freedman, Shaver, & students. *Psychology Today*, 1975, **9**(5).

first question in Table 2-3, you cannot mechanically check off "yes," "no," "agree," or "disagree." For that reason you're likely to read all the options; and there is a good chance that you'll pick the one that best reflects your feelings.

Even when the questions on a questionnaire are carefully devised, the results of a questionnaire study are difficult to interpret for several reasons. First of all, *self-reports* may be inaccurate. Some people deliberately falsify. Some do not care about the topic and respond without thinking. Some attempt to present an image that they like or feel is expected. Still others do not fully understand or recall their own feelings, thoughts, or behavior even though they may think they do. In a study that supports this point, Marian Yarrow and her coworkers compared mothers' memories of their youngsters' nursery school behavior against material in the children's folders and systematic behavioral observations and ratings made at the school three to thirty years earlier. The mothers' observations were systematically biased [14]. There is a second important problem with questionnaire studies. It is usually impossible to tell how well the participants represent the group of interest. The 52,000 people who mailed in their happiness questionnaires, for example, may be sadder or more contented than the majority of *Psychology Today* readers and not representative at all. Interviews, which collect self-reports directly from respondents, have many of the same problems. We will have more to say about interviews as we discuss case studies.

Psychological tests Psychological tests may be designed to measure personality characteristics, motives, moods, beliefs, feelings, opinions, attitudes, abilities, skills, knowledge, and the like. In format some resemble questionnaires, while others present batteries of problem-solving tasks. Tests may ask for written or oral responses. Some are intended for a large group of people; others for a single individual. In Chapters 12 and 13 we will describe tests that attempt to measure intelligence and personality.

Why test? First, testing allows psycholo-gists to increase their knowledge of many characteristics and processes that cannot be directly observed. Consider the personality dimension known as locus of control. *Locus of control* is defined as the degree to which people perceive that the events that happen to them are dependent on their own behavior as opposed to being the result of fate, luck, chance, or powers beyond their personal control [15]. The items in Table 2-4 come from an early version of a test developed to measure this characteristic. Please answer the questions before reading further. So far hundreds of investigators have studied locus of control [16]. By observing people with high and low test scores, behavioral scientists have learned a number of things. Internally oriented people (those who see themselves in charge of their own lives) are more likely than *externally oriented* ones (those who see luck, chance, and other external agents as responsible for their satisfactions and misfortunes) to process information efficiently. Compared with externals, internals tend to exert them-

TABLE 2-4 Items from an Early Version of the Internal-External Scale

Instructions: For each of the five numbered pairs below, choose the one that you believe, or lean toward believing, most strongly. To score your answers, see Answer Keys, Locus of Control, at the end of the chapter.

1. *a.* Promotions are earned by hard work and persist-ence.
   b. Making a lot of money is mostly a matter of getting the right breaks.
2. *a.* In my experience I have noticed that there is usually a direct connection between how hard I study and the grades I get.
   b. Many times teachers' reactions seem haphazard to me.
3. *a.* Marriage is mainly a gamble.
   b. The number of divorces indicates that more and more people are not trying to make their marriages work.
4. *a.* When I am right, I can convince others.
   b. It is silly to think that you can really change another person's basic attitudes.
5. *a.* Getting promoted is really a matter of being a little luckier than the next guy.
   b. In our society, anyone's future earning power depends on ability.

Source: Courtesy of Dr. Julian Rotter.

selves and persist in pursuit of distant goals and to resist the attempts of others to influence them. Externals are more likely than internals to feel depressed and helpless in the face of stress. By testing groups with different backgrounds, psychologists have discovered some influences on these orientations. And locus of control tests have been used to identify children who behave passively in the face of challenges that they are perfectly capable of handling, so that this tendency can be altered [17]. In general, tests can advance psychological knowledge about phenomena that cannot be observed or measured directly.

Tests also further the behavioral scientist's understanding of large populations, institutions, and individuals. By providing measures of abilities, knowledge, skills, attitudes, and personality traits, for instance, tests enable psychologists to answer questions such as these: Are college entrants in 1960 and 1980 similar in their verbal abilities? Does Abraham Lincoln High School equip its students with fundamental arithmetic skills? Do Martha Strauss's interests suit her for a career in electrical engineering? The following account illustrates how tests provide significant information about individuals.

Testing to Understand a Particular Individual: The Case of Mr. M.

Mr. M., twenty-five years old, had come from the Deep South to Syracuse, New York, to live with his relatives. He applied almost immediately for a work-training program as a machinist. During a routine job interview he revealed that he had never learned to read or write. The man was so intensely ill at ease that he could hardly talk either. He answered the interviewer's questions with barely audible yeses and nos. The officials wanted to accept Mr. M. into their program but were uncertain about whether or not he was intelligent enough to complete the training. To resolve that issue, he was referred to a psychologist for an evaluation.

When Mr. M. arrived for his session with the psychologist, he appeared quite tense. The psychologist tried to make him feel more comfortable by engaging him in conversation about his new home, family, schooling, hobbies, and interests. After an hour's chat, Mr. M. appeared much more relaxed and ready for testing. The psychologist administered several tests, including the Weschler Adult Intelligence Scale. This test assesses general information, social know-how, arithmetic reasoning, abstract thinking, and other intellectual skills. (The test is described more fully in Chapter 12.) During the testing the psychologist tried to be encouraging

and supportive. Under these conditions, Mr. M. performed as well overall as most people his own age. His memory and abilities to reason and form concepts were better than average. Skills that require a conventional educational background (sampled by questions such as "Who wrote *The Iliad*?) and those adversely affected by severe anxiety (represented by items such as "Repeat the following digits backward: 9,7,3,5") were worse than average. So the testing furnished a description of Mr. M.'s current intellectual functioning. In the end, incidentally, Mr. M. was accepted into the work-training program, and he completed it successfully.

Case Studies

Case studies involve the collection of detailed information, frequently of a highly personal nature, on the behavior of an individual or group (a family, community, or culture, for example) over a long period. When case studies occur in mental health or medical settings they are labeled *clinical observa-*

tions. Through case studies, psychologists hope to formulate general ideas about the development of inner processes like feelings, thoughts, and personality. Techniques such as interviews, informal observations, and tests are often employed to gather information. Freud used this method. So did Jean Piaget, another famous behavioral scientist who observed the reasoning and problem solving of his own children throughout their infancy and childhood.

Even when scientists observe numerous persons, the case study method has severe limitations. For one thing, the generality of the findings remains in question since it is rarely known whether the subjects were representative of the entire population. Secondly, objectivity is difficult to achieve. Observing clinicians or parents tend to be sympathetic to their "research participants" and invested in their progress. Consequently, their biases are apt to influence their findings. Even when these criticisms are just, case studies, like the following, do generate rich clues about human behavior for further exploration.

Case Studies of the Terminally Ill

Elisabeth Kubler-Ross, a Chicago physician, has studied more than 200 dying hospital patients to "learn more about the final stages of life with all its anxieties, fears, and hopes" and to help people die more comfortably. Kubler-Ross and her students gathered their information largely through extensive interviews with critically ill patients. Potential subjects were always informed of the interview's purpose and nature in advance, and meetings took place only when patients agreed. Participants were free to talk as long or as little as they wished. The interviews varied in content, following the patient's needs. Typically they progressed from general to personal concerns. Kubler-Ross and her students also examined the reactions of people surrounding the ill person. On the basis of these interviews and observations, Kubler-Ross has concluded that terminally ill people pass through a series of stages. In her words: "The outstanding fact . . . is that [people with fatal disorders] are all aware of the seriousness of their illness whether they are told or not. . . . They all sensed a change in attitude and behavior when the diagnosis of a malignancy was made and became aware of the seriousness of their condition because of the changed behavior of the people in their environment. . . . [When told of their disease] all of our patients reacted to the bad news in almost identical ways, which is typical not only of the news of fatal illness but seems to be a human reaction to great and unexpected stress: namely, with shock and disbelief. Denial was used by most of our patients and lasted from a few seconds to many months. . . . This denial is never a total denial. After the denial, anger and rage predominated. It expressed itself in a multitude of ways as an envy of those who were able to live and function. This anger was partially justified and enforced by the reactions of staff and family. . . . When the environment was able to tolerate this anger without taking it personally, the patient was greatly helped in reaching a stage of temporary bargaining followed by depression, which is a steppingstone towards final acceptance. . . . The final acceptance has been reached by many patients without any external help, others needed assistance in working through these different stages in order to die in peace and dignity.

"No matter the stage of illness or coping mechanisms used, all our patients maintained some form of hope until the last moment [18]." ▲

▲ USING PSYCHOLOGY

1. Give two different operational definitions of hunger, sadness, and friendship.

2. Explain whether psychological findings apply to everybody.

3. Suppose that you were interested in observing the tactics adults use during arguments. What are the advantages and disadvantages of laboratory observations? Naturalistic observations? Questionnaire research? Case studies?

Experiments

While a justice of the U.S. Supreme Court, Oliver Wendell Holmes, Jr., declared, "All life is an experiment." He meant that people are continually trying out different courses of action and assessing the consequences. Francine throws jelly beans in her father's coleslaw and observes his reaction. Harold uses a new study technique for a semester while noting changes in his grade-point average. After running an ad on the Late Show, Bargain Basement monitors its sales. In each example, *something is deliberately manipulated (changed or varied) and the effect of the manipulation is assessed*. Scientists do exactly the same thing when they perform an experiment. The only difference is that they do it more methodically; and they attempt to control the influence of *extraneous* (irrelevant) *factors*. Because of this tight control, experiments allow scientists to conclude that something has influenced, changed, or caused something else. Experiments are the only way to establish firmly a cause-and-effect relationship. We look closely now at the basic characteristics of the psychological experiment.

FIGURE 2-5 What sort of individual helps another human being in distress? Through careful research, social scientists have been able to determine many of the personal and situational factors that influence helping behavior. This topic is treated in more detail in Chapter 17. [*Charles Gatewood.*]

The anatomy of a psychological experiment

In March 1964 as Kitty Genovese returned home from work in Queens, New York, at 3:30 A.M., she was assaulted. The young woman screamed, "Oh my God! He stabbed me. Please help me! Please help me!" Thirty-eight neighbors watched from their windows as Kitty struggled against her assailant. The man left the scene then returned and stabbed the young woman twice more—the third time fatally. Kitty's cries and pleas for help continued for about half an hour before she died. Not a single person called the police or came to Kitty's assistance during the assault. Incidents like this one (unfortunately, not an isolated occurrence) are hard to explain. At the time, many social critics assumed that people were adapting to the pressures "caused by the increasing urbanization of life by turning other people into objects, by losing human feeling for them, and by rejecting the moral imperative [obligation] to help another in distress [19]." When Kitty Genovese's neighbors were interviewed in an effort to learn why no one had called the police, many explanations were offered. One response, "I was sure someone else had already called the police," caught the attention of two psychologists who were then teaching at Columbia University. Bibb Latané and John Darley felt that this answer was right on target. Knowing that other people have witnessed an emergency and are in a position to help may reduce each bystander's sense of responsibility for taking action. Think of it like this: If you alone observe an emergency that you can handle, you'll probably feel very guilty if you don't help. But, if you're one of many onlookers, you can easily excuse yourself. "Someone else—someone better qualified—will help." If no one helps, the guilt is easier to bear because it's shared.

Experiments begin with a *hypothesis*. The simplest hypothesis states that one event (called a *variable*) is caused by, and consequently depends on, another. Latané and Darley decided to test the hypothesis, "Perception of the number of other witnesses to an emergency affects people's willingness to help." "Willingness to help" is thought to be caused by, and consequently to *depend* on, one's perception of the number of other witnesses. The dependent variable—willingness to help, in our example—is known as precisely that, the *dependent variable*. In psychological experiments, dependent variables are always some type of behavior or mental act. The other variable, the one that is thought to influence the dependent variable—in our illustration, perception of the number of other witnesses—is called the *independent variable*. Experiments may have several independent and/or dependent variables.

To test the hypothesis, the strength or presence of the independent variable(s) is manipulated and the effect on the dependent variables(s) is measured. Typically, psycholo-

gists observe or assess the responses of many research participants. (Occasionally, one or several subjects are used.) Latané and Darley modeled their experimental situation after the Genovese murder. University students reported individually to a psychology laboratory for an experiment. An assistant there informed all persons that they would be talking over an intercom to one, two, or five other research participants (in actuality, taped voices) about personal problems associated with urban college life. During the course of this rigged "conversation," one "participant" appeared to undergo a serious epileptic-like fit and pleaded for help. Some subjects believed that they were the only witnesses. Others assumed that there were one or four other bystanders. The experimenters measured

FIGURE 2-6 The Latané-Darley experiment on bystander apathy.

HYPOTHESIS: Number of perceived bystanders (independent variable) influences readiness to help in an emergency (dependent variable, operationally defined as speed of reporting an emergency).

SAMPLE: College students

EXPERIMENTAL DESIGN

	RESULTS		
	Average elapsed time before response, seconds	Percentage responding before end of convulsion	Percentage responding by end of experiment
 Experimental group 1 believed one other bystander overheard an emergency.	93	62	85
 Experimental group 2 believed four other bystanders overheard an emergency.	166	31	62
 Control group believed they alone overheard an emergency.	52	85	100

Subjects were randomly assigned to one of the above conditions. They were exposed to uniform experiences (instructions, setting, deception, etc.). Only the perceived number of bystanders varied.

how quickly participants reported the emergency. Speed of response was the operational definition of the dependent variable, willingness to help.

Perceived group size did influence speed of response to the emergency. See Figure 2-6. Latané and Darley theorized that all subjects had been in a state of conflict. On the one hand, they were genuinely worried about the victim's welfare, wanted to help, and felt guilty about not helping. On the other hand, they did not wish to overreact, look foolish, or ruin the study. When students assumed that they were alone with the victim, the first set of factors clearly outweighed the second, and the conflict was quickly resolved. The dilemma took longer to settle when participants believed that other bystanders knew about the convulsion—apparently, because the responsibility for not helping could be passed along to others.

The importance of control in a psychological experiment The most characteristic feature of a scientific experiment is its attempt to *control* all those miscellaneous factors that might keep the investigators from testing whether the independent variable(s) influences the dependent variable(s). In designing their research, psychologists attempt to control the experimental setting, subject characteristics, and experimenter effects. We describe each type of control.

Control of the experimental setting. Suppose that the Latané-Darley study took place at the student lounge on Mondays and at the counseling center on Fridays. Assume that the instructions varied from day to day. Procedural differences like these might affect subjects' responses. Since behavioral scientists are trying to single out the effect of the independent variable(s), they try to expose all participants to the same experiences (situation, procedures, instructions, and tasks).

Even though the subjects' experiences are relatively uniform, specific procedures may affect everyone's behavior in the same way. An experiment conducted by a flirtatious assistant, for example, might yield different results from those obtained when the same study is conducted by a businesslike helper. Because psychologists cannot predict how countless numbers of details will affect the results, they usually create at least two groups of subjects, or *conditions*. The *experimental group* (or groups) is subjected to changes in the independent variable(s), while the *control group* (or groups) is not. In all other respects, participants experience the same events. So any observed differences on the dependent measure(s) are assumed to be due to the independent variables(s). In the Latané-Darley study, two experimental groups and one control group were exposed to the same experimenter, assistant, setting, procedures, and instructions. Only the subjects' perceptions of the number of bystanders witnessing the emergency differed.

Control of subject characteristics. Suppose that the experimental groups in the Latané-Darley study contained mostly young male truck drivers while the control group included mainly middle-aged female nurses. In this case, group differences in speed to report the emergency could be due to sex, age, other personal qualities, and/or perceived number of bystanders. If subjects with particular features are concentrated in one or more groups of an experiment, these personal differences may obscure the effect of the independent variable(s). Because subjects' attributes are influential, investigators try to make sure that all groups of participants are initially equivalent on all significant characteristics, those likely to obscure the effects of the independent variable(s). This may be done in several ways. *Random assignment* (described earlier), which is frequently used to select subject samples for research, is one commonly used procedure. Research participants are chosen for groups in such a way that each person is equally likely to be placed in any condition. *Matching*, putting "equivalent" subjects in each group, is a second way of making research participants similar initially. In studying the effects of a weight-loss treatment, psychologists might match people on pounds overweight, sex, age, and general health. If a forty-year-old man in poor health and approximately 100 pounds overweight is placed in the experimental group, a second such person would be put in the control group. Thus each subject in one group is roughly equivalent on significant characteristics to another in the other group(s).

A third way to be sure that groups are initially comparable is to put precisely the same subjects in both the experimental and control conditions and observe their responses under both sets of circumstances. In an experiment on the effects of extreme heat on learning, people might be asked to master two similar lists of words in a room with the thermostat set first at 100°F and then at 70°F. While the *own control procedure* ensures that research participants are almost perfectly equivalent, boredom, fatigue, or increased proficiency due to practice may alter people's second set of responses. These *repetition effects* can be minimized by putting half the subjects through the control condition first and the other half through the experimental condition first. This tactic is known as *counterbalancing*.

Control of experimenter effects. Investigators sometimes influence the outcomes of their own studies unintentionally, obscuring the effect of the independent variable. We describe several different experimenter effects that have been identified. Consider the Hawthorne effect first. Suppose that several psychologists are studying how different levels of illumination affect rate of widget output in a factory. Our investigators use as control subjects people working under already existing lighting conditions. Experimental participants, in contrast, are informed of the study, placed in a special room with new lighting fixtures, and monitored closely. If differences in widget output between the two groups are found, they could be due to extra attention, variations in lighting, or both. The influence of attention on performance is known as the *Hawthorne effect* [20]. To avoid this problem, careful behavioral scientists pay the same kind and amount of attention to all groups in an experiment. See Figure 2-7.

Sometimes experimenters unknowingly cue subjects, influencing behavior in the direction of their expectations. This phenomenon, known as *experimenter bias*, is illustrated very clearly by the case of Hans. Hans was a horse that answered addition, subtraction, multiplication, and spelling questions by stomping the correct number of times with his right forefoot. Early in the nineteenth century, a prominent German psychologist, Oskar Pfungst, designed a series of ingenious experiments to discover how the horse performed these feats. Pfungst observed that Hans could solve problems with or without his master's presence. But Hans made many errors when he could not see the questioner and when the questioner did not know the answer to the problem. As it turned out, Hans responded to subtle, unintentional visual cues, including almost imperceptible movements of the examiner's head [21].

Harvard psychologist Robert Rosenthal has studied experimenter bias effects systematically. In an early experiment, ten psychology student "researchers" were each assigned twenty subjects for a study. "Researchers" showed participants ten photographs of human faces, one at a time, and asked them to rate the degree of failure or success reflected in each face. All ten "researchers" were told to *read* identical written instructions and were cautioned not to deviate. Supposedly, the purpose of this investigation was to see whether a well-established finding could be duplicated. That well-established finding varied. Half the "researchers" were informed that the faces had been rated "moderately successful." The other half were told that the faces had been rated "moderately unsuccessful." The "researchers"—the real subjects in Rosenthal's experiment—obtained results that agreed with their expectations. See Figure 2-8. Further investigations suggest that behavioral scientists sometimes cue subjects (usually unintentionally) by their facial expressions and vocal tones [22]. The importance of experimenter effects, such as these, can be minimized if instructions are presented by a tape recorder or if the study is run by an

FIGURE 2-7 How did the Hawthorne effect get its name? From 1927 to 1932, F. J. Roethlisberger and William Dickson investigated ways to increase worker productivity in the Hawthorne plant of the Western Electric Company in Chicago. In one two-year study, five women were isolated in the Relay Assembly Test Room (shown in the figure) so that they might be observed as practices such as rest periods, working hours, and pay incentives were systematically varied. Overall, the women's output increased—even when working conditions worsened. While these results have been interpreted in different ways, many social scientists believe that the attention given the workers was the most important independent variable. Not rest periods, working hours, or any other manipulation. Some recent detective work on the Relay Assembly Test Room investigation suggests that direct information about results given the workers and accompanying pay increases for higher production may have been responsible for the improvements [30]. But, whatever the case may be, the term *Hawthorne effect* refers to the influence of attention on performance. [*Harvard University Press.*]

individual who does not know the hypotheses and subjects' condition and is not personally invested in the outcome.

Subtle cues from the investigator tell subjects how they're expected to act. So do other aspects of the study: information provided before the experiment begins, open messages, and hints contained in the experimental procedures. While they may be unaware of it, many people are eager to assist the scientist by "behaving appropriately" and being "good subjects." All cues which convey the experimenter's hypotheses (including the facial expressions, gestures, and vocal tones that signal experimenter bias) are known as *de-mand characteristics*. All laboratory experiments have demand characteristics that cannot be completely eliminated although they may be *standardized*, or kept uniform, for control and experimental groups. In some cases, *placebo conditions* are required for this purpose. Placebos, chemically inactive drugs such as sugar pills or water-filled capsules, are sometimes prescribed for patients whose complaints cannot be handled more effectively. Many people actually feel better after swallowing a placebo—partly because they are soothed by faith in the drug and the expectation of relief. Psychologists use placebo-like practices to control expectations. In studies of

1	2	3	4
Ten "researchers" were assigned to one of two groups.	The "researchers" were given particular expectations about past research results.	Each "researcher" asked twenty different subjects to rate photographs of human faces for the degree of success or failure reflected in each face.	Results

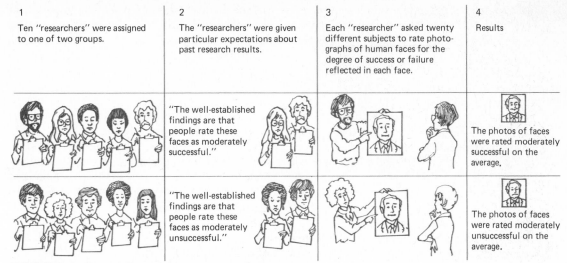

| | "The well-established findings are that people rate these faces as moderately successful." | | The photos of faces were rated moderately successful on the average. |
| | "The well-established findings are that people rate these faces as moderately unsuccessful." | | The photos of faces were rated moderately unsuccessful on the average. |

FIGURE 2-8 Rosenthal's study of experimenter bias.

drug potency, experimental subjects receive the medication of interest, while control participants take placebo medicines of identical appearance. Consequently, both groups begin with similar beliefs. Likewise, in treatment investigations, experimental subjects receive the therapy of interest, while control participants receive a placebo treatment, a different type of therapy. When subjects do not know their condition in an experiment, psychologists say that a *single-blind procedure* has been used. When neither participants nor experimenter know the subject's group, we say that a *double-blind procedure* has been used. While double-blind procedures keep participant and experimenter expectations uniform, they do not eliminate demand characteristics altogether. Subjects being treated for anxieties, for instance, know that they are expected to improve. So they may try harder to cope—knowingly or unknowingly. To see whether demand characteristics are responsible for the observed results, psychologists sometimes create a special type of control group. Subjects in this group may be asked to act as if they have been exposed to the independent variable. In a study of hypnosis, a "blind" experimenter (one who does not know the subject's condition) might test in

random order hypnotized subjects and those pretending to be hypnotized, or *simulators*. If the behavior of the two groups is indistinguishable, then the results are probably due to demand characteristics and not to hypnosis.

The field experiment Laboratory experiments furnish precise, focused, controlled ways to investigate cause-and-effect relationships. But the setting and demand characteristics may distort people's behavior, making it atypical. Another serious problem arises when behavioral scientists attempt to apply laboratory findings to life. We quote psychologist Alphonse Chapanis:

Behavior in the real-world is subject to all sorts of uncontrolled variability. Take automobile driving, for example. All sorts of people drive: the young, middle-aged and old. Men and women drive. So do the quick, the halt and the lame. They drive when they are fatigued or have just taken an antihistamine pill. The cars they drive range from shiny new vehicles to decrepid pieces of machinery scarcely recognizable as automobiles. . . . When we try to extrapolate [generalize] from laboratory experiments on reaction time, or tracking, or steering, to automobile driving what we hope is that the results of the laboratory experiment are large enough to show up when we put them into this huge mélange of real-world conditions. [23]

In other words, what happens in the precisely controlled laboratory setting may not happen in reality where dozens of interacting conditions are the rule.

To avoid artificiality and demand characteristics and to make results more applicable to real-world conditions, experiments are sometimes performed in natural settings—*in the field*, as social scientists put it. Field experiments combine realism with control. Independent variables are manipulated and dependent variables are measured usually without the subjects' knowing that they have participated in a study at all. For example, one field investigation of bystander apathy took place in the New York City subway system. There psychologist Irving Piliavin and his coworkers tested several hypotheses concerning helping behavior. One hypothesis stated, "Type of victim (the independent variable) affects bystanders' frequency and speed of responding to an emergency (the dependent variables)." In this study four student teams, each composed of a male victim, a male model, and two female observers, entered subway trains. The victim, dressed in an Eisenhower jacket and old slacks, stood by the pole in the center of the coach. Some of the time he held a cane and looked sober. At other times he reeked of alcohol and clutched a bottle of liquor wrapped tightly in a brown paper bag. After the train departed, the victim staggered forward, collapsed, and lay on his back on the floor gazing at the ceiling. On some trials the model raised the victim to a sitting position after a certain number of subway stations had been passed. The observers noted the race, sex, and location of all riders and all Good Samaritans and the speed of the first rescue effort. In general, the subway passengers were responsive bystanders. They spontaneously helped the man when he seemed injured on 62 of 65 trials; they aided the apparent drunk on 19 of 38 trials. In this study, time to respond did not increase when more witnesses looked on [24]. (The diffusion of responsibility effect found by Latané and Darley does occur in the field when emergencies are hard to interpret [25].)

To capitalize on both the greater control of the laboratory and the heightened realism of the field, the ideal research strategy probably demands moving from one to the other and back again. ▲

Correlational Studies

Sometimes psychologists are interested in cause-and-effect questions but cannot perform experiments. Suppose that you wanted to know whether high doses of the drug amphetamine cause paranoia or whether a particular type of brain damage produces language difficulties. No ethical human being would consider forming two equivalent groups and subjecting one of them to such harmful experiences. In other cases, practical problems rule

---

▲ USING PSYCHOLOGY

1. Why are experiments said to be the only way to establish cause-and-effect relationships?

2. Think of several informal experiments that you have conducted in real life. Describe the independent and dependent variables, the "experimental design," and the results. Did you make any attempt to control extraneous factors?

3. Design an experiment to test the hypothesis, "Students who have experienced academic success are more likely to perform well on academic tasks than those who have experienced academic failure." What is the independent variable? The dependent variable? How might each variable be operationally defined? Be sure to include controls for experimental setting, subject characteristics, and possible experimenter effects.

out the experimental method. Take the question, "Do dissimilar interests in spouses lead to divorce?" We'd never find people who'd marry to test our hypothesis. There are many other less dramatic issues which cannot be studied by the experimental method. Suppose you wish to find out how age, sex, or race influences conformity. It's impossible to form two groups that are equivalent in *all* important respects and then vary age, sex, race, or any other personal characteristic as experimentation requires. There is no way to change four-year-olds into eight-year-olds, blacks into whites, or females into males. Why can't we just run our experiment on groups of four- and eight-year-olds or blacks and whites or males and females? Because our subjects will not be equivalent on all other important characteristics. Toddlers and adolescents, for example, differ systematically in experiences (such as schooling), maturation of the nervous system, hormone balances, physical size, hand-eye coordination, and in many other ways.

So what can be done in instances like those we have mentioned? Let's assume that we're interested in finding out whether temperature affects crime. Since we can't manipulate the weather, we can't perform an experiment and test our hypothesis as it stands. Let's restate our hunch somewhat differently so that we can check it out. Suppose we suggest, "Weather and crime are related." All we have to do now is pick several representative cities, collect data each day on both number of crimes and average temperature, and figure out whether crime rate and temperature are associated. Suppose that they are. Assume that crime rate tends to be high on hot days and low on cold days. We can now conclude that since the two variables are related, one may be influencing the other. Weather *may* affect crime. Consider a second example. Suppose you wanted to know whether parental interference in romance intensifies love feelings (the Romeo-Juliet effect). You cannot run an experiment. But once again you can test the weaker hypothesis, "Parental interference and intensity of love feelings are

related." Imagine that you interview couples on their wedding day and find that especially ardent pairs had particularly meddlesome parents. Your data support your hypothesis. The two variables are related. Consequently, parental intervention *may* influence passion. These are both examples of *correlational studies*. In each instance we began with a hypothesis which stated that variable A was related to variable B. Then we made measurements and came to a conclusion. Variables A and B have to be either unrelated or related to some degree. If it turns out that they're related, we'll want to know the relationship's (1) strength and (2) direction (that is, as one variable increases, is the other likely to increase or decrease?). Scientists have developed mathematical indices called *correlation coefficients* which give precisely this information. Since you'll be encountering references to correlation coefficients repeatedly throughout this text (and whenever research is presented), we describe basic correlational concepts now in some detail. While there are a number of different types of correlation coefficients, they all share the characteristics specified here.

Correlation coefficients To calculate any correlation coefficient, data on variables A and B must be inserted into the appropriate mathematical formula. Computations will yield a number ranging from -1.00 to $+1.00$, for example $+.23$, $+.49$, $-.32$, and $-.67$. What do such numbers mean? First consider the *sign*. The plus or minus sign describes the *direction of the relationship* between the two sets of scores. Positive correlations, those preceded by plus signs, indicate that the two groups of measurements *vary in the same direction*. When one score is high, the other tends to be high. If one is middle-of-the-road, the second is apt to be middling. Similarly, low scores are associated with low scores. There is a positive correlation between weight in infancy and adulthood. Fat infants tend to grow into obese adults and thin babies into slender men and women. Drug use in parents and children correlate positively. Parents who smoke or drink alcohol are more likely than those who do not to have children who experiment with drugs. <u>*Negative* correlations</u>, those preceded by minus signs, show that measurements *vary in the opposite direction*. You might think of a negative correlation as something like a seesaw. When the score on one variable is high, the score on the other tends to be low. Alcohol intake is negatively correlated with efficiency at work. The more drinks downed, the less competent one's performance. Amount of smoking is negatively correlated with grade-point average. Chain smokers tend to make low marks while nonsmokers and occasional smokers more frequently shine academically. (See Figure 2-9.)

The *size* of the correlation coefficient describes the *strength* of the relationship between the two sets of scores, the probability that any pair of scores in the group will be related. A correlation coefficient of +1.00 or −1.00 means that the relationship between the two sets of scores is perfect. It holds true for every pair of scores. A correlation coefficient of 0.00 indicates that two sets of scores vary haphazardly. There is no consistent relationship between them. The stronger the correlation (the closer it is to +1.00 or −1.00), the more accurately scientists can predict the relationship between any single pair of scores. The weaker the correlation (the closer it is to 0.00), the more likely the prediction will err. Suppose you know that scores on an aptitude test and grade-point average in college are positively correlated. If Juan made a nearly perfect score on the test and Amanda came in near the bottom, we might predict that Juan will make dean's list and Amanda will be lucky to graduate. If the correlation is strong, there's a high probability that we'll be right. If it's weak, we'll have less confidence in our prophecy, though it's still better than a random guess. *Note:* Except when correlations are +1.00 or −1.00, predictions are not error-free. They may be dead wrong for any single individual.

The meaning of correlation coefficients. In practical terms, what do correlation coefficients mean? They tell us that two sets of measurements vary systematically in a particular direction with a specific degree of certainty. They do *not* say that one variable causes the other. Even if there is evidence that some influence is involved, correlation coefficients cannot tell us which variable is cause and which is effect. Suppose that the newspaper informs us that income is moderately positively correlated with happiness. That means people who make a lot of money tend to be quite happy. Any of three different inferences, or assumptions, about causation are equally plausible—at least in theory:

1. Variable A (income) may influence variable B (happiness).
2. Variable B (happiness) may influence variable A (income).
3. Additional variables (in this case, general optimism or a pleasant childhood) may influence both variables A and B (income and happiness).

FIGURE 2-9 Positive and negative correlations are illustrated. If weight tended to decline as height increased, the two would be negatively correlated (a). In actuality, of course, height and weight are positively correlated (b). [*Redrawn from* Statistical thinking *by John L. Phillips, Jr. W. H. Freeman and Company. Copyright © 1973.*]

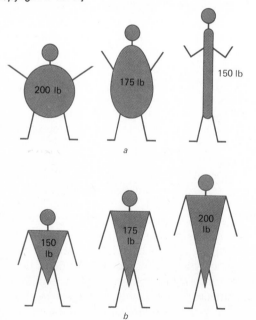

Figure 2-10 presents a second example of inferences about causation.

When trying to establish that phenomenon A causes phenomenon B, experiments are preferable to correlational studies because they can control irrelevant factors and demonstrate whether or not independent variables truly influence dependent variables. The correlational strategy is useful when experimentation is impossible. It can verify the existence of relationships and permit prediction in the real world. Although correlational studies cannot establish cause-and-effect relationships by themselves, they can be used in conjunction with other evidence to support a causal explanation.

HANDLING RESEARCH FINDINGS

After observing, surveying, interviewing, testing, or experimenting, psychologists emerge with findings that are usually in numerical form. Mathematical procedures

FIGURE 2-10 People who undergo a lot of stresses tend to develop physical problems. In other words, amount of stress and number of illnesses are positively correlated. Any of three different inferences about causation is equally plausible in theory.

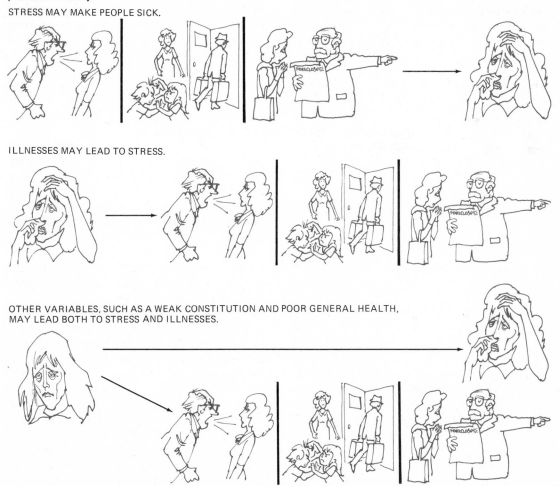

STRESS MAY MAKE PEOPLE SICK.

ILLNESSES MAY LEAD TO STRESS.

OTHER VARIABLES, SUCH AS A WEAK CONSTITUTION AND POOR GENERAL HEALTH, MAY LEAD BOTH TO STRESS AND ILLNESSES.

called *statistics* are used to organize, describe, and interpret the data. In reality, statistical ideas guide research from the beginning. They tell behavioral scientists what information needs to be collected to test the hypothesis adequately. After the study, they help the psychologist make sense of the findings. We have treated one important statistical concept, the correlation coefficient. We discuss several other major statistical notions in the appendix at the end of the book.

The research enterprise does not end with data analysis and interpretation. A single study, however superb, does not convince everybody of the validity of a hypothesis. Because each investigation has numerous problems, psychological knowledge builds slowly. Hypotheses must be supported by many investigators using different procedures on varied subject populations under diverse conditions. As psychologists repeat one another's research to make sure the findings hold up (and are not due to error or procedural details) and as they test out related notions, a body of reliable information accumulates. At the same time, theories are built to tie together diverse findings and suggest new research.

ETHICS AND PSYCHOLOGICAL RESEARCH

You may have been surprised to learn that psychologists sometimes observe people without asking their permission, deceive them about their real purposes, and expose them to unpleasant experiences. Perhaps you have been wondering whether behavioral scientists pay any attention at all to moral considerations. They do. Formal ethical guidelines for research involving both human and animal participants have been published by the American Psychological Association. These standards are frequently reviewed and amended. We focus briefly on the principles guiding the use of human subjects.

Psychologists who study people are responsible for assessing the ethical acceptability of any project they undertake. They are sup-posed to seek advice about procedures that are ethically questionable. In addition, they are expected to adhere to these standards:

1. Inform participants in advance about aspects of the research that might influence their decision to take part and answer questions about the nature of the research. (In some cases, investigators ask subjects for permission not to give precise information about the study so that unbiased responses can be obtained.)
2. Inform participants of reasons for any necessary deceptions after the study is over.
3. Respect subjects' freedom to decline or discontinue participation at any time.
4. Clarify the responsibilities of investigator and participant at the beginning.
5. Protect subjects from physical and mental damage, danger, harm, and discomfort. (When these risks exist, the investigator must inform participants and receive their consent before continuing. Research procedures which could cause lasting or severe damage are *never* to be used.)
6. Clarify the nature of the study and remove misconceptions, once the data are collected.
7. Detect and alleviate any long-term aftereffects that exist.
8. Keep information collected about individual subjects confidential [26].

As we have seen in this chapter, investigators don't always follow the guidelines. Field research poses several ethical difficulties. As in the Piliavin subway study, investigators in the field do not establish prior contractual agreement, ask for consent, or debrief participants after the deception. How do people feel about being subjects in field research? A survey in the mid-1970s by psychologists David Wilson and Edward Donnerstein asked Americans this question. Carefully selected field studies were described in detail. Substantial numbers of survey participants (up to 48 percent) judged specific investigations "offensive" and "unjustified by their scientific contribution" [27]. Deception accompanies many, and probably most, laboratory studies with human subjects. The investigation depicted in Figure 2-11 raises several additional ethical issues: Among them, what should be done about children and other populations that are unable to give informed consent?

FIGURE 2-11 The ethical questions raised by psychological research are frequently subtle and controversial. In the study by Albert Bandura and his coworkers pictured here, children watched an adult model behave aggressively toward a Bobo doll. Later the youngsters had an opportunity to demonstrate what had been learned. As you can see, the imitation was unmistakable. This experiment was among the first to show that watching aggression increases aggression. It could be argued that the research was unethical because (1) it taught aggression and (2) it used children, who cannot give informed consent. On the other hand, many behavioral scientists consider the investigation justified by its potential benefit to society. [*Albert Bandura.*]

Some psychologists believe that certain ethical violations are relatively minor and that the potential gain in knowledge outweighs the risks. Others assert that all morally questionable studies are objectionable. In some cases, scientists could even be criminally prosecuted. Because of these various concerns, psychologists are continually searching for better ways to study people. A special set of guidelines may be advisable for field studies, which cannot honor many of the American Psychological Association "rules."

It should be clear by now that ethical issues do concern behavioral scientists. But, for those invested both in advancing psychological knowledge and protecting research participants' welfare, there are no blanket solutions. ▲

▲ USING PSYCHOLOGY

1. Field experiments and correlational studies both occur in natural settings and attempt to pin down cause-and-effect relationships. What advantages do field experiments have? Under what circumstances are correlational studies especially useful?

2. Suppose that there is a strong positive correlation between internal locus of control and years of education. What three causal inferences are equally plausible?

3. Do you believe that field research is ethically acceptable? What guidelines might be advisable for this type of investigation?

4. Consider the commonly held belief "Spare the rod, spoil the child." Which types of research procedures might be used to test this assumption?

5. "In order to behave like scientists we must construct situations in which our subjects are totally controlled, manipulated, and measured," writes D. Bannister in the *Bulletin of the British Psychological Society*. "We construct situations in which [people] . . . can behave as little like human beings as possible and we do this in order to allow ourselves to make statements about the nature of their humanity [28]." Do you agree with this appraisal? How can psychologists escape this paradox?

6. Most human beings are interested in understanding themselves and other people. What is distinctive about the psychologist's approach?

SUMMARY
Psychology: The Scientific Approach

1. Psychological research is a human undertaking that is often slow and halting.

2. Most psychologists endorse the ways of science as the most appropriate ones for achieving a thorough, well-organized body of accurate information.

3. Researching psychologists aim at four basic goals: description, explanation, prediction, and control (in many cases, application).

4. Systematically ordered knowledge produces laws and theories.

5. Psychological research is guided by these principles: precision, objectivity, empiricism, determinism, parsimony, and tentativeness.

6. Before psychologists begin their research, they limit the scope of their questions, operationally define their terms, and select a sample.

7. Psychologists use (*a*) direct observations in laboratory and natural settings, (*b*) assessment devices such as tests and questionnaires, (*c*) case studies, (*d*) experiments, and (*e*) correlational studies to investigate the issues that interest them. The best technique depends on the problem being studied.

8. Psychologists are frequently interested in cause-and-effect issues. Causation can be established only by controlled experiments. In an experiment the strength or presence of the independent variable(s) is manipulated and the effect on the dependent variable(s) is assessed. Extraneous factors which might affect the dependent variable, including setting and subject characteristics and experimenter effects, are controlled.

9. When controlled experiments are impossible to perform because of practical or ethical reasons, psychologists conduct correlational studies. This type of research can establish whether or not relationships between variables exist but does not permit firm conclusions about causation. In correlational studies, measurements of two variables are made, and a correlation coefficient is calculated. The correlation coefficient indicates the strength and direction of the relationship between the two variables.

10. Ethical guidelines for the use of animal and human research participants exist. The use of human subjects who cannot give informed consent, the practice of deception, and the propriety of field studies are currently controversial issues.

A Study Guide for Chapter Two

Key terms description (27), explanation (27), hypothesis (27), prediction (27), control (two meanings, 27, 42), law (28), theory (28), data (28), precision (28), replicate (29), objectivity (29), empiricism (29), determinism (29), parsimony (30), tentativeness (30), population (33), sample (33), direct observation (33) [laboratory (33), naturalistic (34), participant (34)], assessment device (35) [questionnaire (36), test (37)], case study (38) [clinical observation (38)], laboratory experiment (40), field experiment (45), correlational study (46), correlation coefficient (47), statistics (49), and other italicized words and expressions.

Important research floppy-eared rabbits (Thomas), frequently used subject samples in psychological research, naturalistic observations of childbirth (Anderson, Standley, Nicholson), the accuracy of memories of nursery school behavior (Yarrow), locus of control, case studies of the terminally ill (Kubler-Ross), bystander apathy (Latané, Darley), Hans the clever horse (Pfungst), experimenter bias (Rosenthal), helping in the subway system (Piliavin), survey of attitudes to field studies (Wilson, Donnerstein).

Basic concepts the requirements of researchable questions, operational definitions, standards for questionnaire questions, problems of self-reports, reasons for testing, uses and limitations of research tools (laboratory and naturalistic observations, questionnaires, tests, case studies, laboratory and field experiments, and correlational studies), reasons why extraneous factors need to be controlled in an experiment, repetition effect, Hawthorne effect, experimental bias, demand characteristic, placebo condition, single- and double-blind procedures, the meaning of the size and sign of a correlation coefficient, correlation and causation, ethical guidelines and controversies.

Self-Quiz

1. Which problem impeded the study of floppy-eared rabbits?
a. Failure to be tentative
b. Lack of parsimony
c. Slavish allegiance to the scientific method
d. Stereotyped notions

2. What does the goal called control often mean in reality?
a. Application   *b.* Description
c. Explanation   *d.* Prediction

3. Which practice would be most likely to increase objectivity?
a. Arranging for an assistant who doesn't know the experimenter's hypotheses to conduct the study

b. Choosing a natural explanation and rejecting a supernatural one
c. Choosing a simple explanation and rejecting a complicated one
d. Trying to cast one's conclusions in open-minded language

4. Which action most clearly demonstrates an empirical attitude?
a. Basing conclusions on observations rather than on intuition or speculation
b. Emphasizing precision in report writing
c. Insisting that all psychological phenomena have natural causes
d. Remaining open-minded about conclusions

5. What characterizes a parsimonious explanation?
a. Objectivity   *b.* Precision
c. Relative simplicity   *d.* Tentativeness

6. Which is the best operational definition of curiosity?
a. Amount of inquisitiveness
b. Desire to know and understand
c. Extent of interest in diverse subject areas
d. Number of topics rated as interesting from a long list

7. What is the correct term for 200 women who are questioned by investigators to discover how women, in general, feel about abortions?
a. Population   *b.* Random sample
c. Representative sample   *d.* Sample

8. Psychologists, identity concealed, join a submarine crew to study the behavior of men in close quarters. What research tool are they using?
a. An assessment device
b. A correlational study
c. The experimental method
d. A participant observation

9. When compared with direct observation, which major advantage do questionnaires have?
a. Economy   *b.* Empiricism
c. Objectivity   *d.* Precision

10. Which problem do case studies *usually* present?
a. They are superficial.
b. They fail to reach tentative conclusions.
c. They have questionable generality.
d. They lack parsimony.

11. Which research tool can establish cause-and-effect relationships firmly?
a. Case study   *b.* Correlational study
c. Experimentation   *d.* Naturalistic observation

12. A behavioral scientist designs an experiment to find out whether the quantity of psychology learned in the introductory course is influenced by the relative amounts of time devoted to lecture and classroom discussion. What is the dependent variable in this study?
a. The behavioral scientist
b. The introductory course

c. The quantity of psychology learned

d. The relative amounts of time devoted to lecture and discussion

13. The term Hawthorne effect refers to the influence of what on performance?

a. All cues conveying the experimenter's hypothesis

b. Attention

c. Experimenter bias

d. Subjects' expectations

14. What function does a single-blind procedure in an experiment serve?

a. Controls for experimenter bias

b. Equalizes the attention paid to all groups

c. Prevents experimenters from knowing subjects' groups

d. Prevents subjects from knowing their own condition

15. Suppose an investigator finds a strong positive correlation between subjects' scores on a test of aggression and their number of automobile accidents. What conclusion can be reached?

a. Aggression and car-accident proneness have a common cause.

b. Being highly aggressive causes car accidents.

c. Highly aggressive people have fewer car accidents than less aggressive ones.

d. Less aggressive individuals have fewer car accidents than more aggressive ones.

Exercises

1. OPERATIONAL DEFINITIONS. To make certain that you understand the differences between operational and formal definitions, pick out the operational definitions below. If you make many mistakes, reread page 32.

a. *Anger*: blood pressure elevated above normal resting level accompanied by self-report of feeling wronged and wishing to retaliate

b. *Aggression*: numbers of hits, kicks, and pinches

c. *Hope*: feeling of optimism

d. *Love*: high score on the Fitch Love Questionnaire

e. *Hunger*: sensation of emptiness in the stomach

f. *Religious faith*: self-rating of 7 to 9 on a scale, indicating a strong to very strong belief in God

g. *Pain*: removal of hand from cold water

h. *Devotion*: feeling of great caring and concern

i. *Sleep*: record of particular brain-wave pattern

j. *Racial prejudice*: refusal to consider inviting home a member of another race

k. *Serenity*: sense of peace

2. SCIENTIFIC PRINCIPLES. To check your understanding of the principles that guide psychological research, describe the standards that are violated by the statements below. Unless otherwise indicated, choose only one violation per statement. If you make many mistakes, reread pages 28 to 31.

PRINCIPLES: determinism (D), empiricism (E), objectivity (O), parsimony (PA), precision (PR), tentativeness (T)

_____ **1.** The total number of Americans hospitalized in 1980 for mental disorders was very large.

_____ **2.** We hear more and more about pornography and sex crimes on the news, so they're probably both on the rise. (Select two violations.)

_____ **3.** We cannot hope to understand extrasensory perception (ESP).

_____ **4.** A short life expectancy among certain mental retardates is probably due to separation from parents in infancy. That separation results in depression. Eventually, the retardate gives up on life.

_____ **5.** We are studying joy. We will not define it but allow each research participant to interpret the phenomenon in his or her own way.

_____ **6.** The table manners of the Kuscoriads are revolting.

_____ **7.** Only one conclusion can be reached.

_____ **8.** In view of all the evidence, we are absolutely certain that marijuana usage leads to heroin addiction.

_____ **9.** We are born, philosophers tell us, with five basic needs.

_____ **10.** We may feel confident that females are more verbal than males, since child-care experts are unanimous in this verdict.

_____ **11.** People wear clothing because of symbolic guilt resulting from original sin. This guilt appears anew in the consciousness of every human being at birth.

_____ **12.** The awesome precision of these handwriting analysts is illustrated by the case of R. T.

3. RECOGNIZING INDEPENDENT AND DEPENDENT VARIABLES. Psychologists design experiments to test hypotheses—to find out whether independent variables cause or influence dependent variables. Although hypotheses may be phrased in many different ways, they may usually be reworded in the standard form: A change in X [the independent variable(s)] causes a change in Y [the dependent variable(s)]. Rewording a hypothesis so that it follows this standard form provides a way to identify the independent (IV) and dependent variables (DV). Reword each of the following questions in standard hypothesis form and identify the IVs and DVs. If you have difficulty, reread pages 40 to 42.

1. Do ads featuring beautiful people sell more cosmetics than those featuring plain people?

2. Are objects valued more highly when they are worked for than when they are obtained free?

3. Does a neat appearance have anything to do with getting a job?

4. Are frightened people likely to make more mistakes on a simple task than calm people?

4. CORRELATIONS. Use this exercise to evaluate your understanding of correlational concepts. Examine each statement below. If the variables are correlated, give the sign [positive (+) or negative (−)] of the correlation. If there is no correlation between variables, state "none." If you make many mistakes, reread pages 46 to 49.

_____ *1.* Younger children tend to have higher ratings on activity level than older children.

_____ *2.* The more coffee a person consumes, the greater her/his risk of heart attack.

_____ *3.* There is no relationship whatsoever between height and a firefighter's performance.

_____ *4.* Baby booms are associated with more government restrictions on activities, such as curfews and driving bans.

_____ *5.* Drug experimentation among youths increases as their rated happiness decreases.

Suggested Readings

1. Bachrach, A. *Psychological research: An introduction.* (3d ed.) New York: Random House, 1972 (paperback). An engaging introduction to psychological research by the psychologist who wrote, "People don't usually do research the way people who write books about research say they do research."

2. Doherty, M. E., & Shemberg, K. M. *Asking questions about behavior: An introduction to what psychologists do.* (2d ed.) Glenview, Ill.: Scott Foresman, 1978 (paperback). Written in a conversational style, this brief book focuses on psychological research. It uses studies on stress as illustrations.

3. Siegel, M. H., & Zeigler, H. P. (Eds.) *Psychological research: The inside story.* New York: Harper & Row, 1976 (paperback). Some outstanding psychologists describe their own research: "How they work; how they become diverted by apparently irrelevant issues; how they make mistakes; [and] how their plans grow, change, and mature."

4. Golden, M. P. (Ed.) *The research experience.* Itasca, Ill.: Peacock, 1976 (paperback). This collection of articles has two major purposes: to expose students to a wide range of research strategies and to introduce the experiential aspects of the behavioral sciences. Each article is followed by a personal account written by at least one of the researchers involved. The selections have high interest value. They describe investigations of the Watts riots, prejudice based on sex, and the dynamics of selling used cars, for example. The book should help the student appreciate the day-to-day difficulties and joys of psychological research.

5. Runyon, R. P. *Winning with statistics: A painless first look at numbers, ratios, percentages, means, and inference.* Reading, Mass.: Addison-Wesley, 1977 (paperback). Using stories, satire, humor, illustrations from advertisements, and cartoons, Runyon conveys some important insights into statistical concepts.

6. Warwick, D. P. Deceptive research: Social scientists ought to stop lying. *Psychology Today*, 1975, **8**(9), 38ff. Warwick describes several deceptive strategies commonly used in psychological research and questions the ethics of deception. He concludes that behavioral scientists "should put their own house in order with a permanent moratorium on deceptive research."

7. Bakan, D. Psychology can now kick the science habit. *Psychology Today*, 1972, **5**(10), 26ff. After tracing the history of modern psychology, Bakan argues that the time to stop relying on the methods of the natural sciences has arrived. He offers some controversial guidelines for an "authentic psychology."

Answer Keys

Locus of Control

Give yourself 1 point for each of the answers listed below. The higher the score, the more external you seem to be.

1. *b*   **2.** *b*   **3.** *a*   **4.** *b*   **5.** *a*

Self-Quiz

1. *d* (26)   **2.** *a* (28)   **3.** *a* (29)   **4.** *a* (29)
5. *c* (30)   **6.** *d* (32)   **7.** *d* (33)   **8.** *d* (34)
9. *a* (36)   **10.** *c* (39)   **11.** *c* (40)   **12.** *c* (40)
13. *b* (43)   **14.** *d* (45)   **15.** *d* (47)

Exercise 1

a, b, d, f, g, i, and *j* are operational definitions.

Exercise 2

1. PR   **2.** E, PR   **3.** D   **4.** PA   **5.** PR   **6.** O
7. T   **8.** T   **9.** E   **10.** E   **11.** PA   **12.** O

Exercise 3

1. IV, type of ad; DV, cosmetic buying   **2.** IV, the manner in which objects are acquired; DV, value placed on objects   **3.** IV, neat appearance; DV, being hired   **4.** IV, degree of fear; DV, number of mistakes on simple task

Exercise 4

1. negative   **2.** positive   **3.** none   **4.** positive
5. negative

CHAPTER THREE
The Beginning: Heredity, Environment, and the Early Development of the Child

A young father was diapering his six-month-old son dutifully when his wife rebuked him for his lack of interest. "You don't have to be so grim about it, you can talk to him and smile a little," she said. The man responded with apparent irritation, "He has nothing to say to me, and I have nothing to say to him [1]." The father was very wrong. The infant has a lot to say to us, and that's why we're beginning our study of psychology with early development. Throughout this entire chapter, we'll be focusing on the period of time that extends from conception through early childhood. A great deal is happening during this period. The physical changes are striking. Starting as a single cell at conception, the infant will be made up of close to 1,000 billion cells by the time of birth. Psychologists focus on behavior, of course, and not on counting cells. While it's much more difficult to attach numbers to behavioral complexities, conduct too is changing rapidly and dramatically.

In future chapters we will be describing the development—throughout the life span—of specific functions, including perception, thought, language, personality, and social behavior. We focus on adult development and aging in Chapter 14. In this chapter we are concerned with early development and with developmental processes, the hereditary and environmental forces that interact continuously to shape human behavior. We begin by describing a newborn baby.

The Neonate

The *neonate*, as the newborn human baby is called during its first two weeks, weighs about 7½ pounds on the average and measures between 18 and 21 inches. Early philosophers and psychologists characterized the infant as both ugly and inept. The French philosopher Jean-Jacques Rousseau called the young baby "a perfect idiot, an automaton, a statue without motion and almost without feeling [2]." G. Stanley Hall, one of the first American psychologists to study children systematically, perceived the newborn as "squinting, cross-eyed, pot-bellied, and bow-legged" and attributed to it a "monotonous and dismal cry" and "red, shriveled, parboiled skin [3]." The distinguished psychologist William James did not think very highly of infants either. He wrote, "assailed by eyes, ears, nose, skin, and entrails at once, the newborn feels that all is one great blooming, buzzing confusion [4]."

While neonates may appear homely (see Figure 3-1), recent studies have changed psychologists' opinions about their competence. Newborn babies are actually responsive, active, and aware. From the very first, they show a wide range of sensory capabilities. (Keep in mind that when we say neonates have this or that ability, we mean that many do. Human beings vary at birth, as at other times.)

Neonates must smell and taste. We know these capacities exist because of numerous observations. Whiffs of onion- or licorice-like substances, for example, cause changes in activity, respiration, and heart rates. And certain fluids are sucked especially vigorously while others are refused entirely [5]. Although they cannot coordinate

FIGURE 3-1 Though newborn babies are not inept, they may appear homely. At the very least, their heads are likely to seem disproportionately large. The adult's head is about 5 percent of the total body length, while the neonate's head is approximately 25 percent. [*Wayne Miller/Magnum.*]

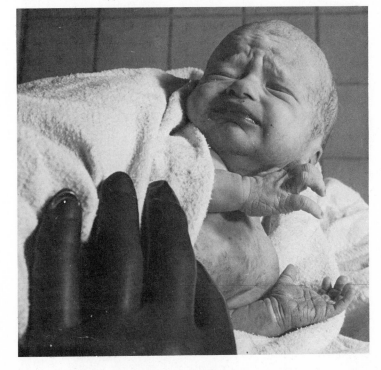

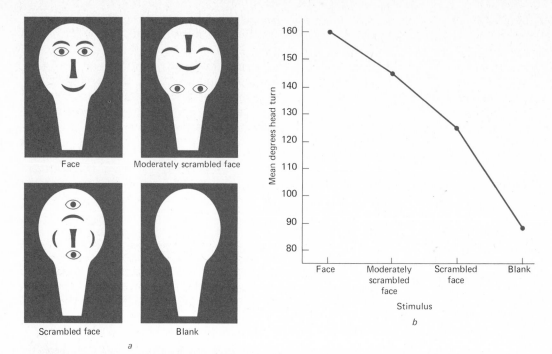

Face

Moderately scrambled face

Scrambled face

Blank

a

b

Mean degrees head turn

Face | Moderately scrambled face | Scrambled face | Blank

Stimulus

FIGURE 3-2 Infants twenty-four hours of age and less were tested with the four figures shown (*a*) to see how avidly they attended to each pattern (operationally defined as how far the infant turned its head to watch the figure). The stimuli were varied randomly and the experimenter did not see them. The graph (*b*) indicates that attention increased as "faceness" increased. [*After Freedman, 1974.*]

both eyes to focus sharply on specific objects, newly born infants must see to some extent because their eyes follow moving targets [6]. Psychologists suspect that babies may be born with preferences for human faces since they exert more effort to look at face representations than at representations of scrambled features or blank heads [7]. See Figure 3-2. Newborns must hear too, for their activity and heart rates accelerate when they are presented with particular sounds, especially high-pitched voices [8]. These observations suggest that the neonate is fashioned to respond to the mother, thus making it likely, perhaps, that

she will find the baby attractive and care for it.

Human beings are equipped at birth with other behaviors that help them survive. They suck to gain nourishment. They cry to motivate caretakers to minister to their needs. Numerous inborn *reflexes* (responses automatically elicited by environmental events) help sustain the baby. When pillows or covers interfere with breathing, infants turn their heads. They close their eyelids to protect their eyes from intense light. They move their limbs or twist their bodies when they encounter painful stimulation. If you touch a baby's cheek lightly, it will turn its head toward the stroked side. This reaction,

called the *rooting reflex*, guides the mouth toward the mother's nipple. Babies possess numerous additional reflexes, many of which are not well understood.

Neonates have another powerful capability that psychologists have discovered only recently. They learn. To be more precise, they alter their responses when doing so leads to pleasurable consequences. Infants several days old will modify sucking or head-turning patterns to increase the milk supply or taste a sweet solution [9]. Shortly after birth, the baby is already showing signs of curiosity. A newborn infant will gaze longer at new targets than at old familiar ones [10].

The neonate is at a beginning and an ending. Birth signals the end of the baby's approximately nine-month sojourn in the uterus. By the time of birth, genes, intrauterine environment, and conditions during delivery have shaped the individual's identity to a significant degree. Birth is the beginning of new influences, including family, social groups, and culture. While neonates are nearly complete (vital organs formed and functioning at least partially), they do not yet possess distinctly human characteristics: language, reason, control, intellect, conscience. They have a lot of developing to do. *Developmental psychologists* investigate the growth of physical structure, behavior, and mental functioning in people and other animals from any point after conception to any time before death.

We turn now to the forces that shape development.

THE ONGOING INTERACTIONS BETWEEN HEREDITY AND ENVIRONMENT

The theme of this chapter is simple: Heredity and environment interact continuously to influence development. Let's start with some definitions. What do psychologists mean by the words "heredity" and "environment"? *Heredity* refers to the physical characteristics transmitted directly from parent to offspring at conception. *Environment* encompasses many influences. Psychologist Donald Hebb has enumerated five that overlap considerably.

1. *The chemical prenatal environment.* Chemical influences which act before birth, such as drugs, nutrition, and hormones.
2. The *chemical postnatal environment.* Chemical influences which act after birth, such as oxygen and nutrition.
3. *Constant sensory experiences.* Events processed by the senses both before and after birth that are normally inevitable for all members of a particular species. After birth, people are ordinarily exposed to changing visual patterns, sounds of human voices, and physical contact with caretak-

ers. Young songbirds universally experience the sight, sounds, and smells of their parents.
4. *Variable sensory experiences.* Events processed by the senses which differ among animals of a particular species, depending on each individual's particular circumstances. Christine, for instance, is surrounded by wealth, attended by servants, and educated at boarding schools. Albert, on the other hand, grows up in a coal-mining town with his widowed mother and is educated in a one-room schoolhouse.
5. *Traumatic physical events.* Experiences that result in the destruction of an organism's cells either before or after birth [11].

We said that heredity and environment interact *continuously* to influence development. The word "continuously" should be emphasized. At conception, heredity programs human potentialities into people. At the same time, the environment is shaping the unborn child. Genetic material operates *within a cell*, while the fetus (roughly, the organism before birth) grows to maturity *within the uterus*. Conditions in either setting may modify the individual. Both heredity and environment *together* continue to shape development as infants grow into childhood and adulthood.

Sometimes students ask, "Is heredity or environment the most important influence?" For centuries scientists have been discussing this *nature-nurture controversy.* It makes no sense to say that heredity or environment is more significant because they are both absolutely essential. The nature and extent of each influence depend on the other's contribution. Consider language. Environment determines whether one converses in Spanish, Russian, Swahili, Italian, English, or some other tongue. But genetics provides people with vocal cords, a high degree of control over the muscles in their lips, a particular type of language-processing brain, and other physical structures necessary for speech. No setting under the sun could produce talking dogs, geese, or gerbils. The question about the roles of genetics and environment must be rephrased if scientists are to make any headway. Instead of the question above, we must ask, "To what extent are behavioral and physical *differences* observed among people or other animals influenced by differences in genetic inheritance? To what extent are they shaped by differences between environments?"

Throughout this chapter, we use Hebb's classification scheme. We turn first to the impact of heredity on development. Then we examine the influence of the chemical prenatal environment and of constant and variable sensory experiences.

HEREDITY AND BEHAVIOR

In the 1860s the prominent British psychologist Francis Galton attempted to investigate how genetics influenced genius. Galton had a similarly eminent cousin named Charles Darwin. According to scientific lore, Galton was struck by family resemblances. Greatness obviously ran in his own family. Did it have a genetic basis? In order to find out, Galton collected data on the family members of celebrated men in science, law, politics, the military, and the ministry. He discovered that these outstanding citizens had a greater number of distinguished relatives than chance alone could account for. He also found that close blood relatives were more likely to be illustrious than distant ones. Minimizing the fact that prominent people often furnished their children with social and educational advantages, Galton concluded that heredity is responsible for brilliance. Despite its shortcomings, Galton's study served as a catalyst, stimulating other investigations of heredity and behavior.

Today psychologists known as *behavior geneticists* use a variety of sophisticated strategies to study (1) the degree to which heredity influences *differences* in the behavior and mental functioning of a specific population and (2) the biological mechanisms by which genes affect the expression of behavior and mental functioning. Keep in mind that saying "genetics influences X or Y" does not mean that X or Y is fixed by heredity or that environment exerts little influence.

Before looking at contemporary behavior-genetic procedures, we review some elementary facts about human heredity. Our summary covers only the most basic essentials. For more detailed information, please consult a biology textbook.

Human Genetics: A Brief Review

1. Technically, each human life begins at conception when one of the father's approximately 360 million *sperm* cells unites with the mother's egg or *ovum*, producing a single fertilized egg cell known as the *zygote*. The egg and sperm are manufactured by reproductive cells called *germ cells*.

2. Genetic information is contained in threadlike structures called *chromosomes*. The chromosomes are found within the *nucleus* (a distinct, centrally located structure) of most bodily cells including germ cells. Human cells contain forty-six chromosomes. Egg and sperm receive only half the full number of chromosomes, twenty-three, from the germ cells. Consequently, when they unite, the zygote contains the complete number, forty-six.

3. The forty-six chromosomes inherited from the mother and father are arranged in twenty-three pairs. One chromosome in each pair came from the father while the other came from the mother. Each pair has a distinctive size and shape, as shown in Figure 3-3. The first twenty-two chromosome pairs match rather closely. The twenty-third pair, which does not always match, determines the sex of the baby. Females receive two large chromosomes, known as X chromosomes. Males receive a smaller chromosome, known as the Y chromosome, and usually one larger X chromosome. One Y is believed to be sufficient to make a male regardless of the number of X's.

4. Each chromosome consists of thousands of smaller particles called *genes*. The gene is considered the basic unit of heredity. Composed of a complex chemical substance, *deoxyribonucleic acid* (*DNA*, for short), genes direct the production of chemical substances called *proteins*. *Structural proteins* form blood, muscle, tissue, organs, and other bodily structures. *Enzymes*, a second type of protein, control physical-chemical reactions within the body (the capture and storage of energy, the breakdown of food, and the timing of development, for example). It is essential to note that organisms do not inherit full-blown behavior patterns. Instead, they are endowed with bodily structures and physical-chemical controls that make a particular range of responses to an environment likely.

5. People and other animals inherit broad *species*

characteristics. Because we acquire opposing thumbs and mobile fingers, we easily learn to manipulate tools. The inheritance of large cerebral cortexes permits the processing of vast amounts of information. At the same time, human beings and other animals inherit unique traits. As an individual you are programmed by your genes with the potential to grow to a certain height and to possess a certain degree of susceptibility to poison ivy.

6. Genes for particular characteristics and functions are located at specific sites called *loci* (singular: *locus*) on particular chromosomes. When the egg and sperm unite, the zygote receives a single gene at each chromosome locus from each parent. Genes on the sex chromosomes (the twenty-third pair) are said to be sex-linked since they are transmitted differently to males and females.

7. If the genes that the zygote receives at a particular locus contain conflicting "orders," one may dominate completely or partially or both may influence the end result.

8. Parents contribute half their chromosomes to each offspring, with each child receiving a somewhat different combination. This means that "each of us is a unique genetic experiment never tried before and never to be repeated again [12]" with one important exception, identical twins, triplets, and the like. *Identical*, or *monozygotic*, offspring come from an unusual event, the splitting of a single zygote into two or more zygotes with identical genes. Most multiple births are *fraternal*, or *dizygotic*. They arise from the union of different egg and sperm cells and resemble one another genetically only as closely as brothers and sisters born at different times. They share about 50 percent of their genes. It should now be clear that people vary greatly in genetic similarity. Monozygotic twins are identical. Members of a family are similar. And unrelated individuals are very different.

9. Scientists' understanding of the genetics of different species varies. Fruitfly heredity is so precisely understood that many traits may be assigned to specific genes on particular chromosomes. Only a small number of human characteristics can be assigned to specific chromosomes, even though geneticists believe that a great many differences among people are influenced by heredity.

10. The heredity of human behavior is difficult to investigate. People are, in many respects, "an unfavorable organism for genetic analysis: experimental crosses [breeding] may not be performed; environmental control may not be imposed; the

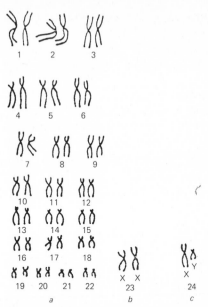

FIGURE 3-3 The first twenty-two pairs of human chromosomes (*a*) look similar regardless of one's gender. The twenty-third pairs of a normal woman (*b*) and of a normal man (*c*) are shown. [*Courtesy of Raymond Turpin.*]

generation interval is relatively long; and the number of offspring per family is relatively small [13]." Moreover, geneticists who study fruitflies and other fairly simple organisms are frequently interested in *discrete characteristics*, those that an animal has or does not have, such as red eyes or curved antennae. When we focus on the *behavior* of simple animals or people, we must deal with *continuous traits*, those that exist in degrees. All normal human beings show some amount of motor coordination and intelligence no matter how ungainly or dull they are. Continuous characteristics like these are thought to be influenced by numerous genes, each one making a small contribution. It is much more difficult to pinpoint many small contributors than to locate one. There is another major obstacle. Continuous characteristics depend on both environment and heredity. Consider athletic prowess. Heredity may contribute a propensity to develop long limbs, a large muscle mass, and acute vision. But if people are malnourished or fail to practice, they will not develop these skills. The same set of genes can produce different results, then, when environments vary.

Studying the Influence of Genetics on Behavioral Differences

We turn now to some of the techniques commonly used to investigate the effects of heredity on human behavioral differences. We focus on *temperament*, defined as a personal style of responding, feeling, and acting. A temperament includes a typical level of activity, sociability, and emotionality.

Twin and adoption studies   Galton introduced the *twin study* method some twenty years after he investigated the families of prominent men. The new strategy was a great improvement over the earlier one. (You may want to review the sections entitled "Experiments" and "Correlational Studies" in Chapter 2 if you have forgotten the technical terms.) We have an experimental group composed of monozygotic twin pairs and a control group made up of dizygotic twin pairs. The independent variable, genetic similarity, is manipulated by nature long before the study begins. In a pair of identical twins each individual has exactly the same genes. Fraternal twins have only 50 percent of their genes in common, on the average. The major extraneous variable, similarity of experiences, is controlled to some extent. Both types of twins have similar experiences. They inhabited the uterus together. Since they are the same age at the same time, they were probably treated alike by family members and friends. To measure the dependent variable, similarity, psychologists test or assess both groups of twins on the characteristic of interest. If the performances of identical twins are more highly correlated than those of fraternal twins, then heredity is probably influencing the differences. If the performances of both types of twins are similar, then genetics does not appear to be especially influential.

Differences in that aspect of temperament called sociability, or friendliness, have been investigated in numerous twin studies. Several research teams have demonstrated that identical twins are more likely than fraternal twins to be similarly *introverted* (shy, reserved, and withdrawn) or *extroverted* (outgoing, friendly, and active) in social situations [14]. Twin studies find that genes contribute to human differences in emotionality, activity, and mental health, as well [15]. If temperament were entirely determined by genetics, identical twins would show perfect agreement. They'd both be introverted to the same degree, for instance. The fact that the temperament-related behavior of identical twins varies quite a bit indicates that experiences shape these differences also. (See Figure 3-4.)

Twin study is far from a perfect natural experiment. The most serious flaw is the assumption that sets of identical and fraternal twins share equally similar environments both before and after birth. Whereas dizygotic twins are usually enveloped in separate inner and outer bags and fed through different placenta in the uterus, monozygotic twins ordinarily share the same outer sac and placenta. And, because they are so similar in physical endowment, one-egg twins are more likely than two-egg twins to be treated in the same way after birth. In short, in addition to having the same heredity, identical twins probably experience a more similar environment than do fraternal twins. To get around this problem, psychologists sometimes compare identical twins reared in separate households (when they can be found) to fraternal twins reared in the same home. The assumption here is that separate households are bound to provide more diverse environments than a single one.

Because identical twins reared apart are exceedingly difficult to find, psychologists turn increasingly to *adoption studies*. An adoption study is a natural experiment, somewhat like a twin study. Adoptees and their parents share a common environment but dissimilar heredity. Natural children and their parents have both similar heredity and similar experiences. If specific behavioral differences are influenced by genetics, then investigators should discover that biological parents and their natural children are more

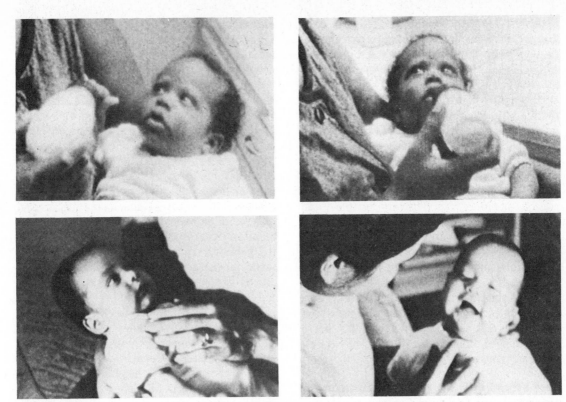

FIGURE 3-4 These male identical and fraternal twins are approximately two months of age. The identical pair (*top*) often displayed similar social responses. Here, both infants fixate on the caretaker's face while being fed. The fraternal set (*bottom*) frequently responded differently to social stimulation. Here, one twin smiles drowsily with his eyes closed, while the other appears alert (both eyes open) and stern. These twins and many others were filmed in numerous situations over an eight-month period for a study conducted by Daniel G. Freedman and his coworkers. Judges rated the filmed behavior of each twin individually, with no judge evaluating both members of a single twin pair. The investigators concluded that monozygotic pairs showed more similar social behavior than did dizygotic ones [98]. [*Courtesy of Daniel G. Freedman, University of Chicago.*]

similar to one another on the characteristics of interest than the adoptees and their adoptive parents. The behavior of adoptees should resemble that of their biological parents more closely than that of their adoptive ones.

Breeding techniques Breeding techniques are frequently employed to study the influence of genetics on differences in animal behavior. The method of *inbred strains* is most commonly used. To produce an inbred strain, related individuals (usually brothers and sisters) are mated for at least twenty generations (in some cases, fifty to one hun-

dred or more) until the animals are practically genetically identical. The behavior of different inbred strains reared under standard environmental conditions is then compared in some test situation. If the response of each strain is distinctive, then we assume that heredity is influencing the behavioral diversity. Inbred laboratory strains of both rats and mice show consistent differences in activity level, in emotionality in new situations, and on other measures of temperament [16]. Purebred dogs, a natural example of inbred strains, demonstrate clear temperament differences too. In a classic series of studies, John Paul

Scott and John Fuller observed five purebred dog strains reared under similar environmental conditions to assess genetic influences on canine social behavior. For one test, emotional reactivity was operationally defined (in Chapter 2) by ratings of distress vocalizations, tail wagging, tremor, investigative behavior, escape attempts, and similar activities. Scott and Fuller compared the animals' reactions at different ages to hearing a bell ring, being left alone, and other experiences. Total emotional reactivity ratings revealed consistent differences. Terriers, beagles, and basenjis were more emotionally reactive than shetland sheepdogs and cocker spaniels [17].

While breeding experiments on people are impossible, of course, human pedigrees can be studied. Such investigations reveal that certain types of neurological diseases show family patterns that support a genetic explanation. Human pedigree studies have not disclosed information about the inheritance of temperament differences.

Investigations of genetic abnormalities Another tactic used to investigate the effects of heredity on behavior is the systematic observation of people and animals with known genetic abnormalities. Several human genetic irregularities are correlated strongly with specific patterns of mental test performance. In 1 out of every 3,000 births, for example, a person inherits a normal X sex chromosome but no second X or Y sex chromosome. This condition is known as *Turner's syndrome*. Individuals with this abnormality resemble females, are short in stature, and impaired in sexual development. Whereas their overall intelligence appears normal, people with Turner's syndrome show poor abilities to visualize three-dimensional objects in space. Some investigations suggest that these spatial abilities may be influenced by heredity [18]. Studies of human beings with known genetic abnormalities have not yielded conclusive evidence of a genetic basis for any temperament differences.

The study of infant differences Another strategy that is sometimes used to

understand how heredity influences behavioral variability is the study of infant differences. Researchers measure the characteristics of newborns before they have been influenced (at least very much) by the social environment, and they continue to assess the same dispositions throughout childhood and adulthood. If a specific pattern persists in large numbers of subjects, we infer that the continuity reflects significant hereditary influence. Observations from this perspective may support or cast doubt on findings from other sources. They are not conclusive for several reasons: (1) a neonate's behavior could be the result of experiences in the intrauterine environment or during delivery; and (2) the persistence of characteristics observed in infancy can be explained in several ways, as we will see.

For centuries mothers have been insisting that their newborn babies differ from one another. Psychologists, in contrast, long viewed neonates as essentially interchangeable. In recent years it has become clear that mothers were right all along. Neonates show stable, measurable, individual differences. Some are easy-going. They sleep, lie quietly in their cribs, or babble softly to themselves most of the time. Others appear to be perpetually upset. They thrash about vigorously, sleep fitfully, and yell loudly for long periods of time [19]. Infants' sensory thresholds differ too. Some babies respond to minimal sensory stimulation. Others are difficult to provoke [20]. Female infants, for instance, flex their toes at lower intensities of electrical current than male babies do, indicating that they are more sensitive to this type of stimulation [21]. Neonates vary qualitatively and quantitatively in their reactions to stress and discomfort. Some infants show relatively intense responses; others, relatively mild ones. When hungry, infants may vomit, flush (because of increased blood pressure), show an elevated heart rate or a rapid change in skin temperature, or break out with a rash [22]. Many behavioral scientists suspect that heredity influences these early differences.

About fifteen years ago three physicians, Alexander Thomas, Stella Chess, and Herbert Birch, began studying the behavioral differences of approximately 140 infants. They wanted to see whether temperament persisted over time and how it was affected by specific experiences. Through interviews with parents, the researchers obtained detailed descriptions of each infant's conduct, beginning at two or three months of age. Checks by trained observers established that such parental reports were reliable. Using these descriptions, Thomas, Chess, and Birch rated each baby on nine temperament dimensions: extent of motor activity (activity level), degree of regularity of functioning (rhythmicity), response to new situations (approach or withdrawal), response to altered situations (adaptability), intensity of reaction, level of stimulation necessary to evoke a response (responsiveness), general quality of mood, distractability, and span of attention and persistence at an activity. At frequent intervals throughout childhood the investigators continued collecting detailed information on behavior to assess these same characteristics.

Thomas, Chess, and Birch distinguished three temperament patterns, which they labeled "easy," "difficult," and "slow to warm up." "Easy" infants gave their parents few problems. They had sunny dispositions. Their eating and sleeping patterns were regular. They were quick to adapt to new routines, foods, and people. These angelic babies continued to be characterized in this way as they grew throughout childhood. Of the sample, 40 percent were classified "easy." "Difficult" infants, in contrast, were rough on their parents. They were disagreeable, fussy, and hard to manage. They slept and ate irregularly. They rejected new foods and withdrew from new situations. Frustration sent them into tantrums. They cried a lot. Above all, they were loud and intense. "Difficult" babies continued to be "difficult" as they grew older. Of the sample, 10 percent were labeled "difficult." A third group of infants was characterized as "slow to warm up." These children were somewhat negative in mood. They adapted slowly to new situations and withdrew when exposed to new experiences. Throughout their childhood they continued to

display these same characteristics. Of the sample, 15 percent were classified in the "slow to warm up" category. It is important to note that more than one-third of the infants were not sufficiently consistent to be included in any one of these groups.

Thomas, Chess, and Birch made an important discovery as they studied their youngsters throughout childhood. Out of forty-two children who required professional attention for behavioral problems, 70 percent had been initially classified "difficult," whereas only 18 percent had been categorized "easy." The child's temperament, as assessed in infancy, related very strongly then, to later adjustment [23]. The Thomas-Chess-Birch investigation supports the notion that temperament differences are at least partly determined by heredity and can be reliably detected early in infancy. Additional studies find that sociability, activity, aggression in males, and passivity in females tend to be fairly stable from childhood to adulthood [24].

The findings that temperament differences are frequently consistent throughout life can be explained by genetics and/or by environmental influences. At the same time that neonates are being shaped, they are molding those around them. An irritable, howling baby who will not be soothed and who resists cuddling (perhaps because of the mother's traumatic pregnancy) will doubtlessly affect parents differently than a serene, infrequently troubled cherub that smiles and clings contentedly. There is evidence, incidentally, that mothers who are stressed emotionally, socially, and economically do produce a disproportionate number of children with difficult temperaments [25]. It takes only a little imagination to see that parental treatment may strengthen children's behavior. Frustrated, angry caretakers are likely to behave harshly, for example, distressing the baby and perpetuating the cycle. The fact that fretful newborns are more apt to be abused than placid ones supports this idea [26].

We have reviewed procedures that are commonly used to study heredity's effects on behavioral differences. We turn now to environmental influences on development. ▲

FIGURE 3-5 This fetus is seventeen weeks old. By the fourth month after conception, fetuses may be sucking their thumbs, as well as turning their heads and pushing with their hands and feet. Prenatal thumbsucking is thought to prepare infants to gain nourishment immediately after birth. Some fetuses suck so vigorously that they're born with a calloused thumb. [*From Rugh and Shettles, with Einhorn, 1971. Used with permission.*]

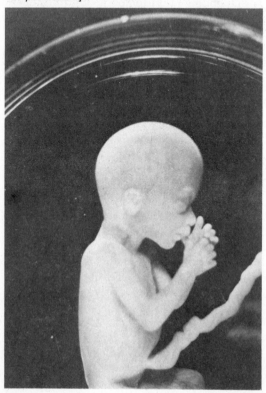

THE INTRAUTERINE ENVIRONMENT AND EARLY DEVELOPMENT

The infant begins life as a single cell, the zygote. The chromosomes duplicate and the cell divides and becomes two. Seventy-two hours after the cell was fertilized, there are thirty-two cells; a day later, seventy. The rapidly multiplying cells pack together tightly in a ball-like mass and soon begin differentiating into organs, muscles, bones, tissues, and other bodily components.

The unborn baby's first forty or so weeks of life are spent within the uterus. The *intrauterine period* (the time spent within the uterus) is usually broken into three phases. The *germinal stage* lasts from conception to about fourteen days; the *embryonic stage* from approximately two to eight weeks. At eight weeks the unborn baby becomes known as a *fetus*. The fetus is active. It turns, kicks, somersaults, squints, smiles, hiccoughs, clenches its fists, sucks its thumb, and responds to tones and vibrations. See Figure 3-5.

In the uterus (*in utero*) the fetus receives *constant sensory stimulation* (in Hebb's terms) from the churning amniotic fluid surrounding it and the mother's beating heart. The mother's daily movements provide *variable sensory experiences*. Maternal health, diet, drug use, and emotional state constitute *chemical prenatal influences* that can destroy cells, functioning as *traumatic events*. In this section we describe the sensitive period concept and examine potentially destructive chemical prenatal influences.

Sensitive Periods

After conception, the organs of the unborn child unfold in a fixed order. Many bodily systems pass through a stage when they are maximally vulnerable to disruption from harmful experiences (including the absence of necessary ones). We call periods of rapid growth during which organisms of a particular species are unusually susceptible to their environment *sensitive periods* (or *critical periods*). Sensitive periods have these important characteristics:

1. Most occur before or soon after birth when the animal is growing rapidly.
2. They last for short periods of time—usually a few hours to a few months—depending on the species and its life span.
3. Certain types of stimulation during these periods have long-lasting effects on the animal's subsequent development. The same stimulation has little or no effect on the animal's growing system if it precedes or follows the sensitive period [27].

The disruptive experiences that we will be describing often occur during sensitive prenatal periods.

The Mother's Health

Diseases, especially when accompanied by fever, can injure the growing fetus. Chronic maternal illnesses, such as diabetes, tuberculosis, syphilis, gonorrhea, and urinary infections, are all associated with birth defects in children. When contracted during the first three months of pregnancy, even comparatively mild maternal disorders, such as mumps, influenza, and rubella (German measles), may damage the developing child. If the mother develops rubella during the early weeks of pregnancy, for example, the baby has a 60 percent chance of being born with some abnormality. Because the heart, nervous system, and sense organs are developing

particularly rapidly at this time, congenital (inborn) heart disease, eye defects, deafness, and mental retardation often result [28]. And fetuses can actually catch illnesses such as smallpox, chicken pox, and mumps from their mothers.

The Mother's Diet

Many authorities feel that inadequate nutrition is the greatest single threat to the child's optimum development in utero. Much research supports the hypothesis that mothers who are seriously malnourished cannot maintain an adequate food supply for themselves or their developing babies. By examining records made during the Dutch famine of 1944–1945 (lasting about six months), Zena Stein and her coworkers found that malnourishment slowed fetal growth [29]. In another study, Harry Ebbs and his associates observed 210 women who were attending a clinic at the University of Toronto. All the mothers-to-be had been on inadequate diets for the first four to five months of their pregnancies. At this late point in time, 90 of the women received supplements to make their diets adequate. The remaining 120 women continued to eat as they had before. Both the pregnancies and the infants of the two groups were compared. Mothers on good diets enjoyed better health than those on inadequate diets throughout the remainder of their pregnancies. They experienced fewer complications, such as anemia, toxemia (a condition of unknown origin characterized by swelling limbs and associated with kidney and circulatory problems), threatened and actual miscarriages, and premature and still births. Their labors were five hours shorter on the average. And the infants of mothers on good diets had better health records than those of mothers on inadequate diets immediately after birth and for the entire first six months of their lives [30].

Autopsies following the death of extremely malnourished humans and other animals suggest that severe malnutrition damages the fetus's nervous system. Early in pregnancy, serious malnourishment may interfere with *myelination* (the growth of critically important insulating fatty sheathes surrounding nerves). Both prenatally and in the first six months of life, when the brain is growing by cell division, severe starvation may decrease the expected number of brain cells drastically (by as much as 40 percent). After six months of age, when brain growth is the product of increased brain cell size, serious malnourishment reduces the ultimate size of brain cells [31]. Currently, scientists do not know whether malnutrition in utero must be extreme to depress intellectual functioning. Nor do they know whether retardation due to malnourishment is reversible after birth [32].

The Mother's Use of Chemicals

Chemicals, such as drugs and food additives, within the mother's bloodstream may affect the developing baby in several ways. They may cross over to the fetus unchanged, influencing it directly. They may produce physical and chemical by-products, or *metabolites*, within the fetus's body. Finally, they may alter the intrauterine environment and influence the infant indirectly. The baby appears to be especially vulnerable to the effects of harmful chemicals in early pregnancy when it is growing most rapidly. The potentially dangerous effects of drugs during pregnancy were brought to public awareness in the late 1950s and early 1960s by the tragic consequences associated with the tranquilizer *thalidomide*. Many women who took this drug soon after conception delivered stillborn or grossly deformed infants.

Unfortunately, the consequences of specific chemicals are difficult to foresee or track down for several reasons.

1. Chemicals which have no effect upon the mother may injure the fetus.
2. The effects of chemical agents depend on (*a*) the dosage, (*b*) the time during development when the substance is administered, and (*c*) the genetically determined susceptibility of the particular fetus.

3. Testing chemical substances on animals is not always conclusive. Creatures of one species (say, rats) may be unaffected by a given chemical agent while members of another (for example, people) may be susceptible.

Despite these problems, scientists have determined that there are a number of potentially destructive substances in common use. We will review some of the most important findings. Preliminary research on oral contraceptives by David Carr suggests that women "on the pill" must be careful about becoming pregnant too soon after discontinuing pill use. Of fifty-four fetuses spontaneously aborted within six months after mothers stopped using birth control pills (in some cases pills had been ingested early in pregnancy), 48 percent showed chromosomal abnormalities. Only 22 percent of 227 spontaneously aborted fetuses whose mothers had not been taking "the pill" showed such defects [33]. The babies of narcotics (heroin, opium, codeine) addicts may become addicted themselves in utero and display acute withdrawal symptoms at birth: irritability, trembling, vomiting, restlessness, sleeplessness, fever, and convulsions. When these symptoms are severe, death may result. Premature births are also associated with narcotics use.

Alcohol is another dangerous drug for pregnant women. Extensive drinking during pregnancy can result in a cluster of infant symptoms, known as the *fetal alcohol syndrome*: retarded physical growth, a small head and subnormal intelligence, problems in motor coordination, heart defects, facial abnormalities, and joint distortions. Even moderate drinking can create severe problems. James Hanson studied seventy-four women who consumed 2 ounces of 100-proof alcohol each day, on the average, before and during pregnancy. He found that 12 percent of their babies showed one or more characteristics of the fetal alcohol syndrome. Fewer than 3 percent of ninety mothers who drank little or no alcohol during pregnancy had babies who showed similar defects [34]. Precisely how alcohol produces these consequences is not well understood.

Cigarette smoking appears to harm unborn infants too. There is a great deal of evidence for this statement. A group of medical researchers headed by T. M. Frazier studied close to 3,000 pregnant women before and after delivery. They found that the rate of premature deliveries varied predictably with the mother's smoking history: approximately 11 percent for nonsmokers, 14 percent for smokers who began during pregnancy, and 19 percent for chronic smokers. As the quantity of cigarettes smoked rose, so also did the *incidence* of premature deliveries. The infants of smokers tended to weigh less than those of nonsmokers too [35]. Women who give up smoking by the fourth month of pregnancy are about as likely as nonsmoking women to bear a baby of normal birth weight [36]. Infants who are small at birth tend to have more deficiencies, difficulties, and abnormalities of all types later on than babies of normal weight (5½ pounds or more). Recently, Neville Butler and his associates have found that children of mothers who smoke during pregnancy are relatively likely to be physically or mentally slow for their ages. The deficiencies are directly associated with the number of cigarettes smoked after the fourth month [37]. Smoking causes uterine and placental vessels to contract, reducing the fetus's nutrition and oxygen supply. Smoking also raises the mother's vitamin A level; in large amounts, vitamin A causes deformities. A by-product of smoking, cyanide, competes with certain nutrients, contributing to the malnourishment of the infant.

Drugs given just prior to and during delivery to anesthetize the mother or reduce her discomfort may have several unfortunate consequences. They pass through the placenta, enter the fetus's bloodstream and tissue, reduce the available oxygen, and affect the child's central nervous system for the first week and probably longer. While neonates whose mothers have been medicated (some 95 percent of American babies) appear healthy at birth, they frequently show relatively little spontaneous motor activity, slow heart and respiration rates, and poor circulation soon afterward. Because their sucking response is somewhat depressed, they are unable to nurse vigorously, and they are unlikely to gain weight as rapidly as they should [38]. The more medication the mother has taken, the less competently the infant performs on tests of muscle tension, vision, maturation, and psychomotor and sensory development [39]. When drugged mothers nurture drugged infants, there may be long-range implications for the parent-child relationship. Alert babies who nurse eagerly probably elicit more parental enthusiasm. Currently, psychologists Yvonne Brackbill and Sarah Broman are checking out another suspicion: drugs in common use during delivery may cause permanent brain damage [40]. In Chapter 10 we will describe the injurious effects of sex hormones on fetuses.

Many other frequently used chemical agents—aspirin, pesticides, and industrial solvents, for instance—are known to affect nonhuman fetuses adversely. The impact of these substances and many others, such as caffeine, nose drops, room fresheners, hair dye, and marijuana, on human infants is not understood.

The Mother's Emotional State

Severely distressed mothers appear to create problems for their unborn children. Like other people, pregnant women respond to emotions, such as rage or anxiety, with a massive outpouring of adrenal hormones. These secretions may enter the fetus's bloodstream. If excessive, they may be injurious. Carefully controlled studies have established a link between maternal stress and fetal damage in certain rat strains. In one such study, psychologist William Thompson stressed female rats by sounding a buzzer and presenting a strong shock. The animals learned to associate the two events and to avoid the shock by opening a door and running to a safe compartment whenever the buzzer sounded. Then the animals were mated. The rats that became pregnant were exposed

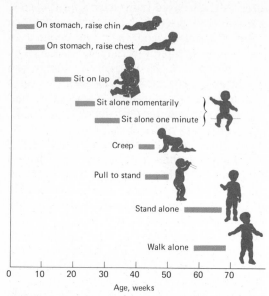

On stomach, raise chin

On stomach, raise chest

Sit on lap

Sit alone momentarily

Sit alone one minute

Creep

Pull to stand

Stand alone

Walk alone

0   10   20   30   40   50   60   70

Age, weeks

FIGURE 3-6   Ages at which human infants developed important motor skills. [*From Shirley, 1931.*]

periodically to the buzzer but were prevented from making the avoidance response. These animals appeared intensely upset. Eventually, they gave birth to fearful, timid offspring. As compared with the pups of mothers that had not been stressed during pregnancy, the rat pups of stressed mothers had trouble learning their way through mazes and reacted with extreme anxiety in new situations [41]. When human mothers undergo emotional crises such as the death or injury of loved ones, the movements of their fetuses increase several hundred percent. If mothers remain upset for several weeks, their babies continue

moving around at the exaggerated tempo [42]. Correlational studies suggest that emotional distress during human pregnancies is associated with irritability, intestinal problems, excessive crying in babies during early infancy, various abnormalities such as cleft palate and harelip (two closely related birth defects caused by the failure of the embryo's palate to fuse completely), and ill health during the school years [43]. These findings suggest, but do not prove, that stress harms human fetuses.

From this brief review, it should be clear that the intrauterine environment may shape the infant's physical and behavioral characteristics significantly. ▲

MATURATION

All over the world the child's behavior develops in much the same order. Almost all normal babies, regardless of circumstances, roll over before they sit with support. A little later they sit by themselves. Later yet they stand while holding on. Very few youngsters sit before rolling over or stand before sitting. Social, language, perceptual, and intellectual abilities tend to appear in a predictable order too. The term *maturation* refers to the emergence of behavior patterns that depend largely on the growth of the body and nervous system. To a large extent, maturation depends on genetics. At the time of conception, heredity programs in certain potentialities for the organism's development. Many of these potentialities are only partially complete at the time of birth and are realized gradually as the animal grows throughout life. Environ-

---

▲ USING PSYCHOLOGY

1. Why should sensitive periods occur more often in early than in later development?

2. Suppose that a very close friend is having a baby and asks for advice. Make a list of dos and don'ts. Next to each item, cite evidence for the recommendation (if possible).

ments play a vital role in maturation also. Before and after birth, chemical, sensory, and traumatic influences, in Hebb's terms, may shape developing capabilities. Special training can slow or speed maturation, for example, but does not alter its sequencing [44].

While many early behavior patterns follow a regular order, individual children reach various milestones at different ages. Occasionally, steps are skipped. Figure 3-6 shows the extent to which a small sample of American youngsters varied in motor development. As you can see, some babies are close to three months ahead of others in achieving specific skills. Curiously, maturation may be a some-what repetitious process, as described and illustrated in Figure 3-7.

In the next sections we focus on constant sensory, or ordinarily inevitable, experiences that influence maturation. We distinguish between sensorimotor and social experiences. By *sensorimotor experiences* we mean (1) opportunities to move about and (2) information taken in by sight, hearing, taste, and other senses. *Social experiences*, a subclass of sensorimotor experiences, involve interactions with others of the same species. Since social experiences always entail sensorimotor experiences, our distinction is an abstract one.

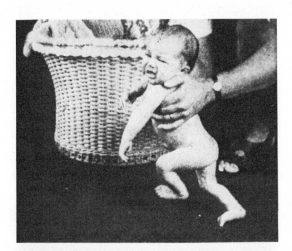

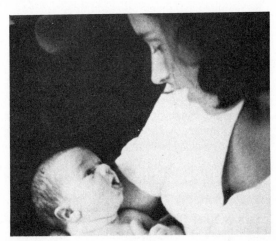

FIGURE 3-7 A six-day-old infant can "walk" (*left*) if supported properly on a flat surface and imitate others' behavior (*below*)—in this case, the mother extending her tongue. These abilities soon disappear and do not resurface until the end of the child's first year. Some basic conceptual capacities vanish and return too. Psychologist T. G. R. Bower has investigated these intriguing repetitions. He believes that infants lose certain motor skills because the skills are not practiced. Decreases in motivation may account for the disappearance of other behaviors. Babies may stop reaching toward sounds, for example, because they learn they have little control over noise. Intellectual repetitions appear to result from changed ways of processing information [99]. [*T. G. R. Bower.*]

UNIVERSAL SENSORIMOTOR EXPERIENCES AND EARLY DEVELOPMENT

Before birth, human infants receive minimal amounts of sensory stimulation within the intrauterine environment. After birth, the baby's senses are bombarded by the sights, sounds, tastes, and odors of the new world. Though the fetus could move about in the uterus, the baby has a lot more freedom of movement and increasingly greater motor capabilities. Psychologists became aware of the importance of sensorimotor experiences from observing the effects of deprivations. To assess the impact of sensorimotor experiences, we examine specific and general sensorimotor deprivations.

Specific Sensorimotor Deprivations

Young animals require all types of sensorimotor experiences to perceive adequately later in life. Numerous investigations support this idea. In one such study, psychologist Henry Nissen and his colleagues reared a chimpanzee until two and a half years of age with cardboard cuffs covering its forearms and lower legs. The animal could move its limbs but could not touch anything. The chimpanzee's later tactile behavior was abnormal. Long after the cuffs were removed, it still sat in peculiar postures, seemed insensitive to pain, and had trouble learning in situations where touch-related cues had to be used [45]. Studies that will be described in detail in Chapter 6 suggest that normal visual skills depend on ordinarily universal visual-motor experiences, including exposure to light and patterns. Sensorimotor experiences after birth appear to be essential, then, for the development of normal sensory capabilities.

General Sensorimotor Deprivation

People, like other animals, appear to require a *minimum level* of sensorimotor stimulation.

How do psychologists know? There are no studies of babies who have been systematically deprived of specific experiences. What we have are naturalistic observations on unfortunate youngsters who happen to have experienced less than ordinary amounts of general sensorimotor stimulation. First, consider premature infants, those born after less than thirty-seven weeks of gestation, weighing below 5½ pounds. Like other low-birth-weight babies, they tend to have deficiencies and difficulties later in life. While such ill effects could be the result of delivery complications and/or parental overprotectiveness, sensorimotor deprivation could contribute. At birth most premature infants who have already missed out on weeks of stimulation in the uterus are placed in incubators called *isolettes*. The isolettes control temperature, humidity, and oxygen and prevent infection. They also isolate the baby from stimulation. Even after the premature infant arrives home, parents may feel reluctant to interact with the "fragile" child. The research of psychologists Sandra Scarr-Salapatek and Margaret Williams supports this hypothesis. Scarr-Salapatek and Williams studied thirty 3- to 4-pound premature infants from severely deprived socioeconomic backgrounds. Some babies received standard incubator care. Others were reared under enriched conditions: removal from incubators for stimulation (feeding, fondling, rocking, and conversation), visual experiences in the incubator (such as a dangling bird mobile) and afterward, visits from social workers until their first birthday, stimulating toys, and child-care instructions to their mothers. While initially slightly behind the control group of traditionally reared premature babies, the enriched infants soon forged ahead. They gained more weight, scored higher on behavioral and neurological tests, and reached nearly normal developmental levels by the age of one year—unlike any other comparable group of premature babies ever tested by the hospital [46]. Similarly promising results have been obtained by providing premature infants with fifteen-minute stroking-massaging-rocking sessions daily [47]. Apparently, inadequate sensorimotor stimulation causes some of the later problems often seen in premature children.

Observations of babies reared in dull, barren orphanages also support the notion that general sensorimotor stimulation is essential for the growth of all types of human capacities. In the mid-1960s two pediatricians, Sally Provence and Rose Lipton, published a particularly careful study of this topic. They compared seventy-five family-reared and seventy-five orphanage-reared infants. The latter had grown up in an institution that was clean, well lit, and adequately heated and ventilated. But, at the institution only one attendant served eight to ten babies for eight hours each day. During the remaining sixteen hours, no one was present except at feeding time when bottles were propped up, formulas heated, and diapers changed. For stimulation each infant had a simple rattle or some beads and occasionally a stuffed toy. No one talked to these babies, rocked them, smiled at them, responded to their crying, or treated them as individuals in any way.

The differences between the infants reared in the orphanage and those raised normally at home became apparent when the babies were about four months old. The institutionalized children rarely babbled, cried, or cooed. When picked up, they felt stiff and wooden—"like sawdust dolls," as one observer put it. By the time they were eight months old, the orphans showed little interest in toys or their surroundings and spent much time rocking back and forth repetitively, perhaps attempting to stimulate themselves. Their expressions were bland and solemn, their movements inhibited and lacking in vigor. When frustrated, they cried or turned away passively, rarely attempting to surmount problems by themselves. By the age of ten months, the orphanage-reared children were very noticeably retarded in many ways [48]. The research of other investigators confirms these observations. Children reared in unstimulating environments during the first year of life often appear retarded in motor skills, language, intellectual development, expression of emo-

tions, and capacity for strong, lasting attachments to people.

Note that there are several types of deficits, including motor, intellectual, and social, and at least two kinds of deprivation, namely sensorimotor and social. What is producing what?

The Link between Sensorimotor Stimulation and Intelligence

It is currently believed that sensorimotor stimulation in infancy is essential for later intellectual development. There are several reasons for this belief. The hypothesis is supported by the observations of the brilliant Swiss psychologist Jean Piaget. Piaget calls the first two years of life, when babies seem to learn primarily through using their senses and moving about, the *sensorimotor stage* in mental development. At this time many information-processing and problem-solving capacities are developing. By using their eyes and ears and acting, babies learn, for example, that their behavior has specific consequences and that objects and people who cannot be seen continue to exist. During this period children also learn a language. If fundamental intellectual abilities are poorly developed, the youngster has a shaky foundation for later mental growth. (More on both Piaget's theory and language development in Chapter 9.) Numerous additional observations suggest that sensorimotor stimulation influences intellectual development. Harvard University developmental psychologist Jerome Kagan and an associate, Robert Klein, studied children as they grew up in a Guatemalan village. Kagan describes the circumstances:

I saw infants in the first years of their lives completely isolated in their homes, because parents believe that sun and dust and air or the gazes of either pregnant women or men fresh with perspiration from the field will cause illness. . . . So the infants are kept in the hut. Now these are bamboo huts, and there are no windows, so the light level in this hut at high noon in a perfectly azure sky is

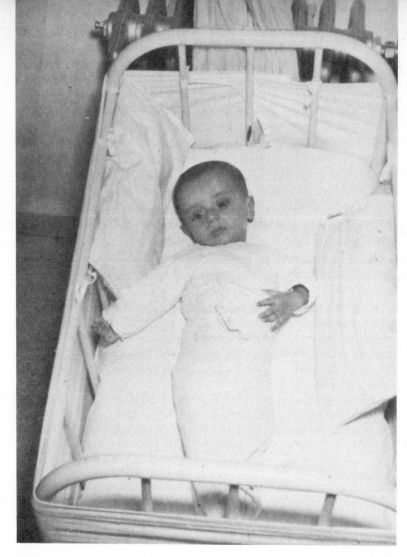

FIGURE 3-8 Here we see an infant raised with minimal sensorimotor and social stimulation in a Lebanese orphanage. Youngsters similarly reared exhibited retardation in many spheres. In this particular institution, sheets covered the sides of the cribs. And there was one caretaker for every ten children. When youngsters remained in the orphanage past the age of two, their intelligence seemed to be depressed regardless of their later experiences. Those who were adopted before the age of two did not generally show permanent deficits. [*From Dennis*, Children of the Creche *1974. Used with permission.*]

what it should be at dusk. Very dark. Although parents love their children—mothers nurse on demand and hold their infants close to their bodies—they don't talk or interact with them. And there are no toys. So at one and one-half years of age, you have a very retarded child. [49]

Lack of sensory variety and restricted opportunities to act and explore during the first year seem to be the critical factors producing the early retardation [50]. Several other observations link intelligence and sensorimotor stimulation. An unusually painstaking investigation by psychologist Leon Yarrow and his colleagues suggests that *kinesthetic stimulation* (providing movement by rocking, jiggling, carrying, and the like) is associated with mental development in infancy. More social types of stimulation, such as vocalizing and eye-to-eye contact, are not linked with cognitive growth at this early stage. Yarrow and his coworkers theorize that kinesthetic stimulation maintains infants in a state of optimal arousal so that they are likely to attend and respond to their surroundings and learn [51]. Finally, consider observations on infants reared from birth under the enriched conditions of Israeli kibbutzim at a time when parental contact was minimal. As compared with children reared in middle-class homes, kibbutzniks generally attained the same and sometimes higher developmental levels intellectually, socially, emotionally, and physically [52]. In sum, numerous observations link sensorimotor stimulation and mental growth.

Sensorimotor Deprivation: Reversible or Irreversible?

Are the effects of early sensorimotor deprivation reversible? Several observations indicate that they often are. Once the Guatemalan children walk, they leave their huts and find stimulation in the outside world. By age ten they are "gay, alert, and intellectually competent children whose performance on memory, perception, and reasoning tests . . . [are] comparable to those of children in the United States [53]." The effects of early deprivation appear to persist only when later experiences are also restrictive and unstimulating, as the following study suggests.

A Radical Experiment in a Home for the Mentally Retarded

In the 1930s Harold Skeels, a psychologist who was then working for a number of state institutions in Iowa, noticed the story of two young orphans. As infants in an Iowa orphanage, the girls had been judged hopelessly defective intellectually and transferred to a home for the mentally retarded. After six months in the new setting, each child had made remarkable and totally unexpected progress. When Skeels investigated further, he found that the girls had been adopted by adoring, mentally retarded "mothers" and "aunts" who played with them, fussed over them, and took them on trips. So the children had received far more affection, attention, and general stimulation in the home than previously in the crowded orphanage. These experiences appeared to have altered their intellectual

functioning. To find out whether that was really the case, Skeels performed a radical experiment. He had thirteen "hopelessly retarded" children (the experimental group) transferred from the orphanage to the home for the mentally retarded. At the time of the move, these youngsters were nineteen months of age and had IQs of about 64, on the average. An IQ this low is considered evidence of retardation. Twelve children, who remained at the orphanage and served as a control group, had an average age of seventeen months and an average IQ of approximately 87, a score within the dull normal range. After roughly a year and a half, both groups of youngsters were retested. Subjects in the experimental group had an average gain of about 29 IQ points and were now functioning in the normal range

of intelligence. The children in the control group had lost 26 IQ points, on the average, and appeared to be intellectually retarded. Eleven of the thirteen experimental children were adopted shortly after this testing. The unfortunate control-group children remained in the institution. More than twenty years later, Skeels checked to see what had happened to his research participants. The thirteen experimental children had fared well. Half had completed the twelfth grade. Eleven had married. None were wards of state institutions. All were either employed or engaged in housework. The twelve control children had been far less successful. Four were still wards of state institutions; one had died in that status. Only half had completed the third grade. Six held jobs, and one had married [54].

Skeel's study suggests that when children are deprived of sensorimotor stimulation at an early age, they retain the capacity for normal intellectual development if their later experiences are enlivening. But should deprivation continue, children are not likely to catch up. Studies by psychologist Wayne Dennis indicate that there may be a sensitive period for these effects. When children from a Lebanese orphanage were adopted into foster homes before the age of two, they appeared to recover almost entirely from earlier retardation. When adopted at ages later than two, some degree of mental deficiency persisted [55]. (See Figure 3-8.)

How Can Sensorimotor Stimulation Affect Intelligence?

Some astonishing studies with rodents suggest that sensorimotor stimulation actually alters the brain. Mark Rosenzweig, a psychologist at the University of California at Berkeley, and his associates have demonstrated this phenomenon with several inbred strains of rats, mice, and gerbils. In an early study, male rats from several litters were randomly assigned at birth to experimental and control groups. Brothers from inbred strains were chosen to control for genetic factors. The late David Krech, who helped initiate this research, described it like this:

Now, the experimental group, almost from the day it was weaned lived in an enriched environment. They lived in a group of about fifteen; they had rat toys; they were given all the food and water they wanted; they were taken out and petted; they were given little problems to solve for sugar, etc. We even encouraged the graduate students to walk around the laboratory playing transistor radios. We stimulated them (the rats, that is!) in every way we could. Their brother rats, meanwhile, although they were fed the same food and water, lived in a very impoverished environment. They were put one in a cage in a dark, soundproof room with no social stimulation. After eighty or ninety days, both groups were decapitated the same day. Their brains were given to the chemist and the neuroanatomist, coded so that neither knew which rat came from the enriched environment and which from the impoverished group. Diamond [the neuroanatomist] and Bennett [the chemist] did their damndest with these rat brains looking for any possible chemical or anatomical differences, and lo and behold, they found lots of them. The rats from the enriched environment had heavier brains; their cortexes were thicker; the blood supply to their brains was better; the cells were larger. [Their brains also contained more enzymes associated with memory and learning.] . . . So here we had definite evidence that the result of an enriched early environment was literally a better brain. [56]

Numerous replications of this study show that the effect is a real one.

More recent research suggests that sensorimotor enrichment is beneficial for rats that have not yet been weaned, for adult rats, and even for brain-damaged ones [57]. Brains do not grow normally when animals are deprived of stimulation early in life, as we shall see. Perhaps human brains also grow larger and manufacture more enzymes associated with learning and memory when they are exercised by a stimulating, complex environment. ▲

UNIVERSAL SOCIAL EXPERIENCES AND EARLY DEVELOPMENT

Under ordinary circumstances many young animals, including people, form strong bonds of attachment to their parents, usually their mothers, during early sensitive periods shortly after birth. The bond ensures that offspring will remain nearby so that they may be nurtured and protected. Many of the initial studies of how these early attachments are formed and what consequences they have for future behavior began on birds and monkeys.

Imprinting in Birds and Other Animals

Within the first hours after birth, birds that walk as soon as they hatch (geese, chickens,

---

▲ USING PSYCHOLOGY

1. Suppose that your one-month-old baby used to imitate certain gestures and then stopped. Is this cause for alarm? Now assume that a friend is upset because his second child is not walking at fifteen months, while his first-born walked at thirteen months. Is this likely to be a sign of a major problem?

2. Explain in your own words why psychologists believe that sensorimotor stimulation in infancy facilitates intellectual development.

turkeys, and ducks, for example) will follow almost anything that moves. This tendency to follow peaks at differing times and then becomes less and less likely. Chickens, for instance, seem most likely to tag along after a moving target at about seventeen hours after birth. At approximately three or four days, they become fearful and will not follow unfamiliar forms. Early following behavior has dramatic future consequences. The nature of the followed target helps determine the animal's later preferences in friends and mates. When turkeys are reared from birth by human beings, for example, they often choose to court people rather than turkeys when they reach sexual maturity. Konrad Lorenz, an Austrian ethologist (a scientist who studies animal behavior in natural settings), named the early following pattern, which reflects a social attachment, *imprinting*. To demonstrate the phenomenon, Lorenz divided the eggs of a greylag goose into two batches. He allowed the mother to hatch some eggs while he nurtured the others in an incubator. Oskar Heinroth, Lorenz's teacher, describes what happens to incubator-reared goslings:

Without any display of fear, [the goslings] stare calmly at human beings and do not resist handling. If one spends just a little time with them, it is not so easy to get rid of them afterwards. They pipe piteously if left behind and soon follow reliably. It has happened to me that such a gosling, a few hours after removal from the incubator, was content as long as it could settle under the chair on which I sat. If such a gosling is carried to a goose family accompanied by goslings of the same age, the result is usually the following: . . . One can . . . rapidly deposit the orphan gosling among . . . [the other geese] and retreat hastily. Aroused as they are, the parents naturally regard the tiny newcomer as their own offspring at first and will attempt to defend it as soon as they see and hear it in the human hand. But the worst is to come: *The young gosling shows no inclination to regard the two adults as conspecifics* [members of the same species]: The gosling runs off, piping, and attaches itself to the first human being that happens to come past; it regards the human as its parent. [58]

Lorenz's incubator-reared goslings tagged along behind him initially, came to regard him

FIGURE 3-9 Ethologist Konrad Lorenz is followed here by goslings that had imprinted upon him. [*Thomas McAvoy, TIME-LIFE Picture Agency.*]

as their parent, and sought him out when frightened. (See Figure 3-9.) The other goslings followed their own mother and formed an attachment to her [59].

Careful studies suggest that imprinting (or an imprinting-like response) is a complicated learned reaction that occurs in certain insects, fish, and mammals, as well as birds. It takes place during a sensitive period after birth which differs from species to species; for mallard ducks, it occurs between thirteen and sixteen hours; for lambs, between one and seven days; for puppies, between three and fourteen weeks. Researching behavioral scientists have been particularly interested in experiences that influence the attachment process. See Figure 3-10. Incidentally, imprinting is not always irreversible. For some animals, later experiences can undo the effects of earlier ones. Mourning doves, imprinted on human beings, for instance, may form social and sexual bonds to other birds after appropriate "adolescent" experiences [60].

a

b

FIGURE 3-10 These photographs show the effects of socialization on the behavior of a fourteen-week-old beagle. (*a*) A pup that had one week of contact with people during the sensitive period for the formation of social attachments follows the psychologist eagerly. (*b*) A frightened dog that had no contact with human beings during the sensitive period refuses to follow [100]. Fears of the strange and unfamiliar develop in infants of many animal species near the close of the sensitive period for imprinting. Such anxieties may interfere with the propensity to follow new targets. As a result, perhaps, the animal's attachment capability may decline drastically. [*Courtesy of Daniel G. Freedman, University of Chicago.*]

Attachment Formation in Monkeys

Monkey infants experience an imprinting-like period early in their development when they form attachments to their parents under ordinary circumstances. In the late 1950s,

psychologist Harry Harlow, working then at the University of Wisconsin in Madison, became interested in the basis for these bonds. At this point in history, most social scientists believed that attachments were rooted in need fulfillment. Psychologists reasoned that parents usually gratify their babies' drives for food, water, warmth, dryness, and the like and are consequently associated with pleasant outcomes. Harlow had different ideas. He had been impressed by the deep attachments that monkeys formed to diaper pads when they were reared from birth without their mothers. These informal observations suggested a classic series of experiments. In these investigations, Harlow and his colleagues examined the importance of bodily contact, nursing, and other associated activities for attaching infants and mothers. Here is Harlow's description of an early study:

[We] contrived two surrogate [substitute] mother monkeys. One is a bare welded-wire cylindrical form surmounted by a wooden head with a crude face. In the other the welded-wire is cushioned by a sheathing of terry cloth. We placed eight newborn monkeys in individual cages, each with equal access to a cloth and a wire mother. . . . Four of the infants received their milk from one mother and four from the other, the milk being furnished in each case by a nursing bottle, with its nipple protruding from the mother's "breast."

The two mothers quickly proved to be physiologically equivalent. The monkeys in the two groups drank the same amount of milk and gained weight at the same rate. But the two mothers proved to be by no means psychologically equivalent. Records made automatically showed that both groups of infants spent far more time climbing [on] and clinging [to] their cloth-covered mothers than their wire mothers. [61] [See Figure 3-11.]

Harlow's findings suggest that bodily contact and the immediate comfort it supplies is more important than nursing in attaching the infant monkey to its mother. Later studies established that nursing, rocking, and warmth (temperature) influence the formation of social bonds in monkeys too.

Harlow's monkey infants were deprived of a *real* mother during the sensitive period for the formation of social attachments (some-

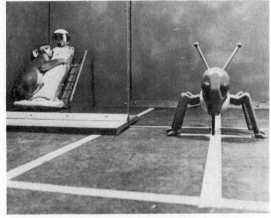

a

b

FIGURE 3-11 (a) Shown here are the wire and cloth surrogate mothers used in the Harlow experiment. (b) A frightened infant monkey snuggles against the cloth mother. Infants nursed by wire mothers did not seek them out for comfort when threatened by fear stimuli, even though they were the only mothers available. [*H. F. Harlow, University of Wisconsin Primate Laboratory.*]

where between three and six months of age in rhesus monkeys). Like the institutionalized children we described earlier, these animals had experienced a minimum of sensorimotor, and almost no social, stimulation. Although they seemed healthy and normal enough to Harlow at the time of this study, they were without question abnormal both socially and sexually as adolescents and adults. They exhibited compulsive habits like moving in circles and rocking back and forth. They showed little interest in other monkeys or in people—very unlike animals reared in the wild. The isolates did not even interact when caged together. In addition, these monkeys were sexual misfits, unable to breed successfully when left to their own devices. When females were eventually impregnated, they became "helpless, hopeless, heartless mothers devoid, or almost devoid, of any maternal feelings [62]." Most of these motherless mothers either ignored or abused their babies [63]. Robert Heath, a Tulane University medical researcher, has found abnormal electrical activity in the brains of such monkey isolates. So there is indirect evidence that social and sensorimotor deprivation during the sensitive period damages the monkey's nervous system [64].

Are the social effects of early isolation reversible for monkeys? Though animals vary, a number of observations suggest that the effects can often be undone. A few of Harlow's motherless mothers that did not succeed in killing their babies were finally won over by the persistent nuzzling and cuddling [65]. In a more recent study at the Wisconsin Primate Center, newborn rhesus monkeys were isolated from other animals during the first six months of life. The monkeys developed the peculiar social habits previously described. This time the isolates were treated by intensive "therapy." Normal infant female monkeys, placed in each cage, gradually approached the isolates, climbed on them, and attempted to play. While it took some time for the socially deprived animals to start reciprocating, they eventually did interact with their "therapists." After twenty-six weeks of this treatment, the isolates were displaying normal monkey social behavior [66].

Attachment Formation in People

Like monkey infants, human babies pass through an imprinting-like period early in life. At the same time, human parents appear to be gradually bonded to their young. Psychologists have begun charting some of the landmarks in these processes. We begin with the parents.

In the late 1960s, psychologists Kenneth Robson and Howard Moss interviewed new mothers to trace their developing feelings toward their infants. About 7 percent of the women described their first reactions as negative ones, while approximately 34 percent reported no or neutral feelings. Close to 59 percent of the mothers responded positively. Still, only 13 percent of these called their feelings "love." First reactions included impressions such as "cute," "pretty," "sweet," "cuddly," "soft," "blah," "like a little doll," "little animals," "a thing," and "a blob." It took most mothers about three weeks to report beginning to love their babies [67].

While human parents may not feel attached to their infants initially, some very interesting studies suggest that physical contact immediately following birth may influence the relationship substantially. In animals like mice, rats, and goats, mother-infant separations at birth may have such disastrous consequences as total rejection or reduced caretaking [68]. Pediatricians Marshall Klaus and John Kennell and their associates have looked into the effects of contact between human parents and children shortly after birth. For one study, the investigators followed the progress of two groups of mother-infant pairs. Pairs in the control group experienced the usual hospital routine following delivery: a glance at the baby near the time of birth, a short visit six to twelve hours later, and twenty- or thirty-minute feeding sessions every four hours daily. Mothers and infants in the experimental group were able to interact for an hour shortly after delivery and several hours daily thereafter. One month later, these mothers were judged to be more attentive, affectionate, and interested in their babies' welfare than those in the control group. More surprisingly, the effects of immediate interaction were still detectable two years later. Observations indicated that mothers in the experimental group asked their children more questions and gave them fewer commands than those in the control group [69]. This study was replicated in Guatemala with two early contact groups. Mothers spent forty-five minutes with their babies either immediately after delivery or twelve hours later. Only the immediate contact group showed the benefits found in the earlier research [70]. Psychologists Peter Vietze and Susan O'Connor and their coworkers are engaged in a five-year experimental investigation of early mother-child interactions on approximately 1,000 participants.

FIGURE 3-12 Potent visual stimulation is presented to increase this critically ill, premature infant's alertness to its surroundings. Josephine Brown, the director of this program, and numerous other psychologists are trying to see that the "human" qualities in high-risk infants, like this one, are developed. Once the baby begins to smile occasionally and to respond to visual and auditory stimuli by fixating and quieting and to relax while being held, parents are brought in. Through exercises, mothers and fathers learn to evoke these social responses. Projects like this one can dramatically improve parent-infant relationships and increase the child's chances of receiving affection and stimulation [101]. High-risk babies are disproportionately often abused, neglected, and abandoned. In these cases, presumably, parental attachments are frequently weak because of long separations and the infant's fragility and unsociability [102]. [*Courtesy of Dr. Ruth Ketler.*]

Preliminary results suggest that immediate contact after delivery reduces the probability of later parenting problems, including abandonment, neglect, and abuse [71].

Why is immediate contact significant? Human beings are probably immature and dependent for basic needs on surrounding adults longer than any other animal. Some behavioral scientists speculate that parents experience a sensitive period soon after birth when they are easily and intensively bonded to the baby. Once such fundamental feelings are established, parents are apt to talk to their infants, hold them, rock them, and attend to their needs more diligently. Social stimulation increases eye contact, babbling, and smiling in the youngster, appealing human gestures that bond parent and child more tightly [72]. In brief, an early tie may ensure better attention and protection from the beginning and throughout the long caretaking period. Still, whether with or without immediate contact, most mothers report feeling strongly attached to their babies by the third month or so [73]. See Figure 3-12.

What about the infant? By six days of age a baby detects and prefers its own mother's odor to another mother's and by the age of twenty or thirty days her voice [74]. By four to six weeks the infant shows more eye contact, smiling, and babbling in the presence of the major caretaker. At about six or seven months of age (sometimes considerably later), there is a clear, well-defined tie. Now children smile at the primary agent frequently. They try to keep her or him within sight and sound. They search visually and auditorally (by listening) when the major caretaker is absent. They display signs of anxiety when the attached person leaves and joy and delight when they are reunited. (See Figure 3-13.) At six to eight months or so, the attachment to the primary caretaker is extended to other familiar people (as illustrated in Figure 3-14). Near this time many children display strong fears of strangers [75]. While behavioral scientists once thought that stranger fears were universal, it is now believed that they depend on specific types of experiences [76].

What factors are involved in bonding

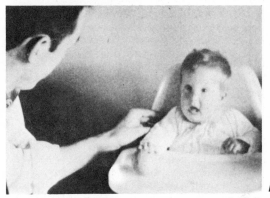

FIGURE 3-13 This girl of seven months smiles fondly at her mother (*a*), but responds quite differently to a stranger (*b*). [*Courtesy of Daniel G. Freedman, University of Chicago.*]

human babies to their parents? Total amount of parental stimulation is positively associated with strong infant attachments. Sustained physical contact with the caretaker is particularly important [77]. The adult's sensitivity to the child's signals, preferences, rhythms, and pacing as it feeds, cries, vocalizes, and smiles is another major factor [78]. Immediate contact after delivery appears to enhance the mother's (and perhaps the father's) responsivity to the baby.

Some psychologists believe that the capacity for social bonding is a product of maturation and that some relationship must occur early in life if the child is to be able to form meaningful ties later on. Children reared during their early years in institutions sometimes show social deficiencies such as exces-

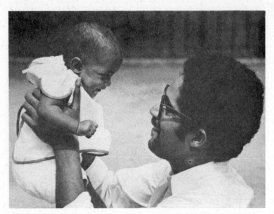

FIGURE 3-14 Though the average American father may spend only about twelve minutes with his offspring on a typical day, fathers are important in their children's lives. Paternal interactions are usually characterized as play-oriented. But men who are present during the birth process tend to show involvement in many child-care activities. Like mothers, fathers may be bonded tightly to their babies by early contact. Young infants, in turn, form strong ties to their fathers, whom they may prefer to their mothers even at the early age of a year. Youngsters with involved fathers show less fear around strangers and in new situations than those with less committed fathers. In preschool boys, paternal nurturance and warmth are associated with intellectual development and a strong masculine identity [103]. [*Bill Anderson/Monkmeyer.*]

sive dependency or coldness. It is possible, of course, that warm, intense social experiences in later childhood, or even adulthood, could compensate.

In sum, sensorimotor and social experiences, which parents ordinarily provide early in life, seem important for the normal development of intellectual and social skills. The *quality* of the sensorimotor and social stimulation that is offered appears to shape the mind and personality of the developing individual in some vital ways, which we describe in the next section. ▲

VARIABLE SENSORY EXPERIENCES: THE CASE OF SOCIALIZATION

Development is profoundly influenced by an individual's varied experiences as a member of a specific family in a particular culture. We focus briefly on socialization, one type of variable sensory experience that molds the developing person. *Socialization* is defined as the process of guiding children toward the behaviors, values, goals, and motives that the culture considers appropriate. All societies hold unwritten but widely shared expectations for their members. Traditional Hopi Indians stress peacefulness, cooperation, hard work, conformity, obedience, and kindness. Middle-class Americans emphasize self-reliance, independence, and achievement. Child-rearing practices reflect these ideals. At an early age youngsters in middle-class American homes, for instance, are taught to walk, control elimination, feed, and dress themselves, read, and write. And they are continually urged to "do their best" so that they can be "first." Parents are the culture's major agents of socialization. They are often advised by authorities on the proper tactics.

Psychologists have been studying the effects of child-rearing practices only since the 1940s. Because it is difficult to obtain systematic and objective data on what parents actually do in raising their children, our findings must be regarded as highly tentative. With this warning, we turn to research

▲ **USING PSYCHOLOGY**

1. Suppose that a new mother confesses to you that she does not love her new baby and asks if she is normal. How should you respond?

2. Argue against hospital practices that separate mothers and infants immediately after childbirth.

3. If you were designing a model orphanage, what specific early sensorimotor and social experiences would be essential? How could these experiences be provided?

findings on several child-care subjects: feeding, toilet training, handling crying, talking to the child, providing social stimulation, and establishing moral behavior. Rewards and punishments will be treated in Chapter 5.

Breast versus Bottle Feeding

For years child-care experts have been debating the relative merits of breast and bottle feeding. In the United States, Canada, and Great Britain, bottle feeding is the more common practice. Breast feeding is more popular in Sweden and China [79]. Breast feeding has several advantages. For human infants, most nutritionists believe, human milk is superior to other types. It protects the child to some degree against many illnesses and is less apt to lead to obesity [80]. Breast feeding has several benefits for mothers too: the faster shrinking of the uterus to normal size and physical pleasure. Still, nursing is not always appropriate. Women must be well nourished to continue the practice past the first few months. They must abstain from certain drugs that degrade the quality of their milk. Babies must suck vigorously, so that milk continues to be produced in ample quantity. Most important, mothers must want to breast-feed. A mother who nurses because she feels she should and does not wish to will feel tense. When mothers are upset, their babies also show signs of distress. Conversely, the babies of relaxed mothers tend to be calm [81]. Currently, psychologists believe that the relationship between mother and infant is far more important than how the baby is fed. One investigator put it well: "The truth is that the emotional health of both mother and baby is best served by whatever generates the most pleasure between the two, the greatest closeness and affection, one for the other [82]."

Toilet Training

Initially, infants automatically release their sphincter muscles as soon as they feel tension from a full bladder or bowel. In many cases,

toilet training is the parent's first major attempt to curb the child's natural inclinations. Asking a youngster to control an involuntary reflex, go into the bathroom, and use the toilet properly may be asking a lot. Children must be ready neuromuscularly. They have to both understand and be able to communicate their needs. Ordinarily, this is impossible until the age of eighteen months or so. Toilet training is usually achieved much later than that [83].

Research indicates that toilet training proceeds most smoothly when parents encourage gradual control and minimize conflict. Waiting until a reasonable age, giving instructions, watching for signs and immediately taking the child to the toilet, allowing the youngster to learn by observing others, and bestowing warmth and approval for success—all seem to make toilet training easier. Rigidity, harshness, coldness, and rejection associated with the toileting routine appear to lead to hostility, chronic bed-wetting, and other behavioral problems [84].

Handling Crying

Crying is one of the infant's major ways of communicating with its parents. But child-care experts, both current and past, have encouraged parents to be wary of responding to their infants' cries. They reasoned that if parents respond immediately whenever babies cry, infants may learn that crying pays off. Later they may become spoiled, fussy tyrants whose continual demands enslave the mother and father. Does responding to a crying infant really have these effects? Until recently, most studies of this topic focused on parental reactions to excessive crying in older children. Psychologists Silvia Bell, Mary Ainsworth, and their colleagues studied twenty-six white, middle-class, American mother-infant pairs to learn more about the effects of this and numerous other practices. Trained behavioral scientists observed the pairs for four-hour intervals once every three weeks throughout the first year of the baby's life. Bell and Ainsworth found that when mothers ignored their young infants' crying,

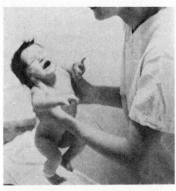 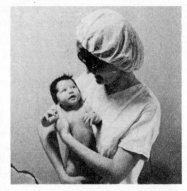 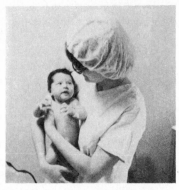

FIGURE 3-15 When parents respond quickly to an infant's crying, the child cries less often later in life. Picking up the baby and initiating close physical contact is frequently effective in soothing the infant. The one-day-old female neonate in these film clips is being consoled for the first time. When picked up, she stops crying almost immediately and looks at her caretaker's face. Some infants, however, may actually respond negatively to physical contact. Most infants will be consistently soothed by something—if not by physical contact, then probably by continuous rhythmic sounds, a sweetened pacifier, gentle rocking, or warmth [104]. [*Courtesy of Daniel G. Freedman, University of Chicago.*]

the babies cried *more* frequently later in their first year. When the parent responded quickly, especially by picking up the infant and initiating close physical contact, the youngster cried *less* often later on. Bell and Ainsworth view the infant's crying as a communication gesture. By responding to the baby's sobs, the parent is answering a request for help and teaching the child, "You are competent. You can affect the behavior of those around you." Accordingly, the baby's communication skills develop more quickly. As soon as they're able, infants begin using more mature modes of expression, notably language [85]. It's important to realize that the responsive mothers in the Bell-Ainsworth study attended to their babies when they were not crying, as well as when they were. If infants are attended to only when they cry, they may very well turn into big crybabies later on. See Figure 3-15.

Talking to the Child

Parents sometimes adopt the adage, "Children are to be seen and not heard." In general, psychologists disagree. Youngsters must be seen, talked to, and heard, or they will not communicate very well later on. Many studies show that talking to children is important for their language development. One investigator found that when working-class mothers read to their children ten minutes a day, their youngsters gained more competence in all areas of speech than children who were not read to [86]. The family's *style* of talking influences the child's later thinking, problem-solving, and learning skills. Some individuals tend to use *restricted codes* of communication. Their sentences are short, simple, unfinished, implicitly understood, and limited both in concepts and information. Other people use *elaborated codes*. Their utterances are precise, particular, and individualized for a specific situation and person. They allow a more complex range of thought. And they discriminate between intellectual and emotional content. Imagine a child playing noisily when the doorbell rings. The parent with a restricted style says, "Be quiet!" The caretaker with an elaborated style says, "Be quiet for a minute. I want to talk to Mrs. Fero, and I won't be able to hear what she's saying unless you stop that racket." In the first instance, the child is asked only to comply. In the second, the youngster is given an opportunity to follow several ideas. There is evidence that these communicative styles shape the child's later mental abilities [87].

Providing Quality Social Stimulation

The quality of the child's early social interactions shape the individual's personality in some important ways. Two types of social stimulation are associated with later competence: (1) responsivity to the child's special needs and tempo and (2) the nurturing of curiosity.

The research of Mary Ainsworth, Alan Sroufe, and several other investigators suggests that parental responsivity is a significant influence on the development of competence. When caretakers react sensitively to the infant's individual needs, rhythms, and tempos (as measured during the early weeks of life), youngsters tend to develop *secure attachments*. Securely attached children will explore in new situations as long as the parent is present. If the parent leaves, the child is distressed. The caretaker's return is greeted with joy; contact is reestablished; and exploration resumes. Youngsters who show this attachment pattern at twelve months tend to show competence at three and a half years of age. In nursery school they are sympathetic, socially active, curious, and interested in learning. Children who have anxious and ambivalent relationships with parents display less competence under the same circumstances. Presumably, responsivity teaches youngsters that they have an impact on the environment and that they can handle new experiences in the presence of the caretaker. That trust in the adult seems to be translated into self-confidence [88].

Psychologist Burton White has found impressive support for the idea that the nurturing of curiosity influences intellectual competence, which he defines as anticipating consequences, planning and carrying out complex projects, understanding language, and dealing capably with problems. White and his colleagues observed thirty-nine households every other week for two years, looking for those parental characteristics that were associated with competence in children at ten to eighteen months (and at older ages). White concluded that the most effective mothers were excellent designers and consultants.

They established a physical world that was suited to nurturing the curiosity of the youngster. It was full of things to manipulate, climb, and inspect. These model mothers tended to interact with their children sporadically during ten- to thirty-second interchanges throughout the day—often when the child had confronted an interesting situation or difficulty. The parent typically responded to most requests for help with aid, shared enthusiasm, or a related idea. Apparently, this "teaching on the fly" at the child's instigation stimulated curiosity. The mothers of less competent youngsters were overprotective. They restricted opportunities for exploration by using high chairs and playpens extensively. They were less available, talked less, and provided less stimulation overall than the mothers of competent youngsters [89].

Establishing Moral Behavior

Children begin learning about right and wrong and helping and hurting at early ages. Two-year-olds may attempt to come to the aid of distressed people, albeit clumsily. Four-year-olds can understand the perspectives of others to some extent [90]. Psychologist Lawrence Kohlberg has proposed some interesting ideas about the development of moral thinking. According to Kohlberg, people pass through stages of moral development (Table 3-1) in an orderly sequence. At each stage, presumably, individuals conform to what is right for different reasons. Please review the table before reading further.

To investigate moral thinking, Kohlberg presented people with stories like this:

Joe is a 14-year-old boy who wanted to go to camp very much. His father promised him he could go if he saved up the money for it himself. So Joe worked hard at his paper route and saved up the $40 it cost to go to camp and a little more besides. But just before camp was going to start, his father changed his mind. Some of his friends decided to go on a special fishing trip, and Joe's father was short of the money it would cost. So he told Joe to give him the money he had saved from the paper route. Joe didn't want to give up going to camp, so he thought of refusing to give his father the money.

TABLE 3-1 Lawrence Kohlberg's Stages of Moral Development

Level and stage	Motive
Premoral level	
Stage 1: Punishment-obedience orientation	Conforms to avoid punishment, deferring to people with superior power. Example: "I don't lie because, if I do, my mother beats me."
Stage 2: Instrumental-exchange orientation	Conforms only to obtain benefits. Example: "If I don't squeal on Joe, Joe won't squeal on me."
Conventional level	
Stage 3: Good-boy, nice-girl orientation	Conforms to please others. Example: "If Dad ever found out I cheated, he'd never trust me again. So I don't cheat."
Stage 4: System-maintaining orientation	Conforms because of concern for the good of the large society, and not simply a personal group. Example: "I obey the law because it's my obligation as a good citizen. It makes life smoother for everyone."
Principled level	
Stage 5: Social-contract orientation	Conforms to maintain the respect of the impartial spectator, judging in terms of community welfare, assuring equal rights for all. Example: "I obey the law because society can't function unless people respect each other's rights."
Stage 6: Universal ethical-principles orientation*	Conforms to avoid self-condemnation and to live up to universal ethical principles. Example: "Violence violates the rights of other human beings. Human life is sacred and must be respected above all else."

*Recently deleted by Kohlberg.
Source: Colby, A., Gibbs, J., & Kohlberg, L. *Standard form scoring manual.* Part I. Cambridge, Mass.: Moral Education Resource Fund, 1978.

After recounting such stories, Kohlberg asked his research subjects questions:

Should Joe refuse to give his father the money? Why? Does his father have the right to tell Joe to give him the money? Does giving the money have anything to do with being a "good son"? Which is worse, a father breaking a promise to his son or a son breaking a promise to his father? Why? Why should a promise be kept?

After analyzing the responses of many people at varied ages, Kohlberg concluded that children and adults make moral judgments fairly consistently at a specific level, regardless of social class and culture. Young children tend to function at the premoral level. Older youngsters and adults tend to think at the conventional level. About one of each four adults reaches one of the principled stages [91]. These ideas are widely accepted, though many studies have failed to confirm Kohlberg's findings [92].

Moral judgments are probably one of many determinants of social conduct [93]. There is some evidence that people who are principled (in Kohlberg's terms) tend to behave ethically in diverse situations, perhaps because they carry their own penalties and rewards inside themselves. Persons at premoral and conventional levels are not consistent in resisting or succumbing to temptations to cheat, lie, or steal. Since people at the first three stages behave ethically for external incentives, such as attaining positive and avoiding negative personal consequences, their moral behavior should depend heavily on their assessment of the circumstances [94].

Three parental practices are rather consistently associated with morality (in thought and behavior) and helpfulness.

1. *Parental warmth and nurturance.* Studies repeatedly find that parental warmth and nurturance are linked with moral behavior in children and adults. In one study, Margaret Bacon and her associates examined anthropological data on forty-eight nonliterate societies in Africa, North and South America, Asia, and the South Pacific. They wanted to see whether child-rearing practices were associated with numbers and types of crimes. Bacon and her coworkers found that societies

▲ USING PSYCHOLOGY

1. Suppose that you were advising new parents. Make a list of suggested child-rearing practices. Explain why psychologists endorse each practice.

2. Says psychologist Burton White, "The vast majority of educated women in this country don't know what the hell they are doing when they have a child. We just don't prepare our women or our men for parenting." Do you agree? Should parents be licensed for parenting? On what basis?

where parents were predominantly nurturant had lower frequencies of theft than those where parents were generally strict. Harsh and abrupt training for independence was associated with high rates of *personal crime*, acts aimed at injuring or killing other people [95].

2. *Parental modeling of helpful and moral behavior.* Parents who set good examples themselves probably contribute mightily to desirable social behavior in their offspring. In one experimental study that supports this notion, Marian Yarrow and her associates had some nursery school children interact with people who talked about helpfulness, but were not particularly helpful. Other youngsters were exposed to adults who stressed helpfulness and were truly helpful as well. In each condition some of the adults were warm and nurturant. Children who interacted with nurturing and helpful models showed significantly more helpfulness consistently in varied settings than the others [96]. Helpful, warm caretakers may teach youngsters firsthand the benefits of considering others. And

their approval may be an especially powerful incentive for moral, humane behavior.

3. *Parental discipline that teaches empathy.* Disciplinary techniques that teach empathy seem to increase socially appropriate conduct. Many studies by psychologist Martin Hoffman and others support this hypothesis. Through discipline, parents encourage children to weigh their desires against the moral requirements of the situation. *Induction techniques* are disciplinary practices that communicate the harmful consequences of the youngster's actions for others. The relatively frequent use of *induction* and the relatively infrequent use of *power assertion* (force and threats) is associated again and again with a high level of moral maturity in children. Induction techniques seem to train people to put themselves in others' positions and consider their welfare before acting. When power assertion practices are employed extensively, youngsters tend to develop external moralities, those based on fears of punishment [97]. ▲

SUMMARY
The Beginning: Heredity, Environment, and the Early Development of the Child

1. Heredity and environment continuously interact to shape development. The term *environment* encompasses five overlapping influences: chemical prenatal environment, chemical postnatal environment, constant sensory experiences, variable sensory experiences, and traumatic physical events.

2. Heredity affects behavior and psychological functioning through its impact on bodily structures such as the nervous system, the muscles, the sensory receptors, and the endocrine glands.

3. A species inheritance gives an animal broad behavioral propensities. An individual inheritance structures unique potentialities.

4. Twin studies, infant studies, and breeding experiments suggest that certain temperament differences (in activity level, sociability, and emotionality, for instance) are influenced by genetics. At least in people, environmental factors, such as parental attitudes and reactions, influence temperament characteristics too.

5. An animal is maximally sensitive to effects of the environment during early brief sensitive periods of rapid growth—both before and after birth. The presence or absence of specific types of stimulation during sensitive periods may have lasting effects.

6. The child's earliest environment is the uterus. Maternal disease, malnutrition, chemical use, and stress may prevent the human infant from achieving its full genetic potential.

7. Normal human babies all over the world develop motor, perceptual, social, intellectual, and language skills in approximately the same sequence. Heredity and environment make organisms physically ready to learn particular behaviors. Then, if minimal opportunities and stimulation are provided, the skills develop.

8. Extreme sensorimotor and social deprivations lead to perceptual, intellectual, and social deficits. In some cases, they may be reversed.

9. Many early child-care practices affect subse-

quent development. The following contribute to children's happiness, competence, humanity, and morality: toilet-training a ready youngster with relaxed nonpunitive techniques, responding to crying infants, talking to babies, being responsive to individual needs, encouraging exploration and curiosity, teaching empathy, being warm, and behaving in a helpful fashion.

A Study Guide for Chapter Three

Key terms neonate (57), developmental psychologist (59), heredity (59), chemical prenatal environment (59), chemical postnatal environment (59), constant sensory experience (59), variable sensory experience (59), traumatic physical event (59), behavior geneticist (60), continuous and discrete characteristics (61), temperament (62), intrauterine period (66), maturation (70), sensorimotor stage (73), imprinting (77), socialization (82), restricted versus elaborated code (84), secure attachment (85), and other italicized words and expressions.

Important research heredity of genius (Galton), facts about genetics, genetics and temperament (Fuller, Scott, Thomas, Chess, Birch, others), rearing practices and temperament, illness during pregnancy, malnutrition during pregnancy (Stein, Ebbs, others), chemicals and pregnancy (Carr, Hanson, Frazier, others), stress during pregnancy (Thompson, others), observations about maturation (Bower, others), sensorimotor experiences and development (Nissen, Scarr-Salapatek, Williams, Provence, Lipton, Kagan, Klein, Yarrow, Skeels, Dennis, Rosenzweig, Krech, others), social experiences and early development (Lorenz, Harlow, Heath, Robson, Moss, Klaus, Kennell, Vietze, O'Connor, others), child-rearing practices and early development (Bell, Ainsworth, Sroufe, White, Bacon, Yarrow, Hoffman, others).

Basic concepts nature-nurture controversy, reasons why human genetics is difficult to investigate, rationales behind and criticisms of behavior-genetic procedures (family study, twin study, adoption study, breeding techniques, genetic abnormality investigations, and study of infant differences), characteristics of sensitive (critical) periods, reasons why chemical effects on the unborn child are difficult to determine, reasons for believing sensorimotor stimulation and intellectual growth are linked (Piaget, others), explanation for the association between parental responsivity and language development and competence (Bell, Ainsworth, Sroufe), stages of moral development (Kohlberg), relationship between moral judgments and behavior.

People to identify Galton, Piaget, Lorenz, Harlow.

Self-Quiz

1. Which phenomenon is part of a person's constant sensory environment?
  a. Attending school
  b. Hearing children's laughter
  c. Hearing human voices
  d. Living in a city

2. How many chromosomes do human beings possess?
  a. 22   *b.* 23
  c. 46   *d.* 92

3. How are discrete and continuous characteristics different?
  a. Discrete characteristics act only at certain times while continuous ones influence the organism throughout its lifetime.
  b. Discrete characteristics are either present or absent while continuous ones exist in degrees.
  c. Discrete characteristics are influenced by the environment while continuous ones are not.
  d. Discrete characteristics are rare while continuous ones are relatively common.

4. Which statement about temperament is true?
  a. All children are readily classified as easy, difficult, or slow to warm up.
  b. Clues about persisting aspects of temperament can be observed soon after birth.
  c. Introversion-extroversion appears to be influenced predominantly by environment.
  d. Temperament patterns in early infancy show a slight relationship to later adjustment.

5. What happened when Canadian social scientists improved the diets of mothers who were malnourished during the first half of their pregnancies?
  a. The babies were healthier but the mothers remained unchanged.
  b. The mothers were healthier but the babies remained unchanged.

c. Only the number of premature births decreased.

d. Both mothers and babies were healthier.

6. Smoking during pregnancy is associated with which condition?

    a. Cleft palate and harelip in infants

    b. Digestive problems in infants

    c. Infectious diseases in infants

    d. Premature deliveries and low-birth-weight infants

7. When a human mother experiences emotional distress during pregnancy, which characteristic is the infant most likely to show?

    a. Irritability and excessive crying

    b. Low birth-weight and prematurity

    c. Mental retardation

    d. Unusual fearfulness

8. The text described a study of a chimpanzee reared with cardboard cuffs covering its forearms and lower legs for its first 2½ years of life. What did this research demonstrate?

    a. Early physical contact between members of a species is important for later social adjustment.

    b. Early sensory experiences are necessary for the full development of sensory capacities.

    c. Early sensory isolation affects the ability to be a caring parent.

    d. Early sensory stimulation influences intelligence.

9. What specific type of maternal stimulation has been shown to be significantly associated with intellectual development in human babies?

    a. Kinesthetic   *b.* Social

    c. Tactile (touch)   *d.* Visual

10. What happens when rats are reared in an enriched environment?

    a. Their brains become larger and heavier.

    b. Their memory is strengthened.

    c. Their sensory capacities become more acute.

    d. They show more concern for their young.

11. How do the majority of mothers respond to their new infants?

    a. Negatively

    b. Neutrally or not at all

    c. Positively, but not lovingly

    d. Lovingly

12. At what age do infants first begin to smile and babble more in the presence of their primary caretakers?

    a. 1 to 2 weeks   *b.* 4 to 6 weeks

    c. 8 to 10 weeks   *d.* 12 to 14 weeks

13. Immediate parent-child contact following delivery has which effect?

    a. Enhanced helping and moral behavior in the child

    b. Increased competence in the child

    c. Reduction in parenting problems such as abuse and neglect

    d. Superior intellectual development in the child

14. What outcome is associated with frequently picking up a crying infant?

    a. Decreased sociability

    b. Less crying later on

    c. More crying later on

    d. Retarded language development

15. How did mothers of competent, coping youngsters differ from those of less competent children?

    a. They designed a home environment with lots of interesting things to see and do and frequently consulted with the child informally for a minute or two about interesting or difficult situations—at the child's instigation.

    b. They devoted the greater part of each day to stimulating the child.

    c. They planned short lessons and spent several hours each day teaching specific skills.

    d. They provided a safe, secure, pleasant environment by confining the child to a playpen or crib located "in the center of the action" and surrounding the youngster with a great many toys.

Exercises

1. HEREDITY: TERMS AND CONCEPTS. The vocabulary and basic ideas of behavior genetics may be confusing to you if this is your first encounter with them. You can test your mastery of the material by working the following exercise. Match the numbered term or concept with the single most appropriate characteristic or definition in the lettered list below. Please review pages 60 to 65 if you make many mistakes.

_____ *1.* Germ cell

_____ *2.* XY

_____ *3.* Zygote

_____ *4.* Nucleus

_____ *5.* Gene

_____ *6.* Structural protein

_____ *7.* Enzyme

_____ *8.* Loci

_____ *9.* XX

_____ *10.* Continuous characteristic

_____ *11.* Turner's syndrome

_____ *12.* Inbred strain

    a. Considered the basic unit of heredity; directs the production of proteins.

    b. Reproductive cell (producing either egg or sperm).

    c. Human zygotes possess forty-six.

    d. Trait that an animal has or does not have.

    e. Chromosome pair identifying normal females.

f. Centrally located structure in a cell; contains chromosomes.

g. Controls the physical-chemical reactions of the body.

h. Produced when sperm and ovum unite.

i. Chromosome pair identifying normal males.

j. Building block for blood, muscle, tissue, and other bodily organs.

k. May be associated with introversion.

l. Exists in degrees; depends on both heredity and environment.

m. Sites on chromosomes where genes are located.

n. Associated with poor spatial ability.

o. Cell body.

p. Related individuals are bred for at least twenty generations until they are practically identical genetically.

q. High scorers on some behavioral measure are bred to one another while low scorers on the same measure are bred to one another.

2. PRENATAL INFLUENCES. In this chapter we described a large number of maternal conditions (chemicals ingested, diseases contracted, etc.) during pregnancy which are either known to influence, or are associated with, physical or behavioral attributes in the unborn child or infant. To make sure you have mastered this information, match the condition on the left with its known or suspected effect(s) on the right. Choose the single most appropriate response. To review this material, see pages 66 to 70.

_____ 1. Cigarette smoking after four months

_____ 2. Smallpox

_____ 3. Medication during labor and birth

_____ 4. Heroin addiction

_____ 5. Rubella (during the mother's first three months)

_____ 6. Cigarette smoking before four months

_____ 7. Alcoholism

_____ 8. Severe malnutrition early in pregnancy

_____ 9. Oral contraceptives

_____ 10. Caffeine

_____ 11. Excessive stress

a. Retarded physical growth, small head, and mental retardation.

b. Prematurity, low birth-weight, later physical and mental defects.

c. Normal birth-weight.

d. Infection may be transmitted to the infant.

e. Reduction in the ultimate size of brain cells.

f. Chromosomal abnormalities.

g. A higher incidence of cleft palate and hare-lip.

h. Unresponsive infant with slow heart and respiration rates and poor circulation; brain damage is possible.

j. Eye and ear problems, mental retardation.

k. Lung disorders.

l. Addiction in the fetus; withdrawal at birth.

m. Decrease in expected number of brain cells and interference with myelination.

n. Not understood.

Suggested Readings

1. Bee, H. *The developing child.* (2d ed.) New York: Harper & Row, 1978; and Papalia, D. E., & Olds. S. W. *A child's world: Infancy through adolescence.* (2d ed.) New York: McGraw-Hill, 1979. These two texts make fine introductions to child development. Both are clear, interesting, up-to-date, and informal in style.

2. McClinton, B. S., & Meier, B. G. *Beginnings: Psychology of early childhood.* St. Louis, Mo.: Mosby, 1978. For more information about early childhood, try this engaging text.

3. Bower, T. G. R. *The perceptual world of the child;* Dunn, J. *Distress and comfort;* Garvey, C. *Play;* MacFarlane, A. *The psychology of childbirth;* Schaffer, R. *Mothering;* Stern, D. *The first relationship: Infant and mother.* These brief paperbacks were published by the Harvard University Press, beginning in 1977. Each book was authored by a distinguished expert. Using a conversational style, in most cases, the writers present current psychological research findings for parents, students, and the general public.

4. Annis, L. F. *The child before birth.* Ithaca, N.Y.: Cornell University Press, 1978 (paperback). This is a concise introduction to the influences on the unborn child. It is written in simple, clear language and filled with fascinating photographs.

5. Thomas, A., Chess, S., & Birch, H. The origin of personality. *Scientific American*, 1970, **223**(2), 102–109. Thomas and his associates describe their research on temperament differences which persist from infancy throughout childhood. They also discuss the practical implications of this work.

6. Scarr, S., & Weinberg, R. A. Attitudes, interests, and IQ. *Human Nature*, 1978, **1**(4), 29–36. The research discussed in this article suggests that heredity influences intelligence, interests, and attitudes. "Biological diversity," write the authors, "is a fact of life and respect for individual differences derives from the genetic perspective."

7. Harlow, H. F., Harlow, M. K., & Suomi, S. J. From thought to therapy: Lessons from a primate laboratory. *American Scientist*, 1971, **59**(5), 538–549. For more information about Harlow's classic studies and their implications, this article is highly recommended.

8. Hess, E. H. 'Imprinting' in a natural laboratory. *Scientific American*, 1972, **227**, 24–31. Hess describes interesting work on imprinting in mallard ducks in both the laboratory and the field.

9. Parke, R. D., & Sawin, D. B. Fathering: It's a major role. *Psychology Today*, 1977, **11**(6), 109–112. This provocative discussion of recent research shows that fathers play a unique role in infant development: chief playmate.

10. Hawkins, R. It's time we taught the young how to be good parents (and don't you wish we'd started a long time ago?). *Psychology Today*, 1972, **6**(6), 28ff. Hawkins argues for compulsory parent training and describes an ideal program that would be beneficial for all would-be parents.

Answer Keys

Self-Quiz

1. *c* (59) **2.** *c* (60) **3.** *b* (61) **4.** *b* (64)
5. *d* (67) **6.** *d* (69) **7.** *a* (70) **8.** *b* (72)
9. *a* (74) **10.** *a* (76) **11.** *c* (80) **12.** *b* (81)
13. *c* (80) **14.** *b* (83) **15.** *a* (85)

Exercise 1

1. *b* **2.** *i* **3.** *h* **4.** *f* **5.** *a* **6.** *j* **7.** *g*
8. *m* **9.** *e* **10.** *l* **11.** *n* **12.** *p*

Exercise 2

1. *b* **2.** *d* **3.** *h* **4.** *l* **5.** *j* **6.** *c* **7.** *a*
8. *m* **9.** *f* **10.** *n* **11.** *g*

CHAPTER FOUR
The Brain, Behavior, and Cognition

The brain has a lot to do with behavior. It determines whether animals move on two legs or four. It dictates the senses that guide perception. Pigs and horses depend primarily on smell, while human beings rely especially heavily on vision. The brain sets communication patterns ranging from grunting and bodily movements to speaking. And it establishes limits on the amount of information that can be absorbed and processed. The brain is unquestionably the single most influential organ of the body. In this chapter we focus on the human brain and its role in behavior and cognition. We begin with the story of a Russian soldier whose life was transformed by a gunshot wound.

The Man with a Shattered World

At the age of twenty-three, a Russian soldier, Sublieutenant Zasetsky, suffered a head injury from a gunshot wound that penetrated the left side of the cranium. This injury produced many abrupt changes in behavior. Zasetsky was treated for approximately twenty-five years by the brilliant Russian psychologist-physician Alexander Luria (1902–1977). During this time Zasetsky kept a journal of his perceptions. We draw on these descriptions now to see how the wound affected some of his capabilities.

One change that Zasetsky experienced was fragmented vision. In his words, "Ever since I was wounded I haven't been able to see a single object as a whole—not one thing. Even now I have to fill in a lot about objects, phenomena, or any living thing from imagination. That is, I have to picture them in my mind and try to remember them as full and complete—after I have a chance to look them over, touch them, or get some image of them."

Parts of Zasetsky's body appeared distorted to him. As he put it, "Sometimes when I'm sitting down I suddenly feel as though my head is the size of a table—every bit as big—while my hands, feet, and torso become very small. When I close my eyes, I'm not even sure where my right leg is; for some reason I used to think (even sensed) it was somewhere above my shoulder, even above my head."

Zasetsky's perception of space was also disturbed. "Ever since I was wounded," he wrote, "I've had trouble sometimes sitting down in a chair or on a couch. I first look to see where the chair is, but when I try to sit down I suddenly make a grab for the chair since I'm afraid I'll land on the floor. Sometimes that happens because the chair turns out to be further to one side than I thought."

Zasetsky's intellectual abilities were profoundly impaired. He lost the capacity to read and write. He had trouble following the meaning of a conversation or understanding a simple story. Although he had been an excellent student and had done research in a number of scientific and technical fields, he could no longer cope with grammar, arithmetic, geometry, or physics. He tried desperately to relearn, beginning from scratch and searching for ways to compensate for abilities that had been lost. But, even though Zasetsky reviewed the same material repeatedly, he had difficulty understanding even the simplest basic concepts. He found that he had to rely on drawings and sketches for information. Without them, explanations didn't "get through" to him.

Wounds heal, but damaged brain cells do not grow back again. (We return to this topic later.) Although Zasetsky worked diligently for more than twenty-five years to recover the abilities he'd lost, he didn't succeed [1].

Zasetsky's poignant story underscores the importance of the brain for behavior. Like other animals, people are composed of billions of cells, each one specialized for a particular role. The nervous system, especially the brain, directs and coordinates the action of these cells so that we see, hear, think, speak, remember, and behave effectively. Damage to the nervous system can disrupt any or all of these capabilities.

The study of the brain and its connection to behavior and cognition lies within the realm of *physiological psychology* (also called *psychobiology* or *biopsychology*). Physiological psychologists investigate the biological foundations of sensation, perception, consciousness, learning, memory, language, motives, emotions, and abnormal behavior. They also conduct research on how genetics, hormones, drugs, brain damage, and illnesses influence, and are influenced by, behavior.

To understand what psychologists have learned about human brain-behavior relationships, you must be acquainted with the overall plan of the nervous system, of which the brain is a part. You must learn about basic research approaches and about the nerve cell, the fundamental functional unit of the brain. After covering these topics, we focus on the brain itself and its roles in behavior and cognition.

AN OVERVIEW OF THE NERVOUS SYSTEM

If you were designing a sophisticated robot, you would want to build in these features:

1. Sensors, to gather information about external surroundings and internal parts
2. A computer, to interpret the information from the sensors, plan appropriate actions, oversee vital functions, and manage energy distribution so that there is sufficient fuel during ordinary conditions and crises
3. Effectors, to enable the robot to move about and make changes in its external and internal environments
4. A communication system linking sensors, computer, and effectors

Though people are far more complicated than any robot, we are fashioned along similar lines. Human sensors are cells called *receptors* (described more fully in Chapter 6). They respond to sound, light, heat, touch, muscle movement, and other stimuli inside or outside the body. Instead of a computer, people have a *central nervous system* (CNS), composed of the brain and spinal cord. The CNS is vastly more powerful in many ways than any computer that has ever been built. The *brain* is the master information-processing, decision-making organ of the body. It receives messages from the receptors, integrates this information with past experiences, evaluates all the data, and plans actions. It directs vital functions, such as circulation and respiration. It oversees the fulfilling of bodily needs, including those for food and sleep, and it manages the body's fuel supply. The *spinal cord* is an extension of the brain, somewhat simpler in organization and function. The cord, as it is often abbreviated, helps protect the body from damage by initiating a great many *reflexes*, very rapid responses to potentially dangerous conditions. Withdrawing the hand from a hot stove is an example of a spinal reflex. The spinal cord is also involved in voluntary movements. The central nervous system acts through *effectors*—in people, cells that control muscles, glands, or organs. Because the receptors and effectors are often located quite far from the CNS, human beings—like robots—need a communication system, a network of information-carrying cables, or *nerves*, to connect the various components. The *peripheral nervous system* serves this function, among others. Just as "peripheral" means "on the border," the peripheral system includes all the nervous system structures bordering, or lying outside, the brain and spinal cord. The system is divided into two major parts. The *somatic nervous system*, composed mainly of nerves which connect the CNS to receptors and skeletal muscles, enables us to perform voluntary actions, to move about and manipulate the external environment. The *autonomic nervous system* contains nerves which relay messages between the CNS and the so-called involuntary muscles, including those that control the heart, kidneys, liver, and other internal organs and glands. The autonomic nervous system functions *autonomously* (on its own), so that our bodies are maintained in proper working order and fuel requirements are met, as environmental demands change. If you have to run across a busy intersection, for instance, the autonomic nervous system speeds the heart and routes blood to the muscles to supply more oxygen and consequently more energy—without any conscious effort on your part. While most people do not directly modify the action of this system, it can be done. Eastern mystics who have learned to slow their hearts or stick pins in their skin without pain or bleeding demonstrate this clearly. (More on the control of the autonomic nervous system in Chapter 5 and more on this system's role in emotion in Chapter 11.)

The autonomic nervous system is further subdivided into two branches: the sympathetic and the parasympathetic divisions. Though they are both active, one ordinarily dominates—functioning somewhat like the accelerator and brake on a car. The *sympa-*

FIGURE 4-1   The overall plan of the human nervous system.

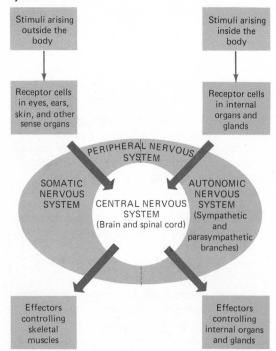

thetic division (the accelerator) usually mobilizes internal resources for vigorous action under special circumstances. The *parasympathetic division* (the brake) generally takes command when a person relaxes so that internal resources may be conserved, maintained, or restored. Figure 4-1 depicts the relationships among various parts of the nervous system. Figure 4-2 pictures the human nervous system.

CAUTION: The nervous system has been simplified to make its broad outlines clear. It would be easy to come away with the impression that the brain is a mere switchboard which becomes active only when the senses are stimulated. That is not true. The brain is active as long as an animal is alive. As people use language, think, solve problems, or recollect—pursuits that are not necessarily initiated by sensory stimulation—the brain is working. It is also diligent in monitoring the internal environment, even while we sleep. Signals from the senses blend into, modify, and are modified by, this ongoing activity. The brain, in turn, has a hand in controlling what the senses bring in. It can allow certain sensory messages access while blocking out others.

RESEARCH APPROACHES: STUDYING THE BRAIN, BEHAVIOR, AND COGNITION

Three general approaches are currently used to explore the role of the brain in behavior and cognition. In this section we look at each technique and the information it provides.

Ablation and Brain Damage

The *ablation* technique, which consists of removing or destroying part of an animal's brain, is frequently used to study the physiological bases of behavior and mental functioning. Scientists study the precise symptoms that result and the exact location of the excised structure or injury, generally by careful microscopic postmortem examinations of brain tissue. Then they draw conclu-

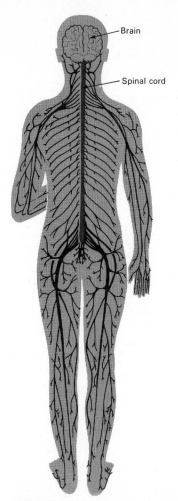

Brain

Spinal cord

FIGURE 4-2 The human nervous system is composed of two divisions: the central and the peripheral nervous systems. The two major components of the central nervous system, the brain and spinal cord, are shown in color. The nerves of the peripheral system connect the effectors and receptors of the body to the brain and spinal cord. Twelve peripheral-system nerve pairs that join the brain directly are not shown.

sions about the area's original role. In the 1930s, for example, Heinrich Klüver, a psychologist, and Paul Bucy, a neurosurgeon, removed the tips of the brain region called the temporal lobes (shown in Figure 4-14) in wild rhesus monkeys. During the surgery, parts of the limbic system (shown in Figure 4-17) were inadvertently damaged. Before the operation the animals had been characterized by short tempers and aggression at the slightest provocation. After the monkeys recuperated from the surgery, Klüver and Bucy noted that their personalities were drastically changed. They were so gentle and peace-loving that they did not aggress even when directly attacked. They showed none of their normal fears, including one of snakes. They exhibited signs of hypersexuality. The males mounted everything in sight, and the females showed unusual sexual receptivity, even to such unlikely suitors as water faucets. The animals' hunger drives were also disordered. Instead of disregarding inedible objects, as normal monkeys do, they attempted to chew up and consume metal bolts mixed with their peanuts [2]. Subsequent research pinpointed which structures were associated with which malfunctions. Damaged limbic system regions had been involved in directing sex, hunger, and aggression [3].

While the ablation approach is *never* used to study people's brains, "experiments of nature" may provide a great deal of insight into the functioning of the human nervous system. Tumors, strokes, and head injuries sometimes damage fairly specific areas of brain tissue. Under rare circumstances, as in cases of severe epilepsy, certain brain regions are removed for therapeutic reasons. All these unfortunate events may provide information about the role of the damaged or excised region. When brains are extensively damaged, as in Zasetsky's case, it is difficult, of course, to know for certain what part contributed to what role. To illustrate how observations of brain damage may furnish information about the mind, we look briefly at the work of Howard Gardner, a psychologist who has examined hundreds of patients with central nervous system injuries, mostly *aphasias* (language disabilities due to brain damage).

Brain Damage: A Window on the Mind

"One of the first lessons gleaned from work with brain-damaged patients is that common-sense notions of the relationships among abilities may be invalid. Take, for example, the set of symptoms encountered in a bizarre but not infrequent condition called *pure alexia without agraphia.* Patients afflicted with this disorder are unable to read text (they are *alexic*) yet remain able to write (they are not *agraphic*). One's immediate thought is that they must be in some sense blind; but in fact the patients can copy or trace out the very letters and words that they fail to read. To complicate the matter even further, the same patients are often able to read numbers. They may even read 'DIX' as '509,' while proving incapable of reading it as 'diks.' They are able to name objects but are frequently unable to name samples of colors shown to them.

"On its own, this syndrome confounds a raft of intuitions about how the mind works. Reading can be separated from writing; verbal symbols differ from numerical symbols; objects are named in a way different from colors. No one completely understands pure alexia, but the major facts of the syndrome described above have been repeatedly described and are widely accepted. . . . Such findings . . . challenge the researcher to devise a model of mind that can account for the bizarre blend of abilities and disabilities. . . . Other syndromes demonstrate precisely the reverse situation; skills usually thought independent of one another [such as doing mathematics and analyzing relationships between objects in space] . . . turn out to be closely related. . . . And so, in this instance, the modeler of mental processes is challenged to unite skills that, on intuitive grounds, may appear quite unrelated [4]."

The study of animals with ablations or of people with natural brain damage poses several problems. First, brain injuries of any type are apt to produce widespread damage throughout the central nervous system. Consequently, the real culprit may go undetected, even though a microscopic analysis of the brain is made during an autopsy. Second, behavior and mental processes depend on the functioning of complex, interconnected chains of cells, as we will soon see. It takes only one broken link to break that chain. But the broken link may not have been doing all the work or even the major work. To cite an extreme example, the Greek philosopher Aristotle believed that the mind was located in the heart because chickens whose heads were cut off continued to run about frantically. When their hearts were removed, all functions ceased immediately.

Recording the Brain's Electrical Activity

Weak electrical signals are generated continuously throughout the nervous system as it performs its many functions. Such activity occurs as long as the brain is alive. Its cessation is one criterion of death. Scientists use a number of recording techniques to "listen in" on the action. All procedures involve *electrodes*, usually small pieces of metal, which pick up electrical signals and send them to amplifying and measuring devices. Recording the brain's electrical activity provides information about which regions are particularly active as animals relax, learn, sleep, or engage in other functions. To record the electrical activity occurring throughout large regions of the brain, electrodes about the size and shape of a dime are taped to the scalp. In this case, the amplifying and recording device is known as an *electroencephalograph* (EEG), and the record that is produced on moving paper is known as an *electroencephalogram*. Figure 4-3 describes how the electroencephalograph can be used to advance knowledge about the brain's role in abnormal behavior. A great many insights into sleep have been generated by EEG investigations, a topic we explore in Chapter 7. While electroencephalographic procedures do not harm the participant, the information obtained is difficult to interpret because the signals originate from all over the brain and reflect many different ongoing activities. To measure the

action of a smaller region of the brain more precisely, scientists insert needlelike electrodes directly into the region of interest. It's even possible to observe the electrical activity of a single cell by implanting tiny *microelectrodes* (less than five-thousandths of a millimeter in diameter) directly into the cell. Since electrode implantation may damage brain tissue, these procedures are used only on laboratory animals or in the course of trying to help human patients with severe brain dysfunctions.

Like the other approaches we have described, recording has problems. Just because a particular nervous system region is especially active doesn't mean it is essential for a particular activity. Suppose, for example, that cats are learning to find their way through a

FIGURE 4-3 This child is being tested for brain function by an electrical recording technique called the Quantitative Electrophysiological Battery (QB). The QB was developed by E. Roy John, a physiological psychologist, and his colleagues at the New York Medical College Brain Research Laboratory to help detect abnormal brain functioning. Patients taking the QB wear a set of electrodes wired to a computer terminal. They are then exposed to a carefully designed series of stimuli, including light flashes, clicks, and taps. As various combinations of stimuli are presented, the computer records about thirty aspects of electrical activity at close to sixty brain sites. The records of the patients are then automatically compared with those of normal people. A number of brain problems produce readily detectable departures from normal patterns. The QB can accurately diagnose strokes, brain tumors, epilepsy, and several other conditions that are often difficult to identify [46]. [*Psychology Today*.]

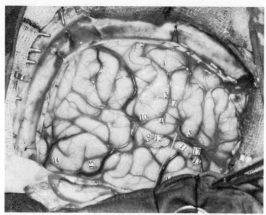

FIGURE 4-4 M. M.'s cerebral cortex is exposed for brain surgery. The numbered labels mark points of stimulation that produced positive responses. Some of those reactions are described in the text. [*Montreal Neurological Institute.*]

maze. At the same time they are learning and recording a memory, they are attending, seeing, hearing, perhaps experiencing hunger or fear, and moving or preparing to move. The nervous system activity that is recorded can reflect any of these processes.

Brain Stimulation

When certain chemicals or mild electrical currents (similar to normally occurring chemical and electrical signals) are applied to specific parts of the brain, they stimulate behavior. We focus on electrical stimulation. Like the recording procedure, electrical stimulation involves electrodes. In this case, mild current is passed through a pair of electrodes which have been placed, usually quite precisely, within a particular area of the brain. By observing the resulting responses, psychologists and other researchers learn about the functioning of the stimulated regions.

Surgery to remove diseased or damaged human brain tissue often takes place under local anesthesia to allow physicians to electrically stimulate tissue in the problem area. By observing patients' responses, surgeons can identify the extent of the damage and the functions served by the injured regions, as well as those nearby. This information enables the surgeon to excise tissue in the most beneficial way. Because there are no pain receptors in the central nervous system, what might sound like a barbaric technique is not. People experience no discomfort even though they are wide awake during the entire procedure. Instead, electrical stimulation elicits or inhibits varied sensations, perceptions, movements, and more rarely, feelings, fantasies, and memories. Wilder Penfield (1891–1976), a Canadian neurosurgeon and one of the pioneers in using this approach, placed numbered labels on the brain's surface to mark the stimulated site (see Figure 4-4), then had the behavior or reported experience recorded. Here is part of Penfield's account of one session with a patient called M. M.

The Case of M. M.

"The patient [M. M.] was a woman of 26 years who was afflicted by recurring cerebral seizures. . . . Electrical stimulation was carried out. . . . [M. M.] was ordinarily warned by the operator each time the [stimulation] . . . was applied. But, as usual, at intervals the warning was given with no stimulus and at other times, stimulation without warning. This serves to eliminate with certainty false or imaginary responses. . . .

[The following responses were obtained from the sensory and motor areas:]

"Stimulation at point 2—sensation in thumb and index finger.

"She called it 'quivering,' 'tingling.'

"3—'same feeling on the left side of my tongue.'

"7—movement of the tongue.

"4—'Yes, a feeling at the back of my throat like nausea.'

"8—She said, 'No.' Then she said, 'Yes, I suddenly cannot hear.' . . .

"The following were the 'psychical' results of stimulating the interpretive cortex. . . .

"11—'I heard something familiar, I do not know what it was.'

"11—[repeated without warning]—'Yes, Sir, I think I heard a mother call her little boy somewhere. It seemed to be something that happened years ago.' When asked to explain, she said, "It was somebody in the neighbourhood where I live.' She added that it seemed that she herself 'was somewhere close enough to hear.'

"Warning without stimulation—'Nothing.'

"11 repeated—'Yes, I hear the same familiar sounds, it seems to be a woman calling, the same lady. That was not in the neighbourhood. It seemed to be a lumber yard.' Then she

added reflectively, 'I've never been around the lumber yard much.'

"This was an incident of childhood which she could never have recalled without the aid of the stimulating electrode. Actually she could not 'remember' it but she knew at once, with no suggestion from us, that she must have experienced it sometime.

"12—'Yes. I heard voices

down along the river somewhere—a man's voice and a woman's voice calling.'

"When she was asked how she could tell that the calling had been 'along the river,' she said, 'I think I saw the river.' When asked what river it was she said, 'I don't know. It seems to be one I was visiting when I was a child [5].'"

Penfield elicited reports of past experiences like these in a small but significant number of patients after stimulating certain parts of the brain (the temporal and parietal lobes, depicted in Figure 4-14). Brain stimulation studies convinced Penfield that:

There is within the adult human brain a remarkable record of the stream of each individual's awareness, his consciousness. It is as though the electrode cuts in, at random, on the record of that stream. The patient sees and hears what he saw and heard in some earlier strip of time, and he feels the same accompanying emotions. The stream of consciousness flows again exactly as before, stopping instantly on removal of the electrode. He is aware of those things to which he paid attention in this earlier period, even twenty years ago. He is not aware of the things that were ignored. The experience evidently moves forward at the original pace. This is demonstrated by the fact that when the music of an orchestra or song or piano is heard and the patient is asked to hum in accompaniment, the tempo of his humming is what one would expect. He is still aware of being in the operating

room, but he can describe this other run of consciousness at the same time.

The patient recognizes the experience as having been his own, although usually he could not have recalled it if he had tried. [6]

The electrical stimulation technique has enabled scientists to draw maps of the human brain showing that certain regions are associated with specific types of behavior. For an example of such a map, see Figure 4-15. Chemical stimulation of the nervous system is described and illustrated in Figure 4-5.

The stimulation approach has its own difficulties. Because the nervous system is interconnected, it is impossible to stimulate one small area of tissue and no other. The introduction of chemicals and electrical currents may also distort brain functioning.

Could a crazed dictator enslave citizens by implanting electrodes within their brains and then stimulating particular behavior, emotions, and motives, like a master puppeteer? We explore this issue briefly.

Brain Control in a Brave New World

Though journalists, science fiction writers, and occasionally psychologists themselves suggest otherwise, brain control is not even remotely possible currently. Physiological psychologist Elliot Valenstein, an expert on this subject, writes, "It has yet to be demonstrated that electrical or chemical stimulation

of any region of the brain can modify one, and only one, specific behavior tendency [7]." While brain stimulation may turn on such behaviors as aggression, eating, drinking, and sexual activity in laboratory animals, the same functions are not always associated with the same area. Eating or drinking, for ex-

ample, may be elicited by stimulating diverse brain regions. On the other hand, stimulating the same area can evoke different behaviors—depending on the individual, the surroundings, and personal history. In some cases, the animal activity that is "consistently evoked" by brain stimulation emerges only after a long period of testing. And precisely what type of response is being elicited is frequently questionable. In a specific instance, brain stimulation may be creating a state of arousal, changing responsivity to different types of events, patterning movements, or arousing motives.

What about people? Brain stimulation is occasionally used to control symptoms in patients suffering from terminal cancer, intractable epilepsy, or psychosis. The human findings are much the same as the nonhuman ones. Patients report different feelings from the stimulation of presumably the same brain region. Moreover, the same person may have different experiences from identical stimulation at different times [8]. The sensations aroused by brain stimulation do not appear to be overwhelmingly positive or negative either, as we see in Chapter 11. The various psychological and physical tortures that people devised long ago to torment one another are probably far more potent weapons for a tyrant. For now, "stimulation techniques have to be considered research tools that have generated interesting, even if highly speculative, guesses about how the brain is organized [9]." See Figure 4-6.

All the brain study tactics that we have discussed have limitations. But each technique provides slightly different information and suffers from slightly different deficiencies. By using all the approaches, psychologists can compensate to some extent for the

FIGURE 4-5 This male rat shows the effects of chemical brain stimulation. In chemical stimulation studies, scientists observe an animal's behavior as minute amounts of chemicals are applied in ingenious ways to specific brain sites while the animal is awake and moving about freely. The rat in this sketch began acting parental soon after the "masculine" sex hormone testosterone was injected into a centrally located brain site near the hypothalamus. First, the animal gathered scraps of paper and fashioned a respectable nest. Then it carried the rat pups to the shelter of the nest, ignoring readily available food pellets. This type of behavior is very unusual for males, which often eat infant rats. Other rats, both male and female, showed similar parental behavior when they received this treatment. The same hormone, injected into a slightly different brain site, made female and male rats react with typical masculine sexual behavior [47]. We will say more about the physical bases of sexuality in Chapter 10. The chemical stimulation technique can provide clues to the function of specific brain regions. But, as with electrical stimulation, interpreting the results is difficult. [*Used with permission of Alan E. Fisher.*]

▲ USING PSYCHOLOGY

1. Try to explain to someone how people and robots are similar in design.

2. Contrast the brain to a telephone switchboard.

3. Do electrical signals arise within the brains of people who lie in a coma near death? Do the brains of hibernating animals show electrical activity?

4. Explain why a tyrant who relied on brain stimulation techniques for controlling citizens' behavior would not get very far.

5. Why do physiological psychologists have to use a variety of techniques to study the brain?

weaknesses of each and gain important insights into brain-behavior relationships. ▲

NEURONS: MESSENGERS OF THE NERVOUS SYSTEM

The human nervous system is an immensely complicated piece of machinery. It consists of billions of nerve cells (estimates range from 12 to 200 billion) and numerous other cells, including blood and glial cells. The nerve cell, or *neuron*, is considered the basic functional unit of the central and peripheral nervous systems. *Glia*, or *glial cells*, which lie amidst the neurons in the central nervous system, actually outnumber the neurons by about 10 to 1. These rather mysterious cells were once thought simply to hold the neurons in place, like the connective tissue in many organs. It now appears that glia serve more active functions. These cells are known to be involved in the healing process when the central nervous system is damaged. And they appear to play a significant role in controlling the

FIGURE 4-6 Reports in the mass media sometimes imply that brain stimulation research has made precise control of behavior possible. These photographs show José Delgado, a famous Spanish neurophysiologist and pioneer in brain stimulation research, in an arena with a ferocious bull—a variety bred to attack people. The bull had a number of radio-controlled electrodes implanted in its brain. Whenever the bull charged, Delgado activated the appropriate electrode, and the animal stopped abruptly. Delgado attributed the bull's behavior to (1) a motor effect forcing the animal to stop and turn to one side repetitively and (2) a reduction of the aggressive drive. Many writers in the popular press overlooked the motor control and emphasized the more dramatic control of aggression. For example, the *New York Times* reported that "the bull's naturally aggressive behavior disappeared. It was as placid as Ferdinand." Aggression, like other complex behavior, is influenced by many different brain circuits. Human beings with electrodes implanted in brain regions similar to those of the bull respond somewhat comparably to stimulation; they often stop whatever they are doing [48]. [*Courtesy of José M. R. Delgado.*]

neuron's activities. According to some scientists, we may discover eventually that glia function during perception and memory.

In this section we focus on the neuron—its anatomy, connections to other neurons, position within the nervous system, and messenger role. We will also see what happens when brain neurons are damaged.

The Anatomy of a Neuron

There are several different types of neurons that vary considerably in size, shape, and function. Still, most nerve cells contain three elements: an axon, a cell body, and dendrites. Neurons, such as the one shown in Figure 4-7, can be distinguished from other bodily cells by their branching fibers (the axon and den-

drites). Like other cells, neurons are filled with a typically colorless, semifluid substance called *protoplasm*; and they are completely covered by a *cell membrane* which regulates everything that passes in and out of them.

The cell body of the neuron, called the *soma*, holds a number of specialized structures that are needed to maintain the cell. The *nucleus*, which is almost always centrally located and somewhat spherical in shape, contains genetic information in the form of *deoxyribonucleic acid* (DNA). DNA determines the cell's makeup and function. Other centers within the protoplasm convert food and oxygen into energy and manufacture proteins and chemical substances called *neurotransmitters* (*transmitters*), which play important roles in the message transmission process.

A typical neuron has one *axon*, a fiber varying in length from less than .05 inch to more than 30 inches. The axon usually carries outgoing information from the cell body to neighboring cells. Sometimes it is surrounded by a fatty covering, known as a *myelin sheath*, which appears to serve an insulating function. Neurons with this covering carry messages faster than those without it. Neurons generally possess *dendrites* too, branching fibers which reach out to gather information from nearby neurons and other cells, such as those embedded in the senses. Most neurons have many dendrites. Recent research indicates that dendrites may occasionally transmit messages [10].

FIGURE 4-7 Neurons vary considerably in structure and function. An idealized neuron is shown here. The elements in the diagram are present in many of the neurons of the nervous system.

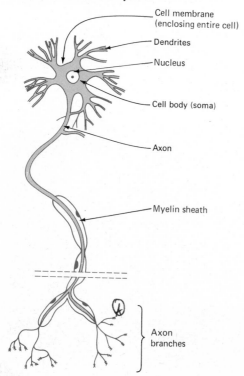

Cell membrane
(enclosing entire cell)

Dendrites

Nucleus

Cell body (soma)

Axon

Myelin sheath

Axon branches

The Neuron Connection: The Synapse

Every neuron links up with at least one other neuron and in most cases, a great many. The number of possible pathways among neurons in a single human brain is staggering, larger than the number of atomic particles that make up the entire universe. The axon of a neuron can make contact with a dendrite, cell body, or axon of a neighboring neuron or with cells in a muscle, gland, or organ. For now, we focus on the neuron in Figure 4-8 and its

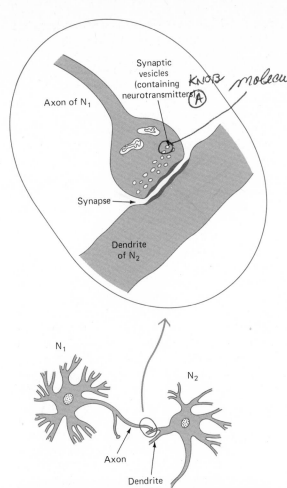

Axon of N$_1$

Synaptic vesicles (containing neurotransmitters)

KNOB *molecules* (A)

Synapse

Dendrite of N$_2$

N$_1$

N$_2$

Axon

Dendrite

FIGURE 4-8 A diagram picturing two interconnected neurons, labeled N$_1$ and N$_2$. The detail of the synapse (shown in the enlargement) is described in the text.

4-9. Most of these endings contain little storage packets called *synaptic vesicles*, which house the neurotransmitter that the cell manufacturers. Current research indicates that each neuron manufactures only one type of transmitter, which is released during communication with an adjacent cell.

From Neuron to Nervous System

The nervous system of a complex animal is highly organized, and not a haphazard collection of specialized cells. How do neurons combine to form the nervous system? First consider the peripheral system. Recall that it is made up primarily of cables, called *nerves* (or *nerve tracts*), which relay messages be-

FIGURE 4-9 Synapses in an *aplysia,* a mollusk known as the California sea hare, photographed by a scanning electron microscope. A large number of the *end feet* (the tiny bulblike swellings at the end of the axon's branches) synapse on a single neuron. The aplysia is often used in neural research because its nervous system contains only 10,000 cells, many of which can be isolated. Then, individual pathways converging on a single cell may be stimulated, and neural transmission may be observed. [*Edwin R. Lewis, Thomas E. Everhart, and Yehoshua Y. Zeevi, American Association for the Advancement of Science.*]

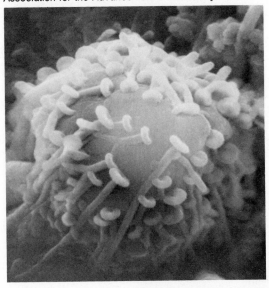

connection to a second cell. Suppose that you looked under a microscope at the junction between the two neurons. Between the axon of the first cell and the dendrite of the second one, you would find a minute gap, about eighteen-millionths of an inch wide, called a *synapse*. You'd see the same gap if you looked at the other possible connections that the neuron could make. People are thought to have about a hundred trillion synapses in their brains. The microscope would also show a slight swelling, or buttonlike structure, at the tip of each of the axon's branches. See Figure tween the central nervous system, effectors, and receptors. The peripheral system contains two distinct types of neurons—sensory neurons and motor neurons. Their structural differences will not concern us here. What is important for our purposes is knowing that *sensory neurons* carry messages from the receptors to the CNS, and *motor neurons* route the orders of the CNS to the effectors. Both types of neurons have relatively long axons. It is these axons (and *only* these axons) that bundle together to form the nerve cables of the peripheral system. These fibers—even those coming from remote regions of the body—run an unbroken course to or from the CNS. In other words, they do not synapse with other cells along the way. The nerves which carry sensory information to the CNS are known as *sensory nerves*, whereas those that route messages from the CNS to the

effectors in the muscles, glands, and organs are known as *motor nerves*. Most nerves are *mixed*; they are formed from the axons of both sensory and motor neurons. Large nerves, such as the ones carrying information to and from the eyes, may contain a million axons, while small nerves hold several hundred. Like the wires that carry messages in telephone lines, each axon works independently of the others. Human beings have forty-three pairs of nerves, one for each side of the body. Branching and rebranching, these nerves put almost every bodily region in direct contact with the central nervous system. The cell bodies connected to all these axons are frequently grouped with other cell bodies which perform similar functions within the peripheral nervous system.

The central nervous system contains the bulk of the neurons that constitute the nervous system. Most of these nerve cells are known as *interneurons*. Once again we will not be concerned with their precise structure except to note that they tend to have short axons and dendrites which branch profusely and that each one tends to be connected to a very large number of other nerve cells. The interconnected organization of the interneurons serves their function: to process and synthesize information and plan action. Within the central nervous system, the neurons are commonly grouped in several ways—in axon "cables" and in cell body and whole neuron clusters.

Neurons as Messengers

We have seen that the nervous system is an elaborate network of interconnected neurons. We focus now on how messages are shuttled along from one point to another throughout this network. To illustrate, we take the very simple example pictured in Figure 4-10. Suppose you're having a medical checkup and the physician taps your leg just below the knee with a little hammer to test the knee-jerk reflex. The tap excites receptors in the tendon that attaches the muscle above the knee to the knee. These receptors, like all bodily receptors, translate the sensation into the

FIGURE 4-10 Some of the nerve pathways involved in the knee-jerk reflex. Note that the brain is not in the circuit (though the spinal cord informs the brain of the event).

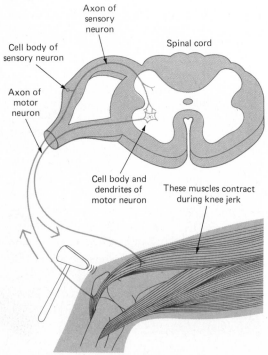

Axon of sensory neuron

Cell body of sensory neuron

Spinal cord

Axon of motor neuron

Cell body and dendrites of motor neuron

These muscles contract during knee jerk

electrical-chemical language that the nervous system uses. If the tap is *sufficiently intense*, as is likely, it will cause the sensory neuron connected to the receptor to conduct a *nerve or neural) impulse.*

Let's stop for a moment and examine several questions.

First, what is a "nerve impulse"? When a neuron is at rest, its cell membrane maintains a delicate balance by keeping certain electrically charged particles inside the cell, barring others from the cell, and allowing others to flow freely in both directions. When stimulated with sufficient intensity, the membrane loses its control for a fraction of a second. In other words, its *permeability* (ability to be penetrated) changes. This fleeting change in permeability begins at the point of contact between the communicating cells—usually at the dendrite of the receiving neuron—and spreads throughout the entire cell. It is accompanied by movements of charged particles across the cell membrane. One byproduct of this movement consists of measurable voltage changes, the electrical signals that scientists record. The *nerve impulse* is defined as the transient (temporary) alteration in the permeability of the membrane *surrounding the axon* and the resulting charge redistribution there. These events usually start at the junction of the axon and cell body and travel *down* the length of the axon.

Now, why did we say that the tap had to be "sufficiently intense" to trigger a nerve impulse? Each neuron has its own *firing threshold*, an excitation level that must be attained before its axon will conduct a nerve impulse. Once that value is reached, the cell fires; in other words, the axon conducts the neural impulse. Like a gun, the neuron either fires or does not fire, so we say that it obeys the *all-or-none law*. Regardless of what stimulated it, the nerve impulse traveling down the axon is the same size and duration. If that is the case, how can people distinguish between a light touch, a punch in the jaw, a clown, a barbecued steak, an operatic aria, and a telephone pole? The events around us are coded in several ways. The receptors themselves are specialized so that they respond to particular types of stimulation. And specific nerves carry their messages to predetermined sites in the brain. Thus, sound and light produce different sensations, in part because of the receptors and neurons they excite and the regions of the brain that receive the message. Firing neurons play a role in coding the intensity of our sensory experiences too. Both the *number* of neurons firing and the *frequency* and *pattern* of their firing vary to signal the properties of a particular object or event.

When the change in permeability and the accompanying charge redistribution reaches the tip of the axon's branches, it generally causes a stored neurotransmitter substance to be released into the synapse(s). The neurotransmitter then combines with highly specific proteins on the surface of the target cell. The union triggers electrochemical responses—in some cases, a neural impulse—in the target cell. Soon afterward, the transmitter substance is destroyed or drawn back into the neuron that it came from for storage and reuse. An accumulation of transmitter substance in the synapse could disrupt communication.

There are about twelve known neurotransmitters. They are sorted into two general categories: excitatory and inhibitory substances. *Excitatory transmitters* tend to make adjacent cells fire. *Inhibitory transmitters* tend to prevent the firing of adjacent cells. Neurons continually monitor the total amount of the two types of transmitters at all their "receiving" synapses, those involved in picking up messages. When the excitatory transmitters at these synapses exceed the inhibitory ones there by a critical amount, the neuron fires.

Let's return to our knee-jerk example. As the knee is tapped, the sensory neuron fires, releasing an excitatory transmitter in sufficient quantity to excite the adjacent cell, a motor neuron, to the firing point. The nerve impulse travels down the axon of the motor neuron. Transmitter substance, again an excitatory one, is released into the synapse of the effector cell in the extensor muscle, causing it to contract and the leg to jerk. The leg relaxes almost immediately because of the further actions of several interconnected neurons, which we will not describe.

Neurotransmitters and Behavior

The neurotransmitters in our bodies are continually in flux. They are constantly being manufactured, secreted, broken down, and recaptured. Drugs, direct electrical stimulation of the brain, disease, and environmental events may raise or lower the amounts of these transmitter substances in specific brain pathways and produce dramatic effects on behavior. Figure 4-11 presents information about a group of neurotransmitters that regulate pain. Here is another illustration.

Dopamine, Parkinson's Disease, Amphetamine Abuse, and Schizophrenia

Parkinson's disease usually strikes susceptible people at about forty to sixty years of age and progressively cripples them. Muscles become rigid. A tremor develops. Initiating movement is exceedingly difficult. Responsiveness to sensory stimulation is reduced. Potent events—an emergency such as a fire, for instance—can elicit relatively normal behavior. Certain brain regions of Parkinson's disease victims show a deficiency in the neurotransmitter *dopamine*. It is currently believed that the illness results, at least in part, from degeneration of dopamine-secreting neurons whose fibers begin at the base of the brain and project to structures in the center of the brain. This cell loss reduces the amount of dopamine available to interact with certain dopamine-sensitive receptor neurons, causing them to function abnormally.

In 1967 the drug *L-dopa* (levodihydroxyphenylalanine), a substance which the body converts into dopamine naturally, was introduced to treat the disorder. The drug is administered orally, travels to the brain, and is transformed into dopamine. (Physicians cannot supply pa-tients with dopamine directly because it will not enter the brain from the blood.) The new supply of dopamine helps make up for the patient's deficiency. In some cases it can reverse the behavioral symptoms, particularly rigidity and slowness of movement. The clinical effects of L-dopa appear to be particularly dramatic when the patient's dopamine-secreting neurons are severely deteriorated. Studies on laboratory animals substantiate the importance of the dopamine-dominated pathways, described above, for normal motor behavior [11]. In Delgado's demonstration (Figure 4-6), the electrodes were located in brain areas which stimulated a dopamine circuit. In this case, you may recall, excess dopamine was associated with repetitive movements and arrested behavior.

Just as dopamine pathways may be stimulated electrically, they may also be stimulated chemically. The drug *amphetamine*, for example, activates certain dopamine brain pathways. Like laboratory animals exposed to the drug, amphetamine abusers generally perform stereotyped acts—in the case of the addict, perhaps, rearranging items on a desk or repeatedly taking apart and reassembling a pencil sharpener. Larger than normal amounts of dopamine appear to heighten sensitivity to perceptual experiences too. Recall that the Parkinson victim is less than normally responsive to such stimulation. Typically, after large doses of amphetamine, addicts hallucinate. They often see vivid, terrifying visions. One amphetamine user reported seeing faces everywhere. His own face "crawled with a dozen others making positive identification impossible [12]."

Currently, some scientists believe that the psychotic condition known as *schizophrenia* is partly caused by dopamine-related abnormalities. Patients diagnosed as schizophrenic frequently show symptoms like those of the amphetamine addict—stereotypic behavior patterns, heightened receptivity to sensory experiences, and hallucinations. Drugs that alleviate these symptoms are known to inhibit dopamine-using circuits. In Chapter 15, we discuss the dopamine hypothesis after looking at schizophrenia in some detail.

The Damaging of the Brain's Neurons

In describing Zasetsky's case early in this chapter, we mentioned that the neurons of the central nervous system do not grow back again, once they've been damaged. Yet, following brain injuries, people often appear to recover—at least to some degree. How can such improvements be explained? In many cases, the individual learns new ways to utilize remaining capacities through persistent hard work, effective instruction, or both. The brain also "repairs" itself to some extent. In the last ten years or so, scientists have discovered that healthy axons in the CNS can sprout new endings. After brain damage, then, the sites vacated by dead axons can be filled by the new growth of neighboring axons. While *sprouting*, as it is called, sounds like a potentially helpful phenomenon, it is not necessarily so. One axon is gaining disproportionate influence, and that could mean trouble. Some recent studies have found that sprouting may be associated with the symptoms of particular brain injuries, and not with recovery [13]. While sprouting may be harmful in some cases, it may prove to be beneficial in others.

Lost abilities may be regained in another way. Some functional deficiencies that are observed immediately after injuries to the brain may be caused by the transient effects of the trauma, such as pressure due to enclosed areas of bleeding and disruption of blood vessels. As the temporary damage is repaired, near-normal brain function may return to that region. Consequently, the individual appears to be recovering from the direct effects of the brain damage, when she or he is merely recuperating from its indirect consequences.

Scientists used to believe that brain damage was less disastrous to animal and human infants because the young brain is more flexible or *plastic*. Physiological psychologist Robert Isaacson has concluded that brain injuries in infancy are, in many instances, more debilitating than those later in life [14].

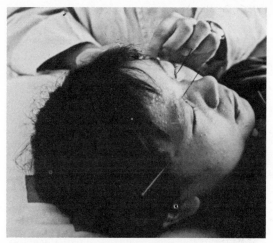

FIGURE 4-11 Pain during surgery and under other circumstances can sometimes be reduced by inserting needles into specific bodily areas, as shown in the figure. This practice, called *acupuncture,* is helping scientists understand the physical bases of pain and pain reduction. Recently discovered brain neurotransmitters called endorphins appear to play a critical role in alleviating pain. The term *endorphin* comes from the words "endogenous" (meaning originating from within) and "morphine." The endorphins and morphine appear to produce their powerful pain-alleviating effects in similar ways. Both activate brain pathways that suppress pain-transmitting neurons in the spinal cord. The endorphins function as part of the brain's natural analgesic system. Evidence linking the endorphins with pain control comes from studies of acupuncture, placebos, and electrical brain stimulation. Scientists believe that acupuncture and placebos both stimulate the production of endorphins because pain relief during both procedures can be partially blocked by the drug *naloxone.* (Naloxone blocks the actions of the endorphins and morphine.) Electrically stimulating certain brain pathways sometimes alleviates chronic severe pain. Recently, it was learned that these brain circuits contain high concentrations of endorphins. Investigators are exploring other experiences that trigger the natural pain-reduction system and individual differences in the ability to activate it [49]. [*Bruno Barbey/Magnum.*]

Because the brain is more plastic shortly after birth, brain damage can result in major structural changes at this time (and only at this time). A generalized reduction in brain size, for example, happens only when brains are damaged in the first few weeks of life. Such a reduction is always harmful. Similarly, following damage to the CNS in infancy, axons may form synapses at unusual sites. Whether such an occurrence is ever beneficial is not known. The brains of young animals do have one potentially useful capability. During infancy and in some cases throughout childhood, *related, healthy* brain tissue which is *not already committed to a specific function because of its immaturity* may serve the functions of a damaged region [15]. Mature tissue loses its capability for reorganization. Injury to the language centers of the brain provides a dramatic example. When such damage occurs in adulthood, it results in specific language-related disabilities, such as those described earlier. When a baby's language centers are damaged, nearby healthy, uncommitted tissue may serve language functions. In later years there may be no apparent language deficits. The individual may even develop superior verbal (language) abilities [16]. ▲

THE BRAIN, BEHAVIOR, AND COGNITION

The human brain, the master organ of the body, looks something like an enlarged 3-pound walnut sitting on top of the spinal cord. We will be talking as if there were a single standard human brain. There is not. Human brains vary quite a bit. We will be describing a typical one. As we have seen, the brain is a collection of neuron groupings. Identifying the "departments" and "chains of command" are among the goals of physiological psychology and other *neurosciences*, those which investigate the nervous system. Because many of the brain's structures are distinct in appearance, have names, and are known to be essential for specific responses, it is easy to fall into the trap of picturing the brain as a set of isolated parts, each with its own specific job, like the separate components of a stereo system. As we have seen, the neurons of the brain are intricately interrelated. Almost every behavior involves interactions between thousands of neuron circuits throughout the brain. The interdependence of the brain's circuits should be constantly kept in mind. As psychologist Richard Thompson has put it:

Abilities, complex behavioral processes, and consciousness do not live in particular pieces of neural tissue. They are the end result of the interrelated activities of the human brain, the most complex machine in the universe and seemingly the only machine that has ever attempted to understand itself. [17]

An Overall Perspective on the Brain

The general organization of the human brain is easier to understand if we examine its development briefly. First, looking at Figure 4-12, you can see that soon after a person is conceived, the brain looks very much like a bumpy tube. It can be divided into three main subdivisions: *forebrain, midbrain,* and *hind-*

▲ USING PSYCHOLOGY

1. Explain in your own words how messages can be transmitted between cells that do not touch.

2. Suppose that someone said to you, "The distribution of neurotransmitter substances within the nervous system remains constant." Correct the person's error. Give several illustrations to make your point more emphatically.

3. Argue both for and against the assertion that brain damage early in life is less injurious than comparable damage in adulthood.

4. Are intellectual deficits that show up immediately after a head injury likely to be permanent ones? Explain your reasoning.

brain. As the unborn infant grows, the *fore-brain* gradually expands until it is far larger than any other region. Now, inspect Figure 4-13, which compares the sizes of the three brain divisions for a number of animal species. Note that as an organism's capacity for processing information increases in quantity and quality, the forebrain enlarges. At the same time, the midbrain decreases in size and the hindbrain remains approximately the same size. This information gives us some clues about the gross functioning of these three regions. The *hindbrain* exerts major control over vital bodily activities such as digestion, circulation, respiration, certain reflex movements, body balance, and equilibrium. Such processes are essential to the functioning of both primitive and sophisticated animals. The *midbrain*, lying between the hindbrain and forebrain, receives some sensory information and controls certain muscles. In people, most of the sensory and motor functions, which were originally controlled by the midbrain (and still are, in lower animals), have been taken over by the *forebrain.* The forebrain serves several additional roles. Centers here seek satisfaction for the body's recurring needs, including those for food, water, sleep, temperature control, fluid balance, and protection for the individual and the species (reproduction). Regions in the forebrain also process the data received from the rest of the body, analyze and integrate that information with previous experiences, and make decisions, allowing people to talk, think, remember, and learn.

We turn now to brain centers that are interesting to psychologists because they play an especially important role in complex behavior and mental processes.

The Cerebral Cortex

Whenever you look at a picture of the human brain, you see mostly *cerebral cortex,* or *cortex.* The cortex (a word meaning "rind" or "bark") covers a vast region of the forebrain and midbrain. The term *cerebrum* is often used when referring to both the midbrain and

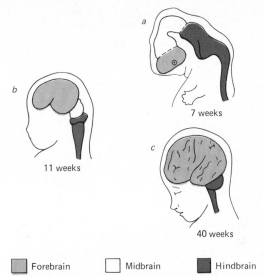

Forebrain   Midbrain   Hindbrain

FIGURE 4-12 The developing human brain grows from a tube of cells. The tube, which is eventually sealed at both ends, pushes out into three main swellings that form the three basic divisions of the brain: forebrain, midbrain, and hindbrain. The figure shows the developing human brain at three stages: (*a*) seven weeks, (*b*) eleven weeks, and (*c*) forty weeks after conception. In (*c*) the midbrain is obscured by the forebrain.

the forebrain. See Figure 4-16. It is the cortex more than any other structure that gives people their enormous information-processing capabilities. The more an organism is capable of intelligent behavior, the more cortex it appears to have. Amphibians (for example, frogs and turtles) and fish have no cortex at all. Birds and reptiles have tiny ones. Mammals (dogs and cats, for instance) have small ones. Primates (such as chimpanzees and human beings) have large ones. Occasionally, people who are born without a cortex or who damage major portions of the cortex may survive—if protected and sheltered. But they make only primitive responses. They do not show the signs of intelligence and consciousness that are considered distinctly human.

The human cortex, a massive structure which contains about three-quarters of the brain's neurons, is approximately one-tenth of an inch thick. It looks wrinkled and folded, as if someone had stuffed into the available space

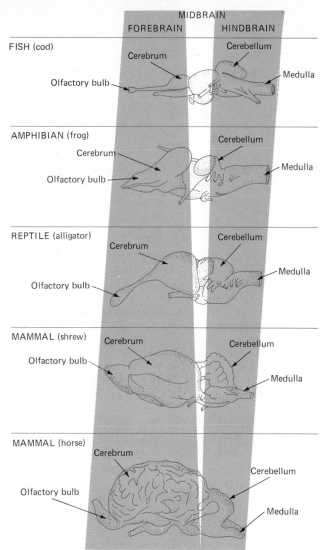

MIDBRAIN
FOREBRAIN HINDBRAIN

FISH (cod)

Cerebrum
Cerebellum
Olfactory bulb
Medulla

AMPHIBIAN (frog)

Cerebrum
Cerebellum
Olfactory bulb
Medulla

REPTILE (alligator)

Cerebrum
Cerebellum
Olfactory bulb
Medulla

MAMMAL (shrew)

Cerebrum
Cerebellum
Olfactory bulb
Medulla

MAMMAL (horse)

Cerebrum
Cerebellum
Olfactory bulb
Medulla

FIGURE 4-13 The evolving brain. From fish to reptile to mammal, the relative amounts of midbrain and forebrain differ very strikingly. [*Adapted from Keeton, 1972.*]

as much "cortical material" as possible. If the cortex were stretched out flat, its surface would cover about 6 square feet. Human cortexes have a similar arrangement of ridges and crevices. Looking down on the brain, as in Figure 4-14, you see a deep crack that divides the brain into the two nearly symmetrical halves called *hemispheres*. Physically, the hemispheres look like mirror images of one another. In general, the right hemisphere receives information from and controls the left

half of the body. The left hemisphere performs these same functions for the right half of the body. More about these arrangements later. Various surface landmarks divide the cortex covering each hemisphere into four subdivisions, called *lobes* (shown in Figure 4-14): frontal, parietal, temporal, occipital.

The lobes are generally organized along similar lines. In each one, vertical columns of neurons in a *primary zone* (or *primary projection area*) either receive and sort a particular

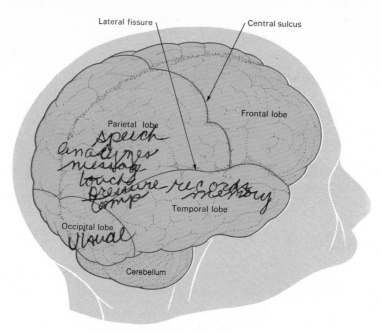

FIGURE 4-14 The cortical lobes of the right cerebral hemisphere.

type of sensory information or control movement. Near each primary sensory or motor zone, one finds *secondary* and, in some cases, *tertiary zones*, which play roles in coordinating and integrating sensory data or motor functions. The secondary and tertiary zones and everything else lying outside the primary zones are known as *association areas*. The association areas make up about 75 percent of the human cortex. People have a higher percentage of association area in their cortexes than any other animals do.

The association areas of the cortex used to be considered "silent." When scientists presented animals with particular types of experiences while recording electrical signals from these regions, neurons there did not respond by firing. In the early 1950s, researchers first began using nondepressing types of local anesthetics during surgery. When such anesthetics were used, the "voices" of these cells began to be heard. Richard Thompson and his colleagues found, for example, that when cats were exposed to shock, flashing lights, and clicks, 82 percent of the monitored neurons in the association areas responded to all three

events. Some cells were more likely to react simply to light, others to sound, and still others to shock. Thompson and his coworkers discovered "*number-coding*" neurons which responded only after a certain number of stimuli (for example, only after each sixth light flash was presented) and "novelty" cells which fired only when new events occurred [18].

How do the lobes of the cortex differ? Here are some of the major ways: The *occipital lobes*, at the rear, receive and process visual information. The *temporal lobes*, above the ears, include regions which record and synthesize auditory data. Recall that some of Penfield's patients reported memories with both visual and auditory components when the temporal and parietal lobes were stimulated. The *parietal lobes*, in the center, contain regions involved in the control of speech. In addition, they hold areas that register and analyze messages from the body's surface (exterior and interior) about touch, pressure, temperature, and muscle movement and position. If a map of the body were drawn on the brain so as to show the size of the cortical area

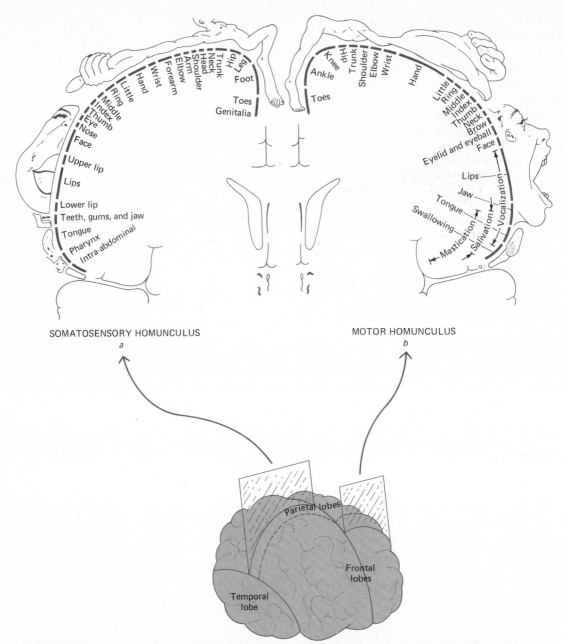

SOMATOSENSORY HOMUNCULUS
a

MOTOR HOMUNCULUS
b

FIGURE 4-15 Two parallel cross sections through the brain are shown. In the distorted caricatures, known as homunculi (singular: homunculus), the size of each body part represents the amount of cortex devoted to controlling the functions associated with that part. As you can see, lips and hands receive high priority from the cortex. It is interesting to note that more cortex is devoted to the motor functions of the hands than to their somatosensory functions. The opposite is true for the lips. [*Adapted from Penfield and Rasmussen, 1950.*]

devoted to the *body sense* (*somatosensory*) functions of each part, the distorted person shown in Figure 4-15a would be created. Looking at this caricature, you can see that the largest number of cortical neurons analyze sensations from our hands and lips, making these regions the most discriminating areas of our bodies. In general, the more cortex that is devoted to receiving the sensations of a particular group of receptors (including those in the skin, the retina of the eye, and the cochlea of the ear), the more sensitive the receptors are. Finally, there are the *frontal lobes*, in the forehead area. These lobes play a particularly important role in higher mental activities such as formulating plans, processing memories, and interpreting language. They are critically involved in sending motor impulses to muscles too. Organized like the body-sense regions, areas of the frontal lobes are assigned in proportion to a muscle's capability for fine, precise movements. Once again, hands and lips are disproportionately represented, as you can see by looking at Figure 4-15b.

The Thalamus

The *thalamus* is a large collection of cell bodies in the forebrain that looks like two small footballs. See Figure 4-16. All incoming sensory information eventually finds its way to this center. One of the main functions of the thalamus is to relay sensory information to the primary sensory zones in the cortex above it. The thalamus plays additional roles that neuroscientists are only beginning to understand. The axons of certain thalamic neurons spread throughout the association areas of the cortex and appear to be involved in arousing the rest of the brain so that it focuses on important events. The thalamus takes an active part in controlling sleep and wakefulness too.

The Limbic System

The *limbic system* is a collection of highly interconnected neuron groupings within the forebrain. It includes the *amygdala*, *hippocampus*, *septum*, and *cingulate gyrus*, and portions of the *hypothalamus* and *thalamus*.

FIGURE 4-16 Two views of the brain, (*a*) as seen through the midline from front to back and (*b*) with two side-to-side sections combined.

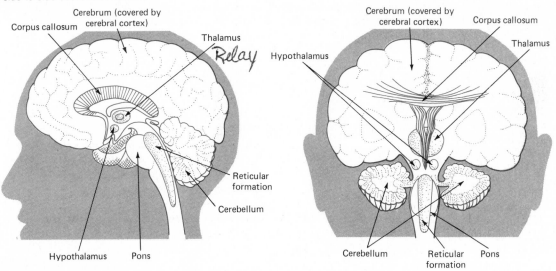

In people the limbic system structures ("limbic" comes from the Latin word meaning "border") lie roughly at the inner borders of the *cerebral hemispheres* (the two halves of the cerebrum), as you can see in Figure 4-17. The limbic centers were among the earliest forebrain regions to evolve. The crocodile's forebrain is just about entirely limbic system—an elaborately complicated one, as ours is. But, unlike ours, the limbic systems of crocodiles and other simple reptiles are primarily engaged in analyzing odors (their intensity, direction, and type), enabling these creatures to mate, approach, attack, or flee at the opportune moment. The human limbic system, in contrast, plays only a very minor role in olfaction (smell). Instead, in combination with the cerebral cortex, circuits in the human limbic system are critically involved in the expression of motivation and emotion. They are known to play essential roles in hunger, thirst, sleep, waking, body temperature, sex, aggression, fear, and docility.

The *hypothalamus*, while no bigger than a peanut in people, appears to be the most central limbic system area. Though small in size, the hypothalamus controls so many vital functions that it is sometimes called the "guardian of the body." The hypothalamus plays a dominant role in regulating the internal environment. Suppose that nourishment, fluid level, or body temperature drops too low. Neuroscientists believe that the hypothalamus senses these changes and works on two levels. At the behavioral level, it causes us to feel hungry, thirsty, or cold and prods us to take action to fill the body's needs. At the physiological level, the hypothalamus activates both the *autonomic nervous system* and the *endocrine system*. The *endocrine system* is composed of ductless glands which secrete chemical substances, called *hormones*, directly into the bloodstream. Once in the blood, these chemical messengers are carried to distant parts of the body to influence responsive target cells. Hormones play important roles in regulating metabolism, growth, sexuality, emotionality, vitality, and motivation. See Figure 4-18. The *pituitary*, the master gland of the endocrine system, lies immediately below the hypothalamus (at the base of the brain) and is physically connected to it by a thin stalk of tissue. The hypothalamus commands the pituitary by chemical signals. When stimulated by the hypothalamus, this gland can release hormones that initiate bodily processes, such as growth. The pituitary may also activate delinquent glands whose hormone production has dropped below normal levels. This latter role gives the hypothalamus its immense influence over the entire endocrine system.

If there is an emergency of any type, one of the hypothalamus's major responsibilities is making sure animals have the energy to confront it. At the physiological level, the hypothalamus switches on the *sympathetic division* of the autonomic nervous system and the *endocrine system*, so that internal energy resources may be redistributed. At the behavioral level, animals frequently respond to challenge by fleeing or fighting. Studies by John Flynn and his colleagues at Yale University suggest that circuits in the hypothalamus play an important role in several different

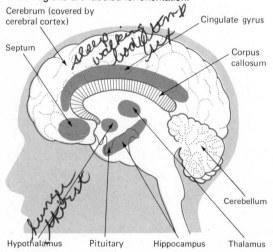

FIGURE 4-17 The approximate locations of the major areas of the limbic system (shown in color). The limbic structures are actually found within the hemispheres and not on the midline. The pituitary and other important brain regions are labeled for orientation.

Cerebrum (covered by cerebral cortex)

Septum

Cingulate gyrus

Corpus callosum

Cerebellum

Hypothalamus   Pituitary   Hippocampus   Thalamus

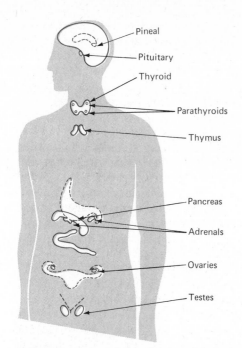

Endocrine gland	Some main functions
Pineal	Processes information about light and dark; imposes a roughly 24-hour rhythm on many bodily processes.
Pituitary	Promotes general bodily growth; raises blood pressure during emergencies; stimulates smooth muscles (for example, during childbirth it excites the uterus to contract; it also activates the mammary glands to produce milk).
Thyroid	Regulates metabolism.
Parathyroids	Control calcium and phosphate levels in the blood.
Thymus	Uncertain.
Pancreas	Regulates the level of blood sugar.
Adrenals	Active in carbohydrate metabolism; promote and maintain secondary sex characteristics and physical conditions necessary for pregnancy; raise blood pressure and blood sugar levels during emergencies.
Gonads	Ovaries (female): Promote and maintain secondary sex characteristics and physical conditions necessary for pregnancy. Testes (male): Promote and maintain secondary sex characteristics.

FIGURE 4-18 The locations of the endocrine glands and the main effects of some of the major hormones secreted. Note that some glands, such as the testes and ovaries, occur in pairs.

types of aggression. Electrically stimulating certain of the cat's hypothalamic pathways results in deadly hunting behavior. Even animals that ordinarily do not kill mice or rats will stalk and quietly bite to death appropriate targets in an unemotional, but highly effective, way. Hunger does not seem to be involved: the animals do not eat their prey [19]. When the electrode is shifted slightly, a different type of aggression occurs. Cats lash out viciously—hissing, growling, snarling, hair on end, backs arched, claws unsheathed—and attack almost anything in range, including the experimenter. A still different type of aggressive reaction called *sham rage* may be elicited by stimulating a region close to the hypothalamus. This time cats look angry, hiss, and extend their claws. But they do not attack, and they may even lap milk, purr, or allow observers to pet them [20].

The hypothalamus also serves the body's needs by conserving energy resources when they are not required. It does this by commanding the *endocrine system* (through the pituitary gland) and by activating the *parasympathetic division* of the autonomic nervous system, which maintains optimal internal conditions for rest during periods of calm.

The hypothalamus is absolutely essential for survival. Without it, animals cannot regulate their essential bodily needs; and they soon die. The other limbic regions, including the septum, hippocampus, and amygdala, appear to influence our emotions and motives indirectly through their interactions with the hypothalamus.

Besides their part in emotion and motivation, the separate regions of the limbic system play some additional roles in behavior. The *hippocampus*, for example, is believed to serve important functions in memory and in organizing information about an animal's location in space, while the *amygdala* has been linked with social behavior.

The Cerebellum

In the hindbrain, behind the cerebral hemispheres which practically cover it, lies a highly convoluted structure about the size of a fist, called the *cerebellum*, shown in Figure 4-16. Similar to the cortex in appearance, this brain region also receives information from all over our bodies—from hundreds of thousands of sensory receptors in the eyes, ears, skin, tendons, muscles, and joints. Instead of entering our awareness and evoking sensations, as in the cortex, this information is used without our consciousness to regulate posture, balance, and movement. Recent research indicates that most of the visual information reaching the cerebellum passes through the *pons* (shown in Figure 4-16). Visual cells in the pons are sensitive mainly to the motion of an image, and not to its shape or orientation in space. Different cells in the pons sense particular types of action and pass the information along to the cerebellum. There the data are used to help coordinate rapid bodily movements [21].

The cerebellum also communicates with the cortex, especially the sensory and motor areas. Some neuroscientists believe that the cerebellum receives advance information from the cortex about motor commands not yet executed. Consequently, it can coordinate highly overlearned, extremely rapid movements, like writing or bowing a violin, that cannot be corrected through ordinary feedback mechanisms. When people sustain damage to the cerebellum, they are likely to develop problems in the force, speed, direction, and steadiness of rapid and intentional movements. It might be difficult, for example, to walk and to grasp a cup a foot away without overshooting it or knocking it down. Tremors during movements, which occur sometimes in old age, appear to be due to disorders of the cerebellum and its connecting regions.

The Reticular Formation

If one hair on the back of your hand moves only 5 degrees, a single nerve impulse may be triggered in a single fiber that terminates at the base of the hair. Yet you may be aware of the sensation. Eyes have the same type of keen sensitivity. On the other hand, we breathe and pump blood every minute of every day and rarely notice the activity unless something goes awry. Similarly, when drowsy, we can drive for several hours and register only a tiny fraction of the sounds and sights along the way. These examples suggest that the nervous system must be selecting and channeling sensory information and controlling our attentiveness to it. The *reticular formation* plays a major role in activating and alerting the cortex. It is a massive network ("reticular" means "netlike" in Latin) of cell bodies and fibers running through the core of the hindbrain into the midbrain and forebrain (up to the thalamus). See Figure 4-16. The reticular formation may be pictured as looking something like a bicycle wheel hub with spokes running in all directions. Its descending tracts extend to the spinal cord and influence muscle tension so that coordinated movements can take place. Its ascending tracts travel up to the cortex (possibly through the thalamus). These circuits alert particular cortical areas so that they may be prepared to react to important sensory signals. There are two ways, then, that sensory information can be routed to the cortex—directly through the thalamus to specific cortical areas or indirectly through the reticular formation. In this latter case, the signals entering the reticular formation arouse the brain in advance. Consequently, the information is especially likely to make an impact.

The ascending tract of the reticular formation plays some role in sleep and wakefulness. When scientists electrically stimulate the ascending system of the cat's reticular formation, animals that have been anesthetized or operated on in such a way as to eliminate all sensory input become attentive immediately [22]. After similar stimulation, normally sleeping cats open their eyes, raise their heads, and look around [23]. When parts of the reticular formation are removed, cats lapse into a coma, a state of inattention which resembles normal sleep [24]. The animal is unlikely to recover if the damage is massive and occurs all at once. Limited damage leads to temporary coma and partial recovery, though deficits in attention remain [25]. Anesthetics such as ether and barbiturates are believed to block the ascending system of the reticular formation. ▲

THE HUMAN BRAIN: TWO BRAINS? OR ONE?

Important biological structures often come in pairs. We have two eyes, two arms, two kidneys, and two cerebral hemispheres. It would actually be more correct to say that the cerebrum has two halves. As we mentioned before, the two sides of the brain are nearly mirror images of one another structurally. Each tends to be associated predominantly with one side of the body. Control of movement from brain to muscles is almost completely crossed. The right side of the brain controls the left side of the body. The left side of the brain dominates the right side of the body. Visual, auditory, and skin sensation systems are crossed to some degree too. This arrangement does not apply to the association areas. They receive messages from both sides of the body. A massive network of axons (some 200 million of them) called the *corpus callosum* (shown in Figure 4-16) permits the two halves to share their resources. In addi-tion to being specialized for controlling the different sides of the body, the cerebral hemispheres may play distinctive roles in information processing and intellectual func-tioning. We explore this topic now in some detail.

People with Split Brains

Severe epilepsy may threaten people's lives or force them to live like vegetables. In some cases, drugs and routine surgical procedures do not help. In the past, as a last resort, surgeons occasionally cut the corpus callosum and several other connecting nerves. Sever-ing this bridge of tissue prevented the trans-fer of the seizure activity from one hemi-sphere to the other. Although the patient emerged from surgery with a split brain, the operation was generally successful in minimiz-ing (and even stopping) the attacks. Sur-prisingly, no symptoms attributable to the surgery were readily apparent. On the sur-face, patients behaved just as they had previ-ously.

In the early 1960s Roger Sperry, a physio-logical psychologist at the California Institute of Technology, and his associates—among them, Michael Gazzaniga and, later, Jerre Levy—began observing a small number of split-brain patients closely. They attempted to find out how the separation of the hemi-spheres affects mental capabilities. Eventual-ly, during the course of extensive research, these investigators discovered that split-brain patients often behaved as if they had two separate brains in their heads. Cats and

▲ **USING PSYCHOLOGY**

1. How are brains and component stereo systems different?

2. How do human brains differ from those of less complicated animals?

3. How do the limbic systems of people and crocodiles differ?

4. Why is the hypothalamus sometimes called the "guardian of the body"?

5. What types of behavioral deficits should result from damage to the cortex alone? Thalamus alone? Limbic system alone? Cerebellum alone? Reticular formation alone? Is any single area by itself likely to be injured? Why?

monkeys whose hemispheres were severed also functioned as if they had two complete brains, each isolated from the other and fully capable of learning and retaining memories [26]. How were these discoveries made?

Sperry and his colleagues frequently used the visual system to test the functioning of their patient's hemispheres. For that reason it is necessary to understand something about its operation. As you look straight ahead, what you see in front of you is called the *visual field*. Objects in the visual field are projected onto the *retina*, the light-sensitive

neural tissue at the back of the eyeball. The retina is connected to nerves that convey visual information to the brain. Imagine that the visual field is divided down the center into two equal parts. The lens of each eye projects the right half of the visual field (right visual field) onto the left side of *each* retina and the left visual field onto the right side of *each* retina. The nerves from the retina are arranged so that both eyes transfer almost all the information in the right visual field to the left cerebral hemisphere and almost all the information in the left visual field to the right cerebral hemisphere, as illustrated in Figure 4-19.

To understand split-brain research, it is also necessary to know that the right and left hemispheres of the human brain frequently differ with respect to language. Scientists have known for about a hundred years that centers which make reading, speaking, understanding language, writing, and other verbal activities possible are often localized on one side of the brain. That side is said to be *dominant* or *major*. The other hemisphere is labeled the *minor* one. People's brains vary a great deal in terms of how they are organized for language functions. In some people, one side (left or right) is dominant. In others, dominance is incomplete (that is, language may be represented in both hemispheres). For most right-handed males, language appears to be controlled by the left hemisphere. The majority of left-handed men show left-hemisphere dominance too, although right-hemisphere and incomplete dominance are much more common among left-handers. Regardless of hand preference, women appear to have less localized language centers than men [27].

Sperry and his colleagues used the experimental test apparatus shown in Figure 4-20 for many of their studies. Patients looked straight ahead at a screen. Then, a picture, written information, or a math problem was flashed in the left or right visual field for a fraction of a second. The time was kept short so that subjects had no chance to move their eyes. Sometimes patients were asked to re-

FIGURE 4-19 The split brain as seen from above. Information in the right visual field is channeled to the left cerebral hemisphere. Information in the left visual field is channeled to the right cerebral hemisphere.

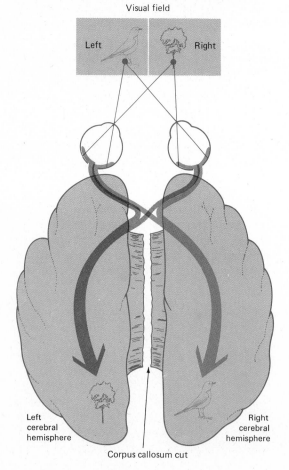

Visual field

Left

Right

Left cerebral hemisphere

Right cerebral hemisphere

Corpus callosum cut

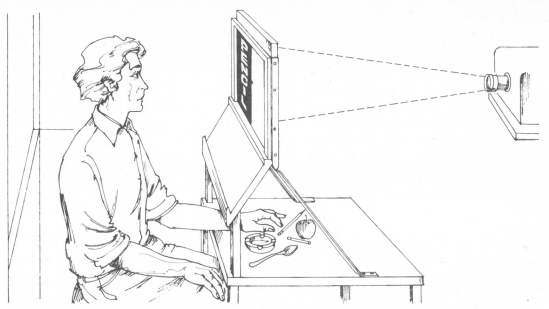

FIGURE 4-20 The experimental apparatus used to test the split-brain patient's responses to visual stimuli.

spond to the visual test items verbally, by naming or describing what had been seen. Sometimes they were asked to react by selecting a matching item by hand. (Hands were hidden from view behind a screen to restrict subjects to tactile information.) For another series of tests, objects were placed in one of the patient's hands, hidden from sight, so that information was channeled primarily to one side of the brain.

When visual or tactile information was directed to the left hemisphere, the dominant one for all the initial split-brain patients, people easily described what had been seen orally or in writing. They had little difficulty reading written messages, performing mathematical calculations, and solving other types of analytic problems—so long as they were presented to the left hemisphere. When similar problems were channeled to the minor hemisphere, split-brain patients behaved as though they were stupid even when doing the simplest tasks. Relying on the right hemisphere alone, people failed to solve any but the simplest mathematical problems. And they could not recall a series of items in order. Using the minor hemisphere by itself, people

could not even identify household objects, or so it seemed. Typically, they made no spoken or written response or ventured a haphazard guess. (A screw driver might be called a "cigarette lighter" or a "can opener.") When Sperry and his associates set up test situations which required less language ability, the right hemisphere proved to be competent at recognizing common objects. Though patients could not describe pictures—say, of a fork— they could retrieve a fork hidden from view, draw a fork, or gesture to show the function of a fork. Curiously, even after correctly identifying an object and while still holding it in their left hands, patients could not name it. These and other tests suggested that the major hemisphere was superior to the minor one for language, processing materials in sequence, analyzing details, and dealing with abstractions [28]. These abilities underlie writing, speaking, calculating, and solving logical problems.

What about the minor hemisphere (the right one for the split-brain patients)? Sperry and other investigators have set up test situations for the minor hemisphere that require minimal or no language ability. People may respond, for example, to pictorial problems by gesturing or drawing. The right hemisphere appears to be centrally involved in perception. Using the minor hemisphere by itself, people are good at visualizing spatial relationships. They are adept, for instance, at arranging blocks in specified designs and drawing pictures of three-dimensional objects. The major hemisphere has trouble with these tasks. See Figure 4-21. The minor hemisphere is more accurate than the major one at making many other types of perceptual judgments. It does well on problems that require recognizing faces and shapes that cannot easily be named and synthesizing details into wholes [29]. Sperry has characterized the consciousness of the minor hemisphere as "holistic and unitary rather than analytic and fragmentary [30]." Apparently, the minor hemisphere plays a vital role in skills that depend on the simultaneous perception of whole phenomena and the synthesis of material.

Several observations have led to speculations that the minor hemisphere plays a significant role in emotionality. Minor hemisphere damage is associated with inappropriate emotional reactions, such as unusual euphoria and depression [31]. And careful laboratory studies find that the minor hemisphere is superior to the major one both for processing emotional information and producing emotional facial expressions in normal subjects [32]. We will describe later how hemispheric research on normal subjects is done. Finally, the minor hemisphere is importantly involved, it appears, in hallucinations and dreams, musical abilities, and constructional skills [33].

The minor hemisphere is not completely without language capabilities. Relying on the right hemisphere, split-brain patients can

FIGURE 4-21 A split-brain patient responds to two requests: to write "Sunday" and to copy two figures. Keep in mind that the right hand was controlled by the left hemisphere and the left hand by the right hemisphere. The right hemisphere had difficulty, as you can see, with language, but showed a clear overall appreciation of the cross and cube. Note that the language-oriented left hemisphere focused on the details of the models' parts. [*Adapted from Bogen, 1969.*]

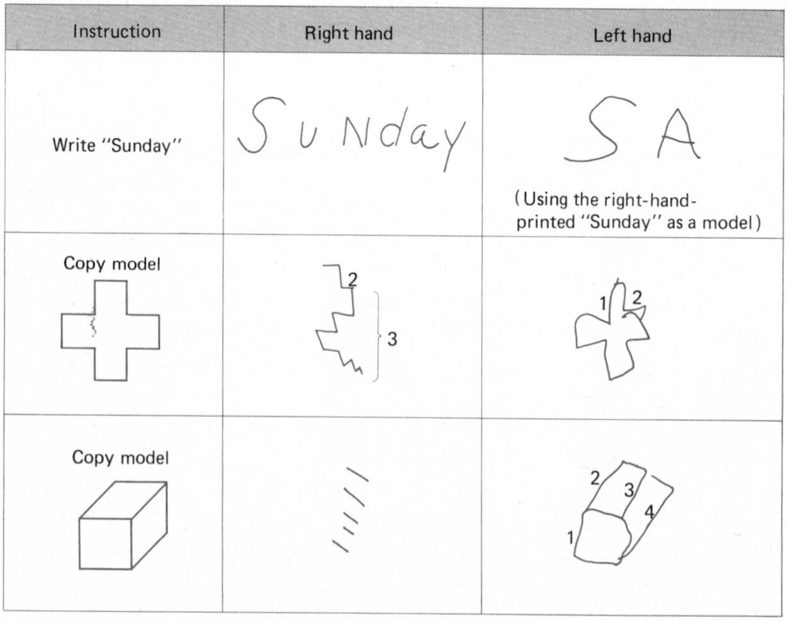

Instruction	Right hand	Left hand
Write "Sunday"	Sunday	S A (Using the right-hand-printed "Sunday" as a model)
Copy model		
Copy model		

recognize simple messages and write simple responses. The minor hemisphere's limit on language varies quite a bit from patient to patient. So far as is known, people cannot speak using the minor hemisphere alone [34]. It should be noted that findings about the minor hemisphere are less than certain because of the extreme difficulty of devising test situations that are entirely free of language.

Do the cerebral hemispheres in split-brain patients take turns processing information? Or do they operate at the same time? Many studies suggests that they operate simultaneously. In one such study, Jerre Levy and her coworkers showed patients composite faces like those in Figure 4-22. One half-face was projected to the left hemisphere, while the other half-face was projected to the right hemisphere. Since each side of the brain was deprived of the conscious experience of the other, patients were totally unaware that they had been shown *two* distinctive half-faces. Evidently, each hemisphere filled in the missing half according to what it saw. When patients were asked to identify the face that had been viewed, their responses varied, depending on the test situation. When asked to *point*, patients overwhelmingly chose the half-face channeled to the right hemisphere. When invited to *say* which face had been seen, most people selected the one routed to the left hemisphere [35].

Informal observations by Michael Gazzaniga and Joseph Le Doux suggest that the parallel information-processing centers of split-brain patients may conflict. Recently these behavioral scientists described the case of P. S., a split-brain patient with considerable language ability on both sides of the brain. P. S. could respond simultaneously to two different problems—one presented to each hemisphere. Even more curiously, P. S. expressed different aspirations for the future, depending on which hemisphere was consulted. When questions about vocational preferences were directed to the major hemisphere, P. S. indicated that he wanted to be a draftsman. Responding in writing with the right hemisphere, P. S. mentioned automobile

FIGURE 4-22 The composite faces for the Levy experiment are shown on the right. The photographs from which the stimuli were made are on the left. [*Courtesy of Dr. Jerre Levy.*]

racing as the work he wanted to go into [36]. Another of Gazzaniga's patients "would sometimes find himself pulling his pants down with one hand and pulling them up with the other. Once, [the man] . . . grabbed his wife with his left hand and shook her violently, while [the right tried] . . . to come to his wife's aid in bringing the left belligerent hand under control [37]." Incidentally, most patients do not appear to be aware of having two separate modes of consciousness, though they may know about them from reading [38].

Hemispheric Function in Normal People

A great many psychologists are presently exploring the functions of the major and minor hemispheres. Some continue to study clinical samples, including patients with split or partially split brains or damage confined to one or the other hemisphere. Split-brain operations are rarely performed now, as less radical surgery appears to provide similar therapeutic benefits.

Currently, most behavioral scientists who study hemispheric function study normal human beings. Some use EEGs to record electrical signals from the intact brain as people work different types of tasks. The records show whether one or the other hemisphere is relatively more relaxed and presumably less involved with the problem [39]. Some psychologists observe eye movements as people solve different types of problems, to see if the gaze is directed to one side or the other. Since each hemisphere controls the capacity to orient toward the other side, the activation of one hemisphere may shift the direction of gaze to the opposite side—a spillover effect [40]. Other investigators test subjects to see if they respond more accurately when information is presented to a specific side of the body. If consistent differences between the sides are seen, psychologists then assume that the hemisphere associated with the superior side is specialized for processing the information involved [41]. The findings on normal samples of children and adults tend to support the observations on split-brain patients.

Implications of Hemispheric Research

What implications can be drawn from hemispheric research on people with split and intact brains? Overall, the literature suggests that normal human brains possess different information-processing systems that operate simultaneously and that these systems are often localized in one or the other hemisphere. One system appears to be specialized for perceiving and synthesizing experiences in three dimensions. Another seems to be tuned for processing sequential information, guiding language, analyzing detail, and conceptualizing. As people behave, these systems (and perhaps others) contribute disproportionately to the responses for which they are specialized. Both hemispheres probably work together most of the time, pooling skills and sharing information. Several observations support this idea.

1. People typically do more than a single thing at the same time. As you type a theme, for instance, you may think about some problem, jiggle your left leg, and read from the paper that you're copying. Both hemispheres have to be involved.
2. Complex activities usually require the specialities of both hemispheres. Reading imaginative stories, for example, probably demands analyzing,

synthesizing, forming imagery, and experiencing emotions—among other activities. EEG studies confirm the hypothesis that both hemispheres are active as people read fanciful material [42].
3. The functions of the hemispheres overlap. As we have seen previously, both the major and minor systems have language abilities; and both may be involved in emotion and in other activities. Many investigators believe that the systems play complementary roles in the same responses.

Hemispheric research provides information about human consciousness, though the message is difficult to decipher. Michael Gazzaniga suggests that the major hemisphere dominates the other subsystems of the brain, imposing its perspectives on conscious awareness [43]. Robert Ornstein, another psychologist active in hemispheric research, believes that each hemisphere of the intact brain is capable of dominating consciousness. Human beings under the control of the major hemisphere, according to Ornstein, behave rationally and analytically; and they use language to express themselves. When the minor hemisphere takes charge, presumably, individuals become intuitive, subjective, spontaneous, and oriented toward fantasy, art, emotion, mysticism, and similar preoccupations. Ornstein speculates that most people alternate between these modes of consciousness. But many individuals (and groups) seem to prefer a single mode. Ornstein has found evidence that lawyers tend to utilize the analytically inclined left hemisphere more extensively than the right in working diverse laboratory tasks. Artists who work with clay, on the other hand, tend to favor the spatially oriented right hemisphere under the same circumstances. Ornstein assumes that the two hemispheres pull people in different directions continually. As a group, Americans seem to neglect right hemisphere functions [44]. Although these ideas may be intuitively appealing, the evidence is not conclusive.

Human beings are thought to be the only animal with a markedly *asymmetrical*, or unbalanced, brain. What is the point of having two different, specialized hemispheres? Some scientists believe that brain asymmetry gives people part of their brain power. Instead of having two identical "computers," we have two distinctive ones. Consequently, each hemisphere may organize itself optimally for maximum efficiency on different types of problems. While this hypothesis sounds logical, it has serious problems. First, some ingenious split-brain research by Jerre Levy and her coworkers indicates that the most competent hemisphere, the one most likely to solve a given problem correctly, does not always take charge [45]. Second, human brains differ in their organization. In actuali-

ty, only about 20 to 25 percent of the population (right-handed males with no immediate left-handed relatives who sustained no birth injuries) are thought to have highly specialized hemispheres. If having a highly specialized brain is so beneficial, Levy argues, evolution would have bequeathed such brains to a higher percentage of people. As we describe influences on masculine and feminine behavior in Chapter 17, we will have more to say about brain organization and evolution. ▲

SUMMARY
The Brain, Behavior, and Cognition

1. The human nervous system consists of the central and peripheral nervous systems.

2. The central nervous system includes the brain and spinal cord.

3. The peripheral nervous system is made up of the somatic and autonomic nervous systems.

4. The somatic nervous system includes sensory nerves that relay messages from the senses to the central nervous system and motor nerves that relay messages from the central nervous system to the muscles.

5. The autonomic nervous system serves internal organs and glands. It includes the sympathetic division, which prepares people to react during emergencies, and the parasympathetic division, which maintains bodily resources at an optimal level when people are relaxed.

6. Psychologists use three general approaches to study the brain's relationship to behavior and cognition: (*a*) observing the behavior of laboratory animals with ablations or of people with specific brain injuries or surgical excisions, (*b*) recording the electrical activity of the brain, and (*c*) stimulating the brain by electrical current or chemicals.

7. The neuron is considered the basic functional unit of the nervous system.

8. A message passing from one neuron to another must cross a synapse.

9. Message transmission throughout the nervous system depends on the firing of the neuron, the conduction of nerve impulses along the axon, and the secretion of neurotransmitters into synapses.

10. Neurotransmitters exert dramatic effects on behavior. Dopamine-related abnormalities are associated with the symptoms of Parkinson's disease, amphetamine abuse, and schizophrenia.

11. Once damaged, the neurons of the central nervous system do not grow back. Some recovery after brain damage may occur. The young brain is more plastic than the adult brain.

12. The brain may be divided into three parts: forebrain, midbrain, and hindbrain.

13. The size and organization of the cerebral cortex distinguish people from other animals.

14. The cortex covering each hemisphere is divided into four lobes: occipital, parietal, temporal, and frontal. Each lobe contains a primary sensory or motor region and association areas that are involved in coordinating and integrating sensory data and motor functions.

15. The thalamus acts as a central relay station for the sensory systems, projecting their information to the appropriate areas of the cortex. The thalamus also plays a role in alertness, sleep, and wakefulness.

16. The circuits of the limbic system help control motives and emotions.

17. The hypothalamus keeps our bodies functioning optimally under ordinary resting conditions and ensures the appropriate redistribution of bodily resources when we confront emergencies. Through its influence on the pituitary, the hypothalamus controls the endocrine system.

18. The cerebellum is concerned with regulating motor coordination, posture, and balance.

19. The ascending tracts of the reticular formation play a major role in activating the cortex; they also function in sleep and wakefulness. The descending tracts influence muscle tension, making coordinated movement possible.

20. The two human cerebral hemispheres function somewhat like specialized, complementary information-processing systems. The major hemisphere tends to take charge of language usage, perception of details, acquisition of sequential information, analysis, and conceptualization. The minor hemisphere plays a particularly important role in processing and synthesizing information about the environment. Under ordinary circumstances, the corpus callosum allows the two sides of the brain to share their abilities and pool their information.

A Study Guide for Chapter Four

Key terms physiological psychology (psychobiology, biopsychology) (93), receptor (93), central nervous system (CNS) (94), brain (94), spinal cord (94), reflex (94), effector (94), nerve (nerve tract) (94), peripheral nervous system (94), somatic nervous system (94), autonomic nervous system (94) [sympathetic (94) and parasympathetic (95) divisions], brain-behavior research procedures [ablation (95), recording technique (97), stimulation strategy (98)], neuron (101), glia (glial cell) (101), neurotransmitter (102), synapse (102), nerve (neural) impulse (105), all-or-none law (105), hindbrain (109), midbrain (109), forebrain (109), cerebral cortex (cortex) (109), cerebrum (109), sensory or motor zone (projection area) (110), association area (111), thalamus (113), limbic system (113), cerebral hemispheres (114), hypothalamus (114), pituitary gland (114), endocrine system (114), hormone (114), cerebellum (116), pons (116), reticular formation (116), corpus callosum (117), major (dominant) hemisphere (118), minor hemisphere (118), brain asymmetry (122), and other italicized words and expressions.

Important research ablation of the "temporal lobes" in monkeys (Klüver, Bucy), observations of aphasia victims (Gardner), electrical stimulation of the brain (Penfield, Valenstein, others), message transmission throughout the nervous system, dopamine-related problems (Parkinson's disease, amphetamine abuse, and possibly schizophrenia), brain damage (Isaacson, others), organization of the cortical lobes, functions of brain circuits in varied regions (cortex, thalamus, limbic system, cerebellum, pons, reticular formation) (Thompson, Flynn, others), functioning of the cerebral hemispheres (Sperry, Gazzaniga, Levy, Le Doux, Ornstein, others).

Basic concepts resemblance between robot and human "nervous systems," differences between the brain and a switchboard, rationale behind and problems posed by brain-behavior study methods (ablation, human brain injury or surgical excision, brain stimulation, brain recording), the threat posed by brain control (Valenstein), differences between the brain and a stereo system, strategies for studying hemispheric function in intact brains, implications of hemispheric research (Gazzaniga, Ornstein, Levy, others).

People to identify Luria, Penfield, Sperry.

Self-Quiz

1. What is a major function of the peripheral nervous system?
   a. Coordinating complex mental processes such as thinking
   b. Governing reflexes
   c. Relaying information to and from the central nervous system
   d. Seeking satisfaction for the body's recurring needs
2. What does the ablation approach consist of?
   a. Chemical stimulation
   b. Electrical stimulation
   c. Recording electrical signals
   d. Removing parts of the brain

3. What does pure alexia without agraphia illustrate?
   a. Brain injuries are likely to produce widespread damage.
   b. Commonsense ideas about how mental abilities are related may be inaccurate.
   c. Language is localized in the minor hemisphere.
   d. Language is localized throughout the brain.

4. When does spontaneous electrical activity occur throughout the human brain?
   a. When an outside event stimulates people's senses
   b. When people are awake
   c. When people dream
   d. Continually, as long as people are alive

5. What function does the dendrite usually serve?
   a. Picking up information
   b. Regulating the passage of electrically charged particles into and out of the cell
   c. Sending information to other cells
   d. Storing neurotransmitters

6. Which two processes are generally required for sending messages throughout the nervous system?
   a. Charge redistribution and release of neurotransmitters
   b. Contraction and excitation of dendrites
   c. Permeability changes and protoplasm redistribution
   d. Release of DNA and inhibitory neurotransmitters

7. In which of the following activities is dopamine likely to be involved?
   a. Initiation of movement
   b. Organization of language
   c. Reduction of pain
   d. Sharpening of memory

8. Which of the following developments occurs after brain damage in infancy and is clearly beneficial?
   a. Formation of unusual neuron connections
   b. Regrowth of damaged axons
   c. Reorganization
   d. Sprouting

9. What do centers in the hindbrain control?
   a. Emotions and motives
   b. Memory
   c. Routine, continually occurring activities
   d. Simple associative processes involving previous learning

10. Which regions comprise 75 percent of the cerebral cortex?
    a. Association   b. Language
    c. Motor   d. Sensory

11. What is the chief function of the human limbic system?
    a. Control of alertness and attention
    b. Control of motives and emotions
    c. Integration of sensory data
    d. Olfaction (smell)

12. Which brain region is considered the guardian of the body?
    a. Amygdala   b. Hippocampus
    c. Hypothalamus   d. Septum

13. Damage to which brain region is associated with shaky movements and problems of motor coordination?
    a. Cerebellum   b. Hypothalamus
    c. Septum   d. Thalamus

14. Suppose that you are testing a right-handed man who has just recovered from split-brain surgery. You flash a picture of a pencil to his left visual field and ask him to identify it. Which of the following responses is most probable?
    a. Abiding confusion and dismay
    b. Describing the pencil (out loud) without naming it
    c. Gesturing to show the pencil's function
    d. Naming the pencil (out loud)

15. In which activity does the minor cerebral hemisphere play an important role?
    a. Complex numerical computations
    b. Language
    c. Logic
    d. Perception of depth

Exercise

THE NERVOUS SYSTEM. The following matching exercises are designed to help you test your knowledge of the nervous system. Match the structure on the left with the appropriate major function, location, description, or illustration on the right. Be sure to read the additional instructions that accompany each part of this exercise.

Part I: Choose the *single most comprehensive* function of each system. To review the material, see pages 93 to 95.

_____ 1. Nervous system

_____ 2. Central nervous system

_____ 3. Peripheral nervous system

_____ 4. Autonomic nervous system

_____ 5. Somatic nervous system

a. Serves the internal organs.
b. Relays sensory messages to the information-processing division and routes its orders to the skeletal muscles.
c. Directs and coordinates the action of *all* cells.
d. Composed of all the nervous system structures lying outside the central nervous system.
e. The information-processing division of the nervous system.
f. Handles emergencies.

Part II: In this exercise, one or more functions or characteristics should be matched with a particular structure. The same attributes may be used for several structures. To review the material, see pages 108 to 117.

_____ *1.* Spinal cord

_____ *2.* Cerebral cortex

_____ *3.* Amygdala

_____ *4.* Septum

_____ *5.* Hippocampus

_____ *6.* Hypothalamus

_____ *7.* Ascending reticular formation

_____ *8.* Descending reticular formation

_____ *9.* Thalamus

_____ *10.* Cerebellum

_____ *11.* Corpus callosum

a. Sensory relay station that looks like two small footballs.

b. Connects the cerebral hemispheres, permitting them to share information and resources.

c. Coordinates certain reflexes as a major role.

d. Network of cells extending from hindbrain to forebrain which influences muscle tension.

e. Most central limbic region.

f. Limbic region that influences hypothalamus.

g. Contains association areas.

h. Fistlike hindbrain structure concerned with regulating motor coordination and body balance.

i. Master decision-making organ.

j. Commands pituitary and autonomic nervous system.

k. Activates cortex.

l. Plays a role in sleep.

Part III: Match the neuron part with its single most appropriate characteristic. To review the material, see pages 101 to 106.

_____ *1.* Axon

_____ *2.* Cell membrane

_____ *3.* Soma

_____ *4.* Neurotransmitter

_____ *5.* DNA

_____ *6.* Protoplasm

_____ *7.* Nucleus

_____ *8.* Dendrite

_____ *9.* Synapse

_____ *10.* Synaptic vesicle

_____ *11.* Nerve

a. Prominent, centrally located body containing DNA.

b. Chemical substance that enables adjacent cells to communicate.

c. A fiber that usually carries information to neighboring cells.

d. Carries genetic information.

e. Manufactures neurotransmitter.

f. Stores neurotransmitter substance.

g. Gap between adjacent neurons.

h. Regulates what passes in and out of cell.

i. Fiber that usually picks up information from other cells.

j. Colorless, semifluid substance.

k. Group of axons.

l. Cell body.

Part IV: Pair each lobe of the cortex with at least one function and one location. The same function may be served by more than one lobe. To review the material, see pages 109 to 113.

LOBES: frontal (F), occipital (O), parietal (P), temporal (T)

Functions:

_____ *1.* Sends motor impulses to muscles.

_____ *2.* Records and synthesizes auditory information.

_____ *3.* Produces memories when stimulated electrically.

_____ *4.* Registers and analyzes somatosensory messages.

_____ *5.* Contains association areas.

_____ *6.* Receives and processes visual information.

Locations:

_____ *7.* Located above the ears.

_____ *8.* Located in the back of the head.

_____ *9.* Located in the front of the head.

_____ *10.* Centrally located between the front and back of the head.

Suggested Readings

1. Schneider, A. M., & Tarshis, B. *An introduction to physiological psychology.* (2d ed.) New York: Random House, 1979. This text introduces physiological psychology to the beginner in an unusually clear way. Schneider and Tarshis provide full, plainly worded explanations and write with a minimal amount of jargon.

2. There are a number of excellent paperbacks about the brain and its roles in behavior. The following are enthusiastic, entertaining, generally accurate, and often provocative. Blakemore's book is beautifully illustrated, in addition. Blakemore, C. *Mechanics of the mind.* Cambridge, England: Cambridge University Press, 1977; Restak, R. M. *The brain: The last frontier.* New York: Doubleday, 1979; Rose, S. *The conscious brain.* (Updated version.) New York: Vintage, 1976; Sagan, C. *The dragons of Eden: Speculations on the evolution of human intelligence.* New York: Random House, 1977.

3. Valenstein, E. S. *Brain control: A critical examination of brain stimulation and psychosurgery.* New York: Wiley, 1973. Valenstein describes and evaluates both brain stimulation and psychosurgery by examining scientific evidence and case histories. If the topic interests you, you'll find this book both accurate and fascinating.

4. Gardner, H. *The shattered mind: The person after brain damage.* New York: Knopf, 1976. Gardner describes the cases of many brain injury victims in detail and includes a number of vivid first-person accounts. The author's aim is "to draw out the implicit lessons concerning our own thought processes, personality characteristics, and sense of self."

5. Snyder, S. H. *Madness and the brain.* New York: McGraw-Hill, 1974. Snyder writes in a lively way about "drugs and the brain and the light they shed on the nature of madness," particularly on the disorder called schizophrenia.

6. Sperry, R. W. Left-brain, right-brain. *Saturday Review,* 1975, **2**(23), 30–33. Sperry describes his research on split-brain patients, providing both historical perspective and more recent observations.

7. Written for the general public—clearly and simply—these articles provide basic information about strategies that are currently used for studying hemispheric functioning in people with intact brains. Kimura, D. The asymmetry of the human brain. *Scientific American,* 1973, **228,** 70–78; Ornstein, R. The split and whole brain. *Human Nature,* 1978, **1**(5), 76–83.

8. Goleman, D. Special abilities of the sexes: Do they begin in the brain? *Psychology Today,* 1978, **12**(6), 48ff. Goleman reviews some controversial research which

suggests that the brains of women and men differ fairly consistently in numerous ways.

9. Cherry, L. Solving the mysteries of pain. *The New York Times Magazine,* Jan. 30, 1977, 12, 13, 50–53. Cherry provides an interesting nontechnical introduction to the topic of pain and its alleviation. He includes material on the discovery of the endorphins and on psychological aspects of pain.

Answer Keys

Self-Quiz

1. *c* (94)   **2.** *d* (95)   **3.** *b* (96)   **4.** *d* (97)
5. *a* (102)   **6.** *a* (104)   **7.** *a* (106)   **8.** *c* (107)
9. *c* (109)   **10.** *a* (111)   **11.** *b* (114)   **12.** *c* (114)
13. *a* (116)   **14.** *c* (119)   **15.** *d* (120)

Exercise

Part I   **1.** *c*   **2.** *e*   **3.** *d*   **4.** *a*   **5.** *b*
Part II   **1.** *c*   **2.** *i, g*   **3.** *f*   **4.** *f*   **5.** *f.*   **6.** *e, j, l*
7. *k, l*   **8.** *d*   **9.** *a, k, l*   **10.** *h*   **11.** *b*
Part III   **1.** *c*   **2.** *h*   **3.** *l*   **4.** *b*   **5.** *d*   **6.** *j*   **7.** *a*
8. *i*   **9.** *g*   **10.** *f*   **11.** *k*
Part IV   **1.** F   **2.** T   **3.** P, T   **4.** P   **5.** F, O, P, T
6. O   **7.** T   **8.** O   **9.** F   **10.** P

CHAPTER FIVE
Fundamental Learning Processes

A tick in a bush may wait weeks for an appropriate host to come by, though the tick is hardly snobbish. It will feast on anybody who meets two modest requirements. The victim must (1) smell of butyric acid, a component of fat, and (2) radiate warmth (98.6°F is warm enough). If the passerby is suitable, the tick drops from its perch, finds an appropriate spot, and begins its meal of blood. If you place a tick on a rock where an overweight person has recently been sitting, the creature will attempt to draw blood from the stone. It will probably persist until it has broken its probos-

cis (protruding mouth adapted for sucking) [1]. The tick does not alter this reflex-like behavior, which is essentially built in by its genes, so long as the environment falls within normal limits. In contrast with the tick's conduct, the behavior of more complex animals—especially people—is continually being molded by their surroundings. In this chapter we discuss three procedures that shape the responses of human beings and many other animals: respondent conditioning, operant conditioning, and observation learning. These simple fundamental learning processes usually occur without a deliberate attempt to change. In most cases, people do not even realize that modifications are taking place. Memorizing, problem solving, and other types of cognitive learning will be examined in Chapters 8 and 9. We begin with a fictionalized account of a "dinner hour."

Some Fundamental Learning at the Dinner Table

Betty Teller smiled at four-year-old Sammy, then glanced nervously at the rest of her family—her husband Bill, eight-year-old Fran, and ten-year-old Mickey. Dinners had been turbulent affairs of late; and no one else was smiling. Bill heaped the plates high with peas and boiled potatoes and deposited a thin pork chop beside the vegetable mounds. In the center of the table there was bread and butter and a pound cake wrapped in plastic. The evening news droned monotonously from a portable TV on the kitchen counter, as the Tellers began eating.

"The bowling league meets tonight, and I've got to be out of this house in twenty minutes," Bill announced suddenly. "Betty, if you want me to drop you off at your sister's as you asked, we don't have time to sit around waiting for Sammy and Mickey. We've got to be done in fifteen minutes. Does everyone hear? . . . The house sure is a mess—toys, books, coats, everywhere you look."

Betty glared at her husband, then muttered, "I just didn't have the time today to straighten up."

"You never have time," Bill snapped.

"That's not fair. Sometimes I do. . . . As a matter of fact, I spent a lot of time picking up your stuff. You left two towels, a washcloth, and a robe on the bathroom floor."

"And his cigarettes," Fran chimed in cheerfully.

"Who asked you? . . . I was in a hurry." (Bill's defense lacked enthusiasm.)

Betty continued to attack, "I picked up two pairs of pants and four shirts in the bedroom. I could understand two shirts. But four shirts? And the kitchen was a mess. Can't you at least put your plates in the sink and run water over them?"

Betty braced herself for what she knew was coming and it came.

"I work hard all day—ten, eleven hours a day, six days a week. And I want peace and quiet when I come home. And I want the house picked up. You're supposed to pick up after *me.* That's why I married you. That's what wives are for. What else do you have to do? . . . Mickey, damnit, why aren't you eating? Sammy isn't eating either. Eat! You have ten minutes."

"I can't cut the meat," Sammy whined.

"Cut it for him," Bill ordered his daughter.

Betty's voice quivered as she spoke: "Oh—I had nothing whatever to do today. After I finished cleaning up after you, I made two lunches, packed two kids off to school, did the dishes, cleaned the kitchen, made the beds, took care of Sammy, ran two loads of laundry, ironed, picked kids up, took Mickey to the dentist, took Fran to Brownies, picked Mickey up, picked Fran up, bought groceries, made dinner. . . . A big nothing!"

Bill wasn't listening. He bellowed at Sammy, "How are you ever going to play football if you don't eat meat and vegetables? I want to see you finish every bite on your plate. Every bite."

"It's too much," Sammy protested.

"You were eating lollipops all day today. You had gum before dinner too, didn't you?" Betty cross-examined him.

"Cut his meat smaller," Bill ordered his wife. "Fran didn't cut it small enough. She never does anything right. . . . Fran, go get your papers."

"I can't. I forgot them."

"That's the fourth time this week," Bill screamed. "I want to see those papers. Bring them home tomorrow—all of them—or you'll spend the whole weekend in your bedroom. And no TV."

Bill looked at his watch, saw it was late, and began eating rapidly. The conversation shifted to a new topic: the mound of peas on Mickey's plate.

"Mickey isn't eating his peas," Fran announced.

"I hate peas."

"Since when?" Bill challenged.

"They made me sick last week," Mickey explained.

"That's ridiculous."

"It's not ridiculous," Betty interrupted. "Remember you forced him to eat his peas last—Friday I think it was—when he had that virus and vomited."

"Peas are like vomit. Just looking at them makes me vomit."

"Eat every pea on that plate,"

Bill ordered. "You're not leaving this table till you've eaten every last pea. I don't care if you choke."

Mickey looked pleadingly at his mother, who offered no aid, though she looked as if she wanted to. "I have five minutes," he protested.

"Four minutes!" Bill roared.

Mickey folded his hands and glowered. After about a minute and a half he piled the peas slowly onto a teaspoon, lifted the spoon to his lips, tilted his head backward, shook the peas into his mouth a few at a time, and attempted to swallow them all at once. The boy gagged and gulped water. The performance was repeated a second time. "I'm going to vomit," Mickey yelled suddenly. He dashed to the bathroom. Bill followed.

Betty turned to Sammy. "Eat, little Sammy," she prodded gently. "It'll make me happy. That's a boy, eat for me."

Sammy attempted to butter a slice of bread. Betty took it from him. "I'll do it," she said. Next she cut up his potato. "Eat, dear, eat for me."

While no one is deliberately teaching, there is a great deal of learning going on in the Teller household during dinner (assuming that this dinner is typical). Simply from *observing others*, people learn many lessons. The Teller children are learning that dinner is an occasion for bringing up grievances and that problems are handled by ignoring them, yelling at and insulting others, and making charges and countercharges. People also learn from the *consequences* of their behavior. We tend to repeat actions that have pleasant results and avoid those that lead to unpleasant ones. Sammy is learning to act helpless because it brings attention. Fran has mastered the art of leaving her papers in school because it minimizes unpleasant comments about her competence. To avoid their father's wrath, all the children are learning to eat too quickly and probably too much. There is a third type of learning going on. Mickey did not always feel nauseated by the sight of peas. Recently, nausea has been "*transferred*" from an illness and from downing too much in a single gulp to peas, so that the vegetable itself now provokes a similar type of queasiness.

Before exploring these types of learning in more detail, we turn to several preliminary issues.

LEARNING: SEVERAL PRELIMINARY ISSUES

How do psychologists define learning? How is learning measured? Do behavioral scientists use the same terminology?

A Definition of Learning

Learning is often defined as a relatively lasting change in behavior that is brought about by experience. Behavioral scientists measure what organisms *do* to get a "handle" on learning. But learning is an activity that occurs inside an organism that cannot be directly observed. In ways not fully understood, learners are changed: They acquire new associations, information, insights, skills, habits, and the like. Subsequently, they may behave—under certain conditions—in measurably different ways. We will have more to say later about precisely what is acquired during conditioning.

Changes in behavior cannot always be attributed to experience, of course. Fatigue, drugs, motives, emotions, and maturation also alter what animals do. In contrast with the effects of learning, those of fatigue, drugs, motives, and emotions tend to be brief. After a night or two of rest, the consequences of a sleepless night usually wear off. The influence of a drug typically vanishes after some fairly well defined period of time. The intertwined effects of motives and emotions are short-lived too. The small child who is hungry may whine and howl until dinner is served. But, once the need is filled, the youngster is likely to settle down.

Now consider maturation (described in Chapter 3). The growth of the body and nervous system facilitates behavior change also. Responses which depend on maturation generally appear at predictable times in development and require *no specific training*.

As long as the environment falls within normal limits, the behavior emerges. At certain ages, for example, children all over the world begin walking and talking. Babies do not need to be taught either skill. They require only those experiences that are ordinarily inevitable, primarily opportunities to move around in the first case and to hear one's own and other voices in the second. So-called instinctive behavior has a similar origin. Though the term *instinctive behavior* is relatively rarely used today, behavioral scientists (especially *ethologists*, students of animal behavior in natural settings) do talk about a similar concept, *fixed action patterns*. Fixed action patterns include responses possessing the following characteristics:

1. Species-specific (observed among all normal same-sexed members of a species)
2. Highly stereotyped (similar whenever executed)
3. Completed, once initiated
4. Largely unlearned (at least independent of specific training)
5. Resistant to modification
6. Triggered frequently by a very specific environmental stimulus

The tick's simple, reflex-like predatory behavior fits into the fixed action pattern category. So do more complicated animal responses such as imprinting (Chapter 3), the song patterns of birds and insects, the nest building of rats, and the mating rituals of fish. Do people exhibit fixed action patterns? Irenäus Eibl-Eibesfeldt, an ethologist, speculates that certain human emotional expressions are, in fact, fixed action patterns. Smiling, laughing, and crying, for instance, are all observed in deaf-blind children who cannot have learned these responses by seeing or hearing them in others. Typically, the behavior is seen soon after birth. In many cultures, flirting and greeting rituals are identical, as shown by slow-action photography (see Figure 5-1). Likewise, in cultures all over the world, bowing and nodding signify submission. Clenching fists and stamping feet communicate anger (perhaps a ritualized attack) almost everywhere [2]. The basic patterns of these emotional responses and other maturation-related behavior patterns are probably programmed by our species-specific genetic inheritance. But the precise form of these acts is certainly shaped by family and culture. These responses are under conscious control and can be modified.

Generally, the more complex the creature, the more impressively learning (experience) contributes to its shaping. Similarly, the more complicated the response, the more learning is apt to have influenced its form. Still, even primitive animals learn to some degree; and learning influences even the simplest responses.

Measuring Learning

The impact of experience on behavior is such an enormously important topic that almost all psychologists are involved in one way or another in trying to understand it. Researchers measure learning by observing changes in behavior (*performance*). Although observing what organisms do is the most practical "yardstick" of learning that is currently available, it is not a completely satisfactory one for several reasons. First, much learning takes place without observable responses. In other words, much learning is *latent* (existing in a concealed, nonvisible form) and becomes evident only when used. During reading, for instance, you pick up information that may or may not affect your conduct at a future time. As you listen to a weather report, you may not say or do a thing that demonstrates the acquisition of the information. But, if rain has been predicted, you're quite likely to dig up your umbrella before venturing outside. Performance is a problematic measure of learning for a second reason. Whenever behavioral scientists design situations to reveal learning—to "force" animals to demonstrate what they have acquired—the performance of the subject may not reflect its learning precisely. For example, many people "freeze" on exams and do badly even though they can reproduce large amounts of material before and after the test. Performance depends, then, on many factors besides learning, including anxiety, fatigue, and motivation. So,

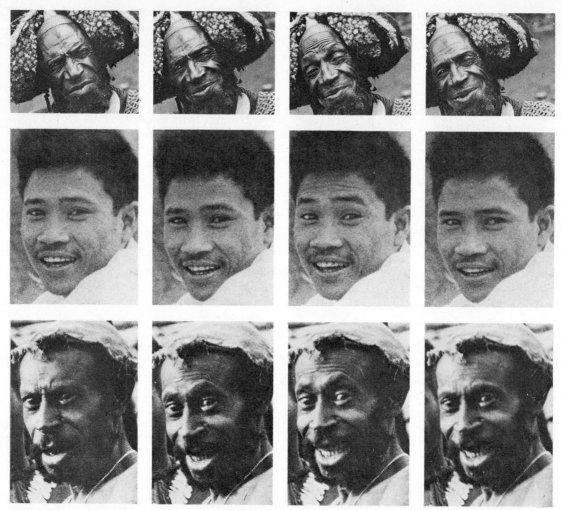

FIGURE 5-1 These film clips show greeting behavior in members of three different cultures. They were taken by ethologist Irenäus Eibl-Eibesfeldt without the subjects' awareness. The similarity, even on tiny details, is striking. In each instance, the greeting person initially smiled and then lifted an eyebrow in a characteristic gesture. These observations and many others suggest that the behavioral patterns associated with certain emotional states are somewhat similar to fixed action patterns [62]. [*From I. Eibesfeldt,* Ethology: The biology of behavior. *Trans. E. Klinghammer. Copyright by Holt, Rinehart and Winston. Used with permission.*]

using performance as a measure of learning is not ideal.

The Vocabulary of Learning

There is another preliminary issue that must be mentioned. Though psychologists generally agree on basic learning principles, terms and definitions in common use do vary somewhat. Your instructor may prefer to use slightly different terminology. If that is the case, be careful to note the corresponding terms that are given when each concept is introduced here.

We turn now to three very basic learning processes, focusing on respondent conditioning first. ▲

▲ USING PSYCHOLOGY

1. Why should ticks persist in sucking blood from stones even though it leads to self-destruction?
2. Is learning always conscious? Always deliberate?
3. When people say that learning has occurred, what have they really observed and what inferences are they making?
4. Why don't human greeting "rituals" (as shown and described in Figure 5-1) fit the category "fixed action pattern"? Can you think of any human responses that fit this category better than the emotional signs mentioned in the text?
5. Think of several measures of learning that teachers might use in place of test performance.

RESPONDENT CONDITIONING

All animals are prewired by their genetic inheritance with automatic responses, which we call *respondents*. What is a respondent? What does it mean to condition a respondent?

Respondents

Respondents are acts that are triggered by events immediately preceding them. The triggering event is known as an *eliciting stimulus*. When something becomes caught in your throat, you gag. The sudden loud report of a rifle produces a startle response. A bright light makes the pupil of the eye constrict.

Respondents include skeletal reflexes (such as startling and withdrawing a hand from a hot stove), *immediate* emotional reactions (such as anger, fear, and joy), and other responses (nausea and salivation, for example) controlled by the autonomic nervous system. Several important characteristics of respondents should be carefully noted.

1. Respondents appear to be involuntary. Most people cannot startle, gag, salivate, or feel nauseated or frightened at will.
2. Respondents seem to be controlled by the events preceding them—the eliciting stimuli that we mentioned before. A forkful of steak in one's mouth, for instance, causes copious salivation.
3. Respondents are not initially learned. All normal animals of a species that have reached a particular developmental stage exhibit the same respondents

automatically when confronted by the appropriate eliciting stimuli. Many respondents appear to be programmed into the body for protection and survival.

Though genes contribute both to respondents and fixed action patterns, the two categories of response are fundamentally different. The respondent is simple and appears involuntary, while the fixed action pattern is relatively complex and clearly under an animal's control.

The Conditioning of Respondents

A respondent can be "transferred" from one situation to another by a procedure called *respondent conditioning*, or *classical conditioning*. Startling, a response frequently made to thunder, is easily "transferred" to the sight that usually precedes thunder, lightning. Feeling nauseated, another respondent, is easily "transferred" from a bout of food poisoning or an illness (in Mickey's case) to the substance that accompanied that experience. When we say "transferred," we mean that a new stimulus acquires the ability to evoke the respondent. The old eliciting stimulus remains effective.

How do such "transfers" take place? Four elements are involved in respondent conditioning.

1. The first element, the *unconditioned stimulus* (US), is an eliciting stimulus that produces a respondent automatically. Let's take a common example. Food in the mouth is an unconditioned stimulus for salivation in people and other animals.

2. The *unconditioned response* (UR) is the respondent that is automatically produced by the unconditioned stimulus—in this case, salivation.

3. A *neutral stimulus* (NS) is defined as an event, object, or experience that does not elicit the unconditioned response at the beginning. The neutral stimulus must be paired with the unconditioned stimulus. Assume that the sound of a bell occurs every day at noon, seconds before one is to eat lunch. The noise of the bell is a neutral stimulus because it does not initially evoke salivation.

4. After the neutral stimulus has been associated with the unconditioned stimulus (occasionally once, usually many times), it may come to evoke a reaction similar to the unconditioned response, called the *conditioned response* (CR). The conditioned response is usually milder and less complete than the unconditioned response. Returning

to our example, if the bell closely precedes lunch every day, the gong itself will eventually stimulate mild salivation. Once the neutral stimulus has begun to elicit a conditioned response, it is called a *conditioned stimulus* (CS). See Figure 5-2.

Let's run quickly through a second example of respondent conditioning, Mickey's conditioned aversion to peas (beginning of this chapter). A specific stomach virus (the unconditioned stimulus) produces nausea (the unconditioned response). Peas, let's assume, begin as a neutral stimulus. After being associated with queasiness during the virus, the mere sight of peas may evoke a conditioned sick feeling. In this and in the previous example, conditioning increases the probability of a particular response. The term *conditioning* is used generally as a synonym for simple types of learning.

FIGURE 5-2 A general model of respondent conditioning using the conditioning of salivation as an illustration.

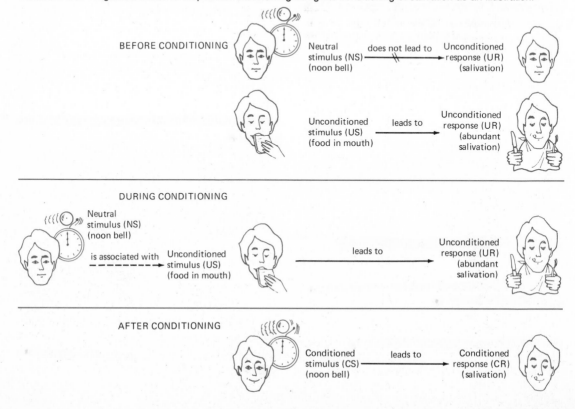

BEFORE CONDITIONING

Neutral stimulus (NS) (noon bell) —— does not lead to ——→ Unconditioned response (UR) (salivation)

Unconditioned stimulus (US) (food in mouth) —— leads to ——→ Unconditioned response (UR) (abundant salivation)

DURING CONDITIONING

Neutral stimulus (NS) (noon bell)

is associated with ------ Unconditioned stimulus (US) (food in mouth) —— leads to ——→ Unconditioned response (UR) (abundant salivation)

AFTER CONDITIONING

Conditioned stimulus (CS) (noon bell) —— leads to ——→ Conditioned response (CR) (salivation)

The History of Respondent Conditioning

Ivan Petrovich Pavlov (1849–1936), the distinguished Russian physiologist, is credited with the discovery of respondent conditioning. Consequently, respondent conditioning is frequently called *pavlovian conditioning*. Pavlov was already an established Nobel Prize winner when he began his conditioning research. In the course of studying the physiology of digestive secretions in dogs, he noted that the animals were salivating to stimuli other than food, such as the feeder's footsteps and the sight of the feeder. These inexplicable salivations, nuisances at first, increasingly occupied Pavlov's attention. Eventually, he and his colleagues set up a simplified version of the situation that had produced the peculiar salivations. They took great care to minimize irrelevant, or *extraneous*, factors insofar as possible. In Pavlov's words:

> To eliminate disturbing factors . . . , a special laboratory was built in Petrograd at the Institute of Experimental Medicine. The Building was surrounded by an isolating trench, and each research room was partitioned with soundproof material into two compartments, one for the animal and the other for the experimenter. [3] See Figure 5-3.

Prior to their studies, Pavlov and his colleagues performed a minor operation on each animal. They made a small incision, usually in

FIGURE 5-3 Ivan Pavlov watches a conditioning experiment taking place in his laboratory in 1934. [*Sovfoto.*]

the dog's cheek, so that the opening of the salivary duct could be transplanted to the outside. Then, a glass funnel was adjusted over the opening so that the saliva could be collected and measured. During a typical conditioning session, dogs stood on a stand and were restrained in a comfortable harness, as illustrated in Figure 5-4. After the animals became accustomed to the situation and seemed relaxed, their salivary reactions to both a meat-cracker mixture in the mouth (the unconditioned stimulus) and a neutral stimulus (in many instances, a tone) were mea-

FIGURE 5-4 Pavlov used experimental apparatus similar to that shown here to condition salivation in dogs. The restraining harness helped keep the animal in place and directed its attention to the experimental stimuli. Note the tube running from the salivary gland in the dog's cheek to a glass container. The device in the lower left recorded the precise amount of salivation.

sured. The animals salivated considerably when given food and negligibly when confronted by a tone—say, the buzzing of an electric bell. At this point, the conditioning trials began. The bell buzzed and a dish of food was given to the dog, often simultaneously or several seconds afterward. Approximately fifty such pairings might occur over the course of several weeks. On *test trials* food was omitted and the bell was presented by itself to see if and when the animal would salivate. Eventually, animals did salivate soon after the onset of the bell. Evidently, the nuisance salivations had arisen from accidental associations between food and other events. Pavlov continued to study respondent conditioning until the day of his death at the age of eighty-seven.

THE PRINCIPLES AND APPLICATIONS OF RESPONDENT CONDITIONING

Russian and American psychologists have been studying respondent conditioning in their laboratories for more than fifty years. Traditionally, they select simple unconditioned stimuli such as puffs of air, food, and mild electric shocks to the leg. These events evoke such simple, unconditioned responses as eyeblinks, salivation, and leg flexion (bending). Characteristically, behavioral scientists also choose simple neutral stimuli; for example, tones, lights, and cards depicting geometric shapes or words. The selection of clearly defined stimuli and responses ensures that procedures may be uniform and that accurate measurements may be made. Researchers study several aspects of the conditioned re-

sponse: *magnitude* (size or amount), *latency* (how long after the conditioned stimulus the response appears), and *reliability* (the percentage of test trials on which the response is elicited). We now describe some basic principles that have been discovered and illustrate each one by examples from everyday life.

Acquisition: The Use of Reinforcement

The pairing of the neutral stimulus with the unconditioned stimulus, usually repeatedly, until a conditioned response appears is called *acquisition* or *acquisition training*. Investigators often present the neutral stimulus at the same time as (or about five seconds or less before) the unconditioned stimulus and terminate both at the same time. This procedure, known as *simultaneous conditioning*, results in a reliable conditioned response and remains the most effective training method for people and less complex animals. Other tactics may be used. In some cases, the neutral stimulus is terminated before the unconditioned stimulus. Occasionally, the neutral stimulus is presented after the unconditioned stimulus, though this procedure rarely results in conditioning. The pairing of the neutral and unconditioned stimuli during acquisition training serves as reinforcement for the conditioned response. The term *reinforcement*, which will be used repeatedly throughout this chapter, roughly means *increaser*. Any event that heightens the probability that a specific response will be made under similar circumstances is known as a *reinforcement* or *reinforcer*. As an example of acquisition training, we consider a controversial experiment that was conducted around 1919.

Little Albert: The Acquisition of a Fear

Newborn human infants are thought to be born with fears of loud noises and pain. Later in the first year, fears of the strange and unfamiliar often de-

velop. These first fears may be genetically programmed into human beings to help them survive. The cries of a terrified infant often bring a concerned

person to remove potential dangers. But how do other fears develop? John Watson, the founder of behaviorism (Chapter 1), and Rosalie Rayner, a graduate student (and later Watson's wife), wanted to see if a young child could learn fears by respondent conditioning. Though hesitant about conducting such a study, Watson and Rayner believed that fears "would arise anyway as soon as the child left the sheltered environment of the nursery for the rough and tumble of home." They also thought that there would be an opportunity to remove any fears that were conditioned.

Watson and Rayner selected as their subject an infant named Albert, the son of a wet nurse employed at a nearby hospital. Albert was a "stolid (unemotional)" child. "His stability was one of the principal reasons for using him as a subject." At the age of approximately nine

months, Albert's fears were tested. He appeared unafraid of a rat, a rabbit, a dog, a monkey, a mask with or without hair, cotton wool, or burning newspapers. The only event that seemed to frighten the boy was a loud sound made by striking a hammer against a steel bar.

Fear conditioning trials began when Albert was about eleven months of age. A white rat was taken from a basket and offered to the boy as he sat on a mattress in Watson's psychology laboratory. Just as Albert reached for the animal, one of the investigators struck a hammer against a steel bar behind his head. Albert "jumped violently and fell forward, burying his face in the mattress." When he reached out again for the rat,

the bar was again struck. This time Albert "jumped violently, fell forward, and began to whimper." There were no further trials that week "in order not to disturb the child too seriously."

A week later, Albert returned to the laboratory, and the conditioning trials resumed. It took five more trials (a grand total of seven) to establish a fear of white rats [4].

This experiment challenged a major psychological principle of the day: that fears necessarily developed because of traumatic *interpersonal* circumstances and were always *symbolic* of complicated conflicts. Watson and Rayner had demonstrated quite clearly that fears were sometimes a matter of simple learning. We return to this case soon.

A second real-life example of acquisition training is presented in Figure 5-5.

Before moving on, it is important to note that the respondent conditioning of fear is often indirect. People do not need frightening experiences with neutral stimuli to acquire fears of them. Since we are cognitive creatures, we often frighten ourselves by what we imagine. Suppose that either the sight of a swimming pool or the words "swimming pool" (neutral stimuli at the beginning) are frequently paired with fear-arousing stories, pictures, warnings, or simply the uneasiness of other people (unconditioned stimuli). Under these circumstances, individuals may develop a conditioned fear response toward pools, as shown in Figure 5-6. Many human fears appear to be established in this vicarious way (through imagined participation). Other prob-

FIGURE 5-5 The basic principles of respondent conditioning have been used successfully to toilet-train human infants. Devices like the one pictured here produce a loud tone whenever a drop of moisture touches a sensor sewn into the youngster's training pants. The tone, the unconditioned stimulus, becomes associated with the neutral stimulus, tension from a full bladder or bowel (the bodily state immediately preceding it). The noise produces an unconditioned response, startling, which alerts the individual to bladder- and bowel-related sensations. Eventually, the child learns to attend to bladder and bowel tension without the tone. We could consider this attention the conditioned response. Once youngsters become aware of the sensations that signal the need to eliminate, they are likely to use the toilet. [*Redrawn from Van Wagenen and Murdock, 1966.*]

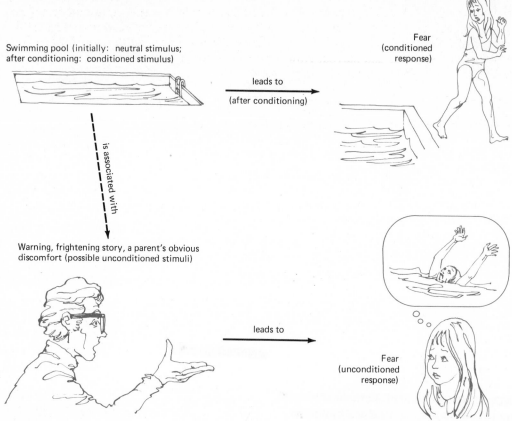

Swimming pool (initially: neutral stimulus; after conditioning: conditioned stimulus)

is associated with

Warning, frightening story, a parent's obvious discomfort (possible unconditioned stimuli)

leads to
(after conditioning)

Fear (conditioned response)

leads to

Fear (unconditioned response)

FIGURE 5-6 The figure shows the major elements involved in the swimming-pool fear example of vicarious respondent conditioning (described in the text). Many human fears appear to be established in this indirect way. Recently, when psychologists studied the fears of youngsters, they found that killers, dying, atom bombs, earthquakes, hurricanes, wars, and plane crashes ranked high [63]. Twenty years ago, lions, tigers, and imaginary animals may have headed such a list. Fears like these are probably acquired vicariously as such words as "killer" and "atom bomb" are repeatedly associated with horrifying images and gruesome stories in the media and in life.

able causes of intense fears, or anxieties, are discussed in Chapters 11 and 14.

Extinction and Spontaneous Recovery

Once a conditioned response has been acquired, it can be expected to persist as long as the conditioned stimulus is associated, at least some of the time, with the unconditioned stimulus. If the conditioned stimulus is presented alone repeatedly, then the conditioned response is no longer being reinforced, and it is likely to decline in frequency until it occurs no more often than it did prior to conditioning. This phenomenon is called *extinction*. How fast extinction takes place depends on the animal, the response, the stimuli, and the number and spacing of conditioning trials. Some conditioned responses diminish very slowly or remain intact for years, even though they are not reinforced.

Conditioned emotional responses often extinguish in real life. Suppose that as a young child you have several violent fistfights with Laura, a girl in your neighborhood. These fights can be seen as unconditioned stimuli. They are likely to elicit pain, fear, and anger as unconditioned responses. Laura begins as a neutral stimulus (in the sense that initial contacts didn't evoke pain, anxiety, or anger). After several fights, the sight of Laura's face or the sound of her voice is likely to elicit a conditioned response of fear and hatred. Now suppose that you see one another for years, but do not fight. Eventually, the fear and hatred may return to preconditioning levels; in other words, the reactions may disappear. Conditioned emotional responses may be deliberately extinguished too, as the following case illustrates.

Peter and the Rabbit: The Extinction of a Fear

Albert's mother withdrew her son from the hospital just before the fear-removal phase of the Watson-Rayner project was scheduled to begin. All subsequent attempts to locate Albert were unsuccessful, so we do not know what happened to him. But the story does not end here. About three years after Albert was conditioned to fear rats, Mary Cover Jones, at the time a graduate student at Columbia University working with Watson, was able to show that fears could be eliminated through conditioning procedures. The participant in this more humane demonstration was a child named Peter, who looked almost like "Albert grown a bit older." At thirty-four months of age, Peter seemed healthy and normal in every way, except for exaggerated fears of rabbits, rats, fur coats, feathers, and cotton wool. In consultation with Watson, Jones planned a treatment strategy for the rabbit fear,

which happened to be particularly intense. Peter was scheduled to play in the laboratory with three children who were unafraid of rabbits. At these sessions the boy was given favorite foods to eat. A rabbit was present in the room for at least part of each period. Peter was encouraged to engage in progressively closer interactions with the animal. Over the course of his treatment, which lasted about three months, Peter passed through the following stages:

A. Rabbit anywhere in the room in a cage causes fear reaction
B. Rabbit 12 feet away in a cage tolerated
C. Rabbit 4 feet away in a cage tolerated
D. Rabbit 3 feet away in a cage tolerated
E. Rabbit close in cage tolerated
F. Rabbit free in room tolerated
G. Rabbit touched when experimenter holds it
H. Rabbit touched when free in room
I. Rabbit defied by spitting at it, throwing things at it, imitating it
J. Rabbit allowed on tray of high chair
K. Squats in defenseless position beside rabbit
L. Helps experimenter to carry rabbit to its cage
M. Holds rabbit on lap
N. Stays alone in room with rabbit
O. Allows rabbit in play pen with him
P. Fondles rabbit affectionately
Q. Lets rabbit nibble his fingers. [5]

By the end of treatment, the boy was on friendly terms with the rabbit. His fears of cotton, fur coats, and feathers had disappeared entirely, while his reactions to rats and a fur rug with a head had greatly improved.

We can explain Peter's new learning by either of two respondent conditioning principles: extinction or counterconditioning (which is described a little later). An extinction explanation is presented in Figure 5-7a. Jones had presented the conditioned stimulus (rabbit) repeatedly without the presumed unconditioned stimulus (frightening experience) until the conditioned response (fear) was reduced to its preconditioning level (when it was probably nonexistent).

Even though a conditioned response may disappear with time, it does not appear to be "erased" entirely. Pavlov discovered this principle when dogs were brought back into his laboratory after extinction and a rest period. When the animals were presented again with the conditioned stimulus, they frequently made a conditioned response. The reappearance of a previously extinguished conditioned response following a rest period is known as *spontaneous recovery*.

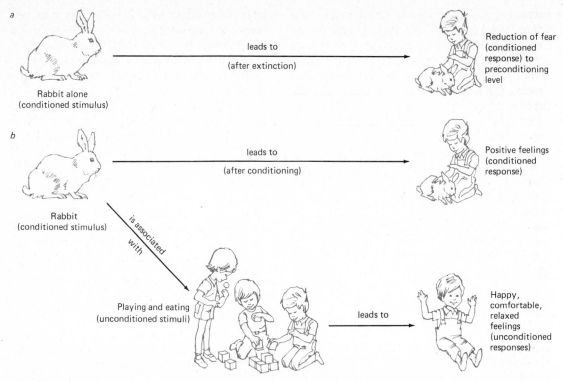

FIGURE 5-7 The major elements in two possible explanations for the success of the procedure which reduced Peter's fear of rabbits. (*a*) The components of extinction; and (*b*) the components of counterconditioning.

Generalization and Discrimination

The spreading of a conditioned response to events that are similar to the conditioned stimulus and to aspects of the situation where the response was initially conditioned is known as *stimulus generalization*, or *generalization*. Suppose that after warm, affectionate contact with a friend, you begin to experience spontaneous joyful feelings whenever you see that person. Imagine that the friend drives a yellow motorcycle. After a while the happy feelings may generalize. You might experience joy, for instance, whenever a yellow motorcycle passes by. When Albert was tested five days after the conditioned fear response had been established, the boy was frightened of a white rabbit, a sealskin fur, cotton wool, Watson's hair, a dog, and a Santa Claus mask. Thirty days later (with only one further conditioning trial), most of Albert's new generalized fears were still intact [6].

Just as animals generalize, they also *discriminate*. They respond to one or more stimuli that were present during conditioning but not to similar stimuli. In the laboratory, the amount of discrimination increases as differences between the original conditioned stimulus and other stimuli increase. In the case of Pavlov's dogs, the animals salivated quite a bit to tones that were a single note higher or lower than the conditioned stimulus and progressively less to increasingly different tones. Discrimination also occurs whenever human fears are conditioned. Suppose that Abe's car skids out of control during a heavy rainstorm. Though Abe is not hurt, he feels frightened after the incident whenever he drives on wet roads, particularly so during storms near the scene of the mishap. Abe's conditioned fear has spread (generalization) to driving during light rain and snow. At the same time, some discrimination is evidenced by two facts: (1) Abe is not afraid of driving in good weather, and (2) Abe's most intense fears are associated with the location and conditions encountered during the accident. Consider one additional example. If Juanita comes down with a stomach virus soon after eating dinner at Bubble's Hamburger Haven, she might feel queasy whenever she sees or smells Hamburger Haven hamburgers, but not Hamburger Haven french fries, and not all hamburgers.

Counterconditioning

During *counterconditioning*, a special type of respondent conditioning, a specific conditioned response is replaced by a new *incompatible*, or conflicting, conditioned response. Several examples should make the meaning of the term *incompatible* clearer. Relaxation cannot coexist with anxiety, so we might say that the two reactions are incompatible. The same is true for joy and misery and for comfort and queasiness. The counterconditioning procedure is straightforward. A second set of acquisition training trials occurs. The conditioned stimulus that evokes the conditioned response that is to be replaced is treated like a neutral stimulus. It is associated with an unconditioned stimulus which elicits an incompatible unconditioned response. After repeated pairings, the conditioned stimulus may come to evoke only the new incompatible conditioned response. As we suggested before, Peter may have had his fear of rabbits counterconditioned. Jones accompanied the conditioned stimulus (rabbit) with new unconditioned stimuli (playing with children and eating). These experiences elicited unconditioned responses (happy, comfortable, relaxed feelings) that were incompatible with anxiety. Eventually, the conditioned stimulus

(rabbit) became associated with a pleasant emotional reaction, a new (and conflicting) conditioned response. See Figure 5-7*b*. In Chapter 16 we describe a counterconditioning procedure, *systematic desensitization*, which is widely used to help people cope with anxieties. Unpleasant types of counterconditioning are sometimes employed in clinic settings as well, to discourage unwanted habits, such as alcoholism, overeating, smoking, and certain sexual deviations. Typically, the bad habit is associated with something aversive—electric shock, for example. Such procedures are used only with the participant's permission. Through association, the bad habit is supposed to become less appealing. Unfortunately, the technique is frequently ineffective for several reasons. First, many people find the treatments so unpleasant that they quit therapy in midstream. Second, positive experiences associated with the bad habit are likely to reexert their influence once people leave treatment. Consequently, the bad habit is quite likely to return. ▲

OPERANT CONDITIONING

We turn now to a second fundamental learning process, operant conditioning, or the conditioning of operants. What are operants? How are they conditioned?

Operants

Operants are actions which animals initiate themselves. Walking, dancing, smiling, kissing, writing poetry, drinking beer, watching television, gossiping, and playing monopoly are common human operants. Although operants appear to be spontaneous and entirely under an animal's control, they are greatly influenced by their consequences.

The Conditioning of Operants

Operant (or instrumental) conditioning occurs whenever the consequences following an oper-

▲ **USING PSYCHOLOGY**

1. Give at least two personal examples of respondent conditioning. Label the elements. Also, find examples from your own experience of extinction, spontaneous recovery, stimulus generalization, and discrimination.

2. What did Watson's and Rayner's experiment on little Albert demonstrate? Do you feel the study was justified? Defend your position?

3. Consider several simple fears of your own. Explain how direct or vicarious respondent conditioning principles may have been involved in their acquisition.

4. Assume that five-year-old Pedro almost drowns while swimming and that he becomes terrified of pools. How could respondent conditioning procedures be used to reduce his fear?

5. Many people experience strong emotions whenever they see or hear about specific symbols (such as the peace sign, the American flag, or a raised clenched fist). How could respondent conditioning account for such reactions?

ant increase or decrease the probability that the operant will be performed in a similar situation. In other words, during operant conditioning the frequency of an action (the operant) is modified. If a given operant is repeatedly followed by outcomes that are pleasing to the learner, the act is likely to be performed more often under similar conditions. If generally followed by unpleasant consequences, the behavior is likely to be repeated less frequently under corresponding circumstances. Throughout our daily lives, operants are continually being conditioned, usually without our awareness. Suppose that as you describe last night's basketball game, your mother (of whom you're fond) fidgets and looks around the room. You're likely to talk less about the game and similar sporting events with your mother. Similarly, if you share your genuine feelings with a friend and the relationship becomes warmer and more interesting, the odds are good that you'll continue to talk personally in this and future relationships. Now assume that a new study technique wins excellent marks. You'll probably keep using it. In each instance, the likelihood that a particular operant will occur in a specific situation has been modified by its consequences.

The History of Operant Conditioning

Many behavioral scientists have advanced our understanding of operant conditioning. We look briefly at the work of two pioneers who have been particularly influential.

Thorndike and his cats: The importance of consequences At about the same time that Ivan Pavlov was working with salivating dogs, an American psychologist, Edward Lee Thorndike (1874–1949), was observing hungry cats to find out how they solved problems. Thorndike placed food-deprived cats in *puzzle boxes*, cages from which the animals could escape by simple acts such as manipulating a cord, pressing a lever, or stepping on a platform. As an incentive to solve the problem, food was placed just outside the cage where it could be seen and smelled (see Figure 5-8). Thorndike observed carefully as numerous cats learned to escape from diverse boxes. Later, he summarized his insights in this way:

When put into the box the cat would show evident signs of discomfort and an impulse to escape from confinement. It tries to squeeze through any opening; it claws and bites at the bars or wire; it thrusts its paws out through any opening and claws at everything it reaches; it continues its efforts when it strikes anything loose and shaky; it may claw at things within the box. It does not pay very much attention to the food outside, but seems simply to strive instinctively to escape from confinement. . . . For eight or ten minutes it will claw and bite and squeeze incessantly. . . . The cat that is clawing all over the box in her impulsive struggle will probably claw the string or loop or button so as to open the door. And gradually all the other nonsuccessful impulses will be stamped out and the particular impulse leading to the successful act will be stamped in by the resulting pleasure, until, after many trials, the cat will, when put in the box, immediately claw the loop or button in a definite way. [7]

Thorndike believed that all animals, including people, solve problems by *trial-and-error learning*. Initially, the creature tries out various "instinctive" responses. Successful behaviors become more frequent. Presumably, they are "stamped in" by the pleasure of success. At the same time, unsuccessful acts become less likely. They are "stamped out" because they do not produce a desirable result. Thorndike was one of the first psychologists to emphasize that consequences are important for learning.

Skinner and operant technology B. F. Skinner (b. 1904), an American psychologist now retired from Harvard University, has probably contributed more than any other single person to our understanding of operant conditioning. Like John Watson, Skinner is known for his behavioristic point of view. He has always insisted that observable behavior is the only appropriate concern of the psychologist. In the late 1920s he began investigating operant behavior. Frequently he trained small groups of food-deprived pigeons or rats to peck a key or press a bar. Each time the hungry animal performed the appropriate action, a food pellet was released into its food cup. Skinner assumed that studying the responses of relatively primitive animals in a distraction-free environment was the most efficient way to determine the *basic laws of operant learning*. The distraction-free envi-

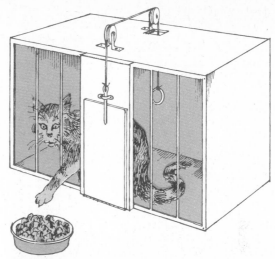

FIGURE 5-8 One of Thorndike's puzzle boxes. To reach the food, a cat had to learn to pull a loop that released the door.

ronment that Skinner used is pictured in Figure 5-9. Known as a *skinner box*, this type of habitat is stock apparatus for a psychology laboratory today. By manipulating the conditions under which food was dispensed, Skinner and his coworkers observed how behavior changed. Exhaustive studies using this simple model enabled Skinner and numerous other behavioral scientists to discover many of the factors that influence operant conditioning.

Operant principles are as relevant for people as for simpler animals. Skinner's science-fiction novel *Walden Two*, about a utopian community based on operant conditioning, was the inspiration for a real commune called Twin Oaks, described in Figure 5-10. Most important, operant conditioning research has led to a sophisticated teaching technology, often called *behavior modification*. This technology is used throughout the world by psychologists, teachers, parents, and others in diverse settings. Before describing the principles of operant conditioning and behavior modification applications, we clarify differences between behavior modification, brainwashing, and other phenomena that are too frequently confused.

What Behavior Modification Is Not

Formal definitions of behavior modification frequently include the following ideas:

1. The goal is the alleviation of human problems.
2. A reeducation effort is involved.
3. The techniques have been derived from, and/or are consistent with, psychological research.
4. The results are systematically evaluated [8].

Unfortunately, many people take the term *behavior modification* at face value and assume that the procedure is used every time behavior is modified. Accordingly, advertising, propaganda, psychosurgery, torture, and brainwashing are frequently lumped into the behavior modification category. In some cases, the media have intensified anti–behavior modification sentiment by portraying the procedures as being inconsistent with freedom and dignity and by associating the techniques with fictional and nonfictional horrors [9]. Considering these circumstances, it is hardly surprising that people feel wary about the whole idea of behavior modification. In a recent experiment by Anita Woolfolk and her coworkers, college students were asked to evaluate a classroom scene. Sometimes the teacher's strategies were labeled and described as being illustrative of "behavior modification" and sometimes as exemplifying "humanistic education training." Subjects responded significantly more favorably to the same vignette under the "humanistic education training" label [10].

While behavior modification can be abused, like any other technology, it is very different from brainwashing and thought control. The techniques used by the Communists in Korea in the 1950s owed much of their strength to what has been called the *DDD syndrome*—debility, dependency, and dread. American soldiers were exposed to conditions of semistarvation, disease, chronic physical pain, and insufficient sleep until they felt terribly *debilitated* (weak). At the same time, the captives were utterly *dependent* on their enemies, the only people who could take care of their needs. The men also lived in constant *dread* of pain, mutilation, never returning home, violence against friends, and death. In this context, techniques similar to conditioning were applied to increase confessions and cooperative responses and to decrease misbehavior [11]. Formal behavior modification procedures *never* utilize debilitation, dependency, or dread to motivate change.

THE PRINCIPLES AND APPLICATIONS OF OPERANT CONDITIONING

We turn now to operant conditioning principles and their applications in human life, particularly in children's learning. Though few people use these "rules" consciously, the laws still operate. Many individuals, like the members of the Teller family (at the beginning of this chapter), teach one another accidentally without realizing that they are doing so. In Chapter 16 we describe how psychologists use these same principles in mental health settings to help adults cope with emotional problems.

Reinforcement

Reinforcement occurs during operant conditioning as during respondent conditioning. In both cases, reinforcement strengthens the likelihood of certain behavior. Several differences between the reinforcement of respondents and operants must be noted. Whereas reinforcement precedes the strengthened act in respondent conditioning, it follows the strengthened act in operant conditioning. The nature of the reinforcement procedure differs for the two types of learning, too. Respondents are reinforced by pairing initially neutral and unconditioned stimuli. Operants are reinforced by the consequences that follow the behavior. Psychologists talk about two types of reinforcement during operant conditioning: positive and negative.

Positive reinforcement Whenever the presentation of an event following an operant *increases* the probability that the operant will occur in similar situations, psychologists call the attention it commanded. Lavishing praise on Edward for being handy around the house is another example of positive reinforcement, if (and only if) the praise makes Edward more likely to keep the house in good repair. If the substitute teacher glares every time Ann clowns around, and Ann shows off increasingly often in this class, glaring is acting as a positive reinforcement. Note that an event that is ordinarily considered unpleasant can function as a positive reinforcer. Since positive reinforcement is defined in terms of its effects, we cannot always predict a priori (in advance) what will operate as a positive reinforcer. We must see what happens in any individual case.

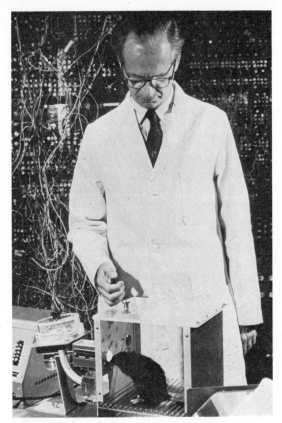

FIGURE 5-9 B. F. Skinner and the training habitat named after him. Rats in skinner boxes like this one have taught Skinner a great deal about operant-conditioning principles. His guiding philosophy has always been, "The subject knows best." In his novel *Walden Two*, Skinner expressed this idea through a character named Frazier. "I remember the rage I used to feel when a prediction went awry. I could have shouted at the subjects of my experiment, 'Behave, damn you! Behave as you ought!' Eventually I realized that the subjects were always right. They always behaved as they should have behaved. It was I who was wrong. I had made a bad prediction [64]." [*Nina Leen*/Life *magazine,* © *1964, Time, Inc.*]

the process and consequences *positive reinforcement*. The consequence is also known as a *positive reinforcer*. The adjective "positive" is used because the event was *presented*. The noun "reinforcement" is used because the frequency of the behavior that preceded the consequence was *increased*. Sammy Teller's helplessness was probably strengthened by

FIGURE 5-10 In his novel *Walden Two*, B. F. Skinner described an ideal human community, also known as Walden Two. The founder of Skinner's utopia believed that behavior is shaped by the environment, so he established conditions that maximized the probability of good behavior and minimized the likelihood of unpleasant conduct. This picture was taken at Twin Oaks, one of several communes inspired by Walden Two. Founded in 1967 in rural Virginia, Twin Oaks today comprises people who hold diverse philosophies. Members share a common belief in cooperation, equality, and nonviolence and a desire to construct a community where people treat one another in a kind, caring, honest, and fair manner. Although Skinner's behavioristic theories are no longer central to the operation of Twin Oaks, the advantages of creating a positive environment and reinforcing desirable behavior in others are still recognized [65]. [*Courtesy of Twin Oaks.*]

Negative reinforcement Whenever the removal of a specific event following an operant *increases* the likelihood that the operant will occur in similar situations, we call both the process and consequence (removal of the event) *negative reinforcement*. The consequence is also known as a *negative reinforcer*. The adjective "negative" is used because an event is *removed*. The noun "reinforcement" is used because the frequency of the response that preceded this consequence was *increased*. Negative reinforcement strengthens behaviors that rid animals of irritating experiences. Psychologists distinguish between two basic types of negative reinforcement: escape conditioning and avoidance conditioning.

During *escape conditioning* the frequency of an operant is *increased* under similar circumstances because it *terminates an ongoing event* (that the organism considers unpleasant). Habits like covering one's ears during thunderstorms to shut out the distressing noise, hanging up the receiver to end annoying phone conversations, and cleaning up messy rooms to stop somebody's nagging are common examples of escape conditioning.

During *avoidance conditioning* the frequency of an operant is *increased* under similar conditions because it *postpones* or *prevents* the occurrence of an event (that the organism anticipates as unpleasant). Fran Teller was able to avoid a lecture on her incompetence by leaving her papers in school, you may recall. Habits such as fastening a safety belt before turning on the car ignition to elude an irritating buzzer, studying to avoid failing marks, obeying parents to forestall a paddling, and obeying laws to prevent accidents, fines, or prison terms are all common examples of avoidance conditioning.

Note: During negative reinforcement, unpleasant events which might by themselves tend to weaken the behavior that they follow are removed. As we will soon see, psychologists call weakeners of behavior *punishers*. So we might say that negative reinforcers strengthen behavior by removing punishers. See Table 5-1.

Varieties of positive and negative reinforcers What is reinforcing during operant conditioning depends on the individual and her or his current circumstances. Biscuits may strengthen the sitting-on-command of some hungry dogs. These tidbits probably won't work well on animals accustomed to stew meat. Praise may be a fine reinforcer for Enrico's coming when called, though it may not strengthen his practicing the flute. Iolanthe may be unlikely to lift her left finger to avoid a tongue lashing, while Jeremy may increase the frequency of any behavior that prevents a mere frown. As we talk about categories of reinforcers, keep in mind that what is reinforcing varies from individual to individual. So any given consequence should be considered a *potential reinforcer* until its effects on a given individual are established.

Positive and negative reinforcers are some-

TABLE 5-1 A Comparison of Reinforcement Procedures

	Reinforcement		
	Positive	**Negative**	
Consequence following behavior	Reinforcement presented	Punisher removed (escape conditioning)	Punisher postponed or avoided (avoidance conditioning)
Effect of consequence	Behavior strengthened		
If training is stopped	Extinction of reinforced response (spontaneous recovery may occur)		

times divided into two general classifications: intrinsic and extrinsic. Reinforcement is said to be *intrinsic* when the behavior to be strengthened is reinforcing *by itself*. In other words, the response alone is a source of pleasurable feelings and the act is automatically strengthened every time it occurs. Several different types of behaviors may be intrinsically reinforcing. Responses which fulfill basic, physiologically based motives (called *drives*), such as drinking when thirsty, eating when hungry, and engaging in sexual activity after a period of abstinence, are intrinsically pleasurable for most animals. Dancing, listening to music, hiking, sculpting, and other activities that provide sensory stimulation are also frequently regarded as ends in themselves. Similarly, pursuits that satisfy curiosity, such as reading, observation, experimentation, and exploration, are innately satisfying for a lot of people. So is the sense of progress or mastery that comes from achieving, attaining competence, or breaking a bad habit. See Figure 5-11. Behaviors that help an animal escape or avoid harm or pain—from fleeing an enemy to spreading soothing lotion on a rash caused by poison ivy—may also be reinforcing by themselves. The intrinsically rewarding activities that have been described are not always reinforcing from the very beginning. Proficiency is required before chess, tennis, guitar playing, or some other skilled activity becomes inherently satisfying.

The majority of behaviors that most people engage in every day are not intrinsically reinforcing but are strengthened by their *external* or *extrinsic* consequences. The rewards are not part of the behavior itself. Psychologists consider three somewhat overlapping categories of extrinsic reinforcers important. Without any prior training, *primary* or *unlearned reinforcers* are powerful in strengthening the behavior that they follow. One does not need to learn to like eating or avoiding pain, of course, as we mentioned before. Intrinsically satisfying events like these can be used to teach *other* habits. Perhaps a small child's willingness to keep a clean room could be strengthened by a reward of raisins. Activities that satisfy curiosity or

FIGURE 5-11 In school programs using operant-conditioning principles, students sometimes record their own academic progress. Self-recording techniques, which focus attention on improvement, may be highly motivating [66]. In some classes pupils also work at their own pace, administering and checking tests and proceeding to new work after achieving a specified level of proficiency. [*Fred Kaplan/Black Star.*]

provide sensory stimulation make extremely useful primary reinforcers for human responses, as depicted in Figure 5-12. In a natural setting, the frequency of using a particular "line" with members of the opposite sex may be increased because it achieves its intended objective, sexual favors. In the laboratory, food, shock escape, and shock avoidance are the most frequently used primary reinforcers of animal behavior.

Extrinsic reinforcers that depend on other people are usually called *social reinforcers*. Common social reinforcers include affection, attention, approval, smiling, laughter (after a joke), recognition, respect, and the removal of rejection, anger, disapproval, and disrespect. Sex could be considered a primary or social reinforcer. While some social reinforcers are probably unlearned, others are definitely learned. It is likely that human beings are born valuing smiles, hugs, and a soothing tone of voice and disliking signs of tension and yelling. At the same time, people learn to cherish words of praise, such as "good" and "excellent." We learn to appreciate signs of status (such as college degrees) too, perhaps

A. Talking
B. Writing
C. Coloring
D. Drawing
E. Reading
F. Swinging feet
G. Record
H. Hugging
I. Dancing
J. Walking
K. Drawing on board
L. Telephoning
M. Puzzle
N. Blocks
O. Jumping
P. Drinking
Q. Using colored pencils
R. Singing
S. Swinging on door
T. Moving chair
U. Erasing blackboard
V. Looking out window

FIGURE 5-12 These items came from a "reinforcement menu." In some classrooms, children select their own reinforcers from such a "menu"—a chart showing enjoyable activities. They earn the right to engage in their selection by completing a specified amount of work. Activity lists might include privileges such as talking, writing, coloring, reading, swinging feet, playing records, hugging, dancing, drawing on the board, telephoning, using colored pencils, singing, swinging on the door, erasing the blackboard, and looking out the window [67]. For young children, activities can function as powerful reinforcers of academic behavior. Earning opportunities in this fashion may teach the individual some important lessons about life. After all, adults must often earn their own privileges too. [*Adapted from Daley, 1969.*]

because they are associated with displays of warmth, appreciation, and respect. Social reinforcers tend to be enormously influential in modifying human behavior.

Secondary or *conditioned reinforcers* acquire their strength through respondent conditioning—by being repeatedly paired with other reinforcers until they become valued. The dollar bill has been associated with the acquisition of food, stimulation, and comforts of all types. Gold stars, points, and report card grades have acquired reinforcing properties because they have been linked with achievement and approval. Learned social reinforcers are sometimes considered secondary reinforcers.

While we have divided the various types of reinforcers into categories, in real life varied intrinsic and extrinsic "rewards" are often found mingled together in the same reinforcing event.

The scheduling of reinforcement B. F. Skinner began investigating reinforcement schedules because of practical problems. As Skinner tells the story:

One pleasant Saturday afternoon I surveyed my supply of dry pellets and, appealing to certain elemental theorems in arithmetic, deduced that unless I spent the rest of that afternoon and evening at the pill machine, the supply would be exhausted by ten-thirty Monday morning. . . . I therefore embarked upon the study of periodic reinforcement. [12]

While the study of schedules began rather modestly, Skinner and C. B. Ferster's early work in this area was anything but casual. They studied a quarter-of-a-billion responses recorded over 70,000 hours. Some schedules that were tested out specified that a certain amount of behavior had to occur for the animal to obtain the reinforcement. Others required that a certain amount of time had to elapse between reinforcers. Some combined both types of requirements. Skinner and Ferster found that the manner of scheduling reinforcement had an important influence on (1) how fast animals learned a response initially, (2) how frequently they performed the behavior that had been learned, (3) how often they paused after reinforcements, and (4) how long they continued to make the response once reinforcement became unpredictable or was stopped. The psychologists also discovered that animals showed a stable characteristic rate and pattern of behavior on a given schedule. The response pattern was so reliable, in fact, that it could be used to measure the influence of drugs, sleep deprivation, hunger, and other phenomena [13].

Reinforcement that is *scheduled continuously* follows every correct response. Continuous reinforcement appears to be the most efficient way to condition behavior initially. Reinforcers seem to be most effective when they come *immediately* after the behavior to be increased. But human beings may also learn from delayed reinforcers, as long as they are periodically reminded that the reinforcer will be forthcoming [14]. Many natural responses are reinforced continuously. Every time you push your foot down on the brake, the car slows down (so long as the vehicle is operating normally). Similarly, whenever you flick a light switch, illumination is increased. And every time you put a forkful of food in your mouth, you get to taste the morsel.

A *partial (intermittent) schedule* is one where some, but not all, correct responses are followed by a reinforcer. This type of schedule results in a more persistent response pattern than a continuous schedule at times when reinforcement becomes erratic (unpredictable) or ceases. A combination of continuous and partial reinforcement is highly desirable in teaching people operant behavior: continuous at the beginning, partial once a response has been established.

Four *basic partial schedules* have been studied extensively in the laboratory. Two specify that the reinforcer should follow a particular *number of correct responses* and are known as *ratio schedules*. On a *fixed-ratio*

schedule, reinforcement occurs after a *definite and unvarying number* of correct responses. When factories pay their workers so much money for producing so many goods, they are using a fixed-ratio schedule. Farm workers are frequently paid to harvest crops on the same type of schedule. Students who take breaks after doing ten pushups, solving twenty math problems, or writing three pages on their term papers are also operating on a fixed-ratio schedule. Note that continuous reinforcement is a fixed-ratio program. Animals (including people) respond at a relatively high overall rate on fixed-ratio schedules, but they usually pause and rest after the delivery of each reinforcer before going back to work. See Figure 5-13*a*.

On a *variable-ratio schedule*, a reinforcer is presented following a *varying number* of correct responses. Now the number of behaviors required for reinforcement changes randomly but averages a particular value, such as 3, 9, 50, 90, or even 120,000. Consider a person receiving a reinforcer on a VR-3 schedule (a variable-ratio schedule with a mean of 3). The individual might be rewarded after five responses first, then after three more, then after one more, and so forth. Slot machines are programmed to pay off on a variable-ratio schedule. Many natural reinforcers, such as achievement, recognition, and profit, approximate the same type of schedule. Variable-ratio schedules produce a high overall response rate which is sustained; animals do not pause. Apparently, the uncertainty of never knowing when the next reinforcer is coming keeps organisms working steadily. (See Figure 5-13*b*.)

Interval reinforcement schedules depend on the *passage of time*. The reinforcer is provided after two conditions are satisfied. First, a particular interval of time must have passed since the previous reinforcement. Second, the response to be reinforced must occur after the interval. On *fixed-interval schedules* the *time period* between reinforcers is *constant*. Looking for the mail is reinforced naturally on an approximately twenty-four-hour, fixed-interval schedule in most parts of the United States. Entering the dining room for dinner

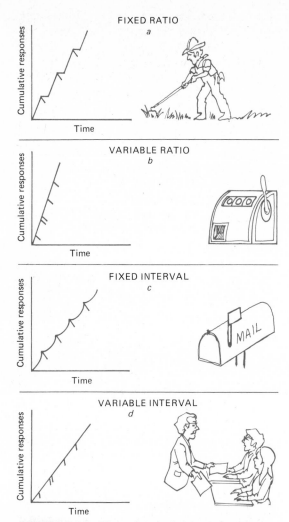

FIGURE 5-13 These characteristic response patterns are associated with each of the four basic reinforcement schedules described in the text. For cumulative records like these, the total number of responses since the start of the experiment is graphed at *each* point. The slashes show when reinforcers were presented. Note that the ratio schedules tend to produce a slightly higher overall response rate than the interval schedules. Notice also that variable schedules produce little pausing, while fixed schedules produce rather long pauses quite predictably—after reinforcement.

may be reinforced every twenty-four hours on another rough "fixed-interval program." A parent might check up on a child every half-hour and pat the youngster on the back as long as he or she is reading. Fixed-interval

schedules produce an uneven rate of responding. After the reinforcer is delivered, the response rate tends to be low. During the interval, the behavior typically increases steadily until it reaches a high level immediately before the next scheduled reinforcer. Because it resembles a scallop (as shown in Figure 5-13c), this response pattern is sometimes called a *fixed-interval scallop*. The overall response rate on a fixed-interval schedule is moderate.

On *variable-interval schedules*, the length of the *time period* between reinforcers *varies* randomly about a mean value. Compliments could be given on a rough variable-interval schedule. After a good performance at a piano lesson (the correct response) every two or three weeks (the variable interval), the teacher might comment. Surprise quizzes every week or so give students the opportunity to be reinforced for studying on a variable-interval schedule. This schedule usually produces a constant but moderate response rate, as can be seen in Figure 5-13d.

In real life, basic schedules are often combined, just as they are in the laboratory. A salesperson, for example, might receive both a base salary and a commission. The salary reinforces regular work hours on a rough fixed-interval schedule. (In actuality, the salesperson may keep regular hours to avoid being fired or losing salary and commission—a negative reinforcement.) The commission, probably a fixed-ratio device, reinforces successful selling efforts. The four basic schedules which have been discussed are also used in escape and avoidance conditioning. ▲

Shaping

Through the appropriate use of a positive reinforcement strategy called *shaping*, or the *method of successive approximations*, people and other animals can learn new operant responses. In the beginning the trainer positively reinforces an act within the organism's current repertoire that only faintly resembles the desired response(s). As this behavior is strengthened, the "teacher" becomes more selective and reinforces only those behaviors that resemble the goal more closely. When this conduct is well established, the trainer becomes even more demanding. The process continues until the goal is reached.

Parents sometimes use shaping intuitively to teach their children. Consider walking (an act that does not need to be taught, but often is). Once a baby stands, its parents no longer fuss over it for simply remaining upright. The child is expected to progress, perhaps to take steps while holding on. After achieving this objective, the toddler may attempt more steps with less support and eventually, of course, walk on its own. After each small accomplishment, parents revise their expectations upward. The youngster must attain more before the parents become excited and enthusiastic. The following case study shows how shaping was used deliberately to treat a serious speech problem in a four-year-old.

Shaping Speech: A Case Study

A troubled four-year-old, whom we call Charles, was referred to the New York State Psychiatric Institute for diagnosis and treatment. At this time the boy could speak only a few words. He was extremely active, negative, and destructive. And he was intensely frightened of people. In the past, Charles had heard very little spoken English because his parents rarely communicated with one another, and when they did, they spoke a mixture of German, Hebrew, and English. Moreover, Charles had heard no voices at all for long periods of time, since he was frequently beaten and locked in his room.

Kurt Salzinger, a psychologist at the psychiatric hospital, and his coworkers established a friendly relationship with Charles. Then they began shaping his language skills during "play" sessions. In the beginning, Charles was reinforced for saying any word at all. The psychologist acted very interested and repeated what had been said. Soon Charles was using his small vocabulary frequently, so a more difficult task could be introduced. At this point Charles had to say, "Gimme . . .," or make some other type of request, when the psychologist showed and named an object. If the boy made the correct response, he recieved praise, candy, and the object itself. Reinforcement was no longer given for simpler verbalizations. After some time at this exercise, Charles became quite skilled at asking for common objects. So the rules of the game were changed once again. This time Charles was shown an object or a picture, and its name was repeated. For imitating the word correctly, Charles received candy, praise, and several minutes of free play. As soon as the boy had mastered the names of many common objects, the psychologist began training a new language skill. The process continued for more than 100 hourly sessions. At the time that Charles was discharged to a new foster home, he spoke entirely in sentences. He had also learned to trust people [15].

Extinction and Spontaneous Recovery

When the reinforcement for a particular response is withdrawn, the behavior gradually declines in frequency until it occurs no more often than it did prior to conditioning. This process is labeled *extinction* in both operant and respondent conditioning. In real life people often learn operants that extinguish if they are not reinforced. Many young children, for example, are taught to be polite. Parents may praise youngsters for using words like "please" and "thank you." If the child's good manners go completely unappreciated later on, they're likely to disappear.

In reality, people often extinguish desirable and reinforce undesirable operants. The Tellers exemplified this pattern. They tended to ignore one another's accomplishments while showering attention on annoyances: sloppi-

ness, helplessness, and verbal attacks. Attention, of course, may serve inadvertently to strengthen the behavior that it is supposed to discourage. Inattention—in this case, removing the reinforcer that is maintaining the behavior—is likely to extinguish the undesired responses.

It is important to note that during the extinction of operants, conditions usually get worse before improving. Initially, after reinforcers are removed, you are likely to see an increase in the rate of the response and in emotional behavior, as well, before the decline. Moreover, just as in respondent conditioning, operants that have been extinguished sometimes reappear again, or show *spontaneous recovery*, after a rest.

The following case study illustrates extinction and spontaneous recovery during operant conditioning.

Extinguishing Tantrum Behavior: A Case Study

A child, whom we call Robert, was seriously ill for the first eighteen months of life. While sick, the boy received more attention than average, and he became quite accustomed to such care. By the age of twenty-one months, Robert had become healthy. He had also become a household tyrant, guarding and defending numerous privileges and comforts. The boy's behavior was especially distressing at bedtime when Robert demanded undivided attention and cried and fussed if his adult companion (parent or aunt) left the room before he had fallen asleep. Because Robert fought sleep as long as he could, a family member usually spent one-half hour to two hours each bedtime sitting with him.

Psychologist Carl Williams helped the family work out a

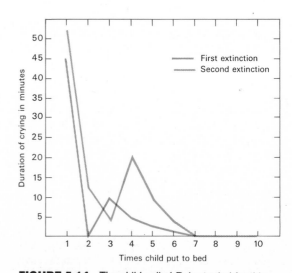

FIGURE 5-14 The child called Robert cried for this amount of time each evening during the course of an extinction program. Shortly after the undesirable crying extinguished, it recovered spontaneously. Consequently, the second set of extinction trials was required. [*Adapted from Williams, 1959.*]

plan to modify Robert's behavior. The parents and aunt were instructed to put the boy to bed cheerfully in a "leisurely and relaxed fashion." After the pleasantries, the adult was to leave the bedroom and close the door. Robert, outraged at this violation of protocol, would cry, scream, and fuss. But the adults were to exercise self-control and ignore him entirely.

As it turned out, the members of Robert's family were able to stick with the plan. It took over a week for Robert to stop crying at bedtime. By the tenth night, the boy had stopped whimpering, fussing, and crying when the adult left the room and was actually smiling.

Unfortunately, about one week after Robert's crying was extinguished, it recovered—apparently spontaneously. In any case, Robert screamed and fussed after the aunt tucked him in. In a weak moment, the woman gave in. She returned to the boy's side and stayed there until he fell asleep. After this incident, it took nine additional sessions of ignoring tantrum behavior to extinguish the response a second time. Figure 5-14 shows how the treatment progressed. Two years after this program a follow-up study indicated that Robert's behavior had changed in a lasting way. The child had staged no further temper tantrums at bedtime [16].

Generalization and Discrimination

Responses strengthened by operant procedures under one set of circumstances tend to spread or *generalize* to similar situations, just as in respondent conditioning. The more alike the setting, the more probable generalization is. If Yolinda praises Michael for being considerate, Michael will probably be thoughtful when he interacts with Lesley and Francesca. If Brigit feels successful after speaking out in one class, she'll probably try voicing her opinions in others.

Animals also form *discriminations*, as responses are reinforced in one situation and not in another. When Boris uses certain slang expressions, his friends act admiring while his parents become angry. Consequently, Boris uses slang with peers, but not adults. Emanuel appreciates Golda's wit but Roger does not, so Golda banters cleverly with certain boys but not with others.

Punishment

If you asked several friends to define punishment, they would probably say that it is a disagreeable disciplinary procedure such as spanking, isolating, or removing privileges. In contrast to common practice, many psychologists define *punishment* as occurring when, and only when, a specific operant is followed by a consequence that *reduces* its frequency in similar situations. The weakening consequence is also known as a *punishment* or *punisher*. Psychologists who accept this definition consider paddling, yelling, "grounding," and similar events as punishments only in those cases where they weaken the preceding behavior. (Although extinction fits our definition of punishment, it is not usually classified as punishment. We will contrast the two procedures a little later.) Just as we differentiated between positive and negative reinforcement, we also distinguish between positive and negative punishment.

Positive punishment *Positive punishment* occurs when the presentation of an event following an operant *decreases* the frequency of the operant in similar situations. The event that is presented is known as a *positive punishment* or *punisher*. As in reinforcement, the adjective "positive" refers to the *presentation* of the consequence. The noun "punishment" refers to the *reduction* in the probability that the behavior will occur. Positive punishment happens naturally much of the time. Horatio dashes out into the new snow without gloves and his hands become painfully cold. After this experience he rarely plays in snow without mittens or gloves. Dorothy reads while on her way to French class, bumps into a wall, and reads less frequently as she travels about the campus. Juan eats without control at a smorgasbord, upsets his stomach, and does not repeat the performance. Positive punishment is often deliberate, of course. Maria's mother slaps her hand every time she gets dirty, and Maria stops playing in the mud.

Negative punishment Negative punishment occurs when the *removal* or *postponement of a reinforcer* following an operant *reduces* the frequency of the behavior in similar situations. As in reinforcement, the adjective "negative" refers to the *removal* of the consequence. The noun "punishment" refers to the *weakening* of the response. Two types of negative punishment are in common use: response cost and omission training. Sometimes conduct is decreased in frequency because it results in the *loss of a reinforcer*, a procedure known as *response cost*. Fines may reduce the probability of parking violations. Docking money from an allowance may weaken a coming-home-late habit. Subtracting points from a grade for late papers may decrease the likelihood of "last-minute-term-paper-syndrome." The probability of a behavior's occurrence may also be decreased by *omission training, postponing a reinforcer* every time the act to be eliminated is initiated. The reinforcer is delivered only if the undesirable response fails to appear during a specific time. If the to-be-eliminated conduct occurs, then the time period begins again. Psychologist Ellen Reese reported this example:

One of our students got his roommate to stop smoking by giving him a dollar for every 24-hour period he went without a cigarette. . . . If the roommate smoked a cigarette at any time during the 24-hour period, even after 23 hours of abstinence, the opportunity to earn a dollar was postponed for a new 24-hour period. The program was so successful that the student's financial resources were depleted at the end of the month. Nonetheless, both roommates were happy at the outcome. In the six weeks following the program, the student reported that his roommate had lighted one cigarette, taken one "drag," and then snuffed the cigarette out. [17]

Table 5-2 contrasts the types of punishment that were described.

Negative punishment versus extinction During extinction and negative punishment, responses are weakened after reinforcers are withdrawn. Though some psychologists do classify extinction as a punishment, the two processes can be distinguished quite easily. Extinction may be said to occur when the specific reinforcer maintaining the response to be eliminated is taken away. Negative punishment occurs, in contrast, when any other reinforcer is removed. Furthermore, to qualify as having been extinguished, a response should diminish to its preconditioning rate. A negatively punished behavior need only decrease in frequency.

Varieties of punishers Like reinforcers, events which function as punishers vary from individual to individual. If the precise effects of an aversive procedure are not known, the consequence should be labeled a *potential punisher*.

TABLE 5-2 A Comparison of Punishment Procedures

	Punishment		
	Positive	**Negative**	
Consequence following behavior	Punisher presented	Reinforcer removed (response cost)	Reinforcer postponed (omission training)
Effect of consequence	Behavior weakened		
If training is stopped	Recovery of punished response (unless suppression has occurred)		

Punishers may be categorized into intrinsic and extrinsic classifications, just as reinforcers are. Some activities are *intrinsically punishing*, or *self-weakening*. Any behavior that necessitates pain or social or sensory isolation for extended time periods is unlikely to persist. Because of its pain-eliciting nature, head banging rarely becomes habitual. Yet youngsters with severe handicaps sometimes find the stimulation of head banging and the attention it attracts more "reinforcing" than the pain is "punishing." In these cases the response can occur at an alarming rate and actually endanger the child's life.

Extrinsic punishers are events which *follow* and *weaken* behavior. Some extrinsic punishers are classified as *primary* or *unlearned punishers* because their ability to weaken the responses that they follow appears to be inborn. Loud noises, pain, and sensory and social isolation can function as primary extrinsic punishers. Other punishers, like the removal of points or stars from a chart, are considered *secondary* or *conditioned* punishers because they have acquired their weakening value through respondent conditioning, that is, by being associated with other punishers. The withdrawal of points, for example, is typically paired with the removal of privileges. Finally, punishers such as ridicule, disapproval, or criticism, which depend on unpleasant human reactions, can be designated *social punishers*. Some are innately aversive, while others acquire their noxious properties. Acquired social punishers can be considered secondary punishers.

Similarities between punishment and reinforcement

Punishment and reinforcement share a number of similarities. Both are defined in terms of their effects on behavior. Both fit into the same positive-negative classification scheme. What about scheduling? Generalization and discrimination? And extinction? Punishment can be scheduled in precisely the same ways that reinforcement is. The response patterns associated with particular schedules of punishment are a lot more variable than those associated with reinforcement schedules. Similarly, just as generalization and discrimination occur when responses are strengthened by reinforcement, they occur when behaviors are weakened by punishment. Three-year-old Tony, for example, took off all his clothing at his friend's house. The behavior was followed by a severe scolding and was subsequently suppressed at friends' houses and in other public places, but not in his own bedroom and bathroom and other private settings. Finally, what happens when punishment is withdrawn? Responses recover if they have not been totally suppressed. In contrast, when reinforcers are withdrawn, behavior extinguishes.

The disadvantages of using potential punishers

Punishers which are presented in positive punishment and withdrawn in negative reinforcement can be powerful [18]. But many potential punishers have harmful side effects which must be carefully considered. We focus on children.

1. Potential physical punishers often get out of hand and damage the recipient. Every year in the United States alone, more than a million children are assaulted brutally by their parents and, in some cases, murdered. Most parents did not intend to hurt their youngsters but were "carried away" as they "punished" them. Potential social punishers, such as ridicule and sarcasm, may be very dangerous too. They may leave lasting psychological scars.

2. Because potential punishers are aversive, children usually try to escape or avoid them. In the process, they frequently learn socially inappropriate responses by negative reinforcement [19]. Fran Teller learned to leave her papers in school and lie about it to avoid humiliation. To escape a spanking, a child may learn to sneak away from the house at certain times or fake illness. Such responses may generalize and become frequent problem-solving maneuvers.

3. Potential physical punishers may elicit an aggressive counterattack. Research indicates that many animals respond to pain with reflex-like aggression [20]. Though children may inhibit themselves in the presence of the punishing agent, they may plan future revenge or attack targets who are physically weaker than they are. (We will have more to say about this and other aggression-related issues in Chapter 11.)

4. Those who use potential physical punishers inevitably model aggressive behavior. Children learn, then, through observation that hurting is an acceptable (and possibly effective) way to handle problems with people [21]. This may be part of the reason that adults who were battered in childhood often batter their own youngsters [22].

5. When potential physical punishers are used frequently, they can respondently condition feelings of hatred and fear to the agent (parent or teacher) and setting (home or school).

Using potential punishers effectively and humanely Psychologists are reluctant to advocate the use of punishers because of their potentially devastating side effects. Generally, behavioral scientists urge teachers of children (including parents) to try other ways of eliminating bad habits and establishing good ones. The training agent can often use some combination of the following to achieve the desired results: positive reinforcement of responses incompatible with the misbehavior, extinction, modeling of appropriate conduct, and instructions. When methods like these fail *after a fair trial* and the problem behaviors are *very frequent* and/or *intensely destructive*, potential punishers may be considered. The following guidelines for using potential punishers with children are based on research findings and are often recommended:

1. Create a warm and friendly relationship with the child, if there isn't one. Disciplinary procedures of all sorts are more effective when there is a strong positive bond between the youngster and adult [23].

2. Choose a mild or moderate potential punisher that will not harm the individual psychologically or physically. Aside from the ethical considerations, mild and moderate punishers are probably more effective for human children over the long run for several reasons. (*a*) They are far less likely to arouse anxiety and anger, which keep the child from utilizing information or prime her or him to strike back. (*b*) They do not demand that the

training agent model violent behavior. (*c*) They are less likely to motivate escape and avoidance stratagems. Finding an effective punisher will probably involve trial and error. The same potential punishers have diverse effects depending on the child's age and temperament, the problem, the relationship, and the context [24].

3. Be certain that you're in good control of yourself before administering the potential punisher [25].

4. Administer the potential punisher consistently for the same response whenever it occurs [26]. At the same time, remove all sources of reinforcement for the response to be eliminated (including attention from other children) insofar as is possible. Though the research literature on scheduling punishment in the laboratory is difficult to interpret (the effects of different schedules seem to depend on the animal and situation [27]), a continuous punishment schedule is more likely to be effective than an intermittent one. If behavior is punished only some of the time, it is also reinforced by its natural consequences some of the time. Partial reinforcement, you may recall, is known for making responses resistant to extinction.

5. Administer the potential punisher at the *onset* of the behavior to be weakened, rather than afterward [28]. This tactic means that anxiety and other unpleasant associations are respondently conditioned to beginning the act. Accordingly, the child is likely to feel uncomfortable as soon as the misdeed is initiated (and likely to stop at this point). Punishment at the onset also establishes the disciplinarian as a person who means business. The further removed the potential punisher is in time and space from the response that is to be eliminated, the less effective the consequence appears to be [29]. But even after delays of several hours, potential punishers may be somewhat effective, if children know *why* they are being disciplined [30].

6. Keep the potential punisher brief. Prolonged physical stimulation, particularly when it is mild, causes adaptation and loses its power [31]. The precise timing depends, of course, on the potential punisher and the child. Isolation for five to ten minutes or less may be more effective than longer stints, which are likelier to build antagonisms and motivate escape and avoidance attempts.

7. Teach the child an appropriate way of behaving that will satisfy the motive that aroused the unwanted response [32]. This alternative behavior may be positively reinforced. Simply punishing bad behavior is rarely an effective tactic because people return to bad habits when they have not established more appropriate ones.

8. Pair the potential punisher with a cue such as "No" or "Don't." Eventually, the cue itself may be conditioned to elicit unpleasant feelings in anticipation of what may follow. Once the association has been established, the cue can be used alone to stop the misbehavior and remind the child to select a more appropriate response.

Some of the guidelines for adminstering punishment are illustrated by the following case study.

Punishment: A Case Study

The escapades of three-year-old Mitch ranged from annoying to exasperating. Staging numerous temper tantrums, pulling clothing from closet and dresser, raiding the refrigerator and spreading the "spoils" on the floor, climbing the furniture, and riding a tricycle around the living room were among Mitch's milder misdeeds. Mitch was capable of far more sophisticated wreckage. He put small objects in the drain pipes; he wrote on the walls; he broke dishes; and he threw rocks and bricks.

Mitch's good moments, which were few and far between, frequently passed unnoticed. He played with his toys about ten minutes a day and picked them up afterward. When his hands were dirty, he washed them. The boy said "please" and "thank you" and helped his mother set the table. At 8 o'clock every night, Mitch went to bed promptly and slept soundly all night long. He was toilet-trained.

Mitch's parents had tried a number of different strategies to cope with their son's misbehavior. Ordinarily, indulgence prevailed. The motto seemed to be: "Appease Mitch at any cost." To minimize property destruction, furnishings likely to be broken were removed or tied down. Rooms were protected by roping the doors "locked." Mitch's parents felt helpless. When they said no, Mitch ordered them to "shut up." On rare occasions when Mitch was spanked, the mischief escalated. Mitch laughed and attempted a more destructive act than the one that had provoked the spanking.

Eventually Mitch's parents contacted Martha Bernal, a psychologist then at the Neuropsychiatric Institute of the University of California in Los Angeles. Bernal and her coworkers made extensive observations and then trained the parents to use these techniques:

1. Every time Mitch was destructive or aggressive, he was removed from the apparently reinforcing circumstances surrounding him (whatever they might be) and taken immediately to a neutral room devoid of interesting objects or people. He was left there by himself for five to ten minutes. After Mitch had served his "sentence," he was released. This potential punisher, called "time out from positive reinforcement" (usually abbreviated "time out"), did function as a punisher. Note that "time out" is a negative punishment that comes closest to fitting the category of "response cost."

2. Every time Mitch had temper tantrums, his parents were to act blind, dumb, and deaf—to extinguish them.

3. Every time Mitch behaved well, his parents were to be affectionate, approving, appreciative, and attentive—to reinforce these behaviors.

Treatment lasted about four months. During this time period Mitch improved greatly. One year later he was still cooperating most of the time. His temper tantrums had stopped almost completely. His destructiveness had decreased from a high of twenty-three incidents in one day to an average of two per day [33].

Conditioning and Complex Behavior

Complex behavior in real life is often at least partially the result of both respondent and operant conditioning. Our discussion of (1) conditioned reinforcers of operants and (2) punishment supported this idea. In some cases, complicated responses are learned bit by bit and then combined or *chained*, as behaviors are associated with one another and

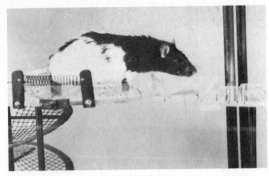

FIGURE 5-15 Barnabus, a trained rat, is shown running through an elaborate performance similar to the one described in the text. Having just climbed a spiral pathway, Barnabus steps on a spring-loaded drawbridge. This lowers the bridge, permitting the animal to cross over the chasm and proceed to the next challenge—climbing a ladder. Chaining procedures were used to teach this routine. [*David Nelson.*]

ascending a ladder to a landing, pulling a chain paw-over-paw to reel in an attached wagon, pedaling the wagon to the bottom of a staircase, climbing the stairs to a platform, squeezing through a glass tube, entering an elevator, pulling a chain to raise a banner as the elevator descended, and running to a lever and pressing it for food after a buzzer sounded [34]. (See Figure 5-15.) This long sequence of events was taught by the chaining procedure. Using food reinforcement, Barnabus was first trained to press a lever after a buzzer cue, the last response in the series. The second-to-last response, riding the elevator, was conditioned next. Barnabus had to learn to ride the elevator to reach the chamber with the bar and buzzer. Subsequently, the ride became a cue for the next response—waiting for the buzzer and bar pressing. These buzzer-awaiting and bar-pressing responses, because they had been associated with the food reinforcer, became conditioned reinforcers for riding. In a similar manner, each new response became a cue for the next one. And, each behavior in the sequence, because it was

with reinforcement. To illustrate chaining, we examine the elaborate routine of a "star" performer named Barnabus, a rat. Barnabus's act included climbing a spiral path after a flashing light appeared, crossing a moat,

▲ USING PSYCHOLOGY

1. Give examples from your own experience of shaping, extinction, spontaneous recovery, generalization, and discrimination during operant conditioning.

2. Plan a shaping strategy to teach social skills to a ten-year-old who rarely interacts with other children.

3. Think of extrinsic punishers that have weakened behaviors of your own. Categorize each as primary, social, or secondary. How was each punisher scheduled? Do you engage in any behaviors that are intrinsically punishing for you?

4. How might teachers use response cost and omission training with fifth-graders?

5. Many parents use potential punishers almost exclusively to modify children's conduct. Describe the disadvantages of this tactic. What practices besides potential punishers may lessen the incidence of tantrums? Teasing? Lying?

6. Explain psychologists' guidelines for using potential punishers to a good parent. Does the parent agree?

7. Give several examples of how operant and respondent conditioning have been combined in your own life.

8. Analyze one of your own social routines or mechanical skills in terms of chaining.

eventually associated with the food reinforcer, began to function as a conditioned reinforcer. Many psychologists believe that work routines, social rituals (for example, dating), and mechanical skills (such as starting a car) are learned step by step in a similar fashion. ▲

THE OPERANT CONDITIONING OF AUTONOMIC RESPONSES

In the early 1950s B. F. Skinner wrote:

We may reinforce a man with food whenever he "turns red," but we cannot in this way condition him to blush "voluntarily." The behavior of blushing, like that of blanching, or secreting tears, saliva, sweat, and so on cannot be brought directly under the control of operant reinforcement. [35]

Skinner appears to have been wrong. A great deal of animal research, beginning in the late 1950s, showed that operant conditioning can modify the responses of glands and internal organs (those controlled by the autonomic nervous system and, for that reason, designated *autonomic* responses) [36]. At about the same time, the claims of Indian yogis about slowing heart and respiration rates and changing skin temperature were verified by physiologists [37]. (*Yogis* are practitioners of Hindu meditation exercises designed to attain union with the Supreme Being or ultimate principle.) Apparently, at least some people could learn significant control of the autonomic nervous system. But were these cases of *direct* control? Or, were human beings and other animals simply making voluntary skeletal responses that altered the autonomic nervous system *indirectly*? You can control hand temperature, for example, by cupping your fingers together or spreading them apart, heart rate by holding your breath and straining downwards to build up pressure in the chest cavity, and the alpha brain rhythm (Chapter 7) by shutting your eyes.

In the late 1960s Neal Miller, a psychologist at Rockefeller University, and his coworkers published accounts of astonishing research on rats which demonstrated conclusively (or so it seemed at the time) that these quite lowly animals could learn to regulate autonomic processes *directly* when reinforced for doing so. Miller and his colleagues used the drug curare to paralyze rats so that they were unable to move their muscles (even to breathe without the help of a respirator). Then, every time the animal made a particular internal bodily response—say, slowed its heart—a powerful reinforcer, a jolt of electricity to the pleasure center in the rat's brain (Chapter 11), was delivered. Subsequently, paralyzed rats learned to control the beating of the heart, contractions of the stomach, the amount of blood in the stomach walls, blood pressure, urine formation within the kidneys, and similar responses [38]. Since later attempts to replicate these findings both in Miller's own laboratory and elsewhere have met with mixed results, it is not clear right now whether autonomic responses can be *directly* controlled by operant conditioning [39]. But careful animal work does show that nonparalyzed rats and monkeys can increase or decrease salivation, heart rate, and blood pressure in some way or another when these responses are systemically reinforced [40]. Note that these laboratory demonstrations blur the distinction between operants and respondents.

Miller's studies accelerated research designed to learn whether or not ordinary people could learn to control internal bodily reactions. The issue of whether control was direct or indirect was deemphasized, as behavioral scientists searched for methods to train people to control autonomic behavior, particularly responses associated with psychological and medical problems. The methods which gradually evolved are known as biofeedback.

Biofeedback

What is biofeedback? The term *feedback* was lucidly defined by the eminent mathematician Norbert Weiner as "a method of controlling a system by reinserting into it the results of its past performance [41]." *Biofeedback* teaches people to control bodily processes by providing systematic information (or *feedback*) about

FIGURE 5-16 Typical biofeedback training apparatus is shown here. Although the form of the equipment varies, certain elements must be present. Participants wear sensors that monitor the action of a specific bodily system; and they receive feedback about that system's performance (in this case, from a flashing light and fluctuating needle). [*John Briggs.*]

what a specific part is doing. This data may be considered a conditioned reinforcer. During biofeedback training, electrical or mechanical sensors respond to some type of physiological activity, such as tension in a particular muscle, surface temperature at a specific area on the skin, brain-wave activity, blood pressure, heart rate, or skin conductivity (essentially a measure of sweat gland output). The signals that are picked up are subsequently amplified, analyzed, and displayed, frequently in auditory or visual form, so that people can "hear" or "see" the physiological activity. See Figure 5-16. As individuals practice with the feedback-generating apparatus, they sometimes begin to notice subtle feelings that precede or accompany the physiological change that is being monitored. They may note the environmental events triggering the physical response too. Participants are typically encouraged to try out different strategies to change the reaction of interest. To increase skin temperature in the extremities, for example, people might picture putting their hands on a warm stove. Behavioral scientists hope that generalization will occur and that biofeedback participants will be able to alter the target autonomic responses in daily life situations without the machinery.

Work with coronary (heart disorder) vic-tims by psychologist Bernard Engel and his coworkers at Baltimore City Hospital is among the most carefully documented biofeedback success stories. By utilizing beat-by-beat information from the heart, patients with *premature ventricular contractions*, or PVCs (premature heart contractions that disrupt the normal beat), can learn to control the problem. During feedback training, people learn to turn PVCs on and off when signaled to do so. In one treatment program, five out of eight patients lowered PVC activity and four kept it relatively low throughout months (in some cases, years) of follow-up observations. The changes were verified by portable electrocardiographic tape recordings. This impressive work has been replicated by independent investigators [42].

Currently, biofeedback techniques are widely employed by psychologists and physicians to help people control many stress-related behavioral and medical problems, including insomnia, anxiety, tension headaches, migraines, chronic pain, epilepsy, obsessions, stuttering, paralyzed muscles, backaches, cerebral palsy, asthma, diabetes, alcoholism, sexual dysfunctions, elevated blood pressure, and heart irregularities [43]. While biofeedback practitioners are enthusiastic, and in some cases downright jubilant, researchers are cautious. Biofeedback research is still at an early experimental stage. It is frequently unclear how results were achieved or how lasting they were. It is possible, for instance, that simple relaxation or positive expectations may be responsible for the observed changes. And there are many dropouts and failures [44]. In short, numerous gaps in knowledge must be filled and a lot of problems solved before biofeedback can be recommended without reservation. Still, the early successes suggest that biofeedback shows a great deal of promise for the future.

CONTROVERSIAL ISSUES IN CONDITIONING

A number of controversies over respondent and operant conditioning are currently unsettled. We describe three of them.

One Type of Conditioning? Or Two?

While we have emphasized the differences between operant and respondent conditioning (summarized in Table 5-3), these fundamental activities share a great many commonalities that could have been stressed. Behaviors conditioned respondently and operantly are in both cases reinforced, extinguished, recovered spontaneously, generalized, and discriminated. The two types of conditioning appear so similar, in fact, that many American and almost all Russian psychologists believe that they may be variants of a single learning process. Some major distinctions between the two types of conditioning are being questioned because of recent research. As we just saw, autonomic responses can be operantly conditioned. Environmental cues paired repeatedly with operants become capable of "automatically eliciting" these voluntary responses [45]. Chaining, mentioned in the previous section, and actions such as stepping on a brake at a red light demonstrate that cues may provoke operants quite reliably in real life. Because of these and other similarities between operant and respondent conditioning and other types of learning, the *monism-pluralism* (one-many) *issue* continues to be widely debated.

What Is Learned during Conditioning?

What is actually learned when a response is conditioned? Some psychologists believe that an *association* between a stimulus and a response is stamped in. Respondents are generally linked with eliciting stimuli; operants, with a particular set of consequences. The association could be acquired because stimuli and responses follow one another closely in time, a position known as *contiguity theory*. Or, the organism's feelings of pleasure or satisfaction may be the key reason that some associations are formed and others are not. This latter viewpoint, endorsed by Thorndike and Skinner, is sometimes called the *law of effect*. A growing number of psychologists take a *cognitive perspective* [46]. They assume that animals formulate hypotheses or expectations about stimuli and responses. During operant conditioning, for instance, a rat might come to understand that bar pressing brings food; a person might learn that behaving graciously brings approval. Later, the animal may act on the information if (and only if) it is motivated—perhaps by deprivation, by an appealing incentive (the potential reinforcer), or by both. Respondent conditioning can be interpreted as a process that teaches organisms about relationships

TABLE 5-3 Some Major Differences between Respondent and Operant Conditioning

	Respondent conditioning	Operant conditioning
What happens before conditioning?	NS —does not lead to→ UR US —leads to→ UR	Frequency of behavior is fairly stable
What happens during conditioning?	NS ⋯is associated with⋯ US —leads to→ UR	Behavior ⋯is followed by⋯ consequences
What happens after conditioning?	(NS) CS —leads to→ CR	Consequences pleasant to learner strengthen behavior. Consequences noxious to learner weaken behavior.
How is the conditioned response perceived?	Involuntary and elicited from learner	Voluntary and initiated by learner
When does reinforcement occur?	Before conditioned response	After conditioned response

between events, helping them understand more about cause and effect in their environment [47].

How General Are the Laws of Learning?

Writing in the early 1970s, psychologist Martin Seligman of the University of Pennsylvania questioned the generality of the laws of learning in these words:

It [was] . . . hoped that in the simple controlled world of levers and mechanical feeders, of metronomes and salivation, something quite general would emerge. . . . [T]he very arbitrariness and unnaturalness of the [operant and respondent conditioning] experiment[s] was assumed to guarantee generality since the situation would be uncontaminated by past experience the organism might have had or by special biological propensities he might bring to it.

Seligman reminded psychologists that:

Any animal—including *homo sapiens*—brings to all situations certain equipment and predispositions more or less appropriate to that situation. It brings specialized sensory and receptor apparatus with a long evolutionary history which has modified it into its present appropriateness or inappropriateness [for that given situation]. . . . [T]he organism [also] brings associative apparatus, which likewise has a long and specialized evolutionary history. [48]

While Seligman was not the first psychologist to achieve this insight (Thorndike himself had been aware of it), these observations raised psychologists' consciousness of the issue. Today, it is widely acknowledged that built-in, species-specific limits on learning must be seriously considered. But, behavioral scientists do not agree about how important these inborn limits are. We look briefly at three areas of research which support the idea that conditioning is limited by species-specific characteristics.

First, consider animal-training efforts. Psychologists Keller and Marian Breland (former students of Skinner's) worked for Animal Behavior Enterprises in Hot Springs, Arkansas. There they trained more than 6,000 individual animals for zoos, museums, depart-

ment store displays, fair exhibits, and the like. In the course of working with some thirty-eight different animal species, the Brelands experienced a number of failures that followed a definite pattern. Chickens being trained to stand on a platform would not stop scratching and had to be billed as "dancing." Raccoons who were learning to deposit money into a piggybank, rubbed the coins together persistently as misers might. Pigs, taught a similar response, exhibited a slightly different problem. Instead of depositing large wooden "coins" cleanly and clearly into a bank, they dropped, rooted, and tossed the discs again and again. Despite near heroic efforts to weaken these patterns, the pigs' dropping-rooting-tossing behavior, like the hens' scratching and the raccoons' rubbing, persisted. All the animals had been food-deprived so that they could be more easily trained. Now they were drifting to natural food-procuring and food-preparing responses, a notion called *instinctive drift*. The Brelands concluded that while operant conditioning often works, animals are not blank slates with insignificant species differences [49].

Research on human fears also suggests that animals are predisposed, or *prepared*, by their evolutionary history (and consequently their inheritance) to learn particular reactions to specific stimuli. Seligman calls this idea *preparedness*. Respondents cannot be conditioned to just any neutral event. Only in science fiction, such as Huxley's *Brave New World*, can infants be conditioned respondently to fear objects like books and flowers. If Watson had paired noises with cloth curtains or blocks of wood, a later study suggests, Albert would not have acquired fears of wood or curtains [50]. Under carefully controlled conditions in the laboratory, people are more likely to acquire lasting fears of snakes than of houses or faces [51]. Like human beings, simpler animals such as rats learn certain fears easily and others with difficulty [52]. Seligman and others speculate that some fears—fears of snakes and heights, for example—helped people survive. Over the course of hundreds of thousands of years, presumably, those genetic variations which make it easier for people to acquire such fears have been built into the human race. Individuals who formed adaptive fears lived longer and reproduced more offspring with similarly healthy propensities than individuals who lacked such fears.

Finally, we consider research by psychologist John Garcia and other investigators on *food aversion conditioning* in rats and other animals. Rats rely on taste and smell, but not on sight, as they sample substances for their meals. For this reason they need to be able to associate the gustatory (taste) and olfactory (smell) correlates of eating with the aftereffects of food. The animals form such associations readily [53]. Should an unfamiliar food be followed by an illness, the rat will form an aversion to the flavor and smell (but not the appearance) of the substance preceding the sickness. The creature may form the association after only one encounter with a food, even when queasiness begins several hours after the meal. Similarly, when substances have beneficial consequences—say, correcting a dietary deficiency—rats come to prefer foods with similar smells and tastes [54]. Quails, guinea pigs, and monkeys that depend on vision as they feed easily associate the consequences of food ingestion with the sight, as well as the smell and taste, of substances [55]. Overall, this research suggests that specific associative mechanisms are "wired into" the brain to equip animals for survival.

Diverse lines of research conclude, then, that learning principles hold within limits. To be ultimately useful, knowledge of conditioning must be blended with an understanding of species-specific behavior (and other characteristics of the organism).

OBSERVATION LEARNING

When an animal's behavior changes in a relatively permanent way as a result of observing another animal's actions, psychologists label the phenomenon *observation learning*, *social learning*, *modeling*, or *imitation*. Both simple and complex organisms learn through observation. The process has been observed in human neonates and is thought to be inborn [56]. (See Figure 3-7.) Albert Bandura, a Stanford University behavioral scientist who has done a great deal of research on this basic process, believes that anything that can be learned directly can be learned *vicariously* by observing others. Observation learning "abbreviates" learning. "If one had to rely solely on one's actions to learn," Bandura has said, "most of us would never survive the learning process [57]." When we use the term *observation learning*, we are not limiting the effect to precise mimicry. In many cases people derive general rules and principles of behavior which permit them to go beyond what they see and hear [58]. Though the Teller children in our introduction may not use the precise expressions of their parents, for example, they are learning interaction styles and grievance-solving strategies. By observing one another, people acquire a vast number of responses, including vocabulary words, styles of talking, physical routines, social etiquette, and role behavior as women and men, workers, marriage partners, and parents. In this section we describe how people learn by observation and who imitates whom. In subsequent chapters we will examine how observation learning contributes to many specific types of behavior.

How People Learn by Observation

How do people learn by observation? The following processes appear to be involved:

1. *Acquisition.* The learner observes a model behaving in a particular way and recognizes the distinctive features of the model's conduct.
2. *Retention.* The model's responses are actively stored in the learner's memory.
3. *Performance.* When the model's behavior is accepted as appropriate for the learner and likely to lead to positive consequences, it is apt to be reproduced.
4. *Consequences.* The learner's behavior meets with consequences which increase or decrease its frequency. In other words, operant conditioning occurs [59].

Observation learning is far more complicated than operant or respondent conditioning. Note that it always involves cognitive activities and frequently considerable time delays as well. Like operant and respondent conditioning, observation learning may be used deliberately in behavior modification. (See Figure 5-17.)

Who Imitates Whom

In 1962 the *Washington Post* reported the case of an eleven-year-old boy who joined a pack of dogs, ran on all fours, and barked with his canine companions each night [60]. When someone mimics the family dog, it's newsworthy because people tend to be much more selective in choosing models. Through experimental studies, psychologists have identified some characteristics that models frequently possess. People who seem successful, glamorous, or high in status are more likely to be imitated than others. Relatively powerful human beings, including parents who often control such important resources as TV, candy, bedtime, and toys, make appealing models. So do individuals with whom we identify, those of the same sex and of similar

FIGURE 5-17 Observation learning principles are sometimes used deliberately to modify maladaptive behavior patterns, such as severe withdrawal in children. In one such project, psychologist Robert O'Connor attempted to teach appropriate social responses to a group of severely withdrawn preschool youngsters. Six shy children (a control group) watched a movie on dolphins. Another six (the experimental group) viewed a film that showed a withdrawn child, a potential model, overcome shyness in eleven different situations. In each scene, the timid film "model" observed other children engaging in some activity and after receiving oncouragement, gradually began participating. From vignette to vignette, the play became more vigorous and the number of people involved increased. After the film session, the children in the experimental group began to interact more frequently and appropriately with other youngsters, while the children in the control group remained withdrawn [68]. [*Sybil Shelton/Monkmeyer Press Photo Service.*]

▲ USING PSYCHOLOGY

1. Why should people be cautious about accepting the merit and utility of biofeedback?

2. Take a stand on the controversies that were described. Do you think that operant and respondent conditioning are different types of learning? What do you believe is learned during conditioning? What limits conditioning? Cite evidence to support your positions.

3. Give several personal examples of observation learning.

4. Considering what social scientists know about who imitates whom, speculate about the possible effects of violent TV models on children. How could this issue be studied? (See Chapter 11 or reference 7 in this chapter's Suggested Readings for information about how psychologists tackle this issue.)

age, socioeconomic background, temperament, education, and values.

Responsivity to a particular model's power is influenced by the learner's emotional state and life-style. *Moderate* emotional arousal, be it fear, anger, or joy, seems to heighten susceptibility to observation learning (and other types of learning). And, people are more prone to imitate behaviors which fit their own life-styles [61]. ▲

SUMMARY
Fundamental Learning Processes

1. During learning there are more or less permanent changes in behavior that can be attributed to experience.

2. A respondent is conditioned by repeatedly associating neutral and unconditioned stimuli during acquisition training.

3. An operant is conditioned when consequences increase or decrease the frequency of the operant in similar situations.

4. Conditioned respondent and operant behaviors show extinction, spontaneous recovery, generalization, and discrimination.

5. During counterconditioning, conditioned respondents are replaced by incompatible respondents.

6. Both positive and negative reinforcements increase the frequency of operant behavior in similar situations. Both positive and negative punishments decrease the frequency of operant behavior in similar situations. Shaping can be used to establish new operants.

7. Intrinsic and extrinsic reinforcers and punishers of operant behavior vary from individual to individual. Reinforcers and punishers may be delivered on continuous or partial schedules.

8. Potential punishers have harmful consequences, so they should be used with extreme care.

9. Complex behavior often results from a combination of operant and respondent conditioning. Chaining establishes complicated sequences of responses.

10. Autonomic behavior may be operantly conditioned. Biofeedback holds promise for helping people gain control over physical and emotional problems.

11. Controversial conditioning issues include these: Are operant and respondent conditioning two aspects of a single process? What precisely is learned during conditioning? To what extent are species-specific characteristics of animals important considerations in applying conditioning principles?

12. Observation learning occurs as people watch one another. It is a complex process involving cognitive activity (evaluation and memory), long time delays, and operant conditioning. People are especially likely to imitate successful, powerful models with whom they identify—particularly if the response fits their life-style. Moderate emotional arousal makes learning more likely.

13. Behavior modification procedures are based on respondent and operant conditioning, observation learning, and other laboratory-based psychological strategies.

A Study Guide for Chapter Five

Key terms learning (130), fixed action pattern (131), respondent (133), respondent (classical, pavlovian) conditioning (133), operant (141), operant (instrumental) conditioning (141), reinforcement (136, 144), extinction (138, 152), spontaneous recovery (139, 152), generalization (140, 153), discrimination (140, 153), positive reinforcement (144), negative reinforcement (146), positive punishment (153), negative punishment (154) [response cost (154), omission training (154)], observation (social) learning (modeling, imitation) (163), and other italicized words and expressions.

Important research tick behavior, human "fixed action patterns" (Eibl-Eibesfeldt), characteristics of respondent conditioning (Pavlov, others), respondent conditioning of fear (Watson, Rayner, Jones), trial-and-error learning in puzzle boxes (Thorndike), negative attitudes to behavior modification (Woolfolk, others), characteristics of operant conditioning (Skinner, Ferster, others), modifying operant behavior (Salzinger, Williams, Reese, Bernal), conditioning autonomic responses operantly (Miller, Engel, others), observations supporting species—specific limits on conditioning (the Brelands, Seligman, Garcia, others), stages during observation learning, conditions favoring observation learning.

Basic concepts reasons why performance is an inadequate measure of learning, vicarious respondent conditioning, differences between negative punishment and extinction, similarities and differences between operant and respondent conditioning, similarities and differences between punishment and reinforcement, disadvantages of potential punishers, guidelines for using potential punishers, questions about the effectiveness of biofeedback, monism-pluralism issue, contiguity theory, law of effect, association learning versus hypothesis/expectation formation during conditioning, instinctive drift (the Brelands), preparedness (Seligman), what is learned by observation (Bandura).

People to identify Pavlov, Watson, Thorndike, Skinner, Miller, Bandura.

Self-Quiz

1. Which phenomenon is defined as being necessary for learning?
a. Attention
b. Conditioning
c. Experience
d. Teaching

2. Which attribute characterizes a fixed action pattern?
a. Difficult to modify
b. Dissimilar whenever executed
c. Largely learned

d. Universally present in the same form in many species

3. Whenever Victor misbehaves, his mother beats him with a belt. The boy has come to fear the sight of the belt. What is the conditioned stimulus?
a. Beating
b. Belt
c. Fear
d. Mother

4. When is the neutral stimulus usually presented during acquisition training in the laboratory?
a. About 60 seconds before unconditioned stimulus
b. About 30 seconds before unconditioned stimulus
c. Less than 5 seconds before or at the same time as unconditioned stimulus
d. About 5 to 10 seconds following unconditioned stimulus

5. Which man is credited with the discovery of respondent conditioning?
a. Pavlov
b. Skinner
c. Thorndike
d. Watson

6. What did the spreading of little Albert's fear to a rabbit and the experimenter's hair illustrate?
a. Acquisition
b. Discrimination
c. Generalization
d. Spontaneous recovery

7. By pairing liquor with illness-producing drugs, positive feelings toward alcohol may be replaced by negative ones in some alcoholics. What role do the drugs play in the counterconditioning process?
a. Conditioned stimulus
b. Neutral stimulus
c. Unconditioned response
d. Unconditioned stimulus

8. Which response is most likely to be learned by operant conditioning?
a. Fearing bees
b. Feeling relaxed while taking tests
c. Liking the color yellow
d. Playing the violin

9. What was the procedure that equipped cats with the skills to escape from puzzle boxes, according to Thorndike?
a. Method of successive approximations
b. Observation learning
c. Positive reinforcement
d. Trial-and-error learning

10. At the grocery, four-year-old Adrian repeatedly screamed, "I want candy!" until his father bought the candy. Whenever Adrian yells, the father acquiesces, and the boy gets his way. What procedure established the father's habit of giving in?
a. Avoidance conditioning
b. Escape conditioning
c. Extinction
d. Response cost

11. Christina gave her daughter Janice a gold star to paste on a chart every time the child put on one article of clothing by herself. Janice soon learned to dress herself. What type of reinforcer did Christina use?

a. Intrinsic   *b.* Primary
c. Secondary   *d.* Social

12. To improve a man's cooking, his family decides to praise the first good meal he cooks each week. What schedule is being used?

a. Fixed-interval   *b.* Fixed-ratio
c. Variable-interval   *d.* Variable-ratio

13. Which of the following guidelines was recommended for punishing a child?

a. Accompany the potential punisher with a cue such as "no."
b. Administer the potential punisher immediately after the response to be eliminated.
c. Make certain that the duration of the potential punisher is fairly long.
d. Use partial punishment. (In other words, use the potential punisher only some times.)

14. What did Miller's operant conditioning work on rats paralyzed by curare appear to demonstrate?

a. Autonomic responses could be operantly conditioned *indirectly*.
b. Autonomic responses *of simple animals* could be operantly conditioned.
c. Autonomic responses could be operantly conditioned *without the subject's awareness*.
d. Autonomic responses could be controlled *directly* by operant conditioning.

15. Which is the last step in observation learning?

a. Acquisition   *b.* Consequences
c. Performance   *d.* Retention

Exercises

1. DISTINGUISHING BETWEEN THE BASIC TYPES OF LEARNING. Students sometimes have difficulty seeing differences between the fundamental learning processes—particularly, between operant and respondent conditioning. If you have this problem, review Table 5-3. Then check your knowledge by identifying the way(s) the italicized response in each of the following examples was learned. Remember that the learning processes frequently occur together. To review, reread pages 133 and 134, 141 and 142, 163 and 164.

LEARNING PROCESSES: observation learning (Ob), operant conditioning (Op), respondent conditioning (R)

_____ *1.* Joy scolds her daughter Nellie, saying, "That's enough! In fact, it's too much!" When Ephraim makes Nellie angry, she reproaches him, *"That's enough! In fact, it's too much!"*

_____ *2.* A dog *runs into the kitchen salivating* every time it hears the sound of a can opener.

_____ *3.* Edgar *feels anxious* every time he sees the horse that threw him.

_____ *4.* Church music evokes a feeling of peace and joy in Susan. Every time she enters the church, she *feels serene and contented*.

_____ *5.* On registration day, Sasha sees a large crowd walking toward a building. He *walks* toward the building too.

_____ *6.* Nine-month-old Margaret says, "Ma." Her parents get very excited. The baby *says "ma"* more and more frequently.

_____ *7.* When Mr. Heinz writes on the board, the chalk squeaks. Every time Pedro sees the teacher pick up the chalk, he *feels uneasy*.

_____ *8.* Angelina studies her spelling list for half an hour. On the spelling test she receives 100. After that, Angelina *reviews half an hour before every spelling test*.

_____ *9.* Young Pam watches "Superman" on TV for the first time. Several days later, Pam's parents discover that she has picked up a new habit—leaping off porch railings.

_____ *10.* Frank, who gets very angry whenever anyone yells, *feels a surge of hostility* every time he sees his mother-in-law, who frequently screams at him.

_____ *11.* Cleo becomes nauseated after drinking five whiskey sours. After this experience, she *feels slightly queasy* whenever she sees a whiskey sour. She even *avoids* the grocery aisle that contains whiskey-sour mix.

_____ *12.* Chip *types the correct letters* automatically, even when he is not concentrating on his typing.

2. ELEMENTS OF RESPONDENT CONDITIONING. To test your understanding of the four basic elements of respondent conditioning, label the unconditioned stimulus (US), the unconditioned response (UR), the conditioned (formerly neutral) stimulus (CS), and the conditioned response (CR) in examples 2, 3, 4, 7, 10, and 11 of Exercise 1. To review, reread pages 133 and 134.

3. PRINCIPLES OF RESPONDENT CONDITIONING. To practice distinguishing the various principles of respondent conditioning, match the following principles with the appropriate examples. A single illustration may be explained by two principles. To review, see pages 136 to 141.

PRINCIPLES: acquisition (A), counterconditioning (C), discrimination (D), extinction (E), generalization (G), spontaneous recovery (SR)

The Tale of Jeff and the Poodles

_____ 1. Every time three-year-old Jeff walks by the Greenfields' house, two miniature poodles bark loudly. The noise frightens the boy, and Jeff becomes afraid of the poodles.

_____ 2. Jeff begins to fear most small dogs.

_____ 3. Jeff is not afraid of a large collie that belongs to his aunt.

_____ 4. For Christmas Jeff receives a miniature poodle puppy. The animal is friendly and affectionate. Soon Jeff begins to like miniature poodles.

The Saga of Sarah and Roy

_____ 5. Sarah and Roy spend a lot of time cuddling and kissing. Each feels a burst of spontaneous joy upon seeing the other.

_____ 6. During a summer separation, their ardor cools. In the fall Sarah and Roy break up. When they see one another occasionally, they do not experience the same sudden happy feeling.

_____ 7. Two years after their romance ended, Sarah and Roy meet unexpectedly on a bus. Both experience an instantaneous surge of happiness.

4. PRINCIPLES OF OPERANT CONDITIONING. You can check your understanding of the principles of operant conditioning by matching the following principles with the appropriate examples. A single illustration may be explained by two principles. To decide how to label an example, ask yourself the following questions: Is the operant behavior, identified by italics, being increased or decreased? Was the consequence presented or removed? If the consequence was removed, did it result in the *withdrawal* of a punisher or reinforcer? Or, did the removal of the consequence *postpone* or *avoid* a punisher or reinforcer? Tables 5-1 and 5-2 should be helpful for this classification exercise. To review more extensively, reread pages 144 to 154.

PRINCIPLES: avoidance conditioning (AC), escape conditioning (EC), extinction (E), omission training (OT), positive punishment (PP), positive reinforcement (PR), response cost (RC), shaping (S)

_____ 1. Every time Philip complains, his brother Joseph leaves the room, depriving Philip of companionship. Philip's *complaining to Joseph* decreases.

_____ 2. When Alberta's father lectures her, she agrees with whatever is said to shut him up. *Agreeing when lectured* has become habitual.

_____ 3. Ovid knows by the look on his mother's face that she is angry and likely to strike out. Whenever he sees that expression, he *goes to a neighbor's home*.

_____ 4. A third-grader named Helga is learning to do homework. She is praised for small amounts of studying regardless of its quality. The requirements for praise become stiffer until Helga is complimented only for *doing an hour of good work*.

_____ 5. Ronald used to attend to Gabriella whenever she pouted. Gabriella began pouting a great deal. Ronald decided to ignore the *pouting*, and it has almost disappeared.

_____ 6. Each time Eve introduces a serious topic of conversation, Peter is sarcastic. Eve rarely *brings up important issues* any more.

_____ 7. To avoid having points docked from her grade, Audrey *refrains from talking to her friend* Ollie for three hours in the morning and three hours in the afternoon. (Ollie and Audrey talk only at noon and after school.)

_____ 8. Each time Remington whines, he gets his way. Remington *whines* a great deal.

_____ 9. Lana confesses that she stole a quarter from George. Her parents lecture her and deprive her of TV for a week. Her *confessions* decrease.

_____ 10. Joseph tells his parents that he failed an important test. They are understanding. Joseph's *confidences to his parents* increase.

_____ 11. Milo is learning to tie his shoelaces. His mother calls him a "clumsy idiot." Milo stops *trying to tie his shoelaces*.

_____ 12. Gina has to refrain from bullying her brother Scott for a week or else her allowance will be removed. This procedure, which is continued for half a year, markedly decreases Gina's *bullying of Scott*.

_____ 13. Gerald hugs Joanne whenever she praises him. Joanne *praises Gerald* increasingly often.

_____ 14. Two-year-old Lilly quiets down—temporarily—whenever her brother Hubert yells. Hubert's *yelling at Lilly* (when she is noisy) has become habitual.

_____ 15. People attend to Julie when she is *mischievous*. Julie progresses from small, relatively harmless deeds to more destructive ones.

_____ 16. Hannah used to listen to her son Gideon talk when he came home from school. Now that

Hannah is busy with her own schoolwork, she rarely pays attention to her son. Gideon has stopped *sharing his feelings with his mother*.

Suggested Readings

1. Reese, E. P., with Howard, J., & Reese, T. W. *Human behavior: Analysis and application.* (2d ed.) Dubuque, Iowa: Brown, 1978. An excellent introduction to operant and respondent conditioning principles. The book is informally written and generously illustrated by vivid human examples.

2. Watson, D. L., & Tharp, R. G. *Self-directed behavior: Self-modification for personal adjustment.* (2d ed.) Monterey, Calif.: Brooks/Cole, 1977. Among the best how-to-do-it books for people who want to use learning principles to modify their own behavior.

3. Patterson, G. R. *Families: Applications of social learning to family life.* (2d ed.) Champaign, Ill.: Research Press, 1975; Macht, J. *Teaching our children.* New York: Wiley, 1975. These paperbacks were written to show parents how to apply behavior modification principles to routine child management issues and family problems. Both are easy to understand, fun to read, and involving. A good supplement to these is Smith, J. M., & Smith, D. E. P. *Child management: A program for parents and teachers.* (Rev. ed.) Champaign, Ill.: Research Press, 1976. The Smiths emphasize parents' roles as models and rule-makers.

4. Skinner, B. F. *Walden II.* New York: Macmillan, 1976 (reissued paperback). Skinner's controversial and provocative novel about a utopian community which shapes its residents' behavior through operant conditioning principles, especially positive reinforcement.

5. Walters, G. C., & Grusec, J. E. *Punishment.* San Francisco: Freeman, 1977 (paperback). Walters and Grusec summarize the psychological research on punishment fairly, including both the rat and child literature.

6. Jonas, G. *Visceral learning: Toward a science of self-control.* New York: Viking, 1972 (paperback). Written by a journalist, this brief book provides an exciting introduction to the operant conditioning of the autonomic nervous system. The case of a stroke victim in biofeedback training is interwoven with an account of Neal Miller's early research and its possible applications.

7. Liebert, R. M., Neale, J. M., & Davidson, E. S. *The early window: Effects of television on children and youth.* New York: Pergamon, 1973 (paperback). TV influences prosocial and antisocial behavior. These psychologists discuss social learning theory and research findings on this important topic.

8. Gustavson, C. R., & Garcia, J. Aversive conditioning: Pulling a gag on the wily coyote. *Psychology Today*, 1974, **8**(3), 68–72. In this article Gustavson and Garcia describe an interesting application of respondent conditioning: controlling the killing habits of coyotes.

9. Gray, F., Graubard, P. S., & Rosenberg, H. Little brother is changing you. *Psychology Today*, 1974, **7**(10), 42–46. This thought-provoking article describes an unusual program in which children were taught to use learning principles deliberately to modify the behavior of teachers, parents, and friends.

Answer Keys

Self-Quiz

1. *c* (130)   **2.** *a* (131)   **3.** *b* (134)   **4.** *c* (136)
5. *a* (135)   **6.** *c* (140)   **7.** *d* (141)   **8.** *d* (141)
9. *d* (143)   **10.** *b* (146)   **11.** *c* (147)   **12.** *a* (149)
13. *a* (156)   **14.** *d* (159)   **15.** *b* (163)

Exercise 1

1. Ob   **2.** R, Op   **3.** R   **4.** R   **5.** Ob   **6.** Op
7. R   **8.** Op   **9.** Ob   **10.** R   **11.** R, Op
12. Op

Exercise 2

2. US, food in mouth; UR, salivation; CS, sound of can opener; CR, salivation
3. US, being thrown; UR, pain, anxiety; CS, sight of horse; CR, anxiety
4. US, music; UR, feelings of peace and joy; CS, church; CR, serene, contented feelings
7. US, squeaking chalk; UR, discomfort; CS, sight of teacher picking up chalk; CR, uneasiness
10. US, yelling; UR, anger; CS, mother-in-law; CR, hostility
11. US, excessive alcohol intake; UR, nausea; CS, sight of whiskey sour; CR, queasiness

Exercise 3

1. A   **2.** G   **3.** D   **4.** C (or E)   **5.** A
6. E   **7.** SR

Exercise 4

1. RC   **2.** EC   **3.** AC   **4.** PR, S   **5.** PR, E
6. PP   **7.** OT   **8.** PR   **9.** PP, RC   **10.** PR
11. PP   **12.** OT   **13.** PR   **14.** EC
15. PR, S   **16.** PR, E

CHAPTER SIX
Perceiving

All creatures live to some degree in a unique world. Members of diverse species occupying the same environment may live in dramatically different realities. Consider the case of a fish and a snail in an aquarium. The snail with its poor visual *acuity* (ability to distinguish details) will be unaware of a hand waved in front of the tank, while the fish will probably see each finger [1]. The eye of the falcon surpasses the human eye in its ability to see at a distance by roughly two and a half times [2]. Flying 60 feet above the ground, the falcon easily spots an insect meal. Though the world is usually a blur to most dogs, they are able to use their noses to locate people buried in an avalanche and to detect gas leaks and drugs of various types. If all creatures were similarly responsive to the same stimuli, we might all be competing for the same food supplies and shelters. Our differing sensitivities allow us to share the same physical environment peacefully.

Even members of a single species differ in their perceptions. People vary somewhat in terms of how they see color and discriminate pitch and in what they smell and taste [3]. During pregnancy and in old age, sensitivities change slightly as the body is altered [4]. Experiences, expectations, motives, and emotions influence what is perceived, too. In sum, perception is a more individualistic process than is ordinarily assumed. In this chapter we focus on perception, especially on vision. We begin with psychologist R. L. Gregory's case history of a blind man whose vision was restored by surgery.

Perceiving the World after Blindness: The Case of S. B.

"[A] man of fifty-two, whom we may call S. B., was, when blind, an active and intelligent man. He would go for cycle rides, with a friend holding his shoulder to guide him; he would often dispense with the usual white stick, sometimes walking into parked cars or vans and hurting himself as a result. He liked making things, with simple tools in a shed in his garden. All his life he tried to picture the world of sight. . . ."

After fifty-one years of being blind, S. B.'s vision was restored through surgery. "When the bandages were first removed from [S. B.'s] eyes, so that he was no longer blind, he heard the voice of the surgeon. He turned to the voice, and saw nothing but a blur. He realised that this must be a face, because of the voice, but he could not see it. He did not suddenly see the world of objects as we do when we open our eyes.

"But within a few days [S. B.] could use his eyes to good effect. He could walk along the hospital corridors without recourse to touch; he could even tell the time from a large wall clock, having all his life carried a pocket watch having no glass, so that he could feel the time from its hands. He would get up at dawn, and watch from his window the cars and trucks pass by. He was delighted with his progress, which was extremely rapid. . . .

"We tried to discover what [S. B.'s] visual world was like by asking him questions and giving him various simple perceptual tests. While still in the hospital, before he became depressed, he was most careful with his judgments and his answers. We found that his perception of distance was peculiar. . . . He thought he would just be able to touch the ground below his window with his feet if he lowered himself by his hands, but in fact the distance down was at least ten times his height. On the other hand, he could judge distances and sizes quite accurately provided he already knew the objects by touch. . . .

"S. B. never learned to read by sight (he read Braille, having been taught it at the blind school) but we found that he could recognize block capital letters, and numbers, by sight without any special training. This surprised us greatly. It turned out that he had been taught upper case, though not lower case, letters at the blind school. . . . Now this finding that he could immediately read letters visually which he had already learned by touch showed very clearly that he was able to use his previous touch experience for his newfound vision."

S. B. did not develop trust in his vision. For the first time in his life, he was terrified, for example, of crossing the street. Gradually, the man became severely depressed. "[He] found the world drab and was upset by flaking paint and blemishes on things. He liked bright colours, but [was saddened] when the light faded. . . . Depression in people recovering sight after many years of blindness seems to be a common feature of the cases. Its cause is probably complex, but in part it seems to be a realization of what they have missed—not only visual experience, but opportunities to do things denied them during the years of blindness. . . . S. B. would often not trouble to turn on the lights in the evening, but would sit in darkness. . . . He gradually gave up active living, and three years later he died [5]."

S. B.'s case raises a number of important issues. When adults view their environments for the first time after a long period of blindness, they don't see as ordinary people do. A cat, for instance, might be described as "something gray, white, and small." Although characteristics like color, shape, and size are recognized, whole objects are not. These observations highlight some critical distinctions between sensation and perception. Our senses may be considered our windows on the world. They bring in information. But we don't simply read off the messages as they are delivered. In the case of vision, for example, we are not aware of the fact that our eyes register impressions upside down and inverted from right to left and that these images change continuously as our eyes move. Nor are we conscious of another curious fact. The brain receives two slightly different pictures—one from each eye. The inputs from our senses are elaborately transformed so that we perceive a meaningful and orderly world. *Perception* is defined as the process of organizing and interpreting incoming sensory data *(sensations)* to develop an awareness of surroundings and self. Perception involves interpretation; sensation does not. In cases such as S. B.'s, sensory capabilities appear to be functional, while perceptual ones are relatively undeveloped.

Do these observations demonstrate that perceptual abilities are learned? No, not necessarily. There are many possible reasons for faulty perception in newly seeing people who have been blind, including damage to the eyes during surgery and degeneration of physical structures due to disuse. Still, as we will see later, certain experiences are vital for normal perceptual development. In this chapter we explore several topics that are suggested by S. B.'s case: What abilities are required for perception? What physiological processes underlie perception? How is perception organized? How adaptable is it? How does it develop? What factors influence perception?

THE NATURE OF PERCEPTION

Perception is an active, complicated operation. In this section we examine its nature more closely. We will see that perception does not mirror reality precisely. We will describe abilities required for perception, focusing especially on the role of attention.

Perception Is No Mirror of Reality

People sometimes assume that perception provides a perfectly accurate reflection of reality. Perception is no mirror. First, our human senses do not respond to many aspects of our surroundings. We cannot hear the high-pitched sounds that bats register or smell the odorous sweat substances that ooze through the soles of shoes and boots, although dogs can. We do not react to magnetic or electrical forces, as certain insects, fish, and birds do [6]. And we are unable to see individual molecules or x-rays. Second, people sometimes perceive stimuli which are not present. Direct electrical stimulation of the brain (Chapter 4) can cause a person to "see" visions or "hear" voices. So can illness, fatigue, monotony, and drugs. Moreover, the physical structure of the brain and sensory systems enables people to convert a rapid series of still photographs into a moving image (a motion picture) and causes them to be aware of faint spots (afterimages) after staring at a bright light. Third, human perceptions depend on expectations, motives, and past experiences, as we mentioned before. The effects of expectations can be demonstrated quite easily. Inspect Figure 6-1 for a moment. What is the middle character in Figure 6-1a? In 6-1b? Your interpretation depends, of course, on whether you read vertically or horizontally. So expectations created by context influence what you see. Next, describe the trees in Figure 6-2. If you see leaves, you are relying on past experiences to interpret the data. There are no leaves on the trees. The branches contain masses of blackbirds, grackles, and starlings. Observations of split-brain patients, described in Chapter 4 (Levy's composite faces experiment, in particular), underscore the creative nature of perception.

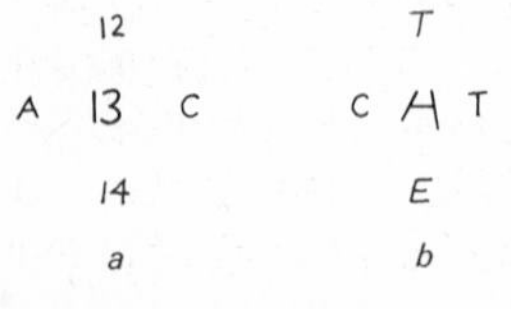

Perception: A Multifaceted Cognitive Capacity

Perception involves numerous cognitive activities. Early in the perceptual process people decide what to *attend* to. As you "read" a textbook, for instance, you might run your eyes over black symbols without meaning, focus on individual letters, or pick up meaningful ideas. While sitting in a classroom, you can concentrate on the noise from a road-blasting operation in the distance, the whis-

FIGURE 6-1 What is the middle character in (a)? In (b)?

	12			T	
A	13	C	C	H	T
	14			E	
	a			b	

pering of students in the back row, your aching feet, or the message of the lecture. Whenever you pay attention, you are more likely to find meaning in the information that you've picked up, associate it with past experiences, and recall it later on. *Consciousness* also influences perception. If you are feeling particularly happy, the distant landscape may look glorious. When you are depressed, the same scene may appear dreary. *Memory* enters into the perceptual process at several points. The senses momentarily store the data that they bring in, as we see in Chapter 8. And, in order to decipher meaning, people continuously compare sights, sounds, and other sensations with memories of similar experiences. *Information processing* takes place during perception too. We decide what data to attend to next, compare past and present situations, and make interpretations and evaluations. *Language* influences our cognitions, molding perception indirectly.

Hypothesis testing is a particularly central information-processing component of perception. Usually, there is only one reasonable interpretation of sensory data, so the "search" for the correct perceptual hypothesis is quick, automatic, and below the level of consciousness. You look across the room, see a glowing object, and know immediately that it is a light bulb, for example. But, suppose that you're driving down a country road and see a small mass several hundred yards in front of you. While your first hypothesis may be "dead rabbit," you accumulate more and more information as you approach. Your hypothesis may change several times before you know what you see—perhaps a brown, crumpled bag. Perception's hypothesis-testing nature becomes particularly clear when we are confronted by certain ambiguous graphics (those capable of being interpreted in more than one way). Consider the scene in Figure 6-3. In this picture, the Dutch artist Maurits Escher created a situation which the brain cannot interpret satisfactorily. Although each individual part of the Escher lithograph is a perfectly acceptable, three-dimensional representation, it is impossible to put all the pieces together to form a coherent whole. As

FIGURE 6-2 During which season of the year was the photograph taken? How do you know? [*Baltimore Sun.*]

we follow along in any one direction, our sensations keep demanding new perceptual hypotheses. Since no single theory completely fits all the data, we entertain one idea and then another. The figure appears to change repeatedly as we vacillate between our hypotheses.

While all cognitive processes are highly interconnected, we are beginning with perception because it may be considered "the point where cognition and reality meet" and "the most basic cognitive activity out of which all others emerge [7]." Information must be taken into the machinery of our minds before anything else can be done with it. In later chapters, we examine consciousness, memory, thought, and language. Since attention precedes perception, we consider this activity now.

Attention: Its Role in Perception

During every waking moment enormous numbers of stimuli compete for our attention. Ordinarily, people and other animals select a small trickle of impressions to attend to. Like a movie camera, we focus first on one experience and then on another. The stimuli that lie in the periphery (boundary) of our attention form a background. This selective openness to a small portion of impinging sensory phenom-

FIGURE 6-3 Are you viewing Escher's building from above? From below? Does the perspective change as you examine the details? [*The National Gallery, Washington.*]

ena is called *attention*. At a party, for example, you listen to one conversation while others blend together forming "noise" of which you are only dimly aware. Should someone call you by name, your attention easily shifts at once to the new focus. Similarly, as you read, you are probably at least vaguely aware of your surroundings, perhaps of the position in which you are sitting, the temperature of the air, the color of the walls, noises, and other people.

What is the nature of attention? Currently, there is disagreement on this issue. Some psychologists see attention as a type of *filter*

that screens out information at different points in the perceptual process [8]. Others believe that people simply *focus* on what they wish to perceive by actively engaging themselves with the experience without directly shutting out competing events [9].

Psychologists are interested in identifying the points in the perceptual process where attention operates. Studies suggest that attention is active at several times: initially when receiving input from a sense organ, and later on when sorting and interpreting sensory data, deciding whether to respond to them, and preparing to act [10].

Attention may be characterized in several ways. First, consider its *intensity*. You may attend to a concert, for instance, avidly or halfheartedly. Attention appears to be *limited in capacity* too, though people can do several tasks at once. According to Daniel Kahneman, an Israeli psychologist who has done a great deal of research on this subject, the capacity of attention depends on the resources demanded by the tasks that are being attempted. If little conscious control and few resources are required, as in the case of driving a car (for an experienced driver) or typing (for an accomplished typist), a person can handle several tasks at once. If the job being tackled is far from automatic—for example, solving a complicated math problem—it may require most of a person's mental resources [11].

There are a great many studies on what *directs* people's attention. Needs, interests, and values have been shown to be important influences on attention. The teacher absorbed in a lecture may scarcely notice the bell signaling the end of class. The student looking forward to lunch and the companionship of friends is keenly aware of the same event. Because of their "construction," people (and other animals) tend to focus on the external environment, not on the internal one. We pay particular attention to events that are novel, unexpected, intense, or changing. This perceptual style has important survival value. It helps us respond to sudden dangers, locate and manipulate objects in space, and move about without collisions. If we attended to everything at once, important survival-related cues could easily be lost amidst the clutter. ▲

THE PHYSIOLOGICAL BASIS OF PERCEPTION

The complex perceptual process depends on both the sensory systems and the brain. The sensory systems detect information, convert (or transduce) it into nerve impulses, process some of it, and send most of it to the brain via nerve fibers. The brain plays the major role in processing sensory data. Perception depends, then, on four operations: detection, *transduction* (the conversion of energy from one form to another), transmission, and information processing. In this section, we examine these roles of the sensory and nervous systems during the perceptual process. Before reading further, you may want to review basic information about the nervous system (in Chapter 4).

Sensory Systems

Our bodies are equipped with specialized information-gathering systems, which we call *senses* or *sensory systems*. They enable us to pick up data so that we can plan and control our behavior and move about [12]. Scientists have cataloged eleven fairly distinct human senses. *Vision*, *hearing*, *taste*, and *smell* are

---

▲ **USING PSYCHOLOGY**

1. Why is it fair to say that every creature lives in its own somewhat unique world?

2. What is the major distinction between sensation and perception?

3. How do psychologists know that perception is no mere copy of reality?

4. Under what conditions can a person attend to more than a single thing at a time? Do Kahneman's conclusions contradict those of Neisser and his colleagues, described in Chapter 1?

5. Needs, interests, values, and novel, unexpected, changing, and/or intense stimuli attract and direct people's attention. Give examples of how elementary school teachers could use this information to catch and keep their students' attention in class.

among the most obvious ones. What used to be called touch turned out to be five separate skin (or *somatosensory*) systems: *physical contact, deep pressure, warmth, cold,* and *pain.* Large numbers of specialized cells responding primarily to one (in some cases, to several or all) of these five sensations are scattered throughout the skin. The somatosensory systems keep us well informed about the characteristics of objects contacting the body's surface. (Incidentally, the cornea of the eye, which does not contain such specialized cells, still registers touch, temperature, and pain [13]. Apparently, specialized cells are not essential for the brain to recognize the varied touch sensations.) People have two additional senses that detect the actions of the body itself: the kinesthetic and vestibular senses. The *kinesthetic sense* depends on receptors in the muscles, tendons, and joints. This system informs human beings about the relative positioning of the body parts during movement. If you close your eyes and bend your fingers, the kinesthetic sense makes you aware of the motion. The *vestibular sense* is sometimes called the *sense of orientation* or *balance.* It tells people about the motion and orientation of their heads and bodies with respect to the earth when they move around on their own and when they are propelled through space by cars, planes, boats, and other modes of transportation. The vestibular sense has been likened to a glass of water securely fastened to the dashboard of a moving car. As the vehicle speeds up, slows down, turns, or stops, the water level in the glass changes accordingly. Similarly, the vestibular organs, located in the bony parts of the skull

in both inner ears, are filled with a fluid that registers changes in speed and direction of movement. People use information provided by the vestibular organs in conjunction with data supplied by the visual and kinesthetic senses to orient themselves in space.

The eleven human senses are sometimes grouped into the five perceptual systems shown in Table 6-1: visual, auditory, somatosensory, chemical, and proprioceptive. These systems work together. You may recall that S. B.'s visual system could utilize material previously acquired through touch immediately after he regained his sight. As normal people perceive, they continually seek, accept, and integrate all types of sensory information.

We see [a man] walk and hear his footsteps, or hear him talk as we watch his face. We look at the things we handle, and experience our own body movements both kinesthetically and visually. In our mouths we feel what we taste and sense the movements of the organs of speech as we hear the sounds of the words we are speaking. [14]

Detection, Transduction, and Transmission

The senses detect, transduce, and transmit sensory information. Each sense has a *detection element* called a *receptor,* a single cell or group of cells that is particularly responsive to a specific type of energy. Certain cells in the ears are especially designed for registering sound, or vibrations in the air, a form of mechanical energy. Cells in the eyes are very sensitive to light, a form of electromagnetic energy. Pressure or vibrations may stimulate the eye too. You can prove this for yourself by closing your eyes and applying gentle pressure to the eyeballs. You are likely to perceive bursts of light. Each receptor is maximally sensitive to a *narrow range* of stimuli. Receptors in our eyes respond to visible light, a tiny fraction of the electromagnetic energy spectrum (which includes radio waves and gamma, infrared, and ultraviolet rays). Although people cannot "see" electromagnetic radiation outside the visible spectrum, they do have a receptor, the warmth sense in the skin, which

TABLE 6-1 Five Perceptual Systems

System	Senses involved
Visual	Sight
Auditory	Hearing
Somatosensory	Touch, deep pressure, warmth, cold, pain (plus combinations like tickle, itch, and smoothness)
Chemical	Taste, smell
Proprioceptive	Vestibular sense, kinesthetic sense

reacts to infrared rays. Similarly, receptors in the ears respond to vibrations of the air in the approximate range of 20 to 20,000 hertz (cycles per second). Vibrations above and below this range frequently occur around us, but we cannot hear them.

Receptors behave like *transducers*. The pickup cartridge on a record player is a transducer that you are probably familiar with. The cartridge converts (transduces) the mechanical vibrations of the needle riding in the record groove into electrical signals. After the signals have been amplified, the speaker (another transducer) transforms this electrical energy back into mechanical vibrations that we can hear. Receptors in our senses convert incoming energy into the electrical-chemical signals that the nervous system uses for communication. If the incoming energy is sufficiently intense, it will trigger nerve impulses that transmit coded information about various features of the stimulus along specific nerve fibers to particular brain regions.

Information Processing: The Case of Vision

Sensory information processing occurs at different locations in the sensory and nervous systems. In the case of vision, processing takes place within the eyes, varied brain regions, and connecting neurons. In this section and throughout the chapter, we use vision to illustrate how perceptual systems operate. There are several reasons for this decision. The visual system gives people a disproportionately large amount of information about their environment. (Not all animals rely so heavily on vision.) Vision may be considered the *dominant* human sense, too. If sensory information conflicts, laboratory studies suggest that people usually believe their eyes. If you touch a cube, for example, while looking at it through a lens that reduces its visible size, you're likely to trust what you see, not what you feel [15]. As S. B.'s case suggested, other human sensory systems may dominate if vision is faulty or inoperative. Furthermore, because the visual system is both important and accessible for study, sci-

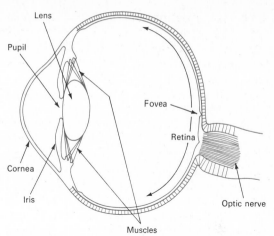

FIGURE 6-4 Some parts of the human eye.

entists understand it better than any other. After describing the anatomy and functioning of the eye, we focus on the visual information processing that occurs in both eyes and brain.

The anatomy of the eye A few basic parts of the human eye, those with which we will be concerned, are shown in Figure 6-4. The eye can be pictured as a dark chamber with an opening in front, the *pupil*, which allows light to enter. When illumination is very dim, the pupil enlarges to admit as much light as possible. When illumination is intense, the pupil decreases in size to limit the amount of incoming light. The pupil's size is controlled by the colored disc surrounding it, the *iris*. The visible part of the eye is covered by a transparent covering, the *cornea*, which protects the eye and helps to focus events in the visual field onto the rear inner surface of the eye, the *retina* (to be described in a moment). The *lens*, located behind the pupil, is also involved in focusing visual images on the retina. The lens operates by changing its shape, becoming thick for close viewing and thin or flat for distant scenes and when at rest. As we age, the lens loses its elasticity. Consequently, bringing nearby objects into focus becomes more difficult.

Because of the way light waves move, images are focused on the retina upside down and reversed from right to left. The retina is composed of several layers of cells, including rods, cones, and sensory neurons. The *rods* and *cones* are receptors which respond to visible light. Whenever incoming light rays are sufficiently intense, the rods and cones initiate nerve impulses, which are transmitted to the *sensory neurons* within the retina. The axons of these sensory neurons are bundled together to form the *optic nerve*, which connects the eye to various brain centers. Each eye contains approximately 120 million rods and about 7 million cones. The *rods* are about a thousand times more sensitive than the cones. In a very dimly lit location, such as a street at night illuminated only by the moon, the rods alone are active. Using pure rod vision, our acuity is poor, and we see only black, white, and shades of gray. When illumination is normal or bright, both rods and cones are active. *Cones* register both color and detail.

Rods and cones are not distributed evenly throughout the retina. Some 50,000 tightly packed cones are concentrated in a small depression within the retina directly in the line of sight, the *fovea*. The organization and density of cones in the fovea make a high degree of visual acuity possible. Rods appear in large numbers in the periphery of the retina and immediately adjacent to the fovea. A faint star (or other dim object) which isn't visible when viewed straight on may sometimes be seen if focused on the more sensitive rods, that is, by looking slightly off to the side.

The movements of the eye Under ordinary circumstances, our eyes are continually in motion. The movement consists of small, rapid, involuntary tremors, called *nystagmus*, and flicks of the eyeball from one position to another, called *saccades*. Because of the eye's unceasing activity, a new retinal image is formed roughly three to five times each second. This motion enables the fovea to range widely over an object or scene so that we can see the details sharply. These movements occur, of course, without conscious awareness. Seeing requires both storing and processing information from successive images on the retina. We discuss the storage aspects in Chapter 8. For now, we examine how the eye itself processes information.

Information processing in the eye
The neurons of the retina do more than simply transduce energy and shuttle messages to the brain. To a greater or lesser degree, depending on the animal, they process visual information for color, shape, detail, contour (boundary lines), and movement. How do we know? Scientists learned about the information-processing functions of the eye by studying cells in the retinas of frogs and other simple creatures. To illustrate, we look briefly at the classic studies of Jerome Lettvin and his colleagues at the Massachusetts Institute of Technology. In the late 1950s these researchers demonstrated that the frog's brain receives information that has been highly processed within the frog's retina. Lettvin and his coworkers presented immobilized frogs with various visual stimuli, such as lines, dots, and checkered patterns. At the same time, they measured "what the frog's eye told the frog's brain" by recording from electrodes inserted directly into the frog's optic nerve. No matter how complex or subtle an event, cells in the frog's retina appear to detect only five distinct pieces of information, which are channeled by the fibers of the optic nerve to the *tectum*, the frog's chief visual brain center. *Stationary-edge detectors* respond to boundaries between light and dark regions. They are probably useful for detecting the general outlines of objects in the frog's surroundings. *Moving-edge detectors* gather information about the movements of boundaries. *Dimming detectors* register the type of darkening that occurs when shadows loom over the frog's visual field, signaling an approaching enemy perhaps. *Dark detectors* react to gradual changes in light intensity. The darker it becomes, the more active these fibers are. *Moving convex-edge detectors* respond when a dark, curved boundary moves within the frog's visual field. This last system, dubbed the "bug catcher," enables frogs to capture flying insects efficiently [16]. In short,

the frog's eye is programmed by heredity to detect, analyze, and extract important survival-related information from the frog's surroundings and send those data to the frog's brain. Similar studies have shown that cells in the retinas of pigeons and rabbits also detect a small number of specific events [17]. Neurons in the eyes of higher animals, such as people, process information too. Such processing keeps the brain from being flooded with data and increases the probability that organisms will attend to survival-related experiences. In human beings and other higher organisms, more information processing takes place in the brain and less in the eyes. Better-informed brains allow more flexible behavior.

Information processing in the brain

In complex creatures, including people, most sensory information processing takes place in various regions of the cortex. Over the past twenty years or so, David Hubel and Torsten Weisel, physiologists at the Harvard Medical School, and many other investigators have been studying how cortical cells respond to different types of basic visual stimuli. Typically, the scientists insert microelectrodes into individual cortical cells of immobilized cats and monkeys. Then they record the cell's responses to stimuli such as flashing lights, slits (bright lines on dark backgrounds), or edges (boundary lines between dark and light regions). Hubel and Weisel have discovered three distinct types of *visual detector cortical cells* within the *occipital lobes* of both cats and monkeys. *Simple cells* respond to only one type of line (say, slit or edge) at a particular orientation (horizontal, vertical, or oblique) moving slowly past a specific region *(receptive field)* of the retina. *Complex cells* operate somewhat like simple ones. But they are primarily sensitive to rapidly moving stimuli and to a larger receptive field. It is believed that these neurons receive and abstract information from a large number of simple cells. *Hypercomplex cells* fire only in response to very short stimuli and to corners. These neurons are thought to process the information that is received from the complex cells [18].

Scientists believe that the cortexes of different mammals are organized along similar lines. The cortex appears to be composed of vertical columns of cells, arranged somewhat like a beehive. The cells in a single column process information from a specific sense and a particular area of the body. Many columns in the occipital lobes of the cortex deal with visual information. Simple, complex, and hypercomplex cells in a single column take care of a restricted region of the retina. Each cell in the column appears to have its own special job: to detect a particular type of stimulus in a specific orientation moving at a certain speed. Vertical cell columns in other cortical regions deal in a similar way with other types of sensory information. Each column has its own incoming and outgoing communication "lines." Yet all are highly interconnected with one another and with other brain regions [19].

There is evidence that the cortex also contains specialized neurons which detect complicated types of visual information. You may recall that psychologist Richard Thompson and his colleagues discovered some cells in the cat's cortex which fired after a certain number of specific events had taken place and other cells which responded to unfamiliar experiences. More recently, Charles Gross and his associates have discovered neurons in the monkey's temporal lobes that react most vigorously to very specific, complex features, such as a hand [20].

Colin Blakemore has speculated that two classes of cortical cells analyze visual data. *Universal feature detectors* (such as simple, complex, and hypercomplex cells) extract separate elements of information (including timing, spacing, orientation, direction of movement, and color) from any type of stimulus. Neurons of this type seem to be present in the visual systems of almost all animals. *Species-specific feature detectors* (such as the hand detectors in monkeys) analyze images for frequently encountered or crucially important information. These cells are thought to be specific to particular animal groups [21].

Because microelectrodes cannot be used to study the human visual system (they can damage the brain), psychologists have devised ingenious tasks to determine how people's brains respond to visual stimulation. Understanding this research requires a great deal of specialized mathematical background, so we will not describe it. It is sufficient to know that these investigations support the idea that people have cortical detectors for information about orientation, intensity, motion, and probably color [22].

Every time the roving eyes bring in new images, specific cells throughout the cortex alter their firing patterns. Somehow the representations are stored, integrated with inputs from other sensory systems, and compared with memories of past experiences almost instantaneously. These processes underlie the ability to extract visual information about ourselves and our surroundings. ▲

THE ORGANIZATION OF VISUAL PERCEPTION

If the image projected onto the retina by the "camera"—our eye—were examined by an optician used to high standards, he would be disgusted. There is more blurring at the edges than with a cheap pair of child's binoculars; straight lines look curved, and the outlines fade away under irridescent haloes. [23]

Despite the poor quality of the retinal image, we see clear, distinct objects meaningfully related to one another in three-dimensional space. And even though the eye is constantly jumping around, the environment appears uninterrupted. How is this possible? The data that our senses supply are continually being *organized*. Ordinarily, the process is so rapid and automatic that we are completely unaware of it. In this section, we turn to some of the principles that underlie the organization of visual perception. Some of the "rules" apply to other perceptual systems, as well as sight. A number of these principles were studied by the early gestalt psychologists (Chapter 1). First we examine the visual perception of objects, then of depth and distance. The sensory-neural approach that we just described cannot currently explain these perceptual abilities.

Perceiving Objects

People use several processing strategies to interpret visual information about objects: among them, constancy, figure-ground, and grouping.

Constancy A woman does not seem to shrink as she walks away from us. A giraffe does not appear to grow larger as it approaches. Nonetheless, in both cases, the viewer's retinal image changes size. When you view a round clock-face from the side, you continue to think of it as being circular, even though it projects an elliptical retinal image. Similarly, white sheets in a dimly lit room continue to look white, though they reflect less light than in bright sunlight. These are all examples of constancy. In general terms, *constancy* means that objects viewed from different angles, at various distances, or under diverse conditions of illumination are still perceived as retaining the same shape, size, and color. Without constancy, our worlds would have an Alice-in-Wonderland quality, with objects changing almost continually. Constancy gives a great deal of stability to our perceptual worlds. There are numerous theories about how constancy is achieved [24]. In ways that are not fully understood, people use knowledge derived from past experience, without

FIGURE 6-5 Which cues did Escher manipulate to create unusual figure-ground effects? [*The National Gallery, Washington.*]

making any effort or having any awareness of the process, to complement the images that the retina picks up.

Figure-ground The black letters of the text stand out from the white page. A picture stands out from the wall on which it is hung. Whenever we look around, we tend to see objects (or *figures*) against a background (or *ground*). The same object may be seen as figure or ground, depending on how you direct your attention. The stimuli that seem figure-like appear to own the boundary or contour that is common to figure and ground and to be in front of the ground. Figures are seen as vivid and definitely shaped, as well. In the Escher lithograph, reproduced in Figure 6-5, you can see how unusual effects can be created by the clever manipulation of the cues that determine figure-ground relationships.

As long as our senses and brains are operating normally, the same stimulus cannot be seen as both figure and ground at the same time. Notice how Figure 6-6 fluctuates. Sometimes we see two red faces on a vague white background. At other times we see a vase on a featureless red background. The reversals occur spontaneously and are hard to control. Still, although we alternate between the two interpretations, only one dominates at any single time. While we generally see figures

FIGURE 6-6 If you stare at this picture, your perceptions of figure and ground should flip back and forth spontaneously.

FIGURE 6-7 Even when the visual field lacks clear boundaries and visual stimuli run into one another, people usually manage to extract figures—a tree frog, in this case—from the background. [*New York Zoological Society*.]

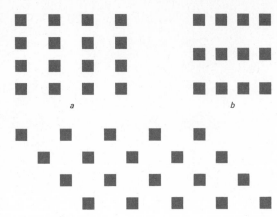

FIGURE 6-9 How do you organize the squares in (*a*)? In (*b*)? In (*c*)? [*From Dember, 1960.*]

emerge from backgrounds, we may not do so immediately—particularly when looking at distant scenes [25] or camouflaged objects, as in Figure 6-7.

The figure-ground principle appears to be basic to all object perception. Something

cannot be seen as an object until it has been separated from its background. This particular "rule" appears to be largely inborn, as we will see.

Grouping The following principles are among those that govern the way we group elements of incoming visual information.

1. *Similarity.* Visual elements with *similar color, shape,* or *texture* are seen as belonging together. In Figure 6-8*a* you are likely to see alternating rows of dark and light squares, rather than forty-nine squares. In Figure 6-8*b*, you are apt to see alternating rows of triangles and squares, rather than forty-nine red shapes. We tend to group elements that *move in a similar direction,* too. Consequently, our eyes unify dancers leaping along parallel paths in a ballet, giving order to what would otherwise be a chaotic collection of single individuals.

2. *Proximity.* Visual elements near one another are seen as belonging together. In Figure 6-9, proximity leads us to organize pattern (*a*) into columns, pattern (*b*) into rows, and pattern (*c*) into diagonals.

3. *Symmetry.* Visual elements that form regular, simple, well-balanced shapes are seen as belonging together. When viewing Figure 6-10, for example, most people report seeing two overlapping squares rather than two irregular shapes and a triangle.

4. *Continuity.* Visual elements that permit lines, curves, or movements to continue in a direction already established tend to be grouped together.

FIGURE 6-8 How do you organize the forty-nine forms in (*a*)? In (*b*)? Do you think of the picture as composed of forty-nine objects? Or, do you see separate rows or columns?

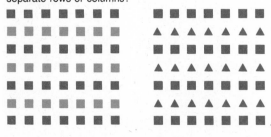

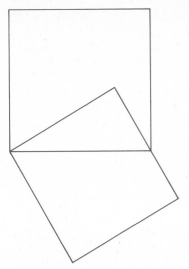

FIGURE 6-10 What shapes do you see?

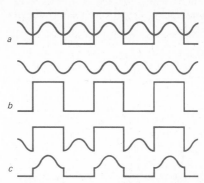

FIGURE 6-11 Which elements make up (*a*)? Choose either (*b*) or (*c*). [*From Wertheimer, 1923.*]

This principle causes us to see the pattern in Figure 6-11*a* as consisting of the two configurations shown in Figure 6-11*b*. It might logically be composed of the two lines in Figure 6-11*c*.

5. *Closure.* Incomplete objects are usually filled in and seen as complete, a tendency known as closure. Our brains supply information that the sense organ may not have provided, particularly when we are familiar with the object represented (as in Figure 6-12).

It is important to note that several grouping principles contribute to our impressions in many of the examples that have been presented and in most real situations. Sometimes the "rules" work together. In Figure 6-9, proximity, similarity, and continuity produce the impression of vertical, horizontal, or diagonal lines. In Figure 6-7, the frog is somewhat difficult to see, primarily because the overall similarity and continuity of tree and frog together mask the frog's own internal similarity and continuity. Grouping principles can conflict. In Figure 6-13, similarity of shape clashes with proximity. The dissimilar shapes (circles and squares) are comparatively close together. Similar shapes (circles or squares) are relatively far apart. In this case, proximity tends to dominate, and you are likely to see three vertical columns. Still, by concentrating on the similarly shaped forms, you should be able to see horizontal rows.

Perceiving Depth and Distance

Like a movie screen, the retina registers images in two dimensions: left-right and up-down. Yet people (and other animals) perceive a three-dimensional world. How do we

FIGURE 6-12 What do you see? By the age of three, (*a*) is almost always identified as a dog. Only at age fifteen does almost everyone see (*b*) as a crouching or sprinting person. Very few three-year-olds see (*b*) as a meaningful stimulus. Research by psychologist Norman Livson suggests that the completion of incomplete representations increases with age until it peaks in adolescence. For unknown reasons, the tendency to use closure declines steadily with increasing age after adolescence [76]. [*From Thurstone, 1944.*]

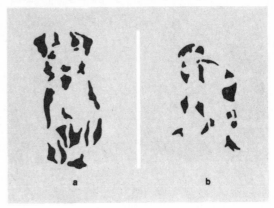

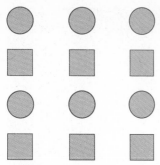

FIGURE 6-13 Do you see four rows containing either circles or squares? Or three columns of mixed forms? Does the organization change?

manage to do it? We use physiological, motion-related, and pictorial cues to see depth and distance.

Physiological cues Several common physiological depth cues depend on the operation of both eyes, so they are called *binocular*

FIGURE 6-14 What pictorial cues inform us of depth in this photograph? [*Paul Siquerira/Rapho Photo Researchers.*]

depth cues. Because our eyes are located in different positions, each retina records a slightly different visual image. This phenomenon is known as *binocular disparity.* Somehow animals use information contained in the two two-dimensional images provided by the eyes to reconstruct a three-dimensional world. Recent experiments by John Ross and his associates in Australia show that the information from both images must be received within a 50-millisecond time period to be utilized for determining depth [26]. *Convergence* provides another binocular physiological depth cue. As our eyes fixate on a nearby object, they turn in toward one another. The resulting kinesthetic feedback from the eye muscles gives us some idea about how distant the object is. Convergence cues are primarily useful for distances less than about 30 feet.

Even without two eyes, people and other animals still perceive distance. They use *monocular depth cues*, those that require the operation of only one eye. We will describe physiological, motion-related, and pictorial monocular depth cues. First consider *accommodation*, a physiological monocular depth cue. As you look at any object in the visual field, the lens system of the eye automatically focuses the incoming light rays onto the retina. During this process, known as accommodation, the eye muscles make the lens bulge to focus nearby objects or flatten to focus distant ones. In each case, the brain receives different kinesthetic sensations from the eye muscles. These sensations provide information about distance. Because only minimal changes in accommodation occur beyond a few feet, this monocular depth cue is mainly effective for estimating short distances.

Motion-related cues Some cues about depth come from the perceiver's own actions. Whenever we move, for example, retinal images of the visual field change. Objects that are close to us appear to sweep by with greater speed than distant ones. This important monocular depth cue is known as *motion parallax*. Motion parallax is vivid when driving down a highway. Fence posts and telephone poles beside the road seem to fly by at high speed, while those far away drift past slowly. The relative motion of objects provides reliable information about their distance.

Pictorial cues   A two-dimensional retinal image of an actual scene contains a great deal of information about distance. People rely on such picture-related, or *pictorial*, cues continually, usually without being aware of doing so. Six categories of these *monocular depth cues* are particularly useful:

1. *Familiar size.* Whenever we see a familiar object, we roughly gauge its distance by noting the size of our retinal image. When the image is relatively large, we assume that the object is near. When the image is relatively small, we infer that the object is distant. We use this principle to judge the relative distances of the cars in Figure 6-14. Note that the same information is also taken into account to achieve size constancy.

2. *Linear perspective.* Linear perspective is a special case of familiar size. It is most easily understood by considering an example. Assume that you are looking down rows of file cabinets, as in Figure 6-15. The actual scene would produce roughly the same image on your retina as the photograph. If we measured the cabinets on the photograph, we'd find that those toward the center are smaller, closer, and higher. Past experience tells us that the actual cabinets are not smaller, closer, and higher. We have seen the apparent narrowing of parallel structures in viewing the sides of roads, railroad tracks, streams, rooms, and buildings often enough to know that their funnel-shaped appearance signifies distance, and not convergence. So every time we see what we believe to be parallel lines converge, we make an interpretation. We assume that the gradually changing retinal image means that the converging end of the structure is farther away. This cue is called *linear perspective.*

3. *Light and shadow.* When light from a specific source such as the sun strikes a three-dimensional object, it illuminates the side(s) facing the light source and leaves the other side(s) in shadow. The pattern of light and shadow helps define contours and gives information about solidity, depth, protrusions, and indentations, as you can see in Escher's lithograph in Figure 6-5.

FIGURE 6-15   Does the aisle between the file cabinets narrow? [*Herbert Gehr*/Life *magazine, © 1947, Time, Inc.*]

4. *Texture gradient.*   Objects in the visual field show a gradual change in texture with distance. They appear clear, detailed, and coarse nearby and less distinct farther away. In Figure 6-16, the rocks on Mars near the observer (the camera, in this case) stand out separately in striking detail. Those farther away tend to blend together, and detail is not discernible.

5. *Aerial perspective.*   Haze, usually present in

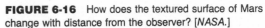

FIGURE 6-16   How does the textured surface of Mars change with distance from the observer? [*NASA.*]

FIGURE 6-17 Identify the varied ways that William Hogarth misused depth cues in this engraving entitled *False Perspective* (1754). [*National Gallery, London.*]

the atmosphere, makes distant objects appear bluish, as well as blurred and indistinct. Accordingly, hazy stimuli, like some of the buildings in Figure 6-14, appear far away.

6. *Interposition.* Whenever one object obstructs our view of another, the complete object is seen as closer than the obstructed one. In Figure 6-17, for instance, we assume that the man in the three-cornered hat is in front of the barrel that he partially conceals and that the barrel is in front of the building which it blocks from view. Note that the artist has deliberately misused depth cues to achieve novel effects. The banner on the building, for example, is partly obstructed by the distant trees.

Artists have long used pictorial cues to depict scenes as they would be captured by the retina witnessing the actual situation. The pictorial cues appear to be learned. We compare images on the retina with memories of past experiences, contrasting dimensions such as size, shape, sharpness, and completeness. These comparisons permit us to extract information about both the objects themselves and their relationships with one another in space. ▲

PERCEPTUAL ADAPTATION

For human beings, perception is a flexible activity that can deal with changing inputs. In the course of ordinary living, people's perceptions continually adapt to their surroundings. If you sit in the front row of a movie theater, for example, the performers will appear too tall and thin at first—as if the screen were a distorting mirror in an amusement park. After a short period, you'll probably stop noticing the peculiarities. A television screen produces a poor picture. Straight lines are often crooked, circles lopsided, and figures and scenery lacking in detail. But most of us learned long ago to compensate for these imperfections, and we continue to do so

▲ **USING PSYCHOLOGY**

1. Find several new examples of constancy, figure-ground relationships, and the grouping "rules" (similarity, proximity, symmetry, continuity, and closure).

2. Find an example which shows that grouping principles can work together. Find another example which shows that the principles can conflict.

3. Make a list of monocular and binocular depth cues. Then try to demonstrate for yourself how each cue operates in daily life.

4. Find a location where you can see a long distance. Identify some near and some far objects to study. Figure out which cues inform you about distance. Locate examples of familiar size, linear perspective, light and shadow, texture gradients, aerial perspective, and interposition.

without realizing it. If you wear glasses, probably they initially distorted your view of your surroundings but became comfortable after an adjustment period lasting several hours to a few days. Psychologists have been studying the adaptability of perception for almost a hundred years. Less complicated animals, such as newts and chickens, do not possess this flexibility. Their perception is fixed by their heredity [27]. You may recall that S. B. appeared to have lost some of his perceptual adaptability. How much can normal people adapt? How do they do it? We focus again on vision.

Adapting to Visual Distortion

In the 1890s George Stratton, a psychologist at the University of California, made the first systematic observations on perceptual adaptation. For one study, Stratton (using himself as a subject) wore spectacles containing lenses and mirrors that turned the world upside down and reversed it left to right. To obtain some idea of what he saw, hold a photograph upside down in front of a mirror. Stratton wore his special inverting lenses about eleven hours every day for eight days, removing them only before going to sleep. On the first day, things looked upside down, unstable, and in motion. As we'd expect, Stratton had a hard time moving around. He wrote:

Almost all movements performed under the direct guidance of sight were laborious and embarrassed. Inappropriate movements were constantly made. . . . At table the simplest acts of serving myself had to be cautiously worked out. The wrong hand was constantly used to seize anything that lay to one side. . . . The unusual strain of attention in these areas, and the difficulty of finally getting a movement to its goal, made all but the simplest movements extremely fatiguing. [28]

Stratton found it progressively easier to get around. After eight days, in fact, he had adjusted so well to his topsy-turvy world that he had problems readapting to ordinary reality.

Since Stratton's early adventures with in-verting lenses, psychologists have found that people can adjust, in time, to many kinds of extreme visual distortions. We can get used to a visual field that is both upside down and backward and to one that is tilted or shifted left, right, up, or down. We can accustom ourselves to a world where straight lines curve and right angles are obtuse or acute and even to split worlds that are blue on one side and yellow on the other or compressed on one side and expanded on the other.

What is meant by the term "adjust"? Gradually, people become accustomed to the new look of things, and they learn to use information automatically. They might see a chair displaced on the right, for example, and without conscious effort, make the correct bodily adjustment to avoid bumping into it. Some research participants slip back into a fairly normal routine. Then, when they first remove the lenses after a long period of time, they feel dizzy and disoriented. The old world looks strange. Objects may appear tilted, highly illuminated, or moving. Consequently, people must adjust once more.

How People Adapt

How are people able to adapt? Since subjects in psychological experiments initially feel some conflict between vision and the other sensory systems, we believe that one or more systems must change during adaptation. What changes? As we noted before, a number of laboratory studies suggest that vision dominates when sensory information conflicts. Suppose that you see your hand in one place while feeling it in another. Proprioception (the sense of the body's position) will likely give way. You will actually begin to *feel* that the hand is where you *see* it. Somehow, vision may reeducate the other perceptual systems.

There is evidence that vision may change too after an experience with distorting lenses, particularly when people have moved about actively or seen parts of their own bodies or familiar objects whose orientations are known, such as vertical buildings. Psychologist Irwin Rock suggests that after putting on distorting lenses, subjects initially compare their new visual perceptions with images of preexperimental conditions and information about the spatial properties of objects seen in the normal way. Adaptation may occur, then, as people build up new memories based on their new visual experiences (which include new information about how their limbs move and how objects are arranged in space). Participants in psychological studies seem to learn that what looks tilted or upside down must not be, because it is aligned with their bodies and other objects [29]. The ability to radically change comparison standards contributes to perceptual adaptability.

THE DEVELOPMENT OF VISUAL PERCEPTION

Perceptual processes develop gradually in many animals, including people. How soon do perceptual abilities appear? Are they present at birth? S. B. did not see after the age of two months until his vision was restored about fifty years later. Did S. B. actually see during these early months somewhat as adults do? Young babies do see, to some degree. In this section, we describe the newborn's visual capabilities and the development of early object and depth perception. Note the ingenious strategies that psychologists use to study perceptual development.

The Visual World of the Newborn Baby

At birth the human baby's retina is incomplete and the neural circuits underlying vision are only partially developed. Yet psychologists are certain that neonates see, though probably quite differently than adults do. Near the time of birth, infants appear to see objects located about 9 to 12 inches from their faces most clearly. For unknown reasons, they do not use the lens for focusing [30]. By adult standards, the infant's vision is probably quite fuzzy. A letter that a person with good vision can see sharply 150 feet away will not be detected at distances of more than 20 feet by a young baby. Many neonates show far less

acuity than this [31]. Even though the newborn's vision is likely to be blurred most of the time, children of five weeks already prefer sharp images. Laboratory studies show that they will actually work hard (by changing their sucking patterns) to bring indistinct motion pictures into focus [32]. It takes about six months for acuity to approach adult levels [33].

The vision of newborns is unusual in many other respects. For example, infants lack the muscular ability to coordinate the movements of both eyes; and they probably see only shades of black, white, and gray until at least several weeks after birth [34]. Are the visual sensations of infants organized into objects and patterns from the day of birth?

Early Form Perception

Cortical cells which detect features, such as slits, in the visual field are present at birth in animal infants [35]. Numerous studies suggest that these detectors operate at the beginning too. Human neonates may even see objects. At birth, babies will track moving forms with jerky eye movements [36], demonstrating that they separate figures from backgrounds, one prerequisite for seeing objects. Motion pictures of the precise location of infants' fixations (points where the eye is aimed) show that newborns scan external outlines, concentrating on high contrast areas such as the hair-skin or skin-garment borders of a human figure. Babies spend relatively little time looking at interior features until they are six weeks of age [37], perhaps because they can handle only a small amount of sensory data at a time.

In addition to responding to contour, neonates react to curvilinearity (the curvature of lines) and complexity, as studies by psychologist Robert Fantz demonstrate. In the early 1950s, while at the University of Chicago, Fantz and his coworkers began investigating the development of form perception in neonates. For studies of human infants, an apparatus called a *looking chamber*, similar to the one pictured in Figure 6-18, was used. One at a time, babies were placed in the looking

chamber in front of two test patterns attached to a background uniform in color and illumination. The investigators watched the infants' eyes through peepholes. When tiny mirror images of one of the patterns appeared over the baby's pupil, the researchers knew that the child was looking directly at that form. Fantz reasoned that if infants spent a longer period of time gazing at one of the patterns, they must be able to see some difference between the two and prefer the one to the other.

In an early study, Fantz and his coworkers tested thirty babies of one to fifteen weeks of age. They presented the four pairs of patterns, shown in Figure 6-19, in a random order to the infants. The total time that the child looked at each pattern was recorded. As you can see from the graph, infants spent more time gazing at the complex pairs and at the more complicated stimulus of each pair

FIGURE 6-19 Babies appear to prefer looking at complex patterns rather than simple ones. When two patterns are of roughly similar complexity, infants spend more time gazing at curved- rather than straight-line designs. The results shown here were obtained from ten weekly tests on twenty-two children. [*Adapted from* The origin of form perception *by R. L. Fantz. Copyright © 1961 by Scientific American, Inc. All rights reserved.*]

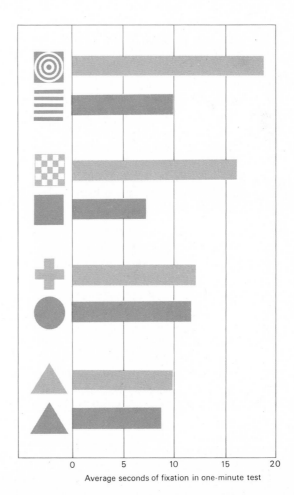

Average seconds of fixation in one-minute test

[38]. Recent research suggests that curvilinearity, and not complexity, produced the preference for the bull's eye over the stripes [39]. Combining these findings with several others (namely, that newborns prefer looking at three-dimensional to flat objects, moving objects to stationary ones, and face-like patterns to others [40]), we may speculate that human babies may be born with preferences for gazing at their caretakers. This perceptual preference could increase the neonate's social responsivity and, consequently, its appeal and the probability of good care.

Early Depth Perception

How early do babies perceive depth? Among the first investigators of this subject were psychologists Eleanor Gibson and Richard Walk, working then at Cornell University. They constructed a simulated (imitation) cliff like the one shown in Figure 6-20. As you can

see, a board spans the center of a heavy glass table top. On one side, checkerboard material extends flush with the under surface of the glass and the side appears solid. On the other side, the same patterned material lies against the floor, causing the surface to appear to drop off like a cliff. The sheet of glass eliminates the danger of injury as well as tactile information, air currents, and echoes that might otherwise warn the infant of the drop. The apparent drop-off is signaled only by visual cues, hence the name *visual cliff*.

Turtles, birds, rats, sheep, goats, lions, tigers, dogs, chimpanzees, humans, and many other animals have been tested on this apparatus using the same general procedure. The animal, usually an infant, is placed on the center board between the deep and shallow sides of the cliff. Consistent avoidance of the "drop" means that depth is perceived and its danger feared. Land animals stay clear of the deep side of the cliff at very early ages—in

FIGURE 6-20 The drawing shows the parts of the visual cliff. The baby on the visual cliff in the photograph appears to prefer the shallow side. Human infants who are just beginning to crawl are not consistent in avoiding the deep side of the cliff. [Diagram: *From Walk and Gibson, 1961*; photograph: *Lawrence Rothblat*.]

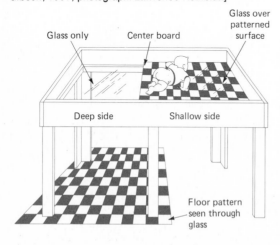

some cases, even when there has been no opportunity to learn about depth. Rat infants reared in darkness and confronting their very first visual experience, for example, alight on the shallow side of the cliff consistently. Several hours after birth when mountain goats first walk well enough to be tested, they too stay away from the deep side of the cliff. In general, it appears that animals whose environments require depth perception for survival avoid the drop on the laboratory cliff as soon as they can move about. Animals for whom depth perception is less critical do not show fears of the drop-off until somewhat later. Nonland animals, such as ducks and sea turtles, do not hesitate to cross the deep side of the visual cliff [41]. Experiments designed to isolate the depth cues that are used to avoid the apparent drop have produced contradictory results. It is known that animals wearing a patch over one eye perform in the same way as those using both eyes, so monocular depth cues must be sufficient [42].

We humans are also land animals. Do our young perceive and fear heights as soon as they can move about? Recent visual cliff studies by psychologist Joseph Campos and his colleagues suggest that while depth perception appears very early in human infancy, fear of heights may have to be learned. One study involved babies of about eight weeks. Since they were too young to move about, they were placed on the deep and shallow sides of the cliff while their heart rates were monitored. The infants' hearts generally slowed down on the deep side and speeded up on the shallow side. These results were surprising because fear is associated with an increased heart rate. The experimenters offered a plausible explanation. Earlier studies had shown that when adults pay close attention to an event, their heart rates tend to decrease. Babies on the deep side of the cliff were in a novel situation. Perhaps they were simply attending to it. If that was the case, their heart rates should decelerate. Infants on the shallow side of the cliff were in a perfectly ordinary situation, so they should be bored and restless, moods associated with heart rate

acceleration [43]. If Campos's interpretation is correct, the study supports the idea that babies perceive depth by eight weeks.

Later research by Campos and his coworkers suggests that fear of heights is not innate. Older infants were tested on the visual cliff just after learning to crawl and retested at approximately two-week intervals until they refused to cross over the deep side twice in a row. After first becoming mobile, only about one-third of the youngsters feared the deep side of the cliff sufficiently to refuse to crawl over it when called by their mothers using an appealing toy as lure. (Almost all the children who refused to cross had been crawling two or three weeks before the test. Those who tackled the cliff, generally had a shorter crawling history.) By the age of nine months, all the babies showed a fear of heights. Interviews with parents suggested that infants passed through an early period when they were not frightened of falling. In fact, they were likely to crawl off the edges of sofas, beds, stairs, and the like if not rescued in time [44].

Do infants younger than eight weeks perceive depth? Studies by psychologist T. G. R. Bower and his colleagues indicate that they do. At ten days of age, newborns in an upright position react defensively as objects are brought closer to their faces. They widen their eyes, retract their heads, and position their hands between the object and their faces. Experiments indicate that the defensive reaction is produced by the child's *visual* perception [45]. In sum, it is probably safe to conclude right now that babies do organize their world in three dimensions shortly after birth. ▲

ENVIRONMENTAL INFLUENCES ON PERCEPTION

Visual form and depth perception appear soon after birth, before infants have had much time to learn. Apparently, then, heredity, which shapes the sensory and nervous systems, affects certain aspects of the perceptual process. But perceptual systems are not complete at birth. They require time to mature and gain precision in handling large amounts of complicated data. Early in infancy and later in life, specific environmental events have an important influence on perception. We examine the impact of four environmental factors on visual perception: ordinarily inevitable sensorimotor experiences during infancy, short periods of sensory deprivation after infancy, states of mind, and cultural environments.

Ordinarily Inevitable Sensorimotor Experiences during Infancy

Many environmental conditions that are ordinarily inevitable during infancy are absolutely essential for the growth of mature perceptual competencies. During sensitive periods (Chapter 3) early in life, harmful experiences (including the absence of necessary ones) may permanently disrupt the development of normal capabilities. The times of maximum susceptibility to disruptions depend on the perceptual ability and the animal. Cats are believed to be most vulnerable to visual damage during the first four months, monkeys during the first eighteen months, and people during the first six years [46]. S. B., of course, experienced massive visual deprivation at a critical time. Observations of such natural perceptual impairments, and especially of very specific ones, provide information about the link between early environmental conditions and the development of normal perceptual abilities [47]. We examine the effects of light, patterned visual experiences, and active movement.

Light Light is important for the growth of numerous visual skills. The early studies of psychologist Austin Riesen are among many that support this hypothesis. In the 1940s Riesen and his colleagues raised two newborn chimpanzees in darkness for sixteen months. When the animals emerged from darkness, they were visually incompetent. They failed to respond to complex patterns of light until they had spent many hours in illuminated surroundings. They did not react visually to toys, feeding bottles, and other familiar objects unless these stimuli actually touched their bodies. Nor did they blink when threatening motions were made [48]. As it turned out, the disuse due to prolonged darkness had resulted in the loss of many retinal neurons [49]. Note that some skills could be recovered through learning. (See Chapter 4 for an explanation of how functions can be recovered after brain damage.)

The effects of light deprivation depend on many factors including species, type and timing of deprivation, and involvement of one or both eyes [50]. Physical damage does not necessarily occur when treatment is short or when the animal's vision has already matured. Some of S. B.'s problems probably were the result of cell destruction due to disuse.

Patterned visual experiences Darkness isolates animals from patterned visual experiences. Does the pattern deprivation by itself have destructive consequences? A great deal of research suggests that it does. In a classic study on this subject, British researchers Colin Blakemore and Grahame Cooper raised two newborn kittens under carefully controlled conditions. Most of the time the infants were in complete darkness, but, for a few hours daily, each one was placed in a different chamber for visual stimulation. The chambers were designed so that one kitten was exposed only to vertical stripes while the other was exposed only to horizontal stripes. A neck ruff kept each animal from seeing its own body. After about five months' exposure to stripes of a single orientation, the cats were tested. The cat deprived of horizontal-stripe experiences navigated around vertical obstacles with ease but slammed into horizontal ones. The cat denied vertical-stripe experiences cruised around horizontal obstacles and crashed into vertical ones. Using Hubel's and Weisel's microelectrode technique, Blakemore and Cooper discovered that nearly all the tested neurons in the brains of the two cats responded best to lines in orientations similar to those to which they had been exposed early in life. Neurons in the brain of the vertical-deprived cat exhibited very little response to lines in vertical orientations. Similarly, neurons in the brain of the horizontal-deprived cat responded poorly to lines in horizontal orientations [51]. More refined studies have confirmed the finding that the early environment can affect the responsiveness of visual neurons to stimuli of particular orientations [52]. During the early weeks of a cat's life, as little as one hour's total exposure to stripes of a specific orientation may alter the preferences of cortical neurons.

Blakemore speculates that each neuron may select as its preferred stimulus the feature it has seen most often during early infancy. Such an arrangement would allow animals to build themselves visual systems optimally matched for their visual worlds [53].

What about people? Studies of infants with various visual problems suggest that experience can alter human brain cells. Consider children with *astigmatisms*, abnormalities of the lens causing lines in some orientations to appear blurred. Unless astigmatic children receive corrective lenses at an early age, they always see lines in some orientations better than in others [54]. Presumably, experience alters the cells that detect line orientation. Deprivation of patterned visual stimulation may have been one of the factors contributing to S. B.'s visual readjustment problem too.

Active movement   Moving around actively is necessary for the development of visual-motor skills. In a classic study of this subject, psychologists Richard Held and Alan Hein raised pairs of kittens in darkness until one member of the pair, the "active" kitten, had sufficient strength and coordination to pull the other kitten, the "passive" one, in the gondola apparatus pictured in Figure 6-21. Both animals were then exposed to the same visual patterns and both moved about. But only the active kitten, the one pulling the gondola, was given the opportunity to coordinate vision and movement. The animals were tested after

FIGURE 6-21   The active and passive kittens in the Held-Hein study received the same types of visual stimulation. But only the active kitten developed normal sensorimotor skills during the course of the experiment. [*Ted Polumbaum.*]

experiencing these conditions three hours a day for ten days. The active kittens showed normal perceptual skills. They chose the shallow side of the visual cliff. They blinked at approaching objects. They extended their forepaws when moved gently downward toward the table's edge. The passive kittens had not developed these normal responses. The skills were recovered within forty-eight hours when the passive kittens were allowed to move about freely [55]. These findings have been replicated [56].

Active movement is considered important for people too. S. B.'s peculiar notions about distance may have had something to do with his inexperience in coordinating movement and vision early in life.

Note: Precisely how early deprivations disrupt the perceptual apparatus is not clear. Certain types of experiences may be necessary for fine tuning or sharpening the system, nurturing its development, and/or simply sustaining it [57].

Sensory Deprivation after Infancy

Jails and prisoner-of-war camps sometimes subject human beings to extremely restricted sensory environments. So do certain routine military, civil, and industrial jobs where workers may do little more than watch pointers, press buttons, and turn dials for eight hours at a time. Does prolonged exposure to such monotonous, relatively unpatterned sensory environments affect the organization of perception? In the early 1950s, psychologist Donald Hebb began systematically investigating this question. In one study, Hebb and his associates paid subjects to lie on a foam-rubber pillow on a comfortable bed in a lighted cubicle. To screen out patterned visual stimulation, participants in the study wore plastic visors. Cotton gloves and cardboard cuffs restricted the sense of touch. The only sound that the participants heard was the humming of an exhaust fan. Brief excursions to the toilet and time out for meals were the only relief from the dull routine. Would you like to

earn $75 a day by lying in bed under these conditions? You may be surprised to learn that most of Hebb's subjects found the "job" exceedingly difficult and unpleasant. In fact, many of them refused to continue with the experiment after two or three days.

Hebb and his colleagues found that the monotonous sensory environment affected behavior, physiology, and perception. After several days of sensory isolation, approximately two-thirds of the participants in the study reported seeing simple images, such as flashes of light, dots, and geometrical patterns. One-third reported complex images and scenes; for instance, "a procession of squirrels with sacks over their shoulders marching purposefully across a snowfield and out of the field of vision [58]." Perhaps this was the body's way of providing more stimulation for itself.

Many of Hebb's subjects reported temporary perceptual distortions even after emerging from sensory isolation. For some participants, the entire room seemed to be in motion. In some cases, vertical and horizontal edges curved, colors glowed, and/or objects changed shape and size [59]. There have been hundreds of investigations of sensory deprivation in adulthood since Hebb's early research. Many psychologists find that visual, auditory, and tactile perceptions are often temporarily altered when people are exposed to a monotonous, relatively unpatterned sensory environment [60]. Long-distance truckers and pilots on intercontinental flights report hallucinations too [61]. Evidently, continual patterned stimulation is important for normal perception.

It should be noted that sensory deprivation affects people differently. Length of time and precise conditions during deprivation are significant. So are the participant's personal characteristics. As we will see in Chapter 10, people vary in their needs for sensory stimulation. What constitutes optimal and unendurable sensory levels varies accordingly. Expectations influence the meaning of sensory deprivation experiences too. Individuals who anticipate beneficial effects may find brief sensory deprivation periods pleasant and, in some instances, helpful for fighting bad habits such as smoking and overeating [62].

States of Mind

Personal motives, emotions, values, goals, interests, expectations, and other mental states influence what people perceive. More than twenty years ago, psychologists Albert Hastorf and Hadley Cantril provided solid evidence for this hypothesis. They observed students' perceptions of an important football game. Samples of undergraduates from the participating schools, Dartmouth College and Princeton University, were shown a film of the game. The students were asked to identify rule violations and rate each one "mild" or "flagrant." Princeton students saw the Dartmouth players make twice as many violations as their own players and rated most of them "flagrant." The Dartmouth men saw the two teams make the same number of violations and rated half their own infractions "mild" [63]. Apparently, motives, emotions, values, and goals caused subjects to emphasize those incidents that had personal significance for them.

It's hardly surprising that people perceive complex, emotionally charged interpersonal encounters subjectively. Certainly, arguments, accidents, love affairs, and crimes are similarly perceived. We will have more to say about person-related perceptions in later chapters. In general, our expectations probably influence our perceptions in several ways. We tend to emphasize aspects of the data that are in harmony with our beliefs. Expectations also influence our actions, which affect the conduct of the perceived persons, in turn.

What about the simple incidents of every-day life? A great deal of research shows that state of mind influences perceptions of these events as well. When we value something, we tend to see it as bigger than it is [64]. We recognize things that interest us more quickly than those that bore us [65]. We often see what we expect to see. Figure 6-22 provides a vivid demonstration of this concept.

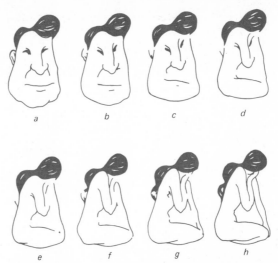

FIGURE 6-22 Can (e) be seen as a man's face? Can (d) be perceived as a woman's body? This series of sketches can be used to demonstrate the effects of expectations on perception. Find several volunteers who haven't seen the figures before. Show the series in order to half your subjects, beginning with (a). Show the series to the other half in reverse order, beginning with (h). Be sure to expose only one figure at a time, keeping the remaining ones covered. For each stimulus, ask, "What is it?" Each participant's first response will probably create persistent expectations that influence responses on (d) and (e). [From Fisher, 1967.]

Culture

Experiences in a particular culture can influence how visual information is processed. Consider the BaMbuti pygmies who live in dense tropical forests in the Congo where distant views are rare. The longest distance most BaMbutis ever see is about 100 feet—from the tops of trees to the ground. One young pygmy named Kenge traveled with a visiting anthropologist, Colin Turnbull, to an open plain where Kenge saw miles into the distance for the first time in his life. Here is Turnbull's account of this event:

Kenge looked over the plains and down to where a herd of about a hundred buffalo were grazing some miles away. He asked me what kind of insects they were, and I told him they were buffalo, twice as big as the forest buffalo known to him. He laughed loudly and told me not to tell such stupid stories, and asked me again what kind of insects they were. He then talked to himself, for want of more intelligent company, and tried to liken the buffalo to the various beetles and ants with which he was familiar.

He was still doing this when we got into the car and drove to where the animals were grazing. He watched them getting larger and larger, and though he was as courageous as any Pygmy, he moved over and sat close to me and muttered that it was witchcraft. . . . Finally, when he realized that they were real buffalo he was no longer afraid, but what puzzled him still was why they had been so small, and whether they really had been small and had so suddenly grown larger, or whether it had been some kind of trickery. [66]

Why didn't Kenge show size constancy? In one study bearing on this issue, psychologist Marshall Segall and his colleagues presented the visual illusions shown in Figure 6-23 to groups of people living in American · and European cities and in African and Philippine villages. Each subject was asked to judge which of the two equally long gray lines (those labeled 1 and 2) was longer. The Americans and Europeans were very susceptible to the

obtuse- and acute-angled illusions (*a*) and (*b*), and only moderately responsive to the horizontal-vertical illusions (*c*) and (*d*). Native Africans and Philippinos showed the opposite pattern.

One plausible explanation for these findings is differential experiences. Because Americans and Europeans live in a world of rectangles, they may unknowingly interpret acute- and obtuse-angled configurations as representing parts of three-dimensional rectangular forms. Consider illusion (*a*) in Figure 6-23 first. The arrow-like figures of the Müller-Lyer illusion resemble the skeletons of building corners. Pattern 1 corresponds to a nearby corner, like the one shown in Figure 6-24*a*. Pattern 2 corresponds to a distant corner, like the one shown in Figure 6-24*b*. Since the "corners" of Figure 6-23*a* project lines of identical size on the retina, city dwellers may automatically draw on past experiences and assume unconsciously that the distant "corner" (pattern 2) is longer. Now consider illusion (*c*) in Figure 6-23. Native Africans and Philippinos live on open, flat plains and often see roads or paths extending

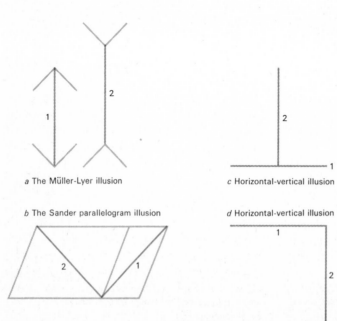

a The Müller-Lyer illusion

b The Sander parallelogram illusion

c Horizontal-vertical illusion

d Horizontal-vertical illusion

FIGURE 6-23 The four optical illusions used in the Segall study. In each illusion, pick the gray line (1 or 2) that looks longer. [*From Segall, Campbell, and Herskovitz, 1963.*]

a

b

FIGURE 6-24 The arrow-like figures of the Müller-Lyer illusion may remind people of nearby (*a*) and distant (*b*) building corners. [*John Briggs.*]

into the distance. They may unconsciously associate the vertical line in illusion (*c*) with such pathways and assume that the line is longer than it looks [67]. To gauge the size of an unfamiliar form, in other words, people may draw on past experiences in a particular environment to complement the size of the retinal image. If size constancy depends on past experience, Kenge's reactions in a strange situation become understandable. Culture influences the use of pictorial depth cues too. For an interesting discussion of this

topic, see reference 8 in this chapter's Suggested Readings. ▲

EXTRASENSORY PERCEPTION

Up until now we have been concerned with perceptual processes that depend on known sensory systems. We turn to the question, Do other types of perception exist? We begin with an anecdote that was reported by *This Week* magazine.

▲ **USING PSYCHOLOGY**

1. Suppose that you hear of two cases of gross deprivation. A child is confined to a dark room for the first six years of life, and an adult prisoner is left in a dark cell for six years. Who is likely to have the most severe perceptual problems? Explain.

2. Have you ever experienced brief periods of sensory deprivation? How did you respond? Speculate about the determinants of your reaction.

3. Describe instances where your own perceptions were influenced by motives, emotions, goals, and/or expectations.

4. Design an experiment testing the hypothesis, "Expectations influence visual perceptions," using the sketches in Figure 6-22. Conduct informal observations using the figure to see if the hypothesis is supported.

Fighting Crime with ESP

A young woman was returning home along a country road when a man leaped out from behind a stone storehouse and assaulted her with a hammer. The police immediately contacted a psychic named W. H. C. Tenhaeff to ask if he could help identify the criminal. Tenhaeff went at once to the police station, accompanied by his friend Gerard Croiset, another psychic.

There Croiset picked up the hammer that the police had found at the scene of the crime, squeezed its handle, and concentrated very hard. "The criminal," he announced, "was tall, dark, and about thirty years old, with a somewhat deformed left ear." Croiset added that the hammer belonged to another man living nearby in a small, white cottage.

A few months later the police arrested a tall, dark, twenty-nine-year-old man on a different charge. Noticing his scarred and swollen left ear, the police questioned the suspect about the attack on the young woman. Eventually the man admitted his guilt. He had borrowed the hammer from a friend who lived in a white cottage, the police later discovered [68].

Evaluating Anecdotal Evidence

Is this incident a bona fide instance of extrasensory perception (ESP)? To verify the facts, C. E. M. Hansel, a British psychologist, contacted the burgomaster (major civil official) of the village where the crime had occurred. Hansel found large discrepancies between the magazine story and the real one. The psychic was not immediately contacted by the police. He was approached some six weeks after the incident by a group of concerned townspeople. By this time the crime had been highly publicized, and the police had already identified a local suspect (who eventually confessed to the assault). Croiset made many predictions. Some turned out to be correct and others did not. The criminal, for example,

was young but he had two perfectly normal ears. And no one ever found out where the hammer came from. In short, even seemingly reliable personal accounts of extrasensory perception are not necessarily trustworthy.

Some of Croiset's statements were accurate. There is no debating that. But we cannot logically assume that extrasensory perception is the most appropriate explanation until four more likely alternatives—*chance, rational inference, acute sensory perception,* and *fraud*—have been ruled out [69]. First, it is entirely possible that Croiset made a lucky guess. A guess of "dark" and "young" will be right on some occasions. After all, criminals have to be light, medium, or dark and young, middle-aged, or old. It's somewhat like guessing the toss of a coin. If you say "heads," you'll be right 50 percent of the time. Predictions, truly based on extrasensory perception, should have a higher probability of being correct than random guesses. Unfortunately, we don't know anything about Croiset's "ESP batting average." Rational inference could also account for Croiset's successful predictions. It hardly requires extraordinary ability to know that women and old men rarely commit violent crimes. Acute sensory perception could explain Croiset's success in other situations. Like many fortune-tellers and mind readers, Croiset perhaps excelled at interpreting ordinary sensory cues including facial expressions that signal tension, joy, fear, and anger. Recall Hans, the horse described in Chapter 2 that made correct responses by noting almost imperceptible movements of the examiner's head. Both people and less complex animals can be quite sensitive to sensory cues. Fraud is another possibility that must be considered carefully. Croiset might have heard about the suspect from conversations with townspeople. Before we can conclude that extrasensory perception is responsible for a particular judgment in any situation, we have to eliminate likelier possibilities. Controlled observations are the only way to do this.

Evaluating Laboratory Investigations

A small number of scientists scattered throughout the world are currently investigating extrasensory perception and other *parapsychological* (psychic-related) phenomena. Joseph Banks Rhine, formerly a botanist, has been one of the most productive of American parapsychological researchers. Rhine became interested in studying extrasensory

perception under carefully controlled conditions in the early 1920s. In 1940 Rhine founded the Parapsychology Laboratory at Duke University, one of the largest centers of its kind in this country. Rhine's studies established model experimental procedures for parapsychological investigators. For many observations Rhine and his associates used a special deck of twenty-five cards. There were five cards showing five symbols: cross, star, circle, wavy lines, and square. See Figure 6-25. In the studies, the cards were shuffled, often mechanically. Then the participant was given twenty-five "trials." In studies that dealt with *telepathy* (the ability to read the thoughts of others), the behavioral scientist chose a card and looked at it before the subject "guessed" the symbol. In research on *clairvoyance* (the ability to see beyond the range of natural vision), the investigator selected a card and placed it face downward on the table without looking at it. Then the participant "guessed" the symbol. For investigations of *precognition* (the ability to foretell the future), the subject "guessed" the symbol that would appear before the experimenter selected the card.

Contemporary investigations of parapsychological phenomena use many types of stimuli besides cards, including flashing lights, slides of emotionally charged events, and paintings. Generally, strict precautions are taken to avoid cheating. The results are carefully compared with what is expected by chance. In "card-reading" studies, people should be able to make five correct responses out of every twenty-five, for example, simply by guessing. To demonstrate ESP, investigators must find people who consistently score above chance. While the number of hits among people who perform well is typically

FIGURE 6-25 Cards used in extrasensory perception studies.

small (perhaps seven out of twenty-five in a card study), some subjects do surprisingly well [70]. Individuals who believe that ESP exists tend to make slightly higher scores on laboratory tests than skeptics [71]. Curiously, task performance is sometimes enhanced by feedback about previous hits and misses [72].

Have laboratory studies established the existence of extrasensory perception? So far behavioral scientists are not convinced that researchers have eliminated all sources of error [73]. Problems can occur even in very

sophisticated studies, such as the one described in Figure 6-26. There are many good reasons for caution about accepting the existence of ESP.

1. Foremost, perhaps, is the point argued by Donald Hebb. "Personally," Hebb wrote, "I do not accept ESP for a moment, *because it does not make sense* [italics added]. . . . My own rejection . . . is—in the literal sense—a prejudice [74]." Parapsychological phenomena strain our rationality because they seem to work against physical laws. Many believers, incidentally, assume that psychic

FIGURE 6-26 In the mid-1970s, physicists Russell Targ and Harold Puthoff of the Stanford Research Institute in California conducted several extremely careful parapsychological investigations. In one series of tests, the Israeli "psychic" Uri Geller "received" and reproduced target pictures that had been drawn at remote locations. As you can see, five of Geller's reproductions were astonishingly accurate. How did he do it? Numerous precautions were taken to rule out explanations besides clairvoyance. Geller was placed in a visually, acoustically, and electrically shielded room. Target pictures were chosen and drawn after he had been sequestered. He did not know the identity of the persons selecting the target nor the method of target selection. To guard against biased scoring, the target pictures and Geller's drawings were submitted to two independent scientists for matching. All ten of Geller's reproductions were matched with the correct target [77]. Despite the experimenters' elaborate care, other scientists and magicians have pointed out how Geller's spectacular performance could have been accomplished by deceptive and distractive strategies and assorted forms of trickery [78]. Consequently, the "demonstration" remains controversial. [*From Targ and Puthoff, 1974.*]

▲ USING PSYCHOLOGY

1. List several good reasons for skepticism about ESP. Include reasons why anecdotes are, by themselves, insufficient proof.

2. Some people claim that animals have extrasensory perception and cite, as evidence, cases where pets react to the death of a master or mistress by dying, show an awareness (in advance) of an unexpectedly returning mistress or master, or exhibit intense restlessness before an earthquake. How else might each of these phenomena be explained?

abilities have natural explanations which will eventually be discovered.

2. Psychologists have been put off by the zeal and enthusiasm of many ESP investigators (scientists are supposed to be neutral) and by the dishonesty and deceit that have sometimes accompanied "demonstrations" of psychic phenomena [75].

3. Finally, a number of technical problems keep dubious psychologists skeptical. Experimental findings are usually inconsistent. Subjects may obtain high scores on some occasions but not on others, with some procedures but not with others, and under some investigators but not under others. In addition, as controls are tightened, the scores of

"psychics" frequently drop. Ordinarily, better methodology in psychological research results in more conclusive demonstrations. All too often, the reporting of parapsychological studies is haphazard, omitting important features of the laboratory setting or presenting discrepant versions of the methods used.

What can we conclude? At this time, about the only thing that behavioral scientists agree on is that extrasensory phenomena have not been disproved. Because the topic is so potentially important, ESP warrants further carefully designed, controlled studies. ▲

SUMMARY
Perceiving

1. Perceiving involves sensation, attention, consciousness, memory, information processing, and language.

2. Attention appears to have a limited capacity. Needs, interests, and values, as well as novel, unexpected, intense, and changing environmental events frequently direct people's attention.

3. Animals' bodies are equipped with specialized information-gathering sensory systems. Eleven human senses have been identified. They contain receptors which receive and transduce energy. While human senses interpret some information, they send most of the data to the brain for processing.

4. People and other animals use processing strategies to organize perception. In viewing objects, human beings (*a*) assume that color, size, and shape are constant, (*b*) discern figure-ground relationships, and (*c*) group separate elements into patterns. To perceive depth and distance, people

rely on physiological, movement-related, and pictorial cues.

5. Without realizing it, human beings continually adapt to distorted perceptual inputs.

6. Human babies process visual information about form and distance shortly after birth before learning is likely to have occurred. Some aspects of perception appear to be at least partially determined by heredity.

7. Experience influences perception too. Many ordinarily inevitable sensorimotor experiences during infancy are necessary for the normal development of certain perceptual skills. Limited periods of sensory deprivation after infancy can produce temporary perceptual distortions. States of mind influence perception. So does the cultural environment.

8. Scientists do not assume that extrasensory perception accounts for particular events until chance, rational inferences, acute sensory perceptions, and fraud have been ruled out. Laboratory research has not definitively established the existence of parapsychological phenomena.

A Study Guide for Chapter Six

Key terms sensation (172), perception (172), attention (173), sense (175), receptor (176), transduction (175), universal and species-specific detector (179), grouping principles (182) [similarity (182), proximity (182), symmetry (182), continuity (182), closure (183)], binocular depth cue (184) [binocular disparity (184), convergence (184)], monocular depth cue (184) [accommodation (184), motion parallax (184), pictorial cue (185)], pictorial depth cue [familiar size (185), linear perspective (185), light and shadow (185), texture gradient (185), aerial perspective (185), interposition (186)], extrasensory perception (197) [telepathy (199), clairvoyance (199), precognition (199)], parapsychology (199), and other italicized words and expressions.

Important research attention (Kahneman, others), information processing within the eyes (Lettvin, others), organization of the visual cortex (Hubel, Weisel, Thompson, Gross, others), perceptual adaptation (Stratton, others), form and depth perception in infancy (Fantz, Gibson, Walk, Campos, Bower, others), ordinarily inevitable sensorimotor influences (Riesen, Blakemore, Cooper, Held, Hein, others), sensory deprivation (Hebb, others), states of mind and perception (Hastorf, Cantril, others), culture and perception (Turnbull, Segall, others), ESP investigations (Hansel, Rhine, others).

Basic concepts distinction between sensation and perception, hypothesis-testing nature of perception, evidence that perception is an inexact mirror of reality, organizing principles of perception (constancy, figure-ground, grouping), explanation of perceptual adaptation (Rock), reasons for caution about ESP.

Self-Quiz

1. Which statement about sensation and perception is *true*?
- *a.* Sensation concerns objects, places, and events, while perception deals with categories such as quality and intensity.
- *b.* Sensation does not provide a mirrorlike view of reality, while perception does.
- *c.* Sensation involves bringing in information, while perception entails organizing and interpreting the data.
- *d.* Sensation requires perception, while perception does not require sensation.

2. How many human sensory systems are known to exist?
- *a.* 7   *b.* 9
- *c.* 11   *d.* 13

3. What does a transducer do?
- *a.* Carries information from one region to another.
- *b.* Converts energy from one form to another.
- *c.* Integrates information.
- *d.* Speeds up information processing.

4. In which situation are the rods *alone* most likely to be active?
- *a.* Driving in traffic on a sunny day
- *b.* Reading the fine print in an insurance policy
- *c.* Walking in the country on a moonlit night
- *d.* Watching a color TV in a dark room

5. During tests of the visual systems of cats and monkeys, which cortical cells responded as one type of line at a particular orientation moved slowly past a specific region of the retina?
- *a.* Complex   *b.* Hypercomplex
- *c.* Simple   *d.* Species-specific detector

6. You perceive a mailbox as having the same shape regardless of the angle from which it is viewed. Which perceptual organizing principle is illustrated?
- *a.* Constancy   *b.* Continuity
- *c.* Grouping   *d.* Similarity

7. What characterizes the ground in a figure-ground relationship?
- *a.* Definite shape   *b.* Farther distance
- *c.* "Ownership" of the contour   *d.* Vivid quality

8. Which cue is a binocular depth cue?
- *a.* Convergence   *b.* Linear perspective
- *c.* Motion parallax   *d.* Texture gradient

9. An artist draws a picture of a car driving down a long, straight highway. The distant lane markers on the road are sketched closer together than the near ones in order to suggest distance. Which depth cue is the artist using?
- *a.* Aerial perspective   *b.* Convergence
- *c.* Interposition   *d.* Linear perspective

10. A chair is perceived as being in front of a table which it partially blocks from view. Which pictorial depth cue is being used to judge the chair's distance?
- *a.* Aerial perspective   *b.* Interposition
- *c.* Light and shadow   *d.* Texture gradient

11. What did tests of human infants on the visual cliff show?
- *a.* Infants fear heights as soon as they begin to move about by themselves.
- *b.* Infants fear heights as soon as they can perceive depth.
- *c.* Infants do not perceive depth or fear heights until about nine months of age.
- *d.* Infants perceive depth and move about before they develop fears of heights.

12. What were the consequences of exposing a dark-reared kitten to vertical stripes (and only vertical stripes) for about six months?

a. After a brief adjustment period the cat showed normal vision.

b. The cat's retina did not function normally.

c. The cat behaved as if it did not see horizontal stripes.

d. While the cat saw stripes of all orientations, it showed a strong preference for vertical stripes.

13. How did several days of monotonous, relatively unpatterned surroundings influence human perception?

a. No effects during the deprivation period; temporary perceptual distortions following it

b. Hallucinations during the deprivation period; nothing following it

c. Hallucinations during the deprivation period; temporary perceptual distortions following it

d. Hallucinations during the deprivation period; permanent perceptural distortions following it

14. Which conclusion about the effects of mental states on perception is supported by research?

a. Mental states affect all types of perceptions.

b. Mental states affect sensations but not perceptions.

c. Mental states alter only interpersonal perceptions.

d. Expectations, motives, and emotions affect perceptions, but interests do not.

15. What did the reactions of a BaMbuti pygmy upon seeing distant buffalo for the first time suggest?

a. Expectations influence perception.

b. Experience in a particular culture influences perception.

c. Motives influence perception.

d. Perceptual principles are largely inborn.

Exercises

1. THE ANATOMY OF THE EYE. Match each part of the eye with its single most appropriate characteristic. To review this material, see pages 177 and 178.

_____ *1.* Cone

_____ *2.* Cornea

_____ *3.* Fovea

_____ *4.* Iris

_____ *5.* Lens

_____ *6.* Pupil

_____ *7.* Retina

_____ *8.* Rod

a. Region of the retina containing densely packed cones

b. The opening through which light is admitted

c. Controls the size of the pupil

d. Transparent covering that protects the eye; helps in focusing

e. Involved in accommodation; loses its elasticity with age

f. Prime receptor for color and detail

g. Rear inner surface of the eye upon which images are projected

h. Prime receptor in dim light

2. PERCEPTION OF OBJECTS. Match the perceptual principles with the appropriate example(s). The same examples may be explained by several principles. You may use the same principle more than once. Your answers will depend to some extent upon your visualization of the scene that is described. If your responses differ from those in the Answer Keys, check your reasoning carefully. To review the material, see pages 180 to 183.

PRINCIPLES: closure (C), constancy (CS), continuity (CT), figure-ground (F), proximity (P), similarity (SI), symmetry (SY)

_____ *1.* As a high school marching band parades around a stadium, trombone players standing shoulder to shoulder in rows form distinct moving lines.

_____ *2.* You see a distant airplane pass behind a cloud and reappear a few moments later. Though too far away to be identified, the position of the emerging plane and its direction of motion have led you to conclude that a single airplane is involved.

_____ *3.* A store has a display of cheeses in the window. The cheeses at the front obstruct our view of those toward the back. Though we cannot see these half-hidden cheeses in their entirety, we perceive them as spheres, cubes, cylinders, and other regular forms.

_____ *4.* Although you're close enough to see the individual red, white, and purple tulips in a floral display, you perceive a "tulip flag" with red and white stripes and white stars on a blue background.

_____ *5.* A tree silhouetted against the sky stands out from its blue surroundings.

_____ *6.* Looking closely at a newspaper photograph, we see that it's really just a collection of small black dots, yet we perceive it as a complete picture.

_____ *7.* After the sun sets over Elsie, our favorite red cow, our eyes signal shades of gray. Yet we continue to perceive Elsie as red.

3. PERCEPTION OF DEPTH AND DISTANCE. Check your understanding of depth and distance cues by matching each one with the *single most appropriate* example or definition. Indicate whether the cue is a monocular (M) or binocular (B) one. To review the material, see pages 183 to 186.

CUES: accommodation (A), aerial perspective (AP), binocular disparity (BD), convergence (C), familiar size (FS), interposition (I), light and shadow (LS), linear perspective (LP), motion parallax (MP), texture gradient (TG).

_____ *1.* Hazy blue mountains seem more distant than green or brown ones.

_____ 2. While riding in a train, the trees near you appear to move by more quickly than those in the distance.

_____ 3. A cat that partially blocks your view of a dog is assumed to be closer than the dog.

_____ 4. Seeing several friends approaching, you judge their distance by the size of the retinal images which they cast, without any conscious effort.

_____ 5. Information from muscles controlling the direction of the eyes enables you to determine the distance of a glass of water on the dinner table, as you eat.

_____ 6. The railroad tracks in a photograph converge but you assume that they're parallel.

_____ 7. As you stand on a shag rug in the center of a large room, the individual strands at your feet appear clear and distinct. The strands by the wall blur together.

_____ 8. Your brain combines slightly different images of the same scene cast on each retina so that a single three-dimensional image is seen.

_____ 9. With the sun behind you, the brighter side of a house seems closer.

_____ 10. The thickness of the lens in each eye changes as you shift your focus from wristwatch to shoelace.

4. PICTORIAL DEPTH CUES. For practice in identifying pictorial depth cues, describe those that William Hogarth misused in Figure 6-17 and those that Maurits Escher manipulated in Figures 6-3 and 6-5. To review the material, see pages 185 and 186.

Suggested Readings

1. Kaufman, L. *Perception: The world transformed*. New York: Oxford University Press, 1979. This text provides an excellent comprehensive introduction to perception. Using ordinary language, focusing on discoveries about the perceptual processes, and generously illustrated, the book covers all the sensory systems.

2. Gregory, R. L. *Eye and brain: The psychology of seeing*. (2d ed.) New York: McGraw-Hill, 1973 (paperback). This interesting, easily read introduction to vision discusses topics such as visual illusions, the evolution of the eye, color vision, and the role of learning in seeing.

3. Droscher, V. B. *The magic of the senses: New directions in animal perception*. New York: Harper & Row, 1971 (paperback). This fascinating account of recent research on the perceptual systems of animals includes discussions of the auditory system of bats and the navigational systems of birds and bees.

4. Bower, T. G. R. *Development in infancy*. San Francisco: Freeman, 1974 (paperback). More than half this brief book focuses on perception in infancy. Bower writes clearly and straightforwardly about his own research and that of many other psychologists.

5. Robinson, J. O. *The psychology of visual illusions*. London: Hutchinson University Library, 1972. Robinson's book provides an excellent summary—balanced and well-written—of over a hundred years of research on visual illusions, including observations on the probable causes of many of them.

6. Bartley, S. H. *Perception in everyday life*. New York: Harper & Row, 1972 (paperback). This small, informal book describes the various perceptual systems and gives many down-to-earth examples of their functioning in life situations, including motion sickness, bicycling, and seeing under water.

7. Teuber, M. L. Sources of ambiguity in the prints of Maurits C. Escher. *Scientific American*, 1974, **231**(1), 90–104; and Ranucci, E. R., & Teeters, J. L. *Creating Escher-type drawings*. Palo Alto, Calif.: Creative Publications, 1978. This article and book are recommended if you would like to see more of Escher's lithographs or learn more about his technology and deliberate use of perceptual experimental findings.

8. Deregowski, J. B. Pictorial perception and culture. *Scientific American*, 1972, **227**(5), 82–88. Deregowski describes intriguing research which suggests that pictures are perceived quite differently in various cultures because of differences in experience.

9. Melzack, R. The perception of pain. *Scientific American*, 1961, **204**(2), 41–49. Pain perception is one of the most fascinating perceptual puzzles. Melzack writes in a lively way about research on such subjects as the influences of early experience, attention, and culture on pain. He also describes phantom limb pain in amputees.

10. Land, E. H. The retinex theory of color vision. *Scientific American*, 1977, **237**(6), 108–128. Land describes how the visual system may extract reliable color information from the everyday world.

11. Beloff, J. Why parapsychology is still on trial. *Human Nature*, 1978, **1**(12), 69–74. This brief survey of recent ESP research describes some reasons why psychologists remain skeptical.

Answer Keys

Self-Quiz

1. *c* (171) **2.** *c* (175) **3.** *b* (175) **4.** *c* (178)
5. *c* (179) **6.** *a* (180) **7.** *b* (181) **8.** *a* (184)
9. *d* (185) **10.** *b* (186) **11.** *d* (191) **12.** *c* (192)
13. *c* (194) **14.** *a* (195) **15.** *b* (195)

Exercise 1

1. *f* **2.** *d* **3.** *a* **4.** *c* **5.** *e* **6.** *b* **7.** *g*
8. *h*

Exercise 2

1. P, SI, CT **2.** CT **3.** SY, C, CT **4.** SI, P
5. F **6.** C, P **7.** CS

Exercise 3

1. AP (M) **2.** MP (M) **3.** I (M) **4.** FS (M) **5.** C (B)
6. LP (M) [correct, but less appropriate: FS (M)]
7. TG (M) **8.** BD (B) **9.** LS (M) **10.** A (M)

Exercise 4

To check responses that you feel uncertain about, talk
with your teacher.

CHAPTER SEVEN
Consciousness

At any single point in time, people are aware to some degree of what is happening inside and/or outside themselves. Often they are in touch with a flowing, meandering mixture of thoughts, feelings, fantasies, memories, and perceptions. This chapter focuses on the subject of consciousness. One characteristic of consciousness is its diversity. As William James recognized more than eighty years ago:

Our normal waking consciousness, rational consciousness as we call it, is but one special type of consciousness, whilst all about it, parted from it by the filmiest of screens, there lie potential forms of consciousness entirely different. We may go through life without suspecting their existence; but apply the requisite stimulus, and at a touch they are there in all their completeness. [1]

We begin with several first-person accounts which illustrate the varieties of consciousness.

The Varieties of Consciousness: Several Personal Descriptions

In the novel *Ulysses*, James Joyce provides this glimpse into his heroine's waking stream of consciousness. "I love flowers Id love to have the whole place swimming in roses God of heaven theres nothing like nature the wild mountains then the sea and the waves rushing then the beautiful country with fields of oats and wheat and all kinds of things and all the fine cattle going about that would do your heart good to see rivers and lakes and flowers all sorts of shapes and smells and colors spring up even out of the ditches primroses and violets nature it is as for them saying theres no God I wouldnt give a snap of my two fingers for all their learning why dont they go and create something [2]."

Waking from sleep, a participant in a laboratory study related this experience. "I was observing the inside of a pleural cavity [a part of the lung]. There were small people in it, like in a room. The people were hairy, like monkeys. The walls of the pleural cavity are made of ice and slippery. In the midpart there is an ivory bench with people sitting on it. Some people are throwing balls of cheese against the inner side of the chest wall [3]."

A deeply hypnotized person reported, "It felt like my eyes were turned around and I could see inside myself . . . as though my eyes and head were not part of my body but suspended on

the ceiling. I was completely unaware of any other part of my body [4]."

During meditation Turkish dervishes (members of a Muslim sect) whirl in circles. A participant observer recorded this experience: "The circles moved faster and faster until I (moving in the outer circle) saw only a whirl of robes and lost count of time. Now and then, with a grunt or a sharp cry, one of the dervishes would drop out of the circle and would be led away by an assistant to lie on the ground in what seemed to be an hypnotic state. I began to be affected and found that, although I was not dizzy, my mind was functioning in a very strange and unfamiliar way. The sensation is difficult to describe and is

probably a complex one. One feeling was that of lightening; as if I had no anxieties, no problems. Another was that I was a part of this moving circle and that my individuality was gone; I was delightfully merged in something larger [5]." (See Figure 7-9.)

A man under the influence of peyote described these perceptions to behavioral scientists. "Sensations were acute. I heard, saw, felt, smelled, and tasted more fully than ever before (or since). A peanut butter sandwich was a delicacy not even a god could deserve. . . . To touch a fabric with one's fingertip was to simultaneously know more about one's fingertip and the fabric than one had ever known about either [6]."

In this chapter we explore ordinary waking consciousness and the altered forms of consciousness that occur during sleep, hypnosis, meditation, and marijuana intoxication. We turn first to several preliminary matters.

CONSCIOUSNESS: PRELIMINARY ISSUES

How is consciousness defined? How is it investigated?

Defining Consciousness

The term *consciousness* has multiple meanings [7]. We use the word to refer to a person's (1) total awareness and/or (2) normal waking state. States besides the ordinary waking one are usually considered *altered states of consciousness*. These forms may be produced naturally (by sleep and disease, for example) or deliberately. For thousands of years people all over the world have been experimenting with consciousness-altering procedures, including chanting, whirling,

fasting, breathing rapidly, concentrating intensely, smoking, and ingesting drugs. See Figure 7-1.

Studying Consciousness: Past and Present

You may remember that Wilhelm Wundt, the founder of scientific psychology, advocated that behavioral scientists concentrate on the elementary processes of human consciousness. He and his followers gathered data by asking people to look within, or *introspect*, and describe their sensations. William James, the distinguished functionalist psychologist, was intensely curious about the operation of the human mind, too. But with the rise of John Watson's behaviorism in the 1930s, psychologists turned their attention away from consciousness and other mental functions, since these phenomena could not be observed and measured objectively. Intellectual activities of all types were considered unsuitable topics for serious study. "Respectable" behavioristic investigators focused al-

FIGURE 7-1 A religious dance ceremony on the island of Bali dramatizes the triumphs of gods and goddesses over evil. In many such ceremonies, dancers and audience tend to become so involved in chanting and in acting out the stories that they enter a trancelike state. Why do people in different cultures all over the world utilize consciousness-altering procedures? Andrew Weil, a psychiatrist who has studied drug use extensively, believes that human beings are born with a drive to alter their awareness and transcend their self-centered way of looking at life [86]. Students of the American drug scene mention less exotic motives, such as curiosity, pressure from peers, and escape from personal problems. Psychologist Robert Ornstein believes that alternative forms of consciousness, especially meditation, are attractive to people for three reasons. (1) They deepen awareness of the sensory, aesthetic, and emotional aspects of life. This sensitivity is often missing in our language- and logic-oriented society. (2) They produce feelings of unity which are particularly comforting today when survival seems to depend on solving worldwide problems, including famine, pollution, and nuclear weaponry. (3) They provide moments of peace and quiet—rare experiences in contemporary life [87]. [*Thomas Hopker/Woodfin Camp.*]

most exclusively on stimuli and responses, and they ignored the internal activities that intervened between the two. In the 1950s, attitudes began changing. Currently, most behavioral scientists consider it essential to gain an understanding of such long neglected activities as consciousness, memory, thought, language, and other cognitive functions.

Since no one has access to anybody else's cognitions, consciousness (like other mental functions) has to be studied indirectly. Whenever possible, investigators rely on the scientific procedures emphasized by the behavioristic tradition. Three strategies are commonly used in consciousness studies: gathering self-observations and self-reports, observing behavior, and measuring physiological func-

tions. We look briefly at the advantages and limitations of each approach. Later we see how these procedures are applied to specific issues. Self-observations and self-reports (including ratings and questionnaire and interview responses) are heavily employed in consciousness research because they are the only strategy that provides information about awareness itself. The general problems of this procedure have been mentioned before. In this case, research participants may represent their consciousness falsely because of a desire to project a certain image or because of lack of effort or insight. Though it is certainly difficult to describe ordinary consciousness, it is much harder to describe unusual states. Because language was developed to communicate about experiences occurring during ordinary waking consciousness, words frequently seem inadequate for characterizing impressions that arise at other times. In some conditions (sleep or meditation, for example), it is impossible to communicate about awareness during the experience itself. Consequently, people have to rely on memory, a notorious distorter of information. These measurement problems are compounded by the phenomenon known as *state-dependent learning*. As we see in Chapter 8, human beings who learn something in one state—perhaps under the influence of a drug—recall the material better in a similarly altered condition than in their usual one. It may be asking for the impossible, then, to expect anyone to remember accurately sensations experienced during another state of awareness. Because self-observation and self-report data have so many problems, investigators often turn to behavioral and physiological observations. Though less prone to bias, these procedures have limitations of their own. Knowing that a certain type of consciousness is associated with a particular problem-solving approach or a specific blood pressure pattern, for instance, may be quite interesting and important. But it doesn't shed light on consciousness itself. Once again, the strategy of combining varied methods appears most likely to advance our understanding.

ORDINARY WAKING CONSCIOUSNESS

Like James Joyce's heroine, waking people engage in running internal monologues. The "conversations" vary from individual to individual and from moment to moment in the same human being. Most of the time, consciousness is probably more chaotic than Joyce's portrayal. Besides thoughts, there are perceptions, memories, images, and feelings. The flow moves rapidly and often in an extremely disjointed and incoherent fashion. In this section we describe theory and research on waking consciousness, considering several basic issues. How is ordinary waking consciousness studied? What is its nature? What influences it?

Investigating Ordinary Waking Consciousness

How do psychologists study ordinary waking consciousness? In general, they try to use procedures that minimize the subject's need to remember or rely on global impressions. Sometimes investigators invite research participants to think aloud in the laboratory. In other cases, they call upon people to describe or rate specific attributes of their awareness (the strangeness of their thoughts, for example). They may also ask subjects to record mechanically—say, by pressing a lever—special events, perhaps shifts in thinking. This strategy probably minimizes self-consciousness and reduces the observer's influence. One promising tactic is known as *thought sampling*. Individuals are asked periodically for a report or rating of their mental content as they work tasks in the laboratory or go about their daily lives. Unfortunately, there is no known way to verify what a specific participant reports. And the process of reporting must necessarily distort to some degree the ongoing stream. There is another serious limitation that should be kept in mind. Current ideas about ordinary awareness have been derived largely from comparatively few observations and have yet to be verified.

The Nature of Ordinary Waking Consciousness

While behavioral scientists view waking consciousness as multidimensional, they divide it in different ways. Psychologist Ernest Hilgard distinguishes between *active* and *receptive* aspects of consciousness. Planning, initiating, and monitoring actions and exerting other types of control over behavior are considered active functions. Receptive operations include simple awareness of thoughts, emotions, sensations, images, and the like. Hilgard and many other psychologists speculate that consciousness is influenced by parallel brain subsystems, including those that underlie memories, emotions, dreams, and fantasies. Presumably, the varied systems actively register and process information independently and without awareness of one another. At any given moment one subsystem assumes control [8]. Research on hemispheric functioning, reviewed in Chapter 4, supports this type of analysis. You may recall that we described two specialized brain systems that were active under different conditions. Recent case studies by L. Weiskrantz, coworkers, and others suggest forcefully that systems of which people are unaware may influence ordinary waking consciousness. For instance, one patient, called D. B., had sustained highly specific damage to the occipital lobe of the brain. He reported being unable to see with one eye. But, at some level, visual information was being registered by the "blind" eye. D. B. could "guess" with great accuracy what the "nonseeing" eye had been shown. The man could distinguish the location of a spot of light and detect differences between red and green, crosses and circles, and horizontal and vertical lines by "feelings." He was not directly aware of any visual input in these instances [9].

Attention (discussed in Chapter 6) appears to play an important role in directing awareness by admitting or denying specific experiences entry into consciousness [10]. Millions of events occur at any given moment, but only a few slip into awareness. "My experience," in James's words, "is what I agree to attend to [11]." Behavioral scientists who subscribe to the subsystems approach assume that as attention patterns change, different systems take control. During altered forms of consciousness, attention may shift automatically, putting new subsystems in command of behavior.

During the past few years, research has begun to yield some interesting preliminary information about the flow of consciousness under fairly ordinary circumstances. In one series of studies, psychologist Kenneth Pope had college students report on their stream of consciousness for about an hour under different conditions. Some subjects gave verbal reports while others pressed keys to describe various dimensions of their experiences. Some reclined; some sat; others walked about. Pope found that posture influenced people's consciousness in several ways. Reclining subjects concentrated on past and future topics for longer periods of time than others. Shifts in thinking were recorded every five seconds or so, on the average, using the key-press procedure [12]. Psychologist Eric Klinger had normal college student research participants answer questions about their consciousness periodically in the laboratory and in real life for as long as nine months. Outside the laboratory an electronic beeper device reminded participants to report their experiences at random intervals (every forty minutes on the average). Klinger found that most of the reported material was specific, present-oriented, realistic, and related to the ongoing situation. Surprisingly, one out of every five reports concerned strange or distorted experiences. Large individual differences in thinking patterns were apparent [13].

Influences on Ordinary Waking Consciousness

Ordinary waking consciousness is continually changing, often in subtle ways that pass unnoticed. Sometimes our awareness is intuitive. We seem to be attuned to mystery, beauty, music, art, emotion, and sensation. At other times, consciousness is rational and analytic. We focus on intellectual matters, clear expression, facts, and reality. Consciousness changes with variations in fatigue. When you feel drowsy and dull, for example, you might catch yourself staring into space and find that you have not been registering the sights and sounds around you. When you feel alert, in contrast, your impressions of the world may be vivid and clear. Moods, such as depression and joy, color our awareness of reality. Consciousness is also influenced by enduring personal characteristics and by environmental circumstances. Psychologist

Steven Starker has discovered thematic continuities between daytime fantasies and night dreams that appear to reflect more than similar self-report styles. Consistent amounts of positive emotion, fear, hostility, and bizarreness (strangeness) characterize reports about both activities [14]. Presumably, an individual's temperament influences her or his awareness. Bodily rhythms appear to affect consciousness too. Many biological functions follow regular cycles. Hormone levels, heart rate, and body temperature, for instance, change predictably throughout the day. Such rhythmic cycles, or *biological rhythms*, are strongly correlated with subtle changes in waking consciousness. Many scientists believe that the rhythmic bodily activities contribute somehow to conscious experience. There is evidence, for example, that internal temperature helps determine how people feel when they wake up. Body temperature usually drops to a low point between 1 A.M. and 7 A.M. If your temperature begins rising in the morning before you do and reaches a comfortable level by the time you're out of bed, you probably feel alert and clear-headed when you get up. If your temperature is relatively low when you awaken, the chances are good that you'll be groggy and inefficient initially.

When normal women and men record their feelings systematically each day for several months, scientists observe fairly regular cycles of elation, anger, anxiety, depression, lucidity, and drowsiness. These orderly fluctuations, which influence consciousness, are thought to reflect the cycling of biological functions [15]. See Figure 7-2.

Environmental circumstances also shape the contents of consciousness. Earlier, we described the effects of posture. We mentioned that most waking thoughts concern present ongoing activities. This latter observation has been confirmed. Ronald Graef and his coworkers asked research participants to carry electronic paging devices for about a week. The devices beeped seven to nine times a day, reminding participants to answer questions about thoughts, actions, and moods. The psychologists found that about 56 percent of the reported thoughts were "bound" to the activity in which the person was engaged [16]. Attending to the environment, and especially to novel, unexpected, intense, changing, and need-related incidents, has survival value. It enables people to react quickly to dangers and plan appropriate behavior to fulfill basic requirements. Internal focusing serves several complementary functions: keeping people alert when bored or drowsy and helping reduce stress. (We describe the stress-reducing functions of cognitions in detail in Chapter 14.) ▲

FIGURE 7-2 When people travel long distances east-west by jet plane, they have to adjust their sleeping schedules. If the required readjustment is five or more hours, various bodily cycles which are ordinarily synchronized become desynchronized, and the individual experiences *jet lag*. Just as synchronized rhythms appear to influence our consciousness, so do desynchronized ones. Jet lag is characterized by fatigue, changes in mood, inefficiency, and similar complaints. The various desynchronized bodily cycles require different periods of time to adapt. The sleep-waking rhythm takes a few days. Temperature and hormonal patterns need a week or so. Other rhythms require even more time. Until the body is resynchronized, one is likely to continue feeling tired and ineffective. Highly irregular sleep schedules, such as those associated with shift work, produce similar symptoms. There is still a lot to be learned about jet lag and related disturbances, including how they affect health over the long run, why older people suffer more than younger ones, and why a busy schedule and social interactions facilitate the adaptation process [88]. [*British Airways.*]

SLEEP AND DREAMING

Alternating periods of sleep and waking organize the days of our lives. The sleep-waking rhythm interweaves with more than a hundred other roughly twenty-four-hour bodily cycles. Originally, scientists suspected that the great rhythms of the universe, like the sun's daily cycle, set and maintained our individual "clocks." In some cases that may be so. Total darkness, blindness, or continuous light will abolish certain twenty-four-hour hormonal rhythms in animals, but not the sleep-waking rhythm [17]. This cycle seems to be controlled from within. See Figure 7-3. During sleep, consciousness changes drastically, of course. In this section we describe the state called *sleep*, focusing on these questions: How do psychologists study sleep? Are there different types of sleep? Is sleep necessary? Later, we turn to dreaming, the state of consciousness associated with human sleep.

Studying Sleep

Women and men have been speculating about sleep for thousands of years and investigating it scientifically for approximately forty. The invention of the *electroencephalograph* (EEG), an instrument that measures the electrical activity occurring within the neural circuits of the brain, greatly advanced the systematic study of sleep. A sample EEG recording, known as an *electroencephalogram*, appears in Figure 7-4. Researchers use the shapes of the wave forms shown here to identify different sleep and waking states.

Because it takes considerable practice to become proficient at recognizing these wave forms, you will probably have to rely heavily on the verbal descriptions of the sleep states. Still, we will refer repeatedly to this recording.

In 1937, scientists discovered that the brain's electrical activity changed regularly both before and during the course of sleep. Since that time, researchers have been using the EEG and other machines which record eye movements, muscle tension, respiration, heart rate, sweating, and other physiological responses to study sleep as an ongoing, moment-to-moment activity. Sometimes the sleep of animals is monitored. Sometimes human volunteers are paid to spend several nights in a *sleep laboratory*. The first laboratories were established in the 1950s. Today there are more than thirty permanent sleep laboratories scattered throughout the United States. Typically, they contain private, bedroomlike compartments (as shown in Figure 7-5) and extensive electronic equipment for measuring the sleepers' physiological responses (as pictured in Figure 7-6). Knowledge about human sleep comes principally from studying thousands of sleep-laboratory volunteers, frequently college students.

Different Types of Sleep

A picture of sleep has been pieced together slowly by numerous sleep researchers. It is clear now that sleep is not a unitary activity, but a sequence of repeated stages. Each stage

FIGURE 7-3 Sleep researchers Nathaniel Kleitman and B. H. Richardson emerge from Mammoth Cave in 1938 after thirty-two days in a damp, chilly underground chamber. During this time the scientists lived in almost total isolation from the outside world while they attempted to adjust to a twenty-eight-hour daily schedule (nineteen hours awake and nine sleeping). Today many investigators are trying to learn more about the sleep-waking cycle and other bodily rhythms by studying people as they live for weeks in special "time-free" laboratory environments. In these settings, all time cues (including clocks, radios, and the sight of natural daylight and dark) are eliminated. Research participants are free to schedule meals, activities, and rest periods as they like. Most persons eventually settle into *consistent*, individualistic sleep-waking patterns of approximately twenty-four to twenty-six hours [89]. In some cases, people adopt roughly forty-eight-, seventy-two-, or even ninety-six-hour rhythms [90]. Since some studies have lasted as long as five and a half months, it seems unreasonable to attribute the regular patterns to the persistence of simple habits. It is more likely that genes program the body's roughly twenty-four-hour sleep-waking cycle. Ordinarily, people probably use external cues, such as alarm clocks or the rising sun, to "reset" their internal rhythm each day. [*William Dement*, Some must watch while some must sleep. *New York: Norton, 1978.*]

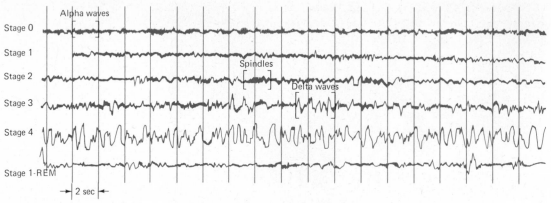

FIGURE 7-4 An electroencephalogram showing the major stages of sleep. The wave forms that characterize specific stages of sleep are labeled. [*W. B. Webb, University of Florida Sleep Laboratories.*]

is characterized by particular types of brain and bodily activity. A presleep stage, called *stage 0*, occurs once as people begin falling asleep. We are still awake at this time, but less responsive than usual to sensory stimulation. Our muscles loosen up, and our brains frequently show a high level of *alpha activity*, brain waves of about 8 to 12 hertz (cycles per second). Alpha waves can be seen on the electroencephalogram in Figure 7-4. This brain-wave activity is sometimes associated with pleasantly relaxed feelings. If aroused during stage 0, people are likely to report thoughts, sensations of floating, images, and dream fragments (such as the second incident in the introduction to this chapter). Most adults average ten minutes or less to attain the state scientists call sleep [18]. See Figure 7-7.

Every night the typical human sleeper experiences two separate and distinct types of sleep: NREM (pronounced non-rem) and REM sleep. *REM* stands for *R*apid *E*ye *M*ovements. As you might expect, bursts of eye movements occur commonly during REM sleep and rarely during NREM sleep. Slowly rolling eye movements may appear during all sleep phases.

NREM sleep People experience four stages of NREM sleep. Each is characterized by a specific type of brain-wave pattern and associated with a number of other physiological and behavioral signs.

Stage 1: Light sleep. As sleep begins, this brief period lasts only a few mintues. Light sleep, at sleep onset, may be considered a continuation of stage 0. People are still falling asleep. They are easy to awaken. If aroused, they are frequently unaware of having been asleep. During this phase, sensations of floating, images, vague thoughts, and dream fragments continue to be common. The body is more relaxed than previously. Brief episodes of stage 1 sleep will recur throughout the night. Fast irregular waves of low amplitude appear on the electroencephalogram, as you can see. (*Amplitude* refers to the heights of the waves and usually reflects voltage.)

Stage 2: Intermediate sleep. During this stage the sleeper is more relaxed and harder to waken than during stage 1. There may be *hallucinations* (sensory experiences without a basis in reality), such as flashes of light, crashes, or shots. A *myoclonic seizure*, a sudden, uncoordinated jerk of the body accompanied by the feeling of falling, is most likely to occur during this stage at the beginning of the sleep cycle. Bursts of 13 to 16 hertz waves lasting between one-half and two seconds, called *spindles*, begin to appear on the electroencephalogram. (See Figure 7-4.)

Stage 3: Deep sleep. As people sink still deeper into sleep, they become relatively unresponsive to sounds and difficult to awaken. At this time, slow (2 hertz or less) high-amplitude waves, called *delta waves*, begin. They are interspersed with spindles and fast, irregular, low-amplitude waves, as shown on the sample electroencephalogram.

Stage 4: Deepest sleep. The sleeper, totally relaxed now, rarely moves and is oblivious to the outside world and extremely hard to awaken. Yet, if sleep irregularities, including sleepwalking or talking, night terrors, or bed wetting occur at all, they are likely to appear during this deepest sleep phase. Delta waves dominate the electroencephalogram, as shown in Figure 7-4.

REM sleep During REM sleep the eyes dart about relatively quickly beneath the closed lids. Typically, there are one or two movements per second in short bursts, not continuously. Vivid dreams occur at this time. Though the research is controversial, there is support for the idea that the eyes move as if they are scanning the visual events of the dream [19]. REM sleep appears to have only one stage and is known as *stage 1 REM* or, because of its seemingly contradictory features, also as *paradoxical sleep*. During this phase scientists record fast, irregular, low-amplitude brain waves similar to those observed during stage 1 NREM (as shown in Figure 7-4). This pattern suggests a lot of cortical activity. Yet the sleeper is as unresponsive to most outside stimulation as during stage 4 sleep. (Interestingly, there is greater activity in the minor hemisphere, the more perceptual, less analytic one. When this hemisphere is damaged, dreaming sometimes ceases [20].) While dreams appear to be "acted out" in the appropriate motor areas of the brain, body movements are inhibited. Although some muscles may jerk and twitch at this time, many—particularly those in the head and neck—are totally relaxed and so lacking in muscle tone that sleepers often report feeling temporarily paralyzed when awakened from this stage. In animals the

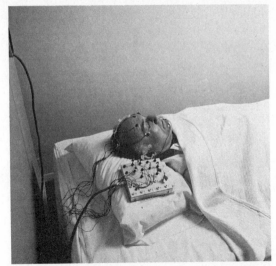

FIGURE 7-5 A sleeper is wired up for the night in a sleep laboratory. Today research about normal sleep is being used to treat people who are suffering from sleep disorders such as insomnia. The term *insomnia* refers to several related problems: taking a long time to fall asleep, waking many times or very early, or sleeping very lightly and unsatisfactorily. When surveyed, more than 14 percent of Americans report persistent insomnia, while about 50 percent report suffering from occasional insomnia. What causes insomnia? If people wrestle with distressing problems before bedtime, they are likely to have trouble falling asleep. Disrupted biological rhythms, mentioned in Figure 7-2, lead to sleeping difficulties. So do the varied drugs which alter sleep patterns, including alcohol, barbiturates, tranquilizers, antidepressants, and stimulants. Aging appears to be associated with unsatisfactory sleep, too. Sleep can also be impaired by illness or a malfunctioning nervous system. Monitoring sleep in a laboratory can help determine the nature of a sleep disturbance so that it can be treated more effectively. Incidentally, healthy adults vary greatly in the amount of sleep they need. The average sleep requirement is a bit more than seven hours. Still, a small but significant percentage of normal adults require more than ten or less than three hours of sleep per night to function well [91]. [*Montefiore Hospital and Medical Center.*]

relaxation is even more general and complete. REM sleep is also characterized by intense variability in the autonomic nervous system. During REM periods, breathing and heart rate are both slightly more rapid and a lot more irregular than during NREM periods.

Similarly, blood pressure is comparatively elevated and erratic. And larger quantities of the adrenal hormones are secreted during REM sleep. In males (even newborns), there are penile erections which last throughout the REM stage. The vaginal tissue of the female shows a corresponding response [21]. This reaction is not necessarily associated with dreams of a sexual nature.

How the sleep stages fit together
Research shows that people wind their way back and forth sequentially through the sleep stages: 1, 2, 3, 4, 3, 2, 1, 2, 3, 4, 3, 2, 1, and so on. Initially, we pass through stage 1 NREM on the way to deeper sleep levels. Subsequent periods of stage 1 sleep are largely stage 1 REM sleep. There are four to six *sleep cycles* within a single night of human sleep. The first cycle lasts from the onset of sleep to the end of the first REM period; the second cycle from this point to the end of the second REM period. Stage 4 sleep is concentrated within the first few hours of the night. (After people reach the age of fifty or so, it may drop out entirely.) The REM stage dominates morning sleep. On the average, young adults (eighteen to twenty-two years of age) spend approximately 5 percent of the night in stage 1 NREM sleep, slightly less than 25 percent in stage 1 REM, roughly 50 percent in stage 2, and the remaining 20 percent in stages 3 and 4. Laboratory observations suggest that each individual has a characteristic sleep pattern that deviates in minor ways from these averages and changes slightly from night to night. See Figure 7-8.

The Purpose of Sleep
How do you feel after staying awake all night? Most people respond, "Sleepy," a term that is usually defined as "uncomfortable, irritable, and less efficient." But is sleep necessary for well-being? One way to find out is to observe people's behavior and monitor their physiological responses before and after sleep deprivation. Many such studies have been conducted. First, consider the behavioral effects of sleep

loss. After missing sleep for several nights, a small minority of individuals (probably fewer than 10 percent) experience *hallucinations* and *delusions* (persistent false beliefs that resist reason). Most people respond to several day's sleep loss with comparatively mild symptoms: inattention (frequent loss of train of thought) misperception, momentary confusion, apathy, and irritation. Human beings work more slowly, take longer to react, and find it more difficult than usual to perform complex or prolonged tasks. Serious psychosis-like symptoms are most likely to occur under several conditions:

When a great deal of energy is being expended, illness or stress is present, or alcohol or drugs are in use

When subject and/or investigator expect dire effects

When the environment is gloomy or depressing

When the subject is emotionally troubled

What about the physical effects of sleep loss? Fine hand tremors, difficulty in focusing the eyes, drooping eyelids, increased sensitivity to pain, and a reduction in alpha activity frequently accompany prolonged sleep loss. After being awake for five straight days and nights, the heart and the respiratory system function somewhat sluggishly. Mild and subtle biochemical changes occur too. The absence of severe symptoms is remarkable, considering the very obvious consequences of sleep loss. At the very least, the person is probably desynchronizing biological rhythms (as in jet lag), expending additional energy to remain awake, and changing dietary habits. After reviewing the existing literature on sleep deprivation, psychologist Wilse Webb has concluded that scientists have yet to find any physiological systems which are seriously disrupted by sleep loss [22]. Nor have the scientists found that sleep loss has any serious long-term consequences. Instead of "hibernating" for days to make up for a long period of sleep deprivation, people usually sleep some twelve to fifteen hours and wake up feeling refreshed. After that long sleep period, human beings perform almost as well on cognitive tests as under normal circumstances. Feelings of fatigue usually persist for two or three days. Mild physiological irregularities may continue for several weeks [23].

Recently, John Pappenheimer of the Harvard Medical School and several Italian researchers have found that the brain of goats and rats produce a "sleep-inducing syrup" when the animals are deprived of sleep for a day or two. If that fluid is slowly introduced into the brains of rabbits and other animals, the recipients' sleep is increased in duration and frequency. Neither the precise composition of the fluid nor its specific effects on the body have been identified yet [24].

Initially, behavioral scientists believed that deprivation studies would suggest reasons why sleep is needed. So far the research has not provided this information. A number of likely hypotheses about the needs sleep serves are currently being investigated. We mention several that pertain to NREM sleep now and examine some that apply to REM sleep later in the chapter. (1) During NREM sleep the body may replenish chemical substances that aid in tissue repair, growth, the synthesis of proteins, and other basic life processes. (2) NREM sleep may allow neural systems involved in higher mental processes (such as learning) to rest [25]. Or, sleep may not serve any physiological needs at all, as Wilse Webb has recently proposed. He speculates that sleep may simply have been programmed into animals' genes by natural selection. Creatures who tended to conserve their energy (and their lives perhaps) by sleeping at times when food gathering and defense against predators were exceedingly difficult were more apt than others to thrive and reproduce similarly inclined offspring [26]. ▲

We focus now on dreaming, the state of consciousness that accompanies human sleep. We explore three questions: Are there different types of dreams? What do people dream about? Why do people dream?

Dreams of REM and NREM Sleep

In the early 1950s, University of Chicago sleep researchers Eugene Aserinsky and Nathaniel Kleitman discovered that people's rapid eye movement periods followed a definite pattern. The activity started about ninety minutes after sleep began, continued about ten minutes, and recurred in increasingly longer bursts at approximately ninety-minute intervals throughout the remainder of the night. The eye movements coincided with a type of brain-wave activity usually associated with an alert, excited state of mind. Aserinsky and Kleitman suspected that the sleeper's eyes might be scanning dream imagery. To find out whether dreams occurred at this time, the investigators woke people up during various phases of sleep and asked them to describe what they had been experiencing. Subjects reported *vivid dreams* 74 percent of the time after awakening from REM sleep and only 7 percent of the time after awakening from NREM sleep [27]. Incidentally, even people who swear they never dream report dreams under these conditions.

▲ **USING PSYCHOLOGY**

1. Suppose that an acquaintance is convinced that increasing alpha brain-wave activity will reduce her unhappiness. Explain the uncertainties and controversies about alpha. (See Figure 7-7.)

2. Explain why sleep cannot be considered a single unitary phenomenon.

3. How are REM and stage 4 sleep similar? Different?

4. Imagine reading about a soldier in a combat zone who reacts severely to prolonged sleep loss. What conditions are likely to have contributed to the response?

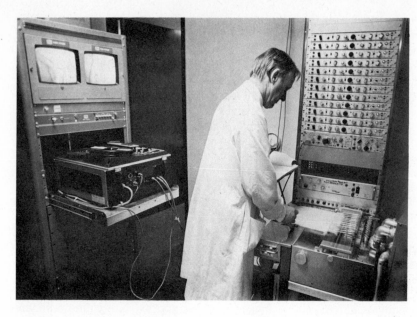

FIGURE 7-6 A sleep researcher is monitoring a night of sleep in a laboratory at Montefiore Hospital and Medical Center in New York. [*Montefiore Hospital and Medical Center.*]

REM sleep is an example of a biological rhythm that cycles on a ninety-minute schedule. Research by Daniel Kripke and David Sonnenschein suggests that emotionally intense, unrealistic fantasies are likely to recur at approximately ninety-minute intervals throughout the day too—both in the laboratory and in real life [28].

Do people dream primarily during REM periods? A later study by psychologist David Foulkes showed that many people remember *fragmentary mental activity* about 75 percent of the time when awakened from NREM sleep. This *dreamlike* material is characterized as less visual, less vivid, less emotional, more controlled, more pleasant, and more thoughtlike than that which appears during REM periods [29]. Apparently, many individuals are mentally active throughout the entire night. The following reports illustrate some typical differences between the mental activity of REM and NREM periods.

[NREM report]: I had been dreaming about getting ready to take some type of an exam. It had been a very short dream. That's just about all that it contained. I don't think I was worried about them.

[REM report]: I was dreaming about exams. In the early part of the dream I was dreaming I had just finished taking an exam, and it was a very sunny day outside. I was walking with a boy who's in some of my classes with me. There was a sort of a, a, break, and someone mentioned a grade they had gotten in a social science exam. And I asked them if the social science marks had come in. They said yes. I didn't get it, because I had been away for a day. [30]

While vivid dreams are most typical of REM sleep, they also occur occasionally during all phases of NREM sleep, particularly during sleep onset [31]. Bizarre images during REM or NREM periods seem to be associated with bursts of high-voltage electrical activity in several brain regions [32].

It is almost certain, then, that all normal human beings dream—probably many times a night. People appear to differ primarily in terms of how well they recall dreams. The reasons for such memory differences are not well understood. Freud believed that upon awakening, people become defensive and block from their awareness those dream elements that mask forbidden impulses or unhappy memories. If he was correct, then people who tend to repress (roughly, to avoid thinking about) anxiety-arousing topics should be infrequent dream recallers. And dream repression should occur more often under psychologically threatening conditions. Careful studies have not confirmed these hypotheses. People do appear to remember most of their dreams when they are awakened and questioned during or immediately following REM periods in a laboratory. Since the biochemical state of the brain during sleep appears to be inappropriate for recording permanent memories, human beings may naturally forget dreams unless they both wake up in the midst of one or soon thereafter and refrain from engaging in distracting activities until they have *rehearsed* (repeated) the dream. There is evidence that recall depends on dream *salience*, or vividness, too. REM dreams, which are more apt to be intense, are more likely than less vivid NREM material to be recalled when sleepers are awakened in the laboratory. Reports of feeling unable to recall a dream after a REM period are correlated with specific physiological events which suggest that the material lacks intensity and emotionality. The dreams of real-life nonrecallers may be less interesting and memorable than those of recallers [33].

Investigating Dream Content

For a long time, dreams were the domain of poets and prophets. Freud, who analyzed his own dreams and those of his psychologically disturbed patients, was one of the first scientists to show a strong interest in dream content. Today, many behavioral scientists investigate this topic. Two methods are used to collect dream reports for analysis. Sometimes psychologists ask research participants to record their dreams in makeshift diaries upon awakening. This procedure allows investigators to collect a vast number of dream reports quickly and inexpensively from subjects sleeping in a natural setting. Unfortunately, when people are responsible for recording their own descriptions, they often procrastinate. Consequently, dream summaries may be composed long after the experience

when forgetting makes imaginative reconstruction necessary and increases the likelihood of inaccuracies.

Researchers in sleep laboratories collect dreams by monitoring physiological responses and awakening people for reports on their mental experiences—usually during or immediately following REM periods. We refer to this procedure as the *laboratory method*. Although more likely than the *diary strategy* to capitalize on memory, the laboratory method is time-consuming and expensive; and it introduces its own distortions. We know that dreams are influenced by the unusual setting because laboratory reports frequently contain references to the unfamiliar environment and electronic paraphernalia. Desires to please the investigator, sound coherent, or present a sane image may also distort these face-to-face responses.

What do people report dreaming about? In the early 1950s, psychologist Calvin Hall conducted one of the first large-scale studies of dream content. Hall had normal people record their dreams upon awakening. He collected and analyzed some 10,000 dreams. The behavioral scientist discovered that by and large the research participants dreamed about engaging in ordinary activities in familiar settings with people they knew. One unexpected finding was that dreams tended to be emotionally negative on balance. Hostile acts outnumbered friendly ones 2 to 1. Anger, apprehension, and fear characterized 64 percent of the dreams. Happy dreams occurred only 18 percent of the time [34].

Research indicates that people experience two distinct types of unpleasant dreams. In a typical *night terror*, the individual awakens, usually from stage 4 sleep, with a blood-curdling scream and may cry out for help. Though remembering little, if anything, about the terror's content, the individual feels panic-stricken and her or his body appears to be handling a dire emergency. Heart rate can triple and respiration rate and amplitude are greatly increased. Night terrors are relatively rare. They are generally confined to very early childhood and often disappear with

FIGURE 7-7 Sitting inside an inflated plastic bubble, these Californians try to produce alpha brain waves using biofeedback instruments. Note the sensing electrodes attached to each person's head (near the occipital lobes of the brain). The alpha rhythm is especially noticeable when the eyes are closed and seems to reflect, at least in part, the activity of the primary visual centers of the occipital region. While many people associate alpha activity with an unusually peaceful yet alert dreamlike state, some individuals find the alpha state unpleasant. Researchers are also divided [92]. Many feel that alpha waves signify little more than the absence of visual activity. Looking into the subjective nature of the alpha experience, David Walsh discovered that serene, contemplative feelings accompanied alpha activity primarily when positive expectations existed [93]. Whatever the case may be, the alpha state has been touted as a uniquely desirable one; and some behavioral scientists have attempted to train people to produce alpha brain waves at will, using biofeedback techniques. Whether human beings can learn to elevate alpha activity significantly is widely disputed [94]. Meanwhile, some manufacturers are marketing cheap biofeedback devices "guaranteed" to help the user attain more alpha waves. Many of these machines are more sensitive to facial tics and eye blinks than to alpha activity. [*Ralph Crane*/Life *magazine*, © 1972, Time Inc.]

maturity. Their cause is not known. Currently, scientists lean toward classifying the terror as a physiological sleep disorder rather than a psychological one.

In contrast to night terrors, *bad dreams*, those which occur during REM sleep and evoke unpleasant feelings like sadness and fear, are common. Almost all children and adults experience bad dreams from time to time. The content of these dreams tends to be remembered. Frequently, several episodes can be recalled. While the body of the sleeper may be somewhat aroused, as is typical during the REM stage, it is operating far less turbulently than during a night terror [35].

What influences the content of people's dreams? The dreams of adults are shaped in part by personally significant life events and motives. Pregnant women dream increasingly about their pregnancies. Current stresses leave their mark on dream content too. So do cultural concerns. Just as the Cuna Indians tend to be less combative than other Nicaraguans, their dreams contain less aggressive imagery. Within our own culture, men's and women's dreams still show the traditional sex-role differences that our rearing instills. Whereas the dreams of American women tend to emphasize friendly interactions, emotions, and home and family themes, those of American men focus on achievement, aggression, physical activity, and sex [36].

Recent laboratory studies find that youngsters' dreams show similar influences. They typically concern realistic situations, activities, and preoccupations, just as adults' dreams do. Observing the development of twenty-six children for five consecutive years (eight or nine times a year), David Foulkes and his associates found that early dreams are quite simple and unemotional. The dreams of children at ages three and four are dominated by animals and impersonal motives, such as hunger, safety, and comfort. As children grow, they report more elaborate, imaginative, and frightening dreams, paralleling their development as waking thinkers. By ages five and six, interpersonal motives predominate and traditional sex differences become apparent [37].

Recent and concurrent environmental events also influence dream content. In one study which supports this notion, William Dement and his colleagues exposed subjects sleeping in a laboratory to varied stimuli near the beginning of REM cycles, including a tone, flashing light, and cold water spray. Though not always successful, the investigators tried not to waken their participants until the end of the REM period. The laboratory stimuli were identifiably incorporated into approximately 25 percent of the reported dreams [38]. Other researchers have sent people to sleep in their laboratories hungry, thirsty, or filled with spicy foods, to determine the effects of these bodily states. Typically, references to hunger or thirst appear in a small but significant portion of the dreams [39]. Similarly, when people wear goggles that tint their surroundings reddish during their waking hours, they report dreaming more frequently about reddish objects than in their pregoggle days [40].

While people have far less control over their sleeping consciousness than over their waking one, there is some evidence that at least a slight degree of control over dreaming is possible [41]. The book and article by Rosalind Cartwright in this chapter's Suggested Readings provide information on this issue.

The Purpose of Dreaming

Why do people dream? Behavioral scientists have approached this question from several angles. Long before anyone knew about REM sleep, Sigmund Freud looked for clues to the purpose of dreaming within the dream. Scanning the fragmented mingling of past and present motives, memories, thoughts and emotions, he concluded that dreams reflect people's unconscious impulses to gratify drives or fulfill wishes that cannot be satisfied in reality. According to him, the dream narrative, or *manifest content*, disguises and dramatizes hidden desires and motives which form the real meaning, or *latent content*, of the dream. The evidence for Freud's explanation came from his psychotherapy sessions. As patients recounted their dreams and conjured up associations for the various dream elements, they frequently discovered impulses and needs that they were not aware of. Does such material really constitute evidence? Probably not. As Freud's critics assert, dreams are vague, easily distorted or embellished, and readily interpreted in many ways. Consequently, people can find in dreams what they expect or want to find. It can also be argued that the purpose of dreaming cannot be discovered simply by analyzing the dream itself. *What* we dream about is not necessarily related to *why* we dream. Memories, motives, thoughts, and emotions may be the subject matter of our dreams for a very simple reason. These are the only phenomena that the brain has to work with during sleep. Still, the idea that dreams help gratify drives has received support, as we will see. And, regardless of whether or not Freud's entire theory of dreams is valid, he was correct in believing that dreams yield insights into drives and motives that have hitherto been unrecognized.

Allan Hobson and Robert McCarley, medical researchers at the Harvard Medical School, have recently proposed an impressive physiological theory of the dream process, the *activation-synthesis hypothesis*. The Hobson-McCarley model assumes that as animals sleep, a clock-trigger mechanism in the neural circuits of the brain stem periodically (every ninety minutes or so in humans) *activates* electrical activity in a random way. The activity reflects sensory, motor, and emotional material that has been processed during wakefulness. At the same time, the activating mechanism arouses higher brain centers but blocks motor output and the pickup of new sensory information. The higher brain centers attempt to *synthesize* the incomplete and chaotic input by searching memory for information which "fits." In other words, during REM periods (and perhaps during NREM periods when vivid dreams appear) higher brain centers are functioning like a computer searching its storage locations for key words, images, and ideas to organize essentially disjointed, fragmentary data. Sometimes the material called forth is unpleasant and conflict-laden; sometimes it isn't. The Hobson-McCarley theory is supported by dramatic parallels in the timing, sequencing, duration, and intensity of neural and dream activity. If the theory is correct, dreams may be the mere psychological accompaniment—a type of by-product—of a specific rhythmic nervous system operation [42].

Many scientists have focused on a related issue: What is the purpose of REM sleep? REM periods are known to be absolutely essential. When people and other animals are deprived of REM sleep in the laboratory, subsequent sleep usually contains longer and more frequent periods of REM sleep. Waking behavior does not appear to be seriously affected, as was once thought, even when people go sixteen days or cats seventy consecutive days without REM sleep [43]. Observations on depressed and anxious people who take prescription drugs which happen to suppress REM sleep (a side effect) for a year and longer confirm this picture. The physical components of the REM stage—the characteristic brain waves, rapid eye movements, central nervous system arousal, and muscle relaxation, for instance—separate from one another and appear in different phases of sleep or during waking. Dreams do not spill over into wakefulness under these conditions. Other behavioral consequences are not observed [44]. These findings suggest that REM sleep may be a conglomeration of separate processes, each serving its own specific functions.

What purposes might REM sleep serve? Any theory must come to grips with several intriguing facts.

1. All mammals seem to experience REM periods.
2. Percentage of time in REM sleep does not correlate with psychological or intellectual complexity. The most primitive of mammals, the living fossil called an oppossum, spends a larger proportion of its sleep time in the REM stage than people

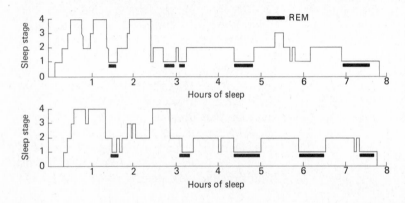

FIGURE 7-8 One person's sleep patterns on two successive nights in the laboratory. The black bars indicate periods of REM sleep. Note the similarity of the records. [*From Webb and Agnew, 1968.*]

do. Cats spend only a slightly smaller percentage of time in REM sleep than humans.

3. Significantly more REM sleep occurs soon after conception and during infancy in most animals (including people) and less during youth and adulthood [45]. The proportion of REM to NREM sleep appears to be negatively related to the maturity of the nervous system. For instance, guinea pigs, born with a fully developed brain, show nearly identical sleep patterns in infancy and adulthood. Newborn human babies and kittens, having relatively undeveloped brains, spend much of their total sleep time in the REM phase at birth and progressively less as their brains develop [46].

Several theories harmonize with these facts. REM sleep may play a role in the development of the central nervous system. Then, once the nervous system has matured, the REM stage may exercise specific brain circuits to keep them in good working order [47]. The rapid eye movements that characterize REM sleep may tune the coordination of both eyes so that binocular vision (Chapter 6) functions efficiently during the waking hours [48]. Laboratory observations on animals suggest that REM sleep may also allow organisms to discharge drives (such as those for sex and aggression) periodically. Otherwise, energy for these motives might accumulate somehow and cause problems [49]. Note that this finding provides partial support for Freud's hypothesis.

It should be clear by now that the purposes of REM sleep have not been established. Despite the claims of many self-styled authorities, scientists do not currently know whether dreams serve a function of their own. Researchers continue to grapple with this challenging question. ▲

THE HYPNOTIC STATE

The word "hypnosis" came from the Greek word for sleep, but the hypnotic state bears little or no resemblance to sleep either behaviorally or physiologically, as we will see. In this section we explore several questions: How do people enter the hypnotic state? How is it measured? What characterizes the hypnotic state? How can it be explained?

Entering the Hypnotic State

How do people enter the hypnotic state? The hypnotist (in self-hypnosis, the subject) uses a *hypnotic induction,* a series of persuasive suggestions. Initially, the induction is likely to encourage concentration, frequently on a small object such as a thumbtack or watch. The induction may suggest that the individual is feeling detached from ordinary preoccupations, calmer, drowsier, sleepier, and/or more comfortable than usual. In some cases, the induction proposes that reality is beginning to change in various ways. The participant may be asked to relinquish control. Willing, cooperative people find themselves responding progressively to increasingly more improbable suggestions [50].

Not everyone appears to be capable of a hypnotic experience, or at least not readily so.

▲ USING PSYCHOLOGY

1. Watch a sleeping dog or cat for REM periods. What characterizes its behavior at this time? If you wanted to see rapid eye movements in a sleeping person, when would be sensible times to watch for them?

2. Explain why Marcus may recall a great many dreams and Julius may claim he never dreams.

3. What are the advantages and disadvantages of the dream collection methods in current use? Can you think of any other ways to gather dream reports?

4. Suppose that the activation-synthesis of dreaming is correct. Explain why analyzing dream content could still further self-understanding.

What percentage of people are susceptible? In the mid-1960s psychologist Ernest Hilgard studied how 533 college students responded to a hypnotic induction. Nearly 25 percent of Hilgard's subjects appeared to achieve a satisfactory hypnotic state. About 5 to 10 percent were totally unresponsive. The rest were moderately susceptible. Roughly one-fourth of those experiencing a satisfactory hypnotic state entered a deep trance where they seemed to be able to hallucinate with their eyes open [51]. Personal impressions of a deep trance are presented in the introduction to this chapter.

What determines how hypnotically responsive a person is? Age is one factor. Children's susceptibility to hypnosis increases up until the age of about ten. Openness to the hypnotic experience may decline as youngsters become less compliant and more worldly [52]. Personality factors appear to be important. Josephine Hilgard, a psychologist and psychiatrist, finds that people who frequently become involved in their own fantasies and in imaginative events are more likely to be particularly responsive to hypnosis. The type of imagination that seems to be required may be appreciated by reading the self-description of one easily hypnotized subject.

When reading a book I get completely involved. . . . I'm somebody who's there. (Invisible?) Yes, they don't know I'm there, but I'm in the middle of the action. Sometimes I identify with the character and then will dream that I'm that character for two or three nights. I continue with the story rather than having it end. . . . In some ways I know I'm myself, I have my own identity, but on many levels I'm that other person—thinking like that person and acting the way that person would act. [53]

Josephine Hilgard has found that certain personal characteristics inhibit hypnotic susceptibility: distractibility, fear of the new and

TABLE 7-1   Tasks from the Creative Imagination Scale

Task	Initial position of subject	Summary of suggestions given to subject
Arm heaviness	Left arm extended and horizontal with palm facing up	Imagine that three heavy dictionaries are being placed on your outstretched hand causing your arm to feel heavy.
Hand levitation	Right arm extended and horizontal with palm facing down	Imagine that a strong stream of water from a garden hose is pushing against the palm of your hand, forcing it up.
Finger anesthesia	Left hand in lap with palm facing up	Imagine that Novocain has been injected into the side of your hand next to the little finger, causing two fingers to feel numb.
Water "hallucination"	Not important	Imagine that you are drinking a cup of cool mountain water.
Olfactory-gustatory "hallucination"	Not important	Imagine that you are smelling and tasting an orange.
Music "hallucination"	Not important	Think back to a time when you heard some wonderful music and try to re-experience "hearing" it.
Temperature "hallucination"	Both hands resting in lap with palms facing down	Imagine that the sun is shining on the top of your right hand, causing it to feel hot.
Time distortion	Not important	Imagine that time is slowing down.
Age regression	Not important	Try to recreate the feeling that you experienced as a child in elementary school.
Mind-body relaxation	Not important	Imagine that you are lying under the sun on a beach and becoming very relaxed.

Source: Wilson, S. C., and Barber, T. X. *The Creative Imagination Scale: Applications to clinical and experimental hypnosis.* Medfield, Mass.: Medfield Foundation, 1976.

different, and unwillingness to accept the authority of the hypnotist or to behave submissively [54].

Measuring the Hypnotic State

During hypnosis the individual's physical responses vary, depending on the hypnotist's specific suggestions and the person's responsivity [55]. The reactions are indistinguishable from those that occur during normal waking consciousness. Since physiological indices cannot differentiate hypnosis from other states, hypnosis must be measured by observing behavior or gathering self-reports. The former strategy is usually preferred, but it leads to a circular definition of the hypnotic state. We say, "Subjects behaved in this or that way because they were hypnotized." When asked how we know that they were hypnotized, we respond, "Because of the way they behaved." Table 7-1 describes tasks that are presented to subjects after a hypnotic induction. Observations of behavior are used to evaluate whether the research participant was hypnotized and to what degree.

The Nature of the Hypnotic State

When the hypnotic induction is successful, consciousness changes in several ways. Heightened suggestibility seems to be the essence of the hypnotic experience. It underlies these commonly observed behavioral effects [56]:

1. *Loss of spontaneity.* Spontaneous feeling and thinking decrease to a low level, perhaps a standstill. People stop planning what to do. They wait instead for suggestions before initiating activity.
2. *Selectivity.* While human beings always select what to attend to, hypnotized individuals are especially selective. They may concentrate, for instance, on the hypnotist's voice and block all other sounds and sights from awareness.
3. *Reduced reality testing.* Under hypnosis, people stop comparing their perceptions with reality, as they ordinarily do. They are even willing to accept gross distortions. Following the hypnotist's

suggestions, participants may hallucinate objects with their eyes open and fail to see real objects in front of their noses.
4. *Enactment of unusual roles.* Hypnotized individuals play unusual roles readily. Under hypnosis, adults may behave as if they were young children or were undergoing traumatic past experiences.
5. *Posthypnotic suggestibility.* Hypnotists sometimes suggest that specific cues will cause particular sensations or behaviors after the trance is over. A hypnotist might tell an obese man that the sight of chocolate cake will make him feel nauseated. Later, when the cue (chocolate cake) appears, the subject responds obediently (with queasiness) without consciously recalling the suggestion. This phenomenon is known as *posthypnotic suggestion*.
6. *Posthypnotic amnesia.* This type of amnesia is closely related to posthypnotic suggestion. It entails temporarily forgetting something that happened during the hypnotic trance until a specific, prearranged signal, like snapping fingers, ends the memory lapse.

Consciousness changes occur most strikingly in people who are highly susceptible to a hypnotic induction. People who are moderately responsive usually feel mildly relaxed, fully in touch with reality, in control, easily able to recall the experience, and quite able to resist the hypnotist's suggestions if they so desire.

Explaining the Hypnotic State

We examine two representative explanations of the hypnotic state. Ernest Hilgard has proposed a *dissociation theory* to clarify the nature of light hypnosis. You may recall that Hilgard believes that the brain contains a number of independent control systems which operate at the same time. The systems record and process information and direct specific activities. Yet they are isolated, or *dissociated*, from one another. These brain systems are arranged in a power hierarchy. Under most waking circumstances, the "normal executive ego system" (conscious voluntary control) governs. Still, the other systems are fully capable of dominating consciousness. During hypnosis, Hilgard suggests, the control shifts and the power of the "normal executive system" is reduced. Because of the "shake-up," normally involuntary capabilities may become voluntary and those ordinarily voluntary may become involuntary. What is usually remembered, for instance, may be forgotten; and what was forgotten may be recalled. When lightly hypnotized individuals are tested for pain threshold in the laboratory, the dominant system seems to be fairly oblivious to pain. At the same time, Hilgard's studies suggest, the "normal executive system" acts like a "hidden observer," processing and storing the unpleasant sensations. He assumes that more radical consciousness changes occur during deep hypnosis [57].

Theodore Barber, a psychologist (and formerly a stage hypnotist), is the most energetic proponent of the view that the hypnotic experience is a product of *suggestibility* and *motivating instructions*. The hypnotic induction, according to Barber, produces a peculiar set of expectations, motives, attitudes, feelings, and imaginings in those people who hold favorable attitudes and expectations toward the experimental or clinical setting and are willing to engage in unusual behavior and play the *hypnotic role* [58]. Barber and his coworkers have done a great deal of research over the past twenty years that has helped to "demystify" hypnosis. They have demonstrated that simple suggestions may produce many "hypnotic" effects (including suspension between two chairs supported only by head and ankles, changes in heart rate and blood glucose level, inhibition of labor contractions, control of dreams, pain reduction, and blister formation). Suggestions are particularly effective when strategies are provided to help people direct their imaginations along the suggested lines, as often happens during

hypnosis. People undergoing pain, for instance, might be asked to imagine that the pain site is dull, numb, and insensitive [59]. Barber argues that during hypnosis people suspend their critical judgment in order to achieve a high degree of cooperation with the hypnotist. Suspended judgment and heightened responsivity allow them to reenact new roles, entertain new ideas, and play by new rules. According to Barber, everyone has these capabilities [60].

Precisely what hypnosis is remains to be demonstrated. But, whatever the final definition, it is clear that hypnosis can be used in therapy to help responsive people overcome many types of personal problems, such as smoking, overeating, and handling excessive anxiety. It can also help susceptible patients gain control over severe pain [61]. Unquestionably, hypnosis deserves to be better understood. ▲

MEDITATION

During meditation, Turkish dervishes whirl in circles accompanied by flutes and drums, as described early in this chapter and pictured in Figure 7-9. Buddhists meditate cross-legged with their eyes closed while they regulate their breathing, pray, chant, or concentrate on a koan. A *koan* is an attention-focusing insoluble puzzle such as "Show me your face before your mother and father met." Many other types of meditation exist. What is meditation? We turn to this question first. Then we look at changes in consciousness and physiology that accompany meditation. Lastly, we try to explain why certain meditative exercises change consciousness.

▲ USING PSYCHOLOGY

1. Do you think that you would be responsive to a hypnotic induction? Have you the attributes that characterize highly susceptible people?

2. Do you believe that light hypnosis involves the dissociation of behavior control systems? Or does Barber's explanation sound more plausible to you?

The Nature of Meditation

Meditation may be defined as a set of diverse exercises that aim at altering consciousness. Generally, meditation shifts awareness "from the active, outward-oriented . . . mode . . . toward the receptive and quiescent mode, and . . . from an external focus of attention to an internal one [62]." In the East, this state is regarded as preparation for achieving comprehensive personal knowledge and is considered a necessary first step for developing qualities such as concentration, awareness, energy, joy, wisdom, and a sense of deep peacefulness and unity. Westerners have adopted many meditative exercises. The techniques fit into two general categories: concentrative and "opening up." In most meditative practices the participant sits alone or with a small group of people in an isolated area and tries to minimize outside stimulation and distractions. *"Opening up" meditative exercises* attempt to heighten awareness of the external environment so that people become unusually alert and sensitive to their daily activities. A Buddhist practice in this category, called "right-mindedness," asks participants to:

Be aware and mindful of whatever you do, physically or verbally, during the daily routine of work in your life, private, public, or professional. Whether you walk, stand, sit, lie down, or sleep, whether you stretch or bend your limbs, whether you look around, whether you put on your clothes, whether you talk, or keep silent, whether you eat or drink—even whether you answer the call of nature—in these and other activities you should be fully aware and mindful of the act performed at the moment. [63]

Concentrative meditative exercises focus awareness on a single, unchanging source of stimulation. Representative practices include gazing continuously at an object or person, dancing as the dervishes do, attending to a bodily process such as breathing, and listening to oneself chant aloud or silently. Once the practitioner has become proficient, the intense concentration is expected to lead to a positive clear feeling, the "void." During this experience all active perceptions and analytic

FIGURE 7-9 The dance of the whirling dervishes is considered a form of meditation. A caller intones a flamenco-like air, often accompanied by flute and drums. Concentric circles of meditators begin revolving slowly in opposite directions. The sheik yells "Ya Haadi" (O guide)! The participants repeat the words, concentrating on them. They chant slowly at first, then faster and faster. The dancers' movements match the repetitions [95], ultimately leading to the state described in the introduction to this chapter. [*Dave Bellack/Jeroboam.*]

thoughts stop. At the same time, the individual feels refreshed and more able to sense life directly. Although the sensation is momentary, meditators report that "the void" has a timeless quality. Throughout this section we focus on concentrative meditation.

Changes during Concentrative Meditation

To study the changes that take place during concentrative meditation, researchers invite people with and without previous experience to meditate under observation. In one such investigation, Edward Maupin recruited student subjects through campus newspaper ads offering ten free lessons in Zen. (Zen is a classical Buddhist meditation which prescribes various concentrative exercises.) During daily sessions over a two-week period, the novices practiced concentrating on the stomach movements associated with normal breathing. After each lesson, they were interviewed about their experiences. Eventually, they were classified as high, moderate, or low responders. *High responders* reported experiencing deep concentration, nonstriving calm, and detachment from feelings and thoughts. *Moderate responders* said that varied bodily sensations, especially those associated with relaxation and breathing, had been intensified. *Low responders* were primarily aware of relaxing and feeling foggy and dizzy [64]. The subjective reports of veteran meditators vary markedly, too. Some view meditation as an extraordinary experience. Others classify it as relaxation.

Does meditation produce the same physiological effects as relaxation? To investigate this topic, Robert Wallace and Herbert Benson asked experienced transcendental meditators to come to their laboratories to rest and to meditate. Twice each day for about fifteen minutes, people practicing *transcendental meditation* (TM) sit in a comfortable position with their eyes closed and concen-

FIGURE 7-10 While this subject meditates, continuous measurements are made of heart rate, blood pressure, and other physiological functions. At ten-minute intervals, samples of arterial blood are drawn by a catheter in the left arm. The blood is analyzed for oxygen and carbon dioxide content, acidity, and lactate production. [*Ben Rose, Scientific American.*]

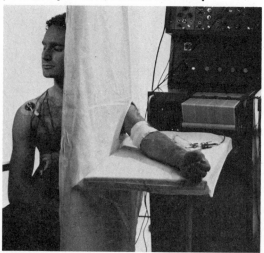

trate on the sound of a special word known as a *mantra*. The meditator reintroduces the mantra whenever it leaves her or his awareness. Other thoughts are not pushed away, so a backlog of partially digested past experiences can enter consciousness for processing. TM is also expected to lead to a joyful oceanic state.

While research participants relaxed or meditated, Wallace and Benson made continuous measurements on their blood pressure, heart rate, body temperature, skin resistance (roughly, a measure of sweat gland activity), and brain waves. They also collected and analyzed samples of blood for information about certain conditions, as described in Figure 7-10. During meditation the body was characterized by an unusual pattern of highly relaxed activity that differed from ordinary relaxation and from REM and NREM sleep. The heart slowed significantly. The metabolic rate was unusually low (oxygen consumption, carbon dioxide elimination, and the rate and volume of respiration were all reduced notably). There were several other physiological signs of tranquility, including relatively large amounts of alpha activity (prominent during sleep onset), a rise in skin resistance, and a low blood lactate level [65]. Although this distinct physiological pattern suggested that TM is a unique state of consciousness, careful follow-up research did not uniformly support these findings. In some cases, the type or magnitude of changes differed [66]. In others, simple rest or relaxation produced essentially the same physiological response pattern as TM [67]. Low metabolic and heart rates and high alpha activity have been observed consistently during concentrative meditation [68].

What about the long-term effects of concentrative meditation? The research findings are mixed and difficult to evaluate. After a meditation training course or years of meditating, many practitioners report large positive changes in physical and mental well-being, mood, personality, and creativity [69]. At the same time, a sizable number of participants say that meditation has some adverse effects, including depression, withdrawal, anxiety, confusion, frustration, insomnia, and hallucinations [70]. Meditators' reports pose two problems in addition to the contradictions:

1. *Demand characteristics* (defined in Chapter 2). Experienced meditators are invested personally in meditation. Accordingly, they are inclined to reflect favorably on the merit of the practice when information is openly solicited.

2. *Self-selection.* People who try meditation are unusual human beings. Experienced meditators, probably fewer than half who begin training, tend to be even less representative of the general population. They have been described, in fact, as particularly committed, motivated, and persistent [71]. Such individuals might report feeling happy and healthy without meditation.

To minimize the influence of motivation and demand characteristics, psychologists use physiological measurements and psychological tests. To reduce the magnitude of the self-selection problem, they compare experienced meditators with less experienced ones. Research along these lines has suggested that certain meditative practices are associated with a healthy response to distress, specific types of creativity (but not others), and distinctive brain-wave patterns that may enhance mental concentration and efficiency [72]. These findings have not been confirmed. A great deal of additional research will be required before the long-range consequences of meditation are clear.

How Concentrative Meditation Alters Consciousness

Three factors, sensory input, relaxation, and expectations, appear to contribute to the effects of concentrative meditative exercises. Consider the sensory input factor first. Numerous laboratory studies have explored the impact of uniform, unchanging visual inputs. Sometimes investigators place halved table-tennis balls over subjects' eyes so that they see a diffuse, featureless visual field called a *ganzfeld*. After about twenty minutes, many people report momentary visual "blackouts."

During these episodes, research participants say that they stop seeing (not that they see nothing). They feel unable to control their eye movements and incapable even of telling whether their eyes are open. It's as if the visual system loses touch with the brain. EEG recordings show that the "blackouts" are associated with bursts of alpha wave activity [73]. The experience known as "the void," which is sought during concentrative meditative exercises, is precisely the same type of phenomenon. Perceptions of the visual world disappear momentarily, and a high level of alpha wave activity occurs simultaneously.

There are relatively little data on how relaxation and expectations alter consciousness during meditation. Both elements are probably important. As we suggested before, concentrative meditation leads to a *relaxed* physical state. Presumably, like regular periods of relaxation, meditation can reduce blood pressure significantly [74]. The low-key awareness characteristic of the relaxed meditative state contrasts dramatically with ordinary waking consciousness too. The contrast may cause people to feel more alert. The *positive expectations* of meditators surely influence the *interpretation* of physiological and psychological sensations. The same experiences that are considered joyful during meditation might be evaluated as neutral in a laboratory and alarming if they happened spontaneously. ▲

MARIJUANA INTOXICATION

People have been taking substances to alter their consciousness for thousands of years. Written accounts of opium use date back to 4,000 years before Christ. We focus now on the changes in awareness that people experience under the influence of one mind-altering drug, marijuana. *Marijuana* ("grass," "pot"), the name for various preparations of the Indian hemp plant *Cannabis sativa*, is generally smoked and more rarely eaten for its effects on consciousness. The use of marijuana in the United States was relatively restricted

▲ **USING PSYCHOLOGY**

1. Does research substantiate claims that meditation leads to creativity, happiness, and mental efficiency?

2. At a rally, an experienced meditator announces that meditation brings people into contact with a life force. How do concentrative meditative exercises appear to change consciousness in reality?

until the early 1960s, when large numbers of college students began experimenting with the drug. Recent polls suggest that some 50 million Americans have tried marijuana at least once and that approximately half that number use it regularly [75]. Though *Cannabis* is smoked by people of all ages, eighteen- to twenty-five-year-olds are by far the most frequent consumers. It is estimated that two of every three college students and more than half of all high school students in the United States have experimented with marijuana at least once or twice. Some 40 percent of college students consider themselves users [76]. In this section we examine the changes in consciousness that occur during marijuana intoxication and the reasons for those changes.

Consciousness Changes during Marijuana Intoxication

To investigate the subjective sensations that a great many people experience during marijuana intoxication, psychologist Charles Tart distributed questionnaires through informal channels. People who had smoked marijuana a dozen times or more were asked to estimate how often more than 200 specific experiences had occurred in the past six months and the smallest degree of intoxication necessary for that outcome. Of approximately 750 questionnaires sent out, about 150 were returned and analyzed. Some of Tart's findings are presented in Figure 7-11. You can see the reported levels of marijuana intoxication at which common consciousness changes frequently begin. At a minimum level of intoxication, many people report feeling restless. This sensation usually disappears within minutes

and is replaced by a sense of calm. At approximately the same time, users say that their sensitivity to other people is keen, creativity is enhanced, and sensations are sharpened. (Reports of acute responsivity resemble the peyote user's impressions presented in the introduction to this chapter.) Spontaneous insights, unusual associations, and novel thoughts commonly arise. Problems are viewed from new perspectives. Once people have reached this level of intoxication, they are likely to report experiencing both positive and negative aftereffects the day following the marijuana session.

If people continue to smoke, they reach a state of strong intoxication. Time seems to slow down while fantasy and imagery are intensified. Though many people experience visual hallucinations at this point, they know that the images are unreal. Thinking drifts off, and the user loses the ability to focus on a specific topic. Feelings of efficiency often give way to doubts and apprehensions. Intense awareness of bodily sensations, such as the beating heart, is likely now.

As the marijuana user moves toward very strong levels of intoxication, the memory span shrinks and contact with the environment fades. Apparently, many people become preoccupied with internal images and mental activities. During this phase of a marijuana "high," feelings of personal identity frequently disappear, intensifying the user's sense of unity with humanity and the world. Mystical experiences may occur too. If smoking continues, nausea and vomiting are probable [77].

Are these reports trustworthy? Do marijuana users really feel what they say they do? Careful experiments in laboratory settings have confirmed some of these self-observa-

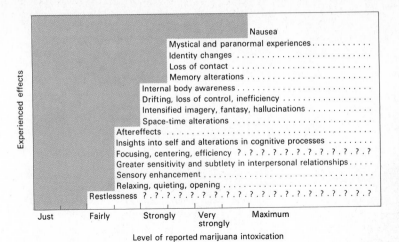

FIGURE 7-11 Some commonly reported consequences of taking marijuana and the level of intoxication at which half the experienced users who were studied reported the initial occurrence of the effect. All experiences except those followed by question marks tend to continue at higher levels of intoxication. [*From Tart, 1971.*]

tions. Systematic studies of marijuana-intoxicated people suggest that they consistently overestimate elapsed time, presumably because time passes slowly for them [78]. When confronted by tasks that involve remembering for a brief time period, thinking in sequence, or keeping long-term goals in mind, intoxicated subjects perform more poorly than sober ones. There is evidence that they can compensate if they try [79]. Many marijuana-intoxicated individuals show significantly reduced driving skills, perhaps because they focus attention on other matters [80]. *Cannabis* also appears to affect sociability. People seem friendly initially, but they tend to withdraw from verbal interactions after continued smoking [81]. Recently, the imagery associated with marijuana and other drugs has been investigated. The findings are described in Figure 7-12.

How Marijuana Alters Consciousness

In the late 1960s, Andrew Weil and his coworkers conducted the first carefully controlled investigation of marijuana's effects. In one series of tests, nine volunteers, who had never tried marijuana before, came to the laboratory on four occasions. During each visit they smoked two cigarettes containing either tobacco (in part to practice inhalation procedures), high-dosage marijuana, low-dosage marijuana, or placebo marijuana. (Placebo marijuana was made from the mature stalks of male *Cannabis* plants which contain no *tetrahydrocannabinol* [THC], a major psychoactive ingredient.) A double-blind procedure (Chapter 2) prevented the novices and experimenters from knowing what type of cigarette was being smoked during the three marijuana sessions. Only one participant, a young man who had been particularly eager to become "high," had an intense experience. The other newcomers reported minimal effects: no euphoria (joy) and no marked perceptual distortions, except for the slowing of time [82]. Why didn't most of the naive subjects become intoxicated? Why do newcomers to marijuana usually require several encounters with the drug before responding to it? One possibility is that sensitivity to the drug has to be learned. People may have to develop both an awareness and an appreciation of the bodily sensations that accompany marijuana use. There is a plausible physiological explanation too. Enzymes in the liver which metabolize a major psychoactive ingredient of marijuana take time to be mobilized, making an initial "waiting period" almost inevitable.

There is a second curious fact to explain. Experienced users sometimes act intoxicated

a

b

FIGURE 7-12 Research by psychologist Ronald Siegel and others indicates that hallucinations originating during epilepsy, psychosis, advanced syphilis, sensory deprivation, electrical brain stimulation, migraine headache attacks, fever, dizziness, and drug intoxication may be similar in form. The figure shows two universal hallucinatory images. For one series of studies, Siegel trained subjects to code visual imagery into form, color, and movement categories. Then, at weekly sessions, they received either a high or a low dose of an hallucinogen, a stimulant, a depressant, or a placebo, not knowing which drug they were taking. During a typical session (of about six hours), subjects lay on beds in a completely dark, soundproof chamber with their eyes open and reported what they saw, using the special code. Several hallucinogens, including a major psychoactive ingredient of marijuana, initially produced symmetrical, regular forms moving in organized, frequently pulsating ways. Though black and white at the beginning, the designs soon turned blue. An hour and a half to two hours after the hallucinogens were administered, lattice-tunnels like those shown in (*a*) were commonly reported. Colors shifted from blue to red, orange, and yellow at about the same time. Movements were still described as pulsating, but appeared more organized within explosive and rotational patterns. Many images included emotionally charged memories. Sometimes the scenes were viewed from unusual underwater or aerial perspectives. The scenes tended to appear first on the border of, or overlying, the lattice-tunnel, as in (*b*). During peak hallucinatory periods, many subjects described feeling fused with their images and dissociated from their own bodies. Highly unusual hallucinations that changed as frequently as ten times a second were commonly reported. The universal nature of many of these images suggests that they may be partly due to the structure of the eye and nervous system. Louis Jolyon West has suggested that hallucinations may occur when sensory input is reduced at a time when the brain is highly aroused. Under these conditions, images originating within the nervous system may be perceived as if they came from the senses [96]. [*Ronald K. Siegel.*]

after smoking placebos [83]. They may simply be acting or succumbing to their expectations. There is a physical explanation for this phenomenon also. Scientists know now that merely inhaling the air in a room where *Cannabis* has been smoked can cause symptoms of intoxication [84]. Moreover, the placebo cigarettes used by many investigators may not have been totally inert, as previously supposed. Until recently, scientists believed that marijuana contained only one important psychoactive ingredient, THC. It now appears that other compounds in *Cannabis*, including *cannibichromene* and *cannabidol*, contribute to the "high."

Ordinarily, marijuana, like other drugs,

FIGURE 7-13 There is still a great deal of controversy about the cumulative long-range effects of frequent marijuana use, and much remains to be learned. It is known that THC is absorbed and stored in the neurons of the brain and that THC buildup occurs in rats and other laboratory animals. How long THC persists and with what results are not known [97]. Animal studies, examinations of people in cultures where the use of high-dosage *Cannabis* has been commonplace for several hundred years, and laboratory investigations of daily marijuana use in the United States for as long as ninety days lead to this conclusion: No abnormalities of mood, thought, behavior, or intellectual ability appear to persist after extended marijuana use [98]. Because it appears to be a relatively safe drug, marijuana's therapeutic potential is currently being explored. *Cannabis* seems to be useful for reducing nausea due to varied types of cancer therapy and for treating glaucoma, an eye disease characterized by pressure within the eyeball and progressive loss of vision [99]. [*Paul Conklin/Monkmeyer Press Photo Service.*]

interacts with the nervous system to create a potential for particular experiences. Then social-psychological factors, such as the setting and the user's mood, past experiences, and personality, help shape the nature of the drug experience. How do behavioral scientists know that social-psychological factors have an impact on marijuana intoxication? One bit of evidence came from a careful study by a team of psychologists and psychiatrists headed by J. H. Mendelson. The participants in this research, both heavy users and casual smokers, were observed in a hospital setting before, during, and after a time period when *Cannabis* was freely available and could be smoked as frequently as desired. The experimenters rated the moods of the participants with and without their awareness. Following marijuana use, the "aware" ratings reflected euphoria, a result consistent, of course, with the drug's reputation. The "unaware" ratings indicated that the user's prevailing mood, whatever it was, intensified [85]. Apparently, *Cannabis*'s influence on mood depends, in part, on expectations and social roles. For information about the long-range effects of marijuana use, see Figure 7-13. ▲

▲ USING PSYCHOLOGY

1. Why do many psychologists question the validity of Tart's conclusions about marijuana's effects? Propose a better way to study marijuana's consciousness-altering consequences.

2. How can scientists explain why novice marijuana users remain sober on high-dosage marijuana cigarettes while experienced users become intoxicated on "mere" placebos?

3. What factors influence the marijuana experience?

SUMMARY
Consciousness

1. Psychologists study consciousness by gathering self-observations and self-reports, measuring physiology, and observing behavior.

2. Ordinary waking consciousness shifts frequently in subtle ways but it is usually focused on present ongoing situations. It is influenced by fatigue, moods, enduring personal characteristics, and environmental circumstances.

3. Sleep is studied as a moment-to-moment process by continually monitoring the electrical activity of the brain and other physical responses as simple animals and human volunteers sleep in laboratories.

4. Human beings and other mammals experience two distinct types of sleep: NREM and REM. Their functions are not known.

5. Vivid dreaming generally accompanies REM sleep and, occasionally, NREM sleep. Fragmentary thoughtlike mental activity occurs during the NREM sleep of many people.

6. Although all normal human beings appear to dream, many do not remember the content of their dreams.

7. Motives, preoccupations, emotions, cultural roles, and recent and concurrent events influence dream content.

8. The purpose of dreaming is not well understood.

9. The hypnotic state is characterized by heightened suggestibility. It frequently results in a loss of spontaneity, perceptual selectivity, reduced reality testing, enactment of unusual roles, posthypnotic suggestibility, and posthypnotic amnesia.

10. About 25 percent of college students appear capable of achieving a satisfactory hypnotic state.

11. Light hypnosis may be explained in several ways.

12. "Opening up" meditative exercises aim at putting people in close touch with their environments. Concentrative exercises lead to moments where perceptions stop and participants feel refreshed and able to sense life directly.

13. During concentrative meditation, people report wide-ranging subjective sensations. Their bodily state is characterized by highly relaxed, waking activity.

14. Sensory input, relaxation, and positive expectations contribute to the effects of concentrative meditative exercises.

15. The long-term effects of meditation are not understood.

16. Marijuana produces changes in sensory perceptions, awareness of time and space, imagery, and mental activity.

17. Marijuana's consciousness-altering effects depend on interactions between drug, nervous system, and social-psychological factors.

A Study Guide for Chapter Seven

Key terms consciousness (207), altered state of consciousness (207), introspect (207), state-dependent learning (209), ordinary waking consciousness (209), thought sampling (209), biological rhythm (211), electroencephalograph (EEG) (212), electroencephalogram (212), stage 0 sleep (214), alpha activity (214), stages of NREM sleep (214), hallucination (214), REM (paradoxical) sleep (215), sleep cycle (216), delusion (216), manifest and latent dream content (221), hypnotic state (223), hypnotic induction (223), meditation (227) [opening up (227), concentrative (227)], tetrahydrocannabinol (THC) (231), and other italicized words and expressions.

Important research nature of and influences on ordinary waking consciousness (Pope, Klinger, Weiskrantz, Starker, Graef, others), sleep stages, effects of sleep deprivation (Webb, Pappenheimer, others), contents of and influences on dreams (Aserinsky, Kleitman, Kripke, Foulkes, Hall, Dement, others), the need for REM sleep, nature of and susceptibility to hypnosis (the Hilgards, Barber, others), psychological and physical changes during meditation (Maupin, Benson, Wallace, others), nature of and influences on marijuana intoxication (Tart, Weil, Mendelson, others).

Basic concepts past and current attitudes toward the study of consciousness (Wundt, James, Watson, others), methods of investigating consciousness (waking, sleeping, dreaming, hypnotic), nature of ordinary waking consciousness (E. Hilgard, James, others), theories about the functions of NREM and REM sleep (Webb, others), hypotheses about dream recall (Freud, others), the purpose of dreams (Freud), activation-synthesis hypothesis (Hobson, McCarley), dissociation theory (E. Hilgard), hypnosis as a product of suggestibility and highly motivating instructions (Barber), purposes of meditation, demand characteristics and self-selection problems in meditation research, determinants of the effects of concentrative exercises, explanation of marijuana's effects.

People to identify Wundt, James, Watson, Freud.

Self-Quiz

1. What percentage of the waking thoughts of normal people appear to be strange or distorted?
- *a.* 50 percent
- *b.* 20 percent
- *c.* 10 percent
- *d.* 2 percent

2. What did visual tests on D. B., a man with occipital lobe damage, demonstrate?
- *a.* Moods influence ordinary waking consciousness.
- *b.* Ordinary waking consciousness is often bizarre.
- *c.* Shifts in ordinary waking consciousness are frequent.
- *d.* Unconscious systems may influence waking consciousness.

3. What typically accompanies stage 0 sleep?
- *a.* Alpha activity
- *b.* Delta activity
- *c.* Fast, irregular, low-amplitude brain waves
- *d.* Spindles

4. In which sleep stage are night terrors most likely to appear?
- *a.* Stage 1 NREM
- *b.* Stage 1 REM
- *c.* Stage 2
- *d.* Stage 4

5. Which stage of sleep is labeled *paradoxical*?
- *a.* Stage 1 NREM
- *b.* Stage 1 REM
- *c.* Stage 3
- *d.* Stage 4

6. In which sleep stage do young adults spend the largest percentage of time?
- *a.* Stage 1 REM
- *b.* Stage 2
- *c.* Stage 3
- *d.* Stage 4

7. What do dreams reflect, according to Sigmund Freud and his followers?
- *a.* Culturally determined roles in a particular society
- *b.* Current stresses
- *c.* Random imagery activated by lower brain centers
- *d.* Unconscious impulses to satisfy unfulfilled wishes

8. When do people experience the largest percentage of REM sleep?
- *a.* Infancy
- *b.* Childhood
- *c.* Adolescence
- *d.* Adulthood

9. Which attribute characterizes hypnotically susceptible people?
- *a.* Distractibility
- *b.* Imaginativeness
- *c.* Liking for the old and familiar
- *d.* Refusal to behave submissively

10. Suppose that during hypnosis a woman is instructed to feel calm whenever she encounters an exam. Over the next few weeks the subject feels relaxed during tests, even though she does not recall the "instruction." Which phenomenon is illustrated?

- *a.* Posthypnotic amnesia
- *b.* Posthypnotic suggestion
- *c.* Reality testing
- *d.* Role enactment

11. Which physiological response usually accompanies concentrative meditation in the laboratory?
- *a.* Delta activity
- *b.* Increased metabolism
- *c.* Increased respiration
- *d.* Slowed heart rate

12. How are meditation and creativity related?
- *a.* Meditation increases feelings of creativity, but does not alter actual creativity.
- *b.* Meditation appears to facilitate certain types of creativity, but not others.
- *c.* Meditation seems to enhance performance on creativity tests that require problem-solving skills, but not on those that require free-associative abilities.
- *d.* Meditation improves all types of creativity.

13. What is the most probable consequence of twenty minutes' exposure to uniform, unchanging visual input?
- *a.* The appearance of short-lived hallucinatory images
- *b.* The momentary disappearance of the visual field
- *c.* A temporary decrease in alpha activity
- *d.* The temporary heightening of concentration

14. Which effect usually begins at a strong level of marijuana intoxication?
- *a.* Feelings of calm
- *b.* Perception of the slowing of time
- *c.* Sense of enhanced creativity
- *d.* Sharpened sensations

15. Which observation most conclusively indicates that social-psychological factors influence experiences during marijuana use?
- *a.* Experienced users achieve "highs" on marijuana "placebos."
- *b.* Experienced users achieve "highs" from marijuana smoke.
- *c.* Naive users generally require two or three sessions to achieve "highs" on *Cannabis*.
- *d.* After smoking marijuana, experienced users rate their moods significantly differently, depending on whether they are aware or unaware of being observed.

Exercise

STAGES OF SLEEP. To test your knowledge of the various sleep stages, match the stage with its characteristics. Each stage may be matched with several characteristics. The same characteristic may fit more than one sleep stage. To review, see pages 212 to 216.

SLEEP STAGES: stage 0, stage 1 NREM, stage 1 REM, stage 2, stage 3, stage 4

_____ *1.* Occupies roughly 5 percent of a young adult's sleep.

_____ *2.* Usually occurs right before stage 4 sleep.

_____ 3. A sleeper aroused from this stage is likely to report thoughts, images, and dreamlike fragments.

_____ 4. Occupies roughly 50 percent of a young adult's sleep.

_____ 5. Alpha activity predominates.

_____ 6. Occupies slightly less than 25 percent of a young adult's sleep.

_____ 7. Most likely time for myoclonic seizures.

_____ 8. Characterized by intense autonomic variability.

_____ 9. Sometimes called light sleep.

_____ 10. Delta waves predominate.

_____ 11. While muscles may jerk and twitch, they usually lack muscle tone.

_____ 12. Spindles first appear at this time.

_____ 13. Usually occurs right after stage 4 sleep.

_____ 14. Upon arousal, vivid dreams or dream fragments are typically reported.

_____ 15. Delta waves first appear and are interspersed with spindles and fast, irregular, low-amplitude waves.

_____ 16. Most likely time for sleep irregularities like sleep walking and night terrors.

_____ 17. Sometimes called intermediate sleep.

Suggested Readings

1. Ornstein, R. E. *The psychology of consciousness.* (2d ed.) San Francisco: Freeman, 1977 (paperback). Through accounts of research, Eastern literature, and personal experience, Ornstein examines what is known about consciousness with an emphasis on meditation and other unusual states. A lucid, broad-ranging book.

2. Cartwright, R. D. *Night life: Explorations in dreaming.* Englewood Cliffs, N.J.: Prentice-Hall, 1977; Dement, W. C. *Some must watch while some must sleep.* (2d ed.) New York: Norton, 1978; Webb, W. B. *Sleep: The gentle tyrant.* Englewood Cliffs, N.J.: Prentice-Hall, 1975. Among many excellent paperback introductions to research on sleep and dreaming, these books, written by well-known sleep investigators, make fascinating reading. Dement's book offers many behind-the-scenes insights into early research. Webb's book emphasizes recent work on sleep and sleep disorders, much of it his own, while Cartwright's book focuses on dreaming.

3. Coates, T. J., & Thoresen, C. E. *How to sleep better. A drug-free program for overcoming insomnia.* Englewood Cliffs, N.J.: Prentice-Hall, 1977 (paperback). This clear and informative book aims to teach people who are sleeping unsatisfactorily to sleep better. Both authors are involved in clinical research with patients who have sleeping problems.

4. Singer, J. L. *The inner world of daydreaming.* New York: Harper & Row, 1975. Singer has spent much of his research life investigating daydreaming. This rather personal book describes how he became interested in, and what he has learned about, the frequency, type, function, and origin of fantasies.

5. Glock, C. Y., & Ballah, R. N. (Eds.), *The new religious consciousness.* Berkeley, Calif.: University of California Press, 1976. This collection of essays by sociologists and theologians analyzes the origin, philosophy, appeal, and types of consciousness encouraged by Hare Krishna, the Healthy-Happy-Holy Organization, the Church of Satan, the Catholic Charismatic Renewal, and other religious movements that began in the 1960s near San Francisco.

6. Goleman, D. *The varieties of meditative experience.* New York: Dutton, 1977. A psychologist-writer who has done research in this area describes the various schools of meditation, their history, and their goals.

7. In *Psychology Today*, December 1978, **12**(7), investigators clearly describe recent dream research for the general public. Three articles should be of interest: McCarley, R. W. Where dreams come from: A new theory (pp. 54ff.); Cartwright, R. D. Happy endings for our dreams (pp. 66–76); and Foulkes, D. Dreams of innocence (pp. 78–88).

8. For more on dissociation theory, see Hilgard, E. R. Hypnosis and consciousness. *Human Nature*, 1978, **1**(1), 42–49. For contrasting views of the nature of hypnosis, see Hilgard, E. R. Hypnosis is no mirage. *Psychology Today*, 1974, **8**(6), 121–128; and Barber, T. X. Who believes in hypnosis? *Psychology Today*, 1970, **4**(7), 20ff.

9. Ornstein, R. E. Eastern psychologies: The container vs. the contents. *Psychology Today*, 1976, **10**(4), 36–43. A provocative critique of transcendental meditation and other self-awareness programs. "TM," says Ornstein, "promotes itself as a synthesizer of East and West. . . . In this case . . . the synthesis is comic: the Eastern lack of rigor with the Western lack of spiritual advancement."

10. Zinberg, N. E. The war over marijuana. *Psychology Today*, 1976, **10**(7), 45ff. This article describes research findings on marijuana's long-term effects and problems that plague marijuana investigations. Yankelovich, D. Drug users vs. drug abusers: How students control their drug crisis. *Psychology Today*, 1975, **9**(5), 39–42. The author discusses patterns of drug use and abuse among college students.

11. Jones, B. M., & Parsons, O. A. Alcohol and consciousness: Getting high, coming down. *Psychology Today*, 1975, **9**(1), 53–58. In describing research on alcohol's consciousness-altering effects, the authors explore some common beliefs including "drinking quickly heightens alcohol's impact" and "women get drunk more easily than men."

Answer Keys

Self-Quiz

1. *b* (210)   **2.** *d* (210)   **3.** *a* (214)   **4.** d (219)
5. *b* (215)   **6.** *b* (216)   **7.** *d* (221)   **8.** *a* (223)
9. b (224)   **10.** *b* (225)   **11.** *d* (228)   **12.** *b* (229)
13. *b* (229)   **14.** b (230)   **15.** *d* (231)

Exercise

1. 1 NREM   **2.** 3   **3.** 0, 1 NREM, 2, 3, 4   **4.** 2
5. 0   **6.** 1 REM, 3 & 4 combined   **7.** 2   **8.** 1 REM
9. 1 NREM   **10.** 4   **11.** 1 REM   **12.** 2   **13.** 3
14. 1 REM, 0, 1 NREM   **15.** 3   **16.** 4   **17.** 2

CHAPTER EIGHT
Memory

Try to imagine for a moment having no memory at all. Our memories operate so swiftly and automatically that few people (memory researchers excepted) notice their pervasive presence. Yet perceiving, being conscious, learning, speaking, and problem solving all require the ability to store information. Perceiving and consciousness frequently depend on comparisons between present and past. Learning demands retention of habits or new information. Speaking requires remembering words and at least a few grammatical rules. Problem solving relies on retaining chains of ideas. Even activities that are ordinarily considered nonintellectual, such as making small talk or washing dishes, depend on the ability to remember. In fact, almost everything people do depends on memory. In this chapter we explore the nature of memory. We begin with the case of S., a man who had an unusual problem—remembering too much.

The Case of S., a Man Who Remembered Too Much

"In [1920] a man came to my laboratory who asked me to test his memory," wrote Alexander Luria, the distinguished Russian psychologist-physician. "At the time the man (let us designate him S.) was a newspaper reporter who had come to my laboratory at the suggestion of the paper's editor. Each morning the editor would meet with the staff and hand out assignments for the day. . . . The list of addresses and instructions was usually fairly long, and the editor noted with some surprise that S. never took any notes. He was about to reproach the reporter for being inattentive when, at his urging, S. repeated the entire assignment word for word. Curious to learn more about how the man operated, the editor began questioning S. about his memory. But S. merely countered with amazement: Was there really anything unusual about his remembering everything he'd been told?"

Luria studied S.'s memory for more than thirty years and was unable to find its limits. "Experiments indicated that S. . . . . had no difficulty reproducing any lengthy series of words whatever, even though these had originally been presented to him a week, a month, a year, or even many years earlier. In fact, some of these experiments designed to test his retention were performed (without his being given any warning) fifteen or sixteen years after the session in which he had originally recalled the words. Yet invariably they were successful." . . .

How did S. form such permanent memories? He reported that he automatically changed words into vivid and stable images which he could see and, in some cases, taste, smell, or touch as well. In S.'s words, "Usually I experience a word's taste and weight, and I don't have to make an effort to remember it—the word seems to recall itself. . . . What I sense is something oily slipping through my hand . . . or I'm aware of a slight tickling in my left hand caused by a mass of tiny, light-weight points."

S. could not "turn off" this word transformation process and having it "turned on" was sometimes very trying. During reading, words produced images which crowded in on one another, masking the meaning of the material. S.'s powerful memory also interfered with his thinking. Because his mind tended to jump from image to image, grasping complicated relationships and abstract ideas was very difficult. On balance, S.'s superb memory caused as many problems as it solved [1].

S.'s case raises many questions about the nature of *memory*, the name psychologists give to the varied processes and structures involved in putting experiences into, and taking them from, storage. How does memory work? Why do most people forget the types of trivia that S. remembered? What causes forgetting? Are there different types of storage? Can ordinary human beings increase their retention? In this chapter we will try to answer these and many other questions as best we can. Though behavioral scientists cannot explain S.'s unusual abilities now, they are beginning to understand many aspects of normal memory. We look first at how normal memory seems to operate.

THE NATURE OF MEMORY

All memory systems, including those used by computers, libraries, people, and rats, require a storage area. An animal's "storehouse" lies in its brain. Memory systems also need procedures to insert information into and remove it from storage. Psychologists believe that the three processes of encoding, storage, and retrieval are necessary for all memory systems. Initially, material headed for storage is encoded. *Encoding* refers to the entire process of readying information for storage. It often involves *embellishing*, or associating, material with past knowledge or experience (a label, an image, or something else) so that data can be found at a later time. Encoding entails *representing* material in a form that the storage system can handle too. For example, as you read, you actually see black "squiggles" on the page. You may encode this information as a pictorial design, as words, or as meaningful ideas. Once an experience is encoded, it will be *stored*, often without any conscious effort, for a varying amount of time. Eventually, you may attempt to *retrieve*, or recover, the information. While psychologists agree on this broad outline, the precise nature of the memory storage structure(s) and input-output processes has not been determined. According to a recent estimate, some fifty models of memory (many of which are similar) are currently being studied [2].

What is a model? A *model* is a simplified system that contains the essential features of a larger, far more complicated system. To be truly useful, a model must allow scientists to make predictions. Tests of these predictions then verify or fail to confirm aspects of the model. This type of systematic exploration leads to improvements in the model, furthering understanding of the large system.

To show how memory is pictured today by a large number of behavioral scientists, we discuss a widely accepted memory model, an amended version of one first described in detail by psychologists Richard Atkinson and Richard Shiffrin [3].

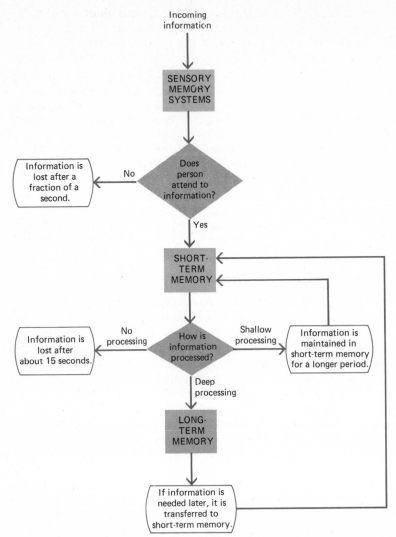

FIGURE 8-1 This diagram summarizing the modified Atkinson-Shiffrin memory model may look confusing initially, but it is actually easy to follow: Begin at the top. The arrows show how the incoming information progresses through the three memory systems, represented here by boxes. The diamonds designate points where the learner has a choice. Select the different options, in turn, and note the results.

A Model of Memory

We will run through the Atkinson-Shiffrin memory model quickly to provide an overview. Later, we will discuss the component systems in detail. Imagine that a friend who collects facts informs you that a human brain weighs approximately 3 pounds, an elephant brain about 13 pounds, and a sperm whale brain roughly 20 pounds. How might this information make its way into your memory? You heard your friend recite the facts. Information that strikes our sense organs seems to be held fleetingly by a storage system (or systems) called the *sensory memory* (SM) or *sensory store*. Materials held by the sensory memory resemble afterimages. They typically disappear in less than a second unless they are immediately transferred to a second memory system, the *short-term memory* (STM), or *short-term store*. To reassign sensory data to the short-term store, a person has to attend to the material only momentarily. If you listened as your friend talked about brain sizes, you'd encode the sounds into meaningful words. The material would then pass into your short-term memory. This system is often pictured as the center of consciousness. According to Atkinson and Shiffrin, the short-term memory holds all the thoughts, information, and experiences that an individual is aware of at any given point in time. The "store" of STM houses a limited amount of material temporarily (usually, for about fifteen seconds). Information can be kept in the short-term system longer by *rehearsing*, or repeating, it. In addition to serving a storage function, the short-term memory also "works" as a central executive. It inserts material into, and removes the data from, a third more or less permanent memory system, the *long-term memory* (LTM), or *long-term store*. Returning to our example, suppose that you just barely listened to your friend's recital of the facts. Or, assume that you thought about the information momentarily. This type of *shallow processing* could hold the facts in the short-term store for a few extra seconds, perhaps even minutes. But it would probably be insufficient to transfer the data to the long-term system. Consequently, this material, like any that is not relocated in LTM, would soon be lost. To move the information into the long-term store, you'd probably have to process it deeply. During *deep processing*, people use *elaborative rehearsal strategies*: They pay close attention, think about meaning, and relate data to items that are already in long-term memory [4]. Simple, mindless repetition appears to be sufficient to transfer information into the long-term store in some cases [5]. The short- and long-term systems communicate continually. Material in the long-term store may be activated and transferred to the short-term store whenever it is relevant.

The short-term system is responsible for retrieving both long- and short-term memories. Suppose someone asks, "Do people have the largest brains of any animal?" seconds after your friend's comments. The necessary information will be in the short-term store and your search will be quick and simple (since STM contains a small amount of material). Now, imagine that the question comes up a year later. In this case, you'll have to comb the long-term store. If you used the information repeatedly or if you learned the facts very well to begin with, the search through LTM may be rapid and essentially effortless. The material will be transferred to the short-term store and used. On the other hand, if you stashed the facts away quickly with little thought and have not sought them out before now, tracking the data down may be a time-consuming and laborious project. And, for a variety of reasons that will be discussed later, you may not be able to find what you're looking for. Figure 8-1 pictures the amended Atkinson-Shiffrin model that has been described.

Are the three memory stores really separate? This issue is quite controversial. Right now many psychologists, including Atkinson and Shiffrin, believe that the short-term system may be some temporarily active part of the long-term system [6]. We will think of STM and LTM as separate processes that may be carried out by a single faculty. Before describing research findings on the three memory systems, we turn to the measurement of human memory.

MEASURES OF HUMAN MEMORY

How is memory measured? We examine one of the earliest studies of human memory and measures of human memory that are commonly used today.

The First Major Investigation of Human Memory

The German philosopher and psychologist Herman Ebbinghaus (1850–1909), pictured in

FIGURE 8-2 This is Herman Ebbinghaus. His book *Concerning Memory* (1885) is thought to have inspired more psychological experiments than any other single source in the entire history of psychology. [*Bettmann Archive.*]

Figure 8-2, published the first systematic investigation of human memory in 1885. To understand the studies, one must know something about Ebbinghaus's assumptions. He believed that the mind stores "ideas" about past sensory experiences. He also thought that events which follow one another closely in time or space become linked to one another. So, memory contains thousands of connected sensory impressions. These views made it sensible to explore the memory of associations. Ebbinghaus was particularly interested in questions such as: When does most forgetting of associations occur? Does retention of associations depend on degree of original learning? Is memory of associations better if practice is crammed into one period or spread out with rest intervals in between? (We look at the answers to these questions later.)

To study memory in a relatively "pure"

form, Ebbinghaus devised *nonsense syllables* (consonant-vowel-consonant combinations such as zik, dag, pif, toc, and jum) to memorize. He thought that the nonsense syllables would be about equally difficult to learn and retain because they were less likely than words to have meaningful associations. In a typical observation, Ebbinghaus served as his own subject. He repeated nonsense syllables from a list until he could recite them without error. Syllables next to one another were naturally linked together. After various time intervals or different study practices, he tested himself in a special way. He observed how many additional times he had to repeat the syllables on the original list before he could recite them again without error. Ebbinghaus was interested in how many practice sessions he could save. In other words, he was measuring memory by the *savings* it provided. If ten repetitions were required to learn a list the first time and two repetitions to master the same list twenty-four hours later, then eight repetitions have been saved (10 − 2 = 8). The number of repetitions saved is usually expressed as a percentage. We divide the number of repetitions saved by the number of repetitions required to learn the original list and multiply the result by 100. (In our example, 8/10 × 100 = 80 percent.)

Measuring savings provides a particularly sensitive gauge of memory. The procedure often shows that previous learning has been retained to some extent, though the person cannot recall or even recognize the material and considers it entirely forgotten.

Ebbinghaus's pioneering studies added to knowledge about memory. Modern experiments have confirmed many of the findings. Today the savings method is still used occasionally to measure memory in the laboratory. Nonsense syllables, on the other hand, have been largely abandoned. As later research showed, they vary in meaningfulness (number of associations) just as words do. In addition to these direct contributions, Ebbinghaus's work stimulated interest in memory and led to a great many further studies.

Current Measures of Human Memory

Modern studies of human memory rely heavily on two measures: recall and recognition. See Figure 8-3.

Recall Who conducted the first major investigation of memory? When did it occur? These questions test *recall*, the ability to remember desired information when prompted with associated material called a *cue*, *probe*, *pointer*, or *prompt*. Psychologists use several types of recall tasks in their research. *Serial recall* tasks ask that material be remembered in a special order, while *free recall* tasks request information in any order. When psychologists use recall measures of memory in the laboratory, they encounter two problems which cloud the interpretation of their results. Suppose that you are taking part in a memory experiment and that you are asked to memorize word associations, including pairs such as "guppy-watermelon" and "violin-daffodil." You know that you must reproduce the items a little later. First, you'll probably feel tempted to repeat the materials to yourself. To eliminate the effects of rehearsal, research participants are often instructed to engage in a distracting task, such as counting backward after encoding. Second, if you learned a long list of verbal materials, you might forget items during the course of reciting what you recall for the investigator. To minimize the possibility of forgetting during recall, a *partial-report* strategy is often used. Subjects are signaled to report one or more items selected at random from the information stored.

Recognition Gustav Fechner was the first major investigator of human memory. Is this true or false? And a multiple-choice question: The first systematic study of human memory was published in (*a*) 500 B.C., (*b*) 1534, (*c*) 1885, (*d*) 1936. These questions test *recognition*, a second commonly used measure of memory. In both examples you are asked to choose the response that has been seen,

FIGURE 8-3 Memory drums, such as the one shown on the table, are often used in memory studies in the laboratory. The drum contains a list of items to be memorized. As the drum turns, each item is exposed through a slit in the front for a precise amount of time. [*Van Bucher, Photo Researchers: Courtesy of Wagner College Department of Psychology.*]

heard, or read before and is consequently familiar. Apparently, people compare the information given with that stored in their memories to see whether they match. Since guessing can influence the results of recognition studies of memory, researchers have devised ways of assessing guessing styles so that they can be taken into account.

How do recall and recognition measures compare with one another? One way to get an intuitive handle on this question is to think about your own experience. Do you prefer multiple-choice or essay tests? Laboratory studies find that people generally do better at recognizing than recalling, even when allowances are made for guessing [7].

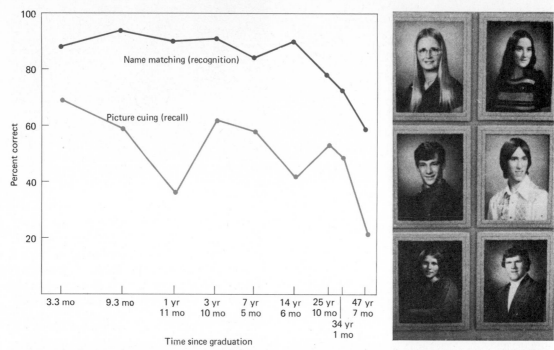

FIGURE 8-4 A memory study by psychologist Harry Bahrick and his colleagues is summarized here. Nearly 400 research participants were tested to see whether they could recognize and recall the faces and names of high school classmates that hadn't been heard or seen for periods varying between two weeks and fifty-seven years. Six different recall and recognition measures of memory were analyzed. In one recognition test, called *name matching*, a photograph of a high school classmate was presented, and subjects had to select the correct name from five possibilities. For *picture cuing*, a recall measure, participants saw a single photograph and had to retrieve the person's name on their own, without additional help. As you can see from the graph, Bahrick and his coworkers found that people do a lot better at recognition than at recall. The investigators also learned that human beings generally recognize faces more easily than names. [*From Bahrick, Bahrick, and Wittlinger, 1975; photograph: Grunzweig/Flash Photo Researchers.*]

Under special circumstances, recall may be easier than recognition [8].

Why is it usually easier to recognize than to recall? Psychologists Geoffrey and Elizabeth Loftus suggest the following reasons:

1. People need complete information for correct recall, but only partial information for correct recognition. The multiple-choice question on the first systematic study of human memory illustrates this point. Even if you hadn't read the chapter, you'd be likely to eliminate options (*a*) 500 B.C., (*b*) 1534, and (*d*) 1936, especially if you remembered anything about experimental psychology's brief history from Chapter 1. Responses (*a*) and (*b*) are improbably distant, while option (*d*) is suspect because of its extreme recency.

2. Recall seems to require two strategies: first, a search of memory to locate the desired information;

and second, a simple recognition test, "Is the material familiar?" During recognition, the information is before you, so you needn't search for it. The recognition test is all that is required.

3. Chance can improve one's score on many tests involving recognition, as mentioned before. On true-false exams, for example, blind guessing usually results in correct answers on about half the questions. Guessing based on a little information is much more powerful. Chance has almost no effect on recall tasks [9]. See Figure 8-4. ▲

We turn now to basic research on the sensory, short-term, and long-term memory systems described earlier. As we explore each store, we will concern ourselves with several questions: What is the system's storage capacity? How is material in the store encoded? Retrieved? And forgotten?

SENSORY MEMORY

Our senses are continually bombarded by huge amounts of information. Suppose that you are lying on your bed reading. Your eyes receive visual information from the words on the page, possibly from a blanket covering the bed, and trees beyond a window, as well. Your ears receive auditory input—maybe a distant conversation or a record on the stereo. Your skin registers temperature, pressure, and pain. The room may be overheated, and one leg may be pressing against the other. Even though a person is not paying attention, information which is taken in by the senses enters a *sensory store*. Recent research suggests that the anatomical location of visual sensory memories may be the retina of the eye [10]. Other sensory stores may be located in the corresponding sensory organs.

The following exercises will give you an intuitive feeling for the types of memory held by the sensory store [11].

1. Hold a pencil by its point at arm's length in front of you. Use a white wall as a background, if possible. While staring straight ahead, wave the eraser end back and forth by moving your wrist rapidly. Note the image outlining the path that the eraser travels.

2. Clap your hands once and note how the distinctness of the sound fades gradually.

3. Gently and for an instant touch a toothpick against the back of your hand. Focus on the sensation that remains momentarily after you remove the point.

As a result of each exercise, a sensory impression—a sight, sound, or feeling—lingers for a fraction of a second. Psychologists call this fleeting impression a *sensory memory*. This brief "shadow" of an experience, persisting for only a moment, is useful in daily life. The visual sensory memory, *iconic memory* (icon means "image"), keeps smooth images before us by filling in visual gaps. You may recall that our eyes are almost constantly moving, bringing us several new scenes for processing every second (Chapter 6). Iconic memory also enables human beings to see a steady flow of action on a movie screen rather than the series of still pictures actually being projected, as shown in Figure 8-5. The *auditory sensory memory* allows precise, immediate recall. A student learning English pronounces the word sun "zun." The teacher makes a correction, "Not *zun*, *sun*." The student can retain a faithful representation of both sounds for a brief period and benefit from the advice.

Psychologists have been aware of the sensory memory capacity since the late 1800s, but systematic investigation has only recently begun. So far, the visual and auditory sensory memories have received the most attention from behavioral scientists. We shall concentrate on the visual sensory memory, iconic memory.

Evidence for Iconic Memory

In the late 1950s psychologist George Sperling, working on his dissertation at Harvard University, began a classic series of experiments which provided a great deal of information about iconic memory. Initially, he was interested in the question, How much can a person see in a very brief period of time?

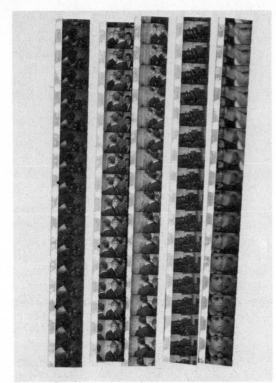

FIGURE 8-5 A motion picture presents a series of still photographs, like these, at a specific speed. Between each picture, people "see" a dark screen for a fraction of a second. Yet the total effect is one of uninterrupted movement. The afterimages that persist for a fraction of a second in iconic memory help human beings fuse the images to produce this illusion, though scientists do not understand precisely how. [*Courtesy of Linda Gutierrez.*]

vised the research tools to check out these reports, and he found evidence that they were correct. In one very important study, he showed subjects *arrays* (groups of letters or numbers arranged in rows or columns), in this case three rows of four letters, for a twentieth of a second (.05 second). Then he signaled the research participants, after varying time delays, to report either the top, middle, or bottom row. From previous work, Sperling had learned that *partial reports* provided more reliable estimates of what had been seen than reports on the whole array. So he worked out a way to communicate to his subjects which part of the array was to be reported. A high-pitched tone signaled the top row; a medium-pitched tone, the middle row; and a low-pitched tone, the bottom row. If the image was really fading little by little, then the number of items identified should decrease gradually to the four or five letters retained (in short-term memory), as the time

FIGURE 8-6 Some of the results of Sperling's study of iconic memory. Research participants in this investigation were shown an array of letters for a twentieth of a second. Then they were signaled by a tone to repeat from memory the letters in one of the lines. The time period when the array was visible is indicated on the horizontal axis (between −.05 and .00 second). The tone was sounded at various times, such as when the array was turned off and .15, .30, and 1.00 second later. The dashed line shows how visual sensory memory decays with time. [*After Sperling, 1960.*]

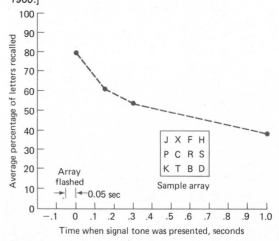

Studies of this topic had been done before. Rows of letters were flashed on a screen. Then, subjects were asked to report what they had seen. No matter how many letters were presented or how the exposure time varied, research participants generally identified four or five letters correctly. Many behavioral scientists assumed that their subjects simply saw four or five letters. When asked about that, the subjects insisted that they had seen more letters but had forgotten them. A number of individuals also asserted that images of the letters faded gradually over the course of a second or so. In other words, the information was available in the form of an image for a very brief period. Sperling de-

delay increased. Figure 8-6 shows that this is precisely what Sperling found [12]. Subsequent studies suggest that iconic images ordinarily persist about 250 milliseconds (a quarter of a second) [13], though they can last longer under special laboratory conditions. If images persisted generally, people would tend to see new scenes superimposed on old ones whenever their eyes moved (because they take in new images every 300 milliseconds or so).

Another of Sperling's experiments suggests that sensory data in the iconic store are *raw*. In other words, they have not been analyzed for meaning. The visual sensory system would preserve C4A8, for example, as a line design, rather than as two letters and two numbers [14]. Recall the distinctions made in Chapter 6 between sensation (the data that our senses bring in) and perception (our interpretations of the material). In these terms, the iconic store holds visual sensations.

The Fate of Material in Iconic Memory

What happens to data in iconic memory? A vast portion of iconic information fades away after approximately 250 milliseconds. Disappearance with the passage of time is known as *decay*. But the information can be preserved, at least temporarily, if people attend to the material and/or interpret its meaning. Attending and/or interpreting cause the material to be automatically transferred into the short-term store. Behavioral scientists call this type of transfer *retrieval from sensory memory*. Research shows that when a new image is presented before an old one has decayed, the most recent one is "written over" the old memory, which is lost [15]. This type of interference is called *masking*.

SHORT-TERM MEMORY

Imagine that a friend is talking to you and your mind wanders to other matters. Somehow you sense that your companion asked a question and is expecting a response. You fumble apologetically and are about to ask, "What did you say?" Suddenly, you realize that you know the precise question. You don't have the foggiest notion of what was said, but somehow you can dredge up the last fifteen to twenty seconds of conversation verbatim (word for word). This type of experience is commonplace. People can recall the most recent words that they themselves have spoken or heard, even though they were barely paying attention. Yet, in almost every case, they aren't able to recall the same few words a minute or two later. *Introspection* (examining personal experiences) suggests, then, that people can store meaningful information for seconds with very little effort. We already know that sensory memory cannot store meaningful material and that it does not hold experiences this long. At the same time, the information does not remain for minutes or longer, as we'd expect if it had been deposited in a permanent store. These observations suggest that some intermediate-length storage system, which behavioral scientists call *short-term memory*, probably exists. We will look at the evidence for the existence of short-term memory and then at the characteristics of the short-term store.

Evidence for Short-Term Memory

Studies of people, such as H. M., who have sustained certain types of brain damage suggest that there is a separate intermediate storage capacity. H. M. was observed by a Canadian psychologist, Brenda Milner.

The Case of H. M.

At age seven H. M. sustained a head injury. Later he began experiencing minor seizures.

These attacks became increasingly frequent and severe until, at twenty-seven, H. M. could no

longer hold a job or lead anything like a normal life. To bring him relief, portions of both temporal lobes, including parts of the cerebral cortex, hippocampus, and amygdala (see Figure 4-17), were surgically removed as a last resort.

Immediately following the surgery, H. M. showed a pronounced memory impairment. He did not recognize members of the hospital staff, except for the surgeon whom he'd known for years. He did not recall and could not relearn his way to the bathroom. Nor could he remember daily happenings around the institution. Other abilities appeared to be intact. H. M.

showed a normal capacity for emotion. His social behavior was appropriate. And his speech was as intelligible as previously.

H. M.'s ability to retain daily occurrences did not improve significantly. When the family moved to a new house, he could not learn the address or find his way home alone. Day after day, he worked the same jigsaw puzzles and read the same magazines. Each time, the contents seemed new and unfamiliar to him.

Yet he remembered his early

past vividly, and he could retain small bits of material for short periods. Observations made during a laboratory test pinpoint the selective nature of H. M.'s memory problem. For one test, he was asked to remember three digits. By making elaborate associations, he managed to retain the numbers for fifteen minutes. But moments later, he could not recall the digits or the train of associations that had helped in recalling them. He could not even remember being assigned the task [16].

The precise interpretation of H. M.'s problem remains controversial [17]. But, whatever the deficit, his short-term capacity was probably not impaired, while his ability to make or use new long-term memories was. Damage to different brain regions may result in contrasting disabilities. An epileptic patient known as K. F. could not repeat brief strings of letters or numbers which he had heard. Yet he could recall one such item correctly. He could remember new letter or number series for long periods of time, too, if they were presented out loud repeatedly. At the same time, his short-term memory for letters or numbers presented visually was approximately normal [18]. While case histories such as these do not prove that the short-term capacity is separate from the long-term one, they suggest that these abilities depend on somewhat different brain mechanisms.

Free-recall studies in the laboratory are a second major source of evidence for the short-term memory. As a subject in a typical free-recall experiment, you'd be presented with words to study (one at a time). Your list might include apple, tiger, finger, soap, umbrella, cigar, bomb, alligator, hat, and automobile. After being given some time to master the items, you'd be asked to recall them in any order at all. Generally, people remember more words from the list's beginning (the *pri-*

macy effect) and end (the *recency effect*). (See Figure 8-7, curve *a*.) Controversy centers on why people in free-recall studies remember the last few words on the list best. Nonbelievers in short-term memory argue that the final items are inserted into the long-term store last and are consequently easiest to retrieve. Believers in STM contend that the last few words are retained because they are still in short-term memory. The two hypotheses can be tested by performing a free-recall experiment and distracting subjects immediately after they have encoded the words. In this case, they won't be able to keep the last few items in short-term memory by rehearsal. The experimental evidence supports the assumptions of the believers in STM. Distraction seems to "flush out" the short-term store so that the last few words are only as likely to be recalled as middle items [19]. (See Figure 8-7, curve *b*.) Though additional observations provide support for a distinct short-term memory [20], the issue is far from settled.

Characteristics of Short-Term Memory

Short-term memory, as mentioned before, is currently pictured as the center of human consciousness. Presumably, it contains what-

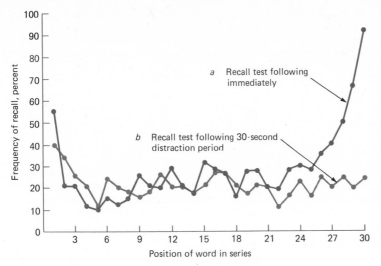

FIGURE 8-7 The results of a typical free-recall study show that, when a recall test immediately follows the memorizing of a list of words, the first and last few items that were mastered have relatively high probabilities of being recalled. These primacy and recency effects are evident in curve (*a*). When a thirty-second distraction period follows the recall test, subjects cannot rehearse and the recency effect disappears, as shown by curve (*b*). [*After Postman and Phillips, 1965.*]

ever thoughts, information, and experiences are in a person's mind at any specific point in time. We described two functions of STM: temporary storage and overall management (selecting materials to maintain momentarily in its own store, transferring experiences to long-term memory for a more permanent record, and retrieving data from the various memory systems). We turn now to research on the storage aspects of the short-term system. Later, we discuss the administrative jobs it performs as we review ways to improve long-term memory.

Capacity of the short-term store How much information can the short-term system hold? To answer this question, investigators present letters, words, digits, sounds, and other stimuli to research participants and ask that they recall as many items as possible. Numerous studies of this sort find that people rarely retain more than seven *chunks* (groupings) of anything [21]. Much of the time, subjects remember only two to five items [22]. How does an upper limit of seven chunks mesh with common experiences, such as being able to hold in mind temporarily the eleven numbers necessary to dial long distance? To manage this feat, most people group the numbers into an area code, a local exchange,

and so on. Similarly, human beings frequently "chunk" letters into words and words into phrases and sentences. To improve the capacity of short-term memory, many individuals convert a relatively large number of low-information items, such as digits, into a smaller number of more meaningful (high-information) items, such as words. A "hot line" agency using this strategy might apply for the phone number 4357. Consequently, clients may dial "H-E-L-P" after dialing the local exchange. In this case, the strategy is so effective that the number is likely to be retained permanently.

Encoding in the short-term store Is material in short-term memory encoded in a specific form? There is evidence that people can represent verbal (language-related) information either *acoustically* (in terms of sound) or *semantically* (in terms of meaning) [23]. What about images, smells, tastes, sounds, or other types of sensory data? It is currently believed that these events are held in the short-term store in the form that they are practiced or rehearsed [24].

Retrieval in the short-term store If information is currently in conscious awareness, it shouldn't take very long to find it.

Material in the short-term store should be retrieved rapidly and efficiently. In the late 1960s psychologist Saul Sternberg found a way to investigate how people locate material in short-term memory. He asked subjects to remember strings of one to six digits, which he called *memory sets*. One series was presented at a time. Then, while the digits were still in the short-term store, a "target" number was introduced. The research participants had to decide whether that digit had been part of the memory set and communicate the decision by pulling a "yes" or "no" lever. As the size of the memory set increased, the time to react lengthened. The subjects seemed to be comparing the target item with each digit that had been stored. They had to search sequentially through STM item by item, in other words. They could not simply "lift out" the targeted information. Each comparison appeared to take about 38 milliseconds [25].

Forgetting in the short-term store

Information in the short-term memory cannot be readily retrieved after some fifteen to

twenty seconds unless it has been rehearsed or deposited in long-term memory. How were the time limits discovered? Psychologists Lloyd and Margaret Peterson presented student subjects with three-consonant groupings, or *trigrams*, one trigram at a time. After each presentation, subjects were asked to count backward by 3's or 4's from a three-digit number, such as 768, to prevent rehearsal of the material. After a specific amount of time had elapsed—3, 6, 9, 12, 15, or 18 seconds, say—the research participants were signaled to stop counting and to recall the trigram. Retention dropped rapidly over an eighteen-second interval. After fifteen seconds there was only about a 10 percent probability of recalling a trigram accurately [26]. (See Figure 8-8.) Subsequent research confirms the notion that material ordinarily disappears from the short-term system in approximately fifteen to twenty seconds [27]. As mentioned before, disappearance with passing time is known as *decay*. Rehearsal can keep information in the short-term store longer.

Just as masking may shorten the storage time of sensory memories, interference may shorten the storage time of short-term memories. Suppose that you are presented with two consonant trigrams—first KGL, and several seconds later, MZQ. Try to recall the first trigram. You're likely to respond with something like "MGL." When new information makes the recollection of past data difficult, *retroactive inhibition* is said to have occurred. The prefix "retro" means backward. In this case new material works backward and interferes somehow with remembering old information. If you had been asked to recall the second trigram instead of the first, you'd probably have responded with something like "MGQ." When past material interferes with retaining new information, *proactive inhibition* is said to have occurred. The prefix "pro" means before. In the case of proactive inhibition, memories of old or earlier experiences somehow disrupt the learning of newer ones. Interference is particularly severe between similar items [28]. For example, you'd probably have a hard time retaining the names of

FIGURE 8-8   The Petersons' study of short-term memory is pictured.

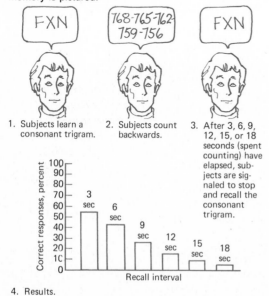

1. Subjects learn a consonant trigram.

2. Subjects count backwards.

3. After 3, 6, 9, 12, 15, or 18 seconds (spent counting) have elapsed, subjects are signaled to stop and recall the consonant trigram.

4. Results.

Jan, Jean, and Jane, three persons to whom you had just been introduced, long enough to address each woman correctly. ▲

LONG-TERM MEMORY

The long-term memory system gives people the ability to recall large amounts of information for substantial periods—hours, days, weeks, years, and in some cases, forever. Your own name, the taste of popcorn, nursery rhymes, and the English alphabet are examples of items that are probably stored in your long-term memory. Psychologists consider this system essentially unlimited in its storage capacity.

Long-term memory is limited by age in a way that is just beginning to be understood. Current research suggests that babies have the capacity for putting experiences into a long-term store beginning near birth [29]. Infants of five to six months appear to recognize targets that have been seen hours, days, and even weeks earlier [30]. If infants store experiences in long-term memory, why don't older youngsters and adults remember the events of their first years? Sigmund Freud suggested that early childhood is filled with conflicts (to be described in Chapter 13). Presumably, people repress early memories to avoid anxiety. Recent research on laboratory animals supports a different hypothesis. Like human infants, rat pups have undeveloped central nervous systems at birth. Correspondingly, these animals, like people, do not retain memories from infancy and "early childhood." Guinea pigs, on the other hand, whose brains are mature at birth, show an adult capacity for forming permanent memories from the very beginning [31]. Long-term memories acquired before the central nervous system is well developed may simply not be retrievable.

Encoding in Long-Term Memory

Ears, eyes, mouths, noses, and skin process information in specialized ways. Do people represent sensory information in long-term memory by a parallel code—visual information by an image, auditory information by a sound, for instance?

We appear to store some visual material as pictures. Observations by psychologist Lionel Standing indicate that people can view enormous quantities of photographs briefly (about five seconds per shot) and recognize them a day and a half or so later. In one study, subjects appeared to be able to correctly identify close to 90 percent of 1,000 vivid photos and 62 percent of 1,000 written words [32]. Apparently, people store vivid images differently and more easily than language in long-term memory. Additional support for this idea comes from the recent laboratory experiments of Roger Shepard and his colleagues. Research participants were shown different target visual materials, including three-dimensional objects and pictures of hands and random geometric shapes, and instructed to form mental images. Later, investigators asked the subjects to pick out the target amidst similar representations. Identifications were made exceedingly quickly and accurately. In many cases, the subjects did just as well using their mental pictures as when using the actual stimulus. When no image or an inappropriate image was formed, reaction time was consistently and significantly increased [33]. Evidently, stored images must resemble perceptions closely.

How is language-related material encoded in long-term memory? Laboratory observations suggest that verbal matter is frequently represented by its meaning, rather than by its sound or appearance [34]. As you read a newspaper, for instance, you probably condense the words into a few ideas that you retain. Few people remember the image of the letters on the page or the exact wording as if they had made a photograph or tape recording. At the same time, careful studies suggest that people do retain word sounds to some extent [35]. And we can store precise wording when it is needed [36], as it is when we're going to recite a poem or act in a play.

There is less research on other methods of encoding long-term memories. Still, experience suggests that people can make accoustic representations of sounds, such as melodies, and odorous representations of smells [37]. In sum, human long-term memory appears flexible in encoding materials. People probably represent some experiences by a summary of the meaning and others in detailed parallel forms (an image for an image, a sound for a sound, and the like) [38].

Retrieval from Long-Term Memory

We retrieve information from long-term memory continuously. According to the Atkinson-Shiffrin model, the short-term system manages the retrieval process. Sometimes the task is easy and automatic. Locating your mother's name or your own current address ordinarily takes no effort. As people perceive, they compare the present with the past, again without deliberate effort. Yet, on some occasions, retrieving long-term memories is an arduous, tedious job.

You've probably experienced that bewildering phenomenon which psychologists call the *tip of the tongue* (TOT) state. You cannot retrieve a word—perhaps a person's name—that you're sure you know and feel just on the verge of remembering. To produce this experience in the laboratory so that it could be studied, psychologists Roger Brown and David McNeill presented college students with definitions of uncommon English words (including apse, nepotism, cloaca, ambergris, and sampan). They asked what word had been defined. More than 200 instances of the TOT state were produced. While people in the TOT state could not retrieve the word they wanted, at least temporarily, they could often "describe" it. They knew the number of syllables, the location of the primary stress, the beginning and end sounds, and words with similar sounds and meanings. When the target word was "sampan," for example, research participants produced these words (in some cases, made up) of similar sound: Saipan, Siam, Cheyenne, sarong, sanching, and sympoon. They gave these words with similar meaning: barge, houseboat, junk. To retrieve words, Brown and McNeill hypothesize, people think about the word's features (sound, spelling, and meaning, for instance). They then use these features as clues to track down the desired word [39]. Note that retrieval under these conditions requires problem solving.

Retrieving facts from long-term memory may also require a problem-solving strategy, which psychologists call *reconstruction, redintegration, refabrication,* or *creative memory.* Let's begin with an example. Suppose someone asks you, "What were you doing two years ago on Monday afternoon in the third week of September?" A response to this question might proceed something like this:

1. Come on. How should I know? (Experimenter: Just try it, anyhow.)
2. OK. Let's see: Two years ago . . .
3. I would be in high school in Pittsburgh . . .
4. That would be my senior year.
5. Third week in September—that's just after summer—that would be the fall term . . .
6. Let me see. I think I had chemistry lab on Mondays.
7. I don't know. I was probably in the chemistry lab . . .

8. Wait a minute—that would be the second week of school. I remember he started off with the atomic table—a big, fancy chart. I thought he was crazy, trying to make us memorize that thing.
9. You know, I think I can remember sitting. . . . [40]

According to memory researchers Peter Lindsay and Donald Norman, people tend to size up "retrieval jobs" without being aware of doing so. We try to decide:

1. Whether the information exists (you wouldn't attempt to retrieve Mozart's phone number, even if you were asked for it).
2. Whether the information has been stored in memory (you probably wouldn't hunt for Jane Fonda's address, even though it exists).
3. How difficult the retrieval process will be (line 1 of our imaginary student's monologue suggests that a lot of trouble was anticipated).

If minimal requirements are met, people begin the retrieval process. We seem to break large questions into small ones and work on one problem at a time. Typically, we remember fragments and fill in details with logical guesses. We emerge eventually with precise responses that are often inaccurate. Classic studies of this topic were done in the 1920s and 1930s by the British psychologist Frederick Bartlett (1886–1969). Frequently, Bartlett asked people to examine, and later reproduce (after several years, in some cases), materials such as stories and drawings. He concluded that after a long time delay, people usually recall striking features which they tend to magnify and distort. Influenced by past experiences and expectations, reconstructions are frequently shortened, simplified, updated, and "glued" together in a logical way. What is most curious is that people are often totally unaware of fabricating at all [41]. Figure 8-9 describes one of Bartlett's studies.

Forgetting in Long-Term Memory

"The horror of that moment," the King went on, "I shall never, never, never forget!"
"You will, though," the Queen said, "if you don't make a memorandum of it." [42]

The problem of too much forgetting is a common one, and it is easy to empathize with the king in *Through the Looking Glass*. While human beings frequently lament their poor memories, a great deal of forgetting may, in fact, be adaptive. People simply do not need to retain lasting impressions of all their experiences. Try to imagine remembering every conversation you have heard and every scene you have viewed. Retaining everything would flood your memory, producing mental paralysis, as in S.'s case. In this section we consider the varied ways of losing materials from the long-term storage system. Failures in encoding, storage, and/or retrieval can be responsible.

Failures during encoding In some cases, forgetting occurs because materials fail to be represented at all in long-term memory. Take the case of the student who complains, "I read, but I don't retain a thing." If one's mind is 10,000 miles away, reading words will not transfer meaningful material into long-term memory. Encoding failures occur when materials are represented inaccurately, too.

Storage failures The commonsense view of forgetting long-term memories is probably a *decay theory*. Long-term memories are likened to newspapers that dry out, yellow, and eventually rot. As more time passes, the memory disintegrates more completely. Is there evidence that decay is a major factor in forgetting from long-term memory? To get a handle on this topic, psychologists study forgetting during sleep when long-term memory appears to be relatively inactive. Subjects learn something, sleep or go about daily routines, and take memory tests periodically. Research of this type shows that a significantly smaller amount of forgetting occurs during sleep than during comparable periods of waking. Most forgetting during sleep seems to take place during REM sleep (see Chapter 7), the time when vivid dreaming is likely [43]. These observations suggest that forgetting from long-term memory may depend more on a person's activities than on time alone.

Original drawing   Reproduction 1   Reproduction 2

Reproduction 3   Reproduction 4   Reproduction 5   Reproduction 6

Reproduction 7   Reproduction 8   Reproduction 9   Reproduction 10

FIGURE 8-9 For one study Frederick Bartlett showed the picture of a stylized owl (the one marked "Original drawing") to a research participant, who was asked to redraw it from memory. That person's drawing was passed along to a second individual who studied and redrew it from memory. A third subject received this new sketch to study and draw from memory. The process continued. As these drawings show, the stylized owl gradually changed into a cat. Studies using different visual materials find essentially identical results. People distort pictorial and verbal materials in much the same way. They retain familiar, commonly recognized elements. They add on appropriate details and simplify. The same general process probably occurs whenever information is filtered through the memories of several people, as on news broadcasts and in rumors. [*From Bartlett, 1950.*]

Just as in the sensory and short-term stores, materials in the long-term system may interfere with one another. A few examples should make it clear that proactive and retro-active inhibition, defined when discussing STM, may both influence long-term memories. These types of interference could operate *during storage and/or retrieval*. If you were raised with the Fahrenheit temperature scale, hearing that today's temperature high will be 30° Celsius is confusing at first. The Fahrenheit scale continues to influence your immediate perception of degrees. Similarly, if you learned to swim free-style as a child, mastering the crawl will probably be a chore. These are both examples of *proactive inhibi-*

tion. When people try to recall a previous zip code or birthday celebration, *retroactive inhibition* often occurs. Even though zip code and birthday festivities were retained clearly perhaps a year or two earlier, they can become very difficult, maybe impossible, to find. Another common example of retroactive inhibition is experienced by many students who learn one language, say Spanish, in high school and a second, perhaps French, in college. If asked for a Spanish word, the equivalent French word is likely to come to mind. Interference is particularly severe when materials are similar. It will be especially difficult to recall a new gym locker combination that has five of the same numbers as your old one. It will also be hard to remember that your professor is Mr. Schleidt, not Mr. Schmidt, whom he replaced.

Retrieval failures Much information that people consider lost from their long-term memories remains but becomes difficult to retrieve. Individuals who have suffered strokes, for example, sometimes revert to "forgotten" behavior such as speaking a language that they haven't spoken, heard, or seen for fifty years. Brain stimulation studies by the late surgeon Wilder Penfield (described in Chapter 4) show that detailed, "long-forgotten" memories can be elicited by direct electrical stimulation of the brain. You have probably had the experience of recovering "lost" information under less dramatic circumstances. You may not remember an acquaintance's name during an encounter on the street, but it may return to you instantly when you meet in class the next day. There will be more on this phenomenon later. *Note:* If all failures in long-term memory (LTM) are due to retrieval problems, as some scientists believe, then LTM is a permanent record that does not decay. There is no firm support for or against this interesting notion. See Figure 8-10.

What occurs during retrieval failures? One piece of information may interfere with another. There are two other likely possibilities: cue-dependent forgetting and motivated for-

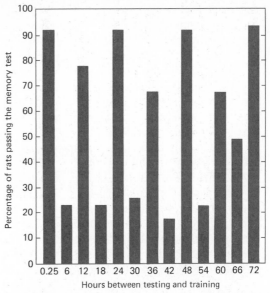

FIGURE 8-10 Laboratory studies with rats suggest that retrieval may be influenced by a biological rhythm. The research results pictured here came from a study by psychologists Frank Holloway and Richard Wansley. Nearly 200 male albino rats were reared on a twenty-four-hour schedule (twelve hours of light and twelve hours of darkness each day). Using electric shocks, Holloway and Wansley trained the animals to fear the darker compartment of a two-chambered cage. Ordinarily, you may recall, rats and many other rodents prefer dark to light places. Later, the animals were tested at one of thirteen different time intervals to see whether they could retrieve the lesson. Any animal who did not enter the dark chamber from a startbox had apparently retrieved the material. Note how the percentages of animals passing the test peaked every twelve and twenty-four hours. This experiment suggests that retrieval may be influenced by a biological rhythm. Whether people show such regular retrieval cycles and what contributes to such cycles are not currently known. [*After Holloway and Wansley, 1973.*]

getting. Consider an example of *cue-dependent forgetting* first. Suppose that an absentminded man at the Complaint Department of Woody's Department Stores files a letter from an unhappy customer under "Dissatisfactions," forgets where the complaint is located, and looks for it under "Complaints." He won't find it, of course. We might conceptualize this problem as using an inappropriate retrieval cue. In other cases, cues may provide access to an excessively large area. Say, the clerk recalls only that the complaint was filed somewhere in the D section, which includes ten separate file drawers. No matter how conscientious the man is, he will probably give up. It's too much like looking for a needle in a haystack. Laboratory studies support the idea that specific cues which are present at the time of encoding make later retrieval easier if they are also available then [44].

Motivated forgetting refers to consciously or unconsciously suppressing a disturbing event or thought. Freud observed that his patients were frequently unable to recall events that had aroused motives such as sex and aggression. He hypothesized that such lapses were the work of *repression*, a mecha-

nism that automatically banishes threatening acts from awareness regardless of the individual's desires. Psychologists disagree about whether this type of forgetting really exists. There is evidence that people tend to recall more pleasant than unpleasant events [45]. Distressing memories that seem to be forgotten can sometimes be restored through procedures such as free association and hypnosis. For these reasons, repressionlike phenomena are sometimes considered instances of retrieval failure. (You will find more on repression in Chapter 14.)

The fact that people do a great deal of forgetting has important practical implications. We consider briefly how this tendency affects our legal system.

Memory and the Law

The legal practice of using eyewitness testimony to convict criminal suspects assumes that people's memories are dependable. But they aren't. When psychologists stage mock crimes to test the reliability of bystanders' reports, they find that most onlookers' memories are highly inaccurate. In one such study, a student attacked a professor in front of 141 witnesses on the campus of California State University at Hayward. After the assault, a sworn statement was collected from each observer. On the average, people overestimated by two-and-a-half times how long the incident took, by 14 percent how tall the "criminal" was, and by more than two years the assailant's age. After seven weeks, only 40 percent of the witnesses identified the guilty person correctly, while 25 percent identified an innocent bystander [46]. Witnesses' memories are faulty for numerous reasons. First, when people encode dramatic events, they

are often highly aroused and confused. Conditions like fatigue and anxiety influence what bystanders perceive [47]. So do expectations. Then, when witnesses retrieve memories, additional problems arise. As noted previously, people tend to recall a few details and reconstruct a logical theory of what happened without being aware of how much they're inventing. Personality, guessing style (tendency to be conservative or liberal about speculating), desire to see justice done, and details reported by others influence retrieved memories. But few people recognize the limitations of their memories. Only 20 percent of the witnesses to a rigged purse-snatching admitted that they did not know who the suspect at a staged lineup was. The remaining witnesses insisted on picking out the culprit, though more than 80 percent of them "identified" innocent people [48]. Figure 8-11 gives a real-life example.

To make matters worse, even subtle biasing practices influence retrieval, as a study by Elizabeth Loftus and John Palmer illustrates. The psychologists showed student subjects a short film about an automobile accident. Then they questioned the research participants about the traffic mishap. Some people were asked, "About how fast were the cars going when they smashed into each other?" Other individuals were queried in a similar way, except "smashed" was replaced by other verbs, including "hit," "collided," "bumped," and "contacted." Research participants who received the "smashed," "collided," or "bumped" versions of the question responded with higher speed estimates than those who received the more neutral "hit" and "contact" questions. To see whether a mere verb had influenced memories, the subjects were invited back to the laboratory a week later and questioned again. If the

FIGURE 8-11 Witnesses of crimes can easily make mistaken identifications. Encoding is done under anxiety-arousing conditions. Retrieval may be biased by police suggestions and by the other factors described in the text. The men on the left and right were picked from police lineups by victims of crime in rape and robbery cases. Later they were cleared. The man in the center was arrested eventually and implicated in both crimes. If the witness remembers only general physical features, striking resemblances between suspects, such as those pictured here, make the identification of criminals nearly impossible. [*Wide World Photos.*]

verb "smashed" had actually changed people's recollections, the accident should be "remembered" as more severe than it had been and fictitious details appropriate for high-speed accidents should be "recalled." The research participants who had heard the verb "smashed" were significantly more likely than those who had heard the word "hit" to respond "Yes" to the question, "Did you see any broken glass?" [49]. No broken glass was shown in the film.

One Memory System? Or Several?

Studies by psychologist Lee Brooks and others suggest that human beings have multiple long-term memory systems which encode, store, and retrieve different types of sensory data. Please perform the tasks described in Figure 8-12 before reading further. Doing so will help you understand Brooks's research.

Whenever people attempt to do two spatial tasks at the same time (as in exercise 4 of Figure 8-12), they tend to move relatively slowly and to make a comparatively large number of mistakes. Similarly, people find it difficult to do two verbal tasks simultaneously (as in exercise 1). Yet we work rather quickly and make few errors when asked to solve concurrently one verbal and one spatial task (as in exercises 2 and 3 [50]). Working two verbal or two spatial tasks may overload the same memory mechanism. Doing a single task of each type does not. Why? The two different exercises may be controlled by separate memory systems which can operate at the same time.

Observations of brain-damaged patients support a multiple long-term memory concept, too. As we saw in Chapter 4, each hemisphere of the human cortex has the ability to learn (encode, store, and retrieve) specific types of material. People whose central nervous systems have been injured may be able to retain spatial data but not language-related information, or visual material but not spatial data [51]. Such clinical

EXERCISE 1. Memorize the sentence: "Rivers from the hills bring fresh water to the cities." Now, time yourself to see how long it takes to go over the sentence word by word in your mind (without looking at it) while simultaneously indicating whether each word is a noun by saying aloud "yes" or "no."

EXERCISE 2. Memorize the sentence: "A bird in the hand is not in the bush." Now, time yourself to see how long it takes to go over the sentence word by word in your mind (without looking at it) while simultaneously indicating if each word is a noun by pointing to a Y (yes) or N (no) on the Sample Output Chart. Move your finger down the lines on the chart as you progress -- first line for first word, second line for second word, etc. The letters in the chart are staggered to force you to monitor your pointing closely.

EXERCISE 3. Memorize the figure on the left. Now, time yourself to see how long it takes to "walk" around the F in your memory, beginning at the asterisk and following the arrow. Each time you come to a corner, indicate whether it is an outside corner by saying aloud "yes" or "no."

EXERCISE 4. Memorize the figure on the left. Now, time yourself to see how long it takes to "walk" around the M in your memory, beginning at the asterisk and following the arrow. Each time you come to a corner, indicate whether it is an outside corner by pointing to a Y (yes) or N (no) on the Sample Output Chart. Move your finger down the lines as you progress --- first line for first corner, second line for second corner, etc.

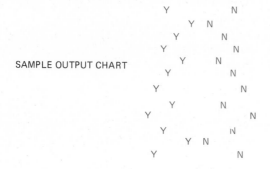

SAMPLE OUTPUT CHART

FIGURE 8-12 Try these four exercises before reading about multiple long-term memory systems. [*From Brooks, 1968.*]

cases support the idea that human beings have a number of physically separate memory capacities. Our descriptions of H. M.'s and K. F.'s deficits suggested that short-term memory is similarly composed of functionally independent subsystems.

This concludes our discussion of the basic processes of sensory, short-term, and long-term memory. Table 8-1 compares the three systems. Throughout the remainder of the chapter we focus on long-term memory: first, on improving it, and then, on the search for its physiological basis. ▲

IMPROVING LONG-TERM MEMORY

When people use the term *learning*, they are usually talking about encoding information in long-term memory and retrieving it. In terms of the Atkinson-Shiffrin model described earlier, learning involves transferring data from the short-term to the long-term store and then back again to the short-term system during retrieval. We now focus on practical ways to improve these processes, with emphasis on academic learning.

TABLE 8-1 Comparison of Sensory, Short-Term, and Long-Term Memories

Distinguishing factors	Sensory memory	Short-term memory	Long-term memory
Material stored by the system	Sensory patterns unanalyzed for meaning	Meaningful interpreted material	Meaningful interpreted material
Length of time material can be stored	Usually about 0.25 second (iconic)	About 15 seconds (minutes, if re-hearsed)	Hours, days, weeks, months, years
Capacity of the system	Large (all the data the sensory organs register)	Maximum: about seven chunks	Essentially unlimited
Attention required to insert data into the system	None	At least a slight amount	Usually a moderate amount
Ways material is encoded for storage	Material encoded in a form parallel-ing the sensory experience	Verbal material frequently encoded by its sound, sometimes by its appearance or meaning; other ma-terial thought to be encoded in the form in which it is practiced	Verbal material frequently encoded in terms of its meaning; may also be encoded in terms of its appear-ance or sound; other types of data may be stored in parallel or sum-mary form
Characteristics of the retrieval process	Data retrieved by attending to them before they vanish; material automati-cally transferred to short-term memory	Data retrieved easily and quickly for about 15 seconds	Varying difficulty in the retrieval process; problem-solving strate-gies often used
Causes of forgetting	Decay, masking	Decay, interference	Failures in encoding (inadequate or inaccurate encoding), storage (decay, interference), or retrieval (interference, cue-related forget-ting, motivated forgetting)

Putting Information into Long-Term Memory

Is memory a skill like weight-lifting that improves with practice? Long ago, the distin-guished American psychologist William James tested this hypothesis by performing a simple experiment on himself and his friends. Each person timed how long it took to learn a specific number of lines of poem A. Next, they all "exercised" their memories by mastering stanzas of poem B. Then came the test. Each person observed how long it took to commit to memory another excerpt, of the same length, from the same poem A. On the whole, no one's memory showed improvement that could be attributed merely to practice [52]. James came to the conclusion that is accepted today. While practicing alone will not strengthen memory, acquiring improved methods of re-cording facts will. Attention, organization, active participation, appropriate spacing of learning sessions, overlearning, and using positive reinforcement can all improve the encoding operation.

FIGURE 8-13 Dichotic listening experiments are often used to demonstrate the importance of attention for learning. During these studies, research participants, like the one pictured here, listen to material through earphones. Each earphone is connected to a single channel of a stereophonic tape recorder so that the subject may hear a different message in each ear. In a recent study of this type, psychologists William Johnston and Steven Heinz compared the performances of students working complex tasks. One group of subjects listened to an audio tape of an unfamiliar passage from a psychology text. At the same time, they pushed a button whenever a signal light brightened. Another group of students confronted a more challenging situation. In addition to monitoring the light and attending to the unfamiliar material, they had to ignore a familiar passage presented simultaneously by the same voice to the other ear. Subjects in the "easy" condition reacted more quickly to the signal light and comprehended the target passage significantly better than those in the "difficult" condition [80]. While attention can be divided, concentration improves performance on complicated tasks. [*Van Bucher/Photo Researchers.*]

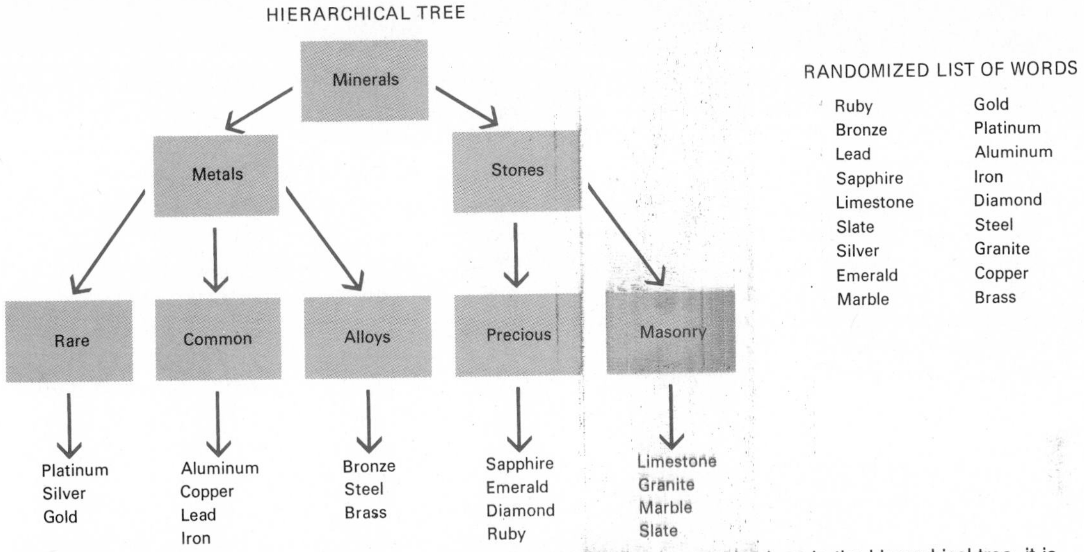

HIERARCHICAL TREE

RANDOMIZED LIST OF WORDS

Ruby	Gold
Bronze	Platinum
Lead	Aluminum
Sapphire	Iron
Limestone	Diamond
Slate	Steel
Silver	Granite
Emerald	Copper
Marble	Brass

FIGURE 8-14 Materials used in the Bower study. When information is organized, as in the hierarchical tree, it is easier to retain than when it is mastered in a random order. [*After Bower, 1970.*]

Attention Some students attempt to learn while simultaneously listening to the radio, talking to friends, and fantasizing about the approaching weekend. They are making the assumption that studying requires only a small amount of attention. But does it? Putting new information into long-term memory demands reading for meaning and using *deep processing (elaborative rehearsal) strategies.* As you may recall, these tactics involve enriching the material by associating it with ideas, images, prior information, and/or past experiences. People cannot perform these activities efficiently without paying attention, a fact underscored by many systematic observations. Research shows that nicotine, caffeine, and amphetamines (drugs which mildly stimulate the central nervous system and function as attention boosters) facilitate retention [53]. Laboratory investigations, such as the one described in Figure 8-13, indicate that when people divide their attention among several difficult activities, performance usually suffers. To succeed on complex tasks like learning, students need to focus their efforts.

Organization When people try to dump facts into their long-term memory without organizing the information initially, they have a hard time remembering the material later. Research by psychologist Gordon Bower supports this hypothesis. He presented words to one group of subjects in random order and to another group in the form of a *hierarchical tree*, as shown in Figure 8-14. All the research participants spent the same amount of time memorizing the items. Those who studied the hierarchical tree averaged a 65 percent recall of the material. Those who tried to master the information haphazardly remembered only 19 percent on the average [54]. Apparently, the hierarchical tree forced people to see the logical organization underlying the words. Many additional studies concur: When students learn merely by rote (memorizing mechanically), they do not retain information as long as when they concentrate on the internal logic of the materials that are being mastered. Similarly, people remember better when they solve problems themselves rather than simply memorize somebody else's solutions [55].

Not only is it important to look for the organization of new materials, but it is also vital to integrate new information with one's existing knowledge, as William James observed so vividly.

The more other facts a fact is associated with in the mind, the better possession of it our memory retains. Each of its associates becomes a hook to which it hangs, a means to fish it up by when sunk beneath the surface. Together, they form a network of attachments by which it is woven into the entire tissue of our thought. The "secret of a good memory" is thus the secret of forming diverse and multiple associations with every fact we care to retain. [56]

It's exceedingly hard to form "diverse" and "multiple" associations with certain types of facts. Suppose that you have to learn the names of a set of bones, the colors on a list, a spelling rule, or vocabulary words. These materials have little or no internal logic and they may not be easy to integrate with previous experiences. *Mnemonics* (or *mnemonic devices*) are organizing strategies for items such as these. They enable us to integrate separate, basically unrelated items into more meaningful, related groupings. (Incidentally, you can remember the term *mnemonic* and its pronunciation, if the word is unfamiliar to you, by using a mnemonic device. Mnemonic, pronounced nē-mon'-ik, rhymes with demonic and it's a demon to pronounce.) We describe several common mnemonic strategies [57].

Mnemonic Strategies: Tricks from the Memory Expert's Bag

Memory experts have used mnemonic strategies for a long time. Psychologists have only recently begun studying and evaluating these techniques in their laboratories. Numerous investigations indicate that mnemonics do improve memory. And at least one study suggests that students who use these devices have higher grade-point averages than those who do not [58]. Mnemonic strategies fall into several categories.

1. *Rhyme.* You may have learned the mnemonic "*i* before *e* except after *c* or when sounded like *a* as in 'neighbor' or 'weigh'." It's almost certain that you learned the mnemonic "Thirty days hath September, ..." Rhymes such as these organize materials by associating them with a particular rhythm and with rhyming words. Since errors usually break the rhythm, destroy the rhyme, or both, they're immediately evident. People tend to repeat jingles again and again, so they

are likely to be thoroughly mastered.

2. *Imagery.* If you picture dignified Mrs. Peck as a gigantic, well-groomed goose pecking for grain, you will easily recall her name. You'll remember Sicily's location longer if you visualize the "boot" of Italy kicking a rock. You can even use images to learn the vocabulary words of foreign languages, as described in Figure 8-15. The *method of loci*, an imagery mnemonic which relates a list of items to a standard set of locations, is useful for remembering lists of errands, geographical facts, points in a speech, customers' orders, and the like. To use this strategy you (*a*) visualize a familiar route, such as walking through your house, (*b*) place an image of each item to be remembered at a distinctive location on the route, and (*c*) take an imaginary walk so that all the items are encountered in order. Say you want to remember a grocery list of three items: eggs, lettuce,

and chicken. You might picture a huge, leafy lettuce replacing the knob on the front door, a sunny-side-up egg plastered to the fireplace, and a hen fluttering its wings in your easychair. A longer list of items requires a longer list of familiar locations. Notice that you are creating some fairly permanent familiar "hooks" to hang material on.

Research shows that recoding verbal information visually (which is what all these imagery devices do) makes the material more memorable than merely repeating it [59]. Combining imagery with repetition appears to be even more effective than using imagery alone. Employing both strategies may give people two separate stores—verbal and visual—to rely on. You may recall that S. converted words into images and other sensory forms automatically.

3. *Recoding.* If you make verbal information that is relatively lacking in meaning more meaningful, your retention will

Russian	Keyword	Translation	Image of interaction of keyword and translation
zvonók	oak	bell	 Oak bearing small brass bells as leaves
západ	zap it	west	 Cowboys in a western shooting at each other with their fingers
durák	two rocks	fool	 Jester standing on two rocks
gorá	garage	mountain	 Steep mountain with garage on top
ósen	ocean	autumn	 Fall trees bordering ocean

FIGURE 8-15 Psychologists Richard Atkinson and Michael Raugh asked students to learn Russian vocabulary words. Some were left to their own devices. Others were instructed to use the *keyword method*, which depends on an imagery mnemonic. The keyword method divides the study of a foreign vocabulary word into two tasks, as illustrated in the figure. First, each spoken foreign word is associated with an English word (keyword) which sounds somewhat like it. Then, a mental image of the keyword interacting with the English translation is formed. The keyword technique appears to be very effective. On one vocabulary test, research participants who used the keyword strategy were correct 72 percent of the time. Students in a control group who spent the same amount of time studying were right only 46 percent of the time. [*From Atkinson and Raugh, 1975.*]

increase. Sometimes the first letter of words to be remembered in order can be converted into a single word. The colors in the spectrum are readily recalled by the name Roy G. Biv (*r*ed, *o*range, *y*ellow, *g*reen, *b*lue, *i*ndigo, *v*iolet). Or words to be remembered may function as the key elements of a story. The following tale makes the names of the cranial nerves more memorable:

"At the *oil factory* (olfactory nerve), the *optician* (optic) looked for the *occupant* (oculomotor) of the *truck* (trochlear). He was searching because *three gems* (trigeminal) had been *abducted* (abducens) by a man who was hiding his *face* (facial) and *ears* (acoustic). A *glossy photograph* (glossopharyngeal) had been taken of him, but it was too *vague* (vagus) to use. He appeared to be *spineless*

(spinal accessory) and *hypocritical* (hypoglossal)."

When subjects in a laboratory experiment used this story-making strategy to learn lists of ten totally unrelated nouns, they recalled almost seven times more words than research participants who did not receive practical instructions on memorizing [60].

Mnemonic strategies make relatively meaningless material

more meaningful and consequently more memorable. To use these devices, you must concentrate and process the information thoroughly. Both practices help retention, of course. Moreover, as you encode the data to be retained, you also encode retrieval cues which will make finding the material easier.

For all these reasons, mnemonics can take the drudgery out of some rote learning and free the user for more interesting tasks.

Active participation Many students think that reading an assignment over once is sufficient for absorbing the content. Numerous laboratory studies show that these expectations are unfounded. Active processing is important for retaining most verbal materials [61]. *Programmed texts* and *teaching machines*, such as those illustrated in Figures 8-16 and 8-17, capitalize on this well-known fact. These devices present learners with relatively small amounts of information. Questions embedded within the material force people to test their understanding before proceeding to new areas. The correct answers are provided immediately to give *feedback*, pointing out facts or concepts requiring further practice or clarification.

Few students have access to teaching machines and most texts are not programmed. Yet students can still participate actively, using standard text materials. Organizing information, as described previously, is one way to be active. A widely used study strategy known as the *SQ3R system* promotes active participation in a systematic manner. The term *SQ3R* (a recoding type of mnemonic) stands for the five steps of the technique: Survey, Question, Read, Recite, Review.

Step 1: Survey. Laboratory studies show that people are better at comprehending complex verbal material when they are informed about its nature in advance [62]. If you understand how a chapter is organized, you know what to expect. You're more likely then to see how the facts fit together and to be able to integrate new materials with those already in long-term memory. To obtain an overview of a chapter in this text, you can look at the outline, the introductory material, and/or the summary.

Step 2: Question. People seem to remember material better when they pause to ask and answer questions. This practice focuses attention on important information and stimulates deep processing. If you're asking and answering questions, you're more likely to

FIGURE 8-16 This set of frames was designed to teach a third- or fourth-grader how to spell the word "manufacture." The six frames are presented to the child, one at a time, in the order in which they appear. Frame 1 asks the learner to copy the word. If the child is successful, frame 2 appears. Now the youngster must identify "fact" as an element in the words "manufacture" and "factory" and copy the root into the appropriate space. Another basic element appears in frame 3. In both frames 4 and 5, the learner must insert the same letters into the word without copying. Finally, in frame 6, the child must spell the word—again without a model—to complete the sentence. Programmed materials like these seem to be especially well suited for teaching basic materials to young children. They are often less effective with older learners. Studies suggest that adults prefer reading units that integrate several facts and ideas and like to proceed at their own pace. Some educators also believe that imagination is stifled by concentrating exclusively on the right answers during advanced types of learning [81]. [*From Skinner, 1958.*]

1. Manufacture means to make or build. Chair factories manufacture chairs. Copy the word here.

☐☐☐☐☐☐☐☐☐☐☐

2. Part of the word is like part of the word <u>factory</u>. Both parts come from an old word meaning <u>make</u> or <u>build</u>.

m a n u ☐☐☐☐ u r e

3. Part of the word is like part of the word <u>manual</u>. Both parts come from an old word for <u>hand</u>. Many things used to be made by hand.

☐☐☐☐☐f a c t u r e

4. The same letter goes in both spaces:

m ☐ n u f ☐ c t u r e

5. The same letter goes in both spaces:

m a n ☐ f a c t ☐ r e

6. Chair factories ☐☐☐☐☐☐☐☐☐☐☐ chairs.

think about the material. Chapter headings may be converted into questions. For example, the first section heading of this chapter, "The Nature of Memory," might be translated into the query, "How do psychologists view the nature of memory?" As you read, try quizzing yourself on the meaning of key terms (often italicized). And you'll learn a lot more by responding to the Using Psychology questions, which ask you to think about, apply, or summarize important materials.

Step 3: Read actively. Many students simply run their eyes down the page while their minds are elsewhere. It is important to read actively, pausing frequently to compose and answer questions.

Step 4: Recite. After reading each section of a text, it is helpful to try to recall out loud or write down (with the book closed) the important information. People retain more material when a given amount of time is divided equally between reading and reciting, rather than between reading and rereading [63]. If you check yourself by going back to the original material (this check is very important [64]), recitation can give immediate feedback about what you don't remember or understand. Then you can correct any problems that exist. Continuing on a wrong course wastes time. Recitation is also important because it provides practice at retrieval, a behavior required for class discussions and exams. Finally, when students recite information out loud that they have been processing visually, they may be depositing that material in a second memory system, thus making retention all the more likely.

Step 5: Review. After reading and reciting the important points under each heading, students should review the chapter as a whole. There are many ways to do that. You might reread underlined passages or notes made during reading. You might turn the headings into questions once again and recite the answers. Or, you might quiz yourself by defining and describing key terms and the like or by tackling the self-quiz and exercises of the Study Guide. Rereading can be a useful way to refresh your memory and reassure

FIGURE 8-17 This child is learning to read through computer-assisted instruction (CAI) in a program directed by psychologist Richard Atkinson at Stanford University. The students received visual and auditory instructional messages from the televisionlike machine and were required to respond actively—by typing responses on a keyboard or by touching correct answers on the screen with a device called a "light pen." Each child's responses were evaluated by the computer, which kept a complete up-to-date record. When the youngster answered a question correctly, the computer introduced appropriate new instructions. When the child responded incorrectly, the computer presented suitable remedial materials. CAI permits individualized instruction. Students may work at their own pace on lessons tailored specifically for their current needs. Well-designed CAI programs are both economical and effective in promoting learning, especially of certain elementary-level materials and basic skills. [*Courtesy of Richard Atkinson.*]

yourself that nothing important has been missed.

The SQ3R method was worked out and thoroughly tested at Ohio State University. Studies indicate that when the method is used conscientiously, it improves the performance of both good and poor students [65].

Massed versus distributed practice
Is it good to cram studying into one long session the night before an exam? Or does spreading out the learning make more sense? Psychologists have investigated this issue indirectly by exploring the effects of massed and distributed practice. *Massed practice* refers to learning in a single period of time with little or no rest; *distributed prac-*

tice, to spacing learning over several "work" periods with rests in between. Current laboratory findings do not uniformly support the superiority of either method [66]. Massed practice appears to be beneficial for mastering a small amount of coherent, organized, or highly meaningful material. It is good for reading stories, memorizing brief speeches, and solving algebra problems. Massed practice immediately before an exam has two advantages for test takers. Since forgetting occurs most rapidly soon after learning, people who review at the last moment are likely to retain more of what they have mastered. People who mass their practice also capitalize on high motivation—so long as they have not begun to panic.

Distributed practice has its own benefits. It is particularly effective for learning motor skills and loosely connected verbal materials, such as the information in the separate chapters of a textbook. When studying for exams, distributed practice has some unique advantages. If learning is spaced out over several weeks, students can closely control several key practices: attention, organization, active participation, and repeated practice, or over-

learning (a topic we take up in a moment). A combination of distributed and massed practice—distributing initial learning and massing the final review—is probably most effective for passing tests.

Overlearning Do the "grinds" who overstudy for each test benefit? Or, are they wasting their time? To put the question more generally, Does practice beyond the point of mastery, or *overlearning,* increase retention of verbal material? In the late 1920s, psychologist William Krueger studied this issue in the laboratory. He asked people to memorize lists of single-syllable nouns. Then he assigned his research participants to one of three groups. Subjects in one group (100 percent overlearning) continued to practice the lists for the same amount of time that had been required to learn them initially. Participants in a second group (50 percent overlearning) continued to study for half again the length of time required to simply memorize the nouns. A third group of subjects (no overlearning) spent no additional time on the items. The research participants were tested after various intervals to see how much they remem-

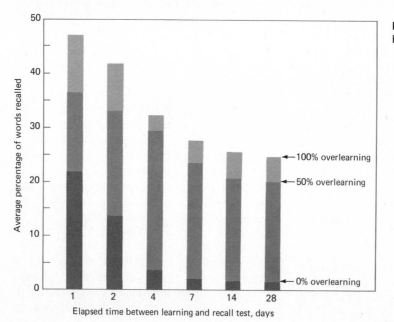

FIGURE 8-18 The results of Krueger's study on overlearning.

bered. The results of the research are summarized in Figure 8-18. Notice that 100 percent overlearning led to superior retention, which was particularly significant on days 4 through 28. Note also that 50 percent overlearning increased retention quite substantially, while additional practice (to 100 percent) improved memory only slightly [67]. These results suggest that there is a point of diminishing returns and that practicing a moderate amount of time beyond the point of bare mastery is the most sensible strategy for students. Discussions, debates, and projects using newly learned material minimize the tedious aspects of overlearning.

Using positive reinforcement Parents frequently try to motivate their children's learning by rewarding good report cards. Such systems fail as often as they succeed for several reasons. The focus tends to be placed too narrowly on the end product, grades, and not enough on the study habits that need to be established. In effect, the rewards encourage cheating as much as learning. In addition, parents frequently demand too much too soon, instead of using a more effective gradual strategy of encouraging and rewarding small steps and asking more as easier goals are achieved.

Still, if used wisely, rewards can increase motivation to learn. In Chapter 5 we distinguished between two general types of positive reinforcers: intrinsic and extrinsic. Positive reinforcers are said to be *intrinsic* when they are the natural and inevitable result of simply engaging in a behavior. In other words, the activity itself is its own reward. Consequently, every time the behavior occurs, it is automatically strengthened. Studying music history because you find the subject fascinating or mastering Chinese to develop conversational skills which make you feel competent are examples of intrinsically reinforced learning. Positive reinforcers are said to be *extrinsic* when they come from outside the behavior. Acquiring knowledge for good grades, a degree, a gold star, a bike, or someone else's approval are illustrations of extrinsically rein-

forced learning. Both types of positive reinforcers can be intertwined.

You may want to consider using reinforcers deliberately to motivate your own learning. Whenever possible, it is best to rely on intrinsic reinforcers, since many extrinsic ones—particularly money and material goods, but even approval—have undesirable side effects. They can encourage habits like hurrying through an activity "to get the goods." They may foster the general attitude, "What do I get out of it?" They may teach excessive dependence on the opinions of others [68]. To increase intrinsic reinforcement, students might look for ways to use their learning. You'll probably feel more interested in mastering Swahili, for example, if you keep in mind a future trip to Africa. Setting small goals, keeping track of progress, and achieving final objectives may give a sense of accomplishment that is intrinsically reinforcing.

Students who fail to find intrinsic reinforcement in learning can systematically use extrinsic reinforcers to increase the likelihood that they will study. You might plan a reasonable daily homework schedule, then allow yourself a five-minute radio break or phone conversation immediately following the completion of a small amount of work. The big problem in self-reinforcement is keeping the reinforcer *contingent* (dependent) on executing the assignment. It's very easy to cheat.

Taking Information out of Long-Term Memory

After encoding, people frequently face a "test." The day comes when information that has been stored must be retrieved and used. Research shows that retrieval is easier under the following conditions:

1. *When the information has been organized during encoding.* If such organization has occurred, the retrieval of one bit of information leads to the recollection of related items.
2. *When internal conditions during encoding and retrieval are similar.* Research shows that if animals (including human beings) are hungry or

"high" on a particular drug or in some other distinctive physiological state as they encode information, they retrieve the material more effectively while in a similar state. This phenomenon, known as *state-dependent learning*, has been demonstrated in the laboratory numerous times. In one such study, psychologist Donald Goodwin and his coworkers had alcohol-intoxicated and sober male medical student volunteers memorize sentences and perform other tasks. Later, the men took recall and recognition tests. Subjects who had encoded the materials while intoxicated retrieved the data better when intoxicated than when sober. Research participants who had both encoded and retrieved the information in a state of sobriety made the fewest mistakes of any group on all measures [69]. Students are well advised, then, to study and take tests in roughly the same physiological condition—preferably sober, well-fed, and rested.

3. *When external conditions (cues) during encoding and retrieval are similar.* You have probably experienced the predicament of seeing an acquaintance in an unfamiliar situation (maybe, a schoolmate downtown) and not being able to recall her or his name. Later, in the familiar setting (the classroom, in this case), the name pops instantly into your mind. What seems to be happening here is that a cue (the setting), which was present when material (the name) was mastered, acts as a reminder. Perhaps it energizes circuits in the brain that were active during learning. Retrieval is usually cued by key words, ideas, or images. If these cues were present initially during encoding, retrieval seems to be easier [70]. Compare the test items "Describe common mnemonic strategies" and "Describe common mnemonic strategies which use rhymes, images, and recoding." The second task provides obvious cues that aid retrieval, especially if the material was originally organized under these headings. To improve test performance, students can provide their own retrieval cues

by organizing the material to be retained under key words and memorizing those words.

4. *When people have practiced retrieving.* The first time you retrieve information from memory (say, details of a past summer's vacation), the process is likely to be slow and laborious. But should the material be required a short time later, it will come to you more readily. Practice at retrieving specific information makes any subsequent search for the same material a lot easier. That's why it makes sense to practice handling potentially difficult situations such as job interviews or public speeches. If you've retrieved the data several times before, you'll sound more fluent, competent, and confident. In studying for a test, practice retrieving material that you think will be needed on the test. If you're going to take an essay exam, try writing short paragraphs. For a vocabulary quiz, drill yourself on the words.

5. *When anxiety is low.* Many people experience anxiety when asked to retrieve what they've encoded. Public speaking and test anxieties are common illustrations of this phenomenon. When anxiety is intense, people's minds sometimes "go blank" and they cannot retrieve the information that they need. We will discuss the nature of anxiety in Chapter 11. In Chapter 16 we describe a behavior modification technique, systematic desensitization, that helps people cope with anxiety. ▲

THE PHYSIOLOGICAL BASIS OF LONG-TERM MEMORY

For centuries scientists have assumed that long-lasting physical changes known as *memory traces*, or *engrams*, are somehow etched in the brain each time a long-term memory is made. While no one knows what engrams look like or how they are made, hundreds of

---

▲ USING PSYCHOLOGY

1. Review the various practices that improve long-term memory. Then describe the procedures that would improve your own study habits.

2. Explain how you could use the method of loci to remember a list of errands. (If you don't have a list handy, use the following: library, shoe repair store, ice-cream parlor, hardware store, dime store, car repair shop, garden center.)

3. Which principles for improving long-term memory have been used in this textbook?

investigators are searching for this information. In this section we focus on how physiological psychologists and others investigate the nature of an engram.

Note: Before reading further, please review the basic physiology of the nervous system in Chapter 4 if the material has not been stored in your long-term memory.

The Search for the Engram

The nervous system is composed of billions of *neurons* and other cells. The neurons, connected to one another at gaps known as *synapses*, form an elaborate communication network. (A single nerve cell may communicate directly with some 80,000 other neurons [71].) The network allows the senses to relay electrical-chemical descriptions of what is happening in the environment to the brain. It permits one brain region to communicate with another so that interpretations and decisions may be reached. It also enables the brain to channel its orders to muscles and glands so that animals act appropriately. Right now, many scientists believe that long-term memories are coded by chemical changes originating within neurons, which subsequently alter communication patterns in the brain. DNA, RNA, and proteins are considered likely to be involved. *DNA (deoxyribonucleic acid)* is the chemical substance that codes information about each individual's genetic inheritance. Acting within the nucleus of the cell, DNA helps determine the structure of *RNA (ribonucleic acid)*, a chemical messenger that transfers information from DNA to the rest of the cell by controlling the production of *proteins. Enzymes*, a type of protein, regulate the operations of the cell. A key function of enzymes is the production and removal of *neurotransmitters*, chemicals involved in communication patterns between neurons. Making a memory might alter some of the links in this complicated chain. We focus on why scientists believe that changes in RNA and protein probably play a role in the formation of long-term memories.

Many studies show that as animals make long-lasting memories, larger quantities and different types of RNA and protein accumulate in their brains. The Swedish biologist Holger Hydén and his associates have performed some ingenious investigations of this topic. In an early study, Hydén and E. Egyházi trained right-pawed rats (that are somewhat like right-handed people) to retrieve food from a narrow glass tube with their left paws. Animals in a control group made the same number of retrieval responses with their preferred paws. Then all the subjects were killed, and single neurons from the right and left sides of each animal's brain were chemically analyzed. Hydén and Egyházi found that learning the new paw preference produced significant changes in both amount and type of RNA in cells on the right side (the one controlling the learning), but not on the left side of the brain. When animals used their right paws, the left side of the brain (the active part) showed only slight increases in amount of RNA and no changes in type of RNA [72].

While alterations in brain RNA or protein may accompany learning, such modifications may not be the basis of memory. They might, for example, reflect attention or sensory processing. So other tests have been devised. Some scientists reasoned that RNA is increased during learning so that it can synthesize (put together) new proteins. The proteins, in turn, might be involved in memory storage. If this is true, the rate of protein formation might be measured and compared with the amount or type of learning that the animal has done. To estimate the rate of protein formation, investigators inject animals immediately before learning with radioactively tagged *precursors*, or forerunners, of the appropriate proteins. The radioactive material makes it possible to measure the degree to which the precursors are incorporated into brain protein during learning. Using this strategy, Hydén's group and several other research teams have found that very specific protein changes accompany precise amounts and types of learning [73].

If protein is important for storing information, then preventing its production should interfere with memory. Because drug inhibitors of protein synthesis often produce side effects, this research tactic is not altogether satisfactory. In any case, a number of investigators have discovered that interfering with protein formation does disrupt memory, at least temporarily. Hydén, for example, inhibited the synthesis of one of two specific proteins that are ordinarily formed as a particular task is mastered. That manipulation kept the learners' performances from improving, as had been usual [74].

All the studies that we have described and many others support the notion that RNA and protein changes accompany retention. Yet no study that we have mentioned completely rules out the idea that modifications in RNA and protein support other biochemical correlates of memory or underlie other aspects of the behavioral mix of which memory is part. Suppose that scientists could transfer specific memories by injecting precise types of brain protein from animals who had learned a task into untrained recipients. This demonstration would provide very strong evidence that

protein itself can either (1) code memory in some animals or (2) alter neurons so that they code memory. Numerous investigators have attempted to transfer learning from animal to animal. The results are contradictory. George Ungar and his associates have conducted some dramatic experiments in this area. In an early series of studies, Ungar presented either an intense noise or an air puff to rats until they became accustomed, or *habituated*, and stopped reacting to the irritation. Then Ungar killed his subjects, extracted protein from their brains, and injected untrained mice (mice were recipients, while rats were donors) with the extract. Mice receiving air-puff–habituated protein showed some habituation to puffs of air but not to noise. Mice receiving noise-habituated protein demonstrated the opposite pattern [75]. The selective nature of these effects rules out the possibility that some general performance-enhancing factor had been passed along. More recently, Ungar and his colleagues actually synthesized a "memory" in a test tube. First, in a fairly typical transfer experiment, they trained rats (that ordinarily prefer dark quarters) to avoid

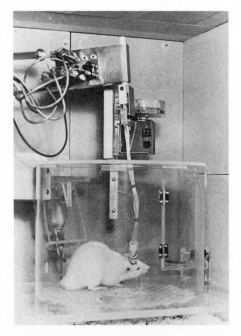

FIGURE 8-19   The late physiological psychologist James Olds developed the technology needed to record the responses of single nerve cells in a learning animal. Microelectrodes implanted permanently within the animal's brain allowed Olds to "listen" to the neurons as the organism moved around. In the study illustrated here, the electrical activity of single neurons throughout the brain was monitored as the rat learned to turn its head toward the food dispenser when a loud sound signaled the delivery of a food pellet [82]. Using a similar approach, Richard Thompson and his coworkers have isolated specific neurons in rabbits' and cats' brains that alter their reactions during several types of respondent conditioning [83]. Many parts of the nervous system are electrically active (and presumably involved) when animals encode, store, and retrieve long-term memories [84]. Initially, wide areas of the cortex seem excited. Then a great deal of electrical activity appears in a number of specific brain system circuits below the cortex, including the reticular formation, the thalamus, and the hippocampus. Later, before any learned response is seen, sensory and motor cortical areas that control the behavior being mastered become active. Finally, distinctive patterns of electrical discharges appear throughout many brain regions. Apparently, the brain must coordinate a great many processes as animals make memories, and numerous parts of the brain are involved. [*J. Olds, Bioelectric Recording Techniques.*]

dim enclosures by shocking the animals whenever they entered one. Then the researchers killed the rats and analyzed their brain chemistry. The investigators found a simple protein in the brains of trained rats which was not present in the brains of untrained animals. They named the substance *scotophobin,* Greek for "fear of the dark." Scotophobin was then injected into naive (untrained) recipient mice (once again mice were recipients, while rats were donors). The mice, who naturally prefer dark surroundings too, avoided a dark chamber. It appeared, then, that fear-related information had been contained in the transferred protein [76]. Going one step further, Ungar's research group synthesized a batch of scotophobin from inorganic chemicals. When this "manufactured" substance was injected

into naive mice, the recipients again avoided dark places [77]. So far, these observations have not been confirmed, so we do not know whether they are the result of memory transfer or uncontrolled factors.

Each research approach which attempts to link RNA, proteins, and engrams has serious weaknesses of its own. But, taken together, the varied tactics provide strong evidence that RNA and protein are involved in altering the structure of the brain so that memories are retained. See Figure 8-19 for information about the parts of the brain that are active as memories are made.

Research on the physiological basis of memory has a great many potential practical applications. We examine one, human memory drugs.

Human Memory Drugs: Science Fantasy? Or, Reality of the Near Future?

Scientists can already increase the retention of certain types of training in animals. To do so, they inject the learner before or soon after training with one of numerous substances [78]. Experiments with memory drugs have recently been begun on human volunteers. Most investigations involve the *peptide hormones* (especially ACTH and vasopressin), proteins secreted naturally by the pituitary gland. The peptide substances are considered very safe, whereas many other memory-enhancing drugs that have been tested on nonhuman animals would be deadly for people. (Incidentally, scotophobin, Ungar's "memory molecule," was a peptide sub-

stance.) In one carefully controlled study at the New York University Medical Center, elderly adults with mild and severe memory impairments received different doses of the peptide ACTH 4-10 for several consecutive days. Either before or after the peptide was administered, research participants received placebos. At the time of an injection, neither experimenter nor subject knew which substance was being dispensed (a double-blind control). No clearcut picture of the drug's activity emerged from this investigation or from several similar ones. ACTH 4-10 produced relatively small effects that depended on the dosage, task, and initial cog-

nitive level of the recipient. For example, a high dose of ACTH 4-10 worsened the visual memory of mildly impaired patients while enhancing the visual memory of severely impaired ones [79].

Memory-drug research is in its infancy and many important questions have yet to be answered. How do the drugs work? How long do they operate? Do they have side effects? What aspects of memory are influenced? Are there more effective substances? The experts believe that we are still years away from clinically useful memory drugs.▲

▲ USING PSYCHOLOGY
If drugs which enhanced or erased memories existed and were widely available, what benefits might they have for you? For society? How might they be abused?

SUMMARY
Memory

1. Memory is fundamental to perceiving, learning, speaking, reasoning, and most other activities.

2. Memory involves three processes: encoding, storage, and retrieval.

3. Ebbinghaus published the first major experimental study of memory in 1885. He used the savings method to measure retention.

4. While the savings method is still used today, psychologists rely primarily on recall and recognition measures of memory.

5. Many psychologists believe that there are three distinct memory systems—sensory, short-term, and long-term. The characteristics of these systems are summarized in Table 8-1.

6. There may be multiple short-term and long-term memory systems.

7. Long-term memory can be improved by practicing particular methods of encoding and retrieval. Paying attention, organizing materials, participating actively, spacing learning sessions appropriately, overlearning, and using positive reinforcement can significantly improve the encoding process.

8. Retrieval is easier when information has been organized during encoding, internal and external conditions during encoding and retrieval are similar, retrieval has been practiced, and anxiety is low.

9. Scientists continue to search for the physiological basis of memory. Changes in RNA and protein appear to be associated with engram making.

A Study Guide for Chapter Eight

Key terms   memory (239), encoding (239), storage (239), retrieval (239), model (239), sensory memory (SM) (240), short-term memory (STM) (241), long-term memory (LTM) (241), shallow and deep processing (elaborative rehearsal strategies) (241), savings (242), recall (243), recognition (243), masking (247), decay (247), interference (250), proactive and retroactive inhibition (250), mnemonic device (262), engram (memory trace) (268), deoxyribonucleic acid (DNA) (269), ribonucleic acid (RNA) (269), proteins (269), and other italicized words and expressions.

Important research   first systematic investigation of memory (Ebbinghaus), iconic memory (Sperling, others), short-term memory (Milner, Sternberg, the Petersons, others), long-term memory (Standing, Shepard, Brown, McNeill, Lindsay, Norman, Bartlett, E. Loftus, Palmer, others), support for the existence of multiple memory systems (Brooks, Milner, others), conditions that improve long-term memory (James, Bower, Krueger, Goodwin, others), learning and RNA (Hydén, Egyházi, Ungar, others), memory drugs.

Basic concepts   Atkinson-Shiffrin memory model, common measures of memory, a comparison of recall and recognition memory measures (the Loftuses), reasons why integration of knowledge aids retention (James), reasons why mnemonic devices are helpful, DNA-RNA-protein chain theory of memory.

People to identify   Ebbinghaus, James.

Self-Quiz

1. Which process is most likely to include embellishing material to be learned with images and past experiences?
   a. Encoding   *b.* Reconstruction
   c. Redintegration   *d.* Retrieval

2. Which system oversees the retrieval of long-term memories, according to the Atkinson-Shiffrin memory model?
   a. Long-term   *b.* Mnemonic
   c. Sensory   *d.* Short-term

3. Which measure of memory did Ebbinghaus use?
   a. Free recall   *b.* Recognition
   c. Savings   *d.* Serial recall

4. Which measure of memory is most influenced by guessing?
   a. Recall   *b.* Recognition
   c. Redintegration   *d.* Savings

5. How often is recall superior to recognition?
   a. Always   *b.* Usually
   c. Rarely   *d.* Never

6. Approximately how long does material ordinarily persist in iconic memory?
   a. 25 milliseconds   *b.* 250 milliseconds
   c. 2.50 seconds   *d.* 15 seconds

7. Which effect supports the existence of a separate short-term memory system?
   a. Primacy effect during free recall
   b. Primacy effect during serial recall
   c. Recency effect during free recall
   d. Recency effect during serial recall

8. Approximately how long does material usually persist in short-term memory if it is not rehearsed?
  a. 1 to 2 seconds   *b.* 15 to 20 seconds
  c. 2 to 3 minutes   *d.* 20 to 25 minutes

9. Which effect illustrates retroactive inhibition?
  a. Confusing a current friend's name with the similar sounding name of a past friend
  b. Experiencing difficulty in learning the words to a new song that has the same tune as "God Bless America"
  c. Failing to remember an old recipe for chocolate-chip cookies after using a new one
  d. Finding a car with a stick shift difficult to drive after learning on a car with automatic transmission

10. Which phenomenon is an example of a retrieval failure?
  a. Habituation
  b. Inaccurate representation of initial information
  c. Memory trace
  d. Motivated forgetting

11. Which phenomenon does the method of loci depend on?
  a. Images   *b.* Recoding
  c. Rhyme   *d.* Rhythm

12. What does the first R in the SQ3R program represent?
  a. Read   *b.* Recite
  c. Reflect   *d.* Review

13. Which advantage does massed practice usually have?
  a. Capitalizes on memory.
  b. Enhances overlearning.
  c. Forces the learner to be active.
  d. Reduces anxiety.

14. Which type of reinforcement was most highly recommended for motivating your own learning?
  a. Extrinsic: material   *b.* Extrinsic: secondary
  c. Extrinsic: social   *d.* Intrinsic

15. Which statement about the effects of human memory drugs is correct?
  a. The drugs tend to help people with mild memory impairments but not those with severe ones.
  b. The effects of these drugs vary and depend on cognitive level and task.
  c. The side effects of the peptides appear to be dangerous.
  d. Though the effects of these drugs are far from uniform, they are usually very dramatic.

Exercises

1. MEMORY STORAGE SYSTEMS. Currently, many psychologists believe that people have three fairly distinctive storage capacities. To make certain that you know the differences between the memory stores, match each description below with the appropriate system. The same attribute may characterize several systems. To review, see pages 245 to 258 and Table 8-1.

SYSTEMS: long-term memory (LTM), sensory memory (SM), short-term memory (STM)

_____ **1.** Holds material for approximately fifteen to twenty seconds.

_____ **2.** Stores sensory patterns unanalyzed for meaning.

_____ **3.** Performs deep processing.

_____ **4.** Stores material for hours and longer.

_____ **5.** Considered the center of consciousness.

_____ **6.** Stores meaningful interpreted stimuli.

_____ **7.** Performs shallow processing.

_____ **8.** Registers whatever strikes the senses.

_____ **9.** Interference or masking produces forgetting here.

_____ **10.** Holds a maximum of about seven chunks of information at a time.

_____ **11.** Access to its information often requires a problem-solving approach.

_____ **12.** Can maintain material for minutes by rehearsal.

_____ **13.** Stores material for a fraction of a second.

_____ **14.** Retrieval here transfers data to STM.

2. MEASURES OF MEMORY. To check your knowledge of the procedures used to measure memory in the laboratory (and their applications), match the measures below with the appropriate examples or descriptions. Use the single most appropriate measure for each example. To review the material, see pages 241 to 244.

MEASURES: recall (R), recognition (RG), savings (S)

_____ **1.** Used by Ebbinghaus.

_____ **2.** Defined as the ability to remember when given only a prompt.

_____ **3.** The most sensitive memory measure, often demonstrating some retention of presumably forgotten materials.

_____ **4.** Rehearsal especially likely to be influential when this method is used in the laboratory.

_____ **5.** Requires both a search and a recognition test.

_____ **6.** Chance should be taken into account when this method is used.

_____ **7.** Has this problem: Subjects may forget when trying to recite a list of items.

_____ 8. Requires only that given information be compared to stored information.

_____ 9. Requires fairly complete information to be correct.

_____ 10. May require remembering items in order.

Suggested Readings

1. Loftus, G. R., & Loftus, E. F. *Human memory: The processing of information*. Hillsdale, N.J.: Erlbaum, 1976 (paperback). A clear, interesting, and well-organized introduction to memory research following the Atkinson-Shiffrin model.

2. Norman, D. A. *Memory and attention: An introduction to human information processing*. (2d ed.) New York: Wiley, 1976 (paperback). A second top-notch, and more informal, introduction to memory research. It contains excerpts from important articles and a particularly outstanding annotated bibliography so that you can explore interesting topics in more depth on your own.

3. Higbee, K. L. *Your memory: How it works and how to improve it*. Englewood Cliffs, N.J.: Prentice-Hall, 1977. A psychologist discusses research on memory and memorizing, taking the viewpoint that memory is a matter of good techniques and can be improved with hard work. Practical and accurate. For a shorter introduction to the same topic, try Bower, G. H. Improving memory. *Human Nature*, 1978, *1*(2), 64–72.

4. Luria, A. R. *The mind of a mnemonist*. New York: Basic Books, 1968. This delightful book describes S., the famous Russian memory expert, whom Luria studied for thirty years.

5. Walter, T., & Siebert, A. *Student success: How to be a better student and still have time for your friends*. New York: Holt, Rinehart Winston, 1976 (paperback). Lively, practical guide to better study habits (and self-development). The book, which advocates a modified SQ3R approach, could be very valuable if your grade-point average isn't what you'd like it to be.

6. Buckhout, R. Eyewitness testimony. *Scientific American*, 1974, **231**(6), 23–31. Buckhout describes the fascinating research literature supporting the idea that eyewitnesses' memories are reconstructions influenced by many factors besides the actual events.

7. John, E. R. How the brain works—A new theory. *Psychology Today*, 1976, *9*(12), 48–52. A prominent physiological psychologist argues that memories are stored by electrical rhythms within the brain.

Answer Keys

Self-Quiz

1. *a* (239) **2.** *d* (241) **3.** *c* (242) **4.** *b* (243)
5. *c* (243) **6.** *b* (247) **7.** *c* (248) **8.** *b* (250)
9. *c* (254) **10.** *d* (255) **11.** *a* (262) **12.** *a* (264)
13. *a* (266) **14.** *d* (267) **15.** *b* (271)

Exercise 1

1. STM **2.** SM **3.** STM **4.** LTM **5.** STM
6. STM, LTM **7.** STM **8.** SM
9. SM, STM, LTM **10.** STM **11.** LTM **12.** STM
13. SM **14.** SM, LTM

Exercise 2

1. S **2.** R **3.** S **4.** R **5.** R **6.** RG **7.** R
8. RG **9.** R **10.** R

Thought and Language

People possess extraordinary cognitive abilities, most obviously, the capacities for thought and language. Though human beings are not the only creatures that think or communicate, they are unquestionably the most sophisticated and skilled thinkers and communicators on this planet. In this chapter we focus on thought and language. We begin with Helen Keller's account of a key language lesson.

The Education of Helen Keller

Helen Keller was born in 1880 in a small northern Alabama town. An illness two years later left her completely blind and deaf. As she grew up, she did not speak, though she learned to make signs to communicate simple desires. A shake of the head meant "No," a nod "Yes," a pull "Come," and a push "Go," for instance. When Helen was about seven, Ann Mansfield Sullivan, a teacher who was partially blind herself, came to live with the Kellers. Miss Sullivan began language instruction almost immediately. About a month later, an important breakthrough occurred. Helen described it vividly in her autobiography.

"One day, while I was playing with my new doll, Miss Sullivan put my big rag doll into my lap, also, spelled 'd-o-l-l' and tried to make me understand that 'd-o-l-l' applied to both. Earlier in the day we had had a tussle over the words 'm-u-g' and 'w-a-t-e-r.' Miss Sullivan had tried to impress it upon me that 'm-u-g' is mug and that 'w-a-t-e-r' is water, but I persisted in confounding the two. In despair she had dropped the subject for the time, only to renew it at the first opportunity. I became impatient at her repeated attempts and, seizing the new doll, I dashed it upon the floor. I was keenly delighted when I felt the fragments of the broken doll at my feet . . . and I had a sense of satisfaction that the cause of my discomfort was removed. She brought me my hat, and I knew I was going out into the warm sunshine. This thought, if a wordless sensation may be called a thought, made me hop and skip with pleasure.

"We walked down the path to the well-house, attracted by the fragrance of the honeysuckle with which it was covered. Someone was drawing water and my teacher placed my hand under the spout. As the cool stream gushed over one hand she spelled into the other the word water, first slowly, then rapidly. I stood still, my whole attention fixed upon the motions of her fingers. Suddenly I felt a misty consciousness as of something forgotten—a thrill of returning thought; and somehow the mystery of language was revealed to me. I knew then that 'w-a-t-e-r' meant the wonderful cool something that was flowing over my hand. That living word awakened my soul, gave it light, hope, joy, set it free! There were barriers still, it is true, but barriers that could in time be swept away.

"I left the well-house eager to learn. Everything had a name, and each name gave birth to a new thought. As we returned to the house every object which I touched seemed to quiver with life. That was because I saw everything with the strange, new sight that had come to me. . . .

"I learned a great many new words that day. I do not remember what they all were; but I do know that mother, father, sister, teacher were among them—words that were to make the world blossom for me, 'like Aaron's rod, with flowers.' It would have been difficult to find a happier child than I was as I lay in my crib at the close of that eventful day and lived over the joys it had brought me, and for the first time longed for a new day to come [1]."

This passage is interesting to psychologists for a number of reasons. You may have noted that Helen Keller considered language and thought closely linked. Language depends on thought; and thought depends to some degree on language. To master a language one has to mentally represent something—say, a chair or a person—by a sound, image, or sign. The user of a language must understand "rules"; for example, words must be strung together in an orderly way. Concepts such as "similarity," "quantity," and "freedom" must be grasped before these words can be used meaningfully.

Thought, in turn, is influenced by language. Words act as a convenient shorthand for experience and help us think, particularly about people and objects that are not present, the past and future, territories ranging from the next room to a distant continent, and abstract ideas. It is important to note that thought can occur without language. Investigations of the problem-solving capabilities of human infants and other animals support this idea. We will describe such studies throughout this chapter.

Words can also constrain, or limit, thinking, as the linguist Benjamen Lee Whorf (1897–1941) observed years ago. Whorf found evidence that we "dissect nature along lines laid down by our native languages." Members of a specific culture build concepts and find significance in situations or events, in Whorf's view, because of their shared language. Anyone who uses twelve different words to describe specific types of snow, as many Eskimos do, is apt to notice and reflect upon differences among snowfalls. English-speaking people, with one word for snow, are less likely to make such distinctions. The Hopi Indians classify their experiences by how long they last. Fleeting events, such as lightning, flames, meteors, and puffs of smoke, are verbs in the Hopi language. This practice probably makes these Indians especially aware of the duration of phenomena [2]. Whorf's observations are controversial and difficult to prove. Still, the idea that language influences thought is consistent with daily experience. Suppose that a friend describes a young woman whom you've never met as a "free spirit." Now imagine that the same young woman is portrayed as a "tramp." The language labels result in very different mental images for the same set of behaviors.

As you read Helen Keller's account of her discovery of language, a number of questions may have occurred to you. Before her tutor arrived, Helen had invented her own gestural language, albeit a crude one. Is that unusual? Do other deaf children invent their own languages? More generally, is there something about being human that makes language likely to be learned? You may also have noted that Helen's first steps in language learning were laborious and deliberate. Is learning a language ordinarily difficult? We will deal with these questions and many others as we explore the nature and development of thought and language.

THOUGHT: PRELIMINARY ISSUES

What is *thought*? Psychologists use this word as a general label for varied mental activities such as reasoning, solving problems, and forming concepts. Thought may be characterized by its goals or its elements.

Undirected versus Directed Thought

During our waking hours, ideas mingle with memories, images, fantasies, perceptions, and associations. Rambling mental activity with no specific goal is sometimes called *undirected thinking*, *stream of consciousness*, or *ordinary waking consciousness*. We described research on this type of thought in Chapter 7. In contrast with undirected thinking, *directed thinking* is aimed at a particular goal, highly controlled, and tied to a specific situation or problem. Moreover, directed thinking can be evaluated by external standards. Reasoning, problem solving, and concept learning are common examples of directed thinking. Though undirected and directed thought have different objectives, they depend on the same basic processes, including memory, imagination, and the formation of associations.

Throughout this chapter we will concentrate on directed thinking.

Elements of Thought

Do people think in words? In images? In some other manner? In diverse ways? While psychologists cannot directly observe anyone's thoughts, of course, they have approached the problem indirectly. In one of the earliest studies of this issue the British psychologist Francis Galton invited people to think about their breakfast table as it appeared earlier that morning. Then he queried his subjects about the clarity of their images. Some individuals reported very vivid pictures. Others recalled none at all.

Mental imagery appears to be an important component of many people's thoughts. Scientists, novelists, and poets often claim to have begun working from "pictures in their minds [3]." The great physicist Albert Einstein discovered relativity (he believed) by imagining himself traveling alongside a beam of light at 186,000 miles per second. What Einstein saw in his mind's eye did not correspond to anything that could be experienced or explained by current theoretical notions. Spoken and written words, so far as Einstein knew, played no role in his thinking [4].

Psychologists have recently begun studying mental imagery in their laboratories in earnest. Experiments demonstrate quite convincingly that people can formulate mental pictures. For answering certain types of questions about an object, such images appear to be just as helpful as having the object itself present. Verbal descriptions are not so useful as mental pictures under the same circumstances [5]. The images that people describe vary considerably in sharpness. And different types of imagery including the visual, auditory, tactual, and gustatory (taste-related) types, appear to accompany thought. S., the man who could not forget (page 238), "saw" and "felt" the sounds of words. People blind from birth learn to rely on nonvisual imagery to make judgments about objects. To compare the themes of the first and second movements

FIGURE 9-1 For most of his life, Jean Piaget, now in his eighties, has been actively involved in observing children. Here he watches children at play. Observations of ordinary play have generated a number of insights into the development of intellectual capabilities [86]. [*Yves Debrainie, Black Star.*]

of Beethoven's Fifth Symphony, you'd probably manipulate auditory images. After becoming completely deaf, Beethoven himself probably used auditory imagery as he composed his glorious Ninth Symphony. In Chapter 8 we described experimental evidence for the existence of varied types of memory imagery.

People frequently characterize their thoughts as an abrupt, incomplete, grammatically messy inner speech, somewhat like the passage from *Ulysses* quoted in Chapter 7. Laboratory observations support the idea that people talk to themselves as they think. During reading (an activity that requires a lot of interpretation), we often make speechlike movements with the lips or throat. These motions seem to help our understanding [6]. When deaf people who are proficient in sign language solve problems, muscle activity in their hands suggests that they may be "signing to themselves" [7]. If research participants in problem-solving studies are instructed to verbalize, say, give a reason for each response out loud, they solve certain types of problems more efficiently and quickly than when they aren't asked to put their ideas into words [8]. All these observations suggest that language is often involved in thought.

In sum, thinking probably depends on imagery of several types, on language, and perhaps on other capabilities which we do not currently understand. Psychologists are just beginning to learn about the elements of thought.▲

THE DEVELOPMENT OF LOGICAL THINKING

The human infant is a creature of reflexes whose thinking appears to be quite limited. The human adult is a subtle and sophisticated thinker. In this section we describe how the capacity for directed thought appears to develop.

Piaget's Theory of Mental Development

The Swiss behavioral scientist Jean Piaget (b. 1896), a giant in the study of the development of thought, has spent more than fifty years mapping out the world of the child's mind. Piaget, pictured in Figure 9-1, became inter-

---

▲ USING PSYCHOLOGY

1. Describe new examples which suggest that language influences thought.

2. Pick some past event to think about—say, your actions last Saturday. Do you use language? Imagery? If imagery is involved, what type is it? How vivid is the imagery?

ested in children's thinking when he noticed that youngsters consistently made certain types of mistakes on intelligence tests. After questioning children about their reasoning, he discovered that they thought *differently*, and not merely less, than adults did. The child's mind used to be pictured as a camera-scrapbook that photographed scenes and accumulated "snapshots." As fresh experiences occurred, new photographs were added. According to this view, the minds of youngsters and adults differ primarily in terms of the number of items stored. Piaget took a *constructionist perspective*. He assumed that people have to use their imaginations to make sense of their experiences. To understand thinking, the scientist had to find out what people take from their experiences and what they add—their "constructions," in other words. Piaget came to believe that as children grow older, their abilities to interpret, or construct, reality progress through a number of stages until their mental capabilities resemble those of adults. We examine Piaget's research methods, assumptions, and stage theory. Then we describe some major points of contention.

Piaget's research methods To collect information about thinking, Piaget used several empirical methods. Sometimes he simply asked children questions such as "Where does the wind come from?" or "What makes you dream?" At other times he observed the progress of individual persons. He closely and astutely watched his own youngsters, for instance. Piaget and his coworkers also conducted miniature experiment-like investigations. For one study, individual children were presented with coins and flowers and asked, "How many flowers can be purchased with six pennies if the price of each flower is one coin?" The observer then questioned each youngster to try to uncover his or her reasoning. This description and dialogue come from Piaget's writings.

Gui [four years; four months] . . . put 5 flowers opposite 6 pennies, then made a one for one exchange of 6 pennies for 6 flowers (taking the extra flower from the reserve supply). The pennies were in a row and the flowers bunched together.

OBSERVER: "What have we done?"
GUI: "We've exchanged them."
OBSERVER: "Then is there the same number of flowers and pennies?"
GUI: "No."
OBSERVER: "Are there more on one side?"
GUI: "Yes."
OBSERVER: "Where?"
GUI: "There (pennies)." [9]

After observing how children deal with numerous questions about causality, space, time, number, speed, and many other matters, Piaget formulated a comprehensive theory about how logical thinking develops. In its broad outlines, this theory is widely accepted.

Piaget's assumptions about inherited functions Piaget believes that human infants, like other animals, are born with both the need and the ability to adapt to their environment. *Adaptation* occurs naturally as organisms interact with their surroundings. They learn to cope; and their mental capacities develop automatically. Adaptation, as Piaget views it, involves two subprocesses: assimilation and accommodation. Most of the time people take in, or *assimilate*, information and categorize it in terms that they already know. The infant's behavior in sucking and mouthing a cup shows assimilation. A very basic response, sucking, which is appropriate for nursing is used to deal with a related situation. Here is another of Piaget's examples of assimilation:

At twenty-one months Jacqueline [Piaget's daughter] saw a shell and said "cup." After saying this, she picked it up and pretended to drink. . . . The next day, seeing the same shell, she said "glass," then "cup," then "hat," and finally "boat in the water." [10]

Occasionally, people encounter situations that cannot be categorized in terms that they already know. In these cases, they must *accommodate*, create new strategies or modify or combine old ones to handle the challenge. Infants who mouth cups eventually accommodate by developing the appropriate drinking strategy. Piaget recorded this additional illustration of accommodation in his son Laurent.

At 16 months, 5 days, Laurent is seated before a table and I place a bread crust in front of him, out of reach. Also, to the right of the child I place a stick about 25 cm long. At first Laurent tries to grasp the bread without paying any attention to the instrument, and then he gives up. I then put the stick between him and the bread; it does not touch the objective but nevertheless carries with it an undeniable visual suggestion. Laurent again looks at the bread, without moving, looks very briefly at the stick, then suddenly grasps it and directs it toward the bread. But he grasped it toward the middle and not at one of its ends so that it is too short to obtain the objective. Laurent then puts it down and resumes stretching out his hand toward the bread. Then, without spending much time on this movement, he takes up the stick again, this time at one of its ends . . . and draws the bread to him. . . . Two successive attempts yield the same result.

An hour later I place a toy in front of Laurent (out of his reach) and a new stick next to him. He does not even try to catch the objective with his hand; he immediately grasps the stick and draws the toy to him. [11]

In addition to the ability to adapt, animals also inherit a tendency to combine two or more separate physical and/or psychological processes into one smoothly functioning system. Piaget calls this capacity *organization*. A young baby can both look and grasp, for instance. Eventually, children coordinate the two actions so that they can grasp specific objects in view. Both adaptation and organization continue to operate throughout development.

As children grow, their general styles of interacting with the environment change. Piaget applies the term *scheme* (or structure) to both observable behaviors and associated concepts which are used to process incoming sensory data. "Looking and picking up" and "sucking" are both considered schemes. These actions proceed from ideas about how to handle sensory events and can be applied in many different situations. While early schemes appear to be composed primarily of reflexes and simple behavior, later ones consist largely of strategies, plans, rules, assumptions, and other mental capabilities. Through assimilation and accommodation, schemes continually change so that individuals can cope more effectively with their surroundings.

Piaget's stage theory Piaget believes that thinking develops in the same fixed sequence of stages in all children. At specific points in development, characteristic schemes appear. The accomplishments of each stage are presumed to build on preceding ones. Though Piaget has emphasized the influence of heredity on the developmental process, he maintains that the social and physical environment may affect the age when specific abilities evolve. We describe the highlights of each developmental period.

Sensorimotor stage (birth to approximately two years). During the first twenty-four months, babies make sense out of their surroundings by seeing, touching, tasting, sniffing, and manipulating. In other words, they rely on their sensory and motor systems. Some fundamental cognitive abilities develop during this time. Children discover that specific behaviors have definite consequences. Kicking gets rid of heavy blankets. Bouncing makes a mobile suspended above the crib dance about. In the beginning, "out of sight" may be equivalent to "nonexistent." Gradually, the baby develops a notion of permanence, an understanding that people and objects exist even when they are not perceived. Peek-a-boo may be delightful to infants because they believe that the adult really vanishes. Consequently, they're genuinely startled (and pleased) to see the person reappear. During the sensorimotor stage, infants develop another ability, the capacity to find new uses for old objects. The game of drop-the-bear-to-watch-father-pick-it-up-again can be exasperating evidence of this capacity. Being able to imitate complex new responses quite precisely, even when the model is absent, is considered another achievement of the sensorimotor period. A youngster who has seen a playmate stage a temper tantrum may "try one out" several days later. To manage this feat, the child must have stored some mental picture of the act. *Delayed imitation* suggests, then, that children begin to form simple representations of events during their first two years. Still, during the sensorimotor period, the child's thought is largely confined to action.

Preoperational stage (approximately two to seven years). During these years, children rely very heavily on their perceptions of reality. They can often solve problems by manipulating concrete objects. But they have a great deal of trouble solving more abstract versions of the same problems. A preoperational child, for example, may easily point out the largest of three boxes. The same youngster can rarely handle the abstract version: "If A is bigger than B, and if B is bigger than C, which is biggest of all?" During the preoperational stage, children become capable of thinking about the environment by *manipulating symbols* (including words) that *represent* the surroundings. The major accomplishments of this stage include (1) using language, (2) forming simple concepts (for example, "Fido, Blacky, and Rover are all dogs"), (3) engaging in imaginative play (a stick may be employed as a sword, a broom as a horse, and a doll as a baby), and (4) making pictures which represent reality. Classification is one type of concept that preoperational children begin to understand. Suppose that a youngster is asked to sort a bunch of cards like those pictured in Figure 9-2. Some cards are white, others red, some small, others large, some circular, others square. A child who understands classification can group the cards by color, size, or shape. Although preoperational children are able to handle this task, they show problems in dealing with relationships between classes. For instance, if given twenty-five toy statues—say, eighteen cows and seven dogs—preoperational children sort the objects into dogs and cows correctly enough. But when asked, "Are there more cows or more animals?" they are stumped. They fail this type of test, according to Piaget, because they cannot conceive of individual items belonging to two different classes at the same time. (A cow cannot be conceptualized as both cow and animal simultaneously.) Youngsters at this stage handle only one dimension at a time, apparently. Piaget also characterizes the thinking of preoperational children as particularly *egocentric*, or self-centered. They tend to see the world largely from their own perspectives. They find it difficult to put themselves in the position of others and understand alternative viewpoints. This humorous example of egocentric thinking is reported in *Winnie-the-Pooh.*

The buzzing-noise means something. You don't get a buzzing-noise like that, just buzzing and buzzing, without it's meaning something. If there is a

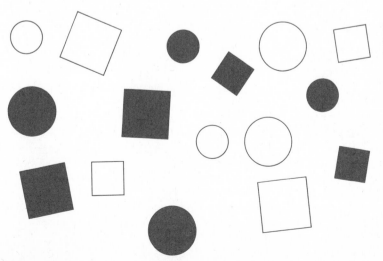

FIGURE 9-2 Cards like these are sometimes used to investigate children's abilities to classify.

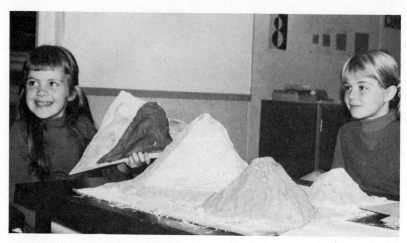

FIGURE 9-3 These girls were shown the three-dimensional mountain models on the table and asked numerous questions about what the model would look like from other vantage points. The preoperational child named Tricia (on the left) is showing how the view would appear from a position slightly to her right side. Generally, Tricia was correct about her own present perspective, but not about the perspectives of other observers. Tricia's older sister (on the right) was able to describe the perspectives of others quite consistently. According to Piaget, preoperational children cannot understand the relativity of their own viewpoints. But children may have difficulty with this task for different reasons. Youngsters have a hard time working abstract problems that have little to do with their daily realities. If a similar perspective task is embedded within a familiar interpersonal situation, the child handles it more accurately [87]. [*Courtesy of Mary Sime. From* A childs eye view. *Thames and Hudson, Ltd., 1973.*]

buzzing-noise, somebody's making a buzzing-noise, and the only reason for making a buzzing-noise that I know of is because you're a bee . . . and the only reason for being a bee that I know of is for making honey . . . and the only reason for making honey is so as I can eat it. [12]

A task used to assess egocentric thinking is described in Figure 9-3.

Stage of concrete operations (approximately seven to eleven years). During this stage children develop the ability to use logic, and they stop relying so heavily on simple sensory information to understand the nature of things. They acquire the capacity to do in their heads what they previously had to do literally. Recall the painstaking matching strategy of Gui, the four-year-old who was asked how many flowers could be purchased for six pennies. Six-year-olds who are able to count typically use the matching tactic when given, say, five sticks and asked for five more. Older youngsters who have acquired some additional cognitive skills, which Piaget calls *concrete operations*, can count the sticks out mentally. As children rely more heavily on reason to solve problems, their ability to categorize and classify objects expands. One important skill that develops during this stage is the capacity to distinguish appearance from reality and temporary from permanent characteristics. If orangeade is poured from a wide, short glass to a thin, tall one (see Figure 9-4), the child using concrete operations concludes that the quantity has remained the same because nothing was taken away. A preoperational child, in contrast, believes that the amount of orangeade has increased because the level is higher. Young children cannot explain a transformation in appearance because they rely primarily on perception instead of using logic. During the orangeade experiment, they tend to center their attention on one aspect of physical appearance, the level of the liquid, and they fail to notice other transformations. The concrete operations child masters the important lesson that sensory characteristics, such as size and shape, can change without affecting more basic properties, such as quantity. While children at the concrete operational level deal logically with objects, they are not yet capable of handling abstract ideas rationally. They can often follow reasoning but can rarely examine it for mistakes. They tend to solve problems by trial and error, rather than by systematically following an efficient strategy such as thinking of several possible solutions and weeding out the inappropriate ones.

Stage of formal operations (approximately eleven to fifteen years). During these years children develop the ability to understand abstract logic—to think about thinking. As one adolescent put it: "I find myself thinking about my future and then I began to think about why I was thinking about my future, and then I began to think about why I was thinking about why I was thinking about my future [13]." Where the youngster who uses concrete operations may come up with a single solution to a problem, the one who uses formal operations is likely to be able to generate many alternatives. When asked why a woman might be lying on the floor, for example, the individual at the formal operations stage of mental development might suggest: "hit on the head," "playing a joke," "drunk," "heart attack," and "accident." People who use formal operations check out alternative solutions to problems mentally. They also examine the logical consistency of their beliefs. A youngster at the formal operations level would be bothered by contradictory notions, such as there being both a kind God and millions of suffering human beings. At this stage people often construct theories, think about the future, understand metaphors, and play the devil's advocate by supporting a position that is contrary to fact. By the end of this period, children possess the same mental capacities that adults do.

Evaluating Piaget's theory Piaget studied mental development, a topic that had long been ignored and unappreciated, imagina-

FIGURE 9-4 This young boy is trying to figure out whether the quantity changes when liquid in the short, wide beaker is poured into the tall, thin one. Preoperational children have difficulty with this task, presumably because they focus on only one sensory dimension, the appearance of the new level. [*Mimi Forsyth/Monkmeyer Press Photo Service.*]

tively and comprehensively. A great many American psychologists were fascinated by his writings and attracted to the vast, unexplored research territories that had been opened up. Currently, numerous investigators are attempting to replicate Piaget's observations, often with tighter controls in the behavioristic tradition (Chapter 1). Many of Piaget's findings have been confirmed and his work is still highly regarded, though certain conclusions are questioned. We sketch some major points of contention.

1. *Are children of particular ages consistent in their mental operations*? A number of studies suggest that youngsters may be quite variable in their intellectual strategies. Four-year-olds, for instance, are not always egocentric. Research shows that they take their audience into consideration when delivering a message, making their communications shorter and simpler for two-year-olds than for adults [14]. Similarly, a particular twelve-year-old may use logic to handle one problem and sensory impressions for another.

2. *Do all children reach the final stage?* Recently, Piaget has amended his theory to suggest that all individuals reach the stage of formal operations by age twenty "according to their aptitudes and specializations [15]." But, there is evidence that formal operational thinking is used by a relatively small fraction (some 15 to 25 percent) of college students [16]. Some psychologists argue that Piaget's theory refers to capacity, and not necessarily to habitual strategy.

3. *Is mental growth irreversible?* In other words, can children lose intellectual capabilities that have been previously attained? As pointed out in Chapter 3, development is often repetitious. Newborn infants mimic during their first few weeks. Then reliable imitation vanishes until the end of the baby's first year or so. Mental abilities may appear, disappear, and reappear during early childhood too [17].

4. *What shapes cognitive capabilities?* Research suggests that children reach various mental milestones at diverse ages and that learning in a particular family and culture has a powerful effect on the time when specific abilities develop [18]. Many behavioral scientists believe that Piaget overemphasized the role of genetics and maturation and underestimated the importance of the youngster's surroundings.

5 *Did Piaget's analysis of children's problem-solving behavior consider language, memory, and perceptual abilities sufficiently?* In general, Piaget's studies did not allow him to differentiate among logical, language, memory, or perceptual inadequacies. Recent research suggests that language, memory, and perceptual deficiencies may be of key importance. Babies may not search for toys that have "disappeared" because they do not remember what they have seen, and not because they lack a concept of object permanence [19]. Older children may have trouble on abstract tasks (such as: A is bigger than B and B is bigger than C. Who is biggest?) because they do not *understand* the language or *remember* the details [20]. And, youngsters may fail conservation problems because they do not *attend to* and *perceive* the relevant dimensions [21]. ▲

PROBLEM SOLVING

Piaget's work focused on the development of directed thinking. We turn now to the nature of one directed-thinking skill, problem solving. Human beings are constantly confronting problems, of course. Every day we handle dozens of difficulties that may run the gamut from inconsequential to momentous. Trivial "dilemmas" (for instance: What should I eat for dinner? What shirt goes with my blue slacks? And should I go to the library tonight?) are solved quickly and easily. We may take years to cope with more complicated questions (for example, What career should I enter? Whom should I marry? And what lifestyle is right for me?). Human *problem solving* is usually defined as an endeavor that involves a goal and obstacles. A person perceives an objective, encounters difficulties, is motivated to achieve the goal, and works to overcome the obstacles [22]. We look first at how psychologists study problem solving, then at how people handle problems, and finally at influences on problem solving.

Studying Problem Solving

Psychologists cannot observe what goes on in people's minds as they work at solving problems, so behavioral scientists usually hone in on what people and other animals *do* as they confront challenges of various types. More often than not the problems are selected by the investigator. Typically, they are straightforward, well-defined tasks. Research participants might be instructed to unscramble letters and make words, work puzzles, play games (such as chess), or figure out the underlying order in a series such as A, B, M, C, D, M, . . . or 1, 1, 2, 3, 5, 8, 13, 21, ... Occasionally, people are given more true-to-life problems with many possible solutions. Psychologists Jerome and Donna Allender, for example, constructed an elaborate game which they called "I am the mayor." Sixth-, seventh-, and eighth-grade children were invited to play the role of chief magistrate and cope with the types of problems that might besiege the mayor of a small town. The youngsters had access to a file containing 250 pages of data (maps, records, plans, calendars, and correspondence) to help them handle the dilemmas that they selected [23].

As research participants struggle with problems, psychologists usually try to make *objective* observations. They may measure the elapsed time, count the number of errors, or list the resources consulted. To get closer to the thinking process itself, behavioral scientists sometimes ask people to reason aloud. In other cases, investigators question participants about their thinking soon after the problem-solving session.

Psychologists have also studied problem solving by analyzing the computer programs created by programming experts working on specific cognitive tasks—for example, developing a general strategy for winning at chess. A computer program is a sequence of operations designed to achieve a particular result. As such, it provides a clear picture of the programmer's approach to the task. When confronted with a difficult problem, a programmer may try various strategies until a successful program (one that solves the problem) is obtained. By studying the final program and the strategies tested along the way, psychologists can reconstruct the human problem-solving approach. For more information on this tactic, see this chapter's Suggested Readings (references 4 and 10).

The Process of Solving Problems

Though different models of the problem-solving process emerge from laboratory research, most share these common features: The problem solver identifies a challenge, prepares to cope, tries to resolve the issue in some way or another, and evaluates the attempt. This model is not meant to be a rigid one. In any single case, steps may be omitted, occur out of order, blur together, or be repeated.

Identifying problems Problems often appear "on their own." Sometimes human beings actively search out challenges. Certain people appear more likely than others to look for problems. When Albert Einstein was asked how he developed certain concepts, he attributed his breakthroughs to "an inability to understand the obvious." Like Einstein, artists, business people, scientists, and many others hunt for problems. Unfortunately, psychologists know relatively little about this initial phase of problem solving.

Preparation A preparation period usually follows the identification of a problem. During this initial analysis phase, people often collect the available data, evaluate the constraints, and define their general goals. This conceptualization of the task determines the mode of attack. Consider the problem of passing a particularly challenging course. You might attribute your difficulty to bad study habits, insufficient background, lack of aptitude, or disinterest. Each possibility dictates a different strategy. The success of your problem-solving efforts depends on analyzing the problem correctly.

Many important real-life problems involve hazy data and constraints. Consider tackling a career choice. You enter college when you're unlikely to clearly understand your own capabilities and needs over the long haul. Any analysis of this problem must be based on a careful consideration of incomplete clues.

Sometimes irrelevant factors are obtrusive and interfere with analyzing a problem effectively. Consider the ring task described in Figure 9-5. Please try to solve the problem before reading further. (You will find the solution in the next section.) The problem has been presented with a great many irrelevant elements. Only those outlined in red are involved in finding the solution. Because the space is cluttered, a great deal of extra time and effort is required to explore the possible

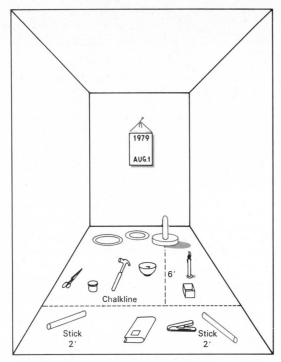

FIGURE 9-5 Work out in your mind how to put the ring on the peg. You can move around the room and use any tools you see. But you must remain behind the chalk line when placing the ring on the peg. The solution to this problem is described in the text. [*Adapted from Problem solving by M. Scheerer. Copyright © 1968 by Scientific American, Inc, All rights reserved.*]

utility of many useless objects. The extra difficulty may cause many people to feel discouraged and give up.

In most laboratory tests, the paraphernalia

TABLE 9-1 Typical Aptitude Test Problems*

Problem 1. You have three shoe boxes. Inside each box there are two glass jars. Each jar contains three coins—a penny, a nickel, and a dime. How much money do you have?
a. $1.92   **b.** $1.12   **c.** $0.96   **d.** $0.56   **e.** $0.48

Problem 2. During a special sale, eight spark plugs cost $2.40 without installation and $6.00 installed. What is the labor charge for installing one plug?
a. $3.60   **b.** $1.80   **c.** $0.50   **d.** $0.45   **e.** $0.40

*See the Answer Keys for correct responses.

that must be used to solve the problem are all there at the same time and in the same place. When the elements of a problem are not present together, analysis is hindered. The pieces of real-life puzzles often turn up helter-skelter—one here, one there. A restless man, for example, may decide to change jobs to solve his problem. After a few months, he may realize that some other aspect of his life—say, his lack of education or his marriage—is the real problem.

Defining a problem adequately requires work. Psychologists Benjamin Bloom and Lois Broder discovered that students who do poorly on aptitude tests designed to measure intellectual capabilities (see Table 9-1) often rush through instructions or skip them entirely [24]. Similarly, psychologist Arthur Whimbey found that people who score low on intelligence tests frequently fail to seek out and use all the information contained in the problems. Poor test performance seems to be at least partially due to failures to take the time to analyze problems effectively. Training in problem analysis, Whimbey found, usually improves intelligence test scores and academic achievement [25].

Resolution How do people resolve problems? It depends on the problem and the problem solver. Let's look at some tasks that psychologists have used in their experiments. Please try the match problem pictured in Figure 9-6 before reading on. How did you handle the puzzle? Many people rearrange the matches visually in their minds to test out various configurations. In other words, they use *mental imagery* to tackle the task. Now try the candle problem in Figure 9-7. When the objects shown in the figure are *labeled*, more people consider the potential uses of the box and work out a solution [26]. *Language* often facilitates the problem-solving process. Now, attempt to resolve the stomach-tumor question posed in Figure 9-8. What *plans* or *strategies* occur to you? Student subjects talked aloud to the investigator as they tried to solve this problem in a laboratory setting. The German psychologist Karl Duncker found that his research participants approached the problem similarly. The students seemed to begin with *functional solutions*, analyses of the problem which included the broad properties of a solution: "If such-and-such could only be achieved, the problem would be solved." Subjects produced these functional solutions to the stomach-tumor problem: "Desensitize the healthy tissue" and "Lower the intensity of the rays on their way through the healthy tissue." The functional solutions showed that the students had grasped and reformulated the problem. These general ideas gave rise to *specific proposals*, such as "Displace tumor toward surface," "Inject desensitizing chemical," and "Give weak intensity in periphery and concentrate in place of tumor." When a specific proposal seemed on target, students searched for *practicable solutions*, concrete ways to apply their specific proposals. One subject suggested, "Send a broad and weak bundle of rays through a lens in such a way that the tumor lies at the focal point and thus receives intensive radiation." When the students ran into difficulties, they usually backtracked; and they sometimes began again with new functional solutions. Strategies in this practical problem-solving situation consisted essentially of organizing and reorganizing the problem in increasingly precise ways [27].

A number of recent laboratory studies suggest that people use diverse strategies to resolve real-life problems. One psychologist, Lee Shulman, asked education students to play the role of a teacher taking over a sixth-grade class in mid-semester. The research participants had to figure out what needed to be done about a great many dilemmas. As in the mayor game mentioned earlier, each "teacher" received material in which the problems were embedded—in this case, an in-basket filled with memos, phone messages, notes, and information about students. Each subject had access to resources including a "principal," a "school secretary," and past records. Shulman found that the participants' initial strategies varied. Some tried to get an overall grasp of all the difficulties. Others worked on the issues one by one. The

You have sixteen matches arranged as shown. Move three (and only three) to create four squares of equal size.

FIGURE 9-6 The solution to the task is presented in the Answer Keys.

Imagine that you are seated before a table on which you see matches, a candle, and a small box filled with thumbtacks. Using these materials, try to fix the candle to the wall and light it.

FIGURE 9-7 The solution to the problem is presented in the Answer Keys. [*After Glucksberg and Weisberg, 1966.*]

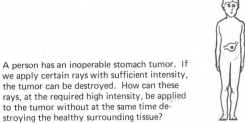

A person has an inoperable stomach tumor. If we apply certain rays with sufficient intensity, the tumor can be destroyed. How can these rays, at the required high intensity, be applied to the tumor without at the same time destroying the healthy surrounding tissue?

FIGURE 9-8 Possible solutions are presented in the Answer Keys. [*After Duncker, 1945.*]

sequencing of efforts also differed. Some people worked on a single dilemma from start to finish before tackling another. Some attempted several similar problems at once. "Branched seekers" began on one issue and took on new and more compelling tasks as their interests and attention shifted [28]. Behavioral scientists James McKenney and Peter Keen found diverse problem-solving styles among business graduate students too. Many subjects used the same type of approach consistently in varied situations. Different styles had different advantages, depending on the issue [29].

Laboratory studies find that skilled problem solvers devote more time and are more thorough in their strategies than less skilled ones. Bloom and Broder discovered that students with low scores on aptitude tests spent relatively small amounts of time trying to answer questions. They often responded on the basis of a few clues, feelings, or impressions, although more information could have been obtained with a little additional energy. And they did not break problems into component subproblems [30]. We will have more to say about the individual differences of problem solvers when we talk about intelligence and creativity in Chapter 12.

In real life, an *incubation period*, a rest ranging from minutes to years when the problem to be solved is put aside and not consciously worked on, may be important. Many scientists and artists have described the necessity of such "hands off" periods. As people continue to work on a task, they often fixate on certain techniques and ideas. After a rest or change of scenery, our thoughts appear to change direction more easily. Laboratory studies on this topic are contradictory and inconclusive [31].

Evaluation Problem solvers often evaluate their solutions to see whether they really work, particularly when the problems have been taxing. Standards for what constitutes an acceptable resolution vary. To prove this point, the gestalt psychologist Wolfgang Köhler presented people with the problem in Table 9-2. Please fill in the missing numbers on the bottom line before reading on. Some research participants considered the issue settled as soon as they had filled in the blanks. Others did not; they strove after a general principle that explained why subtracting each successive square produced a set of odd

TABLE 9-2 A Number Problem

Instructions: Fill in the three missing numbers on the bottom line.

1	4	9	16	25	36	49	64
0	1	4	9	16	25	36	49
	1	3	5	7	9	?	?	?

Source: Köhler, W. *The task of gestalt psychology.* Princeton, N.J.: Princeton University Press, 1969.

numbers [32]. The problem and the problem solver's expertise and personality probably influence whether a specific resolution is acceptable.

Influences on Problem Solving

We examine two influences on problem-solving proficiency: past learning and level of arousal.

Past learning and problem solving Whenever previous experiences help us to learn or solve problems, many psychologists label the effect *positive transfer*. Sometimes past experiences enhance an individual's general problem-solving abilities. In these cases of positive transfer, behavioral scientists say that organisms have acquired a *learning set* or that they have *learned to learn*. Harry Harlow demonstrated this phenomenon clearly in a classic study on monkeys. He presented more than 300 discrimination tasks to his subjects. To solve each problem, the animals had to select one of two small objects—for example, a red cylinder or a blue pyramid. One choice yielded food, the other did not. To obtain the reward on the second trial, the monkeys had to learn to follow the rule: "If correct on the first trial, choose the same object the second time. If incorrect on the first trial, choose the other object the next time." Initially, it took the monkeys many trials to solve each problem correctly. As they practiced, the animals improved gradually. By the hundred and first problem, the monkeys were choosing the correct object on the second trial 85 percent of the time. Their accuracy continued to improve. In the course of problem solving, the animals had obviously mastered some fundamental skills, including how to pay attention and how to figure out and follow rules [33]. See Figure 9-9.

People learn to learn too. After taking exams from numerous teachers, many students become "testwise." They can guess what questions are likely to appear on future exams. They learn general skills, such as how

FIGURE 9-9 This monkey learned general problem-solving skills in Harlow's classic study. The animal had to figure out which of two objects hid food. As monkeys solved more than 300 discrimination tasks of this type, they gradually acquired insights into resolving such problems. [*Harry F. Harlow, University of Wisconsin Primate Laboratory.*]

to eliminate improbable response options on multiple-choice questions and how to write coherent essays. Similarly, with increasing experience, civil engineers become adept at solving sewerage and highway problems, auto mechanics at diagnosing and curing car ailments, and therapists at analyzing human problems and helping people cope.

Learning sets sometimes impede problem solving by making an individual more likely to respond in rigid, stereotyped, or mechanical ways. When past experience retards new learning or problem solving, many psychologists label the effect *negative transfer*. Retroactive and proactive inhibition, described in Chapter 8, can be considered examples of negative transfer.

Negative transfer is often observed when old objects have to be used in new ways to solve problems. The ring problem presented in Figure 9-5 provides a good illustration. To solve the problem, the two sticks must be tied together with a string. Suppose that the function of the string is suggested by its context—say, the string suspends a current calendar. People are likely to see the string as

a support. Consequently, they're not apt to think of using it in a novel way. When the string hangs from the nail by itself, few subjects fail to solve the ring problem [34]. A tendency to see a particular object as fixed in function (largely because of past experiences), and to fail to perceive new and flexible uses for it, is called *functional fixity*. In real life, functional fixity is common. You might not think of using egg yolk, for example, to seal an envelope that won't stay closed when you have run out of conventional paste.

Past experiences sometimes cause people to impose tight restrictions and limit the problem space too closely—another example of negative transfer. Before reading on, try the riddle in Figure 9-10 and the dot puzzle in Figure 9-11. First, consider the riddle. For many people, the assumption that surgeons are men is so firmly established that the possibility of a woman surgeon is never entertained. Recently, a psychologist found that fewer than 20 percent of the male and female subjects who had not heard the riddle before responded correctly (that the surgeon was a woman) [35]. Conventions influence analyses

A doctor and his son were involved in an automobile accident. The doctor was killed, and the son was badly injured. The boy was brought to the hospital for surgery. The surgeon there exclaimed, "I can't operate on him, he's my son!" How is this possible?

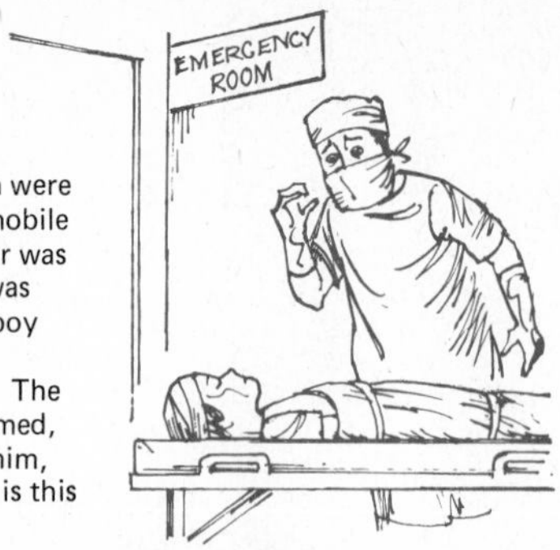

FIGURE 9-10 The solution to this riddle is described in the text.

of the dot problem too. People tend to assume that lines must begin and end at dots. But, in this instance, the problem cannot be resolved if you limit yourself in this way.

Sometimes stereotyped strategies which are established by past experience impede efficient problem solving. Before reading further, please work the water jar problems in Figure 9-12 in order. In a classic study, psychologist Abraham Luchins asked research participants in an experimental group to solve all eight problems in succession. While working on items 2 through 6, many subjects formulated an efficient strategy, "Fill B, then subtract A and twice C (desired volume = B − A − 2C)." Once the participants began using this approach, most of them continued employing it mechanically, even on problems 7 and 8. Here the most efficient solutions are one-step subtraction and one-step addition respectively. Did you solve the last two problems directly? Research participants in a control group, who worked problem 1 and then problems 7 and 8, handled the last two tasks efficiently every time [36].

FIGURE 9-11 The solution to this problem is presented in the Answer Keys.

Connect the nine dots by drawing four straight lines without lifting your pencil from the paper.

Arousal and problem solving In the mid-1940s, psychologist H. G. Birch studied the relationship between hunger and problem solving in young chimpanzees. Birch deprived his subjects of food for various periods—two, six, twelve, twenty-four, thirty-six, or forty-eight hours. Then he observed the animals' performance on problem-solving tasks that required raking in food with a stick. Birch found that when chimpanzees had been without food for short periods, they were easily distracted and often engaged in irrelevant behavior. They simply were not sufficiently interested in the problem to remain with it. Animals who had been deprived of food for very long intervals concentrated so intently on the goal that they frequently failed to see important problem elements. These highly excited chimpanzees screeched and staged temper tantrums more often than the other research participants and seemed utterly unable to endure frustration or failure. The chimpanzees deprived of food for a moderate span of time, in contrast, made flexible, goal-directed responses [37]. This study suggests that *arousal*, or degree of alertness and excitement, has an important impact on problem solving in animals. Numerous studies

FIGURE 9-12 Try to obtain the volume desired by using jars A, B, and C, whose volumes are shown. Please work the problems in order and write down your calculations in each case. Efficient strategies are discussed in the text. [*After Luchins, 1942.*]

Problem	Jar A	Jar B	Jar C	Volume desired
1	29	3		20
2	21	127	3	100
3	14	163	25	99
4	18	43	10	5
5	9	42	6	21
6	20	59	4	31
7	23	49	3	20
8	15	39	3	18

indicate that people behave like Birch's chimpanzees in many learning and problem-solving situations. As arousal (due to focused attention, emotion, needs, or some other reason) increases up to some optimal level, human learning and problem solving are usually enhanced. As arousal increases beyond the optimal level, performance declines [38]. ▲

LANGUAGE: PRELIMINARY ISSUES

We turn now to that distinctively human achievement, language. Psychologists focus primarily on two aspects of language: how it is acquired and how it is used. The study of these subjects is known as *psycholinguistics*. In this section, we explore some preliminary issues: What types of communication do people and other animals use? What is the nature of a language? How are languages different from other modes of communication? Later we will consider how children acquire language and whether chimpanzees and other nonhuman primates can learn a human language. Because language can be observed and recorded directly, it does not present the measurement problems that other cognitive processes do.

Forms of Communication

Most animals, including people, communicate with one another in several ways. Donald Hebb distinguishes between reflexive and purposive modes of communication [39]. *Reflexive communication* consists of stereotyped patterns, such as reflexes, expressive gestures, and signs of emotion, that often convey information, but were not intended expressly for that purpose. Human beings sometimes cry naturally when in pain and smile spontaneously when happy, for instance. Though such signs provide a great deal of information, they were not generated deliberately to communicate specific messages. Similarly, female dogs in estrus secrete a chemical substance that informs male dogs that they are ready and may be willing to mate. The secretion also tells the male where the female is located. Once again, the message is not intentionally generated by the animal.

Purposive communication sets out deliberately to affect the receiver of the information, and its future course depends on the response of the receiver. Dogs may bare their teeth to frighten their enemies. If a foe is intimidated, the animal stops baring its teeth. If not, the dog may attack. People use gestures, facial expressions, movements, and sounds to send many specific messages. By altering your tone of voice, for example, you can express two very different types of information with the same word "terrific." You can say the word with enthusiasm, to convey "Great! I'm really happy," or sarcastically, to deliver the message "Awful! I'm deeply disappointed." Similarly, nodding one's head vertically in our culture says "Yes" or "I understand," while horizontal movements communicate "No" or "I don't understand." In Chapter 17, we describe several additional types of nonverbal

▲ USING PSYCHOLOGY

1. Think of several problems that you solved recently. How did you identify, prepare for, and resolve them? Did you evaluate your solutions? Describe.

2. Review the characteristics of skillful problem solvers. Do you fit into this category?

3. Give personal examples of positive and negative transfer.

4. Think of times when a learning set helped your problem-solving efforts and times when it impeded such efforts.

5. How can students use the knowledge that moderate arousal enhances performance to prepare themselves for exams?

communication (reflexive and purposive). Language is the most sophisticated type of purposive communication.

The Very Special Nature of a Language

Hrugj uryopef erglifds feduxlp. What does this conglomeration mean? You're not likely to go to the dictionary to look up these "words." It's immediately obvious that they're not English terms. Why? Because languages are orderly. A *language* systematically relates symbols (sounds, letters, or signs) to meaning and provides rules for combining and recombining the symbols so that people can speak their minds in an original, appropriate, and coherent way. All utterances are composed of basic sounds, or *phonemes*. English phonemes include vowel sounds like *e*, as in m*e*, consonant sounds like *f*, as in *f*ather, and combination consonant sounds like *sh*, as in *sh*ip, or *th*, as in *th*is. English has forty-five phonemes. Other languages contain between fifteen and eighty-five basic sounds. Languages combine phonemes into units that possess meaning called *morphemes*. English morphemes include words, prefixes (such as un-, anti-, and de-), and suffixes (such as -able, -ing, -ed, -s, and -ly). English has about 100,000 morphemes. A large number of rules, which people are aware of at some level, govern how phonemes and morphemes are combined to form words. Accordingly, you don't have to look up "hrugj" and "uryopef" to see if they are English. On the other hand, you might have been tempted to look up "pog" and "cated," had they been included in our opening "sentence," since they follow the rules for combining phonemes and morphemes. Rules also dictate how words are combined to make phrases and sentences. Once you've picked a word, for example, the words that can follow it are limited by convention. Take the word "I." You would not combine "I teacher," "I the," or "I happy." In English, verbs usually follow nouns. Adjectives usually precede nouns. And there are many other similar standards.

Although language is standardized, it is also incredibly flexible. It provides enormous potential for innovation. Knowing a language means mastering a set of principles that allows the user to generate an almost infinite number of sentences. The nearly 1 million words of English can be combined and recombined, for example, to make more than 100,000,000,000,000,000,000 different twenty-word sentences [40]. So far, the structure, or grammar, of languages cannot be described in a complete way. Psycholinguists define the term "grammar" in a specialized manner: the collection of rules and principles which determine the meaning of every possible sentence that can be formed in a language. In general use, the word "grammar" has a more limited meaning, of course. It refers to rules dealing with the superficial aspects of language, such as appropriate style and correct syntax (rules governing sentence formation).

All known human societies have developed a complete language, while no known nonhuman has. Martin Moynihan of the Smithsonian Institution studied the communication displays of several types of fish, birds, and mammals. He found that none of them used fewer than ten or more than thirty-seven patterns—perhaps the largest number these animals' brains can handle [41]. Each pattern is somewhat like a sentence. It is used in a fairly stereotyped way under specific circumstances. The messages such animals send appear to be quite restricted, then, in the total number of ideas conveyed. Such limits contrast markedly with the almost infinite expressive flexibility of human languages.

THE ACQUISITION OF LANGUAGE

All normal human beings acquire a language. There seems to be something about being human that makes learning a language likely even when children are deaf, as in Helen Keller's case. Ordinarily, the effortlessness of this achievement is remarkable. People who hear a language continually may learn it without any systematic instruction or planning. See Figure 9-13. All over the world, children develop the basics of a language in two short years, usually between the ages of 1½ and 3½. By the age of five, most youngsters use the same language that adults in their environment do. How does this happen? And why?

From Sounds to Words

During their first half-year, almost all babies, regardless of nationality, race, environment, or learning ability, vocalize approximately the same amount and produce similar sounds. As they exercise their muscles, the jaws, tongue, vocal cords, and lips move, producing a variety of random noises. Infants cry when they are uncomfortable. At approximately three months, they begin cooing when they are pleased.

Ordinarily, babies show acute *auditory discrimination*, the ability to differentiate between similar sounds. Long before they acquire language, infants attend to speech and show a readiness to extract information from it. Normal human neonates of only twelve hours move in rhythm with the language spoken around them. They change both the direction and speed of their motions at points marking off segments of adult speech [42]. By one month of age, normal babies can distinguish between consonants like *B* and *P* [43] and between various vowel sounds [44]. Though keen auditory discrimination at an early age is not a uniquely human achievement [45], many of the capacities necessary for developing a language are clearly present in people shortly after birth.

During the second half of the first year, children do a lot of *babbling*. They vary their vocalizations as if they were practicing sounds. The child's earliest communication attempts often use sounds in combination with gazing at a particular person and gesturing (reaching, pointing, waving, and the like) to enlist aid in satisfying a motive. By eight to ten months, babies use particular vocalizations along with gazing and gesturing for specific messages. One boy, for example, said

FIGURE 9-13 These seven-year-old twins are engaged in an English lesson with their speech teacher. They were reared by a German grandmother and rarely exposed to English. As a result, they never learned the language and were classified as retarded. The twins devised their own communication system (as children have done before and since). One conversation proceeded like this: "Dugon, thosh, yom dinckin, du-ah." / "Snup aduk chase die-dapanna." Except for their problems with English, the twins appear to be intellectually normal [88]. Deaf youngsters who are isolated from spoken English and not trained to use signs often devise a surprisingly orderly gestural system for themselves, as Helen Keller did. In some instances, the systems are quite complex [89]. Such cases suggest that human beings have a very strong propensity for communication through language. [*Union Tribune Publishing Company.*]

"mm," "muh," "may," "my," "mow," or "ma" whenever he motioned for something he wanted. The sounds that are used to communicate wishes vary [46].

By their first birthday, children have often mastered several impressive language lessons. They make a distinctive set of vocalizations that mimic the stress and pitch patterns of the language spoken around them. They understand the meaning of several words. They use a simple language that follows orderly patterns. Initially, single words convey whole ideas. The utterance "papa" might mean "Here is Papa," "Come here, Papa," or "Where is Papa?" depending on the situation. Even at this early stage, the child is acquiring some ideas about how to string words together meaningfully and understands simple several-word communications [47].

At the beginning, individual words tend to refer to a broad range of items. The word "mama" might be applied at first to all women. One of the author's young neighbors called all dogs "sams" after the author's Saint Bernard whose name was Sam. Children's pronunciations also follow regular rules. For example, youngsters notice whether words have more than one syllable and the second syllables of two-syllable words are frequently represented by repetition of the first syllable. "Mama" and "papa" are verbal creations of this type which have been incorporated into our language. "Wawa," the term initially used by many children for water, has not received such official sanction.

Recent research by psychologist Katherine Nelson suggests that youngsters acquire their first ten words slowly over a three- or four-month period before about sixteen months of age. The vocabularies of about half the children Nelson studied contained names or classes of objects predominantly. Most of the words used by the remaining youngsters were useful for interpersonal interactions (names of people and feelings). After the first fifty words have been acquired (by about twenty months of age), the child's vocabulary expands rapidly [48].

Cognitive development must precede even this very simple early language. Before verbal communication can become meaningful, babies have to know that objects and people have a certain permanence, that words are stable, and that names represent realities. They must also understand elementary ideas, for example, the notions that objects have locations and can be owned.

From Words to Sentences

All over the world, children of eighteen to twenty-four months begin combining words. Why should speech develop so dramatically at this time? As youngsters start moving around on their own, they interact extensively with their surroundings and encounter many new challenges. Piaget's theory suggests that the toddler's representational skills expand near this time. Word combinations probably help children keep pace with their growing needs to communicate new observations and ideas.

In the late 1960s, Roger Brown, a psycholinguist at Harvard University, and several coworkers who were then graduate students, including Ursula Bellugi-Klima, Colin Fraser, and Courtney Cazden, performed a pioneering study of language development. They worked with three children called Adam, Eve, and Sarah. The youngsters were just beginning to combine words into two- and three-word "sentences" like these: "Sun gone," "Want potty," "More juice," "Sit Adam chair," "Mommy sock," "Hand dirty," "Adam hat," "Sweater chair," "See daddy car," and "That mommy soup." Two psychologists visited the children's home at regular intervals and collected speech samples by tape-recording and taking notes on what was said to and by each child. Later, the youngsters' utterances were analyzed as Brown and his coworkers looked for evidence of rule learning. Though the two- and three-word "sentences" resembled random word combinations on the surface, they proved to be an abbreviated, or *telegraphic*, language that was both incredibly lawful and meaningful. Nouns, verbs, and adjectives were included while other word forms, such as prepositions (in, on), prefixes (un-, dis-), suffixes (-ed, -s), auxiliary verbs (have, will), articles (the, an), and conjunctions (and, or), were excluded. Word order was often preserved. For instance, the possessor came reliably before the object possessed. "Sit Adam chair" may be *expanded*, or translated, into "Sit on Adam's chair." "Sentences" were meaningfully used for a large number of purposes, including the following [49]:

1. To identify and name objects. (Examples: "That mommy soup," "It ball.")
2. To comment on or request that something recur. (Examples: "More juice," "Another bang.")
3. To express possession. (Examples: "Daddy coat," "Adam hat.")
4. To state that something does not exist. (Example: "Not shoe.")

TABLE 9-3 Children's Attempts at Imitation

Model sentence	Eve (25.5 months)	Adam (28.5 months)
1. I showed you the book.	I show book.	[I show] book.*
2. I am very tall.	[My] tall.*	I [very] tall.*
3. It goes in a big box.	Big box.	Big box.
4. Read the book.	Read book.	Read book.
5. I am drawing a dog.	Drawing dog.	I draw dog.
6. I will read the book.	Read book.	I will read book.
7. I can see a cow.	See cow.	I want see cow.
8. I will not do that again.	Do again.	I will that again.
9. I do not want an apple.	I do apple.	I do a apple.
10. Do I like to read books?	To read book?	I read books?
11. Is it a car?	't car?	Is it car?
12. Where does it go?	Where go?	Go?

*Bracketed words are uncertain.

Source: Adapted from Brown, R., & Fraser, C. The acquisition of syntax. In C. N. Cofer & B. Musgrave (Eds.), *Verbal behavior and learning: Problems and processes.* New York: McGraw-Hill, 1963. Pp. 158–201.

5. To express location. (Examples: "Baby high-chair," "Sweater chair.")

6. To indicate someone or something causes an action. (Example: "Mommy go.")

7. To indicate that someone or something has a particular property. (Examples: "Red truck," "Hand dirty.")

8. To indicate that someone or something undergoes a change of state or receives the force of an action. (Example: "Push car.")

Even when youngsters tried to imitate adult speech precisely, they produced similar telegram-like effects, as can be seen in Table 9-3 [50].

Short, abbreviated sentences continue to be used for a year or so. Gradually, the important grammatical gaps are filled and sentences are lengthened. See Figure 9-14. Within a given language domain (such as pronunciation, past-tense formation, and pluralization), grammatical complexities are mastered in a predictable sequence. Though the rate may vary, the order appears to be the same for all children. The most easily understood general rules are usually mastered first. Eventually, rules covering details are acquired. Youngsters initially learn to form the past tense of regular verbs, for example, by adding the terminal "t" sound ("looked," "helped"). Irregular past tenses ("sang," "bought") are

FIGURE 9-14 The average length of a child's utterances increases gradually with age. All over the world, language acquisition occurs in a remarkably similar order. But children progress at different rates, as shown here. The age at which the first signs of language appear and the speed of language acquisition are not correlated in any consistent way with general intelligence. [*From Brown, 1973.*]

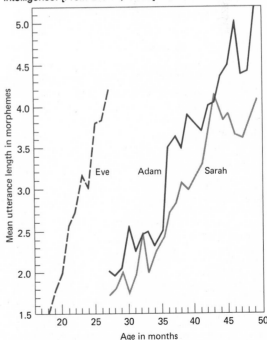

acquired later. Similarly, children form plurals of familiar words by adding the terminal "z" sound ("dogs," "cars") before they master irregular plurals ("oxen," "geese"). By the age of three and a half to four or so, youngsters are putting together two or three clauses to form complex sentences.

Rule Learning: The Essence of Language Acquisition

Sometimes people think of language acquisition as an achievement akin to a tape collection. According to this viewpoint, words, phrases, and sentences are heard, practiced, stored, and later used. But human beings are not storage bins for snippets of tape that "play back" as they were "read in." Language is a very creative function. In the words of Roger Brown, "It is not rare to need to create sentences . . . it is the usual thing. It is constantly necessary to say things that one has never heard in precisely the required form and not at all unusual to need to say something that no speaker of the language has ever said [51]."

The capacity for creative speech depends on knowing and using the set of principles called a grammar to guide speech production. Though no one—no child, adult, or psycholinguist, for that matter—can state precisely all the applicable rules, it is clear that the principles are acquired at a very early age. One imaginative demonstration of this fact came from a linguist, Jean Berko Gleason. Gleason showed 97 four- to seven-year-old youngsters pictures and asked them to complete sentences describing them, as shown in

FIGURE 9-15 The wugs used by Jean Berko Gleason to study children's understanding of grammar. [*After Berko, 1958.*]

This is a wug.

Now there is another one.
There are two of them.
There are two_____.

Figure 9-15. Here are some additional examples:

TENSE: "This is a man who knows how to mot. He is motting. He did the same thing yesterday. What did he do yesterday? Yesterday he _____."

POSSESSIVE: "This is a niz who owns a hat. Whose hat is it? It is the _____ hat."

Gleason found that young children applied grammatical rules to the nonsensical words [52]. A commonly observed type of speech error, called *overregularization* (using general rules when they are inappropriate), also shows that youngsters acquire principles and do not merely parrot fragments that have been heard. Once a child has learned to form a regular past tense by adding a terminal "t" sound, for example, the rule is often misapplied to irregular verbs, producing such classics as "Mary falled down," "Tim goed," and "Spot runned." In many cases, initial rules are wrong. Jennifer, a two-year-old child studied by psychologist Carol Lord, seemed to believe that negatives should be expressed by a high-pitched tone of voice. This youngster assumed that "I want put it on," spoken at a high pitch, meant "I don't want to put it on." Since adults who didn't want Jennifer to do something tended to speak in a higher-pitched tone, the child had apparently concluded that high pitch must be the way to say negative things. Figure 9-16 describes another technique for studying the acquisition of language rules.

Explaining the Acquisition of Language

How can the acquisition of language be explained? Noam Chomsky, a leading linguist at the Massachusetts Institute of Technology, emphasizes the role of genetics in providing basic competencies. Chomsky argues that the material heard by the child often consists of false starts, fragments, errors, and hesitations. Yet, youngsters construct a grammar telling them what is a well-formed sentence and how such sentences can be both used and

FIGURE 9-16 Children learn rules that help them generate new messages. They do not simply "record" and then "play back" the elements of a language. Psychologists Jill and Peter de Villiers are demonstrating this principle here as they study children's abilities to use "tags." A *tag* is a short question (such as "isn't she?" "didn't I?" and "aren't we?") that is added to a sentence to ask that information be confirmed. Tag questions interest psycholinguists because their meaning is simple while their grammatical construction is complex. Tags require the understanding of several grammatical rules. To select the correct tag, a child must be able to identify the subject of the sentence and choose the proper pronoun (suitable gender and number) and the appropriate verb form. Children in this study heard the puppets make several tags. Then the youngsters took on the tag-making role for all kinds of unusual sentences that they had probably never heard before. Linguistically sophisticated children produced the correct tags easily within seconds, showing that people can incorporate general rules and use them quickly without any awareness of the process [90]. [*Frank Siteman.*]

understood. "Children," in Chomsky's words, "develop . . . a very complex and articulated theory of enormous predictive scope and explanatory power—they take . . . an incredible inductive leap [53]." According to Chomsky, the principles of grammar are so deep and abstract that only an organism "informed in advance" about their nature could have discovered them. In other words, human beings may be preprogrammed somehow to work out the rules of language. The following observations all support the notion that people have a built-in propensity for developing language: (1) the similar sequencing of stages in language acquisition all over the world, (2) the infant's extremely early sensitivity to language, (3) the appearance of language-related capacities in deaf infants, and (4) the specialization of the human speech and breathing apparatus and brain.

A number of brain characteristics seem crucial for language development. Cortical motor regions permit fine control of vocal cords, tongue, lips, and other sound-producing mechanisms. Cortical auditory areas allow acute discriminations between sounds. The association regions of the cortex coordinate the motor and auditory activities necessary for speech and give people the capacity to associate auditory representations with visual and tactile impressions, a capability that few other primates possess [54]. The assocation areas also enable human beings to abstract, symbolize, discriminate, generalize, and remember a great deal—mental abilities that make our speech sophisticated. And the separation of language regions from those that control motivation and emotion may play a critical role in what people communicate about. Human beings are probably the only animals that can go beyond emotions and needs to describe (and think about) the world, themselves, and other creatures.

Children's active efforts to master a language support the idea that genetics is linked to language acquisition. Children are enthusiastic users of language and drill themselves without any prodding. Linguist Ruth Weir left a tape recorder in her young son's bedroom which turned on automatically every time the boy, Anthony, talked. He did a great deal of talking just before and after waking from naps, at night, and in the morning. Monologues like the following showed that he practiced speech. Note the rehearsal of negatives in this example: "Not the yellow blanket/ The white/ It's not black/ It's yellow/ It's yellow/ Not yellow [55]." When Weir attempted to record the bedtime monologues of her second child, she found that the baby practiced with Anthony through the wall.

Now let's consider the importance of the child's environment in language acquisition. After all, children with normal hearing end up speaking the language of their family and culture 100 percent of the time. And, on rare occasions when youngsters have spent their lives locked in attics or closets and have heard almost no language at all during childhood, they do not come away from the experience speaking Chinese, Hebrew, Swahili, or some language of their own. Sadly, they are mute [56]. Though learning has to be involved in language acquisition, specific environmental influences have been difficult to pin down.

Currently, psychologists believe that there is a sensitive period (Chapter 3) for language acquisition. Early in development, children need to *hear and speak* a language to master varied language competencies. Case studies are one source of evidence for this hypothesis. Psychologist Breyne Moskowitz has described the history of an asthmatic boy of normal hearing whose deaf parents spoke only in sign language. The boy was confined to his home because of his asthmatic condition. To teach the child English, the concerned parents turned on the television set every day. By the age of three the boy "signed" fluently, but neither spoke nor understood English. Hearing English was not enough. Observations of deaf children support the sensitive period hypothesis too. If deaf youngsters learn sign language and exercise their language capacities *early*, they learn English more easily than

if they acquire English as their first language (as Helen Keller did) in a speech program at a relatively late age. Similarly, adults who learn a foreign language early in life acquire a second foreign language more readily than people who learn only their native tongue [57].

Are specific types of personal interactions especially important for language development? Psychologist Jerome Bruner has observed that language learning involves *solving problems*. Babies have needs and goals—say, obtaining a nearby object, enlisting support for a specific action, or persuading someone to share something desirable. They must learn how to achieve these objectives. After videotaping and studying mother-infant pairs as children acquired language, Bruner, his coworkers, and other investigators have concluded that mothers and infants seem to work together closely on the problem-solving venture. To help the youngster master language, the mother's verbal responses remain closely tuned to, and in some cases, about six months ahead of, the child's present level [58]. Currently, fathers in our culture appear far less involved and much less skilled than mothers in conversing with children [59].

A number of behavioral scientists have focused on the characteristic strategies that the mother uses, especially on her "baby talk" (called *caretaker language* or *motherese*). Typical caretaker language consists of an easy vocabulary, simplified sounds, a high-pitched and exaggerated intonation, short, simple sentences, a high proportion of questions (among mothers) and commands (among fathers), talk about the here and now, and unusually regular patterns. These characteristics appear in Arabic, Commanche, and many other languages as well as in English, and seem to be universal. The high-pitched, exaggerated intonation probably alerts the child to pay attention and often marks what is especially new and/or important. The regularity, simplifications, and here-and-now focus are suited to the child's limited cognitive capacity. As mentioned before, the speech is often adjusted as the child acquires new competencies. Presumably, a consistent, easy language enables the child to begin extracting the structure of the language and formulating general rules.

Many parents seem to realize intuitively that true conversational interactions with the baby are important. But they rarely try to teach language systematically. In one study of this topic, Roger Brown and Camille Hanlon found that parents did not bother to correct the form of their children's utterances but were concerned primarily about the "truth value" of the messages [60]. The parents of a child who said, "Cartoons nine," would be more likely to respond, "The time is eight, not nine," than "Do you mean 'Cartoons will be on at nine'?" In fact, attempts to teach language directly often prove fruitless, as the painstaking effort reported by a father-psycholinguist, Martin Braine, illustrates:

CHILD: Want other one spoon, Daddy.
FATHER: Can you say 'the other spoon'?
CHILD: Other . . . one . . . spoon.
FATHER: Say . . . other.
CHILD: Other.
FATHER: Spoon.
CHILD: Spoon.
FATHER: Other . . . spoon.
CHILD: Other spoon. Now give me other one spoon.

At this point Braine gave up. "Further tuition," he wrote, "is ruled out by the child's . . . protest, vigorously supported by my wife [61]." Katherine Nelson's study, cited earlier, suggests that frequent corrections of pronunciation are actually counterproductive over the short run. Children of parents who corrected inaccurate attempts at pronuncia-

tion developed vocabularies more slowly than youngsters who were not exposed to frequent criticism [62]. In this case, true conversational interactions which help the child acquire language skills appear to be disrupted by the unpleasantness. Since speech errors seem to be generated by the child's current rules, corrections prove useless in most instances. After all, parents don't teach the youngster what is wrong with her or his current grammatical principles. Consequently, the correction is apt to be totally puzzling to the child.

Specific styles of family interactions influence language acquisition too. Competencies are more likely to develop when famiies use language for a wide range of functions [63]. Language that stretches the child's thinking is more apt to encourage mature language usage, as discussed in Chapter 3.

Conditioning principles probably underlie certain aspects of language acquisition. *Observation learning* is likely to be involved. Youngsters often ask, "What's this?" find out, and repeat the label. Research suggests that children spontaneously imitate words that they are already in the process of learning [64]. There is also evidence that babies pick up, presumably through observation, the types of word patterns that they hear a lot [65]. Meaning becomes attached to words as they are repeatedly *associated* with particular objects and events in the natural course of living in a social group. At the same time, speech is automatically *positively reinforced* by its natural consequences much of the time. It gets children things they want, as Bruner suggests. ▲

▲ USING PSYCHOLOGY

1. Make a chart showing the important steps in language acquisition.

2. Observe parents interacting with young children to see whether they use caretaker language. Try to characterize the communication patterns. Do your observations agree with those described in the text?

3. Devise an informal test of grammatical principles based on pictures and sentences, such as those Gleason used. Test several children at different ages to see whether they know how to use grammatical principles.

TEACHING LANGUAGES TO APES

In the seventeenth century René Descartes asserted that language was the critical feature that distinguished human beings from beasts. In his words:

> For it is a very remarkable thing that there are no people . . . so dull and stupid that they cannot put words together in a manner to convey their thoughts. On the contrary, there is no other animal, however perfect and fortunately situated it may be, that can do the same. [66]

The possession of language has long been part of our identity as human beings. Is our capacity for language unique? Or, can other animals learn a language?

Psychologists first began trying to teach language to apes almost fifty years ago. The early efforts were disappointing. In the 1940s, for example, psychologists Keith and Cathy Hayes provided six years of intensive speech training for a chimpanzee named Vicki. But the animal mastered only four recognizable words [67]. In retrospect, these initial attempts seem naive and futile. People and chimpanzees possess extremely dissimilar communication-related capabilities. The two species have exceedingly different vocal apparatus, for example. In the wild, apes communicate extensively, but mostly by gestures. During the mid-1960s, psychologists Allan and Beatrice Gardner took these facts into account and became the first successful teachers of a language-using chimpanzee. They taught a chimpanzee called Washoe (shown in Figure 9-17a) to communicate in *Ameslan*, or *American Sign Language*, the gestural lan-

FIGURE 9-17 (a) Washoe, the first chimpanzee to acquire a language (approximately 200 Ameslan signs), is now teaching her adopted son, Loulis. Eight days after the baby arrived, he made his first sign, imitating Washoe's gesture for George, a trainer. Loulis has also used signs for "food," "drink," "hot," "fruit," "give me," and "hug" (to ask forgiveness after a temper tantrum, in one instance). Washoe's history is described in the text. Sarah (b) and Lana (c) learned languages through positive reinforcement procedures (Chapter 5). Sarah, the Premacks' pupil, was schooled for two years in a plastic-chip language and for more than ten years on cognitive tasks. She has acquired a working vocabulary of roughly 130 symbols. More strikingly, her performance on Piagetian problems suggests that apes, like older children, make inferences and do not depend simply on sensory appearances. Sarah is shown returning "words" after completing a "sentence." Lana types to communicate. Each key of her typewriter contains a different symbol, a white geometric pattern on a colored background standing for a specific "Yerkish" word. A projector attached to the typewriter allows Lana to see the symbols she prints. This chimpanzee combines more than 200 "words" according to fairly strict rules to answer questions and to make requests (such as "Please machine give piece of bread," as shown here). The keyboard arrangement is scrambled frequently so that the animal has to master symbols rather than locations. A computer arranges reinforcers—usually food—for correct and meaningful constructions, registers "word" sequences in a permanent record, and analyzes them. [*Courtesy of Roger Fouts, David Premack, Duane Rumbaugh.*]

a *b* *c*

guage that many deaf Americans use [68]. We will take a closer look at Washoe later. Shortly afterward, David and Ann Premack devised a language using plastic chips of varying sizes, shapes, and colors to represent words. Chimpanzees were taught to manipulate the chips to form sentences [69]. See Figure 9-17*b*. More recently, a research team at the Yerkes Primate Research Center in Atlanta, led by psychologist Duane Rumbaugh, trained Lana, a chimpanzee, to "read" and "write" sentences composed of symbols by pounding the keys of a special computerized typewriter. The automated "Yerkish" system minimizes experimenter bias, which can have a considerable impact on how animals perform in problem-solving situations [70]. See Figure 9-17*c*.

There should be little question at this point that apes can learn to manipulate symbols to communicate. But, do the animals acquire a true language? Before tackling this controversial issue, we'll look more closely at the accomplishments of one chimpanzee, Washoe, to see precisely how apes "talk" and how psychologists teach them. We have chosen to focus on Washoe because she was the first ape to acquire a flexible language and because her language is a natural one that was learned and used within the context of ongoing social relationships, just as human languages always are. As a consequence, Washoe, unlike some other linguistic apes, often "speaks" spontaneously and has a lot to say.

A Closer Look at Project Washoe

Beatrice and Allan Gardner acquired Washoe, a wild-born chimpanzee, when she was about a year old. The Gardners treated the animal like a human child. She lived in their backyard in a trailer that was furnished like a home. At least one, and often two, human companions kept her company during her waking hours. They signed to her and to one another in Ameslan as they interacted in play, at meals, and during "child-care" routines. After about six months of exposure to Ameslan

gestures, Washoe learned some signs. Only a few were acquired merely by *observation learning*. Washoe acquired most of her "words" by a process called *molding*. The chimpanzee's hands, arms, and fingers were placed in the proper signing position in the presence of the object or action that was represented. To teach Washoe the sign for "tickle," for instance, the Gardners put Washoe's hands through the appropriate movements while tickling her. Washoe also learned a number of signs by the operant conditioning technique called *shaping*. For example, every time Washoe wanted to open a door, she held up both hands and banged on the door. The sign for "open" happens to be two open hands held palms down and side by side then moved apart gradually and rotated to turn the palms up. Washoe's banging was actually a beginning. The Gardners waited for her to place her hands on the door and then lift them. Sometimes they prompted her. Then they rewarded the correct approximation by opening the door. Eventually, they shaped a response that resembled the open sign [71].

Washoe's achievements have been quite impressive overall. (Those of other apes promise to be more so as techniques improve, a topic we turn to in a moment.) By 1973, several years after Washoe's intensive training had ceased, the chimpanzee was using a vocabulary of about 160 signs to express herself. There were many more "words" in her receptive vocabulary [72]. Washoe began combining signs to form telegram-like sentences approximately ten months after her training began. Typical sequences were: "Open hurry," "hug come hurry," and "more food gimmee." Washoe uses signs spontaneously to name objects, to make requests (usually for filling physical or social needs or for sensory stimulation), and to conduct simple conversations. The monologue below was recorded by a writer who visited her at her new home, the Institute for Primate Studies at the University of Oklahoma. It conveys some of the flavor of Washoe's spontaneous utterances. At the time Washoe, surrounded by other chimpanzees, was standing on a small island in the midst of a pond. She begged psychologist Roger Fouts, her friend and teacher, to come to her by signing:

Roger ride come gimme sweet eat please hurry hurry you come please gimme sweet you hurry you come ride Roger come give Washoe fruit drink hurry hurry fruit drink sweet please please . . . [A plane flew overhead just then and Washoe signed:] You me ride in plane. [73]

Washoe's language is a creative one. The chimpanzee uses words correctly in new and appropriate contexts. When Roger Fouts refused to take Washoe with him on one occasion, she signed "dirty Roger." Prior to this incident, the "dirty" sign had been used primarily for soiled items and bowel movements. Later, Washoe used the sign for monkeys that irritated her [74]. Certain "errors" reveal Washoe's concepts. She has signed "flower," for example, in the presence of a tobacco pouch and in kitchens with cooking food [75].

Recent Developments

In recent years there have been several interesting developments on the "talking" ape scene. Allan and Beatrice Gardner have used their experience to improve their language-training program. Ameslan lessons begin now at significantly earlier stages of development. Several new chimpanzees were acquired one or two days after birth, and training was started at once during the natural course of caretaking. Fluent signers of Ameslan, including deaf people, are being employed as teachers. The early start and the added expertise seem to produce some important differences. The Gardners' new chimpanzees have taken half as long as Washoe did to acquire their first signs and they are learning significantly more signs at younger ages [76]. Numerous investigators are employing more sophisticated techniques for testing animals and analyzing their sentence structure [77]. At the Institute for Primate Studies at the University of Oklahoma, chimpanzees acquiring the American Sign Language are housed together in colonies to give them a chance to

use their language with one another and to transmit signs to their offspring. So far, observed language use between such animals has been sporadic and is usually limited to requests to "share fruit" or "tickle." Washoe, who lives here, often signs to other chimpanzees. But at the time of this writing, none of the animals appears sophisticated enough to keep pace with her [78]. Highly controlled experiments show that chimpanzees can use language to communicate information about food to one another [79]. Finally, new species—orangutans, pygmy chimpanzees, and gorillas—are learning to "speak" various languages and are being observed closely. These great apes are now thought to be more intelligent than common chimpanzees. After six years of training, Koko, a gorilla tutored by Francine Patterson at Stanford University, has correctly used more than 640 Ameslan words and employs 375 frequently and appropriately. Koko talks about her feelings of sadness, anger, and fear. She correctly uses abstract words such as "imagine," "understand," "curious," "idea," "boring," and "stupid." She jokes, lies, defines words, communicates about past and future, answers "why" questions, insults, argues, expresses empathy, and signs to herself, to other animals including her gorilla companion Michael, and to her dolls. In addition, Koko understands hundreds of English words [80]. Observations in the near future should teach behavioral scientists a great deal about the language and thinking capabilities of these remarkably intelligent animals.

Can Apes Acquire a True Language?

Opinions vary as to whether apes can acquire a true language. If by language one means the use of names or symbols, few psychologists would dispute the ape's "claim." But, if one insists that language requires an ability to recombine words in an infinite number of ways, then the answer is not entirely clear. Those who believe that apes truly possess a language argue that the animals' accomplishments equal young children's. The two species show a number of compelling similarities:

1. Both name the objects and events around them. Average five-year-old children use many more words than five-year-old apes—some 5,000 or so—compared with a "mere" 375 for Koko, the superstar of the linguistic ape world, at the age of seven.

2. The content of their speech is similar. Both note the appearance and reappearance of objects and people and the characteristics of phenomena. Both name locations, report on actions, and ask to have their needs filled.

3. Both grasp elementary abstractions. Sarah, one of the Premacks' early chimpanzee pupils, could work out the problem "If red on green (and not vice versa), then Sarah take red and not green." Apes also master such concepts as those of similarity and difference.

4. Both speak in sentences. Some 78 percent of Washoe's two-word combinations and about 75 percent of young children's utterances fit the meaning categories extracted by Roger Brown from children's speech [81]. Like human youngsters, apes develop rules about words. A chimpanzee named Lucy, for instance, knows the difference between "Roger tickle Lucy" and "Lucy tickle Roger." Lana erases meaningless sentences and fills in the blanks of incomplete sentences in ways that show her understanding of appropriate grammatical constructions. If "Please machine open . . ." is punched on the keyboard, Lana passes up "Banana" and other tempting possibilities and prints "Window." Computer analyses of another chimpanzee's (Nim's) utterances show regularities in his combinations which suggest that he is using structural rules.

5. Both show signs of creativity. Chimpanzees and children use words in appropriate combinations that they have never seen before. Lucy labeled watermelon "water fruit" and radishes the "cry hurt food." The transfer of old words to new situations, as in Washoe's use of the word "dirty," shows that apes use language flexibly. Koko's language usage is often very imaginative.

Critics of the position that apes use a real language maintain that there are important *qualitative* differences between the achievements of children and apes:

1. Apes do not use languages naturally in the wild. Teaching apes to "talk" is an arduous undertaking that requires enormous planning and almost limitless patience and diligence. In contrast, language acquisition appears to be almost inevitable for children.

2. Apes use a narrow range of sentences in specific contexts and it is hard to know whether the animal really understands the sentence and all its parts in the same sense that people do [82]. Powerful grammatical principles, in contrast, allow people to recombine words in almost innumerable ways. Given any utterance at all, we can construct many different forms and ask all types of questions. In the case of "Lucy tickle Roger," for instance, we might ask, "Who tickled Roger?" "When?" "Where?" "How?" "Why?" "Who was Roger tickled by?" And so on. No ape uses language as flexibly as people do.

3. The mental abilities of apes and people differ significantly. It is currently believed that apes do not progress very far beyond the preoperational mental level. However, the apes' capacities are not entirely understood, and there have been some surprises. Koko performs at almost the average level for a human child of her age on commonly used intelligence tests. Sarah has displayed concrete operational abilities [83]. Still, the language of average three- or four-year-old children shows far more sophistication than that displayed by any ape so far. Youngsters between three and five are using abstract nouns such as "place" and "kind," showing that they already possess impressive conceptual abilities. A child of this age constructs complex sentences which demonstrate the capacity to follow a number of ideas at once. The utterance, "When I was a little girl I could go 'geek-geek' like that, but now I can go 'this is a chair' [84]" may not sound like much at first. But study the sentence for a moment. The child is contrasting her past and present language ability, a rather advanced cognitive achievement.

Some people have suggested that the behavioral scientists' preoccupation with "talking" animals is frivolous or juvenile. But the study of linguistic apes can reveal some important lessons about these complex primates and ourselves. If psychologists focus exclusively on human cognition, we will never understand how it is special biologically and how we came by our unusual abilities. To do this, we need to compare. The great apes "are the best comparative material available to us [85]." Research with talking apes has impor-

▲ **USING PSYCHOLOGY**

Do you feel apes have acquired a true language? If so, which arguments seem most persuasive?

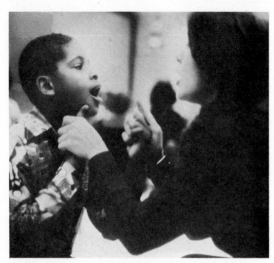

FIGURE 9-18 The various language-instruction strategies for apes have been adapted for people with severe language problems, particularly for mentally retarded, autistic, and cerebral-palsied youngsters and adults with major hemisphere brain damage. Here a teacher shapes an autistic child's hands into a sign for frustration, as the youngster learns sign language at the David School in Chicago. Most autistic children are totally mute or repeat whatever is said in parrotlike fashion. Although they do not appear retarded, they fail to show an interest in exploring their surroundings or socializing with others. Many engage in repetitive rituals such as flapping their arms; some are dangerously self-destructive. Since autism is neither well understood nor easily treated, many victims of this disorder spend their lives in institutions. In a pioneering program at the David School (and in similar projects) autistic children are learning sufficient sign language to make requests and express feelings. Two-thirds of the youngsters in the David School program have learned some speech in addition; and, as a result, nearly all have been able to graduate to less intensive programs. Why sign language is successful with autistic children is not currently known [91]. [*Psychology Today, 1976.*]

tant practical applications for teaching mute people to communicate too, as described in Figure 9-18. ▲

SUMMARY
Thought and Language

1. Thought and language are intricately interrelated.

2. Behavioral scientists often categorize thought as undirected or directed.

3. Thought appears to be composed of images and words.

4. Piaget has taken a constructionist perspective about children's thinking. He assumes that human beings inherit two basic coping tendencies: adaptation (composed of assimilation and accommodation) and organization. He also believes that youngsters progress in a fixed order through the stages of mental growth: sensorimotor, preoperational, concrete operations, and formal operations. While Piaget's observations are highly regarded, certain of his conclusions conflict with research.

5. Psychologists collect both objective observations and introspective data about problem solving. Human problem-solving attempts often involve identifying a problem, preparing to cope, resolving the issue, and evaluating the solution. Past learning can establish learning sets which facilitate or impede problem solving. Functional fixity, imposition of overly strict limits on the problem space, and stereotyped strategies are common examples of negative transfer. Increases in arousal up to some optimal level usually help problem-solving and learning efforts.

6. People and other animals use reflexive and purposive modes of communication. The purposive mode of communication called language is remarkably flexible and innovative.

7. Many of the capacities necessary for language are present in infants shortly after birth. By one year of age children understand the meanings of words and use single words to convey whole ideas. Youngsters of eighteen to twenty-four months begin combining words. Their utterances follow rules. Children of three to four years put together clauses to form complex sentences. The speech of the five-year-old typically resembles the adult's. At early ages children discover language principles (a grammar).

8. Hereditary and environmental influences contribute to language acquisition.

9. Apes can learn to manipulate varied types of symbols to communicate. Still, their use of language is severely constrained by their limited cognitive capacities.

A Study Guide for Chapter Nine

Key terms thought (277), undirected thinking (stream of consciousness, ordinary waking consciousness) (277), directed thinking (277), adaptation (279) [assimilation (279), accommodation (279)], organization (280), scheme (280), sensorimotor stage (280), preoperational stage (281), stage of concrete operations (282), stage of formal operations (283), problem solving (284), positive transfer (288), learning set (learning to learn) (288), negative transfer (289), functional fixity (289), psycholinguistics (291), reflexive and purposive communication (291), language (292), grammar (292), caretaker language (298), and other italicized words and expressions.

Important research elements of thought (Galton, others), research-based criticisms of Piaget's conclusions, problem-solving process (Bloom, Broder, Whimbey, Shulman, McKenney, Keen, Köhler, others), influences on problem solving (Harlow, Luchins, Birch, others), communicative displays in animals (Moynihan), milestones in early human language development (Nelson, Brown, Bellugi-Klima, Frazer, Cazden, others), acquisition of grammar (Gleason, Lord, others), influences on language acquisition (Weir, Moskowitz, Bruner, Brown, Hanlon, Braine, Nelson, others), language acquisition in chimpanzees (the Hayses, the Gardners, the Premacks, Rumbaugh, Patterson, others).

Basic concepts relationship between thought and language (Whorf, others), Piaget's research strategies, constructionist perspective (Piaget), stage theory of mental development (Piaget), methods of investigating problem solving, problem-solving model (identification, preparation, resolution, evaluation), the essence of a language, cognitive prerequisites of early language development, genetics and language learning (Chomsky), problem solving and language acquisition (Bruner), conditioning principles and language acquisition.

People to identify Whorf, Galton, Piaget, Chomsky.

Self-Quiz

1. Which statement about directed thinking is correct?
  a. It is capable of being evaluated by external standards.
  b. It is typically disjointed and rambling in nature.
  c. It is usually loosely controlled.
  d. It lacks direction toward a definite goal.

2. With which viewpoint is Piaget most closely linked?
  a. Behaviorist   *b.* Constructionist
  c. Gestalt   *d.* Humanistic

3. A child encounters an ambulance for the first time and calls it a "fire truck." Which Piagetian concept is illustrated?
  a. Accommodation   *b.* Assimilation
  c. Organization   *d.* Structure

4. During which stage does the development of delayed imitation occur, according to Piaget?
  a. Preoperational stage
  b. Sensorimotor stage
  c. Stage of concrete operations
  d. Stage of formal operations

5. Which statement about mental development is supported by current research?
  a. Almost all children pass through the four Piagetian stages, although the timing varies.
  b. Language and memory are more important than perception and logic for mental development.
  c. Mental abilities sometimes appear, disappear, and reappear during childhood.
  d. A specific child of a particular age is consistent in his or her mental operations.

6. Which is the first stage in strategy formation, according to Duncker?
  a. Evaluation   *b.* Functional solution
  c. Practicable solution   *d.* Specific proposal

7. After handling many complaints, a salesperson becomes very skilled at identifying problems and generating solutions that are satisfactory to all concerned. Which concept is most clearly illustrated?
  a. Functional fixity   *b.* Functional solution
  c. Learning set   *d.* Practicable solution

8. Which phenomenon illustrates negative transfer?
  a. Lack of motivation
  b. Low arousal
  c. Too close limitation of the problem space
  d. Unconventional way of using an old object

9. A cat hisses at a strange dog, but ceases immediately when the dog wags its tail. Which type of communication was exhibited by the cat?

a. Formal *b.* Purposive
c. Reflexive *d.* Telegraphic

10. In which specialized way do psycholinguists use the word "grammar"?

  a. The principles governing all types of communication (including the gestures made by the simplest animals)
  b. The principles governing appropriate style
  c. The principles governing sentence formation
  d. The principles governing the meaning of every possible sentence that can be formed in a language.

11. Which language-related skill would children less than six months old be likely to possess?

  a. Combining sounds in sentence-like intonation patterns
  b. Discriminating the sound of *B* from *P*
  c. Using a specific sound in combination with gazing and gesturing to communicate
  d. Vocalizing the specific sounds of the language spoken around them

12. After learning its first word, how long does a child generally take to learn nine more words?

  a. Several months
  b. Four to six weeks
  c. Two to three weeks
  d. Several days to one week

13. Which language-development theory does Chomsky endorse?

  a. Humans are genetically preset to acquire the principles of a language.
  b. Language is learned primarily through imitation, operant and respondent conditioning, and other types of association learning.
  c. Language acquisition depends on representational processes that develop during the preoperational stage.
  d. The separation of brain functions that underlie thought, on the one hand, and emotions and motives, on the other, give people the power to think about the nature of the world.

14. Which utterance is an example of overregularization?

  a. "Baby highchair"
  b. "He swimmed"
  c. "It's yellow/Not yellow"
  d. "Want other one spoon"

15. In which way do the languages of linguistic apes and children differ?

  a. Apes cannot grasp elementary abstractions such as "similarity" and "difference."
  b. Apes do not use sequences that can be considered sentences.
  c. Apes talk only about their own needs.
  d. Apes use a fairly narrow range of sentences in specific contexts.

Exercises

1. PIAGET'S THEORY. To test your knowledge of Piaget's theory, work through the following matching exercises. You will be pairing functions and stages with appropriate examples. For each illustration, choose the single most appropriate response. To review, see pages 278 to 284.

Part I, Functions: Select the function that is illustrated by each example.

FUNCTIONS: accommodation (AC), adaptation (AD), assimilation (AS), organization (O)

_____ *1.* Combining gazing, gesturing, and vocalizing to communicate

_____ *2.* Seeing snow for the first time and processing it as "thick rain"

_____ *3.* Seeing a Siamese cat for the first time and adding it to the category "cat"

_____ *4.* Encountering a lion for the first time and changing the concept "cat" so that it includes big cats

_____ *5.* Coordinating looking and grasping

_____ *6.* Shaking a new stuffed panda bear as if it were a rattle, a familiar toy

_____ *7.* The name for items 3 and 4 combined

Part II, Stages: Select the stage when the achievements below first appear.

STAGES: concrete operations (CO), formal operations (FO), preoperational (PO), sensorimotor (S)

_____ *8.* Understanding and using abstract logic

_____ *9.* Being able to imitate the words others say

_____ *10.* Learning that kicking removes blankets

_____ *11.* Understanding that the amount of juice remains the same when poured from a tall, thin glass to a short, wide one

_____ *12.* Developing language

_____ *13.* Being able to deal with physical objects in a rational manner, but not being able to handle abstractions in a logical way

_____ *14.* Comprehending that a toy exists even though it cannot be seen

_____ *15.* Speculating about the many possible solutions to a problem

2. LANGUAGE DEVELOPMENT. You can test your knowledge about the times when language abilities first become evident by classifying the *beginning* of the following achievements according to the single most appropriate age range. To review, see pages 292 to 296.

AGE RANGES: 0–6 months, 7–12 months, 13–18 months, 19–24 months, 25–36 months, 37 or more months.

_____ *1.* Moving in rhythm with a spoken language

_____ *2.* Coordinating vocalizing, gazing, and gesturing to present specific messages

_____ *3.* Combining words into two- and three-word "sentences"

_____ *4.* Combining two or three clauses to form complex sentences

_____ *5.* Understanding meaning

_____ *6.* Acquiring the first ten vocabulary words

_____ *7.* Distinguishing between B and P and between various vowel sounds

_____ *8.* Acquiring a distinctive set of sounds that mimic the speech and pitch patterns of the "surrounding" language

_____ *9.* Using single words to convey whole ideas

_____ *10.* Mastering the first fifty words

Suggested Readings

1. Lindsay, P. H., & Norman, D. A. *Human information processing: An introduction to psychology.* (2d ed.) New York: Academic, 1977. This engaging text tries to involve students in learning about how people process information. You will find excellent introductory material about perception, attention, memory, language, problem solving, and thinking. A fine place for a serious student to start.

2. Posner, M. *Cognition: An introduction.* Glenview, Ill.: Scott, Foresman, 1973 (paperback). A brief, clear introduction to research on memory, thinking, problem solving, and other cognitive processes.

3. Ault, R. L. *Children's cognitive development: Piaget's theory and the process approach.* New York: Oxford University Press, 1977; Ginsburg, H. E., & Opper, S. *Piaget's theory of intellectual development: An introduction.* Englewood Cliffs, N.J.: Prentice-Hall, 1979; Phillips, J. L. *The origins of intellect: Piaget's theory.* (2d ed.) San Francisco: Freeman, 1975. Among a number of good introductions to Piaget's work, these paperbacks contain easily understood, concise summaries of Piagetian ideas, many illustrative examples, and discussions of educational implications. The Ault text covers experimental research on cognitive development, as well as Piagetian ideas.

4. Davis, G. A. *Psychology of problem solving: Theory and practice.* New York: Basic, 1973. An informal and lucid introduction to problem solving. Davis examines research designed to understand the nature of problem solving as well as practical applications in business and education. He also describes some interesting training programs that were designed to improve problem-solving skills.

5. Adams, J. L. *Conceptual blockbusting: A guide to better ideas.* San Francisco: Freeman, 1974; Raudsepp, E., & Hough, G. P. *Creative growth games.* New York: Harcourt Brace Jovanovich, 1977. These paperbacks, involving and fun to read, aim at helping people to improve their problem-solving skills.

6. Dale, P. S. *Language development: Structure and function.* (2d ed.) New York: Holt, Rinehart & Winston, 1976 (paperback). An excellent source for information about language development. It covers difficult topics clearly.

7. Miller, G. A. (Ed.) *Communication, language, and meaning: Psychological perspectives.* New York: Basic/ Harper Colophon, 1977 (paperback). In this collection of exceptionally readable essays, distinguished authorities discuss important language and communication topics informally for the general public.

8. Davis, F. *Eloquent animals: A study in animal communication.* New York: Coward McCann & Geoghegan, 1978. A clear and delightful book about communication in animals, including bees, birds, killer whales, and apes. In each instance, Davis visited the research site and provides a personal account.

9. Donaldson, M. The mismatch between school and children's mind. *Human Nature,* 1979, **2**(3), 60–67. This discussion of research on children's thinking takes issue with Piaget's conclusions. Donaldson also explores the practical implications of her findings. "Many children," she feels, "hate school because it is a hateful thing to be forced to do something at which you fail over and over again."

10. Nelson, R. The first literate computers. *Psychology Today,* 1978. **11**(10), 73–80. Nelson describes the efforts of Yale University computer scientist Roger Schank to teach computers to use language appropriately and new ideas about language which have evolved from this research. Schank's computers are programmed to avoid errors like the following: Input: "Now what haven't I added to the cake batter?" Output: "A pound of dog hair and an air filter."

11. Moskowitz, B. A. The acquisition of language. *Scientific American,* 1978, **239**(5), 92–108. A lucid summary of research on language acquisition.

12. Patterson, F. Conversations with a gorilla. *National Geographic,* 1978, **154**(4), 438–465. Accompanied by intriguing photographs, this warm personal account of Koko's training and accomplishments at age seven provides insights into this extraordinary animal.

Answer Keys

Self-Quiz

1. a (277) **2.** b (279) **3.** b (279) **4.** b (281)
5. c (284) **6.** b (287) **7.** c (288) **8.** c (289)
9. b (291) **10.** d (292) **11.** b (293) **12.** a (294)
13. a (296) **14.** b (296) **15.** d (303)

Exercise 1

1. O **2.** AS **3.** AS **4.** AC **5.** O **6.** AS
7. AD **8.** FO **9.** S **10.** S **11.** CO **12.** PO
13. CO **14.** S **15.** FO

Exercise 2

1. 0–6 **2.** 7–12 **3.** 19–24 (beginning at 18 months)
4. 37+ **5.** 7–12 **6.** 13–18 **7.** 0–6 **8.** 7–12
9. 7–12 **10.** 19–24

Table 9-1

Problem 1: (c) $0.96   Problem 2: (d) $0.45

Figure 9-6

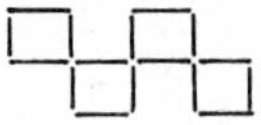

Figure 9-7

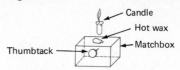

Figure 9-8

Two possible solutions to the stomach-tumor problem:
1. Aim several low-intensity x-ray sources, located at different positions, at the tumor. This will produce high-intensity radiation at the tumor and low-intensity radiation at other body sites.
2. Aim a single x-ray source at the tumor while rotating the body. Consequently the tumor will be exposed to the radiation for a long time while other body sites are exposed only briefly.

Figure 9-11

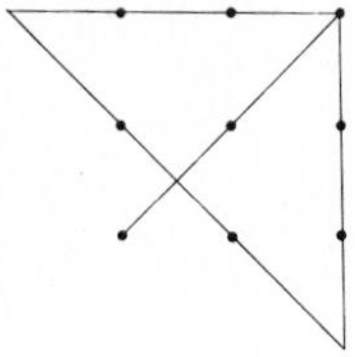

Why does Isaac gamble away his small paycheck every week? Why does Polly spend so much time in the biology laboratory? Why is Clementine almost always eating? Why did Richard Alpert give up wealth and status? "Why" questions of this type are usually questions about motivation, the topic we focus on now. We begin with the case of Richard Alpert. Alpert's story is told by David McClelland, a psychologist who has studied motivation most of his life.

The Case of Richard Alpert

"[Richard Alpert] was born into a wealthy, powerful Jewish family living in a suburb of Boston, Massachusetts. His father was an influential lawyer. . . . Dick Alpert had all the material advantages that wealth could provide plus the knowledge that his family and their connections were in a position to give him powerful assistance in any career he chose. . . . He chose to be a psychologist. . . . His ca-reer in psychology looked very promising. He sums it up as follows:

"'In 1961, the beginning of March, I was perhaps at the highest point of my academic career. . . . I had been assured of a permanent post that was being held for me at Harvard, if I got my publications in order. . . . In a worldly sense I was making a great income and I was a collector of possessions. I had an apartment in Cambridge that was filled with antiques, and I gave very charming dinner parties. I had a Mercedes-Benz sedan, and a Triumph 500 cc motorcycle and a Cessna airplane and an MG sportscar and a bicycle. I vacationed in the Caribbean where I did scuba diving. I was living the way a successful bachelor professor is supposed to live in the American world of 'he who makes it.' I

FIGURE 10-1 As a behavioral scientist, Richard Alpert enjoyed all sorts of material possessions. As Baba Ram Dass, an Indian-style mystic and spiritual teacher, he owned nothing. Richard Alpert had studied human motivation. As Baba Ram Dass, he came to accept the Hindu-Buddhist belief that desire causes suffering and that the goal of life is the renunciation of all motivated striving. Identifying Alpert's motives may be a first step toward understanding his behavior. [*Wide World Photos; Hanuman Foundation and Unity Press.*]

wasn't a genuine scholar, but I had gone through the whole academic trip. I had gotten my Ph.D.; I was writing books. I had research contracts. I taught courses in human motivation, Freudian theory, child development.'

"At this point [Alpert] began taking . . . hallucinogenic drugs in collaboration with another psychologist. . . . Although Alpert took them at first in the genuine spirit of scientific inquiry, their effect on him personally was so powerful that he began to feel they might provide meaning to a life which, though successful, had come to seem empty to him. . . . Eventually, [Alpert] abandoned his position as a psychologist in the 'establishment' in order to spend full-time exploring varieties of drug experiences and setting up environments where people could take drugs without being persecuted by society. After six years of this, he still felt that he had not found what he was looking for. No matter how 'high' he became on drugs for periods of time, he always 'came down.' He was still the old, sad, disillusioned Richard Alpert."

In 1967 Alpert went to India in search of someone to guide him to a more satisfactory life. He encountered a spiritual teacher, experienced a profound conversion, and began to master meditation and yoga. "[Alpert] learned to go without speaking for months, . . . to sit in meditation in a small white room devoid of decoration, to go without food for days, and [to] wander around India as a barefoot sadhu [a holy person]. In the end he changed his way of life entirely—his name, his clothing, above all his worship of the rational mind. His guru [spiritual teacher] took over the direction of his life [1]." (See Figure 10-1.)

How can Alpert's change of identity be explained? We are asking, in essence, what motivated his striking transformation. Like the general public, behavioral scientists often observe behavior and make inferences about motivation. Using this approach, McClelland suggests that Alpert's identity change is not so radical as it appears. The new behavioral patterns seemed to satisfy many of the motives that dominated him previously. As McClelland sees it, Alpert showed the same needs in both identities: needs for attention from an audience, fantasy and a rich inner world of feeling, the opportunity to nurture or help others, guidance and independence, knowledge of the world (the type not provided by academic pursuits), and especially power (the ability to directly influence people).

How do behavioral scientists' efforts to understand motivation differ from everyday attempts? Psychologists, as we will see, have devised careful measures of motivation. And their investigations tend to focus on the factors that shape the strength and persistence of motivated behavior. Typically, behavioral scientists study the physiological mechanisms and environmental conditions that turn motivation on and off. They also explore the malfunctioning of motives. As we examine research findings on motivation for food, sexual activity, and achievement, we focus on topics such as these. But first, we examine several preliminary issues.

MOTIVATION: PRELIMINARY ISSUES

In this section we will try to answer these questions: When did psychologists first begin investigating motives? How are motives defined? How do motives, drives, and instincts differ from one another? What types of motives do behavioral scientists study? How do motives arouse behavior? What problems arise when psychologists study human motivation?

Motivation: A Historical Perspective

At the beginning of the twentieth century, motives became an important topic in psychology largely because of the efforts of William McDougall (1871–1938), a British behavioral scientist. He called motives "instincts" and defined them as irrational, compelling, inherited forces which shape virtually everything people do, feel, perceive, and think. Many early psychologists accepted McDougall's general view and set to work trying to identify the specific instincts which might account for all human actions. McDougall's own list, published in 1908, included curiosity, repulsion, aggression, self-assertion, flight, child rearing, reproduction, hunger, sociability, acquisitiveness, and constructiveness [2]. Many behavioral scientists were dissatisfied with this relatively brief list and proceeded to name literally thousands of instincts, including instincts to be moral, to estimate the age of each passerby in the street, and to avoid eating apples in one's own orchard [3]. It soon became clear that labeling every act an instinct (or motive) was unproductive and did not contribute one iota to any real understanding of why organisms behave as they do. In the words of one critic:

Man is impelled to action, it is said, by his instincts. If he goes with his fellows, it is the "herd instinct" which actuates him; if he walks alone, it is the "anti-social instinct"; if he fights, it is the instinct of pugnacity; if he defers to another, it is the instinct of self-abasement; if he twiddles his thumbs, it is the thumb-twiddling instinct; if he does not twiddle his thumbs, it is the thumb-not-twiddling instinct.

Thus everything is explained with the facility of magic—word magic. [4]

Today psychologists spend relatively little time trying to identify specific types of motives. Most investigators focus on describing and explaining influences on motivated behavior.

Defining Motivational Terms

Psychologists use the words "motive," "need," "drive," and "instinct" in specific ways. All these terms are *constructs*, hypothesized internal processes that appear to explain behavior but that cannot be observed or measured directly. The term *needs* applies to deficiencies which may be based on specific bodily or learned requirements or on some combination of the two. *Motive*, or *motivation*, refers to an internal state which results from a need and which activates, or arouses, behavior that is usually directed toward fulfilling the activating need. Motives which seem to be established largely by experiences are known simply as motives. Those that arise to satisfy basic physiological needs (for food and water, for example) are called *drives*. For research purposes, specific motives and drives are usually defined operationally (Chapter 2) in terms of the procedures used to measure them. What are instincts? The term *instinct* is occasionally used for physiological needs and for complicated behavior patterns that appear to be primarily hereditary in origin. Today many behavioral scientists prefer the term *fixed action pattern* to instinct, since the former expression does not carry the implication that the conduct in question is preset by heredity. Fixed action patterns, as suggested in Chapter 5, are influenced by both genetic and environmental factors.

The Motives Psychologists Study

Psychologists are currently studying motives in the following categories: basic drives, social motives, motives for sensory stimulation (exploration and manipulation), growth motives, and ideas as motives. We describe each category briefly.

Basic drives As we mentioned before, *drives*, or *basic drives*, are motives that activate behavior aimed at satisfying survival-related needs rooted in physiology. Drives arise to fulfill needs for oxygen, water, food, sex, and the avoidance of pain. In a book called *The Wisdom of the Body* (1932), the distinguished American physiologist Walter Cannon described the remarkable manner in which an animal's various bodily systems automatically maintain a properly balanced environment, or *equilibrium* condition. In people, for example, internal temperature is kept within certain critical limits near 98.6°F. Similarly, the concentrations of elements (such as salt, sugar, and calcium) in the blood are automatically maintained at relatively constant levels. The body's self-regulating tendency is known as *homeostasis* (from the Greek words meaning "similar state"). Whenever automatic mechanisms in the body are unable to maintain a balanced state, a need is said to exist. Presumably, a drive is then activated which causes animals to take action to correct the imbalance.

Though drives arise to fulfill bodily needs, the behavior they instigate may be heavily influenced by experience. Consider hunger for a moment. When you feel hungry, you seek out certain foods. Psychological research suggests that early experiences in a specific environment may establish lasting food preferences [5]. The observations of Dorothy Lee, a nutrition expert, make this point clearly:

We do not recognize dragon-flies as human food; the Ifugao do. They eat three species of dragon-fly, as well as locusts which are boiled, then dried, then powdered and stored for food. They eat crickets and flying ants which they fry in lard. They eat red ants and water bugs and a variety of beetles. I doubt that I would recognize these insects as food, however hungry I might be. On the other hand, I regard milk as food, a fluid which some cultural groups regard with disgust and as akin to a mucous discharge. [6]

Keep in mind that drives are often influenced by environmental factors.

Social motives Much human behavior appears to be directed toward satisfying *social motives*, those whose fulfillment depends on contact with other human beings. Social motives arise to satisfy needs for feeling loved, accepted, approved, and esteemed, for instance. From the very first, infants depend on others. If it were possible to design a computer to take care of the baby's basic drives, infants would probably survive. But they would not develop normally without the sensory and social stimulation that other people provide, a topic explored in Chapter 3. Warmth and acceptance appear to be important for successful adjustment. When youngsters feel loved, conditions such as severe poverty, physical handicaps, and harsh discipline, which might otherwise impair development, seem to cause relatively little damage [7]. Human beings who have a great deal of social support (from family and friends) cope more adequately with crises, as we will see in Chapter 14. When people are rejected by the members of their society and socially isolated, they often feel deeply disturbed. Some support for this notion comes from studies of groups of scientists, military officers, and enlisted personnel who gathered scientific data at bases in the Antarctic for approximately a year. Occasionally, when individuals were particularly troublesome, the group ignored them completely. Isolates developed the "long eye" syndrome. They could not sleep. They were prone to crying outbursts. They neglected their personal hygiene and daily routines. And they appeared aimless and apathetic. As soon as the individual was accepted once again by the group, these symptoms of severe depression disappeared [8].

Motives for sensory stimulation People and other animals require stimulation. We often provide our own by daydreaming, whistling, and humming. Some recent research by psychologist Mihaly Csikszentmihalyi suggests that when self-stimulating activities, such as these, are given up, daily routines become tedious and laborious. Irritability, depression, and feelings of being machinelike increase. At the same time, spontaneous creative actions decrease [9]. People appear to operate most effectively with information coming in at a specific rate. If we are understressed or overstressed, our performance deteriorates. When human beings are deprived of sensory experiences for prolonged periods of time or exposed to a constant unchanging environment, as in sensory deprivation studies (Chapter 6) or during activities such as long-distance trucking, they often hallucinate. In these instances, hallucinations appear to provide necessary stimulation. Though everyone requires some stimulation, individuals show consistent differences in how much activity they prefer. Psychologist Marvin Zuckerman has devised a test to measure the degree that human beings seek sensations. Four items from an early version of his sensation-seeking test are presented in Table 10-1. Please answer the questions on the test before reading on.

People classified as high sensation seekers tend to show four related characteristics:

1. Desires to seek excitement in physically risky but socially acceptable activities (such as parachute jumping, diving, fast driving, and the like)
2. Desires to pursue unusual mental and sensual experiences and a nonconforming life-style
3. Preferences for partying, gambling, drinking, and sexual adventures
4. Low tolerance for repetitious or constant experiences [10]

What molds sensation-seeking motivation? Experience appears to influence this motive. Monkeys that live on the outskirts of villages where they are exposed to a rich variety of changing conditions show a definite preference for more complicated visual displays than jungle monkeys on laboratory tests [11]. Neurotransmitter (Chapter 4) and sex hormone levels, which are partially set by heredity, appear to play a role too. The levels of these bodily substances are associated consistently with specific response styles to sensory stimulation [12].

Motivation to explore and manipulate the environment, which is frequently called *curiosity*, is probably related to the need for sensory stimulation. Many animals besides people show this motive. Monkeys, for instance, will solve a puzzle for the intrinsic satisfaction of doing so. When they are confined, they have been observed to work as long as nineteen hours to open a door just to see what is going on outside [13]. See Figure 10-2. Such varied human pursuits as reading novels, climbing mountains, and conducting scientific research could all result from a motive to explore and manipulate. People tend to be attracted to what is new. We investigate novel objects and events to make sense of them [14]. This type of perceptual sensitivity has survival value, as pointed out earlier. Animals that attend to new experiences will be more apt to notice and react competently to unexpected conditions which may require life-or-death decisions.

Growth motives To explain why people strive for mastery or excellence or why they work to perfect a talent in situations where recognition is unlikely, many psychologists assume the existence of basic needs to develop

TABLE 10-1 Items from an Early Version of a Test Measuring Sensation-Seeking Motivation

Instructions: For each item, circle the response (*a* or *b*) that best describes your likes or dislikes.

2. a. I am invigorated by a brisk, cold day.
   b. I can't wait to get indoors on a cold day.

3. a. I get bored seeing the same old faces.
   b. I like the comfortable familiarity of everyday friends.

4. a. I would prefer living in an ideal society in which everyone is safe, secure, and happy.
   b. I would have preferred living in the unsettled days of our history.

9. a. I enter cold water gradually, giving myself time to get used to it.
   b. I like to dive or jump right into the ocean or a cold pool.

Scoring: Count one point for circling each of the following items: 2*a*, 3*a*, 4*b*, 9*b*. Add up your points. The higher the total, the more likely you are to be classified as a sensation seeker.

FIGURE 10-2 Harry Harlow was one of the first psychologists to study curiosity in the laboratory. He and his coworkers found that monkeys would learn merely for the reward of manipulating an object. In the study pictured here, animals repeatedly worked the puzzle of a pin, hook, eye, and clasp without external incentives. Harlow found evidence that puzzles of various types generate a drive to manipulate and explore that acts like other basic physiological drives. Both monkeys and chimpanzees prefer movable objects to fixed ones and gadgets that produce sounds and lights to those that do not change the environment. Young animals consistently display more manipulatory behavior than older ones [102]. [*Harry F. Harlow, University of Wisconsin Primate Laboratory.*]

competence and actualize potential. Presumably, such needs arouse growth motives, which are closely related to those for sensory stimulation, exploration, and manipulation. Robert White was one of the first behavioral scientists to discuss the motive to attain competence. Studies of the exploratory play of children convinced White that the directness and persistence of these efforts provided evidence for the existence of a motive to master the environment [15]. Additional support for the existence of growth motives comes from observations indicating that youngsters all over the world struggle to coordinate bodily movements, communicate, and reason at approximately the same ages, regardless of their special circumstances. Adults strive for mastery too, of course. The achievement motive, which we discuss later, is sometimes considered a growth motive.

Ideas as motives In our own society and in many others, people seek values, beliefs, goals, and plans to guide their behavior. While there is little research on this topic, informal observations suggest that ideas can be intensely motivating. They may even override very fundamental drives. Alpert's ideals were responsible for acts of social isolation and denial of bodily needs. Recently, a popular magazine reported the case of a pastor and a lay person in Tennessee who died in agony after drinking strychnine and water. The men had been testing the notion that true believers may "drink any deadly thing and it shall not hurt them," as stated in the Book of Mark [16]. In this case, the idea of testing one's faith functioned like a motive.

The need for intellectual, or cognitive, consistency often motivates behavior. If cognitions (knowledge, ideas, or perceptions, for instance) conflict with, or contradict, one another, people feel uncomfortable. At the same time, they feel motivated to reduce the *cognitive dissonance* (the anxiety produced by the clash). In such cases, individuals usually seek out new information, change their behavior, or alter their attitudes. Psychologist Leon Festinger has described three common predicaments which activate cognitive dissonance and motivate behavior [17]:

1. Dissonance occurs when personal cognitions are inconsistent with social standards. Put yourself in the following situation. You consider yourself an honest person. But you haven't time to study for a test. So you copy several answers from a friend. You thought you were honest and you cheated. Your own behavior conflicts with a social ideal. You're likely to feel uncomfortable until you resolve the dissonance. You might change your attitude about cheating. ("Cheating is okay under special circumstances.") You might alter your ideas about your own dishonesty. ("I was going to give those answers myself.") You might resolve never to cheat again and attribute your "mistake" to having the flu. Or you might decide cheating pays and cheat in the future. You have a large number of options. The point is this: You're likely to feel motivated to remove the contradiction.

2. Dissonance arises when people expect one event and another occurs. Suppose that Celia promises to meet you at 4 o'clock and doesn't show up. Once again, you're apt to experience anxiety and feel motivated to reduce it. You might demand an explanation or an apology, assuming that your friend had a legitimate excuse, or cross Celia off your list of buddies. In Chapter 2, you may recall, we described a group of religious zealots who predicted that the world would be destroyed by floods and earthquakes on a particular December day and that only a few faithful group members would be rescued beforehand by flying saucers. To reduce cognitive dissonance after the appointed hour passed without event, the group members decided that God had saved the world from destruction because they had succeeded in spreading their faith throughout the world.

3. Dissonance occurs when individuals engage in behavior at variance with their general attitudes. Suppose that you think of yourself as a hater of classical music but find yourself enjoying an opera presented on television. Once again you'll probably feel uncomfortable and motivated to resolve the discrepancy between your former attitude and your new behavior.

There is a great deal of research on the motivating force of cognitive dissonance. Much of the literature suggests that people, especially intellectually oriented individuals, are motivated by a desire to keep their cognitions consistent [18]. ▲

The Operation of Motives

How do motives operate? A number of models attempt to explain the major processes involved when motives activate behavior. We describe a homeostatic model that applies to many basic drives and additional elements that must often be considered.

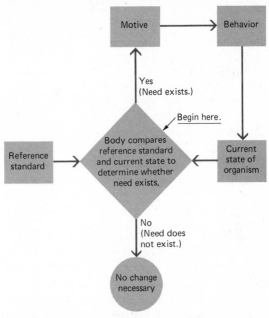

FIGURE 10-3 The homeostatic model of motivation. While this model may look complicated initially, it is not difficult to understand. We are assuming that the body compares its current condition with its optimal state (designated reference standard) to determine if a need exists. To see what happens when a need is found, start at the diamond and follow the arrow marked "yes." To see what happens when no need is found, follow the arrow marked "No."

A homeostatic model Many basic drives appear to follow the model pictured in Figure 10-3. A need arises when the body departs significantly from its optimal, or ideal, state. The reference standard for that optimal state

▲ USING PSYCHOLOGY

1. Identify the types of motives to which five TV or magazine ads attempt to appeal.

2. Make a list of activities that you engage in frequently and consider important. Your list may include such activities as eating, sleeping, and talking to friends. What types of motives probably arouse each behavior?

3. Gather personal examples of behaviors that could be motivated by growth and idea-related motives.

4. Give three new examples of cognitive dissonance (one in each of the categories mentioned in the text). Describe how you would be likely to reduce the dissonance.

is assumed to be set either by heredity or by some combination of heredity and experience. To restore the balance, the need activates a motive. The motive then triggers behavior aimed at returning the equilibrium condition. This model assumes that motives are part of the body's grand scheme for self-regulation, or *homeostasis*. As an example of a motive that fits this model well, consider *specific hungers*. Rats, cats, cows, pigs, chickens, and many other creatures choose a well-balanced diet if they are allowed to pick their meals from a wide range of natural, unsweetened foods. These animals will often actively seek out substances in which their diets are deficient [19]. People exhibit similar self-regulating tendencies, at least under certain conditions. One physician found that when infants chose their diets from a wide assortment of natural foods (harmful foods excluded), they grew and thrived. In some cases, they even compensated for physiological deficiencies [20]. Addison's disease is a condition which progressively destroys the adrenal cortex (a part of the adrenal gland) and prevents the retention of salt. People with this illness frequently experience cravings for foods high in salt, such as ham and sauerkraut. In one case, a thirty-four-year-old man with the disease put an eighth-inch layer of salt on his steak and mixed a half-glass of salt with his tomato juice. Similarly, children with parathyroid deficiencies sometimes eat chalk,

FIGURE 10-4 Various elements that may influence motives are pictured here. We assume that experiences and incentives often alter cognitions and emotions and lead to motivation. Presumably, motivation then arouses behavior. Behavior may alter cognitions and emotions, in turn increasing or decreasing the level of motivation.

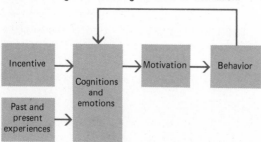

plaster, and other substances high in calcium. People with pernicious anemia may crave and consume enough liver to keep themselves reasonably healthy [21]. In all these cases, a dietary deficiency appears to cause the body to depart from an internal equilibrium, producing a need for a particular substance. Presumably, the need arouses a drive, and the drive activates behavior that may return the body to its balanced state. Certain drug addictions fit this model, too. When introduced into the body at regular intervals, substances like heroin and alcohol create new, artificial chemical equilibria. Then, when this new balance is disturbed because alcohol or heroin are not available soon enough, bodily needs arise and arouse a motive. The motive activates behavior aimed at attaining the substance and restoring the balance.

The influence of incentives, emotions, and cognitions The homeostatic model just described may be helpful for understanding many basic drives. But it does not adequately explain the working of all motives. Consider motivation for sex, sensory experiences, and growth. Equilibrium states do not seem to play a central role in their operation. Instead, *incentives* (which we define as objects, events, or conditions that incite action), *emotions*, and *cognitions* are dominant forces. Incentives stimulate certain cognitions and emotions. Past and present experiences may help establish the value of the incentive. The thoughts and feelings activated by the incentive arouse some level of motivation. The motivation tends to activate behavior aimed at securing the incentive. The actions that are taken probably influence cognitions and emotions, in turn, which then decrease, maintain, or stengthen the motivation. Figure 10-4 shows these important influences on motivation. Since needs generally cannot be distinguished from motives in these cases, the two terms tend to be used interchangeably.

Consider a motive that fits this framework. Suppose that you are an avid movie buff. An enthusiastic film critique could function as an incentive for this type of sensory stimulation, especially if you have enjoyed films that the reviewer praised in the past and you haven't seen a movie in a month. The power of the film critique incentive clearly depends on past and recent experiences. If the film critic has been a dud in your opinion or if you just attended a two-week film festival, the review is unlikely to function as an incentive. If the critique arouses positive feelings and expectations, you will probably feel motivated to see the film—to satisfy your motivation for sensory stimulation.

Incentives, emotions, and cognitions often affect basic drives too. Consider hunger. Seeing a pizza parlor might excite happy memories and produce expectations of a pleasant experience, especially if you haven't eaten recently. These thoughts and feelings may stimulate hunger motivation which arouses behavior, such as entering the pizza parlor and ordering and eating a pizza.

Psychologists sometimes distinguish between *intrinsic* and *extrinsic* incentives in much the same way that they differentiate between intrinsic and extrinsic reinforcers (Chapter 5). You may read, for instance, because of an extrinsic incentive (one *outside* the reading activity itself), such as a good grade or praise. Or, you may read because of incentives that are *built into*, or intrinsic to, the behavior. Reading may be enjoyable and make you feel knowledgeable. What is intrinsically motivating varies, at least to some extent, from person to person, depending on past and current experiences. At the same time, many stimulation- and growth-related activities tend to be intrinsically motivating for a great many human beings. So are many basic drives—hunger and sex, most notably.

A Hierarchy of Motives

The late humanistic psychologist Abraham Maslow proposed that human beings are born with five systems of needs which are arranged in a hierarchy, as pictured in Figure 10-5. People remain "wanting animals" all their lives. As one set of needs is satisfied, a new set replaces it. We work our way up through

FIGURE 10-5 Abraham Maslow's hierarchy of needs.

the various systems in the order shown. We begin with physiological needs—those for food, water, oxygen, sleep, sex, protection from temperature extremes, sensory stimulation, and activity, according to Maslow. These needs, which represent requirements for bare survival, are the strongest, or most compelling, ones. They must be gratified to some degree before other needs can emerge. If only one of these needs remains unfulfilled, it may dominate all the others. In Maslow's words:

For our chronically and extremely hungry man, Utopia can be defined simply as a place where there is plenty of food. He tends to think that, if only he is guaranteed food for the rest of his life, he will be perfectly happy and will never want anything more. Life itself tends to be defined in terms of eating. Anything else will be defined as unimportant. Freedom, love, community feeling, respect, philosophy, may all be waved aside as fripperies that are useless, since they fail to fill the stomach. Such a man may fairly be said to live by bread alone. [22]

Once the physiological needs are satisfied, needs to feel protected, free of danger, and secure become apparent. Children want routines they can depend on. Adults desire stable jobs, savings accounts, and insurance. People may adopt religions and philosophies to organize their lives and give a sense of security. Once the safety needs are achieved, needs for affection, intimacy, and belonging emerge.

FIGURE 10-6   In the late 1960s anthropologist Colin Turnbull studied the Ik, a tribe of hunters in the mountains of northern Uganda. Two Ik children are pictured here. A government decision to create a national park displaced the Ik from their old hunting grounds with disastrous results. The mountain people were deprived of their traditional food supply and forced to farm barren, rocky soil that yielded little. As the Ik began to starve, their social structure deteriorated, providing some gruesome anecdotal support for Maslow's ideas. One motive, hunger, and one behavior, the search for food, dominated the tribe. As Turnbull saw it, the single-minded pursuit of food turned every person against every other. Love and affection were abandoned as "idiotic" and "highly dangerous." "A chilly void" and mutual exploitation remained. Houses were built with low doorways so that intruders searching for food could be speared in the back of the neck. Family sentiment also vanished. Children of three years were routinely abandoned to fend for themselves. Liza, on the left, starved to death while his older brother Murai thrived. Liza would watch his brother eat, showing no malice or hatred, according to Turnbull. As Murai put it, "Surely it is better that one lives than that both should die." In some cases, Ik youngsters who could no longer find food were penned and left to die. Grandparents too were allowed to starve. Life-style changes among the Ik appear to illustrate the enormous strength of unfulfilled primitive drives [103]. [*Colin Turnbull,* The mountain people, *Simon and Schuster. With permission.*]

People seek to love and be loved. In Maslow's view, modern urban life is lonely. The breakdown of traditional family ties, the disappearance of village face-to-face social interactions, and the impersonality of daily activities in big cities interfere with satisfying the love needs. If these needs are filled somehow, needs to be esteemed by oneself and others dominate. People want to feel valued in their community, at work and at home. They want to respect themselves, too. Finally, when all other needs are secured, people search for self-actualization. They struggle to realize their potential capabilities and fulfill their ideals. Maslow believed that actualization needs (growth needs) which enhance and do not merely preserve life predominate in healthy personalities. Yet, according to him, only about 1 percent of the population achieve self-actualization. (We described the traits of self-actualized persons in Chapter 1.) Why do human beings rarely achieve self-actualization? Most of us, Maslow believed, are blind to our own potential. We tend to conform to cultural stereotypes rather than pursue more personal needs. Maslow also believed that safety needs make people fearful of risk taking and likely to close themselves off to new experiences.

Though numerous studies support specific predictions derived from Maslow's theory, no one has found a satisfactory way to investigate the model as a whole. Still, the theory tends to be accepted widely because it is intuitively appealing and fits many informal observations, as seen in Figure 10-6.

The Difficulties of Studying Human Motives

Because they cannot be directly observed or measured, motives are very difficult to study. Psychologists can take animals, deprive them of basic needs, and observe subsequent behavior. To study the sex drive, for example, male and female rats might be isolated from one another for several weeks. Then behavioral scientists might assess how quickly females or males press a bar to gain access to a receptive partner. Psychologists sometimes adopt similar strategies in studying human motives. They may attempt to arouse needs and observe resulting behaviors, such as the choices people make, the persistence or intensity of responses, and the emotional reactions that accompany success or failure to achieve goals. But behavioral observations are hard to interpret for several reasons.

1. A particular behavior can be aroused by several different motives or a combination of motives. Consider the act of watching the evening news on TV. This response might arise from any of several social needs (to comply with orders, to achieve recognition, and/or to avoid failure and subsequent humiliation, for instance). Or, you might watch the news to increase your own understanding, a growth need, and/or for sensory stimulation.
2. Diverse behaviors may satisfy the same need. You might fulfill a need to achieve excellence by becoming a track star, robbing a bank, solving a difficult mechanical problem, or capturing a rare butterfly.
3. Motives do not necessarily produce behavior aimed at satisfying the needs that were aroused.

Consider the plight of a small-town adolescent girl with a need to love and be loved. She may not believe that there are suitable candidates around and spend most of her time daydreaming. Or, although the girl may be fascinated by the town's most eligible bachelor, she may not express her motives outwardly because she is anxious, feels doomed to failure, lacks appropriate skills, or has conflicting needs.

Self-report devices such as interviews, questionnaires, and psychological tests provide an alternative to observation. But, human beings are often unaware of their own motives. Freud believed that we block threatening needs, especially those concerned with sex and aggression, from consciousness. Recently, psychologists Richard Nisbett and Timothy Wilson reviewed a number of studies which had used both self-report and behavioral measures of conduct. Nisbett and Wilson found that people often failed to recognize changes in their own behavior, even though these changes were clear to investigators. When asked to specify why they acted as they did, research participants supplied reasons that seemed to have been inferred from their actions. These observations suggest that people are not in direct touch with their inner experiences [23]. Self-report measures have additional problems that have been mentioned before (Chapter 2).

As we examine research on hunger, sex, and achievement motivation, we will see how psychologists struggle to overcome measurement problems by combining behavioral, physiological, and self-report strategies. ▲

▲ USING PSYCHOLOGY

1. Using the diagrams in Figures 10-3 and 10-4, explain how motives appear to operate. Give new illustrations for each model.

2. Describe a way to test some aspect of Maslow's needs hierarchy theory.

3. Suppose that you were trying to teach impoverished, distrustful third-grade children. How could you apply Maslow's theories so that your students would be more likely to learn?

4. Consider Richard Alpert's conduct (described early in this chapter). Why are his motives so difficult to discern from his behavior?

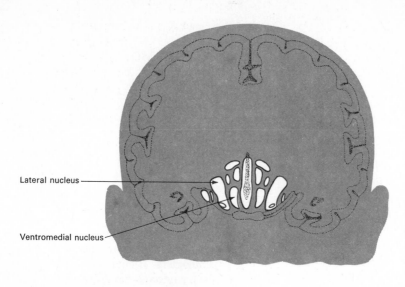

Lateral nucleus

Ventromedial nucleus

FIGURE 10-7 The hypothalamus, consisting of nerve cell groupings in the central portion of the brain, is shown in white.

HUNGER AND EATING

All animals need food to meet their daily requirements for energy, growth, and tissue repair. Although very few organisms consciously regulate their food intake, most man-

FIGURE 10-8 When the ventromedial nucleus of the hypothalamus is removed, animals overeat until they reach a size some two to four times normal. The mechanism behind these dramatic weight changes is not currently clear. [*Dr. Neal E. Miller.*]

age to consume the precise amount of food needed to accomplish these tasks, and no more. This is a rather miraculous feat when you consider what is involved. To maintain a constant body weight, the number of calories an animal takes in each day must balance the number of calories used. (The calorie is the unit expressing the fuel or energy value of food.) Every time a prson consumes approximately 3,500 calories more than is needed for energy, a pound is gained. The person who errs by only 100 calories each day (by eating an extra ounce of cheese or half a chocolate bar or by omitting a twenty-minute walk) may gain 10 pounds each year. That's 50 pounds in five years. How do human beings and other animals know when to eat and when to stop eating? Hunger, as we will see, does not always follow a homeostatic model. It is influenced very strongly by incentives, cognitions, and emotions. We look first at physiological mechanisms that regulate hunger. We then examine environmental influences on the drive. Finally, we see what happens when the motive operates ineffectively and people become obese.

Physiological Mechanisms that Regulate Hunger

Before reading further, you may find it helpful to review the physiology of the nervous system. Many of the physiological and anatomical terms in this and subsequent sections are defined more precisely in Chapter 4 and in the Glossary.

The brain Our brains use signals from the stomach, mouth, throat, blood, and perhaps other sources to make decisions about when we should eat and stop eating. Though a number of brain centers are probably involved in hunger regulation, the dramatic results of early experiments have led researchers to focus on the role of the *hypothalamus*, a group of nerve cells in the central portion of the brain (shown in Figure 10-7). By removing or destroying the *ventromedial nucleus* of the hypothalamus (sometimes called the *satiety center*), physiological psychologists can create rats that eat excessively until they double their weight, as shown in Figure 10-8. When the ventromedial nucleus is stimulated, starving animals do not eat. If cells in the *lateral nucleus* of the hypothalamus (sometimes called the *feeding center*) are removed, appetite loss occurs. Hungry rats reduce their intake so drastically that they die of starvation unless forcibly fed. Stimulation of this site produces feeding even in rats that have just finished gorging themselves [24]. These observations suggest that the hypothalamus contains important hunger-regulating centers. But this may not be the case. Recent research indicates that a number of nerve circuits that merely pass through the hypothalamus, including the trigeminal nerve which we will discuss later, are responsible for these effects. Stimulation or damage to these nerve tracts appears to have caused the overeating and obesity or loss of appetite and starvation that have been seen [25]. Right now, the role of the hypothalamus in regulating hunger is unclear. At the very least, the hypothalamus appears to be responsible for the general arousal that accompanies many motives, including hunger, thirst, and activity [26]. The hypothalamus may play other important roles in motivating feeding.

The stomach Many people link hunger to the growling and groaning of their stomachs, often called "hunger pangs." So did early psychologists, following the lead of the physiologist Walter Cannon. For one ingenious study, Cannon persuaded his research assistant, A. L. Washburn, to swallow a thin rubber balloon at the end of a tube. Once the balloon reached Washburn's stomach, it was inflated so that it touched the stomach walls. Then, whenever stomach contractions occurred, the balloon was pinched and the air pressure at the end of a tube changed. Every time Washburn felt a hunger pang, he pressed a telegraph key. Signals from both the balloon and telegraph key were recorded. You can see Cannon's apparatus in Figure 10-9. Reported pangs coincided quite consistently with stom-

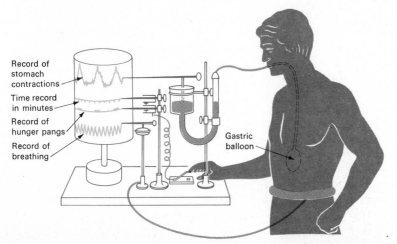

Record of stomach contractions

Time record in minutes

Record of hunger pangs

Record of breathing

Gastric balloon

FIGURE 10-9 Cannon used equipment like this to record stomach contractions and hunger pangs simultaneously. [*After Cannon, 1934.*]

ach contractions. These findings, which were confirmed on additional volunteers, convinced Cannon that the stomach signals the brain whenever the body needs food [27].

Later research suggests that stomach irritation, due to the balloon itself, was partly responsible for the contractions. Still, Cannon was correct in assuming that the stomach helps regulate hunger. Stomach sensations, especially distention after a large meal, are monitored by the brain to judge whether eating should cease [28].

What about hunger pangs? They appear to be partially learned by respondent conditioning (Chapter 5). The stomach must churn food to digest it. When a person eats at regular times each day, the brain seems to anticipate meals approximately an hour beforehand. Accordingly, it sends neural signals to alert the stomach muscles to prepare for action. The muscles then contract, producing the gnawing sensations which are interpreted by other parts of the brain as hunger.

The mouth and throat Messages to the brain from the mouth and throat about chewing, sucking, and swallowing affect how much animals eat [29]. After a reasonable amount of chews, sucks, and swallows and even before any nutritive materials have been absorbed into the bloodstream, the brain signals the person to stop eating. Taste plays a role in limiting food intake, too. The greater the variety of food stuffs available, the more laboratory animals appear to eat [30], a smorgasbord-like effect. A recent program of research by physiological psychologist H. D. Zeigler and anatomist Harvey Karten indicates that the *trigeminal nerve*, which carries information to the brain about the texture and temperature of substances within the mouth, is particularly important in food regulation. When Zeigler and Karten cut pigeons' trigeminal pathways, the birds stopped pecking for food for more than a month. Consequently, they lost enough weight to starve to death, had they not been tube-fed. Even though the birds eventually began pecking for food again, they did not

regain their previous appetites. They ate only about one-tenth to one-twentieth as frequently as before, and remained drastically underweight. Similar deficits were produced in rats by comparable procedures [31]. Oral sensations play at least two roles in controlling feeding. They help the brain to guide and coordinate the specific foods that are eaten. And, along with other inputs to the reticular formation, they help arouse the cortex so that our appetites are stimulated and we feel motivated to eat.

The composition of the blood The composition of the blood provides information about the state of the body's internal environment [32]. The brain takes these data into account too in deciding when to turn hunger on and off. Currently, scientists suspect that the blood provides a number of signals. Both glucose and fat appear to be involved. After a meal, certain powerful *enzymes* in our saliva and stomachs break food down into protein, sugar, and fat molecules which the body can utilize. One type of sugar molecule, called *glucose*, is essential for supplying cells with energy. Experiments suggest that if the glucose level of the blood is high, people and other animals feel full. When the glucose level is low, organisms tend to experience hunger sensations [33]. Besides sensing glucose level, our brains appear to monitor fat-related chemicals or deposits in the bloodstream [34]. Glucose signals seem to help people take in an appropriate quantity of food at meals and as snacks. Fat signals are thought to assist in monitoring weight over long periods. Currently, many behavioral scientists believe that animals have an optimum weight level recorded somewhere within their nervous systems. If the organism is below that standard, signals that monitor fat reserves and reflect current weight inform the brain. Presumably, animals then feel motivated to eat more. When organisms become heavier than their internally set weight level, fat-related signals may pass along this information so that animals feel motivated to eat somewhat less. Nerve cells sensitive to glucose and fat levels have been found in the hypothalamus.

In sum, the brain appears to monitor signals from the stomach, mouth and throat, and blood to help control the hunger drive. Scientists do not understand the hunger-regulating machinery precisely. Nor have they identified the most essential cues that control the system over the short and long runs. In addition to the physical mechanisms that we have described, many others, including hormone levels, body temperature, activity, and disease, influence when people eat and stop eating. To complicate the picture further, environmental influences play an important part in regulating human hunger.

Environmental Influences on Hunger

Children learn a great many lessons about when to eat, how much to eat, and when to stop eating from their families and cultures. The majority of these lessons are subtle ones. Parental practices probably establish how much food constitutes a serving and how many servings to allow per meal. Adults may teach what state of stomach distention to label as "full." "Full" may be associated with a heavy, painful, filled-with-lead sensation or with a much milder feeling. Parents set standards for how frequently and on what occasions eating is appropriate. Children are easily trained to snack after school or before bedtime, for instance. If particular places or activities are associated repeatedly with eating, the places and activities themselves soon begin to elicit hunger, sometimes for the specific foods that have been linked with the setting, by respondent conditioning. Movies and popcorn, baseball games and hot dogs, and TV and potato chips are commonly "connected" by this type of training. Emotions may be tied to eating if youngsters are encouraged to snack when angry, bored, frustrated, or otherwise emotionally troubled. Because eating is usually pleasurable, it is often an excellent distraction, in addition. So intrinsically positive consequences may reinforce the eating-when-upset syndrome, in-

creasing its future probability. An "irresistible impulse" to eat during emotional crises could be the product of both respondent and operant conditioning.

Social conventions influence when people eat too. Still stuffed with breakfast, you might take coffee and a doughnut to be sociable at a coffee break. You might eat dinner because it's six o'clock. Or you might find room for dessert because a refusal might be construed as "rude" or "unfriendly," even though you have eaten recently.

Human hunger, then, is frequently controlled by *external food-related cues* (*incentives*), events which trigger eating even though people are not hungry. The attractive appearance of food, the sight of others eating, the taste or aroma of a favorite dish, and particular times, places, or emotions are all examples of external food-related incentives. We call these conditions "external" because they are unrelated to internal, physiological, hunger-related incentives such as headaches, fatigue, dizziness, and dry sensations in the mouth and throat.

Causes of Obesity

When controls on eating fail to operate as they should and people take in more calories than are needed for current energy requirements, they become obese. The term *obese* is usually applied to individuals who have accumulated an excessive amount of *adipose*, or fat, tissue and are at least 20 percent above their ideal weight. According to a recent estimate, approximately 35 percent of Americans forty and older are obese [35].

Although *obesity* is usually written as a singular noun, it would probably be more accurate to use the plural, "*obesities*." More than a dozen different types of genetically determined obesities have been identified in mice. Mice also become overweight when put on high-fat diets, kept immobile, injected with various chemicals, or altered by surgery. Human obesity is similarly complicated. It runs in families in patterns which suggest that heredity is often involved [36]. Identical twins reared apart, for instance, tend to be closer in weight than fraternal twins reared together. Genes seem to affect both total amount of body fat and distribution of fat in specific tissues. Disease and injury can result in human weight gains, too, sometimes dramatic ones. Still, most experts believe that eating and activity patterns are by far the most important determinants of the current American obesity epidemic. In this section we review major environmental influences on obesity and describe why obesity tends to be self-perpetuating.

Early feeding practices and fat cells
Studies by medical researchers Jerome Knittle and Jules Hirsch suggest that the number of fat cells carried around by adults is determined by their eating habits at an early age. In one experiment Knittle and Hirsch separated the twenty-six offspring of two rat mothers into an "affluent" group of four and a "deprived" group of twenty-two. The rat pups then suckled in the large or small litter throughout their infancy. At the time of weaning, the "affluent" subjects were all consistently fatter than the "deprived" ones. What happened from this point on was less predictable. Although all the rodents were now offered the same quantity of food each day under standard laboratory conditions, the lean animals stayed slim while the stout ones remained fat. Knittle and Hirsch later found that the "affluent" rats had accumulated more fat cells during infancy and that each cell was larger because of greater fat deposits. Once manufactured, the fat cells remained. In other words, the "affluent" adult rats were carrying around the large number of fat cells that had been established at an early age [37].

Like these overweight rat pups, obese two-year-old children have more and larger fat cells than normal-weight youngsters. When babies have been overweight throughout infancy, their fat cells increase in number unusually rapidly throughout childhood too. After age two, weight loss does not seem to alter the number of human fat cells significantly. It primarily affects the *size* of the cells

[38]. So people who were fat babies go through life, it appears, with a permanent excess of fat-storing machinery that probably makes weight reduction especially difficult [39]. Still, obese babies do not always become overweight adults.

Early eating patterns could contribute to a stout physique by a different mechanism. People who were plump infants are likely to have developed the kind of overeating and underexercising habits that keep them fat. Numbers of fat cells in human babies may also be influenced by genetics and/or intrauterine conditions, such as the mother's diet.

External food-related incentives and overeating Overeating, alone or in combination with other factors, is probably the major cause of obesity. But, what causes people to overeat? Studies by psychologist Stanley Schachter and a number of coworkers have provided a tentative answer to this question. In a typical early study, obese and lean subjects came individually to Schachter's laboratory for an experiment—all on empty stomachs (without lunch or dinner). Soon after their arrival (supposedly before the experiment began), half the slim and half the overweight research participants received sandwiches to eat. The rest remained hungry. At this point everybody was told that the psychologists were studying taste. Subjects were to rate crackers for saltiness, cheesiness, garliciness, and the like. They could try as many crackers as they wished before making a judgment. The rating procedure was a ruse. The investigators were really interested in how many crackers were consumed. Slender people tended to eat more crackers when their stomachs were empty than when they were full. On the average, overweight individuals ate the same amount under both conditions [40]. Presumably, the obese people were depending more on external incentives—in this case, the presence of food—than on internal ones, such as gnawing sensations.

Recent research by psychologist Judith Rodin and her coworkers suggests that overweight people tend to be especially sensitive to the external environment [41]. In one series of laboratory studies supporting this idea, the responses of obese and slim subjects were compared in varied situations. The investigators found that overweight individuals tended to be more upset by anxiety-arousing descriptions, more bored by dull materials, more distracted by simultaneous stimulation, and more aroused by erotic movies, for example. Further work by Rodin and her colleagues suggests that an *external orientation* (being especially sensitive to external stimuli) leads directly to overeating even in normal-weight people. The psychologists studied a group of young girls of normal weight who were attending a summer camp. As predicted, campers who tested high in sensitivity to external cues gained more weight at the camp (which provided many tempting high-calorie foods) than less externally oriented campers [42].

How can an external orientation foster overeating? Rodin reasoned that externally oriented people tend to notice and overrespond to food, just as they overreact to other aspects of their surroundings. She and her colleagues found impressive support for this hypothesis. In one laboratory study, an assistant prepared a steak as participants watched, smelled, and heard the sizzling incentive. Externally responsive individuals, regardless of weight, secreted *excessive amounts of insulin*, a hormone which lowers the blood glucose level and makes a person feel hungry. In short, being externally responsive led directly to appetite-augmenting bodily conditions. Note that this research alters the interpretation of Schachter's conclusions. Confronted by crackers, the obese subjects were probably responding to especially strong hunger-related cues.

Rodin's group has begun to explore some of the determinants of an external orientation. Sporadic meals in infancy have been linked to an external orientation to food. When rats eat at random intervals throughout their youth, they show a perpetual interest in food later on, regardless of how recently they have eaten. Similarly, in cultures where food is scarce, people tend to eat whenever they can, again regardless of the timing of their last feeding [43]. Being poor is associated with being overweight [44]. Sporadic meals may be an important contributing factor. Of course, poverty could be linked to human obesity for other reasons. Starchy, fattening foods are cheap and likely to be available when eating habits and taste preferences are being established. And weight watching may seem frivolous and trivial when people are overburdened with the types of stresses that often accompany poverty.

Whatever its origin, an external orientation will make staying thin exceedingly difficult. As you probably know, eating has become a major form of recreation, relaxation, celebration, and hospitality in America. Food cues are abundant and inescapable. With so many temptations, most Americans find it very easy to overeat and become fat.

Underexercising Although contemporary American life is often hectic and tiring, it is rarely physically exerting. In our modern technological society, energy expenditure has become minimally necessary for survival. We tend to drive wherever we go, even to the mailbox. Machinery does most of our labor as we set dials, push buttons, and turn knobs. Jean Mayer, an eminent nutritionist, believes that underactivity is a major cause of obesity. Many behavioral scientists agree that underactivity is a significant contributing factor. As most people realize, exercise burns calories. Mayer's studies suggest that activity serves another extremely important function: keeping weight-regulating mechanisms toned up so that they work properly. Extreme lack of activity among animals leads to overeating and overweight. That is why farmers sometimes pen up hogs or chickens while fattening them for market. When laboratory rats exercise moderately, they maintain their weight quite accurately. But, if rats are forced to remain essentially immobile or intensely active, they tend to overeat or undereat and gain or lose weight accordingly. Mayer and his coworkers have observed that obese people tend to be relatively lethargic. They swim less vigorously and make fewer movements during tennis and volleyball, for example, than normal-weight individuals engaged in the same activities [45]. Lack of sufficient exercise may lead to the breakdown of appetite-regulating mechanisms, overeating, and overweight. Lethargy, on the other hand, may be a *result* of obesity. Since more calories must be expended to move a larger mass, action becomes especially taxing for the fat person.

Obesity: A self-perpetuating phenomenon We have seen that several environmental factors contribute to obesity. The key influences of early feeding practices, overeating, and underexercising tend to interact and augment one another. The same parental feeding tactics that lead to the accumulation of excessive fat cells in infancy result in eating habits that make weight gain likely later on. Practices such as consuming food rapidly in large rather than small portions per feeding and taking in a disproportionate amount of carbohydrates (rather than proteins) are associated with overeating. These same patterns prime the body to store more fat and raise resting levels of insulin, increasing the likelihood of hunger sensations and further eating. Obesity increases the chance of inactivity too. A lethargic life-style, in turn, makes future weight gain all the more probable. Because of

these and other interrelated problems, obesity tends to be self-perpetuating. Once people have accumulated a significant excess of adipose tissue, the mechanisms that ordinarily regulate weight efficiently break down.

Increased understanding of obesity's causes has enabled psychologists to plan more effective weight-control programs. Changing the external environment to make new eating and activity practices probable is the most successful current treatment approach [46]. For more information on this topic, see this chapter's Suggested Readings. ▲

SEXUAL MOTIVATION AND BEHAVIOR

Although people cannot live very long without food, they can easily survive without sex. If they did so, however, the human race would cease to exist. Psychologists usually classify sexual motivation as a basic physiological drive because it is rooted in biology and directed ultimately toward a physical goal—the union between egg and sperm. Of course, the sex drive cannot be understood as resulting simply from reproductive needs. Human sexual motivation, like hunger, is complex. Hormonal and brain mechanisms can "turn on" the drive. So can an attractive partner, an incentive. Experiences influence the specific types of incentives that people find sexually arousing. The role of deprivation is far from

---

▲ USING PSYCHOLOGY

1. Suppose a friend says, "I can tell when I'm hungry because my stomach always growls." Explain why your friend is mistaken.

2. List lessons that you have learned in real life about when to eat and stop eating. How was each lesson learned?

3. What circumstances usually precede your own eating at meals and snacktimes? Which internal and external cues govern your "feedings"?

4. Based on your reading in this textbook, what practices should parents follow to minimize the likelihood that their children will be obese?

5. List information about obesity that could be useful for an adult dieting or trying to maintain her or his current weight.

clear-cut. After long bouts without sexual activity, individuals often seek such experiences. But deprivation is not a requirement for sexual motivation, as it is for many other motives. Human beings frequently engage repeatedly in sexual acts. Cognitions and emotions play a significant role in human sexuality. Guilty thoughts, for instance, produce anxiety which interferes with sexual responsiveness. Explicit erotic fantasies and images, on the other hand, tend to augment sexual motivation in both men and women [47]. In this section we examine the human sexual response and describe some important physiological and environmental influences on sexual behavior.

The Human Sexual Response

Until the late 1940s when Alfred Kinsey published his pioneering interview studies on sexuality, very little was known about sexual customs in America. Kinsey's work, describing "who did what with whom," was an ambitious attempt to understand the sexual practices of average people. Kinsey's research showed that many activities, such as masturbation and premarital and extramarital coitus, which religions and laws often forbade, were widespread. In the early 1950s gynecologist Williams Masters and his colleague Virginia Johnson became the first scientists to attempt to study human sexual behavior in the laboratory on a large scale. Their findings have had enormous practical benefits for people with sexual problems. See Figure 10-10. Initially, Masters and Johnson paid prostitutes to engage in sexual acts (chiefly masturbation) while their physiological responses were recorded. Later, the two researchers studied hundreds of ordinary people during heterosexual intercourse and other activities. Simultaneous physical measurements were made on each individual before, during, and after orgasm.

Although people satisfy the sex drive in diverse ways, the human body exhibits a consistent pattern of physical reactions when

FIGURE 10-10 William Masters and Virginia Johnson are pictured here counseling a couple. Masters and Johnson's research on adequate and inadequate sexual functioning led to the development of highly effective treatment procedures for sexual problems. They view sexual problems as a form of faulty communication which mirrors other communication difficulties. Consequently, treatment is oriented toward improving general as well as sexual communication. Therapists attempt to reduce sexual anxieties and eliminate unhealthy sexual attitudes. Information and instructions are supplied to combat ignorance. Specific sensual and sexual exercises help correct faulty learning. The partners are treated as a unit, and truthful communication between them is stressed. Counselors who use the various techniques developed by Masters and Johnson report high success for varied sexual problems, including premature ejaculation and certain types of impotence among men and orgasmic difficulties in women. A five-year follow-up investigation showed that Masters and Johnson's initial program resulted in an overall success rate of 80 percent. Certain problems were treated successfully 100 percent of the time [104]. [*Levin/Black Star.*]

sexually aroused. Masters and Johnson discerned four stages: excitement, plateau, orgasm, and resolution [48].

Arousal increases at varying rates, beginning within seconds after sexual stimulation. During this *excitement* phase, people breathe more rapidly. Muscles all over the body become tense. The tissues of the genitals and the nipples of the breasts fill with blood. These and other physiological changes ready the body for the sex act.

The *plateau* phase follows. Muscles continue to tighten and blood frequently gathers at the body's surface. Men usually exhibit a single pattern. Their excitement builds to a high point, levels off, and remains for varying lengths of time. Women show several possible responses. They may experience a leveling-off phase as men do, build directly to orgasm, or remain in the plateau stage until resolution without orgasm.

The sensation known as *orgasm*, or climax, lasts several seconds. During this phase males release sperm. Orgasm appears to play the same physical role for both women and men. It brings relief to blood-swollen areas and tightened muscles which might otherwise cause discomfort. Men's climaxes are physiologically similar. According to Masters and Johnson, women experience one type of orgasm too, though it may vary a great deal in duration and intensity. Females may have several orgasms during the same sexual response cycle, while males are limited to one.

The last stage of the sexual response cycle is the *resolution*. During this phase the body returns to its normal state as blood congestion is relieved and tightened muscles relax.

Physiological Mechanisms that Regulate Sexual Behavior

Sexual behavior depends on years of physical development, beginning at the moment of conception.

Early sex differences: Chromosomes and gonads
In the beginning, at conception, the *genetic sex* of the embryo is determined by a single pair of chromosomes, the *sex chromosomes*. (To review genetics, see Chapter 3.) Mothers give their unborn children an X chromosome. If the father contributes a second X chromosome, the newly conceived baby, or *embryo*, develops as a genetic female. If the father contributes a *Y chromosome*, the embryo develops as a genetic male. Genetic sex is only the first step in a long chain. Initially, the unborn child is capable of developing either masculine or feminine *gonads*, or sex glands—the *testes* or *ovaries*. The gonads are part of the endocrine system which is pictured in Figure 4-18. The XX chromosome pattern structures the development of ovaries. The XY chromosome pattern structures the development of testes. After the gonads have formed, they begin producing *sex hormones*, chemical substances that travel throughout the body to affect sexual development and behavior. These hormones then take on the primary role in controlling sexual differentiation.

The sex hormones and early development
Sex hormones are produced in relatively large quantities at certain important stages in sexual development: shortly after conception, around the time of birth, and at sexual maturity, or *puberty*. At puberty the *adrenal glands* also enter the picture. Like the gonads, the adrenals secrete sizable quantities of the sex hormones. Both males and females manufacture "feminine" sex hormones, including *estrogens* and *progestins*, and "masculine" sex hormones, the

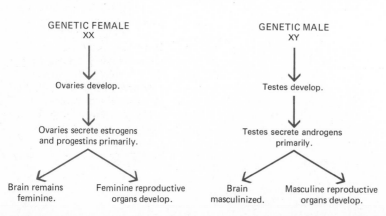

GENETIC FEMALE
XX
↓
Ovaries develop.
↓
Ovaries secrete estrogens and progestins primarily.
↙ ↘
Brain remains feminine.   Feminine reproductive organs develop.

GENETIC MALE
XY
↓
Testes develop.
↓
Testes secrete androgens primarily.
↙ ↘
Brain masculinized.   Masculine reproductive organs develop.

FIGURE 10-11 Some key steps in the differentiation of the two sexes early in development.

androgens. Males produce a relatively large amount of the androgens, while females make relatively large quantities of the estrogens and progestins. The androgens, particularly *testosterone*, which is secreted primarily by the testes, appear to be the most influential sex hormones early in the unborn baby's life. If the androgens are present, they structure the development of masculine genitalia, or *reproductive organs*, and the suppression of feminine ones. In the absence of the androgens, the fetus develops feminine genitalia and masculine ones are inhibited. So females are made automatically unless the androgens are present. Curiously, the androgens may have to be converted into "feminine" sex hormones within the male's body to have a masculinizing effect [49].

The androgens influence not only the reproductive organs, but also the brain and subsequent sexual behavior. The sexual differentiation process is diagrammed in Figure 10-11.

The early presence of the androgens, even in small amounts, appears to alter neural circuits in the *hypothalamus*, either masculinizing or defeminizing them [50]. The androgens produce this effect only during a *sensitive period* (Chapter 3) shortly before or after birth, depending on the species. Subsequently, a masculinized brain makes masculine sexual responses (like mounting and thrusting) probable later in life when animals reach maturity and manufacture large quantities of their own hormones. If female rats, guinea pigs, rabbits, or monkeys receive more than the usual amount of androgen or if males of these species receive less than the normal quantity near birth, they are apt to behave like members of the opposite sex later on. This effect is particularly pronounced if the organisms are injected with the sex hormones of the opposite sex during adulthood. A study that investigated these influences is described in Figure 10-12.

FIGURE 10-12 The study depicted here was one of the first to demonstrate that androgens circulating in an animal's body near the time of birth play an important role in influencing later sex-typed behavior. Carroll Pfeiffer, an endocrinologist, used newly born rat pups as his subjects. In some cases, he removed the rat's gonads (testes or ovaries) and implanted the gonads of the opposite sex in their place. These creatures, then, had the genes of one sex and the gonads and sex hormones of the other. Additional intact newborn rats were given a second set of gonads,

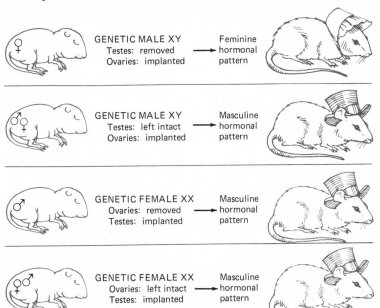

those of the opposite sex. What happened? The androgens exerted the deciding influence on reproductive functioning. Genetic males (XY) without testes tended to show a cyclic hormonal pattern at maturity similar to that of normal females. Genetic males with both testes and ovaries and genetic females (XX) with testes (with or without ovaries) were likely to follow the male pattern—no obvious hormonal cycle—at maturity. Later studies suggested that the hormonal treatment had sex-typed the hypothalamus [105]. (Current research indicates that males do display cyclic patterns. These are, however, far less pronounced and predictable than those of females [106].)

GENETIC MALE XY
Testes: removed
Ovaries: implanted → Feminine hormonal pattern

GENETIC MALE XY
Testes: left intact
Ovaries: implanted → Masculine hormonal pattern

GENETIC FEMALE XX
Ovaries: removed
Testes: implanted → Masculine hormonal pattern

GENETIC FEMALE XX
Ovaries: left intact
Testes: implanted → Masculine hormonal pattern

How does the hypothalamus control sexual behavior? It dominates the *pituitary gland*, the master gland of the endocrine system. The pituitary, in turn, stimulates the gonads and/or adrenals to secrete sex hormones. Special sensor cells in the hypothalamus respond to changing sex hormone levels by exciting varied types of sexual functioning. In some animals, different circuits of the hypothalamus play specific roles in eliciting sexuality. When certain hypothalamic pathways are stimulated directly by testosterone injections, for instance, both female and male rats show masculine sexual responses like mounting. Testosterone injections in another hypothalamic site produce feminine sex-related behavior, such as nest building and pup retrieval in rats [51]. Estrogen injections at specific brain sites can initiate the feminine reproductive cycle in male and female monkeys [52]. Apparently, the neural potential for both feminine and masculine sexual behavior remains intact in certain animals, perhaps including people. Although we call the androgens and estrogens "masculine" and "feminine" sex hormones respectively, it should be clear by now that these labels are oversimplified. Both "feminine" and "masculine" hormones may produce masculine and feminine responses. Other brain structures besides the hypothalamus are involved in sex-typed behavior in ways that scientists are just beginning to understand [53].

Currently, psychologists believe that androgen levels in the human infant shortly before birth alter the brain and affect subsequent behavioral differences between men and women. Why?

Androgens, Human Brains, and Human Sexual Behavior

To understand the influence of the sex hormones on human behavior, psychologists study people with varied sex-hormonal problems. Recently, for instance, Anke Ehrhardt and Susan Baker investigated children with the *adrenogenital syndrome* (AGS). When this genetic disorder occurs, the adrenal cortex produces excessive amounts of androgen during the prenatal period and throughout life in most cases. At birth the genitals of an AGS genetic female appear masculinized. The youngster usually undergoes corrective surgery to normalize the appearance of her reproductive structures. To control the excessive output of androgen, the AGS girl is likely to be treated all her life by the drug cortisone. When AGS occurs in males, cortisone treatment prevents premature sexual development. Ehrhardt and Baker compared AGS children with normal siblings of the same sex. As compared with their sisters, AGS girls had a higher energy level in rough outdoor play, more tomboyish habits, and strong preferences for male rather than female playmates. They showed less interest than their sisters in grooming themselves, playing with dolls, caring for infants, and rehearsing mother and wife roles. As compared with normal brothers, the AGS boys showed a higher energy expenditure during sports and rough outdoor activities [54]. Additional studies on children who have been exposed to excessively high or low sex hormone levels during the sensitive period (because of either genetic defects or drugs) support these findings. Larger than usual amounts of androgen are associated with stereotypically masculine interest and behavior patterns in females and males. Conversely, exposure to reduced levels of "masculine" hormones or to excessive levels of certain "feminine" hormones is associated with stereotypically feminine interest and behavior patterns [55].

Some behavioral scientists believe that differing levels of prenatal androgen may be partially responsible for variations in masculinity and femininity seen in normal individuals and in unusual populations. William Masters and Virginia Johnson found that about a quarter of the male homosexuals whom they studied showed unusually low androgen levels. The same individuals were more likely than other homosexuals to show stereotypically feminine behavior patterns [56]. Perhaps these men had experienced prenatal conditions that blocked the output of androgen. Recent research on rats by psychologist Ingebord Ward

FIGURE 10-13 Barbara Love and Sidney Abbott are coauthors of a book on lesbianism that examines the social, political, and psychological climate of their lives. Recent interview research on 1,500 lesbians and homosexuals by Alan Bell and Martin Weinberg suggests that "gay" people are diverse and do not conform to commonly held stereotypes. Homosexual males do not appear to engage in sexual violence, rape, or seduction as frequently as do heterosexual males. Homosexual teachers seem less likely to make sexual overtures to pupils than heterosexual teachers. Many of the sexual habits of "gay" people are similar to those of heterosexual women and men. Lesbians tend to seek durable, long-term love relationships. Homosexual men are more likely than women to engage in a great many impersonal sexual encounters. On the whole, "gay" people appear to be as well adjusted psychologically as heterosexual people. Most hold steady jobs, value stable friendships, and obey civil laws [107]. [*Chie Nishio, Nancy Palmer Photo Agency.*]

suggests that maternal stress during certain embryological periods may block androgen output at a crucial time. Male rat offspring whose mothers have been stressed have normal anatomy. But they are much more likely than pups from unstressed pregnancies to exhibit homosexual behavior under specific laboratory conditions [57]. As of now, there is no conclusive evidence that certain human homosexuals are the product of a stressful pregnancy, but this possibility is being investigated. See Figure 10-13. Some scientists speculate that *transsexuals* (people who at-

tempt to live like members of the opposite sex) are more likely than members of the general population to have experienced unusual prenatal hormonal conditions as well [58].

It should be noted that generalizing from rats and abnormal human populations poses difficulties. In the case of *hermaphroditic* children (those with ambiguous sexual anatomy), psychologists do not know whether they are seeing the behavioral effects of (1) abnormal prenatal conditions, (2) treatments to counteract specific problems, (3) the excessive sex hormone levels *in utero* (as is assumed),

and/or (4) parental attitudes to an unusual child.

What can we conclude? Right now, most behavioral scientists believe that sex hormone levels during a sensitive prenatal period do influence the brain and sex-related conduct in human beings and other animals. At the same time, there is little agreement on the importance of these effects in people. The environment may be a far more powerful influence than sex hormones. In Chapter 17 we explore social influences on sex-related behavioral differences.

Sex hormones, secondary sexual characteristics, and sex drive The sex hormones, relatively abundant near the time of birth, become scarce until puberty.

Then, beginning at approximately age eleven, the human body begins circulating large amounts of sex hormones once again. The hormones stimulate the development of *secon-*

dary sexual characteristics, those which typify mature male and female bodies and do not exist at birth. Secondary sexual characteristics include breast growth in women and voice deepening in men. The increased hormone levels influence sex drive too.

The sexuality of lower animals is largely controlled by brain-gland relationships. The female rat, for example, enters *estrus* every four or five days for about nineteen hours. At this time, its estrogen level is high and its eggs are ready to be fertilized. If the female comes near a male, it is likely to seek copulation actively by posturing receptively. Aged or immature female rats, which do not manufacture ovarian hormones, do not normally display sexual behavior. They will posture receptively if injected with the appropriate hormones. The sexual behavior of the male rat depends to a large degree on hormones also. Castration (removal of the testes) decreases the frequency of sexual behavior, though the ability to copulate may persist. Injections of either androgens or estrogens will increase the frequency of the male rat's coital behavior [59].

As we move up the evolutionary scale, ties between mating and reproduction loosen. Hormones are less important for sexual activities in higher animals, though they remain influential. The androgens have a particularly dramatic impact on women's sexuality. Rhythmic periods of peak sexual receptivity are sometimes seen in the human female near the time of ovulation, when there is a corresponding rise in testosterone level [60]. When the adrenal gland, the chief supplier of androgens for females, is removed, sexual desires decline [61]. After a hysterectomy (surgical removal of the uterus) or during menopause, women receiving relatively large amounts of testosterone as part of therapy commonly report increases in sexual responsiveness [62].

The case of the human male is similar. Hormones influence his sex drive, but do not control it completely. Even when a man's body is not producing substantial amounts of the androgens, as is the case early and late in the life cycle, many males are fully capable of sexual activity. Castration reduces sexual desire and sexual behavior but does not necessarily abolish them [63]. Drugs that slow down the production of the androgens are sometimes administered to male sex offenders who feel obsessed by their sexuality. Such drugs give the men a "vacation from their sex drives" so that they can learn more adaptive ways of expressing their sexuality [64].

Environmental Influences on Sexual Behavior

Although the human sex drive is inborn, the behaviors which satisfy it are actively shaped by experiences within a particular culture.

Social standards and sexuality In most societies, a tangle of laws, conventions, and taboos regulate sexual conduct and tell people which sexual practices are acceptable and when, where, how, under what circumstances, and with whom sexuality may be expressed. Cultures display enormous differences in the sexual practices that are condoned and condemned. People in the Melanesian islands actively encourage homosexual activity in their adolescent boys. On Mangaia in the central Polynesian islands, older women teach young boys about sexual techniques and provide practice sessions. Among the Trobrianders, Sironon, Duson, and Plains Cree, lovers spend hours grooming and delousing one another as stimulation for sexual intercourse [65].

Within a single society, various subgroups often adhere to specific sexual customs. In the 1940s Alfred Kinsey and his colleagues found that poorly educated, low-income groups tended to view any sexual activity besides coitus as distasteful and perverse. Well-educated, high-income groups experimented widely [66]. The so-called sexual revolution is thought to have established radically new standards for sexual conduct in America. Has it?

The Sexual Revolution in America

During the 1960s a dramatic change, or revolution, in sexual attitudes is supposed to have taken place in the United States. Many groups were trying then (and continue trying) to loosen old sexual stereotypes to accommodate their needs. Young people sought some type of bonding arrangement suited to their extended adolescence. Women searched for liberation from sexual restrictions. Homosexuals and lesbians, transvestites, and bisexuals pursued the freedom to express their preferences openly.

Sexual attitudes have become more permissive, especially among the young. In 1972, 73 percent of both female and male college students in one survey reported having engaged in coitus. Only four years earlier, in 1968, 46 percent of a comparable sample of women and 56 percent of a comparable sample of men reported having experienced sexual intercourse [67]. Do these figures represent changing sexual behavior or simply a new willingness to describe sexual experiences? Probably some combination of both. More recent studies suggest that the percentage of college students reporting intercourse is climbing and may be closer now to 85 percent [68]. While the old double standard that allowed males more sexual freedom than females is still alive today, sexual standards for young women and men appear to be converging [69].

For a long time, sex has been considered a "necessary evil" in our culture. In 1902 a popular medical guide advised mothers to "set before the child the exceeding sinfulness of masturbation, its loathsomeness and vileness, and the horrible consequences that follow in its wake [including nervousness, hysteria, and general worthlessness] [70]." Most Americans would dismiss this advice as absurd. But many people remain convinced, often at a less than conscious level, that coitus and other sex acts are dirty, shameful, and generally unsavory activities tolerable only in the context of marriage. Positive feelings about sexuality exist side by side with negative ones. Conflict and anxiety about sex remain. In the late 1970s, behavioral scientists studied 1,400 parents in Cleveland, Ohio. The sample was selected to represent a cross section of Americans. Less than half the parents had mentioned intercourse to their eleven-year-old children. Most said that questions about sex had essentially stopped when their youngsters were nine or ten. The parents felt that they were perpetuating the patterns of anxiety and ignorance that they had learned from their own parents [71].

Females appear to be particularly conflicted about the new sexual standards. For years our society pictured the "ideal" woman as one who was uninterested in sex and accepted coitus only when it was imposed on her by marriage. Even then she was supposed to consider sexual activity a disagreeable matrimonial duty, somewhat like washing soiled socks. These attitudes continue to influence the lives of many people. After interviewing working- and middle-class couples living in the San Francisco Bay area, psychologist Lillian Breslow Rubin summed up her observations thus:

"Socialized from infancy to experience their sexuality as a negative force to be inhibited and repressed, women can't just switch 'on' as the changing culture or their husbands dictate. Nice girls don't! Men *use* bad girls but marry good girls! Submit, but don't enjoy—at least not obviously so! These are the injunctions that have dominated their lives—injunctions that are laid aside with difficulty, if at all [72]."

Reluctance to use contraception and high rates of pregnancy among teenagers may be at least partially the result of sex-related anxieties. Using birth-control devices requires acknowledging to oneself, one's partner(s), and perhaps the druggist, intentions of engaging in sexual intercourse. Controlled studies suggest that many young people feel guilty about such behavior and are reluctant or unwilling to make this declaration to anyone, including themselves [73]. There are other signs suggesting that our Victorian heritage remains strong: attempts by citizens' groups to limit the civil liberties of people who do not fit the heterosexual mold, negative attitudes toward legitimate sexual research by funding agencies and the general public, and resistance to honest sex education in public schools [74].

FIGURE 10-14 In 1971 the Presidential Commission on Obscenity and Pornography concluded from its research that erotic materials do not appear to promote sexual crimes. These conclusions have been criticized for numerous reasons [108]. Recently, controlled laboratory investigations have linked pornography and aggression [109]. The reasons for the association are not yet known. Certain possibilities have been suggested. Sexual arousal may augment existing anger, increasing the likelihood of striking out. As erotica decreases inhibitions about sex, it may also decrease inhibitions against another forbidden behavior, aggression. In addition, materials that pair sex and violence may respondently condition this new taste. Pornography that depicts the victim enjoying sex in the context of

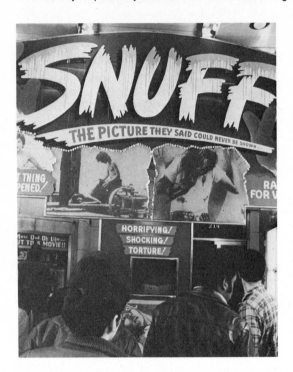

cruelty or pain (sadomasochistic pornography) is becoming increasingly commonplace. A series of laboratory experiments by Seymour Feshbach and his associates suggest that sadomasochistic material may increase the likelihood of aggressive, antisocial sexual conduct. In one study, male college students read a rape story and reported on their sexual arousal. Some subjects were given a mildly sadomasochistic story from *Penthouse* to read before the rape story. Others read a nonviolent version of the *Penthouse* tale. (Previous studies had shown that college students are rarely sexually aroused by rape stories.) After reading the sadomasochistic *Penthouse* story, the men appeared to interpret pain during rape as a sign of the victim's sexual excitement. The more pain the victim experienced, the more sexually aroused the readers felt. Males who read the nonviolent *Penthouse* story showed the opposite pattern—the more pain, the less sexual arousal. A single exposure to sadomasochistic pornography seemed to have altered erotic reactions to the portrayal of rape at least temporarily [110]. Studies like this one raise questions about the impact of repeated exposures to intense sadomasochistic materials, especially on males who are already callous or aggressive. Some presentations are so explicit, Feshbach argues, that they are the equivalent of a how-to-do-it training session. [Leo Choplin/Black Star.]

Learning and sexuality How do societies shape sexual attitudes and practices in their members? One obvious way is *direct teaching.* Parents, peers, educational and religious institutions, and the mass media often provide explicit instructions: "Don't do this" or "This is the way such-and-such is done." Those close to us use approval and disapproval to influence our behavior. Consequently, we tend to move in directions that are supported and abandon those that bring problems and objections. In other words, *operant conditioning* molds sexual practices. What we see in life and in the media may suggest new sexual acts, make us feel freer to express sexual practices that have already been learned, or strengthen already existing sexual behavior. *Respondent conditioning*

makes an important contribution to human sexuality, too. Suppose that a sexually arousing experience is associated with a new "object" (say, a blonde woman, a muscular man, a specific perfume, a leather jacket, brutality, or a young child). Because of the association, the new "object" may subsequently evoke sexual arousal. *Fetishes,* specific objects which some people consider essential for full sexual satisfaction, may acquire their significance when they are accidentally paired repeatedly with a sexually arousing experience. Respondent conditioning, in short, appears to influence the nature of the *incentives* that arouse sexual motivation.

For most people, all four types of learning—instruction, observation learning, and operant and respondent conditioning—

probably teach the same set of sexual attitudes, tastes, and practices. After all, people tend to seek out sexual experiences approved and modeled by the human beings surrounding them. Consider lesbianism and homosexuality. In the mid-1970s, experts estimated that about 6 million Americans regarded themselves as "gay" [75]. While biological variables may be involved in some cases, as suggested before, learning is a plausible explanation for the majority of cases [76]. Many psychologists believe that human beings are capable of choosing individuals of either sex as partners. Less complex animal brains, and maybe human ones as well, retain their capability for both masculine and feminine behavior, as we saw earlier. Studies of bisexuals suggest that people are not immutably fixed in their sexual tastes. Committed homosexuals or lesbians may later have affairs with, or marry members of, the opposite sex. Lifelong heterosexuals with no history of lesbian or homosexual experiences sometimes develop these preferences [77]. Most Americans probably become heterosexual because our society generates strong pressures which move men and women toward their opposite sex. But, assume that sexual experiences with members of the opposite sex are nonexistent, frustrating, or brutal. If sexual contacts with members of the same sex then occur, are satisfying, and fulfill needs for affection, individuals of the same sex may come to be associated with sexual and emotional fulfillment. At the same time, cognitive factors probably enter in. Once a person begins to view himself or herself as homosexual or lesbian, the tag colors self-image and sexual fantasies. It probably influences the person's choice of friends and, consequently, the nature of future relationships. Preferences for a partner of the same sex may be stamped in even more strongly if experiences with the opposite sex remain unpleasant and are consequently avoided. Research supports several aspects of this theory. Lesbians and homosexuals often report early same-sexed sexual contacts [78]. And they frequently describe turning to members of their own sex after unpleasant heterosexual relationships [79]. Figure 10-14 describes how some people may acquire violent sexual tastes. ▲

ACHIEVEMENT MOTIVATION AND BEHAVIOR

I always wanted to be extremely successful and I'm not going to let myself fail. I made up my mind to do it and I'm doing it. [80]

The *achievement motive*, exemplified by this comment, comes from needs to pursue excellence, accomplish lofty goals, or succeed on difficult tasks. This motive is not clearly necessary for survival. Nor is it woven into human physiology in any obvious way. If the satisfaction of personal potentialities is emphasized, the achievement motive may be classified as a *growth motive*. But, if the stress is on competition among people, the achievement motive can be considered a *social motive*. In this section, we focus on several

---

▲ USING PSYCHOLOGY

1. How can the influence of androgens and estrogens on human sexual behavior be investigated without subjecting people to harmful procedures?

2. How do psychologists know that sex hormones are not the only important influence on human sexuality?

3. Make a list of some of your own sexual attitudes. Speculate about how each was acquired.

4. Have you seen evidence that sexual attitudes have become more permissive? That anxieties about sex persist? Explain.

issues: How is the achievement motive measured? What influences the achievement motive and its expression in achievement-related behavior? How do achievement motivation and behavior originate? What are some common obstacles to achievement in our society?

Note: In the case of motives that have no obvious physiological basis, psychologists cannot differentiate needs from motives. Since the distinction is rarely made, the two terms are apt to be used interchangeably. We follow this practice now.

Measuring Achievement Motivation

Assessing the achievement motive was a challenge. Before reading further, try to think of some way to measure achievement motivation. In the 1930s, Henry Murray, a Harvard psychologist, came up with an ingenious approach. Murray assumed that social needs might be accurately mirrored in what human beings think about when they are not pressured to think about anything in particular. But how could these everyday thoughts be

FIGURE 10-15 Ambiguous situations like this one are presented on the Thematic Apperception Test (TAT) designed by Henry Murray.

pinpointed? Murray invited people to tell stories about pictures of situations that could be interpreted in many different ways, like the one in Figure 10-15. Research participants were asked: What is happening in the ambiguous picture? What led up to this situation? What are the individuals in the picture thinking about? What will happen later? As people made up stories, Murray believed, they *projected* their needs, fears, hopes, and conflicts onto their characters. Accordingly, Murray's test, the *Thematic Apperception Test* (TAT), is considered a *projective method* of assessing social motives.

In the 1950s, psychologists David McClelland, John Atkinson, Russell Clark, and Edgar Lowell adapted the TAT for measuring the achievement motive. The investigators tried to arouse the need for excellence in research participants. Then four or five TAT pictures, which could be interpreted as reflecting achievement themes, were presented. A photograph similar to the one shown in Figure 10-16 appeared on one version of the test and inspired the following stories:

"The boy is thinking about a career as a doctor. He sees himself as a great surgeon performing an operation. He has been doing minor first aid work on his injured dog, and discovers he enjoys working with medicine. He thinks he is suited for this profession and sets it as an ultimate goal in life at this moment. He has not weighed the pros and cons of his own ability and has let his goal blind him of his own inability. An adjustment which will injure him will have to be made."

"A young fellow is sitting in a plaid shirt and resting his head on one hand. He appears to be thinking of something. His eyes appear a little sad. He may have been involved in something that he is very sorry for. The boy is thinking over what he has done. By the look in his eyes we can tell that he is very sad about it. I believe that the boy will break down any minute if he continues in the manner in which he is now going." [81]

The first story is dominated by images which reflect competing, striving, winning, accomplishing, and other achievement-related themes. The second story contains no such imagery. The amount of achievement-related imagery is supposed to reflect the intensity of

FIGURE 10-16 Photographs similar to this one are used to measure the achievement motive in the laboratory. [*Rogers/Monkmeyer Press Photo Service.*]

the *need for achievement*, often abbreviated *n-Ach*. McClelland and his associates established precise scoring criteria for evaluating this type of imagery.

The test measuring the achievement motive sounds reasonable. Does it work? It seems to succeed within limits. Different behavioral scientists, following McClelland's rules, score specific stories similarly. There is also evidence suggesting that McClelland's test of achievement motivation measures what it intends to. People who tell stories that contain a lot of achievement imagery are likely to show signs of needing to accomplish excellence in other settings, such as school. Nonetheless, any single story is hard to interpret. The imagery could reflect past personal experiences, last night's TV watching, wishes, or fears, and not motives. In addition, the test shows a built-in bias that you should be aware of. Because of the kinds of situations used to arouse the need for excellence and the types of pictures used to assess the need, McClelland's measure is more apt to detect motives for academic, intellectual, and middle-class career-oriented achievements. The modified TAT does not measure needs for interpersonal accomplishments such as "living well,

laughing often, and loving much." Nor is it likely to assess the kind of achievement motivation that might be expressed on a baseketball court or while building a house.

Influences on Achievement Motivation and Behavior

Hundreds of studies by McClelland, Atkinson, and many other psychologists have helped specify some important influences on motivation and behavior in achievement situations. We know that *incentives* are important. The announcement of a psychology test could function as an incentive for the achievement motive. Incentives, you may recall, appear to arouse *cognitions* and *emotions*. People probably analyze, consciously or unconsciously, *the value of attaining the goal suggested by the incentive*. Is it worth the effort? What are the short- and long-term consequences of success? An A on a psychology test may win self-respect, a friend's approval, or financial rewards from parents. Success may have negative consequences, in addition. It may earn the student a reputation as a grind. In the case of a woman, it may upset male friends who are doing a mediocre job in the same course. Recent research indicates that incentives are more motivating when immediate successes lead to valued future opportunities [82]. If you wanted to be a psychologist, an A on a psychology test would be a small step toward admission to graduate school. Similarly, an A could help make the dean's list or give a competitive edge for a job opening. Incentives arouse *memories* of past performances in similar situations. Memories influence *expectations* about the probability of reaching the goal. If you've done well in academics and feel confident about your abilities, you're likely to anticipate victory on the psychology test and feel positive. If you've done poorly in the past, you may consider failure inevitable. Varied cognitions and associated emotions then evoke some degree of *achievement motivation*. They may elicit *anxieties associated with failure and/or success* too. Motivation and anxiety determine *goal setting*, *diligence*, and *persistence* [83]. Even when motivation is optimally high (too much could create problems [84]) and anxieties are low, success depends to some extent on a person's energy, intelligence, and skills. To predict how a given individual will perform in a specific achievement setting, we must consider all these factors.

Origins of Achievement Motivation and Behavior

Traditionally, Americans value high achievement. William James considered "the exclusive worship of the bitch goddess success . . . our national disease." "Being first" and "getting ahead" are valued accomplishments in our society. More tangible rewards often attend achievement in America: financial gains, power, and high status. Consequently, many American children develop strong achievement needs. Achievement motivation may also be influenced by the tendencies to seek competence and actualize potentialities described earlier.

Families appear to be influential in establishing needs for academic, intellectual, and career-oriented achievements. The parents of boys who score high on tests of achievement motivation stress the importance of success and independence. They reward their sons for accomplishments such as becoming leaders, making friends, attempting difficult tasks by themselves, and persisting without help until victories are attained [85]. The mothers and fathers of boys with strong achievement needs tend to be emotionally involved in their sons' achievement-related performances too. They may be so involved, in fact, that they seem pushy and domineering. These parents set high standards of excellence and raise their expectations as their sons progress. Families of boys with low achievement motivation tend to emphasize different virtues including politeness, cleanliness, and compliance with authority. They are less likely to encourage and support their sons' achievements with any consistency [86].

What about daughters? In the past, academic and intellectual achievements were considered inappropriate for women. Typically, young girls were treated in ways that would discourage this type of achievement motivation. Parents are apt to shelter daughters from danger and reward dependence. They are unlikely to pressure girls to develop separate identities [87]. Even mothers with professional-level jobs hold higher occupational goals for sons than for daughters [88].

Teachers play an important role in establishing achievement-related conduct, too. During the late elementary school years, they appear to use feedback patterns that encourage mastery in achievement situations in boys while discouraging such behavior in girls. Psychologists Carol Dweck and Therese Goetz have observed that teachers are apt to criticize female students for the intellectual characteristics of their work. They tend to chastise male pupils, in contrast, for poor conduct, lack of motivation, and other nonintellectual aspects of their performance. These practices seem to produce *generalized expectations*. When boys meet obstacles in achievement situations, they tend to assume that they need to buckle down and try harder. When confronted by achievement-related difficulties, girls are apt to blame their ability and feel discouraged [89].

Obstacles to Achievement

When people expect failure or fear success, they often stop trying to succeed. Consequently, achievement becomes improbable. We examine these barriers to achievement.

Expectations of failure Many poor children begin school unprepared to sit quietly in their seats and learn. Teachers are apt to feel annoyed and frustrated under these circumstances and their effectiveness is likely to suffer. As a result, pupils may learn little and experience a great many failures. School-related defeats tend to accumulate. Eventually, the deficiencies are massive and seemingly irremediable. Some students drop out. Many just stop trying, perhaps because they feel hopelessly behind and cannot imagine any consequence but failure. Research by psychologist Richard de Charms supports the idea that expectations of failure and feelings of helplessness lie beneath the underachievements of many poor youngsters. The behavioral scientist trained teachers in inner-city elementary schools to help students (1) learn to analyze personal goals and look upon them as challenges, (2) distinguish between outcomes that could and could not be controlled, and (3) set realistic objectives that had a good probability of success. Teaching practices were modified to motivate everyone and provide opportunities for accomplishment. For example, instead of having to compete in traditional spelling matches, each pupil received points for correctly spelling words that were moderately difficult for her or him personally. This way, everyone could contribute points to the team. Most important, of course, was the opportunity for all the youngsters to gain confidence and improve their skills. The results of de Charms's program were impressive. While the academic skills of children in a control group continued to drop below age norms, the skills of the trained students improved significantly on national tests, showing real-life gains that reflected achievement motivation and behavior [90].

Like poor children, a lot of women find it hard to imagine success in academic, intellectual, and career-related situations. These feelings are observable, research indicates, as early as at seven years of age [91]. Several possible reasons have been suggested [92]. (1) Significant people (parents and teachers, primarily) may pass along negative expectations. (2) Women may come to accept cultural stereotypes which portray females as less achieving, striving, active, powerful, intelligent, and independent than males. Once established, low expectations of success may be maintained by how people view their own victories and defeats. If you see success as due to your own abilities and efforts, achievement is under your control, so it makes sense to work for valued goals. Suppose, on the other hand, that you attribute success to luck, some fluke, or having made a superhuman effort. Imagine also that you see failures as due to lack of ability. Such evaluations would be apt to make you feel helpless and unlikely to pursue achievement. There is evidence that women tend to hold this pattern of attitudes [93]. As we suggested before, teaching practices appear to contribute to these cognitions.

Fears about success American women consistently show more anxieties than American men do in achievement-related situations. Matina Horner, one of the first behavioral scientists to investigate these fears, reasoned that besides dreading the negative consequences of failure, women might feel frightened of success because it is considered unfeminine in our culture. In one of Horner's early studies, students at the University of Michigan read a sentence "cue" and constructed a story about it (a modification of the TAT technique). Women responded to the statement, "After first-term finals Anne finds herself at the top of her medical school class." Men reacted to the same cue about John. Horner scored these stories for themes reflecting the *motive to avoid success*, defined as a learned social motive aroused by competitive situations when people fear success will bring negative consequences. The students' fear-of-success imagery was classified into three categories.

Category 1. Success brings strong fear of social rejection. One response in this category read: "Anne doesn't want to be number one in her class. . . . She feels she shouldn't rank so high because of social reasons. She drops down to ninth in the class and then marries the boy who graduates number 1."

Category 2. Success produces guilt, sadness, and doubt about being normal. For example: "Anne feels guilty. . . . She will finally have a nervous breakdown and quit medical school and marry a successful young doctor."

Category 3. Success is denied by changing or distorting the cues so the person is no longer responsible directly for his or her own success. For instance: "Anne is a code name for a nonexistent person created by a group of med students. They take turns writing exams for Anne."

Approximately 65 percent of Horner's female subjects told stories about Anne that fell in one of these three categories. Fewer than 10 percent of the males told stories about John that fit these classifications [94].

Since the late 1960s when Horner's first studies were conducted, an enormous research literature on fear of success has accumulated. Unfortunately, a number of different measures are being used, and the results are at least superficially contradictory and hard to interpret. One initially puzzling finding emerged consistently. Males used a great deal of fear-of-success imagery in writing stories about Anne, the medical student [95]. Currently, many behavioral scientists believe that the unpleasant "Anne" stories of both women and men reflect perceptions of past experiences, and not necessarily personal motivation. Many males are, in fact, rejecting when females perform "too competently" in traditionally masculine achievement arenas [96]. For good reasons, then, women may fear the consequences of deviancy, rather than success. When females believe that success will bring acceptance, they often outperform males in laboratory studies [97]. Like women, men fear nontraditional successes that bring negative consequences, such as feelings of lessened masculinity and social rejection [98].

Women's attitudes toward career-related achievements appear to be changing. In a recent survey, high school girls rated success at work as important as success in marriage. Only 10 percent of them reported simply wanting to be housewives [99]. But research does not support the idea that the new generation has fewer fears of success than the older ones [100]. Women continue to show large individual differences. Those who come from traditional backgrounds often display low career aspirations. Daughters of working mothers appear to be inspired by the example to work toward relatively challenging goals [101]. ▲

▲ USING PSYCHOLOGY

1. Analyze your own need for achievement in your psychology course. Take into account the short- and long-term values of a good mark, expectations about success and failure, and anxieties about success.

2. Make a list of parental and teacher behaviors that do and do not encourage motivation for achievement in academic, intellectual, and middle-class career-related situations. Did your parents and teachers foster high achievement motivation?

3. To what do you attribute academic successes? Academic failures?

4. Do you fear success in any type of achievement situation that you have encountered? Speculate as to why or why not.

SUMMARY
Motivation

1. Psychologists often distinguish between needs (deficiencies), motives (internal arousing states that result from needs and activate behavior), and drives (physiologically based motives).

2. Motives in the following categories are often studied: basic drives, social motives, motives for sensory stimulation (exploration and manipulation), growth motives, and ideas as motives.

3. Many basic drives follow a homeostatic model. They arouse behavior aimed at correcting deficiencies in order to restore optimally balanced conditions. In the case of certain motives and drives, the influence of incentives, emotions, and cognitions must be considered.

4. According to Abraham Maslow, people work their way up through five needs systems: physiological, safety, love, self-esteem, and self-actualization.

5. Motives are difficult to study since (a) they cannot be observed and (b) a specific behavior does not necessarily reflect a particular motive.

6. To regulate the hunger drive, the brain uses information from the stomach, mouth, throat, and blood. The hypothalamus seems to be involved in regulating hunger, but its exact function is not clear currently.

7. Family and culture teach people a great many lessons about when to eat and stop eating.

8. Obesity is caused by a combination of factors including heredity, injuries, early eating practices, overeating because of external food-related cues, and underexercising.

9. Genes structure the development of gonads. The gonads produce sex hormones which influence the development of reproductive structures and the brain. The brain and sex hormones shape sexual motivation and behavior.

10. Social standards have a very strong influence on human sexual conduct.

11. Sexual attitudes and practices are shaped by direct teaching, observation learning, and operant and respondent conditioning.

12. The achievement motive is usually measured by projective tests, such as the TAT.

13. To predict how a given individual will perform in a specific achievement setting, motivation, achievement-related anxieties, expectations of success, the immediate- and long-range values of the goals associated with the incentive, and capabilities must be considered.

14. Societies, families, and teachers shape achievement motivation and behavior.

15. Expectations of failure and fears of success may discourage achievement-related efforts.

A Study Guide for Chapter Ten

Key terms need (311), motive (311), instinct (311), homeostasis (312), basic drive (drive) (312), social motive (312), motive for sensory stimulation (manipulation and exploration) (312), growth motive (313), idea as a motive (314), incentive (316), external food-related cue (incentive) (323), obese (323), sexual response cycle (327), sex hormone (estrogen, progestin, androgen) (328), hypothalamus (321, 329), achievement motive or need (n-Ach) (335), projective test (336), motive to avoid success (339), and other italicized words and expressions.

Important research nature of and influences on basic drives (Cannon, Lee, others), evidence for social motives, evidence for sensory stimulation motives (Csikszentmihalyi, Zuckerman, others), evidence for competence motivation (White, others), evidence for ideas as motives, evidence for specific hungers, physiological influences on hunger and eating (Cannon, Zeigler, Karten, others), environmental influences on hunger and eating, influences on obesities (Knittle, Hirsch, Schachter, Rodin, Mayer, others), sexual response cycle (Masters, Johnson), physiological influences on sexual motivation and behavior (Ehrhardt, Baker, Masters, Johnson, Ward, others), environmental influences on sexual motivation and behavior (Kinsey, others), projective measures of social needs (Murray, McClelland, Atkinson, Clark, Lowell), influences on achievement motivation and behavior (McClelland, Atkinson, others), origins of achievement motivation and behavior (Dweck, Goetz, de Charms, Horner, others).

Basic concepts cognitive dissonance (Festinger), homeostatic motivation model, influences (of incentives, emotions, and cognitions) on complex motives, needs hierarchy (Maslow), reasons for the difficulty of linking specific behaviors to particular motives, "obesity" versus "obesities," reasons why obesity is self-perpetuating, the consequences of the sexual revolution, possible explanations for the development of sexual partner preferences (lesbianism and homosexuality), model for predicting achievement in a specific situation.

People to identify McDougall, Cannon, Maslow, Kinsey, Masters, Johnson, Murray, McClelland.

Self-Quiz

1. How was a drive defined?
 a. A need
 b. An instinct
 c. A physiologically based motive
 d. A social motive

2. What does the term *homeostasis* mean?
 a. A balanced state   *b.* A deprivation
 c. An incentive   *d.* A self-regulating tendency

3. Which statement about the need for sensory stimulation is supported by research?
 a. Giving up self-stimulating activities (such as daydreaming) may result in depression and irritability.
 b. People show needs for approximately the same level of sensory stimulation.
 c. Sensory deprivation does not appear to influence perception.
 d. Sensory stimulation needs are correlated with neurotransmitter levels, but not with sex hormone levels.

4. Which situation is most likely to lead to cognitive dissonance?
 a. You buy an old jalopy for $50, and it rarely starts.
 b. You march for your civil rights beliefs, defying a court injunction, and are arrested.
 c. You see yourself as heterosexual, and a counselor says that you have hidden homosexual tendencies.
 d. Your teacher and parents continually tell you that you're lazy but have a lot of ability.

5. According to Maslow, what needs system is most compelling?
 a. Esteem   *b.* Love
 c. Physiological   *d.* Self-actualization

6. What major role does the stomach play in hunger regulation?
 a. Controls the types of food that are eaten.
 b. Informs the brain when food is needed.
 c. Regulates weight level.
 d. Signals the brain to stop eating.

7. What type of information does the trigeminal nerve convey to the brain?
 a. Number of gulps   *b.* Number of swallows
 c. Taste of food   *d.* Temperature of food

8. What dimension of human fat cells is usually altered by weight loss after the age of two?
 a. Activity   *b.* Metabolism
 c. Number   *d.* Size

9. Which is the third stage of the human sexual-response cycle?
 a. Excitement   *b.* Orgasm
 c. Plateau   *d.* Resolution

10. Which hormone is considered most influential for structuring reproductive organs and sex-typing the brain?
 a. Adrenalin   *b.* Androgen
 c. Estrogen   *d.* Progestin

11. Which of the following practices is likely to be shaped almost entirely by respondent conditioning?
 a. Attitudes toward abortion and contraception
 b. Preferences for green-eyed sexual partners
 c. Rape
 d. Transsexualism

12. Which statement about the consequences of the sexual revolution in America is supported by research?
 a. Most parents (about 80 percent) discuss sexuality openly with their children.
 b. Only a slightly higher percentage of today's teenagers report engaging in intercourse as compared with teenagers of the 1960s.
 c. Reluctance to use contraception among teenagers may reflect sex-related anxieties that persist despite new standards.
 d. Women have adjusted more easily to new sexual standards than men have.

13. Which of the following phenomena was considered especially important for generating achievement-oriented motivation and behavior?
 a. Cognitive dissonance   *b.* Deprivation
 c. Homeostasis   *d.* Incentives

14. Parents of boys with strong achievement needs are most likely to stress which characteristic?
 a. Cleanliness   *b.* Compliance with authority
 c. Independence   *d.* Politeness

15. When does the motive to avoid success arise, according to Horner?
 a. When people attribute success to luck
 b. When people expect to fail
 c. When people fear success will bring negative consequences
 d. When women expect rejection for deviating from traditional sex-role standards

Suggested Readings

1. Cofer, C. N. *Motivation and emotion.* Glenview, Ill.: Scott, Foresman, 1972 (paperback). A good brief introduction to the study of motivation and emotion in people and other animals.

2. Lowry, R. J. *A. H. Maslow: An intellectual portrait.* Monterey, Calif.: Brooks/Cole, 1973. Lowry describes Maslow's beliefs about motivation, self-actualization, values, ideals, religion, science, and other topics. The book is informally written and filled with vital and moving quotations from Maslow's writings.

3. Balagura, A. *Hunger: A biopsychological analysis.* New York: Basic Books, 1973. Balagura, a skillful writer, focuses on many important hunger-related issues, including theories of hunger regulation, specific hungers, malnutrition, and obesity.

4. Stuart, R. S., & Davis, B. *Slim chance in a fat world: The behavioral control of obesity*. Champaign, Ill.: Research Press, 1972 (paperback); Mahoney, M. J., & Mahoney, K. Fight fat with behavior control. *Psychology Today*, 1976, **9**(12), 39ff. For easily understood information and sound advice on applying psychological principles to weight loss, these sources are recommended.

5. Hyde, J. S. *Understanding human sexuality*. New York: McGraw-Hill, 1979. A comprehensive text on sexuality that was written to provide practical information for everyday living as well as material on the biology of sex and psychological theory and research. The book is enjoyable to read, up to date, and thought-provoking.

6. Money, J., & Ehrhardt, A. E. *Man and woman, boy and girl: The differentiation and dimorphism of gender identity from conception to maturity*. Baltimore: Johns Hopkins Press, 1972 (paperback). A good introduction to the research literature on the differentiation of males and females, integrating findings from endocrinology, genetics, embryology, anthropology, and psychology.

7. McClelland, D. C. Managing motivation to expand human freedom. *American Psychologist*, 1978, **33**(3), 201–210. This interesting and provocative article suggests that careful attention to motivational research can lead to correct diagnoses and effective solutions of human problems. It also describes recent attempts to increase achievement motivation and treat alcoholism and hypertension.

8. Zuckerman, M. The search for high sensation. *Psychology Today*, 1978, **11**(9), 38ff. A description of research supporting the idea that people have needs for a consistent level of sensory stimulation which are biologically based and linked to adjustment in our society.

9. Rodin, J. The puzzle of obesity. *Human Nature*, 1978, **1**(2), 38–47. A very clear summary of the research which leads psychologists to believe that obesity has many causes.

10. Feshbach, S., & Malamuth, N. Sex and aggression: Proving the link. *Psychology Today*, 1978, **12**(6), 111ff. The article describes important experiments showing that exposure to sadomasochistic pornography makes college men more likely to find rape sexually exciting. Feshbach and Malamuth summarize the implications of their findings for public policy.

Answer Key

Self-Quiz

1. *c* (311) **2.** *d* (312) **3.** *a* (312) **4.** *c* (314)
5. *c* (317) **6.** *d* (321) **7.** *d* (322) **8.** *d* (324)
9. *b* (327) **10.** *b* (329) **11.** *b* (334) **12.** *c* (333)
13. *d* (337) **14.** *c* (338) **15.** *c* (339)

CHAPTER ELEVEN
Emotion

How does it feel to be anxious? Angry? Happy? In this chapter we focus on emotion. We begin with a student's description of these three feelings. As you read, compare your own reactions.

Feeling Anxious, Angry, and Happy: R. M.'s Personal Account

"When I feel anxious, everything is very tight. I can't relax. I don't sleep well so I constantly feel tired and run-down. I go to the bathroom a lot for some reason, and I snack an awful lot. I keep looking for diverting things to do. But I can't seem to find anything that is relaxing or fun. I don't enjoy anything. Usually I end up watching lots of mindless TV programs and reading magazines I'm really not interested in. Then I feel disgusted about wasting so much time. My thoughts keep returning to the topic that worries me. I'll wish I hadn't gotten myself into the mess, whatever it is. Even when I know that there's really no problem, I keep worrying. It hangs over me.

"I feel tight when I'm angry too. But I also get this overwhelming feeling of wanting to break things or punch something or throw something as hard as I can. My body is tensed up all over—I feel it in my jaws, my arms, my legs, and especially in my temples. And my heart pounds and speeds up. There are moments when I stop thinking and I just have this feeling of rage. It's hard to describe. It's a little like looking into a fire or stubbing your toe, only much more intense. Sometimes I even think about doing violent terrible things that I would never do. The whole time I keep telling myself: 'I shouldn't be doing this. I shouldn't be letting whatever it is get to me this way. It's serving no purpose.'

But I can't seem to help myself.

"You just sort of feel good when you're happy. Loose and warm. It feels good to be alive and very secure. Much of the time I feel very insecure and I worry about things. But when I feel happy, I see what's important in life and what's trivial. It's such a good feeling. You sometimes feel happy on spring days when you're outside and no jobs are pressing down on you and no problems are nagging at you. You feel loose. It doesn't make me want to jump up and down. It's just a warm, relaxed, free sort of feeling."

What characterizes human emotions? Like motives (described in Chapter 10), emotions are *internal states* that can't be directly observed or measured. As people react to their experiences, emotions arise suddenly. R. M.'s description suggests that feelings have an *uncontrollable quality*. They are not easily turned on or off. Though emotions may cause human beings to feel temporarily out of control, they don't really compel behavior. Rather, they increase arousal, reactivity, or irritability. Learning and a particular social context both influence the conduct that occurs. Still, like R. M., people frequently respond to their feelings with thoughts, words, or acts that seem inappropriate, disturbed, irrational, or disorganized.

Emotions have subjective, physiological, and behavioral components that human beings tend to be aware of. First, let's consider the *subjective component*, the cognitions and sensations. When anxious, R. M.'s thoughts kept returning to the worrisome topic. When angered, R. M. contemplated violent, terrible things. The sensation component of an emotion may be evaluated in different ways—by its pleasantness-unpleasantness and intensity, for instance. R. M. perceived anxiety and anger as unpleasant "tight" feelings, while considering happiness a "warm," "good" state. Rage is intense, of course, whereas irritation is mild. See Figure 11-1. Emotions are accompanied by *physiological reactions*, too. You may recall that R. M. reported a pounding heart and bodily tension when angered and gastrointestinal symptoms when anxious. Emotions are also related to changes in *expressive behavior*, such as verbalizations, gestures, postures, facial features, and actions. In response to anger, R. M. felt like attacking but did not. When anxious, R. M. sought out distracting activities.

We are ready now for a definition. *Emotions* (or *affects*) are internal states characterized by specific cognitions, sensations, physiological reactions, and expressive behavior. They tend to appear suddenly and to be difficult to control. After examining the nature of an emotion more closely, we explore three emotional states: anxiety, anger and aggression, and joy. Though we focus on emotion in people, we assume that the lower animals experience basic emotions as well. We draw on animal research whenever it advances our understanding of human emotions.

THE NATURE OF EMOTIONS

In this section we try to answer several general questions: Which emotions arise first? What do psychologists know about the physiological, subjective (sensation and cognition), and behavioral components of emotions? In what order do the components appear? Are emotions generally mingled with one another and with motives? How can the continual changing of emotions be explained?

The First Emotions

Emotions appear soon after birth in close association with motives. Babies cry and seem distressed when needs like hunger arise. Positive reactions similar to joy emerge as infants' needs are satisfied—when they are cuddled or fed, for instance. Newborn babies startle, an early sign of fear. They express interest and disgust. Anger arises during the latter half of the child's first year [1]. Recent

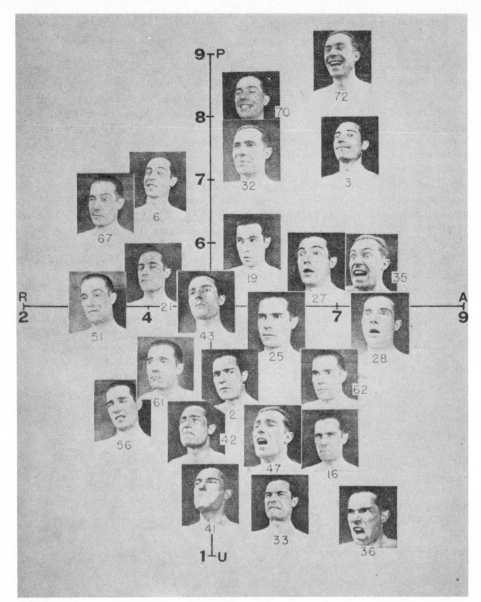

FIGURE 11-1 Psychologist Harold Schlosberg found that many facial expressions can be described reliably in terms of three dimensions: pleasantness-unpleasantness, rejection-attention, and intensity (level of activation). These pictures were among those used in Schlosberg's studies. When research participants rated facial expressions according to the three dimensions, they judged basic emotions similarly. Moving along the vertical axis, the faces display differing degrees of pleasantness-unpleasantness (P-U). Following the horizontal axis, the faces show varying amounts of rejection-attention (R-A). Relatively intense expressions appear at the boundaries; more neutral ones toward the center. As you can see, the facial expressions associated with contempt, happiness, surprise, fear, anger, determination, disgust, and many other emotions can be characterized in terms of the three dimensions [131]. [*H. Schlosberg.*]

observations suggest that the distress cry of one neonate produces a similar reaction in another. Psychologists believe that this response demonstrates the beginning of empathy, the capacity to understand the affects of others by experiencing them directly [2]. Many early emotional reactions function like messages and improve the infant's chances for survival. Crying, for example, is likely to bring a concerned parent to provide some relief. Smiling, as suggested in Chapter 3, appears to strengthen social bonds, leading to better care for the baby.

The Physiological Component of Emotions

More than fifty years ago, the American physiologist Walter Cannon suggested that the physiological responses associated with emotions provide animals with energy to meet emergencies. From his studies, he surmised that situations which evoke pain, rage, or fear produce specific bodily changes that ready organisms to deal vigorously with challenges. If swift action is called for—perhaps wresting food from another animal, fleeing, or

fighting—emotional arousal enhances the likelihood of survival [3].

During affects, physiological reactions are generated by the central and autonomic nervous systems and the endocrine glands. We describe the role of each center briefly. Additional information on these systems appeared in Chapter 4.

1. *The central nervous system.* Circuits within the *central nervous system* arouse, regulate, and integrate the responses that are made during an emotion. The *cerebral cortex,* or *cortex* (see Figure 11-2), is involved in identifying, evaluating, and making decisions about sensory data and subsequent behavior. The thoughts, expectations, and perceptions which arise here play important roles in maintaining or dissolving affects and the behavior that accompanies them.

The *reticular formation,* a network of nerve cells in the brain stem (shown in Figure 11-2), alerts the cortex to important sensory information. As data about potentially emotion-arousing events filter through this system, they are singled out as important. The reticular formation then arouses the cortex, which gives the matter its full atten-

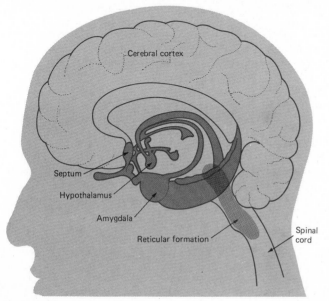

FIGURE 11-2 The parts of the brain that are especially active as people experience emotions: the cerebral cortex, limbic system, and reticular formation. Limbic regions are shown in light red.

tion. To respond appropriately to an emergency, we have to be alert.

The *limbic system*, a group of interrelated circuits deep within the brain's core (see Figure 11-2), plays a regulatory role in both emotions and motives. Though the precise functions of each limbic structure are not as yet clear, it is certain that sensory information passes through the limbic system on its way to the cortex. The cortex, in turn, sends messages down to the limbic system. One limbic structure, the *hypothalamus*, is responsible for activating the sympathetic nervous system during emergencies. The hypothalamus is also involved in fear and rage, as well as in hunger, sex, and thirst. Other limbic centers, such as the *amygdala* and *septum*, play roles in rage, pleasure, pain, and fear.

2. *The autonomic nervous system.* During an intense emotion, people are often aware of internal turmoil—perhaps a pounding heart, rapid pulse, tense muscles, trembling, and similar signs. These responses are called *autonomic reactions* because they are initiated by the *autonomic nervous system* (ANS). You may recall that the ANS consists of nerves that lead from the spinal cord and brain to the smooth muscles of the internal organs, glands, heart, and blood vessels. (See Figure 11-3.) The two branches of the ANS, the sympathetic and parasympathetic systems, maintain an optimal internal environment. The *parasympathetic system* tends to

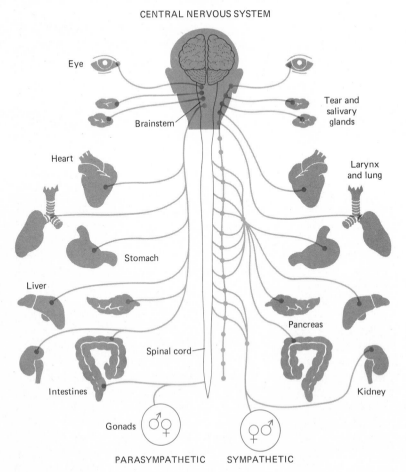

CENTRAL NERVOUS SYSTEM

Eye

Brainstem

Heart

Stomach

Liver

Spinal cord

Intestines

Gonads

Tear and salivary glands

Larynx and lung

Pancreas

Kidney

PARASYMPATHETIC   SYMPATHETIC

FIGURE 11-3 The major connections between the autonomic nervous system and various organs of the body. For clarity, the sympathetic system is drawn on the right and the parasympathetic system on the left. In actuality, each system is linked to organs on both sides of the body. The nerve fibers in the sympathetic system join at centers outside the spinal cord. [*From* A primer of psychobiology: Brain and behavior *by Timothy J. Teyler. W. H. Freeman and Company. Copyright © 1975.*]

be most active when animals are comparatively calm, as they digest their food, sleep, and recuperate from illness, for instance. The *sympathetic system* takes over when emergencies arise (at a time when intense emotion is likely) and mobilizes the body's resources for action. The sympathetic system oversees a number of activities including (1) rerouting blood to the heart, central nervous system, and muscles so that animals may think clearly and act quickly; (2) freeing sugar from reserves in the liver to energize muscles; (3) preparing the blood to clot quickly to heal wounds; and (4) deepening breathing so that additional oxygen is taken into the bloodstream to provide fuel for the body. During crises, the sympathetic system also stimulates the adrenal glands.

3. *The adrenal glands.* The adrenal glands are located on top of the kidneys. (See Figure 4-18.) When emotion-arousing experiences occur, the adrenal glands release the hormones *adrenalin* and *noradrenalin*. These chemical messengers stimulate many of the same centers that the sympathetic nervous system has already activated (including the circulatory and respiratory ones). As long as the body remains highly alert and active—until the crisis has passed or exhaustion sets in—these hormones are continually secreted.

Physiological responses to varied emotions Cannon maintained that physiological responses to pain, rage, and fear are similar. But numerous observations, including subjective impressions, challenge this view. Measurements on a man named Tom by physician Harold Wolff and his coworkers provide support for the idea that specific physiological response patterns underlie particular affects. When Tom was nine years old, he drank a cup of scalding clam chowder and damaged his esophagus. The damage was so severe that part of Tom's stomach lining had to be brought out through an opening in the abdomen so that he could feed himself directly. The surgery left his stomach lining partially exposed. Wolff and his associates studied him during adulthood. They noted that when Tom felt depressed or frightened, his stomach lining became pale and peristaltic contractions (muscle movements associated with digestion) and hydrochloric acid secretions decreased. When he felt angry, his stomach lining reddened and peristaltic contractions and hydrochloric acid secretions increased [4].

Laboratory experiments support the notion that fear and anger elicit different physiological responses. In one study, psychologist Albert Ax wired normal adult volunteers for recordings of blood pressure, heart rate, skin conductance (the skin's ability to conduct electricity, which is largely a measure of sweating), muscle tension, face and hand temperatures, respiration rate, and similar functions. Then each subject was frightened and angered in succession. To produce fear, the experimenter pretended that there was a dangerous high-voltage short circuit in the apparatus wired to the research participant. Anger was elicited by a technician who behaved in an insulting manner. Danger was associated with an increase in the subject's respiration rate and skin conductance, responses which can also be produced by an injection of *adrenalin*. The insulting remarks evoked increased muscle tension, decreased heart rate, and elevated blood pressure, reactions which are typically induced by an injection of both *adrenalin* and *noradrenalin* [5]. Psychologist Gary Schwartz has found that when people think happy thoughts, they produce different facial muscle responses from those produced when thinking sad or angry thoughts. Though the differences cannot be detected by observation, they can be measured [6].

In any given situation, emotions are mingled with other responses—for example, attentive observation and the processing of sensory data. These other behaviors are associated with their own physiological patterns. Attentive observation, for instance, is accompanied by deceleration or stabilization of the heart rate and decreased blood pressure. In measuring physiological signs of emotion, then, investigators must sometimes take into account the distinctive behavioral reactions and associated physiological responses evoked by the entire experimental setting. An extensive research program by psychologist John Lacey and his coworkers demonstrates that people's autonomic reactions to specific circumstances are quite similar [7].

Human differences in physiological responses to the same emotions You probably experience anxiety, anger, and happiness somewhat differently from the way R. M. did. People vary markedly in the type and intensity of their physiological reactions to emotions. Response tendencies often become apparent at early ages. Soon after birth, some infants show intense autonomic changes, while others barely react when stressed [8]. Like adults, individual babies may display a tendency to respond to a specific type of emotion in a particular way [9], predominantly by secreting stomach acid, accelerating heart rate, or elevating body temperature, for example. Human twin studies and research on inbred strains of rats and dogs suggest that individual response patterns may be influenced by heredity [10]. Emotional reactions may be affected by learning, too. Suppose, for example, that a boy is scheduled to take a frightening exam at school. The fear leads to blood-vessel constriction which causes him to look pale and sick. Assume that sympathetic parents keep the youngster home and that the boy's fear diminishes. Because pallor and blood-vessel constriction allow the child to escape an unpleasant experience, they are negatively reinforced. Under similar circumstances, this blood-vessel constriction reaction may become likely. The conditioning of autonomic responses was described in Chapter 5.

A person's physiological response pattern to particular emotions is influenced by age, sex, drugs, diet, personality, and coping style [11]. Studies consistently show that females and males, for instance, react to social pressure with significantly different amounts of adrenalin [12]. Diet may weaken specific bodily systems, such as the heart, altering responses under stress. Particular defenses against anxiety are associated consistently with distinctive hormonal patterns too.

The Subjective Component of Emotions

Suppose that your heart is pounding, your hands are perspiring, and your face is flushed. What emotion are you experiencing? If you have just been insulted, you'll probably label the affect "anger." If you are taking a difficult exam, you'll be likely to attribute your sensations to "fear" or "anxiety." If you've just met an exciting, attractive person, you may call the emotion "love." Many psychologists believe that people's interpretations of the immediate situation determine their emotional labels for quite similar sympathetic nervous system reactions. Because this concept emphasizes cognitions, it is known as the *cognitive theory of emotion*.

A classic experiment by psychologists Stanley Schachter and Jerome E. Singer supports the cognitive theory. Male college-student volunteers came individually to a laboratory. There they were told that they were participating in a study designed to measure how a vitamin supplement called supproxin affected their vision. Research participants were treated in one of four ways. Men in the *informed condition* were given an adrenalin injection and told to expect such side effects as trembling hands, pounding hearts, and flushed faces. Subjects in the *ignorant group* received an adrenalin injection and were not informed about side effects. Participants in the *misinformed condition* received an adrenalin injection but were misled to expect numbness, itching, and a slight headache. Subjects in a *placebo group* were given an injection of a neutral solution that produced no changes, and they were not led to expect any side effects. Consequently, men in the informed group were physically aroused and could explain it. Subjects in the ignorant and misinformed conditions were similarly aroused but could not account for their reactions. Students in the placebo group were not aroused at all. Schachter and Singer predicted that only the aroused research participants without an adequate explanation would seek out an emotional label for their state.

After the injection and explanation, an associate of the experimenters was introduced to each man as a fellow subject in the study. For the research participants in the misinformed group and half of those in each of the other conditions, the stooge tried to create a happy mood. He shot baskets with crumpled wads of paper, sailed paper airplanes, and hula-hooped. For the remaining subjects, the confederate attempted to generate anger by grumbling and complaining about the experiment and showing annoyance with an exasperating questionnaire that everyone had filled out. At the end of the session, Schachter and Singer measured emotional states by observing and rating behavior and by asking for self-reports on a questionnaire.

The psychologists found that research participants in the misinformed and ignorant groups (those who had no reasonable explanation for their state) were more susceptible to the stooge's antics than the others. They behaved more happily and reported more joy when the confederate appeared cheerful. Similarly, they appeared more angry and claimed to feel more hostile when he acted negatively [13]. Presumably, these aroused, uninformed people had actively searched out explanations for their state. The stooge's behavior provided obvious clues that had been accepted. This research is diagrammed in Figure 11-4. The Schachter-Singer investigation is one of many supporting the notion that the sensation component of an emotion may arise when people perceive and label a vague pattern of physio-

logical arousal. This idea remains controversial, as we see a little later.

Though cognitions may or may not trigger the sensations that accompany our affects, they clearly play an important role in maintaining and moderating emotions. Formal and informal observations suggest that people often nurse their feelings, causing them to be prolonged and/or intensified [14]. In one study, psychologists Constance Hammen and Susan Krantz asked depressed and nondepressed women to describe their thoughts about being alone on a Friday night. Depressed research participants tended to report cognitions that would be likely to maintain their misery, such as, "Upsets me and makes me start to imagine endless days and nights by myself." Nondepressed subjects reported experiencing the types of cognitions that would minimize their feelings of rejection, such as, "Doesn't bother me because one Friday night alone isn't that important; probably everyone has spent nights alone." Depressed women also lowered their ratings of self-worth more than nondepressed women after failing an interpersonal task in the laboratory [15]. Presumably, depressed people generate the types of thoughts that further their own unhappiness. In daily life, cognitions continually alter the duration and intensity of emotions. Suppose that you are accused by your mother of being a "sloppy pig." You can feed your anger by concentrat-

FIGURE 11-4 The major events in the Schachter-Singer experiment.

Group	Injection	Expectation	Resulting state	Model	Effect
Informed	Adrenalin	Told precise "side-effects" of adrenalin	Not bewildered, aroused	Happy	No effect
				Angry	No effect
Ignorant	Adrenalin	Told nothing about "side-effects"	Bewildered, aroused	Happy	Relatively happy
				Angry	Relatively angry
Misinformed	Adrenalin	Misled about "side-effects"	Bewildered, aroused	Happy	Relatively happy
Placebo	Neutral solution	Told nothing about "side-effects"	Not bewildered, not aroused	Happy	No effect
				Angry	No effect

ing on the negative aspects of your mother's personality and by cataloging her past indiscretions. Or the anger can be abbreviated or eliminated by numerous strategies. You may put the scene out of your mind. You may excuse your mother because of mitigating circumstances (for instance, "She's frustrated and irritable after a long, hard day at the office"). You may concentrate on her virtues. Sometimes people cope ahead of time by worrying, comforting themselves ("Every-thing will work out"), or trying to relax [16]. There is some evidence that women are more likely than men to try to control their feelings [17].

The Behavioral Component of Emotions

People and other animals respond to their emotions with facial expressions, gestures, and actions. What factors influence these

FIGURE 11-5 What emotion does each face portray? (The answers are in the Answer Keys.) [*Ekman, Universal and cultural differences in facial expression of emotion. In J. K. Cole (Ed.),* Nebraska Symposium on Motivation. *Lincoln: University of Nebraska Press, 1971.*]

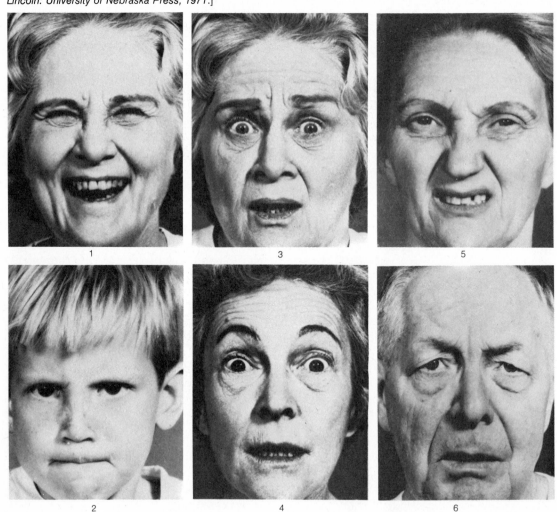

responses? We consider facial expressions first. Before reading further, please try to label the emotions conveyed by the faces in Figure 11-5. Most people can easily identify these particular expressions. Apparently, certain facial patterns communicate basic emotions universally. Human beings all over the world, including the aborigines in New Guinea who have not mixed with modern civilizations, express happiness by smiling or laughing, sorrow by a down-turned mouth, and anger by a red face [18]. These expressions occur spontaneously in young infants. The congenitally blind and deaf (people isolated, beginning at birth, from the sights and sounds of other's emotions) express their affects with the same signs [19]. These observations suggest that certain facial expressions are programmed into people by their genes. Experimental studies by psychologist John Lanzetta and his coworkers show that as people watch the pained facial expressions of another individual, they display signs of physical arousal and report feelings of distress [20]. You may recall that newborn babies are upset by the distress vocalizations of other neonates. Perhaps such internal mimicry occurs during many emotions and helps human beings interpret what others are feeling.

Experience also influences facial expressions. The final form of basic emotional signs (the wideness of a smile or the loudness of a laugh, for example) is affected by social standards and learning. Not all facial expressions and gestures are genetically based, either. Tibetans stick out their tongues as a friendly greeting. In China, people may clap their hands when they are worried and scratch their ears and cheeks when they are happy [21]. In our own culture, members of particular ethnic groups make distinctive gestures in emotion-laden situations [22]. These expressions appear to be acquired largely by observation and imitation.

Now consider variations in the conduct that accompanies emotions. During anger, for example, Bill sulks, Nanny whines and complains, Shawn threatens, Ian yells, Francine destroys, Herman becomes depressed and

self-destructive, and Anna looks for a constructive solution to the problem. Behaviors such as these are probably learned. Observation and imitation are often significant. Reinforcement and punishment strengthen or weaken habits. Sulking, for instance, may be reinforced because it is successful in gaining attention or favors and because it is relatively acceptable to parents (as compared with "mouthing off" or throwing things). Later in this chapter, we explore the determinants of aggression, a behavior that frequently accompanies the affect anger.

Which Component Comes First?

Currently, behavioral scientists don't know how the physiological, sensation, cognition, and behavioral components of emotions are interrelated and whether they arise in a single consistent order. Some psychologists have stressed the triggering role of one or another element. The Schachter-Singer study and others suggest that physiological states precede cognitions and that cognitions precede sensations and behavior at least some of the time. Other investigators have proposed that *appraisal*, a cognitive process, often comes first [23]. One study supporting this position, by T. Symington and his coworkers, involved autopsies on individuals who had died from injury or disease. There were two groups of subjects: those who had not been aware of any crisis and those who had been conscious of their fatal condition. The postmortem examinations showed that certain autonomic indicators ordinarily associated with stressful emotions were absent in the unaware victims. The scientists inferred that people who were unconscious experienced no emotion before dying. The bodies of individuals who were conscious of their fatal condition, in contrast, showed the expected physiological signs of stress [24]. The Symington study suggests that cognitions, which are characteristic of ordinary waking consciousness, must precede feelings of anxiety and associated autonomic responses. But the data on this topic are far

FIGURE 11-6 What emotion does Frank De Vito's face express? [Hackensack Record.]

from consistent. There is evidence that behavior may come before certain physiological responses that attend emotion. Recently, for example, Gary Schwartz found support for the idea that facial expressions precede autonomic reactions [25]. In short, research does not support a single ordering of the emotional components.

In any case, the varied emotional components clearly are interrelated. During an emotion, behavior, like thoughts, may modify sensations. Carefully controlled laboratory experiments by John Lanzetta's group indicate that when subjects deliberately frown, they tend to report feeling angrier than when they project more neutral expressions. Research participants behaved more aggressively after frowning, too. Similarly, when people convey intense pain by their facial expressions, they are apt to report experiencing more pain than when they suppress pain-conveying facial information. Physiological measurements suggested that the self-reports were accurate [26]. Apparently, the varied components of an emotion can alter one another.

The Complexity of Emotions

It is sometimes difficult to detect emotions from facial expressions. Before reading on, please try to identify the emotion expressed by the face in Figure 11-6. Without information about the setting (disclosed in Figure 11-7), the task is difficult. To read feelings in daily life, people often rely on knowledge about the situation that provoked the expression. This additional information may be necessary because feelings are usually mingled with other feelings in real life. As Gary Schwartz has suggested, many situations evoke a number of different emotions, not merely one [27]. This notion is easily demonstrated at an intuitive level by rating several different experiences on the amount of anger, fear, sadness, and happiness that they aroused (or would arouse). Consider being accepted by the college of your choice. The news might arouse little or no anger, a lot of fear, little or no sadness, and a lot of happiness. Accepting a new job in a distant city might evoke little or no anger, a lot of fear, a lot of sadness, and a lot of happiness.

Not only are emotions mingled with one another; they are also tied up with motives, beginning at birth, as we suggested previously. Fulfilling a need, say, hunger, is often associated with specific feelings—in this case, happiness or pleasure. Emotions, in turn, generate motives and behavior. Anger, for example, is often accompanied by a desire to hurt and to behave aggressively, as R. M. (and many others) have noted. You may recall that the limbic brain regions which are centrally involved in motivated behavior play key roles in emotion as well.

Affects seem complex for another reason. They continually change. In general, people are not gripped constantly by violent feelings. More neutral emotions usually prevail. Psychologist Richard Solomon suggests that our brains try to maintain an optimal emotional balance by reducing the intensity of strong positive and negative feelings. Experiences, according to Solomon, may arouse relatively strong emotions. The intensity of these feelings rises to a peak, declines, levels off, and remains steady as long as the input continues. A danger, perhaps a growling, snarling dog, may arouse terror initially. If the danger continues, the terror should decline, perhaps to moderate anxiety. Experience-evoked emotions, Solomon believes, automatically arouse *afterreactions*, defined as emotions very different from the original one. The second feeling gradually opposes, or suppresses, the strength of the affect that triggered it. Thus the model is known as the *opponent-process theory.*

To continue with our dog example, calm may be automatically elicited by anxiety. The emotional state of the organism is determined, Solomon assumes, by the sum total of the two emotional states: the experience-evoked affect and the afterreaction. After an experience ends, the emotion that was directly aroused disappears quickly. Afterreactions, in contrast, tend to linger. If the dog continues to growl and snarl, you are likely to grow accustomed to it and begin relaxing, as the calm afterreaction "neutralizes" your anxiety. If the dog stops growling and snarling, the anxiety will be dispelled quickly. The feeling of relief should remain for a long period. Suppose that similar experiences recur. In this case, Solomon suggests, the intensity of the experience-evoked emotion will weaken. At the same time, the afterreaction will increase in strength and persistence. After working at a kennel, for example, you will probably feel relatively mild anxiety upon hearing a growling dog. After experiencing any strong emotion, Solomon's theory predicts, people return to normalcy only after passing through an essentially opposite feeling. Alcohol, opiate, and other drug addictions follow this model. The euphoria, or intense pleasure, tends to be followed by an unpleasant afterreaction as the drug leaves the person's system [28].

MEASURING EMOTIONS

Psychologists assess human emotions by examining one or more components: the subjective element (cognitions, sensations), behavior, and/or physiology. Studies of the emotions of other animals are limited, of course, to the measurement of behavioral and physiological elements.

To explore the cognitions and sensations that accompany an emotion, behavioral scientists usually administer tests or interview research participants. The items presented in Table 11-1 come from a questionnaire that is

TABLE 11-1 Items from a Scale of the State-Trait Anxiety Inventory

The test taker rates each item: 1 (Not at all), 2 (Somewhat), 3 (Moderately so), 4 (Very much so).

I feel calm	I feel nervous
I am tense	I am jittery
I feel upset	I feel content

Source: Spielberger, C. D. Current trends in theory and research on anxiety. In C. D. Spielberger (Ed.), *Anxiety: Current trends in theory and research.* Vol. 1. New York: Academic, 1972. P. 36.

commonly used to evaluate anxiety in a specific situation. Self-report measures like this one are easy to administer. The questions guide people's responses into a standard format so that they can be quantified and compared with the reactions of others. But, the validity of self-reports is questionable, as has been mentioned repeatedly. Few human beings are acute self-observers who reveal what they see without distortion or falsification.

Sometimes emotions are inferred from direct observations of behavior. To gain insights into anger, for example, investigators might (1) observe and rate the frequency or intensity of trembling and flushing, (2) assess the loudness of the voice, or (3) measure willingness to aggress against the target of the anger. In lower animals, the duration of aggressive acts can be timed. Using behavioral observations as measures of emotion assumes that conduct accurately mirrors feeling. It probably does in some cases. But people's responses are varied, as we have seen. They are influenced by past experiences and perceptions of the immediate setting.

Physiological instruments are also used to assess emotion. Psychologists monitor internal physical reactions that accompany feelings, including changes in heart and respiration rates and muscle tension. Often, several physiological responses are recorded on a *polygraph,* a device that simultaneously records more than one reaction, event, or process. Like other types of data, physiological measurements are somewhat difficult to

FIGURE 11-7 The face of Frank De Vito, a New Jersey plumber, probably expresses a combination of feelings, including joy and surprise. He and his wife had just been informed that he had won $1 million in a state lottery. Because facial expressions often reflect several emotions at once, information about the setting is frequently important for interpreting the face's messages correctly. [Hackensack Record.]

interpret. Typical responses to the specific situation and varied individual differences must be taken into account for accuracy. Figure 11-8 describes the lie detector test, a commonly utilized measure of deception that relies on assessing physiological signs of emotion.

As we describe research on anxiety, anger and aggression, and joy, you will see how varied measurement strategies are combined to provide information about emotions. ▲

ANXIETY

We define *anxiety* as an emotion characterized by feelings of anticipated danger, ten-

---

▲ **USING PSYCHOLOGY**

1. How does your body respond when you're angry? Anxious or fearful? Are the reactions noticeably different?

2. Think of situations where the same physical state could be labeled as two different emotions, depending on the circumstances.

3. What cognitions could magnify the intensity of jealousy? Reduce its intensity? Are you aware of nursing the sensations that accompany your own emotions? Describe specific examples.

4. What would the opponent-process theory predict about the duration of ecstacy associated with romantic love?

5. If you were conducting a study of anxiety, what type(s) of measures would you select? Reject? Why?

sion, and distress and by sympathetic nervous system arousal. You may recall that R. M. characterized the affect as a negative, "tight" one. Anxiety and fear are sometimes distinguished from one another on two dimensions. (1) The object of a fear is easy to specify, while the object of an anxiety is often unclear. (2) The intensity of a fear is proportional to the magnitude of the danger. The intensity of an anxiety is likely to be greater than the objective danger (if it is known). In real life, anxiety and fear are not easy to differentiate, so we will use the two terms interchangeably, as many psychologists do. In this section we examine several questions. What triggers anxiety? What shapes its intensity? How does anxiety influence learning? How does it contribute to health?

Triggers of Anxiety

A number of triggers of anxiety have been described. Freud listed two: (1) real-world dangers and (2) anticipation of punishment for expressing sexual, aggressive, or other forbidden impulses or engaging in immoral behavior. In the first case, anxiety is caused by actual situations which lead to physical pain; in the second case, by cognitions. Behavioral scientists tend to emphasize one or the other source. Cognitive psychologists stress conflicts between expectations, beliefs, attitudes, perceptions, information, conceptions, and the like, which lead to *cognitive dissonance* (described in Chapter 10). Humanistic psychologists focus on mental conflicts too, especially on those that arise while choosing a fulfilling and meaningful life-style. Behavioristic psychologists believe that most anxieties are established by *conditioning*, as an "object" of some type is accidentally associated with an anxiety-arousing experience, often one that may be dangerous. (Chapter 5 treats the conditioning of fear in more detail.) Both cognitive conflicts and potentially perilous situations, then, appear to be able to excite anxiety. Recent research suggests that the two types of anxiety have their own distinct physiological patterns [29].

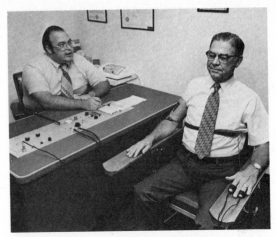

FIGURE 11-8 This photograph shows the administration of a lie detector test. The test is based on the assumption that lying arouses anxiety and that anxiety produces predictable autonomic changes which can be measured. As subjects answer questions, the lie detector (a polygraph) records blood pressure, respiration rate, skin conductance, and heart rate. Other bodily responses can also be recorded. Many business organizations, national security operations, and law enforcement agencies use polygraphs to make decisions about people's integrity. An examiner administering a lie detector test begins by asking control questions to assess the test taker's responses when telling the truth and when lying. These questions are often unrelated to the incident of interest. Knowing the suspect's autonomic behavior under varied conditions helps in evaluating responses to critical questions directly associated with the current investigation. Because crime-related questions may be intensely anxiety-arousing to innocent people, polygraph operators sometimes ask suspects about details that only the true criminal and police would know. How accurate are polygraph results? Estimates vary from no better than chance to perfect. The variability is not entirely surprising since (1) the results depend heavily on the operator's skill and experience and (2) people can learn to control their autonomic responses and "beat the machine" [132]. A relatively new type of truth machine, the voice-stress analyzer, operates on speech samples. It picks up changes in pitch generated by tension. The voice-stress analyzer suffers from many of the same limitations as the polygraph. [*Wide World Photos.*]

Influences on the Intensity of Anxiety

Physical responses to the same threat may be mild or intense. Twin studies and investigations of infant differences, mentioned earlier, suggest that genes influence human reactions to stress. Experiences mold an individual's anxiety level, as well. In rats, too few or too many fear-arousing experiences in infancy are associated with a higher-than-average level of anxiety later in life [30]. Too many stresses during infancy and throughout the life cycle are definitely harmful to human beings. After continuous exposure to danger during combat in World War II, for instance, soldiers reached a point of no return. Responses to stress became exaggerated. When the soldiers returned to civilian life, they reacted to minor pressures (such as loud noises, bright lights, or exercise) as though they were confronting a major emergency. Their bodies recovered slowly. The mechanisms that ordinarily restore equilibrium conditions seemed to have broken down [31].

Although people show characteristic levels of anxiety, responses to any specific event depend to some extent on thoughts and perceptions. There is evidence that both laboratory animals and people experience less tension when they feel in control—when stresses are predictable and coping is possible. Rats, for example, that are shocked immediately after a tone are less likely to develop ulcers, a severe reaction to anxiety, than those that are shocked randomly without warning (but with the same number of shocks). Similarly, rats that can make a response that will terminate a shock develop fewer stomach lesions than animals that are exposed to identical shocks without being able to control them in any way [32].

A sense of control helps people handle stress, too. In one investigation, psychologists David Glass and Jerome Singer and their coworkers studied the effects of noise on forty-eight undergraduate women. Some research participants listened to a tape recording of superimposed sounds: voices of a Spaniard and an Armenian, a typewriter, a desk calculator, and a mimeograph machine. Subjects in one group heard the discordant noise at high volume; those in another group, at low volume. For some individuals in each group,

the clatter appeared at regular (predictable) intervals; for others, at random (unpredictable) intervals. After listening to the tape, the research participants were asked to work paper-and-pencil tasks (some of which were insoluble). Another group of women, who had been spared the noisy experience altogether, tackled the same problems. Students who had been exposed to any noise at all were less persistent on the insoluble tasks than the others. Randomly spaced noise, even at low volume, decreased persistence more than regularly spaced noise. Similar results were obtained on male college students and on city-dwelling residents of both sexes. Later laboratory experiments have shown that when people feel that they can control the presence of noise, its aversive effects are reduced [33]. Unpredictable noise which cannot be regulated may lead to a sense of helplessness that increases anxiety and decreases ability to tolerate frustration and think clearly. In real life, unpredictable, uncontrollable noise adversely affects academic achievement and possibly mental health [34].

Research by James Geer and his colleagues and many other psychologists suggests that it is the *perception of control*, not the actual control, that is of critical importance [35]. He and his coworkers gave student subjects ten painful six-second electric shocks. After each one, the research participants had to press a switch immediately "to provide an index of their reaction time." To assess anxiety, Geer measured the students' sweat-gland activity. After the first series of shocks, half the subjects were told that they could cut the duration of the next ten shocks in half if they reacted quickly enough. These people perceived themselves in control. The remaining research participants were informed merely that the next ten shocks would be shorter. Though all students received the same three-second shocks, those who believed that they were in control showed significantly less sweat-gland activity (and presumably less anxiety) than the others.

Helping people feel that they have control over frightening circumstances is likely to reduce the anxiety level in a great many settings. When patients are prepared for surgery beforehand, for example, they adjust more easily to the tensions of the postoperative period than unprepared patients do. They complain less, require less sedation, and seem to recover more quickly [36].

Anxiety's Effects on Learning

Anxious students sometimes report blocking or choking up on tests and being unable to retrieve information that they know. Anxiety can affect learning at different stages. In terms of our memory model (Chapter 8), anxiety may influence encoding, storage, and/or retrieval. Effects on the various memory processes are not easily separated from one another. In the past, psychologists simply administered different types of learning tasks in the laboratory to people who identified themselves (on tests) as feeling either much or very little anxiety in academic situations. The overall performances of the two groups were subsequently compared. The relationship between anxiety and overall performance under these circumstances appears to be complicated. In general, anxiety seems to facilitate success on simple tasks and to hinder complex achievements [37]. People with high anxiety levels are especially likely to perform poorly on difficult or ambiguous test items (which are apt to be misread or misinterpreted). They do particularly badly in pressured, stressful situations such as important exams [38]. When materials are loosely organized and when rote learning, or memorizing, is required, highly anxious individuals tend to perform worse than less anxious ones, as well [39]. Recent studies suggest that highly anxious people may experience encoding problems that interfere with putting information into memory in the first place. Psychologist John Mueller has found that research participants with high anxiety appear to encode fewer dimensions of the material to be learned than less anxious ones. They use less complicated organizing strategies as they process information. When

adaptability is required, they tend to be less flexible than less anxious people in switching from tactic to tactic [40].

In view of these findings, we would expect highly anxious people to perform rather poorly in school. To investigate this issue, psychologist Charles Spielberger examined the grades and scholastic aptitude test scores of male college students. Anxiety level appeared to have relatively little influence on the academic performance of students with either very high or very low aptitudes. Regardless of reported anxiety level, men who scored low on aptitude tests made relatively poor grades generally. High scorers tended to make relatively good marks. Excessive anxiety did appear to adversely affect the great majority of students, those who scored in the middle range on the aptitude test. Among these middle-aptitude people, high anxiety was associated with low academic performance [41].

A number of techniques can help anxious students cope with their tension. Charles Spielberger and his associates counseled highly anxious university students in groups to increase their sense of control in the classroom. The psychologists focused on practical topics, including studying and preparing for exams, figuring out what the instructor wanted, handling individual academic difficulties, managing dormitory life, and selecting a vocation. This program raised the anxious students' grade points by one-half point on the average [42]. Systematic desensitization, a relaxation technique described in Chapter 16, is frequently successful in helping students lower their anxiety. Jogging and thinking about calm, happy, comfortable experiences appear to be effective tension reducers for anxious students, too [43]. ▲

Anxiety's Effects on Health

Early in his career, the endocrinologist Hans Selye (b. 1907) (pictured in Figure 11-9) discovered that animals responded similarly to many different types of stresses, including intense cold, conflict, injury, bacterial agents,

▲ **USING PSYCHOLOGY**

1. Describe plausible causes of anxiety about sexuality from the viewpoints of psychoanalytic theory, behaviorism, and humanistic and cognitive psychology. (Chapter 1 provides more information on each viewpoint.)

2. Even if you study regularly, surprise quizzes are apt to be more distressing than scheduled ones. Why?

3. Describe a situation where feelings of control helped you cope with anxiety.

4. Do you ever experience test anxiety? Under what circumstances? What symptoms appear? What can you do to reduce this type of tension? How can your feelings of control over exams be increased?

and surgery. The victim, Selye came to believe, experienced a *general adaptation syndrome* (GAS) in three stages:

Stage 1: Alarm reaction. During this stage, the sympathetic nervous system and the adrenal glands mobilize the body's defensive forces. In this way energy production is maximized to handle the emergency—to resist the stressor. If

the tension is prolonged, the body enters a second stage.

Stage 2: Resistance. As an animal fights off a specific stressor, its body remains highly aroused. But a price is paid for this emergency preparedness. Systems responsible for growth, repair, and warding off infection do not operate well under these conditions. Consequently, the organism is in a weakened state and very

FIGURE 11-9 Hans Selye relaxes in his office at the Montreal Institute of Experimental Medicine and Surgery. In recent years, behavioral scientists have been focusing on factors that influence responses to stress. Selye is convinced that coping style is important. "A man of 71 like me," Selye writes, "who has slightly hardened arteries and high blood pressure, might collapse if he took himself too seriously. He might act so defensively in a stressful situation that the increased pumping of his heart and pulsing of his blood might kill him. But if he can learn to moderate his reactions to stressors, he will find that the pressure of life leaves him relatively unharmed [133]." Psychological research supports the idea that coping styles are important. In a recent correlational study, for example, the attitudes of executives who handled a lot of stresses without becoming ill were compared with the attitudes of highly stressed executives who succumbed to various sicknesses. The healthy business people differed from the ill ones in that they (1) tended to feel significantly more in control of and committed to life, (2) believed more strongly in the meaningfulness of existence, and (3) were more actively involved with their surroundings [134]. [*John Olson*/People *weekly.* © 1974, Time, Inc.]

susceptible to other stresses, including disease. If the old stressor continues or new ones arise, the animal enters a third stage.

Stage 3. Exhaustion. The body cannot maintain its resistance indefinitely and gradually shows the signs of exhaustion. After the sympathetic nervous system has depleted its energy supply, the parasympathetic system takes charge. Body activities slow down and may stop altogether. If the stressor continues, the worn-out victim will have great difficulty coping. At this time, continued tension leads to psychological problems, including depression and psychotic behavior, and/or to physical illness or even death [44].

Before looking at some of the health-related implications of Selye's general adaptation syndrome, it is important to know that the model has been amended by subsequent research. The GAS is more apt to occur after a stress of long duration, and not after brief, abrupt strains [45]. Not all prolonged pressures produce the syndrome. Exercise, fasting, and heat, for instance, do not [46]. It is currently unclear whether intense joys activate the response [47]. Moreover, as indicated earlier, physiological reactions during emotion depend on the situation and the organism involved. Diverse stresses produce different reactions. A given stressor—say, electric shock—does not influence all bodily systems that participate in the stress response in the same way. Some systems may be severely taxed, while others are hardly affected or even benefited [48]. Experience and genetics influence the precise responses. In sum, animals undergoing crises probably react somewhat similarly with the core responses Selye described. But a great many individual differences are observed. Figure 11-9 discusses the effect of coping styles on response to stress.

The general adaptation syndrome is a mixed blessing. On the one hand, it offers people and other animals the necessary energy for fighting or fleeing. If action is required, organisms are apt to perform and feel better as the adrenalin level rises [49]. But modern strains, such as crowded highways, tight budgets, social conflicts, and competition, more frequently demand clear thinking over a long period rather than quick action. For this

reason, some scientists believe that our autonomic and hormonal stress-related responses have outlived their usefulness. They are, in fact, often harmful. The sugar summoned from the liver to provide energy, for example, is converted to fat if it isn't used, creating conditions that lead to artery disease. Excessive adrenalin and noradrenalin damage organs and contribute to headaches, sinus attacks, high blood pressure, ulcers, allergic reactions, and many other illnesses. These disorders are often labeled *psychosomatic*. (They are the result of an animal's bodily, or *somatic*, responses to tension, a psychological condition.) Many diseases that were once thought to be caused entirely by physical mechanisms are now believed to be influenced by stress [50]. We examine evidence for this hypothesis.

Disease and stress In the late 1960s, Thomas Holmes, Richard Rahe, Minoru Masuda, and others began a massive research program to explore the connections between personal experiences and health. Initially, these behavioral scientists developed a questionnaire to measure the stressfulness of forty-three common *life changes*. Nearly 400 people were asked to indicate how much readjustment was required by these experiences. Each event had to be compared with marriage (arbitrarily assigned the value 500) and rated accordingly. The ratings of diverse groups were very similar. Table 11-2 shows how representative experiences were evaluated in *life change units* (the average ratings assigned divided by 10). This research has enabled psychologists to explore the question: Is the number of life change units in a specific time period, say one year, associated with later health problems? In one of many studies of this topic, Richard Rahe and his coworkers had 2,500 naval officers and enlisted men fill out a questionnaire reporting significant experiences throughout the preceding six months. As the navy men went about their sea duties, the investigators gathered health information. During the first month of the cruise, the men who had been recently sub-

TABLE 11-2 Representative Experiences and Their Value in Life Change Units

Rank	Life event	Mean value
1	Death of spouse	100
2	Divorce	73
5	Death of close family member	63
6	Personal injury or illness	53
7	Marriage	50
8	Fired at work	47
10	Retirement	45
12	Pregnancy	40
13	Sex difficulties	39
16	Change in financial state	38
17	Death of close friend	37
18	Change to different line of work	36
19	Change in number of arguments with spouse	35
22	Change in responsibilities at work	29
25	Outstanding personal achievement	28
27	Beginning or ending of school	26
29	Revision of personal habits	24
31	Change in work hours or conditions	20
33	Change in schools	20
34	Change in recreation	19
35	Change in church activities	19
38	Change in sleeping habits	16
40	Change in eating habits	15
41	Vacation	13
43	Minor violations of the law	11

Source: Holmes, T. H., & Rahe, R. H. The social readjustment rating scale. *Journal of Psychosomatic Research,* 1967, **11,** 213–218.

jected to a great many readjustments came down with 90 percent more first illnesses than those who had made few such adjustments. For each subsequent month of the voyage, men who had experienced many previous stresses reported more new illnesses than the others [51]. Similar studies find small but significant associations between life changes and heart attacks, cancer, leukemia, asthma, tuberculosis, pregnancy complications, hernias, warts, colds, skin disorders, menstrual difficulties, depression, suicide attempts, anxiety, and schizophrenia [52].

Daily stresses and strains may be just as injurious to health as major life changes are, or even more so. All over the world, poor people exhibit greater health-related problems than more fortunate people [53]. The tension associated with poverty may be an important contributor to ill health. Recent research on black Americans living in urban and rural areas supports this idea. People who had been exposed to a great many daily strains experienced a significantly greater incidence of high blood pressure and related disorders (such as strokes and hypertensive heart conditions) than those leading more stable lives [54]. Though this body of correlational research is far from being airtight proof that stresses of varied types cause illnesses, it has called attention to the consistent relationship between the two phenomena. We look more closely now at peptic ulcers, heart attacks, and sudden deaths and the evidence suggesting that stress contributes to each condition.

Peptic ulcers Peptic ulcers will probably afflict one in every ten Americans now living at some time during the life cycle. A peptic ulcer is essentially a sore in the lining of the stomach or duodenum (the first section of the small bowel). During digestion, hydrochloric acid and enzymes produced by the body break food down into usable components. In the case of the peptic ulcer victim, excessive amounts of hydrochloric acid erode the mucous layer that protects the inner wall of the stomach or duodenum. Then the acid begins to digest the wall itself.

Stress appears to play a major role in the production of excessive secretions of hydrochloric acid. Numerous experimental studies link the ulcers of animals to severe stresses [55]. When people undergo intense, prolonged strains, during migrations, floods, earthquakes, and wars, for example, a relatively high number develop peptic ulcers or other gastrointestinal disorders [56]. Air traffic controllers, burdened every day by life-and-death decision making, have an unusually high rate of ulcers and other stress-related problems [57].

Observations on Tom (the man with the

partially exposed stomach described earlier) suggest that there is a direct connection between tension and ulcers. When Tom became angry, increased acid secretions and rhythmic contractions took place just as though his stomach were full of food that needed to be digested. During two weeks of intense agitation, he secreted excessive quantities of gastric juices and developed bleeding sores in his stomach.

Stresses do not produce ulcers in all laboratory animals or all people. Apparently, ulcer victims are predisposed to respond to tension by increasing gastric secretions. This tendency is associated with a *high pepsinogen level*, a characteristic which appears to be influenced by heredity. (Pepsinogen is a substance secreted by the gastric glands in the stomach and later converted into pepsin, a major ingredient in the gastric juices. Pepsinogen level may be thought of, then, as an index of gastric activity.) Research shows that a high pepsinogen level often precedes the formation of ulcers. In one study supporting this notion, psychologist Herbert Weiner and his colleagues measured the level of pepsinogen in more than 2,000 newly inducted male military draftees. The investigators then selected the men with the highest and lowest pepsinogen levels for further observation. No soldier showed signs of ulcers at the time. When the subjects were reexamined during the eighth and sixteenth weeks of basic training, nine of them were developing ulcers. All nine came from the high-pepsinogen group. A similar association between high pepsinogen level and ulcer formation has been found in children and civilian adults [58]. Presumably, a genetic propensity to secrete gastric juices under stress and prolonged tension combine to produce ulcers. Other factors are undoubtedly involved. Since the mid-1950s, there has been an absolute decline in ulcer cases in the United States. Right now, no one knows the causes of this trend [59].

Heart attacks Heart disorders kill approximately 700,000 Americans every year [60]. The causes of coronary diseases are known to be multiple, but are not well understood. Many studies suggest that the stresses and strains of life are a contributing factor.

The pioneering research of cardiologists Meyer Friedman and Ray Rosenman has related heart attacks to a particular personality pattern, called *type A*. Type A people struggle continually to accomplish too many things in too little time or against too many obstacles. They appear aggressive (sometimes hostile), ambitious for achievement and power, competitive, and compulsive. They are habitually racing against the clock, and they rarely "waste time" by relaxing. Type A college students frequently ignore fatigue as they push themselves in the laboratory. Type A individuals talk loudly, quickly, and explosively. Even when no time constraints exist, they like to act with speed. People with this personality pattern show exaggerated sympathetic nervous system responses to laboratory stresses. Resting measures of the autonomic activity of the type A person are not distinctive [61].

A number of well-controlled, long-term studies suggest that individuals with type A personalities (especially men) are more likely than others to develop cardiac conditions. In a typical investigation, scientists classify the personalities of large numbers of middle-aged males who have no history of coronary problems. The research participants are checked periodically thereafter for signs of cardiac disease. Type A people are more apt to develop heart conditions than others. In one study, for example, 70 percent of the coronary cases had initially been categorized type A [62]. Smoking and other known risk factors cannot account for the findings.

While researchers do not know which aspects of the type A personality pattern are associated with heart trouble or precisely how [63], they speculate along these lines: Type A individuals maximize their daily pressures. The resulting anxiety leads to biochemical changes that precipitate the coronary problems. Genetics might predispose people both to heart attacks and type A personalities. This hypothesis is currently being investigated.

Sudden deaths Every year approximately 400,000 *sudden deaths* are reported throughout the United States [64]. Walter Cannon was one of the first scientists to show an interest in the abrupt deaths which occur without clear medical cause. He examined reports of *voodoo deaths* from all over the world and then visited Africa to investigate firsthand. By asking questions such as "Did the death occur rapidly?" and "Were poisons available?" Cannon tried to rule out alternative causes of death. He concluded that voodoo deaths were legitimate and followed a predictable pattern. The victim, usually a male, was cursed and a "spell" was cast. People surrounding the "target" withdrew their support. Consequently, the individual was alone, isolated, and in many cases, treated as already deceased. The individual expected imminent death and experienced intense anxiety. Death often occurred within twenty-four hours of being "targeted" [65].

In modern civilizations, sudden deaths take place under a wide range of circumstances. Occasionally, chronically ill people in hospitals are thought to "lose the will to live" and to die of no specifiable cause [66]. Individuals in prisoner-of-war camps sometimes "turn their faces to the wall" and give up on life [67]. A substantial number of unexpected deaths follow the loss of a close human relationship, the confrontation of danger, reduced status, lost property, failure, and even triumph [68]. Lesser animals die abruptly under varied conditions too—after fights without injuries or when transferred to unfamiliar locations, immobilized, stimulated excessively, or deprived by death of a mate or master [69].

How can animals, including people, die of psychological causes? Many sudden deaths are thought to result from deadly cardiac irregularities which are more easily triggered after the prolonged sympathetic nervous system arousal that accompanies stresses. Investigations by Bernard Lown and his coworkers support this hypothesis. In one experiment, the scientists allowed some of their dog subjects to rest in their cages while they stressed others. Then, they paced the dogs' hearts artificially in the *ventricular fibrillation pattern*, a lethal irregular rhythm, using progressively stronger currents. The anxious animals were more sensitive to the irregular pattern at lower current intensities [70]. The precise link between sympathetic nervous system activity and irregular heart rhythms is not well understood. ▲

ANGER AND AGGRESSION

We focus now on the emotion of anger and on aggression, a behavior that typically accompanies anger. First we define and describe the relationship between the two phenomena. Then we explore biological and environmental determinants of aggression. We are emphasizing aggression because, being observable, it has been more extensively researched and is

---

▲ USING PSYCHOLOGY

1. Why was the GAS characterized as a mixed blessing?

2. Since life changes and disease are positively correlated, any of three causal inferences are possible (as discussed in Chapter 2). How may life changes produce disease? May illness (before becoming apparent) produce life changes? What factor(s) can account for both life changes and sickness?

3. Suppose a friend says, "If you don't calm down, you'll get an ulcer." Explain why the friend's notion about the causation of ulcers is incomplete.

4. Do you or any of your acquaintances fit the type A pattern? Describe ways that people might be able to combat the syndrome.

5. Explain to a skeptical person how voodoo deaths may occur.

far better understood than anger. We define *anger* as an emotion characterized by a high level of sympathetic nervous system activity and by strong feelings of displeasure which are triggered by a real or imagined wrong. A simple definition—any act at all aimed at hurting people or property—describes most (but not all) cases of *aggression*. Though much human aggression is verbal, we must stress physical aggression since there is little research on verbal aggression. We do know that the two types of aggression often occur together.

The Link between Anger and Aggression

When angry, R. M. (in the chapter's introduction) reported wanting to break, punch, or throw something. He also described having violent, terrible thoughts. Anger is frequently accompanied by an impulse to retaliate by aggression. Laboratory studies confirm the existence of this relationship [71]. Of course, anger and aggression are not always linked. As mentioned before, anger can lead to sullen, withdrawn, depressed, or constructive behavior. Aggression, in turn, can be triggered by incentives (Chapter 10) without any anger whatsoever being present. Though we are making a distinction between *anger-induced aggression* and *incentive-induced aggression*, the two types are often intermingled and impossible to separate.

Anger-induced aggression Many people mistakenly assume that aggression is the only way to temper anger. It isn't. Research by Jack Hokanson and his colleagues supports the hypothesis that an individual's beliefs influence whether a specific tactic reduces the tension accompanying anger. Hokanson's studies suggest that any response at all that has been associated with avoiding aggression from others can diminish anger. In our culture, men generally learn that fighting will help avoid future attacks. Women learn to be passive to discourage aggression. In the laboratory, aggression, rewarding the antagonist,

and even shocking oneself can reduce the arousal accompanying anger, depending on the subject's past learning experiences [72]. Aggression, in any case, is a common response to anger. Frustration, physical pain, taunts, insults, and threats frequently lead to anger and provoke aggression. We describe these provocations briefly.

Frustation. Frustration arises when an obstacle prevents people from reaching a goal, need, desire, expectation, or action. Aggression is one of several frequent reactions to frustration. Boredom can be a treacherous source of frustration. When stimulation is scarce, people, monkeys, and many other animals try to create their own, as we have seen. Some social scientists have suggested that terrorism may be partially a product of the anger of bored middle-class college students. Similarly, the delinquency of poor adolescents may arise, in part, as frustration due to too much free time, meager finances, and a high need for stimulation generates anger [73]. Conflict is another source of frustration and anger. About two-thirds of the murders occurring in the United States today are committed by relatives, friends, or acquaintances, usually during brawls or arguments [74]. People who abuse young children seem to show low tolerance for frustration. Brutal acts of child abuse are sometimes meant simply to quiet crying or suppress other irritating behaviors [75].

Physical pain. Immediately after being shocked, rattlesnakes, snapping turtles, rats, raccoons, foxes, ferrets, cats, squirrel monkeys, and other animals attack almost anything, whether another animal, a stuffed doll, a tennis ball, or a tube, in a reflex-like manner. See Figure 11-10. Intense heat, physical blows, and other sources of pain can also elicit fighting in animals [76]. The response has survival value. It is likely to remove noxious stimulation, increasing the organism's odds of remaining alive. Although people do not handle pain or any other experience by reflexive aggression, they are more likely to report feeling angry and to hurt others after physical punishment than after

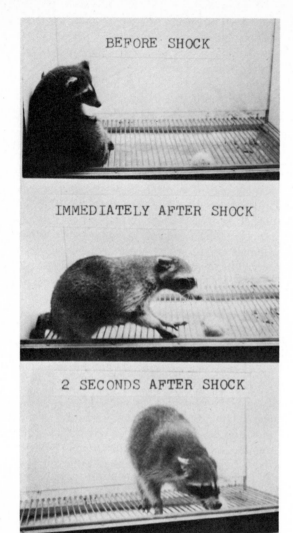

BEFORE SHOCK

IMMEDIATELY AFTER SHOCK

2 SECONDS AFTER SHOCK

FIGURE 11-10 The raccoon in these film clips is responding to shock with reflex-like aggression. Note how the animal attacks the only available target, a tennis ball. [*Nathan Azrin.*]

considerate treatment [77]. The knowledge that pain increases the probability of aggression may be used intuitively to prepare soldiers for battle. One ex-marine observer described his combat training for Vietnam as a combination of torture, terrorism, and humiliation [78].

Taunts, insults, and threats. Taunts, insults, and threats often provoke feelings of intense anger and lead to aggression. Psychologist Hans Toch found that the explosive encounters of assault-prone police officers, parolees, and prison inmates followed a stable scenario. One individual taunted or insulted another before the battle escalated into a physical confrontation [79]. Even mild taunts precipitate aggression in the laboratory if the opportunity presents itself [80]. Inner-city children sometimes insult one another in a game called "the dozens."

One of the tormentors will make a mildly insulting statement, perhaps . . . "I saw your mother out with a man last night." Then he may follow up this with "She was drunk as a bat." The subject, in turn, will then make an insulting statement about the tormentor or some member of the tormentor's family. This exchange of insults continues, encouraged by the approval and shouts of the observers, and the insults become progressively nastier and more pornographic. . . . Finally, one of the participants, usually the subject, . . . reaches his threshold and takes a swing at the tormentor, pulls out a knife or picks up an object to use as a club. This is the sign for the tormentor, and sometimes some of the observers, to go into action. [81]

Incentive-induced aggression Aggression is sometimes provoked by incentives. American soldiers at My Lai murdered defenseless Vietnamese civilians to obey orders, at least in part. In *Little Murders*, a drama by Jules Feiffer, people amused themselves by shooting at one another. Social pressures for aggression increase hostile acts in the laboratory [82] and in real life. Among delinquents in gangs, points are sometimes given for physical assaults that are viewed by club members. Brutality increases stature, respect, and self-esteem. The youth gangs of Chinatown in New York City aggress for money. They can earn more income by terrorism and extortion rackets than through unemployment compensation or menial jobs.

We have described some common provocations to aggression. Biology and experience both influence where, when, and how people aggress.

Biology and the Capacity for Aggression

Is there an aggressive instinct in animals? How does biology influence aggression? We focus on these questions.

Is there an aggressive instinct? Freud believed that people are born with an instinct to kill and destroy. In his words: "[People] are not gentle, friendly creatures wishing for love, who simply defend themselves if they are attacked. [A] powerful measure of desire for aggression has to be reckoned as part of their instinctual endowment [83]." Suppose that human beings were not permitted to express aggression. Freud assumed that aggressive instincts accumulate somehow and eventually overflow, erupting in sudden violence.

Was he correct? Some students of animal behavior believe that he was. Konrad Lorenz, the Austrian ethologist, takes a similar position. In Lorenz's view, all creatures, including people, are born with aggressive instincts that help them survive. Dangerous animals, he believes, inherit inhibitions against seriously injuring members of their own kind. The built-in safeguard keeps each species from wiping itself out. Our ancestors, Lorenz argues, were ineffectual fighters with a meager capacity for destruction. Consequently, there was no need to develop elaborate inhibitory mechanisms. Later, people invented weapons. Ever since, they have been the most potentially destructive beasts of all [84]. Not all students of animal behavior agree with Lorenz's analysis.

Animals fight for numerous purposes [85]:

1. To repulse intruders entering a home territory
2. To attain dominance and exclude members of the same species from desirable objects (such as food) and actions (such as mating)
3. To force other animals to mate and to keep mates from straying
4. To discipline offspring—to keep them close, urge them into motion, break up fights, and encourage weaning, for instance
5. To defend relatives
6. To secure food

But so far, there is no convincing evidence that a need to fight arises *spontaneously* from inside animals. It appears, instead, that aggression must be stimulated. As one behavioral scientist put it, "A person who is fortunate enough to exist in an environment which is without stimulation to fight will not suffer physiological or nervous damage because [of] never fight[ing] [86]."

Are patterns of animal aggression instinctive? Many are probably learned. Even the fighting of "natural enemies"—rats and cats, for instance—is influenced by experience. In a classic series of studies, psychologist Zing-Yang Kuo demonstrated this clearly. Kuo reared some kittens with rat-killing mothers and others with rats as companions; still others were reared alone. About 85 percent of the kittens that had been raised by a rat-killing parent became avid rat killers. Approximately 45 percent of those reared in isolation later attacked rats. Only 17 percent of the kittens brought up with rats later preyed on these rodents. Even under conditions of extreme hunger, only an additional 7 percent of non–rat-killing cats could be induced to kill by special training (witnessing an adult cat kill a rat). After living together from infancy, cats and rats developed such strong attachments that a cat would even crouch over a rat protectively and hiss at a threatening cat [87].

How does biology influence aggression? Although animals may not possess aggressive instincts, their biology supplies aggressive capabilities. We focus on Kenneth Moyer's research-based model of aggression's physiological basis [88]. He contends that there are different neural systems within the brain that control specific types of aggression. (Evidence for this assumption was presented in Chapter 4.) As Moyer sees it, the systems go into action when a particular threshold value is reached. That value varies. In a high-threshold state, brain circuits are insensitive and will not fire even when the animal is provoked. The middle level is the normal one. The neural systems are inactive and only

FIGURE 11-11 Stimulation of certain limbic regions, including sites in the amygdala, may produce rage and increase the likelihood of aggression. One example linking human rage to the amygdala is provided by a tragic incident at the University of Texas. Charles Whitman (shown here) climbed a tower at the school and shot at everyone within range, killing many people. Previously, Whitman had tried to convince a physician that he feared "overwhelming violent impulses." During the autopsy following Whitman's death, a highly malignant tumor in the amygdala was discovered. Though Whitman grew up amidst brutality and guns, the tumor probably contributed to the intense anger that preceded the mass murder [135]. Scar tissue in the amygdala has been linked with "spells" of rage and anxiety in other cases. So has direct stimulation of particular amygdaloid sites. Some surgeons have removed these regions to stop violent episodes that could not be controlled in less radical ways [136]. As we see later (Figure 11-16), this type of surgery has a great many problems. [*Wide World Photos.*]

specific circumstances trigger attacks. At a low-threshold level, the brain systems are spontaneously active. Animals feel restless, perhaps hostile. Still, striking out occurs only when an appropriate target happens along. The various neural systems that control aggression can be activated directly in real life by tumors or scar tissue (see Figure 11-11)

and by electrical or chemical stimulation. Four influences on these aggressive systems are especially noteworthy: genes, other neural systems, blood chemistry, and learning.

1. Genes appear to contribute to the sensitivity of neural systems which regulate aggression. Behavioral scientists can breed fish, birds, rabbits, and dogs that are easy or exceedingly difficult to provoke. Heredity seems to make males of many species readier to fight than females.

2. Brain systems that are not involved in aggression can intensify or inhibit neural circuits controlling aggression. For example, when psychologists stimulate a cat's lateral hypothalamus, the animal will attack a mouse in a stereotyped way. Applying current to the reticular formation results in arousal. If both regions are stimulated simultaneously, the cat's attack is intensified. The same phenomenon seems to occur in people. If an individual is angered and then further aroused, say by heat or noise, aggression is more likely than if either anger or arousal has occurred alone [89]. In simple animals, rage may be inhibited by stimulating the septal area of the limbic system, a region associated with pleasure. In people, there may be a reciprocal relationship between pleasure and violence too, with one inhibiting the other. Psychologist James Prescott speculates that pleasure-oriented human beings display little aggression, while brutal individuals are sometimes incapable of joy and affection. Prescott believes that intense destructiveness, allied with an inability to experience pleasure, may result from brain damage due to lack of sensory stimulation in infancy [90]. While these ideas are plausible in some cases, they have not been confirmed.

3. Blood chemistry (especially sex hormone levels, which are partially set by heredity) affects aggression under some circumstances. When scientists inject rats, roosters, and other animals with *testosterone*, the chief *androgen* (masculine sex hormone), they fight more frequently and more intensely [91]. When testosterone level is reduced, animals usually become gentler. The castrated calf, for instance, grows into a benign steer and not a ferocious bull. Danish sex offenders have sometimes consented to "therapeutic" castrations. The reduction in testosterone level seems to result in "general pacification" [92]. The relationship between aggressive behavior and testosterone is complex and can be modified by social influences [93]. The ovarian hormones also influence animal aggression in ways that are not well understood

[94]. During the premenstrual period when estrogen and progesterone production is low, many human females experience feelings of tension, irritability, and hostility [95]. Women commit a disproportionate number of crimes at this time [96]. Besides acting directly on the central nervous system, hormones may influence aggression indirectly—say, by contributing to size, strength, or "natural weapons" (like antlers in deer). Recent studies suggest that human aggression is consistently correlated with certain levels of brain neurotransmitters (Chapter 4). Whether these transmitter substances play a causative role in aggression is not clear [97].

4. Human beings continually learn about aggression from their experiences in a particular family and culture. Since people are superlative learners, experience plays an immense role in promoting and inhibiting aggression. We focus on this topic now.

Environmental Influences on Aggression

Cultures and families hold standards about aggression which influence the types of lessons children learn. They establish conditions that inhibit or encourage hurting.

Aggression, social standards, and learning "Violence," pronounced H. Rap Brown, the civil rights activist, "is as American as apple pie." A recent survey of representative American adults suggests that Brown was an astute observer. Many people reported owning guns. In fact, the United States has the highest gun-to-population ratio in the world. (Encounters involving guns are apt to result in serious injuries and death more often than those involving other weapons.) Americans approved of aggression in diverse situations. Many felt that wars were justifiable, spouses might hit one another freely, police officers should use physical force, parents and teachers should discipline children by spanking them, and boys should fight [98]. These standards are not universal ones. In central Malaya, the 13,000 Semai have no police force and murder is unknown. Adults do not strike one another and children on the verge of fighting are separated. In

Montana, the Hutterites, who have lived in relatively isolated settlements for about a hundred years, value peace and condemn aggression. Owning their lands in common and working primarily as farmers, they inhabit modest dwellings that are furnished alike. They eat meals in a single dining hall. To preserve the communal way of life, their children are taught to suppress all outward signs of anger. Though that may not be the ideal way to handle irritations, it leads to extremely low rates of murder, arson, physical assault, and rape.

Americans who value aggression teach it to children directly and indirectly. In some cases, youngsters, especially sons, are instructed in "combat" techniques. Aggressive toys, such as the one shown in Figure 11-12, convey the message that hurting is acceptable and perhaps fun. In many cases, learning is

FIGURE 11-12 This toy guillotine swings a blade that cuts the victim in half. Parental demands forced the manufacturer to remove the guillotine from the market. Stores all over the country still sell many types of grizzly alternatives, including dolls armed with bullwhips and steel hooks and automated high-kicking, karate-chopping fighters. Violent toys probably give information about means of aggression while communicating the message "aggression is fun." [*Al Freni.*]

more subtle. For example, winning a skirmish is likely to be met with praise or approval. Parents who discipline their children by striking them probably increase the likelihood that youngsters will use the same strategy to handle interpersonal problems. The conditions for observation learning (Chapter 5) are ideal:

1. The child probably sees aggression working successfully.
2. The lesson is apt to be memorable, since it will probably be accompanied by a moderate amount of fear, shame, and/or anger. (Some arousal is optimal for learning.)
3. Parents are powerful models with whom the child identifies.
4. The pain and frustration produced by assaultive techniques may provoke striking out, as mentioned before.

All these conditions increase the likelihood that aggressive parental behavior will be imitated. Research supports the idea that particularly aggressive parents frequently have especially aggressive children. Brutal delinquent boys are more likely than other children to have come from harsh disciplinarian homes [99]. Societies that use strict, anxiety-provoking measures to control children have higher violent crime rates than those that do not [100]. Parents who abuse their youngsters tend to have been battered themselves [101].

Survey research suggests that the members of an "average American family" witness a lot of aggression. Recently, sociologists led by Murray Strauss interviewed a large representative sample of adults on this topic. They found that over 80 percent of parents of children three to nine years of age had used physical punishment during the survey year. About one of every five adults had struck youngsters with objects. Slightly more than one of every six couples reported a violent episode between spouses during the year of the interview [102]. (A violent episode was defined as any act intending to cause pain and/or injury.) More than a million Americans were, in fact, physically injured because of family aggression in 1976. Schools are often violent places too. In 1976, some 75,000 teachers in the United States required medical attention for student-inflicted injuries. During approximately the same period, more than 300,000 students were casualties of brutality in American schools [103]. All these estimates are considered conservative.

Even when families and schools are peaceable, most American children are exposed to violent models on television. What effects does this exposure have?

Violent Models on Television

American children spend more hours watching television, on the average, than they spend in any other single activity except sleeping. Estimates of the number of violent episodes seen in an average hour of TV viewing vary. Still, they tend to be alarmingly high. According to one recent survey, Saturday morning cartoons average 21.5 aggressive acts per hour [104]. The ingredients for an influential experience are all there. Watching fighting and killing tends to be moderately physiologically arousing, a state that increases susceptibility to the model's influence. Television heroes are usually sympathetic figures whose aggression pays off. Realistic unpleasant consequences, including blood, gore, and grieving relatives, rarely accompany the violence. Learning is especially likely when the pattern fits in with the viewer's values and life-style. This analysis is known as the *social learning hypothesis* because it was derived from observation, or social, learning research. (See Figure 11-13.)

Not all psychologists subscribe to the social learning hypothesis. Long ago, the Greek philosopher Aristotle speculated that witnessing drama can purge people of grief, anger, fear, and other strong emotions. The *catharsis hypothesis*, derived from Aristotle's theory, assumes that the daily frustrations that everyone faces increase the need for aggression. Presumably, this need can be satisfied by aggressing directly, watching others aggress, or indulging in fantasy aggression. According to the catharsis hypothesis, then, witnessing violent television

FIGURE 11-13 While the amount of aggression on television changes somewhat from year to year (dropping in 1977, but rising in 1978, for instance), there is still a great deal of filmed violence both on television and in movies. Much of it has been characterized as "bloodless." In the 1940s western *They Died with Their Boots On*, for example, beatings, shootings, and killings were displayed with negligible signs of suffering on the part of victims and their families. After a "bloodless" mass slaughter, General Custer died with the grace of a dancer. Some behavioral scientists hypothesize that depicting realistic consequences might decrease the attractiveness of modeled aggression. [*New York Public Library.*]

models should reduce assaultive needs and acts.

Let's examine the evidence for these competing theories. Many experiments designed to investigate the influence of violence on television follow a similar pattern. Participants are first exposed to a frustrating experience, such as being insulted by someone. Then they are shown either violent or neutral filmed material. Later, each individual is placed in a situation where aggression is encouraged and measured. For instance, subjects may be given the opportunity to administer shocks to the person who insulted them. The vast majority of studies based on this model find that observing aggression increases willingness to hurt in both adults and children [105].

Since the findings of contrived studies in artificial settings are difficult to interpret, psychologists turned to research in natural situations for confirmation. A great many investigators find significant moderate positive correlations between time spent viewing or preference for violent television programs and aggression. But these observations do not prove that TV is harmful. Though watching violence could increase aggression, being aggressive to begin with may simply create a type of gluttony for observing violence. Experi-

ments in natural situations have helped psychologists distinguish between these interpretations. Aletha Stein and her associates, for instance, worked with ninety-seven preschool children. As part of a summer nursery school program, the youngsters were assigned to television-viewing groups. Three times each week for four weeks, children watched either twenty to thirty minutes of aggressive material (like "Batman"), prosocial programs (such as "Mister Roger's Neighborhood"), or neutral films (those that were neither aggressive nor prosocial). Before, during, and after these experiences, aggression, persistence, self-control, and other characteristics were observed and rated. Differences in socioeconomic class, intelligence, and initial level of aggression were taken into account. Stein and her coworkers found that only children who were above average on aggression initially behaved more destructively toward others after exposure to a steady diet of filmed violence [106]. More recent studies confirm the finding that watching violence increases aggression in real life in a significant number of people [107]. The effect may be a persistent one, too. Nine-year-old boys who prefer (and presumably view) especially many violent TV

programs tend to be more aggressive than others ten years later [108].

It is not clear whether aggressive television heroes generally inspire direct mimicry or simply free people of inhibitions about hurting. Both effects are plausible. Television violence may have an additional unfortunate consequence. As people watch brutality or suffering, they tend to show autonomic nervous system and facial expression signs of pain themselves, as suggested before. The arousal is thought to be a component of empathy that inspires helping. Children who watch TV a great deal show diminished autonomic reactions to new filmed savagery [109]. There is evidence that with increasing exposure, violence may bother youngsters less and less. Children who viewed a violent cowboy movie in the laboratory were more apt to remain passive when confronted by a real fight than those who had not been exposed to the film [110]. In sum, just as television brutality increases the aggression of some youngsters, it probably numbs many others to the consequences of violence.

The compensating benefits of TV aggression have yet to be demonstrated convincingly in the laboratory. Adults' reports of aggressive moods do not, in fact, appear to decline after a steady diet of fighting and killing on television [111]. Most psychologists agree that aggressive television programming has an overwhelming negative impact. Currently, behavioral scientists are studying the factors that increase people's susceptibilities to the ill effects of filmed violence [112]. They are also investigating ways of using television to promote prosocial behavior.

Aggression and social conditions Certain social conditions make aggression likely. We focus on two: anonymity and poverty.

Anonymity. Cities present enormous quantities of sounds, sights, and other types of information. People tend to adapt to the constant overloading of their senses and brains, according to social psychologist Stanley Milgram, by several interpersonal strategies.

1. They give little time to each encounter.
2. They allow only superficial contacts, filtering out involvements which demand an emotional investment.
3. They disregard low-priority inputs. Since they barely have time for important matters, they're unlikely to help a strange woman stranded on the highway with a flat tire or a drunk lying on the sidewalk.
4. They block off their receptivity by looking cold and unfriendly and by such tactics as not listing their phone numbers.
5. They create special institutions, such as charities and welfare, to further reduce the number of inputs that must be handled personally [113].

Sensory and cognitive overload results in an impersonal world where the great majority of people, even in small geographical locations, don't know one another. Moreover, each individual tends to feel *anonymous* (lacking an identity). When human beings feel anonymous, they don't behave as they do when they feel like individuals. Philip Zimbardo, of Stanford University, is responsible for a great deal of the research on this topic. In one of his laboratory experiments, female subjects were asked to administer electric shocks to two victims, confederates of the experimenter. First, the women listened in small groups to taped interviews with each "target." One behaved obnoxiously; the other, sweetly. For the listening sessions, research participants, to be anonymous, wore baggy laboratory coats and face-covering hoods and sat in semidarkness, as shown in Figure 11-14. The subjects in a second "individuated" condition were treated like individuals. They saw one another's faces, wore name tags, and addressed one another by name. After these group interactions, each woman delivered shocks individually to both victims. People in the anonymous condition gave longer shocks than those in the individuated condition. They did not appear to be inhibited by either social conventions or perceptions of the "sweet" victim's virtue [114]. When people feel anonymous, then, they are likely to feel less inhibited by social conventions and less sympathetic toward other human beings than ordinarily. Additional studies support these ideas [115].

Poverty. When children grow up in poverty, aggression is often positively reinforced by its natural consequences. To paraphrase psychologist Boyd McCandless [116]: The young learn to grab while the grabbing is good. If they don't, brothers, sisters, parents, or peers will grab instead. Reason doesn't win street fights nor enable youngsters to keep drunken fathers from beating mothers. With-

FIGURE 11-14 Subjects in the anonymous condition of Philip Zimbardo's experiment are shown listening to tapes of their future "victims." [*Philip G. Zimbardo.*]

out immediate action and intense drive, children may not survive in the tooth-and-claw existence that is essentially routine. Striking, yelling, and pushing cause others to stand back and move people ahead.

Behavioral scientists consider the type of poverty that exists in a rich society like ours especially frustrating. Here in America the distribution of goods in the here and now, and not eternal salvation, is a dominant preoccupation. At the same time, the mass media stimulate desires for a luxurious life-style. But, instead of the American dream, many poor people confront stopped-up toilets,

health problems, worries about food and clothing, distressing heat and cold, unemployment (and the feelings of boredom, futility, and uselessness which accompany it), delapidated housing, rat infestations, and continual fears of bodily harm. Minority racial-group members among the poor face discrimination and injustice in addition. To escape from oppressive realities, perhaps, poor young people in disproportionate numbers turn to violence. The frustration of poverty may prime people for an aggressive life-style. Crowding, another condition associated with poverty, has also been linked to aggression.

Crowding and Aggression

In zoos and in the wild, crowding often results in vicious fighting even among relatively peaceful animals [117]. Rats that are kept amply stocked with food, water, and nesting materials and that lack nothing except space and privacy adjust poorly to dense conditions. Many males engage in senseless, unprovoked aggression. Many females neglect infant care and nest building. Social conventions deteriorate. Miscarriages and premature deaths from stress-related diseases increase, and the population declines drastically [118]. See Figure 11-15.

The effects of human crowding are difficult to investigate neatly. Sometimes psychologists compare two groups of people who live under relatively dense and sparse conditions and are similar in income, education, and religious and racial background. Adult and juvenile crime, mental hospital admissions, mortality rates, and other measures of aggression and stress are collected. High household density is associated consistently with aggression, signs of anxiety, and poor health. High neighborhood density is related to withdrawal

FIGURE 11-15 Medical researcher John Calhoun (on the right) and his coworkers overlook their new mouse universe, constructed specifically to investigate the effects of severe crowding. Confined within a similar enclosure, mice in an earlier study multiplied naturally over the course of about 1,600 days. Resources remained abundant; and disease, predators, inclement weather, and several other mortality-related factors were eliminated. Nonetheless, competition became intense after a few generations, since roles in the large social group were occupied and niches for the young to fill were scarce. At twice the optimal density, breakdowns in parental care, territorial defense, and normal social maturation became apparent. Eventually, the incidence of conception declined, while fetuses were reabsorbed and babies rejected increasingly. Mice who did survive learned little about social conduct: courtship, parenting, and aggression. Both passivity and vicious fighting became commonplace. Finally, the animals stopped interacting and reproducing young, and the population died out completely. [*Courtesy of John B. Calhoun, National Institute of Mental Health; photographer: Lela Garlington, 1978.*]

[119]. Psychologists use laboratory experiments to investigate the effects of crowding, too. Typically, volunteers are assigned to large or small rooms so that some are packed together densely and others are not. Individuals then interact in structured ways or work tasks. Under these conditions, physical discomfort, competition, restricted movement, offensive odors, heat, and the like (ordinary accompaniments of real-life crowd-

ing) are minimized. Though high density does not appear to alter task performance, it can intensify people's current feelings whatever they may be. In many cases, small room size produces discomfort and unpleasant mood states. People like one another less and children interact less often [120]. Sex differences are not consistently reported [121].

The consequences of crowding in real life probably depend

on irritants and on available resources. We would expect more frustration and aggression (if that response has been learned and sanctioned) as oppression increases and available resources decrease. Cognitions play a key role. People are more apt to find crowding frustrating when they feel their lives are out of control, when they believe that their privacy has been invaded, or when they see the conditions as stressful [122].

While aggression and poverty are associated for the reasons we have mentioned, most poor people are not aggressive. Why do only relatively few poor adolescents turn to violent crime? Undoubtedly, there are many contributing causes. Recent research by psychologist Allan Berman and his coworkers suggests that violent delinquents (most of whom are males) show consistent early experiences. In the preschool years, future male delinquents display perceptual and attentional problems. These difficulties tend to be ignored. Parents are likely to be unsupportive and to lack understanding. The child enters school feeling unable to do what is expected. As Berman sees it, the youngster has few adaptive skills, deflated self-esteem, and fears of inadequacy. Yet the boy shows evidence of strong nonacademic abilities. Teachers consider the child a nuisance and punish and ridicule him. Often, to handle the embarrassment of repeated failure, the boy clowns around and disrupts the class. By the fourth or fifth grade, youngsters who fit this description are associating with other underachievers who are out of favor with teachers. Eventually, the future male delinquent is suspended or drops out of school. Frequently by the junior high school years, these youths are roaming the streets in gangs, handling their frustrations by aggression, as previously described. The court system and prison experiences intensify the violent pattern, as will be discussed in Chap-

ter 16. By studying the characteristics that predict which youngsters are at high risk for violent delinquency, psychologists hope to be able to intervene early and prevent the development of this syndrome [123]. ▲

JOY

Psychologists have spent far more time studying the negative emotions (anger, anxiety, depression, and the like) than the positive ones (including joy and love). In any case, we focus briefly on joy. First we explore how physiological psychologists localized brain areas associated with pleasure. Then we discuss an intense type of joy, the "peak experience."

Pleasure Centers

When particular areas of the limbic system are stimulated, people may feel furious and experience strong desires to attack or destroy (as described in Figure 11-11). Are positive emotions also rooted in the brain? Early in the 1950s, physiological psychologists James Olds and Peter Milner were exploring another issue when they accidentally happened on the answer to this question. At the time, Olds and Milner were interested in learning more about *avoidance regions* in the brain. When such areas were stimulated, rats reacted as if they were experiencing sharp pain. They subsequently avoided anything associated with the stimulation. One day Olds and Milner accidentally implanted an electrode in the wrong brain location of one experimental animal. As this subject neared the corner of its cage, the psychologists turned on the current. They expected the rat to step backward, as others had done under apparently identical conditions. Instead, the rat moved forward. Olds and Milner stimulated again. Again the rat advanced. The animal appeared to be thoroughly enjoying itself. What was going on?

When Olds and Milner checked the position of the electrode, they discovered that the needle had been implanted in the limbic system and not in the reticular formation, as they had believed. Evidently, the stimulation of that particular limbic site was pleasurable. Just how pleasurable became clear in later studies. When a lever was connected to an electric stimulator so that rats could send current to particular limbic sites in their own brains by bar pressing, the animals activated the lever as many as 5,000 times in a single hour. The rats preferred particular types of brain stimulation to drinking when thirsty, to eating when starving, and to mating when sexually deprived. They also endured intense pain to have an opportunity to stimulate certain regions of their own brains. In some cases the rodents were so greedy for particular types of brain stimulation that they bar-pressed until they literally collapsed of exhaustion some fifteen to twenty-five hours later [124].

Today psychologists know that many mammals, including people, have numerous brain circuits associated with pleasure scattered throughout the brain, including the frontal lobes of the cortex. We don't know exactly what the sites do or how. Some behavioral scientists believe that animals are genetically programmed to experience at least two distinct types of pleasure. Sensory receptors, which are apparently connected to specific pleasure sites in the brain, are often activated when a biological need, say, hunger or thirst, is present to some degree. Satisfying the need leads at this time to both *relief*, a pale type of pleasure, and *joy*, a vivid one. Expectations of joy can be viewed as a kind of incentive that persuades animals to fill certain bodily deficiencies. Pleasure-center stimulation does not appear to serve need reduction functions all the time. Desire for stimulation at certain pleasure-center sites may (or may not) be influenced by recent deprivations [125]. There is also evidence that pleasure centers are aroused as animals learn and remember. The neurotransmitter dopamine appears to be involved [126].

How do people react to direct stimulation of the pleasure sites? Since the early 1950s, physician Robert Heath has been using brain

FIGURE 11-16 This ex-marine underwent brain surgery to curb his violent behavior. Brain surgery for behavioral change, or *psychosurgery*, is a very controversial practice. Some psychologists are convinced that the procedures are justifiable when people are totally incapacitated by severe rage (and aggression), depression, hyperactivity, and/or pain. Neurosurgeons sometimes claim that stimulating and recording from the brain enables them to identify and destroy the precise trouble-making tissue without damaging matter that serves other functions. Many behavioral scientists question the benefits of psychosurgery for several reasons. (1) Specific brain circuits play multiple roles. Consequently, any destruction inevitably affects many types of functioning. (2) "Maps" of human brain function are crude and incomplete. They are not an adequate guide for complex surgery. (3) Brain surgery is not reversible. Moreover, after surgery, brain circuits are likely to reorganize with unpredictable results (Chapter 4). (4) The long-range consequences of brain surgery are difficult to identify [137]. Several court cases are currently pending on behalf of psychosurgery patients who initially appeared to have benefited but later developed serious problems [138]. (5) Finally, some behavioral scientists worry that psychosurgery may be misused. It may prove to be easier to operate on troublesome social critics than to correct serious societal problems [139]. [*Wide World Photos.*]

stimulation therapeutically to help alleviate severe chronic pain and to gain control over certain types of problematic human behavior. In one instance, Heath and his associates attempted to relieve sudden attacks of deep sleep, muscle weakness, and impulsive activity, the symptoms of two male epileptics. The medical researchers implanted a number of electrodes in the patients' brains. Six months after the men recovered from surgery, observations began. The patients could excite various brain sites by depressing a button on a control unit worn on their belts. Stimulation at one site produced the reaction "feels great." It elicited "sexual feelings" and eliminated "bad thoughts" too. Stimulation in another region evoked the response "cool taste." Stimulation at a third point produced "drunk feelings." Heath's studies and those of other researchers indicate that people are a lot less enthralled by pleasure-center stimulation than rats appear to be. The patients stimulated the pleasure centers for many reasons besides joy. In some cases they wished to pursue a particular memory or alleviate an aggravating symptom. The pleasurable stimulation was not considered as intensely enjoyable as the activities themselves would have been [127]. There seems to be little danger of brain stimulation addiction in people. Figure 11-16 describes the current controversy over this type of surgery.

"Peak Experiences"

The late humanistic psychologist Abraham Maslow coined the term "peak experience" for the happiest moments of life. These intensely pleasant emotions can be reached through love, being an involved parent, undergoing a mystic experience, creating beauty, achieving insight, meeting a challenge, or engaging in other self-fulfilling acts [128]. Recently, Mihaly Csikszentmihalyi has investigated a similar emotion which he calls a "flow experience" [129]. During a "peak (or "flow") experience," human beings feel so intensely aware of their sensations that they may feel united with the world. A rock climber interviewed by

▲ **USING PSYCHOLOGY**

1. In his novel *The Terminal Man*, Michael Crichton describes an "elad," a person who has had electrodes implanted in the pleasure centers of the brain and has become addicted to electrical stimulation. Based on current research, do you think such brain stimulation could be addicting? What problems would such an addiction pose for the individual? For society?

2. Have you ever experienced a "peak (or "flow") experience"? Did it fit Maslow's and Czikszentmihalyi's descriptions? Explain.

3. Describe several observations which suggest that there is a close link between motives and emotions.

Csikszentmihalyi expressed this idea clearly: "You are so involved in what you are doing you aren't thinking of yourself as separate from the immediate activity." During "peak experiences" people feel that they are using their capacities fully, yet their functioning is effortless. Human beings achieve a sense of control and freedom from blocks and fears. They feel spontaneous and natural, "completely here-now," in Maslow's words. To experience emotions of this sort, Csikszentmihalyi believes, people must meet challenges at

the outer limits of their capabilities. Maslow assumed that the feeling was only possible after basic biological, social, and psychological needs were satisfied (Chapter 10). "Peak experiences" convince people that life is worth living, even though it is usually "drab, pedestrian, painful, or ungratifying [130]". We have a vivid description of the emotional state known as the "peak experience." But there is still a great deal to be learned about this and other positive feelings. ▲

SUMMARY
Emotion

1. Different emotions appear to be associated with specific physiological, sensation, cognition, and behavioral components. The varied elements interact with one another.

2. The physiological changes that accompany emotions are triggered by the central and autonomic nervous systems and the endocrine glands.

3. Individuals experiencing the same emotion display physiological reactions that vary in both intensity and type.

4. Emotions are usually mingled with one another and with motives.

5. The opponent-process model assumes that the brain acts to reduce both positive and negative emotions to maintain a balanced state.

6. Anxiety arises when people face mental conflicts and potentially dangerous situations. An enormous range of anxieties may be established by conditioning.

7. Heredity and experience influence an individual's general anxiety level.

8. Cognitions about control contribute to the intensity of anxiety in any specific situation.

9. In general, anxiety facilitates performance on simple tasks and disrupts performance on complex ones. It is particularly debilitating to the academic performance of students who make moderate scores on aptitude tests.

10. Animals respond to numerous stresses with the general adaptation syndrome. Prolonged exposure to stress may contribute to mental problems, disease, and even death.

11. Anger due to frustration, physical pain, taunts, insults, or threats may trigger aggression. Incentives such as status, obedience to orders, money, and social pressure may provoke aggression.

12. Biology gives animals the capacity to hurt one another, though there is no conclusive evidence that an aggressive instinct exists.

13. The threshold level of numerous aggressive brain systems appears to be influenced by heredity, other neural circuits, blood chemistry, and learning.

14. Cultures which sanction aggression tend to have high rates of violent crime. Through operant conditioning and observation learning, people learn when, where, and how to hurt others. Conditions such as anonymity and poverty increase the prevalence of aggression.

15. The stimulation of numerous brain sites is pleasurable for many mammals. These pleasure centers may serve need-regulating, learning, and memory functions.

16. "Peak (or "flow") experiences" occur spontaneously when people meet challenges successfully at the outer limits of their capabilities. Presumably, basic needs must be satisfied before these feelings arise.

A Study Guide for Chapter Eleven

Key terms emotion (affect) (345), cerebral cortex (347), reticular formation (347), limbic system (348), hypothalamus (348), autonomic nervous system (parasympathetic and sympathetic systems) (348), adrenal glands (349), polygraph (355), anxiety versus fear (357), general adaptation syndrome (GAS) (360), psychosomatic disorder (361), peptic ulcer (362), type A personality (363), sudden death (364), anger (365), aggression (anger-induced and incentive-induced) (365), anonymity (372), pleasure center (374), "peak ("flow") experience" (376), and other italicized words and expressions.

Important research early emotions, physiological responses to emotions (Cannon, Wolff, Ax, Schwartz, Lacey, others), cognitions and emotions (Schachter, Singer, Hammen, Krantz, others), behavior and emotions (Lanzetta, others), interactions between components of emotion (Schachter, Singer, Symington, Schwartz, Lanzetta, others), complexity of emotions (Schwartz, Solomon, others), influences on anxiety (Glass, Singer, Geer, others), anxiety-learning relationships (Mueller, Spielberger, others), alleviating test anxiety (Spielberger, others), GAS (Selye, others), disease and stress (Holmes, Rahe, Masuda, Weiner, Friedman, Rosenman, Cannon, Lown, others), provocations to aggresssion (Hokanson, Toch, others), biological basis of aggression (Kuo, Prescott, others), environmental influences on aggression (Zimbardo, Stein, Berman, others), pleasure centers in the brain (Olds, Milner, Heath, others).

Basic concepts the intermingling of emotions (Schwartz), opponent-process theory (Solomon), the ordering of emotional components, strategies for measuring emotion, anxiety triggers. [Freud (psychoanalytic), cognitive, humanistic, behavioristic viewpoints], physiological basis of aggression model (Moyer), pleasure-aggression relationship (Prescott), sensory and cognitive overload (Milgram), reasons for the link between poverty and aggression, social learning and catharsis hypotheses about witnessing aggression.

People to identify Cannon, Freud, Lorenz, Aristotle, Maslow.

Self-Quiz

1. During an intense emotion, which branch of the autonomic nervous system is particularly active?
   a. Central nervous system
   b. Parasympathetic nervous system
   c. Somatic nervous system
   d. Sympathetic nervous system

2. What did Schachter and Singer learn from their classic study of "supproxin's effects on vision"?
   a. Adrenalin is released during an emotion.
   b. Cognitions influence how people label physiological arousal.
   c. Different physiological states produce different emotions.
   d. Individuals show different responses to the same emotion.

3. By what means is the smiling-when-happy response probably acquired?
   a. Genetics
   b. Observation learning
   c. Operant conditioning
   d. Respondent conditioning

4. Which theory assumes that the brain aims at emotional balance by reducing intensely positive and negative emotions?
   a. Balance theory
   b. Cognitive theory
   c. Homeostatic theory
   d. Opponent-process theory

5. What can a polygraph actually record?
   a. Anxiety level   *b.* Facial expressions
   c. Lying   *d.* Physiological responses

6. What source of anxiety do cognitive psychologists emphasize?
   a. Anticipation of punishment for forbidden impulses
   b. Conflicts between beliefs, attitudes, and information

c. Conflicts over leading a good life

d. Real-world dangers

7. How does anxiety usually affect learning?

a. Disrupts the learning of simple tasks.

b. Disrupts the learning of all tasks.

c. Facilitates the learning of simple tasks.

d. Facilitates the learning of complex tasks.

8. Which is the second stage of the general adaptation syndrome?

a. Alarm   *b.* Exhaustion

c. Impairment   *d.* Resistance

9. What characterizes type A personalities?

a. Brutality and hypocrisy

b. Competitiveness and compulsivity

c. Egocentrism and impulsivity

d. Lack of imagination and stubborness

10. What mechanism appears to precipitate sudden deaths?

a. Brain hemorrhages

b. Cardiac irregularities

c. Overactive adrenal glands

d. Respiratory dysfunctions

11. What event consistently alleviates the tension accompanying anger in the laboratory?

a. Engaging in aggression

b. Making any response associated with avoiding aggression

c. Rewarding the antagonist

d. Watching others aggress

12. Which of the following conditions is thought to reduce the probability of aggression?

a. Anticipation   *b.* Arousal

c. Fear   *d.* Pleasure

13. What effect does a reduced testosterone level often have?

a. Decreases aggression   *b.* Decreases anxiety

c. Increases arousal   *d.* Increases pleasure

14. What consequence does anonymity have?

a. Decreases anger   *b.* Decreases anxiety

c. Increases aggression   *d.* Increases empathy

15. Which assumption does the catharsis hypothesis make?

a. Fantasy aggression reduces the likelihood of real aggression.

b. Frustration rarely leads to aggression.

c. Witnessing violence increases aggression.

d. Witnessing violence reduces empathy.

Exercise

PHYSIOLOGY AND EMOTIONS. The brain is very active during emergencies. Use the following matching exercise to test your knowledge of its basic roles. Each function should be paired with the appropriate brain structure. The same region may play several roles. To review, see pages 347 to 349.

BRAIN STRUCTURES: amygdala (A), cerebral cortex (CC), hypothalamus (H), parasympathetic nervous system (PNS), reticular formation (RF), sympathetic nervous system (SNS)

_____ *1.* Controls the cognitive processes associated with an emotion.

_____ *2.* The branch of the autonomic nervous system responsible for rerouting blood to the heart, central nervous system, and muscles for clear thinking and action.

_____ *3.* The part of the limbic system that activates the sympathetic nervous system.

_____ *4.* Stimulates the adrenal glands during an emergency.

_____ *5.* The branch of the autonomic nervous system active during calm periods.

_____ *6.* The central nervous system network that alerts the cortex so that it attends to crises.

_____ *7.* The branch of the autonomic nervous system that is active during an emergency.

Suggested Readings

1. Darwin, C. *The expression of the emotions in man and animals.* Chicago: University of Chicago Press, 1965 (paperback). In this fascinating classic, Darwin describes his studies on the ways people, dogs, cats, horses, and monkeys express emotions. The parallels are fascinating.

2. Malmo, R. B. *On emotions, needs, and our archaic brain.* New York: Holt, Rinehart & Winston, 1975. Malmo interweaves case studies with information about emotions, emphasizing bodily responses during emotions. He takes the point of view that physiological mechanisms that once helped people survive emergencies are being used for long-term social striving and are no longer useful. This book offers an especially enjoyable way to learn more about the physiological bases of affects.

3. Rachman, S. J. *Fear and courage.* San Francisco: Freeman, 1978 (paperback). A research worker and clinician describes studies of fears during combat, theories of fear and fear reduction, physiological aspects of fear, and paradoxes and problems in concepts of fear. Recent research on courage is discussed too. The style is informal.

4. Selye, H. *The stress of life.* (Rev. ed.) New York: McGraw-Hill, 1978 (paperback). Selye describes how he came to formulate his concept of stress and discusses his own research on stress and its practical implications. Selye writes personally and clearly.

5. Barron, R. A. *Human aggression.* New York: Plenum, 1977. This recent survey of research on aggression is both thorough and lively. Barron discusses the impact of heat, noise, crowding, drugs, bystanders, and other potential determinants of aggression. He also explores the prevention and control of aggression.

6. Freedman, J. L. *Crowding and behavior*. San Francisco: Freeman, 1975; Insel, P. M., & Lindgren, H. C. *Too close for comfort: The psychology of crowding behavior*. Englewood Cliffs, N.J.: Prentice-Hall, 1978. These two paperbacks are comprehensive, interesting reviews of research on crowding.

7. Smith, B. M. The polygraph. *Scientific American*, 1967, **216**(10), 25–31. This is a good place to start learning about the lie detector test. The unusually lucid and interesting description includes cases and problems.

8. Ekman, P. Face muscles talk every language. *Psychology Today*, 1975, **9**(4), 35–39. Ekman's research supports the idea that people all over the world share the same neural programming which links certain basic facial muscles to emotions.

9. Routtenberg, A. The reward system of the brain. *Scientific American*, 1978, **239**(5), 154–164. A physiological psychologist describes his research program on the pleasure system of the brain.

10. Furlong, W. B. The flow experience: The fun in fun. *Psychology Today*, 1976, **10**(1), 35ff. Furlong discusses Mihaly Csikszentmihalyi's interview-questionnaire studies which have given some insight into peak experiences.

Answer Keys

Self-Quiz

1. *d* (349)   **2.** *b* (350)   **3.** *a* (353)   **4.** *d* (354)
5. *d* (355)   **6.** *b* (357)   **7.** *c* (359)   **8.** *d* (360)
9. *b* (363)   **10.** *b* (364)   **11.** *b* (365)   **12.** *d* (368)
13. *a* (368)   **14.** *c* (372)   **15.** *a* (370)

Exercise

1. CC   **2.** SNS   **3.** H   **4.** SNS   **5.** PNS   **6.** RF
7. SNS

Figure 11-5: Facial Expressions

1. joyful   **2.** angry   **3.** fearful   **4.** surprised
5. disgusted   **6.** sad

CHAPTER TWELVE

Intelligence and Creativity

You hear so many people talking about IQ. The first time I ever heard the expression was when I was at Empire State School. I didn't know what it was or anything, but some people were talking and they brought the subject up. It was on the ward, and I went and asked one of the staff what mine was. They told me 49. Forty-nine isn't fifty, but I was pretty happy about it. I mean I figured that I wasn't a low grade. I really didn't know what it meant, but it sounded pretty high. Hell, I was born in 1948 and forty-nine didn't seem too bad. Forty-nine didn't sound hopeless. [1]

These words were spoken by a man presumed to be mentally retarded. They suggest that most adults in our culture have heard of the IQ concept, know that the numbers have something to do with intelligence, and value high scores. What is an IQ? More important, what is intelligence? What is creativity? How can psychologists measure these characteristics? What is known about them? In this chapter we will explore these topics. We begin with the case of L.

The Case of L.

L., an eleven-year-old boy, could not follow the regular school curriculum or learn through classroom instruction. During his academic career, he had made meager progress in only a few subjects. At home, the boy displayed no interest in ordinary childhood activities or in socializing with others. Because of these and other problems, L. was taken by his family for a psychological and medical consultation with Martin Scheerer, Eva Rothmann, and

Kurt Goldstein. Over a six-year period, L.'s intelligence and personality were evaluated by specially devised experiments and standard tests. The findings suggested that L. was unable to understand abstractions (cause-and-effect relationships, logic, symbols, concepts, and the like). When asked what was wrong with a picture of a man holding an umbrella upside down in the rain, for example, he responded, "Yes, the man is holding an umbrella, I don't know why, there is a lot of rain there." To the question, "How are a penny and a quarter similar?" L. answered, "Because the penny is big and the quarter is small, because they are different in shape, the penny is down and the quarter is up, high." Existing side by side with these striking intellectual deficits were some remarkable skills. L. could say at once on what day of the week a past or future birth date

(or any other date from 1880 to 1950) had fallen or would fall. This feat was achieved without any understanding of the concept of age. L. judged people born in the early months of the calendar year older than those born in the later months. He made this mistake even when he knew years of birth and/or physical appearance. L. could add twelve two-digit numbers as quickly as they were called out. But he did not understand that 23 was larger than 15. Without knowing, or caring to know, the meaning of many words, he could spell almost any word that was pronounced both forward and backward. And he was musically gifted. He had absolute pitch and played melodies from Dvorak and Beethoven on the piano by ear. He sang operatic arias from beginning to end without mistakes, too.

Scheerer and his associates diagnosed L. as an "idiot sa-

vant," a mentally handicapped person who possesses one or more extraordinary abilities. L.'s puzzling mixture of talents and deficiencies is not understood. Scheerer, Rothmann, and Goldstein assumed that the boy channeled all his energy into perfecting rote memory skills since he had no other abilities to develop. Memory, arithmetic calculations, and music were the "only performance[s] through which L. could actualize himself and come to terms with his surroundings [2]." Psychologists are still baffled by this condition. We know now that idiot savants come from diverse economic and educational backgrounds. Though they display different patterns of mental abilities, they are likely to excel at memory, arithmetic, art, or music [3]. Behavioral scientists know little more.

What does L.'s case tell us about intelligence? We can extract at least one vivid lesson. People may be exceptionally efficient in one mental skill and utterly inept in another. We speak of intelligence as if it were a single entity. Yet, intelligence appears to consist of numerous components. L.'s case brings to mind the old heredity-environment issue discussed in Chapter 3, as well. We have to wonder whether his feats were simply the result of obsessive practice or whether some unusual genetic endowment made these achievements possible. We will explore these issues and many others as we describe psychologists' attempts to define and measure intelligence.

DEFINING INTELLIGENCE

If the many psychologists who research mental functioning were asked to define intelligence, there would be a great many differences of opinion. Some behavioral scientists

propose that intelligence is essentially a single general ability. Others argue that intelligence depends on many separate capacities. Charles Spearman (1863–1945) was a well-known proponent of the "single general ability" view. He concluded that all mental tasks require two qualities: general intelligence and skills specific to the individual item. Solving algebra problems, for instance, demands general intelligence plus an understanding of numerical concepts. Spearman assumed that smart people had a great deal of the general factor [4]. L. L. Thurstone (1887–1955), an American electrical engineer who became a prominent test maker, espoused the "separate capacities" viewpoint. He claimed that Spearman's general intelligence factor was really seven somewhat distinct skills: (1) to add, subtract, multiply and divide; (2) to write and speak with ease; (3) to understand ideas in word form; (4) to retain impressions; (5) to solve complex problems and profit from past experiences; (6) to perceive size and spatial relationships correctly; and (7) to identify objects quickly and accurately. Though Thurstone found that these capabilities were related to some extent, he emphasized their distinctness [5]. Other controversies about the nature of intelligence divide psychologists into opposing camps: Should intelligence be conceptualized as an ability (or abilities) to learn in scholastic situations or to master abstract conceptual materials, or more broadly, as a capacity (or capacities) to adapt to the environment? Should intelligence be viewed as an entirely cognitive faculty or should motivation be taken into account? To what extent does heredity influence intelligence?

Early psychologists were much interested in devising tests that could differentiate between dull and quick students so that they could be assigned to an appropriate school curriculum. For this reason, theoretical issues were easily swept aside. Intelligence came to be defined operationally (Chapter 2) in terms of the tests designed to measure it. In other words, *whatever* the tests measured was called intelligence. Practical concepts like this one have dominated psychological research on intelligence until very recently, when behavioral scientists have begun reexamining their assumptions.

In this chapter we distinguish between measured intelligence and intelligence. By *measured intelligence* we mean performance in a specific testing situation which is always based on achievements: habits and acquired skills. We define *intelligence*, in contrast, as a capacity for mental activity that cannot be directly measured. We will take the view that intelligence consists of many separate cognitive abilities, including those involved in perception, memory, thought, and language. Though all human beings possess these capacities to some degree, there appears to be a great deal of variability in the efficiency of each process. We also assume that intelligence applies to adjustment in *all* spheres of life.

Since investigations of intelligence rely heavily on testing, it is crucial to understand how psychologists have measured mental abilities.

MEASURING INTELLIGENCE

We describe early and more recent efforts to test intelligence, the precise meaning of an IQ, and considerations guiding the development of intelligence tests.

An Early Attempt to Measure Intelligence

The British behavioral scientist Francis Galton was probably the first person to think seriously about testing intelligence. He set up a small laboratory in a London museum expressly for the purpose of making measurements of human abilities (see Figure 12-1). Reasoning that mentally handicapped people lack sensory acuity, he decided that intellectual and perceptual capacities might be highly

FIGURE 12-1 This poster describes the purposes of Galton's Anthropometric Laboratory, among the first to make precise measurements of human mental abilities. [*Cambridge University Press.*]

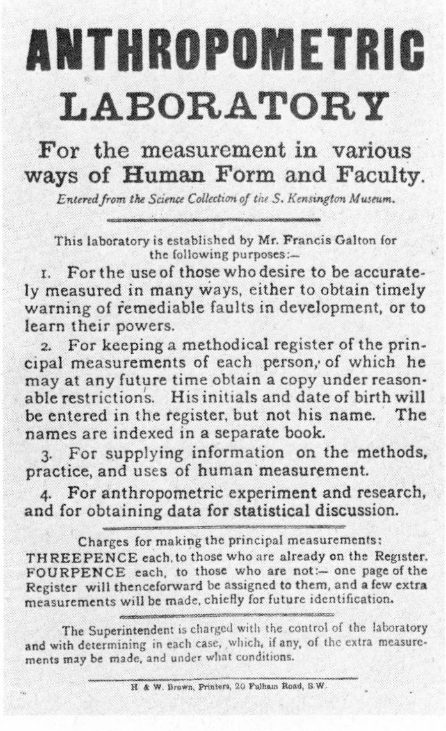

ANTHROPOMETRIC LABORATORY

For the measurement in various ways of **Human Form and Faculty.**

Entered from the Science Collection of the S. Kensington Museum.

This laboratory is established by Mr. Francis Galton for the following purposes:—

1. For the use of those who desire to be accurately measured in many ways, either to obtain timely warning of remediable faults in development, or to learn their powers.

2. For keeping a methodical register of the principal measurements of each person, of which he may at any future time obtain a copy under reasonable restrictions. His initials and date of birth will be entered in the register, but not his name. The names are indexed in a separate book.

3. For supplying information on the methods, practice, and uses of human measurement.

4. For anthropometric experiment and research, and for obtaining data for statistical discussion.

Charges for making the principal measurements: THREEPENCE each, to those who are already on the Register. FOURPENCE each, to those who are not:— one page of the Register will thenceforward be assigned to them, and a few extra measurements will be made, chiefly for future identification.

The Superintendent is charged with the control of the laboratory and with determining in each case, which, if any, of the extra measurements may be made, and under what conditions.

H. & W. Brown, Printers, 20 Fulham Road, S.W.

related. If so, the one might provide an index of the other. Accordingly, Galton began assessing such characteristics as keenness of sight and hearing, color sense, visual judgment, and reaction time. He measured motor activities, including "strength of pull and squeeze" and "force of blow" too [6]. Soon many other psychologists were similarly engaged in trying to devise tests of intellectual capacities. See Figure 12-2.

Alfred Binet's Intelligence Test

Alfred Binet (1857–1911), a prominent French psychologist (pictured in Figure 12-3), created the first practical measure of intelligence. Initially, he and his associates measured sensory and motor skills, as Galton had done.

But they soon realized that such assessments did not provide the desired information. Subsequently, they began evaluating cognitive functions: vividness of imagery, length and quality of attention, memory, aesthetic and moral judgments, logical thinking, and sentence comprehension. Binet gathered mental tasks to appraise these capacities and started testing the items out on Parisian school children.

Binet's test-making project was given a big push in 1904. At that time he was appointed to a government commission which was studying the problems of educating retarded children. The group concluded that mentally handicapped youngsters should be identified and placed in special schools. Binet and his associates began working on a test that would distinguish children who could benefit from

FIGURE 12-2 James Cattell and the Hipp chronoscope, a mental test instrument of the nineteenth century. In the 1890s James Cattell of Columbia University led a group of American psychologists who believed it possible to obtain information about intelligence by measuring reaction time, visual acuity, and other fundamental sensorimotor processes. For the reaction-time test, the examiner presented a visual stimulus to the subject. On seeing the stimulus, the test taker pressed a telegraph key. The Hipp chronoscope recorded the time the subject took to respond. Measurements from tests such as this one did not correlate with school grades or other practical indicators of intelligence or even with other measures of fundamental bodily processes. The sensorimotor approach to testing intelligence was laid away early in the 1900s, though it is revived from time to time. [*Culver Pictures; Archives of the History of American Psychology.*]

ordinary schooling from those who couldn't. For the test, they selected items which differentiated between older and younger children of apparently similar intelligence. (Presumably, youngsters acquired more intellectual skills with age.) Binet and his coworkers chose tasks that picked out apparently brighter from duller children of the same age, as well. Using these general strategies, a large number of discriminatory test items were amassed and arranged in order of difficulty. Tasks at the three-year level included pointing to nose, eyes, and mouth, repeating two digits, and identifying objects in a picture. Items at the seven-year level included pointing to the right hand, describing a picture, executing a series of three commands, and counting coins. (See Figure 12-4.) Binet's test was designed so that children of approximately average ability could solve about 50 percent of the problems at their own age level and most of the tasks at lower levels.

Children took Binet's test individually. Their answers were recorded and graded. The test taker was then assigned a *mental level*,

FIGURE 12-3 Alfred Binet first became interested in measuring higher mental processes when he observed that his daughters, pictured with him here, developed learning skills differently. Madelaine (center) was more methodical and logical than Alice. Eventually, he wrote a book describing his daughters' intellectual functioning. Before devising the first practical intelligence test, Binet observed the thinking processes of many additional children in his laboratory at the Sorbonne in Paris. [*Madame Binet.*]

FIGURE 12-4 Alfred Binet collaborated with a coworker Théophile Simon to develop the first practical intelligence test. These test items appeared on that instrument, known as the Binet-Simon Scale. Five-year-olds were presented with (*a*) and (*b*) and asked "Which is prettiest?" Seven-year-olds had to identify the missing parts in (*c*). [*Binet-Simon Scale, 1905.*]

or *mental age*, as it was eventually called. A ten-year-old who performed like an average ten-year-old received a mental level of ten. A ten-year-old who responded like an average six-year-old achieved a mental level of six. Differences between mental level and chronological age served as the index of intelligence. Children whose mental levels were two years below their chronological ages were considered retarded.

The Meaning of IQ

Lewis Terman (1877–1956), an American psychologist working at Stanford University, produced a widely accepted revision of Binet's test for Americans in 1916. At this time Terman adopted the *intelligence quotient*, or *IQ*, from a German behavioral scientist, as an indicator of intelligence. An IQ is a numerical index describing relative performance on a test. It compares one person's performance with those of others of a similar age. IQs can be computed in different ways. Terman used the IQ to describe the relationship between mental level and chronological age. He rejected Binet's measure, the difference between the two. On the *Stanford-Binet Intelligence Scale*, as Terman's revision was called, the IQ was initially calculated in this way: The test taker received a precise number of months' credit for each correct answer. The points were added and the sum labeled *mental age* (MA). (The point values awarded for each task were chosen so that average people's mental age scores equaled their chronological ages.) The mental age was then divided by the chronological age (CA) and the result multiplied by 100. In other words, IQ = (MA/CA) × 100. A ten-year-old who achieved a mental age score of eleven obtained an IQ of 110 ($^{11}/_{10} \times 100 = 110$). The IQ reflected the assumption that a mental age one year below one's chronological age showed more of a handicap at age five than at age fifteen. Today, IQs on the Stanford-Binet are computed slightly differently. *Note*: Don't make the mistake of equating IQs and intelligence. Intelligence, as we have defined it, is an overall capacity for mental activities. IQ is a number that tells how a person performed on a particular test as compared with others in the same age bracket.

Current Intelligence Tests

Binet's ideas about intelligence testing were generally adopted throughout the world because his model "worked" in a practical sense. It allowed psychologists to assign to intelligence a number that seemed reasonable. And the number could be easily computed by an absolute stranger after interacting with a subject for approximately an hour. Some behavioral scientists tried to improve Binet's scale. Others constructed new tests along similar lines. To save time and money, psychologists developed instruments that could be administered to groups of individuals. Tests were devised for specific categories of people, including infants, adolescents, adults, the blind, and the deaf. Currently, there are nearly a hundred tests of intelligence in use by educators.

The *Wechsler Adult Intelligence Scale* (WAIS) is an example of a modern intelligence test which is widely used today to evaluate adult mental capacities. It was put together by psychologist David Wechsler. Six *verbal subtests* on the WAIS assess abilities that depend on language. Five WAIS *performance subtests* evaluate capacities that rely on thinking without words and practical problem-solving skills. Table 12-1 describes each subtest.

Using standard instructions, a trained examiner administers the WAIS to a single individual. The tasks on each subtest are tackled in order of difficulty from easy to hard. The test taker's precise responses are recorded so that they may be evaluated later against a set of criteria which accompany the test. Scores on each of the eleven subtests show how the subject's performance compares with that of others in the same age bracket. This information makes it possible to construct a profile of intellectual strengths and weaknesses. Eventually, the overall perform-

TABLE 12-1   Subtests on the Wechsler Adult Intelligence Scale

Verbal subtests

Information.   Questions that call for general information; e.g., "How many wings does a bird have?" "Who wrote *Paradise Lost*?" Designed to assess general knowledge.

Comprehension.   Questions that call for knowledge of practical matters; e.g., "What is the advantage of keeping money in a bank?" "What should you do if you see a boy forget his book when he leaves his seat in a restaurant?" Designed to assess the possession of practical information and the ability to make social judgments.

Arithmetic.   Questions that require the manipulation of numbers; e.g., "Three women divided eighteen golf balls equally among themselves. How many golf balls did each individual receive?" Designed to assess abilities to concentrate and reason using arithmetic.

Similarities.   Questions requiring that two items be compared for their essential similarity; e.g., "In what way are a lion and a tiger alike?" "In what way are an hour and a week alike?" Designed to assess logical and/or abstract abilities.

Digit span.   Questions that ask for the repetition of two to nine digits—forward or backward—from memory. Designed to assess attention and rote memory.

Vocabulary.   Questions that ask for definitions of words such as "umbrella" and "conscience." Designed to assess ability to learn verbal information and general range of ideas.

Performance subtests

Digit symbol.   Different symbols must be associated with each of nine digits. Then a series of digits is presented in a random order and the corresponding symbol must be written beneath each one. Designed to assess speed of learning and writing symbols.

Picture completion.   Incomplete pictures are presented. The essential part that is missing must be specified. Designed to assess visual alertness and visual memory.

Block design.   Pictorial designs are presented. Small wooden blocks must be manipulated to duplicate the pattern. Designed to assess the abilities to analyze the whole into its component parts and form abstractions.

Picture arrangement.   Three to six small pictures are presented in a random order. They must be rearranged to make a sensible story. Designed to assess ability to comprehend and size up a social situation.

Object assembly.   Puzzle-like parts of an object are presented. They must be put together quickly. Designed to assess the ability to construct a concrete form from its components.

---

ance of each WAIS taker is compared with the overall performance of a representative sample of people in the same age bracket. A subject who performs as well as 50 percent of the reference group did receives an average IQ—100. An individual who performs better or worse than 50 percent of the reference group obtains a correspondingly higher or lower IQ. Table 12-2 shows the percentage of people in the reference group who fall within each IQ range on the WAIS.

TABLE 12-2   IQ Classifications on the WAIS

IQ	Classification	Percentage included
130 and above	Very superior	2.2
120–129	Superior	6.7
110–119	Bright normal	16.1
90–109	Average	50.0
80–89	Dull normal	16.1
70–79	Borderline	6.7
69 and below	Mental defective	2.2

Source: Wechsler, D. *WAIS manual.* New York: Psychological Corporation, 1955. P. 20.

Constructing Psychological Tests

Traditional intelligence tests, those based on Binet's model, illustrate some important rules of test construction.

Selection of test items Test designers choose problems which satisfy specific criteria. The guidelines used by Binet, Wechsler, and other constructors of traditional intelligence scales include these:

1. The tasks should call for skills within the repertoire of the average individual for whom the test is intended. Accordingly, items that require knowledge of standard English are considered reasonable for testing the intelligence of Americans. Those that require calculus are judged unfair.

2. The problems posed should be fairly interesting so that test takers feel motivated to work at solving them. Success on a task such as "Count backward from 1,000 by 10" might measure the capacity to withstand boredom more than mental ability.

3. The questions must have one or more correct answers so that scoring is straightforward. This policy reduces the probability that the examiner's personal biases will influence the evaluation.

4. The entire set of test items should not favor or discriminate against subgroups of people (for example, rural folk or females) for whom the test is intended. Because nondiscriminatory items are hard to find, test designers often try to balance the bias by providing equal numbers of favored questions for each significant group.

5. In the case of children's intelligence tests, questions are chosen so that the percentage of youngsters giving correct responses increases with age. Any question that is answered correctly by more nine-year-olds than twelve-year-olds in the same IQ range is discarded.

6. Failure or success on a particular item must be positively correlated with performance on the remaining items. (Correlational concepts will be used repeatedly throughout this chapter. To review, see Chapter 2.) Measurement instruments are devised so that a test taker who is right on question 34, for example, is more likely than someone who is wrong on that item to answer later questions correctly. This criterion is based on the assumption that there is something called general intelligence which each item should be measuring to some degree.

Eventually, test items that pass initial screenings are tried out on a large sample of people. This sample is supposed to be similar in age, sex, social class, and other significant attributes to the population for whom the test is intended. This strategy permits psychologists to further evaluate the suitability of each test item.

Objectivity Tests that are reasonably free of examiner bias are said to be *objective*. Generally, intelligence test designers try to increase the objectivity of their measurement instruments by several related strategies:

1. They use questions with one or more correct answers, as we suggested before.

2. They furnish detailed directions, or *standard procedures*, to help ensure that the test is conducted uniformly. When examiners adhere to the specified guidelines, test scores are more likely to reflect the subjects' characteristics rather than the examiner's policies.

3. The test designer develops comprehensive, detailed scoring criteria or supplies correct solutions to the questions. Consequently, every examiner will evaluate all test responses in essentially the same way. If acceptable answers were not spelled out, test takers' performances might be assessed differently, depending perhaps on the examiner's mood and personal biases.

4. Test developers gather *norms*, information on the performance of a large *reference group*. The reference group is supposed to resemble, or represent, the entire population of interest on all significant characteristics—age, sex, race, social class, geographical distribution, and the like. Norms help in interpreting individual test scores. Figure 12-5 presents normative information about the Stanford-Binet. The graph describes the performance of 3,184 native-born, white American children who took an early version of the test. These data, which are still used today, provide a common standard for evaluating individual test performances. If a boy in Indiana achieves a Stanford-Binet IQ of 126, for example, the norms tell psychologists in Maine, Florida, and California that the score is unusually high. Only about 7 percent of the reference group (and presumably, of the entire population) are apt to perform as well or better.

Reliability and validity Eventually, test designers must gather evidence about the instrument's reliability and validity. First, consider *reliability*, a characteristic roughly synonymous with consistency or stability.

Psychologists are interested in several types of reliability, including those suggested by the following questions:

1. When different examiners score the same test, are they consistent in their appraisal?
2. Are items on the test internally consistent? (Is failure or success on a specific item positively correlated with performance on the remaining items? See guideline 6 on page 388.)
3. Do repeated measurements of the same phenomenon with the test, at different points in time, yield similar results?

We focus on the last question, which relates to what is called *test-retest reliability*. If you weigh 150 pounds one morning, you will weigh about the same amount a day later on a reliable scale. Constructors of intelligence tests assume that mental capabilities are similarly stable. Consequently, a person's score should not change much over time,

especially over short periods. When children are tested twice on the Stanford-Binet Intelligence Scale with less than a week intervening between testings, the two scores are usually very strongly positively correlated (approximately .83 to .98) [7].

Test designers strive to produce *valid* tests, those that measure what they were intended to. Measurement instruments may be reliable without being valid. Jessica's history essays, for example, may yield marks near 70 quite consistently. But the grades may reflect the teacher's opinion of Jessica's grammar or conduct, and not her knowledge of history. Psychologists are interested in several types of validity, including those suggested by the following questions:

1. Does overall test score correlate with some *current* performance that requires the same characteristic(s)?

FIGURE 12-5 The distribution of intelligence test scores for a carefully selected group of 3,184 white, English-speaking, native-born American children, aged two to eighteen. This testing provided normative information for the 1937 Stanford-Binet and later versions. When the scale was revised in 1972, information about the test performances of a new reference group was gathered. This time, black and Spanish-surnamed children whose primary language was English were included in the representative sample. Today, youngsters tend to achieve higher mental age scores on the Stanford-Binet than they did in 1937. The test designers assumed that the distribution of IQ scores for children in a particular age range had remained constant—that the 1972 IQ norms should match the 1937 norms. To achieve that result, the relation between mental age and IQ scores was adjusted. The adjustment permits behavioral scientists to directly compare current research findings on IQ with those based on previous versions of the Stanford-Binet. [*From Terman and Merrill, 1960.*]

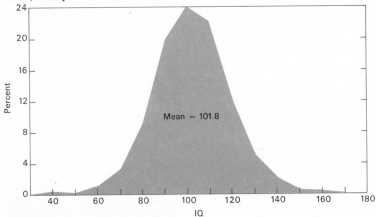

2. Does test performance correlate with some *future* performance that depends on the same characteristic(s)?

To assess an intelligence test's validity, behavioral scientists investigate the question, Does performance on the test correlate highly with other types of intelligent behavior? Unfortunately, there are no clear-cut criteria of intelligence on which everyone agrees. Many psychologists assume that grades in school, scores on achievement tests and other intelligence assessment devices, and college and vocational success reflect intelligent functioning. They reason that if an intelligence test really measures mental abilities, then people who make high IQ scores should excel in these other situations. And vice versa.

Are traditional intelligence tests valid? Psychologists who believe that they are cite these facts: Performances on mental tests frequently agree with the judgments of educators concerning mental retardation and exceptional intelligence. IQs correlate positively (approximately .50, on the average) with measures of academic achievement. People who do well on intelligence tests often receive high grades in elementary and high school and in college. Low scorers tend to make poor marks in these academic situations [8]. Intelligence test performance shows a low positive correlation with occupational proficiency across many types of jobs. In other words, people who score high on intelligence tests frequently do well at work, in their employer's estimation. The converse is true too [9]. Amount of education is correlated positively with intelligence test performance. People who graduate from high school score 110 IQ points on the average. Those who graduate from college attain an average IQ of 120. Individuals who go on to graduate school and earn an advanced degree achieve average IQs of about 130 [10]. Finally, intelligence test performance correlates positively with overall socioeconomic achievements. Adults with high incomes and high-status jobs (such as physicians, lawyers, and scientists) generally make high scores on intelligence tests. Those with low incomes and low-status jobs (such as porters, domestics, and laborers) tend to score low [11]. These findings, which are supported by a great many studies, show that intelligence tests enable psychologists to make predictions about varied academic, social, and vocational achievements. From this point of view, traditional intelligence tests may be considered valid. We return to the validity question shortly. ▲

A number of controversial issues have been raised by research on measured intelligence. We focus now on two related topics. How stable is the IQ? And, to what extent does heredity contribute to scores on intelligence tests?

▲ USING PSYCHOLOGY

1. How do you define intelligence? Be sure to take a stand on these questions: Is intelligence essentially unitary? Is it related primarily to scholastic achievements? Does it depend on motivation? Defend your positions.

2. If ten-year-old Enrico performed like an average fifteen-year-old on the 1916 version of the Stanford-Binet, what IQ score would he achieve? Suppose that Enrico performed like an average five-year-old. Calculate his IQ again. Use the formula IQ = (MA/CA) × 100.

3. How do the computations of IQs on the WAIS, the initial Binet, and the 1916 version of the Stanford-Binet Intelligence Scale differ?

4. Ask several friends to define the term "IQ." Do they confuse IQ and intelligence? Explain the difference.

5. Examine the criteria for choosing items for intelligence tests. Does each one appear sensible to you? Do they reveal an underlying concept of what intelligence is? Explain.

THE STABILITY OF MEASURED INTELLIGENCE

The IQ is essentially a rank which tells how an individual stands in relation to others the same age. Does a person's relative standing on an intelligence test change? Once a child has passed the age of approximately five, the IQ remains rather stable. Youngsters who attain superior IQs at age six usually achieve similarly superior ones at age sixteen. Average and below-average six-year-olds tend to maintain their relative positions too.

Although IQs do not undergo predictable age-related patterns of growth or decline during childhood, IQ changes may occur during this period. In Chapter 3 we saw that an inadequate environment (such as an understaffed orphanage) could depress measured intelligence while an enriched setting (an Israeli kibbutz, for example) could raise IQ scores. How unusual is IQ change? In one study of this topic, Marjorie Honzik and her colleagues tested and retested children at eight different times throughout childhood. (When the same people are tested and retested at two or more points in time, psychologists call the procedure a *longitudinal study*.) Honzik found that the IQs of 85 percent of the subjects varied ten or more points. The scores of nearly 10 percent of the youngsters changed as many as thirty points or more. Whereas some IQs improved, others declined or seesawed up and down [12]. Psychologist Lester Sontag and his coworkers studied 200 youngsters who had been tested every year throughout their childhood. The behavioral scientists looked for personality characteristics that might account for gains and losses in IQ. Both emotional dependence on parents and femininity were related to a declining IQ. Curiosity, emotional independence, verbal aggression, persistence in efforts to solve difficult and challenging problems, and competitiveness in ordinary interactions were all associated with IQ gains [13]. The latter characteristics, which are linked with the masculine role in our society, probably facilitate learning and contribute to habits of intellectual mastery. Findings that American men are more likely than American women to show increases in measured intelligence support this hypothesis [14]. These sex-related differences in personality appear to be shaped by our culture, a topic discussed in Chapter 17.

Psychologists Robert and Pauline Sears and their colleagues recently studied characteristics that are associated with IQ gains and losses during adulthood. The Sears administered tests of various types to a sample of approximately 1,000 adults with exceptionally high IQs (above 140). These research participants had been assessed and questioned throughout their lives to further psychologists' understanding of unusually bright people. The Sears found that gains in measured intelligence among women were associated with high parental occupational and educational levels, cultural interests, and career satisfactions. Gains among men were related to two characteristics that had been assessed during childhood—high achievement motivation and persistence in overcoming obstacles. These findings are consistent with Sontag's. IQ gains in bright adults were not associated with an especially satisfactory life adjustment. The men whose IQ scores decreased were more apt to be people-oriented than those whose scores increased. The male IQ-point losers reported more friendships, happier marriages, and greater joy in living than the IQ-point gainers [15]. Whether these results apply to the entire population or only to exceptional people is not known.

Incidentally, there are no significant overall IQ differences between American men and women. This is partly because items on most traditional intelligence tests were selected initially so that the test would be equally difficult for both females and males. The two sexes do display their own consistent intellectual strengths. In general, men do better on items that require mathematics and visualization of spatial relationships (such as giving directions for right and left turns from a map without rotating it or imagining how a house will look from a blueprint). Women tend to excel on items that require verbal abilities. Reasons for these differences are not currently clear, though both heredity and environment appear to contribute [16]. Females and males mature on distinctive timetables during childhood. Rate of maturation (Chapter 3) has been linked recently with the development of particular mental skills. Early-maturing males are likely to show feminine mental strengths and weaknesses, while late-maturing females are apt to show the masculine intellectual pattern [17].

What ordinarily happens to measured intelligence in middle and old age? Many behavioral scientists have found evidence that deficits in problem solving, memory, and learning appear at predictable times throughout adulthood. Some psychologists believe that these declines reflect deteriorating brain functioning [18]. Not all investigators agree with these conclusions [19]. One reason for discrepant opinions is the difficulty of measuring intelligence in old age. Elderly people tend to feel more bored and humiliated by working seemingly nonsensical tasks than younger ones do. Older individuals may feel more anxious, too, as societal stereotypes assess their mental abilities unkindly. Confusion due to lack of familiarity with research methods may interfere with an accurate assessment. Greater fatigue and lessened motivation must also be considered [20].

Psychologists tend to agree on these findings about intelligence during old age:

1. After age seventy, losses in measured intelligence often appear. Yet, during these late years, IQs may remain constant or even increase [21]. Intellectual losses in old age do not seem to be inevitable, universal, and irremediable. A decreasing IQ in old age is associated with failing health and inactivity. People with a substantial education and comfortable income are more likely than others to maintain their intellectual capacities [22].

2. Elderly people lose the ability to work efficiently at tasks that require speed and hand-eye coordination [23]. Rote learning (memorizing new facts) becomes more difficult. Speed and accuracy in retrieving materials from short- and long-term memories (Chapter 8) decrease [24].

3. Certain abilities decline from one to six years before adults die although these people appear healthy when they are tested [25]. Some psychologists speculate that brain functions may be altered, perhaps by arteriosclerosis, as death nears. See Figure 12-6.

HEREDITY, ENVIRONMENT, AND MEASURED INTELLIGENCE

Both heredity and environment influence differences in measured intelligence. Earlier, we noted that stimulating or impoverished surroundings can change IQ scores in children. The evidence for the effects of heredity on variations in measured intelligence come from two sources. First, there are consistent associations between specific hereditary abnormalities and performance patterns on mental tests. For example, the missing Y or X chromosome in Turner's syndrome (Chapter

FIGURE 12-6 Some elderly people continue to display excellent intellectual functioning. Others vary enormously in their retention of mental skills. Currently, psychologists are investigating cognitive-skill training programs that can help reduce or eliminate age-related deficits. Practice in using mnemonic devices, especially imagery, improves certain aspects of memory. In some cases, counseling to lessen anxiety and/or depression strengthens cognitive capabilities [78]. [*Irene Bayer/Monkmeyer Press Photo Service.*]

3) tends to be linked with above-average verbal abilities and below-average spatial ones [26]. In Down's syndrome (commonly known as mongolism), a specific extra chromosome is associated with moderate intellectual retardation [27]. Second, studies on predominantly white, middle-class English-speaking families support the idea that heredity influences differences in measured intelligence. The greater the genetic similarity between two such people, the more alike their intelligence test scores are apt to be. Figure 12-7 summarizes the results of fifty-two studies on this topic. The correlation coefficients show the degree to which pairs of individuals achieve similar IQ scores. You can see that when the measured intelligence of two genetically unrelated persons reared together are compared, the correlations range from .10 to .35, suggesting that the likelihood of the scores being similar is relatively low. Comparisons of the IQs of identical twins reared apart, in contrast, yield correlations of approximately .60 to .80. These very high correlations indicate that genetically identical individuals quite probably make similar scores on intelligence tests even when they are reared in diverse environments. In fact, average differences in IQ among identical twins reared apart appear to be only a point or two greater than the average IQ differences among identical twins reared together [28]. Recent, carefully controlled adoption studies (Chapter 3) also strongly support the idea that heredity contributes to variations in measured intelligence [29].

Saying that heredity contributes to IQ differences doesn't mean that the environment has little or no impact. Experience can have a huge effect on behavior that is influenced by genes. Hereditary endowment seems to shape *ranges of reactions* to particular circumstances, as discussed previously. It does not fix behavior rigidly.

It must be pointed out that the findings of family studies are not free of problems. Psychologists recently discovered that some of the basic supportive data are untrustworthy. Cyril Burt, an eminent British psychologist who provided a great deal of evidence demonstrating genetic influences on IQ differences, fabricated much of his data [30]. Even legitimate family studies have serious difficulties, as described previously. You may recall that

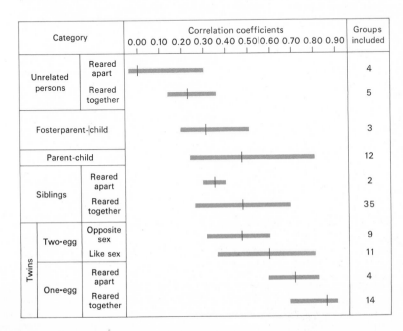

FIGURE 12-7 The correlation coefficients on this table show the extent of IQ similarity found among people of varying degrees of kinship. The data came from fifty-two studies. The horizontal lines show the range, or spread, in the calculated correlation coefficients. The vertical slashes represent medians—the point above which half the correlations fall. [*From Erlenmeyer-Kimling and Jarvik, 1968.*]

as hereditary similarities increase, so usually do environmental ones. Even when identical twins are reared in different homes, they are apt to be brought up under roughly comparable circumstances, since most adoption agencies try to place children in socially and economically advantaged environments. Despite these objections, the bulk of current evidence leads to the conclusion that genes and experience both shape performance differences on mental tests.

In the late 1960s and early 1970s, controversies about how nature and nurture contribute to measured intelligence in specific groups attracted a great deal of attention from the popular press. Scientists argued about two issues: Do poor people have less native ability than middle- and upper-income individuals? Do blacks have less inborn intelligence than whites? We focus in some detail on both these still-controversial questions.

Poverty and IQ

Children and adults from lower-class homes average twenty to thirty IQ points below those living in middle- and upper-class surroundings on intelligence tests [31]. Some psychologists believe that the differences are at least partially genetically determined and that socioeconomic status is, in part, the result of inherited ability [32]. Other behavioral scientists favor an environmental explanation for the differences between the two groups.

There are many ways that the environment could create IQ differences between the poor and others. Numerous intelligence-arresting physical conditions—poor prenatal care, malnutrition, lead poisoning, and disease, for example—are more prevalent among low-income families than among financially advantaged ones. The effects of the social-psychological climate of poverty on intelligence are open to debate. Four somewhat overlapping viewpoints are popular today:

1. Poverty is associated with crowded, noisy, disorganized, tense, and changing living conditions. Under such circumstances, poor youngsters are less likely than their middle-class counterparts

to attend to new information, to detect order, and to learn that their behavior produces predictable results. These activities seem important for developing intelligence [33].

2. Compared with financially advantaged youngsters, economically disadvantaged ones are apt to hear relatively few language labels for their experiences. Such verbal deficits limit thinking and result in lower intelligence [34].

3. If parents are malnourished, unhealthy, tired, uncomfortable, and worried, they are unlikely to take time to help children develop abilities. Parents who desire to help may not know how, especially if their own education was limited and their own capacities were never cultivated.

4. When numerous children are spaced close together in a family (a pattern associated with poverty), each child receives limited intellectual stimulation from adults and older children. It is hardly surprising, then, that youngsters from large, closely spaced families tend to score lower on IQ tests than those from smaller families [35].

The findings of early-education programs support an environmental explanation for the intelligence test differences between poor and middle-income people. After surveying a Milwaukee slum area, behavioral scientists Rick Heber and Howard Garber found that mothers with IQs below 80 (45.5 percent of the sample) reared 78.2 percent of the children with IQs below 80. Heber and Garber hypothesized that low-IQ mothers might somehow be retarding the mental development of normally intelligent offspring. If this hunch was correct, then an enrichment program might counteract the decline. To see if retardation could be prevented, Heber and Garber began an ambitious "total push" program, known as the *Milwaukee project*. They identified forty mothers with IQs below 70 and randomly assigned each one to an experimental or control group. As soon as one of the mothers returned home from the hospital with a newborn infant, treatment began. The mothers in the experimental group received occupation, homemaking, and baby-care training. Their infants took part in an intensive program to stimulate sensory processing, language, and thinking. During the preschool years, the children learned cognitive skills (including language) in small groups. Attention was paid to the individual strengths and weaknesses of each youngster. The children in the control group grew up under ordinary circumstances, except for occasional testing. By age 5½, the differences between the two groups were dramatic. The experimental children averaged IQ scores of 124. Control youngsters averaged only 94 IQ points. Follow-ups at age nine showed that the early training program had lasting effects. The experimental children still showed a lead of 20 IQ points over the control youngsters [36]. Investigators find that poor children make impressive gains on intelligence tests when enrolled in shorter, less intensive programs that emphasize language and cognitive skills too. Early reports on Head Start and similar preschool projects were pessimistic about the durability of the results. But recent research, which includes school-age follow-ups, suggests that many enrichment programs do work. Parental involvement and earlier, longer interventions are best. These projects result in lasting IQ increases of ten points and more. Persistent reading-level gains occur. And "tutored" youngsters are more likely than "nontutored" ones to achieve at grade level and less likely to be set back a year [37]. See Figure 12-8.

The results of early-education programs may be attributed to different causes. Basic intellectual capacities might be expanding. Increased IQs may reflect these underlying gains. Or, children might simply be learning those particular skills which traditional intelligence tests assess, while their mental capacities remain the same. Let's consider the second possibility, that poor children are generally cognitively competent but do not acquire the particular abilities measured by traditional intelligence tests. Behavioral scientists who espouse this viewpoint make the following assumptions: Economically advantaged children begin school with a powerful head start. They have often been taught elementary scholastic tasks (counting and memorizing the alphabet, for example). They are likely to be familiar with academic etiquette (listening, sitting quietly, and obeying

FIGURE 12-8 Today, many preschool education projects attempt to involve parents. Home Start, one offshoot of Head Start, includes programs all over the United States which emphasize the parents' potential contributions as the first and most influential educators. A staff of home visitors (trained community residents) helps families diagnose problems and assess needs; it provides information, support, and direct services as well. In most cases, parents learn about early development and learn to use household materials as educational toys and games, to instruct their children in school-related skills, and to provide positive reinforcement of constructive efforts. [*Home Start Training Center, West Central West Virginia, CAA, Inc.*]

authority figures, for instance). Many lower-class children are handicapped by not having acquired these skills. To make matters worse, school-related capabilities and rules may seem petty and irrelevant to youngsters who are hungry, tired, and tense. The poor child's proficiency at survival (perhaps self-defense and infant care) generally goes unappreciated within the traditional school setting.

The rest of the story is predictable. The middle-class children like the teacher and vice versa. On the whole, these youngsters have relatively positive experiences at school. Teachers and parents believe that they will succeed and encourage efforts in that direction. In contrast, many poor children dislike the alien routines of the classroom which seem to have little meaning. The teacher is apt to perceive economically disadvantaged youngsters unfavorably, in turn. Encouragement within the academic arena is unlikely. Expectations for accomplishment are generally low.

All in all, school is likely to be a frustrating experience for the deprived child.

Soon after children enter kindergarten, socioeconomic status may "seal their fate." The snowball effect is a rapid one. As upper- and middle-class students advance, lower-income pupils slip increasingly further behind on the school-related skills defined as intelligence. Their IQ scores may simply reflect this reality.

A number of investigators report findings that support this theory. Eigel Pedersen and

FIGURE 12-9 The value of testing minority-group children using traditional intelligence tests continues to be debated vigorously. Psychologists Joe Martinez and Robert Williams believe that psychological tests which fail to take cultural differences into account are inaccurate in assessing the abilities of minority-group members. This idea has support. IQ scores predict the future achievements of white middle-class youngsters far better than they predict those of minority-group children. Both Martinez and Williams fear that the use of traditional intelligence tests leads to unfair special educational placements that diminish opportunities for blacks, Chicanos, and others [79]. Not everyone agrees with this analysis. Psychologist Nadine Lambert argues that in most cases teachers demand testing only *after* youngsters are failing. In other words, the tests themselves may simply support special placement decisions. Lambert also points out that black and Chicano children often do better on IQ tests than on other assessments of academic ability, such as the teacher's estimates of intelligence and grade-point averages. Finally, Lambert believes that intelligence tests provide important information about children's special needs [80]. [*Nancy Hays/Monkmeyer Press Photo Service.*]

his coworkers discovered that first-grade teachers exert an enormous impact on children's future scholastic achievements [38]. Robert Rosenthal and his associates have shown that teachers' expectations can alter IQ scores. In the mid-1960s, Rosenthal and Lenore Jacobson gave intelligence tests to children at an elementary school in a poor neighborhood in south San Francisco. Then they randomly chose 20 percent of the children from each classroom, labeled them "intellectual bloomers," and gave their names to teachers. The teachers were led to expect remarkable progress from the "bloomers." The differences between "bloomers" and others was, of course, solely in the teacher's mind. Eight months later, Rosenthal and Jacobson retested the children. The "bloomers," whether low or high in measured intelligence, had all "bloomed" at least modestly. They had gained four IQ points more, on the average, than the others [39]. More than 200 replications of this study have been attempted. A sizable proportion show that expectations produce small but significant effects.

Recent research suggests that teachers translate expectations into behavior without necessarily being aware of doing so. When teachers believe that children have high intellectual potential, they tend to create a warm, stimulating climate. They give more feedback, teach more material, question more, and give more opportunities to respond than usual [40]. When youngsters are considered capable of only average or below-average work, they are apt to be ignored. Should such youngsters achieve—contrary to their teachers' expectations—they may simply be labeled as troublemakers [41]. Poor and black children tend to be negatively perceived by their teachers more frequently than others—even when the teachers themselves are black [42]. Recent longitudinal research by psychologist Virginia Shipman and her coworkers suggests that poor black children who achieve academically tend to be the products of warm, supportive family and school settings [43].

The content of traditional intelligence tests and the standard examining procedures may both contribute to the IQ-score gap between the poor and others. Unlike middle-class children, disadvantaged ones are likely to feel ill at ease with the examiner, uninterested in the school-like tasks of the intelligence test, and unmotivated to perform to the best of their abilities. Youngsters from an inner-city ghetto or a rural slum may not understand the vocabulary words, instructions, or situations that are supposed to be evaluated. A widely used children's intelligence test asks this question: "What would you do if you were sent to the store by your mother to buy something and you found the store didn't have it?" "Go to another store" (the preferred answer) may be the best response for the middle-class child. But the youngster on an Indian reservation may not have another store to go to. For the ghetto child, going to a store on the next block may be dangerous and therefore stupid. For varied reasons, then, many psychologists believe that traditional intelligence tests simply do not tap the insights, skills, and competencies of lower-income people.

Race and IQ

Most investigators of racial differences in IQ find that whites achieve higher scores than blacks on traditional intelligence tests, regardless of social class. The IQ differences between the two races generally range from 1 to 20 points [44]. The reasons for these findings have been heatedly debated in recent years. An educational psychologist, Arthur Jensen, took the position that heredity may be responsible. In a now famous article in the *Harvard Educational Review*, he argued:

1. Studies of blood relatives suggest that heredity determines approximately 80 percent of the differences between people in measured intelligence. Genes are roughly twice as important as experiences in shaping IQs.
2. Blacks score points on intelligence tests differently from whites. They excel at rote learning; whites, at abstract thinking. Jensen speculates that blacks and whites may inherit different types of intellectual capacities.
3. If the measured intelligence of blacks were

merely suppressed by adverse conditions, compensatory education programs should have been able to raise the average IQ of black children to the average IQ level of white children [45].

Jensen continues to believe that existing evidence favors an hereditary explanation for the IQ differences between the races. His interpretations of the intelligence test data have been challenged for numerous reasons, however. We mention some of the most important criticisms:

1. As stated earlier, traditional intelligence tests contain built-in biases. They provide tasks that are unfair to the poor and to racial and ethnic minority groups. In the United States, blacks always fall in one and often in both categories. Before reading on, try the items on the Dove Counterbalance General Intelligence Test which appears in Figure 12-10. This test gives whites some insight into the plight of being evaluated by an instrument that is grounded in the experiences of an unfamiliar culture.
2. Some of the studies that support Jensen's case used inadequate research designs. Much of his evidence rested on Cyril Burt's data which, unknown to Jensen, were fabricated. It appears, therefore, that Jensen's conclusions rest on a weak data base [46].
3. Jensen's interpretation of a statistic called a heritability coefficient is often attacked.

To understand the arguments, you need some background information. In estimating the extent that genetic variations influence observed differences on intelligence tests (or on any other measure), psychologists usually compute a *heritability coefficient*. The coefficient is a number ranging from .00 to 1.00. Formulas for calculating the index vary. So do analyses of its significance. For our purposes, you should know that heritability coefficients have been computed on the IQ scores of predominantly white middle-class people of varying degrees of kinship. Coefficients calculated in traditional ways suggest that somewhere between 50 and 80 percent of observed IQ differences reflect genetic variations.

Jensen's interpretation of the heritability coefficient is criticized for several overlapping reasons. First, he applied the heritability

1. A "handkerchief head" is: (a) a cool cat, (b) a porter, (c) an Uncle Tom, (d) a hoddi, (e) a preacher.

2. Which word is most out of place here? (a) splib, (b) blood, (c) gray, (d) spook, (e) black.

3. A "gas head" is a person who has a: (a) fast-moving car, (b) stable of "lace," (c) "process," (d) habit of stealing cars, (e) long jail record for arson.

4. "Down-home" (the South) today, for the average "soul brother" who is picking cottom from sunup until sundown, what is the average earning (take home) for one full day? (a) $.75, (b) $1.65, (c) $3.50, (d) $5, (e) $12.

5. "Bo Diddley" is a: (a) game for children, (b) down-home cheap wine, (c) down-home singer, (d) new dance, (e) Moejoe call.

6. If a pimp is up tight with a woman who gets state aid, what does he mean when he talks about "Mother's Day?" (a) second Sunday in May, (b) third Sunday in June, (c) first of every month, (d) none of these, (e) first and fifteenth of every month.

7. "Hully Gully" came from: (a) East Oakland, (b) Fillmore, (c) Watts, (d) Harlem, (e) Motor City.

8. If a man is called a "blood," then he is a (a) fighter, (b) Mexican-American, (c) Negro, (d) hungry hemophile, (e) Redman or Indian.

9. Cheap chitlings (not the kind you purchase at a frozen-food counter) will taste rubbery unless they are cooked long enough. How soon can you quit cooking them to eat and enjoy them? (a) 45 minutes, (b) two hours, (c) 24 hours, (d) one week (on a low flame), (e) one hour.

10. What are the "Dixie Humming-birds?" (a) part of the KKK, (b) a swamp disease, (c) a modern gospel group, (d) a Mississippi Negro paramilitary group, (e) Deacons.

11. If you throw the dice and seven is showing on the top, what is facing down? (a) seven, (b) snake eyes, (c) boxcars, (d) little Joes, (e) 11.

12. "Jet" is: (a) an East Oakland motorcycle club, (b) one of the gangs in "West Side Story," (c) a news and gossip magazine, (d) a way of life for the very rich.

13. T-Bone Walker got famous for playing what? (a) trombone, (b) piano, (c) "T-flute," (d) guitar, (e) "Hambone."*

*Those who are not "culturally deprived" will recognize the correct answers are 1. (c), 2. (c), 3. (c), 4. (d), 5. (c), 6. (e), 7. (c), 8. (c), 9. (c), 10. (c), 11. (a), 12. (c), 13. (d).

FIGURE 12-10 The Dove Counterbalance General Intelligence Test. [*Copyright © 1968, Newsweek, Inc.*]

coefficients derived from work with predominantly middle-class Caucasian groups to black Americans. Many psychologists contend that heritability coefficients describe the extent that genes account for differences on a measured trait in a specific population and cannot be fairly applied to other groups. Heritability coefficients computed for black samples are often lower than those for white ones. Presumably, heredity does not determine as much of the IQ variability among blacks as it does among whites [47]. Second, Jensen applied the heritability index to *differences between whites and blacks*. Many behavioral scientists object: Heritability coefficients pertain to the determinants of variability *within* a single group. Even if the 80 percent figure applies to both blacks and whites, it cannot be used to account for differences *between* the two groups. Third, Jensen assumed that high heritability coefficients mean that genetics is the most important influence on the trait under investigation. He was mistaken on this point. Imagine that all the members of a specific group grow up under precisely the same circumstances. In this case, heredity has to be the source of all observed differences in measured intelligence. But even under these impossible conditions (where the heritability coefficient is 1.00), the environment still contributes importantly to mental abilities. If the surroundings are uniformly inadequate, people will develop in ways very different from those developed under consistently stimulating conditions. Many psychologists believe that this particular misinterpretation caused

Jensen to vastly underestimate the impact of contrasting experiences on blacks and whites. Even wealthy black Americans must contend with the long-range cumulative effects of unequal opportunity and social, legal, and political discrimination. Segregated schools still provide inferior education for many blacks. There is evidence that black youngsters frequently expect a bleak future, too [48]. Under these conditions, striving for the types of academic skills that enhance IQ may appear to be pointless. Fourth, Jensen believed that high heritability coefficients mean that genes essentially fix intelligence. Most psychologists reject this notion. Heritability coefficients do not enable scientists to predict how changes in environment will affect a measured trait. In Israel, for example, home-reared Jewish youngsters of European background achieve average IQs of 105, while those from mid-Eastern backgrounds attain average IQs of 85. But, when Israeli babies were raised in the intensely stimulating atmosphere of the kibbutz, both European and mid-Eastern groups averaged the same IQ score, 115 [49]. Knowledge of heritability coefficients could not have helped predict this result. Changing conditions influence the average measured intelligence of blacks in a similar manner. Jensen questioned the effectiveness of preschool educational programs at a time when preliminary results were very discouraging. Evidence that has since accumulated shows that early enrichment projects do raise black children's IQs substantially. Many other environmental changes, including adoption into advantaged white families, have similar results [50].

The existence of authentic differences in measured intelligence between blacks and whites has been challenged by recent research. After controlling social-class effects carefully, psychologists Sandra Scarr and Richard Weinberg found no significant IQ differences between blacks and whites in their adoption studies. The same investigators compared the intelligence test performances of blacks with varying degrees of white European ancestry (as assessed by blood-sample component analyses). There were no significant differences between groups with small and large white genetic backgrounds [51].

Race-IQ findings remain controversial. At present, scientists lack sufficient information to come to firm conclusions about the origins of observed differences between blacks and whites. ▲

▲ USING PSYCHOLOGY

1. Suppose that you were interested in assessing the stability of IQ scores in people seventy years of age and older. Think of several ways to do so. What problems would arise in each case?

2. What do studies of IQ gains and losses suggest about motivational influences on measured intelligence? About the correlation of increased intelligence (as defined by traditional tests) with assessments of a good adjustment?

3. Imagine that you are the director of a well-funded experimental education project. Design an early-education program that is likely to permanently increase the measured intelligence of poor children.

4. Jensen's work does not appear to have been motivated by either racist or political motives. Nonetheless, his conclusions have been distorted, misstated, and dramatized to support racist claims. Should scientists study issues, such as race and intelligence, that have enormous potential for social abuse?

TRADITIONAL INTELLIGENCE TESTS ON TRIAL

Until the mid-1960s, behavioral scientists felt fairly smug about intelligence tests. The instruments were considered one of psychology's greatest successes and were widely used in business, industry, government, the armed forces, and schools. In recent years, intelligence testing has come under attack on numerous fronts. Currently, there are a great many doubts about the validity and usefulness of traditional measures of mental ability [52].

Questionable Validity and Serious Abuses

The validity of traditional intelligence tests has been questioned for several reasons. First, they make a number of controversial assumptions. For example, most tests presuppose that intelligence is either a unitary ability or a group of highly positively correlated capacities. Because of this assumption, tasks that are not strongly associated with overall performance are discarded as the test is refined. Yet, many mental abilities are not highly correlated. L.'s case provided a dramatic example. Capacities that make one an able carpenter or a poet may not be associated at all with the abilities that lead to a brilliant academic career. Tasks on traditional intelligence tests often heavily sample school-based skills, such as vocabulary, general information, and algebra. This bias has caused some critics to classify intelligence tests as glorified achievement tests. Traditional tests also assume that mental ability may be measured by conventional responses to questions that have a single answer or several correct ones. Most real-life challenges probably have more to do with evaluating the relative advantages of several alternatives.

As you may recall, intelligence test performance is positively correlated with educational, social, and vocational success. But the basis for the correlation is unclear. Behavior sampled by mental tests and these life situations may reflect basic competency. There is an equally plausible alternative explanation. Privileged members of our society learn from parents and teachers the skills that permit them to do well on traditional intelligence tests. At the same time, advantaged backgrounds provide access to extensive schooling and well-paid, high-status jobs.

When traditional intelligence tests are used to make decisions about members of disadvantaged groups, serious abuses may arise. A disproportionate number of individuals from minority cultures are usually singled out for special educational and vocational classes. Some psychologists argue that these assignments keep children from developing the skills that are necessary for achieving success in our society. Low IQ scores appear to convince many teachers that the situation is hopeless. Instead of seeing the problem as one of ineffective initial instruction, they tend to blame the child's low ability and give up on teaching [53]. Jane Mercer, a prominent California sociologist, has recently concluded that assessment practices in public schools violate five rights of children: "their right to be evaluated within a culturally appropriate normative framework; their right to be assessed as a multidimensional human being; their right to be fully educated; their right to be free of stigmatizing labels; and their right to ethnic identity and respect [54]." See Figure 12-9.

New Directions

Should psychologists continue trying to measure intelligence? Why not shelve the whole effort? There are a number of reasons for persevering. If a person isn't learning, tests of intellectual functioning may enable teachers to identify the problem. Mental tests can help to evaluate the effects of new educational practices. When brain damage has occurred, tests can pinpoint remaining abilities and guide rehabilitation. The tests have many additional uses. Today, numerous psychologists are trying to define and measure intelligence in new ways that avoid old problems.

For many years, behavioral scientists have

been developing tests in the Binet tradition that are designed to minimize discrimination against particular ethnic and social groups. The instruments are called *"culture-fair" tests.* They honor the spirit that moved Lena Younger in the play *Raisin in the Sun* to declare, "When you start measuring somebody, measure him right, child, measure him right. Make sure you done taken into account what hills and valleys he come through before he got to where he is [55]."

Culture-fair tests provide tasks such as those in Figure 12-11. These items require mental abilities but depend very little on language and school achievement. Of course, even nonverbal exercises require concepts that are developed in a specific culture. One

African tribe, the Kpelle, considers constructing unanswerable arguments the mark of intelligence. When Kpelle individuals take American mental tests, they are apt to strive for original metaphors, instead of solving the problems [56]. Because of their different concept of intelligence, they would be unfairly measured by "culture-fair" mental tests.

Typically, "culture-fair" tests deemphasize speed to avoid pressuring test takers. To reduce the impact of previous experiences, the subjects may often practice the various tasks. An examiner of the same background as the test taker administers the test in a familiar setting, using the subject's native language. In some cases, special norms have been collected so that people can be compared

1. CLASSIFICATIONS
Which one of these is different from the remaining four?

FIGURE 12-11 These items came from a "culture-fair" intelligence test. [*After Cattell, 1968.*]

2. SERIES
Which of the five figures on the right would properly continue the three on the left? That is, fill in the blank.

3. MATRICES
Which of the figures on the right should go into the square on the left to make it look right?

4. TOPOLOGY
In the figure on the left, the dot is outside the square and inside the circle. In which of the figures on the right could you put a dot outside the square and inside the circle?

with others of similar social and cultural backgrounds [57].

Alfred Binet focused attention on intelligence as an end product instead of on the processes involved in making intelligent judgments. The qualitative differences in mental functioning between individuals—the variety of ways people achieved the same scores—tended to be ignored. Today, many behavioral scientists [58] seem to be turning from the question "Who is intelligent?" to the more basic questions "What is intelligence?" and "Which cognitive and adaptive processes make up intelligent behavior?" Instead of focusing on academic types of abilities, many psychologists are attempting to characterize and measure *basic* mental skills [59]. We describe two examples.

In the United States and in other countries, behavioral scientists are constructing mental tests for children based on Jean Piaget's work. As we saw in Chapter 9, Piaget theorizes that children's thinking develops in stages, becoming increasingly more sophisticated with advancing age until adulthood. Piagetian test makers fault traditional intelligence measures for comparing one child with others the same age on "arbitrary" skills and bits of knowledge. They argue that it makes more sense to identify the mental abilities that are being used and the stage of the individual's current reasoning.

To assess intellectual abilities and stages, children are asked to ponder problem situations of various types. An examiner, for example, might show a youngster a nail and ask, "If we put this nail in water, will it go to the bottom, or will it remain on the water?"

The child is then invited to place the nail in a tank of water to see what happens. After the nail sinks, the examiner might ask, "Why does the nail go to the bottom?" By setting up experimental situations like this one and observing children's reasoning fairly directly, some test makers believe that they can come to a better understanding of both the abilities of the individual child and the general processes underlying intellectual functioning [60].

Psychologist Earl Hunt and his associates are attempting to identify some of the cognitive functions underlying verbal and quantitative abilities. College students who have previously taken aptitude tests are observed as they work specific intellectual tasks. Then Hunt analyzes the mental processes that distinguish people with high quantitative and verbal aptitude test scores from those with low scores. He has found that students who do well on quantitative aptitude tests maintain more information in their short-term memories than those who do poorly on these tests. Highly verbal individuals search their short-term memories more rapidly than less verbal ones do [61]. Through research of this type, psychologists hope to be able to identify many fundamental information-processing functions. In the future, intelligence tests may rate people on dozens of specific cognitive operations that have been pinpointed by careful research. Measurement instruments of this sort may yield profiles of individual abilities which will truly help teachers instruct more effectively and permit students to make sounder educational and vocational choices. ▲

▲ USING PSYCHOLOGY

1. Do you consider traditional intelligence tests valid? Argue for and against their validity.

2. Have you personally seen evidence of intelligence test abuses?

3. List the advantages and disadvantages of traditional and new types of intelligence tests. Which do you prefer? Why?

CREATIVITY

Mozart described the process of creating music like this:

When I am, as it were, completely myself, entirely alone, and of good cheer—say, traveling in a carriage, or walking after a good meal, or during the night when I cannot sleep; it is on such occasions that my ideas flow best and most abundantly. *Whence* and *how* they come, I know not; nor can I force them. [62]

Creative artists cannot explain their own inventiveness. Psychologists are only beginning to understand this complex capability. Creativity and intelligence appear to be based on somewhat different mental skills. Intelligence, at least as assessed by traditional intelligence tests, depends on capacities to reason in conventional ways and arrive at single correct solutions to problems. Psychologist J. P. Guilford calls this ability *convergent thinking*. Creativity, in contrast, requires what Guilford calls *divergent thinking*, innovative and original mental activity that deviates from customary patterns and results in more than one acceptable solution to a problem. Capacities for convergent and divergent thinking tend to be only moderately correlated. The measured intelligence of writers, artists, mathematicians, and scientists, for instance, is almost always above average. But IQ does not predict how inventive an individual will be. A biologist with an IQ of 130, for example, may be far more productive than one with an IQ of 180. We consider *creativity* a distinct problem-solving capacity which enables people to produce original ideas or products that are both adaptive (that serve a useful function) and fully developed. We assume that everyone has some degree of this characteristic. Psychologists' efforts to measure creativity, understand its *correlates* (the characteristics associated with it), and train it are examined in this section.

Measuring Creativity

When studying exceptional creativity, psychologists simply pick out people who have made outstanding original contributions. In this case, assessing creativity is relatively straightforward. Much more ingenuity is required to measure the creativity of people who have not produced noteworthy imaginative achievements. Two strategies are currently used. Most frequently, psychologists present tasks that require divergent thinking, such as those in Figure 12-12. Rare and/or clever answers are then counted to arrive at an overall score. The validity of divergent thinking tests has been questioned recently by a number of investigators for three important reasons [63]:

1. When eminently creative people take these tests, they are rarely distinguished by their performance.

2. High scores on divergent thinking measures are correlated with several traits not usually associated with creativity, including conformity, dependence on others, gregariousness, and suggestability.

3. High scores on divergent thinking tests are not consistently linked with traits that are believed to underlie creativity, including curiosity, persistence, involvement, and intelligence.

Some creativity researchers prefer a personality assessment strategy to the divergent-thinking assessment strategy just described. They attempt to measure the extent to which ordinary people possess attitudes, motivations, interests, and other traits that characterize eminently imaginative individuals. For example, psychologist Gary Davis had students produce poetry, short stories, art projects, and ideas for inventions or teaching methods. These projects were rated. The students filled in a questionnaire describing their own personalities, too. In general, individuals who reported having traits that characterize eminently creative people tended to produce the most original work [64]. When combined with measures of actual imaginative achievements, personality tests appear to be a promising way to identify creative persons in the general population.

Correlates of Creativity

While psychologists cannot specify the deter-

VERBAL PROBLEMS

People are asked to solve problems like these.

Possible jobs:

"As the Inter-Planet Express prepared to land on Mars, the tourists were discussing a new custom developed by the Martians. Since the first settlers had arrived from earth, the Martians had taken to wearing emblems to show what each person's job is.

"As the tourists looked through the videoscope, they saw one Martian wearing the emblem shown below. (Line drawing of a shining light bulb within a circle.)

'Electrical engineer,' said one of the tourists. 'Light bulb manufacturer,' said another. 'Maybe a bright student,' a third tourist suggested.

"In this test you will see more of the emblems that the Martians wore. Imagine that you are one of the tourists. Think of as many possible jobs as you can which might be indicated by the emblems. If you are not sure whether one of your ideas is reasonable, write it down anyway and try to think of another idea."

Problems with educational system:

"List below problems you see with our educational system. Do not discuss or solve these problems. Just *list* as many problems as you can think of."

Apparatus test:

"In this test you will be given names of objects that are familiar to everyone. Your task is to suggest two improvements for each of the objects. Do not suggest an improvement that has already been made. You do not need to worry about your ideas being possible, so long as they are sensible.

"It is not necessary to explain your reason for a suggested improvement. Your suggestions should be specific. A suggested improvement like 'The object should be made more efficient,' is too general to be acceptable.

Sample item: "Telephone"

IDENTIFYING SIMILARITIES

Figures such as these are presented and people are asked to find as many similarities as they can.

Two possible answers are *bce* (black) and *abd* (three parts).

CONSTRUCTING OBJECTS

People are asked to combine forms like those on the left to make specific objects. Two responses are shown on the right.

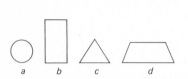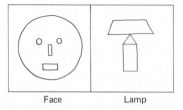

Face   Lamp

FIGURE 12-12 These items came from divergent thinking tests. [Top: *Parnes and Noller, 1973;* center: *Guilford, 1967;* bottom: *Sheridan Psychological Services, Inc.*]

minants of creativity, they know something about the personalities, backgrounds, and environmental conditions associated with imaginative achievements. Much of our knowledge on this subject came from behavioral scientists working at the Institute of Personality Assessment and Research at the University of California in Berkeley. In study after study, psychologists at the Berkeley institute asked artists, business people, writers, mathematicians, scientists, architects, and others to pick out their most creative peers. The outstanding nominees and less creative people in the same field were then invited to the center to be observed, rated, tested, and questioned. In general, eminently creative adults were likely to be characterized by expressions like "ingenious," "courageous," "clear-thinking," "versatile," "individualistic," "preoccupied," and "complicated." Less creative individuals were apt to be described as "appreciative," "considerate," "conventional," "obliging," "sympathetic," "lazy," "easy-going," "shy," "dull," "inhibited," and "weak" [65]. According to more recent research, creative people have needs both for an organized world and for imposing their own structure on experiences [66]. Unusually original artists tend to spend a large amount of time initially exploring and defining problems [67]. Persistence and intense striving, as well as the ability to become childlike and remain open to feelings ordinarily suppressed, are singled out as important attributes of outstandingly imaginative people [68]. Some psychologists (most notably, Abraham Maslow) have associated creativity with mental health. But creative people are not necessarily models of sanity and clean living. Ludwig van Beethoven is often characterized as angry, Jonathan Swift as indignant, Vincent van Gogh as intensely lonely, William Blake as psychotic, Arthur Rimbaud as criminal, and Emily Brontë as despairing. In contemplating these giants, psychologist Frank Barron of the Berkeley institute commented, "If adaptation and maturity in human relations are the essentials of mental health, then the creative genius is frequently not healthy [69]."

To find out whether creative people share certain early experiences, psychologist Donald MacKinnon of the Berkeley institute looked for recurrent themes in the biographies of highly creative adults. The individuals who were studied reported having developed an interest in inner experiences early in life—often because of shyness, unhappiness, loneliness, or sickness. As children, they possessed special abilities that they enjoyed using. They felt encouraged by their families. The parents of outstandingly creative people showed strong interests in aesthetic and intellectual topics. Parents were effective themselves, and they granted their children freedom in decision making. Intense family

closeness and dependency were not cultivated [70].

Classroom conditions may play some role in stimulating creativity. In one study of this topic, hundreds of psychologists and chemists were asked to describe teachers who had facilitated or inhibited their creativity. Many subjects reported that nurturing teachers were informal, well-prepared, unlikely to rely on the assigned text, cordial to contradictory views and other opinions, and rewarding of initiative and originality. Creativity-promoting teachers were perceived as demanding, hard-driving, competent people—good role models, in other words [71].

Though psychologists know something about the personality traits, backgrounds, and climates associated with productivity of an imaginative sort, they do not know which characteristics foster creative thinking or behavior.

Training Creative Thinking

The typical classroom emphasizes the student's digesting materials for examinations and following requirements set by an authority. High marks signifying success at these activities are not associated with creative accomplishments in high school or college [72]. The habits that make imaginative achievement likely may be enhanced, many psychologists believe, by a different type of formal training. Classroom strategies which minimize frustration, competition, and coercion are thought to foster originality. So are teaching tactics that emphasize solving problems and working out conflicts [73]. The Purdue Creativity Program provides an example of the types of learning situations that are believed to encourage creative thinking in elementary school children. Twenty-eight audio tapes first present a principle or idea for improving original thinking. Next there is an eight- to ten-minute story about a famous American pioneer. Printed exercises ask students to practice problem solving. The following exercises come from the tape *The Pony Express*. The first two exercises attempt to improve verbal fluency and flexibility; the third, verbal originality and drawing skills.

1. Suppose that you were a Pony Express rider. You are riding across the country with a bag of mail. It is a warm afternoon. Suddenly, off in the distance on a mountain ridge you see two Indians mounted on horses. They are standing still, looking in your direction. What would you do?

2. Suppose that the telegraph and the railroads had not come along and replaced the Pony Express. The Pony Express would probably have continued to carry the mail. How could the Pony Express Service have been improved? List as many ways as you can think of that would have improved it.

3. Draw a picture of a Pony Express rider crossing a dusty desert. Give your picture as many good and clever titles as you can think of. [74]

To evaluate the Purdue program, pupils in six elementary school classes participated in the creativity instruction project. Pupils in six additional classes at the same grade levels received no training. After the lessons were completed, both groups took creativity and school achievement tests. The experimental students surpassed the controls on verbal and nonverbal originality and language achievement. Later research suggested that the exercises were the most important component of the program.

Divergent thinking skills—fluency, flexibility, and originality—can be taught directly and rewarded in the classroom [75]. But teacher evaluations of creative efforts and tight controls over such efforts may have unfortunate consequences. Research by Teresa Amabile suggests that people who are free of external constraints are more likely to be playful with ideas and material, to explore diverse pathways, and to engage in peripherally related behavior (which may be productive ultimately). Most important, perhaps, Amabile finds that rewards and standards reduce intrinsic motivation and level of artistic creativity, as rated by observers, under diverse circumstances [76].

Two strategies are widely used to train creative thinking in adults: brainstorming and synectics. During *brainstorming*, a technique popularized by Alex Osmond, people, either alone or in groups, are encouraged to produce many ideas about some topic. Participants are usually asked to solve broad problems, such as "How can school be improved?" or "How can energy be saved?" While generating ideas, participants are to defer all judgments. In other words, no one is to be critical or evaluative initially. The point of this policy is to remove inhibitions and stimulate involvement. The emphasis on an abundance of ideas has a purpose too. Osmond assumed that early solutions tend to be commonplace, while unique potentially ingenious solutions occur later in people's "thought chains." Formal studies of brainstorming suggest that the technique leads to *more* ideas, but not necessarily to better ones. Still, the device may be quite useful in specific contexts (such as sharing information about a problem) and in conjunction with other procedures.

Synectics is a more complicated problem-solving strategy, which was developed by W. J. J. Gordon. These are among its most important components: First, people are encouraged to familiarize themselves with all aspects of the problem to be solved ("to make the strange familiar"). Then, they are advised to distance themselves from the problem ("to make the familiar strange"). The question is to be viewed, in other words, from new perspectives. In addition, people are trained to employ specific problem-solving tools. The use of metaphors and analogies (partial similarities between two different phenomena) is often stressed. To solve a parking problem at school, you might examine how bees, squirrels, ants, shoe stores, and automobile factories store things. After generating associations, individuals learn to fit their ideas to the problem. There are many anecdotal and informal reports of the success of synectics. But there are few systematic studies of the procedure by independent investigators [77].

Creativity training programs can increase originality and flexibility. But so far, no one has demonstrated that any type of creativity training leads to serious inventions, products, pictures, poems, scientific breakthroughs, or the like.▲

▲ **USING PSYCHOLOGY**

1. Considering the research on current creativity assessment instruments, devise a creativity measure of your own. How could the validity and reliability of your measure be tested?

2. Do you consider yourself more or less than moderately creative? How do your personality and background match those of eminently creative people?

3. Have you known teachers who encouraged creativity? Did they or their classrooms possess any outstanding characteristics? If so, compare these characteristics with those mentioned in the text.

4. Explain synectics to one friend and brainstorming to another. Then ask each of them to solve some problem. Which method seems more productive? Mention several reasons why you cannot assume your results are general.

SUMMARY
Intelligence and Creativity

1. Definitions of intelligence vary.

2. Early mental tests focused on perceptual and motor capacities.

3. Binet and his coworkers devised the first practical intelligence test. It was designed to distinguish retarded from normal school children.

4. The IQ is essentially a numerical index that describes a test taker's performance on a mental test in relation to others of the same age.

5. Because Binet's model worked, it was adopted throughout the world. Many new intelligence tests were devised along similar lines.

6. The WAIS is widely used today to measure the intelligence of adults.

7. Test designers choose items for their measurement instruments according to fairly definite criteria. They strive to create objective, reliable, valid tests.

8. Though a person's IQ often changes a little, it tends to remain fairly stable throughout childhood. Enriched environments and personality characteristics traditionally associated with the masculine role are correlated with IQ increases.

9. It is not entirely clear what happens to measured intelligence in middle and old age. People show a great deal of variability. Speed, hand-eye coordination, and memory usually decline in old age. Certain mental abilities are depressed shortly before death.

10. Measured intelligence is affected by hereditary and environmental influences.

11. Differences in IQ between diverse socioeconomic classes and racial groups may be attributed largely to hereditary or environmental influences. Both issues remain very controversial.

12. Although traditional tests of intelligence are valid predictors of performance in many academic, social, and vocational situations, they make a number of controversial assumptions. And they may predict for the wrong reasons. Serious abuses often arise when traditional intelligence tests are used with minority-group members.

13. Today, many psychologists are attempting to define and measure intelligence in new ways that avoid old problems.

14. Creativity and intelligence seem to be based on fairly distinct mental abilities.

15. To assess creativity in the general population, psychologists usually measure divergent thinking or the possession of "creative personality" traits.

16. Certain personality, motivational, and experiential characteristics are associated with outstanding creativity.

17. Diverse creative problem-solving programs appear to be able to increase originality and flexibility. But they have not been clearly linked to serious creative achievements.

A Study Guide for Chapter Twelve

Key terms intelligence (383), measured intelligence (383), mental age (385), intelligence quotient (IQ) (386), objectivity (388), standard procedures (388), norms (388), reliability (388), validity (389), longitudinal study (391), heritability coefficient (397), convergent and divergent thinking (403), creativity (403), brainstorming (406), synectics (406), and other italicized words and expressions.

Important research the case of L. (Scheerer, Rothmann, Goldstein), development of the first useful intelligence test (Binet), stability of IQ (Honzik, Sontag, Baker, Nelson, the Sears, others), heredity's influence on differences in measured intelligence, poverty and measured intelligence (Heber, Garber, Pedersen, Rosenthal, Jacobson, others), race and measured intelligence (Jensen, Scarr, Weinberg, others), alternative measures of mental abilities (Hunt, others), measures of creativity (Davis, others), experiential and personality correlates of creativity (MacKinnon, Barron, others), teaching creativity (Amabile, Osmond, Gordon, others).

Basic concepts definitions of intelligence (Spearman, Thurstone), controversies over the definition of intelligence, guidelines for test construction, explanations for the relationship between poverty and measured intelligence, alternative interpretations of the results of early-education programs, criticisms of Jensen's arguments about race and measured intelligence, controversy over the validity and utility of traditional intelligence tests.

People to identify Galton, Binet, Terman, Wechsler, Piaget.

Tests to identify first Binet scale (Binet-Simon Scale), Stanford-Binet Intelligence Scale, Wechsler Adult Intelligence Scale (WAIS), Dove Counterbalance General Intelligence Test, "culture-fair" tests, Piagetian tests, cognitive process tests of intelligence, divergent-thinking tests of creativity, personality tests of creativity.

Self-Quiz

1. What did Galton assess to measure intelligence?
   a. Aesthetic judgments
   b. Logical thinking
   c. Sensory and motor skills
   d. Values (political and social)
2. What was Binet's intelligence test designed to do?
   a. Find out whether intelligence increases with age.
   b. Identify brain damage in children.
   c. Measure current thought level.
   d. Pick out children who could not benefit from ordinary schooling.
3. If fifteen-year-old Loraine receives a mental age of twelve on Terman's 1916 revision of the Stanford-Binet, what is her IQ?
   a. 60   b. 80
   c. 90   d. 125
4. Herman McGee correlates scores on the McGee Intelligence Scale with grades in school. What is he trying to assess?
   a. Normality   b. Objectivity
   c. Reliability   d. Validity
5. With which other term is "reliability" roughly synonymous?
   a. Consistency   b. Objectivity
   c. Simplicity   d. Validity
6. Which characteristic is closely associated with IQ gains?
   a. Cooperativeness   b. Femininity
   c. Independence   d. Obedience
7. On what type of intelligence test tasks do women tend to outperform men?
   a. Logical   b. Mathematical
   c. Spatial   d. Verbal
8. What is a decreasing IQ in old age most likely to be associated with?
   a. Inactivity   b. Inflexibility
   c. Lack of creativity   d. Overambitiousness
9. Which conclusion about the effects of early enrichment programs on the average child is most appropriate, according to current studies that include school-age follow-ups?
   a. There are no lasting gains in IQ.
   b. There are lasting gains of only two to three IQ points.
   c. There are usually lasting gains of twenty to thirty IQ points.
   d. There are lasting reading-level gains.
10. What do heritability coefficients estimate?
   a. The extent to which differences on a measured characteristic can be explained by genetic variations
   b. The extent to which a particular characteristic is determined by heredity
   c. The probability that two groups have similar genetic capabilities
   d. The relative performance of two groups on a genetically dependent ability
11. Which policy is especially characteristic of a "culture-fair" test?
   a. Deemphasis on speed
   b. Delivery of uniform instructions
   c. Focus on specific thinking skills, rather than an overall index
   d. Use of unfamiliar concepts
12. High scores on divergent thinking tests are associated with which characteristic?

a. Curiosity
b. Independence
c. Nonconformity in social situations
d. Suggestability

13. Which trait commonly characterizes eminently creative people?

a. Consideration   b. Inhibition
c. Preoccupation   d. Sympathy

14. Which childhood experience is shared by many eminently creative people?

a. Early interest in inner experiences due to shyness or unhappiness
b. Firm rules structuring most aspects of early life
c. Harsh disciplinary practices that foster escape through fantasy
d. Intense closeness to parents

15. Which practice is particularly closely associated with synectics?

a. Brainstorming
b. Deferring judgment
c. Generating numerous ideas
d. Using metaphors and analogies

Suggested Readings

1. Tyler, L. E. *Individual differences: Abilities and motivational directions*. New York: Appleton-Century-Crofts, 1974. This brief book describes research on relatively lasting psychological characteristics, like intelligence, and emphasizes findings of practical interest. A good introduction to the social significance of psychological tests.

2. Anastasi, A. *Psychological testing*. (4th ed.) New York: Macmillan, 1976. This classic text on psychological tests is very comprehensive in its coverage, including information about tests of intelligence, aptitude, vocational interests, personality, and psychopathology. Anastasi discusses ethical and social implications of testing, too.

3. Vernon, P. E. *Intelligence: Heredity and environment*. San Francisco: Freeman, 1979 (paperback). An overview of the development of intelligence testing and a discussion of environmental and genetic influences on IQ.

4. Willerman, L., & Turner, R. G. (Eds.) *Readings about individual and group differences*. San Francisco: Freeman, 1979 (paperback). Classic and contemporary readings that have shaped our understanding of differences in intelligence, personality, and psychopathology.

5. Loehlin, J. C., Lindzey, G., & Spuhler, J. N. *Race differences in intelligence*. San Francisco: Freeman, 1975 (paperback). A balanced, sound, and thorough treatment of the race-intelligence controversy, showing why the issue cannot currently be settled.

6. Taylor, I. A., & Getzels, J. W. (Eds.) *Perspectives in creativity*. Chicago: Aldine, 1975. Prominent creativity researchers with the longest involvement in the field write about what they thought and did to learn about creativity, how they started, and how their ideas developed and changed. Each investigator describes successes, failures, and future directions as well. Many of the chapters provide interesting insights into creativity research.

7. Rimland, B. Inside the mind of the autistic savant. *Psychology Today*, 1978, **12**(3), 69–80. This fascinating article describes the mental feats of certain autistic children who resemble idiot savants. Rimland discusses the youngster's extraordinary powers and proposes some reasonable explanations.

8. Bogdan, R., & Taylor, S. The judged, not the judges: An insider's view of mental retardation. *American Psychologist*, 1976, **31**(1), 47–52. Psychologists present the personal reflections and life story of a twenty-six-year-old man who was labeled retarded. The article points out vividly how demeaning labels may be and how they influence others' perceptions.

9. Garcia, J. IQ: The conspiracy. *Psychology Today*, 1972, **6**(4), 40ff. This provocative discussion of intelligence testing takes the viewpoint that traditional test instruments were designed to assess the academic intelligence of Anglo-Americans and describes how biases were built into traditional measures.

10. Rosenthal, R. The Pygmalion effect lives. *Psychology Today*, 1973, **7**(4), 56–63. A summary of research on teachers' expectations and their effects on students.

11. Whimbey, A. You can learn to raise your IQ score. *Psychology Today*, 1976, **9**(8), 27ff. A description of problem-solving training programs which help adults make better scores on intelligence and achievement tests.

Answer Key

Self-Quiz

1. *c* (383) **2.** *d* (384) **3.** *b* (386) **4.** *d* (390)
5. *a* (388) **6.** *c* (391) **7.** *d* (391) **8.** *a* (392)
9. *d* (395) **10.** *a* (397) **11.** *a* (401) **12.** *d* (403)
13. *c* (404) **14.** *a* (405) **15.** *d* (406)

CHAPTER THIRTEEN
Personality

Please rate how accurately each of the following statements describes your personality, using this scale: 1 = very accurate, 2 = rather well, 3 = about half right, 4 = more wrong than right, 5 = almost entirely wrong.

1. You have a tendency to be critical of yourself.
2. You have a great deal of unused capacity which you have not turned to your advantage.
3. Disciplined and self-controlled outside, you tend to be worrisome and insecure inside.
4. You prefer a certain amount of change and variety and become dissatisfied when hemmed in by restrictions and limitations.
5. You pride yourself on being an independent thinker and do not accept others' statements without satisfactory proof.
6. Some of your aspirations tend to be pretty unrealistic. [1]

College students, personnel managers, industrial supervisors, and others have served as subjects in some interesting demonstrations. They are given a bogus personality test or a fake astrological reading or handwriting analysis. Later, each research participant receives a personality interpretation, presumably based on the collected information. In actuality, the interpretative sketches are prepared ahead of time and are identical. The six statements on which you just rated yourself are typical of those that appear on the interpretations. When asked to evaluate the accuracy of the sketch, subjects generally see the comments as perceptive [2]. The opening statements, like many of the insights of fortune-tellers and astrologers, rely on a knowledge of common human attitudes, hopes, fear, and experiences. Apparently, people are alike in a great many ways but do not realize it. While psychologists who study personality are interested in the attributes that characterize everyone, they also focus on individual differences, those qualities that make each human being unique. In this chap-

ter we explore the assessment procedures and theories that behavioral scientists have constructed to further the understanding of human personality. We begin with some material on a nineteen-year-old college student: the impressions of an examining psychologist and a self-description.

The Personality of a College Student

The examining psychologist described the subject, whom we call I. S., as "a large, somewhat overweight, 19-year-old male college sophomore." The psychologist continued, "[I. S.'s] general appearance conveys an air of studied indifference to physical appearance. His hair is long, always somewhat mussed, and in need of a washing. His clothes, although clean, are worn very casually and in unusual combinations.

"[I. S.] speaks in a way that is intended to impress others with both his extensive vocabulary and intellectual ability. He attempts to appear above all that is mundane and ordinary and, in general, reflects a desire to be classified as a rebellious intellectual. He is very condescending, in general. . . . The subject is intellectually very bright and not uninteresting to deal with."

During an interview, I. S. described himself like this: "I feel

my general temperament is one of acquiescence. I despise arguments. I don't particularly care for too many people. I think a great deal of my time is wasted on other people. I feel that other people don't deserve my consideration. I very rarely become upset when other people do things not corresponding with my views. I don't particularly like children or the standard concept of what people are supposed to like. I despise girls, among other things. . . . Every girl with whom I've associated with has gotten me in trouble one way or another. . . . I feel myself that I have the average amount of talents. I'm not particularly gifted. I think that in the things I do like, I have great capabilities of becoming good. My temperament lies more in the field of fine arts than it does in the field of science. . . . If you were to ask me what actually I was as other people saw me or as I feel they

saw me, then I would have to say that I am probably generally disliked among my acquaintances because I hold the attitude of intolerance to a lot of things that they express. . . . As far as my feelings toward school . . . I think I am wasting a great deal of time in school because I am lazy, extremely so. . . . I feel that there is a great deal of ignorance that I must more or less wade through to get what I'm after. I won't say that I'm ruthless, if you could use the word. I would say that I strive for the things I want if I want them bad enough but I do take into consideration other people's feelings, for the fact that if one doesn't they'll turn around and they always get you in the end, so it's wise to watch other people. . . . I like a friendly attitude. That's one thing I don't have. I like the ability to laugh at your own troubles. This I do think I have [3]."

Before reading further, try to describe I. S.'s personality. (Please jot down a few notes so that you can refer to your description later on.) We will be returning to I. S. throughout the chapter.

By *personality*, contemporary psychologists usually mean those relatively consistent and enduring patterns of perceiving, thinking, feeling, and behaving that appear to give people separate identities. Personality is a

"summary construct," one that includes thoughts, motives, emotions, interests, attitudes, abilities, and similar phenomena. Almost every topic that we have discussed so far and will treat in future chapters has some bearing on understanding the nature, origin, evolution, or change of personality. *Personality psychology*, then, covers more territory than most other psychological fields. In some way or another, all personality psychologists are engaged in trying to understand the general nature of personality and the differences among individuals. Like other behavioral scientists, personality psychologists tend to specialize. Some are predominantly researchers trying to describe and explain limited aspects of personality, such as anxiety, aggressiveness, need for achievement, or sense of control. Others are principally involved in designing and evaluating tests. Still others are committed to personality theories— teaching old ones and constructing new ones. The vast majority are clinicians who use personality research, theory, and testing to help people understand themselves and solve psychological problems.

In previous chapters, we have dealt with personality-related research, and we will continue to do so. We will treat what could be described as personality problems and personality change in the next few chapters, which focus on adjustment, abnormal behavior, and the treatment of abnormal behavior. In this chapter we look first at personality measurement and then at personality theory.

MEASURING PERSONALITY

To assess personality, psychologists commonly use several tools, often in combination. These include interviews, controlled observations and experiments, and tests.

Interviews

The interview is probably the most popular personality assessment technique in use today. It may be characterized as a *participant observation* (Chapter 2), with the interviewer functioning as both observer and participant. Psychologists in clinics and in educational and vocational settings rely heavily on this procedure to gather information about the personality of individual people. You may have achieved some insights into I. S. through his interview responses. Sometimes interviews follow the interests of those involved and meander informally from question to question. Sometimes they are standardized so that the same questions occur in a particular order each time. Psychologists are even experimenting with computer interviews. People sit behind a terminal and respond to a series of questions that the computer has been programmed to present.

The data obtained from an interview are often handled informally, with experience guiding the interpretations. Interview material can be analyzed more precisely. For example, a person's conduct may be observed and rated through a one-way mirror. Or, an interview may be recorded so that some aspect of behavior—perhaps references to conflicts with a spouse, pauses, sarcastic comments, or a mannerism such as clutching nervously at an article of clothing—can be counted at several points in time to assess change.

Like any other data-gathering technique, interviews have distinct strengths and weaknesses. They are especially useful for investigating personal thoughts, feelings, conflicts, fears, and the like. These aspects of personality cannot be observed directly and are apt to be withheld unless the observer is trusted. Interviews permit behavioral scientists to follow leads and backtrack from dead ends. On the negative side, interviews provide self-report data that may not be accurate. And they suffer from the problems that beset all participant observations. More often than not, the interviewer is likely to influence the behavior being observed, become involved in the relationship (and consequently biased), and rely on impressionistic procedures for information collection and analysis. Ultimately, the effectiveness of the interview strategy depends on the observer's skills in both obtaining and interpreting material.

Controlled Observations and Experiments

Personality researchers frequently elect to observe and measure behavior under carefully controlled conditions, often during the course of an experiment and occasionally in natural settings. This strategy is increasingly popular

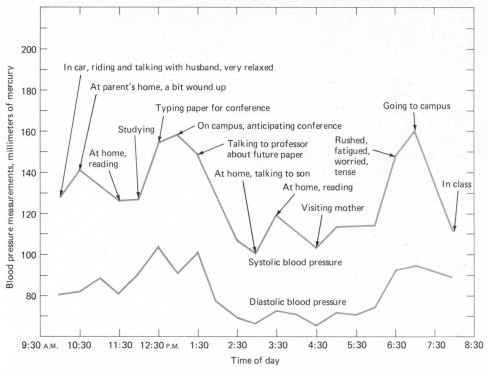

FIGURE 13-1 Certain physiological responses that occur under specific conditions help scientists to understand personality. In this case, a woman patient with hypertension (high blood pressure) wore a portable blood pressure measuring device as she went about daily routines. Periodically, she measured her own blood pressure and noted the activities in which she was engaged. Combining this information, as shown in the graph, helped identify events that particularly distressed the woman. [*From Werdegar et al., 1967.*]

[4]. Physiological responses can be monitored to provide information about personality. You may recall that motives and emotions, in particular, are frequently measured by physiological instruments. (See Figure 13-1.) Facial expressions, movements, verbalizations, and other reactions may be evaluated for insights too. To gain a direct understanding of a personality problem, counseling psychologists sometimes observe the behavior of patients (with permission) in natural settings that tend to be distressing. Controlled observations enable researchers to gather precise information about personality issues. In one recent study, for example, behavioral scientists used a rating approach to investigate the consistency of the personality characteristic of assertiveness in normal men. Judges rated the

behavior of males in pairs upon entering a room, after ten minutes of discussion on a controversial topic about which they disagreed, and after a competitive game. Assertiveness was quite consistent under these varied conditions [5]. We will say more about personality consistency later.

Personality tests are sometimes based on behavioral observations. During World War II, for instance, assessment procedures known as *situational tests* were developed to select men to work behind enemy lines and carry out highly dangerous secret missions for the Office of Strategic Services. For one representative situational test, candidates were assigned the task of building a wooden structure with the "aid" of two assistants. The assistants were members of the assessment staff whose primary job was to obstruct the effort. They asked embarrassing questions, hounded the candidates, ignored instructions, and behaved in a generally clumsy, inept, and disagreeable manner. The candidates' responses to this type of stressful, frustrating predicament were rated and later analyzed [6]. The Peace Corps has used similar tests [7].

Controlled observations and experiments reduce bias and increase precision. But they often put people in artificial and contrived situations where their behavior may not be realistic. And they rarely enlighten psychologists about deeply personal matters.

Personality Tests

Psychologists use varied paper-and-pencil tests to assess personality for counseling, job placement, and research. Personality instruments fall into two categories: objective and projective. We examine representative tests in both categories. You may wish to review the testing concepts discussed in Chapter 12.

Objective tests Instruments classified as *objective* can be scored in essentially the same way anywhere—regardless of who administers the test and analyzes the results. Objective tests, in other words, are minimally influenced by the examiner's biases. Some objective measures have evolved from a personality *theory*. The *Study of Values* test is an assessment device in this category. Developed by psychologists Gordon Allport, Philip

TABLE 13-1 Representative Questions from the Study of Values Test

1. Assuming that you have sufficient ability, would you prefer to be (*a*) a banker? (*b*) a politician?

2. At an evening discussion with intimate friends of your own sex, are you more interested when you talk about (*a*) the meaning of life, (*b*) developments in science, (*c*) literature, (*d*) socialism and social amelioration?

Source: Allport, G. W., Vernon, P. E., & Lindzey, G. *Study of values.* (3d ed.) Copyright © 1960 by Houghton Mifflin Company. Reprinted by permission of Houghton Mifflin Company. All rights reserved.

Vernon, and Gardner Lindzey, the instrument is based on the notion that people hold six types of values: religious (seeking a sense of unity), political (aspiring to power), social (valuing service to and love of other human beings), aesthetic (emphasizing form and harmony), economic (stressing what is practical and useful), and theoretic (searching for truths). The Study of Values test presents multiple-choice questions that ask people to choose the most appealing of several activities. The examples in Table 13-1 are typical. The activity mentioned in each response option reflects a particular value. In item 1, option (*a*) shows economic values and option (*b*), political ones. Answers to the second question reflect these values: (*a*) religious, (*b*) theoretic, (*c*) aesthetic, and (*d*) social. People's total scores on each value are compared with a set of *norms* (the distribution of scores made by a large group of people). If a specific value score is higher or lower than the average score made by the reference group, that value is considered a correspondingly high or low one. Most test takers score high on one or two values. In general, women make higher scores than men on religious, social, and aesthetic values. Men make higher scores than women on theoretic, economic, and political values. Values in college are associated with predictable vocational choices fifteen years later [8]. Apparently, values remain fairly stable, and they probably influence work choices.

Many objective personality tests are said to be *empirically based* because they evolved from observations and were not founded on theoretical preconceptions. The *California Psychological Inventory* (CPI) is a carefully designed objective test of this type. It was developed by Harrison Gough at the University of California in the mid-1950s. The CPI assesses eighteen personality dimensions that are important for social interactions, such as dominance, sociability, self-acceptance, self-control, and flexibility. The test contains more than 450 statements that are to be marked true or false. Here are some examples:

I enjoy social gatherings just to be with people.

I gossip a little at times.
People often expect too much of me.
My home life was always happy.
I love to go to dances.
I like poetry.
Sometimes I feel that I am about to go to pieces.

Obviously, there are no right or wrong answers to these items. To score the test, scales had to be devised. Reference groups—high school and college students considered by their peers high and low on each of the eighteen traits being assessed—took the CPI. Those items that distinguished between high and low groups were selected for each of the scales. Later, the statements were tried out again on new samples considered high and low on each characteristic to substantiate their assessment value. To interpret the CPI, the examiner compares the test taker's performance with the performance of the original reference-group subjects. Suppose that your CPI pattern closely matches that of the highly self-controlled reference-group subjects. You would receive a high score on the self-control scale and you would be considered high on self-control. The test taker is evaluated on each characteristic assessed by the CPI.

While the CPI focuses on social attributes, the *Minnesota Multiphasic Personality Inventory* (MMPI) appraises a wider range of normal personality patterns and personality disturbances. The MMPI, which consists of 550 true-false statements, was devised in the early 1940s by psychologist Stark Hathaway and psychiatrist J. C. McKinley. It consists of a number of scales designed originally to diagnose depression, paranoia, schizophrenia, and other patterns of abnormal behavior. The MMPI scales were developed by administering test items to normal people and to those diagnosed by psychiatrists as suffering from specific psychological problems. Items that differentiated ordinary people from clinical populations make up ten clinical scales. A high score on a specific scale—say, depression—indicates that one is responding like members of a psychiatric population with that diagnosis. A moderate score suggests a less serious problem. Literally hundreds of scales for

measuring different aspects of personality have been derived from the MMPI. The CPI, in fact, took its test questions from the MMPI. MMPI scales also assess carelessness, confusion, and defensiveness so that these phenomena can be taken into account when interpreting the test results. A test report on the MMPI performance of a thirty-seven-year-old man is presented in Figure 13-2. Earlier in the

FIGURE 13-2 This MMPI report was generated by a computer. Note that the computer has been programmed to pay close attention to scales that assess faking and other response characteristics that might invalidate the test findings. There are numerous automated systems for scoring the MMPI. Reports generated by certain systems are considered highly accurate by clinicians [42]. [*From Fowler, 1969.*]

AGE 37 MALE

IN RESPONDING TO THE TEST ITEMS IT APPEARS THAT THE PATIENT MADE AN EFFORT TO ANSWER TRUTHFULLY WITHOUT ATTEMPTING TO DENY OR EXAGGERATE.

THIS PATIENT SEEMS TO BE DEPRESSED, AGITATED AND RESTLESS. HE APPEARS TO BE A PERSON WHO HAS DIFFICULTY IN MAINTAINING CONTROL OVER HIS IMPULSES. WHEN HE DOES ACT OUT IN A SOCIALLY UNACCEPTABLE MANNER HE FEELS GUILTY AND DISTURBED FOR A TIME, ALTHOUGH THE DISTRESS MAY REFLECT SITUATIONAL DIFFICULTIES RATHER THAN INTERNAL CONFLICTS. HE MAY EXHIBIT A CYCLIC PATTERN OF ACTING OUT, FOLLOWED BY GUILT, FOLLOWED BY FURTHER ACTING OUT. FREQUENTLY, HIS BEHAVIOR SHOWS A SELF-DEFEATING AND SELF-PUNITIVE TENDENCY. HE IS PESSIMISTIC ABOUT THE FUTURE AND DISTRESSED ABOUT HIS FAILURES TO ACHIEVE HIS GOALS. HIS INTENTIONS TO IMPROVE SEEM GENUINE, BUT THE PATTERN IS A PERSISTENT ONE, AND THE LONG RANGE PROGNOSIS IS POOR. ASSISTING HIM TO A BETTER ADJUSTMENT WILL PROBABLY REQUIRE A COMBINATION OF FIRM LIMITS, WARM SUPPORT AND ENVIRONMENTAL MANIPULATION.

HE APPEARS TO BE A PERSON WHO REPRESSES AND DENIES EMOTIONAL DISTRESS. WHILE HE MAY RESPOND READILY TO ADVICE AND REASSURANCE HE IS HESITANT TO ACCEPT A PSYCHOLOGICAL EXPLANATION OF HIS DIFFICULTIES. IN TIMES OF PROLONGED EMOTIONAL STRESS, HE IS LIKELY TO DEVELOP PHYSICAL SYMPTOMS. HE IS PARTICULARLY VULNERABLE TO PSYCHOPHYSIOLOGICAL SYMPTOMS SUCH AS HEADACHES, TACHYCARDIA AND GASTROINTESTINAL DISORDERS.

THERE ARE SOME UNUSUAL QUALITIES ABOUT THIS PATIENT'S THINKING WHICH MAY REPRESENT AN ORIGINAL OR INVENTIVE ORIENTATION OR PERHAPS SOME SCHIZOID TENDENCIES. FURTHER INFORMATION WOULD BE REQUIRED TO MAKE THIS DETERMINATION.

HE APPEARS TO BE A RIGID PERSON WHO IS PRONE TO FEARS, COMPULSIVE BEHAVIOR AND OBSESSIONS. DESPITE WORRY AND TENSION, HE IS LIKELY TO BE RESISTANT TO TREATMENT.

HE APPEARS TO BE AN IDEALISTIC, SOCIALLY PERCEPTIVE PERSON WHO IS ESTHETIC AND PERHAPS SOMEWHAT FEMININE IN HIS INTEREST PATTERNS. HE MAY PURSUE ARTISTIC AND CULTURAL INTERESTS AND REJECT COMPETITIVE ACTIVITIES.

THIS PATIENT HAS TEST FEATURES WHICH RESEMBLE THOSE OF PSYCHIATRIC OUTPATIENTS WHO LATER REQUIRE INPATIENT CARE. CONTINUED PROFESSIONAL CARE AND OBSERVATION ARE SUGGESTED.

NOTE: ALTHOUGH NOT A SUBSTITUTE FOR THE CLINICIAN'S PROFESSIONAL JUDGMENT AND SKILL, THE MMPI CAN BE A USEFUL ADJUNCT IN THE DIAGNOSIS AND MANAGEMENT OF EMOTIONAL DISORDERS. THE REPORT IS FOR PROFESSIONAL USE ONLY AND SHOULD NOT BE SHOWN OR RELEASED TO THE PATIENT.

chapter you read about I. S. Like many college students, he scored high on an MMPI scale that reflects intellectual interests. The overall pattern of his responses confirmed the examiner's impression that the young man was "argumentative" and "verbally hostile."

During psychological research, the MMPI is more frequently utilized than any other objective test [9]. Research suggests that both the CPI and MMPI have some *validity* as measures of personality [10]. There is evidence, in other words, that these tests assess what they were intended to.

A *Q-sort* is another type of empirically derived objective test. This device was developed by William Stephenson at the University of Chicago in the early 1950s. A Q-sort invites a person to use words, phrases, or sentences to describe someone—often him- or herself—according to specific rules. You might be asked, for example, to *sort* 100 cards contain-

ing personality descriptions (such as "I anger easily" and "I am thoughtful") into one of eleven piles, according to how closely the description characterizes yourself. Sometimes people are asked to portray their ideal personalities in the same way. Q-sorts are essentially rating procedures. They are often used to obtain a comprehensive picture of the personality strengths and weaknesses of a specific individual. Q-sort results may be analyzed in numerous ways. Frequently, sorts at different points in time are correlated to see whether the test taker's self-concept has changed.

Objective personality tests have some of the same limitations that plague other self-report measures. Test takers may decide not to cooperate with the examiner and consequently withhold the desired information or fake their responses in one way or another. Even cooperative subjects may not be astute

FIGURE 13-3 An inkblot resembling one on the Rorschach is shown on the left. Typical responses appear on the right. For each response, the part of the blot that the subject focused on is indicated and a plausible interpretation is given.

RESPONSE 1. A boat anchor covered with barnacles

Using the whole blot is considered evidence of the subject's capacity to organize and integrate material.

REPONSE 2. A genie in a bottle

Focusing on a part of the blot is thought to show an interest in concrete as opposed to abstract matters.

RESPONSE 3. A headless angel

Referring to an unusual or tiny part of the blot is said to indicate pedantic tendencies (slavish attention to rules and details).

RESPONSE 4. A dog's head

Reversing figure and ground in this way is considered characteristic of negativity and obstinacy.

self-observers. Still, like the MMPI, many objective tests now contain scales designed to expose faking and inconsistencies.

Projective tests Sigmund Freud believed that people continually project perceptions, emotions, and thoughts onto the external world without being aware of doing so. *Projective tests* were designed to disclose this unconscious world of feelings and impulses. Projective instruments ask people to react to relatively unstructured, ambiguous (unclear) stimuli. For example, the test taker may be asked to form associations to words or inkblots, to create a story or picture, or to complete sentence fragments. Though psychologists sometimes use precise guidelines to score projective tests, they are more apt to rely on experience and intuition. In Chapter 10 we described the Thematic Apperception Test (TAT), a storytelling projective technique that is used to assess motivation. We focus now on several other commonly used projective tests.

Hermann Rorschach, a Swiss psychiatrist, was the first person to make a systematic attempt to use inkblots to uncover unconscious thoughts and feelings. When subjects take his test (usually called the Rorschach) today, they are asked to say precisely what they see (a form of free association) as they inspect ten inkblots like the one in Figure 13-3. Five of the blots are black and white, while five contain some color. I. S.'s reactions to several Rorschach inkblots are presented in Table 13-2. After the free association period, the examiner asks the test taker to go through the blots a second time and specify precisely the region of the blot and other details—color, form, texture, and shading, for instance—that led to each impression. Later, the subject's responses are analyzed. Many examiners hypothesize that specific types of perceptions reflect particular personality characteristics. Giving many popular responses is considered a sign of conformity. Seeing a lot of human movement is thought to be associated with creativity, abstract ability, and good intelligence. Being influenced by color is presumed

to indicate responsiveness to the external environment and to be typical of outgoing people. Figure 13-3 presents several additional examples of probable Rorschach interpretations. *Note*: These interpretations may hold for many people, but certainly not all; and no single response demonstrates anything. So, do not conclude that you are unhealthy or negative or anything else from some response that you might make on the Rorschach or on any other psychological test.

Rorschach examiners also search for consistent themes. The psychologist who analyzed I. S.'s Rorschach responses concluded that reactions like "clouds of gloom" and "blobs of color, kinda messy" reflected a negative, dissatisfied, critical, hostile approach to life that was revealed in the interview and on other tests. Clinicians frequently analyze behavior during the test-taking period. The Rorschach test is comparable in some ways to a highly structured interview. Notable hesitancy and qualification of responses are considered signs of anxiety. Repeated attempts to gain reassurance and bids for structure are thought to reflect dependency. A small number of brief responses are likely to be interpreted as symptomatic of defensiveness.

TABLE 13-2 I. S.'s Rorschach Responses

Card IX

1. Looks like two witches dancing around a fire, with some green shrubs in front of them. You're looking at them through the shrubs.

2. From the top it looks like an explosion towards—downwards, perhaps an atomic blast. Viewed from the bottom it also looks like two spectators, ghouls or skeletons would be my guess. Something mysterious is going on above them, have clouds of gloom, and on top of that there is brightness over their heads, representing a good spirit or something like that. (Examiner noted subject's big sigh of relief.)

Card X

Looks just like an artist palette, blobs of color [kinda messy], doesn't seem to have much.

Source: Sarason, I. G. *Personality: An objective approach.* (2d ed.) New York: Wiley, 1972. P. 227.

1. I like *psychedelic drugs.*

2. Back home *is a constant bring down.*

3. What annoys me *is people.*

4. I feel *down.*

5. In high school *I was unhappy.*

6. I am very *bored.*

7. My father *is a dwarf.*

8. I wish *I was always high.*

9. I hate *being down.*

FIGURE 13-4 Selected responses from a sentence-completion test are shown. The respondent, R. T., is an eighteen-year-old male college student. What sort of person is he? See whether your impressions agree with those of the psychologist, whose interpretation is presented in Figure 13-5.

Projective tests involving completing sentences and making drawings are widely used today. *Sentence-completion tests* offer stems, like these, to finish: "I feel . . .," "I wish . . .," "My mother . . .," and "My greatest worry is. . . ." Responses are usually analyzed informally for degree of emotionality, attitudes toward significant life figures and the past, sources of conflict, language style, and personal problems. See Figures 13-4 and 13-5. Some behavioral scientists make inferences about personal characteristics from *human drawings* like those in Figure 13-6. Small-sized figures are thought to indicate feelings of inadequacy. Distortions and omissions are considered expressions of conflict. Heavy lines are said to reflect energy and faint lines lack of drive.

Research-oriented psychologists tend to focus on the limitations of projective techniques:

Although R. T. showed no interest in presenting a socially acceptable front, he was not entirely candid either. The brevity of his responses and his general demeanor suggested less than complete cooperation. R. T. appeared to me to be deliberately generating an image -- member of the campus drug culture.

R. T.'s sentence completions suggest intense unhappiness. This young man seems to vacillate between apathy, hostility, and depression. He has not adjusted to his family ("Back home is a constant bring down." "My father is a dwarf.") nor to others in his environment ("What annoys me is people." "In high school I was unhappy."). As a result R. T.'s social world appears to be a bleak one. R. T. copes, it appears, primarily by escape, particularly through drugs which seem to obsess him ("I wish I was always high." "I like psychedelic drugs." "I hate being down."). It is hard to avoid the conclusion that R. T. is maladjusted and in need of some professional help.

FIGURE 13-5 An excerpt from a test report on R. T. The psychologist who prepared this report had access to forty sentence completions, including the nine presented in Figure 13-4, and to additional test and interview data. Responses to sentence stems by themselves do not provide enough information for a meaningful personality assessment.

1. Diverse examiners often interpret the same responses to a projective test in radically different ways. When several psychologists analyzed the Rorschach responses of Nazi officials awaiting trial at Nuremberg, for example, they concluded that the men were mentally disturbed [11]. Ten Rorschach authorities, asked to evaluate the same responses but not told the subjects' identities, came to different conclusions. They did not find the majority of the war criminals abnormal and did not see any other striking commonalities among the men [12]. Available information, skill, and bias may profoundly influence the interpretation of projective test data. *Reliability* (consistency) among projective test raters, then, is often low. Reliability on two successive projective testings and among adja-

cent items of the same test tends to be low, in addition [13].

2. Studies of the validity of current projective techniques present conflicting conclusions. Some rigorous studies do find projective measures valid for certain purposes, such as assessing degree of psychological disturbance and predicting length of mental hospital stay or appraising cognitive and emotional styles [14].

3. Individual responses on projective tests are difficult to interpret. The tests are readily faked by sophisticated subjects [15]. The theme of a story may be influenced by a recent TV program, a friend's conflict, past experiences, or current personal preoccupations.

FIGURE 13-6 Some behavioral scientists believe that artwork can provide insights into aspects of personality, such as attitudes, self-images, and moods. As part of a study of school desegregation in the South during the early 1960s, Robert Coles had children draw pictures showing how they felt about racial matters and other topics. Ruby, a black youngster living in New Orleans, drew these scenes at age six, while attending a newly integrated school amidst boycotts and riots. Like many other black children, she consistently portrayed white people as large and complete and drew black people smaller and less complete. Such drawings, according to Coles, reflected the black youngsters' painful impressions of vulnerability and inferiority. The validity of artwork tests of personality is highly controversial. [*Coles, 1964.*]

Figure 2
A white girl by Ruby at age 6

Figure 1
Ruby by Ruby at age 6

Although these gloomy research findings are well-known, psychologists continue to use projective tests. Many clinicians believe that they can provide a great deal of information about hidden aspects of personality—if the examiner is an appropriately trained, sensitive, experienced individual [16]. Because there are so many ways to analyze and use projective techniques, the issues are not resolved. Numerous psychologists are currently working to improve these personality measures and devise better ones. ▲

APPROACHES TO PERSONALITY THEORY

Theories have played a prominent role in the study of personality. Many arose from efforts to understand and treat troubled people in clinic settings. Such *clinic-based theories* tend to rely on insights gained from intensive interviews with relatively few disturbed individuals. In some cases, the contacts between behavioral scientist and subject occur almost daily for years. For the most part, hypotheses generated by clinic-based theories are evaluated informally in the course of trying to help human beings overcome problems and achieve satisfactory life adjustments. Personality theories have also grown from controlled observations and experiments in laboratory settings. These *laboratory-based theories* emphasize making precise measurements and using statistical analyses. They are usually supported by studies of comparatively large numbers of normal people (frequently college students). Contacts between behavioral scientists and subjects tend to be brief and impersonal. Nonhuman animals may be used for laboratory studies of personality, too. Clinic-based theories tend to generate broad, general hypotheses. The hypotheses of laboratory-based theories are likely to focus on limited aspects of personality. We examine theories of each type, beginning with several that arose in clinical settings. Personality theories tend to be associated with psychoanalytic, behavioristic, cognitive, and humanistic perspectives, described in Chapter 1. You may wish to review this material.

PSYCHODYNAMIC PERSONALITY THEORIES

Psychodynamic theories attempt to explain the nature and development of personality. They emphasize the importance of motives, emotions, and other internal forces. They assume that personality develops as psychological conflicts are resolved, usually during early childhood. Clinical interviews furnish most of the data for these theories. Sigmund Freud, Carl Jung, Alfred Adler, Karen Horney, Harry Stack Sullivan, and Erik Erikson are among the most famous proponents of psychodynamic concepts. In this section, we explore Freud's psychoanalytic theory in some detail and look briefly at the work of the others.

Sigmund Freud's Psychoanalytic Theory

We described the background of Sigmund Freud (1856–1939) (pictured in Figure 13-7) in depth in Chapter 1. You may recall that as he treated his neurotic patients, he searched for insights that would enable him to understand

▲ USING PSYCHOLOGY

Suppose that you are a psychologist who has been asked to evaluate the personalities of candidates for the post of FBI director. Which type(s) of assessment devices would you use? Why? What are the major strengths and weaknesses of interviews? Controlled observations? Objective tests? Projective tests?

the human personality. He carefully observed himself too. Gradually, he put together a theory, which he called *psychoanalysis*. It explained psychological normality and abnormality and the treatment of the latter. Throughout his life Freud continued to check his ideas against new observations and to revise his notions accordingly.

Freud's concept of the unconscious

Freud came to believe that people are *conscious* of only a small number of thoughts, memories, feelings, and desires. Others are *preconscious*, buried just beneath awareness where they are fairly easy to retrieve. The vast majority are *unconscious*. He believed that this unconscious material enters consciousness in disguised form. It appears in dreams, slips of the tongue, mistakes, accidents, and during free association. (During this type of free association, a person talks about whatever comes to mind and holds nothing back purposefully.) To understand a person's unconscious, presumably, an expert has to scrutinize and analyze the individual's behavior, memories, dreams, errors, and associations over a long period. We describe psychoanalytic assessment procedures in more detail in Chapter 16.

Freud's theories focus on the unconscious aspects of personality. In his view, drives, personality components, memories of early childhood experiences, and painful psychological conflicts tend to be unconscious. *Sexual drives* play an especially important role in Freud's formulations. He used the term "sexual" for all pleasurable actions and thoughts. He used the word "drive" much as psychologists presently use the term *basic drives* (Chapter 10), though he included aggression in this category. Sexual drives, according to Freud, generate a fixed amount of *psychic energy* called *libido* for behavior and mental activity. Psychic energy parallels, but is different from, physical energy. If the sexual drives are not satisfied, psychic energy builds up pressure, like water backed up in a pipe without an open valve. Conflicts may increase the tension. For people to function normally,

the pressure must be reduced. If the pressure can't be discharged, the "pipe" eventually bursts at its weakest point, and people display abnormal behavior.

According to Freud, the personality consists of three important components: id, ego, and superego. The components compete continually for the available psychic energy. The *id* lies at the primitive core of the personality and is the domain of the drives. Freud called the id "a chaos, a cauldron of seething excitement [17]." It has no logical organization, so contradictory impulses may exist here side by side. Drives and repressed experiences (those pushed from consciousness) may remain unaltered indefinitely in the id because it lacks a sense of time. Also, it has no moral values but is dominated, instead, by the *pleasure principle*: It continually presses for the immediate

FIGURE 13-7 Sigmund Freud, the founder of psychoanalysis, formulated ideas that are still controversial. In his day, he was criticized for considering sex a major force in human behavior. Many Victorian contemporaries were extremely upset by the observation that young children are aware of their own sexuality. Today, Freud is acknowledged as an intellectual giant in the history of modern thought. [*Wide World Photos.*]

fulfillment of the drives and cannot tolerate energy buildups. To reduce tension, the id often uses *primary process thinking*. It forms an image of a desired object, one previously associated with drive satisfaction. When hungry, for example, you might visualize a mouth-watering charcoal-broiled steak and find that the image satisfies your need momentarily. Freud considered primary process thinking an infantile form of mental activity. When using this type of thinking, the id cannot distinguish between images and the external world. Nighttime dreaming and hallucinations (sensory experiences without a basis in reality) are clearer examples of primary process thinking. Both dreams and hallucinations may be thought of as wishes in image form that can't be differentiated from reality.

The *ego* emerges in developing children, according to Freud, to handle their daily transactions with the environment as they learn that there is a reality apart from their own needs and desires. The ego was a part of the id which was modified by its closeness to the external world. One of the ego's major tasks is to locate real objects to satisfy the id's needs. The ego must deal, then, with the demands of both id and surroundings and arrange compromises. Unlike the id, the ego is controlled, realistic, and logical. Freud maintained that the ego operates on the *reality principle*. It postpones the gratification of the id's wishes until an appropriate situation or object is encountered. In contrast with the id, the ego uses *secondary process thinking*: It creates realistic strategies to satisfy id drives. The ego may formulate the idea of going to a steak house, for instance, when you're hungry. Daydreaming is an example of secondary process thinking that illustrates how reality-bound the ego is. People rarely mistake fantasies for realities. You might picture the ego as similar to an organized, critical, synthesizing, problem-solving executive. It is the seat of all intellectual processes.

Freud believed that the *superego* is formed from the ego as youngsters identify with parents and internalize their restrictions, values, and customs. It is essentially a conscience. Though once part of the ego, it functions totally independently. It strives for perfection and underlies idealism, self-sacrifice, and heroism. This personality component rewards the ego for acceptable behavior and creates guilt feelings to chastise the ego when actions or thoughts run counter to moral principles. Like the id, the superego lobbies the ego—to attend to moral, not simply realistic, goals and to force the id to inhibit animal impulses. Freud believed that the entire id and parts of the ego and superego are unconscious.

The ego occupies a pivotal position. In Freud's words, "the poor ego . . . has to serve three harsh masters [id, superego, and reality] and has to do its best to reconcile the demands of all three [18]." The more intense the conflicts, the more psychic energy is required to resolve them. Less psychic energy then remains for higher mental functions, such as rational thinking and creativity. Because the ego recognizes the danger of expressing primitive drives, it experiences anxiety when pressed by the id. To reduce anxiety, the ego can banish impulses from awareness, redirect them into acceptable channels, or express them directly. Whenever the ego gives in to the id, the superego punishes the ego by generating a sense of guilt and inferiority. In the course of attempting to cope with the id, superego, and reality, the ego develops *defense mechanisms*, modes of behavior that relieve tension. (Defense mechanisms are described in Chapter 14.) Abnormal symptoms, discussed in Chapter 15, may result from compromises between id impulses, reality, and superego.

Freud's view of personality development Freud believed that personality is shaped by early experiences as children pass through a set sequence of *psychosexual stages*. The term "psychosexual" is used because libido (*sexual* energy) is centered in different bodily regions, as *psychological* development progresses. Three areas (mouth, anus, and genitals), known as *erogenous zones*, are intensely responsive to pleasurable stimulation. At each stage of development, one zone dominates: Persons derive particular pleasure from that zone and seek objects or activities that produce these enjoyable experiences. At the same time, conflicts have to be resolved. If children are overindulged or if they are deprived and frustrated unduly at a particular stage, development is arrested and libido is fixated there. *Fixation* involves leaving a portion of libido—the amount varies with the severity of the conflict—permanently invested at that developmental level. Suppose that a substantial portion of libido is fixated at a particular stage. The individual's adult behavior will be characterized by modes of obtaining satisfaction or reducing tension or by other traits or attitudes that are typical of the stage where the fixation occurred. Freud described four psychosexual stages: oral, anal, phallic, and genital.

The oral stage. During the first year of life, according to Freud, infants derive pleasure primarily from their mouths, from eating, sucking, biting, and similar activities. Libido, in other words, centers on oral joys. Weaning is the major conflict of the *oral stage.* The harder it is for youngsters to leave the breast or bottle and its pleasures (because of overgratification or extreme deprivation), the more libido will be fixated at this stage. If a substantial portion of libido is left here, adults may exhibit oral traits (such as dependency, passivity, and greediness) and oral preoccupations (like eating, gum chewing, smoking, and excessive talking).

The anal stage. During the second year of life, Freud believed, pleasure is obtained primarily from the anal region—initially from expelling feces and later from retaining them. The drive for pleasure (derived primarily from tension reduction following defecation) conflicts with society's constraints. Consequently, children are asked to control natural impulses. Toilet training is the central conflict of the *anal stage.* Some children attempt to "counterattack" by making bowel movements at inopportune times, perhaps after being

removed from the toilet. Other youngsters deliberately retain their feces to manipulate parents, who feel concerned over the child's irregularity. This tactic provides gentle pressure against the intestinal walls, which may be considered pleasurable. If toilet training is either harsh or overly indulgent, a significant portion of libido may be fixated at this stage. Later on, then, adults will use similar strategies for handling general frustrations—messiness and hostile attacks or hoarding, stubbornness, stinginess, and defiance.

The phallic stage. Freud believed that young children discover that the genitals provide pleasure in the third to fifth year during the *phallic stage.* He also thought that most youngsters masturbate. Contemporary psychologists agree that many do. According to Freud, fantasies during masturbation set the stage for a universal crisis. The child loves the opposite-sexed parent excessively and feels intense rivalry toward the same-sexed parent. In the case of the female, the conflict is known as the *Electra complex.* In the male, the conflict is called the *Oedipus complex.* These names come from legendary Greek characters who experienced dramatic conflicts of the same nature.

Let's examine the boy's plight first. The son loves the mother because she gratifies his needs. With the onset of sexual awareness, he directs his erotic fantasies toward her, according to Freud. The boy desires the mother for himself and perceives the father as a rival. He even wishes the father would die and fantasizes about killing him. Sooner or later the child begins to worry. What if the bigger, stronger father should retaliate? The boy particularly fears castration, which would remove the source of the lust. To eliminate this terrifying possibility, the youngster represses his love for the mother and *identifies* with the father (strives to become like him). By this maneuver, the boy eliminates the threat and obtains the vicarious gratification of his sexual impulses. In other words, by identifying with the father, the child shares in the father's sexual privileges in imagination. This identification has far-reaching consequences, according to

Freud. It enables the youngster to adopt masculine sex-typed personality characteristics and the father's superego.

Young girls face a similar crisis at about the same time in their development. Like the son, the daughter loves the mother who has been gratifying her needs. During the phallic stage, the female child discovers that she possesses a cavity, instead of a penis, the "more desirable" sex organ. She assumes that she once had a penis but was castrated. She blames the mother for this misfortune, and her love for the mother decreases. To gain control over the valued organ, the girl temporarily transfers her love to her father. Freud was unable to explain adequately why the daughter should repress her love for the father, identify with the mother, assume feminine sex-typed behavior, and adopt the mother's superego. Eventually, he decided that love for the father and rivalry with the mother simply dissipate slowly with time. Unlike the boy's identification with the father, the girl's with the mother is relatively weak. In Freud's opinion, the lack of a penis accounts for numerous character deficiencies in women. Because of this "deprivation," females develop personality characteristics such as envy and inferiority, and they fail to adopt strong moral standards.

The latency stage. When the phallic stage concludes at approximately the age of five, Freud believed, personalities are essentially formed. For the next seven years or so, the sexual needs become dormant. No important conflicts or personality changes occur. This period is sometimes called the *latency stage.*

The genital stage. At the onset of puberty, according to Freud, sexual interests reawaken. During the *genital stage* (adolescence through adulthood until the onset of senility), people orient toward others as they participate in the activities of their culture. Up to this time, human beings have been absorbed in their own bodies and immediate needs. Now they must form satisfying sexual relationships. Freud believed that a mature heterosexual bond is the hallmark of maturity. If energy is tied up because of excessive gratification or frustration at lower developmental stages, adolescents cannot meet this challenge.

Critical comments Freud's ideas have been exceedingly influential in psychology and psychiatry, as well as in literature, art, philosophy, and related disciplines. Psychoanalytic concepts are widely accepted by the general public too. Terms such as "frustrated needs," "unconscious impulses," "Oedipus complexes," and "oral personalities" have become commonplace. How has Freud's personality theory fared among behavioral scientists? Most agree with him that early experience is important for personality development (see Chapter 3 for the experimental evidence) and that people are often influenced by motives and feelings of which they are unaware. On the other hand, the details of Freud's formulations are debated. Is motivation primarily biological in origin? Are unconscious motives the important ones? Do children pass through oral, anal, phallic, and genital stages? Do women experience penis envy? Are there three parts to the personality? And so forth. From time to time, behavioral scientists try to assess the research support for psychoanalytic ideas. There is little agreement [19]. Authors looking at the same data come to different conclusions, depending apparently on their own theoretical persuasions and sympathies.

Freud is generally criticized for several reasons. He failed to give due weight to social and cultural influences on personality. He assumed, for example, that sexuality is a universal preoccupation, instead of connecting this concern to the practices of his Victorian society. His procedures are challenged as well. Many psychoanalytic ideas are close to impossible to evaluate. How would you measure the id, for example? Freud maintained that clinical observations are the only meaningful way to generate and test theories. Themes that recurred consistently were considered important ones. Theoretical issues were "verified" by consensus (agreement). Ideas were accepted as correct if considered accurate by patients, if symptoms ceased, or if constructive changes occurred. Freud tested principles by seeing how well they explained cultural phenomena such as folktales, too. Because evidence for psychoanalytic ideas comes primarily from case studies, scientifically oriented psychologists consider psychoanalytic research lacking in objectivity and precision. They are upset by the flagrant disregard for *parsimony*, a scientific principle that advocates choosing the simplest explanation that fits the observed facts (Chapter 2). Fixation during the anal stage is not a parsimonious explanation for messiness, for instance. Behavioral scientists assert that Freud also made several logical errors. He observed that boys of four are affectionate to mothers and avoid fathers, for example, and conjectured that rivalry for the mother's sexual favors is the reason. He then replaced the observation with the speculation. Freud confused correlation and causation, as well. Dependent adults often reported being indulged or frustrated when fed in early childhood. Without sufficient evidence, Freud concluded that the one (frustration or indulgence during the oral period) causes the other (dependency).

Though Freud undoubtedly made mistakes, his theories are far from dead. Some psychologists and psychiatrists still subscribe to traditional, or orthodox, psychoanalytic ideas. Historians have used psychoanalytic insights to analyze the diaries and behavior of such figures as Hitler and Nixon [20]. At the same time, many behavioral scientists adhere to *Neo-Freudian ideas*, those modifications and revisions of basic psychoanalytic theories which were introduced by Freud's disciples.▲

Neo-Freudian Theories

Numerous personality theorists, generally drawing on their therapeutic experiences with patients, have amended and extended psychoanalytic ideas.

Carl Jung   Carl Gustav Jung (1875–1961), a Swiss psychiatrist who was considered Freud's heir apparent in the psychoanalytic movement, turned away from Freud in 1912. He is pictured in Figure 13-8. Jung was bothered by the notion that the libido is entirely sexual (pleasure-oriented) and by the emphasis on early childhood. He is associated with the idea that human beings inherit a *collective unconscious*, which holds memories of ancestors, their relationships, and their experiences. These memories, according to Jung, produce images such as the wise old man and the earth mother that inhabit dreams, delusions, and fantasies. Poetic, mythic, and religious statements are presumed to be derived from this source. Jung assumed that people are born with a personal unconscious as well—for repressed individual memories.

Alfred Adler   Alfred Adler (1870–1937), an Austrian psychiatrist (Figure 13-9), was another member of Freud's original group who broke away. Like Jung, he felt that the importance of sexuality had been overestimated. He focused on cultural influences on behavior, assuming that personality is innately social and that inferiority feelings are central to human motivation. In Adler's words:

▲ USING PSYCHOLOGY

1. Are you aware of personality components that might be labeled id, ego, and superego? Are you aware of conflicts between these components? Explain.

2. Which Freudian ideas could be tested by direct observations of some type? Which could not be verified in this way? Suggest other procedures for evaluating these latter ideas.

FIGURE 13-8 In his early years, Carl Gustav Jung worked closely with Freud until personal disagreements arose and the two men parted ways. Jung became increasingly absorbed in studies of cultures and their literatures. One of his most important contributions is the notion of the collective unconscious. Its emotionally charged symbols and images, which Jung called *archetypes*, are presumably shared by all human beings. They emerge, according to Jung, in dreams, fantasies, delusions, and myths. [*Bettmann Archive.*]

I began to see clearly in every psychical phenomenon the striving to superiority. . . . The impetus from minus to plus is never ending. The urge from "below" to "above" never ceases. [21]

Adler believed that inferiority feelings increase in proportion to the magnitude of failures to achieve life goals and that they shape each individual's unique life-style.

Karen Horney The German-born psychoanalyst Karen Horney (1885–1952) (Figure 13-10) studied in Germany under one of Freud's followers and later became influential in American psychoanalytic circles. Like Adler, Horney emphasized the social context of development. She saw classical Freudian ideas as too rigid. She also discarded Freud's drive theory. Horney believed that children's varied experiences resulted in different personality patterns and conflicts. She emphasized the disturbing effects of feelings of isolation and helplessness. These emotions developed, Horney believed, during early parent-child interactions that blocked the youngster's inner growth.

Harry Stack Sullivan Like Adler and Horney, Harry Stack Sullivan (1892–1949), an American psychiatrist (Figure 13-11), emphasized social relationships. He believed that both acceptable and deviant behaviors are shaped by interactions with parents during the socialization process in childhood. Sullivan focused on the evolution of the self-concept as a "good me" and a "bad me." He hypothesized that people were driven by two classes of needs: security-oriented and biological ones.

FIGURE 13-9 In his youth, Alfred Adler worked with Freud's original group. Gradually, he developed a rival approach called *individual psychology*. Despite its name, Adler's psychology emphasized the significance of social influences on personality. Inferiority feelings play a dominant role. Adler believed that all children experience inferiority feelings because they cannot attain important goals and desires. He also felt that the type and intensity of each person's inferiority feelings shape the individual's life-style. [*Wide World Photos.*]

earlier dilemmas were handled. But mental health is not established once and for all. Fortunate and unfortunate later experiences can counteract earlier ones.

During the first year (paralleling Freud's oral stage), infants face a conflict between *trust* and *mistrust*. At this time, the relationship with the mother is all-important. If

FIGURE 13-10 Karen Horney, a highly respected psychoanalyst, believed that, while different experiences produce different personality patterns and conflicts, anxiety feelings due to isolation and helplessness are a core psychological problem. Such feelings arise when early relationships obstruct the child's inner growth and create contradictory needs and attitudes toward other people. [*Bettmann Archive*.]

FIGURE 13-11 Harry Stack Sullivan was a social critic as well as a psychiatrist. Sullivan believed that an imperfect society breeds imperfect people. Human beings can only improve, Sullivan assumed, if the culture that they live in improves. At the core of Sullivan's ideas were personal relationships, especially those that shaped the child early in life. More than any other neo-Freudian thinker, Sullivan was interested in testing ideas empirically and in relating theories to observable propositions so that they could be evaluated. [*Bettmann Archive*.]

Erik Erikson Erik Erikson (b. 1902), an American psychoanalyst with an international background (Figure 13-12), expanded Freud's developmental theories. His formulations stress social and psychological implications and encompass the adult years. Since Erikson's observations have been especially influential, we describe them in some detail.

According to Erikson, personalities form as people progress through *psychosocial* stages throughout life. At each new stage there is a conflict to face and resolve. There is a positive and a negative solution to each dilemma. As Erikson sees it, the conflicts are all present at birth but become dominant at specific points in the life cycle. The positive solution results in mental health, while the negative one leads to maladjustment. The resolution of any conflict depends, in part, on how successfully

FIGURE 13-12 Erik Erikson is known for his developmental theory. He is also recognized for several penetrating psychobiographical studies. Erikson has used his own psychological constructs to analyze the lives of such figures as Gandhi and Martin Luther. Throughout his career Erikson has been particularly interested in adolescent behavior. His identity crisis concept provides an understanding of common adolescent conflicts. [*United Press International.*]

mothers feed babies, keep them warm and cozy, cuddle, play with, and talk to them, youngsters develop feelings that the environment is safe and pleasant (basic trust). When mothers fail to meet these needs, infants develop fears and suspicions (mistrust).

Paralleling Freud's anal stage, during the second year, children face a second challenge, *autonomy* versus *shame and doubt*. At this time, youngsters' capacities are developing rapidly. They like to run, push, pull, hold, and let go. If parents encourage children "to stand on their own two feet" and exercise their own abilities, the young develop control over mus-

cles, drives, environments, and selves (autonomy). If parents demand too much too soon or prevent toddlers from using newly found skills, youngsters experience shame and doubt.

Children three to five years of age are active. They run, fight, and climb. They take pride in attacking problems and conquering the environment. They derive self-esteem from mental powers too—from abilities to use language, fantasies, and make-believe games. At this time, the young face a new conflict: *initiative* versus *guilt* (paralleling Freud's phallic stage). If parents try to understand, answer questions, and accept active play, youngsters learn to approach what they desire, and the sense of initiative is reinforced. When parents are impatient and punitive, considering questions, play, and activities foolish or wrong, children feel guilty and uncertain and become reluctant to act on their own desires.

The six- to eleven-year-old child enters a new world, the school, with its own goals, limits, failures, and achievements. At school, youngsters learn something about being workers and providers as they confront a fourth major challenge, *industry* versus *inferiority*. When children feel less adequate than their peers in achievements, skills, and abilities, they develop a sense of inferiority. Successful children emerge with a feeling of competence and pleasure in work, a sense of industry.

During adolescence (as Freud's genital stage begins), an *identity crisis* occurs. If the crisis is not resolved, young people experience *role confusion*. The teenager must integrate various self-images—as youth, friend, student, leader, follower, worker, woman or man—into one image and choose a career and a life-style. When youths have attained basic trust, autonomy, initiative, and industry, they can achieve an identity more easily. If this crisis is surmounted, individuals emerge with a sense of who they are and what they stand for. Erikson believes that the search for identity explains many typical adolescent behavior patterns. He has written:

Table 13-3 A Comparison of Freud's and Erikson's Stage Theories

Approximate age	Freud's psychosexual stages	Erikson's psychosocial stages
First year	Oral	Basic trust vs. mistrust
2–3 years	Anal	Autonomy vs. shame, doubt
3–5 years	Phallic	Initiative vs. guilt
6 years to puberty	Latency	Industry vs. inferiority
Adolescence	Genital	Identity vs. role confusion
Early adulthood		Intimacy vs. isolation
Middle age		Generativity vs. self-absorption
Later adulthood		Integrity vs. despair

To keep themselves together [young people] temporarily overidentify with the heroes of cliques and crowds to the point of an apparently complete loss of individuality. . . . To a considerable extent adolescent love is an attempt to arrive at a definition of one's identity by projecting one's diffused self-image on another and by seeing it thus reflected and gradually clarified. . . . [C]larification can also be sought by destructive means. Young people can become remarkably clannish, intolerant, and cruel in their exclusion of others who are "different," in skin color or cultural background, in tastes and gifts, and often in entirely petty aspects of dress and gesture arbitrarily selected as the signs of an in-grouper or out-grouper. It is important to understand in principle (which does not mean to condone in all of its manifestations) that such tolerance may be, for a while, a necessary defense against a sense of identity loss. This is unavoidable at a time of life when the body changes its proportions radically, when genital puberty floods body and imagination with all manner of impulses, when intimacy with the other sex approaches and is, on occasion, forced on the young person, and when the immediate future confronts one with too many conflicting possibilities and choices. Adolescents . . . help one another temporarily through such discomfort by forming cliques and stereotyping themselves, their ideals, and their enemies. [22]

During young adulthood a new challenge arises—*intimacy* versus *isolation*. Young adults are ready to form lasting social bonds characterized by caring, sharing, and trust. In Erikson's view, intimacy ideally requires the development of a sexual relationship with a loved member of the opposite sex "with whom one is able and willing to regulate the cycles of work, procreation, and recreation [23]." People who lack a sense of personal identity have a hard time establishing close relationships. Sometimes they isolate themselves. Sometimes they form limited ties that lack spontaneity and genuineness.

The conflicts continue. The middle-aged adult must choose between *generativity* and *self-absorption*. The term "generativity," coined by Erikson, refers to a commitment to the future and to the new generation. He believes that an active concern about young people and their welfare and about making the world a better place enhances the self. Total self-absorption leads to stagnation.

Finally, as life nears its end, the elderly face a last crisis, *integrity* versus *despair*. Integrity arises when people look back, feel contented, and accept their lives as worthy. Despair seizes those who find little meaning and satisfaction in their past and view their lives as wasted. Time seems to have run out and death appears frightening. See Table 13-3.

Critical comments The neo-Freudians contributed acute observations that have been useful to behavioral scientists working in clinical situations with troubled people. Like Freud's theories, neo-Freudian ideas tend to be global ones that are exceedingly difficult to evaluate neatly. Essentially the same sorts of criticism apply to both types of theories. ▲

▲ **USING PSYCHOLOGY**

1. In what ways are Freudian and neo-Freudian ideas similar? How do they differ?

2. Contrast Freud's and Erikson's stage theories of development. Can you see any general problems that are associated with stage theories of development?

3. Suggest a way to test Erikson's idea that all adolescents experience an identity crisis.

4. Assume that Erikson's ideas are correct. What experiences should parents and teachers provide children to increase the likelihood that they will find positive solutions to life conflicts?

FIGURE 13-13 Carl Rogers introduced humanistic concerns into the study of personality. Since the 1960s Rogers has been actively involved in the encounter group movement which he views as a way of facilitating human growth and enhancing human potential. He has attempted to apply his human growth concept within schools and industrial organizations too. Rogers explains his belief in the essential goodness of human nature thus: "I do not have a Pollyanna view of human nature. I am quite aware that out of defensiveness and inner fear individuals can and do behave in ways which are incredibly cruel, horribly destructive, immature, regressive, anti-social, and harmful. Yet one of the most refreshing and invigorating parts of my experience is to work with such individuals and to discover the strongly positive directional tendencies which exist in them, as in all of us, at the deepest levels [43]." [*Bettmann Archive.*]

PHENOMENOLOGICAL PERSONALITY THEORIES

Human beings continually attach meanings to the information that is taken in through the senses, as we saw in Chapter 6. Since people know only what they perceive, each individual's perceptions constitute his or her reality. Inevitably, then, all human beings confront slightly different realities. *Phenomenological* theorists concentrate on trying to understand "selves" and their unique perspectives on life. These behavioral scientists take a holistic viewpoint. They assume that people are integrated organisms that cannot be understood by studying the component parts and "adding up" the findings. The *self* is usually defined as an internal *model* (image, concept, or theory) built up through interactions with the world. This self model influences actions, which in turn affect the self model. Striving toward self-fulfillment is considered the major human motive. The importance of lower physiological drives is played down. Like Freud and the neo-Freudians, phenomenologists often rely on clinical observations and especially on self-reports. Humanistic psychologists are particularly likely to espouse this approach to personality. In previous chapters we have described the ideas of one prominent phenomenological theorist, Abraham Maslow. In this section we focus on the theories of Carl Rogers, another eminent phenomenologist.

Carl Rogers's Self Theory

Carl Rogers (b. 1902) (Figure 13-13) has been trying to help troubled people cope with problems most of his life. His ideas evolved slowly from clinical experiences. In Rogers's words:

I began my work with the settled notion that the "self" was a vague, ambiguous, scientifically meaningless term. . . . Consequently, I was slow in recognizing that when clients were given the opportunity to express their problems and their attitudes in their own terms . . . they tended to talk in terms of the self . . . "I feel I'm not being my real self." [or] "It feels good to let myself go and just be myself here." It seemed clear from such expressions that the self was an important element in the experience of the client, and that in some odd sense his goal was to become his real self. [24]

Rogers defines the "self" or "self-concept" (terms used interchangeably) as an organized, consistent pattern of the perceived characteristics of the "I" or "me," along with the values attached to those attributes.

How does the self-concept develop? Children observe their own functioning, according to Rogers, just as they watch the behavior of others. At early ages, youngsters become aware of consistencies and begin to assign to themselves specific traits—for example, "angering easily" and "having a lot of energy." They attach values to the self-descriptions. "Angering easily" is apt to be perceived negatively; "having energy," positively. Self-concepts evolve slowly as children interact with others and with their surroundings. Rogers assumes that human beings strive to maintain consistency between experiences and self-image. Presumably, people allow situations that agree with the self-concept to enter awareness, and they perceive these events accurately. Conflicting experiences are apt to be prevented from entering consciousness and to be perceived inaccurately.

Rogers views childhood as an especially crucial time for personality development, just as the psychodynamic theorists do. Like many neo-Freudians, he focuses on the lasting effects of early *social* relationships. Everyone needs positive regard, warmth, and acceptance from significant others. Children, in Rogers's opinion, will do almost anything to satisfy this need. To gain parental approval, youngsters often distort or deny their own perceptions, emotions, sensations, and thoughts. In the long run, this strategy leads to problems. People are centrally driven by the motive to fully actualize their own potentialities. Rogers's concept of actualization motivation is much like Maslow's (Chapter 10). Of course, developing one's potential requires self-understanding and a satisfying life-style. People who deny or distort important aspects of themselves hold incomplete, unrealistic self-images. They feel threatened by experiences that conflict with these self-concepts. To shut out disquieting events, maladjusted human beings tend to build rigid defenses. They cannot actualize their own potential because they do not understand it and because they avoid many types of experiences.

Well-adjusted, or "fully functioning," human beings, in contrast, hold realistic self-concepts that include all their own important characteristics. They are accurately aware of their own worlds, open to all experiences, and highly self-regarding. Well-adjusted individuals rely on their own experiences to reach decisions. They feel free because they believe that their choices are self-generated. According to Rogers, fully functioning people live completely in each and every moment and are constantly changing ("moving on in complexity") to make increasingly full use of their varied potentialities.

Though Rogers acknowledges that heredity and environment both limit personality in some ways, he focuses on self-imposed limits that can usually be stretched. To promote growth, he believes, significant others in the environment must accept all aspects of an individual and regard and value the person highly. Under these circumstances, human beings begin accepting themselves, become open to their own experiences, and move in the direction of self-actualization [25].

Research has been important to Rogers and his coworkers. They have focused on clarifying the conditions that facilitate personality growth in counseling situations. The studies often involve tape-recording interviews and analyzing the content systematically to check out hypotheses. Rogers has also endeavored to study the subjective self-image objectively, primarily by using the Q-sort approach discussed earlier. Typically, clients in therapy describe current self-perceptions, then ideal selves. If the two sortings are very discrepant, the individual is thought to be *incongruent* (contradictory, lacking in harmony). Rogers believes that this problem lies at the heart of all psychological disturbances. Therapy is supposed to reduce incongruence. Its success can be evaluated by having the client perform additional Q-sorts after weeks or months of treatment.

Critical comments Many psychologists who counsel others find Rogers's ideas helpful for conceptualizing and treating the problems of mildly troubled people. His faith in human nature is attractive. If people are only allowed to grow naturally, he believes, they will be effective, positive, rational creatures who can be trusted to live in harmony with both others and themselves. Human beings who commit intensely destructive, irrational, or cruel acts are thought to be defensive and closed off to their true inner selves. Rogers's views, like those of the psychodynamic theorists, are criticized for being impossible to test precisely. In addition, many psychologists object to his reliance on what people say about themselves, since self-reports are often inaccurate.▲

We turn now from theories based on clinical observations to those that were built through controlled research procedures.

DISPOSITIONAL THEORIES OF PERSONALITY

Before reading on, please refer to your notes on I. S., the college student with whom we opened the chapter. How did you describe him? To characterize people in daily life, we usually "type" them or enumerate their traits. In both cases, we are attempting to pick out attributes or *dispositions* that seem stable and enduring.

By *traits* psychologists mean single characteristics. You might have described I. S.'s personality by listing traits such as "snobbish," "intellectual," "sloppy," "bohemian," "negative," or "submissive." A trait is a continuous dimension that can be conceptualized as linking two opposite characteristics. People occupy specific positions on the trait between the two extremes. If you were asked to judge a gregarious friend's sociability, for example, you'd probably position the individual somewhere between "almost always socializing" and "almost always isolated"—closer to the former than the latter. Traits may refer to diverse aspects of personality, including temperament, motivation, adjustment, abilities, and values.

Typing people—putting them into personality categories—is another common way to describe personality dispositions. Type approaches differ from trait approaches in several essential ways. (1) Traits tend to refer to specific narrow aspects of personality while types account for an entire personality. (2) Typing assumes that specific traits usually cluster together. An "intellectual type," for example, might be high in "intelligence" and

▲ **USING PSYCHOLOGY**

1. How are Rogers's and Freud's theories similar? How do they differ?

2. Why is Rogers considered a phenomenological theorist?

3. Assume that Rogers's ideas are correct. What child-rearing and teaching policies are important for a youngster's later mental health?

4. Reread the sections describing Maslow's ideas (in Chapters 1, 10, and 11). Why is Maslow classified as a phenomenological theorist?

"snobbishness" and low in "sociability" and "athletic prowess." The Greek physician Hippocrates believed that people possessed one of four temperament types: depressed, optimistic, apathetic, or irritable. Early in his career, Carl Jung, the neo-Freudian theorist whom we just described, classified people as predominantly introverted (shy, preoccupied with their own feelings) or extroverted (sociable, outgoing). Did you type I. S.?

Currently, behavioral scientists are studying the processes underlying ordinary people's type categories in real life. There is a basis in reality for typing human beings. Significant correlations among personality attributes do exist. Talkativeness and activity, for instance, are associated with being outgoing. At the same time, individuals interpret the behavior of others in accordance with preexisting beliefs and expectations. Consequently, many typings reflect the perceiver as well as the perceived [26]. We will describe the person perception process in Chapter 17.

Formal dispositional theories of personality attempt to describe and classify people by traits or types (trait clusters). They carve a whole personality into specific components. Each characteristic is assumed to be relatively enduring over the life span and across different situations. To illustrate how psychologists construct trait and type theories, we turn to the work of Raymond Cattell and William Sheldon.

Raymond Cattell's Trait Theory

Psychologist Raymond Cattell (b. 1905) (Figure 13-14) began defining and measuring the major components of personality in the 1930s. He has continued his personality research and theory development to the present time. Initially, he and his associates collected approximately 18,000 English words which are used to describe people. By omitting rare and overlapping expressions, they reduced the number to approximately 200 items. To compact the list further, Cattell's research team asked varied groups of people to use these

words to describe themselves and friends. The expressions employed were subsequently analyzed by a mathematical technique known as *factor analysis*. In essence, the terms were correlated with one another to see if certain trait words generally occurred together. Sixteen groupings were identified and labeled with letters and, later, trait names. Information from objective tests and ratings of real-life behavior confirmed that these traits were basic dimensions of personality [27]. The sixteen characteristics, shown in Figure 13-15, are known as *source traits*. They appear to be influenced by genetic endowment and are relatively stable throughout life. They are considered the "source" for many superfi-

FIGURE 13-14 Raymond Cattell believes that a personality theory should enable psychologists to predict what a specific person will do in a particular situation. Mathematical methods, Cattell asserts, will some day make the study of personality an exact science. He has devoted his productive career to test construction and to studying genetic and cultural influences on personality. [*Courtesy of Dr. Raymond B. Cattell.*]

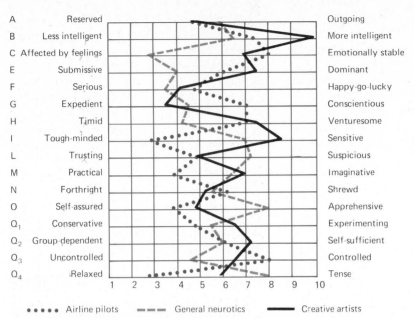

		1	2	3	4	5	6	7	8	9	10	
A	Reserved											Outgoing
B	Less intelligent											More intelligent
C	Affected by feelings											Emotionally stable
E	Submissive											Dominant
F	Serious											Happy-go-lucky
G	Expedient											Conscientious
H	Timid											Venturesome
I	Tough-minded											Sensitive
L	Trusting											Suspicious
M	Practical											Imaginative
N	Forthright											Shrewd
O	Self-assured											Apprehensive
Q₁	Conservative											Experimenting
Q₂	Group-dependent											Self-sufficient
Q₃	Uncontrolled											Controlled
Q₄	Relaxed											Tense

• • • • • Airline pilots   – – – General neurotics   ▬▬▬ Creative artists

FIGURE 13-15 Raymond Cattell's source traits, lettered from A to Q_4, are shown. Personality profiles have been plotted for three groups. [*Institute for Personality and Ability Testing, Champaign, Ill.*]

FIGURE 13-16 William Sheldon, an American physician-psychologist, is known for research which links personality types to specific body types. [*The Biological Humanics Center.*]

cial attributes, or *surface traits*. Source trait "E," defined at one end by "dominance" and at the other by "submissiveness," for example, seems to be responsible for the surface traits "self-confidence" and "boasting."

Besides identifying some of the building blocks of personality, Cattell and his associates have developed a number of self-report questionnaires which are used to characterize the personalities of individuals and groups. In Figure 13-15, you can see the average scores on the sixteen source traits obtained by groups of pilots, neurotics, and artists. Not only do personality test findings allow behavioral scientists to describe the typical member of a particular group; the data also enable psychologists to explain and predict behavior. In one study, for example, Cattell's research team tested happily and unhappily married couples to see whether "birds of a feather live more harmoniously together." Pairs with similar personalities were, in fact, more likely than those with dissimilar personalities to have a stable relationship. It seemed to be especially important for people to be similar on three traits: reserved-outgoing, trusting-suspicious, and group-dependent–self-sufficient. Husbands in relatively contented matches tended to be somewhat more dominant than their wives. This information put Cattell and other investigators in a position to accurately predict which engaged individuals would eventually form successful bonds [28]. In a similar way, Cattell's group has explored the ingredients that enter into academic success, alcoholism, the toleration of contact lenses, and numerous other "achievements." To predict how any single individual will respond in a particular setting, Cattell uses what he calls a *specification equation*. The traits of the person are weighed by their importance for the situation of interest. Relevant traits are given much weight while less relevant traits receive correspondingly less weight. The specification equation permits an employment office, for example, to match an individual's personality with a job's requirements.

William Sheldon's Type Theory

Physician-psychologist William Sheldon (1898–1977) (Figure 13-16) contended that people with particular body types tend to develop specific personality types. He reasoned that human beings are genetically endowed with physical characteristics that determine the activities at which they are apt to excel and consequently find pleasurable. If a man has strong, well-developed muscles, he will probably be good at, enjoy, and engage in athletics. Bodily attributes shape the expectations of others too. Fat people, for instance, are "supposed" to be jolly and even-tempered. As we have seen in previous chapters, expectations influence behavior. People often play the roles that others expect.

Sheldon and his associates found that they could characterize masculine bodies by the extent to which they possess three physical components: *endomorphy*, *mesomorphy*, and *ectomorphy*. Figure 13-17 pictures and

FIGURE 13-17 William Sheldon found support for the notion that these body and personality types are associated with one another.

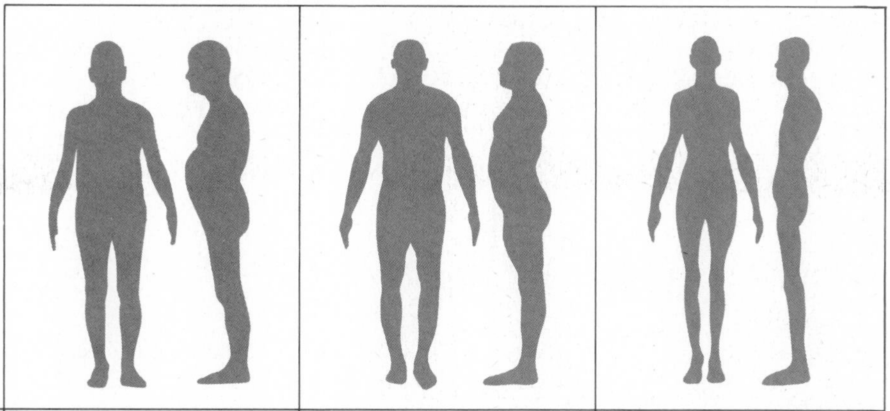

	ENDOMORPHY	MESOMORPHY	ECTOMORPHY
BODY TYPE	Soft, round, overdeveloped digestive viscera	Hard, rectangular, strong, athletic, highly developed muscles	Tall, thin, fragile, large brain, sensitive nervous system
PERSONALITY TYPE	VISCEROTONIA Comfort-loving, sociable, gluttonous, even-tempered	SOMATOTONIA Assertive, aggressive, active, direct, courageous, dominant	CEREBROTONIA Inhibited, restrained, fearful, self-conscious

describes the body types. Because most bodies tend to be mixtures of these characteristics, the investigators developed procedures for rating each component. After devising a reliable way to classify male, and later female, body types, Sheldon's group identified three corresponding personality types: *viscerotonia*, *somatotonia*, and *cerebrotonia* (also described in Figure 13-17). To find out whether personality and body types are, in fact, associated, the *same* researchers rated the bodies and behavior of male college students for five years [29]. Sheldon's team found strong positive correlations (around .80) between the two. In seeking to confirm these findings, later investigators used two sets of trained judges—to prevent unintended experimenter bias. In such cases, one group rated bodies, the other, personalities. Only moderate correlations between body build and personality are detected when this control is used [30].

Critical comments Dispositional theories possess several noteworthy strengths. The formulations are based on careful research with objective measures, so individual insights may be verified or refuted. The test construction that has often accompanied theorizing about dispositions has provided practical fringe benefits. Counselors use the tests to help people gain self-understanding and make school- and career-related decisions. Disposi-

tional theories have a number of liabilities, as well. Some treat people as if they were relatively fixed entities and ignore development and change. Cattell, incidentally, is not guilty of these practices. Many dispositional theories stress inborn determinants of personality and neglect environmental influences. Type theories, in addition, overemphasize a few personality dimensions while ignoring others. We will say more about the trait concept later. ▲

BEHAVIORISTIC THEORIES OF PERSONALITY

Like dispositional theorists, behavioristic ones share a strong dedication to the use of rigorous scientific methods. They are especially likely to emphasize experimentation. Because of their insistence on accurate measurement, behavioristic psychologists usually focus on observable acts, physiological responses, and other phenomena that can be assessed objectively. They sometimes study laboratory animals for insights into fundamental personality processes. In seeking to explain conduct, behaviorists stress learning principles and environmental conditions. We consider two contrasting illustrations of the behavioristic approach: B. F. Skinner's radical behaviorism and Walter Mischel's cognitive social learning strategy.

▲ **USING PSYCHOLOGY**

1. Ask several friends to read about I. S. and write a description of his personality. Do they generally use type and trait approaches? Speculate as to why these approaches tend to be popular. Also speculate about why people rarely "type" themselves even when they "type" almost everyone else.

2. List specific traits that you see in yourself. For each trait, cite several examples of recent behavior which suggest that conduct "generated by that trait" is consistent. Can you think of behaviors that are consistent from your own perspective but do not appear consistent to outsiders?

3. How could you use Cattell's research strategy to predict which of 1,000 seven-year-old boys at Public School 105 are likely to become juvenile delinquents?

B. F. Skinner's Radical Behaviorism

B. F. Skinner (b. 1904), whose work on operant conditioning was described in Chapter 5, is associated with a view of personality known as *radical behaviorism.* He is pictured in Figure 13-18. Personality, in Skinner's opinion, is essentially a fiction. People see what others do and infer underlying characteristics (motives, traits, abilities) which exist primarily in the beholder's mind. Psychologists, he believes, should focus on understanding what organisms do. Inner dispositions are inadequate explanations of behavior. In Skinner's words:

FIGURE 13-18 B. F. Skinner believes that personality theorists should emphasize what people do under specific conditions, and not internal states such as feelings, which he considers mere by-products of behavior. Skinner characterizes the developmental process in terms, not of inner changes, but of environmental variations that alter conduct throughout the life span. As environments vary, he assumes, people adjust appropriately. Life crises arise when the environment has changed but the individual has failed to acquire adaptive behavior and cannot cope with the changes and obtain reinforcements. [*Wide World Photos.*]

When we say that a man eats because he is hungry, smokes a great deal because he has the tobacco habit, fights because of the instinct of pugnacity, behaves brilliantly because of his intelligence, or plays the piano well because of his musical ability, we seem to be referring to causes. But on analysis these phrases prove to be merely redundant descriptions. A single set of facts is described by the two statements: "He eats" and "He is hungry." . . . A single set of facts is described by the two statements: "He plays well" and "He has musical ability." The practice of explaining one statement in terms of the other is dangerous because it suggests that we have found the cause and therefore need search no further. Moreover, such terms as "hunger," "habit," and "intelligence" convert what are essentially the properties of a process or relation into what appears to be things. Thus we are unprepared for the properties eventually to be discovered in the behavior itself and continue to look for something which may not exist. [31]

Skinner believes that behavior may be explained by genetic and environmental forces. He emphasizes experience, especially simple conditioning principles such as reinforcement, extinction, counterconditioning, and discrimination (all described in Chapter 5). As he sees it, an individual's conduct in any setting is controlled by many essentially independent circumstances. Consequently, people should not expect to see a great deal of behavioral consistency from situation to situation. Consider the case of a woman who appears fiercely independent and aggressive on some occasions and warm, passive, and dependent on others. Psychoanalytic or trait theorists might consider such a person basically aggressive with a façade of passivity. Or, they might judge the woman essentially warm, passive, and dependent with aggressive defenses. Skinner and many other behaviorists contend that the woman's behavior at any particular point in time depends on her learning history and on current conditions. If attacking her husband when he nags about financial matters has desirable results, the woman is apt to use aggression in that situation and in similar ones. If a sister takes over the food preparation whenever the woman (who hates cooking) acts helpless in the kitchen, we should expect to see passivity under this and similar circumstances. In sum, Skinner views behavior as specific to a particular situation, or *situation-specific*. He believes that psychologists should perform rigorously controlled experiments to evaluate which conditions contribute to a given response. He sees people as essentially passive organisms, as "loci in which things happen [32]."

Walter Mischel's Cognitive Social Learning Approach

Stanford University psychologist Walter Mischel (b. 1930), pictured in Figure 13-19, has attempted to reconcile the behavioristic view with several other orientations, most notably the phenomenological tradition and cognitive psychology. His *cognitive social learning theory* draws heavily on research in learning, cognition, and social psychology (the

FIGURE 13-19 Walter Mischel is actively involved in both personality theory construction and research. Mischel's studies have furthered understanding of the principles underlying social behavior and cognitive development during childhood. [*Courtesy of Dr. Walter Mischel.*]

study of how human beings interact with and influence one another).

Like Skinner, Mischel believes that behavior is often specific to a particular situation, that it is determined partially by interacting environmental conditions, and that psychologists should use scientific methods to specify what people do, when, and under what circumstances. But, whereas Skinner views human beings as comparatively simple organisms at the mercy of environmental forces, Mischel sees them as complex, uniquely organized, active, aware problem solvers. He finds human beings capable of profiting from an enormous range of experiences and cognitive capacities. He sees them as the active constructors of their own worlds. In Mischel's opinion, predicting behavior requires understanding (1) environmental circumstances, (2) the person involved (including her or his competencies, attitudes, and self-regulating strategies), and (3) the phenomenological impact of the situation (including the individual's interpretations, expectations, values, plans, emotions, and wishes). To gather these types of data, psychologists must place people in specific situations, observe behavior, and collect self-reports. Proceeding in this way, behavioral scientists will eventually accumulate a body of information that allows precise predictions about conduct in particular situations. To decide whether or not an individual can delay the gratification of some desire, for example, one needs certain facts. Mischel's research suggests that one has to know the object awaited, the consequences of not waiting, and the individual's age, sex, self-control strategies, and immediately prior experiences [33].

Mischel believes that a personality theory should be "nourished broadly" by all psychological research. Drawing on empirical studies of social behavior, learning, and cognition, he proposes that the following propositions are currently supportable [34]:

1. People are capable of assessing their own behavior.
2. People are aware of the outcomes of specific responses. This consciousness determines actions and choices in many situations.

3. The same conditions may have radically different effects, depending on how they are conceptualized.

4. Learning is a potent determinant of behavior.

5. All human beings have some internal consistencies but each person is organized in a unique way. For this reason it is close to impossible to generalize automatically from one individual to another.

Critical comments The behavioristic approach to personality stresses precise, careful research above all. While this emphasis is a strength, tightly controlled experiments are too frequently performed in contrived, artificial situations with college students and rats as subjects. Yet investigators often assume that the findings apply to all people. Obviously, field research that doesn't disturb the responses being studied is needed. And human beings from varied backgrounds should be observed. Behavioristic theorists are also criticized for overemphasizing environmental forces. Biologically based influences on personality need to be explored, of course. Some critics argue that Skinner's theory focuses too narrowly on the learning of overt responses and ignores individual differences, in addition. Mischel's approach, on the other hand, is a broad, inclusive one. Incorporating research findings from many perspectives gives the Mischel strategy power and vigor. ▲

CONTROVERSIAL ISSUES IN PERSONALITY

Behavioral scientists are currently debating several controversial personality-related issues.

Is a Single Comprehensive Personality Theory Desirable?

We have reviewed enough personality theories for you to see that psychologists don't share a single orientation. In theory and in research, we find varying emphases on the unconscious, on private experiences, and on overt behavior. Some behavioral scientists concentrate on hereditary and others on environmental influences. Some favor amassing a body of general laws. Others advocate perfecting the assessment instruments that describe and predict an individual's behavior. Each position leads to specific types of research and to particular clinical practices (described in Chapter 16). Some behavioral scientists find the diversity frustratingly chaotic. They contend that a widely shared comprehensive theory would provide researchable questions and help tie together research findings. They argue that the personality area is currently highly fragmented and totally lacking in direction [35]. Not all psychologists are bothered by this "dilemma." Some counter that a single, wide-ranging theory might be nice, but that a meaningful theory cannot be formulated until more knowledge has been accumulated.

Should Psychologists Forget about Traits?

Is the trait construct a useful one? Some behavioral scientists argue that it isn't. If what people do on any single occasion depends on numerous interacting variables and is not primarily the product of general dispositions, then psychologists should focus on those conditions that influence behavior in each and every situation and forget about traits. Not everyone agrees. Many behavioral scientists believe that behavior often depends on persisting dispositions. Researchers have found support for this position. For example, scores on the CPI (page 414) on specific personality characteristics distinguish 81 percent of marijuana users and 81 percent of nonusers. Similarly, strong, consistent relationships exist between socialization scores on the CPI and delinquency [36]. A compromise position has become popular. Current investigations of personality frequently focus on how persons with specific characteristics behave in particular situations [37].

When Are People Consistent?

Although behavior varies somewhat from situation to situation, our daily observations suggest that people often act consistently. Behavioral consistency appears to depend on several factors. *What is being observed* is one important condition. As we saw earlier in this chapter, assertiveness is highly uniform from situation to situation. In previous chapters, we have noted that temperament characteristics (such as persistence, mood, intensity, and attitude to new experiences), needs (such as that for sensory stimulation), and the mental characteristics that enter into intelligent behavior tend to be stable over time. Vocational goals persist for approximately twenty years in many instances and perhaps longer [38]. Consistency depends on *who is observing*, too. From an outsider's point of view, for example, a boy who dresses sloppily most days and neatly for church is behaving inconsistently. But from an internal perspective, the dressing behavior may appear perfectly consistent. The child may be adhering to the value "comfort is to be preferred in all situations unless firmly established conventions demand formal attire and bucking them leads to

problems." In this case, the boy is not consistently neat, but he is uniformly comfort-oriented. Recent research shows that people *vary* in how consistently they behave. Individuals who identify themselves as consistent on traits such as conscientiousness and friendliness, for instance, tend to behave more predictably when rated on these dimensions in diverse situations than do those who see themselves as variable and contradictory [39].

Is Personality Testing Justifiable?

In Houston, Texas, a school board burned the answer sheets to six psychological tests that had been administered to 5,000 ninth graders. Parents objected to specific questions that had been asked. People all over the United States are challenging psychologists' rights to test personality. You may recall that intelligence testing is similarly controversial. Behavioral scientists themselves are divided on the testing issue. Many feel that tests should be used when requested or when people volunteer for research, but only when subjects are fully informed about the project and anonymity is guaranteed. (Test records can be subpoenaed by legal authorities and put into public record.) Others contend that testing is justifiable because it permits sound educational placements and sensitive career guidance—benefits which the general public may not fully appreciate. Powerful arguments can be advanced to support the personality testing of adults. In a complex society like ours, there are trade-offs between the public good and an indivdual's right to privacy to be considered. Personality testing can help psychologists evaluate a person's competency, say, for police work, the military, and political offices. Those who aspire to these and similar roles, it can be argued, should place the public's interest above personal rights to complete privacy. ▲

▲ **USING PSYCHOLOGY**

1. Take a stand on the controversial issues that were raised in this section. (*a*) Do you feel psychologists need a single, comprehensive personality theory currently? (*b*) If you were a personality psychologist, would you find the trait concept a useful one? (*c*) Under what circumstances do you think people behave consistently? (*d*) Do you believe that personality testing is justifiable? Under what conditions?

2. Suppose that you were asked to build your own personality theory. Which of the idea(s) reviewed in this chapter would you try to incorporate into your own formulation?

SUMMARY
Personality

1. To assess personality, psychologists use several tools, often in combination: interviews, controlled observations and experiments, and objective and projective tests.

2. Psychodynamic theories focus on the nature and development of personality. They assume that personality evolves as conflicts between internal forces are resolved. Childhood is often emphasized as the critical period for personality development. Psychodynamic theories rely heavily on clinical observations.

3. Sigmund Freud was the first psychodynamic theorist. His primary beliefs include these: The majority of a person's thoughts, feelings, and desires are unconscious. Three personality components—id, ego, and superego—compete continually for energy generated by biological drives. Sexuality is a dominant drive. Personality develops primarily in early childhood during three psychosexual stages—oral, anal, and phallic. A fourth psychosexual phase, the genital stage, occurs during adolescence and adulthood.

4. Freud's disciples modified and revised his theories. Many of these neo-Freudians stressed social influences on personality and downplayed sexual ones. Jung proposed that people have a collective unconscious. Adler focused on inferiority feelings. Horney described how parental relationships lead to a sense of isolation and helplessness in children. Sullivan emphasized social interactions and the development of the self-concept. Erikson expanded Freud's developmental theory by stressing the social and psychological implications and broadening the scope to encompass adult life.

5. Phenomenological theories concentrate on understanding the self in a holistic way. Self-fulfillment is considered the primary human motive. Phenomenological theories are usually based on clinical observations, especially on people's self-reports.

6. Carl Rogers, a prominent phenomenological theorist, believes that people often distort or deny aspects of themselves during childhood to please parents. As a result, they develop incomplete, unrealistic self-concepts. They build rigid defenses to shut out events that threaten these images. Such people do not understand themselves, and they are closed to a great many experiences. Consequently, they cannot actualize their potential. When individuals feel accepted and valued, they come to accept and value themselves. They open up to their own experiences. They move toward self-actualization.

7. Dispositional theories focus on attributes that seem stable and enduring. Trait theories emphasize single core characteristics, while type theories stress clusters of traits that are thought to be associated with one another. Many of these theories arose from laboratory research.

8. Raymond Cattell, a trait theorist, used mathematical techniques to identify sixteen source traits and to develop personality tests. His research attempts to describe, explain, and predict varied kinds of behavior.

9. William Sheldon, a type theorist, used a rating strategy to assess body and personality types. He found that the two are positively correlated.

10. Behavioristic theories of personality specify that rigorous scientific methods, especially experimentation, are essential for understanding personality. They tend to focus on observable behavior and its environmental determinants, especially conditioning principles.

11. B. F. Skinner, a radical behaviorist, believes that personality psychologists should concentrate on explaining what people do. As he sees it, conduct is situation-specific and inner dispositions are inadequate explanations. Psychologists should look instead for the environmental antecedents and consequences that influence responses. Hypotheses can be investigated formally by precise, controlled experiments.

12. Walter Mischel's cognitive social learning theory attempts to reconcile behavioristic, phenomenological, and cognitive viewpoints. In contrast to Skinner, Mischel believes that psychologists should use personal, social, and phenomenological constructs as well as situational ones to explain behavior.

13. Current controversies in personality center on these questions: Is a single comprehensive personality theory desirable? Are traits useful concepts? Under what conditions are people consistent? Is personality testing justifiable?

A Study Guide for Chapter Thirteen

Key terms   personality (411), psychoanalysis (421), id (421), ego (422), superego (422), psychosexual stage (422), psychosocial stage (427), self model (430), disposition (432) [type (432), trait (432)], source and surface traits (433), body and personality types (435), situation-specific behavior (438), and other italicized words and expressions.

Important research   evidence concerning the reliability and validity of projective tests, development of the source trait concept (Cattell), personality similarity and marital happiness (Cattell), body and personality types (Sheldon), evidence concerning behavioral consistency.

Basic concepts   advantages and disadvantages of personality-assessment tools (interviews, controlled observations and experiments, objective tests, projective tests), clinic and laboratory-based theories, psychodynamic theories, psychoanalytic theory (Freud), neo-Freudian theories, collective unconscious (Jung), psychosocial stages of personality development (Erikson), phenomenological theories, self theory (Rogers), dispositional theories (trait and type), Cattell's trait theory, Sheldon's type theory, behavioristic personality theories, radical behaviorism (Skinner), cognitive social learning approach (Mischel), strengths and limitations of personality theories (psychoanalytic, neo-Freudian, phenomenological, dispositional, behavioristic), controversial personality-related issues.

People to identify   Freud, Jung, Adler, Horney, Sullivan, Erikson, Rogers, Hippocrates, Cattell, Sheldon, Skinner, Mischel.

Tests to identify   *General categories*: situation test, objective test (theory-based, empirically based), projective test. *Specific tests*: Study of Values test (Allport, Vernon, Lindzey), California Personality Inventory (CPI) (Gough), Minnesota Multiphasic Personality Inventory (MMPI) (Hathaway, McKinley), Q-sort (Stephenson), Rorschach test, sentence-completion test, figure-drawing test.

Self-Quiz

1. What is the most essential characteristic of an objective test?
   a. The instrument asks questions about overt behavior.
   b. Measurements made on the same subject at different points in time are consistent.
   c. The same test is scored in essentially the same way by different examiners.
   d. The test measures what it is supposed to.
2. Which test asks subjects to describe a person—often the self or ideal self—according to well-defined rules that may vary?
   a. California Personality Inventory
   b. Minnesota Multiphasic Personality Inventory
   c. Q-sort
   d. Study of Values test
3. How reliable and valid are projective tests, in general?
   a. Highly reliable and valid
   b. Moderately reliable and valid
   c. Low in reliability and consistently valid
   d. Low in reliability and variable in validity
4. Which of the following is associated with the id?
   a. Pleasure principle
   b. Practical problem-solving skills
   c. Reality principle
   d. Secondary process thinking
5. Which personality component "serves three harsh masters"?
   a. Ego   *b.* Id
   c. Libido   *d.* Superego
6. During which stage is sex-role behavior acquired, according to Freud?
   a. Anal stage   *b.* Genital stage
   c. Oral stage   *d.* Phallic stage

7. Which neo-Freudian theorist proposed that people have a collective unconscious?
   a. Adler   *b.* Horney
   c. Jung   *d.* Sullivan

8. Which neo-Freudian theorist focused on inferiority feelings?
   a. Adler   *b.* Horney
   c. Jung   *d.* Sullivan

9. When do people develop a sense of trust or mistrust, according to Erikson?
   a. During the first year of life
   b. Between the ages of three and five
   c. Between the ages of six and eleven
   d. During adolescence

10. Who speculated that young children require positive regard, warmth, and acceptance from significant others and will deny aspects of personality and distort the self-concept to fulfill that need?
   a. Cattell   *b.* Mischel
   c. Rogers   *d.* Sheldon

11. Which type of theory always emphasizes each individual's subjective frame of reference?
   a. Behavioristic   *b.* Dispositional
   c. Phenomenological   *d.* Psychoanalytic

12. Which statement about source traits is correct?
   a. They appear to be influenced by genetic endowment.
   b. They describe superficial attributes.
   c. They refer only to temperament characteristics.
   d. They were discovered by Sheldon.

13. Which attribute is most likely to characterize an ectomorphic man?
   a. An athletic body
   b. A cheerful disposition
   c. An overdeveloped digestive system
   d. A thin, fragile build

14. What does the phrase "situation-specific behavior" mean?
   a. Behavior in any situation depends on the conditions of the situation.
   b. Behavior in similar situations is consistent.
   c. Certain types of behavior, such as assertiveness, tend to be consistent.
   d. Dispositions lead to behavior that is generally consistent across dissimilar situations.

15. Mischel's behavioristic theory reconciles which approaches?
   a. Behavioristic, cognitive, psychoanalytic
   b. Behavioristic, cognitive, phenomenological
   c. Behavioristic, dispositional, phenomenological
   d. Behavioristic, phenomenological, psychoanalytic

Exercises

1. STAGE THEORIES OF FREUD AND ERIKSON. Freud's and Erikson's stage theories both divide personality development into stages, which are summarized in Table 13-3. After studying this material, check yourself by covering up columns 2 and 3 of the table to see if you can identify the corresponding Freudian and Eriksonian stages—both in and out of order. Try to characterize each stage as completely as you can. To check your descriptions, review pages 422 to 424 and pages 427 to 429.

2. COMPARISONS OF FIVE PERSONALITY THEORIES. To test your knowledge of the characteristics of each major type of personality theory, match each of the descriptions below with the single most appropriate theory. If you make mistakes, review pages 420 to 439.
THEORIES: behavioristic (B), phenomenological (PH), psychodynamic (PS), trait (TR), type (T).

_____ *1.* Assume personality develops as people *resolve deep-seated* psychological *conflicts*.

_____ *2.* Focus on what people *do* in particular situations.

_____ *3.* View people as *perceiving, experiencing* beings primarily.

_____ *4.* Concentrate on the degree to which individuals show *single* personality characteristics.

_____ *5.* Stress the importance of precisely controlled *experimental* methods.

_____ *6.* Emphasize *clusters* of traits.

_____ *7.* Assume that behavior is *situation-specific*.

_____ *8.* Use *interviews* and *clinical observations*, but do *not* value simple self-reports.

_____ *9.* Assume that personalities fit into *categories* such as "introvert" and "extrovert."

_____ *10.* Emphasize *self-fulfillment* as the major human motive.

Suggested Readings

1. Liebert, R. M., & Spiegler, M. D. *Personality: Strategies and issues.* (3d ed.) Homewood, Ill.: Dorsey, 1978. A very readable introduction to personality psychology that stresses major strategies and issues. The book covers psychoanalytic, dispositional, phenomenological, and behavioral approaches, integrating assessment tactics with theoretical concepts.

2. Hall, C. S., & Lindzey, G. *Theories of personality.* (3d ed.) New York: Wiley, 1978. This classic text presents major personality theories justly and in detail. A chapter on Eastern concepts of personality has been added to this edition.

3. Nye, R. D. *Three views of man: Perspectives from Sigmund Freud, B. F. Skinner, and Carl Rogers.* Monterey, Calif.: Brooks/Cole, 1975 (paperback). This book is a good brief introduction to three important personality theories. It includes biographical sketches, basic terminology, principal theoretical contributions, and applications. The viewpoints are contrasted and evaluated.

4. Wiggins, J. S., Renner, K. E., Clore, G. L., & Rose, R. J. *The principles of personality*. Reading, Mass.: Addison-Wesley, 1976. This text views human personality from several perspectives and focuses on personality research—on dependency, aggression, sexuality, and competence.

5. Diggins, D., & Huber, J. *The human personality*. Boston: Little, Brown, 1976. This interesting short experimental personality psychology text is oriented toward self-understanding. It is informally written and filled with exercises to involve the reader personally in the various concepts.

6. Kleinke, C. L. *Self-perception: The psychology of personal awareness*. San Francisco: Freeman, 1978 (paperback). This book aims to discuss research "on a topic that is dear to all our hearts: *ourselves*." Kleinke describes psychological studies relevant to daily life.

7. Fancher, R. E. *Psychoanalytic psychology: The development of Freud's thought*. New York: Norton, 1973. A fascinating introduction to Freud's life and the evolution of key psychoanalytic ideas: on hysteria, hypnosis, the mind, sexuality, and instincts. Fancher aims at presenting Freudian theory as evolving in a "proper scientific manner."

8. Evans, E. I. *Carl Rogers: The man and his ideas*. New York: Dutton, 1975 (paperback). Evans's book contains material by and about Rogers, as well as dialogues with him on subjects like the self-concept, psychotherapy, education, drugs, and violence. In one reviewer's opinion, Rogers's "characteristically natural, thoughtful yet direct manner, his uniquely undogmatic style of thinking and speaking, his unfailing respect for and trust in the person" are revealed [40].

9. Skinner, B. F. *Particulars of my life*. New York: McGraw-Hill, 1977 (paperback). This interesting, well-written autobiography reflects Skinner's thinking about human personality. It traces events (rather than feelings and motives) that came together to produce Skinner's behavior throughout life [41].

10. Elms, A. C. *Personality in politics*. New York: Harcourt Brace Jovanovich, 1976 (paperback). Writing for the beginning student in a readable style and with minimal jargon, Elms presents social-psychological perspectives on political behavior, including leadership. He also talks about problems in psychobiographies.

11. Cattell, R. B. Personality pinned down. *Psychology Today*, 1973, **7**(2), 40–46. Cattell describes the development of source and surface trait concepts and related research on predicting academic achievement, creativity, and successful marriages.

12. Gergen, K. G. Multiple identity: The healthy happy human being wears many masks. *Psychology Today*, 1972, **5**(12), 31–35ff. The author describes research which shows how contradictory social behavior may be and how situations often influence how people act.

Answer Keys

Self-Quiz

1. *c* (414)   **2.** *c* (416)   **3.** *d* (419)   **4.** *a* (421)
5. *a* (422)   **6.** *d* (423)   **7.** *c* (425)   **8.** *a* (425)
9. *a* (427)   **10.** *c* (431)   **11.** *c* (430)   **12.** *a* (433)
13. *d* (435)   **14.** *a* (438)   **15.** *b* (438)

Exercise 2

1. *PS*   **2.** B   **3.** PH   **4.** TR   **5.** B   **6.** T   **7.** B
8. PS   **9.** *T*   **10.** PH

Adjustment Throughout the Life Cycle

People are continuously coping with the stresses of everyday life—often without being aware of doing so. If life is a "bowl" of anything, it is a "bowl" of stresses for most individuals. In this chapter we focus on how human beings adjust to varied pressures. We begin with excerpts from the essays of a thirteen-year-old adolescent named Carmen. In the late 1960s she and her classmates at a New York City public school described personal experiences for their teacher, Caroline Mirthes. In these passages Carmen discusses her handling of some major challenges.

Carmen's Essays: On Coping

"First of all I want to introduce myself my name is Carmen. Some people call me Smiley. . . ."

"On February 9, 1955 my mother was 17 years old and I was born. They named me Carmen. . . . My father was really sick in his brain he tried to smash my head with a rock but my mother didn't let him then my father started telling everybody that I wasn't his daughter. And he used to go and leave my mother and go out with other women to dances and he used to let me and my mother suffer.

"Once my mother couldn't take it she told him and my father got mad at her so he hit her bad. And she left my house and left me with my grandmother for two years. I was two years old and my grandmother used to treat me like if I was 12 already. I had to take care of myself when I didn't even learn

445

to talk. She was real cruel to me and my father didn't care about me. My cousins and aunts and uncles use to hit me even my neighbors use to hit me. And nobody use to care for me. . . .

"I have a lot of problems in my family but I don't tell anybody what they are. I always try to look happy and sometimes when I can't stand it and I am just about to cry and scream I laugh and laugh. Sometimes I am laughing but I could be angry or sad inside but I still hold myself. But sometimes I feel like getting into a fight so that they will kill me or I will kill somebody. Then maybe I would get out of this world or get out of the problems. . . . Sometimes I think that the only way of getting out of all my problems is killing myself or running away from home and never coming back. But I want to go to school and college. I want to get a good job so that I could help my mother and father live in peace."

Carmen's teacher, Caroline Mirthes writes: "During spring vacation Carmen got into a very bad fight. She saw a group of older girls shoving and hitting her younger brother, and in an attempt to protect him she attacked one of the girls. Six girls jumped her and forced her to the ground. Later her neck stiffened so that she could hardly

bend it and her whole face turned black and blue. When she went into her house bleeding and crying, her mother yelled at her, 'What's the matter with you? How could you let those girls beat you up. You're a chicken.'"

When Carmen returned to school, she presented Ms. Mirthes with the following essay:

"On May 4th 1968 a girl decided to write about her opinions of ways to fight. I don't mean fist fight but I mean fight with your mind. What I mean by that is when you have a problem you don't fix it by fist fighting. Instead you fight the problem not the person who gives you the problem. Now let me give you a problem as an example of fighting with your mind. If you don't fight with your mind you will have to fight with your hands.

"Here is the problem. You have a mother who was raised on a slum like I'm on now a mother who is a 3rd grade drop-out. She doesn't have understanding for nobody not even her own sons and daughters. Yes she fights but with her hands not with her brain because she was brought up on a slum and she couldn't take it she was weak. The people who were in the slums with her destroyed her brains so she wouldn't use them. But in a way, it was her own fault. She

could have fought with her brain.

"Now here goes. The father was brought up in a family who was very strict and they gave him a good education. But, they forgot to give him a heart. He didn't have a heart to care for a family. So you can tell that this is a problem too. . . . How do you fight it? With your fist? You know that with your fist you will lose your figure, face and many other things. And even if you make believe you know how to do it the fist fighters are not always alone. They can gang up on you.

"These examples of problems I gave you are problems to fight but not with your fist. You must fight with your brain and you have got to know how to do it. You can use your brain differently. Like some kids for example they run away from home. Some get married at the age of 13 and you can imagine what kind of life they have. And some other people just separate themselves from life. But that is not the way to fight your fight with your real brain.

"The first thing you should do is try to understand the way other kinds of people live. Then get a good education and then you can have some peace. And if you do that you recognize that you have won the most important fight in the world [1]."

We define *adjustment* as the process of attempting to meet the demands of self and environment. In the course of trying to adjust, Carmen put up a smiling front, fantasized about suicide and homicide, and attempted to solve problems rationally and deliberately. Other human beings, if in Carmen's shoes, might choose different strategies. What makes one person select one approach and not another? And does the same

individual usually employ varied tactics, as Carmen did? We will examine both these issues later. Carmen's adjustment efforts are frequently viewed as "near-heroic." A number of psychologists consider coping an achievement and find that its success can be evaluated. This is another topic that we will discuss. College and a good job could ease Carmen's life considerably, of course. But they would not take care of her adjustment once and for all. Coping is a never-ending effort at mastery. Even the most fortunate human beings confront disappointments, conflicts, frustrations, pressures, and other types of stress daily, though relatively few face the treacherous conditions that Carmen did. We will have more to say about the environment and its role in adjustment also. As you read, keep in mind that our understanding of adjustment relies very heavily on interview and questionnaire studies, clinical observations, and intuition. It has been difficult to study adjustment-related issues neatly.

We turn first to some general matters: What is frustration? What is conflict? Then we look closely at how people cope. Finally, we explore some important challenges that human beings confront during adolescence and adulthood.

FRUSTRATION AND CONFLICT

Frustrations and conflicts make life challenging for everyone.

Frustration

Psychologists use the term *frustration* as a label for (1) an emotional state that appears whenever an obstacle interferes with the satisfaction of a desire, need, goal, expectation, or action; and (2) the obstacle itself. Because people's desires, needs, goals, expectations, and actions differ, a particular set of circumstances may be frustrating for one individual and not another. *Physical, personal,* or *social* barriers can frustrate. School buildings are sometimes viewed as physical barriers that "imprison" youngsters seven hours a day. A poor mathematics background is a personal weakness that could prevent an otherwise capable and motivated student from obtaining an engineering degree on time. Other people may function as social obstacles. A father, for example, might impose his unrealistically high social standards on his daughter. See Figure 14-1.

Conflict

Conflicts arise in situations where two or more incompatible needs, goals, or courses of action compete and cause an organism to feel pulled simultaneously in different directions with an attending sense of discomfort. Since selecting one option in a conflict precludes choosing the other(s) at least temporarily,

FIGURE 14-1 Registering for classes is one of the many frustrations involved in securing a college education. You might consider the paperwork, lineups, delays, cancellations, and reschedulings as physical barriers. [*Martha Cooper.*]

conflicts are sometimes considered frustrations. Conflicts may be classified as largely internal or external, according to the nature of the options that are involved. In an *internal conflict*, the goals lie within the conflicted individual. A person reared by puritanical parents, for example, may feel caught between strong sexual desires and a strict moral code. *External conflicts* arise when the incompatible options lie outside the person in conflict. On a particular night, for instance, you might find it difficult to choose between two activities: say, a concert and a basketball game. Many conflicts contain both internal and external elements.

Conflicts may also be categorized according to the courses of action involved in resolving them: approach-approach, avoidance-avoidance, approach-avoidance, and double or multiple approach-avoidance. Work by Kurt Lewin and Neal Miller has provided information about these types of conflicts [2].

Approach-approach conflicts occur when people are attracted about equally to two goals, needs, objects, or courses of action and carrying out one means abandoning the other. You might have to choose between buying a car or traveling to Europe, attending a party or a movie, or ordering a sundae or a malted. In each situation there are two attractive, competing options. Research suggests that approach-approach conflicts are easier to resolve than any other type. As a person tentatively nears one goal, its attractiveness rises, and the tendency to draw closer increases. At the same time, the appeal of the other goal diminishes and its attraction weakens. Suppose that you are shopping for a new sweater and you find a couple of suitable candidates. As soon as you tentatively select, say, the brown pullover, you are apt to emphasize its advantages: "warm" "goes with many outfits," and "less expensive." Consequently, the appeal of the brown sweater escalates, the competition loses ground, and the conflict ends. You will generally resolve such approach-approach conflicts rather easily, perhaps because they always result in something pleasant and the alternatives can

frequently be achieved in turn. Returning to our example, you may be able to purchase a second handsome sweater next month.

When a person is simultaneously repelled by two goals, objects, or courses of action and obliged to select one, psychologists label the dilemma an *avoidance-avoidance conflict*. A convicted shoplifter may have to choose several days in jail or a $100 fine. A pregnant teenager may have to bear a child out of wedlock or submit to an abortion. Research shows that as organisms approach an unattractive choice, it becomes more repellent, and the tendency to avoid it increases in strength. Typically, when people embark on one of the undesirable options in an avoidance-avoidance conflict, they find it increasingly repugnant and change directions. As they confront the second option, it too becomes unpleasant, and they change direction again. Avoidance-avoidance conflicts tend to be more difficult to resolve than approach-approach conflicts. People frequently waver between two unpleasant alternatives or try to avoid the conflict altogether. The shoplifter in our example might skip town or withdraw into fantasies.

When a person is simultaneously attracted to and repelled by one option—a goal, need, object, or course of action—we have an *approach-avoidance conflict*. One option, in other words, has a bittersweet quality. An otherwise appealing career may require a lot of education. A luxurious car is costly. A luscious dessert is fattening. Speaking up about a controversial issue may satisfy one's conscience but alienate the powers that be. Intimacy with another person produces vulnerability. *Double approach-avoidance conflicts* involve two goals, each having good and bad points. A young woman, for instance, may have to choose between working and attending college. The only available job, perhaps housecleaning, is dull but will provide income. College will qualify the woman for a meaningful career. But an education is expensive and time-consuming. Approach-avoidance and double approach-avoidance conflicts are usually difficult to resolve. They tend to generate a great deal of discomfort. People are apt to waver back and forth between the options—sometimes indefinitely.

Real-life conflicts do not always fit neatly into one of these categories. Often human beings face more than two choices. And, when examined closely, all options in a conflict appear to entail both positive and negative consequences. At the very least, the selection of any positive option limits other choices, while the adoption of any negative option relieves the discomfort of the conflict itself. So, many—probably even most—real conflicts can be considered *multiple approach-avoidance conflicts*, those between two or more goals where each choice is partly positive and partly negative.

Research suggests that several factors influence decision making in conflict situations. The *strength of the motives* aroused by the options is important. Goals that are aroused by strong motives exert more pull than those that are excited by weak motives. In the case of a boy who cannot decide whether to study or socialize, motives for achievement and affiliation clash. The relative strength of the child's motives will partially determine the outcome. *Distance in time and space* from the options is a second powerful contributor to decision making. The tendency to approach or avoid particular options increases with proximity (closeness). An attractive goal—say, attending a picnic—becomes more compelling as the date of the outing approaches. A dreaded option, such as giving a speech, becomes more repulsive as "zero hour" nears. When options are relatively distant, approach and avoidance tendencies tend to be weak. *Expectations* about options in a conflict also affect the outcome. Individuals consider whether the varied choices are really satisfying. The boy who cannot decide whether to study or socialize may think that the companionship of his acquaintances is worthless. Alternatively, he may conclude that studying for the exam is futile because it won't affect his C average. ▲

COPING WITH FRUSTRATION, CONFLICT, AND OTHER STRESSES

Frustration, conflict, and other stresses are associated with unpleasant emotional states, such as anxiety and anger. When people *cope*, they respond in a way that allows them to avoid, escape, or reduce their distress and/or handle the particular problem. Psychologist Richard Lazarus has been studying how people cope for many years. As Lazarus sees it, there is an orderly pattern. Human beings continually *appraise*, or assess, moment-to-moment interactions with the environment. Events that appear challenging or threatening (potentially harmful) are evaluated further. We ask such question as "What kind of

---

▲ **USING PSYCHOLOGY**

1. Think of several recent instances of physical, personal, and social frustrations. Would the same experiences be frustrating to your mother? Your father? A friend?

2. Give personal examples of (*a*) a largely internal conflict and (*b*) a largely external conflict.

3. Generate two examples of each of these types of conflicts: approach-approach, avoidance-avoidance, approach-avoidance, multiple approach-avoidance.

4. Choose a conflict that occurred recently. Analyze the factors that influenced its resolution (including the strength of the motives involved, distance from the options, and expectations about the options).

action is called for?" and "What resources are currently available?" As new information accumulates, we reassess the situation. Whether we feel alarmed at all and to what extent depend on the estimate of our threat-managing capacities. This judgment is influenced by the situation, past experiences, and personal characteristics. Once we have evaluated an event, we must decide what to do. Such decisions may be made consciously or without much awareness [3].

We explore common behavioral and cognitive tactics that people use as they cope with stress. Though we describe each one individually, keep in mind that adjustment is a complex, changing, ongoing process that requires many responses. Each coping tactic that we discuss might best be considered a component in an overall strategy. After examining the various tactics, we look at what is currently known about their consequences and determinants.

Behavioral Strategies for Coping

Sometimes people adjust by acting—by deliberate problem solving, aggression, regression, withdrawal, and/or escape.

Deliberate problem solving   Human beings often view conflicts, frustrations, and the like as problems to be solved. They evaluate the situation rationally and decide upon appropriate measures. Then they make direct preparations to strengthen their resources and reduce the potential harm. Carmen advocated this approach to life. Many students use this tactic to handle tests. Graduate students confronting comprehensive doctoral examinations were observed by social scientist David Mechanic. As the exams drew near, Mechanic found that most of the students coped with this stress by a deliberate problem-solving strategy. They studied more intensively, reduced recreational activities, modified unrealistic study plans, and devoted less effort to course work and more to preparations for the test [4].

Aggression   As we saw in Chapter 11, frustration and other stresses often lead to anger and aggression. Aggression is rarely, if ever, a productive coping response. As

FIGURE 14-2   Child abuse is a complex, multiply determined problem that appears to be growing in magnitude in the United States. In the late 1970s, experts estimated that more than 2 million American children were at risk for serious physical injuries in a single year. Behavioral scientists have profiled the abusing parent. They believe that social stresses contribute significantly to child abuse. Violence toward youngsters is especially likely in tension-ridden, exceedingly poor (under $6,000 per year) families where the man is employed part-time or unemployed. Abusive parents are likely to hold unrealistic expectations about children's capabilities. They tend to commit injurious acts when angered. The abusive adult comes from a background which taught the use of aggression as a major child-rearing tactic. The cultural milieu sanctions physical punishment. The abusive family tends to be socially isolated—cut off from outside resources that might provide emotional support. Often one child—perhaps a hyperactive, difficult youngster who is viewed as particularly aggravating—is targeted [108]. [*Wide World Photos.*]

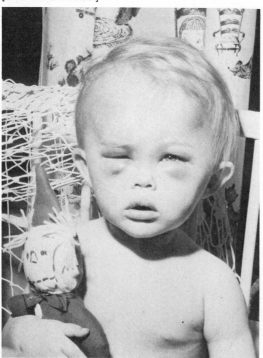

Carmen noted, it can lead to tragic consequences. (See Figure 14-2.) When a threat is vague, hard to pinpoint, powerful, or dangerous, people sometimes *displace* their aggression and attack convenient targets. *Scapegoating*—blaming innocent victims for one's troubles and aggressing against them— is a common example of this practice. It may occur on a personal level. After a humiliating day, one spouse may attack the other with trivial provocation. Scapegoating may take place on a national level too—often with catastrophic results. During the 1930s, at a time of economic stagnation and political tension in Germany, Hitler established Jews as scapegoats for the entire country. In the United States, blacks and Hispanic groups have frequently been blamed for social problems and have borne the brunt of displaced aggression. In Chapter 17 we discuss research suggesting that prejudice may be intensified by frustration.

Regression Sometimes people confront stresses by returning to modes of behavior that are characteristic of younger ages. Children who haven't sucked their thumbs or wet their beds in years commonly react to "crises," such as the birth of a new baby, with these immature responses. Regression may be employed because it offers an escape, returning to past conditions of love and security. Or, the person who uses regression may not have learned more effective responses to the problem and/or may be trying deliberately to attract attention. A classic study by psychologists Roger Barker, Tamara Dembo, and Kurt Lewin showed that regression is a common response to frustration—at least in children. For the Barker-Dembo-Lewin experiment, youngsters came, one at a time, to a room where they found broken and incomplete toys to play with. The children amused themselves as psychologists behind a one-way mirror rated the constructiveness of their behavior. The same youngsters returned to the playroom later for a second session. This time each one was given access to some unusually attractive toys, including a make-believe lake and a large doll's house. After a brief period, a wire room divider was placed so that the child could see the desirable toys but could not play with them (see Figure 14-3). The youngsters were asked to play once again with the original, less desirable toys. Under these frustrating circumstances, the subjects behaved more roughly, destructively, and immaturely than during the initial session; they played at a level characteristic of children about a year and a half younger [5].

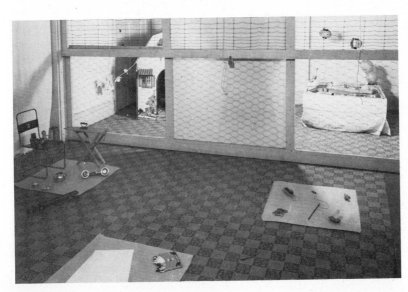

FIGURE 14-3 In the classic Barker-Dembo-Lewin experiment, frustration was generated by having children play in a room (foreground) where they could see but not reach highly desirable toys. [*The University of Iowa Archives.*]

Withdrawal Withdrawal is a common response to threat. When people withdraw, they choose *not* to act. Apathy and depression often accompany this behavior. During the early part of World War II, a physician observed this pattern in fellow American POWs:

Most [prisoners] experienced bouts of apathy or depression. These ranged from slight to prolonged deep depressions where there was a loss of interest in living and lack of willingness or ability to marshal the powers of will necessary to combat disease. An ever-present sign of fatal withdrawal occurred three to four days before death when the man pulled his covers up over his head and lay passive, quiet, and refusing food [6].

The same type of detachment, indifference, and listlessness was noted in Jewish concentration camp victims.

Escape When people feel overwhelmed by a stress, they sometimes try to escape. They may simply leave the situation bodily. Or they may use a less direct method. *Repetitive stereotyped* (or *fixed*) *behavior*, for example, can divert attention from a threat and provide a temporary means of mental escape. Consider the young mother who feels exasperated by her children from time to time but finds the emotion unacceptable. To escape the feeling, she may count cans in the pantry or cracks on the ceiling or whatever else is in sight. Alcohol, heroin, barbiturates, amphetamines, and other chemical substances offer another partial escape route. While drug use is common in our culture, and moderate use in social situations is not associated with adjustment problems, excessive use is [7]. Many heavy drug users see these substances as escapes. "Heroin" in the words of one addict, "is like a finance plan which allows you to consolidate all of your problems into one—Junk! and then the injection in your arm makes them all go away [8]." The incidence of drug dependency is particularly high in city ghettos among young residents who long to escape the bleakness of poverty [9]. We examine alcoholism in some detail.

Alcoholism and Adjustment

Alcoholism, which we define as drinking that impairs adjustment to life, affects an estimated 4 percent of Amerian adults [10]. Its rate is increasing among adolescents. One out of every four high school students now drinks moderately to heavily [11]. Alcohol damages the central nervous system and liver [12] and increases vulnerability to traffic accidents and to a number of serious diseases including heart attacks, cancer, and cirrhosis of the liver. Alcoholism is considered the third major cause of death in the United States [13].

A classic interview study of 2,000 alcoholics by the late E. M. Jellinek suggests that many alcoholics pass through four definite stages, as the problem develops over a time period ranging from several months to several years [14].

1. *Prealcoholic phases.* Potential alcoholics usually begin drinking in conventional social situations. They say that liquor brings relief from tension. Even a relatively small amount of alcohol functions as a *depressant*. It inhibits higher brain centers, reducing their control over lower ones. Paradoxically, people *feel stimulated* because they are freed from inhibitions. Alcohol may also dull perceptions of pain and bring pleasant sensations of warmth and well-being. Eventually drinkers begin using alcohol almost daily, presumably to escape tension.

2. *Early alcoholic phase.* This stage begins almost imperceptibly as alcoholics find that they need to consume more liquor to achieve the desired effects. At this time, spells of amnesia (memory loss), or *blackouts*, become frequent during or immediately following even moderate drinking. Alcoholics are increasingly preoccupied with liquor and worry about getting their next drink. During this period they may begin to stockpile and hide alcohol. While many early alcoholics are troubled about their drinking problem, most feel reluctant to discuss their concern.

3. *True alcoholic phase.* At this point, alcoholics lose control over their drinking. Any liquor at all leads to continued intake until sickness or intoxication occurs. Many drinkers try to justify their behavior. Some attempt to control the problem by changing drinking-related habits—switching from whiskey to wine, for instance. During this stage alcoholics begin withdrawing from jobs, families, and friends. They tend to neglect nutrition and health. They may express grandiose feelings and behave aggressively.

4. *Complete alcohol addiction.* As alcoholics settle into a chronic pattern, they lose their tolerance for liquor. Half the previous allotment will send them into a stupor. At this stage, drinkers often go on prolonged sprees, imbibing alcohol for days at a time until total exhaustion. Fears become persistent. For the first time, drinkers experience the *DTs*, or *delirium tremens*. This reaction may appear after a prolonged bout, during a period of abstinence, or together with an infection or head injury. Typical-

ly, the DTs include the responses of disorientation for time and place, vivid hallucinations (especially of snakes, rats, and roaches), acute fears of these hallucinations, extreme suggestibility, tremors, perspiration, fever, and a rapid, weak heartbeat. But nothing keeps the alcoholic from the bottle for long, and it takes less and less alcohol to produce intoxication.

Research suggests that there are many determinants of alcoholism [15]. The culture influences the initial decision to drink or abstain. While alcohol use occurs in all socioeconomic classes, social environment and life-style seem to contribute to the amount of liquor people consume. See Figure 14-4. Heavy drinking in the United States is more frequent among those who drink in bars (typically poor, working-class men with unstable

employment histories), young unmarried individuals, and blacks—human beings who may face more than an average amount of tension. Alcoholics perceive a great many stresses in their lives. But it is not certain that these troubles precede the dependency, and it is not clear that alcoholics face more stresses than nonalcoholics from comparable backgrounds. Drinkers claim that they use liquor for tension reduction. Careful studies show, however, that alcoholics report more anxiety and depression *following* alcohol consumption than they report beforehand [16]. It is possible, then, that the reputed tension-reducing effects of alcohol occur initially before the dependency develops or that they do not exist at all. So far, there is no conclusive evidence linking alcoholism with any *specific* conflicts, problems, or personality

FIGURE 14-4 While alcoholism occurs at all levels in our society, it tends to be particularly common among certain human groupings. Social customs appear to contribute significantly to the condition. When strong traditions limit drinking to specific times and places, alcoholism tends to be relatively rare. Among orthodox Jews, one group with a low rate of alcoholism, the use of liquor is reserved for religious ceremonies. Other social practices are associated with low alcoholism rates: drinking only around other people, drinking only with meals, and drinking only moderate quantities at a time. When parents drink in moderation, children are likely to follow suit. Certain values and attitudes are also linked with low alcoholism rates: thinking of drink as neither sinful, virtuous, nor proof of adult status or manliness; considering intoxication neither stylish, comical, or even tolerable; and finding abstinence acceptable [109]. [*Gilles Paress/Magnum; Inge Morath/Magnum.*]

traits, though a very large number of such relationships have been hypothesized. The role of physiological mechanisms is also uncertain. Some scientists believe that alcoholics possess a genetic predisposition to develop the problem. The existence of an hereditary propensity could help explain why only some heavy drinkers become dependent. Support for a genetic contribution to alcoholism comes from adoptive studies (Chapter 3). The presence of alcoholism in biological parents predicts later alcoholism far better than does the presence of this disorder in adoptive parents [17].

In sum, alcoholism is a complex phenomenon. It seems to develop, at least initially, as a response to frustration, conflict, anxiety, and depression in physiologically susceptible persons whose culture and background make this avenue of escape apparent and appealing.

Cognitive Strategies for Coping

As we sit safe and comfortable in the midst of plenty, we can conjure up catastrophic scenes and make ourselves miserable. Similarly, our thoughts can make the grimmest of circumstances endurable. This second power underlies a number of *cognitive strategies*, often called *defense mechanisms*, which help people handle conflicts, frustrations, and other stresses. The defense mechanism concept came from Sigmund Freud. He theorized that to protect themselves, people used mental tactics unconsciously to falsify and distort threatening experiences, impulses, conflicts, and ideas. Most information about cognitive strategies comes from clinical observations. The devices are difficult (in some cases, impossible) to study by experimental procedures. Self-deception itself is hard to demonstrate in the laboratory [18]. While many psychologists believe in the existence of these mechanisms, there are numerous disagreements: Are the strategies deliberate or automatic, as Freud specified? Why do individuals use different devices? What do the tactics accomplish? Are they helpful or damaging in the long run? We describe seven cognitive mechanisms. Note that the specific strategies are very similar and that they always involve some degree of self-deception.

Repression *Repression* is defined as the exclusion of anxiety-arousing motives, ideas, conflicts, memories, and the like from awareness. When repression is working, the banished material does not enter consciousness, although it does influence behavior. Certain types of amnesia are considered evidence for the existence of repression. A soldier, for example, who saw a friend die may wander back to his squadron. There he may be unable to describe where he has been or what has happened. Yet he may show unmistakable signs of profound distress. Through the use of techniques, such as hypnosis, to probe the unconscious, the soldier may subsequently recall the incident and come to terms with it.

Repression may occur under less traumatic circumstances as well. Freud attributed forgetting the names of anxiety-arousing people and places (the name, for instance, of a rival lover) to repression. He believed that people repress dreams since they represent unconscious anxiety-arousing wishes. So far, behavioral scientists have not been successful in demonstrating conclusively the existence of repression either in dreams or under any other circumstances [19]. Some repression-like phenomena have been verified. *Suppression*, or *cognitive avoidance* (deliberately putting material out of mind), is often observed in the laboratory. It is also known that many people emphasize the positive aspects of life. There is evidence, for instance, that human beings tend to (1) take longer to recognize unpleasant stimuli than pleasant ones, (2) avoid looking at distressing pictures if possible, (3) communicate good news more frequently than bad, (4) memorize and retrieve positive items more accurately than negative ones, and (5) overestimate the importance of happy events and underestimate the impact of unhappy ones. Psychologist Matthew Erdelyi hypothesizes that cognitive processes selectively favor positive over neutral and negative information during both perception and memory. This phenomenon, sometimes called the *Pollyanna principle* (after a fictional heroine who saw goodness even in the most miserable of circumstances), may be interpreted as defensive. But it is not well understood [20].

Denial of reality   When people *deny reality*, they ignore or refuse to acknowledge the existence of unpleasant experiences (of which they are fully aware) to protect themselves. Denial, as it is usually abbreviated, always involves self-deception. A great deal of research, some of which we examine later, suggests that this strategy is a common one. Unwanted children might insist that parents really love them. An ambitious student might refuse to face an intellectual shortcoming. The following report describes how a female burn victim used denial to make her last few weeks more peaceful.

Within a few days [the patient] developed the attitude that she was not seriously ill at all, but practically well. She then recalled having been afraid of dying immediately after her injury, particularly when she first went to the operating room, but said that when she had survived this ordeal she knew that she would be all right; she felt there was no doubt that she was now practically well, that she would require little further care and would soon be back to a normal family life. . . . She felt that she would be sufficiently improved in a few days so that she would be able to go home and take care of her children. The fact that this patient made such statements calmly and deliberately while she lay helplessly on a Stryker frame—a charred remnant of a woman—had a powerful impact on all observers. [21]

Fantasy   People often "achieve" goals and escape unpleasant, anxiety-arousing, and frustrating events by fantasizing about what might have been. Human beings who daydream a great deal sometimes find their own creations more appealing than reality and withdraw from an active life. In Chapter 15 we see that this is a characteristic feature of schizophrenia. But, in moderation and under conscious control, fantasy appears to be a healthy coping device. Research by Leonard Giambra suggests that normal adults daydream more frequently about solving problems than about sex, achievement, heroism, or other topics. Women report more daytime fantasies than men [22]. Positive daydreams—of relaxing settings such as a beach and of situations that enhance self-esteem—can sometimes reduce the unhappiness accompanying a severe depression [23]. Among normal adults and children, Jerome Singer has found, frequent fantasizing is associated with creativity, flexibility, the capacity to concentrate, and the inhibition of aggression. An active imagination helps in integrating experiences and aids memory. It allows people to "try out" new responses in their heads instead of acting impulsively [24]. Because fantasizing appears to be such a helpful strategy, a number of psychologists have established fantasy training programs for young children. Eli Saltz and his associates taught disadvantaged youngsters in Detroit to play more imaginatively. Subsequently, these children made gains on tests, suggesting that they had acquired more self-control, a longer attention span, and a greater ability to interact with others and to communicate [25].

Rationalization   Rationalization often involves thinking up socially acceptable reasons for behavior to hide the truth from oneself. A boy might tell himself, "I'd have passed that test if the teacher hadn't asked such dumb questions," instead of admitting poor preparation. The executive who is habitually late may blame a busy schedule rather than lack of consideration for others. Rationalization also occurs when people deceive themselves by pretending that a bad situation is really good (the "sweet lemon strategy") or that a good one is really bad (the "sour grapes strategy"). A poor person might adopt the position that poverty is a blessing and wealth makes human beings miserable. Tragedy and suffering may be rationalized as having a worthy purpose. Writing in *Creative Divorce*, Mel Krantzler rationalized, "Through a painful emotional crisis, I have become a happier and stronger person than I was before [26]." Cognitive dissonance (Chapter 10) often results in rationalization.

Intellectualization When people use the device *intellectualization*, they deal with situations that would ordinarily generate strong feelings in a detached, analytic, intellectual way. In other words, they treat potentially stressful experiences as events to study or be curious about, to avoid becoming emotionally involved. Intellectualization enables human beings to reduce the impact of distressing incidents and enhances the ability to respond objectively and dispassionately. A dead body at an autopsy, which tends to arouse a medical student's anxiety, might be treated as an impersonal "learning aid." Physicians and nurses appear to control their distress while working with seriously ill patients by intellectualizing the suffering [27]. Emotional involvement, in this case, would probably interfere with providing good health care. In the following passage a London prostitute describes how she used intellectualization to isolate herself from professional duties:

The act of sex I could go through because I hardly seemed to be taking part in it. It was merely something happening to me, while my mind drifted inconsequentially away. Indeed, it was scarcely happening to me; it was happening to something lying on a bed that had a vague connection with me, while I was calculating whether I could afford a new coat or impatiently counting sheep jumping over a gate. [28]

Reaction formation When people conceal a real motive or emotion from themselves (through repression or suppression) and express the opposite one by attitudes and behavior, they are using *reaction formation*. This device allows an individual to avoid the anxiety associated with having to face disliked personal characteristics. Hatred is sometimes disguised by an exaggerated display of love, a strong sex drive by prudery, and hostility by kindness. The "humane" antivivisectionist who sent the following letter to a research psychiatrist postures as compassionate but appears quite brutal. (An antivivisectionist is a person who opposes medical experiments on animals.)

I read [a magazine article] on your work on alcoholism. . . . I am surprised that anyone who is as well educated as you must be to hold the position that you do would stoop to such a depth as to torture helpless little cats in the pursuit of a cure for alcoholics. . . . A drunkard does not want to be cured—a drunkard is just a weak-minded idiot who belongs in the gutter and should be left there. Instead of torturing helpless little cats why not torture the drunks or better still exert your would-be noble effort toward getting a bill passed to *exterminate* the drunks. . . .

My greatest wish is that you have brought home to you a torture that will be a thousand fold greater than what you have, and are doing to the little animals. . . . No punishment is too great for you and I hope I live to read about your mangled body and long suffering before you finally die—and I'll laugh long and loud. [29]

Projection People who use projection are quick to notice and magnify personal characteristics in others that they don't like and don't acknowledge in themselves. The strategy is thought to reduce anxiety due to facing threatening personal characteristics. Once again, either repression or suppression appears to be involved. Hostile individuals who don't perceive their own anger may be quick to note that trait in others. Human beings who cannot face their own sexuality sometimes see others as "oversexed." Projection can be demonstrated under controlled laboratory conditions [30]. ▲

Consequences of Coping Strategies

Can coping mechanisms reduce anxiety? Which devices lead to a good adjustment? We consider these issues.

Can coping strategies reduce anxiety Freud believed that defense mechanisms help people reduce anxiety as they face threatening information. Psychologist Richard Lazarus and his coworkers have studied the anxiety-reducing effects of denial in the laboratory. In an early investigation, they showed films to male college students. One movie was rather ordinary. The other showed subincision rites in a primitive Australian culture. During subincision rites, which mark the transition from adolescence to manhood, male youths are held down by several men and submitted to a painful operation. The penis is stretched and cut on the underside with a sharpened flintstone. As research participants watched the films, heart rate and skin conductance were monitored as indices of emotion. Afterward, subjects described their reactions. (Some are shown in Table 14-1.) Even though many men denied being anxious (as you can see), they all displayed marked physiological reactions. In this instance, then, denial did not appear to reduce the physical signs of anxiety [31]. In subsequent research, Lazarus and his colleagues demonstrated that defense mechanisms could diminish tension. They showed the same subincision film with three sound tracks. One emphasized the painful and threatening aspects of the operation. The second presented what was happening in a detached intellectual way. The third denied that the operation produced discomfort and stressed the social benefits. A fourth group of subjects saw the film without any sound track. The heart rates and skin conductance of the research participants were greatest when suffering was emphasized. They were lowest when the sound tracks intellectualized or denied the painfulness of the rites [32]. Denial can also reduce anxiety in real life. Physicians

at the Walter Reed Army Medical Center observed mothers and fathers of children with fatal illnesses. Some parents persistently refused to face the fact that their youngsters were dying. Others coped in different ways. Mean urinary 17-hydroxycorticosteroid excretion rates (an indicator of stress) were lower in the denying parents than in those using other strategies [33]. Apparently, denial helped keep anxiety under control. In sum, at least certain cognitive defense mechanisms—notably denial and intellectualization—can diminish the physiological distress associated with anxiety. But they do not consistently alleviate tension in all situations.

Which coping mechanisms lead to a good adjustment? Behavioral scientists can provide only a tentative answer to this question. The response depends inevitably on

TABLE 14-1 Reactions of Six Experimental Subjects to a Stressful Film

Subject	Statement
2	"God, I'm shocked! and nauseated. It made me sick."
3	"I was completely disgusted to the point of almost being ill."
5	"Wished I had never seen it for now I feel extremely tense and nervous."
8	"At first I was curious, then I became very interested in what was going on."
9	"I was bored with the film and felt that watching it was a complete waste of time."
11	"The film was unusual, but it didn't bother me a bit."

Source: Adapted from Lazarus, R. S. *Patterns of adjustment and human effectiveness.* New York: McGraw-Hill, 1969. P. 73.

judgments about what constitutes a good adjustment. Strategies that lead to "inner harmony," for example, may not lead to "creativity" or "efficiency." We examine several attempts to identify the coping mechanisms that lead to some type of good adjustment.

Psychologist Lois Murphy and her colleagues studied how youngsters handle different challenges and pressures throughout childhood. They made observations in controlled natural settings, such as during psychological testings. In addition, they examined behavioral observations recorded during real-life stresses, such as at hospitals and funerals. Murphy and her coworkers found that problem-solving attitudes and an active mastery orientation toward life problems were correlated with various ratings of the capacity to cope with challenges, frustrations, threats, and the like. Characteristics that are related to a problem-solving orientation—including insightfulness, curiosity, attention to detail, and ability to accept substitutes—were linked to a successful adjustment too [34]. Other researchers report similar findings [35].

A problem-solving approach leads to flexible behavior. New challenges demand new solutions. Many psychologists consider flexibility in employing defense mechanisms mandatory. There is convincing evidence for this position. Several behavioral scientists have found, for instance, that people recover more smoothly and rapidly from surgery when they use *avoidant strategies* (ignoring, denying, or evading the problem in some fashion) than attentive or *vigilant* ones [36]. Apparently, when almost nothing constructive can be done, threats are best avoided in some way. Learning about surgical details and focusing on pain probably magnify the discomforts and anxieties. On the other hand, you may recall from Chapter 11, advance preparation for surgery (accurate *general* expectations) aids recuperation. Attentive strategies seem to be helpful under many circumstances. Sailors in the Israeli navy who coped with seasickness in an active, purposive, vigilant manner, for example, were more successful

crewmen than sailors who employed avoidant tactics [37]. To decide what strategy is preferable, then, the specific context and the positive and negative consequences of using a particular maneuver must be examined. Suppression, denial, fantasy, and the like can keep people from being overwhelmed when a threat is unavoidable. When a situation can be mastered or controlled, cognitive mechanisms alone may lead to inaction, which is usually unproductive. Psychologists need more studies of how well-adjusted people cope in real life. Richard Lazarus, who has begun such investigations, believes that successful copers probably use some combination of tactics, including a lot of problem solving and positive thinking and a little self-deception (denial and other avoidant strategies) [38].

Successful adaptation may depend not only on *which* coping devices are used but also on *how* the devices are used. Psychologist Norma Haan believes that similar maneuvers can be used constructively or destructively. She differentiates defense mechanisms from coping strategies. Defense mechanisms such as repression, in Haan's view, tend to be unproductive: they are rigid, past-oriented, distorting of the present, and deceitful. Haan has assigned to each defense mechanism a coping strategy counterpart that she considers healthy, flexible, future-oriented, reality-based, open, and orderly. For example, she considers suppression, which deliberately keeps stressful material temporarily from entering awareness, the coping strategy counterpart of repression. Similarly, she considers playfulness, returning to early ways of thinking and behaving intentionally, the coping strategy counterpart of regression, which she catalogs as a defense mechanism [39].

Determinants of Coping Strategies

Why do people handle challenges and stresses in different ways? We describe how early experiences, cultural beliefs and practices, and cognitive level influence how people adjust.

Childhood events may affect coping behavior in various ways. Parents are powerful models. No matter how much they preach, "Do what I say, not what I do," children often imitate what they observe. At the same time, parents probably punish and reward specific coping styles without realizing they're doing so. If youngsters are generally ignored or abused when discussing negative events, they probably learn to avoid talking about, and perhaps thinking about, unpleasant experiences. When individuals are encouraged to discuss troubles, they're more likely to face up to problems later on. Laboratory studies show that the use of a particular type of coping maneuver can be increased or decreased by reinforcement or punishment [40]. There is also evidence that we, as youngsters, may learn, or fail to learn, to surmount obstacles. The presence of challenges, frustrations, and dissatisfactions *and* parental support in handling these stressors are positively associated with later effectivenss in coping [41]. Psychologist Martin Seligman suggests that when individuals confront a great many threats that cannot be controlled, they learn to believe that they have no control. Accordingly, they respond to later problems by withdrawing, giving up, and/or feeling depressed [42]. Many years ago, psychologists Mary Keister and Ruth Updegraff showed that children can be actively taught to cope constructively. They devised a training program for youngsters who reacted to the frustration of failure by crying, giving up, depending on others, or behaving aggressively. Keister's and Updegraff's pupils were presented with a series of increasingly more challenging tasks and encouraged to persist on each one until they mastered it. At the end of the program, the children were able to confront relatively difficult problems adaptively [43].

Coping styles depend to some extent on the standards and customs of one's culture. Joan Ablon, a medical anthropologist, found support for this notion as she studied how people in a Samoan village handled a disastrous church fire that killed seventeen and injured seventy people. Five years after the catastrophe, Ablon interviewed the survivors, their relatives, physicians, and others who had been in close contact with the victims. The reports suggested that the Samoans had responded stoically to death, pain, and lasting disfigurement. No one had required medication for shock or grief. The patients suffered in silence. When someone died, relatives left quietly after praying. The Samoans, Ablon explains, appear to be closely knit, deeply religious, family-oriented individuals. Because social, family, and religious ties provide emotional supports, the villagers may not have experienced the severe psychological problems that are sometimes associated with disasters [44]. The importance of social supports during coping has been affirmed repeatedly in recent investigations. The Amish, for instance, seem to be able to adjust to death more easily than most other Americans—in part because of their supportive social traditions [45]. Israeli soldiers who have stable interpersonal contacts at home, work, and/or school recover from combat exhaustion more quickly than others [46]. Isolation from people, on the other hand, appears to aggravate stress and to increase the probability of stress-related diseases [47].

Cognitive level influences coping strategies too. Psychologist Walter Mischel and his coworkers find a clear developmental progression in knowledge about strategies for handling life problems. Some of their research focuses on how children delay the gratification of an immediate desire. In laboratory tests, they typically confront youngsters with a choice between a small treat now or a better or larger one later. The delay intervals vary. So does what goes on during the delay. To gain insights into the coping process, the behavioral scientists use interviews and monitor activity choices for the waiting interval. Mischel and his colleagues have found that children of preschool age rarely understand what strategies are effective for helping them delay gratification. Frequently, in fact, these youngsters focus on the immediate lesser reward in ways that intensify their frustration and decrease their ability to wait. By the first grade many children can cope effectively with the situation. They may think about the immediate reward in negative terms, remind themselves about the rules of the game, or engage in distracting activities or thoughts. By the age of eleven or so, many children describe elaborate, detailed plans that they use to control their own behavior [48]. Apparently, growing cognitive competence influences the ability to cope effectively. ▲

ARE THERE ADJUSTMENT STAGES THROUGHOUT THE LIFE CYCLE?

You may recall that Erik Erikson (Chapter 13) divided life into stages. He believed that people face an important conflict during each stage that helps shape their mental health. Four crises occur during adolescence. and adulthood, the period of time that we focus on now: first, identity versus role diffusion; later, intimacy versus isolation; then, generativity (involvement in the world and with future generations) versus self-absorption; and finally, integrity (roughly, acceptance of life) versus despair. Recently, Erikson has expanded his analysis, and other investigators have described a variety of different adult stages [49]. Many psychologists question whether people, especially adults, move through definite, age-linked *adjustment stages*, each one characterized by distinct tasks and by specific outcomes that influence coping at the next "step." Among the most important reasons for skepticism are the following:

1. Development seems to be more continuous during adulthood than during childhood. Preoccupations, conflicts, and challenges occur and recur. Changes tend to be gradual. Individual adults often display quite similar coping responses throughout life. Bernice Neugarten, a University of Chicago psychologist who has specialized in the study of adulthood, conducted a major longitudinal investigation which supports this position. (A *longitudinal investigation* is a study of the same individuals at two or more points in time.) Neugarten and her colleagues interviewed and tested 700 men and women between the ages of forty and ninety over a seven-year period. They found that despite changes in role and status, the subjects were quite consistent over time in adaptive strategies, cognitive abilities, and interpersonal styles [50].

2. The challenges that adults—even in a single culture—face are not universal ones. Because social customs have changed radically in recent years, young Americans growing up today will confront different challenges from those of their parents. Increasingly, people tend to marry at a later age and often more than once, pursue education throughout the life cycle, tackle several careers, look forward to early retirement, and value leisure and personal fulfillment greatly—frequently above work.

3. Individual differences grow with accumulating experiences, so broad generalizations become less appropriate.

We examine common adjustment-related challenges in our culture at different points in the life cycle: during adolescence, young adulthood (emphasizing work and marital adjustment), and middle and old age.

ADJUSTMENT DURING ADOLESCENCE

During *adolescence*, a period of development that extends from approximately ages thirteen to eighteen, people face a number of challenges. The younger adolescent is con-

---

▲ **USING PSYCHOLOGY**

1. Question a friend who seems especially well adjusted about the coping strategies he or she used to handle several recent disappointments. Does the individual cope in a deliberate reality-oriented way? Is the person flexible? Do your findings agree with those reported in the text?

2. Try to identify the factors that influence your own coping strategies. Consider early experiences and cultural beliefs and practices. Do expectations about particular situations affect your choice of coping strategies?

fronted with rapid changes in height and bodily dimensions, sexual maturation, new cognitive capabilities, and different demands and expectations from family, friends, and community. The older adolescent is forging an identity (as described in Chapter 13). Is adolescence usually a time of turmoil? What sorts of problems are likely? How do parents and peers influence adjustment? We explore these questions briefly.

Contrary to popular stereotypes, research shows that adolescence is not necessarily a disruptive period of life. The pre–high school years (ages twelve to fourteen) seem to be the most stormy. These conclusions are supported by the research of psychologists Daniel and Judith Offer and others. The Offers studied middle-class, Midwestern boys and their families intensively during the youngsters' adolescent years. The subjects were classified in three adjustment categories. Almost 25 percent of the boys fit the *continuous growth* pattern. They were realistic in self-image, displayed a sense of humor, and appeared to be relatively happy. About 35 percent of the subjects were characterized as showing a *surgent growth* pattern. During early adolescence, these boys had greater difficulties than the continuous growth research participants in dealing with unexpected stresses. Surgent growth subjects were likely to be unusually angry and defensive during the early crises. Overall, the surgent growth youngsters appeared to be reasonably well adjusted and successful at handling life strains. Roughly 20 percent of the boys displayed a *tumultuous growth* pattern. They experienced intense emotional upheavals and often required counseling. The remaining 20 percent of the Offers' subjects could not be classified neatly, though they resembled youths in the continuous and surgent growth groups more closely than those in the tumultuous growth category [51]. Additional surveys support the idea that relatively few adolescents experience violent mood swings and total loss of self-control [52].

Early in development young boys tend to display more behavioral problems in school and at home than young girls do. Near puberty (sexual maturity) females begin to show many disturbances. In terms of adjustment-related difficulties, females begin catching up with, and may even surpass, males [53]. To learn more about adolescent troubles, psychologists Anne Locksley and Elizabeth Douvan surveyed a random sample of Midwestern urban, lower-middle-class, predominantly Caucasian high school students during the mid-1970s. Boys reported significantly higher degrees of aggression and resentment than girls did. Girls reported significantly higher amounts of tension and psychosomatic symptoms. Locksley and Douvan found evidence that females tend to select inappropriately modest educational and occupational choices. They also report less self-esteem than boys do [54].

How can we account for a relatively good or poor adjustment during adolescence? We consider two major influences: parents and peers. Research by many investigators, including Diana Baumrind and Glen Elder, suggests that parental styles significantly influence the adjustments of male adolescents. *Authoritative* parents involve children in decision making and family affairs. They give reasons for requests. They provide appropriate gradual experiences in assuming independence. Still, they retain ultimate responsibility. The sons of authoritative parents tend to be self-confident, independent, high in self-esteem, and on good terms with their families. *Authoritarian* parents favor punitive, forceful tactics when conflicts arise. They insist on obedience. At the other extreme, *laissez faire* parents are totally egalitarian. All family members are essentially free to do as they wish. These parents rarely make decisions or accept responsibilities. The adolescent sons of authoritarian and laissez faire parents are especially likely to experience adjustment problems [55]. The responses of female adolescents to these parental styles have not been studied yet.

Peers become increasingly influential during adolescence. Research suggests that parental authority is likely to outweigh peer influence when parents are interested, understanding, willing to be helpful, and sharing in family activities [56]. Serious problems, including heavy drinking, drug abuse, and antisocial conduct, become more probable under several conditions: (1) when there are large differences in expectations between friends and families, (2) when peers are more influential than parents, and (3) when friends engage in and support problem behaviors [57]. Undoubtedly, there are other influences on adolescent adjustment which psychologists are just beginning to understand [58].

We turn now to adjustment-related concerns that generally appear first in young adulthood: finding satisfaction at work and in marriage.

TABLE 14-2 Importance of Various Working Conditions (ordered by percentage of subjects responding "very important")

1. The work is interesting.
2. I receive enough help and equipment to get the job done.
3. I have enough information to get the job done.
4. I have enough authority to do my job.
5. The pay is good.
6. My coworkers are friendly and helpful.
7. I have an opportunity to develop my special abilities.
8. The job security is good.
9. I can see the results of my work.
10. My responsibilities are clearly defined.
11. My supervisor is competent.
12. I have enough time to get the job done.
13. I am given a chance to do the things I do best.
14. I am given a lot of freedom to decide how I do my work.
15. The hours are good.
16. My fringe benefits are good.
17. Travel to and from work is convenient.
18. I am given a lot of chances to make friends.
19. Physical surroundings are pleasant.
20. I am free from conflicting demands that other people make of me.
21. I can forget about my personal problems.
22. The problems I am asked to solve are hard enough.
23. I am not asked to do excessive amounts of work.

Source: Adapted from Survey Research Center. *Survey of working conditions: Final report.* Washington, D.C.: U.S. Government Printing Office, 1971. Pp. 55–56.

SATISFACTION AT WORK

Most American adults—in the late 1970s, more than 63 percent—spend the greater part of each weekday working [59]. The Puritan idea that work is a duty, automatically virtuous, and rewarding in and of itself prevailed for a long time. Though this attitude is less visible today (especially among young people), work is still valued. A recent survey suggested that four out of five college students believe that commitment to a meaningful career is a very important part of life [60]. Many individuals value a job for other than monetary reasons and say that they would work even if they inherited enough money to retire [61]. In this section we try to identify factors that lead to a satisfying work experience, considering characteristics of both the job itself and the individual.

The Influence of the Job

Many people find aspects of their jobs unsatisfying. In one recent survey, 41 percent of the men reported having had problems at work. College-educated males were more apt to express job-related concerns than a comparable sample had reported twenty years earlier [62].

What do people want from their jobs? In the early 1970s, investigators at the University of Michigan's Institute for Social Research conducted a nationwide study of working conditions and job satisfaction. More than 1,500 representative full-time workers were interviewed and asked to rate the importance of various aspects of work for job satisfaction. The results are presented in Table 14-2. Interestingly, high pay ranked fifth. So long as working conditions, wages, and benefits meet minimal standards, the psychological satisfactions of work are highly valued by more people than the material rewards [63].

Are certain types of jobs especially unsatisfying? Behavioral scientists find that both too much and too little pressure at work lead to high levels of stress-related hormones, large numbers of psychosomatic complaints (Chapter 11), and hefty absentee rates [64]. As might be expected, tension is also associated with health and safety hazards, work overload, rotating shifts which strain the body (Chapter 7), inadequate supervision, low status, and inadequate or unfair wages and chances for advancement [65]. As you can see from Table 14-3, repetitive, unskilled jobs, which tend to be characterized by many of these conditions, satisfy few people. Only 16 percent of the unskilled auto workers who were questioned reported that they would seek the same jobs again. In contrast, 93 percent of urban college teachers expressed satisfaction with their vocational choices [66]. There are two plausible explanations for the appeal of professional jobs. (1) They offer numerous opportunities for creativity, variety, and achievement, making them intrinsically interesting. (2) They provide prestige, a relatively high income, and other extrinsic benefits as well [67].

Professional-level jobs are far from perfect, of course. Boredom and alienation are associated with certain types of professional work. Poverty-program lawyers, physicians, prison personnel, social workers, clinical psychologists, psychiatric nurses, and other professionals who work extensively with human problems often feel unable to cope continually with distress. Eventually, they may see themselves as "burned out." Psychologist Christina Maslach and her colleagues observed 200 professionals. The behavioral scientists found that many handled "burned-out" feelings by distancing themselves from clients and treating suffering people in detached, dehumanizing ways. As emotions grew increasingly negative, these workers experienced severe tension-related problems including alcoholism. Maslach's research team discovered that opportunities to do less stressful work and high staff-to-client ratios (to minimize overload) reduced the symptoms of "burn out" [68].

In a recent book, psychologist Seymour Sarason questions the one life–one career tradition of our society. A single career, even under ideal conditions, is confining since people have diverse needs and interests that

TABLE 14-3 Percentages of Workers in Various Occupations Who Would Choose Similar Work Again

Occupation	Percent
Professional and white-collar	
Urban university professors	93
Mathematicians	91
Physicists	89
Biologists	89
Chemists	86
Firm lawyers	85
School superintendents	85
Lawyers	83
Journalists (Washington correspondents)	82
Church university professors	77
Solo lawyers	75
White-collar workers (nonprofessional)	43
Skilled trades and blue-collar	
Skilled printers	52
Paper workers	42
Skilled auto workers	41
Skilled steelworkers	41
Textile workers	31
Blue-collar workers	24
Unskilled steelworkers	21
Unskilled auto workers	16

Source: Adapted from Kahn, R..L. The work module—A tonic for lunchpail lassitude. *Psychology Today,* 1973, **6**(9), 39.

change at different times of life. It may be unrealistic, then, to expect a single career to remain satisfying. Human beings may have to seek out several careers over the course of a lifetime [69]. There is some evidence that job change is becoming quite acceptable—at least among relatively well educated, financially advantaged people. A recent survey of more than 20,000 *Psychology Today* readers indicated that a large percentage (approximately 55 percent of professional and 85 percent of semi-skilled respondents) felt "somewhat likely" or "likely" to change jobs in the near future [70]. See Figure 14-5.

The Influence of the Individual

People bring their own unique skills, needs, values, and goals to any job situation. Anyone who is grossly mismatched is apt to feel

FIGURE 14-5 There are no across-the-board arrangements that will enhance everybody's job satisfaction. Increasingly, behavioral scientists talk about the fit between individual and work [110]. But what about unskilled and semiskilled jobs, which may be inevitably repetitive and monotonous? Some experts believe that improving these jobs is impossible. Managers, they suggest, should concentrate, instead, upon facilitating nonwork benefits, such as the freedom to take breaks, talk on the telephone, and socialize while working [111]. Some industrial psychologists advocate increased flexibility in working hours, in rotating between diverse tasks, and even in setting wages, vacations, and fringe benefits. Some stress the need for improved communications and social relationships between managers and workers. Still others believe that low-skill jobs can benefit significantly from *enrichment programs*. Typically, these programs emphasize redesigning jobs to (1) demand a variety of skills, (2) provide start-to-finish experiences so that workers may take pride in a tangible outcome, and (3) increase the laborer's autonomy, decision-making and planning responsibilities, and feedback. In the opinion of many behavioral scientists, model job-enrichment programs have been highly successful. Still, by the mid-1970s, only about 4 percent of corporations had tried enrichment programs. Even these experiments were implemented on a limited scale that affected only a tiny fraction of the total labor force [112]. [*David Hurn/Magnum.*]

unhappy and uncomfortable. But let's assume that the match is reasonably appropriate. Do certain personal characteristics make some individuals more likely than others to find happiness? Research by psychologists Douglas Bray and Ann Howard suggests that job satisfaction is associated with overall life satisfaction. Bray and Howard recently re-

ported on the results of a twenty-year follow-up of more than 200 management-level, middle-aged male employees of the American Telephone and Telegraph Company. The men had been evaluated on managerial, personality, and motivational characteristics in the 1950s, when they joined the company, and again eight years later. Bray and Howard emphasized dimensions of living in their follow-up. They discovered that objective job success was not linked with life satisfaction. Many of the most contented men occupied relatively low management positions. As it turned out, the happiest people were not very evaluative or critical. They rarely ruminated about life's purpose, but accepted their lot and emphasized the positive. These serene men were not hedonistic (pleasure-seeking) or overly dependent on women. A significant number of the satisfied workers scored lower on traditional intelligence tests (though they were all of above-average ability) and were less cynical than the others who were studied. At the same time, the well-adjusted employees were more self-confident, emotionally stable, unselfish, and positive about life than other research participants [71]. These personal traits appear to maximize the likelihood of both job and life satisfaction.

MARITAL HARMONY

When questioned during surveys, most people report that intimacy with other human beings is the single most gratifying aspect of life [72]. After completing a recent interview study of 2,400 respondents chosen to represent the American adult population, psychologist Elizabeth Douvan summarized her perceptions in this way:

While there is plenty of strain in contemporary families, most people nonetheless place their emotional chips there. Most people recognize that life is at best a lonely trip. Those relationships which affirm the self, can survive conflict, and allow expression of the whole self are an enormous help in supplying comfort, meaning, pleasure, gratification, anchors for the self. People have not drastically let that reality slip or lost track of that core area of significance. [73]

In our country, marriage is an important source of intimacy. More than 95 percent of American women and men will probably take wedding vows at some point during their lives—if current trends continue. Though approximately 30 to 35 percent will become divorced, a large percentage will eventually remarry [74].

Marriage is defined variously by different cultures and subcultures at particular points in time. Americans used to enter matrimony for sexual, economic, and social reasons predominantly. Most marry today for companionship and emotional support. Expectations about marriage have changed accordingly. Wedlock in our culture was once viewed (and still is perceived by some) as a permanent and exclusive bond. In this type of marriage, each partner "belongs" to the other, denies having individual needs, maintains a "unified front,"

and follows the roles established by traditional sex-role stereotypes. Today, many young people voice radically different ideals. They may regard marriage as a tentative relationship that should be constantly reevaluated and then dissolved if it fails to fulfill its intended purposes. Honest communication is usually championed. Significant relationships outside the marriage may be encouraged because of the assumption that two individuals cannot fulfill all of each other's needs. Sexual fidelity or infidelity may be negotiated. Rigid sex-role duties are apt to be rejected. Though equality for females and males is emphasized in principle, it is rarely practiced, since sex-role socialization (described in Chapter 17) makes changes difficult—even for the most committed couples. See Figure 14-6. Many of these ideals were described by anthropologists George and Nena O'Neill in

FIGURE 14-6 Many young people find egalitarian marriages appealing. Partners, they feel, should share household, child care, and employment responsibilities fairly. But, despite contracts and intentions, some traditional orientations often persist. "Contrary to popular belief," writes sociologist Joann Vanek, "American husbands do not share the responsibilities of household work. They spend only a few hours a week at it, and most of what they do is shopping." Working wives tend to use weekends to clean and shop while their husbands do odd chores, rest, watch TV, and engage in sports [113]. Breaking traditional role expectations is a major hurdle for both sexes. In a survey during the mid-1970s, researchers found only one of every five women saying that they wanted more household help from husbands. Many female respondents seemed to feel that housework and child care are women's natural responsibilities [114]. Even when both mates have professional careers, studies suggest that the male's work almost always comes first [115]. Is everyone satisfied with the status quo? Probably not. Married women are less likely to report feeling happy than married men. Also, wives are more likely than husbands and single women to complain of the symptoms of mental and physical illnesses [116]. Social critics attribute the married woman's problems to job overload in combination with little power and autonomy. A woman's family status seems to be little altered by long hours of work or professional credentials. A superior income, on the other hand, improves a wife's status considerably [117]. [*Mimi Forsyth/Monkmeyer.*]

their popular book on the open marriage [75]. New perspectives on matrimony coexist, of course, with more traditional views. In this section we explore two topics: common marital problems and correlates of successful marriages. While most research on intimacy focuses on legally married couples, the findings are probably equally applicable to other types of close interpersonal relationships. Chapter 17 will have more to say about liking and loving.

Common Marital Problems

Married people rarely report "living happily ever after." But, as a group, they say that they are satisfied with life more than single individuals do [76]. At the same time, intimate relationships pose problems for even the most stable pairs. In the recent national survey conducted by Elizabeth Douvan and her coworkers (mentioned earlier), close to 60 percent of the men and women admitted having had problems at some time in their marriages. Wives tend to report more dissatisfactions than husbands do, presumably because of the role strains described in Figure 14-6 [77]. Marital difficulties that are commonly cited by clinicians include these [78]:

1. Partners fail to meet each other's needs and expectations.
2. The members of a couple have difficulty accepting real differences in habits, opinions, desires, and values. Major conflicts about money (how to produce and spend it) and children seem to be especially prevalent.
3. Jealousy and possessiveness keep individuals from giving one another sufficient independence.
4. The distribution of power appears unfair to one or both partners.
5. Varied communication failures occur. Many people expect their partners to know what they feel and think although they do not verbalize their concerns explicitly. Individuals are often inept at bargaining, negotiating, and compromising— essential skills for resolving conflicts and frustrations.
6. The members of a pair grow in different directions, pursuing diverse, sometimes incompatible, interests and goals.

Correlates of Successful Marriages

The course of intense relationships, including marriage, rarely runs entirely smoothly. When psychologist George Levinger and his coworkers asked college students to write essays about their closest relationships with friends of the same and opposite sex, the investigators found more involvement and more ups-and-downs in the opposite-sex bonds [79]. Though difficulties may be inevitable in intimate relationships, many people manage to create satisfying ties, those where both partners experience many rewards at a relatively small cost. How are such relationships achieved? To answer this question, psychologists need to intensively study couples in their natural environments at varied times. There are no studies of this type. Most researchers pursue a less demanding, more economical strategy. They administer tests, questionnaires, or interviews on one or more occasions to the members of both happy-stable and unhappy-unstable (or divorced) couples. Comparisons give social scientists some general impressions about the necessary ingredients of solid bonds.

Certain background characteristics are associated again and again with a stable marital relationship: relatively high socioeconomic status; happy parents and being happy oneself; a long, predominantly peaceful courtship; and a "late" marriage (occurring when the male was at least twenty-two and the female at least nineteen) [80]. What do these conditions have to do with marital harmony? We offer some speculations that are consistent with current research findings. High socioeconomic status means fewer frustrations in daily living. Stresses in one domain tend to spill over and strain marriages. Happy parents are good teachers. Presumably, they behaved in ways that perpetuated peace. The children of happy unions are likely to have acquired these productive interpersonal habits through observation learning. There are several plausible reasons for connecting personal happiness with marital harmony. Contented people are probably easy to live with and their joy may be contagious. At the same time, satisfied individuals may emphasize the positive, even though the marriage is difficult. A long, peaceful courtship may signify that partners knew one another well and were prepared to make an intelligent decision about overall suitability. Similarly, a "late" marriage is apt to be built on a solid relationship between people who understand themselves. Such a marriage is less likely to have been precipitated hurriedly by pregnancy. Older people tend to have greater patience than younger ones in working out problems. And "late" marriages are usually helped along by a sounder financial base [81].

The long list of common marital problems, cited earlier, should suggest that a successful relationship requires partners who are both committed to and skilled at problem solving. Research supports this viewpoint. The capacities to communicate thoughts and feelings effectively and to handle tension constructively are both associated with a stable relationship [82]. Members of successful bonds consistently emphasize working very hard to keep their interactions positive [83].

Certain types of partner similarity and complementarity (the meshing of needs) seem to enhance intimate relationships. Personality similarity is linked with a stable marriage, as we saw in Chapter 13. We will say more about these conditions in Chapter 17. ▲

AGING AND ADJUSTMENT

Aging is an inevitable natural process. With the passage of time, the body changes gradually. Skin and blood vessels lose elasticity, fat cells multiply, muscular strength decreases, and the production of sex hormones declines. Complex changes within the nerve cells, including chemical alterations, oxygen deprivation, and cell death (nerve cells, you may recall, do not regenerate), reduce the speed and efficiency of the central nervous system. These various physical processes—and many others—begin at different chronological ages and progress at different rates. The timing varies, depending on the individual's heredity and environment.

Life circumstances also change as people age. There are new roles and new problems to face, often in addition to the old ones. In this section, we focus on some of the current concerns of Americans during their middle and late years. Try to keep in mind that these concerns are not inevitably linked to the aging experience. In youth-oriented countries like our own, elderly individuals frequently feel useless and unwanted. Consequently, as they confront the dreary prospects of middle and old age, depression and anxiety tend to be commonplace [84]. In countries such as China and Japan, the elderly remain active and at the center of life in honored positions; nega-

---

▲ USING PSYCHOLOGY

1. Did your adjustment pattern during adolescence fit one of the categories described in the text? Did your parents display a consistent interactional style? Speculate about the factors that influenced your adjustment during adolescence, taking psychological research into account.

2. What career(s) are you planning to pursue? Evaluate the probable satisfaction of such work by the criteria listed in Table 14-2. Do you anticipate problems due to the job itself, your match with the job, or your personality characteristics?

3. Analyze a long-lasting intimate human relationship with which you are personally familiar. Which common marital problems were troublesome for the partners? If the relationship was happy, try to specify the characteristics that made it so. Be sure to consider those factors mentioned in the text.

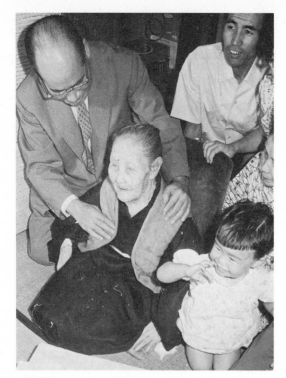

FIGURE 14-7 In Oriental countries, including industrial Japan, the elderly are honored and respected. They receive the best clothing, most respectful forms of address, the first dip in the family bath, and the deepest bows. About 75 percent of Japanese people sixty-five and older live with their children. The Japanese consider caring for an aged parent essential. To neglect a mother or father is a disgrace. In Japan old people participate in community affairs and remain productive within the family. Often they engage in housework, child care, gardening, and/or the family business. They are routinely consulted on major decisions. Although the existence of any causal connection is not clear, it is interesting that babies born in Japan have higher life expectancies than those born in any other industrialized nation [118]. [*Black Star.*]

FIGURE 14-8 A New York executive chins himself on a bar in the doorway of his office. According to Bernice Neugarten's research, males go to more elaborate lengths to preserve health than females do. Presumably, men feel an especially strong sense of physical vulnerability and insecurity. Middle-aged Americans often engage in body monitoring. Large companies frequently accommodate their executives' interests in physical fitness by providing gyms, spas, pools, handball courts, and the like. [*Elliott Erwitt/Magnum.*]

tive feelings are not prominent. See Figure 14-7. As conditions in our culture become more hospitable for aging (as they appear to be in the process of doing), new generations will confront radically different attitudes and roles, and the challenges and concerns of older adults should change.

Coping during the Middle Years

"When more time stretches behind than stretches before one," James Baldwin, the

American writer, said, "some assessments, however reluctantly and incompletely, begin to be made." Bernice Neugarten's longitudinal research on representative samples of American adults confirms Baldwin's observation [85]. Middle-aged people in our culture (those in the forties, fifties, and early sixties) become increasingly introspective and reflective, atuned to what is going on inside themselves. Many people at mid-life think in terms of "time left to live" rather than "time from birth." A sizable percentage report worrying about their bodies. *"Body monitoring"*—the adoption of protective strategies (such as exercising, dieting, or using hair dye or cosmetics) to maintain a stable appearance and to keep physical performance at a desirable level—is widespread. See Figure 14-8. Adults at mid-life mentally rehearse emergencies that they expect to face. Men tend to think a great deal about health changes, especially heart attacks, and death. Although women report some concerns about diseases, such as cancer, and death, they are apt to be more preoccupied by the fear of widowhood. (Most women can expect to be widows.) Middle-aged and older Americans of both sexes become involved in *"the creation of social heirs."* They think a great deal about relationships with young people, including "the need to nurture, the care not to overstep the delicate boundaries of authority relationships, and the complicated issues that relate to one's position, one's power, [and] one's lack of power [86]." Caring for parents, and, in some cases, grandparents is another major concern of many middle-aged people [87].

Some Americans face emotional crises during the middle years. We consider the research on women and men separately.

Mid-Life Crises in Women and Men

Middle-aged women all over the world experience a cluster of physical changes known as the *climacteric*. During the *menopause*, one phase of the climacteric, the ovaries stop producing ripe egg cells and menstruation (sloughing the lining of the uterus in bloody discharges at monthly intervals) stops. Consequently, the reproductive capability ceases. At about the same time, the ovaries begin producing smaller amounts of the "feminine" sex hormones, the estrogens and progestins. (For more information about these hormones, see Chapter 10.) An *estrogen deficiency* causes a number of distressing physical changes that many (but not all) women experience: hot flashes (spells of flushing, perspiration, and warmth), loss of calcium from the bones, backaches, drying of the vaginal lining (which may make the sex act and uri-

nation uncomfortable), and spasms of the esophagus (which can result in an almost continual "lump in the throat"). The estrogen shortage is responsible for striking changes in the woman's appearance too: wrinkles and sagging skin and breasts. In addition, the lack of estrogen appears to cause negative feelings, including anxiety, depression, irritability, and confusion. Support for this idea comes from the finding that estrogen replacement therapy relieves depression and anxiety and is accompanied by a sense of well-being in most cases [88]. Many women face another trial. The climacteric is likely to coincide with the departure of children from home. At mid-life, women frequently contend, then, with physical discomforts, unpleasant moods, an older appearance, and often a substantial role loss. They respond vari-

ously. Some barely notice these changes. Others experience a major crisis. Depression appears to be more common among women who have been socialized traditionally to play the wife-mother role and no other and to see themselves as attractive sex objects and little else [89]. In these instances, aging inevitably brings loss of status and fears of loneliness, isolation, and rejection. Housewives, as one might expect, are more likely to feel depressed during middle age than working women [90]. Yet the middle years of a woman's life offer a striking compensation for all the stresses—freedom. There is evidence that American mothers at mid-life are beginning to appreciate this commodity and are turning toward self-development once the children leave home [91]. There is also support for the idea that the "empty nest" years tend to be happy ones overall for many married women [92].

What happens to men at mid-life? To investigate this issue, Yale University psychologist Daniel Levinson and his co-workers studied forty middle-aged American males: executives, workers, biologists, and novelists. (Note that Levinson's group did not use a representative sample.) Each subject was intensively interviewed. Psychological tests were administered and wives were consulted. Working from approximately 300 pages of tape transcripts per man, Levinson and his coworkers compiled a life history on each individual. Later, this material was analyzed along with biographical information about famous men. Levinson's research team concluded that about 80 percent of its subjects had experienced a moderate to severe crisis between the ages of forty and forty-five. In the following passage, Levinson identifies the common elements of this crisis:

"A number of changes commonly occurring at around 40 intensify the sense of aging. . . . One important change . . . is the decline in bodily and psychological powers. In his late thirties and early forties a man falls well below his earlier peak levels of functioning. He cannot run as fast, lift as much, do with

as little sleep as before. His vision and hearing are less acute, he remembers less well and finds it harder to learn masses of specific information. He is more prone to aches and pains and may undergo a serious illness that threatens him with permanent impairment or even death. These changes vary widely in their severity and their effects on a man's life. Reduced strength and agility may be less distressing to an accountant than to a professional athlete. . . .

"The decline is normally quite moderate and leaves a man with ample capacities for living in middle age. But it is often experienced as catastrophic. A man fears that he will soon lose all the youthful qualities that make life worthwhile. . . . Reminders of mortality are also given by the more frequent illness, death and loss of others. . . .

"Why should the recognition of our mortality be so painful? . . . A primary reason, I believe, is the wish for immortality. [A] man is terrified at the thought of being dead, of no longer existing as this particular person. . . . Beyond the concern with personal survival, there is a concern with meaning. It is bad enough to feel that my life will soon be over. It is even worse to feel that my life has not had—and never will have—

sufficient value for myself and the world. [A man may worry that he] has not fulfilled himself sufficiently and has not contributed enough to the world. . . . As he seeks to modify and enrich his life, he has self-doubts ranging in intensity from mild pessimism to utter panic [93]." Many of the men in Levinson's sample eventually sought out new sources of inner vitality, reoriented toward the future, and began planning a new phase of life.

Are mid-life crises in males common? Behavioral scientists cannot now answer this question authoritatively. Some psychologists consider Levinson's mid-life crisis equivalent to a masculine climacteric and speculate that anxiety and despair in these years may be fed by declining sex hormone levels. (In contrast to women, men do not experience a *drastic* reduction in their major sex hormone, testosterone.) Some behavioral scientists contend that Levinson's mid-life crisis may be a relatively confined cultural phenomenon, one that is primarily troubling to current generations of middle-class American men who grew up in a society that worshiped youth and worldly achievement [94]. Extended bouts of doubt and dissatisfaction do not appear to afflict middle-aged men in all cultures.

Coping during the Late Years

The age of sixty-five, the traditional year of retirement from work in our society, marks the beginning of what is often considered *old age*. Recently, the period of old age has been divided into two segments: *young old age* and *old old age*. The age ranges are not rigidly set.

The young old, generally those in the sixty-five- to seventy-five-year-old range, have a great deal of free time and are concerned about using it meaningfully. They are usually alert mentally. Health may actually improve after retirement [95]. Morale may be high—especially if people live in retirement communities [96]. See Figure 14-9. After the age of seventy-five or so, the beginning of old old age, most people confront a new set of challenges. They must prepare to cope with incapacitating illness and often markedly reduced abilities. And they must face their own death. We describe some of the major tasks and themes from both periods of old age.

In our culture, *renunciation*, or giving up, is an important challenge of old age. The elderly must relinquish work, friends, a spouse perhaps, and a sense of personal competency and authority. Bernice Neugarten and her colleagues find that older Americans experience a conflict (which could be labeled "approach-avoidance"). They desire to remain active to retain a sense of identity and value. At the same time, they wish to withdraw, or *disengage*, from social commitments and to pursue a leisurely, contemplative life. There are several pressures for social disengagement [97]:

1. As retirement begins and circumstances change, people may lose contact with previous social roles and activities.
2. Illnesses and reduced physical and mental capacities lead to self-preoccupation.
3. Younger people in the community tend to withdraw from them.
4. And, as death becomes imminent, the elderly want to push aside matters that are not extremely important.

Older Americans solve this conflict in different ways which reflect lifetime habits, values, and self-concepts. Neugarten and her coworkers have identified several adaptive patterns among adults with diverse personality types. Mature, flexible people with rich inner lives make three satisfying types of adjustment. The *reorganizers* substitute new activities for old ones, often involving themselves in church and community. The *focused* specialize. They concentrate energies on one or more roles or activities, perhaps on being a loving spouse or painting pictures. A third group, the *disengaged*, deliberately abandon social commitments, though they maintain an interest in the world and in themselves—perhaps from their rocking chairs [98].

Though the challenges of old age—

FIGURE 14-9 In the early 1960s, Sweden, among other industrialized countries, pioneered in establishing housing projects for retirees. In America, public housing for the elderly includes subsidized living units and nursing homes for the poor and retirement villages (miniature towns) for the more affluent. The people shown here attend an art class in a retirement village in Croton-On-Hudson, New York. Approximately one in ten retired people can afford a retirement community such as this. While some elderly find the isolation of the retirement village repugnant, residents often like the reality. Frequently, there are convenient facilities for health, recreation, and education. People can engage in stimulating activities and fulfill social needs without feeling that they are burdening their families. [*Miriam Reinhart/Photo Researchers.*]

particularly of old old age—may seem overwhelming to a young person, elderly people often cope successfully with their problems. Psychologist Richard Kalish has suggested a number of reasons for this capability [99].

1. Losses often appear gradually, so the older adult may adapt to slight changes without realizing it.
2. Others of the same age show similar mishaps, so the elderly rarely feel that they are alone.
3. When difficulties are chronic ones, individuals may adjust a little at a time to problems that may initially have appeared catastrophic to them.
4. Losses affect limited aspects of a life. Satisfying substitutes often remain or may be found.
5. As noted before, people rehearse later roles that they will play. Consequently, older individuals may have anticipated and planned for certain discomforts.

A sense of control seems to be very important for adjustment in old age. Even though elderly adults may have to rely on others, they probably need to feel that they have some power and responsibility. A study by psychologists Ellen Langer and Judith Rodin supports this notion. They divided ninety-one nursing-home residents (ages sixty-five to ninety) into two groups by a random procedure. The adults in one group received a pep talk which emphasized the need to take more responsibility in caring for themselves and improving the quality of their lives. Members of this high-responsibility group chose a living plant to maintain by themselves. Patients in a

FIGURE 14-10 In isolated villages of the Caucasus mountains of southern Russia (where this photo was taken) and in Pakistan and Ecuador, inhabitants live a long time. Precisely how long is questionable since reliable birth records do not exist and people exaggerate their ages for added prestige. Still, recent research suggests that these communities hold large numbers of centenarians (people over a hundred)—in one village in Ecuador 300 times more than in the United States. What contributes to longevity? A. Butka (on the right) who boasts of being a hundred and twenty, says he is lively because of his youthful wife Marusia, who is only a hundred and nine. Psychologist Richard Schulz suggests that many environmental factors contribute to longevity: a relatively low caloric intake, a diet lacking in animal fats, an absence of toxins (such as pesticides) and of cigarette smoking, a great deal of strenuous activity from childhood through old age, and a minimal amount of competition and emotional stress. Heredity influences length of life span significantly, too [119]. [*John Ludin/Black Star.*]

second—low-responsibility—group were informed that the staff was there to provide good service. Each individual in this group was given a plant that the nurses cared for. What happened? The members of the high-responsibility group showed significantly more signs of alertness, active participation, and positive feelings than those in the low-responsibility group. Eighteen months later, the differences were still evident. Even more remarkable was the finding that a sense of control appeared to have affected life span. At the time of the follow-up, only 15 percent of the patients in the high-responsibility group had died. About 30 percent of those in the low-responsibility group, in contrast, had passed away [100]. There is evidence that an active mastery approach to life tends to become somewhat more important to women and somewhat less so to men in middle and old age. At this stage of life, both sexes may feel freer to express personal qualities that were suppressed earlier in life during child rearing [101].

In our culture, elderly individuals often orient toward the past, focusing on what they were and what they have accomplished [102]. This "life review" is thought to reflect a need to redefine identity, as fewer options remain and people feel "set aside." Frequently, older adults seek out explanations for events that were not previously understood and work at reconciling themselves to earlier achievements and failures. In some cases, writing a life history may be motivated by the need to come to terms with one's past life.

Eventually, old people must confront death. See Figure 14-10. Psychologists know relatively little about this topic. While the elderly seem to think about death more than younger adults, they appear less frightened of it [103]. Often, older people are preoccupied with the desire to leave some trace of themselves, some contribution for future generations. Psychiatrist Elisabeth Kubler-Ross, a pioneer in the study of dying, described stages that human beings pass through during fatal illnesses like terminal cancer (Chapter 2). Does death follow a pattern? A number of psychologists question this assumption [104]. Dying, they maintain, is influenced by numerous factors: way of life, terminal condition, care, pain, human relationships, setting. To understand a death, then, one has to take into account the particular individual and the specific circumstances. To comprehend the plight of an elderly individual facing death, a young person might try to answer the following questions (suggested by psychiatrist Avery Weisman):

1. If you faced death in the near future, what would matter most?
2. If you were very old, what would your most crucial problems be? How would you go about solving them?
3. If death were inevitable, what circumstances would make it acceptable?
4. If you were very old, how might you live most effectively and with least damage to your ideals and standards?
5. What can anyone do to prepare for [one's] own death, or for that of someone very close?
6. What conditions and events might make you feel that you were better off dead? When would you take steps to die?
7. In old age, everyone must rely upon others. When this point arrives, what kind of people would you like to deal with? [105]

THE QUALITY OF LIFE AND ADJUSTMENT

Throughout this chapter we have focused on how individuals cope with the challenges of living and dying. Because people are limited creatures who do not thrive without favorable conditions, societies too make a powerful contribution to adjustment. They provide circumstances that can make coping relatively easy or close to impossible. What conditions are most likely to improve the quality of human life? Though answers depend to some extent on age and personality, there is a great deal of agreement. When needs are met in the areas of material comforts, health care, rewarding work, and opportunities for active recreation, learning, and creative expression, people are likely to report a sense of overall well-being [106]. An increasing number of psychologists who recognize that adjustment depends on life conditions are working to help people improve their communities: to reduce sources of stress and strain and to establish resources that promote health, both mental and physical. In Chapter 16 we describe the community mental health movement and some of its initial efforts to improve the quality of American life. ▲

SUMMARY
Adjustment Throughout the Life Cycle

1. Adjustment was defined as the process of attempting to meet the demands of self and environment.
2. Physical, personal, and social barriers provide frustration.
3. Conflicts may be classified, according to the nature of the options involved, as largely internal or external. They may also be categorized according to the courses of action required for resolution (approach-approach, avoidance-avoidance, approach-avoidance, double or multiple approach-avoidance).
4. Several factors are known to affect the outcome of a conflict: the strength of the motives aroused by the options, distance in time and space from the options, and expectations about the options.
5. Human beings appear to be continually assess-

ing and reassessing their situations and coping either consciously, automatically, or in both ways. They use various behavioral strategies: deliberate problem solving, aggression, regression, withdrawal, and escape. In addition, they employ numerous self-deceptive cognitive devices, including repression or suppression, denial of reality, fantasy, rationalization, intellectualization, reaction formation, and projection.

6. Denial and intellectualization can reduce anxiety, though not in all situations.

7. Using a combination of coping strategies, including a lot of problem solving and positive thinking and a little self-deception, may be the most effective approach. A successful adaptation probably requires using coping mechanisms deliberately and flexibly in a future-oriented, reality-based way.

8. Early experiences, cultural beliefs and practices, and cognitive level influence coping responses.

9. During adulthood, problems, conflicts, and challenges occur and recur.

10. Adolescence is not necessarily a tumultuous period of life. Problems are more likely when parents are authoritarian or laissez faire and when influential peers engage in and support problem behavior.

11. Too much and too little pressure at work both lead to job dissatisfaction. So long as job conditions, wages, and benefits meet minimal standards, more people value the psychological satisfactions of work more highly than the material rewards. People who go into professional work tend to be happier with their lot than those who take up less skilled occupations. But any single career that spans a lifetime may be perceived eventually as confining.

12. Certain personal characteristics, including overall satisfaction with life, a noncritical attitude, self-confidence, and emotional stability, are associated with job satisfaction.

13. Common marital problems include partners' failures to meet one another's needs and expectations, difficulty in accepting real differences, jealousy and possessiveness, power struggles, breakdowns in communication, and divergent growth patterns.

14. Stable marriages are most likely to be found among spouses of relatively high socioeconomic status who (a) had happy parents, (b) are happy themselves, and (c) married in their early twenties or later after a relatively long-lasting, predominantly peaceful courtship. Other correlates of a stable marital status include the capacities to communicate thoughts and feelings effectively, to handle tensions constructively, and to work hard on the relationship.

15. During the middle years of adulthood, current generations of Americans become increasingly introspective and reflective. They often think in terms of time left to live. They worry about their bodies. They rehearse emergencies that they expect to face. They work out relationships with the young. Women and men in our culture may both face mid-life crises.

16. In old age, adults confront a number of challenges: using retirement time meaningfully, coping with losses, making sense of the past, and accepting death.

17. Environmental circumstances may make adjustment relatively easy or close to impossible.

A Study Guide for Chapter Fourteen

Key terms adjustment (446), frustration (447), conflict (447) [approach-approach (448), avoidance-avoidance (448), approach-avoidance (448), double approach-avoidance (448), multiple approach-avoidance (449)], behavioral strategies for coping (450) [deliberate problem solving (450), aggression (450), regression (451), withdrawal (452), escape (452)], alcoholism (452), cognitive strategies for coping (454) [repression (454), suppression (cognitive avoidance) (454), denial of reality (455), fantasy (455), rationalization (455), intellectualization (456), reaction formation (456), projection (456)], climacteric (469), and other italicized words and expressions.

Important research conflict resolution (Lewin, Miller), behavioral strategies for coping (Mechanic, Barker, Dembo, Lewin, others), alcoholism (Jellinek, others), cognitive strategies for coping (Erdelyi, Giambra, Singer, Saltz, others), anxiety-reducing effects of cognitive strategies (Lazarus, others), coping mechanisms and a good adjustment (Murphy, Lazarus, others), determinants of coping strategies (Seligman, Keister, Updegraff, Ablon, Mischel, others), psychological consistency in adulthood (Neugarten), adjustment during adolescence (the Offers, Locksley, Douvan, Baumrind, Elder, others), work satisfaction (Maslach, Bray, Howard, others), marital harmony (Levinger, others), adjustment during middle age (Levinson, others), adjustment during old age (Neugarten, Langer, Rodin, others), effects of social conditions on individual well-being.

Basic concepts coping model (Lazarus), defense mechanism (Freud), coping versus defense mechanisms (Haan), stage theory of adulthood and alternative views (Erikson, others), criticism of the one life–one career tradition (Sarason), changing ideals of marriage (the O'Neills), activity versus disengagement conflict in old age (Neugarten, others), explanation for the ease of coping with losses in old age (Kalish), the "individual difference" model of dying.

Self-Quiz

1. Under which conditions is the term *frustration* most appropriately used?
   a. Whenever an organism must cope with any challenge
   b. Whenever an obstacle prevents the satisfaction of a need or goal
   c. Whenever a stressful experience can't be handled by previously learned coping strategies
   d. Whenever self-esteem is threatened by some stress

2. Aralia cannot decide whether to visit her grandfather, who is sometimes pleasant and loving but frequently irritable and rejecting. Which type of conflict is she experiencing?
   a. Approach-approach
   b. Approach-avoidance
   c. Double approach-avoidance
   d. Multiple approach-avoidance

3. How are most real-life human conflicts apt to be categorized if they are well understood?
   a. Approach-approach
   b. Approach-avoidance
   c. Double approach-avoidance
   d. Multiple approach-avoidance

4. At which stage of alcoholism are the DTs apt to be observed?
   a. Complete alcohol addiction
   b. Early alcoholic phase
   c. Prealcoholic phase
   d. True alcoholic phase

5. Ten-year-old Eli responds to frustration by behaving as he did when six years old. What type of coping behavior is he displaying?
   a. Displacement   *b.* Reaction formation
   c. Regression   *d.* Withdrawal

6. Edith feels hostility toward her mother. She conceals this feeling from herself and showers the woman with compliments, attention, and gifts. Which coping strategy is Edith using?
   a. Intellectualization   *b.* Projection
   c. Rationalization   *d.* Reaction formation

7. Rudyard does not acknowledge his own prudery and frequently finds other people "hung up about sex." Which coping strategy is he using?
   a. Intellectualization   *b.* Projection
   c. Rationalization   *d.* Reaction formation

8. According to current research, which of the following mechanisms can reduce anxiety?
   a. Denial and intellectualization
   b. Fantasy and repression
   c. Projection and reaction formation
   d. Rationalization and suppression

9. Which aspect of work was rated important by the largest number of workers?
   a. Enough resources to get the job done
   b. Good pay
   c. Interesting tasks
   d. Job security

10. Which personal characteristic was found to be strongly associated with job satisfaction?
   a. Cynical approach to life
   b. Low critical or evaluative tendencies
   c. Relatively high management position
   d. Unusually high performance on intelligence tests

11. Which parental characteristic is correlated with a stable marriage?
   a. Diligence   *b.* Happiness
   c. Resourcefulness   *d.* Responsibility

12. Which experience is most common among current generations of middle-aged Americans?
   a. Body monitoring   *b.* Disengagement
   c. Extroversion   *d.* Memoir writing

13. A shortage of which hormone causes hot flashes, wrinkles and sagging skin, and negative moods during the climacteric?
   a. Androgen   *b.* Estrogen
   c. Progestin   *d.* Testosterone

14. What percentage of American men currently experience a moderate to severe mid-life crisis?
   a. 80 percent   *b.* 60 percent
   c. 40 percent   *d.* Not known

15. What happened when elderly nursing-home residents were made to feel very responsible for their own lives?
   a. They became more achievement-oriented.
   b. They lived longer.
   c. They participated more frequently in vigorous sports.
   d. They showed more intense curiosity about their surroundings.

Exercises

1. CONFLICTS. Check your understanding of conflict terminology by choosing the single most appropriate label for each of the following conflicts. (Try not to add information to the vignettes. Doing so will most probably convert them all into multiple approach-avoidance conflicts.) To review, see pages 447 to 449.

CONFLICTS: approach-approach (A-A), approach-avoidance (A-AV), avoidance-avoidance (AV-AV), multiple approach-avoidance (MA-AV)

_____ 1. Tina can't decide whether to call Josephine or Harriet to baby-sit for the afternoon. She likes both girls.

_____ 2. Hans is failing Spanish. He wants to drop the course but needs the credit to maintain a full load and retain his financial assistance.

_____ 3. For a summer job, Seymour has to choose between waiting on tables and cooking hamburgers. He finds both prospects distasteful.

_____ 4. Trish is selecting a major. She finds chemistry interesting but dislikes the time-consuming labs. Math comes easily to her but doesn't excite her. Pre-med would provide an appealing career and life-style but medical school is expensive.

_____ 5. Mat feels ill. He can't decide whether or not to go to work. He has already used several sick-leave days and wants to conserve those that remain. But his throat is raw and his head is throbbing.

_____ 6. Harriet's marriage isn't working out. She can't decide whether to drag her husband in for counseling, which she has little faith in, or to separate. She sees advantages and disadvantages to both tactics.

2. COPING STRATEGIES. This exercise will give you practice in identifying examples of the cognitive devices for coping. Match each of the following illustrations with the single most appropriate strategy. To review, see pages 454 to 456.

COGNITIVE STRATEGIES: denial of reality (DR), intellectualization (I), projection (P), rationalization (R), reaction formation (RF), repression (RP), suppression (S)

_____ 1. After an upsetting argument, Hilary tries to put the whole scene out of her mind. She goes to a movie for distraction.

_____ 2. Victor, a greedy, materialistic man, continually talks about his generosity and dedication to the welfare of others. He seems to believe his own claims.

_____ 3. Mitchell's father just died. Instead of expressing his emotions, Mitchell walks around like a zombie repeating, "Dad lived a full and productive life, so there's no need for grief."

_____ 4. Al calls his serious car accident a "blessing in disguise."

_____ 5. Matilda feels frustrated by housework but tells everyone, including herself, how happy she is "in the kitchen."

_____ 6. An 8 A.M. class that Juan wanted to take fills up before he can register. He thinks about all the work the course would have involved and how he hates getting up early. He concludes that he's better off without the class.

_____ 7. Dave refuses to believe that an exploratory operation for a "minor back problem" has turned up signs of cancer.

_____ 8. Dorothy, a very bossy person, is quick to see domineering behavior in others, but does not see the pattern in herself.

_____ 9. Margarita maintains that overcoming polio as a child helped her grow spiritually.

_____ 10. After beating his children, Arthur says, "It does me good to get the anger out of my system."

_____ 11. Claudia witnesses a fire that destroys her home. The next day she can't remember anything about the blaze.

_____ 12. Annette won't acknowledge that her son Spiro is retarded. (He is.) She insists that the child is a little slow and will "grow out of it" soon.

_____ 13. Larry, who is very dishonest himself, continually accuses others of cheating and lying.

_____ 14. As the dentist drills on Abbie's teeth (without novocaine), she finds that she can control the pain by imagining that she's an impartial observer describing the sensations accurately to a stranger.

Suggested Readings

1. Coleman, J. C. *Contemporary psychology and effective behavior.* (4th ed.) Glenview, Ill.: Scott-Foresman, 1979. This comprehensive, yet very readable, textbook addresses itself to all types of adjustment-related issues, especially to finding a meaningful, fulfilling life-style. It integrates research with clinical observations.

2. Ray, O. S. *Drugs, society, and human behavior.* (2d ed.) St. Louis, Mo.: Mosby, 1978 (paperback). A psychologist looks at research on drugs, drug abuse, and drug abusers.

3. Rubin, L. B. *Worlds of pain: Life in the working class family.* New York: Basic, 1977 (paperback). To learn more about how people in working-class (and middle-class) families cope with life, look at this book. It provides a "flesh-and-blood" approach to the problems of daily living.

4. Terkel, S. *Working*. New York: Pantheon, 1974. Terkel recorded people's comments about what they do at work and how they feel about it. This is another fascinating "flesh-and-blood" book.

5. Berscheid, E., & Walster, E. H. *Interpersonal attraction*. (2d ed.) Reading, Mass.: Addison-Wesley, 1978 (paperback). This book focuses on the earlier stages of relationships. Scanzoni, L., & Scanzoni, J. *Men, women, and change: A sociology of marriage and family*. (2d ed.) New York: McGraw-Hill, 1980. If you want to learn more about interpersonal relationships, both these books provide engaging, interesting introductions.

6. Conger, J. J. *Adolescence and youth: Psychological development in a changing world*. New York: Harper & Row, 1977. This comprehensive text summarizes current research findings about adolescence.

7. Kimmel, D. C. *Adulthood and aging: An interdisciplinary developmental view*. New York: Wiley, 1980. This text is one of the few that focus on adulthood, describing both theory and research. It includes six histories that help bridge the gap between concepts and "actual adults who are living competent and varied lives in the real world."

8. Kalish, R. A. *Late adulthood: Perspectives on human development*. Monterey, Calif.: Brooks/Cole, 1975 (paperback). An excellent brief introduction to what psychologists know about the many facets of old age. The research is evaluated in a personal way. Many fascinating issues are raised.

9. Schulz, R. *Psychology of death, dying, and bereavement*. Reading, Mass.: Addison-Wesley, 1978 (paperback). A very interesting review and analysis of research on death and related topics. One reviewer called it "a rare jewel among the many books on these topics [107]."

10. Stinnett, N., & Birdsong, C. W., with Stinnett, N. M. *The family and alternate life styles*. Chicago: Nelson-Hall, 1978. This well-written book brings together much of the current research on alternate life-styles, including cohabitation, communes, swinging, group marriage, one-parent families, and extramarital affairs.

11. Janis, I., & Wheeler, D. Thinking clearly about career choices. *Psychology Today*, 1978, **11**(12), 67–76, 121–122. Psychologists describe research on occupational choices and suggest some ways to avoid making career-choice mistakes.

12. Rubinstein, C., Shaver, P., & Peplau, L. A. Loneliness. *Human Nature*, 1979, **2**, 58–65. These social psychologists describe survey research on loneliness. They see loneliness as multiply determined and believe people play a strong role in perpetuating or extinguishing it.

Answer Keys

Self-Quiz

1. *b* (447)   **2.** *b* (448)   **3.** *d* (449)   **4.** *a* (453)
5. *c* (451)   **6.** *d* (456)   **7.** *b* (456)   **8.** *a* (457)
9. *c* (462)   **10.** *b* (464)   **11.** *b* (466)   **12.** *a* (469)
13. *b* (469)   **14.** *d* (470)   **15.** *b* (472)

Exercise 1

1. A-A   **2.** A-AV   **3.** AV-AV   **4.** MA-AV   **5.** A-AV
6. MA-AV

Exercise 2

1. S   **2.** RF   **3.** I   **4.** R   **5.** RF   **6.** R   **7.** DR
8. P   **9.** R   **10.** R   **11.** RP   **12.** DR   **13.** P   **14.** I

CHAPTER FIFTEEN
Abnormal Behavior

What is abnormal behavior? Is it an illness? Does it simply resemble an illness? Or, is it more aptly characterized as a response to problems of living? The answers of the experts vary. We begin our exploration of abnormal behavior with a scene that highlights this issue.

A Diagnostic Interview

"At New York State University's Upstate Medical Center, a routine diagnostic interview is in progress. The patient, a dowdy woman in her late fifties, had been referred for psychiatric evaluation after complaining persistently of a mysterious 'pulling in her head.' In a flat voice she unfolds a life story so filled with disaster, loss, and sudden death that it seems more the stuff of theater than medicine. From time to time, as she answers the questions of the young resident in psychiatry, she cries briefly; and yet, for the most part, she speaks in a curiously emotionless tone, as though telling someone else's story. The senior psychiatrist on the case, Dr. Thomas Szasz, sits quietly to one side, jotting on a yellow note pad. There are some twelve students in the consultation room, all juniors in the medical school. Their expressions range from slight embarrassment to stern scientific interest.

"'Well, what is your diagnosis?' Szasz asks, turning to them after the patient has been escorted from the room. . . . Uncertain, the students look at him without answering.

"'Come now,' he prods ironically. 'You are the doctors and she is the patient, so that means there must be an illness. Otherwise, we wouldn't all be here, would we?'

"'I think,' ventures a young man with a sprouting blond beard, 'that she's in a chronic depression.'

"'Oh, a depression,' says the older man, nodding. 'And you?' he asks, turning to the next student. . . . 'What do you think?'

"'I think that potentially it's a case of involutional melancholia. But for right now, I guess I'd

concur in a diagnosis of chronic, severe depression.'

"Szasz looks at him with interest. 'And how then would you go about treating this condition?'

"There is a pause. 'Er . . . isn't there a drug called Elavil that's good for depression?'

"The psychiatrist blinks several times, parodying extreme amazement: 'So you would treat this sickness she's got with drugs?' There are several uncomfortable, uncomprehending laughs from around the room. 'But what exactly are you treating? Is feeling miserable—and needing someone to talk things over with—a form of mental illness?' Szasz gets to his feet,

walks over to a blackboard and picks up a piece of chalk.

"'I don't understand—We're just trying to arrive at a diagnosis,' protests the student, his voice confused.

"'Of what?' demands Szasz. 'Has she got an illness called depression, or has she got a lot of problems and troubles which make her unhappy?' He turns and writes in large block letters: 'DEPRESSION' and underneath that: UNHAPPY HUMAN BEING. 'Tell me,' he says, facing the class, 'does the psychiatric term say more than the simple descriptive phrase? Does it do anything other than turn "a person" with problems into a "patient" with a sickness?' [1]"

The controversy that Szasz raises is a fascinating one, which we will return to later—after exploring some fundamental issues. A word about our terminology is in order. We will use varied expressions including "abnormal behavior," "abnormality," "psychological problem," "emotional disorder," and "mental illness" (or "disturbance") interchangeably throughout this chapter.

ABNORMAL BEHAVIOR: SEVERAL FUNDAMENTAL ISSUES

In this section we consider several questions. How is abnormal behavior defined? Why classify mental disorders? What difficulties arise when mental disorders are classified? How are psychological problems conceptualized (the "illness" versus "problems in living" controversy)? What are the differences between neurotic and psychotic reactions?

Defining Abnormal Behavior

There are numerous ways to define abnormal behavior. While authorities are not in agreement, the following criteria are often used [2].

1. *Defective cognitive functioning.* When intellectual abilities, such as reasoning, perceiving, attending, judging, remembering, or communicating, are badly impaired, functioning is apt to be labeled "abnormal."

2. *Defective social behavior.* In each society, conduct is regulated by social customs. When behavior deviates grossly from those standards, it is likely to be called "abnormal."

3. *Defective self-control.* Although no individuals have complete control over their own behavior, some exercise very little control. An extreme lack of control is usually considered "abnormal."

4. *Distress.* Distressing feelings such as anxiety, anger, and sadness are normal and inevitable. Handling these emotions inadequately, and consequently suffering in an unusually intense or persistent manner, are thought to be "abnormal."

These criteria have several problems. First, they distinguish abnormality from normality by *degree* of disturbance. In other words, human beings considered psychologically abnormal are said to show *more* cognitive impairment, behave in *less* socially appropriate ways, and/or demonstrate *less* control over their emotions or themselves than so-called normal people do. Not all experts agree that normality and abnormality differ only in degree. Many believe that the distinguishing features are *qualitative* as well as *quantitative*. *Hallucinations* (sensory experiences with no basis in reality), for instance, are probably not merely large amounts of fantasy imagery. We return to this quantity-quality issue a little later.

There is a second significant problem with our criteria for abnormal behavior. When we talk about socially appropriate behavior, as we did in item 2, we are admitting that definitions of psychological abnormality depend on cultural practices. Yet many social standards are artificial and arbitrary. Dirt eating *(geophagy)*, for example, is thought to be a perfectly acceptable activity in certain regions of Siberia, China, Japan, Mexico, Africa, and the United States. The behavior may be motivated by nutritional deficiencies (as described in Chapter 10). But, among the West African group known as the Serer, a dirt-eating compulsion in nonpregnant adults is considered symptomatic of either a terrible moral failure or a fatal illness. When geophagy is accepted by the culture, it is not accompanied by psychological or physical distress. Among the Serer, however, the condition is associated with shame, anxiety, deviousness, dizzy spells, pallor, abdominal swelling and discomfort, weakness, and shortness of breath [3]. Apparently, ridicule, isolation, and disapproval transform dirt-eating into a mental illness. Consider a second example. In most of the Western world, lesbianism and homosexuality have been considered immoral for hundreds of years. Eventually, the moral objections were "medicalized" and the behavior was called "sick." In the early 1970s, homosexuality and lesbianism were removed from the psychiatric illness classification. The change was made because research had demonstrated that sexual preference is not associated regularly with emotional distress or impaired social functioning. The new psychiatric classification system, which we will describe soon, is partially reviving the illness status of same-sex sexual preferences by including a category for "gay" people who feel distressed about their condition and desire to acquire a heterosexual orientation. What is

considered normal and abnormal, then, may depend on the culture, change with the times, and be difficult to justify by absolute standards.

Because of these facts, some mental health professionals strongly object to labeling people abnormal. They worry that nonconformists, eccentrics, rebels, and social critics—particularly if poor and powerless—may come to be viewed as "sick," isolated in institutions, and subjected to treatment [4]. People who opposed the American Revolution were once regarded as suffering from a mental illness called *"revolutiona."* American slaves who ran away from their masters were said to have *"drapetomania."* In practice, many mental health experts avoid using the term "abnormal" and speak instead of *"maladjusted behavior"* or *"maladjustment."* These terms imply that conduct deviates from standards considered appropriate for a specific situation without suggesting that absolute guidelines are being used.

The criteria defining psychological abnormality have a third major problem. They are vague and don't provide clear guidelines for assessing disturbed behavior. As a result, the opinions of psychologists, psychiatrists, and other professionals about a particular person's mental status often differ greatly. Because the standards are hazy, judgments may be readily biased by irrelevant considerations. Recently, psychologists Ellen Langer and Robert Abelson demonstrated that precisely the same behavior in the same individual could be perceived as emotionally healthy or unhealthy by experts, depending on their expectations. Groups of psychologists and psychiatrists saw a videotape on which a young man described job difficulties to an interviewer. The professionals had to judge how psychologically disturbed the interviewee was. Some experts thought that they were seeing an employment interview, while others believed that they were watching a psychiatric interview. The training of the clinicians differed. Some came from a behavioristic background; others, from a psychoanalytic one. Psychologists and psychiatrists who viewed the interaction as a job-centered discussion considered the client reasonably well-adjusted. They described the young man by using terms such as "ordinary," "straightforward," "fairly open," and "somewhat ingenious." Traditional psychoanalytic clinicians who saw the interview as a psychiatric one perceived the young man as more than moderately disturbed. They used adjectives such as "tight," "defensive," "dependent," "frightened," "passive," "rigid," and "hostile" to describe the youth [5]. As we have seen numerous times, expectations color perceptions. This phenomenon has unfortunate consequences on judgments of mental health, which we describe more fully later. See Figure 15-1.

Classifying Abnormal Behavior

Conduct that is considered "abnormal" or "maladjusted" is often classified more precisely in a specific diagnostic category. Most mental health institutions in the United States rely on the system of the American Psychiatric Association, described in the manual entitled *Diagnostic and Statistical Manual of Mental Disorders* (DSM). DSM-II, the edition in use as the author writes in 1979, will

soon be replaced by a new one, DSM-III. Our comments are based on an early draft of DSM-III, which has been in general circulation [6]. The new document is very controversial. We will not discuss the system in detail, but will use its vocabulary as we describe specific syndromes.

Many behavioristic psychologists object to the traditional classification system. Instead of using it, they are likely to assess the varied behaviors that constitute the problem. Why classify abnormal behavior at all? What problems accompany classification?

Why classify abnormal behavior?

Some psychologists believe that the diagnostic categories of the classification system provide insights into (1) causes of a problem, (2) appropriate treatment techniques, (3) symptoms that may eventually become evident, and (4) likely future outcomes. Critics of classification contend that because current understanding is spotty, diagnostic labels do not communicate these types of information adequately. Other behavioral scientists take a middle-of-the-road position. They see classification systems as imperfect but necessary. They believe that the diagnostic labels provide some information and that abandoning classification would retard research. Investi-

FIGURE 15-1 Since the death of her greyhound, Kate Ward has cared for more than 500 dogs. She became the self-appointed guardian of stray canines in the early 1940s and fulfilled the duties of the office for more than 30 years. Do you consider the woman's behavior abnormal? Because criteria of abnormality vary greatly, the opinions of psychologists and other experts often differ. [*Tony Ray Jones/Magnum.*]

gators would fail to notice similarities between disorders that provide critical knowledge. Consider a clear-cut illustration. Phenylketonuria (PKU) is a form of mental retardation that results from an inability to metabolize a particular protein, phenylalanine, and the subsequent accumulation of brain-injuring substances. One effective treatment is a diet low in phenylalanine. But:

. . . had [scientists] taken 100 or even 1,000 people with mental deficiency and placed them all on the phenylalanine-free diet, the response would have been insignificant and the diet would have been discarded as a treatment. It was first necessary to recognize a subtype of mental deficiency, phenylketonuria, and then subject the value of a phenylalanine-free diet to investigation in this specific population. [7]

What problems accompany classification? Any specific classification system is likely to have its own individual problems. DSM-II, for instance, did not provide explicit diagnostic guidelines. Consequently, mental health experts frequently disagreed over how to categorize a specific individual [8]. Though DSM-III promises to minimize this failing, critics argue that it overemphasizes biological causes. They also object to its converting many human problems, habits, and dilemmas (such as "smoking and wanting to quit" and "reacting to a catastrophe") into mental disorders. Another troubling side effect accompanies the use of most—perhaps all—diagnostic systems at this time. Psychiatric diagnoses create harmful expectations. Patients who have been labeled often see themselves as ill and unable to do much about their condition. Friends and relatives, employers, landlords, and other community figures often react adversely. The labels even influence how mental health professionals view people. After being diagnosed as schizophrenic, for example, patients are apt to receive less attention from the experts than before being labeled—perhaps because schizophrenics are sometimes perceived as "beyond help" [9]. The tags may interfere with seeing the patient as an individual. The clinician who believes, for example, that an inability to experience pleasure and to think logically is associated with schizophrenia may look for and find those symptoms even when they aren't present. It is also unfortunate that diagnostic labels tend to stick. A daring and important study by psychologist David Rosenhan highlights some of these shortcomings. We look more closely at this research.

On Being Sane in Insane Places

David Rosenhan arranged for eight reasonably normal people—including several psychologists, a pediatrician, a psychiatrist, a painter, and a housewife—to gain admission to twelve different mental institutions. The "pseudopatients," as Rosenhan called his research participants, complained of hearing voices that were often unclear but seemed to be saying "empty," "hollow," and "thud." "Beyond alleging the symptoms and falsifying name, vocation, and employment, no further alterations of person, history, or circumstances were made. . . . Immediately upon admission to the psychiatric ward, the pseudopatients ceased simulating any symptoms of abnormality. In some cases, there was a brief period of mild nervousness and anxiety, since none of the pseudopatients really believed that they would be admitted so easily." Beyond the ward activities, the research participants spent their time writing notes about the institution, the other patients, and the staff. "Initially these notes were written 'secretly,' but as it soon became clear that no one much cared, they were subsequently written on standard tablets of paper in such public places as the dayroom." Nursing reports confirmed that the pseudopatients exhibited no abnormal indications on the ward. And, when asked, Rosenhan's participants indicated that they no longer experienced any symptoms.

Despite the display of sanity, psychologists, psychiatrists, and other mental health professionals did not detect the faking. With a single exception, the pseudopatients were diagnosed as having schizophrenia and discharged after about nineteen days, on the average, with the diagnosis "schizophrenia in remission." A single hallucinatory experience should not have resulted in the schizophrenia diagnosis. "Having once been labeled schizophrenic, there [was apparently] nothing the pseudopatient [could] do to overcome the tag." The label was so powerful that many normal behaviors were overlooked or misinterpreted. Nursing reports suggested, for example, that the pseudopatients' writing was seen as a manifestation of illness [10].

Many psychologists agree with Rosenhan's major points. Psychiatric labels tend to persist. And, because they are looking for abnormality, clinicians in mental hospitals frequently misinterpret perfectly appropriate responses. You may recall that the Langer-Abelson study supported this notion as well. In concluding his research report, Rosenhan emphasized another point that deserves mention. The labels may be deceptive. They suggest to both the general public and to mental health experts that the disturbed behavior is understood and that everything is under control. Because knowledge of mental disturbances is still very incomplete, complacency is exceedingly premature and potentially very dangerous. We will discuss behavioral problems within the traditional framework. But try not to forget the negative aspects of the classification system. ▲

Conceptualizing Abnormal Behavior

In ancient times the Greeks and Romans believed that evil spirits entered certain people, "possessed" them, and drove them mad. Our ancestors in the Middle Ages held this belief too. As enlightened a man as the German theologian Martin Luther (1483–1546) wrote: "In cases of melancholy . . . I conclude it is merely the work of the devil. . . . Those whom [the devil] possesses corporally as mad people, he has permission from God to vex and agitate, but he has no power over their souls [11]." See Figure 15-2.

Emil Kraepelin (1856–1926), a German psychiatrist who studied psychology under Wilhelm Wundt in Leipzig, helped establish the view that natural forces cause abnormal behavior. Kraepelin noticed that certain mental symptoms tended to occur together. He concluded that each cluster represented a separate and distinct illness, much like measles or small pox. Kraepelin believed that each "mental disease" had a physiological cause which would eventually be discovered.

Medical terminology is often used today to describe psychological problems. In the words of psychologist Brendan Maher:

Abnormal behavior is termed *pathological* and is classified on the basis of *symptoms*, classification

FIGURE 15-2 During the Middle Ages it was commonly believed that evil spirits possessed human beings and drove them mad. The fifteenth-century artist Martin Schongauer illustrated the idea in this engraving, entitled *Saint Anthony Tormented by Demons.* [*The Metropolitan Museum of Art, Rogers Fund, 1920.*]

being called *diagnosis*. Processes designed to change behavior are called *therapies* and are applied to *patients* in *mental hospitals*. If the deviant behavior ceases, the patient is described as *cured*. [12]

Some mental health professionals endorse a *medical model* of abnormal behavior. Like Kraepelin, many believe that mental disorders are specific medical conditions for which biological causes will eventually be discovered. In a relatively small number of cases, a precise infection, nutritional deficiency, genetic defect, hormonal imbalance, or bacterial or viral agent *is known* to cause deviant behavior, as we shall see later on. Many of the experts who endorse a medical model believe that emotional disorders only *resem-*

ble physical ailments. Both types of medical models tend to make the following assumptions:

1. Each psychological disorder, like a disease, consists of a cluster of fairly definite abnormal symptoms that are *qualitatively* different from normal behaviors. Each type of mental problem is viewed as having a specific cause or causes.
2. The expert must identify and treat the underlying cause(s).
3. The patient tends to be viewed as a passive recipient of treatment whose primary responsibility is following the expert's directions.

Thomas Szasz, whom we mentioned at the beginning of the chapter, is a leading critic of the medical model. In his words: "Mental illness is a myth. [Mental health professionals] are not concerned with mental illnesses and their treatment. In actual practice they deal with personal, social, and ethical problems in living [13]." Few clinicians reject the medical model as completely as Szasz does. But a great many believe that medical models often hinder the understanding and treatment of mental problems. Some critics of the medical model endorse a *psychological model* of abnormal behavior, one which generally makes these assumptions:

1. Abnormal behavior is shaped by precisely the same factors that mold normal conduct—cumulative interactions of social, psychological, and biological factors—and is only *quantitatively* different from normal behavior. Similar problems may arise in diverse ways. (Incidentally, many medical conditions follow what we are calling a psychological model. They reflect cumulative interactions between social, psychological, and biological variables and can be developed in different ways. Heart disease, for example, appears to be caused by a genetic predisposition in combination with varied irritants, such as smoking, stress, and diet.)
2. Treatment cannot currently cure mental disorders in the same way that physicians can cure a physical ailment. Today, psychological therapies provide reeducative experiences and medications that help people acquire control over problems and lives.
3. Active patient involvement in treatment is essential. The sufferer must learn to cope productively with various life situations.

While some professionals endorse one model and reject the other, some fail to be convinced of the validity of either one. And many behavioral scientists see no contradiction in using both models. They may perceive disorder X as fitting the psychological framework more closely and disorder Y as fitting the medical framework. As we discuss particular types of abnormal behavior, we will present major research findings and psychoanalytic and behavioristic explanations. You may want to review both personality theories (Chapter 13). Though the correspondence is crude at best, the psychoanalytic viewpoint approximates a medical model while the behavioristic perspective approximates a psychological model.

Differences between Neurotic and Psychotic Behavior

It is common to hear odd behavior labeled "neurotic" or "psychotic." Mental health professionals use these words in specific ways.

Neuroses or *neurotic reactions* were first described by Sigmund Freud. They are disorders that center around anxiety. In some cases, the anxiety is experienced directly and is obvious. In other cases, the anxiety is presumed to be controlled by various maneuvers and is not readily apparent. Persons called neurotic often avoid anxiety-arousing situations, even though their freedom of movement may be constricted severely. While neurotic individuals may find their own behavior bewildering, they typically feel unable to help themselves. As distress and inadequacy increasingly absorb their attention, neurotic persons are apt to feel wasted and unhappy. DSM-II classified the nine different patterns in Table 15-1 as neurotic. Many students of abnormal behavior questioned whether these diverse conditions really belong together. The writers of DSM-III discarded the category of neurosis. They classify behavior which has been traditionally called neurotic under four headings: anxiety, somatoform, dissociative, and affective disorders. We will describe reactions from each of these categories.

TABLE 15-1 Conditions Labeled Neurotic by DSM-II

Condition	Primary symptoms
1. Phobic neurosis	Extreme fear and avoidance of some object that is known to be harmless
2. Anxiety neurosis	Anxiety felt in a large number of situations, though no specific object can be pinpointed
3. Obsessive-compulsive neurosis	Persistent, uncontrollable thoughts or compulsions to repeat specific behaviors
4. Hysterical neurosis, dissociative type	Disorders of awareness including memory lapses, sleepwalking, and multiple personalities
5. Hysterical neurosis, conversion type	Varied sensory disturbances without a physical basis
6. Neurasthenic neurosis	Chronic fatigue and weakness
7. Depersonalization neurosis	Feelings that the world is unreal and estrangement from self and environment
8. Depressive neurosis	Extreme unhappiness brought on by some event
9. Hypochondriacal neurosis	Preoccupation with imagined illnesses and other bodily symptoms

FIGURE 15-3 The objects of the phobic's anxieties are often potentially dangerous ones. The fear of heights is a striking example. Almost all human beings acquire a fear of heights at an early age, as we learned from the visual cliff experiments described in Chapter 6. Currently, many behavioral scientists believe that survival-enhancing fears, such as this one, are preprogrammed into people through evolutionary mechanisms. Why some individuals develop incapacitating fears is not understood. [*Jim Jowers/Nancy Palmer Photo Agency.*]

People are said to have a *psychosis* or to be *psychotic* when their mental functioning is sufficiently impaired to interfere grossly with their capacity to meet ordinary life demands. The problems may result from an inability to recognize reality, alterations of mood, and/or intellectual deficits (in perception, language, memory, and the like). Whereas neurotic people are able to function quite normally in

many ways, psychotic individuals are frequently unable to care for themselves. While neurotics often recognize their symptoms, psychotics are less likely to do so. DSM-III includes psychotic conditions under a number of classifications. We will consider several psychotic patterns, including the bipolar affective, schizophrenic, and organic mental disorders.

The word "*insane*," as it is commonly used, has roughly the same meaning as the term "psychotic." But mental health experts rarely call anybody "insane" today, except in courts of law. (Rosenhan, you may recall, used the word in the popular sense.) Criminal law assumes that people function as free agents and do wrong because they choose to. It is justifiable, then, to punish lawbreakers. Criminals are judged "*insane*" if they appear to have been (1) grossly mentally deficient and/or (2) unable to distinguish between right and wrong at the time that the crime was committed. "Insane" individuals are not punished because they are thought to lack the free will that would justify holding them accountable for their behavior. The usefulness of the criminal insanity concept is highly controversial [14]. ▲

We turn now to varied types of abnormal behavior.

ANXIETY DISORDERS

Phobic, panic, and obsessive-compulsive disorders center around anxiety You may recall that we defined anxiety as an emotion characterized by feelings of anticipated danger, tension, and distress and by sympathetic nervous system arousal. In Chapters 5, 11, and 14, we described the causes and consequences of anxiety and the ways people cope with the emotion. In this section, we focus on abnormal responses to intense anxiety. As in previous chapters, we use the terms anxiety and fear in roughly the same way.

Phobic Disorder

A *phobia* is an excessive or unwarranted fear of a specific object or situation that is handled by persistent avoidance. The person with a phobia, the *phobic*, knows that his or her anxiety is disproportionate to the danger involved but feels unable to control the feeling. Phobias are associated with a wide variety of stimuli, including heights, open or con-fined areas, crowds, being alone, pain, storms, blood, germs, darkness, disease, ridicule, snakes, animals, and fires. Note that many of these phenomena are potentially harmful ones that people may be preprogrammed to learn to fear (a topic discussed in Chapter 5). See Figure 15-3. On the basis of a New England survey, psychologists estimate that approximately 15 million Americans have phobias. But only a small percentage (some 44,000) appear to have crippling fears [15]. Phobias are considered *phobic disorders only* when they are disruptive and disabling, as in the following case.

Martha

Since childhood Martha had been afraid to stay alone in a house. Family discussions of lurid robberies, murders, and rapes had impressed her with the potential dangers and with her own helplessness. The young woman never outgrew the fear. It became particularly troublesome after her husband began working the night shift. Although she attempted to stay by herself at first, she found her life haunted by images of the impending evening. At the time that Martha sought treatment, she was spending the greater part of each day making frenzied arrangements for relatives, neighbors, or friends to stay with her for the evening. The phobia was directing Martha's life.

How does the phobic disorder develop? Psychoanalytic psychologists view phobias as *displaced anxiety reactions*. They assume that fear is shifted unconsciously from an initial anxiety-arousing experience to a harmless object. Consider one of Freud's classic phobic cases. Little Hans, a five-year-old boy, feared that he would be bitten by a horse and did not want to go outside. Using the father's observations, Freud analyzed the boy's behavior. He concluded that Hans loved his mother, desired her sexually, and feared that his rival, the father, might retaliate by castrating him. As Freud saw it, the anxiety due to the Oedipal conflict was transformed subsequently into the horse phobia [16]. Behavioristic psychologists assume that the phobic's anxiety is learned directly. As we saw in Chapter 5, fears can be acquired by respondent conditioning when previously neutral stimuli are associated with anxiety-arousing objects, images, thoughts, and the like. Avoidance behavior may be learned in several ways. Phobics may model the behavior of others. Or a specific avoidance tactic may be adopted because it was successful previously. Whatever behavior diminishes the unpleasant anxiety feelings is likely to be strengthened through operant conditioning principles— even though the long-term consequences may be crippling.

Is there research evidence for the behavioristic analysis? Few people report acquiring phobic disorders directly through fear-eliciting experiences [17]. On the other hand, many phobics say that they engage in anxiety-evoking ruminations when confronting frightening situations [18]. A person with anxieties about airplane travel might think in the midst of flight, "What's that noise? The engines are failing. The plane is probably going to crash. I'm not going to make it." Cognitions of this sort would perpetuate and aggravate phobias.

Why do only some people develop life-disrupting anxieties? Psychoanalytic theorists hypothesize that the phobic's fears reflect deeply rooted unconscious conflicts centering, more often than not, on sex and aggression. Research suggests several alternative possibilities. People whose autonomic nervous systems respond especially swiftly and vigorously to dangers may acquire phobias and other anxiety-related disorders readily. Genetic endowment influences how easily the autonomic nervous system is aroused, how quickly it recovers, and how intensely it responds [19]. Chronic, severe anxiety-arousing experiences, such as combat during war, may also result in an overreactive autonomic nervous system [20].

Panic Disorder

Persons with *panic disorders*, or *anxiety neuroses* as they were formerly called, experience *anxiety* (or *panic*) *attacks*. The attacks are sudden and often begin with an inexplicable, uncontrollable sense of terror. During the panic attack, breathing is difficult. Tremors, nausea, excessive perspiration, heart-rate irregularities, and other autonomic signs of tension are prominent. People with this disorder frequently overreact to minor stresses and strains and appear to be anxious and worried almost continually. The anxiety cannot be traced to specific causes, so it is said to be *free-floating*. Muscle tension, digestive problems, and headaches—the physical accompaniments of anxiety—are common symptoms. Typically, individuals with this condition worry a great deal about the attacks and about other stresses. Worrying interferes with concentration and sleep. Chronic tension and fatigue from insomnia reduce the person's effectiveness and lead to increased anxiety, irritability, and often to depression as well [21]. People with panic disorders (some 10 million Americans are thought to experience this problem [22]) may attempt to escape by drinking, taking drugs, and/or physically avoiding situations where attacks have occurred. The woman in the following case history was diagnosed as suffering from the panic disorder.

Sue

Sue, a recently married, twenty-year-old college student, had been experiencing anxiety attacks for approximately a year when the therapist first saw her. Without warning, her heart began pounding and breathing became difficult. Her hands sweated profusely. Her stomach muscles tightened. Sue also felt flushed and feverish at these times. Although the young woman had frequently experienced these sensations, she could not stop herself from wondering if she was about to die.

Yet, somewhere in the back of her mind Sue knew that when she closed her eyes and rested, she would feel normal again within an hour.

Sue's first anxiety attack occurred as she was leaving a crowded football stadium. The only previous event that could be connected with these feelings was a panicky reaction to a TV story about a nightclub fire which trapped and killed thirty people. Sue's second anxiety attack took place during an argument with her husband about

whether to wear slacks or a dress to a family party. Sue didn't remember the details surrounding the third attack or the fourth or all the others which she had experienced since. The attacks were coming almost every day now—whenever any one disagreed with her, when she encountered strangers, when she drove in congested traffic, when she shopped in crowded stores. Lately, Sue had been trying to avoid the places where the attacks happened most frequently. Consequently, she was spending a great deal of time in her apartment. She ventured into the world primarily to seek help. The many physicians whom Sue consulted found nothing medically wrong, and eventually she was referred to a psychiatric clinic.

What causes the panic disorder? According to Freudian theory, the ego tries to prevent the id from expressing its desires—usually for sex or aggression—in dangerous situations where they are apt to be punished. This unconscious id-ego conflict generates anxiety. Because the person can neither escape nor gratify the id impulses nor come to grips with the conflict (since it is unconscious), the conflict persists and the anxiety continues. Behavioristic psychologists, in contrast, see the causes of the panic disorder as quite similar to those of the phobic disorder. Presumably, the anxiety component of the panic reaction is acquired in the same way that simple fears are—by respondent conditioning. Through stimulus generalization, the anxiety may spread to other situations until it appears to be pervasive. The avoidance response may be learned through observation or personal experience. It is thought to be reinforced by anxiety reduction, at least over the short run. As in the case of the phobic, autonomic nervous system hyperactivity—due to genetic endowment or extensive stresses—may predispose certain people to develop this condition.

Obsessive-Compulsive Disorder

The person with the *obsessive-compulsive disorder* is tyrannized by *obsessions* (recurring, unwanted thoughts) and/or *compulsions* (recurring, unwanted, ritualistic acts). An interview study of eighty-two obsessive-compulsive patients suggests that thoughts and behaviors vary quite a bit and can be categorized in the following ways [23]:

1. *Obsessive doubts.* Worrying persistently about adequately completing a specific task, such as locking the door.
2. *Obsessive thinking.* An endless chain of thoughts, usually centering around a future event. (One pregnant woman ruminated in this way: "If my baby is a boy, he might aspire to a career that would necessitate his going away from me, but he might want to return to me and what would I do because. . . .")
3. *Obsessive impulses.* Urges to perform various actions ranging from trivia to murder.
4. *Obsessive fears.* Worrying about losing control and doing something embarrassing (for example, talking about a sexual problem).
5. *Obsessive images.* Persisting images of a recently seen or imagined event.
6. *Yielding to compulsions.* Performing actions suggested by the obsessive thoughts, such as checking pockets repeatedly for a document.
7. *Controlling compulsions.* Using distractive tactics, such as counting, to control the objectionable thoughts.

Obsessive-compulsive people typically regard their thoughts and/or rituals as morbid or irrational. But they find that intense anxiety arises if the thought or act is prevented. Research supports the idea that obsessions and compulsions reduce anxiety [24]—perhaps by temporarily blocking out fear-arousing ideas or impulses.

A great many psychologically healthy people carry out rituals such as washing the dishes after dinner or checking the doors at night. Similarly, most human beings experience recurring thoughts. The lyrics of a song may run through your mind persistently. Or you may ponder repeatedly a mark in a course, an argument, a rejection, or an eagerly anticipated party. Obsessions and compulsions are considered "neurotic" only when they serve no constructive purpose, are exceedingly distressing, and disrupt life. Estimates of the incidence of the obsessive-compulsive disorder range from 12 to 20 percent of the neurotic population [25].

Psychoanalytic theorists believe that obsessions and compulsions plague individuals who are fixated at the anal stage because of harsh toilet training. The symptoms arise, presumably, during an unconscious conflict between id and ego. The ego uses obsessions and/or compulsions as defense mechanisms to settle the dispute. The ego of an obsessively neat individual, for example, may be utilizing *reaction formation* (concealing a real motive from the self by expressing the opposite one) to resist id impulses to soil. Similarly, the ego might employ a counting ritual to *undo* (or atone for) distressing desires—say, id impulses to masturbate—and consequently cancel or counteract them. Behavioristic psychologists assume that obsessions and compulsions are acquired through reinforcement principles. A person accidentally discovers that performing a particular act or thinking a certain thought blots out a distressing concern and reduces anxiety. The distraction is consequently substituted consciously and deliberately every time the fear arises. Eventually the obsession or compulsion becomes automatic.

Physiological factors may contribute to obsessive-compulsive behavior. Studies of twins indicate that the disorder is influenced by heredity [26]. People with obsessive-compulsive symptoms frequently exhibit neurological problems [27]. Perhaps, a specific property of the nervous system makes some individuals likely to ruminate persistently. If these people also react to stresses with excessive anxiety, they may be particularly likely to develop the obsessive-compulsive disorder.

SOMATOFORM DISORDERS

The *somatoform disorders*, formerly classified as neuroses, are characterized by physical problems. But the symptoms of these disorders have no demonstrable organic basis and appear to be linked to psychological difficulties. We examine one somatoform disorder, the *conversion disorder (conversion reaction)*. People with this syndrome show unusual sensory or motor symptoms, such as paralysis, loss of vision, or insensitivity to pain. The symptoms usually develop in stressful situations and appear suddenly and all at once.

About one of every three patients views the affliction with nonchalance or indifference [28]. (Stoical people view distressing physical conditions in a similar manner.) A medical diagnosis is apt to be rejected for several reasons.

1. In some cases, the symptoms are nonsensical. They do not correspond to any known illness. They may even contradict knowledge about the workings of the body.
2. The symptoms of the conversion disorder may disappear during sleep or hypnosis.
3. The symptoms sometimes handicap the individual selectively. A musician whose paralyzed hand makes violin playing impossible may be able to function quite normally on the tennis court.

How can the conversion disorder be explained? Freud suspected that the condition helps people escape unconscious conflicts that arouse severe anxiety. Behaviorally oriented psychologists see the response quite similarly. A woman who dreads her employer's amorous advances might become blind and find herself "forced" to quit work. A soldier who fears combat duty might develop a paralysis and be "unable" to return to the front. Though faking cannot be ruled out, patients appear to be sincere. The symptoms are thought to be "contrived" at a less than conscious level—perhaps by an unsophisticated, suggestible, melodramatic individual who had little formal education [29]. Some so-called conversion disorders are actually misdiagnosed medical conditions. Recently, investigators followed the progress of conversion reaction patients seven to eleven years after the diagnosis was made. About 60 percent of the subjects had either died of diseases or discovered legitimate medical problems (often involving the central nervous system). These physical disorders may have been present, of course, at the time of the initial diagnosis. Perhaps they had caused subtle disturbances, self-preoccupation, suggestibility, and bids for attention—behavior that contributed to the conversion disorder diagnosis [30]. Findings like these have been reported by other researchers [31]. Because medical assessment is far from perfect at this point in time, the symptoms of a bona fide physical problem can be mistaken for a conversion disorder.

DISSOCIATIVE DISORDERS

Like the somatoform disorders, the dissociative ones were formerly classified as neuroses. *Dissociative disorders* include several syndromes that are characterized by alterations in consciousness—primarily memory lapses. Because injuries and diseases can produce the same symptoms, dissociative disorders are diagnosed only when the problem appears to be produced by a nonmedical condition. Amnesia, fugue, and multiple personality are examples of dissociative disorders. During an *amnesia* the afflicted individual suddenly loses her or his memory for important personal information. The lapse may persist for minutes or for years. A *fugue* occurs when a person not only forgets recent experiences, but also flees to a different locality to begin a new life. The individual with the fugue disorder functions normally in the novel role but cannot remember the previous identity. People with *multiple personality* symptoms show two or more very different personality patterns. Yet, they are aware of only one personality at any specific point in time. The transition from one to another pattern tends to be sudden and is often associated with stress. The multiple personality syndrome is sometimes confused with schizophrenia. People with the dissociative disorder display two or more fairly well-integrated and coherent personalities. Each has its own set of memories, behavior patterns, and friendships, in some instances. Schizophrenics, in contrast, show only one personality that is fragmented and disjointed.

The dissociative disorders are rare. They are more apt to be seen on television soap operas than in psychiatric clinics. So far, only about 200 cases have been documented—mostly by informal clinical observations [32]. Both psychoanalytic and behavioristic psychologists view the dissociative disorders as attempts to escape anxiety-arousing situations. But, as of now, we have a very limited understanding of these problems.

AFFECTIVE DISORDERS

The *affective disorders* are characterized primarily by excessive sadness or its opposite, frenzied excitement and elation. We describe major depressive and bipolar affective disorders and explain what is known about their causes.

Major Depressive Disorder

Major depressive disorder (*depression*, as it is usually abbreviated) includes disturbances that were formerly classified in both the neurotic and psychotic categories, depending on the specific symptoms involved. Depression is considered the "common cold" of psychological problems because it is more widespread than any other. In one recent investigation, 15 percent of a random sample of American adults reported currently experiencing depressive symptoms [33]. Experts estimate that 50 percent of the people in the United States will experience a depression at some point during their lives [34]. Psychologists usually differentiate between depression and sadness. Depression is a more intense and persistent state than sadness. Typically, depressed people feel hopeless and dejected. Time passes slowly, perhaps because depressives fail to experience pleasure. Loved ones, food, sex, hobbies, work, and recreation lose appeal. Consequently, depressed individuals tend to withdraw from former routines and neglect duties and responsibilities. While some depressed people behave in a passive, lethargic way, others appear to be restless and agitated. The conversations of depressed adults suggest that they feel critical of themselves, guilt-ridden, irritable, and unable to control the direction of their lives. Thoughts of death, including suicide, may recur. In proportionately few cases, the depressed person experiences *hallucinations* and *delusions* (persistent irrational beliefs) and shows other signs of psychosis, in addition to the depression [35]. Fortunately, depressions usually dissipate with time—even when individuals receive no treatment at all. The following case illustrates characteristic depressive behavior patterns.

Mr. J.

"Mr. J. was a fifty-one-year-old industrial engineer who, since the death of his wife five years earlier, had been suffering from continuing episodes of depression marked by extreme social withdrawal and occasional thoughts of suicide. His wife had died in an automobile accident during a shopping trip which he himself was to have made but had cancelled because of professional responsibilities. His self-blame for her death, which became evident immediately after the funeral and was regarded by his friends and relatives as transitory, deepened as the months, and then years, passed by. He began to drink, sometimes heavily, and when thoroughly intoxicated would plead to his deceased wife for forgiveness. He lost all capacity for joy—his friends could not recall when they had last seen him smile. His gait was typically slow and labored, his voice usually tearful, his posture stooped. Once a gourmet, he had lost all interest in food and good wine, and on those increasingly rare occasions when friends invited him for dinner, this previously witty, urbane man could barely manage to engage in small talk. As might be expected, his work record deteriorated markedly, along with his psychological condition. Appointments were missed and projects haphazardly started and then left unfinished. . . . Not long [after being referred for psychotherapy] he emerged from his despair and began to feel his old self again [36]."

Bipolar Affective Disorder

Everyone has periodic ups and downs. The individual with the *bipolar affective disorder* (a psychotic condition formerly considered under the category manic-depressive illness) experiences recurring bouts of profound *depression* and *mania* (excited elation). Very few persons have only manic episodes [37]. Since we have already described the symptoms of depression, we focus on those of mania. During a manic episode, individuals appear ecstatic and extraordinarily self-confident. At the same time, they are irritable and easily angered. Speech tends to be rapid. Topics change quickly. Ideas frequently center on grand schemes to obtain wealth, power, and fame. If friends and relatives object, they may be viewed as enemies or traitors. When angered, persons in a manic state are apt to become assaultive. They are physically active and may get in trouble by behaving impulsively and inappropriately—for example, going on outlandish spending sprees, making repeated applications for unsuitable jobs, and engaging in promiscuous sex. Though patients in a manic state appear to have unlimited energy, they are easily distracted and find it difficult to accomplish much of anything. Sleep tends to be fitful and infrequent. The following exchange between a therapist and a patient illustrates features that are typical of the manic episode.

THERAPIST: Well, you seem pretty happy today.
CLIENT: Happy! Happy! You certainly are a master of understatement, you rogue! (Shouting, literally jumping out of seat.) Why I'm ecstatic. I'm leaving for the West Coast today, on my daughter's bicycle. Only 3,100 miles. That's nothing, you know. I could probably walk, but I want to get there by next week. And along the way I plan to follow up on my inventions of the past month, you know, stopping at the big plants along the way having lunch with the executives, maybe getting to know them a bit—you know, Doc, "know" in the biblical sense (leering at therapist seductively). Oh, God, how good it feels. It's almost like a non-stop orgasm. [38]

The incidence of the bipolar affective disorder is hard to estimate because the condition is increasingly treated by drugs while the patient remains in the community. Before effective medicines were discovered, manic attacks might last about three months and depressive episodes approximately six to eight months. The number of depressive and manic episodes varies. So does the rapidity with which they alternate. Depressive symptoms tend to be more common than manic ones [39]. Usually there are normal periods lasting months or even years between attacks. Today, modern drugs can often control manic and depressive symptoms within a week or two. If the medication is discontinued, the symptoms generally return. While some people seem to recover from the bipolar affective disorder, about one in three patients shows a chronic and severe social impairment [40]. See Figure 15-4.

Causes of Affective Disorders

Why do some individuals succumb to severe depressions while others do not? Freud believed that too much or too little gratification during the oral period produces an overly dependent personality. Then, when the individual experiences an *actual loss* (such as the death of a loved one) or a *symbolic loss* (such as rejection), unconscious anger at the other party for "leaving" turns into self-anger and eventually into depression. Behavioristic psychologists assume that depressions occur when sources of customary reinforcements (such as a supportive spouse, a satisfying job, or financial success) are suddenly withdrawn. People respond to the loss by slowing down their activities. If subsequent efforts are not reinforced, the individual may do even less. Sometimes the pattern of inactivity is strengthened by sympathy and attention.

An increasing number of behavioral scientists emphasize the role of cognitions in causing and maintaining depressions. Drawing on clinical observations, psychiatrist Aaron Beck has concluded that depressed individuals often think illogically. He finds that depressives turn relatively unimportant problems

FIGURE 15-4 The brilliant British novelist Virginia Woolf suffered from the bipolar affective disorder. Her adult life was filled with painful bouts of excitability and sadness. Several of Woolf's depressions were precipitated by losses. The author collapsed at her mother's death and again nine years later when her father died. Besides violent alterations in mood, she experienced psychotic symptoms. At times she even babbled incoherently in Greek to imaginary birds. Woolf made several suicide attempts and finally drowned herself in 1941, when she felt she was about to go "mad" again. "I feel we can't go through another of those terrible times. And I shan't recover this time," she explained in a suicide note to her husband [95]. [*Mrs. Ian Parsons, Harcourt Brace Jovanovich.*]

into catastrophes, underestimate accomplishments and strengths, and magnify failures and weaknesses. One of Beck's patients reported the following sequence of events (occurring within a period of half an hour):

His wife was upset because the children were slow in getting dressed. He thought, "I'm a poor father because the children are not better disciplined." He noted a leaky faucet and thought that this showed he was a poor husband. While driving to work, he thought, "I must be a poor driver or other cars would not be passing me." As he arrived at work, he noticed some other personnel had already arrived. He thought, "I can't be very dedicated or I would have come earlier." When he noticed folders and papers piled up on his desk, he concluded, "I'm a poor organizer because I have so much work to do." [41]

Unreasonable self-judgments, in Beck's view, can cause depression [42].

Psychologist Martin Seligman also believes that cognitions play an important role in depression, but he emphasizes a slightly different thought pattern. Seligman believes that past experiences have taught depressives to regard themselves as helpless. When helpless people confront an emergency, they feel inadequate, and depression replaces anxiety. Seligman's early ideas were derived in large part from laboratory research on dogs. Under specific conditions, the animals displayed a depressive pattern: appetite loss, diminished interest in sex, reduced aggression, passivity, and a refusal to cope. This canine pattern, which Seligman called *learned helplessness*, occurred when the dogs were forced to endure shocks without means of escape. Later, the animals were placed in situations where specific escape responses were possible. But the dogs made very few attempts to cope. Dogs who had not been compelled to endure shock readily learned to escape under the same circumstances. Apparently, an initial experience with helplessness affected subsequent coping efforts [43].

Seligman has recently expanded his ideas about depressed human beings. When people feel helpless, he believes, they ask themselves why. The causes to which they attribute the condition determine the generality and persistence of their unhappiness [44]. For example, you could attribute a failure to an *internal* cause—say, lack of ability—or an *external* one—perhaps, an unfair situation. Similarly, you could view a problem as the result of some *global* deficiency, such as limited intelligence, or some *specific* deficit like poor numerical skills. Seligman hypothesizes that people who tend to attribute difficulties to internal and/or global phenomena are more apt to feel dejected than those who attribute troubles to external and/or specific causes.

Research supports the notion that cognitions are involved in depression. But it is not clear that thoughts *precede and cause* the unhappy state. We do know that depressed college students exaggerate personal responsibility for bad outcomes and minimize responsibility for good ones [45]. Clinically depressed adults praise themselves less for successes in the laboratory than nondepressed individuals [46]. Recent studies suggest that depressives may actually be realistic in their appraisals while normal people may be overly generous with themselves [47]. Depressed individuals also report more helpless feelings than those who are not depressed [48].

Physiological problems may contribute to certain affective disorders. Twin studies suggest that heredity is involved in some cases of the bipolar affective disorder and in some depressions that begin at early ages [49]. Different genetic mechanisms are presumed to influence different affective problems. Currently, researchers are studying various biological systems that might precipitate or aggravate depressions. Some are investigating brain neurotransmitters, especially *norepinephrine*. When stresses cannot be actively handled, norepinephrine is depleted. The effectiveness of this neurotransmitter is boosted by certain drugs that alleviate depression and is weakened by certain drugs that induce or exaggerate that state. Scientists are examining brain circuits in the hypothalamus which mediate sex, hunger, aggression, pleasure, and pain (responses that are disordered during a depressive episode) to see whether they are involved in depressions [50]. Researchers are also studying the possibility that disturbed biological rhythms influence moods [51]. Heredity, injury, and/or stress could change physical mechanisms such as these in ways that trigger, intensify, or prolong depression.

Depression and suicide are often associated. We discuss suicide briefly.

Suicide in the United States

It is currently estimated that suicide is responsible for approximately 25,000 deaths each year in the United States. Since many suicides are disguised as accidents, such as drug overdoses and automobile crashes, the actual number may be much higher. For each "successful" act, experts guess that there are five to eight unsuccessful attempts [52]. The suicide rate is comparatively high among single people, especially among the divorced [53]. Males are approximately twice as likely to kill themselves as females, though females make more attempts. In some regions of the United States—notably, California—the suicide rate for women is gradually approaching the one for men [54]. During the last twenty years, the rate of fifteen- to twenty-four-year-olds has tripled [55]. Compared with non-students of the same age, college students are especially likely to kill themselves. In recent years, an alarming number of young urban blacks have been doing so. The suicide rate for American Indian youths is also tragically high [56].

Authorities estimate that about 80 percent of those who kill themselves appear to have been depressed beforehand [57]. Suicide is more highly correlated with feelings of hopelessness than with feelings of sadness [58]. Suicide notes, explanations following unsuccessful attempts, and inferences from case histories suggest that there are a great many reasons for suicide. They include (1) chronic depression or loneliness; (2) guilt, remorse, and desire for self-punishment; (3) shame or fear of punishment for failure or aggression; (4) a desire to manipulate or control others (including a wish to punish somebody); (5) escape from an unbearable situation; (6) entry into a new life, reunion with loved ones, or rebirth; and (7) an impulsive reaction to loss [59].

Why is the suicide rate rising among young people? Experts suspect that declining social supports and increasing pressures for achievement are to blame. As divorce and separation become commonplace and as family members pursue their own individual development, more children experience loneliness and insecurity. There is evidence that youths from broken and disorganized homes are more likely to kill themselves than others [60]. When psychologist Richard Seiden collected data on the personalities of college students who committed suicide, he found that they were described uniformly as "terribly shy, virtually friendless individuals, alienated from all but the most minimal social interactions [61]." Along with reduced social support, young people frequently encounter severe pressures to perform. College students, in particular, face a fiercely competitive job market. Many feel compelled to choose a course of study early and to excel so that

TABLE 15-2 Common Myths about Suicide

1. *People who discuss suicide rarely commit the act.* It is estimated that approximately 75 percent of those who take their lives communicate their intent beforehand. They may talk about suicide, ask for help, threaten, or taunt.
2. *Suicide occurs mainly among the poor.* Wealthy and middle-class people often take their own lives.
3. *People of specific religious affiliations do not generally commit suicide.* Though some religions, such as Catholicism, prohibit suicide, identification with these faiths is no guarantee against the act.
4. *People with terminal illnesses do not commit suicide.* Individuals with fatal conditions sometimes take their own lives, especially when they are suffering great pain or disrupting the lives of loved ones.
5. *Primarily insane people commit suicide.* Suicide *is* relatively common among hospitalized mental patients. But, most people who kill themselves do not appear to be irrational or out of touch with reality, though their social relationships are often described as troubled and their thinking as rigid and extreme.
6. *Suicide is influenced by seasons, latitude, weather fronts, barometric pressure, humidity, precipitation, cloudiness, wind speed, temperature, day of the week, sunspots, and phases of the moon.* There is no evidence that any of these phenomena influences suicide.
7. *An improved emotional state removes the risk of suicide.* Depressed people sometimes commit suicide after their spirits have begun rising.
8. *Suicidal people want to die.* Many suicidal individuals—perhaps all of them—appear to be ambivalent about death. Professionals view suicide attempts as a "cry for help."

Sources: Davison, G. C., & Neale, J. M. *Abnormal psychology: An experimental clinical approach.* (2d ed.) New York: Wiley, 1978. P. 217; Reynolds, D. K., & Farberow, N. L. *Suicide: Inside and out.* Berkeley: University of California Press, 1976; Lester, G., & Lester, D. *Suicide: The gamble with death.* Englewood Cliffs, N.J.: Prentice-Hall, 1971.

they will be admitted to professional programs and "assured"
of an attractive life-style. Such
pressures used to be reserved
for white middle-class males. Increasingly, they affect minority-
group members and women. In
his study of campus suicides,
Seiden found that many of the
subjects had worried intensively
about their grades and about
job-related matters. Table 15-2
lists common myths about suicide.

SCHIZOPHRENIC DISORDERS

The *schizophrenic disorders* (*schizophrenia* or
the *schizophrenias*) are puzzling psychotic
conditions which occur throughout the world.
Behavioral scientists do not agree on what
schizophrenia is and isn't. In 1911 Eugen
Bleuler, a Swiss psychiatrist, introduced the
term *schizophrenia* (Greek for "splitting of
the mind") to characterize the fragmented,
often contradictory, quality of the schizophrenic's thoughts and emotions. Many psychologists consider disturbed thinking the
defining feature of the syndrome. It is estimated that 50 percent of the inmates in
mental hospitals throughout the United
States are currently diagnosed as schizophrenic and that 1 out of every 100 Americans
will develop this problem at some time during
his or her life. According to recent investigations, the rate varies quite a bit from region to
region [62]. Often the disorder recurs. Within
two years following an initial discharge from a
mental hospital, about 50 percent of those
diagnosed schizophrenic reenter institutions
[63]. We focus on symptoms, subtypes, and
possible causes of the schizophrenic disorders.

Symptoms of Schizophrenic Disorders

Although the symptoms of schizophrenia vary
enormously, any individual so labeled is likely
to show several of the following patterns.

1. *Faulty perceptual filtering.* Schizophrenics frequently have trouble focusing their attention. They
report feeling bombarded by incoming sensory
information. One patient observed, "I can't
concentrate. . . . I am picking up different conversations. It's like being a transmitter. The sounds are

coming through to me, but I feel my mind cannot
cope with everything. It's difficult to concentrate on
any one sound [64]."
2. *Disorganized thinking.* Schizophrenics often
have trouble linking thoughts together logically and
solving problems. In the words of a schizophrenic,
"My thoughts get all jumbled up. I start thinking or
talking about something, but I never get there.
Instead I wander off in the wrong direction and get
caught up with all sorts of different things that may
be connected with the things I want to say [65]."
3. *Emotional distortions.* Schizophrenics often
show emotion-related problems. These include an
inability to experience pleasure, flat affect (apathy),
anxiety, ambivalence (strong contradictory feelings
on a particular subject), and/or inappropriate emotional reactions. To explain the latter condition, one
schizophrenic observed: "You see I might be
talking about something quite serious to you and
other things come into my head at the same time
that are funny and this makes me laugh [66]."
4. *Delusions and hallucinations.* Delusions and
hallucinations provide further evidence of disordered thinking, feeling, and perceiving. Here is a
schizophrenic's description of these phenomena:

"Shortly after I was taken to the hospital for the first
time I was plunged into the horror of a world
catastrophe. I was being caught up in a cataclysm
and totally dislocated. I myself had been responsible for setting the destructive forces into motion,
although I had acted with no intent to harm. . . .
   "During the first three weeks of hospitalization I
saw visions at various times. The first type . . . were
entirely projections of inner states of consciousness and appeared before my eyes like a motion
picture. . . . The second type could . . . be called
visual hallucinations and distortions, sometimes
suggested by the play of light and shadow, etc.,
acting upon an overwrought imagination [67]."
5. *Withdrawal from reality.* Schizophrenics frequently feel numbed and apathetic about the real
world and preoccupied with inner fantasies, rever-

ies, and private experiences. Here is a schizophrenic's description of this experience:

"We cannot cope with life as we find it, nor can we escape it or adjust ourselves to it. So we are given the power to create some sort of world we can deal with. The worlds created are as varied as there are minds to create them. Each one is strictly private and cannot be shared by another. It is much more real than reality. For nothing that happens to a sane mortal in the commonplace world of ordinary living can approach the startling intensity of things going on in delusion. There is a sharpness—a shrillness—a piercing intensity which thrusts itself through the consciousness and is so much more convincing than the blunt edge of reason [68]."

6. *Bizarre behavior and disturbed speech.* The schizophrenic's behavior may be quite peculiar and her or his speech jumbled and incomprehensible, as we soon see.

Although schizophrenia may initially appear in childhood or old age, it usually becomes apparent first during adolescence or early adult life. When the condition develops gradually over many years, it is labeled *process schizophrenia*. Process schizophrenics tend to have been sickly, withdrawn, and maladjusted as long as anyone can remember. The symptoms are usually debilitating, and process schizophrenics are not likely to recover. Cases of *reactive schizophrenia*, in contrast, appear to be triggered suddenly by stress. Elements of intense emotional upheaval and confusion are apt to be pronounced. This type of schizophrenic disorder is comparatively mild and the chances of recovery are relatively high.

Subtypes of Schizophrenic Disorders

Schizophrenics, as mentioned earlier, show varied symptoms. From day to day, the same individual may behave in radically different ways, appearing blatantly psychotic on some occasions and relatively normal on others.

Upon first entering a mental institution, sophisticated psychologists may even find it difficult to distinguish certain patients from doctors! During psychotic episodes some schizophrenics show fairly consistent clusters of symptoms, called *subtypes*, for relatively long periods. We will describe four subtypes. You should be aware that a lot of disagreement often exists about diagnosing the subtype of a single individual since symptoms may overlap several categories and change with time [69]. In the past, in fact, the majority of schizophrenic patients were diagnosed as *chronic undifferentiated schizophrenics*. This label signified that their symptoms did not fit any single subtype well.

Paranoid schizophrenia Schizophrenics labeled *paranoid* typically fear that they are being persecuted. Examples of *delusions of persecution* include: "They want to tie me under a bridge and then steal my furniture." "An opium smoker doped me by sticking a needle in my heel." "The manager of the baseball team tried to give me syphilis by putting germs on my sandwich [70]." Like manic individuals, paranoid schizophrenics often report *delusions of grandeur*, beliefs that they are extremely illustrious. They might feel like the richest person in the world, the monarch of England, or Jesus Christ. Paranoid schizophrenics experience vivid auditory and visual hallucinations as well. Increasingly, they center their lives on faulty beliefs and perceptions. They often imagine that natural or impersonal events are communications meant especially for them. A cough or a snowstorm, for example, may be interpreted as a message that the Communists are taking over New York City. Despite these idiosyncracies, many paranoid schizophrenics are somewhat responsive to reality and manage to survive outside of mental institutions. Mel's case illustrates many of these features. Also see Figure 15-5.

FIGURE 15-5 During his trial Sirhan Sirhan, the convicted assassin of Robert Kennedy, was diagnosed paranoid schizophrenic. Shortly before the assassination, Kennedy had proposed sending fifty aircraft to Israel. Sirhan Sirhan harbored intense delusions. He imagined himself a great patriot acting on behalf of the Arab nations. He wrote himself numerous "kill Kennedy" orders. Sirhan's notebooks suggest that he also hallucinated Kennedy's face blotting out his own image in a mirror [96]. [*United Press-International.*]

Mel

Mel, a forty-five-year-old bachelor, lived alone in a rented room. He spent his welfare check as soon as it arrived—mostly on books, drawing supplies, and candy. He had no umbrella and no winter coat. He often went days without eating anything but chocolate bars. Mel's pleasures were simple. He enjoyed lighting matches. He liked to sketch. He was fond of browsing in bookstores. Most of all, he loved sitting in coffee shops talking to college students.

Mel described himself as a free-lance inventor, mathematician, scientist, and philosopher. He claimed to have known Einstein. The list of foreign and American presidents who had consulted him was impressively long. He had spoken before the United Nations. From time to time he advised Standard Oil, General Electric, and similar multinational corporations. Mel's accomplishments were not confined to advice. He had invented color television and the electric can opener. He was on the brink of discovering the cure for lung cancer.

Despite appearances to the contrary, Mel asserted that his inventions had made him rich, a millionaire many times over. But success had brought some heavy burdens. As Mel saw it, the heaviest one was envy. Several jealous state senators were having Mel "tailed" so that they could put him away in a mental hospital.

Catatonic schizophrenia Attacks of *catatonic schizophrenia* tend to occur suddenly and repeatedly over the course of many years. The disorder is characterized most essentially by peculiar motor behavior. Catatonic patients sometimes react with excitement, frenzy, hyperactivity, bursts of talkativeness, and even violence. Most often they are stuporous—passive and uncommunicative. Occasionally, catatonic individuals behave like manikins. Their limbs remain in posed positions for minutes and even hours, a characteristic known as *waxy flexibility*. Self-reports, like the one below, suggest that the catatonic stupor masks intense delusional and hallucinatory experiences.

In the stupor many strange events enter the soul. The soul is bewitched. . . . Everything was polar. . . . In order that the sun should shine, the soul had to have psychic trouble, the trouble corresponding in strength in proportion to the strength of the sun. . . .

If you ask a simple question, I hear it, but it's as if from outside the room. People help but the people become transformed into words, and from words people are transformed into a kinemagraphic picture. . . . Thought stops but for a few fixed points that act as a lighthouse. [71]

See Figure 15-6.

Disorganized (or hebephrenic) schizophrenia

Disorganized, or *hebephrenic*, *schizophrenics* show markedly deteriorated,

FIGURE 15-6 This woman shows the symptoms of catatonic schizophrenia. She maintained this grieving posture for hours while in a stupor. During the trancelike state, the catatonic patient appears to be oblivious to the world: mute, motionless, unresponsive. The sudden catatonic attacks resemble a phenomenon known as tonic immobility. In response to stressful situations, many animals will assume motionless, immobilized postures (*tonic immobility*) that may be maintained for seconds to hours. Behavioral scientists are examining similarities between the two conditions for insights into catatonic schizophrenia [97]. [*Esther Bubley.*]

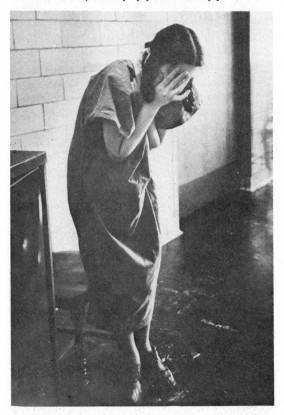

FIGURE 15-7 This man was diagnosed hebephrenic schizophrenic, in part because of his silly grin and inappropriate giggling. [*Benyas/Black Star.*]

bizarre, childlike behavior. The activity of one adult male included "public masturbation, putting fecal matter in his mouth, tying ribbons around his toes, stuffing toilet paper in his nose, wetting his pants, and talking to himself in an unintelligible manner while evidencing a silly, vacant smile [72]." Hebephrenics appear profoundly disoriented. They frequently cannot say where they are, when they arrived, and why they came. Their delusions and hallucinations are disjointed and unreal. Their conversation is difficult to comprehend. Their mannerisms seem silly. Hebephrenic patients do a lot of giggling, posturing, gesturing, and grimacing. Often they spend hours talking to themselves or to imaginary companions. See Figure 15-7. The following dialogue illustrates some typical hebephrenic characteristics.

A Hebephrenic Divorcee

"The patient was a divorcee, 32 years of age, who had come to the hospital with bizarre delusions, hallucinations, and severe personality disintegration and with a record of alcoholism, promiscuity, and possible incestuous relations with a brother. . . .

"DR.: When did you come here?

"PT.: 1416, you remember, doctor (silly giggle).

"DR.: Do you know why you are here?

"PT.: Well, in 1951 I changed into two men. President Truman was judge at my trial. I was convicted and hung (silly giggle). My brother and I were given back our normal bodies 5 years ago. I am a policewoman. I keep a dictaphone concealed on my person.

"DR.: Can you tell me the name of this place?

"PT.: I have not been a drinker for 16 years. I am taking a mental rest after a 'carter' assignment or 'quill.' You know, a 'penwrap.' I had contracts with Warner Brothers Studios and Eugene broke phonograph records but Mike protested. I have been with the police department for 35 years. I am made of flesh and blood—see, doctor (pulling up her dress) [73]."

Simple schizophrenia   To illustrate the wide range of responses that have been classified as schizophrenic, we examine one former subtype, *simple schizophrenia*. This category is no longer included under Schizophrenic Disorders in DSM-III. The defining features of this diagnostic class are quite different from the others that have been described. Simple schizophrenics are not deluded. Nor do they hallucinate or behave bizarrely. They are individuals who have become increasingly apathetic, withdrawn, and disinterested—usually beginning in adolescence. They ask to be left alone to do as they wish (which appears to be very little). Sometimes simple schizophrenics are quite capable of fending for themselves outside of mental hospitals, typically within a sheltered family setting or on skid row.

Causes of Schizophrenic Disorders

Nobody knows the precise conditions that contribute to the schizophrenic disorders at this point in time. It may be that different subtypes have different causes. There may be many ways to acquire the same symptoms. Both psychoanalytic and behavioristic psychologists emphasize environmental determinants of schizophrenia. At the same time, most behavioral scientists assume that a genetic predisposition must also be present.

According to psychoanalytic theory, schizophrenia is the result of a regression to the oral stage—to a period of time before the ego differentiated from the id. Psychoanalytic theorists assume that the schizophrenic lacks an ego to test reality. Presumably, the individual has lost contact with the world and is totally self-absorbed. The regression is attributed to intolerably severe anxiety due to intensely distressing unconscious aggressive and/or sexual impulses. Behavioristic psychologists stress the schizophrenic's entire learning history. Some suggest that patients were reinforced for ignoring the social environment and for "crazy" behavior. Some attribute the schizophrenic's anxieties to respondent conditioning. Research suggests that both hereditary and environmental mechanisms contribute to schizophrenia. We review some highlights from this enormous literature.

The contribution of heredity   Today, few behavioral scientists doubt that heredity plays some role in the development of schizophrenic disorders. The relatives of schizophrenics are significantly more likely to be afflicted with the condition than randomly chosen members of the population. In general, the closer the genetic relationship, the greater the probability that two individuals will be alike, or *concordant*, with respect to schizophrenia. Identical twins, for example, are roughly three to six times more frequently concordant for schizophrenia than fraternal twins [74]. The problems of family and twin studies were described in Chapter 3. The major difficulty is that the more genetically similar people are, the likelier they are to be exposed to common environmental circumstances—pressures, stresses, advantages, routines, and relationships. So the effects of heredity and environment are inevitably intertwined in the findings of family studies. Many researchers have attempted to tease apart the impact of each influence. In a well-controlled recent study in Denmark, Paul Wender, Seymour Kety, and coworkers examined individuals who had been permanently separated from their biological parents early in life (during the first six months, on the average). The babies had been reared by unrelated adoptive parents. The researchers wanted to investigate the strength of two background conditions for predicting the later development of schizophrenic behavior: (1) being born to a schizophrenic parent and reared by a nonschizophrenic foster parent; and (2) being born to a nonschizophrenic parent and reared by a schizophrenic foster parent. Access to extensive Danish records allowed Wender and his associates to select subjects with the appropriate backgrounds, as you can see in Table 15-3. The participants in each group were carefully matched for age, sex, adoption age, and other characteristics.

During adulthood the subjects were interviewed and diagnosed by an experienced examiner who did not know their history. As shown in Table 15-3, heredity turned out to be the best predictor of schizophrenic symptoms. Simply being reared by parents with a schizophrenic diagnosis did not appear to significantly increase the likelihood of the disorder [75]. Many other studies suggest that heredity contributes to at least some schizophrenic conditions [76].

The precise contribution of genetic endowment to schizophrenia is not known. Currently, many behavioral scientists believe that schizophrenics inherit a predisposition, or *diathesis*. The illness, it is assumed, develops in full only under adverse circumstances. Even if this *diathesis-stress model* is accurate, there are still numerous unanswered questions. Among the most significant are these: Are several or many genes involved? Do people inherit something specific for schizophrenia or vulnerabilities to stress? If genetic vulnerabilities to stress are the key, are they uniform? Or do they vary from person to person?

If schizophrenia has a genetic basis, it must be expressed through biochemical abnormalities. Many scientists are investigating possible mechanisms. A leading theory, the *dopamine hypothesis*, assumes that excessive dopamine activity within specific brain cir-

TABLE 15-3 An Adoptive Study of the Genetic Basis of Schizophrenia

Group	Did records contain a schizophrenic or related diagnosis?*		Percentage of adoptees with schizophrenic symptoms
	Biological parents	Adoptive parents	
I	Yes	No	18.8
II	No	No	10.1
III	No	Yes	10.7

*"No" indicates that records did not contain a schizophrenic or related diagnosis. Some parents may have had symptoms that were not observed and reported.

Source: Adapted from Wender, P. H., Rosenthal, R., Kety, S. S., Schulsinger, F., & Welner, J. Cross-fostering: A research strategy for clarifying the role of genetic and experiential factors in the etiology of schizophrenia. *Archives of General Psychiatry*, 1974, **30**, 121–128.

cuits underlies schizophrenia. (The neurotransmitter dopamine was described in Chapter 4.) The dopamine hypothesis is supported by numerous findings, including these:

1. The *phenothiazines*, a family of drugs that are therapeutic for schizophrenia, block the transmission of impulses in brain pathways that use dopamine. The more effectively a specific medication inhibits dopamine action, the more likely it is to reduce schizophrenic symptoms [77].
2. Amphetamines, which appear to make dopamine more available, can worsen the symptoms of schizophrenia. In large doses, amphetamines create a psychotic reaction in normal people that closely resembles paranoid schizophrenia.
3. Medicines that most effectively block amphetamine-induced schizophrenic symptoms are most helpful in alleviating real schizophrenic episodes [78].
4. Schizophrenic individuals appear to have brain cells that are unusually sensitive to the presence of dopamine in several brain regions [79].

Although the dopamine hypothesis looks promising, many behavioral scientists feel cautious. Drugs act on many sites within the brain, and neural circuits are continually interacting. The dopamine-related irregularities and changes that have been observed may be mere side effects or one of many links in a long chain.

The contribution of the environment
If schizophrenia were completely determined by heredity, identical twins would be concordant for the disorder 100 percent of the time. The fact that they are not suggests that environmental factors are operating. Initially, clinicians scrutinized the schizophrenic's family, searching for clues to the condition. Some early investigators blamed the schizophrenic's mother for the disturbance. Mothers were pictured as overly protective, anxious, domineering, weak, rejecting, and/or smothering. Other researchers blamed parents' marital relationships. These were portrayed as tense, emotionally empty, conflicted, destructive, and/or *skewed* [80]. In this latter case, a relatively healthy parent supports the pathology of a distressed one. Psychologists and psychiatrists found faulty communication patterns among family members: peculiar language, blurred meanings, overly precise speech, and *double binds* (confusing messages that pull people in opposite directions and keep them from trusting their own experiences) [81]. For example, a parent might encourage and reject affection simultaneously. Recent studies with appropriate controls have failed to confirm many of these observations [82]. When unusual discord exists, there is evidence that it is generated by the sick individual [83]. In short, domestic stresses have not been shown to precede and precipitate schizophrenia.

Because effects become entangled with causes after people develop a psychotic condition, numerous researchers have begun studying families before children show obvious signs of pathology. For these family studies, investigators select children *at risk for schizophrenia*, those more likely than a random sample to exhibit the illness. Youngsters with schizophrenic parents are usually studied. About 12 to 14 percent of people with a single schizophrenic parent and 35 to 45 percent of those with two schizophrenic parents are likely to develop the disorder [84]. Once families are identified for study, behavioral scientists measure characteristics presumed to be important to see whether these conditions precede the appearance of schizophrenic symptoms. Studies of this nature are necessarily long and time-consuming. So far, only one such investigation (by Sarnoff Mednick and Fini Schulsinger) has been in progress long enough to compare high-risk children who show psychotic behavior to high- and low-risk children who do not. Mednick and Schulsinger have found that the development of schizophrenia in high-risk individuals is associated with experiencing intrauterine or delivery complications, losing a mother early and permanently to a mental institution, and having a seriously disturbed father [85]. Youngsters whose mothers suffer pregnancy and birth complications display signs of an overreactive autonomic nervous system. The findings of severe disturbance in parents could be interpreted as supporting the influence of genetics, stress, or both on schizophrenia.

Besides looking for factors that make schizophrenia likely, a few investigators are exploring protective or corrective environmental circumstances and biological advantages that may offset adverse potentialities [86]. For currently unknown reasons, about 90 percent of the siblings of schizophrenics do not develop the disorder.

This brief review should make it clear that there is still a lot to learn about the causes of schizophrenia.

ORGANIC MENTAL DISORDERS

If the brain is damaged or its biochemical balance disturbed, clinicians often see abnormal behavior. The disorders that result from brain impairments are called *organic mental disorders* because they have a known physical basis. Schizophrenic and bipolar affective disorders are sometimes considered *functional reactions*, in contrast, because they are not *known* to have a physical cause, even though one may be suspected. Organic mental disorders may be triggered by infections (such as syphilis), traumas (such as skull fractures and concussions), nutritional deficiencies (such as pellagra), cerebrovascular diseases (such as arteriosclerosis and brain hemorrhage), tumors, degenerative diseases (such as Huntington's chorea), toxins (such as lead), and endocrine dysfunctions.

The organic mental disorders are characterized by several symptoms. Orientation is usually impaired. People may not know who they are, where they are, and what time it is. Memory losses, especially for recent events, are common. Intellectual deterioration (difficulty in planning, reasoning, and communicating) is likely. Blunted or exceedingly unstable emotional responses are probable.

It is often difficult to distinguish organic disorders from other psychotic illnesses. The patient whose behavior is described below had syphilis. The bacteria responsible for the venereal disease eventually invaded the central nervous system and caused manic symptoms.

M., aged forty-one, a roofing salesman . . . told the office attendant that he was going to give her a million dollars because she was "a nice lady." As he was being questioned for the usual admission data, he began to boast of his wealth, claiming that he had three automobiles, thousands of dollars in the bank, a "diamond watch," and much other valuable jewelry. His son, he said, was lieutenant governor of the state, was soon to be governor, and later would be president of the United States. [87]

PERSONALITY DISORDERS

The most essential feature of the *personality disorders*, according to DSM-III, is a deeply ingrained, inflexible, maladaptive pattern of relating to, perceiving, and thinking about the environment and oneself. The problems are sufficiently severe to cause either significant impairment in adaptive functioning or subjective distress. Personality disorders are generally recognizable by adolescence, and they often persist throughout life. Drug and alcohol dependencies and sexual difficulties used to be included in this category. They now have their own classifications. In this section we focus on one personality disorder, the *antisocial (psychopathic* or *sociopathic) personality disorder.*

Symptoms of the Antisocial Personality Disorder

Psychopathic individuals, as persons with the antisocial personality disorder are called, lack the sense of right and wrong that most people acquire at an early age. Because they have no moral convictions, they typically scheme and manipulate to obtain what they want—without considering anyone else's rights or feelings. Just like very young children, psychopathic people tend to live in the present. They usually act for the immediate gratification of momentary impulses, instead of postponing pleasure when it is appropriate to do so. Psychopaths rarely take pains to conceal misdeeds and appear to be oblivious to consequences. Not surprisingly, they are frequently caught when they behave illegally. But punishment does not teach psychopaths restraint. These individuals seem to experi-

FIGURE 15-8 The Nazi field marshall Hermann Goering showed some characteristic features of the antisocial personality disorder. He seemed to be continually in search of vivid sensations. He was a daring flyer in the air force. He kept his own personal zoo. He ate and drank in Gargantuan fashion. He loved pomp and circumstance. Admittedly having no conscience, he ordered his men to shoot first and inquire later. It was his duty, he felt, to annihilate and exterminate. He introduced the concentration camp idea and is credited with many other acts of barbarous inhumanity. Yet, in social relationships Goering was frequently genial, kindly, and good-natured [98]. [*Wide World Photos.*]

ence few fears and are apt to engage in the same punished acts repeatedly. Some persons with antisocial personalities are described as intelligent, charming, impressive, easygoing, aimless, impulsive, and present-oriented. Others are characterized as somewhat psychotic, suspicious, lacking in empathy, and almost entirely unfeeling [88]. A small percentage of psychopaths end up in mental hospitals and clinics, usually because of court referrals. A larger percentage turn up in prisons and other penal institutions. (The majority of criminals are not classified as having the antisocial personality disorder.) Most psychopathic individuals manage to function in society despite frequent scrapes with the police and other authorities. Donald S.'s case shows characteristic symptoms of the antisocial personality disorder. (Also see Figure 15-8.)

Donald S.

"Donald S., 30 years old, has just completed a three-year prison term for fraud, bigamy, false pretenses, and escaping lawful custody. [He] was the youngest of three boys born to middle-class parents. . . . By all accounts Donald was considered a willful and difficult child. . . . Although he was obviously very intelligent, his school years were academically undistinguished. He was restless, easily bored, and frequently truant. His behavior in the presence of the teacher or some other authority was usually quite good, but when he was on his own he generally got himself or others into trouble. Although he was often suspected of being the culprit, he was adept at talking his way out of difficulty. Donald's misbehavior as a child took many forms including lying, cheating, petty theft, and the bullying of smaller children. As he grew older he became more and more interested in sex, gambling, and alcohol. . . .

"When he was 17, Donald . . . forged his father's name to a large check, and spent about a year traveling around the world. He apparently lived well, using a combination of charm, physical attractiveness, and false pretenses to finance his way. During subsequent years he held a succession of jobs, never staying at any one for more than a few months. Throughout this period he was charged with a variety of crimes, including theft, drunkenness in a public place, assault, and many traffic violations. . . .

"[Donald's] sexual experiences were frequent, casual, and callous. When he was 22 he married a 41-year-old woman whom he had met in a bar. Several other marriages followed, all bigamous. In each case the pattern was the same: he would marry someone on impulse, let her support him for several months, and then leave. . . .

"It is interesting to note that Donald sees nothing particularly wrong with his behavior, nor does he express remorse or guilt for using others and causing them grief. Although his behavior is self-defeating in the long run, he considers it to be practical and possessed of good sense [89]."

Causes of the Antisocial Personality Disorder

The causes of the antisocial personality disorder are not known. Adoption and twin studies indicate that heredity plays a role in this problem [90], but nobody knows what contribution it makes. Several biological deficiencies have been noted. Psychopaths often show specific brain-wave and cardiac irregularities which suggest that their nervous systems make them unlikely to acquire the types of fears that usually restrain wrongdoing [91]. The autonomic responses of psychopaths tend to be fairly weak, indicating that they may be relatively immune to sensory stimulation. Impulsive, excitement-seeking actions could be an attempt to obtain such stimulation [92]. A relatively high need for sensory experiences has been observed in psychopathic juvenile delinquents [93].

There is much speculation about environmental influences on the psychopath's behavior. Psychoanalytic theorists believe that the pattern is caused by unconscious conflicts that prevent the child from identifying with the same-sexed parent and incorporating his or her moral standards. Behavioristic psychologists view psychopathic behavior as learned. Researcher Lee Robins and his coworkers are following samples of children at high risk for psychopathy throughout adolescence and into adulthood. They have found three early-learning–related conditions that are associated with later psychopathic behavior [94]:

1. The fathers of psychopaths are often antisocial. Youngsters may observe and imitate the manipulative, emotionally distant, impulsive, and/or self-indulgent behavior of parents.
2. Psychopaths tend to receive little or inconsistent discipline during childhood, so they may fail to learn prosocial conduct.
3. Psychopaths show a variety of behavioral problems at an early age. They are likely to detest school, fail to learn, act up in class, fight on the playground, be truant a great deal, and exert little effort in the classroom. School-related difficulties may contribute to conflicts at home. To cope with all the hassles, youngsters may learn manipulative tactics.

As you can see, there are numerous plausible explanations of psychopathic behavior. It is likely that this complex personality disorder can be acquired in various ways. ▲

▲ USING PSYCHOLOGY

1. Try to think of movie or TV characters who behaved abnormally. Did they fit any of the categories described in the text? Enumerate the characteristics that influenced your "diagnoses."

2. Consider each disorder described by the text in terms of the medical and psychological models of abnormal behavior. Which model seems most appropriate for understanding each problem? Why?

3. Disorders such as schizophrenia, depression, mania, and multiple and psychopathic personalities are often portrayed in the media. Ask several people to define the characteristics of these syndromes. Do popular notions agree with those provided by the text?

SUMMARY
Abnormal Behavior

1. Abnormal behavior is often defined by these criteria: defective cognitive functioning, defective social behavior, defective self-control, and severe distress.

2. Abnormal behavior is classified in diagnostic categories. Categorization is useful because it communicates some information about causes, treatment, symptoms, and likely outcomes. Unfortunately, diagnostic classifications have negative effects too. They may adversely influence the patient's self-image and the impressions of relatives, friends, community members, and professionals.

3. Abnormal behavior is often conceptualized today in terms of either a medical model or a psychological model. Some mental health professionals use both models, depending on the disorder.

4. Neuroses center on anxiety. Psychoses are more debilitating conditions that are characterized by distortions of reality, profound mood alterations, and/or intellectual deficits.

5. The anxiety disorders include phobic, panic, and obsessive-compulsive problems. Each syndrome has distress and behavioral components.

6. People with somatoform disorders, such as the conversion reaction, show physical problems which have no known organic basis.

7. Dissociative disorders, such as amnesia, fugue, and multiple personality, are characterized by alterations in consciousness.

8. Major depressive and bipolar affective disorders are common affective problems. Heredity may contribute to the development of both disturbances. Losses of varied types often precipitate depressions. Cognitions may initiate, prolong, or aggravate them. Suicide is frequently associated with affective disorders.

9. Common schizophrenic symptoms include faulty perceptual filtering, disorganized thinking, emotional distortions, delusions and hallucinations, withdrawal from reality, bizarre behavior, and incomprehensible speech. Schizophrenic individuals sometimes show symptoms of the paranoid, catatonic, or hebephrenic types. Both hereditary and environmental factors play roles in the development of schizophrenia. The causal mechanisms are still a matter of conjecture.

10. Organic mental disorders result from brain impairments. They are characterized by disorientation, memory loss, intellectual deterioration, and blunted or excessively unstable emotional responses.

11. Psychopaths show manipulative, self-indulgent, impulsive behavior that gets them in trouble with society. Both biological and environmental factors probably contribute to this disorder.

A Study Guide for Chapter Fifteen

Key terms   hallucination (480), *Diagnostic and Statistical Manual of Mental Disorders* (DSM) (481), neurosis (neurotic reaction) (485), psychosis (psychotic reaction) (486), insane (486), anxiety disorder (486), somatoform disorder (490), dissociative disorder (491), affective disorder (491), delusion (491), process versus reactive schizophrenia (497), organic mental disorder (503), personality disorder (503), and other italicized words and expressions.

For each of the following disorders you should be able to describe the major symptoms. In most cases, you should also be able to provide (1) psychoanalytic and behavioristic explanations for, and (2) research-supported findings about, the problem: phobic, panic, obsessive-compulsive, conversion, amnesia, fugue, multiple personality, major depressive, bipolar affective, schizophrenic [paranoid, catatonic, hebephrenic (disorganized), and simple subtypes], antisocial (psychopathic or sociopathic) personality.

Important research   geophagy and abnormality, expectations and judgments about abnormality (Langer, Abelson), shortcomings of the diagnostic system (Rosenhan, others), suicide.

Basic concepts   criteria for defining abnormal behavior and associated problems, "maladjustment" versus "abnormal behavior," advantages and disadvantages of classification, medical and psychological models of abnormal behavior, diathesis-stress theory of schizophrenia, rationale behind studying children at risk for schizophrenia.

People to identify   Luther, Kraepelin, Szasz, Bleuler.

Self-Quiz

1. In the Langer-Abelson study, mental health professionals viewed a videotaped interview and judged the interviewee's mental health. What did this experiment demonstrate?

   a. Criteria for judging abnormal behavior change with time.

   b. Criteria for judging abnormal behavior depend on culture.

   c. Diagnostic labels influence perceptions of psychological health.

   d. Expectations affect judgments about mental health.

2. What did Rosenhan's study of pseudopatients in mental hospitals suggest?

   a. Diagnostic labels affect self-esteem.

   b. Diagnostic labels alienate family.

   c. Diagnostic labels persist.

   d. Diagnostic practices vary greatly from hospital to hospital.

3. Who is credited with establishing the view that natural forces cause abnormal behavior?

   a. Eugen Bleuler   *b.* Sigmund Freud

   c. Emil Kraepelin   *d.* Martin Luther

4. Which of the following assumptions is made by the psychological model of abnormal behavior?

   a. Abnormal behavior is similar in kind, but not in degree, to normal behavior.

   b. The cause(s) of each disorder must be identified and removed.

   c. Each syndrome consists of a cluster of fairly definite symptoms with a consistent specific cause.

   d. The patient should be viewed as a passive recipient of treatment.

5. The term *neurosis* refers to behavioral disorders characterized primarily by what?

   a. Anxiety

   b. Excitement or elation

   c. Impaired cognitive abilities

   d. Maladaptive social behavior

6. Which statement about the phobic disorder is correct?

   a. Even a mild phobia is generally considered an anxiety disorder.

   b. Phobias are usually associated with perfectly safe situations.

   c. The phobic knows that his or her anxiety is disproportionate to the danger involved.

   d. Psychoanalytic psychologists believe that phobias occur only in individuals fixated at the anal stage.

7. Psychoanalytic theorists attribute the panic disorder to which cause?

   a. An actual or symbolic loss experienced by an overly dependent person

   b. Anxiety-arousing experiences during adulthood

   c. Early sexual experiences

   d. Intense unconscious conflicts between the id and ego

8. Which of the following is considered a dissociative disorder?

   a. Bipolar affective disorder

   b. Fugue

   c. Obsessive-compulsive disorder

   d. Antisocial personality disorder

9. How did Seligman produce symptoms of depression in dogs?

   a. By giving them electric shocks over which they had no control

   b. By maintaining them on a nutritionally inadequate diet

   c. By punishing them inconsistently

   d. By rearing them away from their mothers

10. Which condition is suspected of producing or aggravating a depression?

   a. Dopamine deficiency

   b. Norepinephrine depletion

   c. A surplus of dopamine

   d. A surplus of norepinephrine

11. Which type of schizophrenia is characterized as a relatively mild condition brought on suddenly by stress?

   a. Hebephrenic   *b.* Process

   c. Reactive   *d.* Simple

12. Which symptoms are most characteristic of hebephrenic schizophrenia?

   a. Apathy and withdrawal

   b. Bizarre, childlike behavior and giggling

   c. Delusions of grandeur and suspicions

   d. Peculiar motor behavior (frenzy or stupor) and speechlessness

13. Which word is closest in meaning to diathesis?

   a. Environmental   *b.* Genetic

   c. Predisposition   *d.* Stress

14. Mednick and Schulsinger studied individuals at high risk for schizophrenia beginning in early childhood. Which event was found to be most closely associated with the eventual development of psychotic symptoms?

   a. Double binds

   b. Intrauterine and delivery complications

   c. Skewed marriages

   d. Smothering mothers

15. Which possible cause of the antisocial personality disorder (psychopathic behavior) is supported by research?

   a. Brutality and child abuse

   b. Electra or Oedipal conflicts during early childhood

   c. Inconsistent or little discipline

   d. Strong autonomic responses to sensory stimulation

Suggested Readings

1. Coleman, J. C. *Abnormal psychology and modern life.* (6th ed.) Glenview, Ill.: Scott, Foresman, 1980; Davison,

G. C., & Neale, J. M. *Abnormal psychology*: *An experimental clinical approach*. (2d ed.) New York: Wiley, 1978. Both texts are comprehensive, research-oriented, interesting, and illustrated extensively by case history material.

2. Maser, J. D., & Seligman, M. E. P. (Eds.) *Psychopathology: Experimental models*. San Francisco: Freeman, 1977 (paperback). These behavioral scientists describe research programs on diverse human problems including addiction, obesity, depression, psychosomatic disorders, unusual sexual preferences, and schizophrenia.

3. Bernheim, K. F., & Lewine, R. R. J. *Schizophrenia*: *Symptoms*, *causes*, *treatments*. New York: Norton, 1979 (paperback). In this informal, nontechnical book, psychologists describe what is currently known about schizophrenia. They weave together research findings with case history material to explore such topics as causes, chances for recovery, and common treatment strategies.

4. Seligman, M. E. P. *Helplessness*: *On depression*, *development*, *and death*. San Francisco: Freeman, 1975 (paperback). In this engaging book, a psychologist discusses research on helplessness and its relationship to depression, anxiety, death, and other conditions.

5. Becker, J. *Affective disorders*. Morristown, N.J.: General Learning Press, 1977 (paperback). This is a good source for theoretical perspectives and recent research on depression.

6. Kaplan, B. (Ed.) *The inner world of mental illness*. New York: Harper & Row, 1964 (paperback). Essays and excerpts from novels, autobiographies, and other sources provide fascinating insights into how it feels to have various behavior disorders.

7. Szasz, T. S. The myth of mental illness. *American Psychologist*, 1960, **15**(2), 113–118. Szasz argues that there is no such thing as mental illness. He recommends that the phenomena known as mental illnesses be removed from the disease category and be regarded as expressions of the human struggle with the problem of how to live.

8. Rosenhan, D. L. On being sane in insane places. *Science*, 1973, **179**, 1–9. In this very provocative classic essay, Rosenhan describes his controversial study and discusses the depersonalizing aspects of institutionalization.

9. Buchsbaum, M. S. The sensoristat in the brain. *Psychology Today*, 1978, **11**(12), 96–100ff. A biological psychiatrist describes a hypothetical brain mechanism that controls sensory inputs and discusses why its malfunctioning may contribute to problems such as the bipolar affective and schizophrenic disorders.

10. Maddi, S. R. Freud's most famous patient: The victimization of Dora. *Psychology Today*, 1974, **8**(4), 90–100. An existential psychologist discusses one of Freud's most famous cases, explores Freud's interpretation, and presents an alternative explanation. The article provides a perspective on how behavioral scientists with contrasting orientations analyze the same data.

11. Beck, A. T., & Young, J. E. College blues. *Psychology Today*, 1978, **12**(4), 80–92. Clinicians at the University of Pennsylvania Mood Clinic describe and try to explain depression among college students, cognitions that worsen the problem, and therapy for this disorder.

Answer Key

Self-Quiz

1. d (480) **2.** c (482) **3.** c (483) **4.** a (484)
5. a (485) **6.** c (487) **7.** d (489) **8.** b (491)
9. a (494) **10.** b (494) **11.** c (497) **12.** b (499)
13. c (501) **14.** b (502) **15.** c (505)

The Treatment of Abnormal Behavior

Throughout recorded history all societies have attempted to treat psychologically disturbed members. Archeological evidence suggests that about a half-million years ago Stone Age cave dwellers cut holes in people's skulls to free "evil spirits" that were trapped inside. Early civilizations in China, Egypt, and Greece prayed for troubled citizens. They also whipped, starved, and purged emotionally distressed people to force out the "demons."

During the Middle Ages, torture was used as therapy. In Europe and the United States, treatment for psychological problems became more humane near the end of the eighteenth century. See Figure 16-1. Though far from perfect, current techniques are undoubtedly a vast improvement over past ones. We begin our exploration of therapeutic procedures by looking at a "curing" ceremony in another culture.

The Curing of Espanto: The Case of Alicia

A married Guatemalan woman, Alicia, at the age of sixty-three came down with *espanto* for the eighth time. Feeling alternately anxious and lethargic, she neglected her household duties and pottery-making business.

She lost interest in friends and relatives. She complained of pains, fever, and appetite loss, as well.

Rural inhabitants of large areas of Latin America believe that espanto is caused by the escape of the soul during a frightening experience. They assume that people cannot live without a soul indefinitely and must seek the help of an expert curer.

Alicia's curer, whom we call

Manuel, conducted a thirteen-hour ceremony for the patient, attended by her friends and relatives. The group feasted on native dishes and prayed a great deal. Manuel massaged Alicia with eggs (to draw the illness into the eggs). He sprayed her with medicinal potions. He gave assurances that the sickness would disappear.

To bring back Alicia's soul, Manuel led a small delegation of friends and relatives to the river site where Alicia had been frightened and the espanto had presumably occurred. The group made offerings to the evil spirits who were holding Alicia's soul, imploring them to return it. As the delegation returned to the patient's home, people rattled

gourd dishes filled with dirt and stones so that the lost soul would follow them through the darkness.

After the ceremony, Alicia felt happy because she was convinced that her soul had been restored. Her physical complaints and her withdrawal and anxiety symptoms disappeared too—at least temporarily [1].

Although Alicia's therapy may sound strange, folk cures of this sort take place even in the United States today [2]. And many modern treatment procedures use similar elements [3]. A sufferer (sometimes several) seeks help from a trained, socially approved healer—in our society, a mental health expert

(such experts are described in Table 16-1). Generally, the sufferer thinks well of the healer and expects to have the distress alleviated. The two meet—usually regularly—and participate jointly in procedures that are supposed to produce positive changes in the sufferer's behavior, emotions, and thoughts. Later in the chapter we will say more about similarities between diverse therapies and curing rituals. Most of our discussion will concentrate upon the varied procedures currently used in our society to help psychologically troubled people. First we focus on common psychotherapies for nonpsychotic disturbances, then on treatment for chronic psychotic conditions, next on enhancing the mental health of the entire community, and finally on the rehabilitation of criminals.

TABLE 16-1 Mental Health Experts

Title	Degree and education
Psychologist	Ph.D. (usually); postgraduate study in university psychology department plus internship in psychiatric facility
Psychiatrist	M.D.; medical school plus residency in psychiatric facility
Psychoanalyst	M.D. (usually); apprenticeship training in psychoanalysis (generally following medical school and residency in psychiatric facility)
Psychiatric social worker	M.S.W.; postgraduate study in school of social work
Psychiatric nurse	R.N.; training in nursing and psychiatry
Mental health technician	B.A. or A.A.; undergraduate education in psychology, especially mental health
Mental health paraprofessional	No formal educational requirements; orientation program in service facility

These mental health experts are all involved in diagnosis, treatment, and prevention.

TREATING THE EMOTIONALLY DISTRESSED ADULT: OUTPATIENT PSYCHOTHERAPY

We define *psychotherapy*, or *therapy* (the usual abbreviation), as the use of psychological treatment procedures to help mentally troubled people. *Counseling* is described more narrowly: the offering of supportive services to essentially normal individuals with educational, occupational, marital, or other adjustment problems. Psychotherapies may be viewed, in essence, as attempts to construct experiences that will enable the sufferer to cope with life in a more satisfying and produc-

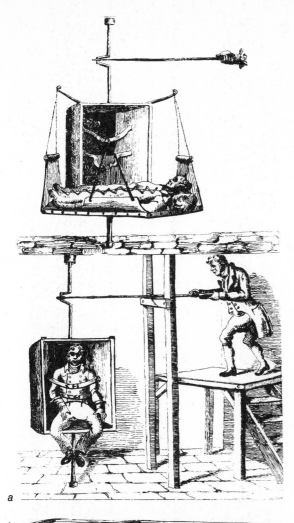

a

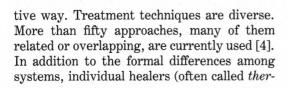

b

c

FIGURE 16-1 During the sixteenth century, special hospitals (called asylums) for treating emotionally disturbed people were established in Britain. The concept spread to Europe and the Americas. Gradually, monasteries and prisons relinquished the care of the mentally ill to these institutions. Conditions and practices in the early asylums were deplorable. Troubled people were often shackled to walls, tormented, and/or tortured as Satanic agents. Near the end of the eighteenth century, humanitarian reforms began in earnest with the work of the French physician Philippe Pinel. Even then, "therapeutic" devices, like those shown here, were widely used to control unmanageable patients. The circulating swing in (a) was designed "to bring back sound reasoning." Authorities believed that no well-regulated institution should be without one. As late as 1882, violent patients were restrained in the crib shown in (b). The tranquilizing chair in (c) was devised by Benjamin Rush, the founder of American psychiatry. Along with this "tranquilizer," he advocated blood letting and purgatives, in addition to tactics which are considered more humane and useful today [75]. [(a) and (b), Bettmann Archive; (c), National Library of Medicine.]

tive way. Treatment techniques are diverse. More than fifty approaches, many of them related or overlapping, are currently used [4]. In addition to the formal differences among systems, individual healers (often called *ther-*

apists or *clinicians*) bring their own distinctive personalities, histories, and philosophies of life to the therapy experience. As a result, the psychotherapy of each expert is unique to some degree.

It is interesting to note that most troubled Americans seem reluctant to use psychotherapy. They are more apt to seek help from clergy, physicians, lawyers, and police [5]. Yet therapy is gradually becoming acceptable. In the last twenty years, the proportion of the adult population reporting actual psychotherapy experiences has nearly doubled, rising from about 14 to 26 percent [6]. Figure 16-2 presents common complaints bringing patients to psychotherapy.

We explore three basic therapy approaches: psychoanalytic, behavior, and humanistic-existential. While all therapies attempt to restore healthy functioning, they differ on (1) conceptions of abnormal behavior, (2) specific goals, and (3) primary procedures. We focus on these features. Our survey will describe psychotherapies designed primarily for non-psychotic adult *outpatients* (patients living outside mental institutions). These therapies may also be applied to children and to psychotic adults.

Psychoanalytic Psychotherapy

Sigmund Freud established the psychoanalytic model of psychotherapy. His ideas about personality, defense mechanisms, and abnormal behavior were described in Chapters 1, 13, 14, and 15. You may want to review this material quickly before reading on. We call Freud's brand of therapy *orthodox psychoanalytic therapy* or *psychoanalysis* to distinguish it from today's many modified versions (*psychoanalytically oriented therapies*). Therapists who use psychoanalysis or psychoanalytically oriented therapies are frequently called *analysts*.

Conception of troubled behavior
Freud believed that neurotic conditions, those characterized by anxiety, are caused by conflicts during the early years of childhood which are repressed (roughly, pushed from awareness) without being resolved. Because

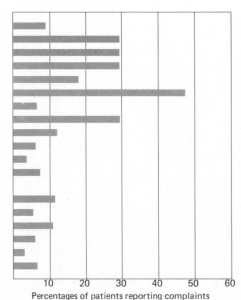

Major complaints bringing patients to therapy

Sexual problems
Physical symptoms
Generalized anxiety
Interpersonal difficulties
Negative self-evaluation
Loss of interest/feel overwhelmed
External cause
Depression-suicide
Phobias and fears
Guilt
Delusions
Concentration problems
Poor judgment/reality testing
Obsessive-compulsive symptoms
Fantasy problems
Work problems
Behavior problems
Psychosis
Unclassifiable

10 20 30 40 50 60
Percentages of patients reporting complaints

FIGURE 16-2 According to a popular misconception, people seek therapy only for severe emotional disorders. Mental health workers, studying outpatient adults at a psychiatric clinic in North Carolina, found that initial complaints are often rather ordinary, as can be seen in the graph. People seeking therapy do report that they experience unusually intense and/or persistent distress. While 30 percent of the patients viewed their problems as long-standing ones, 40 percent reported that the difficulties had existed for less than a year prior to their seeking help. [*Strupp, Fox, & Lessler, 1969.*]

the problem is unconscious, it cannot be explored and mastered. Yet the neurotic person is vaguely aware of incompatible needs or wishes and feels dissatisfied and frustrated. The individual uses defensive, self-deceptive maneuvers to cope. The internal struggles generate anxiety and depression. The defensive strategies interfere with daily functioning. People seek out therapy, then, to relieve their discomfort.

Goals of therapy   Patients complain initially of depression, anxiety, and other symptoms that Freud considered mere superficial expressions of basic unconscious conflicts. To remove the symptoms permanently, the therapist, in Freud's opinion, must help the patient uncover the source of the conflict. But intellectual knowledge by itself is insufficient for a cure. Individuals have to *relive* past experiences as well—to ground insights in a more emotional type of understanding. Once the unconscious conflicts are penetrated and comprehended, the difficult part of the psychoanalytic therapist's job is essentially finished. The analyst will continue to support the patient as he or she resolves current difficulties and masters effective coping strategies.

Psychoanalysis is supposed to provide general resources and insights for dealing with problems throughout life.

Therapy procedures   Freud spent much of his life refining therapy techniques that might be used to probe the unconscious and bring unresolved conflicts into the open. During orthodox psychoanalytic therapy sessions, the patient generally lies on a couch while the therapist sits off to the side or behind, as shown in Figure 16-3. The couch seems to be a direct holdover from hypnosis, a technique Freud employed in his early years to explore unconscious material. The elaborate seating procedures may have been partly motivated by his personal discomfort with face-to-face contacts. Regardless of its origin, the convention offers distinct advantages. The patient is not distracted by books, furnishings, gestures, or facial expressions. The absence of a direct encounter may help the analyst maintain the emotional and intellectual distance necessary for guiding the patient to an objective self-understanding.

The major responsibility of patients in psychoanalytic therapy is *free association*. They must allow their minds to wander

FIGURE 16-3   The analyst, seated somewhat out of the patient's range of sight, is likely to take notes. By studying various aspects of the patient's behavior closely, insights may be gained into unconscious conflicts. [*Jan Lucas/Rapho Photo Researchers.*]

freely—without restraint—while they give a frank running account of all thoughts and feelings. The following excerpt from a psychoanalytic session conveys the flavor of free association:

I feel like a little girl and I see myself as an adult but I'm not quite there. I can see myself loving you and having my warm wonderful feelings about you and then I leave here and I go with Tom and I start over and I have my warm wonderful feelings about him. I see no big problems ahead and our future is wonderful and yet I stay here unhappy.—I always pictured adult life as full of problems. It bothers me that I can't see any problems ahead. I just can't.—My whole life is becoming new. I had a dream about Sally last night. [7]

Presumably, free association allows the patient to put defenses aside and leads to the disclosure of conflict-related material.

The patient in psychoanalytic therapy is usually asked to bring in *dreams* for analysis. Dreams are considered important sources of information about repressed conflicts. Freud believed that the subject matter of the dream, called the *manifest content*, disguised the real meaning, the *latent content*. To establish the dream's latent message, the patient is asked to free-associate to the major dream elements until their significance becomes apparent. Consider an example. A businessman undergoing psychoanalytic therapy dreamed that he had manufactured some crystal and that the therapist angrily broke it. The dream reminded the man of an occasion when his father had in fact smashed a set of glassware because he did not like the design. In the dream, according to the analyst, the patient was reliving the relationship with his deceased father, a domineering man, and showing his own inability to maintain a give-and-take relationship with an authority figure [8].

Without being aware of it, patients participate in their own psychoanalysis through two characteristic responses: resistance and transference. *Resistance* consists of all the patient's actions which interfere with the ther-

apy process. When free-associating, the patient may pause for long periods of time, change the topic suddenly, or forget particular events. Sometimes the individual repeatedly arrives late for the sessions or decides that the psychoanalysis is doing no good and wants to quit. In all these cases, Freud assumed, the patient is resisting. Presumably, she or he has reached repressed material and feels threatened by the pain of facing it. Self-deception has enabled the troubled neurotic to adjust. The defenses were formed over many years and are hard to give up. Analytic therapists believe that they must overcome resistance without pressing too hard. They must persuade the person to search out and examine the painful, conflict-related material.

Often, patients develop strong feelings, such as love or hatred, for the psychotherapist. Freud believed that these emotions arise because people identify the therapist with past authority figures centrally involved in the repressed conflict (usually parents). This phenomenon is known as *transference*. The seating arrangement, incidentally, facilitates transference. It helps the analyst remain in the background so that the patient reacts to fantasies (as opposed to the therapist's real characteristics) and forms a transference relationship. It is essential, according to Freud, that the pathological interactions of early life be reenacted in the transference so that they can be understood and corrected. Before therapy is terminated, patients must give up their childishness and establish mature relationships. Helping the patient understand how the transference relates to past conflicts and current behavior is one of the psychoanalytic therapist's major tasks. The businessman (whose dream was just described) transferred feelings about his father to the therapist. Here is the analyst's description of the patient's transference relationship and its resolution.

The Handling of a Transference Relationship

"From the very start the patient reproduced in the therapeutic situation his combined attitudes toward his father. He wanted rules to be made for him, and scrupulously obeyed one or two that had to be suggested. But his conversation was otherwise designed to impress the analyst with his importance, and whenever the analyst explained anything he quickly began to explain something about which he himself was expert: business or sports. He literally tried to force the doctor to become tyrannical so that he could rebel and compete with him. This attitude was so clear that the analyst undertook to create a corrective emotional experience by behaving in just the opposite fashion. He let the patient take the lead, avoided statements that could be thought arbitrary, admitted the limitations of psychiatry, expressed admiration for the patient's good qualities, took an interest in his business and social activities. Under this treatment the patient became distinctly confused. He plainly thrived in the permissive, encouraging atmosphere, but he was unable to check his competitive feelings and still tried to fight battles with the analyst. This offered the perfect opportunity for crucial interpretations. The patient could not help seeing that his aggression was completely out of relation to the analyst's behavior. His chief overdriven striving was exposed and he became able to enter a more genuine relationship with the doctor. . . . His old role of the now-rebelling, now-submitting son could be outgrown as he found it possible to have a relation of friendly give-and-take with an authoritative person [9]."

By scrutinizing the patient's free associations, dream reports, resistance attempts, and transference relationship, psychoanalytic therapists come to understand the repressed conflicts. They reveal the insights gradually by comments, or *interpretations*, the analyst's chief therapeutic tool. Interpretations are withheld until patients appear receptive. Remarks are then made in such a way that people feel as if they were discovering the unconscious meaning of their own behavior. Because patients resist tracking troublesome patterns back to the beginning, psychoanalysis is a long undertaking. Orthodox psychoanalytic therapy generally requires three to five 50-minute sessions every week for several years.

Psychoanalytically oriented psychotherapies In Chapter 13 we described the ideas of Carl Jung, Alfred Adler, Karen Horney, Harry Stack Sullivan, and other neo-Freudian thinkers. Each of these persons modified Freud's ideas about personality and therapy. Neo-Freudian notions are often incorporated into current psychoanalytically oriented therapies. These modified versions of psychoanalysis tend to be briefer and less intense than orthodox psychoanalysis. They typically focus on present interpersonal experiences while deemphasizing the significance of the early childhood period.

Comments Psychoanalysis has been accepted as the preferred treatment strategy by a great many people (therapists and patients alike). Critics are disturbed primarily by two general shortcomings. First, the concepts of psychoanalysis and psychoanalytically oriented therapies are difficult to define objectively and to investigate by scientific methods. Consider the key therapeutic practice, the interpretation. There is no way to measure the correctness of an interpretation. How can one prove, for example, that a woman in a dream symbolizes a mother? Freud considered controlled observations of little value. Nonetheless, some clinicians are concerned about this issue and are committed to demonstrating the validity of psychoanalytic ideas and practices [10]. Second, orthodox psychoanalytic therapy is very restricted in applicability. Because it requires free association, a transference relationship, insight, and frequent sessions, psychoanalysis is suitable primarily for intelligent, verbal, reality-oriented, emotionally strong, introspective, disclosing, highly motivated, wealthy people. Such individuals have a high probability of improving under any circumstances [11]. Psychoanalytically oriented therapies meet this criticism to some degree. They can be used with a wider variety of patients.

Behavior Therapy

Behavior therapy emerged as an important treatment option in the late 1950s when psychologists began applying research findings to the tasks of understanding and helping distressed human beings. Although behavior therapists vary greatly in their beliefs, they all assume that objective scientific methods and findings should be used in assessing and treating psychological problems [12]. The techniques of behavior therapy are largely a product of controlled laboratory observations, particularly of work on respondent and operant conditioning (Chapter 5).

Conception of troubled behavior

Consider the businessman whose case helped illustrate psychoanalytic techniques. The man complained initially of an irritable and domineering manner that alienated his wife, sexual impotence, and involuntary arm twitches. Whereas the analyst assumed that the problem was an unresolved conflict, the behavior therapist would be likely to treat the symptoms as the problem—the unpleasant social mannerisms, sexual inadequacy, and spasmodic motions. Behavior therapists assume that symptoms, like normal behaviors, are caused by a combination of genetic and environmental factors. Experiences, especially learning, are emphasized. Cognitions may be considered important as well. Behavior therapists usually subscribe to behavioristic personality theories (Chapter 13).

Goals of therapy

The behavior therapist and the patient work together to specify the major goals of therapy. Instead of seeking to uncover a conflict, behavior therapists usually attempt to identify the conditions that have contributed to, and are maintaining, the problem(s) so that these conditions may be modified. Behavior therapists would be apt to speculate that the businessman learned domineering and irritable behavior by observing and imitating his father and that these responses were reinforced by their success. The impotence might be attributed to anxiety about marital problems. While psychoanalytic therapists emphasize discussion and insight, behavior therapists stress action that will improve the patient's current life. Typically, behavior therapists see themselves as instructor-friend figures and focus on teaching. The patient, they assume, must learn or relearn adaptive responses and unlearn maladaptive ones. (*Note:* Some behavior therapists argue that the origins of a disorder are irrelevant to treatment. Even a condition that is caused by heredity may be helped by new learning and, in some instances, environmentally based problems may be alleviated by drugs [13].)

Therapy procedures

The treatment techniques of behavior therapy are derived from research, often on learning. We describe four common procedures.

1. *Respondent conditioning.* In the 1950s a South African psychiatrist, Joseph Wolpe, devised a strategy called *systematic desensitization*, or *desensitization*, to reduce severe anxiety. Desensitization appears to rely on a respondent conditioning principle, *counterconditioning*. You may recall that during counterconditioning an old conditioned response is replaced by a new one. The patient's anxiety is presumed to be a conditioned reaction. Through training, relaxation may replace the old fear. Desensitization works like this. Therapist and patient compile a list of events which provoke the distressing fear (or fears). Let's assume that a patient is intensely upset before and during school examinations. Representative events that arouse the fear are arranged in a hierarchy from weakest to strongest, as shown in Table 16-2. The therapist also trains the patient in deep muscle relaxation. Once the person is able to relax easily and completely, desensitization begins. The patient relaxes and is asked to vividly imagine the weakest item in the hierarchy. If any tension at all is felt while imagining the scene, the patient "blots the picture out" and relaxes again. This basic routine continues until the individual can visualize the weakest anxiety stimulus without discomfort. Then the therapist moves on to the next item on the list, and the process is repeated. At the conclusion of desensitization, the patient should be able to picture the most distressing incident in the hierarchy without feeling uncomfortable. Once people can visualize former fear-arousing items without experiencing anxiety, they often feel confident in confronting actual situations. Many behavior therapists prescribe "homework exercises" as part of the systematic desensitization program. Such exercises ask patients to expose themselves gradually—while relaxing and with additional supports (a trusted friend or a happy thought, for example)—to the actual situation that is feared. These real-life confrontations seem to be valuable.

2. *Positive reinforcement.* The presentation of an event following a behavior can increase the probability that the response will occur in similar situations. Psychologists call this process *positive reinforcement.* Behavior therapists use positive reinforcement principles deliberately to motivate desirable conduct in many treatment situations. Token economies, to be described later, depend on the reinforcement concept. Positive reinforcement is utilized informally with troubled adult outpatients. A woman whose marriage is unsatisfying may be encouraged to provide positive social reinforcement, such as praise and affection, whenever her spouse behaves considerately. A depressed man might be asked to observe his daily activities closely to develop a list of intrinsically positively reinforcing experiences to engage in. Behavior therapists often use their own approval intentionally to encourage constructive efforts in patients.

3. *Observation and imitation.* People learn many behaviors by *observation* and *imitation,* or *modeling.* Problems can occur because individuals observe and imitate maladaptive responses and/or fail to observe and imitate adaptive conduct. In such cases, therapists can function as models. Or they can bring in films or live models to demonstrate appropriate behavior. Observational procedures have been used to teach the mute to speak, to help frightened people cope with fears, and to train new social skills. *Assertion training* is based on observation learning principles. During assertion training, adults who experience severe inhibitions about revealing emotions learn to express themselves more genuinely. Initially, the patient

TABLE 16-2 Selected Items from a Hierarchy of Testing Situations that Arouse Anxiety

Rating	Situation
0	Beginning a new course
15	Hearing an instructor announce a small quiz two weeks hence
35	Trying to decide how to study for an exam
60	Hearing an instructor announce a major exam in three weeks and [describe] its importance
80	Standing alone in the hall before an exam
90	Hearing some "pearls" from another student which you doubt you'll remember, while studying in a group
90	Cramming while alone in the library right before an exam
100	Studying the night before a big exam

A rating of 0 means "totally relaxed," while one of 100 signifies "as tense as you ever are."

Source: Adapted from Kanfer, F. H., & Phillips, J. S. *Learning foundations of behavior therapy.* New York: Wiley, 1970. P. 151.

shows the therapist by *role playing,* or play acting, the way he or she usually behaves in a particularly difficult situation. Eventually, the therapist or model demonstrates appropriate, emotionally expressive behavior. The patient usually practices being assertive in the protected therapy setting and then in the real world in increasingly more challenging contexts. Assertion training is widely used today to teach women to express feelings openly. See Figure 16-4.

4. *Cognitive strategies.* In recent years many behavior therapists have been emphasizing the importance of thoughts in generating and changing behavior [14]. In Chapter 15 we saw that people could aggravate their own phobias and depressions by exaggerating dangers and by focusing on their own helplessness. To cope with thought-related problems, some behavior therapists use a technique called *rational restructuring.* The expert teaches the patient to monitor her or his thoughts and change irrational ones. A man who obsesses about failures at work might be asked to (1) keep a

FIGURE 16-4 Studies by Albert Bandura and his coworkers demonstrate that fears can be diminished through observation learning. The boy in the top row served as a model (on film) for a group of children who were intensely frightened of dogs. A series of brief movies showed the boy interacting with a dog in increasingly more intimate ways. After watching the model, phobic children displayed significant reductions in avoidance behavior around dogs. The gains persisted during follow-up studies. The girl in the lower photographs improved strikingly. Initially terrified of dogs, she displayed mounting boldness around the animals, as shown here. Bandura's research suggests that fear reduction in children is facilitated by viewing several different male and female models of varying ages interacting positively with dogs of diverse sizes and degrees of "fearsomeness" [76]. [*Bandura & Menlove, 1965.*]

list of positive accomplishments and (2) remind himself of at least one of these achievements whenever he downgrades himself. Behavior therapists also teach *problem-solving skills* to people who approach difficulties impulsively or ineffectually. To deal with severe pain, for instance, patients can learn mental relaxation techniques and attention-diverting tactics that reduce their suffering [15].

Generally, the procedures of behavior therapy are used in combination, as in the following case.

The Case of Mrs. S.

"Mrs. S. [aged 29] told the behavior therapist of a life dominated by anxiety and spells of nervous depression. . . . Tension headaches, often precipitated by insomnia, brought almost daily stress and pain. . . . After a half dozen sessions, the behavioral assessment [which included a daily diary in which Mrs. S. recorded important events and her reactions to them] revealed a picture of a woman who had always been underassertive and often anxious in her relations with other people. Mrs. S.'s inability to express her feelings led to her exploitation by others, which in turn bred resentment, hidden anger, intense guilt over her anger, and low self-esteem. Her depression appeared to be tied closely to her negative picture of herself. The therapist also learned that Mrs. S. had never experienced an orgasm. . . .

Since this problem and most of her other problems centered on her marital relationship, Mrs. S. agreed to the therapist's suggestion that they include her husband in the therapy. . . .

"For Mrs. S., as for most complex cases, the therapist forged a multifaceted treatment program. Early on, Mrs. S. began a program of relaxation training to curb her anxiety. . . . In these same early sessions, the therapist started a program of assertion training. . . . After helping her husband adopt a more supportive attitude toward her, the therapist instructed the couple in ways to use assertion strategies at home. In this way

Mrs. S. learned to be assertive outside the therapist's office.

"The third major facet of treatment was a Masters and Johnson-type program aimed at overcoming Mrs. S.'s lack of orgasm. Bolstered by the cooperation and understanding of her husband, Mrs. S. responded well and, after three weeks of treatment, began to have orgasms. This success, coupled with the assertion training, greatly enhanced the quality of their relationship.

"Nevertheless, Mrs. S. still became depressed on occasion and continued to doubt her adequacy as a wife. These reactions appeared to stem from her

unnecessarily low opinion of her own abilities, and the excessively negative interpretation she placed on different life situations. . . . Accordingly, the therapist . . . encouraged Mrs. S. to think up and repeat constructive statements about herself that were incompatible with her feeling of worthlessness. After some initial struggling, she gradually acquired better control over her neurotic thought patterns than she had ever had.

"Approximately four months after getting in touch with the therapist, Mrs. S. reported a dramatic reduction in anxiety and depression [16]."

Comments An impressive body of research suggests that behavior therapy procedures are often effective, especially with well-defined problems [17]. Since behavior therapy is briefer than orthodox psychoanalysis, some clinicians consider its economy another major virtue. It should be mentioned, however, that behavior therapists increasingly intervene in many aspects of their patients' lives and prolong treatment to ensure that gains are sustained. It is not the very brief procedure it once was [18]. Commitment to research is a third important strength. Of course, behavior therapy has critics too. Psychoanalytic theorists argue that behavior therapy does not deal with the real source of the patients' symptoms. They say that symptom removal by itself is a pointless exercise. Presumably, new symptoms will replace the old ones unless underlying conflicts are settled. This idea is known as *symptom substitution*. So far, it has not been experimentally demonstrated [19]. Though behavior therapy is often successful, the reasons for its victories are not clear. Simple conditioning principles cannot account for the extremely complicated learning of troubled outpatients in clinical settings. Terms such as "stimulus," "rein-

forcer," and "respondent conditioning" are used loosely here [20]. For example, the "stimulus" in systematic desensitization, the imagining of a scene, is an enormously complex, uncontrolled event. It is very unlike a light, a tone, or any other typical laboratory stimulus. There is evidence that behavior therapists may be perceived as unusually warm, natural, and involved [21]. The specific, straightforward techniques, which fit in well with commonsense, may inspire great confidence too. In sum, there may be many reasons why behavior therapy works well.

Humanistic-Existential Psychotherapy

Humanistic and existential approaches to psychotherapy are quite similar. We described the *humanistic* philosophy in Chapter 1. *Existential* theories emphasize freedom of choice (in interests, actions, and life-style). They advocate taking full responsibility for existence and striving to achieve self-actualization, or fulfillment. Both humanistic and existential therapies focus on the "*self*"— the purposes, values, concepts, capacity for growth, and subjective experiences of the person. They see human beings as relatively free (controlled by neither the environment nor biological urges). Behavior disorders arise, according to humanistic-existential theories, when something interferes with the achievement of self-actualization. Both views stress the importance of relating to other people openly and warmly and developing self-awareness. We explore two important humanistic-existential treatment approaches: client-centered and gestalt therapies.

Client-centered psychotherapy Client-centered psychotherapy was developed by an American psychologist, Carl Rogers. Rogers's ideas (Chapter 13) were strongly influenced by more than thirty years of clinical experience. In client-centered therapy, the *client* (Rogers's term for patient) is supposed to determine the content and direction of treatment insofar as possible (hence the name "client-centered").

Conception of troubled behavior. According to Rogers, troubled people have neglected their own experiences and have turned from their real selves. The maladaptive patterns usually begin in childhood when the individual learns, probably from parents, that certain impulses (such as hostility and sexuality) are unacceptable. The individual denies these important characteristics in order to win affection. Because maladjusted adults refuse to face significant aspects of their identity, they stop growing psychologically. They are defensive and closed to new experiences. They do not attempt to form intimate relationships. They are not creative. And they think poorly of themselves.

Goals and procedures of therapy. Client-centered therapists try to help people grow in their own self-determined directions so that they may actualize their potential and develop positive self-concepts. Clinicians with a client-centered orientation avoid evaluation and diagnosis. They may not even be interested in the details of the client's past or present life. What really matters, they argue, is the here-and-now encounter between sufferer and healer. If that relationship is characterized by

three important conditions—genuineness, emotional acceptance, and moment-to-moment understanding—therapeutic change should automatically occur.

1. *Genuineness.* Client-centered therapists try to be open to their own experiences and to those of their clients. They attempt to avoid guarded or defensive responses. If clinicians succeed in being genuine, clients will have no need for pretense or deceit and will feel free to be themselves. Therapists of other orientations, although frequently genuine, do not assume that this characteristic leads to therapeutic progress.

2. *Emotional acceptance.* In the past, clients have met with criticism and disapproval. To establish security so that clients can explore their experiences and emotions openly, client-centered therapists strive to accept everything about the client. No conditions are attached to that acceptance. In other words, clinicians try not to evaluate or judge feelings or conduct. While few therapists of any persuasion believe in morally condemning patients, most tend to be more emotionally aloof than the client-centered therapist—at least in theory. Psychoanalytic and behavior therapists are likely to monitor the appropriateness of their patients' conduct. They are also apt to praise adaptive and label maladaptive responses.

3. *Moment-to-moment understanding.* Client-centered therapists are sometimes characterized as *mirrors of feeling*. They verbally reflect the client's emotional experiences to put the individual in touch with those feelings. The following excerpt from a client-centered therapy session illustrates this feature. (*Note:* T stands for therapist; C, for client.)

C: Yeah, I've got feelings. But most of 'em I don't let 'em off.
T: Mhm. Kinda hide them.
C: (Faintly) Yeah. (Long pause) I guess the only reason that I try to hide 'em, is, seein' that I'm small, I guess I got to be a tough guy or somethin'.
T: Mhm.
C: That's the way I . . . think . . . people might think about me.
T: Mm. Little afraid to show my feelings. They might think I was weak, 'n take advantage of me or something. They might hurt me if they—knew I could be hurt.
C: I think they'd try, anyway. [22]

How does the relationship between client and therapist lead to change? Rogers believes that clients and therapists begin at opposite poles. Clients are not genuine. They do not understand or approve of themselves or others. As they find themselves listened to, accepted, and understood, they become increasingly able to attend to themselves and their experiences. They can examine feelings and thoughts that were previously excluded. The warm acceptance and positive regard of the therapist make the individual feel open to him- or herself and able to express all aspects frankly. As insights sharpen, new directions and courses of action become clear. There is a general loosening. Rigidity, immaturity, self-centeredness, and defensiveness disappear. Clients begin to like themselves; and they feel eager to relate to others, share, and grow [23].

Gestalt psychotherapy

The late Frederick (Fritz) Perls, a psychoanalytically trained psychiatrist, introduced gestalt therapy to Americans in the early 1950s. You may recall that the term *gestalt* means shape, pattern, or structure (Chapter 1). The members of the early gestalt movement focused on subjective experience, especially perception, and insisted that the whole is different than the sum of its parts. Gestalt therapy is loosely associated with the ideas of the gestalt viewpoint.

Conception of troubled behavior. Neurotic people, according to gestalt therapists, waste a lot of energy rejecting significant aspects of their nature, such as real needs, and adopting alien characteristics as their own.

Goals and procedures of therapy. The goal of gestalt therapy resembles the goal of client-centered therapy: restoring inherent capacities for growth. To achieve this objective, gestalt therapists break down the pa-

tients' blocks, façades, games, pretenses, and defenses. Then, they foster self-awareness. As a result, fragmented clients should be able to integrate all facets of themselves harmoniously, complete "the gestalt," be what they really are, and live "in the now." Gestalt clinicians observe and analyze speech, vocal tones, gestures, and body language—often in therapy groups. They want to learn what individuals are avoiding and how they are deceiving themselves. Eventually, the clinician uses gestalt exercises to help people recognize their own sensations, perceptions, and emotions (the only "certain" knowledge). Sometimes patients must use the present tense as they speak so that they focus on *current* experiences. When there seems to be an internal conflict—say, between conscience and drives or between masculine and feminine personality components—patients are invited to role-play the viewpoint of each faction in turn, and eventually to accept both. To stress the idea that people are active, responsible beings, another gestalt exercise asks patients to add the phrase "and I take responsibility for it" after comments about feelings and behavior. During "exaggeration" exercises, individuals amplify movements or repeat significant comments increasingly loudly to feel the full impact. Besides using exercises, gestalt therapists interpret dreams within a framework that is very different from the psychoanalytic one. Gestalt clinicians assume that all dream images represent portions of the self. Patients are encouraged to experience the dream from the standpoint of each image—to further self-understanding and self-acceptance. Gestalt therapists also create vivid scenarios, such as the following, to make problems more comprehensible and to motivate behavior change.

A Gestalt Therapy Session

"[During one gestalt therapy session] a husband and wife sat together on a sofa, bickering about the woman's mother. The husband seemed very angry with his mother-in-law, and the therapist surmised that she was getting in the way of his relationship with his wife. The therapist wanted to demonstrate to the couple how frustrating this must be for both of them, and he also wished to goad both of them to do something about it. Without warning, he rose from his chair and wedged himself between the couple. Not a word was said. The husband looked puzzled, then hurt, and gradually became angry at the therapist. [The husband asked the therapist] to move so that he could sit next to his wife again. The therapist shook his head. When the husband repeated his request, the therapist removed his jacket and placed it over the wife's head so that the husband could not even see her. A long silence followed, during which the husband grew more and more agitated. The wife meanwhile was sitting quietly, covered by the therapist's coat. Suddenly the husband stood up, walked past the therapist, and angrily removed the coat; then he pushed the therapist off the sofa. The therapist exploded in good-natured laughter. 'I wondered how long it would take you to do something!' he roared."

The scene had several significant effects. It made the hus-band realize that he felt cut off from his wife by his mother-in-law—just as he had been isolated from her by the therapist's intrusion. The success with the therapist made the husband wonder why he did not take action with the mother-in-law. The wife's extreme passivity was highlighted. Why hadn't she removed the coat? After this session both clients reported feeling in better contact with themselves and each other. They resolved to work actively to change the problematic relationship with the wife's mother [24].

Comments Humanistic-existential psychotherapies have been widely accepted by clinicians who serve troubled people in outpatient settings. They are humane and optimistic treatment approaches that make sense to a lot of people. They are criticized for several reasons. Some behavioral scientists question the evidence for their effectiveness. Gestalt therapists rarely conduct research on the outcome of therapy. They depend instead on testimonials and case histories. Client-centered therapists, in contrast, have done a great deal of research. But they have relied almost exclusively on patients' self-reports about progress. Relatively bright and healthy people do say that they feel better after client-centered therapy with a warm, genuine, empathic clinician [25]. Yet we do not know if behavior really changes or if lives are actually happier. Humanistic-existential approaches have some significant theoretical problems too. They are based on a belief in the essential goodness of human nature and in a master motive, self-actualization. Although appealing, these ideas are nearly impossible to verify. Critics also question the humanistic-existential notion that the extremely diverse neurotic disorders are attributable to a single cause, arrested development. Finally, the goal of humanistic-existential therapies—self-determined psychological growth—is probably impossible to attain because therapists cannot help but influence patients.

Table 16-3 presents a comparison of the three psychotherapy approaches that have been discussed.

The Eclectic Approach

It may have occurred to you that psychoanalytic, behavior, and humanistic-existential therapies each have strengths that might be fruitfully combined. Many clinicians do fashion their own "conglomerate" psychotherapy by adopting and integrating elements from varied approaches. In a recent survey, in fact, investigators found that the majority of responding clinical psychologists regarded themselves as *eclectic* (as using a combination of procedures) [26]. Psychologist Arnold Lazarus has pointed out that no matter how attractive a particular theory is, what the therapist *does* or *does not do* is what affects the patient. Lazarus argues that flexible clinicians who fit responsible and effective technology to the needs and problems of the individual sufferer make the most helpful therapeutic agents [27]. Many psychologists appear to agree with him.

TABLE 16-3 A Comparison of Three Psychotherapies

Distinguishing factors	Psychoanalytic psychotherapy	Behavior therapy	Humanistic-existential psychotherapy
Assumed causes of nonpsychotic disturbances	Repressed conflicts	Maladaptive learning	Aspects of the self not recognized and accepted
Primary goals of therapy	Insight (intellectual and emotional)	Behavior change	Increased self-awareness, self-esteem, and psychological growth
Time orientation of therapy	Early childhood	Present life	Here-and-now (the therapy session)
Aspect of patient emphasized	The unconscious; especially motives, emotions, conflicts, fantasies, memories, and other cognitions	Behavior (sometimes cognitions and emotions such as depression and anxiety)	The self and its conscious subjective perspectives (perceptions, meanings, values, and concepts)
Major tools of therapy	Interpretations of: free associations, dreams, resistance attempts, and transference relationship	Teaching procedures based on experimental psychological findings (especially learning principles and cognitive strategies)	*Client-centered:* genuineness, emotional acceptance, and moment-to-moment understanding *Gestalt:* exercises, dream analyses, and vivid scenarios

Group Psychotherapy

Most psychotherapies can be used with a single troubled person or with a group of disturbed individuals. Some experts feel that therapy in a group, or *group therapy*, is superior to individual therapy for these reasons:

1. It provides a large range of models.
2. Realistic feedback comes from diverse people.
3. Group members give one another a great deal of encouragement and support.
4. Individuals can gain perspective in a group. They are unlikely to be the only ones with a specific problem.
5. Group therapy furnishes real opportunities to practice and improve social skills.
6. By observing how group members interact, the therapist acquires important information about *actual* social behavior.
7. Group therapy is cost-effective. That is, it serves more human beings at a lower cost per person than individual therapy.

In general, research on group therapy is problematic and difficult to interpret [28]. While there is no compelling evidence that group therapy is superior to individual therapy overall, it seems to be especially useful for treating social difficulties (such as trouble in forming or maintaining personal relationships) [29].

Experiential Groups

Experiential groups, those which insist that personal experience is the most important basis of knowledge, have become popular in the past ten years or so. Variously known as *encounter, sensitivity, human relations training*, or *T-groups*, they emphasize different goals. These include increased self-awareness, growth, intimacy with other human beings, and the understanding of group dynamics. Typically, six to twenty people sit in a circle with a leader and talk for a limited number of sessions. Physical contact may be encouraged, in addition. See Figure 16-5. The number and length of sessions, type of participants, and procedures differ. According to Carl Rogers, who has been active in promoting experiential groups, certain

FIGURE 16-5 Experiential groups often use physical exercises to put members in touch with their own bodies and to provide insights into social relationships. Above, a man with his eyes closed trusts other group members to carry him around the room. The individuals in the photograph below were asked to note their sensations when touching and being touched by a stranger. [*W. B. Saunders Company.*]

patterns almost always occur. At first there is apt to be a period of confusion, frustration, and "cocktail party chatter" intermingled with questions about the nature and purpose of the group. Participants begin by revealing their public selves. As trust develops, people gamble on letting the group know deeper facets. Eventually, members openly describe what they are feeling in the immediate moment. Among the first here-and-now attitudes expressed are negative impressions of other group members and/or the leader. Experiential groups demand that individuals reveal current feelings genuinely. While some group members attack façades and defenses, others show a natural capacity for dealing therapeutically with pain and suffering. A sense of warmth and trust increases with time. Participants acquire a great deal of information about how they appear to others; and they learn to accept and be themselves in the group. Many individuals report persisting gains in openness, honesty, empathy, and the like after participating in an experiential group [30].

While people are often enthusiastic about the benefits of experiential groups, caution is well advised. So far, most (but not all) research findings tend to be lukewarm [31]. The changes that occur do not appear to be so great or so long-lasting as those that result from group psychotherapy. Experiential groups may, in fact, be destructive. Recent studies report that from 1 to 47 percent of participants are hurt more than they are helped [32]. Individuals are too frequently left with unresolved problems: new dissatisfactions with spouse or job, for example, or strong sexual or emotional attachments to other group members that may threaten existing relationships. The benefits or costs of the experiential group appear to depend heavily on the leader. Leaders who are seen as warm, adept at conceptualizing and giving meaning to the experience, and moderate in pushing participation and giving orders seem to be most helpful [33].

PSYCHOTHERAPY CONTROVERSIES

Is psychotherapy effective? Is one approach superior to the others? Do successful therapies share key "healing" ingredients? We look briefly at these issues.

Is Psychotherapy Effective?

Until thirty years ago few people questioned psychotherapy's effectiveness. Then, in the early 1950s, Hans Eysenck, a prominent British psychologist, published a paper that ignited a bitter controversy. Eysenck had surveyed the research literature on therapy outcomes and had found that about two-thirds of neurotic people seemed to improve—regardless of whether or not they received formal treatment. If psychotherapy were truly effective, Eysenck argued, it should have a higher success rate than the simple passage of time [34]. In self-defense, behavioral scientists attacked Eysenck's scholarship. They argued, for example, that Eysenck's conclusions were based on a small, nonrepresentative sample of the available evidence. In any case, Eysenck's criticism helped focus psychologists' attention on psychotherapy assessment issues.

Appraising the results of psychological treatment methods is exceedingly difficult for several reasons. First, therapy is a long, enormously complicated, and variable experience that cannot be described precisely. Second, defining and measuring improvement is troublesome. After spending a lot of time (and often money), patients want to believe that they are functioning more capably. Therapists are similarly biased. If they see no improvement, they are admitting failure. Investigators deal with the problems of defining therapy and measuring patient improvement as best they can. Sometimes audio- or videotapes of sessions are analyzed to see what the therapist actually did. Outcomes are generally assessed in multiple ways. In the most careful studies, judges who do not know whether the patient received treatment make relevant behavioral ratings before and after therapy (or no therapy).

Current work suggests that therapy *is* often effective. A recent review of about a hundred outcome studies indicated that treatment was superior to no treatment in 80 percent of the cases. The most rigorously designed research provided even stronger evidence of therapy's value [35]. Unfortunately, psychotherapy, like an experiential group, can be destructive as well as helpful. Allen Bergin and his associates found that deterioration attributable to therapy was observed in about 5 percent of the cases that they investi-

gated. No single profile of therapist characteristics was associated with adverse results [36]. Apparently, what is therapeutic or antitherapeutic depends, to some extent, on the patient and the problem. Some day, it is hoped, research will be able to pinpoint the precise experiences that are most helpful for a specific person.

Is One Type of Psychotherapy Superior?

Comparing the various approaches to psychotherapy fairly is extremely difficult. The problem, of course, is to vary the treatment procedures while controlling significant extraneous, or unwanted, factors including therapist personality, commitment, and experience, and the severity of the patient's symptoms. In one remarkably painstaking comparison study, R. Bruce Sloane and his coworkers had three prominent, experienced behavior therapists and three prominent, experienced psychoanalytically oriented therapists treat nonpsychotic outpatients for several months. Control-group clients with comparable problems were placed on a minimal-treatment waiting list. Tapes of certain sessions were analyzed to pinpoint the therapists' personal characteristics and procedures. Before and after therapy (or no therapy), patients were assessed in an unusually comprehensive way. The appraisal involved psychological tests, ratings on target symptoms, interviews, and reports by informants who had known the subject for an average of twelve years, as well as self- and therapist ratings. About 80 percent of the patients receiving either type of therapy showed improved general functioning that was maintained for a full year. Behavior and psychoanalytic therapies appeared to be approximately equally effective under these conditions [37]. A number of other comparative studies confirm this finding [38]. Apparently, it is hard to demonstrate overall differences in effectiveness among the various major treatment approaches. This perplexing discovery may be explained plausibly in several ways. First, it may be that there are real differences among therapies that depend on the personalities and problems involved. Each therapy, in other words, may score systematic victories and defeats that cancel one another out. Second, any successful therapy may depend to some extent on certain shared ingredients. We examine this second hypothesis more closely.

Do Successful Therapies Share Key Ingredients?

Though we have been emphasizing differences among therapies, the treatment procedures discussed share a number of common elements. Therapy researchers Jerome Frank and Hans Strupp believe that some of these ingredients are the key to successful psychological treatment. Healing rites (such as those used with Alicia) may offer the same types of benefits. Successful therapies typically involve a personal interaction that is characterized by warmth, respect, understanding, trust, and enthusiastic support. This relationship provides the patient with hope and with expectations of positive change. It gives the healer a "power base" for influencing the patient, too. The therapy setting is a secure one where forbidden thoughts and feelings may be expressed freely and accepted—

perhaps for the first time. Therapists usually provide "rational" explanations for the sufferer's problems. These difficulties previously appeared mysterious and distressing. Whether right or wrong, explanations probably allay the client's fears. Clinicians also supply new information and encourage new ways of feeling and behaving. These common elements may be the truly therapeutic ones [39]. Although this position is not widely accepted, it can account for some puzzling findings: namely, why many people improve without the benefit of formal therapy and why novice clinicians are sometimes as effective as more practiced ones. ▲

TREATING THE CHRONIC PSYCHOTIC ADULT

In this section we focus on the treatment of chronic psychotic adults, those who experience recurring psychotic episodes (Chapter 14). The majority of these people have schizophrenic disorders. Typically, family and community ties are meager and chances for a complete recovery poor. In the past, many of these individuals spent their lives in public mental institutions—large, overcrowded, understaffed, bleak places, for the most part. Chronic psychotic patients living in these

---

▲ USING PSYCHOLOGY

1. Suppose that you had a psychological problem that you couldn't handle by yourself. Would you consider psychotherapy? Try to explain your own attitudes to psychotherapy, as well as those of several friends and family members.

2. Do you have a preference for any of the four psychotherapies described in the text? Which one? Why? If you were creating your own brand of psychotherapy, which procedures would you select? Explain.

3. According to a prominent psychologist, the methods of behavior therapy "contradict every major premise of behaviorism [40]." Review Watson's philosophy (Chapter 1). Why might Watson object to behavior therapy if he were alive today?

4. Suppose that a friend asked you, "Which type of therapy is best?" How would you reply? (Be sure to take research findings into consideration.)

5. How was Alicia's healing treatment similar to and different from a modern psychotherapy?

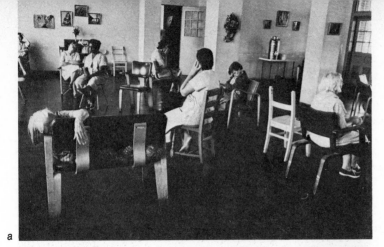

a

b

FIGURE 16-6 In the course of a lifetime, one out of every ten Americans will be hospitalized in a mental institution at least once, if current trends continue [77]. Most mental hospitals in the United States are funded either by the federal or state government. These institutions, often old and bleak, provide little treatment. Patients are apt to be left largely on their own to occupy themselves, as shown in (a). In (b) we see the obviously more favorable conditions of a private mental facility. In the mid-1970s, daily costs for a patient in a private institution, such as this one, were likely to exceed $175, excluding fees for therapy sessions. Specialized, tight-security, prisonlike institutions are reserved for people judged criminally insane. [Zalesky, Clemmer/ Black Star; Burk Uzzle/Magnum.]

institutions are usually heavily medicated. They are often encouraged to work at menial jobs. They may participate in crafts, such as basketweaving and ashtray making. In rare cases, psychotherapy may be available for an hour every week or so. Most of the time, chronic patients are apt to be on their own to occupy themselves as best they can—to wander, watch TV, read old newspapers, play table tennis, and generally kill time. To understand the patient's mental hospital experience firsthand, a number of mental health professionals have pretended to be psychotic and have committed themselves to psychiatric institutions (for details on one such study, see Chapter 14). Clinicians report finding the experience "degrading," "depersonalizing," "dehumanizing," "illness maintaining," and "terribly boring" [41]. See Figure 16-6. We examine the more promising treatment approaches for chronic mental patients, including medical intervention and intensive rehabilitation within institutions and communities.

The Medical Approach

Physicians have tried numerous tactics to alleviate psychotic symptoms. These include special diets, massive doses of vitamins, convulsion-inducing drugs or electric shocks, long periods of sleep, surgery that severs brain connections, and medications. While some of these strategies continue to be employed occasionally (see the Suggested Readings), medication alone is in general use today for treating psychotic disorders. We focus on tranquilizing drugs, the standard medical regime for schizophrenia, the most prevalent psychotic problem.

Chemical agents known as *major tranquilizers* were first used to treat schizophrenia in the United States in 1954. They rapidly became the preferred therapeutic method. By 1970, in fact, more than 85 percent of all state institution patients were taking the major tranquilizing drugs known as the *phenothiazines* [42]. These substances seem to work by blocking impulse transmission in brain pathways that use the neurotransmitter dopamine (Chapter 4). Behavior is dramatically altered. In one very careful drug study, investigators at the National Institute of Mental Health showed that the phenothiazines improved the functioning of approximately 95 percent of the schizophrenic patients who were studied. About 75 percent made marked gains. Appropriate social behavior became more frequent, while delusions, hallucinations, anxiety, confusion, and incoherent speech declined [43]. The major tranquilizers sharpen attentional and perceptual processes [44]. These various gains allow medicated schizophrenics to benefit from psychological treatment and to function—marginally—within the normal community. The widespread use of drugs seems to be largely responsible for the new practice of returning chronic patients to the community (a trend we describe later).

It is important to understand that the major tranquilizers don't cure schizophrenia. Patients must take maintenance doses of the drugs (which have to be readjusted periodically) to continue to derive benefits. Unfortunately, the medications may produce many unpleasant side effects, including drowsiness, lethargy, tremors, and blurred vision. These problems cannot always be controlled. For this reason, some professionals question the value of the drugs. And many patients stop taking medicine once they are on their own. Even when a patient remains on medication, all that can be expected from drugs alone is a poor to borderline adjustment within the

community. Hospital readmission is very likely. Clearly, the major tranquilizers are not the final solution to chronic schizophrenia. At the present time, however, drugs and rehabilitative programs *in combination* appear to be the most effective treatment that can be offered to most chronic mental patients.

Rehabilitation in Institutions: Social Milieu Therapy and Token Economies

Two types of institutional programs show promise for rehabilitating chronic mental patients when used in combination with drugs: *social milieu therapy* and *token economies*. The practices of both rehabilitative programs contrast markedly with traditional institutional policies. Both programs treat the patient as a responsible human being, a "resident." Residents are expected to work, socialize, and follow rules. Concrete realistic behavioral goals (perhaps, managing money, conducting social interactions, holding a job, and solving problems independently) are advocated. Opportunities to learn and practice the relevant skills are provided. As the resident improves, he or she faces increasing demands for independence and responsibility. The ultimate goal is preparing the individual to live in the outside world with support from relatives, friends, and other released residents [45].

During *social milieu therapy*, ordinary hospital wards are converted into therapeutic communities. The physical setting is often remodeled slightly to provide home-style amenities: doors on bedrooms and pictures on walls, for example. Staff and residents dress in street clothes. Each week patients work at jobs, attend psychotherapy sessions, and engage in varied types of recreation. They also participate in "town meetings" where they help make decisions about rules, activities, schedules, problems, and similar matters. Social pressure is the major source of motivation. Staff members treat residents respectfully and "demand" responsible, healthy behavior. As these standards come to dominate hospital life, patients begin expecting adaptive responses from themselves and one another.

The *token economy* is a rehabilitative behavior therapy procedure that uses external incentives—at least initially—to motivate and strengthen productive responses. In essence, token economies specify, "Do X and you will receive Y." The requirements are often tailored to the needs of the individual patient. *Conditioned reinforcers*, such as poker chips, points, buttons, or slips of paper, are given out following constructive behavior. The tokens can be exchanged later for privileges and material goods. Many programs phase out the tokens gradually and substitute natural reinforcers, including a salary for work and praise for appropriate social behavior. The requirements for reinforcement are spelled out precisely so that residents know the rules of the "game." See Figure 16-7 and Table 16-4.

Recently, psychologists Gordon Paul and Robert Lentz compared (1) milieu therapy, (2) social learning therapy (a token economy combined with other behavior therapy interventions), and (3) traditional treatment in one of the best state mental hospitals in Illinois. The severely debilitated chronic schizophrenic

FIGURE 16-7 The Oxnard Community Mental Health Center uses a token economy and other behavior therapy techniques for day-care patients. The program is designed to train residents for community living. Workshop courses teach competent behavior, including skills in grooming, consumer welfare, conservation, recreation, and social interaction. Each patient sets concrete weekly goals which are translated into well-defined behaviors. Adaptive conduct is reinforced by the coupons shown above. They may be redeemed later for privileges. Progress records are kept. Compared with the occupants of a nearby state hospital and residential care facility, patients in this program show more social behavior and less nonsocial behavior [78]. [*Oxnard Community Mental Health Center, California, courtesy of Dr. Robert P. Liberman.*]

TABLE 16-4 Selected Ward Jobs

Job description	Tokens paid
Tooth brushing: Brushes teeth or gargles at the time designated for tooth brushing (once daily)	1
Bed making: Makes own bed and cleans area around and under bed	1
Exercises: Assists recreational assistant with exercises; writes names of patients participating in exercises	3
Commissary: Assists sales clerk assistant; writes names of patients at commissary; records number of tokens patient spent; totals all tokens spent	5

Source: Adapted from Ayllon, T., & Azrin, N. *The token economy.* New York: Appleton-Century-Crofts, 1968. Pp. 246, 250.

patients in each condition were carefully equated on significant characteristics. The same staff ran the social learning and milieu therapy programs on a rotational basis. Both nontraditional treatments provided the same rules, expectations, and structure (stages with increasing requirements and privileges). Both presented a great many focused activities like classes and meetings. The programs were monitored to make certain that the specified procedures were being carried out. For eight years the patients were regularly evaluated. The social learning program was most successful. More than 97 percent of the patients in this type of therapy returned to the community for at least ninety consecutive days. Approximately 70 percent of those in the social milieu program and about 45 percent of those undergoing traditional treat-

FIGURE 16-8 For hundreds of years, mentally ill and mentally retarded patients have been cared for in foster homes within the Belgian town of Gheel. Shopkeepers and townspeople are accustomed to family care patients and treat them well. The project is supervised by the state psychiatric hospital. One patient, Marieke, is shown working with her two "adopted" grandchildren on one of her daily chores, feeding the chickens. Many of the more than 2,000 home-care patients living in private homes in the mid-1970s were old, chronically ill adults. People with schizophrenic, bipolar affective, and psychopathic personality disorders were also represented. Instead of being confined to the lonely, dull, useless existence of the typical nursing home or mental institution, people like Marieke remain actively invested in ongoing responsibilities and challenges [79]. [*James H. Karales.*]

ment were able to meet this criterion [46]. While the Paul-Lentz investigation is a model study in many respects, it is not conclusive. And despite the energetic rehabilitative attempts, no more than 10 percent of the patients *remained* in the community. Most had to be reinstitutionalized at some time during the evaluation period.

Rehabilitation in the Community

While most chronic mental patients are not dangerous to others, they do require help to function minimally within society. Today, treatment projects are being established in increasing numbers in American communities, both to replace and to supplement institutional programs.

Community alternatives to institutionalization Because mental hospitals are so frequently associated with stigma and deterioration, behavioral scientists are exploring alternative arrangements. One important possibility is treating chronic patients in their own homes—if they have homes. Small *home-treatment projects* have been serving chronic psychiatric patients in the United States for about twenty years. Recently, several investigators found that approximately 75 percent of the chronic psychotic individuals whom they studied could be maintained at home with drugs and public health nursing services [47]. See Figure 16-8. *Day-care* is also feasible. Therapeutic programs during the day in hospitals or clinics may serve chronic patients who live in their own communities. A day-care program was described in Figure 16-7. Another alternative to institutionalization is the *halfway house*. Usually located in a city, the house serves as both treatment facility and residence for people fearing that they may need hospitalization (or for those released from institutions). Residence may be limited to four- to eight-month stays. Halfway houses tend to be run by a small, nonprofessional staff, who consult mental health experts regularly. In the typical facility, about ten residents live in a family-style atmosphere. Patients contribute a small fee for room and board. They are expected to keep their rooms clean and to complete chores. They are likely to be encouraged to find jobs. Many consult local psychotherapists. If given appropriate support and supervision, chronic psychotic people can even manage their own halfway houses [48].

Behavioral scientists are currently experimenting with comprehensive, intensive community-based treatment. One outstanding project, the *Training in Community Living Program*, was established in Wisconsin by Leonard Stein and Mary Ann Test. Stein and Test emphasize extensive support within the community at the beginning, when the problems are first noticed. Many of the undesirable side effects of institutionalization—including dependency, the atrophy of skills, and exclusion by family and friends—may thus be avoided. Only people who are suicidal, homicidal, or in need of unusually large doses of medication are excluded from participation in this program (a small percentage of patients). Stein and Test describe the goals and practices of the project in this way:

The Training in Community Living Program

"Since our ultimate goal is to help patients become integrated into the community we have our patients live in independent settings. The patient's 'treatment' consists of participation in a full schedule of daily living activities in the community with pharmacotherapy [medication] utilized where appropriate. More specifically, staff members ('on-the-spot' in patients' residences and neighborhoods) teach and assist them in daily living activities such as laundry upkeep, shopping, cooking, restaurant utilization, grooming, budgeting, and usage of transportation. Additionally, patients are given sustained and intensive assistance in finding a job or sheltered workshop placement, and then staff are in daily contact with patients and their supervisors or employers in aiding with on-the-job problem solving. Furthermore, patients are aided in the constructive use of leisure time and development of effective socialization skills by staff 'prodding' and supporting their involvement in relevant community recreational and social activities. This frequently includes staff members accompanying patients to such functions on a regular basis. In all these activities, a 'can do' philosophy is transmitted from staff to patient, with the assets of patients stressed, and symptomatology *down-played*. Daily, even hourly, contact of staff with patients is emphasized initially and is then gradually diminished based on each patient's progress in the treatment program [49]."

Aftercare in the community The number of resident patients served by mental institutions in the United States has dropped from 559,000 in 1955, a peak year, to 193,000 in 1975 [50]. This decline resulted, in large measure, from a new national *deinstitutionalization policy*, taking chronic patients who don't need custodial care from hospitals and placing them in the community. The practice has been characterized as "a lofty ideal [that] has become something very ugly—a cold methodology by which government washes its hands of direct responsibility for the well-being of its most dependent citizens [51]." All too often, mental patients have been placed in board-and-care facilities, such as nursing or foster homes. In many cases, they have been allowed to drift into skid-row rooming houses and single-room occupancy hotels. Under these circumstances, former mental patients tend to suffer from poor nutrition, ill health, drug abuse, boredom, and exclusion from community life. More often than not, *aftercare* has been inadequate or nonexistent [52]. Yet, most chronic psychiatric patients require continuous aid—

medication, social services, and emotional support—to function in mainstream society [53]. Recently, the National Institute of Mental Health has begun helping states establish community-based aftercare programs, known as *Community Support Systems* (CSSs). The goals of the CSSs include:

1. Providing help for crises and hospitalization when necessary
2. Offering psychological and social rehabilitation (including training in community-living skills in a natural setting—if possible—and opportunities to improve employability and develop social competencies, interests, and hobbies)
3. Finding supportive living and working arrangements of indefinite duration
4. Helping natural community-support agents, such as family and friends, who may be in need of advice

Precisely how each state implements these goals is flexible. The Community Support System idea is considered "experimental" and will be systematically evaluated [54]. If comprehensive aftercare services, such as those envisioned for the CSSs, are readily available, deinstitutionalization may become a humane and effective policy. ▲

ESTABLISHING COMMUNITY MENTAL HEALTH

It became increasingly clear in the 1950s that too few distressed people were benefiting from traditional psychological services. There seemed to be several reasons for the predicament:

1. Outpatient psychotherapy was very expensive.
2. Treatment techniques were geared to the needs of young, verbal, successful people, and not to those of the poor, elderly, and severely disturbed, who needed the help most.
3. Therapy often came very late—after a great deal of suffering.
4. Almost nothing was being done to prevent the occurrence of psychological problems.

In 1963 John Kennedy, then President of the United States, proposed a "bold new approach" and funded hundreds of *community mental health centers*. The centers were supposed to supply quality psychological care inexpensively, as well as consultation and education. Mental health centers were located in the heart of the community, often in storefront buildings. Instead of *waiting* for clients, community mental health workers resolved to *actively seek out* those who needed help. Three somewhat overlapping functions—primary prevention, secondary prevention, and tertiary prevention—were to be served.

Primary prevention refers to all efforts to prevent the occurrence of psychological problems and to foster and strengthen mental health. Anything that improves the quality of life, including government projects to clean up slums and train the jobless, can be considered primary prevention. Since community mental health workers have limited power, their primary prevention undertakings tend to be modest ones. Some workers have established educational and supportive groups to prepare essentially normal people to handle problematic life situations, including difficulties that arise during child rearing, marriage, retirement, and widowhood. Others have organized social action programs, such as voter registrations, block cleanups, and antidrug campaigns. As an illustration of a primary prevention program, we describe a recent project for the elderly.

▲ USING PSYCHOLOGY

1. How are token economies and social milieu therapy similar to one another? Different from one another?

2. Imagine that you develop a chronic schizophrenic condition while in your early thirties. What type of treatment program(s) would you prefer? Explain your preference(s).

Maintaining the Elderly in the Community

Psychologist Thomas Wolff and his associates at the Franklin-Hampshire Community Mental Health Center in Massachusetts were interested in preventing the institutionalization of the elderly by supporting a natural "maintenance system." Accordingly, they engineered a program for women living with or near elderly parents. Clients who might benefit from this service were rounded up by a "natural helper" from the community, Mrs. D. Mrs. D. knew which families were having difficulties. The women met in a group.

When asked about current needs, the group members requested ongoing educational and support sessions. They were also interested in assessments of community issues, such as housing for the aged. The mental health workers tried to honor these requests. They found resource people to conduct educational programs on topics such as alcohol use and hearing loss during old age. At supportive meetings the women were able to share experiences candidly and to assist one another. At one educational ses-

sion, the group learned of impending legislation on a housing development for older adults. The mental health staff aided the women in a lobbying campaign, so that their voices would be heard. Ultimately, the group convinced the county to build relatively small housing units in scattered rural communities, rather than a single centralized high-rise. Overall, then, this rather simple project had a number of significant consequences [55].

The term *secondary prevention* refers to two policies: (1) identifying psychological problems at an early stage and (2) providing immediate treatment to keep situations from deteriorating. To detect psychological problems at the beginning, many community mental health centers work closely with teachers, clergy, family doctors, police officers, and other natural support agents. In some cases, the centers offer educational services to sharpen the insights and skills of the natural agents. Later in the chapter we describe a secondary prevention project for police officers. Community mental health centers provide a wide range of traditional services, including short-term hospitalization and psychotherapy as well. Therapy in the centers tends to be present-oriented and focused on reality. It is usually available at affordable prices during hours convenient for community members without long waiting periods. Many center therapists are paraprofessionals (see Table 16-1) from the local community with on-the-job training. These workers often play unconventional roles. They might make house visits and support clients "on the spot" through traumatic experiences like a death in the family. In addition to providing traditional services, many centers operate twenty-four-hour telephone hotlines for people facing

crises. See Figure 16-9. They are also likely to conduct specialized programs for groups with particular problems—adolescents, divorcees, alcoholics, and drug addicts, for instance.

FIGURE 16-9 In many community mental health centers, telephone hotlines like the one pictured here make psychological services readily available around the clock. In some cases, hotlines specialize in one type of problem, such as potential suicides or drug emergencies. The staff often consists of nonprofessional volunteers supervised by psychologists or psychiatrists. These counselors are trained to listen very closely, to offer emotional support, to evaluate the severity of the problem, and to make suitable referrals to mental health resources within the community. Phone contacts may be followed up by crisis intervention therapy sessions. [*Van Bucher/Photo Researchers.*]

Tertiary prevention, or *rehabilitative, strategies* are designed to correct for the *results* of emotional problems. Most rehabilitative programs stress improving the client's social effectiveness and work skills so that he or she can function more harmoniously in the community. Examples of tertiary prevention include rehabilitative projects for physically handicapped people, chronic psychotic patients (just described), and criminals. In the last section of this chapter we focus on the rehabilitation of criminals.

The community mental health movement has encountered two serious problems. First, financial backing has been minimal. Second, there has been a great deal of internal dissension among mental health workers [56]. Some assume that society is basically benign and reasonable and that the community clinician's chief task is helping maladjusted people adapt. Other workers take the position that most personal problems are the result of misunderstandings. They see effective communication as a major part of the solution. An increasing number of community experts blame individual troubles on society and the practices, values, and/or ideologies of its institutions. These professionals believe that mental health workers should be helping clients change their surroundings through political and social action. In short, community mental health workers are following very different paths toward their goals. Though primary prevention was initially lost in the shuffle, there is growing awareness of its importance and increasing emphasis on implementing this essential role [57]. While community mental health centers have not yet succeeded in making communities psychologically healthy places, they appear to be moving gradually in the right direction. ▲

PRISON, CRIME, AND REHABILITATION

Over the course of a single year about 2½ million Americans (who are thought to represent only a small percentage of lawbreakers) spend time in a jail of some type [58]. In the United States, approximately 97 percent of the prison population is male. A highly disproportionate number are poor and belong to ethnic and racial minority groups [59]. Penal institutions are expected to serve four major functions [60]: (1) to isolate offenders, preventing harm to the community; (2) to make criminals sorry for what they did, a type of revenge; (3) to reduce the likelihood of future crime; and (4) to rehabilitate lawbreakers so that they can function productively in society. What are the effects of prisons? Are there better alternatives for rehabilitation? We examine these issues.

The Effects of Prison

Few experts doubt that prisons are good at confining people and making many of them miserable. Escapes from prison tend to be rare. The pain of imprisonment, though impossible to measure objectively, is probably severe for most. Prisoners are deprived of liberty, autonomy, physical security, genuine human relationships, meaningful work, and contact with the opposite sex. In a typical prison, the inmates gamble and take drugs. Homosexual rape is commonplace. Beatings, torture, and even murder are not rare events [61]. The prison atmosphere is monotonous, constrained, brutal, and lonely. Nor is imprisonment the only penalty that society imposes on people convicted of breaking its laws. Ex-convicts in this country are often denied the right to pursue various occupations [62].

▲ **USING PSYCHOLOGY**

What kinds of primary, secondary, and tertiary prevention programs are needed in your community?

Do prisons reduce the likelihood of future crime? Do they equip offenders to function productively inside society? Since approximately 99 percent of inmates leave prison eventually [63], the answers to both questions are vitally important for everybody's welfare.

Consider the crime-reduction issue first. In Chapter 5, we reported that consistent, brief, moderately aversive experiences at the onset of the behavior to be eliminated or shortly thereafter are most effective in discouraging unwanted acts in children. We also said that incompatible, constructive conduct is most probable when followed by positive reinforcement. Prisons offer inconsistent, lengthy, long-delayed, severe penalties for crime. It is not clear that this tactic is an effective deterrent for the criminal population. Though aversive, the prison experience itself is liable to feed frustration and anger, provide ready access to hundreds of antisocial models, and embed residents in a culture that rewards violent and unlawful behavior. These conditions should increase the probability of future crime. Does research confirm this pessimistic prediction? Investigators who follow the careers of released prisoners find that from 30 to 80 percent return to crime and are rearrested. No one is happy about these statistics. But

the critical question is this: Do conventional prisons result in fewer or more rearrests than other treatment approaches? There are very few controlled studies that come to grips with this issue. For this reason, we conclude that prisons *do not appear* to be successful in reducing crime rates. But we have to withhold final judgment.

Do prisons rehabilitate? Few penal authorities would claim that they do. Less than 5 percent of the billions of dollars spent every year on prison operation and construction goes into job training, education, counseling, and the like [64]. When "vocational training" exists, it is typically menial work that has little relevance to the job market in the outside world. Prison schools are apt to be inadequate and to serve only a small fraction of inmates. Rarely do criminals learn to follow rules or carry out responsibilities in prison. Nor are they likely to receive help with individual problems such as a drug habit, an explosive temper, or anxieties. In addition, prisons probably have a powerful *dehumanizing* effect, reducing awareness of human attributes and compassion. We describe research by psychologist Philip Zimbardo which supports this idea.

The Dehumanizing Effects of Prison Life

With the help of an ex-convict, Philip Zimbardo and several colleagues converted the basement of the psychology building at Stanford University into a mock prison, complete with barred cells and bucket toilets, for a demonstration. Zimbardo's institution was designed to run for two weeks. Prisoners and guards were recruited by newspaper ads offering a modest daily salary for participation. Eventually, twenty-one apparently psychologically and physically healthy male college students were selected for the ex-

perience. Random assignment determined who played guards and who represented prisoners.

The study began dramatically. Each prisoner-subject was unexpectedly picked up by the city police at his home. The arrests were so realistic that some neighbors offered the boys' families sympathy and support. The police frisked and handcuffed each "suspect," then drove him to headquarters for fingerprinting and booking. Later, the subjects were blindfolded and escorted to Zimbardo's prison. There they were ordered to strip and then

skin-searched, sprayed with delousing powder, and dressed in smocks (with numbers) and stocking caps. See Figure 16-10.

Arbitrary rules were designed to make the mock prison experience realistic. During meal and rest periods, for example, prisoners were forbidden to speak to one another. Silence was again enforced when the lights went out at ten o'clock.

The prisoners soon began thinking of ways to escape or subvert the experiment. On the second day, for instance, some

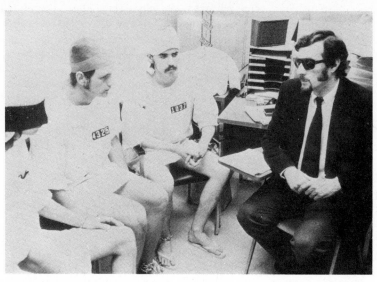

FIGURE 16-10 Inmates at the Stanford mock prison are meeting here with the prison superintendent, Philip Zimbardo. [*Philip G. Zimbardo.*]

men barricaded the door with beds. Others ripped the numbers off their smocks and refused to eat.

The guards behaved with increasing brutality, abusing their wards both verbally and physically. One graduate student guard remarked after the experiment: "I was surprised at myself. I was a real crumb. I made them call each other names and clean out the toilets with their bare hands. I practically considered the prisoners cattle, and I kept thinking I have to watch out for them in case they try something [65]."

As the prison grew more savage, Zimbardo became alarmed. He reported seeing "dramatic changes in virtually every aspect of the subjects' behavior, thinking, and feeling. Human values were suspended, self-concepts were challenged and the ugliest, most base, pathological side of human nature surfaced." Three prisoners had to be released in the first four days because they experienced acute reactions, including hysterical crying, confused thinking, and severe depression. Approximately one-third of the guards became tyrannical, using their power arbitrarily for its own sake. Though some guards merely did their jobs, no one intervened on behalf of the prisoners, told another guard to ease off, or complained to the prison superintendent (the experimenter) about abuse of power by others. "By the end of the week," Zimbardo wrote, "the experiment had become a reality [66]."

While the Zimbardo mock prison study had numerous methodological problems as an *objective* demonstration of the effects of imprisonment, it highlighted the idea that prison is dehumanizing. Seven facets of the prison experience seem to contribute to dehumanization, in Zimbardo's opinion [67]:

1. Steel walls, barbed-wire fences, gun towers, bars, and other physical features establish the prison as a grim, impersonal place where no decent human being would want to live.

2. Prison conditions reduce the inmates' perceptions of their own uniqueness. Offenders wear identical uniforms. All personal possessions are taken away. More important, individuals are treated like numbers without distinctive needs, past experiences, strengths, and weaknesses.

3. The prisoners are required to obey petty, arbitrary prison rules which degrade dignity, destroy trust, and make genuine communication impossible.

4. Prison conditions cause people to distort, inhibit, and/or suppress emotion for several reasons. First, the expression of emotion is dangerous. Those who show feelings are apt to be labeled potential informers and/or targets for rape. Second, being unfeeling minimizes one's suffering and therefore brings a tangible reward.

5. In an all-male prison world, power and control come through superior physical strength. Consequently, offenders frequently play the role of "tough animal." They strive for an image of fearlessness, power, lack of feeling, selfishness, and self-gratification. Such role behavior further reduces the prisoner's individuality.

6. People lose perspective when time creeps, as it does in prison. They find themselves overreacting to minor happenings and failing to plan for major ones.

7. Prisoners lose the right to choose. The sense of self-direction and responsibility is stripped away.

These observations agree with the perceptions of many inmates and penal authorities. Prisons have been likened, in fact, to "warehouses that degrade their baggage" and "factories of crime."

Alternatives to the Prison System

We explore alternatives to the current prison system: crime prevention and community-based rehabilitation.

Preventing crime Many penal authorities believe that massive social reform is the only way to eradicate crime. Violence must be divested of its glamour. The importance of wealth and material possessions must be downplayed. The resources that are truly necessary for a good life must be distributed more equitably. Psychologists are rarely, if ever, in a position to initiate reforms such as these. Typically, their crime prevention efforts involve teaching social agents to handle potential offenders in ways that reduce the probability of their turning to crime. We focus briefly on work with police officers.

Behavioral scientists work with police in several ways. Some attempt to help law enforcement agencies select more suitable officers. Others train police recruits to handle anger more appropriately and to use nonviolent tactics more effectively and frequently [68]. Psychologist Morton Bard, for example,

taught eighteen volunteer police officers to handle family disputes in a therapeutic way. In times of crisis, the poor often call the police. Skills in settling domestic quarrels are highly important because a large proportion of violent acts are triggered by arguments among family members and friends. A sizable number of police fatalities and injuries occur during such scuffles as well. For a month, Bard's police officers, known as the *Family Crisis Intervention Unit* (FCIU), attended behavioral science courses and practiced handling mock disputes staged by professional actors. At the end of the month, the officers reentered the community and began providing twenty-four-hour coverage by radio car to a densely populated Manhattan precinct serving about 85,000 people. The eighteen police officers were essentially "on call' specialists. Two members of the FCIU answered all domestic disturbance calls and attempted to mediate the conflicts. When indicated, they referred families to service agencies in the community; and they followed up on their clients. Psychologists provided consultation each week. Bard's project was a striking success. Although the precinct's homicide rate increased 350 percent overall, there were no homicides among the 962 families visited by the FCIU during the experimental period. Assaults and arrests in the precinct dropped dramatically [69]. Apparently, much crime can be prevented.

Community-based rehabilitation Today, American prisons return offenders to the community with essentially the same resources that they possessed before confinement (plus added anger and increased knowledge of crime). Community-based programs assume, in contrast, that offenders must learn new job, educational, and social skills so that they can have genuinely different options. Currently, many social scientists believe that criminals should be individually studied prior to sentencing, to assess security needs and viable rehabilitation options. Then, people who are not dangerous to society should be treated in a community setting. Between one-half and two-thirds of existing inmate populations have committed nonviolent crimes [70]. In a community-based program, many behavioral scientists reason, lawbreakers can learn to deal more adequately with the realities they must eventually face [71]. Community-based treatment makes a great deal of commonsense, but programs are scattered, unsystematic, and difficult to evaluate because control groups are rarely used. (Control groups are apt to be hard to justify because of budgetary considerations and administrative practices.) We describe a model community-based rehabilitative program for juveniles, an especially important population to reach. Individuals under twenty-six are thought to be responsible for 75 percent of all violent street crimes in the United States. Though the incidence of homicide among the young has declined slightly from peak levels in recent years, it is still astronomical [72].

The Achievement Place Model of Rehabilitation

During the late 1960s and early 1970s, psychologists Montrose Wolf, Elery and Elaine Phillips, Dean Fixsen, and their colleagues developed and refined Achievement Place, a rehabilitation program for predelinquent and delinquent youths. At Achievement Place, houseparents and youngsters live together in a small family-style group, usually within a community. Behavior therapy techniques, especially positive reinforcement and modeling, are used systematically along with support, social pressure, and other teaching techniques to encourage and strengthen prosocial behavior. By the mid-1970s, at least seventy-five group homes around the country were using similar strategies. Research has shown that the Achievement Place approach is very successful in reducing delinquency [73]. Recently, this model was used to restructure Boys Town, a 1,400-acre community in Nebraska. Approximately 400 boys whose parents are either dead or unable to care for them reside here. Many of the children have been in trouble with agencies and courts. The new Boys Town illustrates the key ingredients of Achievement Place.

The massive Boys Town institution was first decentralized into homes for eight to ten youngsters. Each home is run by a married couple living with their own children. Besides being warm and humane, the homey setting is effective for teaching specific survival, job, educational, and social skills. It allows the same adults to be close at hand where they can be responsible for and available to each child.

Upon arrival at Boys Town, each youth is assessed for his deficiencies in family and community living skills. Children are then motivated to acquire these behaviors. Some boys will learn well with natural social reinforcers such as approval and

FIGURE 16-11 The self-government system at Achievement Place is a basic component of the program. In this semidemocracy many, but not all, issues are voted on. The youngsters help make decisions about significant concerns, including curfew hours, fairness of discipline, and interpersonal problems. Family conferences teach the boys to organize ideas, discuss issues in an orderly fashion, negotiate, compromise, and settle problems rationally rather than through physical strength or cunning. [*Courtesy of Dr. Elery Phillips, Boys Town, Nebraska.*]

praise. Youths who require more formal incentives are often placed on a token economy regime. Points are subsequently earned or lost for specific acts and can be exchanged for privileges the following day. In some cases, house parents and child simply keep track of daily behavior and negotiate privileges informally. Ultimately, social reinforcers are used almost exclusively as motivators.

Each home has self-governing procedures to train crucial social competencies: problem solving, negotiating, feedback giving, and criticism taking. The entire "family" meets each day to discuss accomplishments, rules, and problems. Boys take turns being "youth managers," a job which involves settling minor squabbles and making minor decisions, such as when to schedule showers.

The behavior of the teaching parents has proven to be very significant. It is especially important that houseparents provide the following experiences: positively phrased instructions, feedback about what is *right* as well as wrong, reasons for changing, demonstrations of appropriate conduct, practice, affection, and support [74]. Achievement Place principles would probably be useful for rehabilitating many adult offenders. See Figure 16-11. ▲

▲ USING PSYCHOLOGY

1. In what ways are the needs of criminals and chronic psychotic patients similar? In what ways are rehabilitational procedures for both groups alike?

2. First argue for and then against community-based treatment for nondangerous criminals.

SUMMARY
The Treatment of Abnormal Behavior

1. Psychoanalytic, behavior, and humanistic-existential therapies are currently among the most widely used treatments for emotionally troubled outpatients. The essential features of these therapies are described and compared in Table 16-3.

2. Most clinicians combine therapeutic procedures and regard themselves as eclectic.

3. Therapy in a group may have advantages over individual therapy for people with social problems.

4. Experiential groups subscribe to varied goals. Research suggests that effects on participants are mixed and depend heavily on the group leader.

5. While therapy is often effective, it can be destructive occasionally.

6. Comparisons of outpatient psychotherapies have not shown marked overall differences. Particular procedures may be especially suitable (or unsuitable) for specific problems. At the same time, all successful treatments may depend on core experiences. These include establishing a personal relationship with a hopeful authority figure, expressing emotions openly, feeling safe, receiving rational explanations for frightening symptoms, acquiring information, and trying out new responses.

7. Chronic psychotic adults are usually treated by drugs. Token economies and social milieu therapy are useful for rehabilitating institutionalized patients.

8. Promising alternatives to institutionalization include home care supplemented by drug treatment and psychological support, day-care, halfway-house residence, and community living programs. Aftercare within the community is essential for the chronic psychotic individual.

9. Community mental health centers were established throughout the United States to make a large range of psychological services widely available. Three functions—primary prevention, secondary prevention, and tertiary prevention—are served.

10. Prisons appear to be good at confining offenders and making them miserable. Their success at reducing crime rates is questionable. Their record on rehabilitation is poor. Many aspects of prison life make the experience dehumanizing.

11. Psychologists teach community agents, such as police, to interact with potential offenders in ways that reduce the likelihood of violence and crime.

12. Most social scientists believe that nondangerous criminals can, and should be, rehabilitated within communities.

A Study Guide for Chapter Sixteen

Key terms psychotherapy (510), counseling (510), eclectic (522), group psychotherapy (523), experiential group (523), major tranquilizer (528), social milieu therapy (528), token economy (529), home-treatment project (530), day-care (530), halfway house (530), Training in Community Living Program (531), deinstitutionalization policy (531), Community Support Systems (CSSs) (532), community mental health center (532), mental health strategies for prevention [primary (532), secondary (533), tertiary (534)], and other italicized words and expressions.

You should be able to describe (*a*) conceptions of abnormal behavior, (*b*) goals, (*c*) treatment procedures, and (*d*) criticisms of the following therapies: psychoanalytic, behavior, client-centered, and gestalt.

Important research evaluation of group therapy, experiential groups (patterns and evaluations) (Rogers, others), psychotherapy outcomes (Eysenck, Bergin, others), psychotherapy comparisons (Sloane, others), comparison of therapies for chronic psychotic patients (Paul, Lentz), the effects of prison (Zimbardo, others), alternatives to prison (Bard, Wolf, Phillipses, Fixsen, others).

Basic concepts elements common to therapies and "curing" ceremonies, differences between orthodox psychoanalytic (psychoanalysis) and psychoanalytically oriented therapies, existential concepts, humanistic-existential approach to therapy, potential advantages of group psychotherapy, reasons for the difficulty of assessing psychotherapies, elements leading to success in all therapies (Frank, Strupp), similarities between social milieu and token economy therapies, inadequacies of traditional psychological services, problems of the community mental health center movement, purposes of prisons, prison characteristics that lead to dehumanization (Zimbardo), arguments favoring community-based rehabilitation programs for nondangerous criminals.

People to identify Freud, Wolpe, Rogers, Perls.

Self-Quiz

1. What is the primary goal of psychoanalytic therapy?
a. Accepting all aspects of the self
b. Achieving insight into unconscious conflicts
c. Attaining a greater sense of the meaning of life
d. Changing specific problem behaviors

2. What meaning would psychoanalytic therapists be most likely to assign to memory lapses and lateness for therapy appointments?
a. Identification of the therapist with an important past figure

b. Inadequate motivation to complete therapy
c. Reaching repressed material
d. Readiness to leave therapy

3. Which of the following problems may be fairly attributed to psychoanalytically oriented therapy?
a. It does not allow patients to focus on current problems.
b. It leads to symptom substitution.
c. It is difficult to study.
d. It is suitable for only a tiny proportion of all troubled outpatients.

4. Which statement about behavior therapy is true?
a. It emerged as a major treatment approach in the early 1900s.
b. It emphasizes the past history rather than the current life of the patient.
c. It is the by-product of clinical observations.
d. It relies heavily on experimental psychological findings.

5. The learning process on which systematic desensitization relies is:
a. Observation learning
b. Operant conditioning
c. Rational restructuring
d. Respondent conditioning

6. Which of the following is a legitimate criticism of behavior therapy?
a. It is exceedingly time-consuming and consequently uneconomical.
b. It is useless for rehabilitating psychotic patients.
c. It usually leads to symptom substitution.
d. The reasons for its success are unclear.

7. To what does the client-centered therapist attribute psychological disturbances?
a. Failing to acquire adaptive behavior because of faulty models
b. Learning faulty habits
c. Neglecting real experiences
d. Repressing conflicts

8. Which technique do client-centered therapists emphasize?
a. Intellectually analyzing the client's problems and making careful interpretations
b. Modeling desirable behavior
c. Using a lot of positive reinforcement
d. Verbally reflecting the client's emotional experiences

9. Which type of therapist would be most likely to ask a patient to role-play the viewpoints of masculine and feminine aspects of the self so that they may both be fully accepted.
a. Behavior *b.* Client-centered
c. Gestalt *d.* Psychoanalytic

10. Which statement about experiential groups is correct?

    a. The changes produced by experiential groups tend to last longer than those effected by group therapy.

    b. Few people (less than 1 in 500) are adversely affected by experiential groups.

    c. The first here-and-now attitudes expressed in experiential groups are liable to be negative ones.

    d. The most effective leaders of experiential groups are apt to be authoritarians who give the group a great deal of direction.

11. What did studies comparing psychoanalytically oriented and behavior therapies with outpatients find?

    a. Behavior therapy is clearly superior.

    b. Psychoanalytically oriented therapy is clearly superior.

    c. Both therapies help roughly 50 percent of the patients.

    d. Both therapies help roughly 80 percent of the patients.

12. Suppose that you enter a homey ward in a mental hospital and find patients working, participating in therapy, and conducting "town meetings." What type of program are you apt to be observing?

    a. Primary prevention

    b. Secondary prevention

    c. Social milieu therapy

    d. Traditional mental hospital treatment

13. Which of the following programs emphasizes teaching and assisting chronic psychotic patients with a full schedule of realistic daily activities in a natural setting?

    a. Halfway house

    b. Home-treatment program

    c. Token economy

    d. Training in Community Living Program

14. Which of the following is a clear example of a secondary prevention program?

    a. Crisis intervention

    b. Job training for prisoners

    c. Rap sessions for essentially normal teenagers

    d. A senior citizen's action group

15. What was the major purpose of the Family Crisis Intervention Unit?

    a. Consulting with community agencies

    b. Directly mediating disputes

    c. Improving the public image of police officers

    d. Making referrals to community service agencies

Exercise

TYPES OF PSYCHOTHERAPY. This exercise will help you test your knowledge about the varied psychotherapies described in this chapter. Match the appropriate treatment approach(es) with each characteristic. The same characteristic may be applied to more than one therapy. To review, see pages 512 to 522 and Table 16-3.

THERAPIES: behavior (B), client-centered (C), gestalt (G), psychoanalytic (P)

_____ **1.** Believes that therapists should avoid diagnosis and evaluation.

_____ **2.** Uses learning principles deliberately.

_____ **3.** Sees rejection of personal characteristics as the major cause of nonpsychotic disturbances.

_____ **4.** Was developed by Freud.

_____ **5.** Uses exercises and dramatic scenarios to increase awareness.

_____ **6.** Emphasizes the need for careful *objective* research for assessing and treating problems.

_____ **7.** Was developed by Rogers.

_____ **8.** Has roots going back to laboratory research.

_____ **9.** Views the desire to quit therapy as resistance.

_____ **10.** Emphasizes the therapeutic importance of the clinician's moment-to-moment understanding, acceptance, and genuineness.

_____ **11.** Was introduced by Perls.

_____ **12.** Strives to locate sources of unconscious conflicts.

_____ **13.** Asks patients to free-associate.

_____ **14.** Focuses on the self and its subjective viewpoint.

_____ **15.** Assumes that problems consist of maladaptive behavior.

_____ **16.** Emphasizes learning about façades, blocks, and defenses so that all aspects of the self may be integrated harmoniously.

_____ **17.** Assumes that dreams represent alienated portions of the self.

_____ **18.** Focuses on the patient's early childhood.

_____ **19.** Assumes that patients transfer feelings from significant past figures to therapists.

Suggested Readings

1. Corsini, R. J. *Current psychotherapies.* Itasco, Ill.: Peacock, 1973 (paperback). Noted practitioners describe twelve different psychotherapies. Each provides definitions, histories, theories, applications, and case examples.

2. Strupp, H. H. *Psychotherapy and the modification of abnormal behavior.* New York: McGraw-Hill, 1971 (paperback). This brief, clearly written book introduces the reader to major psychotherapy approaches from a research perspective. Strupp assumes that "the clinician must become a better scientist and the scientist a better clinician."

3. Frank, J. D. *Persuasion and healing: A comparative study of psychotherapy.* (Rev. ed.) Baltimore: Johns Hopkins University Press, 1973. Frank discusses features common to psychotherapies as well as placebos, religious revival, and "brainwashing" procedures.

4. Mishara, B. L., & Patterson, R. D. *Consumer's guide to mental health.* New York: Times Books, 1977; Adams, S., & Orgel, M. *Through the mental health maze: A consumer's guide to finding a psychotherapist.* Health Research Group, 1975. If you are contemplating therapy for yourself, such consumer's guides as these two books will provide a good deal of practical information about what to expect. You may also want to look at psychologist N. S. Sutherland's paperback, *Breakdown* (New York: Signet, 1977). Sutherland describes his own depressive episode and the therapy he received. He then discusses other possible treatments along with their problems.

5. Fancher, R. E. *Psychoanalytic psychology: The development of Freud's thought.* New York: Norton, 1973 (paperback). This is an excellent and interesting introduction to Freud's work.

6. Watson, D. L., & Tharp, R. G. *Self-directed behavior. Self-modification for personal adjustment.* (2d ed.) Monterey, Calif.: Brooks/Cole, 1977. This book is highly recommended if you would like some guidance in using behavior therapy techniques to deal with a specific, fairly minor personal problem.

7. Daniels, V., & Horowitz, L. J. *Being and caring.* San Francisco: San Francisco Book Co., 1976. This informal, personal book attempts to synthesize the understandings of Perls, Rogers, Freud, and many others. It emphasizes needs for self-acceptance, self-direction, personal responsibility, and caring. The reader is asked to try exercises that show the relevance of the insights to everyday life.

8. Axline, V. *Dibs: In search of self.* New York: Ballantine, 1964 (paperback). This fascinating case history shows how client-centered therapy techniques are used to treat a troubled child.

9. Kesey, K. *One flew over the cuckoo's nest.* New York: New American Library, 1962. This engaging novel about life in a mental institution shows vividly how unhealthy behavior can be encouraged and healthy behavior discouraged.

10. Bassuk, E. L., & Gerson, S. Deinstitutionalization and mental health services. *Scientific American*, 1978, **238**(2), 46–53. The article discusses the trend toward releasing psychotic patients to the community along with the problems. The authors argue that "neither the hospital nor the community approach is inherently the more humane."

11. Kazdin, A. E. Token economies: The rich rewards of rewards. *Psychology Today*, 1976, **10**(6), 98–105ff. A psychologist describes the use of token economies in different settings and discusses some unresolved ethical and practical issues.

12. Friedberg, J. Let's stop blasting the brain. *Psychology Today*, 1975, **9**(3), 18–23ff.; Gray, J. A. Anxiety. *Human Nature*, 1978, **1**(7), 38–45; Greenberg, J. Psychosurgery at the crossroads. *Science News*, 1977, **111**(20), 314–315ff.; Ross, H. M. Vitamin pills for schizophrenics. *Psychology Today*, 1974, **7**(11), 83–85ff. These popular articles provide nontechnical introductions to medical treatment topics: anxiety control, electroshock treatment, psychosurgery, and vitamin therapies.

13. Schmalleger, F. World of the career criminal. *Human Nature*, 1979, **2**(3), 50–56. Schmalleger, a professor of criminal justice, describes his personal observations on career criminals—about 70 percent of the prison population, in his opinion. Career criminals may regard crime as a vocation and jail as a reunion with old friends. Rehabilitation, he argues, must take the career criminal's special psychological makeup into account.

Answer Keys

Self-Quiz

1. *b* (513) **2.** *c* (514) **3.** *c* (515) **4.** *d* (516)
5. *d* (516) **6.** *d* (519) **7.** *c* (520) **8.** *d* (520)
9. *c* (521) **10.** *c* (524) **11.** *d* (525) **12.** *c* (528)
13. *d* (531) **14.** *a* (533) **15.** *b* (537)

Exercise

1. C **2.** B **3.** C, G **4.** P **5.** G **6.** B **7.** C
8. B **9.** P **10.** C **11.** G **12.** P **13.** P
14. C, G **15.** B **16.** G **17.** G **18.** P **19.** P

CHAPTER SEVENTEEN
Social Bonds, Social Influences, and Social Behavior

Can you imagine a life without other people? Can you picture yourself totally alone in the world? The idea is terrifying to most of us. Human beings are social animals, creatures that group together, depending on one another physically and psychologically throughout life. Close relationships with other human beings appear to be necessities. They are integral to survival and well-being. From the very beginning, the infant is social. Somehow it is preadapted to orient toward its caretakers. They provide for physical needs and supply the sensory and social stimulation that will convert the tiny baby into a perceiving, communicating, thinking person fitted for the culture (described in Chapter 3). Human life is inevitably a group life. People in every region of the world form societies that influence almost everything about them. In this chapter we focus on the distinctly social dimensions of human experience: social bonds, social influences, and social behavior. We begin by looking closely at an incident which suggests that people are entwined in a web of social *norms* (constraints, reference standards, or rules existing within a group).

The Norms of the New York City Subway

"We've recently looked at the subway experience which is so characteristic of New York life," psychologist Stanley Milgram explains. . . . "It is a remarkably regulated situation, and we tried to probe the norms that keep it manageable." At the beginning of his investigation, Milgram asked a class of undergraduates if they would each approach someone on the subway and request his or her seat. The class simply laughed. Not to be discouraged, Milgram suggested the project to his graduate students, "but they recoiled *en masse*." Eventually, "one brave soul, Ira Goodman, took on the heroic assignment, accompanied by [an] observer. Goodman was asked to make the request courteously, and without initial justification, to twenty passengers." He approached fourteen people. About half relinquished their seats. When questioned as to why he had addressed only fourteen and not twenty subjects, Goodman explained, "I just couldn't go on. It was one of the most difficult things I ever did in my life." Milgram guessed that Goodman's behavior might be revealing something important about social conduct in general. So he asked his graduate students to repeat the assignment; and he did not exempt himself. "Frankly," Milgram reports, "despite Goodman's initial experience, I assumed it would be easy. I approached a seated passenger and was about to utter the magical phrase. But the words seemed lodged in my trachea and would simply not emerge. I stood there frozen, then retreated, the mission unfulfilled. My student observer urged me to try again, but I was overwhelmed by paralyzing inhibition. I argued to myself: 'What kind of craven coward are you? You told your class to do it. How can you go back to them without carrying out your own assignment?' Finally, after several unsuccessful tries, I went up to a passenger and choked out the request, 'Excuse me sir, may I have your seat?' A moment of stark . . . panic overcame me. But the man got right up and gave me the seat. A second blow was yet to come. Taking the man's seat, I was overwhelmed by the need to behave in a way that would justify my request. My head sank between my knees, and I could feel my face blanching. I was not role-playing. I actually felt as if I were going to perish [1]."

Social norms, although human beings are often unaware of them, have powerful effects on behavior. In almost all social encounters, not only on subways, we find shared expectations about what to do, say, think, and even feel. Most of the time people honor these norms. We take notes in class, but not at parties or football games. We eliminate bodily wastes in private, though not all people do. Standards about language and conduct are so commonly accepted by the members of a culture that they seem natural. Human beings are apt to feel intensely uncomfortable about violating the rules even though the conventions may be trivial and honoring them may be costly. Reluctance to disregard social norms may lock spouses into hellish marriages. People may even choose to die rather than ignore the standards. If you were naked, for example, you might find it hard to run outside to escape a fire. "If you think it is easy to violate social constraints," Milgram challenges, "get onto a bus and sing out loud. Full-throated song now, no humming. Many people will say it is easy to carry out this act, but not one in a hundred will be able to do it." Throughout this chapter we will describe norms that shape our behavior. See Figure 17-1.

We have entered the realm of *social psychology*. Social psychologists study animals, usually people, as they interact with, and influence, one another directly and indirectly. They search for insights into social processes and principles. The chief measurement problem in social psychology is making *precise* observations on *realistic* social behavior. In Chapter 2 we suggested that it was difficult to achieve both precision and realism. Much social psychological research, as you will see, takes place under rather artificial laboratory conditions. Accuracy is gained while realism is sacrificed. To confirm experimental findings, naturalistic observations must be gathered and field experiments must be conducted.

Since human life is essentially social, we have already touched on many social psychological topics: for example, socialization of children in Chapter 3, sexual behavior in Chapter 10, and aggression in Chapter 11. In this chapter we concentrate exclusively on social psychological issues. We discuss social bonds, social pressures to conform in groups

a

b

FIGURE 17-1 Norms that guide human life often differ greatly from culture to culture. The members of each society tend to view their standards as the "natural" ones. Here we see contrasting group norms about dress. (*a*) Bedouin women near the Sinai desert cover their bodies and faces. The veil convention is being abandoned now in some Middle-Eastern countries after hundreds of years. When first walking on a public street without a veil, many Middle-Eastern women report feeling self-conscious, vulnerable, or even naked [151]. (*b*) A !Kung woman and child are shown. The !Kung are a nomadic people who live on the northern border of the Kalahari desert in Southern Africa. !Kung men, women, and children are comfortable in public with far less clothing than the Bedouins are. Since both groups dwell in hot desert regions, the differences in dress cannot be attributed simply to climatic adaptations. [*Lila Abu Lughod & Mel Kanner / Anthro-Photo.*]

and to obey leaders, and social influences on behavior (particularly sex roles), and on attitudes (especially prejudice).

SOCIAL BONDS: RELATIONSHIPS BETWEEN PEOPLE

People need people. Human beings provide for one another the greatest joys of life and the keenest sorrows as well. That may be the reason we are often observing and trying to figure one another out. In this section, we consider some of the things psychologists have learned about social needs, social perceptions, and social relationships (liking, loving, and helping).

Social Needs

In the late 1950s, psychologist Stanley Schachter began some important investigations on social needs. For one study, female subjects came to Schachter's laboratory and were introduced to Dr. Gregor Zilstein, a gentleman dressed in a white coat with a stethoscope dribbling out of one pocket. Zilstein announced to the group that his experiment was designed to provide information about the effects of intense, but nondangerous, electric shocks. He spent seven or eight minutes solemnly reciting the reasons why the research was significant. At the beginning of a ten-minute delay (presumably to prepare equipment for the study), subjects were asked to indicate whether they preferred to wait alone or with others. Under these anxiety-arousing conditions, more than 60 percent of the women said that they would rather wait together. A second group of female subjects had essentially the same experience except that they were convinced that the shocks would be "more a tickle or a tingle than anything unpleasant." In this case, less than 40 percent of the research participants preferred to wait together [2]. Schachter's findings have held up with different subject populations in diverse settings. When human beings are anxious about physical threats, the majority are eager to be with others [3].

Under what other conditions do people seek human contact? College students were questioned on this matter by social psychologist Patricia Middlebrook. While there was a great deal of variability, many students reported wanting to be near people when in a good mood or very happy, when facing an unfamiliar situation for the first time, when guilt-ridden, and when worried about serious personal problems. Most of the students indicated that they preferred to be alone when physically tired, embarrassed, busy, depressed, wanting to cry (perhaps to save face), and after extensive social interactions [4]. Laboratory studies confirm the notion that people prefer being alone when they fear embarrassment [5]. Research also suggests that human beings differ about when and how often they wish to affiliate. Women, for example, show stronger needs for contact than men do [6].

What is it that people seek from one another? Human beings provide sensory stimulation that keeps life from being dull. They give sympathy, reassurance, and protection from harm. As we saw in Chapter 14, social support actually facilitates recovery from strain and illness. If others are present, individuals placed in a stressful situation show less severe physical reactions [7]. Human beings serve an additional, less obvious need, *social comparison*. Psychologist Leon Festinger has suggested that the presence of *similar* people affords opportunities to evaluate one's own emotions, beliefs, and skills [8]. Apparently, we are all insecure creatures with many self-doubts. We like to know where we stand. The anxious women who were eager to affiliate in Schachter's study may have wanted to

see whether other people were experiencing similar fears.

Person Perception

Because our lives depend so heavily on others, we human beings tend to be people watchers. Behavioral scientists call people watching *person perception*. They have learned quite a bit about how impressions are formed. Like many other complicated activities, the person perception process is a highly individual one. As we have seen before, people hold distinctive biases and expectations that influence their impressions. Teachers, given the false information that specific pupils are especially bright, see the designated students as "bloomers" and provide experiences that encourage intellectual achievement in these "outstanding" youngsters (Chapter 12). Traditional clinicians who anticipate seeing abnormal behavior tend to find it (Chapter 15). People differ in how much they weigh specific pieces of information to form an overall impression [9]. Diverse criteria will be emphasized to judge intelligence, for example. You might give special weight to one or more of such criteria as grade-point average, aptitude scores, course of study, verbal fluency, wit, general knowledge, information about current events, advanced degrees, business or street "savvy," and original scientific discoveries. Human beings vary too in the amount of data they take into account [10]. To evaluate a politician, for instance, you might consider one, several, or all (and then some) of the following dimensions: liberal-conservative, informed-ignorant, candid-defensive, honest-dishonest, effective-ineffective, idealistic-practical, flexible-rigid.

While differing as observers, we show marked similarities also. Research suggests that first impressions often persist in memory and dominate perceptions [11]. Physical appearances are especially influential. Psychologist Karen Dion and her associates have demonstrated that physical beauty biases opinions favorably in diverse situations. For one study, Dion and her coworkers presented student subjects with photographs of people who had been rated high, average, or low in physical appeal. The research participants were asked to judge the figures in the photographs on altruism, sincerity, and other personality traits and to estimate their future marital happiness and occupational success. The subjects rated physically attractive people as having more positive personal characteristics and expected them to be more successful than less attractive people both in marriage and at work [12]. Physically appealing children are judged more positively, as well [13].

In daily interactions, our perceptions of others depend heavily on nonverbal cues. A study by psychologists Dane Archer and Robin Akert supports this notion. Archer and Akert showed 30- to 60-second videotape fragments of natural, unrehearsed encounters and/or conversations to research participants. As subjects watched the short tapes one at a time, they answered questions; for example, whether the woman talking on the phone in Figure 17-2 was addressing a man or a woman. The observers' responses were evaluated against reality. The woman was, in fact, talking to a man. People who saw the videotapes were more apt to be correct on fifteen out of sixteen questions than those in a control group who simply read complete transcripts of the same scenes [14]. Apparently, a person's perceptions of other people are greatly influenced by nonverbal signs of communication, including facial expression, posture, gesture, direction of gaze, and nonverbal aspects of speech (tone, pitch, timing, pauses, and the like). See Figure 17-3.

As human beings observe the behavior of others, they make inferences about causes. Psychologists call the inference dimension of person perception *attribution*. There is a huge body of theory and research on how attributions are formed. Somehow, people have to penetrate company manners, deliberate smoke screens and fronts, defenses, and temporary states due to illness, fatigue, emotion, and other circumstances. While the attribution process is sometimes conscious and delib-

FIGURE 17-2 This picture is from a videotape which was used in an experiment designed to assess the importance of nonverbal signs of communication. During the experiment, subjects in one group watched and listened to videotapes of different human interactions. Subjects in a second group read transcripts of the same scenes. Everyone was asked one question about the social relationships in each interaction. The transcript for the scene of the woman on the phone read: "Oh, well, you can't go because I have . . . You know . . . So . . . Well, 'cause . . . Yeah . . . Yeah . . . Oh, you know. . . . Just awhile . . . Well, because I just had to, you know . . . Yeah, yeah . . . I think you can do it." After watching the videotape or reading the transcript, each subject was asked to guess the gender of the person on the other end of the phone conversation. The woman was talking to a man. Only about 50 percent of the transcript readers were able to answer correctly. (The same percentage would be expected if subjects simply guessed randomly.) Research participants in the videotape group did significantly better, responding correctly about 87 percent of the time. They reported basing their answers on nonverbal cues, such as intensely fond smiles, an affectionate tone of voice, and a coy expression signaled by downcast eyes. [*Dane Archer.*]

erate, research by Ellen Langer and her coworkers suggests that many judgments are made without full awareness [15]. Suppose that someone catches your attention. The only man in a group of women, for example, will stand out. Research suggests that you are likely to exaggerate the man's characteristics. If the same human being had not been singled out—say, the man had been one among many other males—your impression would be more

a

b

FIGURE 17-3 People learn a great deal about one another through nonverbal signs of communication. (*a*) Gazing, for example, often follows fairly well-defined rules (some are universal; others vary from culture to culture). What message is conveyed by the officer? Who will stop looking first? Studies on people and simpler animals support the notion that gazing may function as a threat. During conversations, human beings with high status tend to make longer eye contact than those with low status. Breaking or avoiding another's gaze may signal appeasement or discomfort. (*b*) Facial expressions and gestures are also important sources of information about human beings. What emotional states are conveyed by Charles van Doren? On a quiz show approximately twenty years ago, van Doren—an excellent actor—correctly answered many difficult questions, though his performance turned out to be a hoax. While engaged in deception, individuals frequently give themselves away by drumming their fingers, pausing excessively during speech, making a lot of self-touching gestures, maintaining little eye-to-eye contact, and moving their feet and legs inappropriately [152]. [*Shelley Rusten; Wide World Photos.*]

accurate [16]. Psychologists have pinpointed some of the principles that guide our attributions [17]:

1. We pay close attention to actions that appear to have fairly distinct causes. Imagine that Lem dates a brilliant woman who is cold and dowdy. We are apt to come to the conclusion that brilliance must be very important to him. Now suppose that Lem goes with a brilliant, warm, beautiful woman. There is no single distinct cause for this behavior. Consequently, this action would be unlikely to shape our impressions of Lem.

2. We remember and assign significance to social behavior that is out of the ordinary [18]. We would register the information that Victoria is a vegetarian and lives with an aardvark. We might not recall that she eats three meals every day and drives a car.

3. We weigh behavior in private settings more heavily than public actions. Saul boasts and swaggers about at bars. But, suppose we overhear Saul confide to a friend that he often feels inadequate. We are likely to conclude that Saul is basically insecure.

4. Consistency over time and across diverse situations is another significant influence. Suppose that Winnie has staged tantrums in every conceivable situation for as long as we have known her. We are likely to see her response as motivated by an internal trait—say, a vicious temper. If tantrums were rare, we would probably attribute them to circumstances.

5. We tend to trust attributions that support prior expectations. This is especially true when the judgments are accepted by others.

As far as attributions go, we do not "do unto ourselves as we do unto others." People tend to avoid unpleasant information about themselves [19]. We often see our own unacceptable behavior as due to circumstances [20]. When judging others, we tend to attribute actions to underlying abilities, traits, and motives. We are unlikely to consider the impact of fleeting environmental occurrences [21]. Suppose that I am late. You are apt to blame my selfishness, laziness, and/or lack of consideration for others. If you are late, you will be likely to emphasize an external obstacle—perhaps the car acted up or a storm made driving treacherous. This effect may be due, in part, to differing amounts of information. In many situations, self-observers know their own past history and current circumstances far better than outsiders do. People can evaluate their own acts, then, in a context

that they lack when they assess the behavior of others [22].

If perceptions of people are readily biased, it is not surprising that individuals frequently fail to see eye to eye. Social scientist Richard Niemi studied this issue by interviewing a carefully chosen, representative national sample of more than 500 high school seniors and fathers, mothers, or both parents. He asked each research participant numerous factual and interpretative questions, such as "How many children are there in your family?" and "What are your own and your mother's (father's, spouse's or child's) attitudes toward Jewish people?" The data permitted Niemi to see whether parents, students, wives, and husbands understood one another's perceptions. In a great many instances, they did not [23]. Even when we view people at close range, we apparently see them from our unique vantage point. Though our impressions of human beings are often less than accurate, they are still important because they shape our behavior [24]. And our actions influence the conduct of others. ▲

Liking

Though human beings need others, they are selective. They don't affiliate with anyone and everyone. What attracts us to the individuals we like?

Desirable characteristics Beauty appears to be an important influence on attraction between members of the opposite sex in the initial stages of a relationship. For one study of this topic, psychologist Elaine Walster and her coworkers matched student subjects randomly for blind dates at a dance. Physical attractiveness (as rated by observers taking tickets) turned out to be better than intelligence, personality, or the meshing of needs as a measure for predicting which pairs reported liking one another and wishing to make another date. The most physically appealing individuals were best liked and most sought after [25]. Interestingly, when asked what they value in dates, students are apt to mention intelligence, friendliness, and sincerity rather than beauty [26]. Apparently, human beings are not entirely aware of their own values. People also choose as friends individuals who seem at least moderately competent. At the same time, "perfection" seems to be a "turnoff." "Perfect" individuals, by comparison, may remind people of their own inadequacies [27]. Why should human beings feel attracted to physically appealing and moderately competent persons? There are several plausible explanations. We all learn to value beauty and competence. Individuals with these positive characteristics probably acquire merit by association. A "good catch," in addition, reflects favorably on our own worth and brings the admiration of others. Finally, if the valued person likes us in return, our self-esteem is boosted.

The liking of others Many studies suggest that we feel favorably toward people who like us if we believe that they are sincere [28]. If somebody gradually grows to like you, your attraction is apt to be even stronger than if you had been liked to the same degree all along [29]. People who are initially "hard to get" may appear discriminating, so their affection may be valued especially highly. Flattery, incidentally, often succeeds: Human beings tend to view overevaluations favorably. After reviewing the research on this topic, Ellen Berscheid and Elaine Walster concluded, "The flatterer—who goes too far in shouting our praises—may lose a few points but not many [30]." When we feel sad or

inadequate, we are particularly vulnerable to the charms of those who seem sympathetic [31].

Proximity Physical distance, or *proximity*, is a powerful predictor of who will become friends. In a classic study that supports this idea, Leon Festinger and his coworkers investigated the friendships of couples living in a married-student housing project at the Massachusetts Institute of Technology. The couples, unknown to one another initially, were asked to name their three closest friends in the development. The data showed that even within a single building, people tended to choose companions who lived nearby. Next-door neighbors were more likely to become friends than persons two doors apart. Friendships among individuals four or more doors away were relatively rare [32]. Recent investigations confirm these findings [33]. Proximity may be associated with liking for several reasons. The work of psychologist Robert Zajonc and others shows that with repeated exposure, we find almost anything—paintings, clothing styles, and music, for example—increasingly appealing [34]. Presumably, we are leary of the new, different, or unusual. Repeated contact reduces anxieties and discomforts [35]. Nearness also means that people who like one another may interact often and accumulate mutually satisfying experiences that reinforce the friendship. Proximity alone is not a sufficient basis for harmony, of course. If you find a person objectionable, proximity may make her or him unbearable. Proximity can be overdone, too. When people are continually underfoot, they invade our sense of privacy and become irritating and/or boring.

Similarity We generally like individuals who hold similar attitudes and values and have similar personalities. Donn Byrne's *imaginary stranger strategy* is often used in laboratory studies of this topic. Early in the experiment, information on the subjects' opinions about something—perhaps politics, religion, or sex—are collected. Later, the same research participants are shown question-naires filled in by strangers (imaginary ones) and asked to rate their liking for these individuals. An avalanche of studies in the laboratory, natural settings, and real life suggests that people usually feel more attracted to strangers with similar attitudes than to those with dissimilar ones [36]. Psychologist Zick Rubin and his colleagues have followed the progress of dating couples. They find that pairs who stay together tend to be alike on certain characteristics. They are approximately equally involved in the relationship. They are apt to be similar in age, educational plans, aptitude scores, rated physical attraction, and values related to sex and marriage. They are not necessarily similar on other characteristics, such as religion [37]. Similarity is probably significant for several reasons. It provides a basis for sharing pleasurable activities. It increases each participant's self-confidence. (If we agree, we must both be sensible, superior people.) It reduces bickering as well. Yet, the similarity "law" has exceptions. Men who do not see themselves as fitting the traditional masculine role, for example, are equally attracted to dissimilar and similar female strangers in the laboratory [38]. And there may be such a thing as too much similarity, which makes relationships almost completely predictable and consequently dull.

Complementary personalities If they meet one another's needs, opposites may attract to some extent. Studies of couples in long-term relationships by Alan Kerckhoff and Keith Davis support this idea. Kerckhoff and Davis found that proximity and a similar social background thrust certain college students together initially and made them likely to get to know and like one another. Once pairs began interacting, similar values, attitudes, and interests became important. Finally, scores on a test that measured need complementarity—the gratifying of each other's needs—predicted which couples would remain together for the longest time [39]. Though subsequent research has not always

supported these findings, psychologists continue to believe that need complementarity is significant for relationships. The topic is hard to investigate because some needs are probably best satisfied by similarity and others by complementarity [40].

Overall, attraction between people is sometimes explained by *exchange theory*, a concept introduced into social psychology by John Thibaut and Harold Kelley [41]. In essence, exchange theory assumes that we are attracted to individuals when the rewards of the relationship outweigh the costs. The liking-enhancing characteristics that were just described may be conceptualized as increasing the pleasure of both participants in the relationship. Several other findings fit the exchange theory framework. As we see later, human beings tend to like those who cooperate for mutual benefits and dislike those who compete for valued resources. We even tend to like individuals associated by chance with rewards [42].

Loving

Most people use the term "love" sparingly to describe feelings for a handful of people to whom they are most strongly attracted or attached. It is unclear whether liking and loving are qualitatively different feelings or whether loving is simply a very intense form of liking. In daily life, we distinguish among several different types of love: notably, parental love, romantic and passionate love, love of a friend or companionate love, and love of humanity, country, and God. We focus briefly on *romantic and passionate love*. This emotion was characterized by Elaine and William Walster as a state of intense absorption, associated with strong physiological arousal, and accompanied by longing for and/or ecstacy over the partner and a desire for fulfillment through the partner [43].

Psychologist Zick Rubin attempted to measure something resembling this type of love by administering a questionnaire to several hundred students who were "going together."

The research participants were asked how much they agreed or disagreed with statements about their dating partners (see Table 17-1). Rubin's love scale focuses on three dimensions: *attachment* (needs for the physical presence and emotional support of the other), *caring* (feelings of concern and responsibility), and *intimacy* (desires for close and confidential communication). His questionnaire measure of love appears to have some validity. In other words, it is correlated with other criteria of love. In the laboratory, for example, couples whose love scores are above average gaze into one another's eyes more avidly than those whose love scores are below average. More impressively, pairs with high love scores are more apt to survive as couples than those with comparatively low love scores, especially if both have romantic ideas. Romantic ideas include beliefs that (1) love is reason enough to keep a relationship going and (2) practical considerations, such as personality similarity and economic security, are not critical for the success of the relationship [44].

What are the determinants of passionate love? Psychologists Elaine Walster and Ellen Berscheid suggest that this emotion, like others (Chapter 11), requires two ingredients: (1) physiological arousal and (2) cognitions attributing the tumultuous feelings to passion. In real life, sexual desire, joy, and happiness produce arousal states that often contribute to love. Curiously, physically arousing conditions due to negative emotions (such as anxiety, anger, frustration, jealousy, and even total confusion) appear to be able to intensify passion [45]. There is evidence, for instance, that parental interference heightens romance—the so-called Romeo-Juliet effect [46]. Under carefully controlled experimental conditions, anxiety (due to watching gory automobile accident films or crossing a wobbling suspension bridge over a 230-foot drop to rocks and shallow rapids) enhances sexual arousal and attraction [47].

Certain human beings seem especially susceptible to romantic cognitions. Individuals with high needs for affiliation rate their partners higher on Rubin's love scale than those with lower needs [48]. Persons who believe that fate and other external events control life's rewards are more likely to experience passionate love than those who see themselves in charge of important reinforcements. Contrary to folklore, women seem to be less idealistic and more cynical about romance than men. On the other hand, females experience love's "symptoms" ("wanting to run, jump, and scream" and "feeling giddy and carefree," for example) more intensely than males do [49].

What happens to romantic and passionate love? While it may disappear entirely, affection and friendship may remain. Psychologist Richard Cimbalo and his coworkers found that the longer couples were married, the lower were their average scores on Rubin's love scale. Yet, scores on Rubin's liking scale (see Table 17-1) remained consistently high [50].

What can people expect from love? *Equity theory*, formulated by Elaine and William Walster and Ellen Berscheid, suggests that couples enter into, and remain in, romantic relationships only when the bond is profitable for them both. Individuals may fantasize about partners on pedestals or on white horses. But, in reality, people attract and choose those with similarly desirable social characteristics overall. People who marry tend to be of comparable beauty, mental and physical health, social background, and popularity, for example. Many couples balance and counterbalance strengths and weaknesses. In a marriage between an elderly statesman and a lovely young woman, power and prestige may be traded for youth, beauty, and vitality. Partners seem to feel comfortable when they believe that they get about as much from the relationship as they give to it. If the contribution of one individual is vastly superior to that of the other in many spheres, the tie is apt to generate tension. To resolve the tension, the two people may (1) try to restore equity, (2) attempt to convince themselves that the relationship really is fair, or (3) separate [51].

Helping

In 1964 Kitty Genovese of Queens, New York,

TABLE 17-1   Items Similar to Those on Rubin's Love and Liking Scales

Love scale

1. I trust _____ totally.

2. I would be willing to sacrifice almost anything for _____.

3. No matter what _____ did, I could forgive it.

4. I would find it almost impossible to live without _____.

Liking scale

1. I would recommend _____ highly for an important and responsible position.

2. Most people find _____ admirable.

3. _____ is an extremely likable person.

4. _____ is the type of person whom I would like to resemble.

Not at all true; disagree completely   Moderately true; agree to some extent   Definitely true; agree completely

Respondents are instructed to fill in the blanks with the dating partner's, friend's, or loved one's name and to rate feelings about that individual on a nine-point scale like the one shown.

Source: Adapted from Rubin, Z. *Liking and loving. An invitation to social psychology.* New York: Holt, Rinehart & Winston, 1973. P. 216.

was attacked and stabbed fatally in full view of thirty-eight neighbors who did nothing to help her (Chapter 2). The Kitty Genovese incident and many similar ones stimulated interest in the question, Under what conditions do people help one another? In this section we focus on factors that influence *helping* (also called *altruistic* or *prosocial*) *behavior.*

Child-rearing tactics appear to be a significant influence on helping behavior. Several different disciplinary procedures, which seem to increase empathy, make signs of helpfulness more likely. *Affective explanations* are statements intertwined with (1) emotions, (2) values, or (3) expectations regarding self-control. Examples include: "That makes me very sad to see you hurt someone" and "You must never hurt anyone." Psychologist Carolyn Zahn-Waxler and her coworkers found that if mothers gave a great many affective explanations when the child was distressing, youngsters were apt to try to help out at the early age of eighteen to thirty months [52]. *Induction disciplinary techniques* (Chapter 3)

involve reasoning and explaining the painful consequences of misdeeds. This tactic appears to cultivate consideration for others and prosocial conduct [53]. Preachings about the importance of taking other people's perspectives into account increase generosity in children [54]. Empathy may even be deliberately trained in a school setting, with subsequent reductions in antisocial conduct. Psychologist Norma Feshbach and her colleagues developed exercises designed to sharpen children's abilities to (1) identify emotions felt by others, (2) understand situations from another's perspective, and (3) experience another's emotions personally. In pilot experiments, highly aggressive youngsters trained with these exercises behaved less antisocially than a comparable group of children who did not receive empathy instruction [55]. Observing competent prosocial models strengthens altruism both in the laboratory and in real life. Women and men who worked for black voter registration throughout the southern United States in the 1960s and those who helped Jews escape Nazi Germany, for instance, often came from homes where one or both parents were deeply committed to humanitarian ideals [56].

Several personality characteristics are associated consistently with helping behavior in laboratory research. People who value social relationships highly aid others more often than those who place primary emphasis on other values, such as aesthetic or political ones [57]. Feeling in control of life—believing that one's behavior actually has an impact—is linked with prosocial behavior, too [58]. Good samaritans in *dangerous* real-life situations may be an altogether different breed. Interview studies by Ted Huston and his associates find that these do-gooders are easily angered by minor frustrations, strongly invested in a law-and-order philosophy, prone to risk taking, and familiar and comfortable with violence themselves. Such samaritans tend to be almost exclusively male [59]. Even when danger is not involved, men are more prone than women to provide help during emergencies, a role for which they are trained in our society.

Social conditions also influence helping. To study this topic, psychologists simulate emergencies, involving, for example, a lost child seeking a parent, an injury, a fire, or an epileptic-like fit. Then the responses of the subjects (bystanders) are carefully observed. The clarity of the situation turns out to be an important influence on bystander behavior. If the dilemma is vague and ambiguous, individuals are far less likely to intervene than if it is clear and specific [60]—possibly to avoid an embarrassing mistake. People tend to help when they are alone and cannot pass the responsibility along to someone else (Chapter 2). In the laboratory and in real life, *anonymity* (feeling unknown) increases aggression, while being known to others inhibits it. Townspeople, who are apt to be well acquainted with one another, are far more likely than big-city folk to respond to strangers' pleas for assistance under many different types of circumstances [61]. When people feel known by others and aware of their own personal identity, they may experience shame and guilt

if they allow a fellow human being to suffer without trying to help out.

Field studies suggest that the sufferer's identity is another significant influence on altruism. We tend to come to the aid of those we like and those who depend on us [62]. And we are unlikely to hurt victims whose humanity has been emphasized [63]. Presumably, people experience unusually strong feelings of responsibility and empathy under these circumstances.

Many of the findings that have been described lend themselves to a *cost-reward analysis* [64]. When faced with an emergency, human beings seem to appraise the costs and benefits of alternative actions (effort, danger, and embarrassment, versus self-esteem, reduction of distress, and social and material rewards).

Mood influences prosocial conduct too. In the laboratory and the field, happy children and adults tend to do kind things, such as donate money to charities [65]. Research by psychologist Alice Isen and her coworkers suggests that people in good moods are especially likely to recall pleasant memories. If you focus on the bright side of life, presumably, you are apt to feel optimistic and behave accordingly. Newscasts may affect feelings and helping behavior in the general population. For one study, Harvey Hornstein and his associates exposed research participants to one of two news stories as they waited for an experiment to begin. The first story described a good deed, the donation of a kidney to save a stranger's life. The second described a bad act, an execution-style murder of an elderly person. Though the participants did not seem to be aware of the broadcast's impact, their views of humanity were affected. Individuals were significantly more positive about the human race after hearing about the humane act than after being informed of the deplorable one. Subsequent investigations suggest that newscasts alter conduct too. Adults tend to be especially cooperative and compassionate in the laboratory after hearing reports about kindness. Hornstein speculates that cruel stories disrupt the social bond and cause people to feel alienated from others. Consequently, they are more likely to behave selfishly, distrustfully, and antisocially [66]. ▲

SOCIAL BEHAVIOR IN GROUPS

As social animals, people often gather in family, educational, religious, social, and job-related groupings. Norms, such as those described in the chapter introduction, guide behavior within groups much of the time. Each group that we belong to has its own standards. In your family, you may speak in specific ways and avoid certain topics. Conversation with friends may follow an entirely different code. Dressing up may be dictated by the norms of one group (in church, for instance) and forbidden by those of another (say, in the student union). Human beings seem to feel uncomfortable without norms. When people are placed in novel laboratory situations where no norms exist, they soon create their own rules. These standards tend to persist [67]. Human beings find it taxing to shift to new norms, especially to radically different ones [68]. In Chapter 10, we saw that many people find the new American sexual customs hard to accept. Norms are enforced by pressures to comply. In some cases, pressure is applied by group members; in other cases, by a group leader. In this section we examine conformity and obedience, responses to pressure within groups.

Conformity

Conformity is defined as a change in behaviors and/or attitudes that results from real or imagined group pressure. (Attitudes will be defined formally and discussed later in the chapter. For now, think of an attitude as a learned evaluative concept.) Psychologists often distinguish between conforming behavior (*compliance*) and conforming attitudes (*acceptance*). In any situation, then, we may see one of four possible patterns of conformity: compliance and acceptance, compliance without acceptance, acceptance without compliance, and nonacceptance and noncompliance. Consider an example. Elmer feels pressured to pledge a fraternity. His older brother and his father belonged to Phigma Soo, and many friends are joining. Elmer may join happily (compliance, acceptance). He may comply while feeling that his decision is cowardly (compliance without acceptance). Alternatively, Elmer may decide not to pledge while inwardly longing to join—to please his girlfriend Midge (noncompliance, acceptance). Finally, Elmer may decide for himself that fraternities are destructive and restrictive and remain independent (noncompliance, nonacceptance). Conformity is rarely easy to judge. In any one situation, people may conform to some pressures and not to others. In this section, we try to answer these questions: Is conformity good or bad? How do psychologists study conformity? Why do people conform?

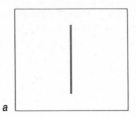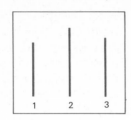

FIGURE 17-4 (*a*) For his studies of conformity, Solomon Asch asked subjects which line on the right matched the line on the left. (*b*) The subject—center—looks perplexed as the experimenter's confederates give wrong responses. (*c*) Despite his confusion, the young man does not comply with the unanimous but incorrect verdict. He gives the correct answer, explaining, "I have to call them as I see them." [*William Vandivert, Scientific American.*]

Is conformity good or bad? Some people feel uncomfortable when standing out in any way at all. You may know someone who hesitates to wear a navy-blue suit when friends are wearing black ones. Another acquaintance may equate conformity with "sinfulness," "selling out," or being "ruled by the mob." Whether conformity is justifiable depends, of course, on the specific context in which it occurs and on the consequences that

follow it. Conformity has led to terribly cruel acts, such as lynchings by mobs. Nonconformity—say, driving down the wrong side of the road—can be disastrous too.

Studying conformity: Solomon Asch's model Psychologist Solomon Asch conducted a classic series of studies on conformity in the 1950s. Many investigations are based on Asch's method, so we examine this early work in some detail. Assume that you are participating in one of his initial studies. When you arrive at the laboratory, the experimenter tells you that the investigation concerns visual perception. You sit around a table with seven other "students," all accomplices of the investigator. The experimenter props up two large cards on a table in the front of the room. One displays a single vertical line; the other, three vertical lines of varying lengths (as in Figure 17-4*a*). Your task is to select the line on the right-hand card that matches the line on the left one. All students are asked to call out their choices in sequence. The first pair of cards is easy; so is the second. Everyone is in agreement, and the task appears dull and routine. On the third set of cards, the initial subject gives a wrong response. You stare at the lines again. Is the person crazy? The next confederate gives the same wrong response. Feeling puzzled, you look again. As the third accomplice agrees with the others, you may wonder if something is wrong with your eyes. If you are wearing glasses, you are apt to remove them. You may tilt your chair backward or move closer to the cards. In any case, you feel alien, strange, and isolated from everyone else. What do you say when your turn comes? You may assume that your perceptions are wrong and comply (compliance, acceptance). Or, you may go along with the crowd while privately believing that everyone else is wrong (compliance, nonacceptance). Or, you may report precisely what you perceive while inwardly believing either that you are mistaken or correct (noncompliance, acceptance, or noncompliance, nonacceptance). See Figure 17-4*b* and *c*.

Asch measured conformity—compliance, in

actuality—by counting how many times people gave incorrect responses in situations where they almost certainly knew the correct answer. He found that a quarter to a third of his subjects did not comply at all. About 15 percent went along with the majority on three-quarters or more of the trials. The typical research participant accepted the group's perceptions a third of the time [69].

You should be aware of the fact that the conformity pressures in Asch's experiments were not entirely representative of real ones. Students are unlikely to feel emotionally involved in the Asch setting, as they do in real groups. Consequently, many may decide to go along with the majority and not "sweat it." The Asch manipulations are well known by now, too. About 75 percent of participants in a recent Asch-type investigation felt wary because they either knew of the ploy or suspected that total unanimity had to be a trap [70]. The Asch setting may be unrealistic for yet another reason. Ordinarily, when responses of group members are unlike our own, we attribute them to personal differences—often in motivation, ideology, or expertise. In Asch's original studies, subjects had difficulty explaining what was happening reasonably. Eventually they had to assume that somebody (either the confederates or themselves) had faulty perceptions. They may have figured, "One person is more likely to be wrong than seven." When the responses of the accomplices in Asch-type experiments can be explained plausibly, people conform significantly less [71].

Influences on conformity Why do people conform? Situational and personality characteristics both appear to be involved in conformity. First, consider situational influences. Research shows that people are likely to yield to groups with certain powers and attributes [72]: (1) a surveillance capacity, the ability to discover who is or is not complying; (2) a coercive capability, the power to impose penalties; (3) cohesiveness, as in a family where membership is not elective; and (4) unanimous opposition. In all these cases,

nonconformity has potentially steep costs—disapproval, rejection, and/or penalties. Conformity, on the other hand, may bring definite benefits—approval, respect, honors, promotions, and/or titles. Conformity to win group support or avoid group rejection is known as *normative conformity*.

Enduring personal qualities may influence the likelihood of conformity. Personality testing allowed the late Richard Crutchfield and his associates to characterize consistently conforming and nonconforming subjects—those especially likely to comply or remain independent in an Asch-type experiment. Conformers subscribed to conventional and socially approved values. They showed less ego strength, tolerance for ambiguity, responsibility, spontaneity, and self-insight than nonconformists. The nonconformists emerged as the heroes of this research. They were described as intelligent, original, capable of coping with stress, self-confident, responsible, and tolerant [73]. Perhaps, traits such as insightfulness, spontaneity, and confidence keep people from abandoning their own beliefs when in conflict with group judgments.

Can we divide the world up into conformers and nonconformers? Probably not. When psychologist Graham Vaughan placed subjects in four *different* group settings, he discovered that only about 20 percent conformed or remained independent consistently [74]. Other investigators find similar results: Most people do not conform regularly. Interactions between situational and personality characteristics must be considered. The individual's status in the group is significant. If people feel exceptionally secure, they tend to speak out. Those who are only marginally accepted also tend to speak out, perhaps because there is little to lose. Individuals with moderate status—those who have the most to lose or gain—are likely to conform [75]. Relative competence is another important consideration. When people feel inadequate, less capable than other group members, or perplexed by an ambiguous or difficult task, they tend to yield to the group's judgments [76]. In all these situations, the group may appear to

Thanks for all the wonderful opportunities which you have provided for us all who are members of this beautiful Socialist family.... We should emulate you and Mother because you are the best Father anyone can have. Mother is the best Mother that we can have.... I have given material things, money and time to the cause, but I will not betray my trust to the cause knowingly. I do not have a commitment to anything but the cause. I know that one is due to obey authority and respect authority. I try daily to be obedient and respectful up until 1959 [when I joined the cause], I was afraid of death and dying, but since then I have thought of death and dying as just going to sleep

FIGURE 17-5 More than 900 men, women, and children died in a suicide-massacre in 1978 at an isolated commune in Jonestown, Guyana. Although information is sketchy, it appears that the decision to die was made by one person—the leader, Reverend Jim Jones. Most of Jones's followers drank flavored water laced with cyanide from the vat shown in the photograph. Like Rosa Keaton, whose letter to Jones appears here, the Jonestown commune residents tended to be extraordinarily obedient. What causes people to surrender their autonomy so completely? Psychologists' informal observations of former members of various cults suggest that cult leaders often use sophisticated tactics that make such unquestioning obedience probable [153]. (1) They tend to recruit especially responsive individuals. Jones, for example, sought out oppressed, powerless, alienated converts—primarily, very poor blacks. (2) Leaders often exploit a charismatic personality to offer members security and a special sense of significance and fellowship. Jones offered membership in an elite, just, egalitarian society, "safety," and communal life. (3) Total obedience is both demanded and exalted. Followers are not permitted to criticize or question. (4) People are isolated from noncult family members and friends. This practice greatly enhances the power of fellow group members. Peer pressure for loyalty is likely to be intense. (5) Followers are subjected to agonizingly long, repetitive lectures about the righteousness of the cause. Such experiences may alter consciousness and increase susceptibility to suggestions—as hypnosis may. (6) Cult leaders demand huge personal sacrifices to cement the commitment. Jones required the members of his group to turn over income and possessions. He demanded confessions of sins. People had to give up privacy and control over all life decisions. Eventually, Jones forced his followers to labor like slaves under conditions of semistarvation. As cult members attempt to rationalize and justify their actions, they probably convince themselves that suffering and self-denial are justified by the importance of the cause. (7) Most groups discourage defections aggressively by pressure and intimidation. Disobedient individuals at Jonestown were subjected to humiliation, psychological and physical torture, and threats of death. [*United Press International.*]

have better information. Conformity to improve the accuracy of information is called *informational conformity*.

Obedience

When we *obey*, we abandon our personal judgments and cooperate with the demands of authorities. As in the case of conformity, submission may be reinforced by positive consequences such as approval, prestige, promotions, and tangible rewards. Submission may also be strengthened by the avoidance of unpleasant consequences such as disapproval, fines, ostracism, imprisonment, beatings, and even death. Many societies, including our own, value obedience. At an early age, most American children learn to take orders—usually from parents, older sisters or brothers, relatives, and teachers. There are rules to honor in almost every group that the youngster encounters. All this practice at obedience probably produces a general tendency to acquiesce, without question, to the powers that be. When everyone follows rules—if they are just and sensible ones—life tends to be safe, orderly, and smooth. But blind obedience can be a dangerous habit. In Nazi Germany, obedient citizens and soldiers slaughtered millions of people. Many other atrocities have been committed in the name of obedience. See Figure 17-5. Less catastrophic conflicts between conscience and obedience occur every day. A football player may have to choose between personal principles and the coach's instructions "to play rough and dirty and win at any cost." A teacher faced with the legitimate needs of a conscientious, but seriously ill, pupil may have to violate (or uphold) an administrative policy which requires that students with more than three absences from class be dropped. When the commands of an authority clash with moral and humane principles, what do ordinary people do? And why? These are the issues that we explore in this section.

Obedience in the laboratory: Stanley Milgram's classic investigation

In the early 1960s Stanley Milgram began investigating questions about obedience. His subjects were men and occasionally women of varied ages and social and educational backgrounds. Imagine that you are a participant in one of Milgram's initial studies. You appear for your session at Yale University along with a pleasant, middle-aged male accountant. He seems to be a second subject but is really the investigator's accomplice. The experimenter is a stern, impassive thirty-one-year-old male biology teacher in a white laboratory coat. He pays you both $4.50 as promised and begins a brief orientation. The study, you are told, concerns the effects of punishment on learning and memory. One person will teach the other a list of word pairs and punish wrong answers by electric shocks. You and the confederate draw straws to see who will be teacher and who will be learner. The drawing is rigged so that you are assigned the instructor role. The learner follows the experimenter to another room where he will memorize word pairs. You tag along and see the man strapped into a chair "to prevent excessive movements." Electrodes are attached to his wrist with electrode paste "to avoid blisters and burns." You learn that the shocks may be "extremely painful" but do not cause "permanent tissue damage." You also learn that the accountant has a slight heart condition. See Figure 17-6*b*. Back in the laboratory, you are given instructions as you sit before an impressively complex, presumably authentic (actually phony) shock generator (pictured in Figure 17-6*a*). Every time the learner makes a mistake, you are to supply the correct response over an intercom and to administer a shock. You are to begin with 15 volts. After every error, you must increase the intensity of the shock by one step. There are thirty steps in all—the last is labeled "450 Volts." The designation "Danger: Severe shock" marks the 375-volt

FIGURE 17-6 (*a*) This is the imposing shock generator used in Stanley Milgram's obedience investigation. (*b*) The learner is strapped into position. [*Stanley Milgram, from the film* Obedience, *distributed by the New York University Film Library.*]

a

b

lever. Other levers have been identified as "Strong shock," "Very strong shock," "Intense shock," "Extreme-intensity shock," and "XXX." In the course of the study the accountant gives a great many wrong answers, and you find yourself delivering increasingly powerful shocks. In actuality, the accomplice receives no shocks at all, though he appears to. You and the other subjects hear the same tape-recorded vocalizations, poundings, and kickings; for example, groans and moans at 75 volts, a demand to be freed at 150 volts, cries that the pain is unendurable at 180 volts, kicking on the wall and a refusal to continue at 300 volts, and pounding on the wall and silence at 315 volts. Like most other participants, you probably want to stop. But, each time you protest, the experimenter orders you to continue with prods such as "Whether the learner likes it or not, you must go on" and "You have no other choice, you must go on." Would you continue? Forty psychiatrists vastly underestimated the number of people who would follow orders in this situation. In the experiment just described, every subject persisted past twenty shocks. Approximately 65 percent of the research participants obeyed until the end.

Reasons for obedience Why did people obey Milgram's experimenter, a man who had no important rewards to offer and would not seek reprisal? Perhaps people were submissive because the study took place at a highly respected university. To check out this possibility, Milgram conducted the research at a run-down shopping center in nearby Bridgeport, Connecticut. Approximately 48 percent of the subjects there followed orders fully. Apparently, Yale's prestige was only partially responsible for the participants' obedience. Milgram ruled out sadism by allowing subjects to choose the shock level themselves. Under these circumstances, most individuals gave relatively low-level shocks and stopped when the victim first indicated that he was uncomfortable. Why, then, was there so much obedience in Milgram's initial experiments? Most human beings, according to Milgram,

assume that legitimate authorities must be obeyed. During the experiment, people see themselves as having duties to "the organization." They want to be polite, to keep their promise, to help out, and to avoid a scene. Values such as loyalty, discipline, and self-sacrifice may blind subjects to the violence of the authority as well. Milgram believes that people are able somehow to "merge their personalities into the institutional structure" and block out the screams and implications.

Influences on obedience Later studies at Yale by Milgram and others show that obedience depends, to some degree, on the characteristics of the situation and the participant. Proximity increases the authority's power. When the experimenter delivers orders over the phone from a distance, subjects obey fully only 22 percent of the time. The placement of the victim is significant too. If the learner is stationed in a distant room, research participants average a maximum shock level of 275 volts. When subjects must physically restrain the man, they average 175 volts maximum. Suppose that participants can easily assign responsibility for hurting the learner to another person: The subject administers the word pairs, while someone else handles the shocks. Under these circumstances, almost everyone continues until the end. On the other hand, only 10 percent persist when they see somebody else defy orders. Enduring personal characteristics may make some individuals especially susceptible to the demands of an authority. Those who obey completely are likely to report a relatively large number of authoritarian attitudes (see Table 17-2). Women and men do not behave in a consistently different manner [77].

An evaluation of Milgram's obedience investigation Some behavioral scientists believe that Milgram's experiments were unethical and/or cruel. There can be little doubt that the studies were upsetting to a lot of participants. In three cases, subjects had uncontrollable seizures. Many other subjects were observed to "sweat, stutter, tremble,

TABLE 17-2 Several Components of Authoritarianism and Items Similar to Those on the Revised Authoritarian Scale

Component of authoritarianism	Items similar to those on Revised Authoritarian Scale
Rigid adherence to middle-class values	"Every decent human being should have a feeling of love, gratitude, and admiration for his/her parents." (Agree)
Exaggerated need to submit to others	"Obedience and respect for parents, teachers, police, and other authorities are the most important characteristics that parents can teach their children." (Agree)
Commitment to severe punishment for people who deviate from conventional values	"The use of the death penalty to punish any crime serves no constructive purpose." (Disagree)
Alignment with powerful figures and a denial of personal weaknesses	"What young people need most is discipline, determination, and a willingness to work and fight for family and country." (Agree)

Test takers are asked to agree or disagree with statements like those in the second column. The responses in parentheses are characteristic of individuals with authoritarian personalities.

Sources: Adorno, T. W., Frenkel-Brunswik, E., Levinson, D. J., & Sanford, R. N. *The authoritarian personality.* New York: Harper & Row, 1950; Cherry, F., & Byrne, D. Authoritarianism. In T. Blass (Ed.), *Personality variables in social behavior.* Hillsdale, N.J.: Erlbaum, 1977. Pp. 109–133.

groan, bite their lips, and dig their finger nails into their flesh [78]."

Yet Milgram's self-defense is persuasive. He maintains that the investigation yielded essential information that could not be learned in any other way and that the ethical issues were handled carefully. At the end of each session, the research was explained. The subjects were reassured that their behavior was entirely normal and that a great many people had responded similarly. Participants were questioned about their feelings toward the study. A psychiatrist interviewed those people most likely to suffer. Less than 2 percent of the subjects polled reported that they regretted taking part in the research. The interviews uncovered no evidence of harmful long-range consequences. Finally, each participant received a detailed report on the objectives and results of the investigation.

Are Milgram's conclusions applicable to real-life settings? While psychologists are not in complete agreement, many feel that the insights gained do apply to situations with strongly pressuring authority figures. The obedience studies suggest that it is potentially disastrous to be unaware of the human capacity for submitting indiscriminately to the commands of a leader. Many subjects came to this realization. One research participant described his new insight in this manner:

What appalled me was that I could possess this capacity for obedience and compliance to a central idea, i.e., the value of a memory experiment, even after it became clear that continued adherence to this value was at the expense of violation of another value, i.e., don't hurt someone who is helpless and not hurting you. As my wife said, "You can call yourself Eichmann." I hope I deal more effectively with any future conflicts of value I encounter. [79]

Milgram's studies have carried this crucial message to a great many people. ▲

▲ **USING PSYCHOLOGY**

1. Think of several recent social situations in which you conformed. Speculate about your reasons for yielding. Consider the influences mentioned by the text.

2. Do you believe that Milgram's obedience study was ethical? Defend your position. Suppose that you had participated in the study and obeyed fully. How would the experience affect you?

3. How might Milgram's research findings be used to advance humanitarian principles by parents? Schools? The military?

SOCIAL BEHAVIOR AND SOCIAL INFLUENCES: THE CASE OF SEX ROLES

Norms regulate social behavior in all societies. They vary with the situation, as mentioned before. They vary also with an individual's age, status, and gender. Standards assigned on the basis of gender are called *sex roles*. In this section we examine the sex roles of our culture. We focus on perceived and actual differences between males and females. We describe the molding of gender-related behavior, especially by social influences. Finally, we look at the costs of maintaining current sex-role standards.

Perceived Sex Roles in Our Culture

Boys make money to buy food. Girls want their children not to make too much noise. Boys work—sometimes help the mother, sometimes play with their children. Mothers they try not to scream. Boys can grow up to be a gardener and girls want their children to be very quiet and good. [80]

This is the way a five-year-old child defines differences between males and females. In our culture, as in most others, women and men are expected to acquire specific personality and social characteristics. More than twenty years ago, sociologists Talcott Parsons and Robert Bales suggested that men play the *instrumental*, or task-oriented, roles in the society. They protect wives and children and represent the family's interests in the outside world by taking charge of political and economic functions. According to Parsons and Bales, females play *expressive* roles. They serve the psychological and physical needs of the family and promote interpersonal harmony [81]. When psychologists ask research participants—college students, parents, children, and clinicians, for instance—about the ideal characteristics of women and men, they find a lot of agreement. In general, people say that women should be gentle, kind, and sensitive to others. They say that men should be dominant, active, achieving, and level-headed [82]. A *stereotype* (discussed more fully later) is essentially an overly simple, rigid generalization about a person or group. While there is less deliberate stereotyping of males and females today, particularly among blacks and the well-educated [83], there is still quite a bit. Males and females at varied ages currently describe themselves in almost identical terms. But they still stereotype (in traditional ways) ideal members of their own sex and especially ideal members of the opposite sex. Adolescents seem especially prone to such stereotyping [84].

The typing of males and females begins early. Psychologist Jeffrey Rubin and his colleagues studied fathers' and mothers' reactions to their babies within the first twenty-four hours of life. While the mothers had held and fed the infants, the fathers had only seen the babies through a nursery display window. The female and male newborns could not be distinguished from one another on the basis of size, color, muscle tone, reflex irritability, or any other obvious physical or neurological dimension. But the parents were already stereotyping them in traditional ways. Men were more extreme in their ratings than women [85]. John and Sandra Condry showed college students a nine-month-old baby on videotape and asked them to judge its emotional responses. The name and presumed sex of the child influenced their judgments significantly. A negative response in a child with a boy's name was perceived as anger, for instance. The same response in the same child identified by a girl's name was apt to be labeled fear [86]. Children probably adopt adult sex-role standards for themselves at early ages. Youngsters of two are already aware of "girl" and "boy" household items and articles of clothing [87].

Before we move on, you should be aware of the fact that the female sex role is considered less valuable than the male sex role in our society and in most others—despite major advances toward equality in the 1970s. Numerous observations can be cited as evidence. Recent surveys show that families prefer to conceive male infants [88]. Competent women in traditionally masculine fields—managers in industry, physicians, and lawyers, for instance—are apt to be devalued by both men and women who hold traditional views about sex roles [89]. Excellence in women, especially in traditionally masculine pursuits, is apt to be attributed to luck or hard work rather than ability. Many females accept this view of themselves [90]. Even clinicians are apt to characterize mentally healthy women by adjectives such as "submissive," "dependent," "not adventurous," "easily influenced," "excitable in a minor crisis," "conceited about appearances," "easily hurt," and "illogical"—characteristics that Americans do not generally admire [91]. As women are valued less, they are paid less. When matched for skill, age, education, experience, and tenure on the job, American women earn, overall, only 58 percent as much in salary as men earn [92].

Actual Behavioral Differences between the Sexes

Many psychologists are engaged in research designed to clarify the actual behavioral differences between the sexes. Because stereotypes about expected conduct are strong, this is a more difficult undertaking than might be suspected. As you examine current findings, keep in mind that differences pertain to *group averages*. Women exhibit a wide range of characteristics, as do men. These ranges overlap. For example, while men may be somewhat more aggressive than women, on the average, we find violent and placid members of both sexes. It is also important to note that many gender-related differences are small ones. And few behavioral sex differences show up consistently throughout the life cycle and in all societies. These observations suggest that many "masculine" and "feminine" characteristics depend, at least partially, on cultural conditions which could change. In Table 17-3 we have listed differences between the sexes for which there is convincing research evidence. The table is a synthesis of the findings of a huge number of investigations. Interpreting the data is difficult and many of the findings remain controversial [93].

Social Influences on Sex-Role Behavior

What accounts for the behavioral differences between the sexes? As we saw in Chapter 10, sex hormones exert different influences on the brains of human females and males long before birth. Though not everyone would agree, many psychologists believe that boys and girls are born with at least a few divergent behavioral propensities. But, it is also clear that society plays a powerful role in shaping sex-related conduct. We examine several types of evidence which support this idea.

Research on masculine and feminine roles in other cultures Investigations of norms in other cultures provide a number of insights into gender-related behavior. Anthropologists and sociologists have learned that biology does not ordain the characteristics considered feminine and masculine in our society. Sex roles vary quite a bit from group to group [94]. In Iran, for example, males are expected to show emotion, to read poetry, and

TABLE 17-3 Differences between the Sexes

Characteristic	Males excel	Females excel
Intellectual abilities	Higher-mathematical and visual-spatial skills	Verbal skills
Health	Mental health (Show fewer psychological problems, such as anxiety and low self-esteem, than females, especially housewives, do)	Physical health (Are less vulnerable than males to disease and abnormal development before and after birth)
Physical abilities	Strength and gross motor skills; visual acuity	Manual dexterity; sensitivities to touch, high-frequency sounds, changes in sound intensity
Personality traits	Activity, aggression, curiosity about nonsocial events and objects, dominance, impulsivity	Compliance, curiosity about social events and people, dependency, empathy, social responsivity

Note: Research findings on sex differences are often inconsistent and almost always difficult to interpret. This is because most studies have significant weaknesses, including bias among raters, the use of small, nonrepresentative samples, and problematic measurement techniques. Psychologists disagree about which data to emphasize. The above list must consequently be regarded as tentative.

Major sources: Maccoby, E. E., & Jacklin, C. N. *The psychology of sex differences.* Stanford, Calif.: Stanford University Press, 1974; Block, J. H. Assessing sex differences: Issues, problems, and pitfalls. *Merrill-Palmer Quarterly*, 1976, **22**, 283–308; Hoffman, M. L. Sex differences in empathy and related behaviors. *Psychological Bulletin*, 1977, **84** (4), 712–722; McGuinness, D., & Pribam, K. H. The origins of sensory bias in the development of gender differences in perception and cognition. In M. Bortner (Ed.), *Cognitive growth and development.* New York: Bruner/Mazel, 1979.

to be sensitive, intuitive, and illogical. Women are supposed to be the coldly practical ones. In certain regions of Africa, females do the heavy work. According to one native, "everybody knows that men are not suited by nature for heavy work, that women are stronger and better workers." Obviously, females and males can learn a wide range of responses.

Sex roles across cultures do show several striking consistencies. In most societies women are socialized to play nurturant, responsible, obedient roles; men, self-reliant, achieving ones. Anthroplogists have not found a single undisputed example of a society where women control the resources [95]. How can these uniformities be explained? Anthropologists remind us that all groups must feed, clothe, and defend themselves and reproduce their own kind to survive. The specific functions that have to be performed are divided among family members. Since women always bear, nurse, and nurture children, they are typically assigned roles near the home base. Notably, they tend the young, cook, gather (berries, fruits, and grains), and keep house.

Men, then, assume the hunting and protective roles. This division of labor puts males in control of a relatively scarce and valued resource, meat. As they distribute meat, they gain political and economic power [96]. Anthropologist Ernestine Friedl has analyzed the data on sex-role patterns among approximately 300,000 people around the world who still hunt and gather their food. Friedl finds that male dominance increases with the amount of meat men supply and distribute. With few exceptions, women enjoy high status when both sexes contribute roughly equivalently to the food supply [97].

Why do the same sex-role patterns persist long after people have ceased to hunt and gather their food? Social and biological factors may both contribute. Some behavioral scientists believe that parents continue to rear males and females along customary lines simply because the traditions are handed down from generation to generation. Males— who have the upper hand—may police the sex-role status quo in order to maintain their power and privileges. Some behavioral scientists feel that there is a physical basis for the social roles of the sexes. Sociologist Alice Rossi argues that females not only bear young and lactate, but also bond to children intensely because of physiological experiences during pregnancy, birth, and nursing. According to Rossi, a woman's biological nature invests her heavily in child and family concerns [98]. Psychologist Jerre Levy contends that sex differences in the brain evolved over the thousands of years that people hunted and gathered, to suit men and women for their predominant social roles [99]. Women's superior verbal fluency was helpful for the largely interpersonal demands of the maternal role. Men's superior spatial abilities and greater aggression were useful for hunting animals and protecting the group. Even if sex differences in behavior are wired into the brain, neural development depends a great deal on experiences (as we saw in Chapters 3 and 6). The treatment of boys and girls can alter both the brain and behavior.

Another question may have occurred to you: Why is the nurturant role consistently less prestigious and powerful? Two hypotheses are generally offered:

1. Men's roles bring power in the outside world. Women's roles, in contrast, limit women's power to the family.
2. Women perform tasks considered natural and unlearned, whereas men handle responsibilities that require training. In all known cultures, learned skills are judged to be more significant and admirable.

Research on people with gender-related disorders

Research on the socialization of females and males with gender-related abnormalities provides additional support for the notion that the social environment has an important influence on sex-role behavior. *Socialization* (Chapter 3) refers to the process of guiding children to the values, attitudes, and behaviors approved by the society. Psychologists John Money and Anke Ehrhardt have described a particularly revealing case: the socialization of a normal male identical twin as a female. Because of a

surgical mishap during circumcision, one member of the pair (the dominant one, in fact) lost his penis at the age of seventeen months. Subsequently, the parents were advised to rear this son as a daughter. The family changed the boy's name. They let his hair grow long. They dressed him in pink slacks and frilly blouses. Without much conscious planning, they established and reinforced radically different standards for his behavior. At the age of four and a half, this twin took pride in his hair, preferred dresses to slacks, did not like being dirty, and appeared "dainty." By the age of six, both twins had established conventional sex-role identities—one female, one male [100]. Money and his co-workers have also studied *hermaphrodites*, genetic males and females who are born with reproductive structures appropriate for both sexes (such as feminine genitalia *and* testes). Hermaphrodites of all types appear to be able to adapt without apparent hardship to whichever sex role is assigned by their families, as long as the role is prescribed near birth [101].

Research on sex-role socialization in the United States

Research on the socialization of normal females and males in the United States provides additional evidence that societies mold sex-related behavior. Two theoretical perspectives have guided most of the investigations. Many behavioral scientists believe that learning principles, especially observation learning and operant conditioning (Chapter 5), are essential for sex-role socialization. This viewpoint is known as *social learning theory*. One proponent, Walter Mischel, takes the position that human beings learn both masculine and feminine behavior by watching the varied models around them. We all learn, for example, "to curse or to fight or use cosmetics or primp in front of mirrors." In most instances, however, we copy models of the same sex. Mischel suggests that we do so because we are encouraged by the approval of parents, peers, teachers, and other societal agents. And we anticipate that approval in advance [102]. The second major perspective is the *cognitive view* advocated by Lawrence

Kohlberg. Kohlberg speculates that cognitions are the crucial ingredient in sex-role socialization. Presumably, children strive to maintain a coherent conception of themselves and their world. They try to keep beliefs, actions, and values consistent. After discovering their gender, Kohlberg argues, youngsters feel motivated to behave as "proper" boys or girls and do "appropriate girl or boy things" [103].

Cognitions, models, and consequences are probably all vital for the development of the child's sexual identity. We review representative research findings which support this idea.

From the very beginning, parents provide different settings and props for sons and daughters. When Harriet Rheingold and Kaye Cook examined the furniture, toys, and decorations in children's rooms, they found—not unexpectedly—that girls' rooms contained more ruffles, lace, and flowers than boys' rooms did. One finding was not anticipated. Girls, for the most part, were limited to dolls and doll-care paraphernalia. Boys had a larger variety of toys to play with, such as trucks and trains, stuffed animals, and action dolls [104]. Other investigators find that parents encouraged children to play with toys appropriate for their gender [105]—regardless, perhaps, of the child's unique interests. Some 80 percent of women recall having been "tomboys" in childhood [106].

There is also evidence that adults condition sex-role behavior subtly, generally without realizing it. Some parents play a *complementary role* and prompt the "correct" behavior from "daddy's little angel" or "mommy's little man" [107]. Boys and girls usually receive different privileges, pressures, and constraints which guide them toward gender-appropriate behavior too. Boys are allowed to roam larger areas and receive less chaperonage than girls [108]. Females may express emotions while males are pressured to inhibit them [109]. Parents and teachers may unintentionally encourage aggression in boys while trying to discourage it. Lisa Serbin and Daniel O'Leary found that preschool teachers responded more than three times as often to boys who misbehaved as to girls who did so.

The teachers scolded boys loudly while rebuking girls softly. In many instances, the public commotion seemed to strengthen the unwanted conduct. (When the "bad" acts were ignored, they extinguished.) These preschool teachers also encouraged independence and mastery in boys by insisting that they persist on difficult tasks and by rewarding them tangibly and socially (with approval) for academic work. Girls received less attention overall and seemed to receive most of it while they were literally or figuratively clinging. The teachers, incidentally, were not aware of treating males and females differently [110]. Other investigators have observed that boys receive more attention from parents and teachers than girls do. It is possible that males commit more misdeeds that cannot be ignored. Or, it may be that adults find boys more interesting because of their personalities and potential [111]. In Chapter 10, you may recall, we described many additional influences on the development of achievement motivation in males and females.

The media in our culture strengthen lessons about sex roles by portraying females and males according to the traditional stereotypes. On popular children's television shows, boys are apt to be shown as active beings. They make and carry out plans; they seek help or information to complete projects. Girls are likely to be punished for being active. They are usually seen following directions—typically, from males. And they are frequently ineffective [112]. Children's books perpetuate similar images. So do adult advertisements and programs [113]. See Figure 17-7.

Costs of Sex Roles

Some behavioral scientists believe that conventional sex-role socialization practices have harmful effects on both women and men. Males, it is argued, are kept from communicating intimately, expressing emotion, showing weakness, yielding to dependency feelings, and looking for personal (and not simply externally evaluated) forms of fulfillment. Men may also experience intense anxieties about being "truly masculine." Some observ-

"All right," said Carol. "But we don't have a grandmother in our family."

"I don't think I want to play house," said Bobby. "Isn't that a girl's game?"

"I don't see why," said Carol. "After all, there has to be a father. A boy can be a father better than a girl can."

"After we play house for a while," said Bobby, "let's play something else."

"All right," said Nancy and Carol. "We'll play one of your games next."

What do you think the children did when they played house? Have you ever played house? What people do you have in your play family?

Is it sometimes hard to think of things to do? What do you like to play?

34

After a while, Bobby said, "I'm tired of playing house. Let's play office. I'll be the boss, like my Dad is. He goes to his office and gives his secretary letters to write."

"What is a secretary?" Nancy asked.

"I'll show you," said Bobby. "Here is a big box for my desk. I send letters to people and do other work. You are my secretary, Nancy. I tell you what to say in the letters, and you write it on your paper. Then you write the letters on a typewriter and mail them. That is what a secretary does."

"Oh, I see," said Nancy.

"All right," said Bobby. "Please take a letter. Dear Mr. Brown . . . " Bobby stopped. Then he said, "I don't know what to say in the letter."

35

FIGURE 17-7 When men and women meet face to face in typical American advertisements, the male is usually shown playing the executive role. (*a*) The occupational status hierarchy confers superior power on the male physician. (*b*) The man assumes the leadership function. Even in ads for household products, males usually play the role of instructor, professional, or celebrity and teach the woman what is to be done. (*c*) In these pages from a child's book, conventional sex-role images appear in both text and illustrations. Although this particular book has long been out of print and such blatant stereotyping is rare today, conventional gender roles still dominate children's literature. Materials such as these probably strengthen beliefs that traditional gender roles are appropriate and desirable. [(a) *and* (b) *Erving Goffman,* Gender advertisements, *Harper & Row, 1979.* (c) *From* I know people *by C. W. Hunnicutt and Jean D. Grambs, illustrated by Guy Brown Wisen. Copyright © 1957 by L. W. Singer Company, Inc. Reprinted by permission of Random House, Inc.*]

ers believe that many males turn to smoking, drinking, and violence to cope with misgivings about their virility [114]. The feminine sex role in our society is similarly constricting and costly. Beginning at a very early age, females tend to develop inferiority feelings and limit their aspirations [115]. As a result, many are denied a complex, diverse life. Women who opt for traditionally masculine careers and life-styles may experience severe conflicts over their femininity.

Can the costs of sex roles be reduced? Some behavioral scientists believe that men and women are inherently and inevitably different behaviorally. What needs to be made equal, they argue, is the value placed on the differences. Other behavioral scientists emphasize the idea that "femininity" and "masculinity" are present in varying degrees in both males and females. For a satisfying life, they maintain, people must acquire the best characteristics of both roles. *Androgeny*—the possession of similar amounts of traditionally masculine and traditionally feminine traits—may be beneficial for most human beings. Research by Sandra Bem and others supports this idea. In the mid- and late 1970s, about a third of the college students who were tested by behavioral scientists saw themselves as androgenous [116]. Bem's studies show that androgenous college students tend to be flexible, readily displaying warmth, nurturance, assertiveness, and independence in the laboratory,

when appropriate. People who fit the traditional gender stereotypes are unlikely to show the same degree of adaptability [117]. As a group, androgenous human beings tend to be especially healthy both mentally and socially. Compared with conventionally sex-typed individuals, for example, the androgenous are apt to possess a high level of self-esteem and to communicate easily with members of the opposite sex [118]. ▲

ATTITUDES AND SOCIAL INFLUENCES

Is androgeny beneficial? Is busing a fair way to achieve racial balance in the schools? Should "gay" teachers instruct young children? Should marijuana be legalized? Should people live together before marriage? By responding to these questions, you are describing attitudes of your own. Human beings hold attitudes toward everything they encounter from mustaches to religious ideas. Our attitudes are shaped by our social experiences. In this section we discuss attitudes and stereotypes and describe how they are acquired and altered. Then we focus on findings about the formation and reduction of one attitude, racial prejudice.

Attitudes and Stereotypes

Attitudes are usually defined as learned evalu-

▲ USING PSYCHOLOGY

1. Make a list of the traits that are considered typical of the ideal male and female. Then rate three women and three men acquaintances as low, moderate, or high on each characteristic. Are the males similar? What about the females? Rate several TV heroines and heros on the same features. Are the media still stereotyping men and women?

2. Did your parents and teachers treat male and female children differently? In what ways?

3. Are you aware of personal costs attributable to your sex role? Describe.

4. Should children be reared so that they acquire the most desirable characteristics of both sex roles? Can our society avoid sex-typing youngsters? How? Make a list of rules and practices to guide parents and teachers.

ative concepts associated with thoughts, feelings, and behavior. Consider the *thought* (cognitive or intellectual) element. People's thoughts about the objects of their attitudes are usually based on experience and information. Typically, people make a few observations and formulate general ideas. As the late psychologist Gordon Allport put it, "Given a thimbleful of facts, [human beings] rush to make generalizations as large as a tub [119]." Because your father and uncles like tinkering with cars, you may jump to the conclusion that all men are mechanically inclined. When generalizations are overly simple and rigid and concern persons or social groups, they are called *stereotypes*. Although the word "stereotype" has negative associations, these generalizations are not always harmful. Sometimes they help order and condense complicated information so that people can act intelligently and quickly. One or two costly encounters with con artists in poker games, for example, might lead an individual to stereotype "card sharks" as potentially dangerous and to behave cautiously around them. Stereotypes are destructive primarily when we forget that they are based on small samples of a population and that they are frequently unjust when applied automatically to other individuals within the population.

The thought component of an attitude is sometimes evaluated in terms of its *complexity*. When asked about her attitude toward protecting environmental resources, Cicely says, "Absolutely essential." Lena responds, "It depends on the resource, its importance, and the jobs created or destroyed by the environmental effort." The thought element of Lena's attitude is obviously more complicated than that of Cicely's.

Psychologists have been particularly interested in the relationship between the thought and behavioral elements of attitudes. Research suggests that the links are not necessarily consistent [120]. People often conduct themselves in ways that are contrary to their thoughts. Tyler may believe in mercy killing but refuse to allow the veterinarian to put his hopelessly ill, suffering, aged dog to sleep. In some cases, thought influences action [121]. Edna believes that abortions are criminal and decides to join the anti-abortion crusade to "put her money where her mouth is." At the same time, the behavioral component may influence the cognitive one [122]. Simon agrees to lead a charitable campaign because he is too embarrassed to refuse. Later, after participating in the fund-raising drive, he might find himself evaluating the cause very sympathetically. Psychologist Daryl Bem suggests that people observe their own behavior when internal (emotional and cognitive) cues are weak or unclear. Presumably, they can make interferences about their own feelings and thoughts, just as they might observe the conduct of others and make attributions [123]. Cognitive dissonance theory (Chapter 10) provides another framework for understanding why behavior may influence the intellectual and emotional aspects of attitudes. If our actions conflict with our ideas, we are apt to feel uncomfortable. We may reevaluate and alter our thoughts to reduce the dissonance.

Occasionally, psychologists assess the *consistency* of the elements of an attitude. Sometimes all components are in harmony. You might hate smoking, avoid smoking yourself, and consider smoking unhealthy. The elements of attitudes can be discordant. You might smoke and like smoking but consider the activity harmful.

Attitude Formation and Attitude Change

People are not born with particular attitudes. We acquire them through observation, operant and respondent conditioning, and cognitive types of learning. Typically, these influences are mingled in a single experience. Though people are continually trying to modify the attitudes of others (big business in our country alone spends billions of dollars each year in advertising for persuasive purposes), attitudes tend to resist change. Psychologist Herbert Kelman suggests a logical reason for our conservatism. Well-established attitudes shape people's experiences with the objects of their attitudes. They affect the information to which individuals expose themselves, the organization of that information, and in the case of interpersonal attitudes, the behavior of the object of the attitude [124]. While attitude change is typically slow, attitudes do shift as people are exposed to new information and experiences. Attitudes are probably altered by the same processes that formed them initially—observation, operant and respondent conditioning, and cognitive types of learning. We focus now on racial prejudice to illustrate how attitudes may be acquired, intensified, and altered.

The Case of Racial Prejudice

The attitude called *prejudice* reflects a negative (or positive) prejudgment about a person or group of people based on stereotypes that exaggerate group characteristics and ignore individual strengths and weaknesses. The target of a prejudice is often a member of a *minority group*, one with subordinate status and power. (A minority group is not necessarily small in number. Though there are more women than men in the world, for example, women are usually considered a minority group.) Prejudice is associated with strong negative (or positive) judgments and feelings and often with *discrimination*. Discrimination is defined as conduct biased against (or for) a person or group of people, based on group membership and not on individual merits or deficiencies. We will be focusing on *negative* racial prejudices and discriminative practices (*racism*) against blacks in the United States. Joel Kovel and Irwin Katz have described several patterns of white racism [125]. *Dominative racists* express violent hatreds of blacks and act out these prejudices even when it means using force and breaking laws. *Ambivalent racists* hold mixed feelings toward black people: sympathy along with hostility. They might consider blacks the victims of grave injustices but resist changes that will improve their lot. *Aversive racists* show subtle signs of prejudice. They consider

themselves liberals and may work to better conditions for blacks. Though they may not recognize their own *aversions*, they are likely to avoid interactions with blacks whenever possible. When contacts occur, aversive racists behave in a friendly, polite manner. (Note that the aversive racist holds complex, discordant attitudes.) Finally, *nonracists* consider race irrelevant and behave accordingly.

Today we see a great deal of ambivalent and aversive racism. Research suggests that stereotypes about black inferiority are fading (see Table 17-4). Antiblack Americans are more likely to object to social, legal, and economic improvements for blacks and personal contact between groups. John McConahay and Joseph Hough call this stance *symbolic racism*. They find the phenomenon rising among affluent and well-educated whites. Typically, symbolic racists complain about fair housing laws, welfare, and black politicians—*symbols* which are thought to represent "unfair advances or demands of blacks at the expense of the values that made this nation great [126]." Table 17-5 shows questionnaire items that are used to assess this attitude.

The formation of racial prejudices By age three, American children are beginning to show consistent attitudes toward people of different races [127]. While few adults set out deliberately to shape prejudices in youngsters, these attitudes are easily established by daily experiences. Observation learning is probably an important influence. Children hear parents talk, say, about "ignorant blacks" (or "honkies"). They see acts of discrimination: perhaps no blacks live in their neighborhood. Until very recently, TV, magazines, and newspapers tended to stereotype minority-group members unfavorably. Black people were often depicted as holding menial jobs, living in poverty, and behaving foolishly—images that "confirmed" their second-rate status. Prejudices are probably conditioned operantly also. Through approval and disapproval, parents, teachers, and peers reinforce attitudes which are consistent with their own and punish those that deviate. After

TABLE 17-4 White Stereotypes about Blacks in the United States

Instructions given to survey participants: "Here are some statements people some-times make about black people. For each statement, please tell me whether you personally tend to agree or disagree with that statement."

	Percentage agreeing		
	1963	**1971**	**1978**
Blacks tend to have less ambition than whites	66	52	49
Blacks want to live off the handout	41	39	36
Blacks are more violent than whites	*	36	34
Blacks breed crime	35	27	29
Blacks have less native intelligence than whites	39	37	25
Blacks care less for the family than whites	31	26	18
Blacks are inferior to white people	31	22	15

Note: These findings come from a series of Louis Harris polls. The 1978 data (partially shown above) were based on a national sample of 1,673 white and 732 black Americans. Although the reported racial prejudices of whites have declined, the majority of black respondents felt that misunderstandings and discrimination persist.

*Not asked.

Source: Harris, Louis, and Associates, Inc. *A study of attitudes toward racial and religious minorities and toward women.* New York: The National Conference of Christians and Jews, 1978.

extensive research, psychologist Thomas Pettigrew concluded that the prejudices of white Southerners are largely acquired in this way [128]. The emotional component of a prejudice is apt to be conditioned by respondent principles. Mark Zanna and his associates have demonstrated that it is not difficult to associate positive and negative emotional responses to words like "light" and "dark." These reactions generalize to the similar terms "white" and "black" [129]. Respondent conditioning is probably commonplace in real life. Let's assume that you're white and often hear of the violent acts of black people. Each report is apt to arouse anxiety and anger. These emotions become associated gradually with the "black villains" and generalize ultimately to most blacks. Blacks, in turn, are apt to associate whites with put-downs and humiliation.

Children may learn prejudice through direct instructions too. In some cases the lessons are persuasive propaganda delivered amid music and fanfare. See Figure 17-8. In general, parents probably communicate subtle messages of rejection. Psychologist Milton Rokeach has suggested that white parents

may unintentionally pass along their prejudices by intimating that black people scorn middle-class values, such as cleanliness, monogamy, diligence, and thrift [130]. David Stein, his colleagues, and other investigators found indirect support for this hypothesis, using the "imaginary stranger" technique (described earlier in this chapter). Stein and

TABLE 17-5 Typical Items Used to Measure Symbolic Racism*

1. Negroes shouldn't push themselves where they're not wanted. (Agree)
2. Over the past few years, Negroes have gotten more economically than they deserve. (Agree)
3. Do city officials pay more, less, or the same attention to a request from a Negro person as from a white person? (More attention)
4. Do you think that Negroes who receive welfare could get along without it if they tried or do they really need this help? (Could get along without it)
5. Streets aren't safe these days without a policeman around. (Agree)

*Racist responses are given in parentheses.

Source: McConahay, J. B., & Hough, J. C. Symbolic racism. *Journal of Social Issues*, 1976, **32**(2), 25.

FIGURE 17-8 Sometimes prejudices are taught to children deliberately. Members of the Ku Klux Klan, for example, are encouraged to bring youngsters to Klan meetings so that they too can learn about the "dangers facing America." Why do people join the KKK? Several reasons have been suggested. Candidates for Klan membership are apt to feel powerless, insignificant, and frustrated by their status. Like other cults, the KKK offers an elite position to its members, "transforming" them into "knights of an invisible empire," "keepers of community morals," and "100 percent Americans." Mysterious language codes, secret calendars, costumes, ceremonies, parades, picnics, field days, and midnight cross-burnings promise to add glamour and excitement to lives that are otherwise dull [154]. [*Brown Brothers.*]

his coworkers asked white high school students to specify the degree to which they agreed with statements about values (for example, "People should be treated as equals"). Two months later, the psychologists asked the same subjects to read the value-scale responses of four fictitious teenaged strangers. Two of the fictitious teenagers (one white and one black) appeared to express nearly identical values. The other two (again one of each race) expressed very different opinions. The subjects indicated how friendly they would feel toward each stranger in varied situations. For casual interactions, research participants seemed to prefer people with similar values, regardless of race. But race clearly affected desires for intimate relationships, as in dating and marriage. Under these circumstances, whites said that they would discriminate against blacks with similar values. These findings have held up in more recent studies [131]. It has also been learned that when people know nothing about an individual except race, many automatically assume that a member of a different race holds dissimilar attitudes, values, and beliefs and that a member of their own race holds similar ones [132]. As Rokeach suggested, parents may communicate these ideas.

The intensification of racial prejudices

In the early 1970s a National Opinion Research Center poll showed that poor whites are more likely than any other American group to exhibit strong prejudices against black people [133]. Similarly, poor, uneducated blacks—more frequently than other blacks—harbor feelings of suspicion, distrust, hostility, and fear towards whites [134]. Poverty, then, appears to be closely linked to prejudice. Although there are probably a number of reasons for the relationship, many behavioral scientists believe that the competition and frustration which often accompany poverty are centrally involved.

Consider *competition* first. When psychologists arrange matches and contests, they find that aggression and bitterness soon appear. In the late 1940s and early 1950s, Muzafer Sherif and his coworkers ran summer camps for children (mostly eleven- and twelve-year-olds) to study the effects of competition in a natural setting. The psychologists divided their homogeneous (healthy, well-adjusted, Protestant, white, middle-class, male) campers into two teams. Each group developed a strong sense of unity as the boys cooked, hiked, swam, worked, and played together.

When Sherif and his associates arranged various tournaments with prizes for the winner, the competitions became increasingly bitter. Eventually both sides "declared war." The members of each group threatened, taunted, and insulted the members of the other. And the boys made one another's lives as miserable as possible [135]. See Figure 17-9. Carefully controlled laboratory research finds that competition for limited resources is associated with aggression too [136]. As you would expect, white prejudices against blacks are most pronounced in regions where blacks and whites compete for the same jobs [137].

Now consider *frustration*, another condition linked with poverty in a prosperous country like the United States. A number of

a

b

FIGURE 17-9 Working with two groups of boys at a summer camp, Muzafer Sherif and his associates demonstrated that competition could generate hostility and aggression. The cabin raids depicted in (a) were one expression of the bitterness between the two groups. In the final phase of the experiment, the social psychologists tried to eliminate the hatred. Both groups were invited to a banquet. The attempt ended in failure, with youngsters hurling food, along with insults, at one another. The social scientists next contrived various emergencies to force the boys to cooperate in order to achieve mutual goals. For example, while the boys were on an outing, the truck in (b) was to pick up lunch in town. When the vehicle broke down, all the campers had to pull together to move it. Joint efforts in situations such as this eventually reduced the friction. In the end, many intergroup friendships developed. [*Muzafer Sherif.*]

investigators have found that frustration leads to aggression, prejudice, and discrimination. In one such study, psychologists Neal Miller and Richard Bugelski gave young men at a camp a long, dull exam that contained very difficult questions. The test ran overtime and forced the subjects to miss a local theater event that they had been eagerly anticipating all week. Before and after the exam, the research participants were asked to check a list of desirable and undesirable traits as being present or absent in either Mexican or Japanese people. After the frustrating experience, the young men checked significantly fewer positive traits and a larger number of negative ones [138]. Presumably, frustration had increased the desire to aggress. Since hostility could not be vented against the experimenters, it was displaced onto a convenient target.

When children are reared by harsh, inconsistent parents, they may be especially apt to develop values and defenses that make prejudice a likely reaction to their troubles as adults. Theodor Adorno and his colleagues found support for this hypothesis as they studied people with *authoritarian personalities.* Authoritarian individuals are characterized as rigid, conventional, intolerant of weaknesses in others and themselves, favorable to punishment, preoccupied with power and toughness, cynical about human nature, awed by authority figures, and convinced of the importance of obedience. Table 17-2 lists items from a test used to measure authoritarianism. Authoritarian persons often hold intense prejudices. Frequently, they report that their parents were cold, unpredictable, and severely punishing. Adorno and his research associates speculated that in childhood, authoritarian people were both frightened of and angry with their parents. But they suppressed these feelings because they feared reprisal. Presumably, they remain insecure and hostile as adults. They handle these emotions by defense mechanisms (Chapter 14). Specifically, they *project* their own inadequacies onto powerless minority-group members and *displace* their anger toward parents

onto these victims [139]. Adorno's analysis may be correct (there is evidence that authoritarian attitudes are associated with prejudice). Still, simple learning principles can also explain how people acquire both authoritarian characteristics and prejudices.

The reduction of racial prejudices

Research on the causes of prejudice have suggested a number of tactics that might be used to diminish prejudice. We describe three general strategies which overlap to some extent. All three approaches rely on a combination of learning principles—modeling non-biased attitudes, respondently conditioning positive emotional responses to people of different races, establishing circumstances that reinforce harmony and cooperation, and communicating favorable information about minority-group members and unfavorable messages about prejudice.

Social norms. People tend to abide by the norms, or standards, of their own group, as we have stated repeatedly. Social norms that favor racial harmony should reduce prejudice. Naturally occurring "experiments" provide evidence that they do. On college campuses, for example, racial prejudice is not fashionable. Investigators find that students' prejudices decrease significantly with increasing time in colleges and universities, even in the deep South [140]. Psychologists Morton Deutsch and Mary Collins found evidence that the social norms of integrated housing may reduce hostility between blacks and whites, too. Shortly after World War II, public biracial housing projects began to spring up in numerous American cities. Deutsch and Collins selected two integrated and two segregated developments in the New York-New Jersey area for study. The norms governing social interactions in the two developments differed substantially. In segregated housing projects where whites and blacks lived in the same development in different buildings, mixing was taboo. Even when blacks and whites had formerly been friends, they refrained from mingling socially because "it wasn't done." In integrated housing units where blacks and whites lived in adjoining apartments, the social norms sanctioned interracial contact and the housing authorities were known to favor it. When Deutsch and Collins conducted interviews, they found that about 60 percent of the white women in integrated housing reported friendly feelings toward their black neighbors. Only 10 percent of those in segregated housing felt that way. Black women reported similar attitudes toward whites [141].

Social norms favoring racial harmony are probably most effective when they permeate home, school, and social settings and begin in the child's early years. Despite the best of intentions, many parents and teachers transmit their own racial prejudices. Studies in the 1970s find that teachers often perceive black children negatively and transmit these biases by calling on and praising black youngsters less and ignoring and criticizing them more than white children [142].

Education. A number of different educational practices can reduce racial hostilities. *Multiethnic curricula* (those that emphasize learning about different groups) and *multiethnic readers* (those that picture people of diverse racial backgrounds) lessen racial prejudices in children [143]. Educational projects dealing with racial attitudes may also decrease hostility between black and white youngsters [144]. Some grade school teachers, for example, have established discriminatory situations in the classroom for short periods of time to provide students with vivid personal insights into the painful costs of prejudice. Group membership is usually determined by some superficial characteristic, such as eye color. Students take turns being in the inferior status group. This type of strategy is described more fully in Figure 17-10.

Thought-provoking messages have been used with some success to promote racial harmony in college students. In one such experiment, Milton Rokeach had more than 300 undergraduates at Michigan State University (about 97 percent white) rank the importance of values such as wisdom, happiness, freedom, equality, a comfortable life,

and mature love. Half the subjects (the control group) were dismissed while the remaining research participants (the experimental group) listened to some potentially disturbing information. The experimental subjects learned that previous students were interested mainly in their own freedom and far less concerned about the freedom of others. Students who valued civil rights efforts, the

FIGURE 17-10 Can brief, controlled experiences with discrimination in a classroom increase children's empathy for the victims of prejudice and decrease discrimination? Research suggests that such experiences are useful. Recently, psychologists Michael Weiner and Frances Wright investigated the "induced discrimination" strategy under controlled conditions. White pupils in a third-grade class were randomly divided into "orange" and "green" people. Status was signaled by the appropriate colored armband. On day 1 of the study, the orange children were treated as superior human beings. The teacher announced that they were smarter, cleaner, and better behaved than green youngsters. They were granted privileges such as dessert with lunch, first place in line, and being door holders; and they were praised at every opportunity. Green youngsters were denied privileges and criticized continually. On day 2, these conditions were reversed. Within only two days, conflicts and strained relationships developed between the children labeled as inferior and superior. The racial attitudes of the youngsters were assessed on day 3 and again three weeks later. Members of the experimental group reported less prejudice and a greater willingness to picnic with black children than third graders who had not participated in the discrimination experience [155]. [*Paul Fusco/Magnum.*]

FIGURE 17-11 Optimal conditions for reducing prejudice include norms that support harmony, contact among people of equal social status, genuinely meaningful encounters, and work toward shared goals. Many group therapy or therapy-like experiences offer these conditions. Therapy group members hold equal status, and they are likely to come from similar social backgrounds. The group demands genuine communication about personal matters. Everyone works toward the same goal, typically deeper knowledge of self and others. Norms encourage interactions between members of different races, understanding, and acceptance. Several research studies support the idea that therapy-like group experiences can reduce prejudice. So far, the durability of the gains and tangible life consequences have not been investigated systematically [156]. [*Dan O'Neill for Editorial Photocolor Archives.*]

behavioral scientist maintained, tended to rank equality much higher. After hearing this message, the experimental subjects were encouraged to reevaluate their own value rankings as well as their own stance on civil rights. Presumably, the self-confrontation and questioning aroused cognitive dissonance, which some of the students reduced by changing their ideas and behavior. Several months later, the National Association for the Advancement of Colored People (NAACP) invited all the research participants to join. Approximately 28 percent of the experimental group members, in contrast to 10 percent of the control group members, accepted the invitation [145].

Contact under conditions of mutual respect. As you may know, merely desegregating housing or schools—putting blacks and whites together—has various effects. In schools, for example, resegregation can occur all over again. Blacks and whites within the same school building may avoid one another and establish separate white and black social groupings, academic curricula, and extracurricular activities. Under adverse conditions such as these, the self-respect and academic achievement of minority-group members may decline [146]. These observations have made it clear that contact *by itself* is not sufficient to overcome racial prejudice—at least in the United States. Gordon Allport suggested many years ago that prejudice might be diminished by putting biased groups in contact with one another under circumstances that enhance mutual respect. Allport believed in the vital importance of several conditions [147]:

1. The norms of the institution have to support harmony and cooperation.
2. The people involved have to be of equal social status.
3. The participants have to work together toward shared, well-defined goals.
4. The encounters have to be genuinely meaningful ones.
5. The setting has to be natural.

Laboratory and field research support the importance of these varied conditions both separately and together [148]. For one such study, Russell Weigel and his colleagues compared (1) traditional lectures and (2) discussion techniques in small, cooperative learning groups in integrated classrooms. In the small-group condition, schoolwork was done by teams of five: three whites, one black, and one Mexican American. This ratio matched the ethnic composition of the school. While films and similar materials were presented to the entire class, gathering and discussion of information tended to occur within groups. Group members reported to one another. Students received rewards for cooperating especially well. The psychologists monitored the project closely to try to minimize the effects of teacher expectations, ensure proper use of the methods, and standardize class content. As compared with children who learned by traditional methods, youngsters exposed to the small-group approach reported feeling friendlier to people of different backgrounds. The teachers' records confirmed these reports. There were far fewer instances of cross-ethnic conflicts and dramatically more instances of cross-ethnic helping and cooperation in the small-group classes than in the conventional ones [149]. This study and others suggest that close contact between races under favorable conditions diminishes hostility. See Figure 17-11. Though much remains to be learned about reducing prejudice, it is clear that social psychologists have identified and are implementing some promising tactics.▲

AN EPILOGUE: GIVING PSYCHOLOGY AWAY

This is probably a good time to pause for a moment and think a bit about how psychology can be useful to you. In 1969 George Miller, who was then president of the American Psychological Association, made some insightful comments about psychology's benefits. He suggested that psychology is not revolutionary in the sense that physics and chemistry can be. In Miller's words, "The real impact of

---

▲ USING PSYCHOLOGY

1. Choose several attitudes of your own for analysis. First, pick out the thought, feeling, and action components in each. Can you see instances where thought influenced behavior? Vice versa? Do the thought elements vary in complexity? Are any of your attitudes discordant?

2. Analyze the racial prejudices of several white Americans. In which of the Kovel-Katz categories do these prejudices fit? Do any of your subjects show symbolic racism?

3. Consider a prejudice of your own. How did you acquire it? Were the factors described in the text involved? Do your expectations influence your interactions with the object of the prejudice? Describe.

4. Based on the research discussed in this chapter, design procedures to integrate minority-group children into a second-grade classroom.

psychology will be felt, not through the technological products it places in the hands of powerful [people], but through its effects on the public at large, through a new and different public conception of what is humanly possible and what is humanly desirable [150]." Miller insisted that behavioral scientists had a responsibility "to give psychology away to the people who need it—and that includes every-

body." You have been exposed to a lot of psychology. Our hope is that the findings and principles presented in this text have provided some important insights about what is humanly possible. And we hope, too, that you will use some of the psychology you have learned, now and in the future, to make your own life and the lives of those around you more satisfying.

SUMMARY
Social Bonds, Social Influences, and Social Behavior

1. Human beings are social animals.
2. Social norms have powerful effects on people.
3. Individuals differ in terms of when they want to be with others. Many like to affiliate when stressed physically, happy, guilt-ridden, worried, or facing unfamiliar situations. We probably seek out others for sensory stimulation, sympathy, protection, comfort, and comparison.
4. Perceptions of others are influenced by the perceiver's personal characteristics. The person perception process shows these uniformities. First impressions persist. Beauty biases judgments. Nonverbal cues are influential. And attributions about the causes of behavior are made lawfully.
5. We tend to like people who (a) are competent and physically attractive; (b) like us; (c) live nearby; (d) hold similar attitudes, interests, and needs; and (d) complement our own needs.
6. Passionate and romantic love can be measured to some extent by a questionnaire. This type of love seems to require two ingredients: physical arousal and cognitions attributing the tumultuous state to passion.
7. Altruistic behavior can be increased through affective explanations, induction techniques, preaching about empathy, empathy training, and the provision of helpful models. Adults are most likely to assist someone in distress under these conditions: The emergency is clear. The victim's humanity is emphasized. The bystander likes and feels responsible for the victim. The bystander's identity is known. The bystander is happy and has positive feelings about the human race. The bystander is alone.
8. People conform to improve the accuracy of their judgments, to gain social, personal, and tangible rewards, and to avoid social, personal, or tangible costs.

9. Most human beings are not consistent in conforming or resisting pressures to conform. Conformity is likely under these conditions: The group is coercive or cohesive. Group members are unanimous. The group is appealing and the person's status is middling. Group members appear relatively competent or tasks seem difficult or ambiguous.
10. When pressures for obedience and the dictates of conscience conflict, many people yield to authority—especially when it is close, the victim is distant, and responsibility for ugly acts may be shifted to someone else.
11. People in our culture tend to see ideal women as gentle, kind, and responsive to others. They see ideal men as dominant, active, achieving, and level-headed.
12. As groups, men and women in our culture show some average differences. These differences are often small ones, and they may not appear consistently throughout the life cycle.
13. Anthropological studies of sex roles throughout the world and research on the sex-role socialization of normal and gender-disordered individuals suggest that many differences between men and women are influenced by social practices.
14. Androgenous people usually appear more flexible and mentally and socially healthier than traditionally sex-typed individuals.
15. Attitudes, including prejudices, are shaped by observation, operant and respondent conditioning, and cognitive learning.
16. In the United States, ambivalent and aversive racial prejudices tend to be more common today than dominative ones. Symbolic racism is particularly prevalent among Americans.
17. Competition and frustration intensify hostility and prejudice.
18. A number of tactics appear to be effective in reducing prejudice. Many successful approaches use social norms, educational efforts, and interpersonal contact under conditions of mutual respect to change attitudes.

A Study Guide for Chapter Seventeen

Key terms social norm (543), social psychology (544), person perception (546), attribution (547), helping (altruistic or prosocial) behavior (553), conformity (555) [compliance (555), acceptance (555), normative (557), informational (558)], obedience (558), sex role (562), socialization (565), hermaphrodite (565), androgenous (568), attitude (568), stereotype (569), prejudice (570), discrimination (570), racism (570), authoritarian personality (574), and other italicized words and expressions.

Important research social norms on the subway (Milgram), social needs (Schachter, Middlebrook, others), the person perception process (Dion, Archer, Akert, Niemi, others), principles guiding the attribution process (Langer, others), interpersonal attraction (E. Walster, Berscheid, Festinger, Zajonc, Byrne, Rubin, Kerckhoff, Davis, others), romantic love (Rubin, Cimbalo, others), helping behavior (Zahn-Waxler, Feshbach, Huston, Isen, Hornstein, others), conformity (Asch) and its influences (Crutchfield, Vaughan, others), obedience (Milgram, others), current sex-role stereotypes (Rubin, Condrys, others), low status of the feminine sex role, anthropological findings on sex roles (Friedl, others), sex-role socialization of gender-disordered people (Money, Ehrhardt), sex-role socialization of normal people (Rheingold, Cook, Serbin, O'Leary, others), costs of sex roles and androgeny (S. Bem, others), formation of racial prejudice (Pettigrew, Zanna, Stein, others), intensification of prejudice (Sherif, Miller, Bugelski, Adorno, others), prejudice reduction (Deutsch, Collins, Rokeach, Allport, Weigel, others).

Major concepts reasons to seek human contact (Festinger, others), imaginary stranger tactic (Byrne), exchange theory of attraction (Thibaut, Kelley), nature of passionate love (the Walsters, Berscheid), equity theory of love (the Walsters, Berscheid), the relationship between mood and helping (Isen, Hornstein), reasons for conformity and obedience, criticisms of the Asch model, ethics of Milgram's obedience investigation, differences between instrumental and expressive sex roles (Parsons, Bales), explanations for sex-role uniformities in different cultures (Friedl, Rossi, Levy, others), social learning principles and sex-role socialization (Mischel), cognitions and sex-role socialization (Kohlberg), costs of sex roles, influence of behavior on attitudes (D. Bem, others), influences on the acquisition and modification of attitudes, resistance of attitudes to change (Kelman), types of racism (Kovel, Katz), symbolic racism (McConahay, Hough).

Self-Quiz

1. Which statement about social norms is correct?
  a. Group members generally shift easily to new norms.
  b. Individuals are often unaware of norms.
  c. It is fairly easy for most people to break norms.
  d. Norms are essentially rigid stereotypes.

2. Under which condition are most people likely to seek out the companionship of others?
  a. Anxiety (about a physical danger)
  b. Depression
  c. Embarrassment
  d. Fatigue

3. To what are people most likely to attribute the behavior of other individuals?
  a. Chance, fate, or luck
  b. Circumstances
  c. Enduring abilities, motives, and traits
  d. Fleeting moods

4. Which characteristic *best* predicted which people would report liking one another and desiring another date at a computer dance?
  a. Enthusiasm and warmth   *b.* Meshing needs
  c. Physical attractiveness   *d.* Similar intelligence

5. Which three dimensions does Rubin's love scale assess?
  a. Attachment, caring, intimacy
  b. Attraction, concern, respect
  c. Caring, excitement, passion
  d. Idealism, intimacy, romance

6. According to current research, which parental practice is associated with helpfulness in young children?
  a. Acceptance of all conduct and unconditional positive regard
  b. Affective explanations when the child causes distress
  c. Church attendance
  d. Physical punishment for aggression and misconduct

7. Who is most likely to conform to an opinion expressed by a group?
  a. People who hold high group status
  b. People who hold low group status
  c. People who perceive the group's task as ambiguous
  d. People who perceive the other group members as less competent than themselves

8. What did Milgram learn about obedience?
  a. Most people assume that legitimate authorities have to be obeyed regardless of their requests.
  b. Most people have sadistic tendencies and obey cruel orders without anguish.
  c. Most people who obey disturbing orders do so only when those orders are supported by powerful, prestigious institutions.
  d. Most people obey inhumane orders even when they see others defy the authority.

9. At which age do children begin to be stereotyped as

masculine or feminine by their parents, according to current research?

   a. At birth

   b. At about six months

   c. At about one year

   d. Between two and five years

10. As a group, women are superior to men on which abilities?

   a. Quantitative   *b.* Reasoning

   c. Spatial   *d.* Verbal

11. Which factor is most crucial for sex-role socialization, according to Kohlberg?

   a. Cognitions

   b. Observation learning

   c. Operant conditioning

   d. Respondent conditioning

12. Which attribute tends to be characteristic of androgenous people?

   a. Difficulty communicating with members of the opposite sex

   b. High intelligence

   c. High self-esteem

   d. A negative self-image

13. Which statement about stereotypes is true?

   a. An individual's stereotypes are generally based on large samples of observations.

   b. Increasing percentages of white Americans stereotype blacks as inferior.

   c. Most stereotypes are complex and fluid.

   d. Stereotypes may be truly useful.

14. By which process is the emotional component of a prejudice apt to be acquired?

   a. Instruction

   b. Observation

   c. Operant conditioning

   d. Respondent conditioning

15. Which statement about integration is correct?

   a. Desegregation under adverse circumstances may lower self-esteem and academic achievement in minority-group members.

   b. Desegregation usually increases racial harmony regardless of circumstances.

   c. Small cooperative learning groups in a desegregated school help minority-group members achieve, but do not promote racial harmony.

   d. Social norms that favor racial harmony decrease student prejudices in integrated colleges all over the United States except in the deep South.

Suggested Readings

1. Aronson, E. *The social animal.* (2d ed.) San Francisco: Freeman, 1976 (paperback); Severy, L. G., Brigham, J. C., & Schlenker, B. R. *A contemporary introduction to social psychology.* New York: McGraw-Hill, 1976. Try one of these for a brief, interesting introduction to social psychology that stresses current social issues. Baron, R. A., & Byrne, D. *Social psychology: Understanding human interaction.* (2d ed.) Boston: Allyn & Bacon, 1977; Wrightsman, L. S. *Social psychology.* (2d ed.) Monterey, Calif.: Brooks/Cole, 1977. For a more comprehensive introduction, these two books are good choices.

2. Berscheid, E., & Walster, E. H. *Interpersonal attraction.* (2d ed.) Reading, Mass.: Addison-Wesley, 1978 (paperback). This delightful book describes research on liking and loving. As one reviewer put it, the authors took "an enormously interesting topic and let its natural values shine through."

3. Walster, E., & Walster, G. W. *A new look at love.* Reading, Mass.: Addison-Wesley, 1978 (paperback). The Walsters describe what psychologists know about varied types of love, using a question-answer format and lively examples, excerpts from popular writing, cartoons, cases, and questionnaires.

4. Mussen, P., & Eisenberg-Berg, N. *Roots of caring, sharing, and helping: The development of prosocial behavior in children.* San Francisco: Freeman, 1977 (paperback). Using a conversational style, these psychologists discuss how human beings acquire social behavior and how altruism may be increased.

5. Milgram, S. *Obedience to authority.* New York: Harper & Row, 1974. Writing clearly and well, Milgram describes his entire obedience research program, offers a theoretical explanation for the findings, and defends his ethics and the generalizability of this exceedingly important investigation.

6. Tavris, C., & Offir, C. *The longest war: Sex differences in perspective.* New York: Harcourt Brace Jovanovich, 1977 (paperback). This is a fine introduction to the topic of sex differences. Tavris and Offir write in a sparkling, often humorous style about real and imagined sex differences, sexuality, explanations for sex differences, and sex-role redefinition "experiments" in Israel, Russia, China, and Sweden. Tavris and Offir do justice to complex issues. They are fair, accurate, and always interesting.

7. Zimbardo, P. G., Ebbesen, E. B., & Maslach, C. *Influencing attitudes and changing behavior: An introduction to method, theory, and applications of social control and personal power.* (2d ed.) Reading, Mass.: Addison-Wesley, 1977 (paperback). These social psychologists provide a student-oriented introduction to attitude change research, with emphasis on practical applications. You will read here about Patty Hearst, Reverend Moon, and others.

8. Allport, G. W. *The nature of prejudice.* New York: Doubleday-Anchor, 1958 (paperback). This is a classic treatment of prejudice that is insightful and a pleasure to read.

9. Kidder, L. H., & Stewart, V. M. *The psychology of intergroup relations: Conflict and consciousness.* New York: McGraw-Hill, 1975 (paperback). This brief book on prejudice has been called "inspired behavioral science which brings to life scientific abstractions with profound implications." Many types of prejudice are cited as examples.

10. Wilcox, R. C. *The psychological consequences of being a black American: A sourcebook of research by black psychologists*. New York: Wiley, 1971 (paperback). A collection of research studies focusing on black experiences in the United States.

11. Kozol, J. *Death at an early age*. New York: Bantam, 1968; Little, M. *The autobiography of Malcolm X*. New York: Grove, 1964; Cleaver, E. *Soul on ice*. New York: McGraw-Hill, 1968. These paperbacks all provide insight into the predicament of being a black American.

12. Ashmore, R. D., & McConahay, J. B. *Psychology and America's urban dilemmas*. New York: McGraw-Hill, 1975 (paperback). Currently, many social psychologists are trying to understand and help resolve serious social problems. With simplicity and clarity, this book covers the psychological theory and research directed at understanding and alleviating varied urban problems, including poverty, education, and criminal justice.

13. Argyle, M. The laws of looking. *Human Nature*, 1978, **1**(1), 32–40. Argyle describes research on gaze patterns during communication in people all over the world. He also discusses the rules that gaze patterns seem to follow.

14. McGuinness, D. How schools discriminate against boys. *Human Nature*, 1979, **2**(2), 82–88. In a provocative essay about sex differences, McGuinness assumes that many sex differences are set by biology and that people must understand their biology to avoid being shackled to it. Schools, she argues, fail to develop girls' abilities and misuse boys' abilities.

15. Aronson, E., with Blaney, N., Sikes, J., Stephan, C., & Snapp, M. Busing and racial tension: The jigsaw route to learning and liking. *Psychology Today*, 1975, **8**(9), 43–50. Traditional teaching methods that stress competition actually increase interracial strife in newly integrated schools. This fascinating article describes a technique which can make integration work.

Answer Key

Self-Quiz

1. *b* (544)   **2.** *a* (545)   **3.** *c* (549)   **4.** *c* (550)
5. *a* (552)   **6.** *b* (553)   **7.** *c* (557)   **8.** *a* (559)
9. *a* (562)   **10.** *d* (564)   **11.** *a* (566)   **12.** *c* (568)
13. *d* (569)   **14.** *d* (571)   **15.** *a* (576)

APPENDIX
Fundamental Statistical Concepts

Collecting the Data

Describing Central Tendency: Means, Medians, and Modes

Describing Variability: Ranges and Standard Deviations

Describing an Individual's Relative Standing: The Normal Distribution

Describing Relationships: Scatter Plots and Correlation Coefficients

Interpreting the Significance of Results: Inferential Statistics

The term *statistics* refers to both the various mathematical methods used to analyze numerical data and to the data themselves. Statistical analyses serve two major functions. *Descriptive statistics* allow psychologists to organize and simplify data. *Inferential statistics* permit behavioral scientists to predict and generalize from their findings. We examine both types of statistics. Our goal is to understand why and when particular statistics are used, not mathematical proficiency.

COLLECTING THE DATA

Assume you're a psychologist with an interest in helping deaf children learn sign language. You want to evaluate a new teaching technique, method A. You decide to test the hypothesis, "Training method A is more effective than training method B (the traditional procedure) for teaching sign language to deaf youngsters." You select twenty deaf two-year-olds at random from a day-care center for deaf children and assign ten of them to an experimental group and ten to a control group—again, randomly. Subjects in the experimental group learn sign language by training method A, while those in the control

group learn the same subject matter by the standard training method. At the end of six months, the children are tested. Their scores are shown in Table A-1. Only a little information can be obtained directly from the data at this point. We can see that some subjects in each group scored well and that others did poorly. It's clear that the *raw data* (findings which have not been transformed in any way) must be summarized more concisely and meaningfully before we can decide whether or not the results support our original hypothesis.

DESCRIBING CENTRAL TENDENCY: MEANS, MEDIANS, AND MODES

One method of simplifying data consists of replacing a group of numbers with a single number—their "average." When we speak of an average, we're referring to a central value around which a group of scores clusters. There are three common measures of this value, known as *measures of central tendency*: mean, mode, and median. Each provides a single summary number which can represent the whole group of scores.

Mean You're probably familiar with the arithmetic average or *mean*, the sum of all scores divided by the number of scores. The mean is the most frequently used measure of central tendency. When the data center around a middle value, a mean is the preferred measure of central tendency usually, because it assigns equal importance to each number. To calculate the mean test score for the deaf children in the experimental group, we just add up the ten subjects' test marks listed on Table A-1 (80 + 50 + 90 + 80 + 30 + · · · + 80) and divide by the number of subjects (10). The mean is 74. Using the table again, please compute a mean for the control group.[1] If the two means are compared, method A appears to be more effective than method B. But we don't know if the difference is significant unless we use inferential statistics, which we'll describe later.

Median A second measure of central tendency is the *median*, the middle number in a group of scores. Half the remaining scores fall above the median and half fall below it. To find the median, one ranks the scores in the group from high to low and then counts down to the middle score. If there are two middle scores, as there are when the number of scores is even, the mean of the two middle scores is computed. The median for the children in the experimental group is 80. Please calculate the median for the youngsters in the control group.[2] It makes some sense to select the median rather than the mean when the numbers pile up at one extreme. Consider the case of a history student with the exam grades of 20, 91, 87, 94, and 92. The median, 91, would yield a more representative summary of the student's performance than the mean, 77. The median keeps the atypical grade, 20, from counting so heavily.

Mode Occasionally, the *mode*, the number that appears most frequently in a group of scores, is used as the measure of central tendency. Modes are valuable when one or

TABLE A-1 Deaf Children's Scores on a Sign-Language Test

Experimental subjects	Control subjects
80	50
50	60
90	60
80	40
30	70
90	30
90	70
80	90
70	70
80	50

The highest possible score is 100.

two scores are extremely frequent in a large group of measurements, and one wishes to talk about the typical score or scores. The mode is inappropriate for our example.

DESCRIBING VARIABILITY: RANGES AND STANDARD DEVIATIONS

Looking at Table A-1, you can see that the test scores of the deaf children in both groups vary quite a bit. Sometimes behavioral scientists are interested in describing *variability*, how much the scores within a group differ from one another. Are they relatively heterogeneous, or dissimilar? Or, do they cluster quite closely together? In other words, are they relatively homogeneous?

The extent that numbers spread out, or the *range*, is one useful measure of variability. The range is defined as the difference between the highest and lowest scores in a group of numbers. The range of scores for the experimental group children is 60: (90−30=60). Please calculate the range of scores for the control group children.[3] The range tells us how much the highest and lowest scores in the group differ. But it doesn't describe how the numbers generally spread out with reference to the central value. The *standard deviation*,

---

[1] The mean for the control group is 59.

[2] The median for the control group is 60.

[3] The range of scores for the control group subjects is also 60: (90−30=60).

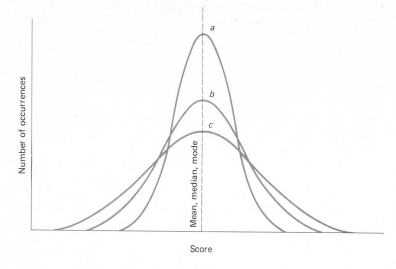

Number of occurrences

Mean, median, mode

Score

FIGURE A-1 Three normal curves. Curve (*a*) has the smallest standard deviation, while curve (*c*) has the largest one.

the most frequently used measure of variability, serves this function. It indicates the extent to which scores vary on the average from the mean. A large standard deviation tells us that the numbers are frequently far from the mean. A small standard deviation indicates that the numbers cluster closely about the mean. Calculating standard deviations involves simple but tedious arithmetic. Since we are concerned more with the concept than the numerical details, we will not compute a standard deviation now.[4]

Variability is often an important bit of information to have. In the case of airline pilots, for example, consistent performance is a matter of life and death. On tests assessing pilots' skills at landing during storms, high means and low standard deviations are essential.

[4] Should you wish to calculate a standard deviation, the formula is

$$s = \sqrt{\frac{1}{N} \sum X^2 - \overline{X}^2}$$

where s = standard deviation
X = each raw score
$\overline{X}$ = mean of raw scores
N = number of raw scores
Σ = mathematical sign for summation

DESCRIBING AN INDIVIDUAL'S RELATIVE STANDING: THE NORMAL DISTRIBUTION

Imagine that you received a letter stating that you scored 545 points on the Soshkish animal energy scale. You'd probably be eager to find out how you did. Was the score about average? Higher than average? Lower than average? More precisely, what percentage of people do better and what percentage do worse than this? To answer questions like these, we must compare your performance on the test with that of a large, representative sample of people. In the course of measuring numerous psychological characteristics, social scientists have discovered that a lot of them (measured intelligence and scholastic aptitude, as examples) are distributed among the general public in a very specific way. The scores of the greatest number of people cluster in the middle range. A small number cluster toward the high and low extremes. The two sides mirror one another precisely. And the mean, median, and mode all coincide. This particular bell-shaped distribution (three are pictured in Figure A-1) is known as the *normal curve* or *normal distribution*. The

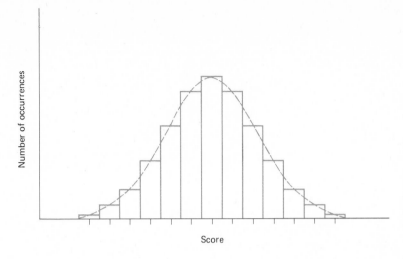

smooth line of the distribution may be visualized as connecting the midpoints of the bars of a histogram (bar graph) with a large number of observations, as is shown in Figure A-2. The normal distribution has these important characteristics:

1. Nearly 68 percent of all scores lie within ±1 standard deviation of the mean.
2. About 95 percent of all scores lie within ±2 standard deviations of the mean.
3. Almost 100 percent (99.9 percent) of all scores lie within ±3 standard deviations of the mean.
4. Approximately 0.1 percent of all scores lie beyond ±3 standard deviations of the mean.

These same percentages hold true for all normal distributions. Once we know, then, that scores on a particular characteristic are normally distributed, we need only two additional bits of information to determine the relative standing of a specific score. We have to know the mean and the standard deviation. Suppose that animal energy is normally distributed, that the mean on the Soshkish scale is 500, and the standard deviation is 15. That would put a score of 545 at +3 standard deviations. In animal energy you rank in the top 0.1 percent of the population. See Figure A-3.

DESCRIBING RELATIONSHIPS: SCATTER PLOTS AND CORRELATION COEFFICIENTS

Suppose you are interested in the question: "Do students who attend class regularly make higher exam grades than those whose attendance is spotty?" In other words, is attendance related to test marks? To see how two sets of measurements change in relationship to one another, we could construct a graph on which both groups of scores are plotted. Each point would represent one pair of scores. Say we choose 20 students at random from 300 enrolled in Botany 101 at Hibiscus College. The students' number of days of attendance and average exam scores are shown in Table A-2. If we plot these data on a grid, we'd come up with a graph like the one in Figure A-4a. Graphs like this one, called *scatter plots*, present a visual representation of the relationship between two scores. Looking at the graph, you can see that grades tend to increase with increasing attendance. If no relationship or a negative relationship existed between marks and attendance, the scatter plots would have looked something like the ones presented in Figure A-4b and c. Eye-

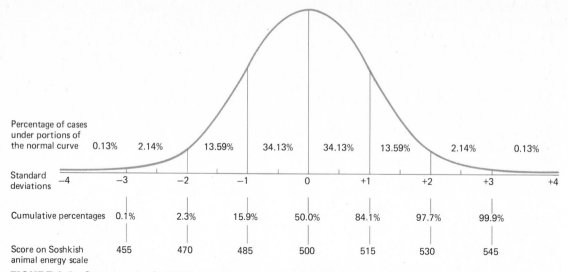

FIGURE A-3 Scores on the Soshkish animal energy scale are distributed normally. You can see the standard deviations, percentages of cases falling within these standard deviations, and corresponding cumulative percentages falling below particular scores. [*Adapted from Psychological Corporation,* Test Service Bulletin, *1955, 49, 8.*]

balling trends is all right for informal purposes, but it leads eventually to problems. Because of its imprecision, bias can easily creep in. If we're emotionally invested in our hypothesis, we may see relationships that don't exist or fail to see ones that do. And eyeballing won't permit estimates of how strong or significant the relationships are. So once again we turn to statistics. To describe relationships between two sets of scores, the statistic called the *correlation coefficient* is used. Recall that correlation coefficients are numbers ranging in value from -1.00 to $+1.00$ and describing in which direction and with what strength two sets of scores are related. If your memory needs further refreshing, please reread the section entitled Correlational Studies, in Chapter 2. Since the various correlation coefficients all involve lengthy computations, we will not describe how to calculate one here. But suppose you did calculate the correlation coefficient known as the Pearson Product Moment Correlation Coefficient, using the data presented in Table A-2. You'd find a correlation coefficient of approximately $+.95$. This value is very close to $+1.00$ and suggests

that our hunch was right. When attendance is regular, students do well on a large percentage of their exams. Conversely, when they attend class infrequently, they generally do rather poorly on their tests. We have to be very careful about how we interpret this relationship. Do not make the mistake of assuming that one event necessarily influences the other. Being present in class could contribute to high exam scores, of course. It is also possible that exam average influences attendance. Doing well on tests could lead to liking the course and few cuts. At the same time, something else, such as high motivation to learn, might lead to both good study habits (and consequently high exam grades) and regular class attendance.

INTERPRETING THE SIGNIFICANCE OF RESULTS: INFERENTIAL STATISTICS

We began our section on statistics with an experimental study. We wanted to test the hypothesis, "Training method A is more effective than training method B for teaching sign language to deaf children." We selected only twenty deaf two-year-olds even though we were interested in all deaf two-year-olds. Invariably, psychologists interested in questions about whole populations select a small portion, or *sample*, to study. Even when ideal sampling strategies are used and large random or representative samples are chosen (as described in Chapter 2), studies on samples will yield somewhat different results from those on entire populations. These differences, called *sampling errors* or *chance factors*, are due to miscellaneous variations in the individuals selected for the research. Try to visualize repeating our study of training methods A and B on 200 or 2,000 young deaf children. You would not expect to obtain *precisely* the same results each time. The word "precisely" is important. While results on different samples will not be identical, they should be rather similar if random or representative samples are relatively large in relation to the population of interest. Because sampling errors are the rule rather than the exception, researchers in the behavioral sciences are faced continually with the questions: Were my results likely to be due simply to sampling errors? If another sample were drawn and the study repeated, would similar results be probable? To answer these questions, psychologists use *inferential statistics*. Inferential statistics help behavioral scientists

TABLE A-2 Exam Grades and Attendance Records of Twenty Students

Student	Average grade	Attendance (total days)
1	89	41
2	77	34
3	65	32
4	68	34
5	92	43
6	67	26
7	72	37
8	57	29
9	82	38
10	69	29
11	84	40
12	78	36
13	98	45
14	93	43
15	60	27
16	67	32
17	56	24
18	85	38
19	90	42
20	79	36

decide whether or not they can *infer* anything about the entire population of interest from the findings on a small sample.

To understand the rationale behind inferential statistics, you need a little insight into the branch of mathematics known as *probability*. Concepts of probability are easier to understand in a concrete context, so we'll consider an example. A man named J. K. claims to

FIGURE A-4 Three scatter plots depicting possible relationships between attendance and exam averages for botany students at Hibiscus College. Figures show (*a*) a positive correlation (using data from Table A-2), (*b*) no correlation, and (*c*) a negative correlation.

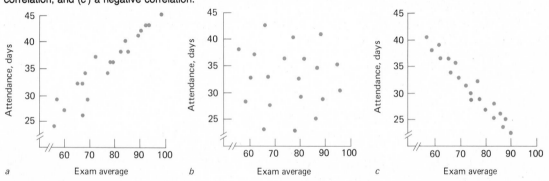

TABLE A-3 Guessing the Outcome of Five Coin Tosses

Number of correct guesses	Percentage of population
5	3.1
4	15.6
3	31.3
2	31.3
1	15.6
0	3.1

have precognition, the ability to know the outcome of events before they occur. Since we're skeptical, we decide to study J. K.'s ability carefully. We will flip one penny five times and ask him to guess—just before each toss—whether it will turn up heads or tails. We begin by gathering data on a large number of ordinary people for comparison purposes. Overall, our subjects guess correctly close to half the time. The scores of individuals vary quite a bit. And, of course, no one makes 2½ correct hits! Our findings are presented in Table A-3. Now that we have a basis for comparison, we test J. K. Suppose he makes three correct guesses. Would we regard his performance as confirmation of precognition? As you can see from Table A-3, 31.3 percent of normal subjects do this well when they merely guess. Three hits isn't a very impressive performance. What if J. K. makes four correct responses? Our decision would be more difficult then, because only 15.6 percent of ordinary mortals do that well by chance. Now suppose J. K. makes five correct predictions. While this perfect performance would not prove that J. K. has precognition, it's a very unusual record. Only 3.1 percent of people do this well simply by chance. Consequently, many individuals would conclude that J. K. may have some unusual skills. (In a real experiment, psychologists would use a lot more coin tosses.)

The problem that we face here is basic to most sciences. Our findings are rarely absolutely certain, so we try to evaluate their probabilities. Whenever experimental or correlational studies are conducted, psycholo-

gists calculate the likelihood that the results are due solely to sampling errors. When the odds are less than 5 in 100 that this could be the case, then the results are considered *statistically significant*. The criterion 5 in 100 is an arbitrary one but has come to be widely accepted in psychology. If J. K. has ordinary sensory capacities, the probability of his guessing five consecutive coin tosses correctly—simply by chance—is less than 5 in 100. For this reason, behavioral scientists would assume that something special is going on. Let's return to our deaf children for a moment. Recall that the youngsters learning sign language by method A averaged fifteen points more on the test than those learning by method B. Could this difference in mean scores be due to sampling errors? If we used an inferential statistical test called a T test, we would find that this fifteen-point difference could be expected less than 5 in 100 times because of sampling errors alone. We'd conclude, then, that the difference between groups is statistically significant.

What does statistical significance mean in practical terms? It indicates that results are reliable (consistent) and likely to be observed again if the study is repeated. Statistical significance does *not* mean that differences or relationships are of practical importance. Training method A, for example, may not produce sufficient benefits to warrant its additional cost. And statistical significance does *not* mean that the hypothesis has been proven correct. Statistically significant findings can be caused by uncontrolled nonrandom factors that were not taken into account in the original study, and not by the variable of interest. The self-proclaimed psychic in our example could be using a weighted coin, and not precognition, to achieve his results. The deaf children, who seem to be learning so well by method A, may really be responding to their teacher's enthusiasm for a new approach. The real proof that conclusions are sound comes when studies are replicated in different laboratories or field settings using diverse samples and procedures and when similar findings accumulate.

Chapter 1

1. Crocker, J., & Taylor, S. E. Theory-driven processing and the use of complex evidence. Paper presented at the annual meeting of the American Psychological Association, Toronto, 1978.

2. Milliard, W. J. Species preferences of experimenters: *Journal of the Experimental Analysis of Behavior. American Psychologist*, 1976, **31**(12), 894–896; Ehrlich, A. The age of the rat. *Human Behavior*, 1974, **3**(3), 24–28.

3. Bustad, L. K. The experimental subject—A choice not an echo. *Perspectives in Biology and Medicine*, Autumn 1970, 14.

4. *Advance*, August–September, 1977, 4.

5. Boneau, C. A., & Cuca, J. M. An overview of psychology's human resources: Characteristics and salaries from the 1972 APA survey. *American Psychologist*, 1974, **29**(11), 821–840.

6. Washburn, S. L. The evolution of man. *Scientific American*, 1978, **239**(3), 194–208.

7. Titchener, E. B. *A beginner's psychology*. New York: Macmillan, 1915. P. 9.

8. Boring, E. G. A history of introspection. *Psychological Bulletin*, 1953, **50**(3), 169–188.

9. Miller, G. A. *Psychology: The science of mental life*. New York: Harper & Row, 1962.

10. Titchener, E. B. *An outline of psychology*. New York: Macmillan, 1896. Pp. 74–75.

11. James, W. *The principles of psychology*. Vol. 1. New York: Holt, Rinehart, 1890. Chap. 9.

12. Watson, J. B. *Psychology from the standpoint of a behaviorist*. Philadelphia: Lippincott, 1919. Pp. 1–3.

13. Watson, J. B. *Behaviorism*. New York: Norton, 1925. P. 82.

14. Wertheimer, M. Max Wertheimer, Gestalt prophet. Address presented at the annual meeting of the American Psychological Association, Toronto, 1978.

15. Freud, S. Fragment of an analysis of a case of hysteria. In A. Strachey & J. Strachey (trans.), *Collected papers*. Vol. 3. New York: Basic Books, 1959. P. 94.

16. Evans, R. I. *The making of psychology*. New York: Knopf, 1976. P. 315.

17. Freud, S. *Psychopathology of everyday life*. New York: Mentor, 1951. Pp. 44–52.

18. Weiss, J. M. Psychological factors in stress and disease. *Scientific American*, 1972, **226**(6), 104–107.

19. Neisser, U. *Cognition and reality: Principles and implications of cognitive psychology*. San Francisco: Freeman, 1976. Pp. 89–92; Hirst, W., Neisser, U., & Spelke, E. Divided attention. *Human Nature*, 1978, **1**(6), 54–61.

20. Bugenthal, J. F. T. The challenge that is man. In J. F. T. Bugenthal (Ed.), *Challenges of humanistic psychology*. New York: McGraw-Hill, 1967. Pp. 5–12.

21. Maslow, A. H. Self-actualization and beyond. In J. F. T. Bugenthal (Ed.), *Challenges of humanistic psychology*. New York: McGraw-Hill, 1967. Pp. 279–280.

22. Maslow, A. H. *Motivation and personality*. (2d ed.) New York: Harper & Row, 1970.

Chapter 2

1. Bachrach, A. *Psychological research: An introduction*. (3d ed.) New York: Random House, 1972. Pp. 19–20.

2. Crutchfield, R. S., & Krech, D. Some guides to the understanding of the history of psychology. In L. Postman (Ed.), *Psychology in the making*. New York: Knopf, 1962. P. 23.

3. Barber, B., & Fox, R. The case of the floppy-eared rabbits: An instance of serendipity gained and serendipity lost. *American Journal of Sociology*, 1958, **54**, 128–136.

4. Skinner, B. F. *Science and human behavior*. New York: Macmillan, 1953. P. 12.

5. McCain, G., & Segal, E. M. *The game of science*. (2d ed.) Monterey, Calif.: Brooks/Cole, 1973. Pp. 176–177.

6. Broadbent, D. E. *In defense of empirical psychology*. London: Methuen, 1973. P. 116.

7. Campbell, D. T. Reprise. *American Psychologist*, 1975, **31**(5), 381.

8. Schultz, D. P. The human subject in psychological research. *Psychological Bulletin*, 1969, **72**, 214–228.

9. Holmes, D. S., & Jorgensen, B. W. Do personality and social psychologists study men more than women? *Representative Research in Social Psychology*, 1971, **2**, 71–76.

10. Hilton, I. Differences in the behavior of mothers toward first- and later-born children. *Journal of Personality and Social Psychology*, 1967, **7**, 282–290.

11. Rosenhan, D. L. On being sane in insane places. *Science*, 1973, **179**(4070), 250–257.

12. Festinger, L., Riecken, H. W., & Schachter, S. *When prophecy fails*. Minneapolis: University of Minnesota Press, 1956.

13. Anderson, B. J. A methodology for observation of the childbirth environment; Nicholson, J. A model of maternal coping with childbirth: Implications for research and methodology; and Standley, K. Psychosocial predictors during pregnancy of obstetrical conditions and events. All three papers were presented at annual meetings of the American Psychological Association: the first, in Washington, D.C., 1976; the others, in Toronto, 1978.

14. Yarrow, M. R., Campbell, J. D., & Burton, R. V. Recollections of childhood: A study of the retrospective method. *Monographs of the Society for Research in Child Development*, 1970, **35** (No. 138).

15. Strickland, B. R. Internal-external control of reinforcement. In T. Blass (Ed.), *Personality variables in social behavior*. Hillsdale, N.J.: Erlbaum, 1977. Pp. 219–267.

16. Lefcourt, H. M. *Locus of control: Current trends in theory and research*. Hillsdale, N.J.: Erlbaum, 1976; Phares, E. J. *Locus of control in personality*. Morristown, N.J.: General Learning Press, 1976.

17. Dweck, C. S. The role of expectations and attributions in the alleviation of learned helplessness. *Journal of Personality and Social Psychology*, 1975, **31**, 674–685.

18. Kubler-Ross, E. *On death and dying*. New York: Macmillan, 1969. Preface and pp. 233–236.

19. Latané, B., & Darley, J. M. *The unresponsive bystander: Why doesn't he help?* New York: Appleton-Century-Crofts, 1970.

20. Roethlisberger, F. J., & Dickson, W. J. *Management and the worker*. Cambridge, Mass.: Harvard University Press, 1939.

21. Rosenthal, R. Clever Hans: A case study of scientific method. In M. S. Gazzaniga & E. P. Lovejoy (Eds.), *Good reading in psychology*. Englewood Cliffs, N.J.: Prentice-Hall, 1971. Pp. 498–518.

22. Rosenthal, R. *Experimenter effects in behavioral research*. (Rev. ed.) New York: Irvington, 1976.

23. Chapanis, A. The relevance of laboratory studies to practical situations. *Ergonomics*, 1967, **10**, 557–577.

24. Piliavin, I. M., Rodin, J., & Piliavin, J. A. Good samaritanism: An underground phenomenon? *Journal of Personality and Social Psychology*, 1969, **13**, 289–299.

25. Solomon, H., & Solomon, L. Z. Bystander intervention and diffusion effects in the field. Paper presented at the annual meeting of the American Psychological Association, Washington, D.C., 1976.

26. Ad hoc Committee on Ethical Standards in Psychological Research. *Ethical principles in the conduct of research with human participants*. Washington, D.C.: American Psychological Association, 1973.

27. Wilson, D. W., & Donnerstein, E. Legal and ethical aspects of nonreactive social psychological research: An excursion into the public mind. *American Psychologist*, 1976, **31**(11), 765–773.

28. Bannister, D. Psychology as an exercise in paradox. *Bulletin of the British Psychological Society*, 1966, **19**, 21–26.

29. Macklin, E. D. Cohabitation in college: Going very steady. *Psychology Today*, 1974, **8**(6), 53–59.

30. Parsons, H. M. What caused the Hawthorne Effect? A scientific detective story. Address presented at the annual meeting of the American Psychological Association, Washington, D.C., 1976.

Chapter 3

1. Stone, L. J., Smith, H. I., & Murphy, L. B. (Eds.), Introduction. *The competent infant: Research and commentary.* New York: Basic Books, 1973. P. 3.
2. Rousseau, J. J. *Émile, or On education* (B. Foxley, trans.) London: Dent, 1911. P. 5.
3. Hall, G. S. Notes on the study of infants. *Pedagogical Seminary*, 1891, **1**, 127–138.
4. James, W. *The principles of psychology.* New York: Holt, 1890. P. 488.
5. Lipsitt, L. P., Engen, T., & Kaye, H. Developmental changes in the olfactory threshold of the neonate. *Child Development*, 1963, **34**, 371–376; Pratt, K. D., Nelson, A. K., & Sun, K. H. *The behavior of the newborn infant.* Columbus: Ohio State University Press, 1930.
6. Wickelgren, L. W. The ocular response of human newborns to intermittent visual movements. *Journal of Experimental Child Psychology*, 1969, **8**, 469–482.
7. Fantz, R. L. The origin of form perception. *Scientific American*, 1961, **204**(5), 66–72; Jirari, C. Form perception, innate form preferences, and visually-mediated head turning in the human neonate. Unpublished doctoral dissertation. University of Chicago, 1970. Cited in D. G. Freedman, *Human infancy: An evolutionary perspective.* Hillsdale, N.J.: Erlbaum, 1974.
8. Lipton, E. L., Steinschneider, A., & Richmond, J. B. The autonomic nervous system in early life. *New England Journal of Medicine*, 1965, **273**, 201–208; Freedman, D. G. Behavioral assessment in infancy. In G. B. A. Stoelinga & J. J. Van Der Werff Ten Bosch (Eds.), *Normal and abnormal development of brain and behavior.* Leiden, Holland: Leiden University Press, 1971. Pp. 92–103.
9. Siqueland, E. R., & Lipsitt, L. P. Conditioned head turning in human newborns. *Journal of Experimental Child Psychology*, 1963, **3**, 356–376; Sameroff, A. J. Can conditioned responses be established in the newborn infant? Unpublished paper, 1969.
10. Friedman, S. Infant habituation: Process, problems and possibilities. In N. R. Ellis (Ed.), *Aberrant development in infancy: Human and animal studies.* Hillsdale, N.J.: Erlbaum, 1975. Pp. 217–239.
11. Hebb, D. O. *Textbook of psychology.* (3d ed.) Philadelphia: Saunders, 1972. Pp. 127–131.
12. McClearn, G. E., & Defries, J. C. *Introduction to behavioral genetics.* San Francisco: Freeman, 1973. P. 312.
13. McClearn, G. E., & Defries, J. C. *Introduction to behavioral genetics.* San Francisco: Freeman, 1973. P. 66.
14. Cattell, R. B., Stice, G. F., & Kristy, N. F. A first approximation to nature-nurture ratios for eleven primary personality factors in objective tests. *Journal of Abnormal*

and Social Psychology, 1957, **54**, 143–159; Vandenberg, S. G. Hereditary factors in normal personality traits (as measured by inventories). In J. Wortis (Ed.), *Recent advances in biological psychiatry.* Vol. 9. New York: Plenum, 1967. Pp. 65–104.
15. Buss, A. H., Plomin, R., & Willerman, L. The inheritance of temperament. *Journal of Personality*, 1973, **41**, 513–524; Gottesman, I. I. Differential inheritance of the psychoneuroses. *Eugenics Quarterly*, 1962, **9**, 223–227; Gottesman, I. I., & Shields, J. Schizophrenia in twins: Sixteen years' consecutive admissions to a psychiatric clinic. *British Journal of Psychiatry*, 1966, **112**, 809–818.
16. Broadhurst, P. L. The biochemical analysis of behavioral inheritance. *Science Progress, Oxford*, 1967, **55**, 123–139.
17. Scott, J. P., & Fuller, J. L. *Genetics and the social behavior of the dog.* Chicago: University of Chicago Press, 1965.
18. Money, J. Two cytogenetic syndromes: Psychological comparison, intelligence, and specific factor quotients. *Journal of Psychiatric Research*, 1964, **2**, 223–231; Bock, R. D., & Kolakowski, D. Further evidence of sex-linked major-gene influence on human spatial visualizing ability. *American Journal of Human Genetics*, 1973, **25**, 1–14.
19. Wolff, P. H. Observations on newborn infants. *Psychosomatic Medicine*, 1959, **21**, 110–118.
20. Bell, R. Q. Relations between behavior manifestations in the human neonate. *Child Development*, 1960, **31**, 463–478.
21. Lipsitt, L. P., & Levy, N. Pain threshold in the human neonate. *Child Development*, 1959, **30**, 547–554.
22. Grossman, H. J., & Greenberg, N. J. Psychosomatic differentiation in infancy. *Psychosomatic Medicine*, 1957, **19**, 293–306.
23. Thomas, A., Chess, S., & Birch, H. The origin of personality. *Scientific American*, 1970, **223**(2), 102–109.
24. Kagan, J., & Moss, H. A. *Birth to maturity.* New York: Wiley, 1962; Schafer, E. S., & Bayley, N. Maternal behavior, child behavior, and their intercorrelations from infancy through adolescence. *Monographs of the Society for Research in Child Development*, 1963, **28**(3), 1–127.
25. Sameroff, A. J. Infant risk factors in developmental deviancy. Unpublished paper, 1974. Cited in N. Garmezy, Vulnerable and invulnerable children: Theory, research, and intervention. Master lecture in developmental psychology presented at the annual meeting of the American Psychological Association, Chicago, 1975.
26. Segal, J., & Yahraes, H. *A child's journey.* New York: McGraw-Hill, 1978.
27. Pryor, G. Malnutrition and the "critical period" hypothesis. In J. W. Prescott, M. S. Read, & D. B. Coursin (Eds.), *Brain function and malnutrition: Neuropsychological methods of assessment.* New York: Wiley, 1975. Pp. 103–112.
28. Emery, A. E. *Heredity, disease, and*

man: Genetics in medicine. Berkeley: University of California Press, 1968.
29. Stein, Z., Susser, M., Saenger, G., & Marolla, F. *Famine and human development: The Dutch hunger, winter 1944–1945.* New York: Oxford University Press, 1975.
30. Ebbs, J. H., Brown, A., Tisdall, F. F., Moyle, W. J., & Bell, M. The influence of improved prenatal nutrition upon the infant. *Canadian Medical Association Journal*, 1942, **46**, 6–8.
31. Winick, M., & Rosso, P. Malnutrition and central nervous system development. In J. W. Prescott, M. S. Read, & D. B. Coursin (Eds.), *Brain function and malnutrition: Neuropsychological methods of assessment.* New York: Wiley, 1975. Pp. 41–52.
32. Stein, Z., Susser, M., Saenger, G., & Marolla, F. *Famine and human development: The Dutch hunger, winter 1944–1945.* New York: Oxford University Press, 1975; Cheek, D. B. Brain growth and nucleic acids: The effects of nutritional deprivation. In F. Richardson (Ed.), *Brain and intelligence: The ecology of child development.* Washington, D.C.: National Education Press, 1973. Pp. 237–256.
33. Carr, D. H. Chromosome studies in selected spontaneous abortions: 1. Conception after contraceptives. *Canadian Medical Association Journal*, 1970, **103**(4), 343–348.
34. Hanson, J. W. Unpublished paper, 1977. Cited in L. F. Annis, *The child before birth.* Ithaca, N.Y.: Cornell University Press, 1978.
35. Frazier, T. M., David, G. H., Goldstein, H., & Goldberg, I. D. Cigarette smoking and prematurity: A prospective study. *American Journal of Obstetrics and Gynecology*, 1961, **81**, 988–996.
36. Butler, N. R., Goldstein, H., & Ross, E. M. Cigarette smoking in pregnancy: Its influence on birth weight and perinatal mortality. *British Medical Journal*, 1972, **2**, 127–130.
37. Butler, N. R., & Goldstein, H. Smoking in pregnancy and subsequent child development. *British Medical Journal*, 1973, **4**, 573–575.
38. Brazleton, T. B. Effects of prenatal drugs on the behavior of the neonate. *American Journal of Psychiatry*, 1970, **126**(9), 95–100.
39. Conway, E., & Brackbill, Y. Delivery medication and infant outcome: An empirical study. *Monographs of the Society for Research in Child Development*, 1970, **35**(4), 24–34.
40. Kolata, G. Behavioral teratology: Birth defects of the mind. *Science*, 1978, **202**, 732–734; Brackbill, Y., & Broman, S. H. Obstetrical medication and development in the first year of life. Unpublished manuscript, 1978.
41. Thompson, W. R. Influence of prenatal anxiety on emotionality in young rats. *Science*, 1957, **125**, 698–699.
42. Sontag, L. W. War and fetal maternal

relationships. *Marriage and Family Living*, 1944, **6**, 1–5.

43. Laken, M. Personality factors in mothers of excessively crying (colicky) infants. *Monographs of the Society for Research in Child Development*, 1957, **22**(64); Strean, L. P., & Peer, L. A. Stress as an etiological factor in the development of cleft palate. *Plastic and Reconstructive Surgery*, 1956, **18**(1), 1–8; Stott, D. H., & Latchford, S. A. Prenatal antecedents of child health, development, and behavior. *Journal of the American Academy of Child Psychiatry*, 1976, **15**(1), 161–191.

44. Zelazo, P. R. From reflexive to instrumental behavior. In L. P. Lipsitt (Ed.), *Developmental psychobiology: The significance of infancy*. Hillsdale, N.J.: Erlbaum, 1976. Pp. 87–104; White, B. L., & Held, R. Plasticity of sensorimotor development in the human infant. In J. Rosenblith & W. Allinsmith (Eds.), *The causes of behavior: Readings in child development and educational psychology*. (2d ed.) Boston: Allyn & Bacon, 1966, Pp. 60–70.

45. Nissen, H. W., Chow, K. L., & Semmes, J. Effects of a restricted opportunity for tactual, kinesthetic, and manipulative experience on the behavior of a chimpanzee. *American Journal of Psychology*, 1951, **64**, 485–507.

46. Scarr-Salapatek, S., & Williams, M. L. The effects of early stimulation on low-birth-weight infants. *Child Development*, 1973, **44**, 94–101.

47. Rice, R. Neurophysiological growth in prematures: Mother's aid in acceleration. Paper presented at the annual meeting of the American Psychological Association, Washington, D.C., 1976.

48. Provence, S., & Lipton, R. C. *Infants in institutions*. New York: International Universities Press, 1962.

49. Kagan, J. A conversation with Jerome Kagan. *Saturday Review of Education*, 1973, **1**(3), 41–43.

50. Kagan, J. The plasticity of early intellectual development. Paper presented at the meeting of the Association for the Advancement of Science, Washington, D.C., 1972.

51. Yarrow, L. J., Rubenstein, J. L., & Pedersen, F. A. *Infant and environment: Early cognitive and motivational development*. Washington, D.C.: Hemisphere, 1975.

52. Kohen-Raz, R. Mental and motor development of the Kibbutz, institutionalized, and home-reared infants in Israel. *Child Development*, 1968, **39**, 489–504; Beit-Hallahmi, B., & Rabin, A. I. The kibbutz as a social experiment and as a child-rearing laboratory. *American Psychologist*, 1977, **32**(7), 532–541.

53. Mussen, P. H., Conger, J. J., & Kagan, J. *Child development and personality*. (4th ed.) New York: Harper & Row, 1974.

54. Skeels, H. M. Adult status of children with contrasting early life experiences. *Monographs of the Society for Research in Child Development*, 1966, **31**(3).

55. Dennis, W. *Children of the Creche*. Englewood Cliffs, N.J.: Prentice-Hall, 1974.

56. Evans, R. I. *The making of psychology*. New York: Knopf, 1976. P. 141.

57. Walsh, R. N., & Cummins, R. A. Neural responses to therapeutic sensory environments. In R. N. Walsh & W. T. Greenough (Eds.), *Environment as therapy for brain dysfunction*. New York: Plenum, 1976. Pp. 171–200; Cummins, R. A., Walsh, R. N., Buditz-Olsen, O. E. Konstantinos, T., & Horsfall, C. R. Environmentally-induced changes in the brains of elderly rats. *Nature*, 1973, **243**(5409), 516–518.

58. Heinroth, O. Cited in K. Lorenz, *Studies in animal and human behavior*. Vol. 1. Cambridge, Mass.: Harvard University Press, 1970. Pp. 125–126.

59. Lorenz, K. *King Solomon's ring*. London: Methuen, 1952.

60. Klinghammer, E. Factors influencing choice of mate in altricial birds. In H. W. Stevenson, E. H. Hess, & H. L. Rheingold (Eds.), *Early behavior: Comparative and developmental approaches*. New York: Wiley, 1967. Pp. 5–42.

61 Harlow, H. F. Love in infant monkeys. *Scientific American*, 1959, **200**(6), 68–70.

62. Evans, R. I. *The making of psychology*. New York: Knopf, 1976. P. 33.

63. Harlow, H. F. The heterosexual affectional system in monkeys. *American Psychologist*, 1962, **17**(1), 1–10; Harlow, H. F., & Harlow, M. K. Social deprivation in monkeys. *Scientific American*, 1962, **207**(5), 136–146.

64. Heath, R. G. Electroencephalographic studies in isolation-raised monkeys with behavioral impairment. *Diseases of the Nervous System*, 1972, **33**, 157–163.

65. Wachtel, M. M. Harlow explains the battered child syndrome. *American Psychological Association Monitor*, 1975, **6**(12), 3.

66. Suomi, S. J., & Harlow, H. F. Social rehabilitation of isolate-reared monkeys. *Developmental Psychology*, 1972, **6**, 487–496.

67. Robson, K. S., & Moss, H. A. Patterns and determinants of maternal attachment. *Journal of Pediatrics*, 1970, **77**(6), 976–985.

68. Scott, J. P. Critical periods in behavioral development. *Science*, 1962, **138**(3544), 949–958.

69. Kennell, J. Jerauld, R., Wolfe, H., Chesler, D., Kreger, N., McAlpine, W., Steffa, M., & Klaus, M. Maternal behavior one year after early and extended postpartum contact. *Developmental Medicine and Child Neurology*, 1975, **16**, 172–179.

70. Hales, D. How early is early contact? Defining the limits of the sensitive period. Paper presented at the meeting of the Society for Research in Child Development, New Orleans, 1977.

71. Vietze, P. M., O'Connor, S., Falsey, S., & Altemeier, W. A. Effects of rooming in on maternal behavior directed towards infants. Paper presented at the annual meeting of the American Psychological Association, Toronto, 1978.

72. Yarrow, L. J., Rubenstein, J. L., & Pedersen, F. A. *Infant and environment: Early cognitive and motivational development*. Washington, D.C.: Hemisphere, 1975; Horn, J. A baby's smile builds a bond. *Psychology Today*, 1974, **8**(4), 22.

73. Robson, K. S., & Moss, H. A. Patterns and determinants of maternal attachment. *Journal of Pediatrics*, 1970, **77**(6), 976–985.

74. Macfarlane, J. A. *The psychology of childbirth*. Cambridge, Mass.: Harvard University Press, 1977.

75. Ainsworth, M. D. S. Patterns of attachment behavior shown by the infant in interaction with his mother. *The Merrill-Palmer Quarterly of Behavior and Development*, 1964, **10**, 51–58.

76. Schaffer, H. R., & Emerson, P. E. Patterns of response to physical contact in early human development. *Journal of Child Psychology and Psychiatry*, 1964, **5**, 1–13; Moss, H. A., Robson, K. S., & Pedersen, F. Determinants of maternal stimulation of infants and consequences of treatment for later reactions to strangers. *Developmental Psychology*, 1969, **1**(3), 239–246; Rafman, S. The infant's reaction to imitation of the mother's behavior by the stranger. In T. G. Decarie (Ed.), *The infant's reaction to strangers*. New York: International Universities Press, 1974. Pp. 117–148.

77. Schaffer, H. R., & Emerson, P. E. Development of social attachments in infancy. *Monographs of the Society for Research in Child Development*, 1964, **29**(3); Ainsworth, M. D. S., & Witting, B. A. Attachment and exploratory behavior of one-year-olds in a strange situation. In B. M. Foss (Ed.), *Determinants of infant behavior*. Vol. 4. London: Methuen, 1969. Pp. 111–136.

78. Ainsworth, M. D. S. Anxious attachment and defensive reactions in a strange situation and their relationship to behavior at home. Paper presented at the biennial meeting of the Society for Research in Child Development, Philadelphia, 1973; Ainsworth, M. D. S. *Infancy in Uganda: Infant care and the growth of love*. Baltimore: Johns Hopkins University Press, 1967.

79. Smart, M. S., & Smart, R. C. *Children: Development and relationships*. (3d ed.) New York: Macmillan, 1977.

80. Baum, J. Nutritional value of human milk. *Obstetrics and Gynecology*, 1971, **37**, 126–130; Jelliffe, D., & Jelliffe, E. F. P. The uniqueness of human milk; An overview. *American Journal of Clinical Nutrition*, 1971, **24**, 1013–1024; Tank, G. Relation of diet to variation of dental caries. *Journal of the American Dental Association*, 1965, **70**, 394–403; Hodes, H. Colostrum: A valuable source of antibodies. *Obstetrics-Gynecology Observer*, 1964, **3**, 7.

81. Kulka, A. M. Observations and data on

mother-infant interactions. *Israel Annals of Psychiatry and Related Disciplines*, 1968, **6**, 70–83.

82. Homan, W. E. Parent and child: Mother's milk or other milk. *The New York Times Magazine*, June 6, 1971, 77; Schmitt, M. H. Superiority of breast-feeding: Fact or fancy. *American Journal of Nursing*, 1970, **70**(7), 1488–1493.

83. Oppel, W. C., Harper, P. A., & Rider, R. V. The age of attaining bladder control. *Pediatrics*, 1968, **42**(4), 614–626.

84. Mussen, P. H., Conger, J. J., & Kagan, J. *Child development and personality*. (5th ed.) New York: Harper & Row, 1979; MacFarlane, J. W., Allen, L., & Honzik, M. P. *A developmental study of the behavior problems of normal children between twenty-two months and fourteen years.* (*University of California Publications in Child Development*, Vol. II.) Berkeley: University of California Press, 1954; Sears, R. R., Whiting, J. W. M., Nowlis, V., & Sears, P. S. Some child-rearing antecedents of aggression and dependency in young children. *Genetic Psychology Monograph*, 1953, **47**, 135–234.

85. Bell, S. M., & Ainsworth, M. D. S. Infant crying and maternal responsiveness. *Child Development*, 1972, **43**, 1171–1190.

86. Irwin, O. C. Infant speech: Effect of systematic reading of stories. *Journal of Speech and Hearing Research*, 1960, **3**, 187–190.

87. Hess, R. D., & Shipman, V. C. Early experience and the socialization of cognitive modes. *Child Development*, 1965, **36**(4), 869–886.

88. Ainsworth, M. D. S., & Bell, S. M. Mother-infant interactions and the development of competence. In K. J. Connolly & J. Bruner (Eds.), *The growth of competence*. New York: Academic, 1974; Sroufe, L. A., & Waters, E. Attachment as an organizational construct. *Child Development*, 1977, **48**, 1184–1199.

89. White, B. L. Fundamental early environmental influences on the development of competence. Paper presented at the Western symposium on learning: Cognitive learning. Bellingham: Western Washington State, 1972.

90. Hoffman, M. L. Developmental synthesis of affect and cognition and its implications for altruistic motivation. *Developmental Psychology*, 1975, **11**, 607–622; Shatz, M. E., & Gelman, R. The development of communication skills: Modification in the speech of young children as a function of listener. *Monographs of the Society for Research in Child Development*, 1973, **38**(5), 152.

91. Kohlberg, L. Stage and sequence: The cognitive-developmental approach to socialization. In D. A. Goslin (Ed.), *Handbook of socialization theory and research*. Chicago: Rand McNally, 1969; Kohlberg, L. Continuities in childhood and adult moral development. In P. B. Baltes & K. W. Schaie (Eds.), *Life-span developmental*

psychology: Personality and socialization. New York: Academic, 1973.

92. Kurtines, W., & Greif, E. B. The development of moral thought: Review and evaluation of Kohlberg's approach. *Psychological Bulletin*, 1974, **81**, 453–470; Hoffman, M. L. Personality and social development. *Annual Review of Psychology*, 1977, **28**, 295–321.

93. Hogan, R. Moral conduct and moral character: A psychological perspective. *Psychological Bulletin*, 1973, **79**, 217–232; Casey, W. M., & Burton, R. V. Moral reasoning, values, and honesty in young children. Paper presented at the annual meeting of the American Psychological Association, Washington, D.C., 1976.

94. Krebs, R. L. Some relationships between moral judgment, attention and resistance to temptation. Unpublished Ph.D. dissertation. University of Chicago, 1967.

95. Bacon, M. K., Child, I. L., & Barry, H. A cross-cultural study of some correlates of crime. *Journal of Abnormal and Social Psychology*, 1963, **66**, 291–300.

96. Yarrow, M. R., Scott, P. M., & Waxler, C. Z. Learning concern for others. *Developmental Psychology*, 1973, **8**, 240–260.

97. Hoffman, M. L. Moral internalization, parental power, and the nature of parent-child interaction. *Developmental Psychology*, 1975, **11**(2), 228–239; Hoffman, M. L. Personality and social development. *Annual Review of Psychology*, 1977, **28**, 295–321.

98. Freedman, D. G. *Infancy: An evolutionary perspective.* Hillsdale, N.J.: Erlbaum, 1974.

99. Bower, T. G. R. Repetitive processes in child development. *Scientific American*, 1976, **235**(5), 38–47.

100. Freedman, V. G., King, J. A., & Elliot, O. Critical periods in the social development of dogs. *Science*, 1961, **133**, 1016–1017.

101. Brown, J. V. Aberrant development in infancy: Overview and synthesis. In N. R. Ellis (Ed.), *Aberrant development in infancy: Human and animal studies*. Hillsdale, N.J.: Erlbaum, 1975. Pp. 269–273.

102. Grobstein, R. Effects of early mother-infant separation. Paper presented at the annual meeting of the American Psychological Association, Washington, D.C., 1976.

103. Kotelchuck, M. The infant's relationship to the father: Experimental evidence. In M. Lamb (Ed.), *The role of the father in child development.* New York: Wiley, 1976; Fein, R. A. Research on fathering: Social policy and an emergent perspective. *Journal of Social Issues*, 1978, **34**(1), 122–135; Parke, R. D. Perspectives on father-infant interaction. In J. Osofsky (Ed.), *Handbook of infancy*. New York: Wiley, 1979.

104. Schaffer, H. R., & Emerson, P. E. Patterns of response to physical contact in early human development. *Journal of Child Psychology and Psychiatry*, 1964, **5**, 1–13; Birns, B., Blank, M., & Bridger, W. H.

The effectiveness of various soothing techniques on human neonates. *Psychosomatic Medicine*, 1966, **28**, 316–322.

Chapter 4

1. Luria, A. R. *The man with a shattered world*. New York: Basic Books, 1972. Pp. 21ff.

2. Klüver, H., & Bucy, B. C. Psychic blindness and other symptoms following bilateral temporal lobectomy in rhesus monkeys. *American Journal of Physiology*, 1937, **119**, 352–353.

3. Ward, A. A. The anterior cingular gyrus and personality. *Research Publications of the Association for Research in Nervous and Mental Disease*, 1948, **27**, 438–445; Schreiner, L., & Kling, A. Rhinencephalon and behavior. *American Journal of Physiology*, 1956, **184**, 486–490; Goddard, G. V. Functions of the amygdala. *Psychological Bulletin*, 1964, **62**, 89–109.

4. Gardner, H. Brain damage: A window on the mind. *Saturday Review*, 1975, **2**(23), 26–29.

5. Penfield, W. *The excitable cortex of conscious man.* Liverpool, England: Liverpool University Press, 1958. Pp. 25–29.

6. Penfield, W. The uncommitted cortex: The child's changing brain. *Atlantic Monthly*, 1964, **214**(1), 79–80.

7. Valenstein, E. S. History of brain stimulation: Investigations into the physiology of motivation. In E. S. Valenstein (Ed.), *Brain stimulation and motivation*. Glenview, Ill.: Scott, Foresman, 1973. P. 32.

8. Valenstein, E. S. *Brain control*. New York: Wiley, 1973.

9. Valenstein, E. S. History of brain stimulation: Investigations into the physiology of motivation. In E. S. Valenstein (Ed.), *Brain stimulation and motivation*. Glenview, Ill.: Scott, Foresman, 1973. P. 32.

10. Shepherd, G. M. Microcircuits in the nervous system. *Scientific American*, 1978, **238**(2), 93–103.

11. Kebabian, J. W., & Calne, D. B. Multiple receptors for dopamine. *Nature*, 1979, **277**, 93–96; Papeschi, R. Dopamine, extrapyramidal system and psychomotor function. *Psychiatria, Neurologia, Neurochirurgia*, 1972, **75**, 13–48; Iversen, S. D., & Iverson, L. L. Central neurotransmitters and the regulation of behavior. In M. S. Gazzaniga & C. Blakemore (Eds.), *Handbook of psychobiology*. New York: Academic, 1975. Pp. 153–200; Poirier, L. J., Bedard, P., Boucher, B., Bouvier, B., Larochelle, L., Olivier, A., Parent, A., & Singh, P. The origin of the different striato and thalamopetal neurochemical pathways and their relationships to motor activity. In F. J. Gillingham & I. M. L. Donaldson (Eds.), *Third symposium on Parkinson's disease*. Edinburgh, Scotland: Livingstone, 1969. Pp. 60–66.

12. Burroughs, W. Cited in S. H. Snyder, *Madness and the brain*. New York: McGraw-Hill, 1974. P. 203.

13. Isaacson, R. L. The myth of recovery

from early brain damage. In N. R. Ellis (Ed.), *Aberrant development in infancy: Human and animal studies.* Hillsdale, N.J.: Erlbaum, 1975. Pp. 1–25.

14. Baisden, R. Behavioral effects of hippocampal lesions after adrenergic depletion of the septal area. Unpublished doctoral dissertation. University of Florida, 1975. Cited in R. L. Isaacson, The myth of recovery from early brain damage. In N. R. Ellis (Ed.), *Aberrant development in infancy: Human and animal studies.* Hillsdale, N.J.: Erlbaum, 1975. Pp. 1–25.

15. Teuber, H. L., & Rudel, R. Behaviour after cerebral lesions in children and adults. *Developmental Medicine and Child Neurology,* 1962, **7,** 3–20; Goldman, P. S. Developmental determinants of cortical plasticity. *Acta Neurobiologiae Experimentalis,* 1972, **32,** 495–511.

16. Smith, A. Differing effects of hemispherectomy on children and adults. Paper presented at the annual meeting of the American Psychological Association, Washington, D. C., 1976.

17. Thompson, R. F. *Introduction to physiological psychology.* New York: Harper & Row, 1975. P. 75.

18. Thompson, R. F., Robertson, R. T., & Mayers, K. S. Commentary on organization of auditory, somatic sensory, and visual projection to association fields of cerebral cortex in the cat. In G. M. French (Ed.), *Cortical functioning in behavior.* Glenview, Ill.: Scott, Foresman, 1973. Pp. 38–44.

19. Levison, P. K., & Flynn, J. P. The objects attacked by cats during stimulation of the hypothalamus. *Animal Behavior,* 1965, **13,** 217–220.

20. Flynn, J. P. The neural basis of aggression in cats. In D. C. Glass (Ed.), *Neurophysiology and emotion.* New York: Rockefeller University Press, 1967.

21. Glickstein, M., & Gibson, A. R. Visual cells in the pons of the brain. *Scientific American,* 1976, **235**(5), 90–98.

22. Moruzzi. G., & Magoun, H. W. Brain stem reticular formation and activation of the EEG. *Electroencephalography and Clinical Neurophysiology,* 1949, **1,** 455–473.

23. French, J. D. The reticular formation. *Scientific American,* 1957, **196,** 54–60.

24. Lindsley, D. B., Schreiner, L. H., Knowles, W. B., & Magoun, H. W. Behavioral and EEG changes following chronic brain stem lesions in the cat. *Electroencephalography and Clinical Neurophysiology,* 1950, **2,** 483–498.

25. Thompson, R. F. *Introduction to physiological psychology.* New York: Harper & Row, 1975.

26. Sperry, R. W. The great cerebral commissure. *Scientific American,* 1964, **210,** 42–62.

27. McGlone, J. Sex differences in functional brain asymmetry. *Cortex,* 1978, **14**(1), 122–128; Levy, J. Lateral specialization of the human brain: Behavioral manifestations and possible evolutionary

basis. In J. Kiger (Ed.), *The biology of behavior.* Corvallis: Oregon State University Press, 1973; Gullahorn, J. E., & Witelson, S. F. Sex-related factors in cognition and in brain lateralization. In J. E. Gullahorn (Ed.), *Psychology and women: In transition.* Washington, D.C.: Winston, 1979. Pp. 9–35.

28. Levy, J. Psychological implications of bilateral asymmetry. In S. J. Dimond & J. G. Beaumont (Eds.), *Hemisphere function in the human brain.* New York: Halsted, 1974. Pp. 121–183.

29. Gazzaniga, M. S. *The bisected brain.* New York: Appleton-Century-Crofts, 1970; Levy, J. Psychological implications of bilateral asymmetry. In S. J. Dimond & J. G. Beaumont (Eds.), *Hemisphere function in the human brain.* New York: Halsted, 1974. Pp. 121–183; Kimura, D., & Durnford, M. Normal studies on the function of the right hemisphere in vision. In S. J. Dimond & J. G. Beaumont (Eds.), *Hemisphere function in the human brain.* New York: Halsted, 1974. Pp. 25–47; Kimura, D. The asymmetry of the human brain. *Scientific American,* 1973, **228**(3), 70–78.

30. Sperry, R. W. Lateral specialization in the surgically separated hemispheres. In F. O. Schmitt & F. G. Worden (Eds.), *The neurosciences: Third study program.* Cambridge, Mass.: MIT Press, 1974. P. 11.

31. Gardner, H. *The shattered mind: The person after brain damage.* New York: Knopf, 1976.

32. Sackeim, H. A., Gur, R. C., & Saucy, M. C. Emotions are expressed more intensely on the left side of the face. *Science,* 1978, **202**(4366), 434–436.

33. Joynt, R. J., & Goldstein, M. N. Minor cerebral hemisphere. In W. J. Friedlander (Ed.), *Advances in neurology.* Vol. 7. New York: Raven, 1975. Pp. 147–180.

34. Gazzaniga, M. S. *The bisected brain.* New York: Appleton-Century-Crofts, 1970; Z lens device aids brain research. *American Psychological Association Monitor,* 1975, **6**(9–10), 19.

35. Levy, J., Trevarthen, C., & Sperry, R. W. Perception of bilateral chimeric figures following hemisphere deconnection. *Brain,* 1972, **95,** 66–78.

36. Gazzaniga, M. S., & Le Doux, J. E. *The integrated mind.* New York: Plenum, 1978.

37. Gazzaniga, M. S. *The bisected brain.* New York: Appleton-Century-Crofts, 1970. P. 107.

38. Levy, J. Variations in the lateral organization of the human brain. Master lecture in brain-behavior relationships presented at the annual meeting of the American Psychological Association, San Francisco, 1977.

39. Galin, D., & Ornstein, R. E. Lateral specialization of cognitive mode: An EEG study. *Psychophysiology,* 1972, **9,** 412–418.

40. Kinsbourne, M. Eye and head turning indicates cerebral lateralization. *Science,* 1972, **176,** 539–541.

41. Kimura, D., & Durnford, M. Normal studies on the function of the right hemisphere in vision. In S. J. Dimond & J. G. Beaumont (Eds.), *Hemisphere function in the human brain.* New York: Halsted, 1974. Pp. 25–47.

42. Ornstein, R. Physiological studies of consciousness. Master lecture in brain-behavior relationships presented at the annual meeting of the American Psychological Association, San Francisco, 1977.

43. Gazzaniga, M. S., & Le Doux, J. E. *The integrated mind.* New York: Plenum, 1978.

44. Ornstein, R. *The psychology of consciousness.* (2d ed.) New York: Viking, 1977; Ornstein, R. The split and whole brain. *Human Nature,* 1978, **1**(5), 76–83.

45. Levy, J. Variations in the lateral organization of the human brain. Master lecture in brain-behavior relationships presented at the annual meeting of the American Psychological Association, San Francisco, 1977.

46. Goleman, D. A new computer test of the brain. *Psychology Today,* 1976, **9**(12), 44–48.

47. Fisher, A. E. Chemical stimulation of the brain. In R. C. Atkinson (Ed.), *Contemporary Psychology.* San Francisco: Freeman, 1971. Pp. 31–39.

48. Valenstein, E. S. *Brain control.* New York: Wiley, 1973.

49. Snyder, S. H. Opiate receptors and internal opiates. *Scientific American,* 1977, **236**(3), 44–56; Blakemore, C. *Mechanics of the mind.* Cambridge, England: Cambridge University Press, 1977; Fields, H. L. Secrets of the placebo. *Psychology Today,* 1978, **12**(6), 172.

Chapter 5

1. Von UexKull, J. V. *Umwelt and innenwelt der tiere.* Berlin: Jena, 1909. Cited in I. Eibl-Eibesfeldt, *Ethology: The biology of behavior.* (E. Klinghammer, trans.) New York: Holt, Rinehart, 1970, and in A. M. Snyder & B. Tarshis, *An introduction to physiological psychology.* New York: Random House, 1975.

2. Eibl-Ebesfeldt, I. *Ethology: The biology of behavior.* New York: Holt, Rinehart, 1970.

3. Pavlov, I. *Conditioned reflexes: An investigation of the physiological activity of the cerebral cortex.* Oxford, England: Clarendon, 1927. In J. Kagan, M. M. Haith, & C. Caldwell (Eds.), *Psychology: Adapted readings.* New York: Harcourt Brace, 1971. Pp. 29–35.

4. J ones, M. C. A laboratory study of fear: The case of Peter. *Pedagogical Seminary,* 1924, **31,** 308–315; Watson, J. B., & Rayner, R. Conditioned emotional reaction. *Journal of Experimental Psychology,* 1920, **3,** 1–4.

5. Jones, M. C. A laboratory study of fear: The case of Peter. *Pedagogical Seminary,* 1924, **31,** 310–311.

6. Watson, J. B., & Rayner, R. Conditioned

emotional reaction. *Journal of Experimental Psychology*, 1920, **3**, 1–4.

7. Thorndike, E. L. Animal intelligence: An experimental study of the associative processes in animals. Doctoral dissertation. Columbia University, 1898. P. 13.

8. Craighead, W. E., Kazdin, A. E., & Mahoney, M. J. *Behavior modification: Principles, issues, and applications.* Boston: Houghton Mifflin, 1976; Bootzin, R. R. *Behavior modification and therapy: An introduction.* Cambridge, Mass.: Winthrop, 1975.

9. Turkat, I. D., & Feuerstein, M. Behavior modification and the public misconception. *American Psychologist*, 1978, **33**(2), 194.

10. Woolfolk, A. E., Woolfolk, R. L., & Wilson, G. T. A rose by any other name. . . . : Labeling bias and attitudes toward behavior modification. *Journal of Consulting and Clinical Psychology*, 1977, **45**(2), 184–191.

11. Farber, I. E., Harlow, H. F., & West, L. J. Brainwashing, conditioning and DDD (Debility, dependency, and dread). *Sociometry*, 1957, **20**, 271–283.

12. Skinner, B. F. A case history in scientific method. *American Psychologist*, 1956, **11**, 226.

13. Ferster, C. B., & Skinner, B. F. *Schedules of reinforcement.* New York: Appleton-Century-Crofts, 1957.

14. Hall, R. V., Axelrod, S., Tyler, L., Grief, E., Jones, F. C., & Robertson, R. Modification of behavior problems in the home with a parent as observer and experimenter. *Journal of Applied Behavior Analysis*, 1972, **5**, 53–64; Brackbill, Z., & Kappy, M. S. Delay of reinforcement and retention. *Journal of Comparative and Physiological Psychology*, 1962, **55**, 14–18.

15. Salzinger, K., Feldman, R. S., Cowan, J. E., & Salzinger, S. Operant conditioning of verbal behavior of two young speech-deficient boys. In L. Krasner & L. Ullman (Eds.), *Research in behavior modification.* New York: Holt, Rinehart, 1965. Pp. 82–106.

16. Williams, C. D. The elimination of tantrum behavior by extinction procedures. *Journal of Abnormal and Social Psychology*, 1959, **59**, 269.

17. Reese, E. P., with Howard, J., & Reese, T. W. *Human behavior: Analysis and application.* (2d ed.) Dubuque, Iowa: Brown, 1978. P. 24.

18. Solomon, R. L. Punishment. *American Psychologist*, 1964, **19**, 239–253.

19. Redd, W. H., Morris, E. K., & Martin, J. A. Effects of positive and negative adult-child interactions on children's social preferences. *Journal of Experimental Child Psychology*, 1975, **19**, 153–164.

20. Ulrich, R. E., & Azrin, N. H. Reflexive fighting in response to aversive stimulation. *Journal of the Experimental Analysis of Behavior*, 1962, **5**, 511–520.

21. Bandura, A., Ross, D., & Ross, S. A. Imitation of film-mediated aggressive models. *Journal of Abnormal and Social Psychology*, 1963, **66**, 3–11; Steuer, F. B., Applefield, J. M., & Smith, R. Televised aggression and the interpersonal aggression of preschool children. *Journal of Experimental Child Psychology*, 1971, **11**, 442–447.

22. Bush, S. Predicting and preventing child abuse. *Psychology Today*, 1978, **11**(8), 97; Steele, B. F., & Pollock, C. B. A psychiatric study of parents who abuse infants and small children. In R. E. Helfer & C. H. Kemp (Eds.), *The battered child.* Chicago: University of Chicago Press, 1968. Pp. 103–133.

23. Parke, R. D. Effectiveness of punishment as an interaction of intensity, timing, agent nurturance and cognitive structuring. *Child Development*, 1969, **40**, 213–235; Sears, R. R., Maccoby, E., & Levin, H. *Patterns of child rearing.* Evanston, Ill.: Row, Peterson, 1957; Carlsmith, J. M., Lepper, M. R., & Landauer, T. K. Children's obedience to adult requests: Interactive effects of anxiety arousal and apparent punitiveness of the adult. *Journal of Personality and Social Psychology*, 1974, **30**, 822–828.

24. Walters, G. C., & Grusec, J. E. *Punishment.* San Francisco: Freeman, 1977.

25. O'Leary, S. G. The use of punishment with normal children. Paper presented at the annual meeting of the Association for the Advancement of Behavior Therapy, New York, 1976.

26. Azrin, N. H., & Holz, W. C. Punishment. In W. K. Honig (Ed.), *Operant behavior: Areas of research and application.* New York: Appleton-Century-Crofts, 1966.

27. Romanczyk, R. G. The use of punishment with children: Procedures and ethics. Unpublished manuscript, 1978.

28. Solomon, R. L., Turner, L. H., & Lessac, M. S. Some effects of delay of punishment on resistance to temptation in dogs. *Journal of Personality and Social Psychology*, 1968, **8**, 233–238; Birnbrauer, J. S. Generalization of punishment effects: A case study. *Journal of Applied Behavior Analysis*, 1968, **1**, 201–211; Walters, R. H., Parke, R. D., & Cane, V. A. Timing of punishment and the observation of consequences to others as determinants of response inhibition. *Journal of Experimental Child Psychology*, 1965, **2**, 10–30.

29. Aronfreed, J. The internalization of social control through punishment: Experimental studies of the role of conditioning and the second signal system in the development of conscience. *Proceedings of the 18th International Congress of Psychology.* Moscow, 1966.

30. Andres, D. H. Modification of delay-of-punishment effects through cognitive restructuring. Unpublished doctoral thesis. University of Waterloo, 1967. Cited in G. C. Walters & J. E. Grusec, *Punishment.* San Francisco: Freeman, 1977.

31. Azrin, N. H., & Holz, W. C. Punishment. In W. K. Honig (Ed.), *Operant behavior: Areas of research and application.* New York: Appleton-Century-Crofts, 1966.

32. Perry, D. G., & Parke, R. D. Punishment and alternative response training as determinants of response inhibition in children. *Genetic Psychology Monographs*, 1975, **91**, 257–279.

33. Bernal, M. Training parents in child management. In R. H. Bradfield (Ed.), *Behavior modification of learning disabilities.* San Rafael, Calif.: Academic Therapy Publications, 1971. Pp. 41–67.

34. Pierrel, R., & Sherman, J. G. Barnabus, the rat with college training. *Brown Alumni Monthly*, February 1963, 8–14.

35. Skinner, B. F. *Science and human behavior.* New York: Macmillan, 1953.

36. Kimmel, H. D. Instrumental conditioning of autonomically mediated responses in human beings. *American Psychologist*, 1974, **29**(5), 325–335.

37. Wenger, M. A., & Bagchi, B. K. Studies of autonomic functions in practitioners of Yoga in India. *Behavioral Science*, 1961, **6**, 312–323; Bagchi, B. K., & Wenger, M. A. Electrophysiological correlates of some Yogi exercises. *Electroencephalography and Clinical Neurophysiology*, 1957, **7**, 132–149.

38. Miller, N. E. Learning of visceral and glandular responses. *Science*, 1969, **163**, 434–445.

39. Miller, N. E., & Dworkin, B. R. Visceral learning: Recent difficulties with curarized rats and significant problems for human research. In P. A. Obrist, A. H. Black, J. Brener, & L. V. DiCara (Eds.), *Contemporary trends in cardiovascular psychophysiology.* Chicago: Aldine-Atherton, 1974. Pp. 312–331; Miller, N. E. Biofeedback and visceral learning. *Annual Review of Psychology*, 1978, **29**, 373–404.

40. Harris, A. H., & Brady, J. V. Animal learning—Visceral and autonomic conditioning. *Annual Review of Psychology*, 1974, **25**, 107–133.

41. Mayr, O. The origins of feedback control. *Scientific American*, 1970, **223**, 111.

42. Engel, B. T., & Bleecker, E. R. Application of operant conditioning techniques to the control of the cardiac arrhythmias. In P. O. Obrist, A. H. Black, J. Brener, & L. V. DiCara (Eds.), *Contemporary trends in cardiovascular psychophysiology.* Chicago: Aldine-Atherton, 1974. Pp. 456–476; Miller, N. E. Biofeedback: Evaluation of a new technique. *New England Journal of Medicine*, 1974, **290**, 684–685.

43. Fuller, G. D. Current status of biofeedback in clinical practice. *American Psychologist*, 1978, **33**(1), 39–48.

44. Miller, N. E. Biofeedback and visceral learning. *Annual Review of Psychology*, 1978, **29**, 373–404.

45. Ivanov-Smolensky, A. G. *Methods of investigation of conditioned reflexes in* *man*. Moscow: Medical State Press, 1933. Cited in N. Schneiderman, *Classical (Pavlovian) conditioning*. Morristown, N.J.: General Learning Corp., 1973.

46. Rescorla, R. A. Pavlovian excitatory and inhibitory conditioning. In W. K. Estes (Ed.), *Handbook of learning and cognitive processes*. Vol. 2: Conditioning and behavior theory. Hillsdale, N.J.: Erlbaum, 1975. Pp. 7–36; Bolles, R. D. Reinforcement, expectancy, and learning. *Psychological Review*, 1972, **79**(5), 394–409; Bandura, A. Behavior theory and the models of man. Paper presented at the annual meeting of the American Psychological Association, New Orleans, 1974.

47. Testa, T. J. Causal relationships and the acquisition of avoidance responses. *Psychological Review*, 1974, **81**, 491–505.

48. Seligman, M. E. P. On the generality of the laws of learning. *Psychological Review*, 1970, **77**(5), 406.

49. Breland, K., & Breland, M. The misbehavior of organisms. *American Psychologist*, 1961, **16**, 681–684.

50. Bregman, E. An attempt to modify the emotional attitude of infants by the conditioned response technique. *Journal of Genetic Psychology*, 1934, **45**, 169–198.

51. Ohman, A., Erixon, G., & Löfberg, I. Phobias and preparedness: Phobic versus neutral pictures as conditioned stimuli for human autonomic responses. *Journal of Abnormal Psychology*, 1975, **84**, 41–45.

52. Allison, J., Larson, D., & Jensen, D. D. Acquired fear, brightness preference, and one way shuttlebox performance. *Psychonomic Science*, 1967, **8**, 269–270.

53. Garcia, J., McGowan, B. K., Ervin, F. R., & Koelling, R. A. Cues: Their relative effectiveness as a function of the reinforcer. *Science*, 1968, **160**, 794–795.

54. Richter, C. P. Total self-regulatory functions in animals and human beings. *The Harvey Lectures*, 1942, **38**, 63–103.

55. Wilcoxon, H. C., Dragoin, W. B., & Kral, P. A. Illness-induced aversions in rat and quail: Relative salience of visual and gustatory cues. *Science*, 1971, **171**, 826–828; Braveman, N. S. Poison-based avoidance learning with flavored or colored water in guinea pigs. *Learning and Motivation*, 1975, **6**, 512–534; Johnson, C., Beaton, R., & Hall, K. Poison-based avoidance learning in non-human primates: Use of visual cues. *Physiology of Behavior*, 1975, **14**, 403–407.

56. Meltzoff, A. N., & Moore, M. K. Imitation of facial and manual gestures by human neonates. *Science*, 1977, **198**(4312), 75–78.

57. Kiester, E., & Cudhea, D. Albert Bandura: A very modern model. *Human Behavior*, 1974, **3**(9), 26–31.

58. Evans, R. I. *The making of psychology: Discussions with creative contributors*. New York: Knopf, 1976. Pp. 242–254.

59. Bandura, A. Analysis of modeling processes. In A. Bandura (Ed.), *Psychological modeling*. Chicago: Aldine, 1971. Pp. 1–62.

60. *Washington Post*, Nov. 1, 1962.

61. Bandura, A., & Walters, R. H. *Social learning and personality development*. New York: Holt, Rinehart, 1963.

62. Eibl-Eibesfeldt, I. *Ethology: The biology of behavior*. New York: Holt, Rinehart, 1970.

63. Mecchi, B., & Parrott, G. L. Children's fears. Paper presented at the annual convention of the Western Psychological Association, San Francisco, 1974.

64. Skinner, B. F. *Walden Two*. New York: Macmillan, 1948. P. 240.

65. A world of difference: B. F. Skinner and the good life. Film aired on "Nova," National Educational Television, January 1979.

66. Farris, H., & Hawkins, R. Cited in E. P. Reese, with J. Howard & T. W. Reese, *Human behavior: Analysis and application*. (2d ed.) Dubuque, Iowa: Brown, 1978.

67. Daley, M. F. The "reinforcement menu": Finding effective reinforcers. In J. D. Krumboltz & C. E. Thoresen (Eds.), *Behavioral counseling: Cases and techniques*. New York: Holt, Rinehart, 1969.

68. O'Connor, R. D. Modification of social withdrawal through symbolic modeling. In K. D. O'Leary (Ed.), *Classroom management*. New York: Pergamon, 1972.

Chapter 6

1. Kalmus, H. Inherited sense defects. *Scientific American*, 1952, **186**(5), 64–70.

2. Fox, R., Lehmkuhle, S., & Westendorf, D. Falcon visual acuity. *Science*, 1976, **192**(4236), 263–265.

3. Kalmus, H. Inherited sense defects. *Scientific American*, 1952, **186**(5), 64–70.

4. Kenshalo, D. R. Aging and touch, vibration, temperature kinesthesis and pain sensations; Schiffman, S. Taste and smell discrimination in obese, pregnant, and aged subjects. Both papers presented at the annual meeting of the American Psychological Association, Chicago, 1975.

5. Gregory, R. L. *Eye and brain: The psychology of seeing*. (2d ed.) New York: McGraw-Hill, 1973. Pp. 194–198.

6. Kalmijn, A. J. The detection of electric fields from inanimate and animate sources other than electric organs. In A. Fessard (Ed.), *Electroreceptors and other specialized receptors in lower vertebrates*. New York: Springer, 1975. Chap. 5; Griffin, D. R. *The question of animal awareness: Evolutionary continuity of mental experience*. New York: Rockefeller University Press, 1976.

7. Neisser, U. *Cognition and reality: Principles and implications of cognitive psychology*. San Francisco: Freeman, 1976. P. 9.

8. Broadbent, D. E. *Decision and stress*. London: Academic, 1971; Broadbent, D. E. The hidden preattentive processes. *American Psychologist*, 1977, **32**(2), 109–118.

9. Neisser, U. *Cognition and reality: Principles and implications of cognitive psychology*. San Francisco: Freeman, 1976.

10. Norman, D. A. *Memory and attention: An introduction to human information processing*. (2d ed.) New York: Wiley, 1976.

11. Kahneman, D. *Attention and effort*. Englewood Cliffs, N.J.: Prentice-Hall, 1973.

12. Lee, D. N. The functions of vision. In H. I. Pick & E. Saltzman (Eds.), *Modes of perceiving and processing information*. Hillsdale, N.J.: Erlbaum, 1978. Pp. 159–170.

13. Lele, P. P., & Weddell, G. The relationship between neurohistology and corneal sensibility. *Brain*, 1956, **79**, 119–154.

14. Neisser, U. *Cognition and reality: Principles and implications of cognitive psychology*. San Francisco: Freeman, 1976. P. 29.

15. Rock, I., & Harris, C. S. Vision and touch. *Scientific American*, 1967, **216**(5), 96–104.

16. Lettvin, J. Y., Maturana, H. R., Pitts, W. H., & McCulloch, W. S. Two remarks on the visual system of the frog. In W. A. Rosenblith (Ed.), *Sensory communication*. Cambridge, Mass.: MIT Press, 1961. Pp. 757–776; Lettvin, J. Y., Maturana, H. R., McCulloch, W. S., & Pitts, W. H. What the frog's eye tells the frog's brain. *Proceedings of the Institute of Radio Engineers*, 1959, **47**, 1940–1951.

17. Blakemore, C. Central visual processing. In M. S. Gazzaniga & C. Blakemore (Eds.), *Handbook of psychobiology*. New York: Academic, 1975.

18. Hubel, D. H., & Wiesel, T. N. Receptive fields and functioning architecture in two nonstriate visual areas (18 and 19) of the cat. *Journal of Neurophysiology*, 1965, **28**, 229–289; Hubel, D. H., & Wiesel, T. N. Receptive fields and functional architecture of monkey striate cortex. *Journal of Physiology*, 1968, **195**, 215–243; Rose, D., & Blakemore, C. An analysis of orientation selectivity in the cat's visual cortex. *Experimental Brain Research*, 1974, **240**, 1–17.

19. Modules of the brain. *Scientific American*, 1978, **239**(3), 97, 100.

20. Gross, C. G., Rocha-Miranda, C. E., & Bender, D. B. Visual properties of neurons in inferotemporal cortex of the macaque. *Journal of Neurophysiology*, 1972, **35**, 96–111; Gross, C. G., Bender, D. B., & Rocha-Miranda, C. E. Infero-temporal cortex: A single-unit analysis. In F. O. Schmitt & F. G. Worden (Eds.), *The Neurosciences: Third study program*. Cambridge, Mass.: MIT Press, 1974. Pp. 229–238.

21. Blakemore, C. Developmental factors in the formation of feature extracting neurons. In F. O. Schmitt & F. G. Worden (Eds.), *The neurosciences: Third study *program*. Cambridge, Mass.: MIT Press, 1974. Pp. 105–113.

22. Eimas, P. D., & Miller, J. L. Effects of selective adaption on the perception of speech and visual patterns: Evidence for feature detectors. In R. D. Walk & H. L. Pick (Eds.), *Perception and experience.* New York: Plenum, 1978. Pp. 307–345.

23. Droscher, V. B. *The magic of the senses: New discoveries in animal perception.* New York: Harper & Row, 1971. P. 3.

24. Epstein, W. (Ed.), *Stability and constancy in visual perception: Mechanisms and processes.* New York: Wiley, 1977.

25. Hochberg, J. Attention, organization, and consciousness. In D. I. Mostofsky (Ed.), *Attention: Contemporary theory and analysis.* New York: Appleton-Century-Crofts, 1970. Pp. 99–124.

26. Ross, J. The resources of binocular perception. *Scientific American*, 1976, **234**(3), 80–87.

27. Sperry, R. W. Mechanisms of neural maturation. In S. S. Stevens (Ed.), *Handbook of experimental psychology.* New York: Wiley, 1951. Pp. 236–280; Hess, E. H. Space perception in the chick. *Scientific American*, 1956, **195,** 71–80.

28. Stratton, G. M. Vision without inversion of the retinal image. *Psychological Review*, 1897, **4,** 344.

29. Rock, I. *The nature of perceptual adaptation.* New York: Basic Books, 1966; Rock, I. *An introduction to perception.* New York: Macmillan, 1975.

30. Salapatek, P., Banks, M. S., & Aslin, R. N. Pattern perception in very young infants: I. Visual acuity and accommodation. II. A critical period of the development of binocular vision. Paper presented at Symposium on the Development of Ocular Abnormalities, Temple University, 1974. Cited in M. M. Haith & J. J. Campos, Human infancy. *Annual Review of Psychology*, 1977, **28,** 251–293.

31. Maurer, D. M. Infant visual perception: Methods of study. In L. B. Cohen & P. Salapatek (Eds.), *Infant perception: From sensation to cognition. Basic visual processes.* Vol. 1. New York: Academic, 1975. Pp. 1–65.

32. Kalnins, J. V., & Bruner, J. S. The coordination of visual observation and instrumental behavior in early infancy. *Perception*, 1973, **2,** 307–314.

33. Marg, E., Freeman, D. N., Pheltzman, P., & Goldstein, P. J. Visual acuity development in human infants: Evoked potential estimates. *Investigative Opthalmology*, 1976, **15,** 150–153.

34. Slater, A. M., & Findlay, J. M. Binocular fixation in the newborn baby. *Journal of Experimental Child Psychology*, 1975, **20,** 248–273; Bornstein, M. H., Kessen, W., & Weiskopf, S. Color vision and hue categorization in young human infants. *Science*, 1975, **191,** 201–202; Peeples, D. R., & Teller, D. Y. Color vision and brightness

discrimination in two-month-old human infants. *Science*, 1975, **189,** 1102–1103.

35. Hubel, D. H., & Weisel, T. N. Receptive fields, binocular interaction and functional architecture in the cat's visual cortex. *Journal of Physiology*, 1962, **160,** 106–154; Thompson, R., Mayers, K. S., Robertson, R., & Patterson, C. J. Number coding in association cortex of the cat. *Science*, 1970, **168,** 271–273.

36. Barten, S., Birns, B., & Ronch, J. Individual differences in the visual pursuit behavior of neonates. *Child Development*, 1971, **42,** 1566–1571.

37. Salapatek, P. Pattern perception in early infancy. In L. B. Cohen & P. Salapatek (Eds.), *Infant perception: From sensation to cognition. Basic visual processes.* Vol. 1. New York: Academic, 1975. Pp. 133–248.

38. Fantz, R. The origin of form perception. *Scientific American*, 1961, **204,** 66–84.

39. Fantz, R. L., Fagan, J. F., & Miranda, S. B. Early visual selectivity as a function of pattern variables, previous exposure, age from birth and conception, and expected cognitive deficit. In L. B. Cohen & P. Salapatek (Eds.), *Infant perception: From sensation to cognition. Basic visual processes.* Vol. 1. New York: Academic, 1975. Pp. 249–345.

40. Jones-Molfese, V. J. Individual differences in neonatal preferences for planometric and stereometric visual patterns. *Child Development*, 1972, **43,** 1289–1296; Gregg, C., Clifton, R. K., & Haith, M. M. A possible explanation for the frequent failure to find cardiac orienting in the newborn infant. *Developmental Psychology*, 1976, **12,** 75–76; Jirari, C. Form perception, innate form preferences, and visually mediated head turning in the human neonate. Unpublished doctoral disertation, University of Chicago, 1970. Cited in D. G. Freedman, *Human infancy: An evolutionary perspective.* Hillsdale, N. J.: Erlbaum, 1974.

41. Gibson, E. J., & Walk, R. D. The visual cliff. *Scientific American*, 1960, **202,** 64–71; Walk, R. D. Depth perception and experience. In H. I. Pick & E. Saltzman (Eds.), *Modes of perceiving and processing information.* Hillsdale, N.J.: Erlbaum, 1978. Pp. 77–103.

42. Wald, R. D. Monocular compared to binocular depth perception in human infants. *Science*, 1968, **162,** 473–475.

43. Campos, J. Heart rate: A sensitive tool for the study of emotional development. In L. Lipsitt (Ed.), *Developmental psychology: The significance of infancy.* Hillsdale, N.J.: Erlbaum, 1976.

44. Campos, J. J., Hiatt, S., Ramsay, D., Henderson, C., & Svejda, M. The emergence of fear on the visual cliff. In M. Lewis & L. Rosenblum (Eds.), *The origins of affect.* New York: Wiley, 1977.

45. Bower, T. G. R., Broughton, J. M., &

Moore, M. K. Infant responses to approaching objects: An indicator of response to distal variables. *Perception and Psychophysics*, 1970, **9,** 193–196

46. Marg, E., Freeman, D. N., Pheltzman, P., & Goldstein, P. J. Visual acuity development in human infants: Evoked potential estimates. *Investigative Opthalmology*, 1976, **15,** 150–153.

47. von Senden, M. *Space and sight.* Glencoe, Ill.: Free Press, 1960. Cited in D. H. Hubel, Effects of distortion of sensory input on the visual system of kittens. *The Physiologist*, 1967, **10,** 17–45.

48. Riesen, A. H. Arrested vision. *Scientific American*, 1950, **183,** 16–19.

49. Chow, K. L., Riesen, A. H., & Newall, F. W. Degeneration of retinal ganglion cells in infant chimpanzees reared in darkness. *Journal of Comparative Neurology*, 1957, **107,** 27–42.

50. Ganz, L. Orientation in visual space by neonates and its modification by visual deprivation. In A. H. Riesen (Ed.), *The developmental neuropsychology of sensory deprivation.* New York: Academic, 1975. Pp. 169–210; Berry, M. Plasticity in the visual system and visually guided behavior. In A. H. Riesen & R. F. Thompson (Eds.), *Advances in psychobiology.* Vol. 3. New York: Wiley, 1976. Pp. 125–192.

51. Blakemore, C., & Cooper, G. Development of the brain depends on the visual environment. *Nature*, 1970, **228,** 477–478.

52. Hirsch, H. V. B., & Spinelli, D. N. Modification of the distribution of receptive field orientation in cats by selective visual exposure during development. *Experimental Brain Research*, 1971, **12,** 509–527; Blakemore, C., & Mitchell, D. E. Research in progress. Cited in C. Blakemore, Developmental factors in the formation of feature extracting neurons. In F. O. Schmitt & F. G. Worden (Eds.), *The neurosciences: Third study program.* Cambridge, Mass.: MIT Press, 1974. Pp. 105–113.

53. Blakemore, C., & Mitchell, D. E. Environmental modification of the visual cortex and the neural basis of learning and memory. *Nature*, 1973, **241,** 467–468; Blakemore, C. Developmental factors in the formation of feature extracting neurons. In F. O. Schmitt & F. G. Worden (Eds.), *The neurosciences: Third study program.* Cambridge, Mass.: MIT Press, 1974. Pp. 105–113.

54. Freeman, R. D., & Thibos, L. H. Electrophysiological evidence that abnormal early visual experience can modify the human brain. *Science*, 1973, **180,** 876–878.

55. Held, R., & Hein, A. Movement produced stimulation in the development of visually guided behavior. *Journal of Comparative and Physiological Psychology*, 1963, **56,** 872–876.

56. Hein, A., Held, R., & Gower, E. C. Development and segmentation of visually controlled movement by selective exposure during rearing. *Journal of Comparative and Physiological Psychology*, 1970, **73**, 181–187.

57. Hein, A., & Diamond, R. M. Independence of cat's scotopic and photopic systems in acquiring control of visually guided behavior. *Journal of Comparative and Physiological Psychology*, 1971, **76**, 31–38; Mitchell, D. E. Effects of early visual experience on the development of certain perceptual abilities in animals and man. In R. D. Walk & H. L. Pick (Eds.), *Perception and experience*. New York: Plenum, 1978. Pp. 37–75.

58. Bexton, W. H., Heron, W., & Scott, T. H. Effects of decreased variation in the sensory environment. *Canadian Journal of Psychology*, 1954, **8**, 70–76.

59. Heron, W., Doane, B. K., & Scott, T. H. Visual disturbance after prolonged perceptual isolation. *Canadian Journal of Psychology*, 1956, **10**, 13–16.

60. Zubeck, J. P. Behavioral and physiological effects of prolonged sensory and perceptual deprivation: A review. In J. Rasmussen (Ed.), *Man in isolation and confinement*. Chicago: Aldine, 1973. Pp. 9–83.

61. Heron, W. The pathology of boredom. *Scientific American*, 1957, **196**(1), 52–56.

62. Kammerman, M. (Ed.), *Sensory isolation and personality change*. Springfield, Ill.: Thomas, 1977.

63. Hastorf, A. H., & Cantril. H. A. They saw a game: A case study. *Journal of Abnormal and Social Psychology*, 1954, **49**, 129–134.

64. Lambert, W. W., Solomon, R. L., & Watson, P. D. Reinforcement and extinction as factors in size estimation. *Journal of Experimental Psychology*, 1949, **39**, 637–641.

65. Postman, L., Bruner, B., & McGinnies, E. Personal values as selective factors in perception. *Journal of Abnormal and Social Psychology*, 1948, **43**, 142–154.

66. Turnbull, C. Some observations regarding the experiences and behavior of the BaMbuti Pygmies. *American Journal of Psychology*, 1961, **74**, 305.

67. Segall, M. H., Campbell, D. T., & Herskovitz, M. J. Cultural differences in the perception of geometric illusions. *Science*, 1963, **139**, 769–771.

68. Harrison, J. P. Crime busting with ESP. *This Week*, Feb. 26, 1961, 21.

69. Hansel, C. E. M. *ESP: A scientific evaluation*. New York: Scribner's, 1966.

70. Rhine, J. B., & Pratt, J. G. *Parapsychology: Frontier science of the mind*. Springfield, Ill.: Thomas, 1957; Wolman, W. B., with Dale, L. A., Schmeidler, G. R., & Ullman, M. (Eds.), *Handbook of parapsychology*. New York: Van Nostrand Reinhold, 1977.

71. Schmeidler, G. R., & McConnell, R. A. *ESP and personality patterns*. New Haven, Conn.: Yale University Press, 1958.

72. Tart, C. T. *Learning to use extrasensory perception*. Chicago: University of Chicago Press, 1976.

73. Horn, J. ESP: The psychologists still want to be shown. *Psychology Today*, 1978, **11**(11), 22–23.

74. Hebb, D. O. The role of neurological ideas in psychology. *Journal of Personality*, 1951, **20**, 45.

75. Rensberger, B. False tests peril psychic research. *The New York Times*, Aug. 20, 1974, 16.

76. Thurstone, L. L. *A factorial study of perception*. Chicago: University of Chicago, 1944; Livson, N. Developmental changes in the perception of incomplete pictures. Unpublished paper, 1962. Cited in D. Krech, R. S. Crutchfield, & N. Livson, *Elements of psychology*. (3d ed.) New York: Knopf, 1974.

77. Targ, R., & Puthoff, H. Information transmission under conditions of sensory shielding. *Nature*, 1974, **251**, 602–607.

78. Randi, J. The psychology of conjuring. *Technology Review*, 1978, **80**(3), 56–63; Asher, J. Geller demystified? *American Psychological Association Monitor*, **7**(2), 1976, 4, 10; Zwinge, J. (The amazing Randi). *The magic of Uri Geller*. New York: Ballantine, 1975.

Chapter 7

1. James W. *The varieties of religious experience*. New York: New American Library, 1958. P. 298.

2. Joyce, J. *Ulysses*. New York: Modern Library, 1961. Pp. 781–782.

3. Vogel, G., Foulkes, D., & Trosman, H. Ego functions and dreaming during sleep onset. *Archives of General Psychiatry*, 1966, **14**, 238–248.

4. Hilgard, E. R. *Hypnotic susceptibility*. New York: Harcourt, Brace, 1965. P. 13.

5. Berg, O. M. In R. W. Davidson (Ed.), *Documents on contemporary dervish communities*. London: Hoopoe, 1966. Pp. 10–11.

6. Masters, R. E. L., & Houston, J. *The varieties of psychedelic experiences*. New York: Holt, Rinehart, 1966. P. 10.

7. Natsoulis, T. Consciousness. *American Psychologist*, 1978, **33**(10), 906–914.

8. Hilgard, E. R. Consciousness and control. Paper presented at the annual meeting of the American Psychological Association. Toronto, 1978; Tart, C. T. *States of consciousness*. New York: Dutton, 1975; Shallice, T. The dominant action system: An information-processing approach to consciousness. In K. S. Pope & J. L. Singer (Eds.), *The stream of consciousness*. New York: Plenum, 1978. Pp. 117–157.

9. Weiskrantz, L., Warrington, E. K., Sanders, M. D., & Marshall, J. Visual capacity in the hemianopic field following a restricted occipital ablation. *Brain*, 1974, **97**, 709–728.

10. Tart, C. T. *States of consciousness*. New York: Dutton, 1975; Csikszentmihalyi, M. Attention and the holistic approach to behavior. In K. S. Pope & J. L. Singer (Eds.), *The stream of consciousness*. New York: Plenum, 1978. Pp. 335–358.

11. James, W. *Principles of psychology*. Vol. 1. New York: Holt, 1890. P. 402.

12. Pope, K. S. How gender, solitude, and posture influence the stream of consciousness. In K. S. Pope & J. L. Singer (Eds.), *The stream of consciousness*. New York: Plenum, 1978. Pp. 259–299.

13. Klinger, E. Modes of normal conscious flow. In K. S. Pope & J. L. Singer (Eds.), *The stream of consciousness*. New York: Plenum, 1978. Pp. 226–258.

14. Starker, S. Dreams and waking fantasy. In K. S. Pope & J. L. Singer (Eds.), *The stream of consciousness*. New York: Plenum, 1978. Pp. 302–319.

15. Luce, G. G. *Body time*. New York: Pantheon, 1971; Parlee, M. B. Diurnal, weekly, and monthly mood cycles in women and men. Paper presented at the annual meeting of the American Psychological Association, Washington, D. C., 1976.

16. Graef, R., Gianinno, S., Csikszentmihalyi, M., & Rich, E., III. The effects of instrumental thoughts and daydreams on the quality of people's everyday life experiences. Paper presented at the annual meeting of the American Psychological Association, Toronto, 1978.

17. Axelrod, J., Wurtman, R. J., & Snyder, S. H. Control of hydoxyindole D-methyltransferase activity in the rat pineal gland by environmental lighting. *Journal of Biological Chemistry*, 1965, **25**, 949–954; Richter, C. P. Sleep and activity: Their relation to the 24-hour clock. In E. M. Blass (Ed.), *The psychobiology of Curt Richter*. Baltimore: York, 1976. Pp. 128–147.

18. Agnew, H. W., Jr., & Webb, W. B. Measurement of sleep onset by EEG criteria. *American Journal of EEG Technology*, 1972, **12**(3), 127–134; Agnew, H. W., Jr., & Webb, W. B. Sleep latencies in human subjects: Age, prior wakefulness, and reliability. *Psychonomic Science*, 1971, **24**(6), 253–254.

19. Dement, W. C. *Some must watch while some must sleep*. San Francisco: Freeman, 1974.

20. Bakan, P. Dreaming, REM sleep and the right hemisphere: A theoretical integration. Second International Congress of Sleep Research, June 30, 1975.

21. Webb, W. B. *Sleep: The gentle tyrant*. Englewood Cliffs, N.J.: Prentice-Hall, 1975; Asher, L. Measuring women's sex arousal during sleep. *Psychology Today*, 1978, **12**(3), 20, 24.

22. Webb, W. B. *Sleep: The gentle tyrant*. Englewood Cliffs, N.J.: Prentice-Hall, 1975; Webb, W. B., & Agnew, H. W. *Sleep and dreams*. Dubuque, Iowa: Brown, 1973.

23. Webb, W. B., & Agnew, H. W. *Sleep and dreams*. Dubuque, Iowa: Brown, 1973.

24. Pappenheimer, J. R. The sleep factor. *Scientific American*, 1976, **235**(2), 24–29.

25. Hartmann, E. *The functions of sleep*. New Haven, Conn.: Yale University Press, 1973.

26. Webb, W. B. Sleep behavior as a biorhythm. In P. Coloquohon (Ed.), *Biological rhythms and human performance*. London: Academic, 1971. Pp. 149–177.

27. Aserinsky, E., & Kleitman, N. Regularly occurring periods of eye mobility and concomitant phenomena during sleep. *Science*, 1953, **118**, 273–274.

28. Kripke, D. F., & Sonnenschein, D. A biological rhythm in waking fantasy. In K. S. Pope & J. L. Singer (Eds.), *The stream of consciousness*. New York: Plenum, 1978. Pp. 321–332.

29. Foulkes, D. Dream reports from different stages of sleep. *Journal of Abnormal and Social Psychology*, 1962, **65**, 14–25.

30. Rechtschaffen, A., Vogel, G., & Shaikun, G. Interrelatedness of mental activity during sleep. *Archives of General Psychiatry*, 1963, **9**, 536–547.

31. Vogel, G., Foulkes, D., & Trosman, H. Ego functions and dreaming during sleep onset. *Archives of General Psychiatry*, 1966, **14**, 238–248.

32. Rechtschaffen, A. The psychophysiology of mental activity during sleep. In F. J. McGuigan & R. S. Schoonover (Eds.), *The psychophysiology of thinking*. New York: Academic, 1973. Pp. 153–205.

33. Cohen, D. B. Toward a theory of dream recall. *Psychological Bulletin*, 1974, **81**(2), 138–154; Goodenough, D. R. Dream recall: History and current status of the field. In A. M. Arkin, J. S. Antrobus, & S. J. Ellman (Eds.), *The mind in sleep: Psychology and physiology*. Hillsdale, N.J.: Erlbaum, 1978. Pp. 113–140; Herman, J. H., Ellman, S. J., & Roffwarg, H. P. The problem of NREM dream recall reexamined. In A. M. Arkin, J. S. Antrobus, & S. J. Ellman (Eds.), *The mind in sleep: Psychology and physiology*. Hillsdale, N.J.: Erlbaum, 1978. Pp. 59–92.

34. Hall, C. S. What people dream about. *Scientific American*, 1951, **184**, 60–63.

35. Kahn, E., Fisher, C., & Edwards, A. Night terrors and anxiety dreams. In A. M. Arkin, J. S. Antrobus, & S. J. Ellman (Eds.), *The mind in sleep: Psychology and physiology*. Hillsdale, N.J.: Erlbaum, 1978. Pp. 533–542; Webb, W. B. *Sleep: The gentle tyrant*. Englewood Cliffs, N.J.: Prentice-Hall, 1975.

36. Van de Castle, R. *The psychology of dreaming*. New York: General Learning, 1971; Breger, L., Hunter, I., & Lane, R. W. *The effect of stress on dreaming*. New York: International Universities Press, 1971; Hall, C. S. What people dream about. *Scientific American*, 1951, **184**, 60–63; Hall, C. S., & Van de Castle, R. *The content analysis of dreams*. New York: Appleton-Century-Crofts, 1966; Winget, D., Kramer, M., & Whitman, R. M. Dreams and demography. *Journal of the Canadian Psychiatric Association*, 1972, **17**, 203–208; Kramer, M., Winget, C., & Whitman, R. M. City dreams: A survey approach to normative dream content. *American Journal of Psychiatry*, 1971, **127**, 1350–1356.

37. Foulkes, D. Children's dreams: The changes in dreaming with age. Paper presented at the annual meeting of the American Psychological Association, Chicago, 1975.

38. Dement, W. C., & Wolpert, E. A. The relationship of eye movement, body motility, and external stimuli to dream content. *Journal of Experimental Psychology*, 1958, **55**, 543–553.

39. Bokert, E. Effects of thirst and a meaningfully related auditory stimulus on dream reports. Unpublished doctoral thesis. New York University, 1965.

40. Roffwarg, H. P., Herman, J. H., Bowe-Anders, C. E., & Tauber, E. S. The effects of sustained alterations of waking visual input on dream content: A preliminary report. In A. M. Arkin, J. S. Antrobus, & S. J. Ellman (Eds.), *The mind in sleep: Psychology and physiology*. Hillsdale, N.J.: Erlbaum, 1978.

41. Cartwright, R. D. *Night life: Explorations in dreaming*. Englewood Cliffs, N.J.: Prentice-Hall, 1977.

42. Hobson, J. A., & McCarley, R. W. The brain as a dream state generator: An activation-synthesis hypothesis of the dream process. *American Journal of Psychiatry*, 1977, **134**(12), 1335–1348.

43. Dement, W. C. *Some must watch while some must sleep*. San Francisco: Freeman, 1974.

44. Wyatt, R., Kupfer, D., Scott, J., Robinson, D., & Snyder, F. Longitudinal studies of the effect of monoamine oxidase inhibitors on sleep in man. *Psychopharmacologia*, 1969, **15**, 236–244; Kales, A., Malmstrom, E., Rickles, W., Hanley, J., Ling Tan, T., Stadel, B., & Hoedemaker, F. Sleep patterns of a pentobarbitol addict: Before and after withdrawal. *Psychophysiology*, 1968, **5**, 208; Dement, W. C. The biological role of REM sleep. In W. B. Webb (Ed.), *Sleep: An active process*. Glenview, Ill.: Scott, Foresman, 1973. Pp. 33–48.

45. Brebbia, D. R., & Paul, R. C. Sleep patterns in two species of bat, *Myotis lucifugus* (little brown) and *Eptesicus fuscus* (big brown). *Psychophysiology*, 1969, **6**, 229–230; McCormick, J. G. Relationship of sleep, respiration and anesthesia in the porpoise: A preliminary report. *Proceedings of the National Academy of Sciences* (U.S.A.), 1969, **62**, 679–703; Snyder, F. The physiology of dreaming. *Behavioral Science*, 1971, **16**, 31–44; Snyder, F. The phenomenology of dreaming. In L. Madow & L. H. Snow (Eds.), *The psychodynamic implication of the physiological study of dreams*. Springfield, Ill.: Thomas, 1970.

46. Jouvet, M. Neurophysiology of the states of sleep. *Physiological Review*, 1967, **47**, 117–177.

47. Hartmann, E. L. *The biology of dreaming*. Springfield, Ill.: Thomas, 1967.

48. Berger, R. J. Oculomotor control: A possible function of REM sleep. *Psychological Review*, 1969, **76**, 144–164.

49. Ellman, S. J., Spielman, A. J., Luck, D., Steiner, S. S., & Halperin, R. REM deprivation: A review. In A. M. Arkin, J. S. Antrobus, & S. J. Ellman (Eds.), *The mind in sleep: Psychology and physiology*. Hillsdale, N.J.: Erlbaum, 1978. Pp. 419–457.

50. Hilgard, E. R. *Hypnotic susceptibility*. New York: Harcourt, Brace, 1965.

51. Hilgard, E. R. *Hypnotic susceptibility*. New York: Harcourt, Brace, 1965.

52. Barber, T. X., & Calverley, D. S. "Hypnotic-like" suggestibility in children and adults. *Journal of Abnormal and Social Psychology*, 1963, **66**, 589–597.

53. Hilgard, J. R. Imaginative involvement: Some characteristics of the highly hypnotizable and the non-hypnotizable. *International Journal of Clinical and Experimental Hypnosis*, 1974, **22**(2), 140, 141.

54. Hilgard, J. R. *Personality and hypnosis: A study of imaginative involvement*. Chicago: University of Chicago Press, 1970; Hilgard, J. R. Imaginative involvement: Some characteristics of the highly hypnotizable and the non-hypnotizable. *International Journal of Clinical and Experimental Hypnosis*, 1974, **22**(2), 138–156.

55. Barber, T. X. Physiological effects of hypnosis. *Psychological Bulletin*, 1961, **58**, 390–419.

56. Hilgard, E. R. *Hypnotic susceptibility*. New York: Harcourt, Brace, 1965; Ruch, J. C., Morgan, A. H., & Hilgard, E. R. Behavioral predictions from hypnotic responsiveness scores when obtained with and without prior induction procedures. *Journal of Abnormal Psychology*, 1973, **82**, 543–546.

57. Hilgard, E. R. A neodissociation interpretation of pain reduction in hypnosis. *Psychological Review*, 1973, **80**, 396–411; Hilgard, E. R. *Divided consciousness: Multiple controls in human thought and action*. New York: Wiley, 1977; Hilgard, E. R. Consciousness and control. Paper presented at the annual meeting of the American Psychological Association, Toronto, 1978.

58. Spanos, N. P., & Barber, T. X. Toward a convergence in hypnosis research. *American Psychologist*, 1974, **29**(7), 500–511.

59. Barber, T. X., & Ham, M. W. *Hypnotic phenomena*. Morristown, N.J.: General Learning, 1974.

60. Barber, T. X., Spanos, N. P., & Chaves, J. F. *Hypnosis, imagining, and human potentialities*. Elmsford, N.Y.: Pergamon, 1974.

61. Chaves, J. F., & Barber, T. X. Hypnotic procedures and surgery: A critical analysis with applications to acupuncture analgesia. *The American Journal of Clinical*

Hypnosis, 1976, **18**(4), 217–236; Hilgard, E. R., & Hilgard, J. R. *Hypnosis in the relief of pain*. Los Altos, Calif.: Kaufmann, 1975.

62. Ornstein, R. E. *The psychology of consciousness*. (2d ed.) New York: Harcourt Brace, 1977. P. 158.

63. Rahula, W. *What the Buddha taught*. New York: Grove, 1959. P. 71.

64. Maupin, E. W. Individual differences in response to a Zen meditation exercise. *Journal of Consulting Psychology*, 1965, **29**, 139–145.

65. Wallace, R. K., & Benson, H. The physiology of meditation. *Scientific American*, 1972, **226**(2), 84–90.

66. Otis, L. S. The facts on transcendental meditation. Part III. If well-integrated but anxious, try TM. *Psychology Today*, 1974, **7**(11), 45–46; Schwartz, G. E. Pros and cons of meditation: Current findings on physiology and anxiety, self-control, drug abuse, and creativity. Paper presented at the annual meeting of the American Psychological Association, Montreal, 1973.

67. Benson, H. *The relaxation response*. New York: Morrow, 1975.

68. Benson, H., Beary, J. F., & Carol, M. P. The relaxation response. *Psychiatry,* 1974, **37**, 37–46; Hirai, T. *Psychophysiology of Zen*. Portland, Ore.: International Scholarly Book Service, 1974.

69. Schwartz, G. E. Pros and cons of meditation: Current findings on physiology and anxiety, self-control, drug abuse, and creativity. Paper presented at the annual meeting of the American Psychological Association, Montreal, 1973.

70. Benson, H., Beary, J. F., & Carol, M. P. The relaxation response. *Psychiatry*, 1974, **37**, 37–46; Hirai, T. *Psychophysiology of Zen*. Portland, Ore.: International Scholarly Book Service, 1974; Hassett, J. Caution: Meditation can hurt. *Psychology Today*, 1978, **12**(6), 125–126.

71. Schwartz, G. E. Pros and cons of meditation: Current findings on physiology and anxiety, self-control, drug abuse, and creativity. Paper presented at the annual meeting of the American Psychological Association. Montreal, 1973.

72. Goleman, D. J., & Schwartz, G. E. Meditation as an intervention in stress reactivity. *Journal of Consulting and Clinical Psychology*, 1976, **44**(3), 456–466; Goleman, D. Meditation helps break the stress spiral. *Psychology Today*, 1976, **6**(9), 82–86, 93; Schwartz, G. E. Pros and cons of meditation: Current findings on physiology and anxiety, self-control, drug abuse, and creativity. Paper presented at the annual meeting of the American Psychological Association, Montreal, 1973.

73. Pritchard, R. M. Stabilized images on the retina. *Scientific American*, 1961, **204**(6), 72–78.

74. Jacob, R., Kraemer, H. C., & Agras, S. Relaxation therapy in the treatment of hypertension: A review. *Archives of General Psychiatry*, 1977, **34**(12), 1417–1427.

75. Gallup Poll, June 1977.

76. Yankelovich, D. Drug users vs. drug abusers: How students control their drug use. *Psychology Today*, 1975, **9**(5), 39–42; Johnston, P. M., Bachman, L. D., & O'Malley, J. G. Drug use among American high school students, 1975–1977. Washington, D.C.: National Institute on Drug Abuse, 1978.

77. Tart, C. T. Marijuana intoxication: Common experiences. *Nature*, 1970, **226**(5247), 701–704; Tart, C. T. *On being stoned: A psychological study of marijuana intoxication*. Palo Alto, Calif.: Science and Behavior, 1971.

78. Weil, A. T., Zinberg, N. E., & Nelsen, J. M. Clinical and psychological effects of marijuana in man. *Science*, 1968, **162**, 1234–1242; Melges, F. T., Tinklenberg, J. R., Hollister, L. E., & Gillespie, H. K. Marihuana and temporal disintegration. *Science*, 1970, **168**(3935), 1118–1120.

79. Melges, F. T., Tinklenberg, J. R., Hollister, L. E., & Gillespie, H. K. Marihuana and temporal disintegration. *Science*, 1970, **168**, 1118–1120; Mendelson, J. H., Rossi, A. M., & Meyer, R. E. (Eds.), *The use of marihuana: A psychological and physiological inquiry*. New York: Plenum, 1974.

80. Klonoff, H. Effects of marijuana on driving in a restricted area and on city streets: Driving performance and physiological changes. In L. L. Miller (Ed.), *Marijuana: Effects on human behavior*. New York: Academic, 1974. Pp. 359–397.

81. Mendelson, J. H., Rossi, A. M., & Meyer, R. E. (Eds.), *The use of marihuana: A psychological and physiological inquiry*. New York: Plenum, 1974.

82. Weil, A. T., Zinberg, N. E., & Nelsen, J. M. Clinical and psychological effects of marijuana in man. *Science*, 1968, **162**, 1234–1242.

83. Jones, R. T., & Stone, G. C. Psychological studies of marijuana and alcohol in man. *Psychopharmacologia* (Berlin), 1970, **18**, 108–117.

84. Science and the citizen. *Scientific American*, 1977, **236**(3), 64.

85. Mendelson, J. H., Rossi, A. M., & Meyer, R. E. (Eds.), *The use of marihuana: A psychological and physiological inquiry*. New York: Plenum, 1974.

86. Weil, A. *The natural mind: A new way of looking at drugs and higher consciousness*. Boston: Houghton Mifflin, 1973.

87. Ornstein, R. E. *The psychology of consciousness*. (2d ed.) New York: Harcourt Brace, 1977. Pp. 186–188.

88. Klein, K. E., & Wegmann, H. M. The resynchronization of human circadian rhythms after transmeridian flights as a result of flight directions and mode of activity. In L. E. Scheving, F. Halberg, & J. E. Pauly (Eds.), *Chronobiology*. Tokyo: Igaku Shoin, 1974; Goldberg, V. What can we do about jet lag? *Psychology Today*, 1977, **11**(3), 69–72.

89. Mills, J. N. Circadian rhythms during and after three months in solitude. *Journal of Physiology*, 1964, **174**, 217–231.

90. Fraisse, P. Temporal isolation, activity rhythms and time estimation. In J. E. Rasmussen (Ed.), *Man in isolation and confinement*. Chicago: Aldine, 1973. Pp. 85–97.

91. Webb, W. B. *Sleep: The gentle tyrant*. Englewood Cliffs, N.J.: Prentice-Hall, 1975.

92. Evans, R. I. *The making of psychology*. New York: Knopf, 1976. Pp. 121–132.

93. Walsh, D. H. Interactive effects of alpha feedback and instructional set. *Psychophysiology*, 1974, **11**(4), 428–435.

94. Travis, T. A., Condo, C. Y., & Knott, J. R. Alpha conditioning: A controlled study. *Journal of Nervous and Mental Disease*, 1974, **158**(3), 163–173; Lynch, J. J., Paskewitz, D. A., & Orne, M. T. Intersession stability of human alpha rhythm densities. *Electroencephalography and Clinical Neurophysiology*, 1975, **36**, 538–540.

95. Berg, O. M. In R. W. Davidson (Ed.), *Documents on contemporary dervish communities*. London: Hoopoe, 1966. Pp. 10–11.

96. Siegel, R. K. Hallucinations. *Scientific American*, 1977, **237**(4), 132–140.

97. Maugh, T. H. Marihuana. Does it damage the brain? *Science*, 1974, **185**(4153), 775–776.

98. Le Dain, G., Lehmann, H., & Stein, J. P. *A report of the commission of inquiry into the non-medical use of drugs*. Ottawa: Information Canada, 1972; Dornbush, R. L. Long-term effects of cannabis use. In L. L. Miller (Ed.), *Marijuana: Effects on human behavior*. New York: Academic, 1974. Pp. 221–232.

99. Cohen, S., & Stillman, R. C. (Eds.), *The therapeutic potential of marihuana*. New York: Plenum, 1976.

Chapter 8

1. Luria, A. R. *The mind of a mnemonist*. New York: Basic Books, 1968. Pp. 7–12, 28.

2. Tulving, E., & Donaldson, W. (Eds.), *Organization of memory*. New York: Academic, 1972.

3. Atkinson, R. C., & Shiffrin, R. M. The control of short-term memory. *Scientific American*, 1971, **224**, 82–90.

4. Craik, F. I. M., & Tulving, E. Depth of processing and retention of words in episodic memory. *Journal of Experimental Psychology*, 1975, **104**(3), 268–294.

5. Mechanic, A. The responses involved in rote learning of verbal materials. *Journal of Verbal Learning and Verbal Behavior*, 1964, **3**, 30–36; Mechanic, A., & Mechanic, J. D. Response activities and the mechanism of selectivity in incidental learning. *Journal of Verbal Learning and Verbal Behavior*, 1967, **6**, 389–397.

6. Atkinson, R. C., Hermann, S. J., & Wescourt, K. J. Search processes in recognition memory. In R. L. Solso (Ed.), *Theories in cognitive psychology: The Loyola symposium*. Potomac, Md.: Erlbaum, 1974. Pp. 101–146; Shiffrin, R. M. Short-term store: The basis for a memory system. In F. R. Restle, R. M. Shiffrin, N. J. Castellan, H. R. Lindman, & D. B. Pisoni (Eds.), *Cognitive theory.* Hillsdale, N.J.: Erlbaum, 1975. Pp. 193–218.

7. Postman, L., & Rau, L. Retention as a function of the method of measurement. *University of California Publication in Psychology*, 1957, **8,** 217–270.

8. Watkins, M. J., & Tulving, E. Episodic memory: When recognition fails. *Journal of Experimental Psychology (General)*, 1975, **104**(1), 5–29.

9. Loftus, G. R., & Loftus, E. F. *Human memory: The processing of information.* Hillsdale, N.J.: Erlbaum, 1975.

10. Sakitt, B. Locus of short-term visual storage. *Science*, 1975, **190,** 1318–1319.

11. Lindsay, P. H., & Norman, D. A. *Human information processing: An introduction to psychology.* (2d ed.) New York: Academic, 1977.

12. Sperling, G. The information available in brief visual presentations. *Psychological Monographs*, 1960, **74,** 1–29.

13. Haber, R. N., & Standing, L. G. Direct measures of short-term visual storage. *Quarterly Journal of Experimental Psychology*, 1969, **21**(1), 43–54.

14. Sperling, G. The information available in brief visual presentations. *Psychological Monographs*, 1960, **74,** 1–29.

15. Sperling, A. A model for visual memory tasks. *Human Factors*, 1963, **5,** 19–39.

16. Milner, B. Amnesia following operation on the temporal lobes. In C. W. M. Whitty & O. L. Zangwill (Eds.), *Amnesia.* London: Butterworth, 1966. Pp. 109–133.

17. Corkin, S. Acquisition of motor skill after bilateral medial temporal lobe excision. *Neuropsychologia*, 1968, **6,** 255–265.

18. Warrington, E. K., & Shallice, T. Neuropsychological evidence of visual storage in short term memory tasks. *Quarterly Journal of Experimental Psychology*, 1972, **24,** 30–40.

19. Glanzer, M., & Cunitz, A. R. Two storage mechanisms in free recall. *Journal of Verbal Learning and Verbal Behavior*, 1966, **5,** 351–360; Postman, L., & Phillips, L. W. Short-term temporal changes in free recall. *Quarterly Journal of Experimental Psychology*, 1965, **17,** 132–138.

20. Rundus, D. Analysis of rehearsal processes in free-recall. *Journal of Experimental Psychology*, 1971, **89,** 63–77.

21. Miller, G. A. The magical number seven, plus or minus two: Some limits on our capacity for processing information. *Psychological Review*, 1956, **63,** 81–97.

22. Broadbent, D. E. The magic number seven after fifteen years. In A. Kennedy & A. Wilkes (Eds.), *Studies in long-term memory.* New York: Wiley, 1975. Pp. 3–18; Glanzer, M., & Razel, M. The size of the unit in short-term storage. *Journal of Verbal Learning and Verbal Behavior*, 1974, **13,** 114–131.

23. Conrad, R. Acoustic confusions in immediate memory. *British Journal of Psychology*, 1964, **55,** 75–84; Shulman, H. G. Semantic confusion errors in short-term memory. *Journal of Verbal Learning and Verbal Behavior*, 1972, **11,** 221–227.

24. Norman, D. A. *Memory and attention: An introduction to human information processing.* (2d ed.) New York: Wiley, 1976; Baddeley, A. D. *The psychology of memory.* New York: Basic Books, 1976.

25. Sternberg, S. Memory scanning: New findings and current controversies. *Quarterly Journal of Experimental Psychology*, 1975, **27,** 1–32.

26. Peterson, L. R., & Peterson, M. J. Short-term retention of individual verbal items. *Journal of Experimental Psychology*, 1959, **58,** 193–198.

27. Reitman, J. S. Without surreptitious rehearsal information in short-term memory decays. *Journal of Verbal Learning and Verbal Behavior*, 1974, **13,** 365–377.

28. Wickens, D. D., Born, D. G., & Allen, C. K. Proactive inhibition and item similarity in short-term memory. *Journal of Verbal Learning and Verbal Behavior*, 1963, **2,** 440–445.

29. Friedman, S. Infant habituation process. In N. R. Ellis (Ed.), *Aberrant development in infancy: Human and animal studies.* Hillsdale, N.J.: Erlbaum, 1975. Pp. 217–240.

30. Fagan, J. F. Infant recognition memory as a present and future index of cognitive abilities. In N. R. Ellis (Ed.), *Aberrant development in infancy: Human and animal studies.* Hillsdale, N.J.: Erlbaum, 1975. Pp. 187–201.

31. Campbell, B. A., & Coulter, X. The ontogenesis of learning and memory. In M. R. Rosenzweig & E. L. Bennett (Eds.), *Neural mechanisms of learning and memory.* Cambridge, Mass.: MIT Press, 1976. Pp. 209–234; Campbell, B. A., & Spear, N. E. Ontogeny of memory. *Psychological Review*, 1972, **79,** 215–237.

32. Standing, L. Learning 10,000 pictures. *Quarterly Journal of Experimental Psychology*, 1973, **25,** 207–222.

33. Shepard, R. N. The mental image. *American Psychologist*, 1978, **33**(2), 125–137.

34. Bransford, J. D., & Franks, J. J. Abstraction of linguistic ideas. *Cognitive Psychology*, 1971, **2,** 331–350.

35. Nelson, T. O., & Rothbart, R. Acoustic savings for items forgotten from long-term memory. *Journal of Experimental Psychology*, 1972, **93,** 357–360.

36. Tieman, D. G. Recognition memory for comparison sentences. Unpublished doctoral dissertation. Stanford University, 1971. Cited in G. R. Loftus & E. F. Loftus, *Human memory: The processing of information.* Hillsdale, N.J.: Erlbaum, 1975.

37. Shepard, R. N. Form, representation and transformation of internal representations. In R. Solso (Ed.), *Information processing and cognition: The Loyola symposium.* Hillsdale, N.J.: Erlbaum, 1975; Hassett, J. Memory and smell. *Psychology Today*, 1978, **11**(10), 45.

38. Norman, D. A. *Memory and attention: An introduction to human information processing.* (2d ed.) New York: Wiley, 1976; Baddeley, A. D. *The psychology of memory.* New York: Basic Books, 1976.

39. Brown, R., & McNeill, D. The "tip of the tongue" phenomenon. *Journal of Verbal Learning and Verbal Behavior*, 1966, **5,** 325–337.

40. Lindsay, P. H., & Norman, D. A. *Human information processing: An introduction to psychology.* (2d ed.) New York: Academic, 1977. P. 372.

41. Bartlett, F. C. *Remembering: A study in experimental and social psychology.* Cambridge, England: Cambridge University Press, 1950.

42. Carroll, L. *Alice's adventures in Wonderland & Through the looking glass.* Cleveland: World, 1946. P. 173.

43. Fowler, M. J., Sullivan, M. J., & Ekstrand, B. R. Sleep and memory. *Science*, 1973, **179,** 302–304.

44. Tulving, E., & Psotka, J. Retroactive inhibition in free recall. Inaccessibility of information available in the memory store. *Journal of Experimental Psychology*, 1971, **87,** 1–8.

45. Matlin, M. W., & Stang, D. J. *The Pollyanna principle: Selectivity in language, memory, and thought.* New York: Schenkman, 1978.

46. Buckhout, R. Eyewitness testimony. *Scientific American*, 1974, **231**(6), 23–31.

47. Mueller, J. H. Individual differences in anxiety and memory. Paper presented at the annual meeting of the American Psychological Association, Toronto, 1978.

48. Buckhout, R. Eyewitness testimony. *Scientific American*, 1974, **231**(6), 23–31.

49. Loftus, E. F., & Palmer, J. D. Reconstruction of automobile destruction: An example of the interaction between language and memory. *Journal of Verbal Learning and Verbal Behavior*, 1974, **13,** 585–589.

50. Brooks, L. R. Spatial and verbal components of the act of recall. *Canadian Journal of Psychology*, 1968, **22,** 349–368; Baddeley, A. D., Grant, S., Wight, E., & Thompson, N. Imagery and visual working memory. In P. M. A. Rabbitt & S. Dornic (Eds.), *Attention and performance.* London: Academic, 1975.

51. Luria, A. R. *The neuropsychology of memory.* Washington, D.C.: Winston, 1976.

52. James, W. *The principles of psychology.* Vol. I. New York: Dover, 1950. (Originally published in 1890.)

53. McGaugh, J. L. Drug facilitation of learning and memory. *Annual Review of Pharmacology*, 1973, **13,** 229–241; Fink, M. Hypothalamic peptides and brain function. In E. Usdin, D. A. Hamburg, & J. D. Barchas (Eds.), *Neuroregulators and psychiatric disorders.* New York: Oxford University Press, 1977. Pp. 296–298.

54. Bower, G. H. Organizational factors in memory. *Cognitive Psychology*, 1970, **1**, 18–46.

55. Jacoby, L. L. On interpreting the effects of repetition: Solving a problem versus remembering a solution. *Verbal Learning and Verbal Behavior*, in press.

56. James, W. *The principles of psychology*. Vol. I. New York: Dover, 1950. P. 662. (Originally published in 1890.)

57. Morris, P. Practical strategies for human learning and remembering. In M. J. A. Howe (Ed.), *Adult learning: Psychological research and applications*. London: Wiley, 1977. Pp. 125–144; Norman, D. A. *Memory and attention: An introduction to human information processing*. (2d ed.) New York: Wiley, 1976; Bower, G. H. Analysis of a mnemonic device. *American Scientist*, 1970, **58**(5), 496–510.

58. Carlson, R. F., Kincaid, J. P., Lance, S., & Hodgson, T. Spontaneous use of mnemonics and grade-point-average. *Journal of Psychology*, 1976, **92**(1), 117–122.

59. Paivio, A. Imagery and long-term memory. In A. Kennedy & A. Wilkes (Eds.), *Studies in long-term memory*. New York: Wiley, 1975. Pp. 57–85.

60. Bower, G. H., & Clark, M. C. Narrative stories as mediators for serial learning. *Psychonomic Science*, 1969, **14**(4), 181–182.

61. Craik, F. I. M., & Tulving, E. Depth of processing and retention of words in episodic memory. *Journal of Experimental Psychology*, 1975, **104**(3), 268–294.

62. Ausubel, D. P. *Educational psychology: A cognitive view*. New York: Holt, Rinehart, 1968.

63. Gates, A. J. Recitation as a factor in memorizing. *Archives of Psychology*, 1917, 6–40.

64. Howe, M. J. A. Learning and the acquisition of knowledge by students: Some experimental investigations. In M. J. A. Howe (Ed.), *Adult learning: Psychological research and applications*. London: Wiley, 1977. Pp. 145–160.

65. Robinson, F. P. *Effective study*. (Rev. ed.) New York: Harper & Row, 1961.

66. Underwood, B. J. Ten years of massed practice on distributed practice. *Psychological Review*, 1961, **68**, 229–247.

67. Krueger, W. C. F. The effect of overlearning on retention. *Journal of Experimental Psychology*, 1929, **12**, 71–78.

68. Lepper, M. R., & Greene, D. (Eds.), *The hidden costs of rewards: New perspectives on the psychology of human motivation*. Hillsdale, N.J.: Erlbaum, 1978.

69. Goodwin, D. W., Powell, B., Bremer, D., Hoine, H., & Stern, J. Alcohol and recall: State-dependent effects in man. *Science*, 1969, **163**, 1358–1360.

70. Tulving, E., & Psotka, J. Retroactive inhibition in free recall: Inaccessibility of information available in the memory store. *Journal of Experimental Psychology*, 1971, **87**, 1–8.

71. Scott, A. C. *Neurophysics*. New York: Wiley-Interscience, 1977.

72. Hydén, E., & Egyházi, E. Changes in RNA content and base composition in cortical neurons of rats in a learning experiment involving transfer of handedness. *Proceedings of the National Association of Science*, 1964, **52**, 1030–1035.

73. Rose, S. P. R., Hambley, J., & Haywood, J. Neurochemical approaches to developmental plasticity and learning. In M. R. Rosenzweig & E. L. Bennett (Eds.), *Neural mechanisms of learning and memory*. Cambridge, Mass.: MIT Press, 1976. Pp. 293–310.

74. Quartermain, D. The influence of drugs on learning and memory. In M. R. Rosenzweig & E. L. Bennett (Eds.), *Neural mechanisms of learning and memory*. Cambridge, Mass.: MIT Press, 1976. Pp. 508–518; Hydén, H. Changes in brain protein during learning. In G. B. Ansell & P. B. Bradley (Eds.), *Macromolecules and behavior*. London: Macmillan, 1973. Pp. 3–26.

75. Ungar, G. Chemical transfer of acquired information. *Proceedings of the Fifth International Congress of the Collegium Internationale Neuropsychopharmacologicum*. Amsterdam: Excerpta Medica, 1967. Pp. 169–175. Cited in A. M. Schneider & B. Tarshis, *An introduction to physiological psychology*. New York: Random House, 1975.

76. Ungar, G., Galvan, L., & Clark, R. H. Chemical transfer of learned fear. *Nature*, 1968, **217**, 1259–1261.

77. Ungar, G., Ho, I. K., Galvan, L., & Desiderio, D. M. Isolation, identification, and synthesis of a specific behavior-inducing brain peptide. *Nature*, 1972, **238**, 196–197.

78. McGaugh, J. L. Drug facilitation of learning and memory. *Annual Review of Pharmacology*, 1973, **13**, 229–241; Fink, M. Hypothalamic peptides and brain function. In E. Usdin, D. A. Hamburg, & J. D. Barchas (Eds.), *Neuroregulators and psychiatric disorders*. New York: Oxford University Press, 1977. Pp. 296–298.

79. Ferris, S. H., Sathananthian, G., Gershon, S., Clark, C., & Moshinsky, J. Cognitive effects of ACTH 4-10 in the elderly. *The neuropeptides. Pharmacology, Biochemistry, and Behavior*. Vol. 5. Supplement, 1976, 73–78.

80. Johnston, W. A. The intrusiveness of familiar nontarget information. Unpublished paper, 1977.

81. Bligh, D. M. Are teaching innovations in post-secondary education irrelevant. In M. J. A. Howe (Ed.), *Adult learning: Psychological research and applications*. London: Wiley, 1977. Pp. 249–266.

82. Olds, J. Multiple unit recording from behaving rats. In R. F. Thompson & M. M. Patterson (Eds.), *Bioelectrical Recording Techniques*. New York: Academic, 1973. Pp. 165–198.

83. Thompson, R. F. The search for the engram. *American Psychologist*, 1976, **31**(3), 209–227.

84. Thompson, R. F. *Introduction to physiological psychology*. New York: Harper & Row, 1975.

Chapter 9

1. Keller, H. *The story of my life*. Garden City, N.Y.: Doubleday, 1954. Pp. 35ff.

2. Whorf, B. L. *Language, thought, and reality*. New York: Wiley, 1956.

3. Shepard, R. N. Externalization of mental images and the act of creation. In B. S. Randhawa & W. E. Coffman (Eds.), *Visual learning, thinking, and communication*. New York: Academic, 1978.

4. Hadamard, J. *The psychology of invention in the mathematical field*. Princeton, N.J.: Princeton University Press, 1945.

5. Shepard, R. N. The mental image. *American Psychologist*, 1978, **33**(2), 125–137.

6. Hardyck, C. D., & Petrinovich, L. F. Subvocal speech and comprehension level as a function of the difficulty level of reading material. *Journal of Verbal Learning and Verbal Behavior*, 1970, **9**, 647–652.

7. Max, L. W. An experimental study of the motor theory of consciousness: IV. Action-current responses in the deaf during awakening, kinesthetic imagery and abstract thinking. *Journal of Comparative Psychology*, 1937, **24**, 301–344.

8. Gagné, R. M., & Smith, E. C. A study of the effects of verbalization on problem-solving. *Journal of Experimental Psychology*, 1962, **63**, 12–18.

9. Piaget, J. *The child's conception of a number*. New York: Norton, 1965. P. 57.

10. Piaget, J. *Play, dreams, and imitation in childhood*. New York: Norton, 1951. P. 124.

11. Piaget, J. *The origins of intelligence in children*. New York: International Universities Press, 1952. P. 335.

12. Milne, A. A. *Winnie-the-Pooh*. New York: Dutton, 1926. P. 6.

13. Mussen, P. H., Conger, J. J., & Kagan, J. *Child development and personality*. (4th ed.) New York: Harper & Row, 1974. P. 314.

14. Gelman, R., & Shatz, M. Appropriate speech adjustments: The operation of conversational constraints on talk to two-year-olds. In M. Lewis & L. Rosenblum (Eds.), *Interaction, conversation, and the development of language*. New York: Wiley, 1977.

15. Piaget, J. Intellectual evolution from adolescence to adulthood. *Human Development*, 1972, **15**, 1–12.

16. McKinnon, J. W., & Renner, J. W. Are colleges concerned with intellectual development? *American Journal of Physics*, 1971, **39**(9), 1047–1052.

17. Bower, T. G. R. Repetitive processes in child development. *Scientific American*, 1976, **235**(5), 38–47.

18. Wallach, M., & Wallach, L. *Teaching*

all children to read. Chicago: University of Chicago Press, 1976; Dasen, P. R. (Ed.), *Piagetian psychology: Cross-cultural contributions.* New York: Gardner, 1977.

19. Bower, T. G. R. The object in the world of the infant. *Scientific American,* 1971, **225**(4), 30–38.

20. Trabasso, T. R. Representation, memory and reasoning: How do we make transitive inferences? In A. D. Pick (Ed.), *Minnesota Symposium on Child Psychology,* 1975, **9,** 135–172; Bryant, P. E., & Trabasso, T. R. Transitive inferences and memory in young children. *Nature,* 1971, **232,** 456–458.

21. Gelman, R. Conservation: A problem of learning to attend to relevant attributes. *Journal of Experimental Child Psychology,* 1969, **7,** 167–187.

22. Vinacke, W. E. *The psychology of thinking.* (2d ed.) New York: McGraw-Hill, 1974.

23. Allender, D. S., & Allender, J. S. *I am the mayor.* Oxford, Ohio: Miami University Press, 1965. Cited in G. A. Davis, *Psychology of problem solving: Theory and practice.* New York: Basic Books, 1973.

24. Bloom, B. S., & Broder, L. *Problem-solving processes of college students.* Chicago: University of Chicago Press, 1950.

25. Whimbey, A. E., & Whimbey, L. S. *Intelligence can be taught.* New York: Dutton, 1975.

26. Glucksburg, S., & Weisburg, R. W. Verbal behavior and problem solving: Some effects of labeling in a functional fixedness problem. *Journal of Experimental Psychology,* 1966, **71**(5), 659–664.

27. Duncker, K. On problem solving. *Psychological Monographs,* 1945, **58**(5).

28. Shulman, L. S. The study of individual inquiry behavior. Paper presented at the annual meeting of the American Psychological Association, Washington, D.C., 1967.

29. McKenney, J. L., & Keen, P. G. W. How managers' minds work. *Harvard Business Review,* 1974, **52**(3), 79–90.

30. Whimbey, A. E., & Whimbey, L. S. *Intelligence can be taught.* New York: Dutton, 1975; de Groot, A. D. *Thought and choice in chess.* The Hague: Mouton, 1965; Bloom, B. S., & Broder, L. *Problem-solving processes of college students.* Chicago: University of Chicago Press, 1950.

31. Adamson, R. E., & Taylor, D. W. Function fixedness as related to elapsed time and to set. *Journal of Experimental Psychology,* 1954, **47,** 122–126; Olton, R. M., & Johnson, D. M. Mechanisms of incubation in creative problem solving. *American Journal of Psychology,* 1976, **89,** 617–630.

32. Köhler, W. *The task of gestalt psychology.* Princeton, N.J.: Princeton University Press, 1969.

33. Harlow, H. F. The formation of learning sets. *Psychological Review,* 1949, **56,** 61–65.

34. Scheerer, M. Problem-solving. *Scientific American,* 1968, **208**(4), 118–128.

35. Goldberg, P. Prejudice toward women: Some personality correlates. *International Journal of Group Tensions,* 1974, **4,** 53–63.

36. Luchins, A. Mechanization in problem-solving: The effect of *Einstellung. Psychological Monographs,* 1942, **54**(6).

37. Birch, H. G. The role of motivational factors in insightful problem-solving. *Journal of Comparative Psychology,* 1945, **38,** 295–317.

38. Yerkes, R. M., & Dodson, J. D. The relation of strength of stimulus to rapidity of habit formation. *Journal of Comparative Neurology and Psychology,* 1908, **18,** 459–482; Atkinson, J. W. Motivation for achievement. In T. Blass (Ed.), *Personality variables in social behavior.* Hillsdale, N.J.: Erlbaum, 1977. Pp. 25–108.

39. Hebb, D. O. *Textbook of psychology.* (3d ed.) Philadelphia: Saunders, 1972.

40. Miller, G. A. Some preliminaries to psycholinguistics. *American Psychologist,* 1965, **20,** 15–20.

41. Moynihan, M. Cited in E. O. Wilson, *Sociobiology: The new synthesis.* Cambridge, Mass.: Belknap, 1975.

42. Condon, W. S., & Sander, L. W. Neonate movement is synchronized with adult speech: Interactional participation and language acquisition. *Science,* 1974, **183,** 99–101.

43. Eimas, P. D., Siqueland, E. R., Jusczyk, P., & Vigorito, J. Speech perception in infants. *Science,* 1971, **171,** 303–306.

44. Trehub, S. E. Infants' sensitivity to vowel and tonal contrasts. *Developmental Psychology,* 1973, **9,** 91–96.

45. Eisenberg, R. B. *Auditory competence in early life: The roots of communicative behavior.* Baltimore: University Park Press, 1976.

46. Carter, A. The transformation of sensorimotor morphemes into words: A case study of the development of "more" and "mine." *Journal of Child Language,* 1975, **2,** 233–250.

47. Moskowitz, B. A. The acquisition of language. *Scientific American,* 1978, **239**(5), 96.

48. Nelson, K. Structure and strategy in learning to talk. *Monographs of the Society for Research in Child Development,* 1973, **38**(1–2, Whole No. 149).

49. Brown, R. *A first language: The early stages.* Cambridge, Mass.: Harvard University Press, 1973.

50. Brown, R., & Fraser, C. The acquisition syntax. In C. N. Cofer & B. Musgrave (Eds.), *Verbal behavior and learning: Problems and processes.* New York: McGraw-Hill, 1963. Pp. 158–201.

51. Brown, R., & Herrnstein, R. J. *Psychology.* Boston: Little, Brown, 1975.

52. Berko, J. The child's learning of English morphology. *Word,* 1958, **14,** 150–177.

53. Shenker, I. Chomsky is difficult to please, Chomsky is easy to please, Chomsky is certain to please. *Horizon,* 1971, **13**(2), 104–109.

54. Premack, D. Language and intelligence in ape and man. *American Scientist,* 1976, **64,** 674–683.

55. Weir, R. *Language in the crib.* The Hague: Mouton, 1962.

56. Curtiss, S. *Genie: A psycholinguistic study of a modern-day "wild child."* New York: Academic, 1977.

57. Moskowitz, B. A. The acquisition of language. *Scientific American,* 1978, **239**(5), 92–108.

58. Bruner, J. A. Learning the mother tongue. *Human Nature,* 1978, **1**(9), 42–49; Snow, C. E., & Ferguson, C. A. (Eds.), *Talking to children: Language input and acquisition.* Cambridge, England: Cambridge University Press, 1977; Phillips, J. R. Syntax and vocabulary of mothers' speech to young children: Age and sex comparison. *Child Development,* 1973, **44,** 182–185; Moerk, E. L. Verbal interactions between children and their mothers during the preschool years. *Developmental Psychology,* 1975, **7**(6), 788–794.

59. McLaughlin, B. Second look: The mother tongue. *Human Nature,* 1978, **1**(12), 89.

60. Brown, R., & Hanlon, C. Derivational complexity and order of acquisition. In J. R. Hayes (Ed.), *Cognition and the development of language.* New York: Wiley, 1970.

61. Braine, M. D. S. On two types of models of the internalization of grammars. In D. I. Slobin (Ed.), *The ontogenesis of grammar.* New York: Academic, 1971. Pp. 160–161.

62. Brown, R. *A first language: The early stages.* Cambridge, Mass.: Harvard University Press, 1973.

63. Wells, G. What makes for successful language development. In R. N. Campbell & P. T. Smith (Eds.), *Recent advances in the psychology of language: Language development and mother-child interaction.* New York: Plenum, 1978. Pp. 449–469.

64. Bloom, L., Hood, L., & Lightbrown, D. Imitation in language development: If, when, and why. *Cognitive Psychology,* 1974, **6,** 380–420.

65. Newport, E., Gleitman, L., & Gleitman, H. A study of mothers' speech and child language acquisition. Unpublished manuscript, 1975.

66. Descartes, R. *Discourse on method and meditations.* (Trans. by L. Lafleur.) Indianapolis: Bobbs-Merrill, 1960. P. 42.

67. Hayes, C. *The ape in our house.* New York: Harper & Row, 1951.

68. Gardner, R. A., & Gardner, B. T. Teaching sign language to a chimpanzee. *Science,* 1969, **165,** 664–672.

69. Premark, A. J., & Premack, D. Teaching language to an ape. *Scientific American,* 1972, **227,** 92–99.

70. Rumbaugh, D. M., Gill, T., & von

Glassersfeld, E. C. Reading and sentence completion by a chimpanzee. *Science*, 1973, **182,** 731–733; Rumbaugh, D. M. (Ed.), *Language learning by a chimpanzee: The LANA project.* New York: Academic, 1977.

71. Gardner, R. A., & Gardner, B. T. Teaching sign language to a chimpanzee. *Science,* 1969, 165, 664–672.

72. Fouts, R. S. Communication with chimpanzees. In E. Eibl-Eibesfeld & G. Furth (Eds.), *Hominisation and Verhalten.* Stuttgart, W. Germany: Gustav Fischer Verlag, 1974.

73. Hahn, E. Washoese. *New Yorker,* 1971, **4** (17, 46–97), (24, 46–91).

74. Fouts, R. S. In *Science Year: World Book Science Annual, 1974.* Chicago: Field, 1973.

75. Gardner, R. A., & Gardner, B. T. Teaching sign language to a chimpanzee. *Science,* 1969, **165,** 664–672.

76. Gardner, R. A., & Gardner, B. T. Early signs of language in child and chimpanzee. *Science.* 1975, **187,** 752–753.

77. Gardner, B. T., & Gardner, R. A. Evidence for sentence constituents in the early utterances of child and chimpanzee. *Journal of Experimental Psychology (General),* 1975, **104**(3), 244–267; Terrace, H. S., Petitto, L., & Bever, T. G. Project NIM: Progress Report, Jan. 30, 1976; Terrace, H. S., & Bever, T. G. What might be learned from studying language in the chimpanzee: The importance of symbolizing oneself. *Annals of the New York Academy of Sciences,* 1976, **280,** 579–588.

78. Fouts, R. S. In *Science Year: World Book Science Annual, 1974.* Chicago: Field, 1973; Gorcyca, D. A., Garner, P., & Fouts, R. Deaf children and chimpanzees: A comparative sociolinguistic investigation. Paper presented at the Speech Communication Association Convention, Houston, 1975.

79. Hans, Sherman, and Austin. *Scientific American,* 1978, **239**(5), 83, 86.

80. Patterson, F. G. The gestures of a gorilla: Language acquisition in another pongoid. *Brain and Language,* 1978, **5,** 72–97; Patterson, F. G. Progress report on project Koko, 1976. *Gorilla,* 1977, **1**(1), 2–4; Patterson, F. Conversations with a gorilla. *National Geographic,* 1978, **154**(4), 438–465.

81. Brown, R. *A first language: The early stages.* Cambridge, Mass.: Harvard University Press, 1973.

82. Brown, R. *A first language: The early stages.* Cambridge, Mass.: Harvard University Press, 1973.

83. Patterson, F. Conversations with a gorilla. *National Geographic,* 1978, **154**(4), 438–465; Woodruff, G., Premack, D., & Kennel, K. Conservation of liquid and solid quantity by the chimpanzee. *Science,* 1978, **202,** 991–994.

84. Limber, J. Language in child and chimp. *American Psychologist,* 1977, **32**(4), 280–296.

85. Mason, W. A. Environmental models and mental modes: Representational processes in the great apes and man. *American Psychologist,* 1976, **31**(4), 284–294.

86. Vandenberg, B. Play and development from an ethological perspective. *American Psychologist,* 1978, **33**(8), 724–738.

87. Donaldson, M. *Children's minds.* New York: Norton, 1979.

88. News and comment. *Human Nature,* 1978, **1**(1), 16.

89. Goldin-Meadow, S., & Feldman, H. The creation of a communication system: A study of deaf children of hearing parents. Paper presented to the Society for Research in Child Development, Denver, 1975.

90. Brown, R., & Herrnstein, R. J. *Psychology.* Boston: Little, Brown, 1975.

91. Offir, C. W. Visual speech: Their fingers do the talking. *Psychology Today,* 1976, **10**(1), 72–78.

Chapter 10

1. McClelland, D. *Power: The inner experience.* New York: Irvington, 1975. Pp. 20–213.

2. McDougall, W. *An introduction to social psychology.* London: Methuen, 1908.

3. Bernard, L. L. *Instinct: A study in social psychology.* New York: Holt, Rinehart, 1924.

4. Holt, E. B. *Animal drive and the learning process.* New York: Holt, Rinehart, 1931. P. 4.

5. Kuo, Z. Y. *The dynamics of behavior development.* New York: Random House, 1967.

6. Lee, D. Cultural factors in dietary choice. *American Journal of Clinical Nutrition,* 1957, **5,** 167.

7. Sears, R. R., Maccoby, E. E., & Levin, H. *Patterns of child rearing.* Evanston, Ill.: Row, Peterson, 1957.

8. Rohrer, J. H. Interpersonal relations in isolated small groups. In B. E. Flaherty (Ed.), *Psychophysiological aspects of space flight.* New York: Columbia University Press, 1961. Pp. 263–271.

9. Csikszentmihalyi, M. *Beyond boredom and anxiety.* San Francisco: Jossey-Bass, 1976.

10. Zuckerman, M. The sensation-seeking motive. In B. Maher (Ed.), *Progress in experimental personality research.* Vol. 7. New York: Academic, 1974.

11. Singh, S. D. Effect of urban environment on visual curiosity behavior in rhesus monkeys. *Psychonomic Science,* 1968, **11,** 83–84.

12. Murphy, D. L. Clinical, genetic, hormonal, and drug influences on the activity of human platelet monoamine oxidase. In Ciba Foundation (Ed.), *Monoamine oxidase and its inhibition.* New York: Elsevier, 1976. Pp. 341–351; Zuckerman, M. Sensation-seeking. In H. London & J. E. Exner, Jr. (Eds.), *Dimensions of personality.* New York: Wiley, 1978. Pp. 487–559.

13. Butler, R. A. Discrimination learning by rhesus monkeys to visual exploration motivation. *Journal of Comparative and Physiological Psychology,* 1953, **46,** 95–98; Berlyne, D. E. Curiosity and exploration. *Science,* 1966, **153,** 25–33.

14. Nunnally, J. C., & Lemond, L. D. Exploratory behavior and human development. In H. W. Reese (Ed.), *Advances in child development and behavior.* Vol. 8. New York: Academic, 1973. Pp. 59–109.

15. White, R. W. *The enterprise of living: A view of personal growth.* (2d ed.) New York: Holt, Rinehart, 1976.

16. Dember, W. N. Motivation and the cognitive revolution. *American Psychologist,* 1974, **24**(3), 161–168.

17. Festinger, L. A. *Theory of cognitive dissonance.* Evanston, Ill.: Row, Peterson, 1957.

18. Bem, D. J. *Beliefs, values and human affairs.* Monterey, Calif.: Brooks/Cole, 1970.

19. Wong, R. *Motivation: A biobehavioral analysis of consummatory activities.* New York: Macmillan, 1976.

20. Davis, C. M. Self-selection of diet by newly-weaned infants: An experimental study. *American Journal of Diseases of Children,* 1928, **36**(4), 651–679.

21. Richter, C. P. The self-selection of diets. In T. Cowles (Ed.), *Essays in biology.* Berkeley: University of California Press, 1943. Pp. 499–507.

22. Maslow, A. *Motivation and personality.* (2d ed.) New York: Harper & Row, 1970. P. 37.

23. Nisbett, R. E., & Wilson, T. D. Telling more than we can know: Verbal reports and mental processes. *Psychological Review,* 1977, **84**(3), 23–259; Wilson, T. D. Awareness and self-perception. Paper presented at the annual meeting of the American Psychological Association, Toronto, 1978.

24. Hoebel, B. G., & Teitelbaum, P. Weight regulation in normal and hypothalamic hyperphagic rats. *Journal of Comparative and Physiological Psychology,* 1966, **61,** 189–193; Anand, B. K., Chhina, G. S., & Singh, B. Effect of glucose on the activity of hypothalamic "feeding centers." *Science,* 1962, **138,** 597–598.

25. Ungerstedt, U. Adipsia and aphagia after 6-hydroxydopamine-induced degeneration of the nigro-striatal dopamine system. *Acta Physiologica Scandinavica,* 1971, suppl. 367, 95–122; Ahlskig, J. E., Randall, P. K., & Hoebel, B. G. Hypothalamic hyperphagia: Dissociation from hyperphagia following destruction of noradrenergic neurons. *Science,* 1975, **190,** 399–401; Gold, R. M. The myth of the ventromedial nucleus. *Science,* 1973, **182,** 448–490.

26. Valenstein, E. S., Cox, V. C., & Kakolewski, J. W. Reexamination of the role of the hypothalamus in motivation. *Psychological Review,* 1970, **77,** 16–31.

27. Cannon, W. B. Hunger and thirst. In C.

Murchison (Ed.), *Handbook of general experimental psychology*. Worcester, Mass.: Clark University Press, 1934.

28. Le Magnen, J. Peripheral and systematic actions of food in the caloric regulation of intake. *Annals of the New York Academy of Science*, 1971, **68**, 332–334; Jordan, H. A. Voluntary intragastric feeding: Oral and gastric contributions to food intake and hunger in man. *Journal of Comparative and Physiological Psychology*, 1969, **68**, 498–506.

29. Janowitz, H. D. Some factors affecting the food intake of normal dogs and dogs with esophagostomy and gastric fistula. *American Journal of Physiology*, 1949, **159**, 143–148; Kohn, M. Satiation of hunger from food injected directly into the stomach versus food ingested by mouth. *Journal of Comparative and Physiological Psychology*, 1951, **44**, 412–422.

30. Le Magnen, J. Effects d'une pluralité de stimuli alimentaires sur le determinisme quantitatif de l'ingestion chez le rat blanc. *Archives of Science and Physiology*, 1960, **14**, 411–419. Cited by S. Balagura, *Hunger*. New York: Basic Books, 1973.

31. Zeigler, H. P. Trigeminal deafferentation and feeding behavior in the pigeon: Sensorimotor and motivational effects. *Science*, 1973, **182**, 1155–1158; Zeigler, H. P., & Karten, H. J. Central trigeminal structures and the lateral hypothalamic syndrome in the rat. *Science*, 1974, **186**, 636–637.

32. Davis, J. D., Gallagher, R. J., Ladove, R. F., & Turausky, A. J. Inhibition of food intake by a humoral factor. *Journal of Comparative and Physiological Psychology*, 1969, **67**, 407–414.

33. Mayer, J. Glucostatic mechanisms of regulation of food intake. *New England Journal of Medicine*, 1953, **249**, 13–16.

34. Kennedy, G. C. Food intake, energy balance and growth. *British Medical Bulletin*, 1966, **22**, 216–220; Kennedy, G. D. The role of depot fat in the hypothalamic control of food intake in the rat. *Proceedings of the Royal Society* (London), 1952, B **40**, 578–592.

35. *Facts about obesity*. Washington, D.C.: U.S. Department of Health, Education, and Welfare, 1976.

36. Seltzer, C. C. Genetics and obesity. In J. Vague & R. M. Denton (Eds.), *Physiopathology of adipose tissue*. Amsterdam: Excerpta Medica, 1969. Pp. 325–334; Clark, P. J. The heritability of certain anthropometric characters as ascertained from measurements of twins. *American Journal of Human Genetics*, 1956, **8**, 49–54.

37. Knittle, J. L., & Hirsch, J. Effects of early nutrition on the development of rat epididymal fat pads: Cellularity and metabolism. *Journal of Clinical Investigation*, 1968, **47**, 2091–2098.

38. Hirsch, J., Knittle, J. L., & Salans, L. B. Cell lipid content and cell number on obese and non-obese human adipose tissue. *Journal of Clinical Investigation*, 1966, **45**, 1023; Knittle, J. Early influences on development of adipose tissue. In G. A. Bray (Ed.), *Obesity in perspective*. Washington, D.C.: U.S. Government Printing Office, 1975.

39. Charney, E., Goodman, H. C., McBride, M., Lyon, B., & Pratt, R. Childhood antecedents of adult obesity: Do chubby infants become obese adults? *New England Journal of Medicine*, 1976, **295**(1), 6–9.

40. Schachter, S., Goldman, R., & Gordon, A. Effects of fear, food deprivation, and obesity on eating. *Journal of Personality and Social Psychology*, 1968, **10**, 91–97.

41. Rodin, J. Obesity: Why the losing battle? Master lecture on brain-behavior relationships presented at the annual meeting of the American Psychological Association, San Francisco, 1977; Rodin, J. Bidirectional influences of emotionality, stimulus responsivity, and metabolic events in obesity. In J. D. Maser & M. E. P. Seligman (Eds.), *Psychopathology: Experimental models*. San Francisco: Freeman, 1977. Pp. 27–65; Rodin, J., Elman, D., & Schachter, S. Emotionality and obesity; Rodin, J. Effects of distraction on the performance of obese and normal subjects. Both in S. Schachter & J. Rodin (Eds.), *Obese humans and rats*. Potomac, Md.: Erlbaum, 1974. Pp. 15–20; 97–109.

42. Rodin, J., & Stochower, J. Externality in the nonobese: The effects of environmental responsiveness on weight. *Journal of Personality and Social Psychology*, 1976, **33**, 338–344.

43. Gross, L. The effects of early feeding experience on external responsiveness. Unpublished doctoral dissertation, 1968. Cited in J. Rodin, Bidirectional influences of emotionality, stimulus responsivity, and metabolic events in obesity. In J. D. Maser & M. E. P. Seligman (Eds.), *Psychopathology: Experimental models*. San Francisco: Freeman, 1977. Pp. 27–65.

44. Stunkard, A. J. *The pain of obesity*. Palo Alto, Calif.: Bull, 1976.

45. Mayer, J. *Overweight: Causes, costs, and control*. Englewood Cliffs, N.J.: Prentice-Hall, 1968.

46. Stuart, R. B., & Davis, B. *Slim chance in a fat world: Behavioral control of obesity*. Champaign, Ill.: Research Press, 1972.

47. Fisher, W. A., & Byrne, D. Sex differences in response to erotica? Love versus lust. *Journal of Personality and Social Psychology*, 1978, **36**, 117–125.

48. Masters, W. H., & Johnson, V. E. *Human sexual response*. Boston: Little, Brown, 1966.

49. McEwen, B. S., Lieburg, I., Chaptal, C., & Krey, L. C. Aromatization: Importance for sexual differentiation of the neonatal rat brain. *Hormones and Behavior*, 1977, **9**, 249–263.

50. Whalen, R. E. Male-female differences in sexual behavior: A continuing problem. In M. B. Sterman, D. J. McGinty, & A. M. Adinolfi (Eds.), *Brain development and behavior*. New York: Academic, 1971.

51. Fisher, A. E. Maternal and sexual behavior induced by intracranial chemical stimulation, *Science*, 1956, **124**, 228–229; Fisher, A. E. Chemical stimulation of the brain. In R. C. Atkinson (Ed.), *Contemporary psychology*. San Francisco: Freeman, 1971. Pp. 31–39.

52. Karsch, F. J., Dierschke, J., & Knobil, E. Sexual differentiation of pituitary function: Apparent difference between primates and rodents. *Science*, 1973, **179**, 484–486.

53. Goldman, P. S. Specificity and plasticity of cortical function in developing rhesus monkeys. Paper presented at the annual meeting of the American Psychological Association, Washington, D.C., 1976; Waber, D. P. The meaning of sex-related variations in maturation rate; Gullahorn, J. E. Sex-related factors in cognition and in brain lateralization. Both in J. E. Gullahorn (Ed.), *Psychology and women: In transition*. New York: Wiley, 1979. Pp. 37–59; 9–35; Levy, J. Variations in the lateral organization of the human brain. Master lecture on brain-behavior relationships presented at the annual meeting of the American Psychological Association, San Francisco, 1977.

54. Ehrhardt, A. A., & Baker, S. W. Fetal androgens, human central nervous system differentiation, and behavior sex differences. In R. C. Friedman, R. M. Richart, & R. L. Van de Wiele (Eds.), *Sex differences in behavior*. New York: Wiley, 1974.

55. Money, J., & Ehrhardt, A. E. *Man and woman, boy and girl: The differentiation and dimorphism of gender identity from conception to maturity*. Baltimore: Johns Hopkins University Press, 1972; Reinisch, J. M. Prenatal exposure of human foetuses to synthetic progestin and oestrogen affects personality. *Nature*, 1977, **266**(5602), 561–562.

56. Money, J. Differentiation of gender identity. Master lecture on physiological psychology presented at the annual meeting of the American Psychological Association, New Orleans, 1974.

57. Ward, I. L. Sexual diversity. In J. D. Maser & M. E. P. Seligman (Eds.), *Psychopathology: Experimental models*. San Francisco: Freeman, 1977. Pp. 387–403.

58. Kessler, S. J., & McKenna, W. *Gender: An ethnomethodological approach*. New York: Wiley-Interscience, 1978.

59. Beach, F. A. Relative effects of androgen upon the mating behavior of male rats subjected to pre-brain injury or castration. *Journal of Experimental Zoology*, 1944, **97**, 249–285; Ford, C. S., & Beach, F. A. *Patterns of sexual behavior*. New York: Harper & Row, 1951; Baum, M. J., & Vreeburg, J. T. M. Copulation in castrated male rats following combined treatment with estradiol and dihydrotestosterone. *Science*, 1973, **182**, 283–285.

60. Money, J., & Ehrhardt, A. E. *Man and woman, boy and girl: The differentiation* *and dimorphism of gender identity from conception to maturity*. Baltimore: Johns Hopkins University Press, 1972; Michael, R. P., Richter, M. C., Cain, J. A., Zumpe, D., & Bonsall, R. W. Artificial menstrual cycles, behaviour and the role of androgens in female rhesus monkeys. *Nature*, 1978, **275**, 439–440; Adams, D. B., Gold, A. R., & Burt, A. D. Rise in female sexual activity at ovulation blocked by oral contraceptives. *New England Journal of Medicine*, 1978, **299**(21), 1145–1150.

61. Money, J. Sex hormones and other variables in human eroticism. In W. E. Young (Ed.), *Sex and internal secretions*. Vol. 2. Baltimore: Williams & Wilkins, 1961. Pp. 1383–1400.

62. Foss, G. L. The influence of androgens on sexuality in women. *Lancet Magazine*, 1951, **1**, 667–669.

63. Bremer, J. *Asexualization*. New York: Macmillan, 1959.

64. Laschat, U. Antiandrogen in the treatment of sex offenders: Modes of action and therapeutic outcome. In J. Zubin & J. Money (Eds.), *Contemporary sexual behavior: Critical issues in the 1970s*. Baltimore: Johns Hopkins University Press, 1973. Pp. 311–319.

65. Davenport, W. Sexual patterns and their regulation in a society of the southwest Pacific. In F. Beach (Ed.), *Sex and behavior*. New York: Harper & Row, 1951; Marshall, D. S. Sexual behavior on Mangaia. In D. S. Marshall & R. C. Suggs (Eds.), *Human sexual behavior: Variations in ethnographic spectrum*. New York: Basic Books, 1971; Ford, C. L., & Beach, F. A. *Patterns of sexual behavior*. New York: Harper & Row, 1951.

66. Kinsey, A., Pomeroy, W., & Martin, C. *Sexual behavior in the human male*. Philadelphia: Saunders, 1948.

67. Bauman, E. K., & Wilson, R. R. Sexual behavior of unmarried university students in 1968 and 1972. *Journal of Sex Research*, 1974, **10**(4), 327–333.

68. Hopkins, J. R. Sexual behavior in adolescence. *Journal of Social Issues*, 1977, **33**(2), 67–85; Peplau, L. A., Rubin, Z., & Hill, C. T. Sexual intimacy in dating relationships. *Journal of Social Issues*, 1977, **33**(2), 86–109.

69. Kaats, C. R., & Davis, K. E. The dynamics of sexual behavior of college students. *Journal of Marriage and the Family*, 1970, **32**, 390–399; Hopkins, J. R. Sexual behavior in adolescence. *Journal of Social Issues*, 1977, **33**(2), 67–85; Peplau, L. A., Rubin, Z., & Hill, C. T. Sexual intimacy in dating relationships. *Journal of Social Issues*, 1977, **33**(2), 86–109.

70. Kellogg, J. H. *The ladies' guide in health and disease*. Chicago: Modern Medicine, 1902. Pp. 144–165.

71. Roberts, E. J., Kline, D. K., & Gagnon, J. The project on sexual development. Cited in C. T. Cory, Parents' sexual silence. *Psychology Today*, 1979, **12**(8), 14, 84.

72. Rubin, L. B. *Worlds of pain: Life in the working class family*. New York: Basic Books, 1977. Pp. 136–137.

73. Byrne, D., Jazwinski, C., DeNinno, J. A., & Fisher, W. A. Negative sexual attitudes and contraception. In D. Byrne & L. A. Byrne (Eds.), *Exploring human sexuality*. New York: Crowell, 1977; Fisher, W. A., Fisher, J. D., & Byrne, D. Consumer reactions to contraceptive purchasing. *Personality and Social Psychology Bulletin*, 1977, **3**(2), 293–296.

74. Sex and Money: An interview with John Money. *American Psychological Association Monitor*, 1976, **7**(6), 10.

75. Broderick, C. B. Homosexuality. *World Book Encyclopedia*. Chicago: Field, 1974.

76. Feldman, M. P., & MacCulloch, M. J. *Homosexual behavior: Therapy and assessment*. Oxford, England: Pergamon, 1971.

77. Blumstein, P. W., & Schwartz, P. Bisexuality: Some social psychological issues. *Journal of Social Issues*, 1977, **33**(2), 30–45.

78. Hedblom, J. H. Dimensions of lesbian experience. *Archives of Sexual Behavior*, 1973, **2**(4), 329–341.

79. Bonnell, C. Preliminary results reported. New Kinsey study may scrap more myths. *The Advocate*, Dec. 18, 1974, 4.

80. Barnard banker: I couldn't get the city out of my system. *Barnard Reporter*, 1977, **8**(6), 3.

81. McClelland, D., Atkinson, J. W., Clark, R. A., & Lowell, E. L. *The achievement motive*. New York: Appleton-Century-Crofts, 1953. Pp. 118, 121.

82. Atkinson, J. W., & Raynor, J. O. *Personality, motivation, and achievement*. Washington, D.C.: Hemisphere, 1978.

83. Atkinson, J. W. Motivation for achievement. In T. Blass (Ed.), *Personality variables in social behavior*. Hillsdale, N.J.: Erlbaum, 1977. Pp. 25–108.

84. Atkinson, J. W., & Raynor, J. O. *Personality, motivation, and achievement*. Washington, D.C.: Hemisphere, 1978.

85. Winterbottom, M. R. The relation of need for achievement to learning experience in independence and mastery. In J. W. Atkinson (Ed.), *Motives in fantasy, action and society*. Princeton, N.J.: Van Nostrand, 1958.

86. Rosen, B. C., & D'Andrade, R. The psychological origins of achievement motivation. *Sociometry*, 1959, **22**, 185–218.

87. Hoffman, L. W. Early childhood experiences and women's achievement motives. *Journal of Social Issues*, 1972, **28**(2), 129–155.

88. Hoffman, L. W. Changes in family roles, socialization, and sex differences. *American Psychologist*, 1977, **32**, 644–657.

89. Dweck, C. S., & Goetz, T. E. Attributions and learned helplessness. In J. H. Harvey, W. Ickes, & R. F. Kidd (Eds.), *New directions in attribution research*. Vol. 2. Hillsdale, N.J.: Erlbaum, 1978. Pp. 157–179.

90. de Charms, R. *Enhancing motivation: Changes in the classroom*. New York: Irvington, 1976.

91. Pollis, M. P., & Doyle, D. C. Sex-role status and perceived competence among first graders. *Perceptual and Motor Skills*, 1972, **34**, 235–238.

92. Parsons, J. E., Ruble, D. N., Hodges, K. L., & Small, A. W. Cognitive-developmental factors in emerging sex differences in achievement related expectancies. *Journal of Social Issues*, 1976, **32**(3), 47–61; Broverman, I. K., Vogel, S. R., Broverman, D. M., Clarkson, F. E., & Rosenkrantz, P. S. Sex-role stereotypes: A current appraisal. *Journal of Social Issues*, 1972, **28**(2), 59–78.

93. Dweck, C. S. Sex differences in the meaning of negative evaluation in achievement situations: Determinants and consequences. Paper presented at the meeting of the Society for Research in Child Development, Denver, 1975; Deaux, K., White, L., & Farris, E. Skill versus luck: Field and laboratory studies of male and female preferences. *Journal of Personality and Social Psychology*, 1975, **32**, 629–636.

94. Horner, M. S. The measurement and behavioral implications of fear of success in women. In J. W. Atkinson & J. O. Raynor (Eds.), *Personality, motivation, and achievement*. Washington, D.C.: Hemisphere, 1978. Pp. 41–70.

95. Tresemer, D. W. *Fear of success*. New York: Plenum, 1977.

96. Peplau, L. A. The impact of fear of success, sex-role attitudes and opposite sex relationships on women's intellectual performance: An experimental study of competition in dating couples. Unpublished doctoral dissertation. Harvard University, 1973. Cited in J. Condry & S. Dyer, Fear of success: Attribution of cause to the victim. *Journal of Social Issues*, 1976, **32**(3), 63–83.

97. Deaux, K. The social psychology of sex roles. In L. S. Wrightsman, *Social psychology*. (2d ed.) Monterey, Calif.: Brooks/Cole, 1977. Pp. 445–473.

98. Cherry, F., & Deaux, K. Fear of success versus fear of gender inappropriate behavior; Janda, L. H., O'Grady, K. E., & Capps, C. F. Fear of success in males and females in sex-linked occupations. Both in *Sex Roles*, 1978, **4**, 97–102; 43–50.

99. Locksley, A. Sex differences in correlates of future plans. Working paper no. 10, Opinions of Youth Project. Ann Arbor, Mich.: Survey Research Center, Institute for Social Research, 1976; Locksley, A., & Douvan, E. Problem behavior in adolescents. In E. S. Gomberg (Ed.), *Gender and disordered behavior: Sex differences in psychopathology*. New York: Bruner/Mazel, 1979.

100. Condry, J., & Dyer, S. Fear of success: Attribution of cause to the victim. *Journal of Social Issues*, 1976, **32**(3), 63–83; Alper, T. G. Achievement motivation in college women: A now-you-see-it-now-you-don't phenomenon. *American Psychologist*, 1974, **24**, 194–203.

101. Berens, A. E. The socialization of achievement motives in boys and girls. Unpublished doctoral dissertation. York University, 1972. Cited in J. Condry & S. Dyer, Fear of success: Attribution of cause to the victim. *Journal of Social Issues*, 1976, **32**(3), 63–83; Frieze, I. H. Women's expectations for and causal attributions of success and failure. In M. T. S. Mednick, S. S. Tangri, & L. W. Hoffman (Eds.), *Women and achievement: Social motivational analyses.* New York: Wiley, 1975.

102. Butler, R. A. Curiosity in monkeys. *Scientific American*, 1954, **190,** 18ff.

103. Turnbull, C. M. *The mountain people.* New York: Simon & Schuster, 1972.

104. Masters, W. H., & Johnson, V. E. *Human sexual inadequacy.* Boston: Little, Brown, 1970.

105. Levine, S. Sex differences in the brain. *Scientific American*, 1966, **214,** 84–90.

106. Doering, C. H., Kraemer, H. C., Brodie, H. K. H., & Hamburg, D. A. A cycle of plasma testosterone in the human male. *Journal of Clinical Endocrinology and Metabolism*, 1975, **40,** 492–500.

107. Bell, A. P., & Weinberg, M. S. *Homosexualities: A study of human diversity.* New York: Simon & Schuster, 1978.

108. Dienstbier, R. A. Sex and violence: Can research have it both ways? *Journal of Communication,*, 1977, **27,** 176–188; Wills, G. Measuring the impact of erotica. *Psychology Today*, 1977, **11**(3), 30–34ff.

109. Donnerstein, E., & Hallam, J. The facilitating effects of erotica on aggression against women. *Journal of Personality and Social Psychology*, in press; Baron, R. A. Heightened sexual arousal and physical aggression: An extension to females. Paper presented at the annual meeting of the American Psychological Association, Toronto, 1978.

110. Malamuth, N. M., Feshback, S., & Jaffe, Y. Sexual arousal and aggression: Recent experiments and theoretical issues. *Journal of Social Issues*, 1977, **33**(2), 110–133; Feshbach, S. Sex, aggression and violence toward women. Paper presented at the annual meeting of the American Psychological Association, Toronto, 1978.

Chapter 11

1. Emde, R. N., Kligman, D. H., Reich, J. H., & Wade, T. D. Emotional expression in infancy: I. Initial studies; Izard, C. E. On the ontogenesis of emotions and emotion-cognition relationships. Both in M. Lewis & L. A. Rosenblum (Eds.), *The development of affect.* New York: Plenum, 1978. Pp. 125–148; 389–413.

2. Sagi, A., & Hoffman, M. L. Empathic distress in the newborn. *Developmental Psychology*, 1976, **12,** 175–176.

3. Cannon, W. *The wisdom of the body.* New York: Norton, 1932.

4. Wolf, S., & Wolff, H. G. *Human gastric functions.* New York: Oxford University Press, 1947.

5. Ax, A. F. The physiological differentiation between fear and anger in humans. *Psychosomatic Medicine*, 1953, **15**(5), 433–442.

6. Schwartz, G. E. Psychosomatic disorders and biofeedback: A psychobiological model of disregulation. In J. D. Maser & M. E. P. Seligman (Eds.), *Psychopathology: Experimental models.* San Francisco: Freeman, 1977. Pp. 270–307.

7. Lacey, J. I. Somatic response patterning and stress: Some revisions of activation theory. In M. H. Appley & R. Trumbull (Eds.), *Psychological stress.* New York: Appleton-Century-Crofts, 1967. Pp. 14–42.

8. Sander, L. W., Stechter, G., Burns, P., & Julia, H. Early mother-infant interaction and twenty-four-hour patterns of activity and sleep. *Journal of the American Academy of Child Psychiatry*, 1970, **9,** 103–123.

9. Lacey, J. I. Somatic response patterning and stress: Some revisions of activation theory. In M. H. Appley & R. Trumbull (Eds.), *Psychological stress.* New York: Appleton-Century-Crofts, 1967. Pp. 14–42.

10. Jost, H., & Sontag, L. W. The genetic factor in autonomic nervous system function. *Psychosomatic Medicine*, 1944, **6,** 308–310.

11. Lazarus, R. S. *Patterns of adjustment.* New York: McGraw-Hill, 1976; Schneider, A. M., & Tarshis, B. *An introduction to physiological psychology.* New York: Random House, 1975.

12. Frankenhaeuser, M. Sympathetic-adrenomedullary activity, behaviour, and the psychosocial environment. In P. H. Venables & M. J. Christie (Eds.), *Research in psychophysiology.* New York: Wiley, 1975. Pp. 71–94; Lundberg, U. Current issues in stress research. Roundtable discussion presented at the annual meeting of the American Psychological Association, Toronto, 1978.

13. Schachter, M., & Singer, J. Cognitive, social and physiological determinants of emotional state. *Psychological Review,* 1962, **69,** 379–399.

14. Henle, M. In search of the structure of emotion. Paper presented at the annual meeting of the American Psychological Association, Montreal, 1973.

15. Hammen, C. L., & Krantz, S. Effect of success and failure on depressive cognitions. *Journal of Abnormal Psychology*, 1976, **85,** 577–586.

16. Lazarus, R. S. A cognitively oriented psychologist looks at biofeedback. *American Psychologist*, 1975, **30**(5), 553–561.

17. Hochschild, A. R. Attending to, codifying, and managing feelings: Sex differences in love. Paper presented at the annual meeting of the American Sociological Association, San Francisco, 1975.

18. Ekman, P. Universal and cultural differences in facial expression of emotion. In T. K. Cole (Ed.), *Nebraska symposium on motivation.* Lincoln: University of Nebraska Press, 1971; Eibl-Eibesfeldt, I. *Love and hate: The natural history of behavior patterns.* New York: Schocken, 1974.

19. Goodenough, F. Expression of the emotions in a blind-deaf child. *Journal of Abnormal and Social Psychology*, 1932, **27,** 328–333.

20. Vaughan, K. B., & Lanzetta, J. T. The observer's facial expressive response in vicarious emotional conditioning. Paper presented at the annual meeting of the Eastern Psychological Association, Philadelphia, 1979.

21. Klineberg, O. Emotional expression in Chinese literature. *Journal of Abnormal and Social Psychology*, 1938, **33,** 517–520.

22. Efron, D. *Gesture, race, and culture.* Atlantic Highlands, N.J.: Humanities Press, 1972.

23. Arnold, M. *Feelings and emotions: The Loyola symposium.* New York: Academic, 1970; Lazarus, R. S. *Patterns of adjustment.* New York: McGraw-Hill, 1976.

24. Symington, T., Currie, A. R., Curran, R. S., & Davidson, J. N. The reaction of the adrenal cortex in conditions of stress. In Ciba Foundation's Colloquia on Endocrinology, Vol. VIII. *The human adrenal cortex.* Boston: Little, Brown, 1955. Pp. 70–91.

25. Schwartz, G. E. Physiological patterning and emotion revisited: Hemispheric-facial-autonomic interactions. Paper presented at the annual meeting of the American Psychological Association, Toronto, 1978.

26. Lanzetta, J. T., Cartwright-Smith, J., & Kleck, R. E. Effects of nonverbal dissimulation on emotional experience and autonomic arousal. *Journal of Personality and Social Psychology*, 1976, **33**(3), 354–370; Colby, C. Z., Lanzetta, J. T., & Kleck, R. E. Effects of the expression of pain on autonomic and pain tolerance responses to subject-controlled pain. *Psychophysiology*, 1977, **14**(6), 537–540; Lanzetta, J T. Facial expressive behavior and the regulation of emotional experience. Paper presented at the annual meeting of the American Psychological Association, Toronto, 1978.

27. Schwartz, G. E. Physiological patterning and emotion revisited: Hemispheric-facial-autonomic interactions. Paper presented at the annual meeting of the American Psychological Association, Toronto, 1978.

28. Solomon, R., & Corbit, J. D. An opponent process theory of motivation: I. Temporal dynamics of affect. *Psychological Review*, 1975, **81**(2), 119–145; Solomon, R. S. An opponent-process theory of acquired motivation: The affective dynamics of addiction. In J. D. Maser & M. E. P. Seligman (Eds.), *Psychopathology: Experimental models.* San Francisco: Freeman, 1977. Pp. 66–103.

29. Davidson, R. J. Specificity and patterning in biobehavioral systems: Implications for behavior change. *American Psychologist*, 1978, **33**(5), 430–436; Glantzmann, P., & Laux, L. The effects of trait anxiety and two kinds of stressors. In C. D. Spielberger & I. G. Sarason (Eds.), *Stress and anxiety.* Vol. 5. Washington, D.C.: Hemisphere, 1978. Pp. 145–168.

30. Levine, S. Stress and behavior. In

R. C. Atkinson (Ed.), *Contemporary psychology*. San Francisco: Freeman, 1971. Pp. 51–56.

31. Malmo, R. B. *On emotions, needs, and our archaic brain.* New York: Holt, Rinehart, 1975.

32. Weiss, J. M. Psychological factors in stress and disease. *Scientific American*, 1972, **226**, 104–113.

33. Glass, D. C., & Singer, J. E. *Urban stress*. New York: Academic, 1972.

34. Cohen, S., Glass, D. C., & Singer, J. E. Apartment noise, auditory discrimination, and reading ability in children. Unpublished manuscript. University of Texas at Austin, 1972; Napp, N. Noise to drive you crazy: Jets and mental hospitals. *Psychology Today*, 1977, **11**(1), 33.

35. Geer, J. H., Davison, G. C., & Gatchel, R. I. Reduction of stress in humans through nonveridical perceived control of aversive stimulation. *Journal of Personality and Social Psychology*, 1970, **16**, 731–738; Perlmuter, L. C., & Monty, R. A. The importance of perceived control: Fact or fantasy? *American Scientist*, 1977, **65**, 759–765.

36. Egbert, L., Battit, G., Welch, C., & Bartlett, M. Reduction of post-operative pain by encouragement and instruction of patients. *New England Journal of Medicine*, 1964, **270**, 825–827; Vernon, D. T. A., & Bigelow, D. A. Effect of information about a potentially stressful situation on responses to stress impact. *Journal of Personality and Social Psychology,* 1974, **29**, 50–59.

37. Farber, I. E., & Spence, W. K. Complex learning and conditioning as a function of anxiety. *Journal of Experimental Psychology,* 1953, **45**, 120–125; Ganzer, V. J. Effects of audience presence and test-anxiety on learning and retention in a serial learning situation. *Journal of Personality and Social Psychology*, 1968, **8**, 194–199.

38. Spielberger, C. D., Goodstein, L. D., & Dahlstrom, W. G. Complex incidental learning as a function of anxiety and task difficulty. *Journal of Experimental Psychology*, 1958, **56**, 58–61.

39. Gaudry, E., & Spielberger, C. D. *Anxiety and educational achievement.* Sydney, Australia: Wiley, 1971; Sieber, J. E., O'Neil, H. F., & Tobias, S. *Anxiety, learning, and instruction.* Hillsdale, N.J.: Erlbaum, 1977.

40. Mueller, J. H. Individual differences in anxiety and memory. Paper presented at the annual meeting of the American Psychological Association, Toronto, 1978.

41. Spielberger, C. D. The effects of manifest anxiety on the academic achievement of college students. *Mental Hygiene*, 1962, **9**, 195–204.

42. Spielberger, C. D., Denny, J. P., & Weitz, H. The effects of group counseling on the academic performance of anxious college freshmen. *Journal of Counseling Psychology*, 1962, **9**, 195–204.

43. Driscoll, R. Anxiety reduction using physical exertion and positive images. *The Psychological Record*, 1976, **26**(1), 87–94.

44. Selye, H. *The stress of life.* (Rev. ed.) New York: McGraw-Hill, 1978.

45. Mahl, G. F. Physiological changes during chronic fear. *Annals of the New York Academy of Sciences*, 1953, **56**, 240–249; Mahl, G. F. Relationship between acute and chronic fear and the gastric acidity and blood sugar levels in *macaca mulatta* monkeys. *Psychosomatic Medicine*, 1953, **14**, 182–210.

46. Mason, J. W. A re-evaluation of the concept of "non-specificity" in stress theory. *Journal of Psychiatric Research*, 1971, **8**, 323–333.

47. Selye, H. *Stress without distress.* Philadelphia: Lippincott, 1974.

48. Weiss, J. M. Psychological factors in stress and disease. *Scientific American*, 1972, **226**, 104–113.

49. Frankenhaeuser, M. Man in technological society: Stress, adaptation, and tolerance limits. Reports from the Psychological Laboratories. University of Stockholm, Suppl. no. 26, 1974.

50. Weiss, J. H. The current state of the concept of a psychosomatic disorder. In Z. J. Lipowski, D. R. Lipsitt, & P. C. Whybrow (Eds.), *Psychosomatic medicine.* New York: Oxford University Press, 1977. Pp. 162–171.

51. Rahe, R. H. Epidemiological studies of life change and illness. In Z. J. Lipowski, D. R. Lipsitt, & P. C. Whybrow (Eds.), *Psychosomatic medicine.* New York: Oxford University Press, 1977. Pp. 421–434; Rahe, R. H., Mahan, J., & Ransom, A. J. Prediction of near-future health change from subjects' preceding life changes. *United States Navy Medical Neuropsychiatric Research Unit Report*, 1970, No. 70–18, 401–406.

52. Liem, J. H., & Liem, G. R. Life events, social support resources, and physical and psychological dysfunction. Unpublished report, 1976; Dohrenwend, B. S., & Dohrenwend, B. P. (Eds.), *Stressful life events: Their nature and effects.* New York: Wiley, 1974.

53. Carstairs, G. M., & Kapur, R. L. *The great universe of Kota: Stress, change, and mental disorder in an Indian village.* Berkeley: University of California Press, 1976; Kolb, L. C., Bernard, V. W., & Dohrenwend, B. P. (Eds.), *Urban challenges to psychiatry: The case history of a response.* Boston: Little, Brown, 1969.

54. Gregg, G. Hypertension: Another burden for blacks. *Psychology Today*, 1976, **10**(4), 25, 26.

55. Weiss, J. M. Psychological factors in stress and disease. *Scientific American*, 1972, **226**, 104–113.

56. Senay, E. C., & Redlich, F. C. Cultural and social factors in neuroses and psychosomatic illnesses. *Social Psychiatry*, 1968, **3**(3), 89–97.

57. Grayson, R. R. Air controllers syndrome: Peptic ulcer in air traffic controllers. *Illinois Medical Journal*, 1972, **142**(2), 111–115.

58. Mirsky, I. A. Physiologic, psychologic, and social determinants in the etiology of duodenal ulcer. *American Journal of Digestive Diseases*, 1958, **3**, 285–314; Weiner, H., Thaler, M., Reiser, M. F., & Mirsky, I. A. Etiology of duodenal ulcer: I. Relation of specific psychological characteristics to rate of gastric secretion. *Psychosomatic Medicine*, 1957, **19**, 1–10.

59. Smith, M. P. Decline in duodenal ulcer surgery. *Journal of the American Medical Association*, 1977, **237**(10), 987–988.

60. Golenpaul, A. (Ed.), *1975 Information please almanac.* New York: Dan Golenpaul Associates, 1974. P. 725.

61. Glass, D. C. *Behavior patterns, stress and coronary prone behavior.* Hillsdale, N.J.: Erlbaum, 1977; Dembrowski, T. M. Biobehavioral factors; Glass, D. C. Current issues in stress research. Papers presented at the annual meeting of the American Psychological Association, Toronto, 1978.

62. Friedman, M., & Rosenman, R. H. Type A behavior pattern: Its association with coronary heart disease. *Annals of Clinical Research*, 1973, **3**, 300–317; Zyzansky, S. J. Association of type A behavior and coronary heart disease. Paper presented at the annual meeting of the American Psychological Association, Toronto, 1978.

63. Herd, J. A. Physiological mechanisms. Paper presented at the annual meeting of the American Psychological Association, Toronto, 1978.

64. Lown, B., Verrier, R., & Corbalan, R. Psychologic stress and thresholds for repetitive ventricular response. *Science*, 1973, **182**, 834–836.

65. Cannon, W. B. "Voodoo" death. *American Anthropologist*, 1942, **44**(2), 169–181.

66. Weisman, A. D., & Kastenbaum, R. *The psychological autopsy: A study of the terminal phase of life.* New York: Behavioral Publications, 1968.

67. Engel, G. L., & Schmale, A. H. Psychoanalytic theory of somatic disorders. *Journal of the American Psychoanalytic Association*, 1967, **15**, 344–365.

68. Engel, G. L. Sudden and rapid death during psychological stress: Folk lore or folk wisdom. *Annual of Internal Medicine*, 1971, **74**, 771–782.

69. Seligman, M. E. P. *Helplessness: On depression, development, and death.* San Francisco: Freeman, 1975.

70. Lown, B., Verrier, R., & Corbalan, R. Psychologic stress and thresholds for repetitive ventricular response. *Science*, 1973, **182**, 834–836.

71. Dengerink, H. A. Personality variables as mediators of aggression. In R. G. Geen & C. O'Neal (Eds.), *Perspectives on aggression.* New York: Academic, 1976. Pp. 61–98.

72. Hokanson, J. E., Eillers, K. R., & Koropsak, E. The modification of autonomic responses during aggressive interchange. *Journal of Personality*, 1968, **36**, 386–404; Hokanson, J. E. Psychophysiological evaluation of the catharsis hypothesis. In E. I. Megargee & J. E. Hokanson

(Eds.), *The dynamics of aggression*. New York: Harper & Row, 1970.

73. Farley, F. H. A theory of delinquency. Paper presented at the annual meeting of the American Psychological Association, Montreal, 1973.

74. Lunde, D. T. *Murder and madness*. San Francisco: Freeman, 1975.

75. Steele, B. F., & Pollock, C. B. A psychiatric study of parents who abuse infants and small children. In R. E. Helfer & C. H. Kempe (Eds.), *The battered child*. Chicago: University of Chicago Press, 1968. Pp. 103–147.

76. Azrin, N. H., Hutchinson, R. R., & Hake, D. F. Attack, avoidance, and escape reactions to aversive shock. *Journal of the Experimental Analysis of Behavior*, 1967, **10,** 131–148; Azrin, N. H. Pain and aggression. *Psychology Today*, 1967, **1,** 27–33.

77. Azrin, N. H., Hutchinson, R. R., & Hake, D. F. Attack, avoidance, and escape reactions to aversive shock. *Journal of the Experimental Analysis of Behavior*, 1967, **10,** 131–148.

78. Eisenhart, R. W. You can't hack it, little girl: A discussion of the covert psychological agenda of modern combat training. *Journal of Social Issues*, 1975, **31**(4), 13–23.

79. Toch, H. *Violent men*. Chicago: Aldine, 1969.

80. Dengerink, H. A., & Bertilson, H. S. The reduction of attack-instigated aggression. *Journal of Research in Personality*, 1974, **8,** 254–262.

81. Berdie, R. Playing the dozens. *Journal of Abnormal and Social Psychology*, 1947, **42,** 120.

82. Borden, R. J. Aggressive behavior and aggressive feelings in the presence of others. Paper presented at the annual meeting of the American Psychological Association, Chicago, 1975.

83. Freud, S. *Civilization and its discontents*. (Trans. by Joan Riviere.) London: Hogarth, 1957. Pp. 85–86.

84. Lorenz, K. *On aggression*. New York: Harcourt, Brace, 1966.

85. Wilson, E. O. *Sociobiology: The new synthesis*. Cambridge, Mass.: Belknap, 1975.

86. Scott, J. P. *Aggression*. Chicago: University of Chicago Press, 1958.

87. Kuo, Z. Y. *The dynamics of behavior development*. New York: Random House, 1967.

88. Moyer, K. E. *The physiology of hostility*. Chicago: Markham, 1971.

89. Konecni, V. J. Annoyance, type and duration of postannoyance activity, and aggression: The "cathartic effect." *Journal of Experimental Psychology (General)*, 1975, **104**(1), 76–102.

90. Prescott, J. W. Body pleasure and the origins of violence. *The Futurist*, 1975, **9**(2), 64–74; Prescott, J. W. Early somatosensory deprivation as an ontogenetic process in abnormal development of the brain and behavior. In E. I. Goldsmith & J.

Moor-Jankowski (Eds.), *Medical primatology*. Basel, Switzerland: Karger, 1971. Pp. 357–375.

91. Levy, I. V., & King, I. A. The effects of testosterone propionate on fighting behavior in young C57 BL/10 mice. *Anatomical Record*, 1953, **117,** 562; Allee, W. C., Collias, N., & Lutherman, C. A. Modification of the social order among flocks of hens by injection of testosterone propionate. *Physiological Zoology*, 1939, **12,** 412–420.

92. LeMaire, L. Danish experiences regarding the castration of sexual offenders. *Journal of Criminal Law and Criminology*, 1956, **47,** 25–310.

93. Eaton, G. G. The social order of Japanese macaques. *Scientific American*, 1976, **235**(4), 97–106.

94. Payne, A. P., & Swanson, H. H. Hormonal control of aggressive dominance in the female hamster. *Physiology of Behavior*, 1971, **6,** 355–357.

95. Hamburg, D. A. Effects of progesterone on behavior. In R. Levine (Ed.), *Endocrines and the central nervous system*. Baltimore: Williams & Wilkins, 1966.

96. Dalton, K. *The premenstrual syndrome*. Springfield, Ill.: Thomas, 1964.

97. Brown, G. Paper presented at the annual meeting of the American Psychiatric Association, Atlanta, 1978. Cited in L. Asher, The brain: The chemistry of violence. *Psychology Today*, 1978, **12**(6), 46, 124.

98. Stark, R., & McEvoy, J. Middle class violence. *Psychology Today*, 1970, **4**(6), 52ff.

99. Welsh, R. S. Severe parental punishment and delinquency: A developmental theory. *Journal of Clinical Child Psychology*, 1976, **5**(1), 17–21.

100. Bacon, M. K., Child, I. L., & Barry, H. III. A cross-cultural study of some correlates of crime. *Journal of Abnormal and Social Psychology*, 1963, **66,** 291–300.

101. Steele, B. F., & Pollock, C. B. A psychiatric study of parents who abuse infants and small children. In R. E. Helfer & C. H. Kempe (Eds.), *The battered child*. Chicago: University of Chicago Press, 1968. Pp. 103–147.

102. Strauss, M. A., Gelles, R. J., & Steinmetz, S. K. *Violence in the American family*. New York: Anchor/Doubleday, 1979.

103. Dietz, P. E. Victim consequences and their controls. Paper presented at the annual meeting of the American Psychological Association, Toronto, 1978; National Institute of Education. *Violent schools—Safe schools. The safe school study report to the congress*. Vol. I. Washington, D.C.: U.S. Government Printing Office, 1978.

104. Stein, A. H., & Friedrich, L. K. Television content and young children's behavior. In J. P. Murray, E. A. Rubinstein, & G. A. Comstock (Eds.), *Television and social behavior*. Vol. II: *Television and social learning*. Washington, D.C.: U.S. Government Printing Office, 1972. Pp. 202–317;

Slaby, R. R., Quarfoth, G. R., & McConnachie, G. A. Television violence and its sponsors. *Journal of Communication*, 1976, **26,** 88–96.

105. Liebert, R. M., & Schwartzberg, N. S. Effects of mass media. *Annual Review of Psychology*, 1977, **28,** 141–173.

106. Stein, A. H., & Friedrich, L. K. Television content and young children's behavior. In J. P. Murray, E. A. Rubinstein, & G. A. Comstock (Eds.), *Television and social behavior*. Vol. II: *Television and social learning*. Washington, D.C.: U.S. Government Printing Office, 1972. Pp. 202–317.

107. Parke, R. D. A field experimental approach to children's aggression: Some methodological problems and some future trends. In J. de Wit & W. W. Hartup (Eds.), *Determinants and origins of aggressive behavior*. The Hague: Mouton, 1974. Pp. 499–508; Wells, W. D. Television and aggression: A replication of an experimental field study. Unpublished study cited in *Television and growing up: The impact of televised violence*. Report to the Surgeon General. Washington, D.C.: U.S. Public Health Service, 1972.

108. Eron, L. D., Huesmann, L. R., Lefkowitz, M. M., & Walder, L. O. Does television violence cause aggression? *American Psychologist*, 1972, **27,** 253–263.

109. Cline, V. B., Croft, R. G., & Courrier, S. Desensitization of children to television violence. *Journal of Personality and Social Psychology*, 1973, **27**(3), 360–365.

110. Drabman, R. S., & Thomas, M. H. Does media violence increase children's toleration of real-life aggression? *Developmental Psychology*, 1974, **10,** 418–421.

111. Loye, D. TV's impact on adults: It's not all bad news. *Psychology Today*, 1978, **11**(12), 87–94.

112. Geen, R. G. Observing violence in the mass media. In R. G. Geen & C. O'Neal (Eds.), *Perspectives on aggression*. New York: Academic, 1976. Pp. 193–234.

113. Milgram, S. The experience of living in cities: A psychological analysis. *Science*, 1970, **167,** 1461–1468.

114. Zimbardo, P. G. The human choice: Individuation, reason, and order versus deindividuation, impulse, and chaos. In W. J. Arnold & D. Levine (Eds.), *Nebraska symposium on motivation*. Lincoln: University of Nebraska Press, 1969.

115. Diener, E., Esteford, K. L., Dineen, J., & Fraser, S. D. Beat the pacifist: The deindividuating effects of anonymity and group presence. Paper presented at the annual meeting of the American Psychological Association, Montreal, 1973.

116. McCandless, B. R. *Children: Behavior and development*. (2d ed.) New York: Holt, Rinehart, 1967. P. 587.

117. Zuckerman, S. *The social life of monkeys and apes*. New York: Harcourt-Brace, 1932.

118. Calhoun, J. B. A "behavioral sink." In E. L. Bliss (Ed.), *Roots of behavior*. New York: Harper & Row, 1962.

119. Sundstrom, E. Crowding as a sequential process: Review of research on the effects of population density on humans. In A. Baum & Y. M. Epstein (Eds.), *Human response to crowding.* Hillsdale, N.J.: Erlbaum, 1978. Pp. 31–116.

120. Sundstrom, E. Crowding as a sequential process: Review of research on the effects of population density on humans. In A. Baum & Y. M. Epstein (Eds.), *Human response to crowding.* Hillsdale, N.J.: Erlbaum, 1978. Pp. 31–116.

121. Freedman, J. L. *Crowding and behavior.* San Francisco: Freeman, 1975.

122. Verbrugge, L. M., & Taylor, R. B. Consequences of population density: Testing new hypotheses. Revised version of a paper presented at the annual meeting of the American Psychological Association, Washington, D.C., 1976; Rodin, J., Solomon, S., & Metcalf, J. The role of control in mediating perceptions of density. Unpublished paper, 1976; Worchel, S. Crowding: An attributional analysis. In A. Baum & Y. M. Epstein (Eds.), *Human response to crowding.* Hillsdale, N.J.: Erlbaum, 1978. Pp. 327–351.

123. Berman, A. Neuropsychological aspects of violent behavior. Paper presented at the annual convention of the American Psychological Association, Toronto, 1978.

124. Olds, J., & Milner, P. Positive reinforcement produced by electrical stimulation of septal area and other regions of the rat brain. *Journal of Comparative and Physiological Psychology,* 1954, **47,** 419–427; Olds, J. Differential effects of drives and drugs on self-stimulation at different brain sites. In D. E. Sheer (Ed.), *Electrical stimulation of the brain.* Austin: University of Texas Press, 1961. Pp. 350–366.

125. Olds, J. Differential effects of drives and drugs on self-stimulation at different brain sites. In D. E. Sheer (Ed.), *Electrical stimulation of the brain.* Austin: University of Texas Press, 1961. Pp. 350–366.

126. Routtenberg, A. The reward system of the brain. *Scientific American,* 1978, **239**(5), 154–164.

127. Heath, R. G. Electrical self-stimulation of the brain in man. *American Journal of Psychiatry,* 1963, **120,** 571–577.

128. Maslow, A. H. Peak experiences as acute identity experiences. *The American Journal of Psychoanalysis,* 1961, **21**(1), 254–260; Maslow, A. H. Fusion of facts and values. *The American Journal of Psychoanalysis,* 1963, **23,** 117–181.

129. Czikszentmihalyi, M. *Beyond boredom and anxiety.* San Francisco: Jossey-Bass, 1976.

130. Maslow, A. Cognition of being in the peak experience. *Journal of Genetic Psychology,* 1959, **94,** 43–66.

131. Schlosberg, H. The description of facial expressions in terms of two dimensions. *Journal of Experimental Psychology,* 1952, **44,** 229–237; Schlosberg, H. Three dimensions of emotion. *Psychological Review,* 1954, **61,** 81–88.

132. Corcoran, J., Lewis, M. D., & Garver, R. Cited in Lie detection: Beating the polygraph at its own game. *Psychology Today,* 1978, **12**(2), 107.

133. Selye, H. They all looked sick to me. *Human Nature,* 1978, **1**(2), 63.

134. Kobasa, S. C. Stressful life events, personality, and health: An inquiry into hardiness. *Journal of Personality and Social Psychology,* 1979, **37**(1), 1–11.

135. Johnson, R. N. *Aggression in man and animals.* Philadelphia: Saunders, 1972.

136. Mark, V. H., & Ervin, F. R. *Violence and the brain.* New York: Harper & Row, 1970. Pp. 97–108.

137. Kling, A. Effects of amygdalectomy on social-affective behavior in nonhuman primates. In B. E. Eleftheriou (Ed.), *The neurobiology of the amygdala.* New York: Plenum, 1972. Pp. 511–536.

138. Dickson, D. Psychosurgery supporters sued for malpractice. *Nature,* 1979, **277,** 164–165.

139. Chorover, S. L. The pacification of the brain. *Psychology Today,* 1974, **7,** 59–69.

Chapter 12

1. Bogdan, R., & Taylor, S. The judged, not the judges: An insider's view of mental retardation. *American Psychologist,* 1976, **31**(1), 49.

2. Scheerer, M., Rothmann, E., & Goldstein, K. A case of "idiot savant": An experimental study of personality organization. *Psychological Monographs,* 1945, **58**(4).

3. La Fontaine, L. The idiot savant. In B. Blatt (Ed.), *Souls in extremis: An anthology on victims and victimizers.* Boston: Allyn & Bacon, 1973. Pp. 223–230.

4. Spearman, C. E. *The abilities of man.* New York: Macmillan, 1927.

5. Thurstone, L. L. Primary mental abilities. *Psychometric Monograph,* 1938, 1. Chicago: University of Chicago Press.

6. Galton, F. *Memories of my life.* London: Methuen, 1908. Pp. 245–246.

7. Terman, L. M., & Merrill, M. A. *Stanford-Binet Intelligence Scale: Manual for the 3d revision. Form L-M.* Boston: Houghton Mifflin, 1973.

8. McNemar, Q. Lost: Our intelligence? Why? *American Psychologist,* 1964, **19,** 871–882.

9. Ghisselli, E. E. *The validity of occupational aptitude tests.* New York: Wiley, 1966.

10. Cronbach, L. J. *Essentials of psychological testing.* (3d ed.) New York: Harper & Row, 1970.

11. Anastasi, A. A. *Differential psychology.* New York: Macmillan, 1958.

12. Honzik, M., & MacFarlane, J. W. Personality development and intellectual functioning from 21 months to 40 years. In L. F. Jarvik, C. Eisdorfer, & J. E. Blum (Eds.), *Intellectual functioning in adults.* New York: Springer, 1973.

13. Sontag, L. W., Baker, C. T., & Nelson, V. L. Mental growth and personality development: A longitudinal study. *Monographs of the Society for Research in Child Development,* 1958, **23**(2).

14. Haan, N. Proposed model of ego functioning: Coping and defense mechanisms in relationship to IQ change. *Psychological Monographs,* 1963, **77**(8); Matarazzo, J. D. *Wechsler's measurement and appraisal of adult intelligence.* (5th ed.) Baltimore: Williams & Wilkins, 1972.

15. Sears, P. S., & Sears, R. R. From childhood to middle age to later maturity: Longitudinal study. Invited address presented at the annual meeting of the American Psychological Association, Toronto, 1978.

16. Maccoby, E., & Jacklin, C. M. *The psychology of sex differences.* Stanford, Calif.: Stanford University Press, 1974.

17. Waber, D. P. The meaning of sex-related variations in maturation rate. In J. E. Gullahorn (Ed.), *Psychology and women: In transition.* Washington, D.C.: Winston, 1979. Pp. 37–59.

18. Horn, J. L., & Donaldson, G. On the myth of intellectual decline in adulthood. *American Psychologist,* 1976, **31**(10), 701–719; Arenberg, D., & Robertson-Tschabo, E. A. Learning and aging. In J. E. Birren & K. W. Schaie (Eds.), *Handbook of the psychology of aging.* New York: Van Nostrand Reinhold, 1977.

19. Schaie, K. W., & Baltes, P. B. Some faith helps to see the forest: A final comment on the Horn and Donaldson myth of the Baltes-Schaie position on adult intelligence. *American Psychologist,* 1977, **32**(12), 1118–1120.

20. Hulicka, I. M. Cognitive functioning of older adults. Master lecture on the psychology of aging, presented at the annual meeting of the American Psychological Association, Toronto, 1978.

21. Honzik, M. P. Predicting IQ over the first four decades of the life span. Paper presented at the biennial meeting of the Society for Research in Child Development, Philadelphia, 1973; Blum, J. E., Fosshage, J. L., & Jarvik, L. F. Intellectual changes and sex differences in octogenarians: A twenty-year longitudinal study of aging. *Developmental Psychology,* 1972, **7,** 178–187.

22. Neugarten, B. L. The psychology of aging: An overview. Master lecture on developmental psychology, presented at the annual meeting of the American Psychological Association, Chicago, 1975.

23. Savage, R. D., Critton, P. G., Bolton, N., & Hall, E. H. *Intellectual functioning in the aged.* New York: Barnes & Noble, 1975.

24. Craik, F. I. M. Age differences in human memory. In J. E. Birren & K. W. Schaie (Eds.) *Handbook of the psychology of aging.* New York: Van Nostrand Reinhold, 1977; Fozard, J. L., & Popkin, S. J. Optimizing adult development: Ends and means of an applied psychology of aging. *American Psychologist,* 1978, **33**(11), 975–989.

25. Jarvik, L. F., Eisdorfer, C., & Blum,

J. E. (Eds.), *Intellectual functioning in adults*. New York: Springer, 1973.

26. Money, J. Two cytogenetic syndromes: Psychological comparison, intelligence, and specific factor quotients. *Journal of Psychiatric Research*, 1964, **2**, 223–231.

27. Bayley, N. L., Rhodes, L., Gooch, B., & Marcus, N. A comparison of the growth and development of institutionalized and home-reared mongoloids: A follow-up study. In J. Hellmuth (Ed.), *Exceptional infant*. Vol. II. *Studies in abnormality*. New York: Brunner-Mazel, 1971.

28. Scarr-Salapatek, S. Genetics and the development of intelligence. In F. D. Horowitz, E. M. Hetherington, S. Scarr-Salapatek, & G. M. Siegel (Eds.), *Review of child development research*, IV. Chicago: University of Chicago Press, 1975. Pp. 1–57.

29. Scarr, S., & Weinberg, R. A. The influence of "family background" on intellectual attainment: The unique contribution of adoptive studies to estimating environmental effects. Unpublished paper, Stanford, 1977. Cited in S. Scarr, Genetic effects on human behavior: Recent family studies. Master lecture on brain behavior relationships, presented at the annual meeting of the American Psychological Association, Washington, D.C., 1977.

30. Dorfman, D. D. Cyril Burt? New findings. *Science*, 1978, **201**, 1177–1186; Kamin, L. J. *The science and politics of IQ*. Potomac, Md.: Erlbaum, 1974.

31. Tyler, L. E. *The psychology of human differences*. New York: Appleton-Century-Crofts, 1956.

32. Herrnstein, R. J. I. Q. in the meritocracy. Boston: Little, Brown, 1973; Scarr, S. Genetic effects on human behavior: Recent family studies. Master lecture on brain-behavior relationships, presented at the annual meeting of the American Psychological Association, Washington, D.C., 1977.

33. Murphy, L. B. Individualization of child care and its relation to environment. In C. A. Chandler, R. S. Lourie, A. D. Peters, & L. L. Dittman (Eds.), *Early child care: The new perspectives*. New York: Atherton, 1968. Chap. 5; Hunt, J. M. Environmental programming to foster competence. In R. N. Walsh & W. T. Greenough (Eds.), *Environment as therapy for brain dysfunction*. New York: Plenum, 1976, Pp. 201–255.

34. Murphy, L. B. Individualization of child care and its relation to environment. In C. A. Chandler, R. S. Lourie, A. D. Peters, & L. L. Dittman (Eds.), *Early child care: The new perspectives*. New York: Atherton, 1968. Chap. 5; Tulkin, S. R., & Kagan, J. Mother-child interaction in the first year of life. *Child Development*, 1972, **43**, 31–41.

35. Zajonc, R. B. Family configurations and intelligence. *Science*, 1976, **192**, 227–236.

36. Heber, R., & Garber, H. An experiment in the prevention of cultural-familial mental retardation. Unpublished paper, 1970; Trotter, R. Intensive program prevents retardation. *American Psychological Association Monitor*, 1976, **7**(10), 4ff.

37. Palmer, F. H. Final report: The effects of minimal early intervention on subsequent IQ scores and reading achievement. Unpublished paper, 1976; Hess, R. D. Effectiveness of home-based early education programs. Paper presented at the annual meeting of the American Psychological Association. Washington, D.C., 1976; Warren, J. Found: Long-term gains from early intervention. *American Psychological Association Monitor*, 1977 **8**(4), 8.

38. Pedersen, E., Faucher, T. A., & Eaton, W. W. A new perspective on the effects of first-grade teachers on children's subsequent adult status. *Harvard Educational Review*, 1978, **48**(1), 1–31.

39. Rosenthal, R., & Jacobson, L. *Pygmalion in the classroom*. New York: Holt, Rinehart, 1968.

40. Rosenthal, R. On the social psychology of the self-fulfilling prophecy: Further evidence for Pygmalion effects and their mediating mechanisms. In M. Kling (Ed.), *Reading and school achievement: Cognitive and affective influences*. Eighth Annual Spring Reading Conference, Rutgers University, 1973.

41. Rosenthal, R., & Jacobson, L. *Pygmalion in the classroom*. New York: Holt, Rinehart, 1968.

42. Leacock, E. Cited in R. Rosenthal, The Pygmalion effect lives. *Psychology Today*, 1973, **7**(4), 56–63.

43. Shipman, V. C. Project report. Disadvantaged children and their first school experiences: Notable early characteristics of high and low achieving black low-SES children. Princeton, N.J.: Educational Testing Service, 1978.

44. Loehlin, J. C., Lindzey, G., & Spuhler, J. N. *Race differences in intelligence*. San Francisco: Freeman, 1975.

45. Jensen, A. R. How much can we boost IQ and scholastic achievement? *Harvard Educational Review*, 1969, **39**, 1–123.

46. Kamin, L. J. *The science and politics of IQ*. Potomac, Md.: Erlbaum, 1974.

47. Scarr-Salapatek, S. Race, social class, and I.Q. *Science*, 1971, **174**, 1285–1295.

48. Ogbu, J. U. *Minority education and caste: The American system in cross-cultural perspective*. New York: Academic, 1978.

49. Bloom, B. S. Letter to the editor. *Harvard Educational Review*, 1969, **39**, 419–421.

50. Scarr, S., & Weinberg, R. A. IQ test performance of black children adopted by white families. *American Psychologist*, 1976, **31**(10), 726–739.

51. Scarr, S. Genetic effects on human behavior: Recent family studies. Master lecture on brain-behavior relationships, presented at the annual meeting of the American Psychological Association, Washington, D.C., 1977; Scarr, S., & Weinberg, R. Intellectual similarities within families of both adopted and biological children. *Intelligence*, 1977, **1**, 170–191; Scarr, S. & Weinberg, R. Attitudes, interests, and IQ. *Human Nature*, 1978, **1**, 29–36.

52. Tyler, L. E. The intelligence we test—an evolving concept. In L. B. Resnick (Ed.), *The nature of intelligence*. Hillsdale, N.J.: Erlbaum, 1976. Pp. 13–26; Tyler, L. E. *Individuality: Human possibilities and personal choice in the psychological development of men and women*. San Francisco: Jossey-Bass, 1978.

53. Brody, E. B., & Brody, N. *Intelligence: Nature, determinants, and consequences*. New York: Academic, 1976.

54. Mercer, J. R. *Sociocultural factors in educational labeling*. Cited in E. Opton, Two views . . . from California. *American Psychological Association Monitor*, 1977, **8**(4), 5.

55. Hansberry, L. *Raisin in the sun*. New York: Random House, 1969. (Originally published in 1958.)

56. Wober, M. *Psychology in Africa*. London: International African Institute, 1975.

57. Mercer, J. R. *System of multicultural pluralistic assessment*. New York: Psychological Corporation, 1977. Described in Psychology briefs. *American Psychological Association Monitor*, 1976, **7**(5), 13.

58. Resnick, L. B. Introduction. Changing conceptions of intelligence. In L. B. Resnick (Ed.), *The nature of intelligence*. Hillsdale, N.J.: Erlbaum, 1976. Pp. 1–10.

59. Neisser, U. General academic and artificial intelligence. In L. B. Resnick (Ed.), *The nature of intelligence*. Hillsdale, N.J.: Erlbaum, 1976. Pp. 135–146; Glaser, R., & Pellegrino, J. W. Cognitive process analysis of aptitude: The nature of inductive reasoning tasks. *Bulletin de Psychologie*, in press; Sternberg, R. J. The nature of mental abilities. *American Psychologist*, 1979, **34**(3), 214–230.

60. Green, D. R., Ford, M. P., & Flamer, G. B. (Eds.), *Measurement and Piaget*. New York: McGraw-Hill, 1971.

61. Hunt, E., & Lansman, M. Cognitive theory applied to individual differences. In W. K. Estes (Ed.), *Handbook of learning and cognitive processes*. Hillsdale, N.J.: Erlbaum, 1975; Hunt, E., Lunneborg, C., & Lewis, J. What does it mean to be "high verbal?" *Cognitive Psychology*, 1975, **7**(2), 194–227.

62. Mozart, W. A. In E. Holmes, *The life of Mozart including his correspondence*. London: Chapman & Hall, 1878. Pp. 211–213.

63. Vernon, P. E. How to spot the creative. *New Society*, 1973, **25**(564), 198–200; Nicholls, J. G. Creativity in the person who will never produce anything original and useful: The concept of creativity as a normally distributed trait. *American Psychologist*, 1972, **27**(8), 717–726.

64. Davis, G. A. Predicting true college

creativity with attitude and personality information. Unpublished paper, 1974.

65. MacKinnon, D. W. IPAR's contribution to the conceptualization and study of creativity. In I. A. Taylor & J. W. Getzels (Eds.), *Perspectives in creativity*. Chicago: Aldine, 1975. Pp. 60–89.

66. Welsh, G. A. *Creativity and intelligence: A personality approach*. Chapel Hill, N.C.: Institute for Research in the Social Sciences, 1975.

67. Getzels, J. W., & Csikszentmihaly, M. *The creative vision: A longitudinal study of problem finding in art*. New York: Wiley, 1976.

68. Barron, F. *Creative person and creative process*. New York: Holt, Rinehart, 1969; Martindale, C. Primitive mentality and the relationship between art and society. *Scientific Aesthetics*, 1976, **1,** 5–18.

69. Barron, F. The psychology of imagination. *Scientific American*, 1958, **199**(3), 151–166.

70. MacKinnon, D. W. IPAR's contribution to the conceptualization and study of creativity. In I. A. Taylor & J. W. Getzels (Eds.), *Perspectives in creativity*. Chicago: Aldine, 1975. Pp. 60–89.

71. Chambers, J. A. College teachers: Their effect on creativity of students. *Journal of Educational Psychology*, 1973, **65,** 326–334.

72. Wallach, M. A. *The intelligence/creativity distinction*. New York: General Learning Press, 1971.

73. Taylor, I. A. An emerging view of creative actions. In I. A. Taylor & J. W. Getzels (Eds.), *Perspectives in creativity*. Chicago: Aldine, 1975. Pp. 297–325.

74. Feldhusen, J. F., Treffinger, D. J., & Bahlke, S. J. Developing creative thinking: The Purdue Creativity Program. *The Journal of Creative Behavior*, 1970, **4**(2), 85–90.

75. Dirkes, M. A. The role of divergent production in the learning process. *American Psychologist*, 1978, **33**(9), 815–820.

76. Amabile, T. M. Effects of external evaluation on artistic creativity. *Journal of Personality and Social Psychology*, 1979, **37**(2), 221–233.

77. Stein, M. I. *Stimulating creativity*. Vol. 2. *Group procedures*. New York: Academic, 1975.

78. Fozard, J. L., & Popkin, S. J. Optimizing adult development: Ends and means of an applied psychology of aging. *American Psychologist*, 1978, **33**(11), 975–989.

79. Williams, R. L. A position paper on psychological testing of black people. Paper presented at the annual meeting of the American Psychological Association, Toronto, 1978; Kaye, H. Joe Martinez: Looking at another psychology. *American Psychological Association Monitor*, 1978, **9**(12), 9.

80. Lambert, N. M. Legal challenges to testing—Larry P. A case in point. Paper presented at the annual meeting of the American Psychological Association, Toronto, 1978.

Chapter 13

1. Stagner, R. The gullibility of personnel managers. *Personnel Psychology*, 1958, **11,** 348.

2. Ulrich, R. E., Stachnick, D. J., & Stainton, N. R. Student acceptance of generalized personality interpretations. *Psychological Reports*, 1963, **13,** 831–834; Snyder, C. R. Why horoscopes are true: The effects of specificity on acceptance of astrological interpretations. *Journal of Clinical Psychology*, 1974, **30**(4), 577–580.

3. Sarason, I. G. *Personality: An objective approach*. (2d ed.) New York: Wiley, 1972. Pp. 224–226.

4. Sundberg, N. D., Snowden, L. R., & Reynolds, W. M. Toward assessment of personal competence and incompetence in life situations. *Annual Review of Psychology*, 1978, **29,** 179–221.

5. Gormly, J., & Edelberg, W. Validity in personality trait attribution. *American Psychologist*, 1974, **29**(3), 189–193.

6. Office of Strategic Service Assessment Staff. *Assessment of men*. New York: Holt, Rinehart, 1948.

7. Dicken, C. Predicting the success of Peace Corps community development workers. *Journal of Consulting and Clinical Psychology*, 1969, **33,** 597–606.

8. Allport, G. W., Vernon, P. E., & Lindzey, G. *Study of values*. (3d ed., rev.) Boston: Houghton Mifflin, 1970.

9. Gynther, M. D., & Gynther, R. D. Personality inventories. In I. B. Weiner (Ed.), *Clinical methods in psychology*. New York: Wiley, 1976. Pp. 187–279.

10. Kleinmuntz, B. *Personality measurement: An introduction*. Homewood, Ill.: Dorsey Press, 1967.

11. Miale, F. R., & Seltzer, M. *The Nuremberg mind: The psychology of the Nazi leader*. New York: Quadrangle, 1975.

12. Harrower, M. Were Hitler's henchmen mad? *Psychology Today*, 1976, **10**(2), 76–80.

13. Buros, O. K. (Ed.), *The sixth mental measurements yearbook*. Highland Park, N.J.: Gryphon, 1965.

14. Anastasi, A. *Psychological testing*. (4th ed.) New York: Macmillan, 1976; Karon, B. P., & O'Grady, P. O. Quantified judgments of mental health from the Rorschach, TAT, and clinical status interview by means of a scaling technique. *Journal of Consulting and Clinical Psychology*, 1970, **34,** 229–234; Gerstein, A. I., Brodzinsky, D. M., & Reiskind, N. Perceptional integration on the Rorschach as an indicator of cognitive capacity: A developmental study of racial differences in a clinic population. *Journal of Consulting and Clinical Psychology*, 1976, **44,** 760–765.

15. Holmes, D. S. The conscious control of thematic projection. *Journal of Consulting and Clinical Psychology*, 1974, **42,** 323–329.

16. Wade, R. D., & Baker, T. B. Opinions and use of psychological tests: A survey of clinical psychologists. *American Psychologist*, 1977, **32**(10), 874–882; Karon, B. P. Projective tests are valid. *American Psychologist*, 1978, **33**(8), 764–765.

17. Freud, S. *New introductory lectures on psychoanalysis*. New York: Norton, 1933. P. 104.

18. Freud, S. *New introductory lectures on psychoanalysis*. New York: Norton, 1933. P. 108.

19. Eysenck, H. J., & Wilson, G. D. *The experimental study of Freudian theories*. New York: Barnes & Noble, 1974; Fisher, S., & Greenberg, R. P. *The scientific credibility of Freud's theories and therapy*. New York: Basic Books, 1977.

20. Abrahamsen, D. *Nixon vs. Nixon: An emotional tragedy*. New York: Farrar, Straus, 1977; Binion, R. *Hitler among the Germans*. New York: Elsevier, 1976.

21. Adler, A. Individual psychology. In C. Murchison (Ed.), *Psychologies of 1930*. Worcester, Mass.: Clark University Press, 1930. P. 398.

22. Erikson, E. *Identity, youth and crisis*. New York: Norton, 1968. Pp. 132–133.

23. Erikson, E. *Childhood and society*. (2d ed.) New York: Norton, 1963. P. 266.

24. Rogers, C. A theory of therapy, personality, and interpersonal relationships, as developed in the client-centered framework. In S. Koch (Ed.), *Psychology: A theory of a science*. Vol. 3. New York: McGraw-Hill, 1959. Pp. 184–256.

25. Rogers, C. *Client-centered therapy: Its current practice, implications, and theory*. Boston: Houghton Mifflin, 1951; Evans, R. I. *The making of psychology*. New York: Knopf, 1976. Pp. 213–226.

26. Mischel, W. On the interface of cognition and personality. Address delivered at the annual meeting of the American Psychological Association, Toronto, 1978.

27. Cattell, R. B. *Abilities: Their structure, growth and action*. Boston: Houghton Mifflin, 1971.

28. Cattell, R. B., & Nesselroade, J. R. Likeness and completeness theories examined by sixteen personality factor measures on stably and unstably married couples. *Journal of Personality and Social Psychology*, 1967, **7**(4), 351–361.

29. Sheldon, W. H., in collaboration with Stevens, S. S. *The varieties of temperament: A psychology of constitutional differences*. New York: Harper & Row, 1942.

30. Tyler, L. E. *Individual differences*. Englewood Cliffs, N.J.: Prentice-Hall, 1974.

31. Skinner, B. F. *Science and human behavior*. New York: Macmillan, 1953. P. 31.

32. Skinner, B. F. Cited in The long view: Looking at the life span. *American Psychological Association Monitor*, 1977, **8**(7), 6–7.

33. Mischel, W. Toward a cognitive social learning reconceptualization of personality. *Psychological Review*, 1973, **80**(4), 252–283.

34. Mischel, W. On the future of personality measurement. *American Psychologist*, 1977, **32**(4), 246–254.

35. Sechrest, L. Personality. *Annual Review of Psychology*, 1976, **27**, 1–27.

36. Hogan, R., DeSoto, C. B., & Solano, C. Traits, tests, and personality research. *American Psychologist*, 1977, **32**(4), 255–264.

37. Magnussen, D., & Endler, N. S. (Eds.), *Personality at the crossroads: Current issues in interactional psychology*. Hillsdale, N.J.: Erlbaum, 1977; Mischel, W. On the interface of cognition and personality. Address delivered at the annual meeting of the American Psychological Association, Toronto, 1978; Bem, D. J., & Funder, D. C. Predicting more of the people more of the time: Assessing the personality of situations. *Psychological Review*, 1978, **85**, 485–501.

38. Campbell, D. P. Stability of interests within an occupation over thirty years. *Journal of Applied Psychology*, 1966, **50**, 51–56.

39. Bem, D., & Allen, S. On predicting some of the people some of the time: The search for cross-situational consistencies in behavior. *Psychological Review*, 1974, **81**, 506–520.

40. Kinget, G. M. He keeps making a difference. *Contemporary Psychology*, 1977, **22**(3), 220–221.

41. Skinner, B. F. Cited in The long view: Looking at the life span. *American Psychological Association Monitor*, 1977, **8**(7), 6–7.

42. Lachar, D. Accuracy and generalizability of an automated MMPI interpretation system. *Journal of Consulting and Clinical Psychology*, 1974, **42**, 267–273.

43. Rogers, C. *On becoming a person: A therapist's view of psychotherapy*. Boston: Houghton Mifflin, 1961. P. 27.

Chapter 14

1. Mirthes, C. *Can't you hear me talking to you?* New York: Bantam, 1971. Pp. 23–25ff.

2. Lewin, K. *A dynamic theory of personality*. (K. E. Zener & D. K. Adams, trans.) New York: McGraw-Hill, 1959; Miller, N. E. Liberalization of basic S-R concepts: Extensions to conflict behavior, motivation, and social learning. In S. Koch (Ed.), *Psychology: A study of a science*. Vol. 2. New York: McGraw-Hill, 1959.

3. Lazarus, R. S. The self-regulation of emotion. Paper delivered at symposium, Parameters of Emotion, Stockholm, Sweden, 1973.

4. Mechanic, D. *Students under stress*. New York: Free Press, 1962.

5. Barker, R. G., Dembo, T., & Lewin, K. Frustration and regression: An experiment with young children. In R. G. Barker, J. S. Kounin, & H. F. Wright (Eds.), *Child behavior and development*. New York: McGraw-Hill, 1943. Pp. 441–458.

6. Nardini, J. E. Survival factors in American prisoners of war of the Japanese. *American Journal of Psychiatry*, 1952, 109, 241–248.

7. Kandel, D. B. (Ed.), *Longitudinal research on drug use: Empirical findings and methodological issues*. Washington, D.C.: Hemisphere, 1978.

8. Vaillant, G. E. The natural history of narcotic drug addiction. *Seminars in Psychiatry*, 1970, **2**, 486–498.

9. Clark, K. B. *Dark ghetto: Dilemnas of social power*. New York: Harper & Row, 1967.

10. U. S. Department of Commerce, Bureau of the Census. *Statistical abstract of the United States*. 98th Annual Edition. Washington, D.C.: U.S. Government Printing Office, 1977.

11. Research Triangle Institute. Report on Project 23 U-891. Cited in P. Horn, Our wayward youth—Drinking, drugs and smoking are on the increase. *Psychology Today*, 1976, **9**(12), 33, 34.

12. Lieber, C. S. The metabolism of alcohol. *Scientific American*, 1976, **234**(3), 25–33.

13. Miller, W. R., & Muñoz, R. F. *How to control your drinking*. Englewood Cliffs, N.J.: Prentice-Hall, 1976. P. 188.

14. Jellinek, E. M. Phases of alcohol addiction. *Quarterly Journal of Studies on Alcohol*, 1952, **13**, 673–678.

15. Amor, D. J., Polich, J. M., & Stambul, H. B. *Alcoholism and treatment*. New York: Wiley, 1978.

16. Cappell, H. An evaluation of tension models of alcohol consumption. In R. J. Gibbins, Y. Israel, H. Kalant, R. E. Popham, W. Schmidt, & R. G. Smart (Eds.), *Research advances in alcohol and drug problems*. Vol. 2. New York: Wiley, 1975.

17. Goodwin, D. *Is alcoholism hereditary?* New York: Oxford University Press, 1976.

18. Gur, R. C., & Sackeim, H. A. Self-deception: A concept in search of a phenomenon. *Journal of Personality and Social Psychology*, 1979, **37**, 147–169.

19. Holmes, D. S. Investigations of repression. *Psychological Bulletin*, 1974, **81**, 632–653; Cohen, D. B., & Wolfe, G. Dream recall and repression: Evidence for an alternative hypothesis. *Journal of Consulting and Clinical Psychology*, 1973, **41**(3), 349–355.

20. Matlin, M. W., & Stang, D. J. *The Pollyanna principle: Selectivity in language, memory, and thought*. New York: Schenkman, 1978.

21. Hamburg, D. A., Hamburg, B., & de Goza, S. Adaptive problems and mechanisms in severely burned patients. *Psychiatry*, 1953, **16**, 9.

22. Giambra, L. Cited in M. Marcus, We daydream about our problems. *Psychology Today*, 1977, 11ff.

23. Schultz, K. D. Fantasy stimulation in depression: Direct intervention and correlational studies. Unpublished doctoral dissertation. Yale University, 1976. In J. L. Singer, Experimental studies of daydreaming and the stream of thought. In K. S. Pope & J. L. Singer (Eds.), *The stream of consciousness: Scientific investigations into the flow of human experiences*. New York: Plenum, 1978. Pp. 187–223.

24. Singer, J. L. *The child's world of make-believe: Experimental studies of imaginative play*. New York: Academic, 1973; Singer, J. L. *The inner world of daydreaming*. New York: Harper & Row, 1975.

25. Saltz, E. Stimulating imaginative play: Some cognitive effects on preschoolers. Paper presented at the annual meeting of the American Psychological Association, Toronto, 1978.

26. Krantzler, M. *Creative divorce*. New York: Signet, 1975.

27. Hay, D. H., & Oken, D. The psychological stresses of intensive-care unit nursing. *Psychosomatic Medicine*, 1972, **34**, 109–118.

28. Cousins, S. (pseud.). *To beg I am ashamed*. New York: Vanguard, 1938. Pp. 150–151.

29. Masserman, J. *Principles of dynamic psychiatry*. Philadelphia: Saunders, 1961. P. 38.

30. Bramel, D. A dissonance theory approach to defensive projection. *Journal of Abnormal and Social Psychology*, 1962, **64**, 121–129.

31. Lazarus, R. S., & Speisman, J. D. A research case history dealing with psychological stress. *Journal of Psychological Studies*, 1960, **11**, 167–194; Lazarus, R. S., Speisman, J. C., Mordkoff, A. M., & Davison, L. A. A laboratory study of psychological stress produced by a motion picture film. *Psychological Monographs*, 1962, **76**(34, Whole No. 553).

32. Speisman, J. C., Lazarus, R. S., Mordkoff, A. M., & Davison, L. A. Experimental reduction of stress based on ego-defense theory. *Journal of Abnormal and Social Psychology*, 1964, **68**(4), 367–380.

33. Wolff, C. T., Friedman, S. B., Hoffer, M. A., & Mason, J. W. Relationship between psychological defenses and mean urinary 17-hydroxycorticosteroid excretion rates. 1. A predictive study of parents of fatally-ill children. *Psychosomatic Medicine*, 1964, **26**, 576–591.

34. Murphy, L. B., & Moriarty, A. E. *Vulnerability, coping, and growth: From infancy to adolescence*. New Haven, Conn.: Yale University Press, 1976.

35. Spivack, G., Platt, J. J., & Shure, M. B. *The problem-solving approach to adjustment*. San Francisco: Jossey-Bass, 1976.

36. Cohen, F., & Lazarus, R. S. Active coping processes, coping disposition, and recovery from surgery. *Psychosomatic Medicine*, 1973, **35**, 375–389.

37. Gal, R. Coping processes under seasickness conditions. Manuscript submitted for publication, 1975. Cited in R. S. Lazarus, A cognitively-oriented psychologist looks at biofeedback. *American Psychologist*, 1975, **30**(5), 553–561.

38. Lazarus, R. S. Current issues in stress research. Roundtable discussion held at the annual meeting of the American Psychological Association, Toronto, 1978.

39. Haan, N. A tripartite model of ego functioning: Values and clinical and research applications. *Journal of Nervous and Mental Disease*, 1969, **148**, 14–30.

40. Dulany, D. C., Jr. Avoidance learning of perceptual defense and vigilance. *Journal of Abnormal and Social Psychology*, 1957, **55,** 333–338; Eriksen, C. W., & Kuethe, J. L. Avoidance conditioning of verbal behavior without awareness: A paradigm of repression. *Journal of Abnormal and Social Psychology*, 1956, **53,** 203–209.

41. Murphy, L. B., & Moriarty, A. E. *Vulnerability, coping, and growth: From infancy to adolescence.* New Haven, Conn.: Yale University Press, 1976.

42. Seligman, M. E. P. *Helplessness: On depression, development, and death.* San Francisco: Freeman, 1975.

43. Keister, M. E., & Updegraff, R. A study of children's reactions to failure and an experimental attempt to modify them. *Child Development*, 1937, **8,** 243–248.

44. Ablon, J. Reactions of Samoan burn patients and families to severe burns. *Social Science and Medicine*, 1973, **7,** 167–178.

45. Bryer, K. B. The Amish way of death: A study of family support systems. *American Psychologist*, 1979, **34**(3), 255–261.

46. Teichman, M., & Frischoff, B. Combat exhaustion: An interpersonal approach. In C. D. Spielberger & I. G. Sarason (Eds.), *Stress and anxiety.* Vol. 5. Washington, D.C.: Hemisphere, 1978. Pp. 349–353.

47. Cobb, S. Social support as a moderator of life stress. *Psychosomatic Medicine*, 1976, **38,** 300–314.

48. Mischel, W. On the interface of cognition and personality. Address presented at the annual meeting of the American Psychological Association, Toronto, 1978; Yates, B. T., & Mischel, W. Young children's preferred attentional strategies for delaying gratification. *Journal of Personality and Social Psychology*, 1979, **37,** 286–300.

49. Erikson, E. H. (Ed.), *Adulthood.* New York: Norton, 1978; Levinson, D. J. *The seasons of a man's life.* New York: Knopf, 1978; Gould, R. The phases of adult life: A study in developmental psychology. *American Journal of Psychiatry*, 1972, **129**(5), 521–531.

50. Neugarten, B. L., and associates. *Personality in middle and late life.* New York: Atherton, 1964.

51. Offer, D. *The psychological world of the teen-ager: A study of normal adolescent boys.* New York: Basic Books, 1969; Offer, D., & Offer, J. *From teenage to young manhood.* New York: Basic Books, 1975.

52. Douvan, E., & Adelson, J. *The adolescent experience.* New York: Wiley, 1966.

53. Gove, W. R., & Herb, T. R. Stress and mental illness among the young: A comparison of the sexes. *Social Forces*, 1974, **53,** 256–265.

54. Locksley, A., & Douvan, E. Problem behavior in adolescents. In E. S. Gomberg (Ed.), *Gender and disordered behavior: Sex differences in psychopathology.* New York: Bruner/Mazel, 1979.

55. Baumrind, D. Authoritarian vs. authoritative control. *Adolescence*, 1968, **3,** 255–272; Elder, G. H., Jr. Structural variations in the child rearing relationships. *Sociometry*, 1962, **25,** 241–262; Blum, R. H. *Horatio Alger's children.* San Francisco: Jossey-Bass, 1972; Offer, D., & Offer, J. *From teenage to young manhood.* New York: Basic Books, 1975.

56. Larson, L. E. The relative influence of parent-adolescent affect in predicting the salience hierarchy among youth, 1970. Cited in J. J. Conger, Current issues in adolescent development. Master lecture on developmental psychology presented at the annual meeting of the American Psychological Association, Chicago, 1975.

57. Jessor, R., & Jessor, S. L. *Problem behavior and psychological development: A longitudinal study of youth.* New York: Academic, 1977.

58. J. Adelson (Ed.), *Handbook of adolescent psychology.* New York: Wiley-Interscience, 1979.

59. Council of Economic Advisers. *Economic indicators.* Washington, D.C.: U.S. Government Printing Office, 1978.

60. Yankelovich, D. *The changing values on campus: Political and personal attitudes on campus.* New York: Washington Square, 1972.

61. Morse, R., & Weiss, N. The function and meaning of work and the job. *American Sociological Review*, 1955, **20,** 191–198; Renwick, P. A., Lawler, E. E., & the *Psychology Today* staff. What you really want from your job. *Psychology Today*, 1978, **11**(12), 53–65ff.

62. Dubnoff, S. J., Veroff, J., & Kulka, R. A. Adjustment to work: 1957–1976. Paper presented at the annual meeting of the American Psychological Association, Toronto, 1978.

63. Survey Research Center. *Survey of working conditions: Final report.* Washington, D.C.: U.S. Government Printing Office, 1971.

64. Frankenhaeuser, M. Man in technological society: Stress, adaptation, and tolerance limits. *Reports from the Psychological Laboratories.* Suppl. no. 26. Sweden: University of Stockholm, 1974.

65. Kasl, S. V. Epidemiological contributions to the study of work stress. In C. L. Cooper & R. Payne (Eds.), *Stress at work.* New York: Wiley, 1978. Pp. 3–48.

66. Kahn, R. L. The work module—A tonic for lunchpail lassitude. *Psychology Today,* 1973, **6**(9), 35–39ff.

67. Weaver, C. N. Occupational prestige as a factor in the net relationship between occupation and job satisfaction. *Personnel Psychology*, 1977, **30**(4), 607–612.

68. Maslach, C. Burned-out. *Human Behavior*, 1976, **5**(9), 16–22.

69. Sarason, S. B. *Work, aging, and social changes: Professionals and the one life-one career imperative.* New York: Free Press, 1977.

70. Renwick, P. A., Lawler, E. E., & The *Psychology Today* staff. What you really

want from your job. *Psychology Today,* 1978, **11**(12), 53–65ff.

71. Schaar, K. Vermont: Getting through the adult years. *American Psychological Association Monitor*, 1978, **9**(9–10), 7ff.

72. Norton, A. J., & Glick, P. C. Marital instability: Past, present, and future. *Journal of Social Issues*, 1976, **32**(1), 5–20.

73. Douvan, E. The marriage role: 1957–1976. Paper presented at the annual meeting of the American Psychological Association, Toronto, 1978.

74. Bernard, J. *The future of marriage.* New York: Bantam, 1973; Carter, H., & Glick, P. C. *Marriage and divorce: A social and economic study.* (Rev. ed.) Cambridge, Mass.: Harvard University Press, 1976.

75. O'Neill, N., & O'Neill, G. *Open marriage.* New York: Evans, 1972.

76. Campbell, A., Converse, P. E., & Rodgers, W. L. *The quality of American life.* New York: Russell Sage, 1976.

77. Bernard, J. *The future of marriage.* New York: Bantam, 1972; Gove, W. The relationship between sex roles, mental illness, and marital status. *Social Forces*, 1972, **51,** 34–44; Gove, W. R., & Tudor, J. F. Adult sex roles and mental illness. *American Journal of Sociology*, 1973, **78,** 812–832; Knupfer, G., Clark, W., & Roorn, R. The mental health of the unmarried. *American Journal of Psychiatry*, 1966, **122,** 842–844; Douvan, E. The marriage role: 1957–1976. Paper presented at the annual meeting of the American Psychological Association, Toronto, 1978.

78. Coleman, J. C., Hammen, C. L., & Fox, L. J. *Contemporary psychology and effective behavior.* Glenview, Ill.: Scott, Foresman, 1974; Scanzoni, L., & Scanzoni, J. *Men, women, and change.* New York: McGraw-Hill, 1974.

79. Levinger, G. Models of close relationships: Some new directions. Paper presented at the annual meeting of the American Psychological Association, Toronto, 1978.

80. Udry, J. R. *The social context of marriage.* (2d ed.) Philadelphia: Lippincott, 1971; Renne, K. S. Correlates of dissatisfaction in marriage. *Journal of Marriage and the Family*, 1970, **32,** 54–67; Wilson, W. Correlates of avowed happiness. *Psychological Bulletin*, 1967, **67,** 294–306; Furstenberg, F. F. Premarital pregnancy and marital instability. *Journal of Social Issues*, 1976, **32**(1), 67–86.

81. Furstenberg, F. F. Premarital pregnancy and marital instability. *Journal of Social Issues*, 1976, **32**(1), 67–86.

82. Dean, D. G. Emotional maturity and marital adjustment. *Journal of Marriage and the Family*, 1966, **28,** 454–457; Mudd, E., Mitchell, H., & Tauber, S. *Success in family living.* New York: Association Press, 1965.

83. Levinger, G. Models of close relationship: Some new directions. Paper presented at the annual meeting of the American Psychological Association, Toronto, 1978.

84. Gurin, G., Veroff, J., & Feld, S. *Americans view their mental health.* New York: Basic Books, 1960.

85. Neugarten, B. L. Personality changes in adulthood. Master lecture presented at the annual meeting of the American Psychological Association, Toronto, 1978; Neugarten, B. L. The psychology of aging: An overview. Master lecture presented at the annual meeting of the American Psychological Association, Chicago, 1975.

86. Neugarten, B. L. The psychology of aging: An overview. Master lecture presented at the annual meeting of the American Psychological Association. Chicago, 1975. P. 8.

87. Neugarten, B. L. Personality changes in adulthood. Master lecture presented at the annual meeting of the American Psychological Association, Toronto, 1978.

88. Kantor, H. I., Michael, C. M., Boulas, S. H., Shore, H., & Ludvigson, H. W. The administration of estrogens to older women, a psychometric evaluation. *Seventh International Congress of Gerontology Proceedings*, June 1966. Cited in J. M. Bardwick, *Psychology of women: A study of bio-cultural conflicts.* New York: Harper & Row, 1971; Klaiber, E. L., Broverman, D. M., Vogel, W., Kobayashi, Y., & Moriarty, D. Effects of estrogen therapy on plasma MAO activity and EEG driving responses of depressed women. *American Journal of Psychiatry*, 1972, **128**, 42–48.

89. Williams, J. H. *Psychology of women: Behavior in a biosocial context.* New York: Norton, 1977.

90. Bart, P. Depression in middle-aged women. In V. Gornick & B. K. Moran (Eds.), *Woman in sexist society.* New York: Basic Books, 1971.

91. Rubin, L. B. *Worlds of pain: Life in the working class family.* New York: Basic Books, 1977.

92. Campbell, A., Converse, P. E., & Rodgers, W. L. *The quality of American life.* New York: Russell Sage, 1976.

93. Levinson, D. J. *The seasons of a man's life.* New York: Knopf, 1978. Pp. 213–217.

94. Neugarten, B. L. Personality changes in adulthood. Master lecture presented at the annual meeting of the American Psychological Association, Toronto, 1978.

95. Shanas, E. Health and adjustment in retirement. *Journal of Gerontology*, 1970, **10**, 19–21.

96. Martin, W. C. Activity and disengagement: Life satisfaction of inmovers into a retirement community. *Gerontologist*, 1973, **13**, 224–227.

97. Havighurst, R. J., Neugarten, B. L., & Tobin, S. S. Disengagement and patterns of aging. In B. L. Neugarten (Ed.), *Middle age and aging.* Chicago: University of Chicago Press, 1968.

98. Neugarten, B. L., Havighurst, R. J., & Tobin, S. S. Personality and patterns of aging. In B. L. Neugarten (Ed.), *Middle age and aging.* Chicago: University of Chicago Press, 1968.

99. Kalish, R. A. *Late adulthood: Perspectives on human development.* Monterey, Calif.: Brooks/Cole, 1975.

100. Langer, E. J., & Rodin, J. The effects of choice and enhanced personal responsibility for the aged: A field experiment in an institutional setting. *Journal of Personality and Social Psychology*, 1976, **34**, 191–198.

101. Gutmann, D. The cross-cultural perspective: Notes toward a comparative psychology of aging. In J. E. Birren & K. W. Schaie (Eds.), *Handbook of the psychology of aging.* New York: Van Nostrand Reinhold, 1977.

102. Butler, R. N. The life review: An interpretation of reminiscence in the aged. *Psychiatry: Journal of the Study of Interpersonal Processes*, 1963, **26**, 65–76.

103. Kalish, R. A., & Reynolds, D. K. Death and bereavement in a cross-ethnic context. Unpublished manuscript, 1975. Cited in R. A. Kalish, *Late adulthood: Perspectives on human development.* Monterey, Calif.: Brooks/Cole, 1975.

104. Kastenbaum, R., & Costa, P. T. Psychological perspectives on death. *Annual Review of Psychology*, 1977, **28**, 225–249.

105. Weisman, A. *On dying and denying.* New York: Behavioral Publications, 1972. P. 157.

106. Flanagan, J. D. A research approach to improving our quality of life. *American Psychologist*, 1978, **33**(2), 138–147.

107. Carp, F. M. Briefly noted. *Contemporary Psychology*, 1978, **10**, 780.

108. Parke, R. D. Theoretical models of child abuse: Their implications for prediction, prevention and modification. In R. Starr (Ed.), *Prediction of abuse.* In press, 1979; Rappaport, R. Mixed views: A national conference on child abuse. *American Psychological Association Monitor*, 1979, **10**(1), 4–5.

109. Bacon, S. D. Social settings conducive to alcoholism. In American Medical Association, *A manual on alcoholism*, 1962. Pp. 61–73; National Center for Prevention and Control of Alcoholism. *Alcohol and alcoholism.* Washington, D.C.: U.S. Government Printing Office, 1967; Keller, M. The great Jewish drink mystery. *British Journal of Addiction*, 1970, **64**, 287–296.

110. Cooper, C. L., & Payne, R. (Eds.), *Stress at work.* New York: Wiley, 1978.

111. Schrank, R. *Ten thousand working days.* Cambridge, Mass.: MIT Press, 1978.

112. Van Maanen, J. (Ed.), *Organizational careers: Some new perspectives.* New York: Wiley, 1977.

113. Vanek, J. Time spent in housework. *Scientific American*, 1974, **231**, 116–120.

114. Osmond, M. W., & Martin, P. Y. Sex and sexism: A comparison of male and female sex-role attitudes. *Journal of Marriage and the Family*, 1975, **37**, 744–758.

115. Heckman, N. A., Bryson, R., & Bryson, J. B. Problems of professional couples: A content analysis. *Journal of Marriage and the Family*, 1977, **39**, 323–330.

116. Douvan, E. The marriage role: 1957–1976. Paper presented at the annual meeting of the American Psychological Association, Toronto, 1978.

117. Lipman-Blumen, J., & Tickamyer, A. R. Sex roles in transition: A ten-year perspective. *Annual Review of Sociology*, 1975, **1**, 297–337.

118. Bradbury, W. *The adult years.* New York: Time-Life, 1975.

119. Schulz, R. *The psychology of death, dying and bereavement.* Reading, Mass.: Addison-Wesley, 1978.

Chapter 15

1. Scarf, M. Normality is a square circle or a four-sided triangle. *The New York Times Magazine*, Oct. 3, 1971, 16, 17.

2. Page, J. D. *Psychopathology: The science of understanding deviance.* (2d ed.) Chicago: Aldine, 1975.

3. Beiser, M., Burr, W. A., Collomb, H., & Ravel, J. L. Pobough Lang in Senegal. *Social Psychiatry*, 1974, **9**, 123–129.

4. Ehrlich, A., & Abraham-Magdamo, F. Caution: Mental health may be hazardous. *Human Behavior*, 1974, **3**(9), 64–70.

5. Langer, E. J., & Abelson, R. P. A patient by any other name . . . : Clinical group difference in labeling bias. *Journal of Consulting and Clinical Psychology*, 1974, **42**, 4–9.

6. The Task Force on Nomenclature and Statistics of The American Psychiatric Association. *DSM-III Draft.* Jan. 15, 1978.

7. Mendels, J. *Concepts of depression.* New York: Wiley, 1970.

8. Schmidt, H. O., & Fonda, C. P. The reliability of psychiatric diagnosis: A new look. *Journal of Abnormal and Social Psychology*, 1956, **52**, 262–267.

9. Stuart, R. B. *Trick or treatment: How and when psychotherapy fails.* Champaign, Ill.: Research Press, 1970.

10. Rosenhan, D. L. On being sane in insane places. *Science*, 1973, **179**(4070), 1–9.

11. Luther, M. Colloquia mensalia. Cited in J. C. Coleman, *Abnormal psychology and modern life.* (5th ed.) Glenview, Ill.: Scott, Foresman, 1976. P. 34.

12. Maher, B. A. *Principles of psychopathology: An experimental approach.* New York: McGraw-Hill, 1966. P. 22.

13. Szasz, T. *The myth of mental illness.* New York: Dell, 1961. P. 296.

14. Herbert, W. States ponder notion of criminal insanity. *American Psychological Association Monitor*, 1979, **10**(4), 8–9.

15. Agras, S., Sylvester, D., & Oliveau, D. The epidemiology of common fears and phobias. Unpublished manuscript, 1969. Cited in G. C. Davison & J. M. Neal, *Abnormal psychology: An experimental clinical approach.* (2d ed.) New York: Wiley, 1978.

16. Freud, S. Analysis of a phobia in a five-year-old boy. In *Collected papers.* Vol. 10. London: Hogarth Press, 1957. Pp. 5–149.

17. Lazarus, A. A. *Behavior therapy and beyond.* New York: McGraw-Hill, 1971.

18. Rimm, D. C., & Somervill, J. W. *Abnor-*

mal psychology. New York: Academic, 1977.

19. Slater, E., & Shields, J. Genetic aspects of anxiety. In M. H. Lader (Ed.), *Studies of anxiety.* Ashford, England: Headley Broteis, 1969; Vandenburg, S. G., Clark, P. J., & Samuels, I. Psychophysiological reactions of twins: Heritability factors in galvanic skin resistance, heartbeat, and breathing rates. *Eugenics Quarterly,* 1965, **12**, 7–10.

20. Malmo, R. B. *On emotions, needs, and our archaic brain.* New York: Holt, Rinehart, 1975.

21. Prusoff, B., & Klerman, G. L. Differentiating depressed from anxious neurotic outpatients: Use of discriminant function analysis for separation of neurotic affective states. *Archives of General Psychiatry,* 1974, **30**, 302–309.

22. Pitts, F. N., Jr. The biochemistry of anxiety. *Scientific American,* 1969, **220**, 69–75.

23. Akhtar, S., Wig, N. N., Varma, V. K., Pershad, D., & Verma, S. K. A phenomenological analysis of symptoms in obsessive-compulsive neurosis. *British Journal of Psychiatry,* 1975, **127**, 342–348.

24. Roper, G., Rachman, S., & Hodgson, R. An experiment on obsessional checking. *Behaviour Research and Therapy,* 1973, **11**, 271–277.

25. Coleman, J. C. *Abnormal psychology and modern life.* (5th ed.) Glenview, Ill.: Scott, Foresman, 1976.

26. Gottesman, I. I. Differential inheritance of the psychoneuroses. *Eugenics Quarterly,* 1962, **9**, 223–227.

27. Grimshaw, L. Obsessional disorder and neurological illness. *Journal of Neurology, Neurosurgery, and Psychiatry,* 1964, **27**, 229–231.

28. Stephens, J. H., & Kamp, M. On some aspects of hysteria: A clinical study. *Journal of Nervous and Mental Disease,* 1962, **134**, 305–315.

29. Rimm, D. C., & Somervill, J. W. *Abnormal psychology.* New York: Academic, 1977.

30. Slater, E. T. O., & Glithero, E. A follow-up of patients diagnosed as suffering from "hysteria." *Journal of Psychosomatic Research,* 1965, **9**, 9–13.

31. Whitlock, F. A. The aetiology of hysteria. *Acta Psychiatrica Scandinavica,* 1967, **43**, 144–162.

32. Abse, D. W. *Hysteria and related mental disorders.* Baltimore: Williams & Wilkins, 1966.

33. Secunda, S. K. Special report: The depressive disorders. National Institute of Mental Health, 1973. Cited in J. Becker, *Affective disorders.* Morristown, N.J.: General Learning Press, 1977.

34. Gallant, D. M., & Simpson, G. M. (Eds.), *Depression: Behavioral, biochemical, diagnostic and treatment concepts.* New York: Spectrum, 1976.

35. Becker, J. *Affective disorders.* Morristown, N.J.: General Learning Press, 1977.

36. Davison, G. C., & Neale, J. M. *Abnormal psychology: An experimental clinical approach.* (2d ed.) New York: Wiley, 1978. P. 191.

37. Abrams, R. Unipolar mania: A preliminary report. *Archives of General Psychiatry,* 1974, **30**, 441–443.

38. Davison, G. C., & Neale, J. M. *Abnormal psychology: An experimental clinical approach.* (2d ed.) New York: Wiley, 1978. P. 192.

39. Page, J. D. *Psychopathology: The science of understanding deviance.* (2d ed.) Chicago: Aldine, 1975.

40. Carlson, G. A., Kotin, J., Davenport, Y. B., & Adland, M. Follow-up of 53 bipolar manic-depressive patients. *British Journal of Psychiatry,* 1974, **124**, 134–139.

41. Beck, A. T. *Depression: Clinical, experimental, and theoretical aspects.* New York: Hoeber, 1967. P. 235.

42. Beck, A. T. *Depression: Causes and treatment.* Philadelphia: University of Pennsylvania Press, 1970.

43. Seligman, M. E. P. *Helplessness: On depression, development, and death.* San Francisco: Freeman, 1975.

44. Abramson, L. Y., Seligman, M. E. P., & Teasdale, J. D. Learned helplessness in humans: Critique and reformulation. *Journal of Abnormal Psychology,* 1978, **87**(1), 49–74.

45. Rizley, R. Depression and distortion in the attribution of causality. *Journal of Abnormal Psychology,* 1978, **87**(1), 32–48.

46. Lobitz, W. C., & Post, R. D. Parameters of self-reinforcement and depression. *Journal of Abnormal Psychology,* 1979, **88**, 33–41.

47. Mischel, W. On the interface of cognition and personality. Address presented at the annual meeting of the American Psychological Association, Toronto, 1978.

48. Abramson, L. Y., & Sackeim, H. A. A paradox in depression: Uncontrollability and self-blame. *Psychological Bulletin,* 1977, **84**, 839–851.

49. Cadoret, R. J., & Winokur, G. Genetics of affective disorders. In M. A. Sperber & L. F. Jarvik (Eds.), *Psychiatry and genetics.* New York: Basic Books, 1976. Pp. 66–75.

50. Becker, J. *Affective disorders.* Morristown, N.J.: General Learning Press, 1977.

51. Asher, L. Speeding up the depressive night of the soul. *Psychology Today,* 1979, **12**(10), 22–24; Buchsbaum, M. S. The chemistry of brain clocks. *Psychology Today,* 1979, **12**(10), 124.

52. Shneidman, E. S., & Mandelkorn, P. How to prevent suicide. In E. S. Shneidman, N. L. Farberow, & R. L. Litman (Eds.), *The psychology of suicide.* New York: Science House, 1970.

53. Yolles, S. F. *The tragedy of suicide in the U.S.* Washington, D.C.: U.S. Government Printing Office, 1965.

54. Allen, N. H. Suicide in California, 1960–1970. State of California Department of Health, 1973. Cited in N. L. Farberow, *Suicide.* Morristown, N.J.: General Learning Press, 1974.

55. Williams, D. A. Teen-age suicide. *Newsweek,* Aug. 28, 1978, 74–77.

56. Frederick, C. J. Suicide, homicide, and alcoholism among American Indians. Washington, D.C.: U.S. Government Printing Office, 1973.

57. Farberow, N. L. *Suicide.* Morristown, N.J.: General Learning Press, 1974.

58. Lester, D., Beck, A. T., & Mitchell, B. Extrapolation from attempted suicides to completed suicides: A test. *Journal of Abnormal Psychology,* 1979, **88**, 78–80.

59. Page, J. D. *Psychopathology: The science of understanding deviance.* Chicago: Aldine, 1971.

60. Seiden, R. H. Suicide among youth: A review of the literature, 1900–1967. A supplement to the *Bulletin of Suicidology.* Washington, D.C.: National Clearinghouse for Mental Health Information, 1969.

61. Seiden, R. H. Campus tragedy: A study of student suicide. *Journal of Abnormal and Social Psychology,* 1966, **71**, 389–399.

62. Torrey, E. F. *Schizophrenia and civilization.* New York: Jason Aronson, 1979, in press.

63. Gunderson, J. G., Arutry, J. H., Mosher, L. R., & Buchsbaum, S. Special report: Schizophrenia, 1973. *Schizophrenia Bulletin,* 1974, **2**, 15–54.

64. McGhie, A., & Chapman, J. S. Disorders of attention and perception in early schizophrenia. *British Journal of Medical Psychology,* 1961, **34**, 104–106.

65. McGhie, A., & Chapman, J. S. Disorders of attention and perception in early schizophrenia. *British Journal of Medical Psychology,* 1961, **34**, 108.

66. McGhie, A., & Chapman, J. S. Disorders of attention and perception in early schizophrenia. *British Journal of Medical Psychology,* 1961, **34**, 109–110.

67. Anonymous. Autobiography of a schizophrenic experience. *Journal of Abnormal and Social Psychology,* 1955, **51**, 677–689.

68. Jefferson, L. *These are my sisters.* Tulsa, Okla.: Vickers, 1948. Pp. 51, 52.

69. Blashfield, R. An evaluation of the DSM-II classification of schizophrenia as nomenclature. *Journal of Abnormal Psychology,* 1973, **82**, 382–389; Chapman, L. J., & Chapman, J. P. *Disordered thought in schizophrenia.* New York: Appleton-Century-Crofts, 1973.

70. Kisker, G. W. *The disorganized personality.* (2d ed.) New York: McGraw-Hill, 1972. P. 314.

71. Luce, G. G. *Body time.* New York: Pantheon, 1971. Pp. 245–246.

72. Rimm, D. C., & Somervill, J. W. *Abnormal psychology.* New York: Academic, 1977.

73. Coleman, J. C. *Abnormal psychology and modern life.* (5th ed.) Glenview, Ill.: Scott, Foresman, 1976. P. 306.

74. Rosenthal, D. *Genetics of psychopathology.* New York: McGraw-Hill, 1971.

75. Wender, P. H., Rosenthal, R., Kety, S. S., Schulsinger, F., & Welner, J. Cross-fostering: A research strategy for clarifying the role of genetic and experiential factors in the etiology of schizophrenia.

Archives of General Psychiatry, 1974, **30,** 121–128.

76. Kety, S. S., Rosenthal, D., Wender, P. H., & Schulsinger, F. The types and prevalence of mental illness in the biological and adoptive families of adopted schizophrenics. In D. Rosenthal & S. S. Kety (Eds.), *The transmission of schizophrenia..* Elmsford, N.Y.: Pergamon, 1968.

77. Seeman, P. Current status of the dopamine hypothesis of schizophrenia. Invited address presented at the annual meeting of the American Psychological Association, Toronto, 1978.

78. Snyder, S. H. *Madness and the brain.* New York: McGraw-Hill, 1974.

79. Owen, F., Crow, T. J., Poulter, M., Cross, A. J., Longden, A., & Riley, G. J. Increased dopamine-receptor sensitivity in schizophrenia. *Lancet*, 1978, **2**(8083) 223–225.

80. Fontana, A. Familial etiology of schizophrenia: Is a scientific methodology possible? *Psychological Bulletin*, 1966, **66,** 214–228.

81. Wynne, L., & Singer, M. Communication deviance scores in families of schizophrenics. Intramural Research Program, NIMH. Cited in L. R. Mosher & J. G. Gunderson, with S. Buchsbaum, Special report: Schizophrenia, 1972. *Schizophrenia Bulletin*, 1973, **7,** 12–52; Bateson, G., Jackson, D. D., Haley, J., & Weakland, J. Toward a theory of schizophrenia. *Behavioral Science*, 1956, **1,** 251–264.

82. Garmezy, N. Vulnerable and invulnerable children: Theory, research, and intervention. Master lecture on developmental psychology presented at the annual meeting of the American Psychological Association, Chicago, 1975; Mishler, E. G., & Waxler, N. E. *Interaction in families: An experimental study of family processes and schizophrenia.* New York: Wiley, 1968; Hirsch, S. R., & Leff, J. P. *Abnormalities in parents of schizophrenics.* London: Oxford University Press, 1975.

83. Liem, J. H. Effects of verbal communications of parents and children: A comparison of normal and schizophrenic families. *Journal of Consulting and Clinical Psychology*, 1974, **42,** 438–450.

84. Garmezy, N. Vulnerable and invulnerable children: Theory, research, and intervention. Master lecture on developmental psychology presented at the annual meeting of the American Psychological Association, Chicago, 1975.

85. Mednick, S. A., & Schulsinger, F. Some premorbid characteristics related to breakdown in children with schizophrenic mothers. In D. Rosenthal & S. S. Kety (Eds.), *The transmission of schizophrenia.* Elmsford, N.Y.: Pergamon, 1968; Mednick, S. A. Breakdown in individuals at high-risk for schizophrenia. *Mental Hygiene*, 1966, **50,** 522–535.

86. Wynne, L. C. Family relationships and communication: Concluding comments. In L. C. Wynne, R. L. Cromwell, & S. Matthysse. (Eds.), *The nature of schizophrenia: New approaches to research and treatment.* New York: Wiley, 1978. Pp. 534–542.

87. Kolb, L. C. *Noyes' modern clinical psychiatry.* (8th ed.) Philadelphia: Saunders, 1973. P. 229.

88. Schalling, D. Psychopathy-related personality variables and the psychophysiology of socialization. In R. D. Hare & D. Schalling (Eds.), *Psychopathic behavior: Approaches to research.* New York: Wiley, 1978. Pp. 85–106.

89. Hare, R. D. *Psychopathy: Theory and research.* New York: Wiley, 1970. Pp. 1–4.

90. Schulsinger, F. Psychopathy: Heredity and environment. *International Journal of Mental Health*, 1972, **1,** 190–206; Eysenck, H. J., & Eysenck, S. B. G. Psychopathy, personality, and genetics. In R. D. Hare & D. Schalling (Eds.), *Psychopathic behavior: Approaches to research.* New York: Wiley, 1978. Pp. 85–106.

91. Hare, R. D. Electrodermal and cardiovascular correlates of psychopathy. In R. D. Hare & D. Schalling (Eds.), *Psychopathic behavior: Approaches to research.* New York: Wiley, 1978. Pp. 107–143.

92. Fenz, W. D. Heart rate responses to a stressor: A comparison between primary and secondary psychopaths and normal controls. *Journal of Experimental Research in Personality*, 1971, **5**(1), 7–13.

93. Orris, J. B. Visual monitoring of performance in three subgroups of male delinquents. *Journal of Abnormal Psychology*, 1969, **74,** 227–229.

94. Robins, L. N. *Deviant children grown up.* Baltimore: Williams & Wilkins, 1966; Robins, L. N. Aetiological implications in studies of childhood histories relating to antisocial personality. In R. D. Hare & D. Schalling (Eds.), *Psychopathic behavior: Approaches to research.* New York: Wiley, 1978. Pp. 255–271; Robins, L. N. Sturdy childhood predictors of adult antisocial behavior: Replications from longitudinal studies. In J. E. Barnett, R. M. Rose, & G. L. Klerman (Eds.), *Stress and mental disorders.* New York: Raven, 1979.

95. Bell, Q. *Virginia Woolf: A biography.* New York: Harcourt Brace, 1974.

96. Diamond, B. L. Sirhan B. Sirhan: A conversation with T. George Harris. *Psychology Today*, 1969, **3**(4), 48–56.

97. Gallup, G. G., Jr., & Maser, J. D. Tonic immobility: Evolutionary underpinnings of human catalepsy and catatonia. In J. D. Maser & M. E. P. Seligman (Eds.), *Psychopathology: Experimental models.* San Francisco: Freeman, 1977. Pp. 334–357.

98. Bluemel, C. S. *War, politics, and insanity.* Denver: World Press, 1948.

Chapter 16

1. Gillin, J. Magical fright. *Psychiatry*, 1948, **11,** 387–400.

2. Wintrob, R. M. Influence of others: Witchcraft and rootwork as explanations of behavior disturbances. *Journal of Nervous and Mental Disease*, 1973, **156**(5), 318–326.

3. Frank, J. D. *Persuasion and healing: A comparative study of psychotherapy.* (Rev. ed.) Baltimore: Johns Hopkins University Press, 1971.

4. Harper, R. A. *Psychoanalysis and psychotherapy: 36 systems.* Englewood Cliffs, N.J.: Prentice-Hall, 1959; Harper, R. A. *The new psychotherapies.* Englewood Cliffs, N.J.: Spectrum, 1975.

5. Lowen, A. *A practical guide to psychotherapy.* New York: Harper & Row, 1968.

6. Kulka, R. A. Seeking formal help for personal problems: 1957 and 1976. Paper presented at the annual meeting of the American Psychological Association, Toronto, 1978.

7. Dewald, P. A. *The psychoanalytic process. A case illustration.* New York: Basic Books, 1972. Pp. 514–515.

8. White, R. W., & Watt, N. F. *The abnormal personality.* (4th ed.) New York: Ronald Press, 1973.

9. White, R. W., & Watt, N. F. *The abnormal personality.* (4th ed.) New York: Ronald Press, 1973. P. 263.

10. Nash, E. H., Hoehn-Saric, R., Battle, C. C., Stone, A. R., Imber, S. D., & Frank, J. D. Systematic preparation of patients for short-term psychotherapy. II. Relation to characteristics of patient, therapist, and the psychotherapeutic process. *Journal of Nervous and Mental Disease*, 1965, **140,** 374–383.

11. Strupp, H. H. *Psychotherapy and the modification of abnormal behavior: An introduction to theory and research.* New York: McGraw-Hill, 1971.

12. Franks, C. M. Conditioning, cognition, and the role of behaviorism in the evolution of present day behavior therapy. Paper presented at the annual meeting of the American Psychological Association, Toronto, 1978.

13. London, P. The end of ideology in behavior modification. *American Psychologist*, 1972, **27**(10), 913–920.

14. Goldfried, M. R., & Davison, G. C. *Clinical behavior therapy.* New York: Holt, Rinehart, 1976; Meichenbaum, D. *Cognitive-behavior modification: An integrative approach.* New York: Plenum, 1977.

15. Turk, D. C. Application of coping skills training to the treatment of pain. In C. D. Spielberger & I. G. Sarason (Eds.), *Stress and anxiety.* Vol. 5. Washington, D.C.: Hemisphere, 1978. Pp. 383–392.

16. Wilson, G. T., & Davison, G. C. Behavior therapy: A road to self-control. *Psychology Today*, 1975, **9**(5), 57–60.

17. Gomes-Schwartz, B., Hadley, S. W., & Strupp, H. H. Individual psychotherapy and behavior therapy. *Annual Review of Psychology*, 1978, **29,** 435–471.

18. Franks, C. M., & Wilson, G. T. *Annual review of behavior therapy: Theory and practice.* Vol. 4. New York: Brunner/Mazel, 1976.

19. Paul, G. L. *Insight vs. desensitization in psychotherapy.* Stanford, Calif.: Stanford

University Press, 1966; Lang, P. J., Lazovik, A. D., & Reynolds, D. J. Desensitization, suggestibility and pseudotherapy. *Journal of Abnormal and Social Psychology*, 1965, **70**, 395–402.

20. Breger, L., & McGaugh, J. L. Critique and reformulation of "learning theory" approaches to psychotherapy and neurosis. *Psychological Bulletin*, 1965, **63**, 338–358.

21. Sloane, R. B., Staples, F. R., Cristol, A. H., Yorkston, N. J., & Whipple, K. *Psychotherapy vs. behavior therapy*. Cambridge, Mass.: Harvard University Press, 1975.

22. Truax, C. B., & Carkhuff, R. R. *Toward effective counseling and psychotherapy: Training and practice*. Chicago: Aldine, 1967. P. 57.

23. Rogers, C. R. Client-centered psychotherapy. In A. M. Freedman & H. I. Kaplan (Eds.), *Comprehensive textbook of psychiatry*. Baltimore: Williams & Wilkins, 1967. Pp. 1225–1228.

24. Davison, G. C., & Neale, J. M. *Abnormal psychology: An experimental clinical approach*. (2d ed.) New York: Wiley, 1978. P. 486.

25. Truax, C. B., & Carkhuff, R. R. *Toward effective counseling and psychotherapy: Training and practice*. Chicago: Aldine, 1967.

26. Garfield, S. L., & Kurtz, R. Clinical psychologists in the 1970s. *American Psychologist*, 1976, **31**(1), 1–9.

27. Lazarus, A. A. *Multimodal behavior therapy*. Vol. 1. New York: Springer, 1976.

28. Zander, A. The psychology of group processes. *Annual Review of Psychology*, 1979, **30**, 417–451.

29. Parloff, M. B., & Dies, R. R. Group psychotherapy outcome research 1966–1975. *International Journal of Group Psychotherapy*, 1977, **27**, 281–319; Piper, W. E., Debbane, E. G., & Garant, J. Group psychotherapy outcome research: Problems and prospects of a first-year project. *International Journal of Group Psychotherapy*, 1977, **27**, 321–341.

30. Rogers, C. R. *Carl Rogers on encounter groups*. New York: Harper & Row, 1970.

31. Lieberman, M. A., Yalom, I. D., & Miles, M. B. *Encounter groups: First facts*. New York: Basic Books, 1973; Smith, P. B. Controlled studies of the outcomes of sensitivity training. *Psychological Bulletin*, 1975, **82**, 597–622; Zander, A. The psychology of group processes. *Annual Review of Psychology*, 1979, **30**, 417–451.

32. Hartley, D., Roback, H. B., & Abramowitz, S. I. Deterioration effects in encounter groups. *American Psychologist*, 1976, **31**, 247–255.

33. Lieberman, M. A., Yalom, I. D., & Miles, M. B. *Encounter groups: First facts*. New York: Basic Books, 1973.

34. Eysenck, H. J. The effects of psychotherapy: An evaluation. *Journal of Consulting Psychology*, 1952, **16**, 319–324.

35. Meltzoff, J., & Kornreich, M. *Research in psychotherapy*. New York: Atherton, 1970.

36. Bergin, A. E. The evaluation of therapeutic outcomes. In A. E. Bergin & S. L. Garfield (Eds.), *Handbook of psychotherapy and behavior change*. New York: Wiley, 1971. Pp. 217–270.

37. Sloane, R. B., Staples, F. R., Cristol, A. H., Yorkston, N. J., & Whipple, K. *Psychotherapy vs. behavior therapy*. Cambridge, Mass.: Harvard University Press, 1975.

38. Di Loreto, A. O. *Comparative psychotherapy: An experimental analysis*. Chicago: Aldine-Atherton, 1971; Luborsky, L., Singer, B., & Luborsky, L. Comparative studies of psychotherapies: Is it true that "everyone has won and all must have prizes"? *Archives of General Psychiatry*, 1975, **32**, 995–1008.

39. Frank, J. D. *Persuasion and healing: A comparative study of psychotherapy*. (Rev. ed.) Baltimore: Johns Hopkins University Press, 1973; Strupp, H. H. On the basic ingredients of psychotherapy. *Journal of Consulting and Clinical Psychology*, 1973, **41**(1), 1–8.

40. Lazarus, A. A. Has behavior therapy outlived its usefulness? *American Psychologist*, 1977, **32**(7), 550.

41. Goldman, A. R., Bohr, R. H., & Steinberg, T. A. On posing as mental patients: Reminiscences and recommendations. *Professional Psychology*, 1970, **1**, 427–434; Rosenhan, D. L. On being sane in insane places. *Science*, 1973, **179**(4070), 1–9; Sarbin, T. R. On the futility of the proposition that some people are labeled "mentally ill." *Journal of Consulting Psychology*, 1967, **31**, 445–453; Goffman, E. *Asylums*. Garden City, N.Y.: Doubleday, 1961.

42. Davison, G. C., & Neale, J. M. *Abnormal psychology: An experimental clinical approach*. (2d ed.) New York: Wiley, 1978.

43. Cole, J. O. Phenothiazine treatment in acute schizophrenia: Effectiveness. *Archives of General Psychiatry*, 1964, **10**, 246–261.

44. Spohn, H. E., Lacoursiere, R. B., Thompson, K., & Coyne, L. Phenothiazine effects on psychological and psychophysiological dysfunction in chronic schizophrenics. *Archives of General Psychiatry*, 1977, **34**, 633–644.

45. Paul, G. L. The chronic mental patient: Current status—Future directions. *Psychological Bulletin*, 1969, **71**, 81–94.

46. Paul, G. L., & Lentz, R. J. *Psychosocial treatment of chronic mental patients: Milieu vs. social learning programs*. Cambridge, Mass.: Harvard University Press, 1977.

47. Davis, A. E., Dinitz, S., & Pasamanick, B. *Schizophrenics in the new custodial community: Five years after the experiment*. Columbus: Ohio State University Press, 1974.

48. Fairweather, G. W., Sanders, D. H., Maynard, H., & Cressler, D. L. *Community life for the mentally ill: An alternative to institutionalization*. Chicago: Aldine, 1969.

49. Stein, L. I., & Test, M. A. Training in community living: An alternative to the mental hospital. Paper presented at the annual meeting of the American Psychological Association, Toronto, 1978. Pp. 4–5.

50. Bassuk, E. L., & Gerson, S. Deinstitutionalization and mental health services. *Scientific American*, 1978, **238**(2), 46–53.

51. Santiestevan, H. Deinstitutionalization: Out of their beds and into the street. Washington, D.C.: American Federation of State, County, and Municipal Employees, 1975.

52. Segal, S. P., & Aviram, U. *The mentally ill in community-based sheltered care: A study of community care and social integration*. New York: Wiley, 1978.

53. Davis, A. E., Dinitz, S., & Pasamanick, B. *Schizophrenics in the new custodial community: Five years after the experiment*. Columbus: Ohio State University Press, 1974.

54. Turner, J. C., & TenHoor, W. J. The NIMH community support program: Pilot approach to a needed social reform. *Schizophrenia Bulletin*, 1978, **4**(3), 319–348.

55. Wolff, T., Crisci, G., Hutchison, E., Levine, J., & Peterson, J. Developing consultation and education programs with an emphasis on primary prevention. Paper presented at the annual meeting of the American Psychological Association, Toronto, 1978.

56. Rappaport, J. *Community psychology*. New York: Holt, Rinehart, 1977.

57. Snow, D., & Newton, P. Task, social structure and social process in the community mental health center movement. *American Psychologist*, 1977, **31**, 582–594; Goldston, S. E. Emerging primary prevention programs: 1978. Paper presented at the annual meeting of the American Psychological Association, Toronto, 1978.

58. Goldfarb, R. L., & Singer, L. R. *After conviction*. New York: Simon & Schuster, 1973.

59. Geller, W. The problem of prisons—A way out? *The Humanist*, 1972, **32**(3), 24–33.

60. Cressey, D. Cited in E. Goffman, *Asylums*. Garden City, N.Y.: Doubleday, 1961. P. 83.

61. Jones, D. A. *The health risks of imprisonment*. Lexington, Mass.: Heath, 1974.

62. Banks, H. C., Shestakofsky, S. R., & Carson, G. Civil disabilities of ex-offenders. A team project report sponsored by the John Hay Whitney Foundation, 1975.

63. Glaser, D. *The effectiveness of a prison and parole system*. Indianapolis: Bobbs-Merrill, 1964.

64. Chaneles, S. Prisoners can be rehabilitated—Now. *Psychology Today*, 1976, **10**(5), 129–134.

65. Faber, N. I almost considered the

prisoners as cattle. *Life*, Oct. 15, 1971, **71,** 82–83.

66. Zimbardo, P. G. Pathology of imprisonment. *Society*, 1972, **9**(4), 4–6.

67. Zimbardo, P. G. The dehumanization of imprisonment. Unpublished paper, 1973.

68. Bard, M. Police selection: Impact of administrative, professional, social, and legal considerations. Paper presented at the annual meeting of the American Psychological Association, Washington, D.C., 1976; Meichenbaum, D., & Novaco, R. Stress innoculation: A preventative approach. In C. D. Spielberger & I. G. Sarason (Eds.), *Stress and anxiety*. Vol. 5. Washington, D.C.: Hemisphere, 1978. Pp. 317–330; Toch, H. *Peacekeeping: Police, prisons, and violence*. Lexington, Mass.: Lexington, 1976.

69. Bard, M. Alternatives to traditional law enforcement. In F. Korten, S. W. Cook, & J. I. Lacey (Eds.), *Psychology and the problems of society*. Washington, D.C.: American Psychological Association, 1970. Pp. 128–132.

70. National Council on Crime and Delinquency. Prisons: The price we pay. Cited in J. Horn, Prisons—We pay too much for too little. *Psychology Today*, 1978, **11**(8), 14, 18.

71. Mills, R. B. Planning a community-based corrections program. Paper presented at the annual meeting of the American Psychological Association, Montreal, 1973.

Sarason, I. G. *Abnormal psychology*. (2d ed.) Englewood Cliffs, N.J.: Prentice-Hall, 1976; Wolfgang, M. E., Figlio, R. M., & Sellin, T. *Delinquency in a birth cohort*. Chicago: University of Chicago Press, 1972; Easterlin, R. A., Wachter, M. L., & Wachter, S. M. Demographic influences on economic stability: The United States experience. *Population and Development Review*, 1978, **4**(1), 1–22.

73. Shah, S. A., & Lalley, T. L. Achievement Place: The NIMH perspective. Paper presented at the annual meeting of the American Psychological Association, Washington, 1976; Braukmann, C. J., Fixsen, D. L., Kirigin, K. A. Phillips, E. A., Phillips, E. L., & Wolf, M. M. The dissemination of the teaching-family model. Paper presented at the annual meeting of the American Psychological Association, Chicago, 1975.

74. Fixsen, D. L., Phillips, E. L., Baron, R. L., Coughlin, D. D., Daly, D. L., & Daly, P. B. The Boys Town revolution. *Human Nature*, 1978, **1**(11), 55–61.

75. Coleman, J. C. *Abnormal psychology and modern life*. (5th ed.) Glenview, Ill.: Scott, Foresman, 1976.

76. Bandura, A. *Principles of behavior modification*. New York: Holt, Rinehart, 1969.

77. Atthowe, J. M. Treating the hospitalized person. In W. E. Craighead, A. E. Razdin, & M. J. Mahoney (Eds.), *Behavior modification: Principles, issues, and applications*. Boston: Houghton Mifflin, 1976.

78. Liberman, R. P., DeRisi, W. J., King, L. W., Eckman, T. A., & Wood, D. Behavioral measurement in a community mental health center. In P. O. Davidson, F. W. Clark, & A. Hamerlynck (Eds.), *Evaluation of behavioral programs in community, residential, and school settings*. Champaign, Ill.: Research Press, 1974. Pp. 103–140.

79. Coleman, J. C. *Abnormal psychology and modern life*. (5th ed.) Glenview, Ill.: Scott, Foresman, 1976; Campbell, R. *The enigma of the mind*. New York: Time-Life, 1976.

Chapter 17

1. Tavris, C. The frozen world of the familiar stranger. *Psychology Today*, 1974, **8**(1), 71, 72.

2. Schachter, S. *The psychology of affiliation*. Stanford, Calif.: Stanford University Press, 1959.

3. Strumpfer, D. Fear and affiliation during a disaster. *Journal of Social Psychology*, 1970, **82,** 263–268; Kissel, S. Anxiety, affiliation and juvenile delinquency. *Journal of Clinical Psychology*, 1967, **23,** 173–175.

4. Middlebrook, P. N. *Social psychology and modern life*. New York: Knopf, 1974.

5. Sarnoff, I., & Zimbardo, P. Anxiety, fear and social affiliation. *Journal of Abnormal and Social Psychology*, 1961, **62,** 356–363.

6. Wheeler, L. Social comparison and selective affiliation. In T. L. Huston (Ed.), *Foundations of interpersonal attraction*. New York: Academic, 1974. Pp. 309–329; Teichman, Y. Affiliative reaction in different kinds of threat situations. In C. D. Spielberger & S. G. Sarason (Eds.), *Stress and anxiety*. Vol. 5. Washington, D.C.: Hemisphere, 1978. Pp. 133–144.

7. Berscheid, E., & Walster, E. H. *Interpersonal attraction*. (2d ed.) Reading, Mass.: Addison-Wesley, 1978.

8. Festinger, L. A theory of social comparison processes. *Human Relations*, 1954, **7,** 117–140.

9. Harvey, O. J., Hunt, D. E., & Shroder, H. M. *Conceptual systems and personality organization*. New York: Wiley, 1961.

10. Jackson, D. N., & Messick, S. Individual differences in social perception. *British Journal of Social and Clinical Psychology*, 1963, **2,** 1–10.

11. Luchins, A. S. Primacy-recency in impression formation. In C. I. Hovland (Ed.), *The order of presentation in persuasion*. New Haven: Yale University Press, 1957. Pp. 33–61; Lingle, J. H. Retrieval selectivity in memory-based impression judgments. *Journal of Personality and Social Psychology*, 1979, **37**(2), 180–194.

12. Dion, K. K., Berscheid, E., & Walster, E. What is beautiful is good. *Journal of Personality and Social Psychology*, 1972, **24,** 285–290.

13. Clifford, M., & Walster, E. The effect of physical attractiveness on teacher expectation. *Sociology of Education*, 1973, **46,** 248.

14. Archer, D., & Akert, R. M. Words and everything else. Verbal and nonverbal cues in social interpretation. *Journal of Personality and Social Psychology*, 1977, **35,** 443–449.

15. Langer, E. J. Rethinking the role of thought in social interaction. In J. H. Harvey, W. Ickes, & R. F. Kidd (Eds.), *New directions in attribution research*. Vol. 2. Hillsdale, N.J.: Erlbaum, 1978. Pp. 35–58.

16. Taylor, S. E., Crocker, J., Fiske, S. T., Sprinzen, M., & Winkler, J. D. The generalizability of salience effects. *Journal of Personality and Social Psychology*, 1979, **37**(3), 357–368.

17. Kelley, H. H. The processes of causal attribution. *American Psychologist*, 1973, **28**(2), 107–128; Jones, E. E., & Davis, K. E. From acts to dispositions. In L. Berkowitz (Ed.), *Advances in experimental social psychology*. Vol. 2. New York: Academic, 1965. Pp. 219–266.

18. Hastie, R., & Kumar, P. A. Person memory: Personality traits as organizing principles in memory for behaviors. *Journal of Personality and Social Psychology*, 1979, **37**(1), 25–38.

19. Skolnick, P. Reaction to personal evaluations: A failure to replicate. *Journal of Personality and Social Psychology*, 1971, **18,** 62–67; Bradley, G. W. Self-serving biases in the attribution process: A reexamination of the fact or fiction question. *Journal of Personality and Social Psychology*, 1978, **36,** 56–72.

20. Jones, E., & Nisbett, R. *The actor and the observer: Divergent perceptions of the causes of behavior*. New York: General Learning Press, 1971.

21. Jones, E. E. The rocky road from acts to dispositions. *American Psychologist*, 1979, **34**(2), 107–117.

22. Eisen, S. V. Actor-observer differences in information inference and causal attribution. *Journal of Personality and Social Psychology*, 1979, **37**(2), 261–272.

23. Niemi, R. G. *How family members perceive each other: Political and social attitudes in two generations*. New Haven, Conn.: Yale University Press, 1974.

24. Messé, L. A., & Stollak, G. E., Larson, R. W., & Michaels, G. Y. Interpersonal consequences of person perception processes in two social contexts. *Journal of Personality and Social Psychology*, 1979, **37**(3), 369–379.

25. Walster, E., Aronson, V., Abrahams, D., & Rottman, L. Importance of physical attractiveness in dating behavior. *Journal of Personality and Social Psychology*, 1966, **4,** 508–516.

26. Vreeland, R. Is it true what they say about Harvard boys? *Psychology Today*, 1972, **5**(8), 65–68.

27. Aronson, E., Willerman, B., & Floyd, J. The effect of a pratfall on increasing interpersonal attractiveness. *Psychonomic Science*, 1966, **4,** 227–228.

28. Berscheid, E., & Walster, E. H. *Interpersonal attraction.* (2d ed.) Reading, Mass.: Addison-Wesley, 1978.

29. Aronson, E., & Linder, D. Gain and loss of esteem as determinants of interpersonal attractiveness. *Journal of Experimental Social Psychology*, 1965, **1,** 156–171.

30. Berscheid, E., & Walster, E. H. *Interpersonal attraction.* (2d ed.) Reading, Mass.: Addison-Wesley, 1978. P. 56.

31. Walster, E. The effect of self-esteem on romantic liking. *Journal of Experimental Social Psychology*, 1965, **1,** 184–197.

32. Festinger, L., Schachter, S., & Back, K. *Social pressures in informal groups: A study of human factors in housing.* New York: Harper & Row. 1950.

33. Segal, M. W. Alphabet and attraction: An unobtrusive measure of the effect of propinquity in a field setting. *Journal of Personality and Social Psychology*, 1974, **30,** 654–657; Nahemow, L., & Lawton, M. P. Similarity and propinquity in friendship formation. *Journal of Personality and Social Psychology*, 1975, **32**(2), 204–213.

34. Zajonc, R. B. Attitudinal effects of mere exposure. *Journal of Personality and Social Psychology Monograph Supplement*, 1968, **9,** 1–27.

35. Smith, G. F., & Dorfman, D. D. The effect of stimulus uncertainty on the relationship between frequency of exposure and liking. *Journal of Personality and Social Psychology*, 1975, **31,** 150–155.

36. Byrne, D. *The attraction paradigm.* New York: Academic, 1971; Griffitt, W., & Veitch, R. Preacquaintance attitude similarity and attraction revisited: Ten days in a fall-out shelter. *Sociometry*, 1974, **37,** 163–173.

37. Rubin, Z. *Research Report*, 1975, **2**(1).

38. Grush, J. E., & Yehl, J. G. Marital roles, sex differences, and interpersonal attraction. *Journal of Personality and Social Psychology*, 1979, **37**(1), 116–123.

39. Kerckhoff, A. C., & Davis, K. E. Value consensus and need complementarity in mate selection. *American Sociological Review*, 1962, **27**(3), 295–303.

40. Tharp, R. G. Psychological patterning in marriage. *Psychological Bulletin*, 1963, **60,** 97–117; Murstein, B. I. *Who will marry whom: Theories and research in marital choice.* New York: Springer, 1976.

41. Thibaut, J. W., & Kelley, H. H. *The social psychology of groups.* New York: Wiley, 1959.

42. Lott, A. J., & Lott, B. E. The role of reward in the formation of positive interpersonal attitudes. In T. L. Hudson (Ed.), *Foundations of interpersonal attraction.* New York: Academic, 1974. Pp. 171–189.

43. Walster, E., & Walster, G. W. *A new look at love.* Reading, Mass.: Addison-Wesley, 1978.

44. Rubin, Z. *Liking and loving: An invitation to social psychology.* New York: Holt, Rinehart, 1973.

45. Berscheid, E., & Walster, E. H. *Interpersonal attraction.* (2d ed.) Reading, Mass.: Addison-Wesley, 1978.

46. Driscoll, R., Davis, K. E., & Lipetz, M. E. Parental interference and romantic love: The Romeo and Juliet effect. *Journal of Personality and Social Psychology*, 1972, **24,** 1–10.

47. Dutton, D., & Aron, A. Some evidence for heightened sexual attraction under conditions of high anxiety. *Journal of Personality and Social Psychology*, 1974, **30,** 510–517; Hoon, P. W., Wincze, J. P., & Hoon, E. F. A test of reciprocal inhibition. Are anxiety and sexual arousal in women mutually inhibitory? *Journal of Abnormal Psychology*, 1977, **86,** 65–74.

48. Centers, R. Evaluating the loved one. The motivational congruency factor. *Journal of Personality*, 1971, **39,** 303–318.

49. Kanin, E. J., Davidson, K. D., & Scheck, S. R. A research note on male-female differentials in the experience of heterosexual love. *Journal of Sex Research*, 1970, **6,** 64–72; Dion, K. L., & Dion, D. D. Correlates of romantic love. *Journal of Consulting and Clinical Psychology*, 1973, **41**(1), 51–56.

50. Cimbalo, R. S., Faling, V., & Mousaw, P. The course of love: A cross-sectional design. *Psychological Reports*, 1976, **38,** 1292–1294.

51. Walster, E., Walster, G. W., & Berscheid, E. *Equity: Theory and research.* Boston: Allyn & Bacon, 1978.

52. Zahn-Waxler, C., Radke-Yarrow, M., & King, R. A. Child rearing and the development of children's altruism. Paper presented at the annual meeting of the American Psychological Association, Toronto, 1978.

53. Hoffman, M. L. Moral internalization, parental power, and the nature of parent-child interaction. *Developmental Psychology*, 1975, **11**(2), 228–239; Hoffman, M. L. Personality and social development. *Annual Review of Psychology*, 1977, **28,** 295–321.

54. Eisenberg-Berg, N., & Geisheker, E. Content of preachings and power of the model/preacher. The effect on children's generosity. *Developmental Psychology*, 1979, **15**(2), 168–175.

55. Feshbach, N. D. Empathy training: A field study in affective education. Invited address presented at the American Educational Research Association meeting, Toronto, 1978.

56. Hornstein, H. A. The influence of social models on helping; Rosenhan, D. The natural socialization of altruistic autonomy; London, P. The rescuers: Motivational hypotheses about Christians who saved Jews from the Nazis. All in J. Macaulay & L. Berkowitz (Eds.), *Altruism and helping behavior: Social psychological studies of some antecedents and consequences.* New York: Academic, 1970; Eisenberg-Berg, N., & Geisheker, E. Content of preachings and power of the model/preacher. The effect on children's generosity. *Developmental Psychology*, 1979, **15**(2), 168–175.

57. Krebs, D. L. Altruism: An examination of the concept and a review of the literature. *Psychological Bulletin*, 1970, **73,** 258–302.

58. Gergen, K. J., Gergen, M. M., & Meter, K. Individual orientations to prosocial behavior. *Journal of Social Issues*, 1972, **28,** 105–130; Midlarsky, M., & Midlarsky, E. Additive and interactive status effects on altruistic behavior. Paper presented at the annual meeting of the American Psychological Association, Honolulu, 1972.

59. Huston, T. L., Geis, G., Wright, R., & Garrett, T. Good samaritans as crime victims. In E. Viana (Ed.), *Crimes, victims, and society.* Leiden, Holland: Sijthoff, 1976.

60. Clark, R. D., III, & Word, L. E. Where is the apathetic bystander? Situational characteristics of the emergency. *Journal of Personality and Social Psychology*, 1974, **29,** 279–287.

61. Altman, D., Levine, M., Nadien, M., & Villena, J. Trust of the stranger in the city and the small town. Unpublished research, 1969. Cited in S. Milgram, The experience of living in cities: A psychological analysis. *Science*, 1970, **167**(3924), 1461–1468; Takooshian, H. Helping responses to a lost child in city and town. Paper presented at the annual meeting of the American Psychological Association, Washington, 1976.

62. Berkowitz, L., & Daniels, L. R. Affecting the salience of the social responsibility norm: Effects of past help on the response to dependency relationships. *Journal of Abnormal and Social Psychology*, 1964, **68,** 275–281; Pandey, J., & Griffitt, W. Attraction and helping. Paper presented at the annual meeting of the Midwestern Psychological Association, Chicago, 1973.

63. Bandura, A., Underwood, B., & Fromson, M. E. Disinhibition of aggression through diffusion of responsibility and dehumanization of victims. *Journal of Research in Personality*, 1975, **9,** 253–269.

64. Middlebrook, P. N. *Social psychology and modern life.* New York: Knopf, 1974.

65. Rosenhan, D., & White, G. M. Observation and rehearsal as determinants of prosocial behavior. *Journal of Personality and Social Psychology*, 1967, **5,** 424–431; Isen, A. M., Shalker, T. E., Clark, M., & Karp, L. Affect, accessibility of material in memory, and behavior: A cognitive loop. *Journal of Personality and Social Psychology*, 1978, **36**(1), 1–12.

66. Hornstein, H. A. *Cruelty and kindness: A new look at aggression and altruism.* Englewood Cliffs, N.J.: Prentice-Hall, 1976.

67. Sherif, M. *An outline of social psychology.* New York: Harper, 1948.

68. Whittaker, J. O. Parameters of social influence in the autokinetic situation. *Sociometry*, 1964, **27,** 88–95.

69. Asch, S. E. *Social psychology.* Englewood Cliffs, N.J.: Prentice-Hall, 1952.

70. Glinski, R., Glinski, B., & Slatin, G. Nonnaivety contamination in conformity experiments: Sources, effects, and implications for control. *Journal of Personality and Social Psychology,* 1970, **16,** 478–485.

71. Ross, L., Bierbrauer, G., & Hoffman, S. The role of attribution processes in conformity and dissent: Revisiting the Asch situation. *American Psychologist,* 1976, **31**(2), 148–157.

72. French, J. R. P., Morrison, H. W., & Levinger, G. Coercive power and forces affecting conformity. *Journal of Abnormal and Social Psychology,* 1960, **61,** 93–101; Festinger, L. Laboratory experiments: The role of group belongingness. In J. G. Miller (Ed.), *Experiments in social process.* New York: McGraw-Hill, 1950. Pp. 31–46; Asch, S. Effects of group pressure upon the modification and distortion of judgment. In M. H. Guetzkow (Ed.), *Groups, leadership, and men.* Pittsburgh: Carnegie Press, 1951. Pp. 117–190.

73. Crutchfield, R. S. Conformity and character. *American Psychologist,* 1955, **10,** 191–198.

74. Vaughan, G. M. The trans-situational aspect of conforming behavior. *Journal of Personality,* 1964, **32,** 335–354.

75. Dittes, J., & Kelley, H. Effects of different conditions of acceptance upon conformity to group norms. *Journal of Abnormal and Social Psychology,* 1956, **53,** 100–107.

76. Wiesenthal, D. L., Endler, N. S., Coward, T. R., & Edwards, J. Reversibility of relative competence as a determinant of conformity across different perceptual tasks. *Representative Research in Social Psychology,* 1976, **7,** 35–43.

77. Milgram, S. *Obedience to authority.* New York: Harper & Row, 1974; Kelham, W., & Mann, L. Level of destructive obedience as a function of transmitter and executant roles in the Milgram obedience paradigm. *Journal of Personality and Social Psychology,* 1974, **29,** 696–702.

78. Milgram, S. Behavioral study of obedience. *Journal of Abnormal and Social Psychology,* 1963, **67,** 375.

79. Milgram, S. *Obedience to authority.* New York: Harper & Row, 1974. P. 54.

80. Mischel, W. *Introduction to personality.* New York: Holt, Rinehart, 1971. Pp. 268–269.

81. Parsons, T., & Bales, R. F. *Family socialization and interaction process.* Glencoe, Ill.: Free Press, 1955.

82. Spence, J. T. Traits, roles, and the concept of androgeny. In J. E. Gullahorn (Ed.), *Psychology and women: In transition.* Washington, D.C.: Winston, 1979. Pp. 167–187; Cicone, M. V., & Ruble, D. N. Beliefs about males. *Journal of Social Issues,* 1978, **34**(1), 5–16.

83. Komarovsky, M. Dilemmas of masculinity in a changing world. In J. E. Gullahorn (Ed.), *Psychology and women: In transition.* Washington, D.C.: Winston, 1979. Pp. 71–82; Scanzoni, J. H. *Sex roles, life styles and childbearing: Changing patterns in marriage and the family.* New York: Free Press, 1975.

84. Urberg, K. A. Sex role conceptualizations in adolescents and adults. *Developmental Psychology,* 1979, **15**(1), 90–92.

85. Rubin, J. Z., Provenzano, F. J., & Luria, Z. The eye of the beholder: Parents' views on sex of newborns. *American Journal of Orthopsychiatry,* 1974, **44,** 512–519.

86. Condry, J., & Condry, S. Sex differences: A study of the eye of the beholder. *Child Development,* 1976, **47,** 812–819.

87. Thompson, S. K. Gender labels and early sex role development. *Child Development,* 1975, **46,** 339–347.

88. Hoffman, L. W. Changes in family roles, socialization, and sex differences. *American Psychologist,* 1977, **32,** 644–657.

89. Hagen, R., & Kahn, A. Discrimination against competent women; Spence, J. T., Helmreich, R., & Stapp, J. Likeability, sex-role congruence of interest, and competence: It all depends on how you ask. Both in *Journal of Applied Social Psychology,* 1975, **5,** 362–376; 93–109.

90. Deaux, K. *The behavior of women and men.* Monterey, Calif.: Brooks/Cole, 1976.

91. Broverman, I. K., Broverman, D. M., Clarkson, F. E., Rosenkrantz, P. S., & Vogel, S. R. Sex-role stereotypes and clinical judgments of mental health. *Journal of Consulting and Clinical Psychology,* 1970, **34,** 1–7.

92. Levitin, T. E., Quinn, R. P., & Staines, G. L. A woman is 58% of a man. *Psychology Today,* 1973, **6,** 89–92.

93. Maccoby, E. E., & Jacklin, C. N. *The psychology of sex differences.* Stanford, Calif.: Stanford University Press, 1974; Block, J. H. Issues, problems, and pitfalls in assessing sex differences: A critical review of the psychology of sex differences. *Merrill-Palmer Quarterly,* 1976, **22**(4), 283–308; Mednick, M. T. S. The new psychology of women: A feminist analysis. In J. E. Gullahorn (Ed.), *Psychology and women: In transition.* Washington, D.C.: Winston, 1979. Pp. 189–211; McGuinness, D., & Pribram, K. H. The origins of sensory bias in the development of gender differences in perception and cognition. In M. Bortner (Ed.), *Cognitive growth and development.* New York: Bruner/Mazel, 1979.

94. Hall, E. T. *The silent language.* New York: Fawcett, 1959; Albert, E. The roles of women: A question of values. In S. M. Farber & R. H. L. Wilson (Eds.), *The potential of woman.* New York: McGraw-Hill, 1963. Pp. 105–115.

95. Bamberger, J. The myth of matriarchy. In M. Z. Rosaldo & L. Lamphere (Eds.), *Women, culture, and society.* Stanford, Calif.: Stanford University Press, 1974. Pp. 263–281; Barry, H., Bacon, M. K., & Child, I. I. A cross-cultural survey of some sex differences in socialization. *Journal of Abnormal and Social Psychology,* 1957, **55,** 327–332.

96. Sanday, P. R. Toward a theory of the status of women. *American Anthropologist,* 1973, **75,** 1682–1700.

97. Friedl, E. *Women and men: An anthropologist's view.* New York: Holt, Rinehart, 1975.

98. Rossi, A. S. Essay: The biosocial side of parenthood. *Human Nature,* 1978, **1**(6), 72–79.

99. Levy, J. Variations in the lateral organization of the human brain. Master lecture on brain-behavior relationships presented at the annual meeting of the American Psychological Association, San Francisco, 1977.

100. Money, J., & Ehrhardt, A. A. *Man and woman: Boy and girl.* Baltimore: Johns Hopkins University Press, 1972.

101. Money, J., Hampson, J. G., & Hampson, J. L. An examination of some basic sexual concepts: The evidence of human hermaphroditism. *Bulletin of the Johns Hopkins Hospital,* 1955, **97,** 301–319; Money, J., Hampson, J. G., & Hampson, J. L. Sexual incongruities and psychopathology: The evidence of human hermaphroditism. *Bulletin of the Johns Hopkins Hospital,* 1956, **98,** 43–57.

102. Mischel, W. Sex-typing and socialization. In P. H. Mussen (Ed.), *Carmichael's manual of child psychology.* Vol. 2. New York: Wiley, 1970. Pp. 3–72.

103. Kohlberg, L. Stage and sequences: The cognitive-developmental approach to socialization. In D. A. Goslin (Ed.), *Handbook of socialization theory and research.* Chicago: Rand McNally, 1969. Pp. 347–480.

104. Rheingold, H. L., & Cook, K. V. The contents of boys' and girls' rooms as an index of parents' behavior. *Child Development,* 1975, **46,** 459–463.

105. Will, J., Self, P., & Datan, N. Paper presented at the annual meeting of the American Psychological Association, New Orleans, 1974. Cited in C. Tavris & C. Offir, *The longest war: Sex differences in perspective.* New York: Harcourt Brace, 1977.

106. Rosenberg, B. G., & Hyde, J. S. Female development revisited. Unpublished paper, 1973.

107. Mussen, P. H., & Rutherford, E. Parent-child relations and parental personality in relation to young children's sex-role preferences. *Child Development,* 1963, **34,** 589–607.

108. Block, J. H. Another look at sex differentiation in the socialization behaviors of mothers and fathers. In F. Denmark & J. Sherman (Eds.), *Psychology of women: Future directions of research.* New York: Psychological Dimensions, 1978.

109. Block, J. H. Another look at sex differentiation in the socialization behaviors of mothers and fathers. In F. Denmark & J. Sherman (Eds.), *Psychology of women:*

Future directions of research. New York: Psychological Dimensions, 1978; Hoffman, L. W. Changes in family roles, socialization, and sex differences. *American Psychologist*, 1977, **32**, 644–657.

110. Serbin, L. A., O'Leary, K. D., Kent, R. N., & Tonick, I. J. A comparison of teacher response to the preacademic and problem behavior of boys and girls. *Child Development*, 1973, **44**, 796–804.

111. Maccoby, E. E. Sex differentiation during childhood development. Master lecture on developmental psychology presented at the annual meeting of the American Psychological Association, Chicago, 1975.

112. Sternglanz, S. H., & Serbin, L. A. Sex role stereotyping in children's television programs. *Developmental Psychology*, 1974, **10**, 710–715.

113. *Dick and Jane as victims: Sex stereotyping in children's readers*. (2d ed.) Princeton, N.J.: Women on Words and Images, 1975. *Channeling children: Sex stereotyping on primetime TV*. Princeton, N.J.: Women on Words and Images, 1975.

114. Harrison, J. Warning: The male sex role may be dangerous to your health. *Journal of Social Issues*, 1978, **34**(1), 65–86.

115. O'Leary, V. E. Some attitudinal barriers to occupational aspirations in women. *Psychological Bulletin*, 1974, **81**, 809–826; Ollison, L. Socialization: Women, worth, and work. Cited in C. Tavris & C. Offir, *The longest war: Sex differences in perspective*. New York: Harcourt Brace, 1977.

116. Spence, J. T. Traits, roles, and the concept of androgyny. In J. E. Gullahorn (Ed.), *Psychology and women: In transition*. Washington, D.C.: Winston, 1979. Pp. 167–187; Bem, S. L. The measurement of psychological androgyny. *Journal of Consulting and Clinical Psychology*, 1974, **42**, 155–162.

117. Bem, S. L. Sex-role adaptability: One consequence of psychological androgeny. *Journal of Personality and Social Psychology*, 1975, **31**(4), 634–643; Bem, S. L., & Lenney, E. Sex-typing and the avoidance of cross-sex behavior. *Journal of Personality and Social Psychology*, 1976, **33**, 48–54.

118. Donelson, E. Development of sex-typed behavior and self-concept. In E. Donelson & J. E. Gullahorn (Eds.), *Women: A psychological perspective*. New York: Wiley, 1977; Ickes, W., & Barnes, R. Boys and girls together—and alienated: On enacting stereotyped sex roles in mixed-sex dyads. *Journal of Personality and Social Psychology*, 1978, **36**(7), 669–683.

119. Allport, G. *The nature of prejudice*. Garden City, N.Y.: Doubleday, 1958. P. 9.

120. Wicker, A. W. Attitude versus action: The relationship of verbal and overt behavioral responses to attitude objects. *Journal of Social Issues*, 1969, **25**(4), 41–78.

121. McGuire, W. J. The concept of attitudes and their relations to behaviors. In

H. W. Sinaiko & L. A. Broedling (Eds.), *Perspectives on attitude assessment: Surveys and their alternatives*. Champaign, Ill.: Pendleton, 1976; Kahle, L. R., & Berman, J. J. Attitudes cause behaviors: A cross-lagged panel analysis. *Journal of Personality and Social Psychology*, 1979, **37**(3), 315–321.

122. Kelman, H. C. Attitudes are alive and well and gainfully employed in the sphere of action. *American Psychologist*, 1974, **29**, 310–324.

123. Bem, D. J. *Beliefs, attitudes, and human affairs*. Monterey, Calif.: Brooks/Cole, 1970.

124. Kelman, H. C. Attitudes are alive and well and gainfully employed in the sphere of action. *American Psychologist*, 1974, **29**, 310–324.

125. Kovel, J. *White racism: A psychohistory*. New York: Pantheon, 1970; Katz, I., Glass, D. C., & Cohen, S. Ambivalence, guilt, and the scapegoating of minority group victims. *Journal of Experimental Social Psychology*, 1973, **9**, 423–436.

126. McConahay, J. B., & Hough, J. C. Symbolic racism. *Journal of Social Issues*, 1976, **32**(2), 23–45.

127. Katz, P. A. The acquisition of racial attitudes in children. In P. A. Katz (Ed.), *Towards the elimination of racism*. Elmsford, N.Y.: Pergamon, 1976. Pp. 125–154.

128. Pettigrew, T. Social psychology and desegregation research. *American Psychologist*, 1961, **16**, 105–112.

129. Zanna, M. P., Kiesler, C. A., & Pilkonis, P. A. Positive and negative attitudinal affect established by classical conditioning. *Journal of Personality and Social Psychology*, 1970, **14**(4), 321–328.

130. Rokeach, M. *Beliefs, attitudes, and values*. San Francisco: Jossey-Bass, 1968.

131. Stein, D. C., Hardyck, J. A., & Smith, M. B. Race and belief: An open and shut case. *Journal of Personality and Social Psychology*, 1965, **1**(4), 281–289; Silverman, B. I. Consequences, racial discrimination, and the principles of belief congruence. *Journal of Personality and Social Psychology*, 1974, **29**, 497–508.

132. Wilson, W. Rank order of discrimination and its relevance to civil rights priorities. *Journal of Personality and Social Psychology*, 1970, **15**, 118–224.

133. Greeley, A. M., & Sheatsley, P. B. Attitudes toward racial integration. *Scientific American*, 1971, **225**(6), 13–19.

134. Turner, C. B., & Wilson, W. J. Dimensions of racial ideology: A study of urban black attitudes. *Journal of Social Issues*, 1976, **32**(2), 139–152.

135. Sherif, M. Experiments in group conflict. *Scientific American*, 1956, **195**(5), 54–58.

136. Rocha, R. Children's aggression as a function of competition and reward. Paper delivered at the annual meeting of the American Psychological Association, Washington, 1976.

137. Greeley, A. M., & Sheatsley, P. B. Attitudes toward racial integration. *Scientific American*, 1971, **225**(6), 13–19.

138. Miller, N., & Bugelski, R. Minor studies of aggression: II. The influence of frustrations imposed by the in-group on attitudes expressed toward outgroups. *Journal of Psychology*, 1948, **25**, 437–452.

139. Adorno, T. W., Frenkel-Brunswik, E., Levinson, D. J., & Sanford, R. N. *The authoritarian personality*. New York: Harper & Row, 1950.

140. Caffrey, B., Anderson, S., & Garrison, J. Changes in racial attitudes of white southerners after exposure to the atmosphere of a southern university. *Psychological Reports*, 1969, **25**, 555–558.

141. Deutsch, M., & Collins, M. E. *Interracial housing: A psychological evaluation of a social experiment*. Minneapolis: University of Minnesota Press, 1951.

142. Rubovits, P. C., & Maehr, M. L. Pygmalion black and white. *Journal of Personality and Social Psychology*, 1973, **25**, 210–218; Leacock, E. Reported in R. Rosenthal, The Pygmalion effect lives. *Psychology Today*, 1973, **7**(4), 56–63.

143. Forehand, G., Ragosta, M., & Rock, D. *Conditions and processes of effective school desegregation, Final Report*. Princeton, N.J.: Educational Testing Service, 1976; Lichter, J. H., & Johnson, D. W. Changes in attitudes toward Negroes of white elementary school children after use of multi-ethnic readers. *Journal of Educational Psychology*, 1969, **60**, 148–152.

144. Forehand, G., Ragosta, M., & Rock, D. *Conditions and processes of effective school desegregation, Final Report*. Princeton, N.J.: Educational Testing Service, 1976; Weiner, M. J., & Wright, F. E. Effects of undergoing arbitrary discrimination upon subsequent attitudes toward a minority group. *Journal of Applied Social Psychology*, 1973, **3**, 94–102.

145. Rokeach, M. Long-range experimental modification of values, attitudes, and behavior. *American Psychologist*, 1971, **26**, 453–457.

146. Gerard, H. B., & Miller, N. *School desegregation: A long-range study*. New York: Wiley, 1975.

147. Allport, G. *The nature of prejudice*. Garden City, N.Y.: Doubleday, 1958.

148. Cook, S. W. The effect of unintended interracial contact upon racial interaction and attitude change. Final Report. August 1971; Slavin, R. E., & Madden, N. C. School practices that improve race relations: A reanalysis. Unpublished paper, 1978; Slavin, R. E. Effects of biracial learning teams on cross-racial friendship and interaction. *Center for Social Organization of Schools. Report No. 240*. November 1977; Aronson, E. *The social animal*. (2d ed.) San Francisco: Freeman, 1976.

149. Weigel, R., Wiser, P., & Cook, S. The impact of cooperative learning experiences on cross-ethnic relations and attitudes. *Journal of Social Issues*, 1975, **31**(1), 219–244.

150. Miller, G. A. Psychology as a means of promoting human welfare. *American Psychologist*, 1969, **24,** 1063–1075.

151. Fernea, E. W., & Fernea, R. A. A look behind the veil. *Human Nature*, 1979, **2**(1), 68–77.

152. Burgoon, J. K., & Saine, T. *The unspoken dialogue: An introduction to nonverbal communication*. Boston: Houghton Mifflin, 1978; Argyle, M. The laws of looking. *Human Nature*, 1978, **1**(1), 32–40.

153. Mass psychology and church research. *American Psychological Association Monitor*, 1979, **10**(1), 11, 40; Singer, M. T. Coming out of the cults. *Psychology Today*, 1979, **12**(8), 72–82.

154. Chalmers, D. M. *Hooded Americanism: The first century of the Ku Klux Klan, 1865–1965*. Garden City, N.Y.: Doubleday, 1965.

155. Weiner, M. J., & Wright, F. E. Effects of undergoing arbitrary discrimination upon subsequent attitudes toward a minority group. *Journal of Applied Social Psychology*, 1973, **3**(1), 94–102.

156. Weissbach, T. A. Laboratory controlled studies of change of racial attitudes. In P. A. Katz (Ed.), *Towards the elimination of racism*. Elmsford, N.Y.: Pergamon, 1976. Pp. 157–182.

Glossary

Note: Italicized terms in definitions are described in separate entries.

ablation Research approach for studying the role of the *brain* in behavior and *cognition*. Involves removal or destruction of part of the brain.

abnormal behavior Behavior characterized by grossly defective cognitive or social functioning or self-control or by uncontrollable distress.

accommodation Process by which the *lens* of the eye either thickens or flattens to focus incoming light rays onto the *retina*. Also, Piaget's term for the creation of new strategies or modification or combination of old ones to handle new challenges.

acuity Ability to distinguish details.

adaptation According to Piaget, the development of mental capacities as organisms interact with and learn to cope with their surroundings. Composed of *assimilation* and *accommodation*. (Also see *adjustment*.)

adjustment Process which involves attempting to meet the demands of self and environment.

adolescence A period of human development that extends from approximately ages thirteen to eighteen.

adoption study Research strategy used to investigate whether, and to what extent, *heredity* influences human differences on a particular characteristic. Involves comparison of the similarities between (1) natural parents and children and (2) adoptive parents and adoptees.

adrenal gland One of a pair of *endocrine system glands* located on top of each kidney. They produce *adrenalin* and *noradrenalin*, *sex hormones* (beginning at *puberty*), and additional *hormones* that regulate other bodily functions.

adrenalin A *hormone* secreted by the *adrenal glands* during periods of stress to prepare the body to handle an emergency.

aerial perspective A *monocular depth cue*: as distance increases, colors become grayer and outlines within an image become blurred.

affect See *emotion*.

affective disorder *Abnormal behavior* characterized primarily by excessive sadness or frenzied excitement or elation.

aggression An act aimed at hurting people or property.

alarm reaction Stage 1 of the *general adaptation syndrome*, during which the *sympathetic nervous system* and *adrenal glands* mobilize the body's defensive forces to resist the *stressor*.

alcoholism Drinking that impairs *adjustment* to life.

alpha activity (alpha waves) Brain waves of about 8 to 12 *hertz*, often associated with pleasantly relaxed feelings.

altered state of consciousness A type of awareness different from *ordinary waking consciousness*. Appears during *hypnosis*, *meditation*, and marijuana intoxication, for instance.

ambiguous Unclear.

Ameslan (American Sign Language) (ASL) The gestural *language* used by many deaf Americans.

amnesia Disorder involving sudden loss of memory of important personal information. The lapse may persist for periods ranging from minutes to years.

amygdala Part of the *limbic system*; plays a role in rage, pleasure, pain, and fear.

anal stage According to Freud's theory, the second *psychosexual stage* during which pleasure is focused on the functions of elimination. If toilet training is harsh or if elimination is associated with extreme pleasure, Freud believed, the individ-

ual will show anal characteristics such as messiness or excessive orderliness as an adult.

analyst Person who conducts *psychoanalytic psychotherapy*.

analytic introspection A rigorous type of self-observation requiring intensive training; used by advocates of *structuralism*.

androgen(s) "Masculine" *sex hormones* that regulate *primary* and *secondary sex characteristics* and modify the sex *drive*. During an early *sensitive period*, they alter the *nervous system* and influence subsequent hormonal and behavioral patterns.

anger *Emotion* characterized by a high level of *sympathetic nervous system* activity and by strong feelings of displeasure which are triggered by a real or imagined wrong.

anonymity Lack of an identity; feeling of being unknown.

antisocial personality disorder (psychopathic or sociopathic personality disorder) A *personality disorder* characterized by behavior patterns that bring people into conflict with society. Psychopathic persons neglect others' rights, behave like con artists, act for their own immediate gratification, and appear to be oblivious to the consequences of their conduct.

anxiety Emotion characterized by feelings of anticipated danger, tension, and distress and by *arousal* of the *sympathetic nervous system*.

anxiety disorder Any of three *abnormal behavior* patterns centering around *anxiety*: the *phobic, panic,* and *obsessive-compulsive* disorders.

anxiety neurosis See *panic disorder*.

apparent movement Perceived motion where none is present in actuality.

approach-approach conflict A *conflict* that occurs when a person is simultaneously attracted to two goals, objects, or courses of action and the achievement of one means the abandonment of the other.

approach-avoidance conflict A *conflict* that occurs when a person is simultaneously attracted to and repelled by the same goal, object, or course of action.

arousal An alert or excited state. The term is often applied to *sympathetic nervous system* activity that underlies the state.

arteriosclerosis Disease of the arteries, often seen in elderly people; characterized by thickening and inelasticity of blood-vessel walls and decreased blood flow.

assertion training A type of *behavior therapy* during which adults with severe inhibitions about revealing *emotions* learn to express themselves more genuinely. The training depends on *observation learning* principles.

assimilation Piaget's term for the process of taking in information and categorizing it in terms of what is already known.

association areas Regions of the *cerebral cortex* that integrate incoming information and coordinate the decision-making process. These areas lie outside the cortical regions that receive *sensory* information and control movement.

astigmatism Abnormality of the *lens* of the eye, causing lines in some orientations to appear blurred.

attention Selective openness to a small portion of impinging *sensory* phenomena.

attitude A learned evaluative concept associated with *thoughts*, feelings, and behavior.

attribution An inference about the cause(s) of behavior.

auditory Pertaining to hearing.

autonomic nervous system (ANS) A division of the *nervous system* composed of *nerves* that lead from the *brain* and *spinal cord* to the smooth muscles of the internal organs, glands, heart, and blood vessels; comprises the *parasympathetic* and *sympathetic nervous systems*.

autonomic response (reaction) Reaction (including a rapid pulse, trembling, and tense muscles) controlled by the *autonomic nervous system*.

avoidance-avoidance conflict A *conflict* that occurs when a person is simultaneously repelled by two goals, objects, or courses of action, one of which must be selected.

avoidance behavior Conduct that is learned because it is successful in evading something unpleasant, such as *anxiety* or *punishment*.

avoidance conditioning A type of conditioning during which the frequency of an *operant* is increased under similar conditions because it postpones or prevents an event.

avoidant strategies *Cognitive strategies* that involve ignoring, denying, or evading a problem in some fashion.

axon A branching fiber which protrudes from the *neuron*; its primary function is transmitting information to other neurons, muscles, and *glands*.

babbling The production of meaningless sounds. Ordinarily, children do a lot of babbling during the second half of their first year.

basic drive See *drive*.

behavior genetics The study of (1) the degree to which *heredity* influences differences in the behavior and mental functioning of a specific population and (2) the biological mechanisms by which *genes* affect the expression of behavior and mental functioning.

behavior modification A set of reeducative procedures used to help alleviate human problems. The techniques have been derived from, and/or are consistent with, psychological research; the results are evaluated systematically. These procedures are used in *behavior therapy*.

behavior therapy A type of *psychotherapy* that assumes that psychological problems are caused by social, biological, and environmental factors. It involves modifying those conditions that appear to be maintaining the problem. Typically, techniques from the experimental psychology laboratory are employed to help people unlearn maladaptive behavior and learn or relearn adaptive behavior.

behavioral scientist Specialist in the *science* of behavior, often a psychologist.

behaviorism A psychological movement founded by John Watson. The early behaviorists insisted that psychologists should study observable behavior and use *objective* methods. (See *neobehaviorism*.)

behavioristic Pertaining to *behaviorism*.

binocular depth cue A *depth cue* that depends on the operation of both eyes.

binocular disparity A *depth cue* that occurs because the eyes are located in different positions, causing each *retina* to register a slightly different visual image.

biofeedback Procedure used to teach control of a *physiological* process by providing a learner with systematic information about the operation or state of the bodily part.

biological rhythm(s) Bodily cycles that vary from fractions of a second to a year and even longer (example: the sleep-waking cycle).

bipolar affective disorder A *psychotic* condition (formerly classified as a manic-depressive illness) characterized by recurring bouts of profound *depression* and *mania*.

bizarre Very strange.

body monitoring A widespread activity among *middle-aged* Americans involving the adoption of protective strategies designed to maintain a stable appearance and keep physical performance at a particular level.

brain The master information-processing, decision-making organ of the body.

brainstem *Brain* area containing regions between the medulla (the part of the *hindbrain* connected to the *spinal cord*) and *thalamus*.

case study Collection of detailed information, frequently of a highly personal nature, on the behavior of an individual or group over a long period. (See *clinical observation*.)

cell membrane Thin covering that regulates whatever passes in and out of a cell.

central nervous system (CNS) One of two major subsystems of the *nervous system*; the central information-processing component, consisting of the *spinal cord* and *brain*.

cerebellum A *hindbrain* region that helps regulate posture, balance, and movement.

cerebral cortex A part of the *brain*; the outer covering of the *cerebrum* which receives and processes *sensory* data, integrates present and past information, controls *cognitions*, and directs movement.

cerebral hemisphere A part of the *brain*; one of two nearly symmetrical halves of the *cerebrum*. The right hemisphere controls the left half of the body while the left hemisphere controls the right side of the body.

cerebrum The *midbrain* and *forebrain*.

chemical postnatal environment Chemical influences which shape development after birth.

chemical prenatal environment Chemical influences which shape development before birth.

chromosome Threadlike structure within the cell *nucleus* which contains *genetic* information.

chronic Recurring.

circuit Pathway.

clairvoyance A form of *extrasensory perception*; seeing something in the past, present, or future that cannot be processed by the known *senses*.

classical conditioning See *respondent conditioning*.

client Term for "patient," used in *client-centered psychotherapy*.

client-centered psychotherapy (therapy) A *psychotherapy* approach that assumes that psychological problems occur when people are forced to deny aspects of their own identity and cease to grow. Therapy aims at restoring the *self-concept*

and renewing the growth process. It consists of an intimate here-and-now relationship with a genuine, warmly accepting, and *empathic* psychotherapist.

climacteric Cluster of physical changes experienced by women during *middle-age*. One change is called the *menopause*.

clinical observation A *case study* that occurs in a mental health or medical setting.

clinical psychologist A specialist who studies normal and abnormal psychology and diagnoses and treats emotional problems.

clinician A person who works with troubled people, counseling and conducting *psychotherapy*.

closure Principle that organizes *perception* so that incomplete objects tend to be seen as complete.

CNS See *central nervous system*.

cognition The process of knowing. The term is used by psychologists for mental activities such as using *language*, thinking, reasoning, solving problems, conceptualizing, remembering, imagining, and learning complex materials.

cognitive Pertaining to *cognition*.

cognitive dissonance Tension aroused by conflicting *cognitions*. People attempt to reduce dissonance by seeking new information, changing *attitudes*, altering behavior, or rearranging the environment.

cognitive psychology An approach to the study of psychology used by psychologists who rebelled against the *behavioristic* notion that the mind's operations could be ignored. Cognitive psychologists try to acquire precise knowledge about how mental processes operate during daily life.

cognitive strategy A mental device, or *defense mechanism*, that helps people cope with stress. Also, a procedure used in *behavior therapy* to change maladaptive thinking and problem solving.

community mental health center Clinic designed to bring a wide range of psychological services to people within their own communities.

compulsion A ritualistic behavior that recurs despite a person's attempts to resist the impulse.

concentrative meditation *Meditation* exercise focusing awareness on a single, unchanging source of stimulation.

concordant In agreement.

concrete operations, stage of Piaget's name for a developmental stage (between the ages of seven and eleven, approximately) during which children develop the ability to use logic and stop relying heavily on *sensory* information to understand the nature of things.

conditioned Learned by *operant* or *respondent conditioning*.

conditioned reinforcer See *secondary reinforcer*.

conditioned response In *respondent conditioning*, a response evoked by a *conditioned stimulus* that is similar to, but milder than, the *unconditioned response*.

conditioned stimulus In *respondent conditioning*, the *neutral stimulus* after it has been *conditioned* to evoke a new *response*.

conditioning Term used synonymously with simple types of *learning*, especially *operant* and *respondent conditioning*.

conductance See *skin conductance*.

cone *Receptor* in the *retina* of the eye which responds to visible light, registering both color and detail.

conflict A situation in which two or more incompatible needs, goals, or courses of action compete, causing an organism to feel pulled in different directions with an attending sense of discomfort.

conformity A change in human behavior and/or *attitudes* that results from real or imagined group pressure.

conscious Aware.

consciousness Total awareness; normal waking state.

constancy Principle that organizes the process of *perception*; objects viewed from different angles, at various distances, or under diverse conditions of illumination are still perceived as retaining the same shape, size, and color.

constant sensory experience Events processed by the *senses* both before and after birth that are normally inevitable for all members of a particular species; an important influence on development.

constructionist perspective Viewpoint, associated with Piaget, that people use imagination (constructions) to make sense of experiences.

contingent Dependent.

continuity Principle that organizes *perception*; visual elements that form smooth regular patterns are seen as belonging together.

continuous reinforcement In *operant conditioning*, *reinforcement* that occurs after every correct response.

continuum A continuous series of values.

control A powerful test of a *hypothesis*, in which the conditions thought to cause a behavior or mental process are altered to see whether the phenomenon changes accordingly. Also, a method used to keep *extraneous* factors from interfering with or obscuring the influence of the *independent variable(s)* in an *experiment*.

control group *Subjects* in an *experiment* exposed to the same experiences as the experimental subjects, except the *independent variable*. Differences in performance between these groups are attributed to the independent variable.

convergence A *depth cue* provided by *kinesthetic* feedback from the eye muscles.

convergent thinking Ability to reason in conventional ways and arrive at a single, correct solution to a problem.

conversion disorder (conversion reaction) A type of abnormal behavior in which the sufferer shows unusual *sensory* or motor symptoms, such as paralysis, loss of vision, or insensitivity to pain.

cope Handle a problem in some fashion, often by avoiding, escaping, or reducing the distress aroused.

cornea Transparent covering that protects the eye and helps focus events in the *visual field* onto the *retina*.

corpus callosum Massive network of *axons* joining the two halves of the brain and enabling them to share skills and resources.

correlate *Verb:* To conduct a correlational study that investigates whether, to what extent, and in what manner two sets of scores are associated with one another. A *correlation coefficient* is calculated to determine whether the two sets of scores are significantly related. *Noun:* A phenomenon that is significantly correlated with another.

correlation coefficient (correlation) A *statistic* describing the strength and direction of the relationship between two *variables*, based on two sets of scores. A positive correlation coefficient indicates that high, middling, or low scores on one variable are associated with correspondingly high, middling, or low scores on the other. A negative correlation coefficient suggests that high scores on one variable are associated with low scores on the other.

cortex See *cerebral cortex*.

cortical Pertaining to the *cerebral cortex*.

counterconditioning A special type of *respondent conditioning* in which a specific *conditioned response* is replaced by a new, incompatible conditioned response.

creativity Distinct problem-solving capacity which enables people to produce original ideas or products that are both adaptive and fully developed.

curiosity *Motivation* to explore and manipulate the environment.

data Facts; information; *statistics*; findings.

day-care In the field of mental health, a therapeutic program attended during the day by *chronic* mental patients living in their own communities.

decay Disappearance of a memory with the passage of time.

deep processing (elaborative re- **hearsal strategies)** Information-processing practices (e.g., paying close attention, thinking about meaning, and relating data to items already in *long-term memory*) which are likely to transfer material to long-term memory.

defense mechanism Sigmund Freud's term for *cognitive strategies*. According to Freud, the ego uses these devices without the person's awareness to falsify and distort threatening experiences, impulses, *conflicts*, and ideas in order to relieve tension.

delusion Persistent false belief that resists reason.

demand characteristics All cues in an *experiment* which convey the investigator's *hypotheses*; may include facial expressions, gestures, and vocal tones.

dendrite A branching fiber attached to the *soma* of the *neuron*; usually picks up information from nearby neurons.

denial of reality (denial) A *cognitive strategy* in which a person ignores or refuses to acknowledge the existence of an aversive experience in order to alleviate distress.

deoxyribonucleic acid (DNA) Chemical substance that codes information about each individual's *genetic* inheritance.

dependent variable In an *experiment*, the *variable* whose state is caused by, and therefore depends on, changes in another variable, called the *independent variable*.

depression See *major depressive disorder*.

depth cue Information received through the eyes that signals depth or distance.

desensitization See *systematic desensitization*.

determinism Belief that all events have natural causes and may eventually be explained. Determinism should not be confused with fatalism (a belief that behavior is established in advance by outside forces beyond a person's control).

developmental psychology A branch of *psychology* which investigates the evolution of physical structure, behavior, and mental functioning in people and other animals from any point after conception to any point before death.

Diagnostic and Statistical Manual of Mental Disorders (DSM) Manual that describes different types of *abnormal behavior*; used widely for classifying mental disorders.

diathesis Predisposition.

directed thinking *Thought* aimed at a particular goal, highly controlled, and tied to a specific situation or problem.

discrimination In *respondent conditioning*, responses to one or more *stimuli* that were present during *conditioning*, but not to similar stimuli. In *operant conditioning*, responses *reinforced* in a specific situation spread to some circumstances, but not to similar ones. The cognitive process of distinguishing between similar phenomena. Also, conduct biased against or for a person or group of people, based on their group membership and not on individual merits or deficiencies.

displace Relocate. The term is often applied to *aggression*.

displaced aggression *Aggression* which results from *frustration* and is directed at available targets, instead of at the source of the frustration.

disposition Attribute of *personality*.

dissociation theory Explanation of light *hypnosis* which makes these assumptions: People have independent mental control systems operating at the same time to record and process information and direct activities. Each system is isolated from the others. During light hypnosis, control may shift from systems that ordinarily dominate to those that are usually controlled.

dissociative disorder Disorder that includes several *abnormal behavior* syndromes that are characterized by alterations in *consciousness*, primarily memory lapses, including *amnesia*, *fugue*, and *multiple personality*.

divergent thinking Innovative and original mental activity that deviates from customary patterns and results in more than one acceptable solution to a problem.

dizygotic (fraternal) A characteristic of offspring delivered near the same time yet originating from the union of different *ova* and *sperm* cells. Dizygotic siblings resemble one another *genetically* only as closely as brothers and sisters born at different times.

DNA See *deoxyribonucleic acid*.

dominant hemisphere (major hemisphere) The side of the *brain* where centers which make *verbal* activities possible are *localized*.

dopamine *Neurotransmitter* that seems to be related to Parkinson's disease, amphetamine abuse, and *schizophrenia*; involved in movement and pleasure.

dopamine hypothesis The hypothesis that excessive *dopamine* activity within specific *brain* circuits underlies *schizophrenia*.

double approach-avoidance conflict A *conflict* involving two goals each of which has good and bad points.

double-blind procedure A tactic used in an *experiment* to prevent both the experimenter and the *subject* from knowing the subject's group.

drive *Motive* that arises to satisfy basic *physiological* needs.

DSM See *Diagnostic and Statistical Manual of Mental Disorders*.

DTs (delirium tremens) Reaction in an alcoholic that may appear after a prolonged spree on alcohol, during abstinence from alcohol, or accompanying an infection or head injury. Includes disorientation for time and space, vivid *hallucinations* and fears of them, extreme suggestibility, tremors, perspiration, fever, and a rapid, weak heartbeat.

eclectic Using a combination of approaches.

EEG See *electroencephalograph*.

effectors Cells that control muscles, *glands*, or organs.

ego According to Freud, a *personality* component that emerges in developing children to handle transactions with the environment. One of its major tasks is locating real objects to satisfy the *id*'s needs.

egocentric Self-centered.

elaborative rehearsal strategies See *deep processing*.

Electra complex According to Freud's *personality theory*, the *conflict* experienced by young girls during the *phallic stage*; females presumably turn against their mothers and desire their fathers sexually.

electrode Usually a needle or flat piece of metal that conducts electricity.

electroencephalogram A recording of electrical activity within *neural* circuits of the *brain*.

electroencephalograph (EEG) Instrument which measures electrical activity within *neural* circuits of the *brain*.

eliciting stimulus The triggering event in *respondent conditioning*, known as the *unconditioned stimulus*.

embryo An unborn baby during early stages of development; a human two to eight weeks after conception.

emotion Internal state characterized by specific *cognitions*, sensations, *physiological* reactions, and expressive behavior. Emotions tend to appear suddenly and to be difficult to control.

empathy Ability to experience another's thoughts and *emotions*.

empirical (empirically based) Pertaining to *empiricism*.

empiricism Philosophical doctrine asserting that *sensory* experiences, particularly *experiments* and observations, are the best source of knowledge.

encoding Process of readying information for memory storage. Encoding often involves associating material with past knowledge or experience, and also entails representing material in a form that the storage system can handle.

endocrine system (endocrine glands) Coordinating system composed of ductless *glands* that secrete *hormones* into the bloodstream, regulating an animal's internal environment.

engram Long-lasting physical change that takes place within the *nervous system* as a memory is made.

enzymes Types of *proteins* that regulate the operations of the cell.

escape conditioning Process during which the frequency of an *operant* is increased under similar circumstances because it terminates an ongoing event (considered unpleasant).

estrogen(s) "Feminine" *sex hormones* that influence the development of *secondary sex characteristics* and regulate the *estrus cycle*. A deficiency causes distressing physical changes that many, but not all, women experience during the *menopause*: hot flashes, loss of calcium, drying of the vaginal lining, and spasms of the esophagus.

estrus cycle The hormonal cycle in the female related to reproduction.

ethologist Scientist who studies the behavior of animals in natural settings.

excitatory neurotransmitter *Neurotransmitter* that tends to make adjacent *neurons fire*.

exhaustion The third stage of the *general adaptation syndrome* when the body shows signs of exhaustion. After the *sympathetic nervous system* exhausts its energy, the *parasympathetic nervous system* may take over. If the stress continues, severe psychological or physical problems or even death may result.

existential theory A *theory* that emphasizes freedom of choice and advocates taking full responsibility for one's own existence and striving to achieve *self-actualization*.

experiment A powerful method for studying causal relationships. During an experiment, the effects of a deliberately manipulated *variable* are assessed. The characteristic feature of the experimental method is its attempt to *control* all *extraneous* factors that can obscure or interfere with the effect of the manipulation.

experimenter bias Phenomenon

occurring when an experimenter unknowingly cues *subjects*, influencing the responses in the direction of his or her expectations.

extinction In both *operant* and *respondent conditioning*, the gradual decrease in frequency of the *conditioned response* until it occurs no more frequently than it did prior to *conditioning*. Extinction takes place when the *reinforcement* for the response is withdrawn.

extinguished Reduced in frequency through *extinction*.

extraneous Irrelevant. In an *experiment*, investigators attempt to control the influence of extraneous *variables*.

extrasensory perception (ESP) *Perception* through means other than the known *senses*.

extrinsic reinforcer (reinforcement) A *reinforcer* that is not the natural and inevitable result of simply engaging in a task; a reinforcer coming from a source other than the behavior being strengthened.

familiar size A *depth cue*, pictorial in nature, used to estimate the distance of a well-known object by noting the relative size of the image on the *retina*.

fantasy A *cognitive strategy* used by people to achieve needs or goals in imagination while escaping unpleasant, anxiety-arousing, or frustrating realities.

fetus The unborn infant in the later stages of development; in humans, the period from eight weeks after conception until birth.

field experiment *Experiment* that takes place in a natural setting.

figure-ground relationship A principle that organizes *perception*; an object (figure) tends to be seen standing out from a background (ground).

fire Conduct a *nerve impulse*.

firing threshold Excitation level that must be attained before an *axon* will conduct a *nerve impulse*.

fixation Freudian term that means the permanent investment of a portion of *libido* at a *psychosexual* stage of development.

fixed action pattern A *response*

that is *species-specific*, highly *stereotyped*, completed once initiated, largely independent of training, resistant to modification, and often triggered by a specific environmental *stimulus*.

forebrain Part of the *brain* that is involved in processing data and satisfying recurring bodily needs in people.

formal operations, stage of Period from approximately eleven to fifteen years of age when children develop the ability to understand abstract logic (think about thinking), according to Piaget.

fovea A small depression within the *retina* of the eye directly in the line of sight where tightly packed *cones* are concentrated.

fraternal See *dizygotic*.

free association The process of allowing one's mind to wander freely while giving a completely frank running account of thoughts and feelings; a type of *undirected thinking*.

free recall Task used in memory *experiments* asking that the subject *recall* material in any order at all.

frontal lobe Part of the *cerebral cortex* (near the forehead) that plays a particularly important role in higher mental activities.

frustration (1) The emotional state that results when an obstacle prevents the satisfaction of a desire, *need*, goal, expectation, or action; (2) the obstacle itself.

fugue Syndrome of *abnormal behavior* in which a person forgets recent experiences and flees to a different locality to begin a new life.

functional fixity A tendency to see a particular object as fixed in function largely because of past experience and to fail to perceive new and flexible uses for it.

functionalism A psychological movement of historical interest that concentrated on the functioning of mental processes, especially as they help people survive in a dangerous world.

GAS See *general adaptation syndrome*.

gender Sex.

gene The basic unit of *heredity*,

composed of deoxyribonucleic acid. It directs the production of *proteins* and makes up the *chromosomes*.

general adaptation syndrome (GAS) A pattern of *physiological* responses to continued stress; it consists of three stages: *alarm reaction*, *resistance*, and *exhaustion*.

generalization In *respondent conditioning*, the spreading of a *conditioned response* to events similar to the *conditioned stimulus* and to aspects of the situation where the response was initially *conditioned*. In *operant conditioning*, the spreading of a *conditioned response* strengthened under one set of circumstances to similar situations. Also, the cognitive process of inferring trends, conclusions, or similarities.

genetic (genetically) Pertaining to the *gene*.

genetic sex The *gender* of an organism, determined by a single pair of *chromosomes*, the *sex chromosomes*.

genital stage In Freud's *personality theory*, the final *psychosexual stage* when sexual interests shift from the self to others.

gestalt Shape, pattern, or structure (from the German word *gestalt*).

gestalt psychology A psychological movement of historical interest, founded by Max Wertheimer and his colleagues. Its members argued that psychologists should study whole phenomena and focus primarily on people's *subjective* experiences.

gestalt psychotherapy (therapy) A *psychotherapy* approach that assumes that problems occur when people waste energy rejecting significant aspects of their nature and adopting alien characteristics as their own. Therapy aims at restoring inherent capacities for growth. Therapists use exercises, dream interpretations, and vivid scenarios for this purpose.

gland Cell, cell group, or organ which secretes a chemical substance.

glia (glial cells) Cells lying amidst the *neurons* in the *central nervous system*. Their precise functions are currently unknown.

global General; pertaining to the whole; impressionistic.

glucose Type of sugar molecule.

gonads Sex glands (the *testes* and *ovaries*).

grammar As defined by *psycholinguists*, the collection of rules and principles which determine the meaning of every possible sentence that can be formed in a *language*. As commonly used, rules that deal with superficial aspects of language, such as appropriate style and correct sentence formation.

ground Abbreviation for background.

group psychotherapy *Psychotherapy* in a group.

grouping principles Principles that organize *perception*. Separate visual elements are unified into patterns according to these "laws."

growth motive *Motive* to attain mastery, excellence, or competence.

habituate Become accustomed to.

halfway house A residence that is also a treatment facility, and thus, an alternative to institutionalization for mental patients.

hallucination *Sensory* experience without a basis in reality.

Hawthorne effect The influence of attention on performance during an experiment.

hemisphere One of two nearly symmetrical halves of the *brain*.

heredity The physical characteristics transmitted directly from parent to offspring at conception.

hermaphrodite Person born with masculine and feminine reproductive structures.

hertz Cycles per second; a measure of frequency.

hierarchy System where persons or things are ranked in a specific order, one above another.

hindbrain Part of the *brain* that exerts major control over vital bodily functions in people and many other animals.

hippocampus A *limbic system* region which serves important functions in memory and in organizing information about spatial location.

homeostasis The body's self-regulating tendency.

homosexual Male who prefers members of his own sex as sexual partners.

hormone A chemical substance secreted directly into the bloodstream by the *endocrine* glands.

humanistic psychology An approach to psychology that emphasizes viewing people as whole beings, focusing on *subjective* awareness, investigating significant human problems, and enriching human life.

hypnosis *Altered state of consciousness*, produced by a series of persuasive suggestions, during which people feel unusually responsive to the influence of the hypnotist.

hypothalamus A central *limbic system* region that is responsible for activating the *nervous system* during emergencies and controls so many other vital functions that it is sometimes known as the "guardian of the body."

hypothesis A *tentative* explanation that can be tested by an *experiment*; a statement positing the existence of a relationship between two or more *variables*.

iconic memory Visual *sensory memory*.

id *Personality* component, according to Freud, lying at the primitive core of the person; the domain of basic *drives* that seek immediate gratification.

identical See *monozygotic*.

identify Freudian term meaning to strive to become like someone else.

idiot savant A mentally handicapped person who possesses one or more extraordinary abilities.

imitation See *observation learning*.

imprinting An early following pattern seen in many young animals that reflects a social attachment.

in utero During the *intrauterine period*.

incentive Object, event, or condition that incites action.

independent variable In an *experiment*, the *variable* which, when manipulated, causes changes in the *dependent variable*.

induction disciplinary technique A parental practice involving reasoning with children and explaining the painful consequences of their misdeeds.

inhibitory neurotransmitter *Neurotransmitter* that tends to prevent the firing of adjacent *neurons*.

insane The term used by professionals primarily in courts of law to imply that people lacked the free will that would justify holding them accountable for their own behavior. As commonly used, the word is roughly equivalent to the term *psychotic*.

instinct The term occasionally used for *physiological needs* and complicated behavior patterns that are influenced heavily by *heredity*. Today, *behavioral scientists* are likely to talk about *fixed action patterns* rather than instincts.

instrumental conditioning See *operant conditioning*.

insulin Hormone that lowers blood *glucose* level and stimulates hunger.

intellectualization A *cognitive strategy* that treats situations that would ordinarily generate strong feelings in a detached, analytic, intellectual manner.

intelligence A capacity for mental activity that cannot be directly measured; also see *measured intelligence*.

intelligence quotient (IQ) Numerical index describing relative performance on a test of mental abilities, comparing the performance of one person with others of similar age.

interference The "collision" of items of information with one another that somehow hampers retention and causes memory failure.

interneuron The type of nerve cell predominating within the *central nervous system*; has short *axon* and *dendrites* which branch profusely.

interposition A *monocular depth cue*, causing a complete object to be perceived as closer than an obstructed one.

interpretation In *psychoanalytic psychotherapy*, the comments made by *clinicians* as they gradually reveal the insights they have gained while coming to understand patients' *repressed conflicts*.

intrauterine period Time spent within the uterus.

intrinsic reinforcer (reinforcement) The type of *reinforcer* that occurs when the behavior to be strengthened is a source of pleasurable feelings and the act is automatically strengthened every time it occurs.

introspect (introspection) The process of looking within oneself and examining personal experiences.

iris Colored disc surrounding the *pupil* of the eye; controls the pupil's size.

kinesthetic sense Sense that depends on *receptors* in muscles, tendons, and joints; informs animals about the relative positioning of body parts during movement.

language System relating symbols to meaning and providing rules for combining and recombining the symbols for communication.

latency stage A period between the *phallic* and *genital stages* when sexual needs become dormant, according to Freud, and no *personality* changes or *conflicts* occur.

latent Existing in an *unconscious* or nonvisible form.

latent content Freudian term for the dream's real meaning.

law Statement that describes regular, predictable relationships.

learned helplessness Syndrome produced by subjecting laboratory animals to shocks that cannot be escaped; the condition is characterized by appetite loss, diminished interest in sex, reduced *aggression*, passivity, and a refusal to cope.

learning Relatively lasting change in behavior brought about by experience.

learning to learn See *learning set*.

learning set A case of *positive transfer* when organisms acquire general problem-solving abilities.

lens The eye structure, behind the *pupil*, that helps in focusing visual images on the *retina*.

lesbian Female who prefers members of her own sex as sexual partners.

lesion Change in tissue because of disease, injury, or surgery; usually harmful.

libido Freudian concept denoting a fixed amount of energy generated by *sexual drives* for behavior and mental functioning.

light and shadow A picture-related *monocular depth cue*. When light from a specific source, such as the sun, strikes a three-dimensional object, it illuminates the side(s) facing the light source and leaves the other side(s) in shadow, giving information about solidity, depth, protrusions, and the like.

limbic system Group of interrelated *neuron* circuits deep within the *brain's* core which play a regulatory role in both *emotions* and *motives*. Includes the *amygdala*, *hippocampus*, *septum*, cingulate gyrus, and portions of the *hypothalamus* and *thalamus*.

linear perspective A *monocular depth cue* related to *familiar size*.

lobe One of four subdivisions of the *cerebral cortex*: *frontal*, *parietal*, *temporal*, and *occipital* lobes.

localized Located in a particular place.

longitudinal investigation A study measuring the same *subjects* on particular characteristics at two or more points in time.

long-term memory (LTM), long-term store More-or-less permanent memory system.

major depressive disorder A type of *abnormal behavior* characterized by an unusually intense and persisting state of sadness. Includes disturbances formerly classified in both *neurotic* and *psychotic* categories.

major hemisphere See *dominant hemisphere*.

major tranquilizer Chemical agent that has a calming effect; used to treat *schizophrenia*.

maladjusted (behavior) Term implying that conduct deviates from standards considered appropriate for a specific situation, without suggesting that absolute guidelines are being used.

mania *Abnormal behavior* characterized by excited elation.

manifest content Freudian term for the superficial subject matter of a dream.

matching *Control* for *extraneous subject variables* in an *experiment*; subjects who are equivalent on significant characteristics are assigned to each group in the experiment.

maturation The emergence of behavior patterns that depend primarily on the development of body and *nervous system* structures.

mean A *measure of central tendency*; arithmetic average.

measure of central tendency A measure of the central value around which a group of scores clusters.

measured intelligence Performance in a specific mental testing situation which is always based on achievements—habits and acquired skills.

median A *measure of central tendency*; the middle score in a group of scores; the point at which 50 percent of the scores are higher and 50 percent of them are lower.

medical model Model of *abnormal behavior*; assumes that either (1) mental disorders are specific medical conditions for which biological causes will eventually be discovered or (2) emotional disorders closely resemble physical ailments.

meditation Diverse exercises that aim at altering *consciousness*, usually by inducing a receptive, quiet mode and an internal focus.

memory trace See *engram*.

menopause One phase of the *climacteric* which occurs in women during middle age; the *ovaries* stop producing ripe *ova* and menstruation stops.

mental age Measure of *intelligence* computed in diverse ways on different mental tests.

microelectrode A tiny *electrode* that enables scientists to observe the electrical activity of a single *neuron*; can be implanted directly into a single cell.

midbrain Part of the human *brain*

receiving some *sensory* information and controlling certain muscles.

middle age Period of time when people are in their forties, fifties, and early sixties.

minor hemisphere *Hemisphere* of the *brain* that does not handle *verbal* functions; important in skills depending on the simultaneous *perception* of whole phenomena and the synthesis of material.

mixed nerves Nerves formed from the *axons* of both *sensory* and *motor neurons*.

mnemonic devices Strategies enabling people to integrate separate, basically unrelated items with little or no internal logic into meaningful related groupings so that they are easier to retain.

mode A *measure of central tendency*; the score that appears most frequently in a group of scores.

model Simplified system that contains the essential features of a larger, more complex system. Models usually allow scientists to make *predictions*; tests of these predictions verify or disprove aspects of the model.

modeling See *observation learning*.

monocular depth cue *Depth cue* that depends on the operation of only one eye.

monozygotic (identical) A characteristic of offspring who come from the splitting of a single *zygote* into two or more zygotes with identical *genes*.

motion parallax A *monocular depth cue*; close objects seem to move with greater speed than distant ones.

motive (motivation) Internal state which results from a *need* and incites behavior, usually directed toward fulfilling the activating need.

motor nerves Bundles of *axons* which carry information from the *central nervous system* to *effectors* in the muscles, *glands*, and organs.

motor neurons *Neurons* which carry messages from the *central nervous system* to *effectors* in the muscles, *glands*, and organs.

multiple approach-avoidance conflict A *conflict* between two or more goals where each choice is partly positive and partly negative.

multiple personality A type of *abnormal behavior* pattern in which an individual shows two or more very different *personalities* yet is aware of only one personality at any specific moment.

myelin sheath Fatty covering surrounding the *axon* that appears to serve an insulating function.

naturalistic observation An observation made in a real-life setting to gather information about realistic behavior.

need A deficiency that may be based on specific bodily or learned requirements or on some combination of the two.

negative correlation coefficient See *correlation coefficient*.

negative reinforcement (reinforcer) The process and consequence occurring whenever the removal of a specific event following an *operant* increases the likelihood that the operant will occur in similar situations.

negative transfer Effect that is said to occur when previous experiences retard new *learning* or problem solving.

neobehaviorism A modern version of *behaviorism* that has become increasingly concerned with complex human processes. The neobehaviorist insists on asking precise, well-delineated questions, using the *scientific method*, and performing careful, accurate research.

neo-Freudian Pertaining to modifications and revisions of basic Freudian (or *psychoanalytic*) ideas.

neonate Newborn human infant.

nerve impulse Temporary alteration in the permeability of the membrane surrounding the *axon* and the resulting charge redistribution there.

nerves (nerve tracts) Network of information-carrying cables (composed of *axons*) which relay messages among the *central nervous system*, *receptors*, and *effectors*.

nervous system Internal coordinating system that organizes the functioning of all living organisms; includes the *central* and *peripheral nervous systems*.

neural Pertaining to the *neuron*, *nerves*, or *nervous system*.

neuron A nerve cell; the basic unit of the *nervous system*.

neurosis (neurotic reaction) A behavioral disorder that centers on *anxiety*. Neurotic people typically have difficulty handling anxiety. They frequently react by *avoidance behavior*. More often than not, they lack insight into the causes of their symptoms and persist in the same maladaptive responses. As they become increasingly preoccupied with anxieties, inadequacies, and symptoms, work and interpersonal relationships suffer. Consequently, neurotics usually feel unhappy and out of control.

neurotransmitter Chemical substance which plays an important role in message transmission throughout the *nervous system*.

neutral stimulus In *respondent conditioning*, any experience or object that is paired with an *unconditioned stimulus* and does not initially elicit the *unconditioned response* evoked by the unconditioned stimulus.

noradrenalin See *norepinephrine*.

norepinephrine One of about a dozen *neurotransmitters*. When animals are prevented from actively handling stresses, this substance becomes depleted.

norm(s) Information on the test performance of a large *reference group* which allows an examiner to interpret an individual score. Also, a constraint, reference standard, or rule governing behavior within a group.

NREM sleep Sleep characterized by the absence of rapid eye movements; includes stage 1 NREM and stage 2, stage 3, and stage 4 sleep.

nucleus A distinct, centrally located structure within a cell which contains *chromosomes*.

nystagmus Small, rapid, involuntary tremors of the eye.

obedience Abandonment of personal judgments and cooperation with the demands of an authority.

obese Possessing an excessive amount of fat; descriptive of individuals who are at least 20 percent over their ideal weight.

objective Free of bias. Research methods and test results are said to be objective when the procedures used minimize the influence of the experimenter's or examiner's biases. Tests classified as objective can be scored in essentially the same way anywhere.

observation learning (imitation, modeling, social learning) Learning that occurs when relatively enduring changes in behavior result, in large part, from observing another's conduct.

obsession A *thought* that repeatedly occupies *attention* although the person prefers to be rid of it.

obsessive-compulsive disorder *Abnormal behavior* characterized by *obsessions* and/or *compulsions* that disrupt life.

occipital lobe Region at the rear of the *cerebral cortex* that receives and processes visual information.

Oedipus complex The *conflict* that occurs during the *phallic stage*, according to Freud's *theory*, when a young boy displays (1) desires to possess his mother sexually and (2) intensely rivalrous feelings toward his father.

old old age Period of life when a person is more than seventy-five years old.

opening up meditation *Meditation* exercise that attempts to heighten awareness of the external environment.

operant An action which animals initiate themselves.

operant conditioning (instrumental conditioning) Conditioning that occurs whenever the consequences following an *operant* increase or decrease the probability that the operant will be performed in a similar situation.

operational definition A precise definition relating a concept or object to the procedures used to observe or measure it.

optic nerve *Axons* of *sensory neurons* connecting the eye to various *brain* centers.

oral stage According to *psychoanalytic theory*. the first *psychosexual stage*, during which the child's pleasure centers on oral activities, such as eating and sucking.

ordinary waking consciousness Rambling mental activity with no specific goal; the type of awareness that accompanies being awake and functioning normally, when *perceptions* mingle with *thoughts*, feelings, memories, and the like.

organic mental disorder *Brain* impairment that results in *abnormal behavior*.

organization A term applied to *perception* because numerous principles appear to structure the process. Also, a Piagetian term for the tendency to combine two or more separate physical or psychological processes into one smoothly functioning response system.

orthodox Traditional.

orthodox psychoanalytic psychotherapy See *psychoanalytic psychotherapy*.

outpatient Psychiatric patient who lives outside a mental institution.

ovaries Feminine sex *glands*.

overlearning Practice beyond the point of mastery.

ovum (*plural:* ova) The mother's egg cell; it combines with the father's *sperm* to form a *zygote*.

panic disorder (anxiety neurosis) *Abnormal behavior* characterized by almost continuous *anxiety* and tension; anxiety attacks are sudden and unexpected.

paradoxical sleep See REM sleep.

parapsychological Pertaining to *extrasensory perception*.

parasympathetic nervous system (division) A subsystem of the *autonomic nervous system*; most active during periods of comparative calm in controlling the performance of routine duties that build up and conserve the body's store of energy.

parietal lobe Region in the central

part of the *cerebral cortex* which is involved in the control of speech and in registering and analyzing information about events at the body's interior and exterior surfaces (touch, pressure, temperature, and muscle movement and position).

parsimony A philosophical doctrine stating that the best explanation is the simplest one that fits the observed facts.

partial reinforcement schedule *Schedule of reinforcement* where some, but not all, correct *responses* are followed by a *reinforcer* during *operant conditioning*.

partial report strategy Used in memory experiments; *subjects* are signaled to report one or more items selected at random from the information they have learned.

participant observation A *naturalistic observation* made while scientists participate in the event or activity being studied.

pavlovian conditioning See *respondent conditioning*.

peptic ulcer A *lesion*, usually in the stomach or duodenum lining, produced by the excessive secretion of hydrochloric acid.

perception (perceptual system) Process of organizing and interpreting incoming *sensory* data to develop an awareness of self and surroundings. It includes visual, auditory (hearing), *somatosensory*, chemical (taste-smell), and *proprioceptive* perceptual systems.

perceptual adaptation Flexibility in handling changing *sensory* inputs.

performance Behavior measured to assess whether *learning* occurred.

peripheral nervous system One of two major subsystems of the *nervous system*; composed of the *autonomic nervous system* and the *somatic nervous system*.

peristaltic contraction Muscle movement associated with digestion.

personality A distinct identity that appears to be formed of relatively consistent and enduring patterns of perceiving, thinking, feeling, and behaving.

personality disorder Deeply in-grained, inflexible, maladaptive pattern of relating to, perceiving, and thinking about the environment and oneself, causing an impairment in adaptive functioning and/or *subjective* distress.

phallic stage The third *psychosexual stage*, according to Freud's *theory*, when pleasure is focused on the genitals and the *Electra* and *Oedipus complexes* arise.

phenomenological theory *Theory* that concentrates on trying to understand a person's *self*, emphasizing the importance of unique *subjective* perspectives on life.

phenothiazines A type of major tranquilizer used to treat *schizophrenia*.

phobia (phobic disorder) An excessive or unwarranted fear of an object or situation that is handled by persistent avoidance. Considered a phobic disorder only when the condition is disruptive and disabling.

physiological Pertaining to the physical functions of living organisms or any of their parts.

physiological psychologist Specialist who studies relationships between behavior and biology; also known as a psychobiologist.

pictorial cue A picture-related *monocular depth cue*.

pituitary gland The master gland of the *endocrine system*. It may initiate bodily processes, such as growth, and activate delinquent glands whose *hormone* production has dropped below normal levels; it is commanded by the *hypothalamus*.

placebo An inert drug or "neutral" treatment used to equalize the expectations of groups in an *experiment*.

plastic Flexible.

pleasure center Area in the *brain* which, when stimulated directly, seems to arouse pleasant feelings. Many pleasure centers exist throughout the brains of mammals—including people.

polygraph An instrument used to measure several *physiological responses*, such as heart rate, respiration rate, and muscle tension, at the same time.

pons A *brain* region which helps coordinate rapid bodily movements; located in the *hindbrain*.

population The entire group under study.

positive correlation coefficient See *correlation coefficient*.

positive reinforcement (reinforcer) The process and consequence that take place whenever the presentation of an event or object following an *operant* increases the probability that the operant will occur in similar situations.

positive transfer Effect that is said to occur whenever previous experiences help animals *learn* or solve problems.

posthypnotic amnesia Temporary forgetting of something that happened during a hypnotic trance until a specific prearranged signal, such as snapping fingers, ends the memory lapse.

posthypnotic suggestion Phenomenon occurring when a hypnotist suggests to a *subject* that a specific cue will cause particular sensations or behaviors after the hypnotic trance has ended and the subject obeys without any conscious awareness of the suggestion.

potential reinforcer A consequence that is suspected of being able to *reinforce* an *operant*.

precision Exactness, clarity, and accuracy in definitions and descriptions.

precognition A form of *extrasensory perception*; knowledge of a future event that cannot be logically inferred.

preconscious Freudian concept; certain *thoughts*, memories, feelings, and desires are buried, presumably, just beneath awareness where they are fairly easy to retrieve.

prediction A powerful test of a *hypothesis*; if a hypothesis is correct, it should be able to predict what will happen in related situations.

prejudice Negative or positive prejudgment about a person or group based on *stereotypes* that exaggerate group characteristics and ignore individual strengths and weaknesses.

preoperational stage Period from approximately ages two to seven, when children rely heavily on *perceptions* of reality to solve problems, according to Piaget.

primary prevention In mental health care, helping essentially normal people to utilize their full potential and develop satisfying, effective ways of adjusting to life.

primary reinforcer (unlearned reinforcer) *Reinforcer* that is powerful in strengthening an *operant* without prior training.

primary sex characteristic(s) Sex organ(s): in females, *ovaries*, vagina, and uterus; in males, *testes* and penis.

primary zone (primary projection area) Region of the *cerebral cortex* that (1) receives or sorts a particular type of *sensory* information or (2) controls movement.

proactive inhibition Process that occurs when previously acquired information interferes with retaining new information.

problem solving An endeavor involving a goal and obstacles. Problem solvers perceive an objective, encounter difficulties, are motivated to achieve the goal, and work to overcome the obstacles.

process schizophrenia A type of *schizophrenia* that develops gradually over many years. Persons with this disorder tend to have been sickly, withdrawn, and maladjusted all their lives. Symptoms are severe and the *prognosis* is poor.

progestin(s) "Feminine" *sex hormone(s)* whose primary function is preparing the uterine lining for pregnancy.

prognosis Likelihood of recovery.

projection A *cognitive strategy* occurring when people assign their own undesirable characteristics, problems, impulses, desires, or *thoughts* to others—presumably to reduce their own *anxiety* at having to recognize these qualities as their own.

projective test (projective tech-

nique) A type of measurement instrument that is designed to disclose *unconscious* feelings and impulses, based on the idea that people project *perceptions*, *emotions*, and *thoughts* onto the external world without being aware of doing so. Projective instruments ask people to react to relatively unstructured, *ambiguous* stimuli.

proprioceptive Pertaining to the *vestibular* and *kinesthetic senses*.

protein Chemical substance that forms blood, muscle, tissue, and organs and controls physical-chemical reactions within the body.

protoplasm Typically, a colorless semifluid substance that fills the *neuron* and other cells.

proximity A principle that organizes *perception*; visual elements near one another are seen as belonging together.

psychiatrist A physician who has specialized in the diagnosis and treatment of behavioral disorders.

psychic See *parapsychological*.

psychoanalysis See *psychoanalytic psychotherapy*.

psychoanalytic psychotherapy (psychoanalysis, orthodox psychoanalytic psychotherapy) A *psychotherapy* approach assuming that psychological problems are caused by *repressed* conflicts. The cure consists of a lengthy, intensive exploration of the person's mental life, past and present. *Psychoanalytic therapists* analyze their patients' *free associations* and dreams; they also look for and interpret *resistance* and *transference*. Through the psychoanalysts' *interpretations*, patients gain insight into their *unconscious conflicts*. The insight is assumed to lead automatically to a more constructive *adjustment*.

psychoanalytic theory The general name for Sigmund Freud's *theories* about *personality*, *abnormal behavior*, and *psychotherapy*.

psychoanalytically oriented therapy Modified version of *psychoanalytic psychotherapy*; tending to be briefer and less intense, it focuses on present interpersonal experiences.

psychodynamic theory A type of

theory that aims at describing how *personality* develops and explaining how underlying processes interact to determine behavior. It emphasizes the importance of internal forces such as impulses, *motives*, and *emotions* and assumes that personality develops as people resolve *conflicts* between these forces.

psycholinguist A psychologist who focuses on how *language* is acquired and/or used.

psychological model A *model* of *abnormal behavior* assuming that (1) abnormal behavior is similar in kind, though not in degree, to normal behavior; (2) treatment is rarely syndrome-specific; and (3) active patient involvement in treatment is important.

psychology Usually defined today as the *science* that studies behavior and mental processes.

psychopathic See *antisocial personality disorder*.

psychosexual stage Freud's term for periods during early development when *libido* centers on different bodily regions and *personality* is formed.

psychosis (psychotic reaction) A type of *abnormal behavior* that is characterized by severely impaired cognitive and behavioral functioning. Moods may be profoundly altered. People with psychotic disorders are frequently absorbed in their disturbances, out of contact with reality, and unable to care for themselves for long periods. They are also likely to have little or no perspective about their symptoms.

psychosocial stage A stage, according to Erik Erikson, wherein people must face and resolve social *conflicts*. The solutions shape mental health.

psychosomatic (disorder) A physical disorder, such as peptic ulcers or high blood pressure, that results from the body's response to stress.

psychotherapy (therapy) The various psychological (as opposed to biological) treatment procedures designed to help troubled people solve personal problems.

psychotic Pertaining to a *psychosis*.

puberty Beginning of sexual maturity; at this time *sex hormones* are produced in relatively large quantities.

punishers (punishment) Technically, weakeners of behavior; the process that occurs when an *operant* is followed by a specific consequence that reduces its frequency in similar situations is called punishment.

pupil Opening in the front of the eye through which light enters.

racism Negative *prejudice* based on race.

random assignment Selection of *subjects* for groups in an *experiment* so that each person is equally likely to be placed in any condition.

random sampling Picking *subjects* for a study in such a way that each and every individual in the *population* under consideration has an equal chance of being selected for the research. If the *sample* is large, it will mirror the population.

range A measure of *variability* computed by subtracting the lowest score from the highest score.

rationalization A *cognitive strategy* including two devices: (1) People think up socially acceptable reasons for past, present, or contemplated behavior to hide real *motives* from themselves, and (2) they pretend that a bad situation is really good or that a good situation is really bad.

reaction formation A *cognitive strategy* that occurs when people conceal a real *motive* or *emotion* from themselves and express the opposite one by *attitudes* and behavior—presumably to avoid *anxiety*.

reactive schizophrenia A type of *schizophrenia* that is triggered suddenly by stress. It seems to be a relatively mild disorder characterized by intense emotional upheaval and confusion. Recovery is more likely than in *process schizophrenia*.

recall Measure of memory that asks people to *retrieve* particular information when prompted with associated material.

receptor Single cell or group of cells that is particularly responsive to a specific type of energy.

recognition Measure of memory that asks *subjects* to choose a familiar response from several presented.

recording Measurement of the weak electrical signals that are generated by the *brain* to learn more about its relationship to behavior or cognition.

reference group The *sample* that is tested to provide information about a psychological measure; the reference group should resemble the entire *population* of interest on all significant characteristics.

reflex (reflexive behavior) Behavior automatically elicited by an environmental *stimulus*; rapid, consistent, unlearned *response* that is not ordinarily subject to voluntary control.

regression Coping behavior that occurs when persons handle threats by returning to immature modes of behavior.

rehabilitation See *tertiary prevention*.

rehearse Repeat.

reinforced Strengthened; see *operant* and *respondent conditioning*.

reinforcement (reinforcer) Any object, event, or process that increases the probability that a specific *response* will be made under similar circumstances; used during *respondent* and *operant conditioning*.

reliability A term roughly synonymous with consistency or stability. Several types of test reliability interest psychologists: (1) Is the scoring of different examiners consistent? (2) Are test items internally consistent? (3) Do repeated measurements of the same phenomenon with the same test at different times yield similar results?

REM sleep (paradoxical sleep) Sleep that is accompanied by rapid eye movements.

replicate Repeat a study either to disclose errors or to confirm previous results.

representative sample A *sample* that mirrors the important characteristics of the *population* under study.

repression Exclusion of anxiety-arousing *motives*, ideas, *conflicts*, memories, and the like from awareness. When repression is working, the banished material does not enter *consciousness*, although it does influence behavior. Also see *suppression*.

reproductive organs Genitals.

resistance In Freud's view, acts that disturb the therapy process when patients reach repressed material and feel threatened by the pain of facing it. Stage 2 of the *general adaptation syndrome* is also called resistance; during this stage, the body remains highly aroused and systems responsible for growth, repair, and resisting infection are shut down.

respondent Automatic reaction such as a skeletal *reflex*, immediate emotional response, or other acts controlled by the *autonomic nervous system*.

respondent conditioning (classical conditioning, pavlovian conditioning) A *learning* procedure that occurs when a *respondent* is transferred from one situation to another so that a new *stimulus* acquires the ability to elicit the respondent. The old stimulus remains effective.

response A behavior elicited by a *stimulus*; sometimes used for any behavior.

reticular formation A massive network of *neuron* cell bodies and fibers running through the core of the *hindbrain* up to the *thalamus*; plays a central role in coordinating movements and in regulating attention, sleep, and wakefulness.

retina Light-sensitive *neural* tissue at the back of the eyeball; composed of layers of cells.

retrieve Recover information from memory storage.

retroactive inhibition Process that occurs when new information makes the recollection of previously learned material difficult.

rod Sensitive *receptor* in the *retina* that responds to visible light.

Rorschach test A *projective test* asking people to respond to inkblots.

saccade Flick of the eyeball from one position to another.

sample The portion of a *population* that is actually studied in a research investigation. (Also see *representative sample*.)

savings An especially sensitive measure of memory; even though people cannot *recall*, or even *recognize*, previously learned materials, they may be able to master the same information more quickly than originally; the demonstrated savings suggests that something was retained.

scapegoat An innocent victim who is blamed for one's troubles and aggressed against—an example of *displaced aggression*.

schedule of reinforcement In *operant conditioning*, "rules" that tell when and how *reinforcement* is administered following a particular response; reinforcement schedules have predictable effects on behavior.

scheme Piagetian term for both observable behaviors and associated concepts used to process incoming *sensory* data.

schizophrenia(s) (schizophrenic disorder) A puzzling group of *psychotic* disorders likely to include several of the following patterns: faulty perceptual filtering, disorganized thinking, emotional distortions, *delusions* and *hallucinations*, withdrawal from reality, *bizarre* behavior, and jumbled, incomprehensible speech.

science (scientific method) Strategies used to evaluate evidence, verify principles, and amass a systematic body of internally consistent information; includes goals (such as precise description and explanation), procedures (such as experimentation), and principles (such as *objectivity*).

secondary prevention In mental health care, the identification of a psychological problem in its early stages and the provision of immediate treatment before the difficulty becomes serious.

secondary reinforcer (conditioned reinforcer) *Reinforcer* that acquires its strength through *respondent conditioning*; becomes valued because of being repeatedly paired with other reinforcers.

secondary sex characteristic(s) *Gender*-related bodily characteristics developing at *puberty*, including facial and bodily hair and deepened voices in young men and breast and hip enlargement in young women.

self (self-concept) An internal model, image, concept, or theory built up through interactions with the world.

self-actualization Self-fulfillment.

self-report (self-report measure) Data based on what people say about themselves.

self theory Carl Rogers's theory of *personality*; focuses on the *self-concept* and its development.

semantically Pertaining to meaning.

sensation Data taken in by the *senses* which have not been interpreted.

sense (sensory system) Information-gathering system enabling animals to pick up data about themselves and their surroundings so that they can plan and control their behavior and move about effectively. (Also see *perception*.)

sensitive period (critical period) A time when a developing system is maximally vulnerable to the impact of the environment, usually occurring early in the animal's life.

sensorimotor experience(s) Opportunities to move about and take in information through vision, hearing, taste-smell, and other *perceptual systems*. (See *perception*.)

sensorimotor stage Period from birth to about two years of age when babies make sense of their surroundings by relying on *sensory* and motor systems, according to Piaget.

sensory Pertaining to the *senses*.

sensory deprivation Restriction of input to the *senses*.

sensory memory (SM), sensory store Memory system that holds *sensory* information generally for a fraction of a second unless the material is immediately transferred to another memory store.

sensory nerves Bundles of *axons* which carry *sensory* information to the *central nervous system*.

sensory neurons *Neurons* which carry messages from the *receptors* to the *central nervous system*.

sensory stimulation Information received through the senses. People seem to operate most efficiently when *sensory* information comes in at a specific rate. Too much or too little sensory data cause performance to deteriorate.

sensory system See *sense*.

septum Part of the *limbic system* of the brain that plays a role in rage, pleasure, pain, and fear.

serial recall Memory task requiring that material be *recalled* in a special order.

sex chromosomes *Chromosomes* that determine the *gender* of the organism; females receive an X from both parents, while males receive an X from the mother and a Y from the father.

sex glands See *testes* and *ovaries*.

sex hormone(s) *Hormone*(s) produced by the *gonads* which travel throughout the body to affect sexual development and behavior; they include *androgens*, *estrogens*, and *progestins*.

sex role Standards assigned on the basis of *gender*.

sexual drive *Motive* for sex; in Freudian *theory*, a *drive* for all pleasurable actions and thoughts.

shallow processing Information processing that is usually insufficient to transfer data to the *long-term memory*.

shaping (method of successive approximations) In *operant conditioning*, a *positive reinforcement* strategy for teaching new responses; reinforcement is *contingent* upon the *subject*'s making closer approximations to the desired behavior.

short-term memory (STM), short-term store Memory system holding all the material that individuals are aware of at any given time; houses a limited amount of material for about fifteen seconds ordinarily.

similarity A principle that organizes *perception*; visual elements with the same color, shape, or texture are seen as belonging together.

simulate Pretend.

single-blind procedure A tactic used in an *experiment* to prevent the *subject*'s knowing his or her condition.

situation-specific A *behavioristic* concept maintaining that conduct in any given situation is controlled by many essentially independent causes and conditions, especially current circumstances and past *learning*.

skin conductance A measure of the skin's ability to conduct electricity; largely assesses amount of sweating.

skinner box Distraction-free environment designed by B. F. Skinner and used to study the behavior of laboratory animals primarily during *operant conditioning experiments*.

social experience A type of *sensorimotor experience* involving interactions with others of the same species.

social learning theory A type of *theory* that draws heavily on research in *learning* and *social psychology*, often emphasizing *observation learning* and *operant conditioning*. The term social learning is sometimes used synonymously with observation learning. Some proponents of social learning theories stress *cognitions* also.

social learning therapy See *behavior therapy*.

social milieu therapy A set of procedures that is used to turn a hospital ward into a therapeutic community.

social motive *Motive* whose fulfillment depends on contact with other human beings.

social psychology Study of animals, usually people, as they interact with and influence one another.

social reinforcer (reinforcement) *Reinforcer* that depends on other people.

social scientist A professionally trained person who studies society or social behavior, including psychologists, sociologists, anthropologists, and historians.

socialization Process of guiding children toward the behavior, values, goals, and *motives* that the culture considers appropriate.

sociopathic personality disorder See *antisocial personality disorder*.

soma The cell body of the *neuron* and other cells.

somatic nervous system The division of the *nervous system* containing *sensory* and *motor nerves* which carry messages to and from the *central nervous system*.

somatoform disorder *Abnormal behavior* characterized by physical problems without a demonstrable organic basis; the symptoms appear to be linked to psychological difficulties.

somatosensory Relating to the five separate *sensory systems* of the skin: physical contact, deep pressure, warmth, cold, and pain. Areas of the *parietal lobes* of the *cerebral cortex* register these messages.

species-specific Observed among all normal, same-sexed members of a species.

specific hunger Hunger that causes animals, including people, to seek out substances in which their diets are deficient.

sperm Male reproductive cell that unites with the *ovum* to produce a *zygote*.

spinal cord Extension of the *brain* but somewhat simpler in organization and function; one of its major roles is protecting the body from damage by initiating *reflexes*.

spontaneous recovery The reappearance of a previously *extinguished conditioned response* following a rest period during *respondent* or *operant conditioning*.

sprouting The action of developing new endings which occurs in healthy *axons* of the *central nervous system* after *brain* damage.

standard procedures Detailed directions for administering a test.

state-dependent learning Learning that occurs when human beings or other animals who are intoxicated or in some other distinctive physical state as they *encode* information *retrieve* the material more effectively when in a similar condition.

statistic(s) Various mathematical techniques which provide ways of organizing, describing, and interpreting numerical *data*; also, data themselves.

statistically significant result(s) Findings occurring less than 5 in 100 times simply because of chance and suggesting that the same results are likely to be seen if the study is repeated; they do not mean that the *hypothesis* was proven or that differences are of practical importance.

stereotype Overly simple, rigid *generalization* about a person or group.

stereotyped Showing fixed behavior; similar whenever executed.

stimulation A technique for studying the relationship between (1) the *brain* and (2) behavior or *cognition*; chemicals or mild electrical currents are applied to specific brain regions to learn more about their functions.

stimulus (plural: stimuli) An event, object, or situation that evokes a response.

stream of consciousness See *ordinary waking consciousness*.

stressor Disturbing event.

structuralism An early psychological movement founded by Edward Titchener; the structuralists believed that psychologists should study the elements of *consciousness*, using *analytic introspection*.

subject Research participant.

subjective (experience) Meaning that human beings impose on the objects and events of the world.

superego *Personality* component, according to Freud, formed from the *ego* as youngsters *identify* with parents and internalize restrictions, values, and customs; essentially, a conscience.

suppression (cognitive avoidance) Act of deliberately putting material out of mind; this *cognitive strategy* is frequently observed in the laboratory.

symmetry A principle that organizes *perception*; visual elements that form regular, simple forms are seen as belonging together; also, balance or correspondence in arrangement, parts, or other properties.

sympathetic nervous system (division) A subsystem of the *autonomic nervous system*; most active during periods of intense *emotion* when it mobilizes the body's resources for action.

symptom substitution The *psychoanalytic* idea that new psychiatric symptoms replace old ones unless *unconscious conflicts* are settled during *psychotherapy*.

synapse Minute gap separating adjacent *neurons* from one another.

synaptic vesicle Storage packet housing the *neurotransmitter* manufactured by the *neuron*.

systematic desensitization (desensitization) A *behavior therapy* procedure relying on *respondent conditioning* principles to reduce incapacitating *anxiety*; relaxation is paired with the imagination of anxiety-arousing situations until the patient no longer feels upset by these situations.

TAT See *Thematic Apperception Test*.

telegraphic Abbreviated.

telepathy A form of *extrasensory perception*; knowing the thoughts of another without using known *senses* to pick up the information.

temperament Personal style of responding, feeling, and acting.

temporal lobe Part of the *cerebral cortex* located above the ear; regions here record and synthesize *auditory* data.

tentative(ness) The scientific attitude of being open-minded and ready to reevaluate and revise conclusions if warranted by new evidence.

tertiary prevention (rehabilitation) Mental health programs designed to correct for the results of emotional problems.

test-retest reliability A type of *reliability* that is determined by seeing whether repeated measurements of the same phenomenon with the same test at different times yield similar results.

testable Capable of being evaluated by *empirical* methods that confirm or disprove the contention(s); usually applied to a *theory* or *hypothesis*.

testes Masculine sex *glands*.

testosterone "Masculine" sex *hormone*; a major *androgen*.

texture gradient A *pictorial depth cue*; gradual change in texture with distance.

thalamus Large collection of *neuron* cell bodies in the *forebrain*; in people, all incoming *sensory* information is eventually routed here.

Thematic Apperception Test (TAT) A story-telling *projective technique* used to assess *motivation* and other aspects of *personality*.

theory Possible explanation of experimental findings.

therapist Abbreviation for psychotherapist, a person who conducts *psychotherapy*.

thought General label for varied mental activities such as reasoning, solving problems, and formulating concepts.

token economy A *behavior therapy* procedure that systematically motivates and rewards adaptive behavior.

trait Single *personality* characteristic.

transcendental meditation (TM) *Concentrative meditation* exercise.

transducer Device that converts energy from one form to another.

transference In *psychoanalytic psychotherapy*, the patient's identification of the *therapist* with a person who was significant in the past (usually a parent).

traumatic physical events Experiences that result in the destruction of an organism's cells either before or after birth.

trigeminal nerve *Nerve* that carries information to the *brain* about the texture and temperature of sub-

stances within the mouth; thought to be important in food-intake regulation.

Turner's syndrome A *genetic* abnormality that causes individuals to resemble females. They are short in stature and impaired in sexual development. The problem is caused by the inheritance of a normal X *sex chromosome*, but no second X or Y sex chromosome.

twin study A naturally occurring *experiment* that helps *psychologists* determine whether and to what extent *heredity* influences differences on a particular characteristic. The study involves comparison of the similarity between *identical* and *fraternal* twin pairs on the characteristic of interest.

type A *personality* category to which a person is sometimes assigned. Typing assumes that several related personality *traits* commonly occur together.

unconditioned response In *respondent conditioning*, the *respondent* that is automatically elicited by the *unconditioned stimulus*.

unconditioned stimulus In *respondent conditioning*, any event, object, or experience that automatically elicits a particular *respondent*.

unconscious Unaware; Freud believed that people are unaware of most of their thoughts, feelings, and desires and cannot become aware of this unconscious material without the help of a trained specialist.

undirected thinking See *ordinary waking consciousness*.

valid(ity) The extent to which a test or measure appraises what it is intended to; a test's validity is assessed by correlating its results with other measures of the same characteristic; also, general soundness.

variability A concept describing how widely the scores in a group deviate, or vary, from a central value.

variable Anything that can change or take on different values or characteristics.

variable sensory experiences Events processed by the *senses*;

they differ among animals of a particular species, depending on each individual's circumstances.

verbal Language-related.

vestibular Pertaining to the sense of orientation or balance.

vicarious Through imagined participation; by observing others.

vigilant strategies Attentive *cognitive strategies* that involve focusing on a problem, rather than ignoring, denying, or avoiding it.

visual cliff An apparatus used to test depth *perception*; simulates the visual conditions of a steep drop.

visual field The entire view registered by the eye when gazing in any one direction.

withdrawal Choosing not to act in the face of stress.

young old age The sixty-five to seventy-five-year-old age range.

zygote A single cell produced at conception by the union of the father's *sperm* and mother's *ovum*.

Acknowledgments

FIGURES AND TABLES

Chapter 1

Table 1-2 Adapted from C. A. Boneau & J. M. Cuca. An overview of psychology's human resources: Characteristics and salaries from the 1972 APA survey. *American Psychologist*, 1974, **29**(11), 821–840.

Figure 1-3 Adapted from C. A. Boneau & J. M. Cuca. An overview of psychology's human resources: Characteristics and salaries from the 1972 APA survey. *American Psychologist*, 1974, **29**(11), 821–840.

Figure 1-12 J. M. Weiss. Psychological factors in stress and disease. *Scientific American*, 1972, **226**(6), 104–107.

Chapter 2

Table 2-2 Adapted from B. J. Anderson & K. Standley. Manual for naturalistic observation of the childbirth environment. *JSAS Catalog of Selected Documents in Psychology*, 1977, **8**, 6. (Ms. No. 1413.) Copyright © 1977 by the American Psychological Association.

Table 2-3 J. Freedman, P. Shaver, & students. What makes you happy? A PT questionnaire, *Psychology Today*, 1975, **9**(5), 67, 68, questions 1 and 15–30. Copyright © 1975 by Ziff-Davis Publishing Company. All rights reserved.

Table 2-4 J. B. Rotter. External control and internal control. Reprinted from *Psychology Today*, 1971, **5**(1), 37–40ff. Copyright © 1971 by Ziff-Davis Publishing Company.

Figure 2-6 B. Latané & J. M. Darley. *The unresponsive bystander: Why doesn't he help?* Copyright © 1970. P. 97. Used by permission of Prentice-Hall, Inc., Englewood Cliffs, N.J.

Figure 2-9 Redrawn from J. L. Phillips, Jr. *A structural approach to statistical thinking.* San Francisco: Freeman, 1973.

Chapter 3

Figure 3-2 From D. G. Freedman. *Human infancy: An evolutionary perspective.* Hillsdale, N.J.: Erlbaum, 1974. Adapted by permission of the author.

Figure 3-6 Adapted from M. M. Shirley. *The first two years: A study of twenty babies.* Minneapolis: University of Minnesota Press, 1931.

Chapter 4

Figure 4-13 Adapted from W. T. Keeton. *Biological science.* (2d ed.) New York: Norton, 1972.

Figure 4-15 Adapted from W. Penfield & T. Rasmussen. *Cerebral cortex of man.* New York: Macmillan, 1950.

Figure 4-21 Adapted from J. E. Bogen. The other side of the brain. I, II, III. *Bulletin of the Los Angeles Neurological Societies*, 1969, **34**(3).

Chapter 5

Figure 5-5 Adapted from R. K. Van Wagenen & E. E. Murdock. A transistorized signal-package for toilet training of infants. *Journal of Experimental Child Psychology*, 1966, **3**, 312–314. Reproduced by permission.

Figure 5-12 Adapted from M. F. Daley. The reinforcement menu. Finding effective reinforcers. In J. D. Krumboltz & C. E. Thoresen (Eds.), *Behavioral counseling: Cases and techniques.* New York: Holt, Rinehart and Winston, 1969. P. 44.

Figure 5-14 Adapted from C. D. Williams. The elimination of tantrum behavior by extinction procedures. *Journal of Abnormal and Social Psychology*, 1959, **59**, 269. Copyright © 1959 by the American Psychological Association. Used by permission.

Chapter 6

Figure 6-9 Adapted from W. N. Dember. *The psychology of perception.* New York: Holt, Rinehart and Winston, 1960.

Figure 6-12 L. L. Thurstone. *A factorial study of perception.* Copyright 1944 by The University of Chicago. Adapted by permission.

Figure 6-19 Adapted from R. L. Fantz. The origin of form perception. *Scientific American*, 1961, **204**, 66–84. Copyright © 1961 by Scientific American, Inc. All rights reserved.

Figure 6-20 Adapted from R. Walk & E. J. Gibson. A comparative and analytical study of visual depth perception. *Psychological Monographs*, 1961, **75** (Whole No. 519).

Figure 6-22 Adapted from G. H. Fisher. Preparation of ambiguous stimulus materials. *Perception and Psychophysics*, 1967, **2**(9), 422.

Figure 6-23 M. H. Segall, D. T. Campbell, & M. J. Herskovitz. Cultural differences in perception of geometric illusions. *Science*, 1963, **139**, 770. Copyright © 1963 by the American Association for the Advancement of Science.

Figure 6-26 R. Targ & H. Puthoff. Information transmission under conditions of sensory shielding. *Nature*, 1974, **251**, 602–607.

Chapter 7

Table 7-1 Adapted from S. C. Wilson & T. X. Barber. The Creative Imagination Scale: Applications to clinical and experimental hypnosis. Medfield, Mass.: Medfield Foundation, 1976.

Figure 7-4 W. B. Webb, University of Florida Sleep Laboratories.

Figure 7-8 W. B. Webb & H. W. Agnew, Jr. In L. E. Abt & B. F. Riess, *Progress in clinical psychology*, Vol. 8. New York: Grune & Stratton, Inc., 1968. P. 17.

Figure 7-11 C. Tart. *On being stoned: A psychological study of marijuana intoxication.* Palo Alto, Calif.: Science and Behavior Books, 1971. P. 20.

Chapter 8

Figure 8-4 Adapted from H. P. Bahrick, P. O. Bahrick, & R. P. Wittlinger. Fifty years of memory for names and faces: A cross-sectional approach. *Journal of Experimental Psychology (General)*, 1975, **104**(1), 66.

Figure 8-6 Adapted from G. Sperling. The information available in brief visual presentations. *Psychological Monographs: General and Applied*, 1960, **74**(11) (Whole No. 498).

Figure 8-7 Adapted from L. Postman & L. W. Phillips. Short term temporal changes in free recall. *Quarterly Journal of Experimental Psychology*, 1965, **17**, 135.

Figure 8-8 Adapted from L. R. Peterson & M. J. Peterson. Short-term retention of individual verbal items. *Journal of Experimental Psychology*, 1959, **58**(3), 195.

Figure 8-9 F. Bartlett. *Remembering: A study in experimental and social psychology.* Cambridge, England: Cambridge University Press, 1950. P. 180.

Figure 8-10 Adapted from F. A. Holloway & R. Wansley. Multiphasic retention deficits at periodic intervals after passive-avoidance learning. *Science*, 1973, **180**, 209.

Figure 8-12 Adapted from L. R. Brooks. Spatial and verbal components of the act of recall. *Canadian Journal of Psychology*, 1968, **22**(5), 349–368.

Figure 8-14 Adapted from G. H. Bower. Organizational factors in memory. *Journal of Cognitive Psychology*, 1970, **1**, 18–46. Used by permission of the author and the publisher, Academic Press.

Figure 8-15 Adapted from R. C. Atkinson & M. R. Raugh. An application of the mnemonic keyword method to the acquisition of a Russian vocabulary. *Journal of Experimental Psychology: Human Learning and Memory*, 1975, **104**(2), 126–133.

Figure 8-16 B. F. Skinner. Teaching machines. *Science*, 1958, **128,** 969–977.

Chapter 9
Table 9-2 Adapted from W. Kohler. *The task of gestalt psychology.* Copyright © 1969 by Princeton University Press: Princeton 1972. P. 150. Used by permission of the publisher.

Table 9-3 Adapted from R. Brown & C. Fraser. The acquisition of syntax. In C. N. Cofer and B. Musgrave (Eds.), *Verbal behavior and learning: Problems and processes.* New York: McGraw-Hill, 1963. Pp. 158–201.

Figure 9-5 Adapted from M. Scheerer. Problem solving. *Scientific American*, 1968, **208**(4), 118–128.

Figure 9-7 Adapted from S. Glucksberg & R. W. Weisberg. Verbal behavior and problem-solving: Some effects of labeling in a functional fixedness problem. *Journal of Experimental Psychology*, 1966, **71**(5), 659–664. Copyright © 1966 by the American Psychological Association. Used by permission of Princeton University Press.

Figure 9-8 Adapted from K. Duncker. On problem-solving. *Psychological Monographs*, 1945, **58**(5). Copyright 1945 by the American Psychological Association. Used by permission.

Figure 9-12 Adapted from A. S. Luchins. Mechanization in problem-solving: The effect of Einstellung. *Psychological Monographs*, 1942, **54**(6). Copyright 1942 by the American Psychological Association.

Figure 9-14 R. Brown. *A first language: The early stages.* Cambridge, Mass.: Harvard University Press, 1973. P. 57.

Figure 9-15 From J. Berko. The child's learning of English morphology. *Word*, 1958, **14,** 150–177. Used by permission of Johnson Reprint Corporation.

Chapter 10
Figure 10-9 W. B. Cannon. Hunger and thirst. In C. Murchison (Ed.), *Handbook of general experimental psychology.* Worcester, Mass.: Clark University Press, 1934. (Reprinted by Russell and Russell, 1969).

Chapter 11
Figure 11-3 Redrawn from T. J. Teyler. *A primer of psychobiology.* San Francisco: Freeman, 1975. P. 36.

Chapter 12
Figure 12-5 L. M. Terman & M. A. Merrill. *Stanford-Binet Intelligence Scale: Manual for the 3rd revision.* Form L-M, 1960. P.

18. Reproduced by permission of the publisher, Houghton Mifflin Company.

Figure 12-7 L. Erlenmeyer-Kimling & L. F. Jarvik. Genetics and intelligence: A review. *Science*, 1963, **142,** 1478. Copyright © 1963 by the American Association for the Advancement of Science.

Figure 12-10 From The Chitling Test, *Newsweek*, July 15, 1968. Copyright © 1968 by Newsweek, Inc. Reprinted by permission.

Figure 12-11 Adapted by permission of the Institute for Personality and Ability Testing, University of Illinois, Champaign, Ill.

Figure 12-12 Adapted from S. J. Parnes & R. B. Noller. *Toward supersanity: Channeled freedom.* Copyright © 1973. Used by permission of D.O.K. Publishers, Buffalo, N.Y. Pp. 41ff. J. P. Guilford. *The nature of human intelligence.* New York: McGraw-Hill. P. 144. Copyright © 1967; Making objects test. Used by courtesy of Sheridan Supply Company.

Table 12-1 Adapted from the Wechsler Adult Intelligence Scale and paraphrased test items supplied by The Psychological Corporation, New York, N.Y.

Table 12-2 D. Wechsler. *Manual for the Wechsler Adult Intelligence Scale.* New York: Psychological Corporation, 1955. P. 20. Reproduced by permission. Copyright © 1955 by The Psychological Corporation, New York. All rights reserved.

Chapter 13
Table 13-1 G. W. Allport, P. E. Vernon, & G. Lindzey. *Study of values.* (3d ed.) Copyright ©. 1960 by Houghton Mifflin Company. Reprinted by permission of the publisher. All rights reserved.

Table 13-2 Excerpted from I. G. Sarason. *Personality: An objective approach.* (2d ed.) New York: Wiley, 1972. Pp. 226–227.

Figure 13-1 D. Werdegar, M. Sokolow, D. B. Perloff, W. F. Riess, R. E. Harris, T. Singer, & H. W. Blackburn, Jr. Portable recording of blood pressure: A new approach to assessments of the severity and prognosis of hypertension. *Transactions of the Association of Life Insurance Medical Directors of America*, 1967, **51**, 103.

Figure 13-2 R. D. Fowler, Jr. The current status of computer interpretation of psychological tests. *American Journal of Psychiatry*, 1969, **125**, 21–27.

Figure 13-6 R. Coles. *Children of crisis: A study of courage and fear.* Boston: Little, Brown, 1964.

Figure 13-15 Reproduced by permission of the Institute for Personality and Ability Testing, Champaign, Ill.

Chapter 14
Table 14-1 Adapted from R. S. Lazarus. *Patterns of adjustment and human effec-*

tiveness. New York: McGraw-Hill, 1969. P. 73.

Table 14-2 Adapted from Survey Research Center. *Survey of working conditions: Final report.* Washington, D.C.: U.S. Government Printing Office, 1971. Pp. 55, 56.

Table 14-3 Adapted from R. L. Kahn. The work module—A tonic for lunchpail lassitude. *Psychology Today*, 1973. **6**(9), 39.

Chapter 15
Table 15-3 Adapted from P. H. Wender, R. Rosenthal, S. S. Kety, S. Schulsinger, & J. Welner. Cross-fostering: A research strategy for clarifying the role of genetic and experiential factors in the etiology of schizophrenia. *Archives of General Psychiatry*, 1974, **30**, 121–128.

Chapter 16
Table 16-2 Adapted from F. H. Kanfer & J. S. Phillips. *Learning foundations of behavior therapy.* New York: Wiley, 1970. P. 151.

Table 16-4 Adapted from T. Ayllon & N. Azrin. *The token economy.* New York: Appleton-Century-Crofts, 1968. Pp. 246, 250.

Figure 16-2 Adapted from H. H. Strupp, R. E. Fox, & K. Lessler. *Patients view their psychotherapy.* Baltimore: Johns Hopkins University Press, 1969. P. 59.

Chapter 17
Table 17-4 Adapted from Louis Harris and Associates, Inc. A study of attitudes toward racial and religious minorities and toward women. New York: The National Conference of Christians and Jews, 1978.

Table 17-5 Adapted from J. B. McConahay & J. C. Hough. Symbolic racism. *Journal of Social Issues*, 1976, **32**(2), 25.

TEXT QUOTATIONS

Chapter 1
P. 16 R. I. Evans. *Dialogue with Erich Fromm.* New York: Harper & Row, 1966.

P. 21 A. H. Maslow. Self-actualization and beyond. In J. F. T. Bugenthal (Ed.), *Challenges of humanistic psychology.* New York: McGraw-Hill, 1967. Pp. 279–280.

Chapter 2
Pp. 26–27 B. Barber & R. Fox. The case of the floppy-eared rabbits. *American Journal of Sociology*, **54,** 128–136. Copyright © 1958 by the University of Chicago Press.

P. 29 From G. McCain & E. M. Segal. *The game of science* (3d ed.). Copyright ©

1977 by Wadsworth Publishing Company, Inc. Reprinted by permission of the publisher, Brooks/Cole Publishing Company, Monterey, Calif.

P. 39 E. Kubler-Ross. *On Death and dying.* Copyright © 1969 by Elisabeth Kubler-Ross.

P. 45 A. Chapanis. The relevance of laboratory studies to practical situations. *Ergonomics*, 1967, **10**, 557–577.

Chapter 3
Pp. 73–74 A conversation with Jerome Kagan. *Saturday Review of Education*, April 1973, **1**(3), 41–43.

P. 76 D. Krech. In R. I. Evans (Ed.), *The making of psychology.* New York: Knopf, 1976. P. 141. Reprinted by permission of the publisher and the author's wife.

Chapter 4
Pp. 92–93 From A. R. Luria. *The man with a shattered world: The history of a brain wound (translated from the Russian by Lynn Solotaroff).* Copyright © 1972 by Basic Books, Inc., Publishers, New York.

P. 96 H. Gardner. Brain damage: A window on the mind. *Saturday Review*, Aug. 9, 1975. **2**(23), 26–29.

Pp. 98–99 W. Penfield. *The excitable cortex of conscious man.* Liverpool, England: Liverpool University Press, 1958. Pp. 25–29.

P. 99 W. Penfield. The uncommitted cortex: The child's changing brain. *Atlantic Monthly*, **214**(1), 77–81. Copyright © 1964 by The Atlantic Monthly Company, Boston, Mass. Reprinted with permission of the publisher.

Chapter 6
P. 171 R. L. Gregory. *Eye and brain: The psychology of seeing.* (2d ed.) New York: McGraw-Hill, 1973. Pp. 194–198.

P. 176 U. Neisser. *Cognition and reality: Principles and implications of cognitive psychology*, P. 29. Copyright © 1976 by W. H. Freeman & Co.

Pp. 195–196 C. Turnbull. Some observations regarding the experiences and behavior of BaMbuti pygmies. *American Journal of Psychology*, 1961, **74**, 305. Used with permission of the University of Illinois Press.

Chapter 7
Pp. 206–207 J. Joyce. *Ulysses.* New York: Modern Library. Copyright © 1961 by Random House, Inc.

P. 207 R. E. L. Masters & J. Houston. *The varieties of psychedelic experiences.* New York: Holt, Rinehart and Winston, Inc., 1966. P. 10.

P. 218 A. Rechtschaffen, G. Vogel, & G. Shaikun. Interrelatedness of mental activity during sleep. *Archives of General Psychiatry*, 1963, **9**, 536–547. Copyright © 1963 by the American Medical Association.

P. 224 From J. R. Hilgard. Imaginative involvement: Some characteristics of the highly hypnotizable and non-hypnotizable. Quoted from *International Journal of Clinical and Experimental Hypnosis*, April 1974. Copyright © 1974 by the Society for Clinical and Experimental Hypnosis.

P. 227 W. Rahula. *What the Buddha taught.* New York: Grove Press, 1959. P. 71.

Chapter 8
Pp. 238–239 Excerpted from A. R. Luria. *The mind of a mnemonist: A little book about a vast memory (translated from the Russian by Lynn Solotaroff).* Pp. 7–12. 28. Copyright © 1968 by Basic Books, Inc., Publishers, New York, and Jonathan Cape, Ltd.

Pp. 252–253 P. H. Lindsay & D. A. Norman. *Human information processing: An introduction to psychology.* (2d ed.) New York: Academic, 1977. Reprinted by permission of the authors and the publisher.

Chapter 9
Pp. 275–276 H. Keller. *The story of my life.* Garden City, N.Y.: Doubleday, 1954. Used by permission of the publisher.

P. 279 Adapted from J. Piaget. *The child's conception of number.* New York: Norton, 1965. Used by permission of the Humanities Press, Inc., and Routledge & Kegan Paul, Ltd.

P. 279 J. Piaget. *Play, dreams, and imitation in childhood.* New York: Norton, 1951. Used by permission of W. W. Norton & Company, Inc., and Routledge & Kegan Paul, Ltd.

P. 280 J. Piaget. *The origins of intelligence in children.* New York: International Universities Press, 1952. P. 335. Used by permission of the publisher.

Pp. 281–282 From *Winnie-the-Pooh*, by A. A. Milne. Copyright 1926 by E. P. Dutton; renewal © 1954 by A. A. Milne. Reprinted by permission of the publisher.

Chapter 10
Pp. 309–310 D. C. McClelland. *Power: The inner experience.* Copyright © 1975 by Irvington Publishers, Inc., New York: Reprinted by permission of the publisher.

P. 311 Excerpts from E. B. Holt. *Animal drive and the learning process*, 1931. P. 4. Reprinted by permission from Holt, Rinehart and Winston, Inc.

P. 312 D. Lee. Cultural factors in dietary choice. *American Journal of Clinical Nutrition*, 1957, **5**, 167.

P. 317 A. Maslow. *Motivation and personality.* (2d ed.) New York: Harper & Row, 1970. P. 37.

P. 336 D. McClelland, J. W. Atkinson, R. A. Clark, & E. L. Lowell. *The achievement motive.* New York: Appleton-Century-Crofts, 1953. Pp. 118, 121.

P. 340 M. S. Horner. The measurement and behavioral implications of fear of success in women. In J. W. Atkinson & J. O. Raynor (Eds.), *Personality, motivation, and achievement.* Washington, D.C.: Hemisphere, 1978. Pp. 41–70.

Chapter 12
P. 406 J. F. Feldhusen, D. J. Treffinger, & S. J. Bahlke. Developing creative thinking: The Purdue Creativity Project. *Journal of Creative Behavior*, 1970, **4**(2), 85–90.

Chapter 13
P. 410 R. Stagner. The gullibility of personnel managers. *Personnel Psychology*, 1958. **11**, 347–352.

P. 411 I. G. Sarason. *Personality: An objective approach.* (2d ed.) New York: Wiley, 1972. Reprinted by permission of the author.

P. 429 Reprinted from E. H. Erikson. *Identity, youth and crisis.* New York: Norton, 1968. Pp. 132–133. Used by permission of W. W. Norton & Company and Faber and Faber, Ltd.

P. 431 C. Rogers: A theory of therapy, personality and interpersonal relationships, as developed in the client-centered framework. In S. Koch (Ed.), *Psychology, A theory of a science.* Vol. 3. New York: McGraw-Hill, 1959.

P. 437 B. F. Skinner. *Science and human behavior.* New York: Macmillan, 1953. P. 31.

Chapter 14
Pp. 445–446 Excerpts from C. Mirthes & the Children of P.S. 15. *Can't you hear me talking to you?* Copyright © 1971 by Bantam Books, Inc. Used by permission of the publisher.

P. 452 J. E. Nardini. Survival factors in American prisoners of war of the Japanese. *The American Journal of Psychiatry*, 1952, **109**, 241–248. Copyright 1952 by the American Psychiatric Association.

P. 455 D. A. Hamburg, B. Hamburg, & S. de Goza. Adaptive problems and mechanisms in severely burned patients. *Psychiatry*, 1953, **16**, 9.

P. 456 J. Masserman. *Principles of dynamic psychiatry.* Philadelphia: Saunders, 1961. P. 38.

P. 470 D. J. Levinson. *The seasons of a man's life.* New York: Knopf, 1978. Pp. 213–217.

P. 473 A. Weisman. *On dying and denying.* New York: Human Sciences Press, 1972. P. 157.

Chapter 15

Pp. 478–479 M. Scarf. Normality is a square circle or a four-sided triangle. Copyright © 1971 by Maggie Scarf. Reprinted by permission of Brandt and Brandt.

P. 482 J. Mendels. *Concepts of depression.* New York: Wiley, 1970.

Pp. 482–483 D. Rosenhan. On being sane in insane places. *Science,* 1973, **179,** 250–258. Copyright © 1973 by the American Association for the Advancement of Science.

P. 492 G. C. Davison & J. M. Neale. *Abnormal psychology: An experimental-clinical approach.* (2d ed.) P. 191. Copyright © 1978 by John Wiley & Sons, Inc. Reprinted by permission of the publisher.

P. 492 G. C. Davison & J. M. Neale. *Abnormal psychology: An experimental clinical approach.* (2d ed.) P. 192. Copyright © 1978 by John Wiley & Sons, Inc. Reprinted by permission of the publisher.

P. 496 A. McGhie & I. Chapman. Disorders of attention and perception in early schizophrenia. *British Journal of Medical Psychology,* 1961, **34,** 104–106ff.

P. 496 G. G. Luce. *Body time: Physiological rhythms and social stress.* Copyright © 1971 by Pantheon Books, a Division of Random House, Inc.

P. 500 J. C. Coleman. *Abnormal psychology and modern life.* (5th ed.) Copyright © 1976, 1972, 1964, by Scott, Foresman and Company. Reprinted by permission.

P. 503 L. C. Kolb. *Noyes' modern clinical psychiatry.* (8th ed.) Philadelphia: Saunders, 1973. P. 229.

Pp. 504–505 R. D. Hare. *Psychopathy: Theory and research.* Pp. 1–4. Copyright © 1970, John Wiley & Sons, Inc. Reprinted by permission of the publisher.

Chapter 16

P. 514 P. A. Dewald. From *The psychoanalytic process: A case illustration.* Pp. 514–515. Copyright © 1972 by Basic Books, Inc., Publishers, New York.

P. 515 R. W. White & N. F. Watt. *The abnormal personality.* (4th ed.) New York: Ronald Press, 1973. Pp. 262–264.

Pp. 518–519 G. T. Wilson & G. C. Davison. Behavior therapy: A road to self-control. Reprinted from *Psychology Today* magazine. Copyright © 1975 by Ziff-Davis Publishing Company.

P. 520 C. B. Truax & R. R. Carkhuff. *Toward effective counseling and psychotherapy: Training and practice.* Chicago: Aldine, 1967. P. 57.

Pp. 521–522 G. C. Davison & J. M. Neale. *Abnormal psychology: An experimental-clinical approach.* (2d ed.) New York: Wiley, 1978. P. 486.

P. 531 L. I. Stein & M. A. Test. Training in community living: An alternative to the mental hospital. Paper presented at the annual meeting of the American Psychology Association, Toronto, 1978. Pp. 4–5.

Chapter 17

Pp. 543–544 C. Tavris. The frozen world of the familiar stranger. Reprinted from *Psychology Today,* 1974, **8**(1), 71, 72. Copyright © 1974 by Ziff-Davis Publishing Company.

Page numbers in *italic* indicate illustrations or tables.